THE FISKE 2002
GUIDE TO
COLLEGES

Also by Edward B. Fiske

The Fiske Guide to Getting into the Right College (with Bruce G. Hammond)

Smart Schools, Smart Kids: Why Do Some Schools Work? (with Sally Reed and R. Craig Sautter)

Get Organized! (with Phyllis Steinbrecher)

Using Both Hands: Women and Education in Cambodia

When Schools Compete: A Cautionary Tale (with Helen F. Ladd)

THE FISKE GUIDE TO COLLEGES 2002

EDWARD B. FISKE

former Education Editor of
The New York Times
with Robert Logue
and
The Fiske Guide to Colleges Staff

SOURCEBOOKS, INC.
NAPERVILLE, ILLINOIS

Published by Sourcebooks, Inc.
P.O. Box 4410
Naperville, Illinois 60567-4410
(630) 961-3900 • FAX: (630) 961-2168
www.sourcebooks.com

ISBN 1-57071-765-6
Eighteenth Edition

Your comments and corrections are welcome.
Please send them to:

The Fiske Guide to Colleges
P.O. Box 287
Alstead, NH 03602
Fax: (603) 835-7859
Email: editor@fiskeguide.com

Printed and bound in the United States of America
DR 10 9 8 7 6 5 4

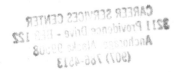

To Sunny

Index by State

The colleges in this guide are listed alphabetically and cross-referenced for your convenience. Below is a list of the selected colleges grouped by state. Following this listing you will find a second listing in which the colleges are categorized by the yearly cost of attending each school.

Iowa
Cornell College
Grinnell College
Iowa State University
Iowa, University of

Kansas
Kansas, University of

Kentucky
Centre College
Kentucky, University of

Louisiana
Louisiana State University
Loyola University New Orleans
Tulane University
Xavier University of Louisiana

Maine
Atlantic, College of the
Bates College
Bowdoin College
Colby College
Maine, University of–Orono

Maryland
Goucher College
Hood College
Johns Hopkins University, The
Maryland, University of–College Park
St. John's College
St. Mary's College

Massachusetts
Amherst College
Babson College
Boston College
Boston University
Brandeis University
Clark University
Gordon College
Hampshire College
Harvard University
Holy Cross, College of the
Massachusetts Institute of Technology
Massachusetts, University of–Amherst
Mount Holyoke College
Northeastern University

Smith College
Tufts University
Wellesley College
Wheaton College
Williams College
Worcester Polytechnic Institute

Michigan
Albion College
Alma College
Calvin College
Hope College
Kalamazoo College
Michigan State University
Michigan, University of

Minnesota
Carleton College
Gustavus Adolphus College
Macalester College
Minnesota, University of–Morris
Minnesota, University of–Twin Cities
St. John's University, and St. Benedict, College of
St. Olaf College

Mississippi
Millsaps College

Missouri
Missouri, University of–Columbia
Saint Louis University
Truman State University (formerly Northeast Missouri State University)
Washington University in St. Louis

Montana
Montana Tech of the University of Montana

Nebraska
Nebraska, University of–Lincoln

New Hampshire
Dartmouth College
New Hampshire, University of

New Jersey
College of New Jersey, The
Drew University

New Jersey Institute of Technology
Princeton University
Rutgers University
Stevens Institute of Technology

New Mexico
New Mexico Institute of Mining and Technology
New Mexico, University of
St. John's College

New York
Alfred University
Bard College
Barnard College (Columbia University)
Clarkson University
Colgate University
Columbia College
Cooper Union
Cornell University
Fordham University
Hamilton College
Hartwick College
Hobart and William Smith Colleges
Houghton College
Ithaca College
Manhattanville College
New School University–Eugene Lang College (formerly New School for Social Research)
New York University
Rensselaer Polytechnic Institute
Rochester Institute of Technology
Rochester, University of
St. Lawrence University
Sarah Lawrence College
Skidmore College
SUNY–Albany
SUNY–Binghamton University
SUNY–Buffalo
SUNY–Geneseo
SUNY–Purchase College
SUNY–Stony Brook
Syracuse University
Union College
Vassar College
Wells College

North Carolina
Davidson College
Duke University

Guilford College
North Carolina State University
North Carolina, University of–Asheville
North Carolina, University of–Chapel Hill
North Carolina, University of–Greensboro
Wake Forest University

Ohio
Antioch College
Case Western Reserve University
Cincinnati, University of
Dayton, University of
Denison University
Hiram College
Kenyon College
Miami University
Oberlin College
Ohio State University
Ohio University
Ohio Wesleyan University
Wittenberg University
Wooster, The College of

Oklahoma
Oklahoma, University of
Tulsa, University of

Oregon
Lewis and Clark College
Oregon State University
Oregon, University of
Reed College
Willamette University

Pennsylvania
Allegheny College
Bryn Mawr College
Bucknell University
Carnegie Mellon University
Dickinson College
Drexel University
Franklin and Marshall College
Gettysburg College
Haverford College

Lafayette College
Lehigh University
Muhlenberg College
Pennsylvania State University
Pennsylvania, University of
Pittsburgh, University of
Susquehanna University
Swarthmore College
Ursinus College
Villanova University
Washington and Jefferson College

Rhode Island
Brown University
Rhode Island School of Design
Rhode Island, University of

South Carolina
Charleston, College of
Clemson University
Furman University
Presbyterian College
South Carolina, University of
Wofford College

Tennessee
Rhodes College
South, University of the (Sewanee)
Tennessee, University of–Knoxville
Vanderbilt University

Texas
Austin College
Baylor University
Dallas, University of
Rice University
Southern Methodist University
Southwestern University
Texas A&M University
Texas Christian University
Texas Tech University
Texas, University of–Austin
Trinity University

Utah
Brigham Young University
Utah, University of

Vermont
Bennington College
Marlboro College
Middlebury College
Vermont, University of

Virginia
George Mason University
Hampden-Sydney College
Hollins University (formerly Hollins College)
James Madison University
Mary Washington College
Randolph-Macon Woman's College
Richmond, University of
Sweet Briar College
Virginia Polytechnic Institute and State University
Virginia, University of
Washington and Lee University
William and Mary, College of

Washington
Evergreen State College, The
Puget Sound, University of
Washington, University of
Whitman College

West Virginia
West Virginia University

Wisconsin
Alverno College
Beloit College
Lawrence University
Marquette University
Ripon College
Wisconsin, University of–Madison

Canada
British Columbia, University of
McGill University
Queen's University
Toronto, University of

Index by Price

PUBLIC COLLEGES AND UNIVERSITIES

Inexpensive—$

Alabama, University of–Tuscaloosa, AL

Arizona, University of, AZ

Arizona State University, AZ

British Columbia, University of, Canada

Evergreen State College, The, WA

Florida State University, FL

Florida, University of, FL

Iowa, University of, IA

Kansas, University of, KS

Louisiana State University, LA

McGill University, Canada

Montana Tech of the University of Montana, MT

New College of the University of South Florida, FL

New Mexico Institute of Mining and Technology, NM

New Mexico, University of, NM

North Carolina State University, NC

North Carolina, University of–Asheville, NC

North Carolina, University of–Chapel Hill, NC

North Carolina, University of–Greensboro, NC

Oklahoma, University of, OK

Utah, University of, UT

West Virginia University, WV

Moderate—$$

Arkansas, University of, AR

Auburn University, AL

California, University of–Irvine, CA

California, University of–Los Angeles, CA

California, University of–Riverside, CA

California, University of–Santa Barbara, CA

California, University of–Santa Cruz, CA

California, University of–San Diego, CA

Charleston, College of, SC

Clemson University, SC

Colorado, University of–Boulder, CO

George Mason University, VA

Georgia, University of, GA

Georgia Institute of Technology, GA

Hawaii, University of–Manoa, HI

Iowa, University of, IA

Iowa State University, IA

James Madison University, VA

Kentucky, University of, KY

Mary Washington College, VA

Miami University, OH

Nebraska, University of Lincoln, NE

Ohio State University, OH

Oregon, University of, OR

Oregon State University, OR

Purdue University, IN

Queen's University, Canada

South Carolina, University of, SC

Tennessee, University of–Knoxville, TN

Texas A&M University, TX

Texas, University of–Austin, TX

Toronto, University of, Canada

Truman State University, MO

Virginia Polytechnic Institute and State University, VA

Washington, University of, WA

Wisconsin, University of–Madison, WI

Expensive—$$$

California, University of–Berkeley, CA

California, University of–Davis, CA

Illinois, University of–Urbana-Champaign, IL

Indiana University, IN

Maine, University of–Orono, ME

Maryland, University of–College Park, MD

Minnesota, University of–Twin Cities, MN

Missouri, University of–Columbia, MO

New Jersey Institute of Technology, NJ

Ohio University, OH

Pittsburgh, University of, PA

Rhode Island, University of, RI

SUNY–Albany, NY

SUNY–Binghamton University, NY

SUNY–Buffalo, NY

SUNY–Geneseo, NY

SUNY–Purchase College, NY

SUNY–Stony Brook, NY

St. Mary's College, MD

Vermont, University of, VT

Virginia, University of, VA

Very Expensive—$$$$

Colorado School of Mines, CO

Connecticut, University of, CT

Delaware, University of, DE

Massachusetts, University of–Amherst, MA

Michigan, University of, MI

Michigan State University, MI

Minnesota, University of–Morris, MN

New Hampshire, University of, NH

New Jersey, The College of, NJ

New Jersey Institute of Technology, NJ

Pennsylvania State University, PA

Pittsburgh, University of, PA

Rutgers University, NJ

Texas Tech University, TX

St. Mary's College of Maryland, MD

Vermont, University of, VT

William and Mary, College of, VA

PRIVATE COLLEGES AND UNIVERSITIES

Inexpensive—$

Agnes Scott College, GA
Albertson College, ID
Alma College, MI
Alverno College, WI
Austin College, TX
Baylor University, TX
Birmingham-Southern College, AL
Brigham Young University, UT
Calvin College, MI
Centre College, KY
Cooper Union, NY
Dallas, University of, TX
Dayton, University of, OH
Deep Springs College, CA
DePaul University, IL
Florida Institute of Technology, FL
Gordon College, MA
Guilford College, NC
Hampden-Sydney College, VA
Hendrix College, AR
Hollins University, VA
Hope College, MI
Houghton College, NY
Howard University, DC
Loyola University New Orleans, LA
Marquette University, WI
Millsaps College, MS
Morehouse College (Atlanta
   University Center), GA
Presbyterian College, SC
Prescott College, AZ
Principia College, IL
Randolph-Macon Woman's College,
   VA
Rice University, TX
St. John's University, and St.
   Benedict, College of, MN
Spelman College (Atlanta
   University Center), GA
Sweet Briar College, VA
Texas Christian University, TX
Trinity University, TX
Tulsa, University of, OK
Wells College, NY
Wheaton College, IL
Xavier University of Louisiana, LA

Moderate—$$

Albion College, MI
Alfred University, NY
Antioch College, OH
Atlantic, College of the, ME
California Institute of Technology,
   CA
Case Western Reserve University,
   OH
Catholic University of America,
   The, DC
Cornell College, IA
Denver, University of, CO
DePauw University, IN
Drexel University, PA
Eckerd College, FL
Fordham University, NY
Furman University, SC
Grinnell College, IA
Gustavus Adolphus College, MN
Hiram College, OH
Hood College, MD
Illinois Institute of Technology, IL
Illinois Wesleyan University, IL
Ithaca College, NY
Kalamazoo College, MI
Knox College, IL
Manhattanville College, NY
Marlboro College, VT
Mills College, CA
Northeastern University, MA
Oglethorpe University, GA
Pacific, University of the, CA
Redlands, University of, CA
Rhodes College, TN
Richmond, University of, VA
Ripon College, WI
Rochester Institute of Technology,
   NY
Rose-Hulman Institute of
   Technology, IN
St. Olaf College, MN
Saint Louis University, MO
San Francisco, University of, CA
Santa Clara University, CA
South, University of the (Sewanee),
   TN

Southern Methodist University, TX
Southwestern University, TX
Stetson University, FL
Susquehanna University, PA
Syracuse University, NY
Wabash College, IN
Washington and Jefferson College,
   PA
Washington and Lee University, VA
Wofford College, SC

Expensive—$$$

Allegheny College, PA
American University, DC
Babson College, MA
Barnard College (Columbia
   University), NY
Bates College, ME
Bennington College, VT
Beloit College, WI
Boston College, MA
Bucknell University, PA
Carnegie Mellon University, PA
Claremont McKenna College
   (Claremont Colleges), CA
Clark University, MA
Clarkson University, NY
Colorado College, CO
Cornell University, NY
Davidson College, NC
Denison University, OH
Earlham College, IN
Fairfield University, CT
Goucher College, MD
Harvey Mudd College (Claremont
   Colleges), CA
Holy Cross, College of the, MA
Lafayette College, PA
Lake Forest College, IL
Lawrence University, WI
Lewis and Clark College, OR
Macalester College, MN
Miami, University of, FL
Muhlenberg College, PA
New School University–Eugene
   Lang College, NY
Notre Dame, University of, IN

Occidental College, CA
Ohio Wesleyan University, OH
Puget Sound, University of, WA
Rhode Island School of Design, RI
Rochester, University of, NY
Rollins College, FL
St. John's College, NM
Scripps College (Claremont Colleges), CA
Smith College, MA
Southern California, University of, CA
Stevens Institute of Technology, NJ
Ursinus College, PA
Villanova University, PA
Wake Forest University, NC
Whitman College, WA
Whittier College, CA
Willamette University, OR
Wittenberg University, OH
Wooster, The College of, OH
Worcester Polytechnic Institute, MA

Very Expensive—$$$$
Amherst College, MA
Bard College, NY
Boston University, MA
Bowdoin College, ME
Brandeis University, MA
Brown University, RI
Bryn Mawr College, PA

Carleton College, MN
Chicago, University of, IL
Colby College, ME
Colgate University, NY
Columbia College (Columbia University), NY
Connecticut College, CT
Dartmouth College, NH
Dickinson College, PA
Drew University, NJ
Duke University, NC
Emory University, GA
Franklin and Marshall College, PA
George Washington University, DC
Georgetown University, DC
Gettysburg College, PA
Hamilton College, NY
Hampshire College, MA
Hartwick College, NY
Harvard University, MA
Haverford College, PA
Hobart and William Smith Colleges, NY
Johns Hopkins University, The, MD
Kenyon College, OH
Lehigh University, PA
Massachusetts Institute of Technology, MA
Middlebury College, VT
Mount Holyoke College, MA
New York University, NY

Northwestern University, IL
Oberlin College, OH
Pennsylvania, University of, PA
Pepperdine University, CA
Pitzer College (Claremont Colleges), CA
Pomona College (Claremont Colleges), CA
Princeton University, NJ
Reed College, OR
Rensselaer Polytechnic Institute, NY
St. John's College, MD
St. Lawrence University, NY
Sarah Lawrence College, NY
Skidmore College, NY
Stanford University, CA
Swarthmore College, PA
Trinity College, CT
Tufts University, MA
Tulane University, LA
Union College, NY
Vanderbilt University, TN
Vassar College, NY
Washington University in St. Louis, MO
Wellesley College, MA
Wesleyan University, CT
Wheaton College, MA
Williams College, MA
Yale University, CT

The Best Buys of 2002

Following is a list of 40 colleges and universities that qualify as Best Buys based on the quality of the academic offerings in relation to the cost of attendance.

Public

University of Colorado–Boulder
The Evergreen State College
Georgia Institute of Technology
University of Illinois–Urbana-Champaign
University of Iowa
University of Kansas
Mary Washington College
Miami University (OH)
University of Minnesota–Twin Cities
New College of the University of South Florida
University of North Carolina–Asheville
University of North Carolina–Chapel Hill
University of Oregon
St. Mary's College of Maryland
SUNY–Binghamton University
SUNY–Geneseo
University of Texas–Austin
University of Virginia
University of Washington
College of William and Mary
University of Wisconsin–Madison

Private

Baylor University
Beloit College
Birmingham-Southern College
Brigham Young University
Calvin College
Centre College
Cooper Union
Deep Springs College
Gustavus Adolphus College
Hendrix College
Millsaps College
Morehouse College
Presbyterian College
Rice University
University of Richmond
St. John's University and College of St. Benedict
Spelman College
University of the South (Sewanee)
Stetson University
Trinity University (TX)
Washington and Jefferson College
Wofford College

Introduction

THE FISKE GUIDE TO COLLEGES—AND HOW TO USE IT

The 2002 edition of *The Fiske Guide to Colleges* is a revised and updated version of a book that has been a best-seller since it first appeared two decades ago, and is universally regarded as the definitive college guide of its type. Features of the new edition include:

- Updated write-ups on more than 300 of the country's "best and most interesting" colleges and universities
- A section entitled "Sizing Yourself Up," with a questionnaire that will help you figure out the kind of school that is best for you
- A Guide for Preprofessionals that lists colleges and universities strong in nine preprofessional areas
- A list of schools with strong programs for students with learning disabilities
- Designation of the 43 schools that constitute this year's Best Buys
- Statistical summaries that give you the numbers you need, but spare you those that you do not
- Authoritative rankings of each institution by academics, social life, and quality of life
- The unique "If You Apply…" feature, which summarizes the vital information that you need about each college's admission policies including deadlines and essay topics
- A section on the top Canadian universities in response to the fact that a growing number of students and families in the United States have become aware of the educational bargains that are lurking just across the border to the north. These Canadian universities offer first-rate academics—easily the equivalent of the flagship public institutions in the U.S.—and they do so at a fraction of the cost.

Picking the right college—one that will coincide with your particular needs, goals, interests, talents, and personality—is one of the most important decisions that any young person will ever make. It is also a major investment. One year of college now costs at least $8,000 at a typical public university and $21,000 at a typical private college, and the tab at the most selective and expensive schools tops $30,000. Obviously, a major investment like that should be approached with as much information as possible.

That's where *The Fiske Guide to Colleges* fits in. It is a tool to help you make the most intelligent educational investment you can.

WHAT IS *THE FISKE GUIDE TO COLLEGES*?

The Fiske Guide to Colleges mirrors a process familiar to any college-bound student and his or her family. If you are wondering whether to consider a particular college, it is logical to seek out friends or acquaintances who go there and ask them to tell you about their experiences. We have done exactly that—but on a far broader and more systematic basis than any individual or family could do alone.

In using *The Fiske Guide*, some special features should be kept in mind:

- The guide is *selective*. We have not tried to cover all four-year colleges and universities. Rather, we have taken over 300 of the best and most interesting institutions in the nation—the ones that students most want to know about—and written descriptive essays of 1,000 to 2,500 words about them.
- Since choosing a college is a matter of making a calculated and informed judgment, this guide is also *subjective*. It makes judgments about the strengths and weaknesses of each institution, and it contains a unique set of ratings of each college or university on the basis of academic strength, social life, and overall quality of life. No institution is right for every student. The assumption underlying *The Fiske Guide* is that each of the colleges chosen for inclusion is the right place for some students. Like finding the right husband or wife, college admissions is a matching process. You know your own interests and needs; *The Fiske Guide* will tell you something about those that each college seems to serve best.
- Finally, *The Fiske Guide* is *systematic*. Each write-up is carefully constructed to cover specific topics, from the academic climate and the makeup of the student body to the social scene, in a systematic order.

This means that you can easily take a specific topic, such as the level of academic pressure or the role of fraternities and sororities on campus, and trace it through all of the colleges that interest you.

HOW THE COLLEGES WERE SELECTED

How do you single out "the best and most interesting" of the more than 2,000 four-year colleges in the United States? Obviously, there are many fine institutions that are not included. Space limitations simply required that some hard decisions be made.

The selection was done with several broad principles in mind, beginning with academic quality. Depending on how you define the term, there are about 175 "selective" colleges and universities in the nation, and by and large these constitute the best institutions academically. All of these are included in *The Fiske Guide*. In addition, an effort was made to achieve geographical diversity and a balance of public and private schools. Special efforts were made to include a good selection of three types of institutions that seem to be enjoying special popularity at present: engineering and technical schools, those with a religious emphasis, and those located along the Sunbelt, where the cost of education is considerably less than at their Northern counterparts. This current edition also includes several colleges that in recent years have significantly increased their academic quality and appeal to students.

Finally, in a few cases we exercised the journalist's prerogative of writing about schools that are simply interesting. The tiny College of the Atlantic, for example, would hardly qualify on the basis of superior academic program or national significance, but it offers an unusual and fascinating brand of liberal arts within the context of environmental studies. Likewise, Deep Springs College, the only two-year school in the *Guide*, is a unique institution of intrinsic interest.

HOW *THE FISKE GUIDE* WAS COMPILED

Each college or university selected for inclusion in *The Fiske Guide to Colleges* was sent a packet of questionnaires. The first was directed to the administration, and covered topics ranging from their perception of the institution's mission to the demographics of the student body. Administrators were also asked to distribute a set of questionnaires to a cross-section of students.

The questions for students, all open-ended and requiring short essays as responses, covered a series of topics ranging from the accessibility of professors and the quality of housing and dining facilities, to the type of nightlife and weekend entertainment available in the area. By and large, students responded enthusiastically to the challenge we offered them. The quality of the information in the write-ups is a tribute to their diligence and openness. American college students, we learned, are a candid lot. They are proud of their institutions—but also critical in the positive sense of the word.

Other sources of information were also employed. Administrators were invited to attach to their questionnaires any catalogs, in-house research, or other documents that would contribute to an understanding of the institution and to comment on their write-up in the last edition. Also, staff members visited many of the colleges, and in some cases additional information was solicited through published materials, telephone interviews, and other contacts with students and administrators.

The information from these various questionnaires was then collated by a staff of journalists and freelance writers and edited by Edward B. Fiske, former Education Editor of *The New York Times*.

THE FORMAT

Each essay covers certain broad subjects in roughly the same order. They are as follows:

Academics	**Housing**
Campus setting	**Food**
Student body	**Social life**
Financial aid	**Extracurricular activities**

Certain subtopics are covered in all of the essays. The sections on academics, for example, always discuss the departments (or, in the case of large universities, schools) that are particularly strong or weak, while the sections on housing contain information on whether the dorms are coed or single-sex and how students get the rooms they want. Other topics, however, such as class size, the need for a car, or the number of volumes in the library, are mentioned only if they constitute a particular strength or weakness at that institution.

The drinking age is 21 in most states, and we paid particular attention to what effect that has on campus life. Also, we noted efforts some schools' administrations have been making to change or improve the social and residential life on campuses by such measures as banning fraternities and constructing new athletic facilities.

BEST BUYS

One of the lesser-known facts of life about higher education in the U.S. is that price and quality do not always go hand in hand. The college or university with the jumbo price tag may or may not offer a better education than the institution across town with much lower tuition. The relationship between the cost paid by the consumer and the quality of the education is affected by factors ranging from the size of an institution's endowment to judgments by college officials about what the market will bear.

In the face of today's skyrocketing tuition rates, students and families in all economic circumstances are looking for ways to get the best value for their education dollar. Fortunately, there are some bargains to be found in higher education; it just takes a bit of shopping around, with a little guidance along the way.

Since its inception more than a decade ago, *The Fiske Guide* has featured an Index by Price that groups public and private institutions into four price categories, from inexpensive to very expensive. Now we have gone one step further: we have combined the cost data with academic and other information about each college and university, and have come up with 43 institutions—21 public and 22 private—that offer remarkable educational opportunities at a relatively modest cost. We are calling them Best Buys, and they are indicated by a Best Buy graphic next to the college name. (A list of the 2002 Best Buys appears on page xiv.)

All of our Best Buys fall into the inexpensive or moderate price category, and most have four- or five-star academic ratings. But there are bargains to be found among all levels and types of institutions. For example, some of the best values in American higher education are public colleges and universities that have remained relatively small, and offer the smaller classes and personalized approach to academics that are typically found only in expensive private liberal arts colleges. Half a dozen of these are included as Best Buys.

STATISTICS

At the beginning of each write-up are basic statistics about the college or university—the ones that are relevant to applicants. These include the address, type of location (urban, small town, rural, etc.), enrollment, male/female ratio, SAT or ACT score ranges of the middle 50 percent of the students, percentage of students receiving need-based financial aid, relative cost, whether or not the institution has a chapter of Phi Beta Kappa, the number of students who apply and the percentage of those who are accepted, the percentage of accepted students who enroll, the number of freshmen who graduate within six years, and the number of freshmen who return for their sophomore year. For convenience, we include the telephone number of the admissions office and the school's website and mailing address.

Unlike some guides, we have intentionally not published figures on the student/faculty ratio because colleges use different—and often self-serving—methods to calculate the ratio, thus making it virtually meaningless.

A word about several of these items:

> You will sometimes encounter the letters "N/A." In most cases this means that the statistic was "not available." In other cases, however, such as schools that do not require standardized tests, it means "not applicable." The write-up should make it clear which meaning is the relevant one.

> We have included information on whether the school has a chapter of Phi Beta Kappa because this academic honorary society is a sign of broad intellectual distinction. Keep in mind, though, that even the very best engineering schools, because of their relatively narrow focus, do not usually qualify under the society's standards.

> Tuition and fees are constantly increasing at American colleges, but for the most part, the cost of various institutions in relation to one another does not change. Rather than put in specific cost figures that would immediately become out of date, we have classified colleges into four groups ranging from inexpensive ($) to very expensive ($$$$) based on estimated costs of tuition and fees for the 1999–2000 academic year. Separate scales were used for public and private institutions, and the ratings for the public institutions are based on cost for residents of the state; out-of-staters should expect to pay more. If a public institution has a particularly low or high surcharge for out-of-staters, this is noted in the essay. The categories are defined as follows:

	PUBLIC	PRIVATE
$$$$	More than $5,000	More than $23,000
$$$	$4,000–$5,000	$20,000–$23,000
$$	$3,000–$4,000	$17,000–$20,000
$	Less than $3,000	Less than $17,000

We also include an index that groups colleges by their relative cost (see pp. xi–xiii).

SAT and ACT SCORES

A special word needs to be said about SAT and ACT scores. Some publications follow the practice of giving the median or average score registered by entering freshmen. Such figures, however, are easily misinterpreted as thresholds rather than averages. Many applicants forget that if a school reports average SAT-Verbal scores of 500, this means that, by definition, about half of the students scored below this number and half scored above. An applicant with a 480 would still have lots of company.

To avoid such confusion, we report the range of scores of the middle half of freshmen—or, to put it another way, the scores achieved by those in the 25th and 75th percentiles. For example, that college where the SAT-Verbal average was 500 might have a range of 440 to 560. So if you scored within this range, you would have joined the middle 50 percent of last year's freshmen. If your score was above 560, you would have been in the top quarter and could probably look forward to a relatively easy time; if it was below 440, you would have been struggling along with the bottom quarter of students.

The reporting of ranges rather than a single average is an increasingly common practice, but some colleges do not calculate ranges. These are indicated by "N/A." Keep in mind, as well, that score ranges (and averages, for that matter) are misleading at colleges such as Bates, Bowdoin, and Union, which do not require test scores from all applicants. These are indicated by "N/R."

Unfortunately, another problem that arises with SAT and ACT scores is that, in their zeal to make themselves look good in a competitive market, some colleges and universities have been known to be less than honest in the numbers they release. They inflate their scores by not counting certain categories of students at the low end of the scale, such as athletes, certain types of transfer students, or students admitted under affirmative action programs. Some colleges have gone to such extremes as reporting the relatively high math scores of foreign students but not their relatively low verbal scores. Aside from the sheer dishonesty of such practices, they can also be misleading. A student whose own scores are below the 25th percentile of a particular institution needs to know whether his profile matches that of the lower quarter of the student body as a whole or whether there is an unreported pool of students with lower scores.

Even when dealing with a range rather than a single score, keep in mind that standardized tests are an imprecise measure of academic ability, and comparisons of scores that differ by less than 50 or 60 points on a scale of 200 to 800 have little meaning. According to the laws of statistics, there is a chance of only one out of three that the SAT score you receive is within about 30 points—either higher or lower—of your "real score," or the average score that you would receive if you took the test an infinite number of times. On the other hand, median scores offer some indication of your chances to get into a particular institution and the intellectual level of the company you will be keeping—or, if you prefer, competing against. Remember, too, that the most competitive schools have the largest and most sophisticated admissions staffs, and are well aware of the limitations of standardized tests. A strong high school average or achievement in a field such as music will usually counteract the negative effects of modest SAT or ACT scores.

SCHOLARSHIP INFORMATION

Since the first edition of *The Fiske Guide to Colleges* appeared, the problems of financing college have become increasingly critical, mainly because of the rising cost of education and a shift from grants to loans as the basis for financial aid packages.

In response to these developments, many colleges and universities have begun to devise their own plans to help students pay for college. These range from subsidized loan programs to merit scholarships that are awarded without reference to financial need. Most of these programs are aimed at retaining the middle class.

We ask each college and university to tell us what steps it has taken to help students pay their way, and their responses are incorporated in the write-ups. Also indicated is whether a candidate's inability to pay the full tuition, room, and board charges is a factor in admissions decisions. Some colleges advertise that they are "need-blind" in their admissions—meaning that they accept or reject applicants without reference to their financial situation, and then guarantee to meet the "demonstrated need" of all students whom they accept. Others say they are need-blind in their admissions decisions but do not guarantee to provide the financial aid required of all those who are accepted. Still others agree to meet the demonstrated need of all students, but they package their offers so that students whom they really want receive a higher percentage of their aid in the form of outright grants than in repayable loans.

"Demonstrated need" is itself a slippery term. In theory, the figure is determined when students and families fill out a needs-analysis form, which leads to an estimate of how much the family can afford to pay. Demonstrated need is then calculated by subtracting that figure from the cost at a particular institution. In practice, however, various colleges make their own adjustments to the standard figure.

Students and parents should not assume that because their family has even a six-figure income they are automatically disqualified from some kind of subsidized financial aid. In cases of doubt, they should fill out a needs-analysis form to determine their eligibility. Whether they qualify or not, they are also eligible for a variety of awards made without regard to financial need.

Inasmuch as need-based awards are universal at the colleges in this guide, the awards generally singled out for special mention in the write-ups in *The Fiske Guide to Colleges* are the merit scholarships. We have not mentioned awards of a purely local nature—restricted to residents of a particular county, for example—but all college applicants should search out these awards through their guidance offices and the bulletins of the colleges that are of interest to them. Similarly, we have not duplicated the information on federally guaranteed loan programs that is readily available through both high school and college counseling offices, but we cite novel and often less expensive variants of the federal loan programs that are offered by individual colleges.

RATINGS

Much of the controversy that greeted the first edition of *The Fiske Guide to Colleges* revolved around its unique system of rating colleges in three areas: academics, social life, and quality of life. In each case, the ratings are done on a system of one to five, with three considered normal for colleges included in *The Fiske Guide*. If a college receives a rating higher or lower than three in any category, the reasons should be apparent from the narrative description of that college.

Students and parents should keep in mind that these ratings are obviously general in nature and inherently subjective. No complex institution can be described in terms of a single number or other symbol, and different people will have different views on how various institutions should be rated in the three categories. They should not be viewed as either precise or infallible judgments about any given college. On the other hand, the ratings are a helpful tool in using this book. The core of *The Fiske Guide* is the essays on each of the colleges, and the ratings represent a summary—an index, if you will—of these write-ups. Our hope is that each student, having decided on the kind of configuration that suits his or her needs, will then thumb through the book looking for other institutions with a similar set of ratings.

The categories are defined as follows:

Academics

This is a judgment about the overall academic climate of the institution, including its reputation in the academic world, the quality of the faculty, the level of teaching and research, the academic ability of students, the quality of libraries and other facilities, and the level of academic seriousness among students and faculty members.

Although the same basic criteria have been applied to all institutions, it should be evident that an outstanding small liberal arts college will by definition differ significantly from an outstanding major public university. No one would expect the former to have massive library facilities, but one would look for a high-quality faculty that combines research with a good deal of attention to the individual needs of students. Likewise, public universities, because of their implicit commitment to serving a broad cross-section of society, might have a broader range of curriculum offerings but somewhat lower average SAT scores than a large private counterpart. Readers may find the ratings most useful when comparing colleges and universities of the same type.

In general, an academics rating of three stars suggests that the institution is a solid one that easily meets the criteria for inclusion in a guide devoted to the top 10 percent of colleges and universities in the nation.

An academics rating of four stars suggests that the institution is above average even by these standards, and that it has some particularly distinguishing academic feature, such as especially rich course offerings or an especially serious academic atmosphere.

A rating of five stars for academics indicates that the college or university is among the handful of top institutions of its type in the nation on a broad variety of criteria. Those in the private sector will normally attract students with combined SAT scores of at least 1300, and those in the public sector are invariably magnets for the top students in their states. All can be assumed to have outstanding faculties and other academic resources.

Social Life

This is primarily a judgment about the amount of social life that is readily available. A rating of three telephones suggests a typical college social life, while four telephones means that students have a better-than-average time socially. It can be assumed that a college with a rating of five is something of a party school, which may or may not detract from the academic quality. Colleges with a rating below three have some impediment to a strong social life, such as geographic isolation, a high percentage of commuting students, or a disproportionate number of nerds who never leave the library. Once again, the reason should be evident from the write-up.

Quality of Life

This category grew out of the fact that schools with good academic credentials and plenty of social life may not, for one reason or another, be particularly wholesome places to spend four years. The term "quality of life" is one that has been gaining currency in social science circles, and in most cases the rating for a particular college will be similar to the academic and/or social ratings. The reader, though, should be alert to exceptions to this pattern. A liberal arts college, for example, might attract bright students who study hard during the week and party hard on weekends, and thus earn high ratings for academics and social life. If the academic pressure is cutthroat rather than constructive, though, and the social system manipulative of women, this college might get an apparently anomalous two bullets on quality of life. By contrast, a small college with modest academic programs and relatively few organized social opportunities might have developed a strong sense of supportive community, have a beautiful campus, and be located near a wonderful city—and thus be rated four bullets for quality of life. As in the other categories, the reason can be found in the essay to which the ratings point.

IF YOU APPLY...

An extremely helpful feature is the "If You Apply..." section at the end of each write-up. This is designed for students who become seriously interested in a particular college and want to know more specifics about what it takes to get in.

This section begins with the deadlines for early admissions or early decision (if the college has such a program), regular admissions, and financial aid. If the college operates on a rolling admissions basis—making decisions as the applications are received—this is indicated.

"If You Apply..." gives a snapshot of the institution's financial aid policies. It indicates whether the college or university guarantees to meet the demonstrated need (see above) of applicants and, if so, the percentage of students whose financial need is actually met. The phrase "guarantees to meet demonstrated need" means that the institution for all practical purposes makes every effort possible to come up with the aid for which all of its students qualify.

Colleges have widely varying policies regarding interviews, both on campus and with alumni, so we indicate whether each of these is required, recommended, or optional. We also indicate whether reports from the person doing the interview are used in evaluating students or whether, as in many cases, the interview is seen only as a means of conveying information about the institution and answering applicants' questions.

This section also tells what standardized tests—SAT, ACT, or achievement—are required, and whether applicants are asked to write one or more essays. In the latter case, the topics are given.

The admissions policies of most colleges are fairly similar, at least among competing clusters of institutions. In some cases, however, a school will have its own special priorities. Some don't care that much about test scores. Others are looking for students with special talent in math or science, while others pay special attention to personal characteristics such as leadership in extracurricular activities. We asked each institution to tell us if its admission policies are in any ways "unique or unusual," and their answers are reported.

Finally, "If You Apply..." lists the institution's biggest "overlaps"—that is, the colleges and universities to which its applicants are also applying in greatest numbers and which thus represent its major competitors. Keep in mind that overlapping does not necessarily work both ways. College A might list College B as an overlap, but College B's biggest competitors might be Colleges X, Y, and Z. This is especially true in the case of institutions that are considered "safety" schools by students who also apply to more selective colleges and universities.

CONSORTIA

Many colleges expand the range of their offerings by banding together with other institutions to offer unusual programs that they could not support on their own. These options range from foreign-study programs around the world to semesters at sea, and keeping such arrangements in mind is a way of expanding the list of institutions that might meet your particular interests and needs. The final section of *The Fiske Guide* describes 15 of these consortia and lists the member institutions.

Students will find *The Fiske Guide* useful at various points in the college-selection process—from deciding whether to visit a particular campus to selecting among institutions that have accepted them. To make it easy to find a particular college, the write-ups are arranged in alphabetical order in the index. Indexes by state and price can be found on pages vii–ix and xi–xiii, respectively.

While most people are not likely to start reading at Agnes Scott and keep going until they reach Yale (though some tell us they do), we encourage you to browse. This country has an enormously rich and varied network of colleges and universities, and there are dozens of institutions out there that can meet the needs of any particular student. Too many students approach the college-selection process wearing blinders, limiting their sights to local institutions or the pet schools of their parents or guidance counselors, or to ones they know only by possibly outdated reputations.

But applicants need not be bound by such limitations. Once you have decided on the type of school you think you want—a small liberal arts college, an engineering school, or whatever—we hope you will thumb through the book looking for similar institutions that might not have occurred to you. One way to do this is to look at the "Overlaps" of schools you like and then check out those schools' overlaps. Many students have found this worthwhile, and quite frankly, we view the widening of students' horizons about American higher education as one of the most important purposes of the book. Perhaps the most gratifying remark we hear comes when the student tells us, as many have, that she is attending a school that she first heard about while browsing through *The Fiske Guide to Colleges*.

Picking a college is a tricky business. But given the current buyer's market, there is no reason why you should not be able to find the right college. That's what *The Fiske Guide to Colleges* is designed to help you do. Happy college hunting.

Sizing Yourself Up

The college search is a game of matchmaking. You have interests and needs; the colleges have programs to meet those needs. If all goes according to plan, you'll find the right one and live happily ever after—or at least for four years. It ought to be simple, but today's admissions process resembles a high-stakes obstacle course.

Many colleges are more interested in making a sale than they are in making a match. Under intense competitive pressure, many won't hesitate to sell you a bill of goods if they can get their hands on your tuition dollars. Guidance counselors generally mean well, but they are often under duress from principals and trustees to steer students toward prestigious schools regardless of whether the fit is right. Your friends won't be shy with advice on where to go, but their knowledge is generally limited to a small group of hot colleges that everyone is talking about. National publications rake in millions by playing on the public's fascination with rankings, but a close look at their criteria reveals distinctions without a difference.

Before you find yourself spinning headlong on this merry-go-round, take a step back. This is your life and your college career. What are you looking for in a college? Think hard, and don't answer right away. Before you throw yourself and your life history on the mercy of college admissions officers, you need to take some time to objectively and honestly evaluate your needs, likes and dislikes, strengths and weaknesses. What do you have to offer a college? What can a college do for you? Unlike the high school selection process, which is usually predetermined by your parents' property lines, income level, or religious affiliation, picking a college isn't a procedure you can brush off on dear ol' Mom and Dad. You have to take some initiative. You're the best judge of how well each school fits your personal needs and academic goals.

We encourage you to view the college selection process as the first semester in your higher education. Life's transitions often call forth extra energy and focus. The college search is no exception. For the first time, you'll be contemplating a life away from home that will unfold in any direction you choose. Visions of majors and careers will dance in your head as you sample various institutions of higher learning, each with hundreds of millions of dollars in academic resources; it is hard to imagine a better hands-on seminar in research and matchmaking than the college search. The main impact, however, will be measured by what you learn about yourself. Piqued by new worlds of learning and tested by the competition of the admissions process, you'll be pushed as never before to show your accomplishments, clarify your interests, and chart a course for the future. More than one parent has watched in amazement as an erstwhile teenager suddenly emerged as an adult during the course of a college tour. Be ready when your time comes.

DEVELOP YOUR CRITERIA

One strategy is to begin the search with a personal inventory of your own strengths and weaknesses and your "wish list" for a college. This method tends to work well for compulsive list makers and other highly organized people. What sorts of things are you especially good at? Do you have a list of skills or interests that you would like to explore further? What sort of personality are you looking for in a college? Mainstream? Conservative? Off-beat? What about extracurriculars? If you are really into riding horses, you might include a strong equestrian program in your criteria. The main problem won't be thinking of qualities to look for—you could probably name dozens—but rather figuring out what criteria should play a defining role in your search. Serious students should think carefully about the intellectual climate they are seeking. At some schools, students routinely stay up until 3:00 A.M. talking about topics like the value of deconstructing literary texts or the pros and cons of free trade. These same students would be viewed as geeks or weirdos on less cosmopolitan campuses. Athletes should take a hard look at whether they really want to play college ball, and if so, whether they want to go for an athletic scholarship or play at the less-pressured Division III level. Either way, intercollegiate sports require a huge time commitment.

Young women have an opportunity all to themselves—the chance to study at a women's college. *The Fiske Guide* profiles 14 such campuses, a vastly underappreciated resource on today's higher education scene. With small classes and strong encouragement from faculty, students at women's colleges move on to graduate study in significantly higher numbers than their counterparts at coed schools, especially in the natural sciences.

Males seeking an all-male experience will find two options in the *Guide*, Hampden-Sydney College and Wabash College.

Students with a firm career goal will want to look for a course of study that matches their needs. If you want to major in aerospace engineering, your search will be limited to schools that have the program. Outside of specialized areas like this, many applicants overestimate the importance of their anticipated major in choosing a college. If you're interested in a liberal arts field, your expected major should probably have little to do with your college selection. A big purpose of college is to develop interests and set goals. Most students change their intentions regarding a major at least two or three times before graduation, and once out in the working world, they often end up in jobs bearing no relation to their academic specialty. Even those with a firm career goal may not need as much specialization as they think at the undergraduate level. If you want to be a lawyer, don't worry yourself looking for something labeled prelaw. Follow your interests, get the best liberal arts education available, and then apply to law school.

Naturally, it is never a bad idea to check out the department(s) of any likely major, and occasionally your choice of major will suggest a direction for your search. If you're really into national politics, it may make sense to look at some schools in or near Washington, D.C. If you think you're interested in a relatively specialized field, say, oceanography, then be sure to look for some colleges that are a good match for you and also have programs in oceanography. But for the most part, rumors about top-ranked departments in this or that should be no more than a tie-breaker between schools you like for more important reasons. There are good professors (and bad ones) in any department. You'll have plenty of time to figure out who is who once you've enrolled. Being undecided about your career path as a senior in high school is often a sign of intelligence. Don't feel bad if you have absolutely no idea what you're going to do when you "grow up." One of the reasons you'll be paying megabucks to the college of your choice is the prospect that it will open some new doors for you and expand your horizons. Instead of worrying about particular departments, try to keep the focus on big-picture items like "What's the academic climate?" "How big are the freshman classes?" "Do I like it here?" and "Are these my kind of people?"

KEEP AN OPEN MIND

The biggest mistake of beginning applicants is hyper-choosiness. At the extreme is what we call the "perfect-school syndrome," which comes in two basic forms. In one category are the applicants who refuse to consider any school that doesn't have every little thing they want in a college. If you're one who begins the process with a detailed picture of Perfect U. in mind, you may want to remember the oft-quoted advice that "two out of three ain't bad." If a college seems to have most of the qualities you seek, give it a chance. You may come to realize that some things you thought were absolutely essential are really not that crucial after all. The other strain of perfect-school syndrome is the applicant who gets stuck on a "dream" school at the beginning and then won't look anywhere else. With those 2,200 four-year colleges out there (not counting those in Canada), it is just a bit silly to insist that only one will meet your needs. Having a first choice is okay, but the whole purpose of the search is to consider new options and uncover new possibilities. A student who has only one dream school—especially if it is a highly selective one—could be headed for disappointment.

As you begin the college search, don't expect any quick revelations. The answers will unfold in due time. Our advice? Be patient. Set priorities. Keep an open mind. Reexamine priorities. Be patient. To get the ball rolling, move on the Sizing-Yourself-Up Survey.

FISKE'S SIZING-YOURSELF-UP SURVEY

With apologies to Socrates, knowing thyself is easier said than done. Most high school students can analyze a differential equation or a Shakespearean play with the greatest of ease, but when it comes to cataloging their own strengths, weaknesses, likes, and dislikes, many draw a blank. But self-knowledge is crucial to the matching process at the heart of a successful college search. The 30-item survey below offers a simple way to get a handle on some crucial issues in college selection—and what sort of college may fit your preferences.

In the space beside each statement, rate your feelings on a scale of 1 to 10, with 10 = Strongly Agree, 1 = Strongly Disagree, and 5 = Not Sure/Don't Have Strong Feelings. (For instance, a rating of 7 would mean that you agree with the statement but that the issue is a lower priority than those you rated 8, 9, or 10.) After you're done, read on to Grading Yourself to find out what it all means.

_____ 1) I enjoy participating in many activities.

_____ 2) I would like to have a prominent place in my community.

_____ 3) Individual attention from teachers is important to me.

_____ 4) I learn best when I can speak out in class and ask questions.

_____ 5) I am undecided about what I will study.

_____ 6) I want to earn a Ph.D. in my chosen field of study.

_____ 7) I learn best by listening and writing what I hear.

_____ 8) I would like to be in a place where I can be anonymous if I choose.

_____ 9) I prefer devoting my time to one or two activities rather than many.

_____ 10) I want to attend a college that most people have heard of.

_____ 11) I am interested in a career-oriented major.

_____ 12) I like to be on my own.

_____ 13) I prefer a college in a warm or hot climate.

_____ 14) I prefer a college in a cool or cold climate.

_____ 15) I want to be near the mountains.

_____ 16) I want to be near a lake or ocean.

_____ 17) I prefer to attend a college in a particular state or region.

_____ 18) I prefer to attend a college near to my family.

_____ 19) I want city life within walking distance of my campus.

_____ 20) I want city life within driving distance of my campus.

_____ 21) I want my campus to be surrounded by natural beauty.

_____ 22) I like to be surrounded by people who are free-thinkers and nonconformists.

_____ 23) I like the idea of joining a fraternity or sorority.

_____ 24) I like rubbing shoulders with people who are bright and talented.

_____ 25) I like being one of the smartest people in my class.

_____ 26) I want to go to a prestigious college.

_____ 27) I want to go to a college where I can get an excellent education.

_____ 28) I want to try for an academic scholarship.

_____ 29) I want a college with as much diversity as possible.

_____ 30) I want a college where the students are serious about ideas.

Grading Yourself

Picking a college is not an exact science. People who are total opposites can be equally happy at the same college. Nevertheless, particular types tend to do better at some colleges than others. Each item in the survey is designed to test your feelings on an important issue related to college selection. Sizing Up the Survey (below) offers commentary on each item. Taken together, your responses may help you construct a tentative blueprint for your college search.

Statements 1–12 deal with the issue of size. Would you be happier at a large university or a small college? Here's the trick: Add the sum of your responses to questions 1–6. Then make a second tally of your responses to 7–12. If the sum of 1–6 is larger, you may want to consider a small college. If 7–12 is greater, then perhaps a big school would be more to your liking. If the totals are roughly equal, you should probably consider colleges of various sizes.

Statements 13–21 deal with location. The key in this section is the intensity of your feeling. If you replied to number 13 with a 10, does that mean you are going to look only at schools in warm climates? Think hard. If you consider only schools within a certain region or state, you'll be eliminating hundreds of possibilities. By examining your most intense responses—the 1s, 2s, 9s, and 10s—you'll be able to create a geographic profile of likely options.

Statements 23–30 deal with big-picture issues related to the character and personality of the college that may be in your future. As before, pay attention to your most intense responses. Read on for a look at the significance of each question.

Sizing Up the Survey

1) **I enjoy participating in many activities.** Students at small colleges tend to have more opportunity to be involved in many activities. Fewer students means less competition for spots.

2) **I would like to have a prominent place in my community.** Student Council Presidents and other would-be leaders take note: It is easier to be a big fish if you're swimming in a small pond.

3) **Individual attention from teachers is important to me.** Small colleges generally offer more one-on-one with faculty both in the classroom and the laboratory.

4) **I learn best when I can speak out in class and ask questions.** Students who learn from interaction and participation would be well-advised to consider a small college.

5) **I am undecided about what I will study.** Small colleges generally offer more guidance and support to students who are undecided. The exception: students who are considering a preprofessional or highly specialized major.

6) **I want to earn a Ph.D. in my chosen field of study.** A higher percentage of students at selective small colleges earn a Ph.D. than those who attend large institutions of similar quality.

7) **I learn best by listening and writing what I hear.** Students who prefer lecture courses will find more of them at large institutions.

8) **I would like to be in a place where I can be anonymous if I choose to be.** At a large university, the supply of new faces is never-ending. Students who have the initiative can always reinvent themselves.

9) **I prefer devoting my time to one or two activities rather than many.** Students who are passionate about one activity—say, writing for the college newspaper—will often find higher quality at a bigger school.

10) **I want to attend a college that most people have heard of.** Big schools have more name recognition because they're bigger and have Division I athletic programs. Even the finest small colleges are relatively anonymous among the general public.

11) **I am interested in a career-oriented major.** More large institutions offer business, engineering, nursing, etc., though some excellent small institutions do so as well (depending on the field).

12) **I like to be on my own.** A higher percentage of students live off campus at large schools, which are more likely to be in urban areas than their smaller counterparts.

13) **I prefer a college in a warm or hot climate.** Keep in mind that the Southeast and the Southwest have far different personalities (not to mention humidity levels).

14) **I prefer a college in a cool or cold climate.** Consider the Midwest, where there are many fine schools which are notably less selective than those in the Northeast.

15) **I want to be near the mountains.** You're probably thinking Colorado or Vermont, but don't zero in too quickly. States from Maine to Georgia and Arkansas to Arizona have easy access to mountains.

16) **I want to be near a lake or ocean.** Oceans are only on the coasts, but keep in mind the Great Lakes, the Finger Lakes, etc. Think about whether you want to be on the water or, say, within a two hour drive.

17) **I prefer to attend a college in a particular state or region.** Geographical blinders limit options. Even if you think you want a certain area of the country, consider at least one college located elsewhere just to be sure.

18) **I prefer to attend a college close to home.** Unless you're planning to live with Mom and Dad, it may not matter whether your college is a two-hour drive or a two-hour plane ride.

19) **I want city life within walking distance of my campus.** Be sure to check out the neighborhood(s) surrounding your campus. Urban campuses—even in the same city—can be wildly different.

20) **I want city life within driving distance of my campus.** Unless you're a hardcore urban-dweller, a suburban perch near a city may beat living in the thick of one. Does public transportation or a campus shuttle help students get around?

21) **I want my campus to be surrounded by natural beauty.** A college viewbook will take you only so far. To really know if you'll fall in love with the campus, visiting is a must.

22) **I like to be surrounded by free-thinkers and nonconformists.** Plenty of schools cater to students who buck the mainstream. Talk to your counselor or browse *The Fiske Guide* to find some.

23) **I like the idea of joining a fraternity or sorority.** Greek life is strongest at mainstream and conservative-leaning schools. Find out if there is a split between Greeks and non-Greeks.

24) **I like rubbing shoulders with people who are bright and talented.** This is perhaps the best reason to aim for a highly selective institution, especially if you're the type who rises to the level of the competition.

25) **I like being one of the smartest people in my class.** If so, maybe you should skip the highly selective rat race. Star students get the best that a college has to offer.

26) **I want to go to a prestigious college.** There is nothing wrong with wanting prestige. Think honestly about how badly you want a big name school and act accordingly.

27) **I want to go to a college where I can get an excellent education.** Throw out the *U.S. News* rankings and think about which colleges will best meet your needs as a student.

28) **I want to try for an academic scholarship.** Students in this category should consider less selective alternatives. Scholarships are more likely if you rank high in the applicant pool.

29) **I want a diverse college.** All colleges pay lip service to diversity. To get the truth, see the campus for yourself and take a hard look at the student body statistics in the *Guide*'s write-ups.

30) **I want a college where students are serious about ideas.** Don't assume that a college necessarily attracts true intellectuals merely because it is highly selective. Some top schools are known for their intellectual climate, and others for their lack of it.

Putting It All Together

We hope the survey will help you get started on a thorough self-assessment that will continue throughout the college search. After thinking about your priorities, the time is right to begin looking at the colleges. Hundreds of them await!

Use the state-by-state index to search geographically if you like; or simply browse to find those that interest you. When you find a likely candidate, look to the Overlaps at the end of the article to find additional possibilities.

A Guide for Preprofessionals

The lists that follow include colleges and universities with unusual strength in each of nine preprofessional areas: engineering, architecture, business, art/design, drama, music, dance, communications/journalism, and film/television. The lists are suggestive but by no means all-inclusive, and there are other institutions in *The Fiske Guide to Colleges* that offer fine programs in these areas. Nevertheless, we hope the lists will be a starting place for students interested in these fields. We also recommend that you shop for a school that will allow you to combine preprofessional training with an adequate dose of liberal arts. For that matter, you might consider a double major (or minor) in a liberal arts field to complement your area of technical expertise. If you allow yourself to get too specialized too soon, you may end up as tomorrow's equivalent of the typewriter repairman. In a rapidly changing job market, nothing is so practical as the ability to read, write, and think.

ARCHITECTURE

Private Universities Strong in Architecture
Carnegie Mellon University
Columbia University
Cooper Union
Cornell University
Howard University
Lehigh University
Massachusetts Institute of
   Technology
University of Notre Dame
Princeton University
Rensselaer Polytechnic Institute
Rice University
Tulane University
Washington University in St. Louis

Public Universities Strong in Architecture
University of California–Berkeley
University of Cincinnati
Georgia Institute of Technology
University of Illinois–Urbana-
   Champaign
University of Kansas
Miami University (OH)
University of Michigan
State University of New
   York–Buffalo
University of Oregon
Pennsylvania State University
University of Texas–Austin
Virginia Polytechnic Institute and
   State University
University of Washington

A Few Arts-Oriented Architecture Programs
Barnard College
Bennington College
Pratt Institute
Rhode Island School of Design
Wellesley College
Yale University

ART/DESIGN

Top Schools of Art and Design
Art Center College of Design
California Institute of the Arts
Cooper Union
Maryland Institute, College of Art
Massachusetts College of Art
Moore College of Art and Design
North Carolina School of the Arts
Otis Institute of Art and Design
Parsons School of Design
Pratt Institute
Rhode Island School of Design
School of the Art Institute of
   Chicago
School of Visual Arts

Major Universities Strong in Art and Design
Boston University
Carnegie Mellon University
University of Cincinnati
Cornell University
Harvard University
University of Michigan
New York University
University of Pennsylvania

University of Rochester
Washington University in St. Louis
University of Washington

Small Colleges and Universities Strong in Art and Design
Alfred University
Bard College
Brown University
Furman University
Hollins College
Kenyon College
Lake Forest College
Manhattanville College
State University of New
   York–Purchase
Randolph-Macon Woman's College
University of North
   Carolina–Greensboro
Scripps College
Skidmore College
Smith College
Williams College

BUSINESS

Private Universities Strong in Business
Carnegie Mellon University
Case Western Reserve University
Emory University
Georgetown University
Howard University
Massachusetts Institute of
   Technology
New York University
University of Notre Dame

University of Pennsylvania
Rensselaer Polytechnic Institute
University of Richmond
University of Southern California
Tulane University
Wake Forest University
Washington University in St. Louis

Public Universities Strong in Business

University of Arizona
University of California–Berkeley
University of Florida
University of Illinois–Urbana-
 Champaign
Indiana University
Miami University (OH)
University of Michigan
State University of New
 York–Albany
University of North
 Carolina–Chapel Hill
University of Vermont
University of Virginia
College of William and Mary
University of Washington

Small Colleges and Universities Strong in Business

Babson University
Bucknell University
Claremont McKenna College
DePauw University
Fairfield University
Franklin and Marshall College
Gettysburg College
Hendrix College
Lehigh University
Lewis and Clark College
Morehouse College
Ohio Wesleyan College
Skidmore College
Trinity University (TX)
Washington and Lee University

COMMUNICATIONS/ JOURNALISM

Major Universities Strong in Communications/Journalism

American University
Boston University

University of California–Los Angeles
University of Florida
University of Georgia
University of Illinois–Urbana-
 Champaign
Indiana University
University of Michigan
University of Missouri–Columbia
University of North
 Carolina–Chapel Hill
Northwestern University
Ohio University
University of Southern California
Stanford University
Syracuse University

ENGINEERING

Technical Institutes

California Institute of Technology
Colorado School of Mines
Cooper Union
Florida Institute of Technology
Georgia Institute of Technology
Harvey Mudd College
Illinois Institute of Technology
Massachusetts Institute of
 Technology
New Mexico Institute of Mining
 and Technology
Rensselaer Polytechnic Institute
Rochester Institute of Technology
Rose-Hulman Institute of
 Technology
Stevens Institute of Technology
Worcester Polytechnic Institute

Private Universities Strong in Engineering

Carnegie Mellon University
Case Western Reserve University
Columbia University
Cornell University
Duke University
The Johns Hopkins University
Northwestern University
University of Notre Dame
University of Pennsylvania
Princeton University
University of Southern California
Stanford University
Tufts University

Tulane University
Vanderbilt University
Washington University in St. Louis

Public Universities Strong in Engineering

University of California–Berkeley
University of California–Los
 Angeles
Clemson University
University of Illinois–Urbana-
 Champaign
Iowa State University
University of Michigan
Michigan State University
State University of New
 York–Buffalo
Pennsylvania State University
Purdue University
Rutgers—The State University of
 New Jersey
Texas A&M
University Virginia Polytechnic
 Institute and State University
University of Washington

Small Colleges and Universities Strong in Engineering

Brown University
Bucknell University
Calvin College
Clarkson University
Dartmouth College
Lafayette College
Lehigh University
University of the Pacific
University of Redlands
Rice University
Smith College
Swarthmore College
Trinity College (CT)
Tuskegee University
Union College

FILM/TELEVISION

Major Universities Strong in Film/Television

Arizona State University
Boston University
University of California–Los Angeles
University of Cincinnati

University of Florida
University of Kansas
University of Michigan
New York University
Northwestern University
Pennsylvania State University
University of Southern California
University of Texas–Austin

Small Colleges and Universities Strong in Film/Television

Bard College
Beloit College
Brown University
Evergreen State University
Hampshire College
Hofstra University
Ithaca College
State University of New York–Purchase
Occidental College
Pitzer College
Pomona College
Sarah Lawrence College

PERFORMING ARTS—MUSIC

Major Universities Strong in Music

Boston University
University of California–Los Angeles
Carnegie Mellon University
Case Western Reserve University
University of Cincinnati
University of Colorado–Boulder
Harvard University
Indiana University
Ithaca College
University of Miami (FL)
University of Michigan
University of Nebraska–Lincoln
New York University
Northwestern University
Rice University
University of Southern California
Vanderbilt University
Yale University

Small Colleges and Universities Strong in Music

Bard College

Bennington College
DePauw University
Illinois University
Lawrence University*
Manhattanville College
Mills College
Oberlin College*
St. Mary's College of Maryland
St. Olaf College
Sarah Lawrence College
Skidmore College
Smith College
Stetson University
Wesleyan University
Wheaton College (IL)
*Has a conservatory

PERFORMING ARTS—DRAMA

Major Universities Strong in Drama

Boston College
Boston University
University of California–Los Angeles
Carnegie Mellon University
The Catholic University of America
DePaul University
Fordham University
Indiana University
New York University
Northwestern University
University of North Carolina–Chapel Hill
University of Southern California
Southern Methodist University
Syracuse University
University of Washington
Yale University

Small Colleges and Universities Strong in Drama

Bennington College
Connecticut College
Ithaca College
Kenyon College
Lawrence University
Macalester College
State University of New York–Purchase
Princeton University

Rollins College
Sarah Lawrence College
Skidmore College
Vassar College
Whitman College

PERFORMING ARTS—DANCE

Major Universities Strong in Dance

Arizona State University
University of California–Irvine
University of California–Los Angeles
Case Western Reserve University
Florida State University
Indiana University
New York University
Ohio University
Southern Methodist University
University of Texas–Austin
University of Utah
Washington University in St. Louis

Small Colleges and Universities Strong in Dance

Amherst College
Barnard College
Bennington College
Connecticut College
Dartmouth College
Goucher College
Kenyon College
Princeton University
Sarah Lawrence College
Smith College
State University of New York–Purchase

ENVIRONMENTAL STUDIES

Allegheny College
College of the Atlantic
Bowdoin College
University of California–Davis
University of California–Santa Barbara
Colby College
University of Colorado–Boulder
Dartmouth College

Deep Springs College
The Evergreen State College
Middlebury College
University of New Hampshire
University of North
   Carolina–Greensboro
Oberlin College
Prescott College
St. Lawrence University
Tulane University
University of Vermont
University of Washington
University of Wisconsin–Madison

INTERNATIONAL STUDIES

American University
Austin College
Claremont McKenna College
Colby College
Connecticut College
Dartmouth College
Dickinson College
Georgetown University
George Washington University
Goucher College
Hiram College

The Johns Hopkins University
Kalamazoo College
Lewis and Clark College
Macalester College
University of
   Massachusetts–Amherst
Middlebury College
Occidental College
Princeton University
Reed College
St. Olaf College
Sweet Briar College
Tufts University
College of William and Mary

Learning Disabilities

Services for students with learning disabilities have proliferated in recent years. Following is a list of major universities and small colleges with strong support for such students.

Major Universities with Strong Support for Students with Learning Disabilities

American University
University of Arizona
University of California–Berkeley
Clark University
University of Colorado–Boulder
University of Denver
DePaul University
University of Georgia
Hofstra University
Purdue University
Rochester Institute of Technology
Syracuse University
University of Vermont
University of Virginia

Small Colleges with Strong Support for Students with Learning Disabilities

Bard College
Bradford College
Curry College
Landmark College
Loras College
Lynn University
Marist College
Mercyhurst College
Mitchell College
Muskingum College
University of New England
St. Thomas Acquinas College (NY)
Southern Vermont College
Westminister College (MO)
West Virginia Wesleyan College

THE FISKE GUIDE TO COLLEGES 2002

Agnes Scott College

141 East College Avenue, Atlanta/Decatur, GA 30030

Agnes Scott College, founded in 1889, continues to be the South's leading women's institution. An academically challenging liberal arts college across the board, Agnes Scott is highly acclaimed for its science and mathematics programs. Along with its commitment to higher education, the college is loved by its students for its caring atmosphere. One student claims, "Agnes Scott is special because of the attention it lavishes on its students." This outward expansion has brought about the development of new facilities, programs, and a tighter connection to the opportunities provided by the neighboring city of Atlanta.

The school, comprised of a combination of Gothic and Victorian architecture, is located on 100 acres of beautifully wooded Georgia landscape nestled in a historic district of Decatur. Donated rare shrubs, bushes, trees, and gardens decorating the campus, and one of the largest per-student endowments in the country are evidence of the school's strong alumni support. Renovations and new facilities include expansion and renovation of McCain Library, a new campus center, new building for the Campbell Science Hall, new parking structure, newly purchased apartment complex, newly purchased property for the Offices of Telecommunications and Facilities, renovated dining hall, and new Public Safety office.

The relationship between professors and students at Agnes Scott is a close one. "The teaching is amazing," claims one freshman. The professors are not just available in the classroom; professors have been known to invite students to their house for dinner. "All of my professors know who I am and they are always available to talk to," says a psychology major. A sophomore adds that the counselors are "great" and "always willing to help, or even just talk." Some of ASC's best departments include English, psychology, biology, history, and economics. The nationally acclaimed foreign language department has had five of its German majors named Fulbright scholars in the past six years. The fine and performing artists have their own modern facility, and the scientists have their own small observatory. Creative writers get the chance to rub elbows with real-life practitioners each spring, when the college sponsors a writers' festival. Would-be Heideggers can philosophize at ASC's own regional Undergraduate Philosophy Conference, or those more inclined to science can attend the Spring Annual Research Conference.

Agnes Scott is primarily a liberal arts college. First-year students are required to take two semesters of English composition and reading. In addition, everyone must take at least one course each in a variety of areas, including literature, math, historical studies and classical civilization, and fine arts. They must also complete a foreign language through the intermediate level and two semesters of physical education and science. ASC is affiliated with the Presbyterian Church, and one course in religion and philosophical thought is mandatory. There is also a new "social and cultural analysis" standard. The average class size is 15, and students are lavished with personal attention from the faculty. The downside of ASC's size is that some courses are taught only every other year, and scheduling conflicts are sometimes a problem.

The popular Return to College program enables women of any age to complete an interrupted degree in the same classes as traditional students, and the Atlanta Semester Program concerns the issues of women, leadership, and social

Website: www.agnesscott.edu
Location: Urban
Total Enrollment: 887
Undergraduates: 879
Male/Female: 0/100
SAT Ranges: V 580–680 M 530–640
ACT Range: 24–29
Financial Aid: 65%
Expense:
Phi Beta Kappa: Yes
Applicants: 688
Accepted: 77%
Enrolled: 45%
Grad in 6 Years: 70%
Returning Freshmen: 85%
Academics: ✍ ✍ ✍
Social: ☎ ☎
Q of L:
Admissions: (404) 471-6285 or (800) 868-8602
Email Address: admission@agnesscott.edu

Strongest Programs:
English
Psychology
Biology / Biochemistry
History
Economics

change. Those with an international bent can go abroad under the auspices of the Global Awareness Program, or the Global Connections Program, which gives students a semester of cross-cultural study before sending them out to all corners of the world. "The study abroad program is terrific," says a sophomore. Southerners who want a taste of the California lifestyle can spend a semester at all-female Mills College in Oakland, California, while engineers and architects may complete their degrees in a 3–2 program with Georgia Tech or in a 3–4 program with Washington University in St. Louis. The library has about 208,000 volumes, access online to digital library resources, and even a cozy spot on the main floor where students can curl up in front of a fireplace. As part of the Atlanta Regional Consortium for Higher Education, Agnes Scott shares facilities and resources with 19 other Atlanta-area schools through a cross-registration program.

The student body hails mainly from the Southeast, with 50 percent of them native Georgians. Most students share conservative upbringings but champion many liberal causes. Approximately 78 percent of them are from public high schools, and African Americans, Hispanics, and Asian Americans make up 27 percent of the student body. "The great thing about ASC is that there are no outcasts here. All these diverse people can peacefully coexist," confides a religious studies major. An honor system, which is strictly enforced by the Honor Court student judiciary, allows for self-scheduled exams and unmonitored tests, and is frequently cited as the cornerstone of the college. Agnes Scott awards merit scholarships ranging from $6,000 to a full ride based on academic performance, demonstrated leadership, or musical ability.

Linked by tree-lined brick walks, dorms at Agnes Scott are large and spacious. Students rate the housing as "unrivaled," and three older dorms, prized for their high ceilings and hardwood floors, still wear their original and impressive Victorian facades. Freshmen are assigned to places in two of six dorms which tend to be more "chummy," or a modern apartment complex. The students can grab a bite at the snack bar or dine in the newly expanded and renovated dining hall.

ASC women tend to spend their weekends "trying to meet guys" at monthly TGIFs (a euphemism for beer blasts). Every October, students invite the men of their choice to a formal dance known as Black Cat. The dance follows a weeklong festival of class competitions that marks the end of the new-student orientation period. Other quaint old traditions survive, such as throwing anyone recently engaged into the alumnae pond. Seniors who have been accepted into graduate schools or found jobs climb the stairs of the college's bell tower to ring the bell, sharing their good news. But for the most part, those looking for fun travel to Georgia Tech. The "Agnes Scott Convent" has no sororities, but with only 800 or so students, the college itself is a close-knit sisterhood. Alcohol policies are covered under the honor code, but some underage students still find a way to drink. "The policies and enforcement are not so strict that people can't get around them," a junior says.

By popular demand, the college initiated a shuttle and taxi service to Emory and other locations in the Atlanta area. The city's public transportation is also convenient to campus, and lures students to the symphony or art museum, as well as to haunts traditionally more popular with males. All in all, the bustling city of Atlanta is a "big plus" to this little college in Decatur. Varsity sports are improving with a step up from NAIA to NCAA Division III and the addition of cross-country, soccer, volleyball, softball, swimming, and basketball as intercollegiate sports. The tennis team is definitely a standout. Intramural activities are popular and include the standard roundup of sports, plus a few more exotic ones, such as studio dance.

Would-be Heideggers can philosophize at ASC's own regional Undergraduate Philosophy Conference, or those more inclined to science can attend the Spring Annual Research Conference.

The Agnes Scott experience comes complete with its small-town Southern heritage, interest in Georgia Tech football, love of Emory U beer, and of course, a desire to immerse yourself in friendship and learning. As one sophomore puts it, "We are self-confident, hard working, poised, well articulated, independent individuals." The women of Agnes Scott see themselves as the leaders of the twenty-first century."

Overlaps

University of Georgia, Emory, Spelman, Hollins, Randolph-Macon Woman's College.

If You Apply To ➤ Agnes Scott...Early decision: Nov. 15. Regular admissions and financial aid: Mar. 1. Campus interviews: recommended, evaluative. Alumni interviews: optional, informational. SATs or ACTs: required. SAT IIs: optional. Accepts the Common Application and electronic applications. Essay question: issues of concern; most significant event; or most significant cultural work; topic of choice.

University of Alabama

Box 870132, Tuscaloosa, AL 35487-0166

Tuscaloosa, Alabama, still boasts the historical novelties that have faded from many Southern cities: well-preserved antebellum homes, Dreamland barbecue, and world renowned blues music. But the University of Alabama is possibly its most famous landmark. And don't forget, 'Bama's powerful football team, the Crimson Tide. "When the Tide plays, the whole city stops to watch the game," one student claims. Although tradition reigns here, the university is hardly resistant to change. With the election of a pro-education governor and the ongoing administration of UA president Andrew Sorensen, the school has positioned itself to tackle the challenges of the 21st century.

'Bama's campus combines classical, revival-style buildings (several of which survived the 1865 burning of the university by Union troops) with modern facilities and technologically advanced classrooms. One of the most stunning in the South, the campus wraps around a shaded quadrangle. On the quad stand the main library and "Denny Chimes," a campanile carillon that rings the Westminster Chimes on the quarter hour.

The University of Alabama supports eight undergraduate colleges and schools. The Culverhouse College of Commerce and Business offers excellent programs in marketing, business administration, world business, and accounting. Mary Hewell Alston Hall, an imposing classroom-administrative building features state-of-the-art instructional technology for budding tycoons. The Bruno Business Library and Bashinsky Computer Center provide access to online databases and programs in architecturally elegant surroundings. The College of Communication and Information Sciences boasts one of the top ten journalism schools in the country. In addition, the College of Human Environmental Sciences offers several respected programs including food, nutrition, and hospitality management.

Alabama's Center for Materials for Information Technology is the only National Science Foundation Materials Research Science and Engineering Center in the South. The School of Music is a regional standout and has attracted guest artists like Jean Pierre Rampal, the Guarneri String Quartet, Stephen Hough, and

Website: www.ua.edu
Location: Small city
Total Enrollment: 18,744
Undergraduates: 14,645
Male/Female: 48/52
SAT Ranges: V 480–620 M 480–610
ACT Range: 20–26
Financial Aid: 64%
Expense: Pub $
Phi Beta Kappa: Yes
Applicants: 7,433
Accepted: 90%
Enrolled: 36%
Grad in 6 Years: 55%
Returning Freshmen: 80%
Academics: ✐ ✐ ✐
Social: ☎ ☎ ☎
Q of L: ★ ★ ★
Admissions: (205) 348-5666
Email Address: admissions@ua.edu

Strongest Programs:
   Accounting
   Communications
   Creative Writing

Alabama's Center for Materials for Information Technology is the only National Science Foundation Materials Research Science and Engineering Center in the South.

The College of Communication and Information Sciences boasts one of the top ten journalism schools in the country.

Midori. The library's online databases provide students with access to needed material and the ability to search for and retrieve information from a wide variety of sources. Strong programs include communications, engineering, creative writing, and music, while students say the math department needs improvement.

For those wishing to flex their academic muscle, the Alabama University Honors Program is open to academic award recipients and those who score at least 28 on the ACT or 1240 on the SAT. Honor students get small classes, better professors, and the chance to write a senior thesis. Additionally, 20 talented students of any major—although most are engineers—enroll in the Computer-Based Honors Program in which they are paid as research fellows to devise computer applications in their field of study. Students in the International Honors Program combine the study of languages and travel with their majors. The College of Arts and Sciences offers the Blount Undergraduate Initiative, a living-learning curriculum which includes a common residency for freshmen, a faculty director, and faculty fellows. Innovative courses have spilled over into 'Bama's Weekend College, a division of continuing education that has attracted a large undergraduate following, as has the popular interim term in May, when students may take one indepth course for credit. Students may also take correspondence courses for up to 24 percent of their work toward a bachelor's degree.

About 20 percent of Alabama freshmen take part in the College of Arts and Sciences' Mentoring Program, which pairs them with faculty mentors who help in the adjustment to college through informal counseling and enriching activities (concerts, movies, or lectures). Enrollment in the Academic Potential Seminar is open to all students, but was designed to meet the needs of freshmen in particular. The two-credit course covers self-assessment, motivation, personal responsibility, time management, memory, textbook reading, note-taking, and test preparation. However, the only course 'Bama requires students to take their first year on campus is a two-term English composition sequence. Before graduation, though, students must take courses in writing, natural sciences, math, humanities and social sciences, and either two semesters of a foreign language or one of computer science. UA's core curriculum has been streamlined, reducing the math requirement from six hours to three. Students say the academic climate can be competitive. "You have to work hard to stay ahead of the game," says a senior. Another student adds, "The classes here are challenging and the students do compete with each other as far as grades are concerned, but students are still willing to help each other out." Students characterize the professors as "qualified" and "capable." "I have fully enjoyed the teaching at the University of Alabama," says a civil engineering major. "The professors here are intelligent, accessible, and caring." Still, some complain about the huge size of lecture classes, which can hold several hundred students. For a publicly supported institution, 'Bama goes for scholarships in a big way. The success of the university's five-year capital campaign increased the number of academic scholarships and strengthened the endowments supporting hundreds more. Almost 500 scholarships are earmarked for athletes, and more than 4,200 for academic achievement, ranging from $300 to $14,216.

Seventy-eight percent of 'Bama's students are homegrown, but Alabama leads Southern flagship universities with 16 percent minorities in its student body. Hispanics and Asian Americans register at just 1 percent each, while African Americans make up 14 percent of the campus community. "Relations are quiet, but that is because the different racial and ethnic groups do not mix," notes an economics major. "The students value diversity so long as it doesn't affect them."

Most Alabama students live in apartments in the Tuscaloosa area and 70 percent make their homes in the dorms or on-campus Greek houses. 'Bama offers various living arrangements, from apartments to private rooms and suites. Students' opinions of the dorms vary. "The dorms are roomy and comfortable and many have just been renovated," says an advertising/public relations double major. Another student disagrees. "The dorms are fair but there's a lot of room for improvement." Six dorms have cafeterias, and the student union building also has dining facilities. The 21 percent of the women and 16 percent of the men who belong to the Greek system can live and dine in their own houses. Participation in the Greek system has been steady in recent years, and although fraternities and sororities are no longer allowed to have parties on campus, some say they still rule. The range of other campus organizations is impressive: everything from the Society for Creative Anachronism (medievalists) to Bible study groups to the sailing club. "The Strip," located a half-mile from the center of campus, is prime stomping ground for students who wish to go non-Greek for a night. UA also offers its students a free trolley service which connects the campus to the downtown restaurants and clubs. City Fest, featuring music, food, beer, and a German theme, is a popular annual event. Road trips to Mississippi, Louisiana (for Mardi Gras), Florida, and Atlanta are another diversion.

Football rides the crest of the Tidal wave of student enthusiasm, and the annual Auburn-Alabama game—the Iron Bowl—is the highlight of the school year. One student says, "The Auburn-Alabama rivalry is one of the most intense in all of college sports." Men's basketball and baseball are among the understudies to the mighty gridiron dwellers. Women's gymnastics, softball, and soccer are also competitive.

Although Alabama's football fame attracts many students, the university is making changes to see that as many now come for the academic program. By instituting numerous innovative programs and increasing the number of merit-based academic scholarships, UA is attempting to make what happens in the classrooms and laboratories the university's top priority. One student claims their mission has already been a success. "Alabama is finally gaining recognition as fine research/academic institution rather than simply as a party school."

> *The Culverhouse College of Commerce and Business offers excellent programs in marketing, business administration, world business, and accounting.*

Overlaps

Auburn, University of Georgia, Florida State, University of Tennessee, University of Florida.

If You Apply To ➤ 'Bama...Regular admissions: Aug. 1 with April 1 priority. Financial aid and housing: Mar. 1. Campus interviews: optional (required for applicants with high test scores and low grades or low test scores and high grades), evaluative. Alumni interviews: optional, informational. SATs or ACTs: required. SAT IIs: optional. No essay question.

Albertson College

Caldwell, Idaho 83605

As Idaho's oldest four-year university, Albertson College of Idaho offers students a solid liberal arts education in a small-town environment. Its strengths are natural sciences and preprofessional areas, but the college is placing a greater emphasis on computer technology and interdisciplinary courses. While requiring most students to take a structured curriculum, Albertson allows its best incoming

Website: www.albertson.edu
Location: Small town
Total Enrollment: 763
Undergraduates: 763

students to bend the rules a bit and choose their own requirements. Outside class, the school's scenic environs allow sports and nature enthusiasts to experience the playground that is so much of this unspoiled state.

The college is located in the small town of Caldwell where the atmosphere is calm and serene. For those looking for a little excitement, the state capitol of Boise is a short drive from campus. Also nearby are some of Idaho's most scenic locations such as beautiful mountains, deserts, and whitewater rivers. The school, originally a Presbyterian college, first planted roots in downtown Caldwell in 1891, then moved to its present site in 1910, where its 21 buildings now inhabit 43 acres. For more than 80 years, it was called the College of Idaho. But officials changed the college's name to honor the Albertson family, which gave $13.5 million for new facilities. Recent additions to the campus include the McCain Center, a $3-million student union that features a snack bar, coffee shop, student theater, movie theater, and outdoor eating area.

Most classes at Albertson have 25 or fewer students, and all are taught by full professors. Students agree its small size is the school's strongest asset. One sophomore raves, "The quality of teaching is phenomenal." Students enjoy being able to get to know their professors. "The professors here are personable and friendly," says one psychology major.

The school's academic schedule is composed of 12-week semesters, spring and fall, separated by a 6-week winter session, during which students can assist professors with research, take an internship, volunteer, or travel abroad. The general education requirements include writing, mathematics, and physical education. In addition, students must choose courses from areas such as humanities, social sciences, fine arts, and natural sciences. Although there are no first-year requirements, freshmen usually take composition, mathematics, western civilization, biology or chemistry, and a foreign language. Freshmen demonstrating leadership potential are invited to a series of seminars to draw them into the Leadership Studies program, a minor in the business department. The two libraries, with a combined stock of 178,000 volumes, are adequate and accessible 24 hours a day via computer.

Biology and English are recommended by students as particularly strong programs, as well as history and business. Preprofessional majors, such as premed, prevet, and prelaw, are also popular and strong. Weaker departments are the smaller departments, as they offer fewer class choices, and include foreign languages and music. The college cooperates with Columbia University, the University of Idaho, Boise State University, and Washington University in St. Louis to offer a five-year course of study in engineering. For those who want to venture abroad (physically or mentally), the International Education Program offers several options, including attending a foreign university, traveling overseas during the summer and winter breaks, and taking international studies on campus. Travel abroad has really taken off, with 25 percent of students accepting opportunities to such places as Greece, Germany, Ireland, and England. Advising is available to help students make good academic choices. "Each student is assigned a professor within their area of interest who guides them and makes sure they are maintaining expectations," says one freshman.

Although college students will always lament rising prices and declining aid, the school's price tag is far lower than those of most private colleges. The school offers an unlimited number of merit scholarships ranging from $75 to $16,300, as well as 79 athletic scholarships to members of the basketball, baseball, soccer, ski, golf, volleyball, and tennis teams. Also, "the financial aid office is reasonable and fairly generous," notes a philosophy major. The student body is hardly diverse;

The school's academic schedule is composed of 12-week semesters, spring and fall, separated by a 6-week winter session, during which students can assist professors with research, take an internship, volunteer, or travel abroad.

only 25 percent are from out of state (most of those are from nearby Oregon, Washington, and California), and 2 percent are foreign.

Recently, the college spent $4.5 million to renovate five residence halls. Each room now has individual heating and cooling, and individual hookups for computer access to electronic mail, the Internet, and other campus offerings. In addition, each hall has a computer lab. New carpeting, painting, furniture, and fixtures round out the project. Twenty-five percent of men and women participate in the Greek system, which dominates campus social life. Annual social highlights include Winterfest and Spring Fling, events that bring bands, games, and food to eagerly awaiting students. Caldwell, with 24,000 people, is not a great college town. Nearby Boise is a popular destination for shopping, dining, and cultural events. Students agree that its offerings are an important part of an Albertson student's life. "Most leisure time is that is spent off campus is usually spent in Boise which is about 30 minutes away," says one student. Many students take advantage of hiking, kayaking, and skiing in the surrounding area. The week-long break every six weeks creates many opportunities for road trips and other activities most other college students save for spring break.

Basketball is the crowd-pleaser here, and the team has made Albertson students proud, chalking up victories in NAIA Division II competition. The men's baseball team won the 1998 NAIA Division II national championship, and the women's ski team competed for the national championship during the 1999–2000 season. For those who enjoy the game but might not make the team, there is an active intramurals program, including Frisbee football, volleyball, basketball, and softball. Students enjoy the athletic facilities in the J. A. Albertson Activities Center, a 75,000-square-foot center with a large gym, swimming pool, and weight and aerobics rooms. Beyond sports, extracurricular activities include Bible study, theater, student publications, student government, choir, an environmental club, and a rejuvenated Hispanic club.

Albertson College and its students have a big appetite, and not just for potatoes! The students receive a solid liberal arts education and personal academic attention. For many college-bound students, that's a winning combination. As one student puts it, "Plain and simple, ACI is a second home in every way."

Overlaps

University of Idaho, Boise State, Whitman, Willamette, Puget Sound.

If You Apply To ➤ | **Albertson**...Early decision: Nov. 15. Regular admission: June 1. Financial aid: Feb. 15. Does not guarantee to meet demonstrated need. Campus and alumni interviews: optional, informational. SATs or ACTs: required. SAT IIs: optional. Accepts the Common Application and electronic applications. Essay question: experience or achievement, important issue, influential person.

Albion College

Albion, MI 49224

Leadership and public service are the hallmarks of an Albion education. The school's motto, "Liberal arts at work," emphasizes the importance Albion places on combining learning with hands-on experience. Students at Albion often participate in role-playing exercises and attend leadership seminars. And when the work is through, students here enjoy a close-knit social life. "The students are the

Website: www.albion.edu
Location: Small town
Total Enrollment: 1,529
Undergraduates: 1,529

(Continued)

Male/Female: 45/55

SAT Ranges: V 520–630 M
530–640

ACT Range: 22–28

Financial Aid: 62%

Expense: Pr $ $

Phi Beta Kappa: Yes

Applicants: 1,413

Accepted: 84%

Enrolled: 35%

Grad in 6 Years: 58%

Returning Freshmen: 84%

Academics: ✐ ✐ ✐

Social: ☎ ☎

Q of L: ★ ★ ★

Admissions: (800) 858-6770

Email Address:
admissions@albion.edu

Strongest Programs:
Economics and
Management
History
Chemistry
English
Biology
Visual Arts

Albion was the first private college in Michigan to have a Phi Beta Kappa chapter (1940), and has produced three Rhodes Scholars.

biggest reason I have enjoyed Albion College," admits a junior. "There is a friendly atmosphere that bonds our students together."

The campus, founded in 1835 by the Methodist Church, is located near the banks of the Kalamazoo River. In addition to its newer Georgian style architecture, Albion has retained and restored several of its 19th-century buildings. The campus is spacious with statuesque oaks and a beautiful nature center. Robinson Hall, the campus centerpiece, houses myriad departments, including the Ford Institute for Public Service, the Gerstacker Liberal Arts Program in Professional Management, and the Anna Howard Shaw Women's Center. The campus continues to expand with the complete renovation of campus dining facilities.

Academically, Albion is as sound as its buildings. It was the first private college in Michigan to have a Phi Beta Kappa chapter (1940), and has produced three Rhodes Scholars. Students are required to take core courses distributed among the humanities, natural sciences, social sciences, fine arts, and math. They must also satisfy requirements in environmental science, gender and ethnicity studies, and complete a writing proficiency requirement. First-Year Seminars are also available, and are designed to provide a "stimulating learning environment" in a small class setting. Albion offers a number of interdisciplinary majors, such as international studies and mathematics/economics, and allows students to design their own majors. Freshmen must take a first-year seminar, and seniors participate in a capstone experience. The speech communication and physical education departments are reported by students and administrators to need improvement.

Albion's most distinguishing feature is the emphasis that is placed on citizenship and service. The Gerald R. Ford Institute for Public Service takes a unique approach for future civic leaders. Students participate in a simulation of city government in which they play the roles of community leaders. Visiting speakers include senators and congressmen, governors and state legislators, and interest group representatives. The Sleight Leadership Program offers qualified students the opportunity to participate in weekly leadership seminars, national leadership conferences, awards, and honors. The premedical and predental programs draw dedicated undergrads, and the English and history departments are well respected. Another option is the Albion Research Fellows program, which offers 20 freshman $1,200 grants each semester to conduct original research with faculty members. As a member of the Great Lakes College Association,* the school cosponsors study abroad programs on six continents. The academic climate at Albion is described as competitive but not cutthroat. "Courses are hard but not killers," says a senior math and economics major. "It sounds weird, but we are competitive and laid back." Top-notch academic and career counseling and low student/faculty ratios help keep students on track and motivated. Class size varies, but the average class is under 25 students. Professors are interested not only in students' academic performance, but also in their emotional well-being. One senior Spanish and English double major asserts, "Professors will take students on field trips and invite students to their homes." Teaching assistants are used for tutoring, not teaching. Albion's libraries feature computer facilities, a listening lab for language or music study, computerized card catalogs, and a helpful staff. The interlibrary loan service is also useful, as are weekly bus trips to the University of Michigan libraries in Ann Arbor. About 35 percent of students participate in an off-campus study program, either within the country or abroad. Another 25 percent complete an internship.

Albion continues to attract an ambitious, bright bunch of students, 84 percent of whom are from Michigan, with most of the rest from surrounding states. There is little deviation from the white, upper-middle-class norm. One senior notes that "Albion is a fairly homogeneous town," while another insists that "diversity is celebrated and appreciated." African Americans make up only 3 percent of the student population, but a new host family program matches students of color with people of color from the community. There are a number of merit scholarships worth between $3,500 and full tuition, based on academic records, extracurricular involvement, and demonstrated leadership abilities. There are no athletic scholarships.

Ninety-six percent of Albion students reside in the residence halls, which are comfortable and well-maintained. The entire freshman class inhabits Wesley Hall, which is described as "beautiful and full of heritage". During their sophomore year, many students move to Seaton or Whitehouse halls. Fiske, the beautiful on-campus home of a past college president, houses upperclass students. Dorms are coed by hall or floor, and rooms are assigned by lottery. One student claims, "The dorms fit all of the students' needs and are very well maintained." Other housing options include a limited number of apartment annexes and co-ops, and the fraternity houses. (Sororities do not have houses; they hold their meetings in lodges.) Two large dining rooms feed campus residents on an "eat all day" meal plan, but many students supplement their diet with fare from nearby Loud's Ice Cream or the 115 truck stop, which caters to the 3:00 A.M. munchies crowd.

Forty-five percent of the men and 44 percent of the women belong to one of Albion's five national fraternities and six sororities, respectively. Greek parties draw large crowds—Greek and non-Greek—making them one outlet for social life. But controlling student alcoholic intake has become a priority of the administration. One student says that although alcohol policies are enforced, "underage drinking is very easy." Those who insist on imbibing can do it at Charlie's or Cascarelli's, popular pizza-and-beer joints.

Road trips are a big part of weekends for many students. Jackson and Battle Creek are frequent destinations, as are Ann Arbor and East Lansing. A well-run Union Board organizes all sorts of activities—films, lectures, plays, comics, and concerts—to keep students occupied in their spare time.

Still, students complain that there are not many social outlets available at Albion. Students focus some of their energy on work for groups supported by the Student Volunteer Bureau; in fact, half the students volunteer on a regular basis. Some of the more traditional events help to liven up the remaining time, including the Festival of the Forks, an activities carnival called the Briton Bash, Special Olympics, International Week, and a student talent night.

The varsity football team has won nine conference championships in the past decade and a Division III national title. Men's track, baseball, and golf, along with women's soccer and swimming, also receive a lot of attention on campus. Hope College is a most hated rival, as is Alma College.

"Can do!" pride permeates every facet of life at Albion College, and students and professors alike enjoy the Albion experience. Professors are accessible and interested; academics are challenging without being overwhelming and preprofessional without being vocational. One student sums it up like this: "Albion's students are unique because of the togetherness and friendliness."

The Sleight Leadership Program offers qualified students the opportunity to participate in weekly leadership seminars, national leadership conferences, awards, and honors.

Overlaps

Michigan State, University of Michigan, Alma, Kalamazoo, Hope.

If You Apply To ➤ Albion...Early decision: Dec. 10. Financial aid: Feb. 15. Does not guarantee to meet demonstrated need. Campus interviews: recommended, evaluative. No alumni interviews. SATs or ACTs: required. SAT IIs: optional. Accepts the Common Application and electronic applications. Essay question: significant experience; issue of personal, local, or national concern; influential person; personal interest.

Website: www.alfred.edu
Location: Rural
Total Enrollment: 1,468
Undergraduates: 1,174
Male/Female: 49/51
SAT Ranges: V 470–580 M 530–650
ACT Range: 23–28
Financial Aid: 76%
Expense: Pr $ $
Phi Beta Kappa: No
Applicants: 1,371
Accepted: 85%
Enrolled: 25%
Grad in 6 Years: N/A
Returning Freshmen: 78%
Academics: ✎ ✎ ✎
Social: ☎ ☎ ☎
Q of L: ★ ★ ★
Admissions: (607) 871-2115 or (800) 541-9229
Email Address:
admssn@bigvax.alfred.edu

Strongest Programs:
Ceramic Engineering
Art and Design
Business
Psychology
Chemistry
Biology
English

Ceramic engineering (the development and refinement of ceramic materials) is the undisputed king of the academic castle and the program that brings Alfred international recognition.

When you think of ceramics, what comes to mind? Sculptures or semiconductors? Either way, Alfred University has a top-notch program to satisfy your educational needs. This small school boasts highly respected programs in art and design, as well as ceramic engineering. Innovation not only influences the curriculum, but also has a profound effect on campus life. Small classes and friendly competition support this diversity while encouraging individuals to succeed. With just under 2,500 students, Alfred isn't a bustling academic factory; it's a quiet, cloistered, self-described "educational village" in a tiny town wholly dedicated to the "industry" of learning.

Alfred's campus consists of a charming, close-knit group of modern and Georgian brick buildings, along with a stone castle. The Kanakadea Creek runs right through campus, and the town of Alfred consists of two colleges (the other is the Alfred State College) and a main street with one stoplight. There are a few shops and restaurants, but certainly no malls, parking lots, or tall buildings. Recent campus additions include the Miller Performing Arts Center, the Robert E. McComsey Career Development Center, and the Allen Steinheim Museum.

The university and its students share a no-nonsense approach to education. Although prospective students apply directly to one of four colleges and declare a tentative major, half of all requirements for a bachelor's degree are earned in the liberal arts college. Requirements are quite different in each school. However, the mix usually includes coursework in oral and written communication, foreign language and culture, social sciences, history, literature, philosophy, and religion.

Alfred, though private, is actually the "host" school for the New York State College of Ceramics, which is a unit of the state university system. Ceramic engineering (the development and refinement of ceramic materials) is the undisputed king of the academic castle and the program that brings Alfred international recognition. The school is the site of a great deal of superconductivity research, as well as the Ceramic Corridor, a research project involving Corning Enterprises. In fact, students talk about the excellence of the ceramic engineering program regardless of their personal majors or interests, and the clay artists often earn the fond nickname "cement heads." The art department, with its programs in ceramics, glass, printmaking, sculpture, video, and teacher certification, is also highly regarded. The School of Art and Design offers an unusual graphic design major in which students use electronic and computer equipment. The business administration school also gets rave reviews from students, and provides undergraduates with work experience through a small-business institute where students have real clients. Many majors also offer a co-op program that alternates semesters of work and study. According to students, foreign languages, mathematics, and computer science are the weakest links in Alfred's curricular chain, but history, English, communications, and environmental studies are strong departments within the College of Liberal Arts and Sciences.

The College of Business has added a major in health planning and management, and within the School of Ceramic Engineering, material sciences engineering has replaced ceramic engineering sciences (whew!). The major in foreign language and culture sponsors trips abroad, and exchange programs are available in England, Germany, Italy, France, Japan, China, and the Czech Republic. The Track II program enables students to design their own interdisciplinary majors with personal guidance from top faculty members. Whatever their major, all students enjoy very small classes (average size is 18 students), and the quality of teaching is described as very high. "All the professors bring a great deal of knowledge into the classroom," notes a sophomore. All classes are taught by full professors, with graduate students and teaching assistants helping out only in lab sessions.

The university stresses its commitment to helping undergrads plan their future, and the academic advising and career planning services are strong enough for Alfred to deliver on its promise. Students say faculty members really want to see them succeed, both in class and in the "real world." "The advisors are great," says a student. "They really help you get your schedule right."

Two-thirds of the students at Alfred are from New York State, and 35 percent graduated from high school in the top fifth of their class. The campus is mostly white, with minority enrollment nearly steady at 4 percent black, 4 percent Hispanic, and 1 percent Asian American. "We must all learn to be sensitive to each other's life situations," says a freshman. Students praise the financial aid packages they receive, and the university is holding freshman tuition steady under the "Alfred Plan." Outstanding students can apply for merit scholarships ranging from $1,000 to a full ride, and National Merit finalists receive Alfred's Award of Merit. There are no athletic scholarships.

No one seems to mind the two-year on-campus residency requirement, since the rooms are large and comfortable, and the dorms are equipped with lounges, kitchens, and laundry facilities; some even boast such extras as computers and saunas. Upperclassmen have a choice of coed-by-floor dorms, with single rooms, suites, or apartments. Freshmen enjoy their own housing divided into doubles. The favorite freshman dorm is Barresi. Seventy percent of the students choose to stay on campus all four years, but some juniors and about half of the seniors opt to live off campus. The school has two dining halls and a choice of a 15- or 21-meal plan. Freshmen and sophomores are required to subsist on cafeteria cuisine, which features an enormous variety of regular buffets, plus a salad bar, a deli line, and daily international lines. Campus security is adequate, according to most. "I feel more safe on this campus than I do at my own house," admits a business major.

Alfred's location in the Finger Lakes region, almost two hours from Buffalo and an hour and a half from Rochester, is isolated. Social life is difficult due to the rural atmosphere, but the Student Activities Board brings many events to campus, including musicians, comedians, lecturers, and movies. Favorite road trips are to Letchworth and Stony Brook state parks, and to Ithaca, Rochester, Buffalo, and Toronto, Canada. Many students are skiing, hunting, camping, and rock-climbing enthusiasts. Friendly games of hackeysack, Frisbee, football, softball, and other sports can often be found somewhere on campus. Fraternities and sororities (12 of them) provide much of the spark for Alfred's social life, and claim 15 percent of the men and 10 percent of the women. The alcohol policy is enforced on the campus, but students say it is not impossible to get alcohol. "I tend to think of Alfred as a 'semi-dry' campus," says a senior. "You can find alcohol readily available if you really want to." Because Alfred shares the town with Alfred State University, the dominant student population makes Alfred a good "college town." The downtown scene provides students with an adequate number of movie theaters and eateries. Every spring brings the annual Hot Dog Weekend, a big fundraising event that fills Main Street with game booths, bands, and lots and lots of hot dog stands. Alfred's Division III Saxons are ominous opponents on the football, soccer, and lacrosse fields.

If you want to spend four years concentrating on learning the ABCs (that's

The university and its students share a no-nonsense approach to education. Although prospective students apply directly to one of four colleges and declare a tentative major, half of all requirements for a bachelor's degree are earned in the liberal arts college.

arts, business, or ceramic engineering), then small, secluded Alfred University is a good choice. But bring your heavy coat and gloves, because upstate New York winters can be brutal!

If You Apply To ➤ **Alfred...**Early decision: Dec. 1. Regular admissions: Feb. 1. Art and Design Portfolios: Feb. 15. Financial aid and housing: May 1. Campus interviews: recommended, evaluative. No alumni interviews. SATs or ACTs: required. SAT IIs: recommended (writing, for placement only). Essay question: develop a product or idea; comedy skit proposal; take standard piece of paper and be creative; contributions to Alfred.

Allegheny College

520 North Main Street, Meadville, PA 16335

Website: www.alleg.edu
Location: Small town
Total Enrollment: 1,886
Undergraduates: 1,886
Male/Female: 47/53
SAT Ranges: V 540–650 M 550–650
ACT Range: 22–27
Financial Aid: 77%
Expense: Pr $ $ $
Phi Beta Kappa: Yes
Applicants: 3,014
Accepted: 75%
Enrolled: 25%
Grad in 6 Years: 72%
Returning Freshmen: 90%
Academics: ✍ ✍ ✍
Social: ☎ ☎ ☎
Q of L: ★ ★ ★
Admissions: (800) 521-5293
Email Address:
admiss@admin.alleg.edu

Strongest Programs:
Chemistry
Biology

Allegheny College seems to pull off the collegiate trifecta—strong academic programs, lots of personal attention, and a fun enjoyable atmosphere. Those attending "Agony College" know it's a place with a highly charged academic program that demands dedication in order to survive. Although there are a few drawbacks, such as its far-from-everywhere location and dreary winter weather, Allegheny is a school that has students saying things like, "The thing that made it stand out for me was the rapport between the students and professors. It's a unique atmosphere of friendliness, common ambitions, and different perspectives."

Allegheny College is nestled in the picturesque rolling hills of northwestern Pennsylvania. The school features ivy-covered buildings and redbrick streets on 72 acres, including a $14.5 million science complex and renovated dance studios. In addition, the college owns a 182-acre outdoor recreational facility and a 283-acre nature preserve.

The academic climate at Allegheny is indeed intense, as evidenced by high acceptance rates in medical, law, and business schools. "Allegheny is a highly competitive school, and the courses are challenging and require many, many hours of outside-of-class preparation," says a student. The psychology and English programs reign supreme at Allegheny. Biology, history, political science, and foreign languages are also strong programs. The environmental studies program is consistently strong, and students say this program emphasizes hands-on learning and encourages a multidisciplinary approach to solving problems. There is a 3–2 cooperative program leading to double BS degrees in engineering, a seven-year bachelor's/doctoral program in nursing, and 3–1 programs in medical technology. Administrators added the Allegheny College Center for Experiential Learning (ACCEL) to give students better-organized access to internships, service learning, and overseas study.

Allegheny maintains a 15-week semester calendar in an academic year.

Accompanying this schedule is a comprehensive general education program that requires students to complete 128 credits. These requirements include courses in each of three major divisions (humanities and the natural and social sciences), and a minor in a topical area outside the division of the major. All freshmen take a sequence of two courses called the First Course and the Freshman Communication Seminar. These are followed by a Sophomore Communication Seminar the next year. According to the administration, the courses are "united and connected by an emphasis on the processes of writing and speaking as they relate to the development of critical thinking skills central to success in both college and life after college." Students rarely have problems getting into classes, and the majority graduate in four years.

The faculty receives accolades from students for their passion, knowledge, and accessibility. "Professors are amazing," a senior gushes. "The class sizes are small enough that the professors get to know you as a person and a friend." You won't find a TA at the lectern in any Allegheny classroom, and most classes have fewer than 25 students. The college has an honor code that allows students to take unproctored exams. Allegheny College attracts serious-minded students who are willing to work extremely hard to get good grades.

For a break from the standard grind, Allegheny offers study in several U.S. cities or abroad, a popular on-campus independent study option, and semester internships or "externships" (a chance to observe a professional at work during the winter vacation). Allegheny offers a 3- or 4-week term after spring semester for study abroad and internships not available during the school year. The library claims nearly 600,000 volumes and offers an impressive collection of 300-plus computer workstations. *The Chronicle of Higher Education* calls the productivity of Allegheny's computer programs "staggering," given the institution's size and limited technical resources.

Sixty-five percent of Allegheny students dive right into the business world after graduation, while 35 percent continue to pursue academic aspirations. Sixty-one percent of the student body hails from Pennsylvania, and sizable contingents come from nearby New Jersey, upstate New York, and New England. Although minority students make up only 5 percent of the student body, Allegheny seems committed to increasing awareness of and appreciation for diversity. Still, some claim that students of color remain isolated. "Once a diverse community is achieved, how do we get everyone to interact and cooperate?" asked a plaintive studio art major.

Allegheny is need-blind in admissions, meeting the full demonstrated need of nearly all entering students. The rest receive about 90 percent of need. "I wouldn't be here if it wasn't for Allegheny's excellent financial aid," says one environmental studies major. Over 1,000 merit scholarships, ranging from $6,000 to $10,000, are offered to freshmen each year, based on academics alone or a combination of academics, success in activities, and/or active volunteer involvement. There are no athletic scholarships.

Ten dorms and 20 houses (complete with TV and study rooms) accommodate undergraduates in relative style and comfort, and offer a variety of living situations: all-freshmen dorms, coed and single-sex halls, small houses, and single, double, and triple rooms and suites. Students agree that while the dorms are generally well maintained and comfortable, adequate space is sometimes a concern. Everyone who wants a dorm room can have one, and 73 percent choose to stay on campus. The most popular student housing choice is the new, townhouse–style College Court complex, accommodating 80 students in suites that each have four single bedrooms. The school's cuisine is generally considered

(Continued)
Premed
Prelaw
English
Psychology
Computer Science
Environmental Studies

As for Allegheny traditions, there's the somewhat suspect 13th Plank ritual, which states that all freshman women must be kissed on the 13th plank of the campus bridge by an upperclassman in order to be considered a "true Allegheny coed."

average. Campus security receives high marks from students, and one senior describes Meadville, referred to lovingly as Mudville, as a "safe, low- incident community."

Greek organizations claim 18 percent of the men and 28 percent of the women, and while they don't quite have a lock on the social scene, they do provide a great deal of nightlife. Three fraternities enjoy their own housing, while the four sororities are relegated to special dorm suites. On-campus activities also abound: The center for student activities attracts comedians, ventriloquists, and live bands, and provides a weekly showing of a popular movie. "Social life on campus is pretty mixed," says one junior. "If you want to find parties, they are easy to find, but if you want to stay in, that's easy to do also." The campus is technically alcohol-free, but most students say it's pretty easy to get alcohol "if a student is thirsty enough." The winter carnival helps students shake the winter blues, and features a unique obstacle course: "The fastest person with the least amount of clothing wins," says a senior. The Spring Fest welcomes the much-awaited seasonal explosion of campus color and beauty. Downtown Meadville is a 10-minute walk from campus, and offers a four-screen movie theater and several community playshops. Many find their way downtown when they do volunteer work (Alleghenians total over 20,000 hours of volunteer time annually).

When the thought of bumming in Meadville is too much to bear, students have the option of some great road trips. The nearest getaways are Conneaut Lake and Lake Erie, and there are ski areas, beaches, and shopping malls within an hour's drive. As for Allegheny traditions, there's the somewhat suspect 13th Plank ritual, which states that all freshman women must be kissed on the 13th plank of the campus bridge by an upperclassman in order to be considered a "true Allegheny coed." Of course, a group of freshman men steal the plank every year at the beginning of the first semester to prevent that from happening. Athletics play a big role in Allegheny life, and the addition of a $13-million sports and fitness complex has given students new reason to cheer. Men's football, golf, and baseball consistently place in the national top 20, as do women's swimming, cross-country, and softball.

With its caring faculty and emphasis on lifelong learning, Allegheny College is making the grade with its students as well: "Allegheny provided me with the supportive environment I needed to try new challenges, and the people at Allegheny provided me with the inspiration to explore and develop my potential as a leader and a student."

Overlaps

Penn State, Washington and Jefferson, Bucknell, Pittsburgh, Miami University (OH).

If You Apply To ➤   **Allegheny…**Early decision: Jan. 15. Regular admissions, financial aid, and housing: Feb. 15. Does not guarantee to meet demonstrated need. Campus interviews: recommended, informational. Alumni interviews: optional, informational. SATs or ACTs: required. SAT IIs: optional (English and subjects of possible major). Accepts the Common Application and electronic applications. Essay question: significant experience; important issue; or person of significant influence.

Alma College

Alma, MI 48801

Students seeking a liberal arts education with an international emphasis need look no further than Alma College. Located at the center of Michigan's lower peninsula, Alma's focus is on the world. Off-campus study options are wildly popular here, and the annual Highland Festival, featuring kilt-wearing bagpipe players and traditional Scottish competitions, has led some to dub the school "Scotland, USA." But it's the personal attention that students seem to love most. Says a sophomore, "I wouldn't trade it for anything."

On Alma's residential campus, 24 buildings surround a scenic central mall. Prairie-style architecture combines red brick with limestone capstones. "The campus has lots of trees and open places to sit," says one student. "It looks like a picture on a postcard." Top facilities include the McIntyre Center for Exercise and Health Science, the Colina Library Wing, and the Heritage Center for the Performing Arts.

The academic climate is described as competitive and challenging. "Students come to Alma expecting a good education and most of them work hard to get one," says a sophomore. General distribution requirements cover a variety of coursework including literacies, arts and humanities, social sciences, and natural sciences. Students must also complete one college-level mathematics course in addition to showing basic computational proficiency. In addition, students are required to take English 100 and up to five more English courses thereafter. Education is the most popular major, followed by business, biology, exercise and health science, and psychology. Up-and-coming departments include biochemistry, music, and theatre and dance, while foreign languages are cited as weaker than most.

Twenty-four percent of Alma's students major in the life sciences, and the college has a strong reputation for graduate placement in those fields. A popular exercise and health science major deals with a wide variety of health-related professions including health and wellness intervention programs, public health, and rehabilitation therapies. In all academic disciplines, students may design independent coursework in their major or craft an entire program of emphasis. Alma's Service Learning Program links classroom instruction with community service and offers students the opportunity to work in public or private nonprofit economic development or with educational, environmental, and health agencies. The annual Honors Day features presentations of scholarly work from nearly 10 percent of the student body.

One of Alma's big selling points is its numerous opportunities for study abroad. During Alma's one-month spring term, students enroll in only one intensive course at a time which often includes study off campus. For example, past programs involved Pacific Rim corporate approaches in Australia, language and culture in Paris, and archeological fieldwork in Israel. Alma also offers formal foreign study programs in France, Germany, Mexico, Scotland, and Spain.

Faculty members are highly praised by students. "The professors are well educated and definitely show a true interest in helping their students succeed," says an elementary education major. "They really care about their students," says a senior business major. "They don't let you slack off (at least not for too long)." Faculty advising is also deemed "excellent." Class size is fairly intimate—the average is 21 students—and getting into a required course is seldom a problem. "Most

Website: www.alma.edu
Location: Rural
Total Enrollment: 1,383
Undergraduates: 1,383
Male/Female: 42/58
ACT Range: 22–28
Financial Aid: 89%
Expense: Pr $
Phi Beta Kappa: Yes
Applicants: 1,366
Accepted: 83%
Enrolled: 30%
Grad in 6 Years: 72%
Returning Freshmen: 86%
Academics: ✍ ✍ ✍
Social: ☎ ☎ ☎
Q of L: ★ ★ ★
Admissions: (800) 321 ALMA
Email Address:
    admissions@alma.edu

Strongest Programs :
    Art and Design
    Biology
    Business Administration
    Chemistry
    Communications
    Education
    English
    Exercise and Health Science

Almost all Alma students celebrate St. Paddy's Day with Irish Pub, a thunderous festival sure to rouse the leprechauns for a celebratory toast.

students are able to graduate in four years if they stay on track," observes one student.

The Alma student body is composed mostly of Michiganders; 95 percent are from inside state lines and most graduated from a public high school. Minorities make up only 6 percent of the student body. While the recruitment of minority students remains a focus of the admissions department, faculty members have really targeted adding diversity to the campus through several program options, including the Urban Life Center in Chicago and the Philadelphia Center Internship Program. For those concerned about the cost of higher learning, Alma awards an unlimited number of merit scholarships ranging from $200 to full tuition.

Twenty-four percent of Alma's students major in the life sciences and the college has a strong reputation for graduate placement in those fields.

Eighty-four percent of the students live on campus in residence halls, which are described by residents as "cozy." One student says, "For the most part, they are kept up, and the halls and bathrooms are cleaned every day." Freshmen are assigned rooms in single-sex and coed dorms, while upperclassmen play the lottery and usually end up in suites. Two coed international houses, a multicultural house, and fraternities and sororities round out the housing options. Everyone subscribes to either a 14- or 19-meal-a-week plan and chows down at the Commons. All-you-can-eat service is offered on a daily basis, featuring a salad bar, deli bar, pizza, grill, and dessert. Students can also opt to eat in Joe's Place, a snack bar. Campus security is effective, according to most students. "You see security walking around, especially in the dorms," says one student. "That adds to the secure feeling."

Alma students depend mainly on the Greeks for social activities. "Going Greek is a big issue here," says a junior. "There's a tremendous pressure to join one of the fraternities or sororities." Other campus events are sponsored by the student-run Union Board. "Social life at Alma is what you make it," says one student. "There's always something going on. You just have to look for it." Twenty-three percent of men and of women join Greek organizations. The campus alcohol policy (no one under 21 can drink) has been enforced by students and administrators alike through campaigns that promote responsible drinking, but alcohol is not in short supply. One sophomore says, "Alcohol is widely available. If you want it, you can usually get it."

Alma is described as a "little town with a big heart." The townsfolk and the students here have accepted each other and work together to improve their community. "Many students volunteer all over town and the people of Alma appreciate everything the students do for them," says a communication major. One annual event the students look forward to is the Highland Festival, which features ubiquitous bagpipe playing and Scottish dancing. If your fantasies include wearing a kilt, you should join the marching band, whose members sport the traditional garb in the colors of the McPhearson plaid. Almost all Alma students celebrate St. Paddy's Day with Irish Pub, a thunderous festival sure to rouse the leprechauns for a celebratory toast. Students who need excitement more often through the year make the 45-minute trip to East Lansing or the 20-minute jaunt to Mt. Pleasant. Ski slopes are an hour away, and for warm-weather diversions, students can hit the "pits," old gravel pits filled with water and surrounded by beach areas. For the sports-minded, there is the annual Alma-Albion rivalry to cheer about, as well as an active intramural program. Top varsity teams include softball, women's golf, and men's soccer.

For the individual who doesn't want to trade traditional disciplines for preprofessional training, Alma offers a unique compromise. Students here delve into the liberal arts without neglecting the practical considerations of today's job market. It's a friendly atmosphere; Alma College truly seeks to offer its students the best of both worlds.

If You Apply To ➤

Alma... Rolling admissions. Early action: Nov. 1. Financial aid: Feb. 15. Housing: May 1. Meets demonstrated need of 91%. Campus interviews: recommended, informational. No alumni interviews. ACT: required. SAT IIs: optional. Accepts electronic applications. Optional essay question: creatively introduce yourself.

Alverno College

3401 South 39th Street, P.O. Box 343922, Milwaukee, WI 53234-3922

Try as you might, you will never earn an A at Alverno College. That's because letter grades are a thing of the past at this Roman Catholic women's college. In place of letter grades, students are required to show "mastery" in a range of liberal arts courses, as well as demonstrated ability in eight broad areas: communications, analysis, problem solving, values in decision making, social interaction, global perspectives, effective citizenship, and aesthetic responsiveness. Students move through interdisciplinary progressive levels toward a degree by being "validated" in these areas. For example, a course in sociology might contribute to validation in communication and social interaction, as well as to validation in making independent value judgments. Students demonstrate their competence all the while in a noncompetitive, though intense, atmosphere that emphasizes the relationship between liberal and religious traditions and everyday life. "The ability-based curriculum," says one junior, "is the most positive thing Alverno has to offer." "The courses are time consuming and tough, but the academic and real-life education received is amazing," adds a science major.

Alverno is located in a quiet, well-kept residential area. The parklike 46-acre campus is just 15 minutes from downtown Milwaukee and a 10-minute walk from shops and restaurants. Its three main academic buildings, of 1950s and '60s vintage, feature brick and stone exteriors and stained-glass windows. The new Teaching, Learning, and Technology Center houses 73,000-square-feet of science labs, multimedia production areas and computer facilities.

Alverno is really two colleges rolled into one. There is a regular weekday program that attracts mostly traditional college-age women, the majority of whom are from Milwaukee. The Weekend College allows women, most of them older with full-time jobs, to earn a degree in four years by attending classes every other weekend. Students in weekday may earn credit by spending four to eight hours a week in internships related to their field of study. First-year students take an orientation seminar, two introductory integrated arts and humanities courses, two integrated science courses, and introductory courses in psychology and sociology. They also take integrated communication seminars and two math courses that combine the study of mathematics with other discipline courses. The student body is diverse—in age, ethnic background, and religion. Religious studies aren't

Website: www.alverno.edu
Location: Suburban
Total Enrollment: 1,872
Undergraduates: 1,754
Male/Female: 0/100
ACT Range: N/A
Financial Aid: 91%
Expense: Pr $
Phi Beta Kappa: No
Applicants: 564
Accepted: 71%
Enrolled: 57%
Grad in 6 Years: 57%
Returning Freshmen: 82%
Academics: ✍ ✍ ✍
Social: ☎
Q of L: ★ ★ ★ ★
Admissions: (414) 382-6100
Email Address:
admissions@alverno.edu

Strongest Programs:
Nursing
Education
Business and Management
Psychology
Science Education
Professional Communication
Interdisciplinary Arts and Humanities

In place of letter grades, students are required to show "mastery" in a range of liberal arts courses, as well as demonstrated ability in eight broad areas: communications, analysis, problem solving, values in decision making, social interaction, global perspectives, effective citizenship, and aesthetic responsiveness.

The most striking quality about Alverno, other than its unique curriculum, is its quiet feminism.

required, but for those who seek it, a Catholic liturgy is available on a daily basis.

Alverno's business and management programs are solid and well established. Students praise the professional communications and teacher education programs, and the school is noted for its strong nursing program. Newer majors include the international business major and the master of arts. The library holds 350,000 titles, and for major research projects students can use the online library/media center catalog made available through a consortial arrangement with five Milwaukee colleges. Bali, Paris, Tokyo, and London are just a few of the places where students have taken advantage of the schools study-abroad program.

Faculty members at Alverno are teaching oriented; this is a "teach or perish" school—not publish or perish. Students note that the quality of teaching is "outstanding" and "superb." Says a sophomore, "The instructors here are very knowledgeable and have a lot of experience." Academic counseling and individual attention run throughout students' academic careers to keep them on track, resulting in high retention and graduation rates. The career advising services have been described as "awesome."

Many students are older than typical college age and quite a few have children. There are dozens of student groups and cultural groups, like Women of Color, active on campus. Alverno students have diverse cultural backgrounds, and there's a prevailing sense of pride in race and ethnicity on this peaceful campus. One psychology senior attributes this to Alverno's focus on global perspectives: "We learn to understand things that are outside of our little world. I think this cuts down on the narrow-mindedness associated with many racial problems." The vast majority of the students receive financial aid, and merit scholarships ranging from $1,500 to $7,000 are awarded based on a personal evaluation of each incoming student.

A three-day orientation program serves freshmen, transfer, resident, and commuter students. The majority of students are commuters. The residence halls offer clean, spacious rooms with fully equipped lounges, laundry, and cooking facilities available on each floor. "The residence halls are well maintained and provide a feeling of home and belonging," says one nursing major. Male visitors are allowed, but they must sign in and be out by midnight on weekdays and 2:00 A.M. on weekends.

"Most of the social life takes place off campus at local clubs, bars, coffee bars, and nearby colleges, but the student union, called the Pipeline, frequently offers on-campus activities. "We've had everything from bands and comedians to magicians and hypnotists at the Pipeline," says one sophomore. The campus also has an on-site day care center, a fitness center, and a jogging track, and sponsors dance and theater groups. Milwaukee offers myriad parks and shopping centers, a Performing Arts Center, professional sports teams, ethnic festivals, and free outdoor concerts. On-campus parties frequently draw students from Marquette and the Milwaukee School of Engineering. "As a result of being located in a residential area, it's much more difficult to find places to drink, let alone areas that will serve minors," says a student. There are no organized athletics, varsity or intramural, but students don't appear to miss the thrill of athletic rivalry. Nonsporting annual events include Student Seminar Day, which allows students and faculty to change places so that students can "share their experiences" with the Alverno community.

Perhaps the most striking quality about Alverno, other than its unique curriculum, is its quiet feminism. By background and training, Alverno students are rarely political activists, but there is among teachers and students an underlying determination to further the role of women in American society and to support one another in the process.

Overlaps

Milwaukee Area Technical College, University of Wisconsin, Cardinal Stritch, Carroll.

<table>
<tr><td>

If You Apply To ➢

</td><td>

Alverno…Regular admissions: Aug. 1. Financial aid: Apr. 1. Housing: June 1. Does not guarantee to meet demonstrated need. Campus and alumni interviews: optional, informational. ACTs: required. Accepts the Common Application and electronic applications. Essay question: recent activities and/or work history; academic goals and abilities; and most important reason for applying to Alverno.

</td></tr>
</table>

American University

4400 Massachusetts Avenue NW, Washington, DC 20016-8001

No one in Washington, D.C., wants to admit to having clawed their way to the top, but if you're a student at American University, there's no getting around it: their mascot, a bird named Clawed, is everywhere. Still, school spirit is hardly what keeps AU's Eagles soaring—the academic climate can seem pretty heady when you're living and learning in the exciting, international atmosphere of D.C. Not surprisingly, international studies and journalism are top-notch programs, providing classroom training in addition to a wealth of field opportunities to prepare students for real careers. Reports one regal Eagle, "Students here aren't just going to college, they're working in Congress, government agencies, and businesses. The 'real-world' connections that AU brings into and outside the classroom make the education very valuable."

AU's 84-acre residential campus is located in the northwest corner of Washington, D.C., just minutes from downtown; free shuttle buses transport students to the nearby subway station. Most buildings are a blend of classical and modern architecture, though the residence halls are high-rises. Recent construction includes a new fitness center and renovations that wire all classrooms.

With an extensive government internship program, unlimited professional and volunteer opportunities in the nation's capital, and courses on seemingly every politically related topic imaginable, American University truly takes advantage of its prime location. The university has established ties with more than 900 private, nonprofit, or government institutions, through which many students obtain nearby internships for credit during the semester. The school also uses these connections in its Washington Semester* and co-op programs, available in a wide range of majors. "AU realizes what type of students come to Washington, D.C., and so we have very strong programs in public affairs, communications, and political science," reports one senior.

Other subjects of note include foreign languages, business, and the social sciences. Theater, math, and the hard sciences are seen as weaker programs. American has a reputation for attracting respected professors who are well known outside academia, as well. "Professors are experts in their fields and active with academic and professional pursuits," says one senior. Freshmen are almost always taught by full professors, and the profs in general are described as "truly outstanding, almost without exception," according to a political science major. Students say academic advising is sufficient but not magnificent, and that career advising is infinitely stronger. In keeping with its international theme, AU offers a wide range of study abroad programs that attract approximately a quarter of the student body to cities around the globe. Notably, AU is also strong in support services to disabled students. New programs include a BS in design/multimedia and a degree in physics and computing.

Website: www.american.edu
Location: Urban
Total Enrollment: 10,894
Undergraduates: 5,533
Male/Female: 40/60
SAT Ranges: V 550–650 M 530–630
ACT Range: 23–29
Financial Aid: 81%
Expense: Pr $ $ $
Phi Beta Kappa: Yes
Applicants: 7,554
Accepted: 74%
Enrolled: 26%
Grad in 6 Years: 65%
Returning Freshmen: 85%
Academics: ✍ ✍ ✍
Social: ☎ ☎ ☎
Q of L: ★ ★ ★
Admissions: (202) 885-6000
Email Address: afa@american.edu

Strongest Programs:
International Affairs
Political Science
Communications
International Business
Economics
History

All American undergraduates must follow a general education program that requires a total of 30 credit hours from five areas: the creative arts, traditions that shape the Western world, international and intercultural experience, social institutions and behavior, and the natural sciences. Students choose two courses, one foundation course and one second-level course, in the same cluster in each of the five curriculum areas. All general requirements are designed for completion during the first two years to allow for ample time to study abroad or participate in an internship or co-op. Students say that AU is challenging academically, but not overshadowed by a competitive edge. "Students strive to do well individually and tend to work together," says one sophomore.

AU prides itself on drawing students from every state and more than 130 foreign countries. In fact, only 6 percent of the student body hail from the District of Columbia. Eight percent of the undergraduate student body are black, 6 percent are Hispanic, and 4 percent are Asian American. Unlike many college campuses where apathy seems to reign, AU is very active politically, and all ideas are welcome, as the mission of the school is to turn these ideas into action and then into service. After all, this is Washington, D.C., and causes are what this city is all about.

AU provides a solid financial assistance program, which includes merit scholarships ranging from $6,000 to full tuition. Nearly 200 athletes in ten sports are also awarded athletic scholarships.

Students have mixed emotions about on-campus housing, although all of the dorms have been renovated in the past six years. Rooms are average size, with carpeting, self-controlled heating and air-conditioning, plenty of storage space, and built-in closets and bureaus. Boarders may choose from a range of meal plans or cook on their own using dorm kitchen facilities. Approximately two-thirds of students live in on-campus housing. The rest of the student population resides off campus, however. "Many students prefer living off-campus because it is much cheaper," says one sophomore. Another student recommends living off campus because dorms are "overcrowded and small." Students report that campus security is helpful and "visible on campus."

Social life at AU is mostly found off campus, though there are dorm and frat parties. Greek life occupies the time of 17 percent of the student body, but fraternities and sororities do not dominate the social scene. "Being in D.C. means the social life is never lacking," says one sophomore. A classmate adds, "Washington, D.C., is the college town of America. It never stops or shuts off for the night." Most of the social life tends to occur off campus, where students enjoy bar-hopping and yes, monument-hopping in the D.C. area. Although popular road trips include Baltimore, Annapolis, and Ocean City, students tend to remain on their extended campus. "You just jump on the Metro to get anywhere in the city," says one communications major. Students of legal drinking age may imbibe at AU's popular Tavern; otherwise, the campus is officially dry. One annual event enjoyed by all students is Ward Weekend, which brings games, rides, and popular bands to the campus and includes a carnival on the quad. Homecoming, Spring Concert, Winter Ball, and various free concerts are also campus favorites.

American competes in Division I, but sports are an afterthought to most AU students. There is no football team, but, "AU football: undefeated" is a popular T-shirt around campus. Without football, the students spend the autumn months preparing for Eagles basketball. Games against James Madison and the Naval Academy top the basketball schedule. Men's soccer and tennis also have good squads.

Students generally agree that location makes AU stand out. "The experiences here can be found nowhere else," a senior points out. And for that reason, AU appeals to a certain type of student: the career-minded individual who knows how to make good grades and job contacts in a city where the advantages (and possible distractions) are plentiful. American University students take it upon themselves to make their college experience something special, and most leave the school with an enormous sense of pride. The most popular slogan at AU? "Once an Eagle, always an Eagle."

If You Apply To ➢ **American**...Early decision: Nov. 15. Regular admissions: Feb. 1. Financial aid: Mar. 1. Housing: May 1. Does not guarantee to meet demonstrated need. Campus and alumni interviews: optional, informational. SATs: required. SAT IIs: recommended. Apply to particular program. Essay question: cover story for a 2025 national newsmagazine; event of personal significance.

Amherst College

Amherst, MA 01002-5000

Amherst College, a consensus pick for one of the top liberal arts colleges in the nation, offers its students much more than just higher education. One of the major benefits of Amherst is the "freedom to explore." The focus here is on learning, not competing for grades, as students have no standardized curriculum. "You don't come to Amherst to get A's," says a student. "You come to Amherst to stretch your abilities, to question your beliefs, and to engage your mind." Students center on academics, with little time left over for partying or playing games, yet somehow they are able to do the impossible—squeeze in time for these crucial collegiate releases even if they have to sacrifice sleep to do so.

Situated on a hill overlooking the picturesque town of Amherst and the Pioneer Valley, the 964-acre campus offers a panoramic view of the Holyoke Range and the Pelham Hills. The college is roughly divided into thirds: the academic and residential buildings, athletic fields and facilities, and a plot of open land that houses a wildlife sanctuary and a forest. Variations on traditionalism also permeate the campus architecture. While Amherst's predominant style is still 19th-century academia—red brick is the key—everything from a "pale yellow octagonal structure to a garish, modern new dorm" can be found here. But whether or not students approve of the structural growth, no one complains about the ideal setting of luscious green knolls and valleys and enough large, healthy trees to produce a thick multicolor blanket of leaves each fall.

In keeping with the school's established emphasis on the inquiring mind, Amherst's curriculum is guided by the philosophy that education is a process and an activity, not a body of knowledge. The only college-wide required course is a first-year seminar to be taken in the fall of one's freshman year. The seminars are taught by two or more professors from different disciplines and are designed to foster thinking across many lines of traditional study. The freedom also means the academic climate at Amherst is basically laid-back, one student reports. The only requirement is that students settle on a major, fulfill the departmental program requirements, and perform satisfactorily on comprehensive exams in their major

Website: www.amherst.edu
Location: Small town
Total Enrollment: 1,664
Undergraduates: 1,664
Male/Female: 52/48
SAT Ranges: V 650–760 M 650–740
ACT Range: 27–33
Financial Aid: 43%
Expense: Pr $ $ $ $
Phi Beta Kappa: Yes
Applicants: 5,190
Accepted: 19%
Enrolled: 43%
Grad in 6 Years: 96%
Returning Freshmen: 97%
Academics: ✍ ✍ ✍ ✍ ✍
Social: ☎ ☎ ☎
Q of L: ★ ★ ★ ★
Admissions: (413) 542-2328
Email Address: N/A

Strongest Programs:
English
Psychology
Political Science
History

Junior-year study abroad finds Amherst students in 35 countries, ranging from a math program in Budapest to analyzing architecture in Rome.

field. Of this approach to college education, the administration says that "a student should be free at this stage to make choices—even foolish choices. "The students place demands on themselves to think hard and think well," an anthropology major says. "At the same time, the atmosphere at Amherst is warm, supportive, and non-competitive."

The most popular majors—economics, English, political science, psychology, and history—are top-notch, and students are able to mix and match among these subjects to create their own dual-degree, interdisciplinary programs. The dance program is also strong, and the Spanish department now includes language and cultural studies. Students can create their own course in Special Topics classes if the subject is not being taught. A weaker spot in the Amherst arsenal of majors is philosophy, which students claim lacks the enthusiasm of other departments. The ethnic studies field, which does not have its own department, also needs a financial boost, students say. Amherst has more than its share of prelaw, prebusiness, and premed candidates, and the last group reports that the natural science departments are strong but cruel. To house all these programs, Amherst has spent millions over the past few years renovating facilities with updated technologies and improved spaces for study, exhibits, performances, and sports.

On such a small campus, interaction with professors is constant and friendly, students say. "The quality of teaching should be one of the biggest draws for prospective students," a senior says. "Outstanding" and "pretty fantastic" describe the professors, who are always willing to meet with students outside of class time. One junior says, "A student's learning does not begin and end in the classroom. It spills over into a discussion with a professor in his/her office, a dinner at a professor's home, or students debating an issue brought up in class over a pizza at 3:00 A.M."

Every aspect of Amherst life is immeasurably enhanced by its memberships in the Five College Consortium.* Amherst also belongs to the Maritime Studies Program* and the Twelve College Exchange.* With three other liberal arts colleges and a major state university a brief shuttle-bus ride away, cross-registration in any one of a host of fields—like basic accounting at UMass or "something experimental" at Hampshire—is a godsend about the middle of sophomore year. All-female Smith and Mount Holyoke also add to the social life (ask any Amherst man), and there are numerous cultural and artistic events open to Amherst students at each of the other schools. Amherst offers several study abroad options with one-third of the junior class taking advantage of them, including one in Kyoto, Japan, where one of the college's Colonial-style buildings has been duplicated. During the three-week January interim, there are no formal courses offered and no grades or academic credits given, but the college keeps its facilities open so that students may pursue individual research projects or even teach courses to fellow students if they wish.

Amherst is working hard to shake off its image of a homogenous, elitist school. Though students say most of their peers are well-off, diversity is working its way into the student body. The college dealt a major blow to the old-boy network with the abolition of fraternities in the mid-'80s. Students from public high schools now account for more than half of the student body, and minority enrollment includes 6 percent African Americans, 7 percent Hispanics, and 12 percent Asian Americans. Students seem generally appreciative of diversity, yet realistic about their own community. Many students feel that race relations and homosexuality are big issues on campus, as are the political issues surrounding Tibet and North Korea. Still, one self-described conservative complains, "Open-mindedness here often means acceptance and tolerance of absolutely anything...as long as it's liberal." Amherst guarantees to meet the financial needs of applicants—a good thing considering there are no merit nor athletic scholarships.

Housing at Amherst is first-rate, but you'll have to wait a while before you hit the housing jackpot. One student describes the dorms this way: "Freshmen—horrible. Sophomore—half great, half horrible. Junior and senior—great." The freshman dorms are crowded and noisy, which should not be a shocker. Upperclassmen usually get singles, and choose from several options, including suites in nicer and less noisy residence halls, apartment-like social dorms, and best of all, converted fraternity houses that were once Victorian mansions and come complete with ballrooms, pianos, hardwood floors, and stained-glass windows. Everyone who lives on campus (97 percent of undergrads), and anyone else who wants to, eats in Valentine Hall, which includes a state-of-the-art central serving station and five dining rooms. It is no secret among students that the food is not great, but options are provided.

The legacy of beer-drenched partying has lingered even after the demise of the frats. "In theory, the rules are the same as Massachusetts' state law," a religion major says. "In practice, there is no big deal about it. If you want it, you can get it, and you won't be hassled about it. There is no sick, puritanical concern over it." Thursday Night TAP (The Amherst Party), complete with kegs, dancing, and security monitors, is the place to go to see and be seen, with popular theme nights such as Madonna TAP and Motown TAP.

While much of the social life is on campus, students also take advantage of the other schools in the area. The biggest party of the year, thrown every February, is Casino Night, which includes gambling with real money. Another festivity is Bavaria, a spring festival complete with pig roast and big-wheel joust. Perhaps the biggest change on the Amherst social scene in the past decade or so is the addition of the Campus Center, a handsome building that includes outdoor terraces, a formal living room, an enlarged game room, snack bar, a small theater, and a student-run co-op coffeehouse, open three nights a week, with live entertainment. The town of Amherst is described by one student as a "quaint, small New England town, but it caters to the mass of students in the area with restaurants, coffee shops, and book and music stores. For the many outdoorsy types, good skiing is not far, and Boston (an hour and a half) and New York (almost four) are close enough to make a road trip or two a semester.

Amherst's idyllic setting seems to bring out the athlete in everyone; sports are taken seriously, as both varsity sports and intramurals attract a healthy number. Amherst competes in Division III, but the strong baseball team takes on Division I opponents as well. The women's tennis team recently won the NCAA national championship. Other standouts include men's basketball and soccer, as well as women's volleyball and lacrosse. In any sport, the annual showdown with archrival Williams is inevitably the biggest game of the season, drawing out fans from all corners of campus.

Amherst provides the best of all worlds for its students. The close-knit campus is personal, while students are able to relish the opportunities for study and fun from the network of nearby colleges. Students are granted the freedom to carve their own academic niches while enjoying solid courses and excellent professors to guide them on their way. Though it may be difficult at first for some students to make heads or tails of the academic array, the college fully supports each student in their quests. And with parties, traditions, sports and cultural attractions available for the choosing, Amherst students get a college experience that stays with them well beyond graduation day.

Some Amherst dorms are a bit unexpected: converted fraternity houses that were once Victorian mansions come complete with ballrooms, pianos, hardwood floors, and stained-glass windows.

Overlaps

Yale, Brown, Harvard, Stanford, Dartmouth.

Antioch College

795 Livermore Street, Yellow Springs, OH 45387

Website: antioch-college.edu
Location: Rural
Total Enrollment: 650
Undergraduates: 650
Male/Female: 35/65
SAT Ranges: N/A
ACT Range: N/A
Financial Aid: 91%
Expense: Pr $ $
Phi Beta Kappa: No
Applicants: 600
Accepted: 80%
Enrolled: 35%
Grad in 6 Years: N/A
Returning Freshmen: 83%
Academics: ✍ ✍ ✍
Social: ☎ ☎
Q of L: ★ ★ ★ ★
Admissions: (800) 543-9436
Email Address:
admissions@
antioch-college.edu

Strongest Program:
Cooperative Education

Close relationships often develop between students and faculty, and representatives of both groups sit on several of the influential governing committees.

You say you want a revolution? Well, Antioch College may be the perfect place to start your own. Founded in 1852 by abolitionist and social reformer Horace Mann, Antioch remains a haven for outspoken and independent students who thrive under the rigors of a refreshingly nontraditional education. Antioch pioneered the idea that students should alternate time in the classroom with jobs in the "real world," and this idea has remained the foundation for Antioch's unique approach to training students. Under the college's famed co-op program, students spend nearly half of their college years out in the "real world," be it selling fresh-squeezed orange juice on a street corner in California, studying Buddhism in India, or working in a Fortune 500 company in New York City.

The atmosphere on this architecturally eclectic campus is more reminiscent of a 1960s commune than a small Midwestern college. The students, many of them products of "alternative" high schools, discuss feminism, gay rights, and nuclear proliferation over vegetarian meals, and they are more likely to take road trips to Washington for an environmental rally than show up at a neighboring school's fraternity party. One student cheerfully reports that after students were jailed for taking part in a peaceful protest, the dean of students bailed out all participants. In class, written faculty evaluations take the place of grades, and students are required to submit self-evaluations of their class performance. "Students who aren't self-starters tend to have academic difficulties," notes a senior. A sophomore adds, "The academic program is demanding, engaging, and personalized toward the individual."

In completing Antioch's 32-credit general education program, students spend their first year pursuing a core of courses that blends the traditional liberal arts with examination of the "social, historical, philosophical, and economic" nature of work. In addition, there are distribution requirements in the humanities, social and behavioral sciences, natural sciences, and cultural studies. Physical education is also required. Students report that the academic climate is laid-back yet rigorous. Because classes are usually no larger than 20, students must always be prepared to participate. Close relationships often develop between students and faculty; representatives of both groups sit on several of the influential governing committees, including the administrative council, the housing board, and the community council. "There's a lot of personal attention, everyone knows each other by first names, and discussion dominates," says a student. Each student is also assigned a co-op advisor to help with the nearly continuous job hunt, and a network of alumni offering jobs is one major resource that students can depend on in their search.

Antioch's trimester system lasts 15 weeks, with co-op terms lasting 16 weeks.

The college helps place students in co-op programs, and credit is earned after the student completes a paper or project demonstrating what he or she learned during the co-op experience. Antioch's mission lies in its "commitment to undergraduate experiential learning, and to preparing students to face the challenges and opportunities of the 21st century." In order to receive a "cross-cultural" experience, Antioch has all students spend 3 to 12 months in a significantly different cultural environment. In addition to those offered by the school, study abroad options are available through the Great Lakes College Association.* There is a downside to this: Students blame the high attrition rate on the rigors of the co-op program. One student explains that "students often move every three or six months because of co-op—this is both financially and emotionally draining." Friendships and involvement in extracurricular activities at the Yellow Springs campus often suffer because of the on-again, off-again attendance schedules.

Antioch's trimester system lasts 15 weeks, with co-op terms lasting 16 weeks.

Antioch's traditional academic programs are somewhat uneven. Although there are only eight official majors, each allows for concentration in a more specialized area. The major in physical sciences has traditionally been strong, especially with its heavily stocked research laboratory. Concentrations in political science, psychology, and many of the arts offerings are also established strongholds. Environmental and life sciences is excellent, in part because of the proximity of a 1,000-acre forest preserve, Glen Helen, and a nature museum. Students complain mostly about the history department. The communications program benefits from a major public radio station operated by Antioch, which gives students experience in the broadcasting field.

Being different may be the only thing Antioch students have in common, and diversity is a given on this campus. "We have a reputation for being socially-conscious, eccentric, and non-conformist," says a student, "and there is a lot of truth to this reputation." Twenty percent of the students come from Ohio; the rest hail from points throughout the nation. Five percent of students are African American, 2 percent are Asian American, and 4 percent are Hispanic. A variety of merit scholarships are renewable for four years.

Ninety-five percent of the students are housed on campus in apartment-style dorms. "To get financial aid you have to live on campus," says one resident. In contrast to the college's democratic creed, room assignments are determined by the whim of "a much-courted administrator." Coed and single-sex dorms are available, and all come equipped with kitchens. Everyone is guaranteed on-campus housing if they want it, and students can choose from a number of special options that include a quiet hall, a moderate-noise hall, and even a substance-free hall, which bars smoking and drinking. The Spalt International Center, just a few years old, houses 60 students in foreign language living/learning halls. Seven- and 19-meal-a-week plans are available at the Caf, which features vegetarian entrées, a salad bar, and a popcorn machine. Since the dorms all have kitchens, many students choose the 7-meal plan and form a co-op with friends for the rest.

Without Greek organizations, social life tends to be spontaneous and mellow, and limited to on-campus activities. There is a student coffeehouse, which "is the best hangout space," while stargazers frequently congregate on the roof of the science building. Dance aficionados cut the rug twice a week at campus dances, which one student characterizes as "sweaty celebrations of good energy." "Some students are quite the socialites and others are bookworms," notes a senior, "but there tends not to be any animosity between opposing groups." Many student organizations, including the Anarchist Study Group and Third World Alliance draw widespread student interest. A noteworthy tradition on this untraditional campus is the Quasi-Prom, an annual dance put on by the Lesbian/Gay Center.

One aspect in which the students take pride is their own governance, the Community Government.

Traditionally considered taboo, varsity sports have nevertheless enjoyed a rousing comeback, thanks to the women's rugby team. Gym classes are offered in kayaking, rafting, and horseback riding. Camelot, a 100-lap bicycle race, is an annual event: A team of two races around a muddy track while the audience slings at them yogurt, mud, and "anything else that isn't hard." The 1,000-acre nature preserve ("the glen") across the street "lets you forget the boring flatlands of Ohio." Behind the glen is John Bryan State Park. A nearby reservoir is a popular place for swimming and windsurfing, and Clifton Gorge offers rock climbing.

The town of Yellow Springs is "a bubble of liberalism in Bible Belt Southern Ohio," according to one student. The town hosts a variety of health-food stores, a pizza joint that makes its pies with whole-wheat crust, and an assortment of bars and restaurants. Yellow Springs may become limiting for some students, but that problem is usually solved by the next co-op trimester.

Antioch offers a unique opportunity for students to discover themselves in both the working world and among the college's bright, opinionated, and cooperative student body. "My own sense is that Antioch is on an upswing," says a sophomore, noting the school's "socially active student body, great faculty, and cooperative education program which sends students out into the world to test what they learn in the classroom." Horace Mann once implored his students to "be ashamed to die until you have won some victory for humanity." The Antioch community takes this message to heart.

Overlaps

Oberlin, Evergreen State, Hampshire, Bard, Earlham.

If You Apply To ➤ **Antioch**...Recommended deadline of Feb. 1 for summer or fall regular admissions. Financial aid: Mar. 1. Housing: July 1. Does not guarantee to meet demonstrated need. Campus interviews: recommended, informational and evaluative. Alumni interviews: optional, informational and evaluative. SATs: optional. SAT IIs: optional. Essay question: important experience; significant personal, local, or national issue; what you see yourself doing in 10 years; or portfolio. Looks for those willing to take risks.

Arizona State University

Box 870112, Tempe, AZ 85287-0112

Website: www.asu.edu
Location: Urban
Total Enrollment: 44,215
Undergraduates: 33,948
Male/Female: 47/53
SAT Ranges: V 490–600 M 490–620
ACT Range: 21–26
Financial Aid: 41%
Expense: Pub $
Phi Beta Kappa: Yes
Applicants: 17,082

You've no doubt heard about the postcard that reads, "Weather beautiful, wish you were here." Though this usually applies to some remote vacation spot, it could just as well apply to Arizona State University. Perennial sunshine and balmy afternoons make for a gorgeous academic setting. Add rigorous academics, top-notch facilities, and caring faculty to the mix, and you can see why students at ASU seem so pleased. Says a student, "If you want something at ASU, you will be able to find it."

The ASU campus is a beautiful blend of palm-lined walkways, desert landscapes, and public art displays. Campus architecture ranges from the decidedly modern to turn-of-the-century historic, including the newly renovated Old Main with its Territorial Romanesque style. The campus is officially listed as an arboretum, and ASU groundskeepers tend to more than 115 species of trees that thrive in Arizona's arid climate.

Despite all the pleasant outdoor diversions, ASU students definitely find time to study, and some report the academic climate is challenging. A fifth of the students enter the college of business administration, which is one of the largest in the country and ranks second in placing graduates in the Big Eight accounting firms. Business is ASU's most popular major, followed by psychology and education. There are nine undergraduate schools: business, liberal arts and sciences, engineering and applied sciences, architecture and environmental design, education, fine arts, nursing, public programs (justice studies, leisure studies, communication, public affairs), and social work. The fine arts program features outstanding facilities, an innovative child drama program, and nationally recognized programs in art, music, and dance. Engineering programs, especially microelectronics, robotics, and computer-assisted manufacturing, are sure bets; the facility for high-resolution microscopy allows students to get a uniquely close-up view of atomic structures. ASU students also can specialize across several disciplines. For example, specialization in computer sciences and technology crosses the business, engineering, education, and liberal arts and sciences colleges. The brightest students attend the four-year-old Honors College, which gives them a challenging living/learning experience that culminates in a senior thesis. There are also undergraduate research apprenticeship programs offered in numerous areas. Students who want to leave ASU for a semester or a year may choose to experience London, Latin America, Germany, or numerous other domestic and foreign special programs.

In the liberal arts, the sciences (including solar energy, physical science, geology, and biology) and social sciences are strong and boast first-class facilities, notably the largest university-owned meteorite collection in the world. Planetary science is out of this world; students have the opportunity to collaborate on projects with NASA. Anthropology is a strong department, and Donald C. Johnson, the discoverer of the 3.2-million-year-old fossil skeleton named Lucy, has moved his Institute of Human Origin to the ASU campus. The less technically minded may enjoy the interdisciplinary opportunities in such areas as film studies, urban planning, and Islamic studies. The Walter Cronkite School of Journalism and Telecommunication finished fourth in the Hearst annual writing competition, and Cronkite makes it a point to visit the campus to lecture every year. Among the social sciences, psychology is the standout. Students cite the statistics and sociology departments as weak. Under the general studies program, all students must meet core requirements by choosing courses from five disciplines—literacy and critical inquiry, numeracy, humanities and fine arts, social and behavioral sciences, and natural sciences—as well as from three awareness areas—global, historical, and U.S. cultural diversity. The more than 33,000 undergrads register for class using the "Intouch" telephone system. Students can usually get into a full class if they need to with a faculty override. With ASU's size also come charges of delays and trouble finding the answers to everyday questions. Despite this, students maintain that ASU is a "user-friendly" campus. The library, a noteworthy facility, contains more than 3.1 million volumes, 4.1 million microforms, and almost 30,000 magazine subscriptions.

Arizona State's admissions policy says out-of-state students must either rank in the top quarter of their class or have a 3.0 GPA, cumulative SAT score of 1110, or ACT of 24 in order to enjoy automatic admission. Nearly a quarter of each freshman class comes from out of state, including many Chicagoans fleeing miserable winters. In-state students need to be in the top half of their class or have a 2.5 GPA, as well as a total SAT score of 1040 or an ACT of 22. ASU offers hundreds of athletic scholarships, as well as 1,200 merit scholarships that range from $1,000 to $9,000. Of the student body, Hispanics make up the largest minority group at

(Continued)
Accepted: 80%
Enrolled: 43%
Grad in 6 Years: 47%
Returning Freshmen: 75%
Academics: ✍ ✍ ✍
Social: ☎ ☎ ☎ ☎ ☎
Q of L: ★ ★ ★ ★ ★
Admissions: (480) 965-7788
Email Address:
  ugradINQ@asu.edu

Strongest Programs:
  Accountancy
  Planetary Science
  Engineering
  Business
  Anthropology
  Journalism
  Geology

The Walter Cronkite School of Journalism and Telecommunication finished fourth in the Hearst annual writing competition, and Cronkite makes it a point to visit the campus to lecture every year.

Anthropology is a strong department, and Donald C. Johnson, the discoverer of the 3.2-million-year-old fossil skeleton named Lucy, has moved his Institute of Human Origin to the ASU campus.

11 percent, while African Americans and Asian Americans combined make up 8 percent. While social and political issues touch on everything from race to gender to religious freedom, overall, "ASU has quite a mellow and laid-back attitude," reports a communication major.

The single-sex and coed dorms are generally well maintained and spacious, but they can accommodate only 16 percent of the student body, and there is a waiting list. Because returning students receive priority, prospective freshmen should return their housing applications to be ensured a room. Those who get into campus housing are especially pleased to be placed in one of the three residence halls that boast their own swimming pools and volleyball courts. Off-campus living possibilities are made more accessible through a special service known as the ASU Tenants/Commuters Association, which issues updated vacancy information and will forward it to out-of-staters. The university's Grand Marketplace, a collection of eight "theme" dining centers, may well have the best institutional food in the country.

Many students own cars, and the university has three parking structures to alleviate the parking crunch. A car also puts Colorado mountains, California beaches, Vegas slots, and real Mexican food all within a day's reach. The Grand Canyon is also a popular road trip. Although small in numbers (8 percent of the men and 6 percent of the women), the Greeks have some say on campus, and there are plenty of Greek and non-Greek parties to go around for those who aren't road tripping on the weekends. "The social life at ASU is great," says a senior. "There are so many activities going on that the problem is deciding which one to go to." The ban on alcohol for students under 21 is strictly enforced on campus, but students sometimes get around the rules by attending off-campus parties or procuring a fake ID.

ASU football and basketball fans turn out in droves to cheer on various Division I Sun Devil teams, and the "Fork 'em Devils!" rallying cry often reverberates around campus. The football team really gave them something to cheer about recently when they played in the Rose Bowl. The men's baseball, wrestling, badminton, archery, and gymnastics teams and the men's and women's golf teams are national powerhouses. Intramurals alone feature more than 60 different sports.

Despite the university's massive size, the atmosphere at Arizona State is not overbearing. In fact, ASU students praise all the resources provided to them and revel in the "diversity of opportunity," as one student calls it, including nationally recognized undergraduate programs. For those attending this sun-drenched university, ASU offers a "devil" of a good time.

Overlaps

University of Arizona, Northern Arizona, UCLA, University of Southern California, San Diego State.

If You Apply To ➤

ASU...Rolling admissions. Early action: Nov. 1. Financial aid: Mar. 1. Guarantees to meet demonstrated need. Campus interviews: recommended, informational. No alumni interviews. SATs or ACTs: required. SAT IIs: optional. Accepts electronic applications. No essay question.

Robert L. Nugent Building, Tucson, AZ 85721

With a campus that's encircled by mountain ranges and the beautiful Sonoran Desert, lined with palm trees and cacti, and set against a backdrop of stunning Tucson sunsets, it's no surprise that students at the University of Arizona love to hang out at the mall. Of course, we're not referring to the shopping center but to a huge grassy area in the middle of campus where nearly 35,000 Wildcats gather between classes. Judging by numbers alone, that's enough people to fill a medium-sized town. But students here claim that UA really has a strong sense of community and offers a genuinely friendly campus. "Nobody else has a huge central meeting place like we do," says a senior marketing major. "I always see familiar and friendly faces around the mall area." With all the natural beauty that surrounds them, it's no wonder that the Wildcats simply purr through four satisfying years.

Architecturally, the UA campus distinguishes itself from the city's regiment of adobe buildings with a design that seems a study in the versatility of red brick. Old Main, the university's first building, is into its second century, but others verge on high-tech science facilities. Sciences are unquestionably the school's forte—the astronomy department is among the nation's best, helped by those clear night skies. Students have access not only to leading astronomers, but also to the most up-to-date equipment, including a huge 176-inch telescope operated jointly by the university and the Smithsonian. A $28-million aerospace and mechanical engineering building has a state-of-the-art subsonic wind tunnel and rocket combustion test facility. The facility emphasizes the department's strengths in fluid dynamics and hydrodynamics.

The history and English departments are standouts, as are several of the social science programs. Eager shutterbugs can pore through photographer Ansel Adams's personal collection, and the Center for Creative Photography offers one of the leading photographic collections in the world. Students in the popular business and public administration school can pick racetrack management as their area of expertise, while interested anthropology students can delve into garbage research. Areas getting low marks from students are the language programs and journalism department.

Under the core curriculum, students take 10 general education courses in common. They fall under the broad categories of arts, humanities, traditions and cultures, natural sciences, and individuals and societies. In addition, almost everyone gets a healthy dose of freshman composition, math, and foreign language. Academic competition, according to most students, is left up to both the individual and the specific concentration. "The courses can range in difficulty from somewhat challenging to impossible," explains one senior. The University Honors Center offers one of the nation's largest and most selective honors programs (students must maintain a GPA of 3.5 to remain in the program). In addition to offering 200 honors courses per year, the center features smaller classes, personalized advising, special library privileges, and great research opportunities. The Undergraduate Biology Research Program also has a national reputation. Teaching is well regarded, with some freshman courses taught by graduate students. "Each of the professors and TAs have something special to bring to the classes and show an exceptional amount of enthusiasm," a sophomore says.

Despite tougher admission standards, the administration cites a sharp

Website: www.arizona.edu

Location: Urban

Total Enrollment: 34,327

Undergraduates: 26,157

Male/Female: 48/52

SAT Ranges: V 490–610 M 490–610

ACT Range: 20–26

Financial Aid: 70%

Expense: Pub $

Phi Beta Kappa: Yes

Applicants: 17,595

Accepted: 82%

Enrolled: 36%

Grad in 6 Years: 52%

Returning Freshmen: 80%

Academics: ✍ ✍ ✍

Social: ☎ ☎ ☎ ☎

Q of L: ★ ★ ★ ★

Admissions: (520) 621-3237

Email Address: APPINFO@arizona.edu

Strongest Programs:
Management Information Systems
Nursing
Astronomy
Pharmacy
Creative Writing
Aerospace Engineering

increase in freshman applications over the past few years, especially out-of-staters who constitute 28 percent of the student body. The competition has always been much tougher for those who hail from beyond the sunny Arizona boundaries, and some colleges—nursing, pharmacy, and architecture, for example—are virtually closed to them. In addition to various merit scholarships, all the athletic scholarships allowed by the NCAA are available. Hispanics account for 15 percent of the enrollment, African Americans for 3 percent, and Asian Americans for 5 percent. A diversity action council, a newly developed student minority advisory committee, and cultural resource centers help students deal with race relation issues. An active and popular student government runs a free legal service and a tenants' complaint center, and the university has instituted many programs to help those with learning disabilities.

Dorm rooms tend to be small but well maintained, the major problem being getting a room rather than living comfortably in it. "It's important to send your housing application in early," advises a veteran. Only 19 percent of undergraduates live in the dorms, while most upperclassmen flock to the abundant and inexpensive apartments near the school. The best way to enjoy the excellent food service at the student union's seven restaurants is to use the university-issued All Aboard credit card, which helps students take advantage of the wealth of different gustatory options and frees them from carrying cash.

Despite the high percentage of off-campus residents, students stream back onto campus on weekends for parties, sports, and cultural events. Fifteen percent of the men and 14 percent of the women belong to fraternities or sororities. The campus is technically alcohol-free, though some question whether the frats have realized that yet. Still, most social life takes place off campus. There are a lot of different dance clubs around town and some do have after hours for underaged people. Those who feel they must go elsewhere need only head to the Mexican town of Nogales (one hour away), where there is no drinking-age limitation. Many students are content remaining in Tucson because it offers "the most incredible sunrises and sunsets, and delightful temperatures year-round."

One of the UA's most time-honored traditions is Spring Fling, described as the largest student-run carnival in the country. Athletics is also somewhat of a tradition here. The basketball Wildcats have been among the nation's leaders in recent years. Division I football and baseball enjoy national prominence, generate lots of money for other men's and women's sports teams, and provide great weekend entertainment, especially when the opposing team is big-time rival Arizona State. UA's battle cry "Bear Down!" frequently heard at sporting events, dates back to the 1930s, where a campus football hero, fatally injured in a car crash, whispered his last message to his teammates: "Tell them, tell them to bear down." More than 60 years later, the enigmatic slogan still appears on T-shirts and in a gym on the central campus.

The University of Arizona offers a wide variety of academic opportunities, and enough diversions to make it no place for those who need coddling or individual guidance. As for the spectacular weather, prospectives are warned to honestly evaluate how it will affect their ability to concentrate. UA is the place to go to engage in the pursuit of truth, knowledge, and a good tan. Just don't put too much emphasis on the tan.

Overlaps

Arizona State, Northern Arizona, UCLA, University of Colorado.

<table>
<tr><td>**If You Apply To** ➤</td><td>**Arizona**...Early decision: Oct. 1. Regular admissions: Apr. 1. Financial aid and housing: Mar. 1. Campus interviews: optional. Alumni interviews: optional, informational. SATs or ACTs: required. SAT IIs: optional. No essay question.</td></tr>
</table>

University of Arkansas

200 Hunt Hall, Fayetteville, AR 72701

If you're planning to attend the University of Arkansas, you'd better start practicing your wildest and craziest hog call. Although this behavior might seem silly at some universities, it's practically mandatory when the pride and joy of this university, the Razorbacks, play. And don't think that Bill and Hillary Rodham Clinton haven't contributed their share of pig calls—both of them served on the law school faculty of U of A. Whether you're interested in poultry science or creative writing and translation (both of which are ranked among the best programs in the country), let down your inhibitions and bring your loudest hog cheer to one of the most spirited schools in the South.

Nestled among the mountains, lakes, and streams of the Ozarks, the University of Arkansas is located in the extreme northwest corner of the state. The campus architecture has been characterized as "mismatched towers," and indeed, walkways connect the modern concrete and WPA-vintage buildings. A bit of Hollywood Boulevard–style nostalgia can be found on the Senior Walk; the concrete sidewalk is engraved every year with the name of every student who made it through to graduation. The focal point of the campus is the stately brick Old Main building, which used to house the entire university. A new center for space and planetary science is in the works, and the renovations at Razorback Stadium are still underway.

Established as a land-grant institution in 1871, the University of Arkansas has since expanded its scope of educational responsibilities from solely agricultural and mechanical arts to a broad spectrum of academic offerings in eight colleges and professional schools. If you are of the fowl-mooded type, you may want to roost in the school's Poultry Health Center, one of the nation's laboratories for the containment and research of poultry epidemics. But research isn't the only game in town; U of A offers more than 150 undergraduate degree programs. The Dale Bumpers College of Agriculture Food and Life Sciences offers directed study and internships at the Scottish Agricultural College in Edinburgh, Scotland, while business administration students take advantage of study abroad options around the globe. The university boasts a fine English department, and a history department strong in Southern history. Other academic strengths include physics, chemistry, engineering, and architecture. Students say, however, that the biology and sociology departments need improvements. A BA in American Studies, Ph.D. in public policy, and MS in applied physics have recently been added.

Every student must take the required university core curriculum, which includes courses in English, U.S. history or government, math, natural sciences, fine arts or humanities, and social sciences. Arts and sciences students must also achieve proficiency in a foreign language. The honors program gives

Website: www.uark.edu

Location: Small city

Total Enrollment: 15,167

Undergraduates: 12,240

Male/Female: 51/49

SAT Ranges: V 500–650 M 520–650

ACT Range: 21–27

Financial Aid: 35%

Expense: Pub $ $

Phi Beta Kappa: Yes

Applicants: 4,452

Accepted: 88%

Enrolled: 54%

Grad in 6 Years: 45%

Returning Freshmen: 77%

Academics: ✎ ✎ ✎

Social: ☎ ☎ ☎ ☎

Q of L: ★ ★ ★

Admissions: (501) 575-2000

Email Address:
uafadmis@comp.uark.edu

Strongest Programs:
Engineering
Agricultural Law
Poultry Science
Business Marketing
Accounting
Architecture
Creative Writing

undergraduates a chance for independent study, self-designed courses, and individual research. The prevailing academic atmosphere is fairly relaxed. "There's a certain level of competitiveness here but not enough to put undue stress on anyone," says an environmental science major. Students rate their professors highly and report they're enthusiastic about teaching. "I have the highest respect for all of my professors," says a senior.

Students at the U of A are of the small-town, 1950s Main Street variety. Arkansas residents make up 88 percent of the student body. Only 6 percent of the students are African American, 1 percent Hispanic, and another 3 percent Asian American. "There is some tension between races, but for the most part, people are civil to each other," says a political science/European studies double major. Arkansas is prime Bible Belt territory, so vocal fundamentalist groups are in no short supply. Campus dress ranges from upscale to down-home, though the Greeks are known for wearing "ties, oxfords, and dresses," presumably not all at once. Approximately 900 merit scholarships are available, ranging from $500 to $15,000. The university also gives out athletic scholarships to 216 bristling young Razorbacks in a wide variety of sports.

All freshmen who are single and under 21 are required to live in on-campus housing, which is abundant and relatively well maintained. All the dorms are single-sex, except one that is coed by floor. Students recommend Gregson and Holcombe halls for freshmen. Dining facilities are adequate—a few prize salad bars are to be found on campus for those willing to seek them out. The 25 Greek societies (26 percent of the women and 21 percent of the men join) are the most prominent social presence on campus, to the dismay of many. Campus-sponsored activities include theme parties, such as Casino Night or Holiday on the Hill, but a crackdown on campus drinking has stanched the flow of alcohol. For entertainment off campus, George's and José's are popular weekend nightspots. Fayetteville is a quiet, reasonably crime-free town that provides most of the necessities of student life. Bluegrass festivals, craft fairs, and good fishing are among the regional charms.

And then there's sports. "The Hogs rule" is how one student describes their role on campus. There are Razorback logos on T-shirts, napkins, book covers, license plates, and on game day, on the cheeks of ecstatic fans. The influx of spectators on game weekends in the fall "makes the campus look like midtown New York," one student comments. The school's indoor track, outdoor track, and cross-country teams boast a coach who has won more NCAA championships than any coach in the history of the NCAA. The volleyball and basketball teams boast recent conference championships as well. A well-equipped recreation center provides more than adequate facilities for less serious jocks of both sexes.

In 1840, a local store clerk wrote that Fayetteville "has become one of the most lawless and uncivilized places in all creation…shooting, stabbing, knocking down and dragging out appear to be the order of the day in this place. Almost everyone you see is armed to the teeth at all times." Well, things seem to have calmed down a bit now. The town, students note, has grown up and around the campus. Although there are still a number of students who try to reenact Fayetteville's unruly past, most come to the University of Arkansas to get a solid education at a bargain price.

Arkansas…Rolling admissions. Financial aid: Mar. 1. Meets demonstrated need of 49%. Campus interviews: optional, evaluative. Alumni interviews: optional, informational. ACTs or achievement test (writing): required. Accepts the Common Application and electronic applications.

Atlanta University Center

Atlanta is viewed as the preeminent city in the country for bright, talented, and successful blacks. It became the capital of the civil rights movement in the 1960s—the town whose leaders said was "too busy to hate"—and today it is a place where middle-class blacks can savor "the black experience."

At the heart of this extraordinary culture is the Atlanta University Center, the largest black educational complex in the world, replete with its own central library and central computing center. The seven component institutions have educated generations of black leaders. The Reverend Martin Luther King, Jr. went to Morehouse College; his grandmother, mother, sister, and daughter to Spelman College. Graduates spread across the country in a pattern that developed when these were among the best of the few colleges to which talented blacks could aspire. Even now, when the options are almost limitless, alumni continue to send their children back for more.

The center consists of three undergraduate colleges (Morris Brown, Morehouse, and Spelman) and three graduate institutions (Clark Atlanta University, the Interdenominational Theological Seminary, as well as the Morehouse College of Medicine) on adjoining campuses in the center of Atlanta three miles from downtown. Students at these affiliated schools can enjoy the quiet pace of their beautiful magnolia-studded campuses or plunge into all the culture and excitement of this most dynamic of Deep South cities. The six original schools—all but the medical school—became affiliated in 1929, using the model of California's Claremont Colleges, but they remain fiercely independent. Each has its own administration, board of trustees, and academic specialties, and each maintains its own dorms, cafeterias, and other facilities. There is cross-registration among the institutions (Morehouse students, for example, go to Spelman for drama and art courses) and with Georgia State and Emory University as well. The governing body of the consortium, the Atlanta University Center, Inc., administers a center-wide dual degree program in engineering in conjunction with Georgia Tech—and it runs campus security, a student crisis center, and a joint institute of science research. There is also a center-wide service of career planning and placement where recruiters may come and interview students from all six of the institutions.

Dating and social life at the coeducational institutions tend to take place within the individual schools, though Morehouse, a men's college, and Spelman, a women's college, maintain a close academic and social relationship. The Morehouse-Spelman Glee Club takes its abundance of talent around the nation, and its annual Christmas concert on the Spelman campus is a standing-room-only event.

Morehouse and Spelman (see full write-ups below) constitute the Ivy League of historically black colleges. Following are sketches of the other two institutions offering undergraduate degrees.

Clark Atlanta University. (www.cau.edu)

Formed by the consolidation of Clark College, a four-year liberal arts institution, and Atlanta University, which offered only graduate degrees, CAU is a comprehensive coeducational institution that offers undergraduate, graduate, and professional degrees. The university draws on the former strengths of both schools, offering quality programs in the health professions, public policy, and mass communications (including print journalism, radio and television production, and filmmaking). Graduate and professional programs include education, business, library information studies, social work, and arts and sciences.

Morris Brown College. (www.morrisbrown.edu)

An open-admission, four-year undergraduate institution that is related to the African Methodist Episcopal

Church. Its most popular programs are education and business administration. Students receive considerable personal attention, and those arriving with poor academic preparation are provided with special help. Morris Brown also offers evening courses for employed adults as well as a program of co-op work-study education. Only a small percentage of Morris Brown graduates continue their formal education beyond the baccalaureate. Enrollment: 600 men/870 women.

Morehouse College

830 Westview Drive, Atlanta, GA 30314

Website: www.morehouse.edu
Location: Urban
Total Enrollment: 3,012
Undergraduates: 3,012
Male/Female: 100/0
SAT Ranges: V 440–680 M 470–680
ACT Range: 19–32
Financial Aid: N/A
Expense: Pr $
Phi Beta Kappa: Yes
Applicants: 2,785
Accepted: 65%
Enrolled: 41%
Grad in 6 Years: 56%
Returning Freshmen: 85%
Academics: ✍ ✍ ✍
Social: ☎ ☎ ☎
Q of L: ★ ★ ★
Admissions: (404) 215-2632 or (800) 851-1254
Email Address: apattillo@morehouse.edu

Strongest Programs:
Economics
Business
Biology
Political Science
Psychology

Founded in 1867, Morehouse College has the distinction of being the nation's only historically black, four-year, liberal arts college for men. If its sister school, Spelman, was once the "Vassar of black society," Morehouse was the Harvard or Yale, attracting male students from the upper echelons of society around the country. Top students come to Morehouse because they want an institution with a strong academic program and a supportive atmosphere in which to cultivate their success orientation and leadership skills without facing the additional barriers they might encounter at a predominantly white institution. "Morehouse is a college of young, assertive, ambitious black men," says a psych major. Notable alumni include the Reverend Martin Luther King, Jr., Dr. David Satcher (U.S. Surgeon General), Samuel L. Jackson, Spike Lee, and Dr. Louis Sullivan, current president of the Morehouse School of Medicine and former U.S. Secretary of Health and Human Services.

Located near downtown Atlanta, the 61-acre Morehouse campus is home to 35 buildings, including the Martin Luther King, Jr., International Chapel. In the past decade, the college has enriched its academic program, conducted a successful multimillion-dollar national fund-raising campaign, increased student scholarships and faculty salaries, doubled its endowment, improved its physical plant, and acquired 12 additional acres of land.

The general education program includes not only 68 semester hours in four major disciplines (humanities, natural sciences, math, and social sciences), but also the study of "the unique African and African-American heritage on which so much of our modern American culture is built." In fact, appreciation of this culture is one of the college's main drawing cards. "Many students are here to get a greater understanding of their heritage and to promote it," attests one student.

Undergraduate programs include the traditional liberal arts majors in the humanities and social and natural sciences. While the sciences have been traditionally strong at Morehouse, business courses have risen in prominence, and the college has obtained accreditation of the undergraduate business department by the American Assembly of Collegiate Schools of Business. The most popular major is business administration. Engineering, which trails shortly behind in popularity, is actually a 3–2 program in conjunction with Georgia Tech and other larger universities. The school also runs a program with NASA that allows students to engage in independent research. Programs that receive less favorable reviews from students are English, art, and drama, and the administration admits that physical education and some of the humanities offerings could use some strengthening. Study abroad options include programs offered through the Associated Colleges of the South consortium.* The school also offers courses and additional resources as a member of the Atlanta Regional Consortium for Higher Education.* The academic climate at the House can get intense, with students learning and challenging themselves for the sake of learning and not just to bust a curve. "Morehouse offers an academic structure that is both competitive and rigorous," states a freshman.

Counseling, including career counseling, is considered quite strong, and one senior says, "My professors tend to develop personal relationships/friendships/mentorships with the students."

Seventy-three percent of Morehouse students come from outside the state, with a sizable number from New York and California. Sixty-seven percent graduated in the top quarter of their high school class. Merit scholarships are available, many providing full tuition. And there are more than 100 scholarships for athletes in football, basketball, track, soccer, and tennis.

There's limited housing, leaving a large part of the student body to make do on their own. Half the students search for off-campus quarters. For freshmen, students recommend Graves Hall, the college's oldest building, built in 1889. Those who do get campus housing sometimes wish they hadn't. Complaints range from "too small" to "not well maintained." Most upperclassmen live off campus. The meal plan at Morehouse is mandatory for students living on campus, and draws its share of complaints.

Morehouse's Homecoming, the centerpiece of Spike Lee's movie, *School Daze*, is a joint effort between Morehouse and Spelman. The queen elected by Morehouse men has traditionally been a Spelman woman, as are the cheerleaders and majorettes. The four fraternities, which sign up a very small percentage of the students, hold popular parties; "drinking is not a big deal here," most students concur. Going out on the town in Atlanta is a popular evening activity, and on-campus football games, concerts, movies, and religious programs all draw crowds. In its early years, Morehouse left much to be desired in the area of varsity sports, but it now competes well in NCAA Division II. Track, cross-country, tennis, basketball, football, and soccer are all strong, but it is the strong intramural program that "allows students a chance to become the Dr. J. that we all have lurking inside us," notes one incognito superstar. During football season, Morehouse men road-trip to follow the games at Howard, Hampton, and Tuskegee universities.

Morehouse is well equipped to serve the modern heirs of a distinguished tradition. Morehouse students don't just attend Morehouse. They become part of what amounts to a network of men who share the bonds of having had the Morehouse experience, and graduates find previous alumni stand ready and willing to help them with jobs and other needs.

While the sciences have been traditionally strong at Morehouse, business courses have risen in prominence.

Overlaps

Clark Atlanta, Howard, Georgia Tech, Hampton.

If You Apply To ➤ **Morehouse...**Early action: Nov. 1. Regular admissions: Feb. 15. Financial aid: Apr. 1. Does not guarantee to meet demonstrated need. Campus and alumni interviews: recommended, informational. SATs or ACTs: required. SAT IIs: optional. Essay question: greatest influence on your life; why Morehouse?

Spelman College

350 Spelman Lane, Atlanta, GA 30314

Website: www.spelman.edu
Location: Urban
Total Enrollment: 1,937
Undergraduates: 1,937
Male/Female: 0/100
SAT Ranges: V 500–590 M 480–570
ACT Range: 20–24
Financial Aid: N/A
Expense: Pr $
Phi Beta Kappa: No
Applicants: 2,972
Accepted: 50%
Enrolled: 34%
Grad in 6 Years: N/A
Returning Freshmen: 88%
Academics: ✍ ✍ ✍
Social: ☎ ☎ ☎
Q of L: ★ ★ ★ ★
Admissions: (800) 982-2411
Email Address: admiss@spelman.edu

Strongest Programs:
Engineering
Natural Sciences
Premed
Prelaw

As one of only two surviving black women's colleges in the United States, Spelman College is far and away the most prestigious. And it's certainly found a friend in comedian Bill Cosby. His $20-million gift helps keep tuition low and quality academics available. Cosby is not alone in his generosity; Spelman recently completed a campaign that raised $144 million, which is said to be the largest amount ever raised by a historically black university. These contributions—as well as a strong academic department—are sure to produce promising young black women who will become leaders in fields ranging from science to the arts.

Founded in 1881 by two white women from New England (it was named after John D. Rockefeller's mother-in-law, Mrs. Harvey Spelman), the school was traditionally the starting point for teachers, nurses, and other black female leaders. Today's emphasis is on getting Spelman grads into the courtrooms, boardrooms, and engineering labs. Honing women for leadership is the main mission, and that nurturing takes place on a classic collegiate-green 32-acre campus with a $140-million endowment.

These are heady times for Spelman. Although the college finds itself competing head-on with the Seven Sisters and other prestigious and predominantly white institutions that are eager to recruit talented black women, the college is none the worse for wear. Students still flock here for that something special that the predominantly white schools lack: an environment with first-rate academics where black women can develop self-confidence and leadership skills before venturing into a world where they will once again be in the minority.

The college offers a well-rounded liberal arts curriculum that emphasizes the importance of critical and analytical thinking and problem solving. Usually by the end of sophomore year, students are expected to complete 34 credit hours of core requirements, including English composition, foreign language, health and physical education, mathematics, African diaspora and the world, African American women's studies, and computer literacy. In addition, freshmen are required to take First Year Orientation, and sophomores must take Sophomore Assembly. Spelman's liberal arts program introduces students to the principal branches of learning, specifically languages, literature, English, the natural sciences, humanities, social sciences, and fine arts.

Spelman's established strengths lie in the natural sciences (especially biology) and the humanities, both of which have outstanding faculties. Over the last decade, the college has greatly strengthened its offerings in math and the natural sciences; extensive undergrad research programs provide students with publishing opportunities, and many end up attending grad school to become researchers. Many students have discarded the popular majors of the early '70s—education and the fine arts—in favor of premed and prelaw programs, and these programs remain strong. The dual degree program in engineering (in cooperation with Georgia Tech) is also a standout. The Women's Research and Resource Center specializes in black women's studies and community outreach to black women.

Individual attention is the hallmark of a Spelman education. About 70 percent of the faculty have doctorates, and many are black and/or female—and thus excellent role models, ones the students find very accessible. One political science major reports that the majority of instructors are "very well learned. Their lectures are tactful and effective," and she is "often challenged to put forth the best effort." Except for some of the required courses, classes are small; most have fewer than 25 students. Students who want to spread their wings can venture abroad through a variety of programs, or try one of the domestic exchange arrangements with Wellesley, Mount Holyoke, Vassar, or Mills. The school also offers courses and additional resources as a member of the Atlanta Regional Consortium for Higher Education.*

Spelman's reputation continues to attract black women from all over the country, including a high proportion of alumnae children. All but 17 percent of the students come from outside Georgia. Students represented here include high achievers looking for a supportive environment, and those women with high potential who performed relatively poorly in high school. Only about 4 percent of the student body are not African American. Spelman does not guarantee to meet the financial need of all those admitted, but it does offer a variety of merit scholarships. There are no athletic scholarships.

Housing is "well kept and quite comfortable," reports a mathematics major. Because Spelman is an old school and it has tried to keep up the original buildings, most of the dorms are relatively old. But that certainly can add to the school's historical charm, and students report having little trouble in getting a room. There are 11 dorms, and students recommend that freshmen should check out the Howard Harreld dorm. About a third of the students elect to live off campus in a nearby residential area. The meal plan is mandatory for campus dwellers.

Largely because of the Atlanta University Center, students also have plenty of chances for social interaction with other nearby colleges. "Students mingle in the student centers of all four schools all the time, especially on Fridays," a veteran explains. "Atlanta is a great college town!" gushes one junior. "If there is any place that a student can be academically enriched, it is here." Spelmanites do take advantage of the big-city nightlife; they attend plays, symphonies, and the hot Atlanta nightclubs such as Ethiopian Vibrations, Fat Tuesdays, and Lenoxx. Sororities are present but only in small numbers—3 percent of the students go Greek. The attitude on drinking leans toward the conservative. Says one student, "No alcohol on campus—period." The most anticipated annual events include sisterhood initiation ceremonies and the Founders Day celebration. Although varsity sports are not the highlight here, the school boasts fine volleyball, basketball, and tennis teams; synchronized swimming is the specialty, however. Athletic facilities are poor, but there are several organized intramurals, including flag football and bowling.

Spelman College has spent a century furthering the education and opportunities of black women. It has adapted its curriculum to meet the career aspirations of today's youth, built up its bankroll, and successfully met the challenge posed by affirmative action in other universities. Still an elite institution in black society, Spelman is staking its future on its ability to provide a unique kind of education that allows its graduates to compete with anyone.

The Women's Research and Resource Center specializes in black women's studies and community outreach to black women.

Overlaps

Clark Atlanta, Tuskegee, Hampton, Howard, Xavier.

If You Apply To ➤ **Spelman...**Early action: Nov. 15. Regular admissions: Feb. 1. Does not guarantee to meet demonstrated need. Campus interviews: optional, informational. No alumni interviews. SATs or ACTs: required. SAT IIs: optional. Essay question: personal statement reflecting achievements, interests, personal goal; or issue of personal, local, or national concern. Seeks women who are active in school, church, or community.

College of the Atlantic

105 Eden Street, Bar Harbor, ME 04609

Website: www.coa.edu
Location: Small town
Total Enrollment: 287
Undergraduates: 283
Male/Female: 32/68
SAT Ranges: V 580–680 M
   550–640
ACT Range: 20–27
Financial Aid: 63%
Expense: Pr $ $ $
Phi Beta Kappa: No
Applicants: 242
Accepted: 49%
Enrolled: 50%
Grad in 6 Years: 67%
Returning Freshmen: 80%
Academics: ✑ ✑ ✑
Social: ☎ ☎
Q of L: ★ ★ ★
Admissions: (800) 528-0025
Email Address:
   inquiry@ecology.coa.edu

Strongest Programs:
   Human Ecology
   Marine Biology
   Environmental Studies
   Public Policy
   English Literature

Each student, with the help of advisors and resource specialists, designs an individual course of study that draws from different programs.

The founders of College of the Atlantic cast a worried eye on destruction of the environment, pollution, troubled inner cities, and the harmful effects of job automation, and they decided to do something about it by creating a "mission-oriented" college that would address those issues. The school's curriculum is centered around a core study of human ecology—the relationship between humans and their natural and social environments. "COA students are really concerned about what is happening to the world," says a senior.

Set upon the island of Mount Desert, along the shoreline of Frenchman Bay and adjacent to Acadia National Park, the 26-acre campus is covered in old flowers, vegetable gardens, and oceanside lawns. The most recent addition to the campus is a new building for the Natural History Museum.

Though the college's only major is human ecology, most courses focus on a single aspect of man's relationship to the world. There are not traditional academic departments, but rather three broad resource areas: environmental science, arts and design, and applied human studies. A course on creativity, for instance, might pair a scientist and a poet to examine parallels in scientific and artistic thought. Under the umbrella of human ecology, many students choose to concentrate on more narrowly defined topics, such as marine studies, biological and environmental sciences, public policy, creative arts, environmental design, consciousness and culture, education, and writing. Each student, with the help of advisors and resource specialists, designs an individual course of study that draws from different programs. The sciences still stand out as the ruling orientation, with excellent instruction available in ecology, zoology, and marine biology. The most recent addition to the curriculum is the creation of a more formal video and performance art program. "The academic climate at COA is fairly laid-back, but courses are very rigorous," says a junior. "Professors ask a lot, and students give a lot." Students have an opportunity for hands-on research at Allied Whale, the school's marine research arm, as well as in a course that prepares exhibits for the college's natural history museum. COA also offers more than 90 courses from the Human Studies resource area, with significant concentrations in literature, public policy, philosophy, economics, history, law, education, and anthropology.

Most of student life at COA is intense and semicommunal, beginning with a rugged five-day wilderness orientation occurring before a student's first semester. Students must also complete a 10-week off-campus internship, participate in a student-run problem-solving workshop, and support at least one "campus-building" activity, such as the student government or newspaper. Freshmen take a human ecology course and a writing course, and all must complete a survey course in Western civilization. Juniors must write a human-ecology essay and expand it during their senior year, until it grows into their senior project, a major work of independent study.

With fewer than 30 full-time professors, students develop close relationships with their teachers. Students receive written evaluations of their work (although they may request a grade), and they must reciprocate with their own evaluation of the course and their performance in it. Written work usually boils down to a term paper. The unusual advising system (a three-person student-faculty team chosen by the advisee), described as "extremely personable," further promotes close student-faculty contact.

COA's library was destroyed in a disastrous fire in 1983, but a tremendous group effort quickly produced an almost total replacement collection of books. An updated library was erected, complete with everything the old one had plus a computer center. There are only 31,000 volumes on hand, but COA belongs to OCLC, a national consortium that gives students access to over 18,000 libraries.

Students attracted to the quirky College of the Atlantic and its unique curriculum are often bright and idealistic, with 36 percent in the top tenth of their high school class. The school is predominantly white, with African American, Hispanics, and Asian Americans combining to make up 3 percent of the population. "People here are very interested in gay rights, women's rights, animal rights, the environment, the free Tibet movement, recycling, and a million other things," says a freshman. "Almost all students have strong opinions and are willing to fight for what they believe in." Numerous merit scholarships are available to qualified students, ranging from $1,000 to $3,000. There are no athletic scholarships.

Most students live in nearby Bar Harbor; freshmen have first priority in on-campus housing, and the 40 percent that live on campus enjoy small cooperative houses with 5 to 20 others, as well as a fairly new dorm that houses 60 students. Some students, particularly the older ones, prefer to "seek out special places to live" in the nearby countryside. The college provides 15 meals during the week, including the popular vegetarian alternative, but students fend for themselves on the weekends.

Though the college's only major is human ecology, most courses focus on a single aspect of man's relationship to the world.

Though the tiny tourist town of Bar Harbor is packed with visitors during the summer, it rolls up its sidewalks during the winter. But most students at COA prefer a more laid-back lifestyle to the often-frenetic pace of typical undergraduate social life and enjoy Bar Harbor's cozy atmosphere. "It gets to the point where you know everyone in the grocery store in town during the winter," says a senior. Few students leave campus on the weekends—after all, Boston, the nearest urban center, is five and a half hours away. Campus social functions revolve around nature and the seasons, including biking, hiking, boating, cross-country skiing, skating, and rock climbing. Not surprisingly for a school that prides itself on its "tree-hugger" and "granola" image, there are no fraternities or sororities, but students still can kick back at off-campus house parties. Although students say that most students under 21 are respectful of underage drinking prohibitions, they also acknowledge that alcohol is available for those who want it. The school is mostly female, with men making up only about one-third of the population. Two new additions to COA's extracurricular life are men's and women's soccer teams known as the Blackflies and nicknamed the "Swarm." Though relatively new, they have earned strong student support.

COA students seem to have few gripes. Though the close quarters and tiny student population can be stifling at times, students appreciate the rich curriculum and tight community that is found here. In short, the school is finding ways to help those who want to help the world.

Overlaps

Marlboro, Colby, Colorado College, Cornell University, Reed.

If You Apply To ➤ **COA**...Early decision I: Dec. 1. Early decision II: Jan. 1. Regular admissions: Mar. 1. Financial Aid: Feb. 15. Housing: May 1. Guarantees to meet demonstrated need. Campus interviews: recommended, evaluative. Alumni interviews: optional, evaluative. SAT I or ACT: optional. SAT IIs: optional. Accepts electronic applications. Essay question: introduce a new idea or material thing to primitive culture; comment on natural environment versus urban setting; how you fit into COA's idea of self-government; comment on quote from book; open essay. Looks for students with commitment to improving the quality of life on this planet.

Auburn University

202 Mary Martin Hall, Auburn, AL 36849

Website: www.auburn.edu
Location: Small town
Total Enrollment: 22,120
Undergraduates: 19,327
Male/Female: 52/48
SAT Ranges: V 480–590 M 500–600
ACT Range: 20–26
Financial Aid: 28%
Expense: Pub $ $
Phi Beta Kappa: No
Applicants: 10,542
Accepted: 88%
Enrolled: 40%
Grad in 6 Years: 66%
Returning Freshmen: 81%
Academics: ✍ ✍
Social: ☎ ☎ ☎
Q of L: ★ ★ ★
Admissions: (334) 844-4080
Email Address:
admissions@auburn.edu

Strongest Programs:
Agriculture
Architecture
Engineering
Pharmacy
Veterinary Medicine
Prehealth Programs
Economics
Fisheries

Pharmacy and veterinary medicine are highly regarded, as are the biological sciences; the premed major is popular as are psychology, civil engineering, mechanical engineering, and education.

Good ol' Alabama is known for much more than its rich Southern culture. It's home to more than 20,000 football-crazy socialites at Auburn University. Aside from its impressive and renowned football team and record, Auburn is also known for its successful agricultural and technical fields. With many strong departments and programs, Auburn offers more to its students than just an exciting football experience.

"On the rolling plains of Dixie, 'neath its sun-kissed sky," begins Auburn's alma mater, and most students think the campus couldn't be lovelier. Huge mossy trees, lush lawns, and majestic colonnades grace the nearly 2,000 sprawling acres, though most of the "mellow" redbrick Georgian and modern academic buildings are grouped in a compact central location. The town of Auburn, whose namesake is depicted in an Oliver Goldsmith poem as the "loveliest village of the plain," grew up amid miles of forest and farmland largely to serve the university.

As a public land-grant institution, Auburn's traditional academic strengths have been in the agricultural sciences. But architecture, business, and engineering are also strong. Pharmacy and veterinary medicine are highly regarded, as are the biological sciences; the premed major is popular as are psychology, civil engineering, mechanical engineering, and education. Math and sciences are particularly avoided by many students. Auburn also offers a freshwater fisheries program that ranks among the strongest offered anywhere.

The university's common core of courses requires 10 quarter hours of composition (including 5 for freshmen and 5 taken at the junior or senior level), 10 quarter hours of literature and science, 5 quarter hours of math and philosophy, 9 quarter hours of social science and history, and 3 quarter hours of fine arts. Two upper-level writing reinforcement classes are required components of each student's concentration. There is an optional (and popular) freshman seminar called the Auburn Experience, which serves as an introduction to university resources and transition into the college environment. Whereas engineering and premed are intense, many other areas are fairly casual. "There are both competitive and laid-back courses. In general, a spirit of teamwork pervades," says one engineering junior. The co-op option, which provides pay and credits in several professional fields, is increasingly popular, as is the campus ROTC program. An honors program offers greater academic challenge to those who want it. The faculty receives praise from students, but TAs teach many of the lower-level classes. "The quality of teaching increases greatly once you start taking the classes for your major," one senior admits.

Two-thirds of the undergraduates are homegrown Alabamians. Blacks account for only 7 percent of the undergraduates. The conservative tone of this Bible Belt campus fosters many Christian groups, and Auburn is home to one of the largest branches of the Campus Crusade for Christ movement in the United States. Each year the school awards over 1,500 merit scholarships and offers hundreds of athletic scholarships and its own non-need-based loan program.

Fourteen of Auburn's 25 dorms have been renovated, but only 16 percent of the students reside in them. There is only one coed dorm, and visiting hours are restricted to weekends. The best dorms for women are on the quad; for guys, it's the Carolyn Draughon Village Extension. Seventeen percent of the men join one of the 27 fraternities, and 27 percent of the women join sororities, which have space in the choicest dorms. Freshmen must request housing when they apply for admission, and compete on a first-come, first-served basis with returning students. There are five cafeterias and several snack bars on campus; fraternity men have the option of eating in their houses. Once they set aside their books, Auburn students revel in old school traditions such as football rivalries and tailgating parties.

Seldom are students so bored by their bucolic surroundings that they have to hightail it out of town the minute their last Friday class ends, but they do enjoy supporting their football team, no matter where the destination. Reports one fan, "The best trips are to college football games—away." The Greek system plays a major role in keeping the social scene lively, but "by no means does not being Greek mean not being social," says one socialite. Plays, concerts, pep rallies, parties, and traditional festivities such as the Burn the (Georgia) Bulldogs Parade present additional diversions. Once a year, these students, in the spirit of Southern hospitality, celebrate Hey Day, when everyone wears a nametag and walks around saying, "Hey!" The proximity of I-85 is very convenient, putting Montgomery (where Auburn has a branch campus) just an hour away and Atlanta, Birmingham, and the inviting Gulf Coast beaches just a couple of hours farther off. Auburn is traditionally a football powerhouse, and the time-honored rallying cry, "War Eagle!" reverberates through the stadium every time an Auburn back runs to daylight. This hearty cry symbolizes the pride and joy of Auburn—just ask alumni athlete Bo Jackson. A popular pastime centers on composing catchy slogans for football rallies and parades, and whenever there's a football victory, one can be sure that Toomer's Corner (in downtown Auburn) is going to be rolled with toilet paper. Although swimming and track draw nowhere near the rabid crowds of their pigskin-crazy peers, these sports produce teams that are just as impressive. Auburn's resurgent men's basketball team is now drawing record crowds. Intramurals are popular, especially among Greeks, who compete for the coveted All-Sports trophy every year.

Students affirm that Auburn is, without doubt, "truly the friendliest campus you will ever set foot on." History, tradition, and high spirits make feeling of genuine warmth contagious.

Once a year, these students, in the spirit of Southern hospitality, celebrate Hey Day, when everyone wears a nametag and walks around saying, "Hey!"

A popular pastime centers on composing catchy slogans for football rallies and parades, and whenever there's a football victory, one can be sure that Toomer's Corner (in downtown Auburn) is going to be rolled with toilet paper.

Overlaps

Florida State, University of Georgia, Mississippi State, University of Tennessee, Georgia Tech.

If You Apply To >

Auburn…Rolling admissions. Early decision and early action: Dec. 31. Regular admissions: Jul. 7. Does not guarantee to meet demonstrated need. Campus and alumni interviews: optional, informational. SATs or ACTs: required. SAT IIs: optional. Accepts electronic applications. No essay question.

900 North Grand Avenue, Sherman, TX 75020-4440

Website: www.austinc.edu

Location: Small town

Total Enrollment: 1,257

Undergraduates: 1,233

Male/Female: 45/55

SAT Ranges: V 550–670 M 550–660

ACT Range: 24–30

Financial Aid: 62%

Expense: Pr $

Phi Beta Kappa: No

Applicants: 1,003

Accepted: 74%

Enrolled: 41%

Grad in 6 Years: 66%

Returning Freshmen: 83%

Academics: ✍ ✍ ✍

Social: ☎ ☎ ☎

Q of L: ★ ★ ★

Admissions: (800) 442-5363

Email Address:
admission@austinc.edu

Strongest Programs:
Health Sciences
The Austin Teacher Program
International Studies
Religion
Philosophy

Students at Austin must take one communications course and three in the heritage of western culture, all in the name of undergirding the overall liberal arts program.

Only an hour away from the ten gallon hats and gleaming skyscrapers of Dallas is Austin College, a small but warm institution where students know their professors personally and take advantage of a broad array of majors. With about 1,200 undergraduates, no one is just a number at Austin. Students are encouraged to learn about themselves and the world. "Everyone is able to learn what they need to succeed," one sophomore says. Professors here even serve their students breakfast at 10:00 P.M. the night before finals. It's just another example of the personal style that is typical of this charming Southern institution.

Austin's 65-acre campus is located in a residential area outside the city of Sherman. The campus is designed in the traditional quadrangle style and hosts beige sandstone buildings, tree-lined plazas, decorative fountains, and an impressive 70-ton sculptured solstice calendar. Dorms are conveniently located approximately 200 yards from most classrooms.

Austin College challenges its students, but the atmosphere is far from cutthroat. One psych major analyzes the situation this way: "The students are competitive with themselves, instead of with each other." But classes are not a breeze. "Austin is definitely an academically intensive institution with a student body of future leaders," says a physics/computer science double major. The core curriculum begins with a freshman seminar called Communication/Inquiry. Each professor who teaches the course becomes the mentor for the 20 freshmen in his or her class. Next is a three-course sequence on the Heritage of Western Culture. Then comes a slew of optional courses in eight categories, including formal reasoning, language and written expression, and historical or social perspectives. Two-thirds of all classes have 25 students or less, and no class has over 100. Students report that they rarely have problems getting the classes they want, but sometimes it's necessary to plan early.

Preprofessional areas are Austin College's specialties. When it comes time to apply to grad school, premed and predental students at this little college have one of the highest acceptance rates of any Texas school, and aspiring lawyers also do well. AC's five-year teaching program grants students both a bachelor's and a master's degree. Science and education receive high marks from students, as do international studies and political science. Business is among the school's most popular majors. The Jordan Language House boards 48 students studying French, German, Japanese, and Spanish along with a native speaker of each language. Students can also earn a double major or combine three of the school's 26 majors into an interdisciplinary degree. A cooperative engineering program links the college with other schools, and a number of minors—some interdisciplinary—have been added, such as environmental studies and gender studies.

A January term option lets students take an "experiential learning" course, usually outside their major, on a pass/fail basis. An international studies concentration provides opportunities to study abroad. The college also offers its students independent study, directed research, junior year abroad, and departmental honors programs. The Leadership Institute is open to just 15 students of each entering class, five more can get in after their first year. Participating students enjoy a suite of privileges, from study abroad options to working with mentors outside the college. Austin also provides three research areas located in Grayson

County: The Barry Buckner Biology Preserve, The Lee Harrison Bratz Field Laboratory, and The Clinton and Edith Sneed Environmental Research Area.

Ninety-one percent of Austin students hail from the Lone Start State. Hispanics and blacks comprise 6 and 4 percent of the student body, respectively, and Asian Americans make up 8 percent. Hot political issues include abortion and homosexuality, and one junior reports that the campus is "very open-minded and liberal compared to other institutions in the South." Austin has been tied to the Presbyterian Church in the United States since 1849; this affiliation manifests itself in the emphasis on values in the core courses, participation in service activities, and limited residence-hall visitation hours. Students are beginning to chafe under that latter rule, one student says. AC offers merit scholarships, ranging from $2,000 to full tuition.

As for dorm life, there are six residence halls, and 74 percent of undergraduates live in this traditional dorm housing. (Only juniors and seniors are permitted to live in apartment-style buildings owned by the college.) One sophomore says the dorms are "better than your average state school," but a junior notes that Luckett Hall is usually not that clean. One AC dorm is coed, one houses language-studies students, two are men-only, and two are women-only. Dean (the only coed residence hall) seems to be a popular choice for freshmen, despite (or perhaps because of) its reputation as loud and social. Others say Clyce is the best bet for freshman women, and Luckett for freshman men. Residence hall access is computerized, and security officers are on duty 24 hours a day. Nearly all students take advantage of the three-meal-a-day plan, though not all take advantage of the all-you-can-eat option. Then there's the Pouch Club, an on-campus joint that serves beer and wine for those students 21 and over.

"Most of the social life is either on or near campus, with the Greeks taking the lion's share of credit. Thirty-three percent of the men and 30 percent of the women belong to fraternities and sororities, but the Greeks are not school-funded and are not allowed to advertise off-campus parties without the college's permission. Not everyone depends on the Greek system for a good time. Students get an eyeful during the Baker Bun Run in which the men of Baker Hall strip to their boxers and cavort around the campus on the Monday night before finals. Whew. Students can have alcohol in dorm rooms only if they are 21 or over, and school policy prohibits booze at campus organization events. Popular weekend excursions are the drive to Dallas or to the college's 28-acre recreational spot on Lake Texoma (a half-hour north). Some students say having a car is an absolute must. "Sherman is not a great college town," a psychology major laments. "The population is rather elderly and there's little nightlife." Even without athletic scholarships, varsity sports are generating increasing support. The school's teams compete in Division III and the women's basketball, soccer, and volleyball teams have each won recent championships.

At Austin, the teachers are inspiring and the atmosphere familial. Upon graduation, students know they are prepared for the big leap into the real world. "The concepts of learning, leadership, and lasting values are stressed," a sophomore says. The school's small size is one of its greatest assets, notes another. "It's easy to adjust to and the closely interacting faculty and students make it a good place."

For all the prospective teachers out there, Austin's College Teacher Program offers a five-year program in which students receive a masters in teaching as well as their bachelors' degree.

Overlaps

Baylor, University of Texas, Texas A&M, Texas Christian, University of North Texas.

Babson College

Babson Park, MA 02457-0310

Website: www.babson.edu

Location: Suburban

Total Enrollment: 3,431

Undergraduates: 1,701

Male/Female: 64/36

SAT Ranges: V 540–630 M 590–670

Financial Aid: 40%

Expense: Pr $ $ $

Phi Beta Kappa: No

Applicants: 2,582

Accepted: 45%

Enrolled: 35%

Grad in 6 Years: 81%

Returning Freshmen: 90%

Academics: ✍ ✍ ✍

Social: ☎ ☎

Q of L: ★ ★ ★

Admissions: (781) 239-5522 or (800) 488-3696

Email Address:
ugradadmission@babson.edu

Strongest Programs:
Entrepreneurial Studies
Finance
Economics

Theories are fine, but in the world of big business there's no substitute for experience. That's why Babson College integrates classroom theory with a large dose of real-life, hands-on training. The curriculum focuses on putting students into complex business scenarios and giving them the skills to make sound management decisions. Savvy professors and small classes allow students ample opportunity to express themselves. For many, the first step up the corporate ladder begins in the halls of Babson College.

Founded in 1919, Babson sits on a 450-acre campus nestled in the sedate Boston suburb of Wellesley, and features open green spaces, gently rolling hills, and heavily wooded areas. The school's 1.2 million square feet of buildings represent a mix of neo-Georgian and complementary modern architecture. The atmosphere is one of peace and tranquillity, with trees gently shading buildings and parking lots relatively hidden. Recent additions to the campus include the F. W. Olin Graduate School building, the Richard W. Sorenson Center for the Arts, the Donald W. Reynolds student center, and the Arthur M. Blank Center for Entrepreneurship.

The college's general education requirements emphasize field experiences. The curriculum focuses on the importance of five competencies: rhetoric; numeracy; ethics/social responsibility; international/multicultural perspectives; and leadership/teamwork/creativity. In addition, major emphasis is placed on the Integrated Management Core (IMC), a sequence of three expanded courses that helps students develop sound managerial decision-making skills. These courses include Perspectives in Management, Management Diagnosis and Analysis, and Managing Business Complexity, and each creates realistic business scenarios of increasing complexity and responsibility. Freshmen are required to take the Foundation Management Experience, composition, quantitative methods, history and society, law, speech, statistics, arts and humanities, and economics. There is also a mandatory post-acceptance evaluation program that assesses each student's abilities in math, computers, writing, and technology.

The three most popular majors are entrepreneurial studies, accounting, and economics, followed by finance and investments. The competitive entrepreneurial studies program brings prominent venture capitalists and entrepreneurs to campus for how-to lectures. "The curriculum is designed so school is a full-time job," says a senior. "Students at Babson are goal-oriented, motivated, and energetic." Accounting is highly touted, while liberal arts and science departments receive less than stellar critiques from students.

Upperclassmen get priority in course registration, but most students report little difficulty getting into necessary and desired classes. The computer center houses more than 250 public access workstations, and has five computer labs, a LAN lab, and even a 24-hour quiet lab, where group projects are not allowed. The labs are equipped with Pentium PCs capable of network and stand alone printing. The Horn Library contains thousands of volumes, and Babson is a member of the WEBnet consortium with Pine Manor and Regis College libraries, giving Babson students access to 300,000 volumes online. "The teaching is amazing because most profs have been out in the field—so when they teach they bring real life experience into the classroom," says one student. Courses are usually taught by the case-study approach, in which specific business situations are covered in class and students perform in groups or little pseudo-corporations. In the Foundation Management Experience course, first-year students have $3,000 seed money to launch, manage, and liquidate a business. All profits from these businesses are used to support community service projects. This type of learning requires frequent out-of-class group meetings and a lot of study schedule coordination. "The faculty advisors are very involved from day one," notes one senior.

Although diversity is an issue, the campus remains mostly white and mostly male: Blacks, Asian Americans, and Hispanics make up only 2, 6, and 4 percent of the student body, respectively. Forty-three percent hail from Massachusetts, and 19 percent are foreign. Need-based financial aid is available, and the school offers a wide variety of financing options, including payment plans and parent loan programs. There are no athletic scholarships, but the presidential merit scholarship can offer the best and brightest of Babson a $5,000 to $7,000 grant each year.

Freshmen are guaranteed housing, but upperclassmen must contend with the whims of a lottery based on points per credit hour. With 85 percent of the students on campus, there is high demand for dorm rooms, but all students are guaranteed housing. There is one male-only dorm and women-only floors and wings. The remaining coed halls, students report, are well maintained. "Dorms are mostly comfortable and well-maintained," says one student. Everyone uses one of three meal plans at the dining hall. Every Wednesday is gourmet night, when the menu fluctuates between such delicacies as fresh lobster, Italian cooking, and turkey dinners.

Wellesley is described as a dry, quiet town where students get involved in volunteer work. "Most of social life is on campus," says one senior. Campus safety is rated highly. One student claims "it's so safe, they have nothing better to do than give us parking tickets." Boston, only 14 miles away, affords plenty of opportunity for fun. A subway stop is only 2 miles from campus and connects students all over the Boston area. Those with cars have easy access not only to Boston but also to Cape Cod and the New Hampshire ski slopes. Many students choose to stick around for entertainment, with several mentioning campus parties as a guaranteed good time. "If you choose to stay on campus, most of the social activities revolve around alcohol and school-sponsored events," reports one student. Other options include an all-school party at the auditorium or a semiformal sponsored by a residence hall or a Greek organization. Although only 10 percent of the women and 9 percent of the men go Greek, the four fraternities and two sororities end up hosting more than their fair share of parties, including follow-ups (room parties) after the regular 9:00 P.M. to 1:00 A.M. school events. The $50 fine for underage drinking and $25 fine for open containers has cut down on drinking but there are parties sponsored by school administration where alcohol is served to students of age.

Lest you think the career-oriented students rarely take a break, be informed that some of the best-attended functions are sponsored by the marketing club, whose members presumably know how to stir up participation. Extracurricular

Courses are usually taught by the case-study approach, in which specific business situations are covered in class and students perform in groups or little pseudo-corporations.

In the Foundation Management Experience course, first-year students have $3,000 seed money to launch, manage, and liquidate a business. All profits from these businesses are used to support community service projects.

activities include Oktoberfest Weekend, the Harvest Ball, and Founder's Day, which celebrates entrepreneurship.

In sports, Babson competes in Division III. Women's basketball and lacrosse are very competitive teams, as is soccer. Top men's teams include the soccer squad, golf, and basketball. Competition against archrival Bentley heats up the Babson campus, and the annual soccer games against Brandeis and Colby are the spectator events of the year. Intramural athletics are popular and very competitive.

It seems that everything at Babson—the heavy academic load, cooperating on group projects, dorm life—combines to hone students' skills at earning the very best. These "Beavers" are proud of their school's reputation for excellence, and they don't mind carrying its heavy load for four years. Babson means business.

If You Apply To ➤

Babson...Early decision and early action: Dec. 1., Jan.1. Regular admissions: Feb. 1. Guarantees to meet demonstrated need. Campus and alumni interviews: recommended, evaluative. SATs or ACTs: required. SAT IIs: required (composition and math I or II). Accepts the Common Application and electronic applications. Essay question: significant experience or achievement; personal, national or international concern; significant person.

Bard College

Annandale-on-Hudson, NY 12504

Website: www.bard.edu
Location: Rural
Total Enrollment: 1,427
Undergraduates: 1,233
Male/Female: 47/53
SAT Ranges: V 550–700 M 540–670
Financial Aid: 60%
Expense: Pr $ $ $ $
Phi Beta Kappa: No
Applicants: 2,508
Accepted: 47%
Enrolled: 30%
Grad in 6 Years: 65%
Returning Freshmen: 90%
Academics: ✐ ✐ ✐ ✐
Social: ☎ ☎ ☎
Q of L: ★ ★ ★ ★
Admissions: (914) 758-7472
Email Address:
admission@bard.edu

Strongest Programs:
Film

It's almost impossible to imagine Bard College when it was founded back in 1860. Its first class consisted of 12 men studying to enter the seminaries of the Episcopal Church. Those folks would no doubt be surprised at the eclectic mix of students that now populate Bard, as well as the wealth of diverse academics available at this iconoclastic institution. The professors are highly praised and the courses are rigorous, but don't fuel intense competition. "Bard is a place where I feel free to think and learn and make mistakes," a film major says. "Students here care about learning for the sake of learning."

Bard was once known mainly as a school for the performing arts, and creative types have flocked to its lovely campus, which occupies 600 well-landscaped acres, for more than seven decades. The hodgepodge of architectural styles leaves each ivy-covered brick building with a character all its own, especially the dorms, which come in every variety from cottages in the woods, to one Russian Colonial–style dorm. Construction has begun on the $40 million performing arts center designed by renowned architect Frank O. Gehry, slated for completion in 2002. Other improvements include a multi-use campus center and a new 70-student dorm.

Students can get a taste of Bard's individualized approach to higher education before they are even admitted if they choose to participate in a daylong seminar/interview known as the Immediate Decision Plan, after which they receive an immediate acceptance or denial. Freshmen show up three weeks before classes start for a unique, required Workshop in Language and Thinking, organized around the quaint notion that good writing and clear thinking are necessary tools for higher learning. Designed to "provide a balanced encounter between classical and progressive traditions," Bard's general education requirements include a year-long multidisciplinary freshman seminar. At the end of their second year, all students write their educational autobiography and declare a major program of study. These are presented before a board of professors in the relevant area and discussed with the student. Junior year includes a tutorial in preparation for the senior project, and during senior year students do the project, equivalent to an undergraduate dissertation—an original work that could materialize in the form of a critical analysis of literature, a portfolio of artwork, a dance, a novel, or a research project.

"The academic climate at Bard is challenging but the competition is more internal than with other students. "Students do excessive work in every class they take, but the atmosphere is pretty laid back," a literature major says. "You just know that you have to do the work in order to do well." Independent studies and tutorials are the soul of the curriculum. Students have the opportunity to draw up their own course description, find a professor to sponsor it, and produce a custom-designed program. Bard also makes a point of recognizing visual and performing arts as equals among academic disciplines, and all faculty members are full professors. "The professors are amazing," a film major gushes.

With distinguished authors such as John Ashbery, Mona Simpson, Chinua Achebe, and Bradford Morrow teaching seminars in creative writing, it is no wonder that some students feel the best divisions at the school are literature and writing. Natural sciences and physics are surprisingly good for their size, and the distinguished-scientist scholars program offers full tuition to the top students in the Division of Natural Science and Mathematics. Students say that the history and dance departments need improvement. A new collaborative program with Rockefeller University allows Bard undergrads to students to study at this premier science research institution. Students also complain about inadequate library resources—only 190,000 volumes, slim for the amount of research that success at Bard requires.

Science junkies can get their fix through a new program with The Rockefeller University, which will host Bard students interested in the impact of scientific inquiry on society.

Bard offers combined programs with other schools in engineering, architecture, city planning, social work, public health, business and public administration, forestry, and environmental science. Students can study abroad in far-off places including India, Russia, South Africa, France, and countries in South America. The winter field period comes at the end of December and lasts six weeks: a chance to take in-depth courses on or off campus, pursue internships, travel, or just experience life while remaining a student. A few of the research opportunities include the summer Archaeology Field School, and a science scholars program that carries a $1,500 stipend for summer research.

Diversity, be it racial, ideological, or even regarding fashion, is a hallmark at Bard. "Students are extremely open-minded, tolerable, intelligent, off-beat, self-motivated, curious, and bizarre," says a sophomore. Minorities comprise 16 percent of the student body, though only 2 percent are African American. Most students are from out-of-state, and one-third attended private school. In terms of political correctness, "Half the people make it an issue, the other half make an issue of rebelling against it," an art major sighs. Hot debate issues range from gay rights to racism, biodevastation and abortion. In terms of dress code, according to one student, "There are those who wear Izods and flannel nighties, those with nose clips and purple hair. You see everything from Arab robes to three-piece suits." Although Bard does not guarantee financial aid for all four years, 60 percent of the students receive some form of financial assistance. Bard offers up to 20 merit scholarships of $500 to $20,000. Under Bard's unique Excellence and Equal Cost program, high school students in their class's top 10 can apply to Bard at the cost of their state university's tuition. Admission to this program is not automatic; about 200 students vie for 40 spots. Bard's current endowment of about $83

The hammers are flying as Bard continues construction on a new $40 million performing arts center designed by renowned architect Frank O. Gehry. The facility is slated to open in 2002.

million may not seem noteworthy until you realize that it was less than $4 million in 1986.

Freshmen are required to live on campus in dorms, which range from cabins on stilts in a ravine to converted mansions. "Housing at Bard is all about luck," a sophomore says. One student boasts, "My room has four diamond-paneled bay windows that face west, sunsets like a Monet painting. It has oak walls, carved ceilings, and its own bathroom with a marble shower." The room draw system can be chaotic, driving some students to rent rooms off-campus. That option can be less expensive, but it does require transportation. All residential students eat on campus and food quality has improved with a new food service.

Social life at Bard is far from an endless party, but Bardians enjoy films, concerts (a lot of indie rock and hip-hop), dances, student art exhibits, and lectures as well as local coffee shops. There are no fraternities or sororities on campus. Bard's Winter Carnival raises money to fight world hunger while offering a weekend of outdoor winter games, an auction of faculty memorabilia, and a formal dance. Drag Race, which happens on Parents' Weekend, is a cross-dressing, performance-based extravaganza bearing the theme "Dress in Drag or Don't Dress At All."

In athletics, although soccer, tennis, cross-country, fencing, basketball, squash, and women's volleyball are popular, Bard is virtually devoid of dedicated jocks. "But there are plenty of pseudo-jocks and intellectuals in good shape," reports one student. There's always Ultimate Frisbee in the fall and intramural softball competition is "a staple in the spring," for which most majors—and faculty and staff—form teams. Nearby, there are five miles of trails through the woods along the Hudson that are perfect for myriad outdoor activities, from raspberry picking to skiing, jogging, or hiking.

Having a car on this lovely but rural campus does much to prevent occasional attacks of claustrophobia. Some students say Bard's hometown of Annandale-on-Hudson is "in the woods." But the town is less than 20 miles away from great shopping in Woodstock, and within striking distance of ski slopes in the Catskills or Berkshires. Plus, New York City is just a two-hour Amtrak ride away. Students also cite the Upstate Films movie theater in Rhinebeck as one of the best cinematic experiences around.

Students at Bard have the unique opportunity to discover what it is they want to learn, how they want to learn it, and the ways in which they'll use that information to create a life after college. The environment is warm and students have a great deal of freedom to mold their educations. "Bard is special because of the open-minded atmosphere," says one sophomore, who adds slyly, "You can get away with anything. But in a good way."

Overlaps

NYU, Vassar, Oberlin, Wesleyan, Brown.

If You Apply To ➤

Bard...Early action: Nov. 1. Regular admissions: Jan. 15. Financial aid: March 15. Meets demonstrated need of 90%. Campus interviews: recommended, informational. Alumni interviews: optional, informational. SATs and ACTs: optional. SAT IIs: optional. Accepts the Common Application and electronic applications. Essay question: important issue and intellectual development. Students tend to be "active in political or social causes outside of school."

Barnard College

3009 Broadway, New York, NY 10027-6598

Students at Barnard College claim to have the best of both worlds. As a small liberal arts institution, Barnard offers women an intense, personalized liberal arts education that is designed to address the needs of today's urban, cosmopolitan student. And as an affiliate of Columbia University, students have access to vast resources for research and study. It's a winning combination that attracts students from around the world. Add indefatigable New York City, and the school is nearly irresistible to any modern, academically-oriented woman.

The tiny campus, dwarfed by its Manhattan surroundings, consists of architecturally diverse buildings that are notably more modern than Columbia's. Although Barnard is situated in one of the most cosmopolitan cities in the world, lawns, trees, and other greenery abound on the campus itself. Springtime sunbathers on the lawn can look through a lovely brass fence onto Broadway, and, across the street, Columbia. First-year students share an orientation program with Columbia, where they are mixed together, put into small groups, and led around campus and the city. Students can also enjoy COOP, a preorientation backpacking expedition.

Barnard offers the intimate attention of a small, independent women's college and the resources of a major research university. English, creative writing, political science, economics, art history, architecture, and the cutthroat premed program are particularly strong subjects. "Barnard women are serious about academics," reveals a sophomore. "It is competitive in the sense that everyone is trying to be the best." The experimentally oriented psychology department is dubbed excellent, and the women's studies program also ranks high, although majors in this field must have a concentration in another department as well. Barnard students must trek across the street if they want to major in computer science, though the school does have an adequate computing center. The math department is tiny, and anyone who's survived a math course here would not recommend this school for serious mathematicians. In most subject areas, Columbia's departments have more offerings, and with cross-registration Barnard students can take full advantage of them. Many students cite the low faculty-student ratio as one of the more appealing aspects of the school. Barnard really takes care of its students. "It's like a supportive community within the larger framework of Columbia University," explains a political science major.

Barnard also offers several interdisciplinary majors unique within the university, including medieval and Renaissance studies and urban affairs. An arts program offers women the chance to concentrate on their particular specialty—dance, music, theater, visual arts, or writing—while completing a program in liberal arts. Thanks to a reciprocal agreement between the schools, music students can also take classes at Juilliard and the Manhattan School of Music.

The school's new curriculum requirements are designed to reflect the changing nature of our technological society, and the fact that more and more of its graduates are going into law, business, and other professions rather than academic careers. The curriculum includes a traditional freshman writing course and a freshman seminar taught by a senior faculty member on some broad theme such as "the modern idea of freedom" or "the rise of possessive individualism." Other requirements include courses in areas such as Reason and Value, Cultures in Comparison, Quantitative and Deductive Reasoning, and Literature. While these

Website: www.barnard.edu

Location: Urban

Total Enrollment: 2,318

Undergraduates: 2,318

Male/Female: 0/100

SAT Ranges: V 620–710 M 610–690

ACT Range: 26–30

Financial Aid: 57%

Expense: Pr $ $ $

Phi Beta Kappa: Yes

Applicants: 3,883

Accepted: 37%

Enrolled: 39%

Grad in 6 Years: 82%

Returning Freshmen: 95%

Academics: ✑ ✑ ✑ ✑ ✑

Social: ☎ ☎ ☎

Q of L: ★ ★ ★

Admissions: (212) 854-2014

Email Address: admissions@barnard.edu

Strongest Programs:
English
Biology
Psychology
Political Science
History
American Studies
Environmental Science
Theater

An arts program offers women the chance to concentrate on their particular specialty—dance, music, theater, visual arts, or writing—while completing a program in liberal arts.

requirements guarantee Barnard grads intellectual breadth, the mandatory senior thesis project or comprehensive examination ensures them of academic depth. To add to their academic career, Barnard's students, like Columbia's, can take graduate courses throughout the university and sign up for a variety of dual-degree programs.

A joint-degree program with the Jewish Theological Seminary is also available. The Senior Scholars program enables academically advanced students to substitute a single extensive research project for a semester or year of classes, and 10 especially able students of any class are awarded stipends of $2,500 to be spent on an independent project under the Centennial Scholars program. While Barnard's small 169,000-volume library accommodates both "lookers and gabbers" and the more studious ("You can find quiet stacks and not see anyone for hours"), the many gaps in the collection are easily filled by trips across the street, where the Columbia University library system boasts a whopping 6 million volumes.

Barnard professors enjoy the proximity of a research institution almost as much as undergraduates do, and each year one-third of the full-time faculty teaches in the graduate departments throughout the university. But students, not research, are given top priority by faculty members. "The professors here are unbelievably committed to Barnard students' education," gushes an American Studies major. First-year students can have access to top professors, and upper-level seminars guarantee intimate access once you're seriously into a subject. Students say they appreciate the high proportion of female faculty members and the strong academic and career counseling services.

Ninety-six percent of Barnard students are from the top quarter of their high school class. Asian Americans make up 23 percent of the student body, while blacks and Hispanics make up another 10 percent. Thirty-five percent are natives of New York, and there are plenty of wealthy East Siders. A hefty 37 percent went to private schools. Still, a political science major claims, "We're definitely an eclectic bunch. We have Orthodox Jews, prep-school WASPs, punk rockers with purple hair, and lots of 'regular' college students, too." Barnard is also one of the most politically liberal colleges in the nation, and students are seldom shy to rally and protest. The annual Take Back the Night rally, for example, draws thousands of women.

Barnard now competes head to head with Columbia in admissions. A large percentage of the women who are accepted decide to enroll, which shows that Barnard is still the first choice of many students, though the cross-street rivalry doesn't appear to be dying down any time soon. In general, women looking for a more traditional college experience should head for Columbia, while those seeking a more "go your own way" atmosphere might do better at Barnard. Barnard "promotes women getting ahead, and stresses the small-school experience with all the social and academic benefits of an Ivy League university," says a junior.

Barnard's housing has come a long way since the college was primarily a commuter school, and with New York's notorious rent prices, demand for on-campus housing remains high. Eighty-six percent of all Barnard students live on campus, though the housing is reported as "no frills." The college guarantees housing. In addition to the 18-story Barnard dormitory tower, the college has one dorm complex and five off-campus apartment buildings. Two coed dorms are shared with Columbia, though as Columbia women increase in number, there is less and less space.

Lest anyone attempt to exist on a diet of coffee, de Beauvoir, and Derrida, students who reside in Barnard's on-campus dorms must buy a full meal plan, and the meal cards can be used at Columbia's John Jay cafeteria.

While Barnard has had difficulty in the past trying to keep its students on campus on the weekends, this is certainly not a problem anymore, even with the best of New York nightlife right outside the school's gates. "Social life takes place both on and around campus and all over New York City," says an economics major. One senior laughs, "Barnard doesn't have a whole lot of traditions that made it past the tumultuous '60s and '70s," so the newly revived Greek games are extra popular with both students and locals. Certainly Barnard students have much to choose from; on any given night there are movies or lectures by everyone from the Kathy and Mo comedy team to Sean Lowery from the New York City Ballet. Barnard also hosts a continuous series of readings by women poets, and women in the arts are celebrated in the annual Winterfest. Students are not too heavily monitored by the administration. This may be due to the students' high levels of responsibility. "This is a very politically aware campus and there is absolutely no peer pressure to drink," notes one veteran. Off campus, of course, there is New York City. "Anyone can get drunk in New York City unless they look ten," says a senior.

Women athletes from both sides of Broadway compete on joint teams. The fencing team is strong, as are archery and basketball. Other strong teams include tennis, volleyball, and cross-country. Barnard women are welcome to take advantage of Columbia's marvelous gym and the numerous coed intramurals. Spectator sports evoke little interest.

"Sometimes I feel like I'm missing out on the true collegiate experience," says a women's studies major. "People at Barnard don't often throw raucous beer bashes and don't get pumped up for big games." But they do get a crash course in self-reliance from a college that makes sure they have everything they need to make it, and then leaves them at the doorstep. Life at Barnard can be intense and bewildering, but independent women who thrive on challenge rarely regret coming here.

If You Apply To ➤ **Barnard**...Early decision: Nov. 15. Regular admissions: Jan. 15. Financial aid: Feb. 1. Housing: Second Friday in June. Guarantees to meet demonstrated need. Campus interviews: recommended, evaluative. Alumni interviews: optional, evaluative. ACTs or SATs and SAT IIs: required (writing or literature and two others). Accepts the Common Application. Essay question: describe summer activities; how a form of art influenced you; personal statement.

Bates College

23 Campus Avenue, Lewiston, ME 04240

Founded by abolitionists in 1855, Bates College has a long history of providing a haven for those seeking guidance and knowledge. This small school offers a wealth of programs at home and abroad that provide students with a well-rounded, liberal arts education. Students say the academic climate is hardly cutthroat, but hitting the books is a popular pastime. "Expect to work hard," says a political science major. Though the library is a campus hotspot during the week, folks at Bates are always striving for new ways to have fun.

The Bates campus features an intriguing mix of Georgian and Federal

Website: www.bates.edu
Location: Small city
Total Enrollment: 1,706
Undergraduates: 1,706
Male/Female: 49/51
SAT Ranges: V 630–700 M 630–700

(Continued)

Financial Aid: 42%

Expense: Pr $ $ $

Phi Beta Kappa: Yes

Applicants: 3,860

Accepted: 33%

Enrolled: 38%

Grad in 6 Years: 87%

Returning Freshmen: 93%

Academics: ✑ ✑ ✑ ✑

Social: ☎ ☎ ☎

Q of L: ★ ★ ★

Admissions: (207) 786-6000

Email Address:

admissions@bates.edu

Strongest Program:

Liberal Arts and Sciences

Check out Bates' rhetoric program and national-level debate team, and argue with your new classmates.

buildings and Victorian homes, all spread out over grassy lawns. The campus seems to be an oasis in the New England industrial city of Lewiston. Situated near Boston (about two and a half hours) and Maine's picturesque coast, Lewiston is an old mill town that provides plenty of internships and part-time jobs, a distinct vocational advantage not always found at such small colleges. "Almost all second-through sixth-graders at a nearby elementary school have mentors from Bates," one freshman notes.

True to its ancestry, this very selective school remains open-minded academically as well. SAT scores are not required of applicants, and a unique 4–4–1 calendar saves some of the most interesting, unconventional learning experiences for the end of the school year. But don't think Bates is home to the easy A. "Courses are very rigorous," a sophomore says. "Once you start getting to upper level classes, be ready to hit the books." Professors make the hard stuff fun. "Even my calculus teacher made class entertaining," one student raves.

Bates features a traditional liberal arts curriculum that is as strong as the pressure to achieve within it. Students cite chemistry, biology, physics, and geology as solid in the sciences, and English, history, psychology, and economics as standouts on the humanities side. Weaker departments include art and theater. The philosophy program appears to be rising steadily as student interest in such courses as Contemporary Moral Disputes climbs. The music and art departments benefit from the Olin Arts Center, which houses a performance hall, gallery, recording studio, art studios, and practice rooms. Bates also boasts a rhetoric program and a national-level debate team that is great for prelaw students. These academic offerings are enhanced by a challenging independent studies program, the junior year abroad for top scholars, and the Washington Semester.* A fall semester program is open to first-year students (in fact, preference is given to new students) and includes home stays with families and tours throughout the country. Fall semester programs have included study in France, Ecuador, and Japan.

The 4–4–1 calendar at Bates is also conducive to studies abroad at the end of the college year, and trips to China, India, or South America are there for the taking. While the spring short-term courses may be more relaxed, students nonetheless find them worthwhile. After all, what could be more valuable than the ever popular *Philosophy of Star Trek?* Or how about Cult and the Community, which led two students to a five-week tour with the Grateful Dead? One student cites an Arts and Artists course, which took him to several major U.S. cities, as having greatly influenced his view of the art world. While only two short-term courses are required for graduation, many students take more. In addition, students have access to the 10-college Venture Program* and the American Maritime Studies Program at Mystic Seaport*—two unusual and attractive options for students seeking real-world experience. Students also benefit from the Ladd Library, with more than 500,000 volumes, an all-night study room, a typing room, and "an audio room with everything from Bach to Bruce Springsteen."

Eighty-five percent of the students come from outside Maine, many from Massachusetts, Connecticut, and New York. Many students decry the lack of diversity on campus—it's 84 percent white—but administrators are working hard to change that. "It feels like Bates got all the rich, smart, and popular kids from high school," a freshman says. True to form for this crunchy locale, environmental issues are hot at Bates. Students also are involved in fighting for equal rights for women, homosexuals, and marginalized groups in society. The college guarantees to meet the demonstrated need of almost all students, but no athletic or merit scholarships are awarded.

Campus dwellers are spread out among student centers, upperclass dorms, and charming old Victorian houses for 10 to 30 students. Maid service once a week makes living in Bates housing an even more pleasant experience. Housing space has been tight, but is guaranteed. There is a lottery. Smith, once an all-freshmen dorm, is reportedly loud and lots of fun. Upperclassmen who want singles will probably have to settle for the single-sex dorms or houses. All boarders eat in the Commons, where they enjoy near-restaurant-quality food. A few adventurous or penurious souls take to cheaper off-campus living as one way to beat the increasing cost of education.

Most students don't stray far from campus to find their weekend hangouts because there's simply not much to do in Lewiston. Campus parties are hardly dry affairs, considering the college isn't draconian in its policies. "As long as the party isn't too loud or destructive, they won't bother to break it up," a freshman says. Getting served at local bars isn't an impossible feat, but drinking on campus can seem that way. "College policies are strict regarding campus-wide events," a sophomore says, "but dorm parties still rock." Other social activities at Bates are far more wholesome. There's the annual Winter Carnival, with ice skating, snow sculpting, and a semiformal dance. And there's the Puddle Jump on St. Patrick's Day, when "students of Irish descent and all those who want to be Irish for the day cut a hole in the ice on Lake Andrews and jump in," a student explains. Leaving Lewiston can be a relief, especially when the driveable destinations include Portland, Boston (and Fenway Park), and Montreal. Skiing is a common passion, and excellent slopes, including Sugar Loaf, are just over an hour away.

Most students stick around when their varsity teams—especially basketball, football, and lacrosse—are playing, despite their unexceptional records. The Bates teams that do excel are the women's volleyball, the men's and women's ski, the men's and women's lacrosse, and the women's and men's cross-country. As for rivalries, Colby or Bowdoin fans should tread lightly at Bates. The intramural program, organized by the students and supervised by faculty members, is "strong and spirited," complete with lively dorm rivalries.

So it's cold up there, and Lewiston isn't exactly hopping with activity. But Batesies are a dedicated bunch: dedicated to taking advantage of enthusiastic professors, camaraderie and the gorgeous scenery of New England. "Bates has a strong sense of community, and students here look out for one another, socially and academically," says a political science major. One freshman is sold. "It's a fun place," the student says. "People just seem happy here."

> *Students of Irish descent, and those seeking a thrill, get mighty chilly at the Puddle Jump on St. Patrick's Day when they cut a hole in the ice on Lake Andrews and jump right in.*

Overlaps

Bowdoin, Colby, Middlebury, Dartmouth, Williams.

If You Apply To ➢

Bates…Early decision: Nov. 15, Jan. 1. Regular admissions: Jan. 15. Guarantees to meet demonstrated need. Campus and alumni interviews: recommended, evaluative. SATs and ACTs: optional. SAT IIs: optional. Accepts the Common Application and electronic applications. Essay question: Why Bates? Encourages applicants to send additional material.

Website: www.baylor.edu

Location: Center city

Total Enrollment: 13,334

Undergraduates: 11,472

Male/Female: 42/58

SAT Ranges: V 520–630 M 540–650

ACT Range: 22–27

Financial Aid: 67%

Expense: Pr $

Phi Beta Kappa: Yes

Applicants: 7,212

Accepted: 87%

Enrolled: 44%

Grad in 6 Years: 69%

Returning Freshmen: 83%

Academics: ✍ ✍ ✍

Social: ☎ ☎ ☎

Q of L: ★ ★ ★

Admissions: (254) 710-3435

Email Address:

Admission_Serv_Office@ baylor.edu

Strongest Programs:

Arts & Sciences

Business

Education

Engineering & Computer Science

Marketing

Biology

Management Information Systems

Psychology

The Honors and University Scholars Programs offer more freedom in course study and independent research opportunities for superior students.

With its solid Christian heritage and dynamic academics, Baylor University offers its students a powerful set of tools for lifelong success. Traditions at this Baptist institution are religiously observed, but one eye is always kept on the future. In fact, not long ago, the president signaled an end to Baylor's unwritten but long-standing ban on dancing by giving his wife a whirl in public (albeit to the tasteful strains of Beethoven). At Baylor you'll find rigorous classes taught by a friendly faculty in an environment that supports growth—both intellectually and spiritually.

The university sits upon 432 acres adjoining the historic Brazos River near downtown Waco (population: 110,000) in central Texas, right between Dallas and Austin and about 100 miles from each. Students love hopping onto Interstate 35 for the trek north to Dallas or south to Austin. The campus, nicknamed Jerusalem on the Brazos, is constructed in the gracious tradition of the Old South and is well maintained. The central part of campus, called the quadrangle, was built when Baylor moved from Independence, Texas, in 1886.

Waffling on a major? Not to worry. Except for those admitted to the school of music, all freshmen must enter the college of arts and sciences. They then must complete an interdisciplinary core curriculum before moving into their majors—either in arts and sciences or one of Baylor's six schools: business, education, engineering, computer science, music, and nursing. All degree students must take two religion courses, as well as two semesters of Chapel Forum, a series of lectures and meetings on various issues or Christian testimonies. The Honors and University Scholars Programs offer more freedom in course study and independent research opportunities for superior students.

Education is the school's most popular major, followed by marketing and biology. Accounting is a good program, and the school of music is also strong. Classes are described as "challenging" and "competitive," while the atmosphere is considered "laid-back." Drama and artsy majors, such as interior design and home economics, receive unfavorable reviews from student critics.

The 158,000 square-foot McLane Student Life Center was opened in 1999. Within this state-of-the-art complex students will find a complete fitness and sports center, including the tallest rock-climbing wall in Texas, as well as a computer lounge, snack bar, and Health Services. Special programs at Baylor include church-state studies and museum studies, and the institutes of environmental studies and childhood learning disorders are also available. The archeology and geology departments utilize fossil- and mineral-rich Texas prairies, but those who tire of the Southwestern scenery may migrate toward one of Baylor's programs in England, Mexico, Costa Rica, Brazil, and many other countries. Newer programs include forensic science, bioinformatics, and biochemistry.

The friendly, family-style atmosphere of the school is one of Baylor's biggest strengths. Students say the professors are always available to help them out. "There's always a friendly, caring faculty member nearby to answer questions," says one junior. Students do, however, complain that getting into necessary classes is no mean feat, although the situation seems to be improving. Academic counseling receives high marks from many students.

Students are mostly middle- to upper-middle-class Christians. Eighty percent are Texans, and most are quite conservative, although administrators say student attitudes are beginning to diversify. Minorities total 19 percent of the student body, with Hispanics the largest group at 8 percent, Asian Americans at 5 percent, and African Americans at 6 percent. Several programs address social issues on campus, and students cite growing diversity among the student population.

The university administers more than $67 million in financial aid, and students describe the packages as "adequate" and the school a "great buy." There are also full-tuition scholarships available to National Merit finalists who name Baylor as their first choice; athletic scholarships are available in many men's and women's sports, including football, basketball, baseball, and track.

All dorms are single-sex, and restrictive visitation privileges can be frustrating. A junior comments that these "absurd visiting hours and inane dorm rules" cause many upperclassmen to move off campus, but adds that on-campus housing is "comfortable and well maintained." A classmate adds, "The dorms have beautiful lounges, gyms, and computer labs." "Getting a private room in the dorms is difficult," says a senior majoring in business journalism, which probably explains why the dorms house only 30 percent of the student body. Freshmen are urged to live on campus, and are assigned rooms when they are admitted. Students say campus dining is palatable, and there's even a "lite line" for students counting calories.

Nineteen percent of the men and 30 percent of the women belong to a fraternity or sorority, but no Greek housing is permitted. These groups engage in community service projects when not throwing parties. Despite several other student organizations, though, "much of the school's social life revolves around the frats." Students agree Waco is not a college town, leading many who live nearby to spend their weekends at home. Baylor's campus is officially dry, but while a senior says the alcohol policies are strictly enforced, a psychology major claims, "Alcohol is always present at nonschool-sponsored events." A management major adds, "Anything that stirs the Southern Baptist convention stirs Baylor." But most students don't mind the parental concern of Baylor's faculty and administrators, crediting it with removing the temptations that could stand in the way of their success. Campus police and call boxes are part of Baylor's improving safety program. Besides, "Waco doesn't have many threats," says a sophomore.

The university maintains a small marina for leisure activities like swimming and paddle boating, and there are several lakes with good beaches nearby. Special events include the Halloween Monster Bash (complete with a scary ghost story told by the president of the university), and Dia del Oso (Day of the Bear) in the spring, when the whole campus takes on a carnival atmosphere and classes are canceled. "Baylor is huge on tradition," says a proud senior. "We have the largest collegiate homecoming parade in the world." As for nightlife, students seek variety in Austin or Dallas, each about two hours away. Needless to say, a set of wheels is a big help, if not a necessity.

And what about football? C'mon, this is Texas. Football dominates at Baylor. "Sic 'em Bears!" cheers one student. The 10,000-seat Ferrell Center provides a great setting for indoor athletic and special events and the Casey Athletic Center provides facilities for the football team and offices for the coaches. Construction is currently underway on several other athletic facilities, including the addition of skyboxes and a new pressbox to Floyd Casey Stadium. While there is an intramural sports program, religious groups draw more devotees: chapters of Campus Crusade for Christ and the Fellowship of Christian Athletes are alive and well.

Baylor's Baptist history is its strongest selling point; current students and alumni alike are devoted to their alma mater because of its dedication to the maintenance of traditional moral values. Many students cite the Christian

The Armstrong Browning Library houses the largest collection of books, papers, and personal belongings of Victorian-era poets Robert and Elizabeth Barrett Browning.

heritage of Baylor as its finest quality. Add to that a variety of academically solid departments and a bargain price tag, and it's easy to see that Baylor truly does offer all-around good value.

If You Apply To ➤ | **Baylor**…Rolling admissions. Priority, Mar. 1. Does not guarantee to meet demonstrated need. SATs or ACTs: required. SAT IIs: optional. Campus interviews: optional, informational. No alumni interviews. Accepts electronic applications. Essay question: Discuss how your system of values would help you succeed as a Baylor student and throughout your lifetime. Looks for students who want a "Christian education with academic excellence."

Beloit College

BEST BUY

700 College Street, Beloit, WI 53511

Website: www.beloit.edu
Location: Small city
Total Enrollment: 1,223
Undergraduates: 1,223
Male/Female: 41/59
SAT Ranges: V 590–690 M 550–660
ACT Range: 24–29
Financial Aid: 73%
Expense: Pr $ $ $
Phi Beta Kappa: Yes
Applicants: 1,495
Accepted: 67%
Enrolled: 30%
Grad in 6 Years: 68%
Returning Freshmen: 91%
Academics: ✎ ✎ ✎
Social: ☎ ☎ ☎
Q of L: ★ ★ ★ ★
Admissions: (800) 356-0751
Email Address:
  admiss@beloit.edu

Strongest Programs:
  Anthropology
  Biochemistry
  Biology
  Chemistry
  Modern languages

With academic requirements that stress foreign language, culture and international relations courses, Beloit encourages its undergraduates to drink deeply of today's global society. The worldly student body is drawn from around the globe–only 21 percent of the undergraduates are from in-state. One senior says Beloit is "an island in the heart of the Midwest."

This small northeastern-style outpost is nestled on a 40-acre campus, an hour's drive from Madison and Milwaukee. Beloit's campus has two distinct sections, with academic and administrative buildings on one side and residence halls on the other. The campus also has two dominant architectural themes, characterized by one student as, "1850s Colonial and obtuse 1930s buildings." Four campus buildings are on the National Register of Historic Places. Recent renovations were completed on Morse-Ingersall Hall, the college's main classroom and office building; the Wright Art Museum; and Strong stadium. Four dorms also underwent an $8 million renovation—air-conditioning at last!

All freshmen must complete a First Year Initiative seminar, with last year's focus on Local/Global issues and a choice of topics such as "Hurtin' Leavin' and Longin'" in Comparative Perspective." Beloit's nurturing educational environment does not end with the freshman year's one-on-one advising. The Sophomore Year Program is an extension of the journey, with a retreat, Exploration Week, and the charting of a Comprehensive Academic Plan. In their junior and senior years, students can participate in field terms, language institutes, and an annual campus-wide symposium. One sophomore raves, "There are so many resources for academic and career counseling that I don't have time to take advantage of them all!"

All students must take a writing-intensive course and interdisciplinary courses, such as American Values and Institutions in Contemporary Cinema. In addition, there's an extensive list of distribution requirements in the natural sciences, social sciences, and humanities. Students are supportive of one another, and many form informal study groups. A senior English major boasts that Beloit students are inventive and creative. "They are interested in the culture of the college, in the arts, in diverse, eclectic things. It's not strange to have a music and chemistry double major."

Teaching is the faculty's first priority. "The professors are always welcome to criticism and advice for change," one sophomore says. Most classes have fewer than 15 students, and all are taught by full professors. Beloit's anthropology and geology departments—often weak areas at other small liberal arts colleges—are two of the strongest courses of study here, thanks to excellent facilities and faculty and numerous field trips. The English department brings in a visiting writer to teach every year, and the unusual Museum Studies minor is one of the finest in the country. The Philosophy and Religion department offers three minors in philosophy, philosophy and religion and religion. One of the more interesting majors on campus is Rhetoric and Discourse, in which students are asked to reflect on the discourses shaping nonfiction writing while they produce prose of their own. The Student Symposium encourages students to conduct research and present their findings in the annual campus-wide symposium. Eighty percent of students conduct independent study.

Students take advantage of many off-campus programs, including school-arranged jobs, internships, and summer positions. The World Outlook Program provides overseas study opportunities as well as special-problems courses, which lets up to three students work with professors on research in areas of common interest. An exchange program sends five Beloit students and a faculty member to the Fudan University in China; their counterparts come to the United States. Other options include student teaching in Britain or Australia and studying marine biology at the University of the French Pacific in Tahiti. About 50 percent of the students study abroad through the College's World Affairs Center. Other exotic destinations include Cameroon, Nepal, Senegal, Tanzania and Zimbabwe. The Center for Language Studies complements Beloit's good foreign language programs with intensive summer study in Chinese, Japanese, Russian, Hungarian, and English as a second language. Beloit is also a member of the Associated Colleges of the Midwest* consortium.

Beloit's alternative programs and educational strengths attract an independent and diverse student body from 49 states and 48 countries. Race relations are relaxed among on this campus, where 12 percent of students are minorities, though women's issues, censorship, multiculturalism and homosexuality are hot topics. "We are a different breed," says one junior. "Students are quite individual and for the most part extremely accepting of others, although there's somewhat of a split between the jocks, the hippies, and the nerds." Renewable merit scholarships worth $10,000 are offered to eligible students, though athletes in search of scholarships will have to look elsewhere.

Ninety-three percent of students at Beloit live on campus, which leads to a strong sense of community, students say. Students compete for space in three prized dorms—Haven Hall, Wood Hall, and 815 Hall—that now have carpeting, new furniture, and centralized air-conditioning and heating. Dormies are compelled to consume Chapin Hall's cafeteria food, but the toss-up dining can even help some students expand their tastes—like it or not. "I have found that it has enhanced my creativity when figuring out what to eat," one sophomore says. Alternatives come in the form of four fraternities, two sororities, or one of the specialty houses—the arts co-op, women's center, foreign language houses, or veggie dining.

Movies, dances, and all- campus parties tie up Friday and Saturday nights, and there are two all-campus festivals each year. The first is the Folk and Blues Fall Music Festival, which brings jazz, reggae, folk, and blues bands to campus, and the other is Spring Day, when classes are canceled and bands are brought in so that everyone can kick back and enjoy the (finally!) warmer weather. There are

(Continued)
English
Geology
Psychology

All freshmen must complete a First Year Initiative seminar, with last year's focus on Local/Global issues and a choice of topics such as Hurtin', Leavin', and Longin' in Comparative Perspective.

The English department brings in a visiting writer to teach every year, and the unusual Museum Studies minor is one of the finest in the country.

several student-frequented bars in town. Students say that the school's alcohol policy is lax, and that "for the most part, we all like it this way and have few problems." Another student is quick to add that the policies "do not promote an environment for drinking, but rather encourage students to make responsible decisions." Sixteen percent of the men and 8 percent of the women go Greek; their parties are great but don't dominate the social scene.

At Beloit, having wheels will definitely raise your social standing, though laundromats, drugstores, Italian restaurants, and quiet country roads are all within walking or biking distance. Popular road trips include Chicago, Milwaukee, and the excellent college town of Madison. There is bus service to Chicago and Madison for a few bucks each way. As a college town, Beloit is "pretty scarce," one senior says. A blue-collar industrial town, there is the ever-popular Wal-Mart to satisfy late-night room decor flights of fancy, as well as a movie theater and coffee shops. "The campus is pretty self-contained and students don't venture out too often," one psychology major says. "We refer to campus as the "Beloit Bubble," because people seldom leave its parameters." Sports are played more for fun than glory, but women's softball, track, and volleyball, and basketball teams and men's baseball, football, basketball and track are most popular.

In many ways, Beloit is an academically rigorous East Coast liberal arts institution blended with the freer spirit and slower pace of life of the Midwest. The school tends to draw students who are looking for their own path, but who want to make sure that path is lined with solid academics and interesting friends.

Overlaps

Oberlin, Macalester, Grinnell, Carleton, Lawrence.

If You Apply To ➤ **Beloit**...Early decision: Dec. 1. Rolling admissions: Feb. 1. Guarantees to meet demonstrated need. Campus interviews: recommended, informational. Alumni interviews: optional, informational. SATs or ACTs: required. SAT IIs: optional. Accepts the Common Application and electronic applications. Essay question: personal statement or topic of your choice.

Bennington College

Bennington, VT 05201

Website: www.bennington.edu
Location: Rural
Total Enrollment: 571
Undergraduates: 447
Male/Female: 30/70
SAT Ranges: V 560–670 M 500–610
ACT Range: N/A
Financial Aid: 76%
Expense: Pr $ $ $
Phi Beta Kappa: No
Applicants: 782
Accepted: 60%

The most important principle at Bennington College is learning by practice, an idea that underlies every major facet of the school. Academically, the college has undergone a major period of restructuring. In an attempt to "reinvent" itself, trustees eliminated all academic departments and cut the size of the faculty by a third, causing much commotion and controversy. Today, Bennington prides itself on nontraditional structures. In addition to teaching specific disciplines, the faculty has organized itself into faculty program groups (FPGs) in which scholars, artists, and scientists with converging interests create programs of study for students and faculty. As the first liberal arts school in the nation to grant the arts equal status with other disciplines, Bennington College offers its students a unique learning experience taught by practitioners in their fields. It's an innovative approach that's revived the once-struggling college and given students reason to sing.

Founded in 1932 and set on 550 acres at the foot of the Green Mountains in picturesque southern Vermont, Bennington offers students a true New England setting accentuated by the latest high-tech innovations in learning. The campus was once an active dairy farm, and the main classroom and administration space is a converted barn. The Elizabeth Harrington Dickinson Science Building offers students the latest technology for intensive study of chemistry, biology, environmental sciences, and genetics, and is the home of the Computer Center, as well as the Center for Language Technologies, a media lab dedicated to the learning of foreign languages. At the Community Farm, students work with full-time farmers to cultivate some 90 varieties of vegetables as well as to conduct intensive agro-ecological studies.

The entire academic structure at Bennington is far different than a typical school. Each student designs his or her own major, and, rather than grades, all students, except premed and prevet, get written comments in each class twice a term. There are few academic requirements. Freshmen must take a First Year Seminar, which focuses on a variety of topics related to studies in the arts and sciences. In addition, every January and February, students must complete a seven-week internship related to an academic or career interest in a location of their choice. At Bennington, close faculty attention (the student/faculty ratio is less than 10 to 1) is a must: each faculty member is assigned fewer than a dozen students, with whom he or she must meet on a weekly basis. The faculty gets rave reviews, and students truly appreciate all their professors have to offer: "The quality of teaching is impeccable," says one junior, "led by the professors' obvious dedication to offering the student body a complete and sensual education."

"The academic climate is pretty much what you want it to be," reports a mathematics and childhood studies double major. A classmate describes the climate as "liberal," "artsy," and "very experimental." The school requires every student to own a computer with a full complement of software; the school offers the package at minimal cost and, when applicable, figures it into the student's financial aid.

In the absence of academic departments, the Core Faculty works as a whole to provide students with well-rounded academic programs; since the school's size limits the standard course offerings, more than 175 tutorials fill in the gaps. The most popular area of study is visual and performing arts. Another popular area of study, literature and language, has changed its focus (once critical analysis and creative writing) and is now being taught by poets, novelists, short-story writers, essayists, and playwrights, marking the school's return to learning-by-doing. Indeed, do-it-yourself interdisciplinary majors, including such unlikely combinations as biology and set design, are the second-most popular route here. Several newer programs include Culture, Community and Environment, Study of Experience, and Mind, Body and Behavior. And as for foreign languages, Chinese, French, German, Japanese, Russian, and Spanish are offered.

Bennington's "fluid and free-form" climate appeals to certain types of students. "If you hated high school and really wanted to guide your own education, this place is for you," explains one student. A senior adds, "I have never been as academically motivated as I am now." Eight percent of the students are from Vermont, and 9 percent are from other countries. Blacks, Hispanics, and Asian Americans account for 6 percent of the student body. Still, Bennington is known for its liberal students. "People here are all pretty much politically correct without ever really thinking about it," says a senior playwriting and media studies double major. "We are all about art—about individual freedom and artistic license," adds a classmate. Some students do report that, like anywhere else, there are cliques. "The social life here is pretty incestuous," says one. Bennington offers merit scholarships and, after an enrollment crisis several years ago, enrollment is on the upswing.

(Continued)

Enrolled: 30%
Grad in 6 Years: 65%
Returning Freshmen: 79%
Academics: ✍ ✍ ✍
Social: ☎ ☎ ☎
Q of L: ★ ★ ★ ★
Admissions: (800) 823-6845
Email Address:
admissions@bennington.edu

Strongest Programs:
Literature
Writing
Music
Dance
Drama
Architecture
Sciences

In addition to teaching specific disciplines, the faculty has organized itself into faculty program groups (FPGs) in which scholars, artists, and scientists with converging interests create programs of study for students and faculty.

Filmmaking is quite popular on campus, and is headed up by actor and director Alan Arkin.

There are no dorms per se at Bennington; the majority of the students live in 15 white New England houses and three modern row houses, in which "rooms are to die for!" states a satisfied sophomore. All housing is coed, right down to the bathrooms, and students of the opposite sex can share a room if both parties request it. First-year students are assigned to doubles, but most upperclassmen can get singles. The houses have their own living rooms, fireplaces (with wood delivered to the door), and "personalities," and each holds between two and three dozen students and elects a house chairperson.

Although the atmosphere on campus is sophisticated and cosmopolitan, the surroundings are rural New England at its best. Quaint towns, good hiking country, and ski slopes are all close by, and just off campus students can meet for a good, inexpensive meal at the Blue Benn Diner. Downtown Bennington, about four miles from campus, offers little more than movies and ice cream, and some feel the tension between Bennington "townies" and students. Many student feels that there is simply "bad karma" between the two, while another explanation is that the town "might tend to be wary of what might appear to be freaky students with strange lifestyles." The college offers a multitude of student performances, exhibitions, and recitals, and the annual Ben Belitt lectures draw famous literary figures. Periodic major social events, such as the late-spring music jamboree and Sunfest, add life to the social calendar. On weekends, there is the possibility of a theme party, a film on Saturday, and a coffee hour with House Chairs on Sunday. Tradition does not play a large role in the social life here.

Bennington's recreational options are numerous given the landscape of the area and the facilities available. The college's facilities consist of a clay tennis court, a fitness center, outdoor basketball courts and volleyball space, and during the colder months, part of the huge Visual and Performing Arts complex can be used for indoor basketball and volleyball and as a roller skating arena. Weekend activities include varied college-organized trips such as hiking, canoeing, rock climbing, caving, and camping. The college competes in an intramural coed soccer league composed of colleges in the Northeast.

Students here seem to break the mold when it comes to the typical college coed. But that doesn't seem to bother them one bit. Says one sophomore, "This school allows you to be who you are. You can be liberal or conservative–you can have fuchsia hair, fluorescent nail polish, and multiple body piercing or you can be your average Joe." If you are a resourceful, inventive, eager student committed to the challenges and joys of independence, then Bennington could be the place for you.

Overlaps

Bard, Sarah Lawrence, Reed, Amherst, Hampshire.

If You Apply To ➤ **Bennington**…Early decision: Nov. 15. Regular admissions: Jan. 1. Financial aid: Mar. 1. Does not guarantee to meet demonstrated need. Campus interviews: recommended, evaluative. Alumni interviews: optional, evaluative. SATs or ACTs: required. SAT IIs: optional. Accepts the Common Application. Essay question: important experience; relationship between passion and compassion; respond to proposition by Sherlock Holmes; when is imagination encountered? Recently graded analytical essay required. Encourages students to send samples of papers, photographs, tapes, etc.

Binghamton University, NY—See SUNY–BINGHAMTON UNIVERSITY

Birmingham–Southern College

Box A18, Birmingham, AL 35254

Birmingham-Southern College's tradition of service continues to flourish, effectively preserving the school's image as a strong liberal arts institution with its own brand of community involvement and conservative values. More than half the student body participates in community service through Southern Volunteer Services, as well as claiming active membership in fraternities and sororities. Caring and attentive faculty add to a sense of commitment to both personal and community growth. Says a junior: "'Southern has this incredible atmosphere in which students meet great friends, delve into different areas of academics, become involved in the community, and feel proud of their school."

Known as the Hilltop because of its hilly environment, BSC is the result of the 1918 merger of two smaller colleges: Birmingham College and Southern University. The campus, a green and shady oasis in an urban neighborhood, contains a pleasing hodgepodge of traditional and modern architecture, all surrounded by a security fence that controls access and increases security. A $9-million physical fitness center featuring a pool, track, and handball and racquetball courts is the newest addition to the campus.

The academic climate at BSC is described as rigorous by most. "Students can generally handle the workload," says a sophomore, "but must remain dedicated and diligent in their studies to succeed." Each student is assigned a faculty member who serves as his or her academic advisor from freshman convocation to graduation, an arrangement that students praise for its effectiveness. "My faculty advisor was fantastic in helping me with my schedule," says one senior. Equal praise goes out to faculty in the classrooms, where classes rarely have more than 25 students. "The professors here are extremely intelligent and compassionate," says an accounting major. "They sincerely care about their students and are committed to helping them reach their goals." Thirty percent of the students go on to professional or graduate school. English is one of the school's strongest programs, and premeds cite the strong biology program as a major drawing card. The Stephens Science Laboratory gives this program, as well as the chemistry and physics departments, a further boost. About a quarter of the students major in business, a division that includes programs ranging from accounting to international issues. The art, drama, dance, and music programs are all among the best in the South. One group of students traveled to Florida to help conceptual artist Christo wrap an island, while back at 'Southern, students stage several major productions each year, often including American and world premieres.

All liberal arts majors must complete a general education program that includes courses in writing, mathematics, a foreign language, and seven different liberal arts areas. BSC, a member of the Associated Colleges of the South* consortium, also offers a wide variety of special programs. The January term allows students to explore new areas of study from cooking lessons to travel in China. In addition, this extensive program focuses on-campus energies into culturally diverse opportunities via project experiences, social activities, ethnic food fairs, and many other projects. The international studies program offers students the chance to study abroad in several different countries, and the honors program allows 25 exceptional first-year students to take small seminars with one or more professors. The most recent curricular change was the addition of The Expanded Paradigm, an enhancement for the liberal arts program. This concept was awarded

Website: www.bsc.edu
Location: Urban
Total Enrollment:: 1,477
Undergraduates: 1,395
Male/Female: 40/60
SAT Ranges: V 540–660
  M 530–650
ACT Range: 24–29
Financial Aid: 47%
Expense: Pr $
Phi Beta Kappa: Yes
Applicants: 885
Accepted: 98%
Enrolled: 35%
Grad in 6 Years: 72%
Returning Freshmen: 94%
Academics: ✐ ✐ ✐
Social: ☎ ☎ ☎
Q of L: ★ ★ ★
Admissions: (205) 226-4696
Email Address:
  admission@bsc.edu

Strongest Programs:
  Biology
  English
  Business
  Humanities

The most recent curricular change was the addition of The Expanded Paradigm, an enhancement for the liberal arts program. This concept was awarded a $100,000 Hewlett Foundation grant to fund course expansions and development.

a $100,000 Hewlett Foundation grant to fund course expansions and development. America's Project is a cohesive, multidisciplinary program that examines the society, culture, and history of North, South, and Central America as a whole.

Seventy-six percent of the students are homegrown Alabamians, and practically all the rest hail from Deep South states, many with family ties to 'Southern. Though moderate by Alabama standards, the student body is quite conservative. Thirty-eight percent of the students belong to the Methodist Church, and the school chaplain heads the personal counseling program. Despite their geographic homogeneity, students of color do exist at BSC: 3 percent are African American, 1 percent are Hispanic, and 4 percent are Asian American. "Birmingham-Southern is a conservative Southern school," says a student. "There is not a great amount of mixing of ideas, but there is no obvious racism, homophobia, or anything of the sort." In addition to need-based awards, BSC offers various merit scholarships, ranging from $1,000 to $23,100. National Merit Scholars who list 'Southern as their first choice receive an automatic scholarship of $500 to $2,000, and up to 10 get full-tuition awards. Athletes compete for scholarships in baseball, basketball, soccer, and tennis.

Eighty-five percent of the students live on campus, including many of those whose families reside in Birmingham. Coed housing hasn't filtered down to 'Southern yet, so all seven dorms are single-sex, with a variety of visitation policies, depending on student preferences. North Hall and New Mens are generally the most desired men's residences, while Margaret Daniel is the preferred choice for women. "The rooms are not large, but more than adequate," says a student. Campus security is quite visible and students praise its effectiveness in keeping the campus safe.

Sixty-five percent of the men and women are members of Greek organizations, which means that much of the social activity at BSC revolves around the Greek system. "Fraternity row is always hoppin' for Greeks and independents," says one socializer. "We often have jazz and blues bands on Sunday afternoon on the Dorm Quad, and the SGA sponsors fall and spring concert weekends as well," a history major reports. As for alcohol, it's not allowed on the quad, and elsewhere it must be in an opaque container, a policy most students find reasonable. The biggest social event of the year is Southern Comfort, a four-day festival that is "always a wild time," notes one satisfied customer. When social opportunities on campus dry up, many students take advantage of what the city of Birmingham has to offer in the way of nightlife—cultural events, bars, and the rather bohemian (at least for Alabama) South Side. Beaches and mountains are less than five hours away, accessible for weekend trips.

In a state where the late Bear Bryant of 'Bama is practically a saint, BSC is a school without a football team. Men's basketball partially fills the void, as does the baseball team, which at one point, had 20 winning seasons in a row. The men's soccer team is also top-notch, and both the men's and women's tennis teams are of championship caliber. Beyond that, however, "women's sports are virtually nonexistent," one student complains. Intramurals are popular, though dominated by the Greeks.

BSC offers a career-oriented education in a fairly social and individual-attentive setting. Because the vast majority of students are from the Deep South, those from other areas of the country run the risk of spending four years as outsiders. But for students who fit the mold, BSC's conservative and friendly climate can offer four happy and prosperous years.

Overlaps

University of Alabama, Rhodes, University of Alabama–Birmingham, Auburn, Stamford.

Boston College

140 Commonwealth Avenue, Devlin Hall, Room 208, Chestnut Hill, MA 02167

Boston College is a study in contrasts. Academics are well respected, but so are the athletic teams. The environment is safely suburban, but barely 20 minutes from Boston, the hub of the Eastern seaboard. The Jesuit influence on the college, the largest Roman Catholic school in the country, really does provide a guiding spirit for campus life, but the social opportunities still seem endless. If you're looking for the best of all possible worlds, you just might find it here.

Don't let the name fool you. Boston College is actually a university with nine schools and colleges. It has two campuses: the main campus at Chestnut Hill and the Newton campus a mile and a half away. The dominant architecture of the main campus (known as "the Heights") is Gothic Revival, with modern additions over the past few years, including new dining-hall facilities and Fulton Hall for the Carroll School of Management. There's lots of grass and trees, not to mention a large, peaceful reservoir (perfect to jog around) right in the front yard.

The college's mission is to "educate skilled, knowledgeable and responsible leaders within each new generation." To accomplish this goal, the Core Curriculum requires not only literature, science, history, philosophy, social science, and theology, but also writing, mathematics, the arts, and the study of other cultures, in addition to specific requirements set by each undergraduate school. "Core Curriculum forces you to take classes you might not want to take but end up enjoying," says a senior. Students in arts and sciences must also show proficiency in a modern foreign language or classical language before graduation. Freshmen are required to take a writing workshop, in which each student develops a portfolio of personal and academic writing and reads a wide range of texts. Seniors participate in the University Capstone program, a series of seminars aiming to give a "big-picture" perspective to the college experience.

The climate here is challenging. "I feel it is very competitive between students," reports a junior. A senior adds, "The courses are rigorous but intellectually stimulating." Professors are described as "top-notch" and "excellent." The Jesuits on BC's faculty (about 60 out of 900) exert an influence out of proportion to their numbers. "The philosophy, theology, and ethics departments are the most important in setting the tone of the campus, because they keep the students encouraged to be open-minded," says a freshman. Another student says, "Our teachers are dedicated to students and scholarly research, and they are easily accessible through regular office hours." Registration is made painless through a computerized system and students report that getting required classes is "never much of a problem."

The schools of arts and sciences, management, nursing, and education award bachelor's degrees. In the College of Arts and Sciences—the largest undergraduate

Website: www.bc.edu

Location: Suburban

Total Enrollment: 14,700

Undergraduates: 8,900

Male/Female: 47/53

SAT Ranges: V 600–680 M 610–690

ACT Range: N/A

Financial Aid: 46%

Expense: Pr $ $ $

Phi Beta Kappa: Yes

Applicants: 16,680

Accepted: 38%

Enrolled: 33%

Grad in 6 Years: N/A

Returning Freshmen: N/A

Academics: ✍ ✍ ✍

Social: ☎ ☎ ☎ ☎

Q of L: ★ ★ ★

Admissions: (617) 552-3100

Email Address: N/A

Strongest Programs:
  Chemistry
  Music
  Art
  Drama

division—English, biology, and psychology are popular. Future Massachusetts politicians will benefit from the strong political science program. Outside the traditional classroom, at the Boston College Museum of Art in Devlin Hall, students find exhibitions, lectures, and gallery tours. The Music Guild sponsors professional concerts throughout the year, and music students emphasizing performance can take advantage of facilities equipped with Steinways and Yamahas. Theater majors find a home in the 600-seat E. Paul Robsham Theater Arts Center, which produces eight student-directed productions each year.

Students searching for out-of-the-ordinary offerings will be happy at BC. The student-run PULSE program provides participants with the opportunity to fulfill their philosophy and theology requirements while engaging in social service fieldwork at any of about 35 Boston organizations. Perspectives, a four-part freshman program, attempts to illustrate how great thinkers from the past have made us who we are. There's also a Freshman-Year Experience program, which offers seminars and services to help students adjust to college life and take advantage of the school and the city. An honors program allows students to work at a more intensive pace and requires a senior thesis.

Thirty percent of BC students come from the greater Boston area, and Catholics comprise about 80 percent of the student body. Blacks now constitute 4 percent of the student body, while Asian Americans make up another 8 percent, and Hispanics 5 percent.

According to a marketing major, BC's "biggest problem is the lack of minorities on campus." Still, the Jesuit appeal for tolerance means that students can find support and interaction even when approaching hot-button issues that Catholicism will not condone.

Housing is plush compared to most colleges. When students are admitted, they are notified whether they will get on-campus housing for three or four years, and most juniors with three-year guarantees live off campus or study abroad that year. The city of Boston has a fairly reliable bus and subway system to bring distant residents to campus; if students want to drive to school, there's a lottery for parking stickers. Another lottery system determines where on-campus residents hang their hats. Freshman dorms are described as "not great and not very modern" but accouterments in upper-class suites include private baths, dishwashers, and full kitchens. Students pay in advance for a certain number of dining-hall meals, served a la carte.

BC students are serious about their work, but not excessively so. There is time and plenty of places to party. Yet BC's reputation as a hard-core party school is diminishing, now that no kegs or cases of beer are allowed on campus grounds. Those of legal age can carry in only enough beer for personal consumption. Bars in Boston ("The best city!" gushes a freshman, when asked how Boston rates as a college town) are a big draw because it's easier to get served there. On weekends, especially in the winter, the mountains of Vermont and New Hampshire beckon outdoorsy types who like to hike and ski. The campus is replete with sporting events, movies, festivals, concerts, and plays. And as far as social life is concerned, "BC is not a dating school," laments one lonesome student. As at other Jesuit institutions, there is no Greek system at BC.

Athletic events become social events too, with tailgate and victory parties common. Although the Doug Flutie era is over, football games remain a big draw–the annual contest with Notre Dame is jokingly referred to as the "Holy War," and the Eagles recently beat Kansas State in the Aloha Bowl. The football program has been recognized for achieving the highest graduation rate in the College Football Association, and the women's field hockey team made it to the quarterfinals of the NCAA Tournament. The Silvio O. Conte Forum Sports Arena can seat the entire undergraduate student body indoors. Basketball games are also well attended, and BC meets fierce competition from Big East rivals Georgetown, Syracuse, Pitt, Villanova, and Miami. Students even get the day off from classes to line the edge of campus and cheer Boston Marathon runners up "Heartbreak Hill." Intramural sports are huge here, and students rave about BC's marvelous recreational complex.

BC students spend four years fine-tuning the art of the delicate balance, making old-fashioned morals relevant to life in the '90s, and finding time for fun while keeping an eye on their academic averages.

If You Apply To ➤ | **BC**…Early action: Oct. 15, Nov. 1. Regular admissions and housing: Jan. 1, Jan. 15. Financial aid: Feb. 1. No campus or alumni interviews. SATs or ACTs: required. SAT IIs: required (English, math, and one other). Apply to particular schools or programs. Meets demonstrated need of 94%. Essay question: why Boston College; a flash of revelation you have had; how a piece of art impacted you; or an important issue facing today's teens.

Boston University

121 Bay State Road, Boston, MA 02215

Between cheering cold-nosed at hockey games, exploring bustling Boston on the T, and burning the midnight oil for competitive classes, the close to 30,000 students at Boston University are busy bees. BU is a seriously academic school. With some of the most noted performance arts and communications programs in the country, BU's strengths in music, film and television, journalism, drama, and art and design all contribute to its solid standing as a thriving university. Pre-medical programs prep budding doctors at the Sargent College of Health and Rehabilitative Sciences while concierges-in-waiting practice their accommodation skills at the School of Hospitality Administration.

Like its close cousins George Washington University and NYU, the BU campus is practically indistinguishable from the city that surrounds it. A six-lane thoroughfare runs through the middle, and students looking for grassy courtyards and Frisbee games are more likely to find themselves plastered to the hood of a fast-moving automobile. BU's hodgepodge of nondescript high-rises and large Gothic buildings are woven into the city streets alongside fast-food restaurants and various shops. A measure of relief from the urban bustle can be found on the tree-lined side streets, which feature quaint Victorian brownstones. The newest addition to campus is an 18-story apartment-style student residence.

Boston University is one of the largest private universities in the nation and has a growing reputation as a research institution. Look no further than The Photonics Center, for engineering students, and the recently added School of Management, one of the most technically advanced classroom buildings in the country, to get an eyeful of academia. At the undergraduate level, the best of BU is generally found in preprofessional programs. The College of Arts and Sciences, the largest of the colleges, has recently been strengthened by the appointment of several outstanding professors and the College of Communication is popular and nationally known. Its curriculum comprises a healthy mixture of theory and hands-on training, and it houses the nation's only center for the study of political disinformation. "One of the professors I have lives in D.C. and works as an

Website: www.bu.edu
Location: Center city
Total Enrollment: 28,487
Undergraduates: 18,018
Male/Female: 40/60
SAT Ranges: V 590–680 M 590–680
ACT Range: 26–29
Financial Aid: 67%
Expense: Pr $ $ $ $
Phi Beta Kappa: Yes
Applicants: 28,090
Accepted: 55%
Enrolled: 27%
Grad in 6 Years: 68%
Returning Freshmen: 86%
Academics: ✍ ✍ ✍ ✍
Social: ☎ ☎ ☎ ☎
Q of L: ★ ★ ★
Admissions: (617) 353-2300
Email Address: admissions@bu.edu,
international admissions: intadmis@bu.edu

Strongest Programs:
University Professors

advisor to CNN," says an American Studies major. "I like being taught by people who are still active in their fields." The School for the Arts contains a strong theater department and a renowned music program, augmented by a concert hall, Tsai Performance Center, in which students are taught by members of the Boston Symphony Orchestra. The Sargent College of Health and Rehabilitation Sciences now offers a nutritional science program with two curricular options in nutritional sciences and dietetics.

The School of Management has added a four-year honors program and the College of Engineering has its own lab for robotics and biomedical engineering. The School of Hospitality Administration has received renewed support from the university; companies are supporting scholarships, and students now can find internships in Belgium and London as well as stateside. Serious liberal arts students can enroll in the honors program through invitation only. Also intriguing is the University Professors Program, which begins with a two-year integrated core of courses focusing on major authors and central themes of Western thought. As juniors and seniors, UPP students create their own interdisciplinary programs that are not limited by neat departmental divisions. The College of General Studies provides an alternative path into BU for late bloomers who might not otherwise qualify for admission. After a two-year introduction to college academics, successful students can move to one of the other divisions. Students with a sweet spot for teeth can take advantage of a Seven-Year Liberal Arts/Dental Education Combined Degree Program, which combines courses in the College of Arts and Sciences with the curriculum of the Henry M. Goldman School of Dental Medicine.

Each school within the university sets its own general education requirements, but all undergraduates take at least a few core courses in the College of Liberal Arts. There's also the Boston University Collaborative Degree Program, which allows students to earn two bachelor's degrees from any two schools in the university, such as Classics and Nutritional concentrations. Study abroad semesters and exchanges are available in many areas, including Grenoble, Madrid, London, Ecuador, Russia/Eastern Europe, Greece, Israel, and Venice, and now students can choose internships in the Pacific Rim/Australia area or in Moscow. For those who want to leave dry land, there is the Sea Semester.*

The academic climate at BU requires students to hit the books, but is laid-back enough that they don't hit each other. "The climate here is moderately competitive," says a senior. "The courses I've taken require a good amount of reading and effort." The toughest course to get into is taught by Nobel laureate Elie Wiesel, which requires signing up at least a year in advance. Lecture classes are predictably large, and students say that about half their classes have 50 students. Smaller sections are offered in subjects such as English. Students cite the College of Engineering as being the most competitive. As for academic advising: "Every student at BU has an academic advisor in their field," says a junior. "Students are required to meet with their advisor before they register." But one management information systems major complains that there is a lot of red tape to navigate when dealing with the campus administration. "They say that the first two letters of bureaucracy are BU."

Diversity extends from academics to the student body at BU. About 67 percent of the students hail from outside Massachusetts, and about 8 percent come from foreign countries. Seventy-two percent attended public high schools, and an equal proportion finished in the top fifth of their graduating class. BU has a local reputation as a rich kids' school. Yet students are adamant that they, as a whole, are diverse. African Americans and Hispanics together comprise 10 percent of the

The Sargent College of Health and Rehabilitation Sciences now offers a nutritional science program with two curricular options in nutritional sciences and dietetics.

student body, and Asian Americans account for 14 percent. "Boston University is so diverse that there is no 'typical' student image," one graduate student says.

Admissions criteria vary for each of the 10 undergraduate schools. Students apply to one school but may indicate a second, and usually less selective, choice. Among top students, BU tends to be a back-up school to more prestigious competitors. Many apply just because they want to be in Boston, sometimes without knowing what they're getting into. Besides the almost 250 athletic scholarships—a quarter for women, primarily in basketball, swimming, field hockey, and track and field—the university awards over 2,000 merit awards ranging from $500 to full tuition. Several alternative financing programs are also available to meet tuition costs. "BU became cheaper than my state's colleges because of my financial aid," says a physical therapy major. "You get constant aid as long as you keep up your grades."

BU's diversity extends to on-campus housing, which is guaranteed for all four years. Warren Towers, a high-rise that houses about 1,600 students, is says to be the best place for freshmen. Sophomores move into the smaller dorms or three-story brownstones. Upperclassmen compete in separate lotteries for special-interest floors or for a room in another dorm. Macintosh computer labs have been added to residence halls. "Our dorms range from adequate to beautiful," one student reports. "We have high-rise buildings with doubles to brownstones that have been renovated to their original condition." Thirty-six percent of the undergraduates live off campus. Flexible food plans are available to all, and there are a number of cafeterias to choose from, including a veggie dining room.

Social life is divided mainly between on-campus parties, local bars and nightclubs (many of which are just around the corner from the dorms), and parties at neighboring colleges. Fenway Park is just a short walk across Kenmore Square, and the Green Line of the Boston subway system, which squiggles through the center of the campus, puts the city right at students' fingertips. A senior boasts, "Boston is College Town, U.S.A. 'Nuff said." But BU students do more than keep the bartenders and baristas in beers and coffee beans. "Students are a major part of the labor force and they give a lot back to the city through community service," says one graduate student. Three percent of the men and 4 percent of the women belong to the Greek system, and there are well over 250 clubs and organizations on campus. Drinking is fairly common, though BU strictly enforces liquor laws on campus and Boston's college town reputation makes merchants wary of selling to those under 21.

The annual Beanpot hockey tournament, which pits BU, Boston College, Harvard, and Northeastern against one another, is the athletic highlight of the school year. With a championship hockey team, BU often wins. The the Head of the Charles regatta, which starts at BU's crew house, draws national attention. The men's soccer, track, cross-country, hockey, tennis, and wrestling squads as well as women's tennis, track, field hockey, cross-country, swimming, softball, and crew squads are also popular. Sadly for pigskin fans, the Boston University football program was terminated.

With 250 degree programs and a campus centered in a major city, it would probably be easy to get lost in the crowd at BU. Here, it takes a lot of energy to be bored. It's all up to the student to find their place and make the most of their college experiences. One student sums it up this way: "From the challenging academics to the diversity among its students to the wide range of extracurricular activities, life at BU offers boundless opportunities for growth."

Overlaps

New York University, Boston College, Tufts University, Northeastern, George Washington University.

BU…Early decision: Nov. 1. Regular admissions: Jan. 1. Financial aid: Feb. 15. Meets demonstrated need of 67%. Campus interviews: optional, informational (required, evaluative for some programs). Alumni interviews: optional, informational. SATs or ACTs: required. SAT IIs: required (vary by program). Apply to particular program.

Bowdoin College

Brunswick, ME 04011

Website: www.bowdoin.edu
Location: Medium-size town
Total Enrollment: 1,608
Undergraduates: 1,608
Male/Female: 48/52
SAT Ranges: V 640–720 M 640–710
Financial Aid: 37%
Expense: Pr $ $ $ $
Phi Beta Kappa: Yes
Applicants: 3,942
Accepted: 32%
Enrolled: 37%
Grad in 6 Years: 90%
Returning Freshmen: 94%
Academics: 🖉 🖉 🖉 🖉 🖉
Social: ☎ ☎ ☎
Q of L: ★ ★ ★
Admissions: (207) 725-3100
Email Address:
admissions@henry.bowdoin.edu

Strongest Programs:
Chemistry
Biology
Anthropology
Economics
English
Government
Sociology
Asian Studies

Bowdoin College can not only boast of such prestigious graduates as Longfellow and Hawthorne, but its students take pride in the fact that when they sign in, they write their names in the matriculation book at Hawthorne's very desk.

Since it was founded in 1794, it has been the college's mission to consider nature, art, the world of books, and friendship as a part of every student's experience. Bowdoin has developed a reputation for excellence in practically every academic pursuit and is one of those "quiet places" that ranks among the best liberal arts colleges in the country.

Bowdoin's compact campus covers 200 acres, and includes a patchwork of pine groves, athletic fields, and a congenial mix of over 90 buildings. The architecture has been called "a mosaic of styles", and includes buildings of the German Romanesque, Colonial, Medieval, neoclassic, neo-Georgian, modern, and postmodern era. New additions include a state-of-the-art theater and experimental theater, renovations to student housing, an addition to the dining hall, a new squash court facility, and athletic turf field. Bowdoin was the first institution in the country to make SAT scores an optional part of the admissions process, thereby shifting the college's emphasis from relying primarily on hypothetical evaluation to regarding the student as a whole. Although students at Bowdoin take their studies seriously, the academic climate is considered laid-back. "Academics are the number one reason students are here but the competition is not against other students, it's against yourself," says a government and environmental studies major. "The students here aren't always checking to compare grades on every assignment," adds a computer science major. "If they do, it's only so they can judge how they are doing themselves." The professors here receive high marks. "I've been extremely impressed by my professors," says a junior. "They have a passion for teaching and are dedicated to their students." Another student adds, "Bowdoin's number one resource is its professors."

Bowdoin is notable among top liberal arts colleges because some of its strongest programs are in the sciences. Chemistry receives rave reviews, and biology and environmental studies are also very strong. All three have top-of-the-line equipment and outstanding faculty; the microscale organic chemistry lab was developed and advanced at Bowdoin. In keeping with the school's mascot of the polar bear (and its Maine location) Bowdoin offers courses in Arctic Studies. Students also praise the government department for its distinguished professors, impressive speakers, and extensive document selection in the library. Students cite the music and theater departments as weak. However, after the renovation of one theater and the construction of another, there's a renewed focus on the arts at the college. Recent curriculum changes include a minor in gay and lesbian studies.

Self-designed and double majors have become increasingly popular on the long list of options for Bowdoin undergraduates. Inexpensive study abroad options include semesters at Bowdoin's affiliated programs in Sri Lanka, South India, Rome, and Sweden, participation in the Maritime Studies Program* and opportunities to travel to Cape Town, South Africa; Quito, Ecuador; and London, England through its partnership with Bates and Colby. Bowdoin also participates in the Twelve-College Exchange,* which allows students to study for a year at other highly selective liberal arts schools in New England. In addition, the college offers the Writing Project, a peer tutoring program that assigns specially trained writing assistants to students in a variety of courses. About 60 percent of juniors and seniors conduct independent study projects with one or more faculty members, often publishing their results. Students can also elect unusual research opportunities, such as participation in Arctic archeological research in Labrador or ecological research at Bowdoin's Kent Island Scientific Station in the Bay of Fundy, Canada.

To graduate, students must complete 32 courses, including two in natural science and mathematics, social and behavioral sciences, and humanities and fine arts. They also must complete two semester courses in non-Eurocentric studies and spend at least four semesters in residence. The freshman orientation program at Bowdoin gives a standard introduction to college life, plus optional preorientation canoeing, hiking, and climbing trips that attract about half the entering class. Freshmen also have their choice of over 70 seminars, each limited to 16 students, which emphasize improving students' reading and writing skills. The Quantitative Skills Development Program is designed to encourage all students to develop competence and confidence in using quantitative information. You won't find monster classes at Bowdoin; 92 percent have 50 students or fewer and the majority of students get the classes they want without much hassle. "If you do have trouble getting into a class, I've always found that some good, solid groveling will get you in," says one student.

Bowdoin students tend to look and act similarly (L.L. Bean's 24/7 factory store is just down the road); most are "clean-cut and somewhat conservative." Though luring minorities to rural Maine is no easy task, Bowdoin's nonwhite and international enrollment has increased in recent years to nearly 20 percent. "We do pretty well...considering we're a small school in Maine, but I think Bowdoin would be a better place with more racial, ethnic, and economic diversity," admits a senior. Although no merit scholarships are offered, all students may work on campus, and a special program allows students working on independent projects to apply for research stipends in lieu of a campus job.

"Housing is one of the most exceptional aspects of life at Bowdoin," says a sophomore. "Freshman dorms are very comfortable and the on-campus apartments for upperclassmen are actually semiluxurious." Another student adds, "Everyone always comments on how huge the rooms are here." That's good news, considering that 85 percent of the school's undergraduates live on campus. Freshmen live in coed dorms or theme houses, and upperclassmen who do well in the very competitive room lottery make a beeline for on-campus apartments. Bowdoin's liberal housing policy includes coed suites with four rooms adjoining a common living room. The school also offers "chem free" dorms, in which smoking and alcohol are prohibited. Off-campus house-sitting accommodations along the scenic Brunswick shore are available at low, off-season rates, and some hardy souls even live on nearby islands. The food gets a four-star rating and the chefs even put on succulent lobster bakes twice a year.

Brunswick is Maine's largest town—population 22,000—but by no means its

Bowdoin was the first institution in the country to make SAT scores an optional part of the admissions process, thereby shifting the college's emphasis from relying primarily on hypothetical evaluation to regarding the student as a whole.

In keeping with the school's mascot of the polar bear (and its Maine location) Bowdoin offers courses in Arctic Studies.

largest city. "The town of Brunswick goes to bed by 10:00 P.M. so it's up to the students to make their own nightlife," says computer science major. Another student disagrees: "Brunswick is a great location for a small liberal arts college because it's so colorful and offers students many opportunities to play." If students do get a case of the Brunswick blahs, Portland is only a half-hour drive away and offers good shopping, restaurants, nightlife, an art museum, and a symphony. Boston is two and a half hours away, and there are several ski slopes within an 80-mile radius. Bowdoin has also instituted a shuttle program so that students without cars can have access to nearby cities.

As for social life, a new college house system replaces the traditional Greek scene. The new system, managed by a group of upperclass student leaders, randomly assigns each new student to a college house. Bowdoin's alcohol policy is very strict, requiring the registration of all campus parties, but alcohol is still available. According to one chemistry major, "The social life revolves around drinking."

On-campus activities include, concerts, lectures, movies, and dances. Festivals, such as Winter's Weekend, Ivies Weekend, and Spring Fling spice up the social calendar. And when hockey season starts, things really get rolling. The Polar Bears, longtime ECAC East, formerly Division III, winners, always play to a packed house. The long-standing rivalry with Colby gets Bowdoin students riled up. "The most school spirit typically surfaces at hockey games, particularly those against Colby, when rowdy Bowdoin students have been known to toss grilled-cheese sandwiches onto the ice," says a veteran. The women's track, basketball and cross-country teams and the men's cross-country and field hockey teams have also enjoyed winning seasons. Students love the athletic facility, with its 16-lane swimming pool and a field house boasting a 200-meter track, tennis courts, and exercise rooms. A fitness center also houses freeweights, Cybex weight stations, and 20 aerobic stations.

Bowdoin takes pride in tradition, and its excellence stems from its personalized approach to a multifaceted education. Though some may bristle at the tough Maine winters, many will find the academic climate warm and hospitable. "This place really pulls together and makes it happen," says a satisfied senior. Another student sums it up this way: "Bowdoin is a challenging, rigorous, academic program in a beautiful and safe New England setting."

About 60 percent of juniors and seniors conduct independent study projects with one or more faculty members, often publishing their results.

Overlaps

Dartmouth, Williams, Middlebury, Colby, Brown.

If You Apply To ➤ **Bowdoin**...Early decision: Nov. 15. Regular admissions: Jan. 1. Financial aid: Nov. 15. Guarantees to meet demonstrated need. Campus and alumni interviews: recommended, evaluative. SATs: optional. SAT IIs: optional. Accepts the Common Application and electronic applications. Essay question: your greatest challenge; influential work of art, book, or experience. Places less emphasis on test scores than do comparable colleges.

Brandeis University

Waltham, MA 02454-9110

Website: www.brandeis.edu
Location: Suburban

The only nonsectarian Jewish-sponsored college in the country, Brandeis University was founded to provide educational opportunities to those otherwise discriminated against and has always had a reputation for intense progressive thought. Now, it's also being recognized as a rising star among research institutions. Although it continues its struggle to maintain its historic Jewish identity and its need to attract a well-rounded, eclectic group of students, Brandeis is fast becoming one of the nation's leading research institutes.

Set on a hilltop in a pleasant residential neighborhood nine miles west of Boston, Brandeis's attractively landscaped 270-acre campus boasts many distinctive buildings. The music building, for example, is shaped like a grand piano; the theater looks like a top hat. The Carl and Ruth Shapiro Admissions Center, built in a stunning "international style," welcomes and informs campus visitors. Plans are in the works for a new campus center and art gallery expansion and construction is underway on a new women's studies resource center.

At Brandeis, biochemistry, chemistry, neuroscience, and physics are top-notch, benefiting from the $41.5-million Volen Natural Center for biological, cognitive, and computational research. Several other departments, including English, history, theater arts, music and political science, offer nationally ranked graduate programs. Dedicated premeds are catered to hand and foot, with special advisors, internships, and their own Berlin Premedical Center, with specialized laboratories designed to provide would-be MDs with research opportunities. Psychology, biology, and economics are the most popular majors here; prelaw and premed students dominate.

With the largest faculty in the field outside of Israel, the university is virtually unrivaled in Near Eastern and Judaic studies; Hebrew is a Brandeis specialty. The school's East Asian Studies Program gives students a broad yet intimate knowledge of the history, politics, economics, art, and language of the major areas of East Asia. A wide variety of interdisciplinary programs, including Latin American, medieval, Russian, peace, and women's studies, add spice to the academic menu. New interdisciplinary programs include International Economics and Environmental Studies. Journalism is also offered as an interdisciplinary program, approaching the field from the broad liberal arts perspective instead of the pre-professional. A joint program in comparative religion brings together students from Brandeis and College of the Holy Cross. Brandeis also maintains a commitment to the creative arts, with strong theater offerings and a theory-based music program founded by the late Leonard Bernstein. Students rave about the natural sciences—biology, chemistry, physics—but a senior says anthropology and sociology could "use some help." The great majority of classes have 19 or fewer students.

The Brandeis core curriculum is rooted in a commitment to developing strong writing, foreign language, and quantitative reasoning skills from an interdisciplinary perspective. One part of the core requires a "cluster" of three interrelated courses, from at least two of the university's four schools, designed to introduce the multidisciplinary study of a particular topic, theme, problem, region, or period. Currently, there are more than 45 clusters, including The City, Film and Society, and Medicine, Health and Social Policy. The combination of topics, and benefits of cross-disciplinary study, is limited only by a student's imagination. Students must also take the University Seminar in Humanistic Inquiries, through which they explore fundamental questions about human existence and meaning. In addition, during the summer before their arrival, all freshmen read an assigned book, which they discuss with faculty members during orientation.

The student body at Brandeis is 27 percent in-staters and heavily bicoastal otherwise, with sizable numbers of New York, New Jersey, and California residents. The group is also very bright; 95 percent graduated in the top quarter of their high school class, and professors want them to keep working hard. Students

(Continued)

Total Enrollment: 4,527
Undergraduates: 3,112
Male/Female: 44/56
SAT Ranges: V 610–710 M 610–710
Financial Aid: 50%
Expense: Pr $ $ $ $
Phi Beta Kappa: Yes
Applicants: 5,792
Accepted: 52%
Enrolled: 27%
Grad in 6 Years: 81%
Returning Freshmen: 92%
Academics: ✑ ✑ ✑ ✑
Social: ☎ ☎ ☎
Q of L: ★ ★ ★
Admissions: (781) 736-3500
Email Address:
  sendinfobrandeis.edu

Strongest Programs:
  Neurosciences
  Biochemistry
  East Asian Studies
  Politics
  Psychology
  English
  Near Eastern and Judaic Studies
  Biology

With the largest faculty in the field outside of Israel, the university is virtually unrivaled in Near Eastern and Judaic studies; Hebrew is a Brandeis specialty.

say the academic climate here is intense. "Brandeis takes its academic integrity seriously," notes a creative writing and English major. "Our programs are highly competitive and professors here expect great things from their students. Classes here are designed to challenge, and they do." There is an out, though; the Flex 3 option allows students to take three classes one semester if an especially rough course is required, and five the next, to stay on track for four-year graduation.

Though the student body at Brandeis is 55 percent Jewish, there are three chapels on campus—Catholic, Jewish, and Protestant—built so that the shadow of one never crosses the shadow of another. It's an architectural symbol that students say reflects the realities of the campus community. African Americans make up 2 percent of the student body, Hispanics another 3 percent, and Asian Americans 10 percent. "Everyone at Brandeis wants others, even those different from them, to feel accepted and comfortable," says a senior. Gays and lesbians have an established presence, and throw some of the liveliest parties. The unofficial fraternities and sororities that have colonized at Brandeis are clamoring for recognition from the school. Other hot-button issues include political correctness, rape awareness, and environmental causes. As might be expected, "The major political issues deal more with the Middle East than any American social or political issues," says a senior.

Even with one of the highest tuition rates in the country, Brandeis does not guarantee to meet each student's full demonstrated need, but help is generally available to those who apply on time. The level of support remains fairly constant over four years, students report. The university also offers over 700 merit scholarships, in amounts from $750 to $19,000. The six-day freshman orientation program is one of the most extensive in the nation, including a broad spectrum of events, such as Boston Harbor cruise and special programs for minority, international, commuter, and transfer students.

As befits its mold-breaking heritage, Brandeis is the only school in the nation where you can live in a replica of a Scottish castle with pie-shaped rooms and stairways leading to nowhere. More pedestrian housing options include traditional quadrangle dormitories, where freshmen and sophomores live in doubles, juniors in singles. "North Quad is the newest area and very well maintained," reports a junior. "On the other side of campus is Mossel, a quad with a very peaceful pond in the middle." The Foster Living Center, or the "Mods," are coed, university-owned town houses reserved for seniors. According to a junior, "Ziv Quad, with its air-conditioning and modern suites, is the hope of many sophomores." Freshmen and sophomores are guaranteed housing, while upperclassmen play the lottery each spring. Eighty-five percent of students live on campus, and the remaining 15 percent find affordable off-campus housing nearby. Brandeis boasts the best college food in the Boston area, as well as the most appetizing setups, students say, thanks to a decision to outsource dining services. Campus meal tickets buy lunch or dinner in a fast-food joint, the pub, a country store, a kosher dining hall with vegetarian selections, or the Boulevard, a cafeteria where "the salad bars are huge."

Social life at Brandeis offers lots of options for those ready to relax. There are 207 campus clubs to keep students busy, but "Brandeis is not the type of school where there are parties at every corner," a student adds. Weekends begin on Thursday, with live entertainment at the on-campus Stein pub. Students can party at will in the dorms so long as they don't get too rambunctious, but suites are officially "dry" unless a majority of the residents are over 21. Major events on the campus calendar include a Tropics Night dance (where beachwear is required in February), the massive Bronstein Weekend festival just before spring finals, and the "Screw Your Roommate" dance, where dormies set up their roommates on blind dates. Also well attended are the Homecoming soccer match and the annual lacrosse tilt against cross-town rival Bentley College. The possibilities for off-campus diversion are nearly infinite, thanks to the proximity of Boston and Cambridge, which are accessible by the free Brandeis shuttle bus or a nearby commuter train. (A car is more trouble than it's worth.) And what about Waltham, Brandeis's host town? Well, a new movie theater opened last summer to rave student reviews, and "We have a hugely successful volunteer/community service program called the Waltham Group," says a senior. But, quips a history major, "Waltham is a blue-collar town containing a university of students with champagne backgrounds and caviar aspirations. Another student sees it differently: "There's a lot of fun things to do in Waltham. You just have to look for them."

Though the school does not field a football team, Brandeis has developed strong men's baseball, basketball, tennis, soccer, track and cross-country squads and women's basketball, track and cross-country, and fencing squads, all of which have taken regional championships in recent years. The athletic program gets a boost from its membership in the University Athletic Association, a neo–Ivy League for high-powered academic institutions such as the University of Chicago, Johns Hopkins, and Carnegie Mellon.

Brandeis's sports facilities include the 70,000-square-foot Gosman Sports and Convocation Center, reportedly the largest multipurpose indoor athletic facility in the East.

Brandeis University is proud of its Jewish heritage, although it does tend to cause some friction. Still, few private universities have come as far as Brandeis in just 50 years, evolving from a bare 270-acre site with the leftovers of a failed veterinary school to a modern research university of more than 100 buildings and a $300-million endowment. Landscaping, dining services, health services, and the campus computer network have all been dramatically improved in the past few years, students say, adding to their feelings of pride in the school. One student sums it up this way: "Brandeis is not only an awesome place to get an education, it's also an open, accepting place where anyone can feel at home."

A wide variety of interdisciplinary programs, including Latin American, medieval, Russian, peace, and women's studies, add spice to the academic menu.

Overlaps

Tufts, Brown, Harvard, University of Pennsylvania, Boston University.

If You Apply To ➢   **Brandeis**…Early decision: Jan. 1. Regular admissions and financial aid: Jan. 31. Meets demonstrated need of 94%. Campus and alumni interviews: recommended, evaluative. SATs or ACTs: required. SAT IIs: required (writing and two others). Essay question: significant experience or achievement with special meaning; issue of personal, local, national or international concern; or influential person. Accepts the Common Application and electronic applications.

Brigham Young University

ASB A153, Provo, UT 84602

You don't have to be a Mormon to attend Brigham Young University, but it helps. Affiliated with the Church of Jesus Christ of Latter-Day Saints, BYU provides its students with a challenging academic environment that is rooted in the Mormon faith. In return, students must honor a strict code of ethics, which can be tough for those without the religious commitment to back it up. Still, most students agree that the school's commitment to the Mormon belief is why they chose BYU

Website: www.byu.edu
Location: City outskirts
Total Enrollment: 32,161
Undergraduates: 29,386
Male/Female: 47/53

(Continued)

ACT Range: 24–29
Financial Aid: N/A
Expense: Pr $
Phi Beta Kappa: No
Applicants: 8,524
Accepted: 71%
Enrolled: 80%
Grad in 6 Years: 62%
Returning Freshmen: 87%
Academics: ✍ ✍ ✍
Social: ☎ ☎ ☎
Q of L: ★ ★ ★ ★
Admissions: (801) 378-2507
Email Address:
   admissions@byu.edu

Strongest Programs:
   Accounting
   Law
   Languages
   Chemical, Electrical, and
   Computer Engineering
   Computer Science
   Geology
   Economics
   Elementary Education
   Music
   Zoology

Everyone must complete an extensive 36- to 50-hour general education program that includes work in the natural sciences, social sciences, arts and letters, mathematics, and foreign languages (there are 54 to choose from).

in the first place. "BYU is a fine institution where all ideas are discussed," says a student, "but our religion is the core."

Mormon values of prosperity, chastity, and obedience pervade all aspects of life on the 638-acre campus, where the utilitarian buildings, like everything else, are "clean, modern, and orderly." Recent campus additions include the Ezra Taft Benson Science Building, and additions to the law library and dairy products lab.

The day begins on the well-kept campus at 6:00 A.M. when the campus bell peals the first four bars of the Mormon hymn "Come, Come Ye Saints" to rouse students for another day. Students are required to take the equivalent of about one religion course per term to graduate, and offerings include study of the Book of Mormon. In addition, everyone must complete an extensive 36- to 50-hour general education program that includes work in the natural sciences, social sciences, arts and letters, mathematics, and foreign languages (there are 54 to choose from). These courses are designed to "improve a student's ability to think and communicate clearly, respond to beauty with sensitivity and discrimination, make moral judgments, and act wisely," says the administration.

BYU has more full-time students than any other church-sponsored university in the nation, and academic offerings run the gamut from traditional liberal arts courses to novelties such as range management. Travel and tourism and clothing and textiles, two of the more unique programs, are also two of the weakest. Programs in the sciences are especially strong, as are accounting, law, and philosophy. The foreign language programs are greatly aided by multimedia labs. There is a large study abroad program that offers travel to Vienna, London, Jerusalem, and elsewhere at relatively low cost. Only 46 percent of the students graduate within five years because 95 percent of the men and 14 percent of the women interrupt their studies to fulfill the traditional two-year stint as a missionary. This is typically done after the freshman year.

An honors program, open to highly motivated students, offers small seminars and allows students much interaction with professors. The faculty members, who are addressed as "Brother" or "Sister," are both accessible to students and loyal to mainline Mormonism. Advisement is also given the thumbs-up. One of the most popular course offerings at BYU is ballroom dancing, partly because many participants aspire to join BYU's award-winning dance team. Most classes at BYU are kept to 25 or 30 students, though required courses can be larger, and some in the social sciences can soar well into the hundreds. Though BYU is a bona fide mega-university, massive registration lines are one headache students are spared because of telephone registration. However, students do say that they have a hard time getting all the courses they want to take each term. Exceptions are made, one student reports, "if you're a senior." The libraries have good resources and contain 2.3 million volumes.

One-third of BYU students are from Utah, another quarter are from California and Idaho, and the remainder includes about 1,500 foreign students, who speak a total of 70 different languages and testify to the effectiveness of the far-ranging Mormon missionary effort. Only 6 percent of the students belong to minority groups. "Political correctness is a huge issue because many people oppose it," notes a business major; students here tend to be extremely conservative.

Brigham Young annually awards a whopping 7,000 merit scholarships, which range from $400 to full tuition, as well as offering full-tuition loans, with terms similar to those for Guaranteed Student Loans, to anyone. About 350 scholarships are reserved for varsity athletes. Tuition for church members is $950 lower than that for nonmembers because Mormon families contribute to the university through their tithes. At freshman orientation, students are divided into groups of perhaps a dozen, headed by an upperclassman, and participate in various activities, including a reception with the president.

Freshmen live either in the single-sex dorms or in no dorms at all. Although the rents in Provo have gotten steeper, most upperclassmen still opt for nearby apartments, which are also single-sex (remember the honor code?). To promote a more intimate social life, the campus is broken into geographic "wards," and then again into smaller "home evening groups" of about 15 students. "It's an effective way of shrinking the big-university atmosphere," a student explains. An unusual program is Freshman Academy: Students housed in specific dorms attend classes together and eat meals with their instructors. BYU's three cafeterias get high marks. Shopping is within walking distance, and for other needs there is a bus to the mall in Orem.

The town of Provo, 45 miles south of Salt Lake City, leaves the students with little inspiration. The nearest excitement is in Salt Lake City. But one needn't look far for sights of beauty and tranquillity. The campus, which lies at an elevation of 4,600 feet between the shores of Utah Lake and Mount Timpanogos, offers breathtaking sunsets and easy access to magnificent skiing, camping, and hiking areas. As for activities, the dances are frequent, as are concerts, plays, and sports events. Dating is common, within Mormon bounds of proper behavior. Also in accordance with Mormon belief, alcohol is banned, as are drinks that contain caffeine. There are no fraternities and sororities. The droves of clubs and organizations to join include everything from "astronomy and bagpipes to zoology and folk dancing."

Physical fitness is big here, and the intramural program is rated as one of the best in the country, with indoor and outdoor jogging tracks and facilities for tennis, swimming, racquetball, handball, golf, and just about any other athletic activity you might want. Also important are varsity sports, and the philosophy of obedience seems to work wonders here. The BYU football team has national prowess as well as numerous conference trophies. Other recent WAC champions include the women's cross-country, soccer, and volleyball teams. Annual contests with the University of Utah transform the typically mild-mannered BYU student body into the gracious but raucous BY Zoo (hence their nickname, "Zoobies"). One student mentions "devotionals every Tuesday at 11:00 A.M." and "the bell tower playing hymns and ringing every hour" as other favorite campus traditions.

BYU might seem like a 1950s time-warp to most Americans. Indeed, BYU may appear, in one student's words, to be a "clean-scrubbed complacency farm that churns out nice, quiet students." But its students seem to thrive on the university's caring, albeit squeaky-clean, atmosphere. The combination of the social code and the tightness of the community can make the school seem a little unreal and isolated from the rest of the world, but most BYU students see this as a small price to pay for an education that will serve them all their lives and then some.

BYU has more full-time students than any other church-sponsored university in the nation, and academic offerings run the gamut from traditional liberal arts courses to novelties such as range management.

Ninety-five percent of the men and 14 percent of the women interrupt their studies to fulfill the traditional two-year stint as a missionary. This is typically done after the freshman year.

Overlaps

Ricks College, University of Utah, BYU–Hawaii, Utah State, Arizona State.

If You Apply To ➢

BYU…Regular admissions: Feb. 15. Financial aid: Apr. 15. Housing: No deadline, but apply one year in advance. Does not guarantee to meet demonstrated need. Campus and alumni interviews: optional, informational. ACTs: required. Essays: two, both related to significant experience. Looks for college prep courses versus overall GPA.

British Columbia, University of Canada—See CANADIAN UNIVERSITIES

Brown University

45 Prospect Street, Providence, RI 02912

Website: www.brown.edu
Location: City center
Total Enrollment: 7,782
Undergraduates: 6,112
Male/Female: 46/54
SAT Ranges: V 640–750 M 650–750
ACT Range: 27–32
Financial Aid: 38%
Expense: Pr $ $ $ $
Phi Beta Kappa: Yes
Applicants: 15,489
Accepted: 17%
Enrolled: 55%
Grad in 6 Years: 93%
Returning Freshmen: 96%
Academics: 🖋 🖋 🖋 🖋 🖋
Social: ☎ ☎ ☎ ☎
Q of L: ★ ★ ★ ★ ★
Admissions: (401) 863-2378
Email Address:
admission_undergraduate@ brown.edu

Strongest Programs:
History
Geology
Computer Science
Religious Studies
Film and Television
Engineering
Art and Design
Writing
International Relations

With a growing number of applications and an overwhelming number of happy students, Brown University finds itself a perennial "hot college." Students not only receive the prestige and quality of an Ivy League education, but they have a chance to explore their creative sides at a liberal arts college that does not emphasize grades and preprofessionalism. This unique environment has drawn both praise and criticism over the years, but Brown students say they thrive on this discussion and on lively debate. "The freedom of shaping one's own education is both frightening and exhilarating, since the possibilities for good and ill are almost endless," says one student.

Located atop College Hill on the east side of Providence, Brown's 140-acre campus affords an excellent view of downtown Providence that is especially pleasing at sunset. Campus architecture is a composite of old and new: plenty of grassy lawns surrounded by historic buildings that offer students refuge from the city streets beyond. One student describes it as a "melting pot of architecture's finest. We have a building that resembles a Greek temple [and] buildings in the Richardsonian tradition." The neighborhoods that surround the campus lie within a national historic district and boast beautiful tree-lined streets that are full of ethnic charm.

Brown's faculty has successfully resisted the notion that somewhere in their collective wisdom and experience lies a core of knowledge that every educated person should possess. As a result, aside from completing courses in a major, the only university-wide requirements for graduation are to demonstrate writing competency and complete the 30-course minimum satisfactorily. (The assumption is that students will take 4 courses a term for a total of 32 in four years.) Freshmen have no requirements. Those with interests in interdisciplinary fields will enjoy Brown's wide range of concentrations that cross departmental lines and cover everything from cognitive science to public policy. Indeed, there are bona fide departments in cognitive and linguistic sciences and media and modern culture. Students can also create their own concentration from the array of goodies offered. Brown also offers group independent-study projects, a popular alternative for students with the gumption to take a course they have to construct primarily by themselves. Particularly adventurous students can choose to spend time in one of Brown's 20 study abroad programs (including Brazil, Great Britain, France, Tanzania, Japan, Denmark, and Egypt). Closer to home, students can cross-register with Rhode Island School of Design, which is also located on College Hill, or participate in the Venture Program.*

Students can take their classes one of two ways: either for marks of A, B, C, or No Credit; or Satisfactory/No Credit. The NC is not recorded on the transcript, while the letter grade or Satisfactory can be supplemented by a written evaluation from the professor. A habit of NCs, however, lands students in academic hot water. Any fewer than seven courses passed in two consecutive semesters makes for an academic "warning" that does find its way onto the transcript, and means potential dismissal from the university. To some extent, Brown is still trying to live down its curriculum, which is the source of both its popularity and its inferiority complex.

Among traditional departments, history and geology are some of the university's best, and students also praise computer science, religious studies, and applied math. Other top-notch programs include comparative literature, classics, modern languages, and the writing program in the English department. Among the sciences, engineering and the premed curriculum are standouts. Future doctors can try for a competitive eight-year liberal medical education program where students can earn an MD without having to sacrifice their humanity. The political science department is said to be rapidly improving, as is the international relations concentration. Sociology, psychology, and math, however, still receive thumbs down from students. Scientific technology–related fields have very good facilities, including an instructional technology center, while minority issues are studied at the Center for Race and Ethnicity.

Brown prides itself on undergraduate teaching and considers skill in the classroom as much as the usual scholarly credentials when making tenure decisions. Younger professors can receive fellowships for outstanding teaching, and the administration's interest in interdisciplinary instruction and imaginative course design help cultivate high-quality instruction. The advising system reflects the administration's commitment to treat students as adults. The lack of a set of predetermined requirements is supposed to challenge students, so "no one is going to tell you what to take." The advising system pairs each freshman with a professor and a peer advisor, and resident counselors in the dorms are also available to lend an ear. "As an Asian, I have an Asian advisor as well as a woman's peer counselor, a resident counselor, a minority counselor, and a head counselor who lived on my floor in the dorm," reports one well-counseled student. Sophomores utilize special advising resources, upperclassmen are assigned an advisor in their concentration, and a pool of interdisciplinary faculty counselors is on hand for general academic advising problems.

Brown offers more than 100 freshman courses via the Curricular Advising Program (CAP), and the professors in these courses officially serve as academic advisors for their students' first year. This program receives mixed reviews, but some professors are highly praised by students for their abilities and availability. "They are very casual about open office hours, and welcome students to pop in for a chat." Upper-level classes are usually in the teens, CAP courses are limited to 20, and only 13 percent of intro lectures have more than 50 students. Especially popular courses are usually jammed with students, and often there aren't enough teaching assistants to staff them effectively. Some popular smaller courses, especially writing courses in the English department and studio art courses, can be nearly impossible to get into, although the administration claims that perseverance makes perfect—in other words, show up the first day and beg shamelessly. Compared with the other Ivies, Brown's academic climate is relatively casual, or at least seems to be. "Students are self-motivated, study often, and learn a great deal, because they want to do the work, not compete with others," one student says.

With a small percentage of the students hailing from Rhode Island, geographical diversity is one of Brown's hallmarks. Politically, there is also a lively mix. "We are very diverse," writes one student, "from your local beer-guzzling frat partyer to the lesbian/gay/bisexual alliance." Brown is one of the few remaining hotspots of student activism in the nation; nary a semester passes without at least one demonstration about the issue of the day.

Blacks make up 6 percent, Hispanics 6 percent, Asians 15 percent, and foreigners 7 percent of the student body, and minorities rarely miss an opportunity to speak out on issues of concern. The gay and lesbian community is also prominent. "They throw the best dances on campus," says one science major.

The only university-wide requirements for graduation are to demonstrate writing competency and complete the 30-course minimum satisfactorily. (The assumption is that students will take 4 courses a term for a total of 32 in four years.)

Future doctors can try for a competitive eight-year liberal medical education program where students can earn an MD without having to sacrifice their humanity.

Ninety-seven percent of students were in the top quarter of their high school class, and 40 percent hail from private or parochial schools.

Brown admits 95 percent of the students on a need-blind basis, and although it doesn't offer athletic or academic merit scholarships, it does guarantee to meet the full demonstrated need of everyone who is admitted. "The most contentious issue is making Brown a need-blind institution," says one student. According to the administration, a worldwide capital campaign is currently under way to raise the endowment and the alumni consciousness to eventually provide need-blind admissions for all students. Fifteen Starr National Service scholarships, ranging from $1,000 to $2,000, are also awarded each year to students who devote a year or more to volunteer public service jobs. About 120 other "academically superlative" students, called University Scholars, will find their financial aid package sweetened with extra grant money.

Freshmen arrive on campus a few days before everyone else for orientation, which includes a trip to Newport, and there is also a Third World Transition Program. About half the freshmen are assigned to one of the eight coed Keeney Quad dorms, in "loud and rambunctious" units of 30 to 40 with several sophomore or junior dorm counselors. The other half live in the quieter Pembroke campus dorms or in a few other scattered locations. After the freshman year, students seeking on-campus housing enter a lottery. The lottery is based on seniority, and sometimes the leftovers for sophomores can be a little skimpy, though there are some special houses set aside to give them a chance at some decent rooms.

The dorms themselves are fairly nondescript. "There are no fireplaces or engraved wood trim a la Princeton," observes one student, but nevertheless there are many options from which to choose, including apartment-like suites with kitchens, three sororities, two social dorms, and three coed fraternities. Brown guarantees housing all four years, and a dorm with suites of singles ensures that there is room for all. A significant number of upperclassmen get "off-campus permission." Places nearby are becoming more plentiful and more expensive as the area gentrifies. Brown's food service, which gets high marks from students for tastiness and variety, offers meal plans ranging from 7 to 20 meals a week. Everyone on a meal plan gets a credit card that allows the student to do what students at every other school only wish they could: use the meal ticket for nocturnal visits to snack bars should they miss a regular meal in one of Brown's two dining halls. Campus security is described as "very good." Says a junior, "I feel safer here than I do at home."

Providence is an old industrial city that recently underwent a renaissance. It is still the butt of student jokes—"Be prepared to wear your proletarian disguise," cautions one—but extensive renovations of the downtown area have had a positive impact. Providence is Rhode Island's capital, so many internship opportunities in state government are available, as are a few good music joints, lively bars, and a number of fine, inexpensive restaurants. For the couch potato set, there are plenty of good things right in the neighborhood. "Downtown is a 10-minute walk, but why bother when you can buy anything from Cap'n Crunch to cowboy boots on Thayer Street, which runs through the east side of campus," a philosophy concentrator explains. For a change of scenery, many students head to Boston or the beaches of Newport, each an hour away.

The few residential Greek organizations are generally considered much too unmellow for Brown's taste (only 10 percent of the men and 2 percent of the women sign up), and hence freshmen and sophomores are their chief clientele. The nonresidential black fraternities and sororities serve a more comprehensive student-life function. Tighter drinking rules have curtailed campus drinking somewhat. The university sponsors frequent campus-wide parties, and plays, concerts, and special events abound. Funk Nite every Thursday night at the Underground, a campus pub, draws a mixed bag of dancing fools. The biggest annual bash of the year is Spring Weekend, which includes plenty of parties, and a big-name band. Strong theater and dance programs, daily and weekly newspapers, a skydiving club, political organizations, "even a Scrabble club and a successful croquet team," represent just a few of the ways Brown students manage to keep themselves entertained. One other is the campus student center, which has been thoroughly renovated. For those interested in community outreach—and there are many at Brown who are—the university's nationally recognized public-service center helps place students in a variety of volunteer positions. The Brown Community Outreach, in fact, is the largest student organization on campus.

Brown isn't an especially sports-minded school, but a number of teams nevertheless manage to excel. Of the 36 varsity teams, recent Ivy League champions include men's and women's crew, men's soccer, and women's ice hockey. The football team, once noted for "choking" in big games, gained new respect thanks to a strong showing in the 1998 Ivy League championship. Athletic facilities include an Olympic-size swimming pool and an indoor athletic complex with everything from tennis courts to weight rooms. There's also a basketball arena for those trying to perfect their slam dunks. The intramural program is solid, mixing fun with competitiveness.

Ever since the days of Roger Williams, Rhode Island has been known as a land of toleration, and Brown certainly is a 20th-century embodiment of this tradition. The education offered at this university is decidedly different from that provided by the rest of the Ivy League, or for that matter, by most of the country's top universities. Brown is content to gather a talented bunch of students, offer a diverse and imaginative array of courses, and then let the undergraduates, with a little help, make sense of it all. It takes an enormous amount of initiative, maturity, and self-confidence to thrive at Brown, but most students feel that they are up to the challenge. "You get four years of choice," says one student. "Deal with it."

Overlaps

Harvard, Yale, Stanford, Cornell University, Princeton.

If You Apply To ➤

Brown...Early action: Nov. 1. Regular admissions: Jan. 1. Financial aid: Jan. 20. Guarantees to meet demonstrated need. Campus and alumni interviews: optional, evaluative. SATs or ACTs: required. SAT IIs: required (any three). Essay question: personal statement in your own handwriting.

Bryn Mawr College

101 North Merion Avenue, Bryn Mawr, PA 19010-2899

Founded in 1885, Bryn Mawr has prospered as a welcome haven for students seeking a solid, single-sex education. Adjectives abound when Bryn Mawr students attempt to define their school's populace. They are studious and compassionate, disciplined and friendly, organized and ethereal. And all agree that the women of this small college are some of the best and brightest they'll ever meet. "The only common thread is that we are all very smart women," a junior says. "Besides that, we are all over the map." And with it's near-perfect acceptance rate at law schools and average-breaking production of science majors, Bryn Mawr is a gem.

Website: www.brynmawr.edu
Location: Suburban
Total Enrollment: 1,779
Undergraduates: 1,256
Male/Female: 0/100
SAT Ranges: V 610–710 M 600–680

(Continued)

Financial Aid: 54%

Expense: Pr $ $ $ $

Phi Beta Kappa: No

Applicants: 1,596

Accepted: 58%

Enrolled: 35%

Grad in 6 Years: 81%

Returning Freshmen: 90%

Academics: ✍ ✍ ✍ ✍ ✍

Social: ☎ ☎ ☎

Q of L: ★ ★ ★

Admissions: (610) 526-5152

Email Address:

admissions@brynmawr.edu

Strongest Programs:

Archaeology

Art History

Classics

Foreign Languages

Sciences

Students are encouraged to do independent research during their senior year, and faculty in fields including anthropology, geology and sociology often take students along during summertime field research studies.

Bryn Mawr's lovely suburban campus is a path-laced oasis, peaceful and self-contained. Just a 20-minute train ride to downtown Philadelphia, Bryn Mawr provides the perfect blend of a country setting with a vital and exciting city nearby. The predominant architecture is collegiate Gothic, a style that Bryn Mawr helped to introduce to the United States. Ten of Bryn Mawr's buildings are listed in the National Register of Historic Places. The M. Carey Thomas Library, which was named after the school's first dean and second president, a pioneer in women's education, is also a National Historic Landmark. Variations on the collegiate Gothic theme include a sprinkling of modern buildings, such as Louis Kahn's slate-and-concrete residence hall and the redbrick foreign language dormitory. All of this is set among trees (each carefully labeled with Latin and English names) and lush green hills, perfect for an afternoon walk, bike ride, or jog.

Even though students are prohibited from discussing their grades, students at Bryn Mawr all work hard. "The classes are rigorous and everybody puts in a good amount of work," an English major says. "But I don't even know my best friend's GPA." Most departments are strong, especially the sciences, classics, archaeology, art history and the foreign languages, including Russian and Chinese. The fine arts department, however, is criticized as one of the weakest because of its small size. Mawrtyrs who want to major or do serious work in music, art, photography, or astronomy hike over to coeducational Haverford, Bryn Mawr's nearby partner in the "bi-college" system. Bryn Mawr handles the theater, dance, creative writing, geology, art history, Italian, and Russian programs for the two colleges, and the departments of German and French are joint efforts.

Bryn Mawr also offers a rich variety of special programs. Approximately one third of students study overseas during their junior year through one of the 50 study abroad programs approved by the college. A variety of interdisciplinary programs are offered including environmental sciences, neural and behavioral sciences, Africana Studies, and feminist and gender studies. As for general education requirements, all students must complete two classes in each of the three divisions (social sciences, natural sciences, and the humanities), one semester of "quantitative" work, an intermediate level of competency in a foreign language, and also must fulfill the requirements of a major. Students are also required to take eight half-semesters of physical education and must also pass a swimming test. In addition, all freshmen are required to take two College Seminars to develop their critical thinking, writing, and discussion skills.

The quality of teaching at Bryn Mawr is unquestionably high. "Because of the close faculty-student ratio, students get a lot of opportunities to work closely with professors," a Russian major says. A political science major raves that "all professors make themselves available and love to talk to students and answer questions." Freshmen are initiated to the Bryn Mawr experience during Customs Week, which includes a variety of seminars and workshops as well as a tour of the campus and town. To help first-year students acclimate, Bryn Mawr has developed the OWLS (Orientation Workshop Leaders) program, which begins during orientation and continues throughout the first year. A wide range of topics, from going home for the first time to the honor code and dealing with stress, are discussed by first-year and upper-class students, administrative staff, and faculty. For those looking ahead to see what the steep tuition will buy in the long term, the campus has a career resource center that offers information on interviewing and building a résumé. It also brings recruiters to campus, offers mock interviews, and keeps students posted on internships.

The student body is fairly diverse—African Americans make up 4 percent, Hispanics 3 percent, and Asian Americans 17 percent. To encourage diversity and harmony on campus, as part of orientation, freshmen can take an intensive four-hour session on pluralism, which teaches students to examine assumptions about class, race, and sexual orientation. The college also has added an assistant director in the Office for Institutional Diversity to support student cultural groups and opened a Multicultural Center providing meeting and office space for the groups.

Even though the much-prized fireplaces do not operate, housing at Bryn Mawr is "beautiful," says one student. "Almost all rooms have nice perks: hardwood floors, a window seat, a nice view, a bay window," a senior says. The college has added dining halls to two dorms and the rooms have high-speed Internet access. Dorms have quotas for students from all four classes, so freshmen mix freely with upperclassmen. Though housing is a little tighter than it was a few years ago, it is still guaranteed for four years, and most students can expect singles after freshman year. All those who live on campus—97 percent of the student body—must subscribe to the 20-meal-a-week plan, and most seem to really like it. In fact, the food service has even received a national award from *Restaurants and Institutions Magazine*.

Bryn Mawr is located on suburban Philly's wealthy Main Line (named after a railroad), and the campus is two blocks from the train station. "The people who live here are yuppies with BMWs," a freshman notes. "Bryn Mawr equals suburbia." Shopping at national chain stores is nearby, and there are cute places to eat, but, like college students around the world, Mawrtyrs duck out of town and head to the city for nightlife. The 20-minute train ride provides students with easy access to cultural attractions, as well to social and academic events at the nearby University of Pennsylvania.

The social life at Bryn Mawr is, well, different due to the fact that it is a women's college. There's little pressure to "go with any flow," a senior says. Students usually need to travel for parties, which take place off campus at Swarthmore, Haverford, or Penn. What social life there is at Bryn Mawr generally includes Haverford men. Tradition is a very important part of the social scene on campus, and the college holds many welcomed traditional ceremonies and celebrations. The medieval-style May Day festivities are held the Sunday after classes end in May. Everyone wears white, eats strawberries, and watches Greek plays. Students are known to skinny-dip in the fountains and drink champagne on the lawn. The presentation of lanterns and class colors to incoming freshmen on Lantern Night, and regal pageants, such as Parade Night, Hell Week, and Step-Sings, fill life with a Gothic sense of wonder and school spirit. Says a student, "They play a big role in united all four classes and give students a role in the greater history of the college."

As for athletics, cross country, volleyball and field hockey are very competitive. And, of course, there's always the national champion badminton team. Sports, however, do take a second role to academics.

Shipping off to Bryn Mawr presents students with a unique opportunity to revel in an all-women environment while taking advantage of nearby testosterone havens and cultural activities. But all that is secondary to the real experience of being a Mawrtyr, many students say. "The Bryn Mawr community is unlike anything I have ever encountered," a political science major explains. "Finding your niche here is very personal, but the environment makes it inevitable. I have grown so much as a person even in the last year. Bryn Mawr has a way of encouraging you."

Bryn Mawr students share a host of symposia, lectures, and parties as part of a consortium with Haverford and Swarthmore colleges.

Tradition reigns supreme at Bryn Mawr, with the annual Parade Night, Lantern Night, and the torturous Hell Week, in which seniors teasingly torment freshman for seven days.

Overlaps
Wellesley, Smith, Swarthmore, Mt. Holyoke, Brown.

Bryn Mawr…Early decision: Nov. 15, Jan. 1. (application and financial aid). Regular admissions, financial aid, and housing: Jan. 15. Guarantees to meet demonstrated need. Campus and alumni interviews: recommended, evaluative. SATs: required. SAT IIs: required (English and two others). Accepts common and electronic applications. Essay question: describe a course you believe should be part of liberal arts education; balancing advantages and disadvantages of modern advances; discuss something you thought you knew for sure but now question.

Bucknell University

Lewisburg, PA 17837

Website: www.bucknell.edu
Location: Rural
Total Enrollment: 3,560
Undergraduates: 3,403
Male/Female: 52/48
SAT Ranges: V 570–650 M 590–680
ACT Range: 26–29
Financial Aid: 51%
Expense: Pr $ $ $
Phi Beta Kappa: Yes
Applicants: 7,011
Accepted: 44%
Enrolled: 29%
Grad in 6 Years: 89%
Returning Freshmen: 94%
Academics: ✑ ✑ ✑ ✑
Social: ☎ ☎ ☎ ☎
Q of L: ★ ★ ★
Admissions: (570) 577-1101
Email Address:
admissions@bucknell.edu

Strongest Programs:
Humanities
Engineering
Business
English
Music
Theater
Psychology
Interdisciplinary Studies

Strong in business management, engineering, and natural sciences, Bucknell is a secluded slice of Utopia, drawing hardworking, hard-partying students to its idyllic location in central Pennsylvania. The school attracts a preprofessional crowd, but stresses the individual—in keeping many of its classes small and stressing quality time with faculty members. The academic climate keeps Bucknellians on their toes, but offers a broad array of social scenes to let them kick off their shoes and relax, whether than means moshing at a frat or aspiring to be Arnold Palmer on the campus's own 18-hole golf course.

In addition to being comfortable and friendly, Bucknell is physically beautiful. Located on a hill just south of Lewisburg, Pennsylvania, the campus overlooks the scenic Susquehanna River valley and features a landscape of leafy nooks and grassy expanses of playing fields. Greek Revival architecture dating from the 19th century provides a picture-book setting, but blends with modern residential complexes, a magnificent science center, a performing arts center, and Davis Gym. Renovations of the 488-seat University Theater include all the trappings of a state-of-the art lighting and sound system. A $14-million, 304-bed residence hall has opened and older residence halls are continually renovated.

Academics come first for most students at Bucknell, according to a senior psychology major. "The courses are demanding, but not impossible," says the student. Many academic programs are lauded, including the extremely demanding engineering and natural science departments, humanities, English, music, theater, and interdisciplinary studies such as international relations. Biology, management, and economics are the most popular majors, followed by civil engineering and education. The liberal arts emphasis means students take a wide variety or classes, sometimes to their dismay. "Usually, non-science majors are very afraid of any science classes, even the basic ones," admits one senior.

All freshmen in the College of Arts and Sciences take Interdisciplinary Foundation seminars taught by faculty advisors, designed to strengthen crucial skills like library research, computing, and writing. Degree candidates in the College of Arts & Sciences also must complete at least 32 credits, while engineering students complete at least 34, including 4 half-credit courses. Additionally, Arts and Sciences students fulfill distribution requirements consisting of four courses in the humanities, two in social science, and three in natural science and mathematics. Two more courses address "broadened perspectives" on the natural and fabricated world, and on human diversity; team-taught interdisciplinary options to fulfill this requirement were introduced. All students enrolled in engineering have a common first semester, including a special course designed to provide an engineering perspective and an active learning experience in all five engineering disciplines.

Finally, along with major-related requirements, each student completes a capstone project during the senior year and must meet the writing-competency standard to graduate. Recently, the civil, chemical, and mechanical engineering curricula were revised to provide greater flexibility and to balance the courseload more evenly over the program's four years.

Once they have fulfilled Bucknell's many requirements, students select from a variety of courses, including the popular Management 101, where students create and sell a product whose earnings go to charity. Thirty-seven percent of each graduating class studies abroad, with semesters in England, France, or Barbados led by Bucknell professors; universities in 62 countries sponsor Bucknellians. Back on campus, rarely do more than 50 students occupy a classroom, and students report it's extremely rare to be shut out of a course. Independent research projects often pair students and professors with common interests, especially during the summer. The unique, two-summer Institute of Leadership in Technology and Management, for example, provides engineering and management students with an opportunity to learn new approaches to problem-solving while enhancing their critical thinking, teamwork, and communication skills. On-campus study the first summer is followed by an off-campus internship during the second. Government, corporate, and local grants are also available to spend summers studying physics, astronomy, geology, biology, and the environment. The students are close with the faculty, most of whom have their doctorates. "It is very common to be friendly with profs and get invited to their homes or invite them to yours," a chemistry major says.

Sixty-five percent of Bucknell's students hail from out of state, and 71 percent attended public high school. Eighty-five percent ranked in the top quarter of their class. The student body is not terribly diverse, with only 3 percent African American, 4 percent Asian American, and 3 percent Hispanic, though the administration is reportedly working to change this. The campus is highly conservative and major issues include alcohol abuse and the Greek system. One senior International Relations and Japanese Studies double major says Bucknellians are socially aware. "Students here seem to vary drastically in their values and beliefs."

All first-year students are required to live in the dorms, and housing is guaranteed for upperclassmen who want it. Eighty-six percent of the student body stay on campus, and seniors who want to move off campus must apply for the privilege. "The housing is definitely cleaner and well-kept than any other I have seen in my four years," one student reports. A residential college option draws about 25 percent of each entering class to one of the six more intellectually-focused "colleges": Environmental, Global, Social Justice, Humanities, Arts, and Society and Technology. Some upperclassmen are integrated into the colleges, but most enter a lottery based on seniority for space in the dorms. There also are five residential apartments housing more than 300 upperclassmen. Most boarding students take their meals in a central dining hall, where they rate the food above average. Bison, a popular food-and-recreation center, as well as Larison Dining Hall, are other university-run dining options.

When they tire of institutional fare, Bucknellians head into downtown Lewisburg, which has a few quaint shops and restaurants, coffeehouses, a theater, and one bar, the Bull Run Inn. "It is amazing how much the town has grown since I was a freshman," says a senior. "But it is not a college town. It is a good place to go to school because there are not many off-campus distractions." There are, however, many opportunities for community service, including work at the local

All freshmen in the College of Arts and Sciences take Interdisciplinary Foundation seminars taught by faculty advisors, designed to strengthen crucial skills like library research, computing, and writing.

hospital and projects spearheaded by B.I.S.O.N., or Bucknellians In Service to Our Neighbors. Students often road-trip to New York City, Atlantic City, Philadelphia, and Washington, D.C.; Penn State's main campus is an hour away. Due to Lewisburg's relative lack of social options, 38 percent of the men join fraternities, and 43 percent of the women join sororities. "Social life is very monotonous," a student says. "It tends to be the same thing a lot, which can be good or can get boring fast!" Bucknell's 10-point program to reduce alcohol abuse stresses education, counseling, the development of alternative social programming and stricter sanctions. Some students report that it's still fairly easy for underage drinkers to be served. "If students want a drink, they'll find a way," a senior says. For those who choose not to imbibe, a new substance-free student organization, with the longest acronym ever seen, moved into a former fraternity house in the fall of 1995: C.A.L.V.I.N. and H.O.B.B.E.S., which means Creating a Lively, Valuable, Ingenious, and New Habit of Being at Bucknell and Enjoying Sobriety. Every spring, House Party Weekend is a carefully planned and structured enterprise that enables everyone to go bananas. Tent Party Weekend is the celebratory weekend of graduation, when the university gathers under a huge tent to dance and socialize all night long with friends, family, faculty, and administrators. Homecoming Weekend, sporting and multicultural events, and the Greek system's annual Bid Day are also eagerly awaited. The arts center hosts ballet and jazz ensembles, and philharmonic orchestras.

A five-time winner of the Patriot League Presidents Cup for overall athletic excellence in the league, Bucknell boasts successful men's cross-country, baseball, and lacrosse teams and regular season titles in volleyball, women's indoor track and field, women's soccer, and women's basketball. Intramurals are available in almost every imaginable sport, and participation is enthusiastic. The college also introduced two new women's sports: water polo and golf.

The relative isolation on campus can be a boon or a drag depending on the student. "It sometimes seems like it's out in the middle of nowhere, but that depends on the student and what they want to do to enforce or deconstruct that feeling/sense," a senior reasons. Bucknellians are a tight-knit group, probably from bonding over snow shovels or commiserating about the proliferation of parking tickets giddily issued by campus police officers. "There are amazing people who truly care and become your family," an English and education double major says. "You cannot slip through any cracks at Bucknell."

If You Apply To ➤

Bucknell...Early decision: Nov. 15, Dec. 15. Regular admissions and financial aid: Jan. 1. "Need-aware" for last 15% of students admitted, and does not guarantee to meet demonstrated need of other students. Campus interviews: recommended, evaluative. Alumni interviews: optional, evaluative. SATs: required. Accepts the Common Application and electronic applications. Essay question: significant experience or achievement; issue of personal, local, or national concern; or influential person.

California Institute of Technology

Mail Code 163, 515 South Wilson, Pasadena, CA 91125

Caltech is not a school for cowards. Small in size, gigantic in reputation, it is in a class by itself: a student/faculty ratio of 3 to 1 for just 907 undergraduates; an average combined SAT score flirting with 1500 for entering freshmen (tops in the nation); and 27 Nobel Prize winners among its faculty members and alumni. Check out the opportunities: rigorous training in math, science, and engineering; research from sophomore year on with world-class professors; a phenomenally successful honor system that makes integrity the unbroken rule in and out of the Caltech classroom; and sure job offers at top dollar from private industry and the federal government at the end of four years. But there is a catch: intense academic pressure that is matched by few if any other undergraduate programs and will slap many students with the first C's of their lives.

Old Spanish-mission-style buildings and a few "typical block institutional moderns" along with courtyards and arcades make up the 124-acre Caltech campus, which is isolated from the show-biz/hot-tub scene that many people think of as La La Land culture. The campus features lots of greenery, including olive trees, lily ponds, and plenty of flowers. Recent additions include a new bookstore.

Though it takes a while for students to get acclimated, most soon become devoted to Caltech. "Everyone is horribly bright here," says one student, and it's taken as gospel on this campus that Caltech offers the best overall scientific education in the country, no matter what students at a certain school in Massachusetts might think. "Caltech students possess a deep love of science," says a senior chemistry major. The school's mission, according to one official, is "to train the creative type of scientist or engineer urgently needed in our educational, governmental, and industrial development."

After all, it was at Caltech that Albert Einstein abandoned his concept of a static cosmos and endorsed the expanding-universe model; it's also where physicist Carl Anderson discovered the positron.

But for the mere mortal undergraduate, most of the first year and some of the second are devoted to fulfilling the school's scientific requirements: two years of math, two years of physics, one year of chemistry, one year of biology, and a number of labs. Lectures are large but break into recitations of about 20 students each that are often led by other faculty members. The pass/fail grading system in the freshman year goes a long way toward easing the high-powered atmosphere for new arrivals. Each term, a course in the humanities and social sciences is also required to round out the core.

Caltech first made its reputation in physics, and this subject is still a premier attraction. Engineering (especially electrical engineering), chemistry, and biology are standouts. Planetary science, astronomy, and geology are also strong. In fact, just about everything outside of the humanities/social science division (in which students must take a third of their courses) is excellent. Students seriously interested in the humanities or social sciences are often frustrated by the limited course offerings. "Caltech is not the school to attend if you plan to major in a humanities subject," says a junior, "unless you also want an intense science background." Now that's an idea.

Most students can access the campus computer system from their dorm rooms, and one student boasts that Caltech has "the best computer/student ratio in the nation." Speaking of the best, among Caltech's facilities are the Beckman

Website: www.caltech.edu
Location: Suburban
Total Enrollment: 1,889
Undergraduates: 907
Male/Female: 70/30
SAT Ranges: V 700–780 M
750–800
Financial Aid: 67%
Expense: Pr $ $
Phi Beta Kappa: No
Applicants: 2,894
Accepted: 18%
Enrolled: 45%
Grad in 6 Years: 82%
Returning Freshmen: 96%
Academics: 🖎 🖎 🖎 🖎 🖎
Social: ☎
Q of L: ★ ★ ★
Admissions: (626) 395-6341
Email Address:
ugadmissions@caltech.edu

Strongest Programs:
Engineering
Physics
Applied Science

Caltech offers the best overall scientific education in the country, no matter what students at a certain school in Massachusetts might think. Its mission, according to one official, is "to train the creative type of scientist or engineer urgently needed in our educational, governmental, and industrial development."

Institute, a center for fundamental research in biology and chemistry, and the Keck telescope, the largest optical telescope in the world. Recently added to the campus is the Moore Laboratory with 90,000 square feet filled with high-tech equipment for engineering and communications majors.

In spite of a few geniuses who are either impossible to understand or impossibly demanding, the professors tend to be good teachers. They are described by students as "fantastic," "approachable," and "top-notch." Of course, they are usually more interested in research than in classes, but then again, so are most of their students. For many, summertime is the time to go SURF-ing, as in Summer Undergraduate Research Fellowships, which are grants that give 311 undergraduates a chance to get a head start on their own research under a faculty sponsor. Some 20 percent of them publish their work in scientific literature, the administration estimates. Research is so much in the air, in fact, that many students agree that "the focus definitely leans toward research and the graduate population," which is slightly larger than the undergraduate.

After four years in high school as the resident math/science genius, most freshmen show up at Caltech a little wet behind the ears. Bragging about being first in your high school class will impress no one at Caltech; you're just joining the club. But Techers, despite their academic preoccupations, vociferously deny that they prefer computers to people. "Despite what you might think, there is a social life here," confirms one biology and history major. "People tend to hang out and talk, go out to eat, go to movies, or go to campus parties. The campus is very close for the most part, and the house system encourages you to make a lot of very close friends that last all four years." One-third of the student body comes from California, but the rest are drawn from all over the nation. Asian Americans account for less than one-third of each class, with African Americans and Hispanics at 6 percent combined. This seeming lack of diversity was recently highlighted by the fact that, among the nation's elite institutions, Caltech was the only one to admit no black freshmen in the 1999 academic year. The school guarantees to meet the full demonstrated financial need of every admit, and there are merit scholarships awarded to students at the beginning of sophomore year.

Perhaps the most distinctive attribute of Techers is their commitment to one another, a supportiveness sustained by an honor system that a recent student poll rated as the best aspect of life at Caltech. Based on the principle that "no one shall take unfair advantage of any other member of the Caltech community," it is maintained through four years of grueling academic pressure that, though intense, is curiously enough not competitive. "Everyone in the Caltech community trusts each other," notes a student. Faculty gives take-home exams, and if the instructions say the exam is three-hour closed book, then the students all follow these instructions to the letter. Students rule themselves, and if violations of the honor code are suspected, "students decide if a violation was indeed made," describes one student.

There are no fraternities or sororities, but the seven coed on-campus houses inspire a loyalty worthy of the Greeks. The four older houses, which have been renovated, offer mostly single rooms, while the three newer dorms have doubles that have also been refurbished. Freshmen select their house during Rotation Week, when they spend an evening of partying at each one, indicating at week's end the four they like the most. Resident upperclassmen take it from there in a professional-sports-type draft that places each freshman in one of his or her top choices. For those business-minded types, there's Avery House, a dorm whose residents embody the spirit of entrepreneurship. Each dorm's dining hall serves, on a mandatory basis, standard institutional food from a central kitchen (a new food service has improved quality a bit), but other than for meals, students loyally support their home bases. Eighty-eight percent of the entire student body live in one form of university housing or another.

The houses are the emotional center of Caltech life. Site of Caltech parties, they are also the scene of innumerable practical jokes perpetrated on staff members and seniors. "Caltech is definitely known for its pranks," notes a junior. On Ditch Day, seniors barricade their dorm rooms using everything from steel bars to electronic codes, leave clues as to how to overcome the obstacles, and disappear from campus. Underclassmen spend the day figuring out how to break in and claim the awaiting reward, which can range from the edible to…well, anything is possible. Perhaps the most unforgettable student prank was orchestrated during the 1984 Rose Bowl game. UCLA was playing Illinois, and a group of Caltech whiz kids were playing with the scoreboard. They spent months devising a radio-control device that would allow them to take control of the scoreboard in the second half and flash pictures of their school's mascot, the beaver, as well as a new version of the score that had Caltech leading MIT by a mile.

A Caltech student's idea of fun is likely to be a little offbeat and creative. For example, the annual Pumpkin Drop (on Halloween, of course) involves immersing a pumpkin in liquid nitrogen for several days and then dropping it from the library roof so it shatters into a zillion frozen pumpkin shards. During finals week, stereos blast "The Ride of the Valkyries" at 7:00 each morning, just the thing to get you going after that all-nighter. Although Pasadena has become a hip, trendy place for up-and-coming yuppies to hang out, L.A. is the original all-night city for Caltechers with a car—and even rarer—a free evening. As one stressed-out Techer notes, "When I have free time, I go to sleep."

When it comes to athletics, physical education, and recreation, Caltech sponsors a well-balanced and broad-based program. The program consists of 18 NCAA sports including men's and women's cross-country, men's soccer, women's volleyball, water polo, men's and women's basketball, men's and women's fencing, baseball, golf, men's and women's tennis, and men's and women's track and field. Caltech has a large and varied program of physical education classes and boasts an excellent program of both undergraduate and graduate student intramural sports, with an 80 percent participation rate.

Although studying at one of the world's most renowned schools for scientific research is an exhilarating experience, the downside is the accompanying stress. One electrical engineering major reflects, "You can play a sport that you hadn't heard of a year ago, you can be an actor in the winter play, or write for the newspaper. You can do it all if you don't let your studies take over your life." At this high-powered and demanding college, that may be easier said than done.

It was at Caltech that Albert Einstein abandoned his concept of a static cosmos and endorsed the expanding-universe model; it's also where physicist Carl Anderson discovered the positron.

Overlaps

MIT, Harvard, Stanford, UC–Berkeley, UCLA.

If You Apply To ➢ | **Caltech**…Early action: Nov. 1. Regular admissions: Jan 1. Guarantees to meet demonstrated need. No campus and alumni interviews (information sessions conducted on campus). SATs: required. SAT IIs: required (writing, math, and either physics, biology, or chemistry). Looks for math/science aptitude as well as motivation toward research or unusual academic potential.

California Colleges and Universities

California's three-tiered system of colleges and universities has long been viewed as a model of excellence by other public higher education institutions nationwide and even around the world. Many have attempted to emulate its revered status, which offers a wealth of educational riches including world-class research universities, enough Nobel Prize winners to fill a seminar room, and colleges on the cutting edge of everything from film to viticulture. Underlying the creation of this remarkable system was a commitment to the notion that all qualified Californians, whatever their economic status, were entitled to the benefits of a college education. In pursuing this ideal, California led the nation in opening up access to higher education for African Americans, Hispanics, and other previously disenfranchised groups.

Unfortunately, in the early 1990s, this golden dream started fading due to the state's recession, population growth, and many other contributing factors. As a result, California's public universities and colleges received reduced tax support, student charges and user's fees shot up, student/faculty ratios increased, fewer classes were offered, and, in some cases, entire academic programs were eliminated. Although it still remained relatively lower than most states, tuition started to climb. The good news is that California has made major adjustments to counteract this quandary and to restore some stability to the financing of the University of California, which expects its total enrollment to swell by 60,000 students over the next decade. System leaders struck a deal with the Governor that calls for an annual 4 percent increase in state outlays along with additional funds tied to enrollment growth, maintenance, capital outlays, and other new projects. In return, the systems have promised to slow increases in tuition and fees, to cut costs, and to devote more resources to teacher training.

The system is composed of the 9 combined research and teaching units of the University of California (UC), with a 10th campus, UC Merced, expected to open in 2005, and 23 state universities and colleges (CSUC), including the newest CSU campus at Channel islands, which focus on undergraduate teaching. It also includes 106 two-year community colleges that offer both terminal degrees and the possibility of transferring into four-year institutions.

Admissions requirements to the three tiers and the institutions within them vary widely. Community colleges are open to virtually all high school graduates. The top third of California high school graduates (as measured statewide by a combination of SAT scores and grade point average) may attend units of the state university and college system; all applicants must have taken a course in the fine or performing arts to be considered for admission. In the past, students in the top 12.5 percent of their class have been eligible to attend the University of California. Under a controversial new policy, only those students graduating in the top 4 percent of their high school class will be guaranteed admission to UC. The proposal is part of a broader plan to revise current admission standards by giving more weight to grade-point averages and SAT II achievement tests and placing less emphasis on the SAT I test. Out-of-state students continue to face ferocious competition for a limited number of spots and still pay more.

The University of California is the undisputed star of the state's public education system, comprising some of the nation's best research universities. Although technically one school, the nine campuses each do their own thing in the best Western tradition, and they do it extremely well.

Berkeley was founded first (in 1868) and remains best known. Most of the other schools began as specialized branches: San Francisco opened in 1873 as a graduate institution in the health sciences, San Diego focused on marine biology, Riverside was a citrus research station, and Davis ran a farm for agriculture students. Los Angeles and Santa Barbara joined the troupe in 1919 and 1944, respectively. In the '50s and '60s, all these campuses gradually changed from strictly vocational schools to full-fledged universities. UC's great leap forward came in 1965, when the economic boom of the '60s and the Great Society ideals led to the opening of two more campuses: Irvine and Santa Cruz.

UC has become a lightning rod for controversy as it struggles with issues that plague California—and the nation—as a whole. A 1995 vote by the UC Board of Regents abolished all race-based preferences in student admissions and as it stands, UC no longer uses "race, religion, gender, color, ethnicity, or national origin" as criteria in its admissions decisions. Many feel this threatens UC's legendary diversity and have vocalized this by staging rallies and sit-ins. UC contends that programs, such as the Educational Opportunity Program, which assists low-income or educationally disadvantaged students with promising academic potential, are already in place to counteract these issues. The intense affirmative action debate, however, rages on.

To apply for admission to the University of California, complete the electronic application available at UC's PATHWAYS Application Center or submit the printed version to UC's Undergraduate Application Processing Service. Prospective students may apply to as many as eight UC campuses using the same application form. It should be noted that UC does not base admission on the applicant's campus choice so students cannot request a campus preference. However, it is possible to be accepted at more than one school; and in that case, the applicant is free to choose between those campuses. Each of the major undergraduate UC campuses receives a full-length summary in the following pages.

The California State University and Colleges is totally separate from the University of California; in fact, the two institutions have historically competed for funds as well as students. The largest system of senior higher education in the nation, Cal State focuses on undergraduate education; while its members can offer master's degrees, they can award doctorates only in collaboration with a UC institution. Research in the state university system is severely restricted, a blow to Cal State's national prestige but a big plus for students. Unlike UC, where the mandate to publish or perish is alive and well, teachers in the state system are there to teach. Cal State's biggest problem is the success of UC, and its frequent lament—"Anywhere else we'd be number one"—is not without justification.

The 23-campus system caters to more than 350,000 students a year, most of them commuters, many already in the work force or married. While a solid liberal arts education is offered, the stress is usually on career-oriented professional training. Size varies dramatically, from about 30,000 students at San Diego and Long Beach to fewer than 6,000 at several other branches. Each campus has its own specific strengths, although in most cases a student's choice of school is dictated by location rather than by academic specialties. For those with a wider choice, some of the more distinctive campuses are profiled below. A few of the schools have built up residential populations.

Chico (enrollment: 14,983), situated in the beautiful Sacramento Valley, draws a large majority of its students from outside a 100-mile radius. The on-campus undergraduate life is strong and the partying is great. Bakersfield (5,594) and San Bernardino (12,000), boast residential villages along with more conventional dorms. The former is in a living/learning center with affiliated faculty members; the latter has its own swimming pool. California Polytechnic at San Luis Obispo is the toughest state university to get into. It provides excellent training in the applied branches of such fields as agriculture, architecture, business, and engineering. Enrollment: 16,735. Fresno is the place to go for wine and cheese. Situated in the verdant Central Valley, it has the only viticulture school in the state outside of Davis, and undergraduates can work in the school winery. Yosemite, Kings Canyon, and Sequoia national parks are nearby. Enrollment: 18,113.

San Diego State is the biggest and balmiest of the campuses, and since it has a more residential and outdoorsy, campus-oriented social scene, it appeals more to traditional-age undergraduates. "You could go for the weather alone—some do," says one former student. Contrasted with other state schools, athletics are very important, and the academic offerings are almost as oriented to the liberal arts as at its UC neighbor at San Diego. Enrollment: 30,776. Humboldt State is perched at the top of the state near the Oregon border in the heart of the redwoods. Humboldt's forestry and wildlife departments have national reputations, and the natural sciences are, in general, strong. Students have the run of excellent laboratory facilities and Redwood National Park. Most in-staters come here to get away from Los Angeles and enjoy the rugged coastline north of San Francisco. Enrollment: 7,475. Dominguez Hills in East Los Angeles is especially strong in management and business, fine arts, and computer science. Individual attention is available through the Small College, a school-within-a-school, in which students may design their own curriculums with the assistance of a faculty advisor. Primarily a commuter school, Dominguez Hills has opened a few dorms. Enrollment: 12,054.

To apply to California State University, complete either the electronic application available at their website, which will be routed to the campus of the applicant's choice or the paper application, which should be mailed to the admissions office of the campus to which the applicant is applying. The prospective student can list a first and alternate campus choice on the application. If the first choice can't accommodate the applicant, it automatically sends the application to the alternate campus.

Website: www.berkeley.edu

Location: Urban

Total Enrollment: 31,347

Undergraduates: 22,705

Male/Female: 49/51

SAT Ranges: V 580–710 M 620–730

ACT Range: N/A

Financial Aid: 48%

Expense: Pub $ $ $

Phi Beta Kappa: Yes

Applicants: 31,108

Accepted: 27%

Enrolled: 43%

Grad in 6 Years: 83%

Returning Freshmen: 94%

Academics: ✍ ✍ ✍ ✍ ✍

Social: ☎ ☎ ☎ ☎

Q of L: ★ ★ ★

Admissions: (510) 642-3175

Email Address:

ouars@uclink4.berkeley.edu

Strongest Programs:

Engineering

Architecture

Business

Theoretical Physics

Molecular and Cell Biology

Political Science

English

If you want a quick indicator of Berkeley's academic prowess, look no farther than the parking lot. The campus is dotted with spots marked "NL"—spots reserved for resident Nobel laureates. The last time anyone counted, Berkeley boasted 7 Nobel Prize winners, 140 Guggenheim fellows, and a bevy of Pulitzer Prize recipients, MacArthur fellows, and Fulbright scholars. Is it any wonder that this radical institution of the '60s still maintains the kind of reputation that makes the top private universities take note? Engineering, architecture, and business are a few of the best of the fine programs at this mother of UC schools. The social climate is not as explosive as it once seemed to be, but don't expect anything tame on today's campus. Flower children and granola chompers still abound, as do fledgling Marxists, young Republicans, and body-pierced activists.

Spread across 1,200 scenic acres on a hill overlooking San Francisco Bay, the Berkeley campus is a parklike oasis in a small city. The sometimes startlingly wide variety of architectural styles ranges from the stunning classical amphitheater to the modern University Art Museum draped in neon sculpture. Large expanses of grass dot the campus and are just "perfect for playing Frisbee or lying in the sun." The oaks along Strawberry Creek and the eucalyptus grove date back to Berkeley's beginnings nearly 130 years ago.

Like everything else, the academic side of Berkeley can be overwhelming. With over 22,000 undergraduate overachievers crammed into such a small space, it is no wonder that the academic climate is about as intense as you can get at a public university. "Everyone was the top student in his or her high school class so they can't settle for anything less than number one," says one student. A classmate concedes that "it can be a stressful environment, especially during the first years." Another says tersely, "Expect very little sleep." Some introductory courses, particularly in the sciences, have as many as 800 students, and professors, who must publish or perish from the university's highly competitive teaching ranks, devote a great deal of time to research. After all, Berkeley has made a large part of its reputation on its research and graduate programs, most of which rank among the best in the nation.

And while the undergraduate education is excellent, students take a gamble with the trickle-down theory, which holds out the promise that the intellectual might of those in the ivory towers will drip down to them eventually. As a political science major explains, "This system has allowed me to hear outstanding lectures from amazing professors who write the books we read, while allowing far more personal attention by the graduate student instructors." Another student opines, "It's better to stand 50 feet from brilliance than five feet from mediocrity." Evidence of such gravitation is seen in the promising curriculums designed specifically for freshmen and sophomores that include interdisciplinary courses in writing, public speaking, and the history of civilization, and an offering of small student seminars (enrollment is limited to 15) taught by regular faculty. Despite these attempts at catering to undergraduates, the sheer number of students at Berkeley makes it difficult to treat each student as an individual. As a result, such things as academic counseling suffer. "Advising? You mean to tell me they have advising here?" asks one student.

Each college or school has its own set of general education requirements, which are generally not extensive, and many can be fulfilled through advanced placement exams in high school. All students, however, must take English composition and literature, and one term each of American history and American institutions. Also, undergrads have an American Cultures requirement for graduation–an original approach (via courses offered in several departments) to comparative study of ethnic groups in the United States.

Most of the departments here are noteworthy and some are about the best anywhere (like engineering and architecture). Sociology, mathematics, physics, chemistry, history, and English are just a handful of the truly dazzling departments. Engineering is also strong, and Berkeley offers a 3-2 engineering program with UC–Santa Cruz. The biological sciences department integrates several undergraduate majors in biochemistry, biophysics, botany, zoology, and others into more interdisciplinary programs such as integrative biology and molecular and cell biology. The College of Natural Resources has streamlined its eight departments into four and established an Institute for Natural Resource Systems.

Special programs abound at Berkeley, though it's up to the student to find out about them. "Our class enrollment system is much like playing a low-risk lottery," opines one undergrad. "Maybe you'll win, or maybe you won't. If anything, adding courses will definitely toughen up any person." Students may study abroad on fellowships at one of 50 centers around the world, or spend time in various internships around the country. If all you want to do is study, the library system, with over 8 million volumes, is one of the largest in the nation and maintains open stacks. The system consists of the main library (Doe-Moffitt) and more than 20 branch libraries, one of which (Bancroft) houses rare books and Western Americana.

Applications to Berkeley have been at record levels. The acceptance rate of minority students, however, has declined sharply since the implementation of Proposition 209, which banned the use of racial preferences in admissions decisions. Forty-five percent of the student population is Asian American, 4 percent African American, and 9 percent Hispanic. The Coalition for Excellence and Diversity in Mathematics, Science and Engineering, which provides women and minorities with undergraduate mentors in these fields, received the Presidential Award for Excellence in Science, Mathematics, and Engineering in 1998. The university also provides a variety of other programs to promote diversity, including Project DARE (Diversity Awareness through Resources and Education), the Center for Racial Education, and a Sexual Harassment Peer Education Program. Despite Berkeley's liberal reputation, the recent trend is away from the legacy of the free speech movement, and business majors and fraternity members increasingly outnumber the young Communists and peaceniks, though the school does boast a large number of Peace Corps volunteers.

The main issue concerning every group on campus? Cost. In the past few years, outrageous fee hikes and severe budget cuts had some students wondering if a first-rate, affordable education had gone the way of the dinosaurs. Things look brighter though as lawmakers are expected to introduce bills to finance a new round of tuition cuts at state universities. In addition, the passage of Proposition 1A, will provide $2.5 billion to California public higher education institutions for new facilities or renovations of older ones, some of which will assist Berkeley in its effort of the seismic rehabilitation of many of its structures.

Though dorms have room for only a quarter of the students, freshmen are guaranteed housing for their first year. After that, the Community Living Office is a good resource for finding an apartment in town. Many students live a couple of miles off campus, where "apartments are cheaper," says one student. About two-thirds of the university's highly prized dorm rooms are reserved for freshmen, and

The Coalition for Excellence and Diversity in Mathematics, Science, and Engineering, which provides women and minorities with undergraduate mentors in these fields, received the Presidential Award for Excellence in Science, Mathematics and Engineering in 1998.

Engineering is also strong, and Berkeley offers a 3-2 engineering program with UC–Santa Cruz.

The College of Natural Resources has streamlined its eight departments into four and established an Institute for Natural Resource Systems.

the few singles go to resident assistants. Doubles are likely to become crowded triples, albeit at a reduced fee. Losers in the May lottery automatically go on a long waiting list to vie for rooms in subsequent monthly lotteries. In the absence of a mandatory meal plan, everybody eats "wherever and whenever they wish," including in the dorms.

The biological sciences department integrates several undergraduate majors in biochemistry, biophysics, botany, zoology, and others into more interdisciplinary programs such as integrative biology and molecular and cell biology.

Though the housing shortage can get you down, the beautiful California weather will probably take your mind off it in time. The BART subway system provides easy access to San Francisco, by far one of the most pleasant cities in the world and a cultural and countercultural mecca. The Bay Area boasts myriad professional sports teams, including the Oakland A's and the San Francisco 49ers. From opera to camping, San Francisco has a wide variety of activities to offer. Get yourself a car, and hike in Yosemite National Park, ski and gamble in Nevada, taste wine in the Napa Valley, or visit the aquarium at Monterey. But be advised that a car is only an asset when you want to go out of town: Students warn that parking in Berkeley is difficult, to say the least.

"Social life at UC–Berkeley is killer!" exclaims one geography major. Weekends are generally spent in Berkeley, hanging out at the many bookstores, coffeehouses, and sidewalk cafés, heading to a fraternity or sorority party, or taking advantage of the many events right on campus. Berkeley is a quintessential college town ("kind of a crazy little town," opines one anthropology major), and of course, there's always the people-watching; where else can an individual meet people trying to convert pedestrians to strange New Age religions or revolutionary political causes on every street corner? Nearby Telegraph Avenue is famous (infamous?) for such antics every weekend. More than 300 student groups are registered on campus, which ensures that there is an outlet for just about any interest and that no one group will ever dominate campus life.

Despite all this activity, many students use the weekend to catch up on studying. Greeks have returned in force, with 9 percent of the men and 6 percent of the women in a fraternity or sorority, and there is a certain amount of tension between them and the independents. Varsity athletics are also on the rise, strengths lying in the men's gymnastics and crew teams, and a surge in popularity for the basketball team probably has to do with its great performance in the PAC 10. And just about everyone turns out for the "Big Game," where the favorite activity on the home side of the bleachers is badmouthing the rival school to the south–Stanford. Intramurals are popular, and the personal fitness craze is fed by an extensive recreational facility.

The common denominator in the Berkeley community is academic motivation, along with the self-reliance that emerges from trying to make your mark among upward of 22,000 peers. Beyond that, the diversity of town and campus makes an extraordinarily free and exciting college environment for almost anyone. "It makes one feel free to dress, say, think, or do anything and not be chastised for being unorthodox," explains a student. "At Berkeley, it is worse to be dull than odd."

Overlaps

UCLA, Stanford, UC–San Diego, UC–Davis, Harvard.

If You Apply To ➤

Berkeley...Regular admissions: Nov. 30. Financial aid: Mar. 2. Guarantees to meet demonstrated need of in-state students. No campus or alumni interviews. SATs or ACTS: required. SAT IIs: required (writing, math I or II, and one other). Essay question: personal statement. Apply to particular school or program.

175 Mark Hall, Davis, CA 95616

Looking for the good life? Want to get back to life's simple pleasures: the rich land, the innocent animals, some good wine? UC–Davis may be your Eden. At Davis, where environmental studies and most everything that has to do with agriculture or biological science is noteworthy, the Aggies' cup truly runneth over. Of course, they might be talking about their winemaking class (yes, a winemaking class). Originally known as the University of California Farm, the campus maintains its sprawling, verdant beauty, replete with native and imported forestry, charming bike paths, and mooing cows. But lest you assume this environmentally oriented university is full of quaint country folk, think again. Davis has become an international leader in the agricultural, biological, biotechnical, and environmental sciences.

Located 15 miles west of Sacramento and 72 miles north of San Francisco, the 6,000-acre campus is in the middle of a stretch of flat farmland that even Dorothy and Toto could mistake for Kansas and features nearly 1,000 buildings with a blend of architectural styles, from traditional dairy barn to modern concrete. The hub of the university is a central area known as the Quad, one of many grassy open spaces on campus. New facilities include the Center for Comparative Medicine and a variety of seismic renovations.

Though it has added programs in many disciplines over the past few years—including Chinese, Japanese, food engineering, and biological systems engineering—its biological and agricultural science departments are still the ones that shine. Animal science and engineering are strong departments, and the botany program is one of the best in the country. The school is "the number one choice for any prevet," and it isn't bad for premeds, either. The food sciences major is also stellar, and not for the faint of heart or those afraid of chemistry. It was Davis food scientists who gave us the square tomato (better for packing into boxes), as well as more useful things such as the method for creating orange juice concentrate. Studio art, boasting several internationally known artists, is also among the top in the nation while history and English are generally good but not up to par with the sciences. Noteworthy special programs include the Inter-Disciplinary Electronics Arts (IDEA) Lab, which allows students to create electronically based productions by integrating photography, video, digital editing, and the Internet. Internships and co-op programs are well established, which is why many students remain for more than four years.

Faculty members here are expected to do top-level research as well as teach, so Davis is charged with both education and research. These two are uniquely blended when undergraduate students contribute to first-class research groups as paid technicians or volunteer interns. Davis also offers the innovative Washington Program, which gives undergraduates academic credits for internships in Congress, at federal agencies, and the like. Many introductory courses are quite large, but Davis also offers 40 freshman seminars taught by the best instructors. The academic advising system gets generally high marks, but you must seek out their assistance. "They helped me plan a four-year college schedule and always kept me on track."

General education requirements stipulate that all students take courses in three broad areas: topical breadth, social-cultural diversity, and writing experience. These areas include courses in the arts and humanities, science and

Website: www.ucdavis.edu

Location: Small city

Total Enrollment: 25,092

Undergraduates: 19,517

Male/Female: 44/56

SAT Ranges: V 510–630 M 550–650

ACT Range: 21–27

Financial Aid: 51%

Expense: Pub $ $ $

Phi Beta Kappa: Yes

Applicants: 22,766

Accepted: 63%

Enrolled: 27%

Grad in 6 Years: 76%

Returning Freshmen: 89%

Academics: ✍ ✍ ✍ ✍

Social: ☎ ☎ ☎

Q of L: ★ ★ ★ ★

Admissions: (530) 752-2971

Email Address:
thinkucd@ucdavis.edu

Strongest Programs:
Environmental Studies
Botany
Animal Science
Viticulture
Agricultural Sciences
Studio Art
Biological Sciences
Engineering

Davis recently added two new graduate programs: the Native American studies department and the medical infomatics master's program.

engineering, and the social sciences. Students may elect to take a general education theme option (sets of general ed courses that share a common intellectual theme).

The academic demands are intense, and the students are high achievers. Many students describe the atmosphere as competitive if not cutthroat (especially in the biological sciences). "It is not rare to find many students in the library on Saturday night," testifies one student. Another student reports, "Professors expect students to learn vast amounts of information in a 10-week span." For students who still want more, the Davis Honors Challenge is designed for highly motivated, academically talented first- and second-year students who want to enhance their education through special courses. A famous campus saying claims that "Davis students take notes at graduation." Maybe they're taking notes for job interviews: 59 percent of Davis students get jobs after college and 32 percent prefer taking more notes in graduate school. African Americans account for 3 percent of the students, Asian Americans 35 percent, and Hispanics 10 percent. Students are slightly more "conservative" than in past years, but most are characterized as "friendly and open-minded." Campus hot topics include fair labor practices and political correctness can be found in abundance. In its pledge to foster awareness of diversity issues, the university has established an Office of Campus Diversity and a Cross-Cultural Center. UC–Davis boasts the highest graduation rate in the UC system. Davis awards merit scholarships but there are no athletic awards.

Virtually all freshmen inhabit campus housing, which is well maintained and includes a number of theme houses. The vast majority of upperclassmen live off campus in nearby houses or apartments. Housing is guaranteed for freshmen and transfer students if applications are received by the deadline. Six different meal plans for the dining halls are available, and one student says, "The dorm food is very good (better than at most colleges)." A variety of nearby eating establishments serve the student clientele, but a car can come in handy if you are looking for a good meal in Sacramento (15 minutes) or a great one in San Francisco (little more than an hour). Beaches are a two-hour drive from the campus, and the ski slopes and hiking trails of Lake Tahoe and the Sierra Nevada are a little closer. But if you feel, as most Davis students do, that studies are too important to be abandoned on weekends, the town has restaurants, activities, and entertainment enough to keep the stay-at-homes happy.

In between quizzes and cram sessions, the outlying countryside offers a welcome change of pace. The town of Davis itself is small, about 50,000, and students make up half the population. If some call it a cowtown, others call it peaceful, with its tree-lined streets and quiet nights. The relationship between college and town is one of rare cooperation (partly because the students are a significant voting bloc in local elections). Health and energy consciousness runs high in town and on the vast, architecturally diverse campus, where bicycles are the main form of transportation on the incredible 46 miles of bike paths that crisscross the campus and environs. "Bicycles are the norm at Davis. Don't come without one," advises one psych major. The university has encouraged environmental awareness by sponsoring solar energy projects, and promoting such novelties as contests between dorms for the lowest heating and electric bills.

On-campus activities are varied, and many university-sponsored events fill the calendar. One rhetoric major points out that "social functions are hard to avoid at Davis." Active drama and music departments provide frequent entertainment, and there is plenty of room for homegrown talent in the coffeehouses, which offer mellow live entertainment and poetry readings on a regular basis. Fraternities and sororities attract 7 percent of the men and 6 percent of the women. Alcohol is allowed in the dorms for those over 21 years old; those too young to imbibe have trouble finding booze, unless it's supplied by peers. Major annual social events include Picnic Day, in which alumni join current students in a massive outdoor shindig; African-American Week, and the Whole Earth Festival, "an earthy, tie-dyed sort of event" in celebration of the '60s. But people "just interested in partying often find Davis dull," warns an engineering student.

The university's varsity athletic teams compete in Division II and attract relatively scant attention compared to those at most other state universities. Nevertheless, Davis won the Sears Directors' Cup, a trophy symbolic of overall excellence in intercollegiate athletics, and cross-country, basketball, and track and field have brought home NCAA championships. The annual Causeway Classic against rival Sacramento State does create a measure of excitement. Intramurals, however, are much more popular than spectator sports, with 65 percent of students participating. On this outdoor campus almost everyone does something athletic—jogging, softball, tennis, swimming, or Frisbee—if only to break up the monotony of studies with a different kind of competition. A versatile in-line skating rink, the first in the state, now makes available four different recreational activities.

Proud of its small-town atmosphere, Davis is not for the lazy or faint of heart. As one man says, "There's no free ride. You are going to have to work for everything you get." And most students get a lot out of their four or more years at Davis. It's the ideal spot to combine high-powered work in science and agriculture with that famous easygoing California lifestyle.

If You Apply To ➤ **Davis**…Regular admissions: Nov. 30. Financial aid: Mar. 3. Does not guarantee to meet demonstrated need. No campus or alumni interviews. SATs or ACTs: required. SAT IIs: required (writing, math, and one other). Accepts the Common Application and electronic applications. Essay question: personal statement. Apply to particular program.

UC–Irvine

260 ADM, Irvine, CA 92697

On the surface, UC–Irvine's calm, clean, concrete campus appears to be home to some of the most conventional students in the UC system—students who study diligently in the busy library, wear sensible shoes to biology lab, resist that double shot of espresso at the local coffeehouse. But that image starts to dissipate as soon as you hear that bizarre noise: "Zot! Zot! Zot!" Then a UCI student explains that "it's the sound that an anteater supposedly makes when it swipes an ant with its tongue." Hey, any school that has an anteater as a mascot can't be completely straight-laced. The university is, however, straight on its reputation as a strong school with stellar programs in biology and creative writing. The current academic climate can be quite serious and challenging, but as one UCI student swears, the Anteaters are "also surprisingly cooperative."

Located in the heart of Orange County, UCI (founded in 1965) is among the newest of the UC campuses. Although enrollment is up and the administration has dreams of further expansion, "it is the perfect size," says one English major. UCI occupies 1,500 acres liberally supplied with trees and shrubs from all over the

Website: www.uci.edu
Location: Suburban
Total Enrollment: 19,277
Undergraduates: 15,361
Male/Female: 47/52
SAT Ranges: V 495–600 M 540–655
ACT Range: N/A
Financial Aid: 52%
Expense: Pub $ $
Phi Beta Kappa: Yes
Applicants: 22,157
Accepted: 60%

(Continued)

Enrolled: 27%

Grad in 6 Years: 75%

Returning Freshmen: 91%

Academics: ✍ ✍ ✍

Social: ☎ ☎

Q of L: ★ ★ ★

Admissions: (949) 824-6703

Email Address:

oars@uci.edu

Strongest Programs:

Biology

English

Dance

Chemistry

Computer Science

UCI has added three new majors: African American Studies, Asian American Studies, and European Studies, while the Russian major has been dropped.

The university also houses the Reeve-Irvine Research Center, which supports the study of spinal cord trauma and disease with emphasis on finding a cure.

world. Futuristic buildings are arranged in a circle around a large park, "giving it the appearance of a relaxed art school," says one observer. Undergraduates have long quipped that UCI stood for "Under Construction Indefinitely," and current campus construction does little to challenge the moniker: new additions include a student recreation center and new drama and music buildings.

A "premed mentality" reigns at Irvine, since the School of Biological Sciences is the best and most competitive academic division. The School of Arts offers nationally ranked programs in dance, drama, music, and studio art as well as a minor in digital arts. The popular interdisciplinary School of Social Ecology offers courses combining criminology, environmental and legal studies, and psychology and social behavior and strongly emphasizes teacher-student relationships. Like most of the other UC campuses, UCI is on a 10-week quarter system so the pace is fast and furious. Students should face registration with the same determination, too; it's a tough fight to get into the science classes of choice as a sophomore.

Languages are strong at UCI, as are the biggest nonbiology majors: English, economics, political science, psychology, and a fiction-writing program that is gaining national recognition. The Information and Computer Science Department recently added a computer lab, complete with more than 150 new and upgraded computers and dozens of software packages. UCI has added three new majors: African American Studies, Asian American Studies, and European Studies, while the Russian major has been dropped.

"UCI is fairly competitive and the courses are moderately rigorous," says a junior. Students may be overwhelmed by the size of most classes. Even seniors find their classes packed with 100 undergrads, which leaves little time for personal attention. "Graduate students teach lower division writing courses," says one student, adding that "most classes are overcrowded leaving little room for personal attention." The Center for Health Sciences focuses on five areas of research including neuroscience, genetics, cancer, infectious diseases, and aging. The university also houses the Reeve-Irvine Research Center, which supports the study of spinal cord trauma and disease with emphasis on finding a cure. The "breadth requirement" means that students must take three courses each in writing, natural sciences, social and behavioral sciences, and humanities in order to graduate. There is also a language requirement, though students can substitute linguistics, logic, math, or computer science, and requirements in multicultural and international/global issues. Honors programs are available in humanities, economics, psychology, and political science.

Ninety-eight percent of the student body are in-staters, the majority from Southern California and many of those from wealthy Orange County. The students are in general "much more conservative than at the other UC campuses," says one applied math major. Minorities account for well over half the student body, with Asian Americans at 55 percent, while African Americans and Hispanics combine for 13 percent of the undergrads. "Cultural groups seem to segregate from each other more than I really like," says a senior.

Condominium-style dorms, both single-sex and coed, are "exceptional compared to the high-rise dormitories of other institutions," says one senior. Others agree that the homey campus dwellings provide a good experience for freshmen, though finding a room can be a challenge. "If you really want on-campus housing," warns a student, "you need to make sure you meet the deadlines." Newly added housing, including those with academic themes and ones especially for fraternities and sororities, opens more rooms for students, but most opt to move off campus after their first year. Currently, 40 percent of the students live off campus—many on the beach—giving the campus a commuter-school atmosphere. One student laments, "You have to find the social life on this campus. It won't find you."

Still, the Greek scene is vigorous. There are 13 sororities and 17 fraternities, and each has something going on every weekend. As for booze, "UCI is a dry campus and students say finding a drink on campus without proper ID is difficult. Irvine touts many festivals that seem to attest to a celebration of diversity: the Rainbow festival (cultural heritage), Asian Heritage week, Black History month, Cinco de Mayo, and rush week. The one event that brings everybody out is the daylong Wayzgoose, when the campus is transformed into a medieval fair complete with mimes, jugglers, and performers dressed up in medieval costumes.

But if life on campus is slow, life off campus is not. That's because the campus is located just 40 miles from L.A., 5 miles from the beach, and a little over an hour from the ski slopes. Catalina Island, with beaches and hiking trails, is a quick boat trip off Newport Harbor; Mexico is two hours away. While some students treasure the quiet setting of Irvine, others lament its "lackluster, homogeneous communities". Notes one student, "UCI and the city of Irvine seem like completely different entities; the former is slightly liberal while the latter is ultra-conservative."

Irvine fields 20 athletic teams and competes in Division I of the NCAA. Tennis and cross-country are perennial Big West powerhouses and men's water polo has been ranked in the top 5 nationally for 23 of the last 31 years. There is no football team, but intramurals are extremely popular, as is the 5,000-seat multipurpose gym.

What lures students to UCI is its top-name professors, innovative academic programs and the chance to be a part of its cutting-edge research. For the students who come here prepared to keep their heads buried in a book for a few years, the ultimate reward will be an exceptional education.

> ### Overlaps
>
> **UCLA, UC–San Diego, UC Santa Barbara, UC–Berkeley, University of Southern California.**

> ### If You Apply To ➤
>
> **Irvine**…Regular admissions: Nov. 30. Financial aid: Mar. 2 (priority). No campus or alumni interviews. SATs or ACTs: required. SAT IIs: required (English composition, math, and one other). Essay question: autobiographical statement.

UC–Los Angeles

1147 Murphy Hall, 405 Hillgard Avenue, Los Angeles, CA 90095

With stellar programs in music, film and television, journalism/communication, dance, and drama, you'd think UCLA was some kind of incubator for truly talented and gifted people. Or with alumni such as Kareem Abdul-Jabbar, Troy Aikman, and Arthur Ashe, maybe UCLA's some sort of farm that grows superstar athletes. Well, UCLA is all that and more. A superb faculty, a reputation for outstanding academics, and a powerful athletics program make this university the ultimate place to study. "There are endless opportunities and unlimited resources because of the size of this university," says an English major. "There's nothing you can't do at UCLA."

UCLA's prime location—sandwiched between two glamorous neighborhoods

> **Website:** www.ucla.edu
> **Location:** Urban
> **Total Enrollment:** 36,351
> **Undergraduates:** 24,668
> **Male/Female:** 45/55
> **SAT Ranges:** V 570–680 M 600–720
> **ACT Range:** 23–29
> **Financial Aid:** 53%

(Continued)

Expense: Pub $ $

Phi Beta Kappa: Yes

Applicants: 35,681

Accepted: 29%

Enrolled: 40%

Grad in 6 Years: 80%

Returning Freshmen: 97%

Academics: ✍ ✍ ✍ ✍

Social: ☎ ☎ ☎

Q of L: ★ ★ ★

Admissions: (310) 825-5754

Email Address:
ugadm@saonet.ucla.edu

Strongest Programs:
Music
Film and Television
Journalism/Communications
Premed
Drama
Engineering
Dance
Political Science

As befits a university next door to Hollywood, the School of Film, Theater, and Television is first-rate, and its students have the opportunity to study in Verona, Italy, with the theater overseas program.

(Beverly Hills and Bel Air) and a short drive away from Hollywood, the Sunset Strip, and downtown Los Angeles—makes it appealing for students who want more from their college experience than what classes alone can offer. The university's beautifully landscaped 419-acre campus features a range of architectural styles, with Romanesque/Italian Renaissance as the dominant motif, providing only one of a number of reasons students also enjoy staying on campus. A wealth of gardens—botanical, Japanese, and sculpture—adds a touch of quiet elegance to the campus. Planned facilities include additional student apartments, a physics and astronomy building and the Luck Center, which will house research activities in orthopedics and related fields.

Strong programs abound at UCLA, and many are considered among the best in the nation. The School of Engineering and Applied Science, especially electrical engineering, is generally regarded as the leading department. As befits a university next door to Hollywood, the School of Film, Theater, and Television is first-rate and its students have the opportunity to study in Verona, Italy, with the theater overseas program. The dance and drama departments are excellent and the popular music department offers a course in jazz studies. The biological sciences are also highly regarded. Research opportunities abound at UCLA, and the university ranks seventh in the nation in federal funding for research. In the Student Research Program, over 1,400 undergrads work side-by-side with professors on cutting-edge research. Students say that the math department doesn't add up to the sum total of its parts.

Freshmen are encouraged to participate in a three-day summer orientation, which provides workshops, counseling, and a general introduction to the campus and community. During their first two years, most students take required core classes that are sometimes jammed with 300 to 400 people. But administrators are quick to point out that nearly two-thirds of all undergraduate classes have less than 50 students. Savvy students come to UCLA with advanced courses in their high school backgrounds and test out of the intro courses. First-year students are required to take a course involving quantitative reasoning unless they hit 600 or higher on their math SAT and English Composition requirements should also be met during the freshman year. Lab science and a language requirement are also required for a liberal arts degree. To bring UCLA's graduation requirements more in line with other campuses in the UC system, the upper division minimum unit requirement has been reduced from 72 to 60 units. Simply getting into classes here can be a big challenge. Students register by phone in a sequence of two scheduled "passes" based on their class standing. UCLA's academic environment is extremely intense. "The academic calendar here is based on the quarter system, which makes it easy to get behind in your work," says a senior. The faculty is also very impressive. "My professors have been dynamic and inspirational and genuinely interested in the student's success," says an English major. On the other hand, there is a widespread sense here that undergraduate teaching is often sacrificed on behalf of scholarly research. "Some professors considered their research primary and teaching their students secondary," says a mechanical engineering major. The UCLA library ranks in the top ten of all research libraries, public or private, and actually consists of the College Library and nine specialized libraries containing more than 7.2-million volumes. The campus newspaper, the *Daily Bruin,* is the third-largest daily in all of Los Angeles.

In 1995, Proposition 209 abolished admissions decisions based on affirmative action in California. The long-term effect on minority enrollment remains to be seen. The administration contends that many policies and programs are already in place to counteract this issue, including the Academic Advancement Program, which assists low-income and educationally disadvantaged students with promising academic potential. At this time, Asian Americans account for 38 percent of UCLA's student population, Hispanics make up 15 percent, African Americans 5 percent, and Native Americans 1 percent. "Affirmative action and minority representation are the largest political issues on campus," says a sophomore.

UCLA has several student-run newsmagazines as alternatives to the *Daily Bruin,* including the feminist *Together* and the Asian-American newsmagazine *Pacific Ties.* UCLA is also one of the few universities in the nation with a gay fraternity and a lesbian sorority. These groups, as well as GALA (Gay and Lesbian Association) and *TenPercent,* the self-described "UCLA's Queer Newsmagazine," have helped foster a rising feeling of empowerment among the campus's gay and lesbian students and faculty.

Freshmen are guaranteed housing, but for everyone else it's strictly a waiting list. "Dorm life is awesome!," says one student. "It spawns lifelong friendships." Overcrowding is a concern, though future housing construction should give students a bit more elbow room. The campus is philosophically divided into North and South. North attracts more liberal arts aficionados, while those in math and science tend to favor South. Fifteen dining halls, restaurants, and snack bars serve average meals.

UCLA has won a nation-leading number of collegiate championships, including 82 NCAA titles. The men's football, basketball, baseball, and tennis teams are the undeniable superstars as is the women's gymnastic and water polo teams. Beating USC is the name of the game in any sport; UCLA fans regard their intracity rivals with passionate feelings. ("Bruins are forever, but a Trojan is good only once.")

If you would rather be a doer than a watcher, the opportunities awaiting you are superb. "UCLA has an awesome social setting!" exclaims a junior. "Since we're based right here in L.A., there's too much to do." The hopping Westwood suburb, which borders the university, has at least 15 movie theaters and scores of restaurants but the shops cater to the upper class. UCLA's Ocean Discovery Center, located on the Santa Monica Pier, is an innovative, hands-on ocean classroom for students and the public. The beach is five miles away and the mountains only a short drive. Although public transportation is cheap, it's also inconvenient, making a car almost a necessity for going outside of Westwood. Unfortunately, parking is expensive and difficult to obtain. The easiest solution is to live close to campus and bike it. With all the attractions of the City of Angels at its doorstep, the campus tends to empty out on the weekends (except when the football Bruins have a home game). Eleven percent of the men and 9 percent of the women join one of UCLA's 50 fraternities and sororities. The university's alcohol policy is similar to that of other UC schools—open consumption is a no-no. But according to one student, "It is extremely easy for undergrads to be served, especially at fraternities."

Once a year the entire school gets together for Mardi Gras, a carnival-type event held to benefit UniCamp, UCLA's official charity, which takes underprivileged children from the inner city camping during the summer. Top-name entertainers, political figures, and speakers of all kinds come to the campus; film and theater presentations are frequent, and the air is thick with live music, usually every week.

A leading research center, UCLA's broad range of innovative academic programs, distinguished faculty members, and outstanding athletics make it one of the most prestigious universities in the nation. In order to make the most of this university, a student must have stamina, self-reliance, and willpower.

Freshmen are encouraged to participate in a three-day summer orientation, which provides workshops, counseling, and a general introduction to the campus and community.

Overlaps

UC–Berkeley, UC–San Diego, UC–Irvine, UC–Santa Barbara, USC.

If You Apply To ➤

UCLA…Regular admissions: Nov. 30. Housing: May 1. Does not guarantee to meet demonstrated need. No campus or alumni interviews. SATs or ACTs: required. SAT IIs: required (writing, math I or II, and one other). Apply to particular school or program. Accepts electronic applications. Essay question: personal statement.

UC–Riverside

Riverside, CA 92521

Website: www.ucr.edu
Location: City outskirts
Total Enrollment: 11,600
Undergraduates: 10,120
Male/Female: 46/54
SAT Ranges: V 440–570 M 480–620
ACT Range: 18–24
Financial Aid: 69%
Expense: Pub $ $
Phi Beta Kappa: Yes
Applicants: 16,316
Accepted: 84%
Enrolled: 17%
Grad in 6 Years: 66%
Returning Freshmen: 86%
Academics: ✐ ✐ ✐ ✐
Social: ☎ ☎
Q of L: ★ ★ ★
Admissions: (909) 787-3411
Email Address: N/A

Strongest Programs:
   Biomedical Sciences
   Dance
   History
   Political Science
   Creative Writing

The University Honors Program offers exceptional students further academic challenges, in addition to extracurricular activities.

Lacking the big-name reputation and booming athletic programs of the other UC schools, UC–Riverside has chosen to place its emphasis on something that not all institutions consider to be an important component of higher education: the student. Riverside offers one of the lowest student/faculty ratios in the UC system, strong programs with personalized attention, and a sense of academic community that seems to have been forgotten at other UC schools. "Students are well taken care of and get personal attention," says one satisfied senior. Though part of the UC system, UC–Riverside is a breed apart.

Located 60 miles east of Los Angeles, UCR is surrounded by mountains on the outskirts of the city of Riverside. The beautifully landscaped campus consists of mainly modern architecture, with a 160-foot bell tower (48-bell carillon) marking its center. Wide lawns and clusters of oaks are spread out over 1,200 acres, creating "a veritable botanical garden," where students and faculty enjoy relaxing between classes. New facilities include a science library, fine arts building, and entomology building.

Years ago, researchers at UC–Riverside decided the regular orange had too many seeds and was hard to peel, so they perfected the navel orange. Riverside still specializes in the plant sciences, but all the sciences, as well as math, statistics, and computer science, are excellent. The biomedical sciences program, unique in California, is UCR's most prestigious and demanding course of study and its students can earn a seven-year BS/MD with UCLA. Other notable majors include Asian studies, women's studies, and creative writing. One of the few undergraduate environmental engineering programs is at UCR as is a doctoral program in dance history and theory. Academic weaknesses include psychology and some languages. The University Honors Program offers exceptional students further academic challenges, in addition to extracurricular activities, and special seminars for participating freshmen.

All students are required to meet extensive "breadth requirements" that include courses in English composition, natural sciences and math, and humanities and social sciences, ethnicity, as well as fluency in a foreign language. In addition, students are required to take American History and Institutions, must fulfill a unit requirement and also must meet a minimum residence requirement of three-quarters. Students do not encounter much difficulty in getting the courses they want. "Underclassmen have more of a struggle for classes that may be popular with upperclassmen," explains a biology major. The library has an impressive 1.5 million volumes and what Riverside doesn't have can probably be found at UCLA's massive collections; a daily shuttle bus runs students back and forth to the UCLA campus. Research is an institutional priority for faculty, but unlike those at other UC schools, Riverside professors dedicate much of their time and attention to their students. Plus, UCR has a tradition of undergraduate and faculty interaction with a wide range of undergraduate research grants available during the academic year. "The teachers at UCR are superb," says one student. "They present material through the latest technological devices and are very knowledgeable about their subjects." This may be why one in six graduates goes on to get a Ph.D. to become faculty members themselves.

Ninety-nine percent of the UCR student body are from California, mainly the L.A., San Diego, and Bay areas. Ninety-four percent of the students graduated in the top tenth of their public high school class. Asian Americans account for 42 percent of the students, and Hispanics and African Americans 21 percent and 5 percent, respectively. As part of the UC commitment to diversity, Riverside upholds policies prohibiting sexual harassment, hazing, and physical and verbal abuse, and supports a Women's Resource Center as well as programs in ethnic studies. A senior English major declares, "There is not necessarily a distinct separation among the minority groups, but definitely a separation between them and the Caucasians on campus." Numerous merit scholarships, ranging from $750 to $2,000, are doled out every year, as well as athletic scholarships in baseball, softball, basketball, tennis, volleyball, track and field, and water polo. National Merit Scholars are guaranteed a $750 award each year they attend, and scholarships are available for engineering students.

Housing is a breeze—reasonably priced and reasonably easy to obtain. Thirty percent of the students live in the well-maintained dorms, where freshmen and continuing dorm residents are guaranteed a spot. About 30 percent of the students live in off-campus apartments, and another third commute from home. Dorms, all of which are coed, are clean and comfortable and provide a social context as well as a living atmosphere. Social life is relatively tame, since so many of the students commute. The administration claims "a quiet atmosphere, conducive to serious study"; students say it's boring but friendly. "Social life is quite dull," says a senior. "The campus is quiet after 5:00 P.M." Fraternities lure 4 percent of the men, and sororities 4 percent of the women. The groups usually hold campus-wide parties once a quarter. "Any campus with 10 fraternities does its share of partying," observes a math major. But "it is becoming harder for undergrads under 21 to drink," says a theater major. And in general there is "no wild party action here," reports one slightly disappointed student. A campus hangout known as the Barn has live bands, comedy nights, and movies. Every Wednesday the campus can enjoy a "nooner," where live bands play during lunch. "We're not on the beach and don't have a football team, so we don't have jocks and air-headed blondes," reports one serious student. Scots Week is a festival of athletic and other activities; clubs vie to see who can stage the best prank, and individuals engage in a pie-eating/throwing contest.

Homecoming is also a big to-do, and sports generate a considerable amount of interest at UCR. Both the male and female karate teams are among the best in the nation, and the men's basketball consistently performs at championship levels. Men's tennis and cross-country are also strong contenders. Among women's sports, the national championship volleyball team draws big crowds. For weekend athletes, intramurals are a popular antidote to too many hours in the library. People have been known to camp outside the sign-up office for a night in order to make sure their team gets a place in the intramural league.

Most students agree with a physics major who says, "The thing I like least about Riverside is the city of Riverside," which is "an hour from everywhere, in the middle of nowhere." A suburb is about the nicest thing it gets called, but the

Research is an institutional priority for faculty, but unlike those at other UC schools, Riverside professors dedicate much of their time and attention to their students.

weather is wonderful three seasons a year (the smog is terrible in the summertime). Near the campus there are a few bars and nightclubs, but farther down the road lies a run-down neighborhood. Luckily, Los Angeles, Palm Springs, the beaches, and (if you go for horned toads, Gila monsters, and rattlers) the desert are all within an hour's drive of the campus. Big Bear and Mountain High ski resorts are also within easy reach.

All in all, coming to Riverside is a trade-off. Some students complain that course offerings are limited, and others that the school lacks history, tradition, and culture. But the intimate, personalized style is unique in the UC system and especially cherished by the homesick. Academics are serious and demanding, but on-campus social life and extracurriculars are on a strictly do-it-yourself basis. It can't do what Berkeley or UCLA does, but then it doesn't try. Comparing Riverside to schools 10 times its size really doesn't work; it's a little like comparing apples and, well, navel oranges.

Overlaps

UC–Irvine, UCLA, UC–San Diego, UC–Santa Cruz, UC–Santa Barbara.

If You Apply To ➤   **Riverside**…Regular admissions: Nov. 30. Financial aid: Mar. 2. Housing: June 1. Guarantees to meet demonstrated need. No campus or alumni interviews. SATs or ACTs: required. SAT IIs: required (writing, math, and one other). Essay question: personal statement.

UC–San Diego

9500 Gilman Drive, Department 0021-A, La Jolla, CA 92093-0021

Website: www.ucsd.edu
Location: Suburban
Total Enrollment: 19,918
Undergraduates: 16,230
Male/Female: 48/52
SAT Ranges: V 550–650
  M 590–690
ACT Range: 22–27
Financial Aid: 51%
Expense: Pub $ $
Phi Beta Kappa: Yes
Applicants: 32,539
Accepted: 41%
Enrolled: 25%
Grad in 6 Years: 70%
Returning Freshmen: 93%
Academics: ✍ ✍ ✍ ✍
Social: ☎ ☎ ☎ ☎
Q of L: ★ ★ ★ ★
Admissions: (619) 534-4831
Email Address:
  admissionsinfo@ucsd.edu

Some say that looking good is better than feeling good, but at UC–San Diego, they're doing a lot of both. Set against the serene beauty of La Jolla's beaches, students catch as much relaxation time as they do study time. But it's not all fun and games around this campus. The research star of the UC system, UCSD's faculty is rated number one nationally among public institutions in science productivity. And within each of the five undergraduate colleges, a system that offers undergraduates more intimate settings, students are honing their minds with the classics and the cutting edge in academics. Sure, San Diegans tend to be more mellow than the average Southern Californian, and UCSD students follow suit. But beneath the frown-free foreheads and bright smiles, UCSD's bubbling with intellectual energy and the healthy desire to be at the top of the UC system.

San Diego's tree-lined campus sits high on a bluff overlooking the Pacific in the seaside resort of La Jolla. Each of the five colleges has its own flavor, but the predominant architectural theme is contemporary, with a few out-of-the-ordinary structures, including a library that looks like an inverted pyramid. Another tinge of the postmodern is the nation's largest neon sculpture, which wraps around one of the high-rise academic buildings and consists of seven-foot-tall letters that spell out the seven virtues superimposed over the seven vices.

UCSD's programs in science and engineering are "not for the faint of heart," says one student. Engineering requires a B average in entry-level courses for acceptance into the major. The Scripps Institute of Oceanography is also excellent, due to the university's advantageous location. Computer science and chemistry also get strong recommendations, but you really can't go wrong in any of the hard sciences. Although the humanities and social sciences are not as solid in comparison, political science and psychology get strong backing from students. The math department, however, is less than adequate. In addition, the university lacks a full-fledged business program, and the administration states that UC–San Diego is not the place to go for practical or career-oriented courses. Imaginative interdisciplinary offerings include computer music, urban planning, ethnic studies, and a psychology/computer science program in artificial intelligence, as well as majors devised by students themselves.

Like most of the UC campuses, San Diego operates on the quarter system, which makes for a semester's worth of work crammed into 10 weeks. Science students find the load intense. "The courses here are challenging and intellectually stimulating, but there are also a lot of fun classes too," says one senior. Students have a choice of six libraries, some good for research, others better for socializing. Despite the quality of research done by the faculty, half a dozen of whom are Nobel laureates, students find that the typical scenario of research over teaching seen at most large research universities is not as common at UC–San Diego. "Professors here are brilliant and conduct research throughout the year, but they also have a desire to share their knowledge with their students," says a communication major.

UC–San Diego's five undergraduate colleges, each of which (except the newest) has about 3,000 students, have their own sets of general education requirements, their own personalities, and differing ideals upon which they are based. Prospective freshmen apply to UC–San Diego—the admissions requirements are identical for each college—but students must indicate their college preference. Revelle College, the oldest, is the most rigorous and mandates that students become equally acquainted with a certain level of coursework in the humanities, sciences, and social sciences, as well as fulfill a language requirement. Muir allows more flexibility in the distribution requirements. "Generally, Muir students are considered dumb blondes, while Revelle students are considered nerdy," says a recent graduate. Thurgood Marshall College was founded to emphasize and encourage social awareness; like Revelle, it places equal weight on sciences, social sciences, and humanities. However, it stresses a liberal arts education based on "an examination of the human condition in a multicultural society." Warren has developed a highly organized internship program that gives its undergraduates more practical experience than the others do. The newest college, Eleanor Roosevelt College ("Fifth"), devotes its curriculum to international and cross-cultural studies.

A theater major notes that UCSD's academic intensity "does not mean that all the students here are nerdy. They enjoy athletics and extracurricular activities, but academic excellence is their priority." A short walk to the beach, however, reveals the student body's wild and crazy half-surfers and their groupies, who celebrate the "kick back." Students jumping curbs on skateboards are common on this campus. Yet these beach babies are no scholastic slouches. Virtually all of them placed in the top 10 percent of their high school class, and they had an average GPA of 3.8. The average student pulls a 3.0 GPA while at UCSD. Many students here choose to take five years to graduate in order to gain a higher GPA, and many of the scientists continue their studies after graduation. UCSD also ranks high among public colleges and universities in the percentage of graduates who go on to earn a Ph.D. and in the percentage of students accepted to medical school. Most of the 3 percent from out of state are from the other Southwestern states. Minority representation is high, with 35 percent of the student body Asian American, 10 percent Hispanic, and 2 percent African American. Affirmative action programs have been abolished in the UC system, but "UCSD is still shaping

(Continued)
Strongest Programs
Biology
Psychology
Applied Mechanics &
Engineering
Economics
Political Science
Oceanography
Communications

The Scripps Institute of Oceanography is excellent due to the university's advantageous location.

its new admissions policy to maintain ethnic diversity on campus," notes the administration—perhaps a response to all the student protests against the passing of the anti-affirmative action initiative.

Each of the university's colleges has its own housing complex, with either dorms or apartments. Eighty percent of the freshmen live on campus and are guaranteed housing for their first two years. "The residence halls are very nice with all the amenities including Ethernet hook-ups in every room," says an animal physiology major. By junior year, students usually decide to take up residence in La Jolla proper or nearby Del Mar, often in beachside apartments; only 36 percent of all the students live on campus. But that can be costly: the price ends up being inversely proportional to proximity to the beach. If you are willing to relinquish the luxury of a five-minute walk to the beach, a short commute will bring you relatively affordable housing.

The immediate surroundings of UCSD, however, are definitely not affordable. "La Jolla," says a student, "is a wealthy, ritzy beach community. In no way is it a college town." Cars are, of course, an inescapable part of Southern California life, and owning one—many people do—makes off-campus living even more pleasant. Unfortunately, trying to park on campus can be difficult, though at least one student says that "parking is not nearly as bad here as it is at other schools." Dorm residents are required to buy a meal card, which gets them into any of the four campus cafeterias as well as the campus deli and burger joints.

The university is dry, so most of the real socializing seems to take place off campus. "Most students hang out at the dance clubs, jazz bars, and great restaurants in the Gaslamp Quarter," says a senior. Annual festivals include the Open House, Renaissance Faire, UnOlympics, and the Reggae Festival. Another annual festival pays tribute to a hideously loud and colorful statue of the Sun God, which is the unofficial mascot for this sun-streaked student body. Ten percent of both the men and the women try to beat the blahs by joining a fraternity or sorority. Alcoholic parties are banned in the residence halls, though students say lax RAs and good fake IDs make for easy underage drinking. Although campus life is relatively tame, students rely heavily on the surrounding area—but not La Jolla—for their entertainment. Students go to nearby Pacific Beach, and downtown San Diego with the zoo, Sea World, and Balboa Park, is only 12 miles away. Torrey Pines Natural Reserves are great for outdoor enthusiasts. Mexico—and the $5 lobster—is a half-hour drive (even nearer than the desert, where many students go hiking), and the two-hour trip to Los Angeles makes for a nice weekend jaunt.

Although San Diego is the farthest thing imaginable from a rah-rah school, it is rapidly becoming a Division III powerhouse, most notably in women's sports. Women's volleyball and tennis teams have won numerous national championships, and the water polo team has done nearly as well. Women's and men's soccer have also won titles, and golf and baseball have recently placed in the top five. For weekend competitors, classes are available in windsurfing, sailing, scuba diving, and kayaking at the nearby Mission Bay Aquatic Center. Everyone participates in one intramural league or another, and if you're not on a team, "you're not a true UCSD student." The recent opening of RIMAC, an impressive sports facility for students, has gotten even the couch potatoes off their BarcaLoungers.

The students at UCSD are exceptionally serious and out for an excellent education. But the pace (study, party, relax, study more) and the props (sun, sand, Frisbees, and flip-flops) give the rigorous curriculum offered by UCSD's five colleges an inimitable flavor that undergraduates would not change. Indeed, many believe they have the best setup in higher education: "a beautiful beach-front environment that eases a life of academic rigor."

Overlaps

UC–Berkeley, UCLA, UC–Santa Barbara, Stanford, San Diego State.

UC–Santa Barbara

Santa Barbara, CA 93106

For students at UC–Santa Barbara, California's famed beaches serve as both classroom and playground. On weekends, sun-worshipping students don surfboards and bikinis and head for the water to have some serious fun. During the week, students found walking the shore are likely to be studying technology rather than tan lines. UCSB provides a comfortable mixture of work and play that is unique to the UC system and draws praise from its students. Says a senior, "I love the fact that I am getting a highly rated UC education in such a relaxing location."

Located just a stone's throw from the beach, UC–Santa Barbara's 989-acre campus is bordered on two sides by the Pacific Ocean, with a clear view of the Channel Islands. On the landward side are a nature preserve and the predominantly student community of Isla Vista (I.V.), and five miles to the north lie the Santa Inez Mountains. "The environment is really unique, especially Isla Vista," says a student. "It is almost all college students and is close-knit and self-sufficient." The campus itself features mainly 1950s Southern California architecture with a Southern California atmosphere to match.

Not surprisingly, the marine biology department capitalizes on the school's aquatic resources and stands out among the university's best. Other favorites include physics, ecology, engineering materials, and chemistry. The accounting program is also very strong and the courses are geared toward taking and passing the CPA exam, so graduation is usually followed by a mass recruitment by California's big accounting firms. In addition, history, English, communications, and geological sciences are solid, but students say political science and math are considerably weaker. The College of Creative Studies, described as "great if you can get in," offers an unstructured curriculum to about 160 self-starters ready for advanced and independent work in the arts, math, or the sciences. An interdisciplinary program called the Global Peace and Security Program combines aspects of physics, anthropology, and military science. The National Science Foundation provides funding for the $5.5-million National Center for Geographic Information and Analysis program. NCGIA has put Santa Barbara on the map as a leader in geographic information systems, which combines cartography with computer technology to create a powerful approach for analyzing spatially distributed data. Sounds serious, and it is. Yet it's only one of eight national research centers on campus, where students work alongside researchers on projects that hold vast potential for enhancing both the quality of life for all Californians and the economic competitiveness of the entire nation.

For those who crave time away, Santa Barbara is the headquarters of the UC system's education abroad program, which sends students to any one of 100 host universities worldwide. In order to graduate, all students must take courses in

Website: www.admit.ucsb.edu
Location: City outskirts
Total Enrollment: 19,360
Undergraduates: 17,059
Male/Female: 47/53
SAT Ranges: V 520–620 M 540–650
ACT Range: 22–27
Financial Aid: 67%
Expense: Pub $ $
Phi Beta Kappa: Yes
Applicants: 23,697
Accepted: 58%
Enrolled: 23%
Grad in 6 Years: 72%
Returning Freshmen: 89%
Academics: ✍ ✍ ✍
Social: ☎ ☎ ☎ ☎
Q of L: ★ ★ ★ ★
Admissions: (805) 893-2881
Email Address:
appinfo@sa.ucsb.edu

Strongest Programs:
Marine Biology
Physics
Engineering
Chemistry
Geology
Religious Studies
Accounting
Environmental Studies

The College of Creative Studies, described as "great if you can get in," offers an unstructured curriculum to about 160 self-starters ready for advanced and independent work in the arts, math, or the sciences.

English Composition, American History and Institutions, must fulfill a unit requirement, and must also meet the requirements of their individual majors. In addition, students must be registered at UCSB for a minimum of three regular quarters. "The climate is very laid back," notes a senior. "There is a strong feeling of camaraderie among the students." Professors are highly praised. "The professors here are very accessible and do what they can to help their students succeed," says a biology major. Another student adds, "I think the quality of teaching I have received has been fantastic."

Besides possible earthquakes, congestion is UCSB's biggest problem. The libraries are "overcrowded at midterms and finals; it is almost impossible to find a spot to study!" says one student. Many classes overflow with 150 or more students, but according to the administration, 96 percent of the classes still have fewer than 30 students. Merit scholarships and various athletic scholarships are available for those who qualify.

UCSB students are traditionally public spirited; 50 percent serve as volunteers in the community, and the campus is a steady supplier of Peace Corps volunteers. Like everything else about UCSB, dress is casual. "If there were a campus uniform, it would be a pair of shorts and a sweatshirt, sunglasses optional," says an English major. Another student notes that political attitudes "are liberal on subjects like sex and parties, and conservative on subjects like El Salvador." Minorities make up 35 percent of the student body, and Asian Americans and Hispanics are the largest groups, with 16 percent and 13 percent, respectively. One student notes, "UCSB's ethnic population is definitely increasing and students value diversity very much." A classmate adds, "The politically correct way to act on the campus is to be totally accepting while at the same time being as unconventional as possible."

Not surprisingly, the marine biology department capitalizes on the school's aquatic resources and stands out among the university's best.

University housing, which includes both dorms and privately run residence halls, is comfortable, well maintained, and much sought after. "The dorms are clean and have spectacular views," boasts a psychology major. Unfortunately, there is a waiting list to get into the dorms, which house only 23 percent of the students, most of whom are freshmen. The rest must fend for themselves in the overpriced college towns of Isla Vista and Goleta. One student notes, "Isla Vista is the accompanying small town next to the campus. It is fun to live among so many students in your own apartment." Meals in the dorms are available to residents and nonresidents alike, and are, according to one student, "reasonable, with four entrées and always a large salad bar. This is California, remember?"

"Lots of parties!" is how one man describes the UCSB social life. In fact, one economics major explains that UCSB really stands for "You Can Study Buzzed." With alcohol banned in public places on campus, affairs in Isla Vista (a.k.a. "Party Town") are a social staple. The local bars are off-limits to those under 21, but when the long-awaited birthday arrives, students celebrate with a quaint little ritual known as the State Street Crawl, imbibing at all the numerous establishments up and down the "main drag" of Santa Barbara. "[The] good weather and beautiful setting really encourages students to get out and be active," says a senior. Movies and concerts are also available, and the mountains, Los Padres National Forest, and L.A. are all an easy drive away. The "big enchilada" of the social season is the annual Halloween festival, which draws 20,000 people from far and wide for a night of revelry in Isla Vista.

The National Science Foundation provides funding for the $5.5-million National Center for Geographic Information and Analysis program.

Fraternities and sororities draw 8 percent of the men and 10 percent of the women. Although the Greeks are strong and growing, there's an ample selection of other organizations from which to choose. A never-ending rotation of intramurals is available on and off the beach; 36 percent of the students participate on one team or another. The most successful varsity teams include water polo, baseball, volleyball, swimming, and basketball. All of UCSB's varsity teams compete in the NCAA's Division I. Ultimate Frisbee is also quite popular, as well as nationally competitive.

If asked what they like best about their college, most students would agree with the political science major who says, "Location, location, location." Though academic standards are always on the rise here, it is almost a matter of pride among UCSB'ers to maintain the university's free-and-easy atmosphere. To be totally happy at UCSB, one must revel in its "casual, kicked-back feeling toward life"—and get along without brunettes.

If You Apply To ➤ | **Santa Barbara**…Regular admissions: Nov. 30. Financial aid: Mar. 2. Does not guarantee to meet demonstrated need. No campus or alumni interviews. SATs or ACTs: required. SAT IIs: required (English, math I or II, and one other). Essay question: personal statement.

UC–Santa Cruz

1156 High Street, Santa Cruz, CA 95064

UC–Santa Cruz, still a baby in the UC system, grew up during the radical '60s when it reigned as the ultimate alternative school. The founding vision of an integrated learning environment remains to this day and every undergraduate affiliates with one of the residential colleges. Overcrowding has become a problem, especially in terms of housing and the school's innovative Narrative Evaluation System. Still, progressive thought continues to flourish as does an excellent academics program devoted to undergraduate education and students still come to UCSC to do their own thing.

The campus, among the most beautiful in the nation, is set on a 2,000-acre expanse of meadowland and redwood forest overlooking Monterey Bay. Bike paths and hiking trails wind throughout the campus and the beach is only a few minutes away. The buildings range from 1860 Cowell Ranch farm structures to the multi–award-winning modern colleges, whose styles range from Mediterranean to Japanese to sleek concrete block. Thanks to a unique building code, nothing can be built taller than two-thirds the height of the nearest redwood tree. Newest additions include the Bay Tree Bookstore and the Seymour Marine Discovery Center.

The surroundings are deceptive. "Courses are very rigorous in my experience," warns one undergrad. Santa Cruz's academic offerings range as widely as its architecture, and feature both traditional and innovative programs. In an effort to become what one official calls a "near-perfect hybrid" between the large university and the small college, campus life revolves around the residential colleges, each of which includes between 900 and 1,300 students and specializes in a broad academic area. Whatever one's specialty, the curriculum is demanding. Led by marine sciences and biology, the sciences are Santa Cruz's strongest suit, and frequently give students the opportunity to coauthor published research with their professors. Science facilities include state-of-the-art laboratories, the Institute of Marine Sciences, which boasts one of the largest groups of experts on marine

Website:
http://admissions.ucsc.edu
Location: Suburban
Total Enrollment: 11,302
Undergraduates: 10,269
Male/Female: 43/57
SAT Ranges: V 520–640 M 520–640
ACT Range: 21–26
Financial Aid: 60%
Expense: Pub $ $
Phi Beta Kappa: Yes
(Continued)
Applicants: 14,485
Accepted: 77%
Enrolled: 22%
Grad in 6 Years: 68%
Returning Freshmen: 85%
Academics: ✍ ✍ ✍ ✍
Social: ☎ ☎ ☎
Q of L: ★ ★ ★ ★ ★
Admissions: (831) 459-4008
Email Address:
admissions@cats.ucsc.edu

Led by marine sciences and biology, the sciences are Santa Cruz's strongest suit, and frequently give students the opportunity to coauthor published research with their professors.

mammals in the nation, and the nearby Lick Observatory for budding stargazers. Santa Cruz boasts the top linguistics division in the country and the psychology department is also praised. In the past, computer engineering wasn't up to par but that has changed with the addition of the Jack Baskin School of Engineering, which was developed to accommodate the growing needs of engineering students. UCSC has recently added an Italian studies major.

While the majority of students now pursue traditional majors, the possibility is still there for eclectically minded students to pursue just about anything they can get a faculty member to OK. One of UCSC's most unique features is that professors provide written evaluations for each student in their class and also provide letter grades to every undergraduate student who requests them. UCSC boasts more than the average number of interdisciplinary programs, including environmental, community, and women's studies; creative writing; and modern society and social thought. Field and independent study are encouraged. Overall, the emphasis is on the liberal arts, and students will find few programs with a vocational emphasis.

To meet general education requirements, students must complete courses in quantitative methods, ethnic/Third World studies, arts, writing, humanities and arts, natural sciences, social sciences, and three topical courses. In addition, American History and Institutions and English composition are required as is a senior thesis or comprehensive exam. The main library, McHenry, houses more than a million books and 13,000 periodicals, and students have access to books at other UC campuses through an online catalog system and interlibrary loans. The science library houses an additional 300,000 volumes.

Though the curriculum is demanding and the quarter system keeps the academic pace fast, the atmosphere is emphatically noncompetitive. Such competition as there is tends to be internalized. "The NES and the setting may appear casual, but there is a strong pressure for individual achievement," says one history major. The majority of the students eventually go on to graduate study. All UC campuses insist on faculty research, but most Santa Cruz professors are there to teach. "I've been very impressed with how accessible professors are," says a sophomore. "Whether it's via email or regular office hours, I feel very comfortable approaching and talking to all of my professors."

Santa Cruz and its students are more conservative than in the past. "Before I came here I was told that UCSC was a 'hippie dippie' college," says a student, "but this is not true at all." Still, it remains the most liberal of the UC campuses, and, according to one student, "still a school with a social conscience." Ninety-six percent of the students are Californians, though Santa Cruz has managed to lure a few Easterners. One-quarter of the students are members of minority groups, with Asian Americans accounting for 11 percent of the students, Hispanics 13 percent, and African Americans 2 percent. "Racial, ethnic, and cultural diversity is celebrated and strongly encouraged by the majority of the students here," reports a politics major. Santa Cruz offers over 200 merit scholarships ranging from $2,000 to $12,000 but there are no athletic scholarships.

UCSC also has two new majors: Information Systems Management and German Studies.

Half of the student population live in the residential colleges. Overcrowding is a problem but new housing is on the way. Until then, the school has devised a few ingenious ways to accommodate its students, including converting lounges into dorm rooms and offering students the option of living in an on-campus trailer park. "I lived in the trailer park for two years and loved it," says a language studies major. "It was a tight-knit community complete with potluck dinners." Some dorms have their own dining halls with reasonably good food; students may also opt to join a food co-op. Freshmen and transfer students are guaranteed on-campus housing and are free to choose among the colleges. Upperclassmen can take their chances in the lottery or move off campus, though higher enrollment means that nearby apartments are becoming increasingly scarce and expensive in this "tourist" town.

The beach and resort town of Santa Cruz, with its boardwalk and amusement park, are only 10 minutes away from campus by bike. Those looking for city lights will have no trouble getting to San Jose (35 miles away) or San Francisco (75 miles) by public transportation. If you have a car, places like Carmel, Big Sur, the Napa Valley, and the Sierras are easily accessible.

There are a dozen fraternities and sororities as well as countless established student groups to provide an active social life. One senior boasts, "With eight colleges, you have eight times as many opportunities for concerts, dances, films, speakers, and so on." Although Santa Cruz fields only a few varsity teams, students love the school mascot, Sammy the banana slug. The men's tennis team is nationally ranked and won the NCAA Division III championship last year, as did the men's swimming team. Participation in intramurals ("Friendship Through Competition" is the motto) is widespread, with rugby in particular growing in popularity. The student recreation department sponsors everything from white-water rafting to cooking classes.

Santa Cruz is a progressive school where the main priority is the education of undergraduates. Many students are concerned that UCSC is growing too fast and with powerful lures such as a gorgeous campus and innovative academic programs, that's likely to continue. Still, as the student population grows, so does the college itself. As long as UCSC retains its belief in "to each his or her own," it will always remain uniquely Santa Cruz.

Science facilities include state-of-the-art laboratories, the Institute of Marine Sciences, which boasts one of the largest groups of experts on marine mammals in the nation, and the nearby Lick Observatory for budding stargazers.

Overlaps
UC–Santa Barbara, UC–San Diego, UC–Davis, UC–Berkeley, UCLA.

If You Apply To ➤ | **Santa Cruz**…Regular admissions: Nov. 30. Financial aid: Mar. 2. Housing: May 1. Does not guarantee to meet demonstrated need. Campus and alumni interviews: not available. SATs or ACTs: required. SAT IIs: required (writing, math I or II, and one other). Essay question: personal statement.

Calvin College

3201 Burton, Grand Rapids, MI 49546

It should be no surprise to incoming students that Calvin College places a high premium on Christianity. Students are asked to define their religious beliefs on the admissions application. And a spiritual mentorship program offers to link students with "wise Christian friends" such as professors and staff. Religion also permeates the classroom environment. Says one senior, "Professors teach their material, but then ask students to think about this material from a Christian point of view. I have enjoyed being able to talk about my faith in the classroom and with my professors." Along with Wheaton College in Illinois, Calvin is regarded as one of the country's top two evangelical colleges.

The educational wing of the Christian Reformed Church in North America, Calvin was founded in 1876. After outgrowing its first home, the college bought a large tract of land on the city's edge and built the present campus of more than 370 beautifully landscaped acres that encompass three ponds, playing fields, and

Website: www.calvin.edu
Location: Suburban
Total Enrollment: 4,309
Undergraduates: 4,263
Male/Female: 43/57
SAT Ranges: V 540–650 M 530–670
ACT Range: 23–29
Financial Aid: 65%
Expense: Pr $
Phi Beta Kappa: No

(Continued)

Applicants: 1,870
Accepted: 99%
Enrolled: 56%
Grad in 6 Years: 69%
Returning Freshmen: 86%
Academics: ✑ ✑ ✑
Social: ☎ ☎ ☎
Q of L: ★ ★ ★ ★
Admissions: (616) 957-6106 or
  (800) 688-0122
Email Address:
  admissions@calvin.edu

Strongest Programs:
  English
  History
  Philosophy
  Music
  Math
  Engineering
  Teacher Education
  Natural Sciences

Calvin graduates have few problems getting accepted to graduate schools of law, medicine, or business.

Class size is small—most have fewer than 25 students—and faculty members, all of whom must be committed to Christian teachings, are especially helpful.

a nature preserve. The campus includes a 174-acre woodland and wetland nature preserve that is used for classwork, research, and recreation. Campus facilities are less than 35 years old and were designed by a pupil of architect Frank Lloyd Wright. The school is located in suburban Grand Rapids, which one student describes as "a very happening town."

Calvin students describe the overall academic environment as "challenging but supportive." The emphasis is less on enforcing rigid codes of conduct than on creating and conveying a Christian sense of scholarship. Every subject, the school believes, can be approached from a Christian perspective, integrating faith and learning. For instance, every student must take a course titled Christian Perspectives on Learning during his or her first year. The Communication Arts and Sciences department is highly respected for its reformed Christian perspective on the mass media and popular culture.

Calvin undergrads face general education requirements that mandate six courses in history, philosophy, and religion; three courses in literature, music, and art; two courses each in a foreign language at the second-year level and the natural sciences; one course each in mathematics, written rhetoric, physical education; and a course in spoken rhetoric. Strong high school preparation and advanced-placement tests can reduce the number of required core courses.

Traditionally, the school's strongest programs have been English and history, and the departments of music, math, and the natural sciences are outstanding. Calvin graduates have few problems getting accepted to graduate schools of law, medicine, or business. Students also recommend the education, social work, and nursing programs, as well as the engineering and communication arts departments. Students cite the languages as weak. Students in the general business program can opt for a wide range of specializations, including marketing, human resources management, operations management, finance, and economics. Internships and small business consulting opportunities are also integral parts of a student's program—Calvin is a member of the Christian College Consortium*— and there's a five-year co-op plan. The bachelor's degree in accounting has resulted in students passing the CPA exam at rates of 15 to 20 percent above the national average. Education is the most popular major.

Class size is small—most have fewer than 25 students—and faculty members, all of whom must be committed to Christian teachings, are especially helpful. "The profs here really want you to learn and develop academically," says a senior, "but they also give you help if you need." There are no teaching assistants, and professors are expected to reserve about 10 hours per week for advising outside of class, but most devote more time than that to their students. Students use the interim month of January to pursue a variety of creative, low-pressure alternatives both on and off campus. For those who opt for travel, there are opportunities for studying art and theater in England, and languages in Germany, Canada, and the Dominican Republic. Students who stay on campus can take such courses as Shakespeare's Greatest Hits or the provocative Toward a Theology of Wealth and Possessions. Another feature of the month is the January Series, an award-winning lecture series that brings nationally known speakers to campus.

The administration reports that more than half of Calvin students are members of the Christian Reformed Church, though that number is dwindling. While many students are committed to the strong Dutch heritage, there is the sense that the school needs to be more ethnically diverse. The population is 86 percent white; African Americans account for less than 1 percent, Hispanics 1 percent, and Asian Americans 2 percent. The college administration continues to be strongly committed to the Entrada program, which has been successful in bringing high school students from ethnic minority to campus for a residential summer program. Calvin is basically a khakis-and-loafers, young Republican school, not a ready home to unconventional types. The school offers 1,500 merit scholarships, and a tuition gift certificate program that allows families to prepay tuition years in advance. There are no athletic scholarships.

Freshmen and sophomores under the age of 21 who do not live at home with their parents must live on campus. "The dorms are great," says a Spanish major. "All are well-maintained and fairly comfy." Commons areas, including meditation chapels, are open to all. Each residence hall and two apartment buildings have computer rooms in their basements. The "MOSAIC Community" provides on-campus students with the choice of living in an intentionally multicultural residence hall. "Project Neighborhood" places Calvin students and two adult mentors in a college-owned house located in a core neighborhood in Grand Rapids.

Calvin's social life includes on-campus concerts and Thursday open-mike nights at Cave Cafe. There are no fraternities or sororities, and many of the social activities revolve around the housing units. Road trips include the beaches of Lake Michigan (a one-hour drive) or Chicago and Detroit (three hours distant). A popular annual event is Chaos Day, when each dorm (both the male and female wings) competes in athletic games. The huge Airband lip-sync competition in February is also a favorite activity, as are athletic contests versus Hope College. Several students mention on-campus drinking as a concern. Calvin maintains a dry campus, and "for the most part, these rules are obeyed," says a senior.

While the Knights don't field a football squad, students love almost all other sports competitions, with men's soccer, cross-country, and track, and women's cross-country, softball, volleyball, and field hockey strong and well supported. The softball and men's basketball teams both earned recent NCAA postseason bids. Intramural competition never fails to get Calvinites' juices flowing.

Calvin's sense of community and the opportunity to serve meshes well with the strong Christian faith of most students. They come here looking for an environment that would combine faith-based learning with academic rigor, and they find it. As one senior says, "Students at Calvin tend to be very bright, intensely spiritual, and committed to transforming the world."

> *Strong high school preparation and advanced-placement tests can reduce the number of required core courses.*

Overlaps
Hope, Grand Valley State, Dordt College, Wheaton (IL), University of Michigan.

If You Apply To ➤ | **Calvin**…Rolling admissions. Financial aid: Feb. 15. Housing: May 1. Campus interviews: optional, informational. No alumni interviews. ACTs: required. SAT IIs: optional. Essay question: state your religious beliefs; personal statements.

Canadian Colleges and Universities

Horace Greeley told ambitious young men of his generation to "go West." Today his admonition to young men and women seeking a quality college education at a fraction of the usual cost would probably be to "go North"— to Canada. A growing number of American students are discovering the educational riches that lie just above their northern border in this huge land of 30 million people known for its rugged mountains, bicultural politics, spirited ice hockey and cold ale. What's drawing them is easy to discern.

The top Canadian universities are the academic equals of most flagship public universities and many leading privates in the United States, but the expense of a bachelor's degree is far lower, even taking travel into account. Canadian campuses and the cities in which they are located are safe places, and, unless one opts for a French course of study, there are no language and few cultural barriers. Canadian schools are strong on international exchange programs, and their degrees carry weight with U.S. graduate schools.

Canada has 90 institutions of higher learning ranging from internationally-recognized research universities to the small undergraduate teaching institutions in the country's more rural areas; the country ranks second after the U.S. in the percentage of citizens attending university. Most of the larger universities are located in highly urban centers, but some are situated in smaller towns where they dominate the life of the community. Most are almost literally next door to the States, within 100 miles of the Canada–U.S. border. In this guide we feature four of Canada's strongest universities: the University of British Columbia, McGill University, Queen's University and the University of Toronto.

Institutions of higher learning in Canada were established from the earliest days of French settlement in the mid 17th Century, making them some of the oldest in North America. The precursors to the public universities in Canada were the small, elite, denominational colleges that sprang up in Quebec, in the Maritimes and later in Ontario. A few private denominational colleges and universities still exist in Canada, but most have been subsumed into affiliations or associations with the larger universities. Education in Canada, including university education, became the exclusive jurisdiction of provincial governments, and as the Canadian West was developed the large Western provinces of British Columbia, Alberta, Manitoba and Saskatchewan set up provincially-chartered universities similar to land-grant colleges in the U.S.

One of the key differences between Canadian and U.S. universities, is that Canadian universities (and this is what they are, not "colleges") are primarily funded from public monies. Despite steady tuition increases in the past five years, the average Canadian student still only pays on average about $2,500 in Canadian dollars, or U.S. $1,700. Although non-Canadians may be charged up to six times the domestic rate, most costs are still lower than out-of-state tuition in the U.S. Tuition at the four universities described below ranges from U.S. $5,500 to $9,200.

Canadians have come to expect easy and affordable access to a uniformly high-quality of education whether they live in Halifax or Vancouver. After diminishing government funding in the past several years, a now booming economy, a large government surplus and with it new federal initiatives grants for innovations and scholarships, combined with universities' own aggressive fund-raising campaigns bode well for the continued growth and quality of Canadian higher education in the immediate future.

Federal and provincial loans and grants that are readily available to Canadian students are generally not available to students from the U.S. and other countries. However, the majority of universities with competitive admissions, particularly those featured in *The Fiske Guide*, offer merit-based awards and scholarships to students of all nationalities. American students who attend leading Canadian schools can apply their U.S. student assistance funds, including Stafford Loans and Pell Grants as well as the recently implemented HOPE Scholarship and Lifetime Learning tax credits.

The requirements for obtaining a degree are set by each institution, as are the admission requirements and prerequisites. Unlike the U.S., Canada does not offer nor require its own students to take a Canadian college entrance test. Some Canadian universities admitting students from the United States will require the results of SAT or ACT scores along with high school marks from academic subjects in the last two or three years of high school. In general, top universities are about as selective as their American counterparts.

Application fees vary by institution, as do deadlines. Canadian universities are aware of the May 1st deadline operative in the U.S. and try to accommodate. Applications to the University of Toronto and Queens University in Ontario are handled centrally through the Ontario Universities' Application Service. McGill handles applications directly and accepts both web-based and paper applications. British Columbia has its own application, which can be mailed, but encourages students to apply online. Canadian universities differ widely in the amount of credit and/or advanced standing they offer for Advanced Placement Examinations or International Baccalaureate Higher Level Examinations.

The following admission requirements apply to applicants from an American school system: The University of British Columbia bases admission decisions on the average on 8 full-year academic courses over the last two years of high school, and there are also specific program requirements for students entering the science-based faculties. SAT test results are not required, but if students submit them, the results can be helpful in the evaluation process. McGill bases its assessment of American high school graduates on the overall record of marks in academic subjects during the final three years of high school, class standing, and results obtained in SAT I and SAT II and/or ACT

tests. Queens wants applicants with a minimum score of 1200 on SAT I (with at least 580 in the verbal section and 520 in the mathematical one) and looks at class rank. There are also program specific requirements for programs where mathematics and/or biology, chemistry and physics are a requirement. Toronto's Arts and Science faculties want a high grade point average and good scores on the SAT I and on three SAT II subject tests. ACT and CEEB Advanced Placement Examination scores are also considered.

It is hard to beat Canadian universities for the quality of student life. Although many students commute, most of the universities in Canada offer on-campus housing; some even guarantee campus housing for first year students. Universities offer active intramural and intercollegiate sports programs for both men and women, and the usual student clubs, newspapers and radio stations provide students with opportunities to get involved and to develop friendships. As in the United States, student-run organizations are active participants in university life, with leaders serving on university committees and lobbying on issues ranging from creating more bicycle paths to keeping tuitions low. Few Canadian campuses are troubled by issues of student safety or rowdiness. In the larger urban centers Canadian campuses reflect the rich cultural diversity of Canada's cultural mosaic, and most encourage their students to gain international experience by spending a term or a full year abroad.

Americans wondering about the currency of a Canadian degree in the U.S. should be reassured that top American and multinational countries—the likes of Archer Daniels Midland, Chase Manhattan, IBM, Microsoft, Nortel Networks and Solomon Smith Barney—actively recruit on Canadian campuses, as do American graduate schools. According to the Institute of International Education in New York, more than 7,000 Canadians are currently enrolled in graduate schools in the United States.

The one thing that is different for U.S. and other international students intending to study in Canada is that they will have to obtain Student Authorization, equivalent to a visa, from Canadian immigration authorities. Getting a Student Authorization is fairly straightforward for American citizens, but this slight bureaucratic hurdle is a reminder that Canada, for all of its similarities in language and culture with the United States, is still another country. For many American students who have chosen to study in Canada, this is part of the draw—they get to enjoy all the excitement of studying abroad in a foreign country with few of the cultural and none of the linguistic barriers to overcome. One of the most pleasant differences American students soon discover is how far their American dollar goes in Canada with the favorable exchange rate.

The Association of Universities and Colleges of Canada has a website at http://www.aucc.ca/en/acuindex.html. Another good source of scholastic information is the website of the Canadian Embassy in Washington D.C. at http://www.canadianembassy.org/studyincanada.

Canadian universities are currently playing host to about 3,000 American students on their campuses, and as a result of funding cutbacks and internationalization policies in the early 1990s they have become increasingly active in recruiting students from south of the border. This is but one more reason why it makes sense for more young Americans to check out the "Canadian option." Canada, eh?

University of British Columbia

Vancouver, British Columbia, Canada V6T 1Z1

What do two prime ministers of Canada, three provincial premiers, an astronaut, a world-renowned opera singer, and a Nobel Prize winner have in common? Give up? They are all graduates of the University of British Columbia, one of Canada's elite institutions. Founded in 1908, UBC offers students solid programs in business and science, ready access to beaches and mountains, and a diploma with instant name recognition. Though the massive campus can sometimes feel isolating, students are nevertheless happy to be here. After all, not everyone can lay claim to such illustrious company.

Located just 25 minutes from downtown Vancouver, UBC's striking Point Grey campus covers a peninsula that borders the Pacific Ocean and is bounded by

Website: www.ubc.ca
Location: Suburban
Total Enrollment: 35,502
Undergraduates: 29,146
Male/Female: 43/57
SAT Ranges: N/A
ACT Range: N/A
Financial Aid: N/A
Expense: Pub $

(Continued)

Phi Beta Kappa: No

Applicants: 18,642

Accepted: 41%

Enrolled: 53%

Grad in 6 Years: 87%

Returning Freshmen: 88%

Academics: ◿ ◿ ◿ ◿

Social: ☎ ☎

Q of L: ★ ★ ★

Admissions: (604) 822-8999

Email Address:

international.reception@
ubc.ca

Strongest Programs:

Economics

Microbiology

Business Administration

Computer Science

Computer Engineering

Asian Studies

International Relations

Qualified students can take advantage of Science One, featuring team-taught courses in biology, chemistry, math, and physics.

Minorities are well-represented on campus (Asians make up the largest contingency) and the university encourages diversity through a series of special programs.

an old growth forest. Mountains—perfect for skiing—loom in the distance. Architectural styles are a mix of Gothic and modern, and students can enjoy a leisurely stroll through the university's botanical gardens. Recent campus additions include the Chan Centre for the Performing Arts, the Centre for Integrated Computer Systems Research, and the $50 million Forest Sciences Centre.

According to the UBC administration, the university's mission is to "offer students an intellectually challenging education...that prepares them to become citizens of...the 21st century through programs that are international in scope, interactive in process, and interdisciplinary in content and approach." Strong programs include microbiology, international relations, economics, and business administration. Asian studies is highly regarded and theatre majors benefit from the new Chan Centre for the Performing Arts. Other popular majors include psychology and computer science. The administration admits that some home economics and agricultural science courses could be strengthened, and one student grumbles about his 8:00 A.M. philosophy lecture: "Who can focus on the big questions at that time of the morning?"

Freshman benefit from a wide array of first-year programs, including Imagine UBC, a first-day orientation. Arts Foundation is a series of three courses that offers an enriched, integrated approach to broad interdisciplinary themes in arts and humanities. Qualified students can take advantage of Science One, featuring team-taught courses in biology, chemistry, math, and physics. Student exchange programs are available through 83 partner universities around the globe, and co-op programs in engineering, science, arts, commerce, and forestry give students an opportunity to earn while they learn. In addition, honors and double honors programs are available to super-brains and budding geniuses.

The academic climate is exactly what you would expect from a university of UBC's stature. "The academic climate is very competitive," says a senior. "Courses are, for the most part, intense and rigorous." Most classes have less than 50 students, though mammoth lectures are not uncommon for freshmen. Faculty receive mixed reviews, depending largely on the department. "Most profs are focused on their students and will help whenever possible," says a senior. A junior, however, grumbles that many professors "are either too old and need to be retired...or too young and without experience." Academic advising is praised by most, as is the library, which houses 10 million books, journals, and microforms.

With nearly 40,000 students attending, it's no surprise that UBC's student population is a melting pot. "Everyone can fit in because the student body is so diverse and large," says a senior. The typical UBC student is bright, hardworking, and gregarious. Though government subsidies make UBC a relatively affordable institution, at least one student says "those with tons of money" will fit in best. A history major divides his classmates into two categories: commuters "who come in their fancy new cars with cell phones" and "those who live on campus and enjoy the community spirit." Minorities are well-represented on campus (Asians make up the largest contingency) and the university encourages diversity through a series of special programs. Hot political issues include homosexual rights, abortion, and sexual harassment. UBC offers 75 merit scholarships to qualified students and athletic scholarships in 17 varsity sports.

Only 5 percent of the students—mostly freshmen and sophomores—live in college housing, which is described as "quite nice and well maintained." The rest must fend for themselves against Vancouver's pricey rental market or commute from home. On-campus options include coed complexes (primarily for freshmen), university apartments, and family units for upperclassmen. Theme houses are another alternative and offer like-minded students the opportunity to mingle.

Dorm food encourages dieting, although "there are a couple of low cost/good food places that are always busy," reports a senior. Security is adequate, and features a walking escort service and nightly shuttle, though "most people just walk to where they want to go."

On such a large campus, isolation is a real threat. "You need to get in touch with other students quickly when you get here or you could feel lost on such a big campus," says a freshman. A senior adds, "To get the full value of UBC, you must willingly seek out clubs to join. Otherwise, you can feel lost and alone." Social life largely "depends on the crowd you hang with," according to one student. For partying types, there are the requisite beer bashes and toga parties, courtesy of UBC's small but active Greek scene—one of the few places where underage drinkers can sneak a sip of booze. Alcohol-free alternatives include university-sponsored events, such as movies and guest speakers. Popular campus events include Storm the Wall, long boat racing, and the Arts County Fair.

Vancouver offers students countless opportunities for fun and contribution. "We can do anything we want in Vancouver," says a senior. "Most people go downtown for social events, bars, and shopping." Beautiful weather draws students outdoors and to nearby beaches and mountains for in-line skating, snowboarding, and swimming. Varsity and intramural competition are favorite pastimes; popular sports include soccer, basketball, hockey, volleyball, and skiing.

"If you're not confident and outgoing...you might be lost or lonely [at UBC]," admits a junior. Indeed, spending four years at this mammoth university can be isolating for the shy student. But for those willing to take control of their social lives, UBC offers an impressive academic milieu.

On-campus options include coed complexes (primarily for freshmen), university apartments, and family units for upperclassmen. Theme houses are another alternative and offer like-minded students the opportunity to mingle.

Overlaps

McGill University, University of Toronto, University of Washington, Simon Fraser, UC–Berkeley.

If You Apply To ➤ **British Columbia**...Early admission: Jan. 28 (domestic). Regular admissions: Apr. 30. Financial aid: Apr. 15. Housing: June 1 (for non-Canadians). Does not guarantee to meet demonstrated need. No campus or alumni interviews. SATs: recommended. SAT IIs: optional. No essay question.

McGill University

Montreal, Quebec, Canada H3Z 2E2

Strong preprofessional programs and a diverse student body are just two of the drawing cards of McGill University, one of Canada's premiere institutions. But beware: this is not a place for those in need of attention. "McGill is a very independent school," says a senior. "It is not a place for the student who needs lots of personal contact." Though Montreal's freezing weather and the university's impersonal atmosphere can leave some feeling cold, those who are willing to boldly go forward can expect to fit right in. With such notable alum as singer Leonard Cohen, musician Burt Bacharach, and actor William Shatner (*Star Trek's* Captain Kirk), it's easy to see why enterprising men and women from around the world flock to McGill University.

A junior describes McGill's 88-acre campus as "an oasis in the heart of the city." Located in downtown Montreal, amidst the hustle and bustle, the campus provides students with ample greenspace and a welcome respite from the decidedly urban atmosphere of the city. Campus buildings range from "Gothic-like"

Website: www.mcgill.ca
Location: City center
Total Enrollment: 28,711
Undergraduates: 21,939
Male/Female: 43/57
SAT Ranges: N/A †
ACT Range: N/A
Financial Aid: 35%
Expense: Pub $
Phi Beta Kappa: No
Applicants: 13,405
Accepted: 60%

(Continued)

Enrolled: 50%

Grad in 6 Years: N/A

Returning Freshmen: N/A

Academics: ✍ ✍ ✍ ✍

Social: ☎ ☎ ☎ ☎

Q of L: ★ ★ ★ ★

Admissions: (514) 398-3910

Email Address:
admissions@aro.lan.mcgill.ca

Strongest Programs:
Medicine
Law
Engineering
Management
Environmental Studies
Music

Freshmen must accumulate 6 to 12 credits in three of four disciplines, including languages, math and science, social sciences, and humanities, and declare a major before their sophomore year.

structures with vines growing up the sides to more modern (read: ugly) constructions ("You can ignore them if you try hard," says a senior). Trees and greenery dot the campus landscape, and mountain ranges rise into the sky to the north and south. Recent construction projects include a new student services building (opened in 1999) and renovations to the engineering complex.

Though the most popular majors are psychology and English, there is no denying that the university's strengths lie in preprofessional programs such as medicine, law, and engineering. The management program is renowned, and students cite political science, religious studies, and philosophy as sure bets. The sciences receive uniform praise, and the school has recently opened its School of Environment, where environment-related courses are under development. For those who want to escape Montreal's brutal winter weather, there are internships, field studies in Barbados, exchange programs with more than 500 partner universities around the world, and study abroad options via the Canadian University Study Abroad Program (CUSAP). Students cite visual arts as less than adequate.

To fulfill the university's general education requirements, students must first choose which discipline (or faculty) to enter; popular choices include management, engineering, religious studies, art, music, and agriculture. A senior says, "It is important to consider the university on the basis of which faculty you would be interested in, because they vary greatly and operate almost as independent units." On average, students must earn 120 credits to graduate with a four-year degree. Freshmen must accumulate 6 to 12 credits in three of four disciplines, including languages, math and science, social sciences, and humanities, and declare a major before their sophomore year. Upon entering their major, students have a menu of course options that includes honors programs and double majors.

Regardless of the major, students can expect classes to be demanding. "McGill definitely keeps you on your toes," says a sophomore. Classes tend to be large—especially for freshmen—and students must be willing to seek out professors and advisors. "Students looking for small classes and personalized education...would not fit in at McGill," warns a political science major. "In many undergrad programs, classes are huge," agrees a psychology major. "However, classes are often accompanied by smaller tutorial sessions where students get more focused attention with professors or teaching assistants." Professors receive high marks for their knowledge and accessibility outside of class. "The quality of teaching is tremendous," says a student. "Our first two weeks of classes are the best because the institution is so big you can 'shop' for the best professors." Academic advising is a bureaucratic tangle—"My suggestion is to get to know a professor in your area and ask him or her your questions," says a student. McGill's 3.1 million library holdings are reportedly adequate, though "not outstanding."

McGill students are a diverse lot—more than 40 countries are represented here–and the only common thread among students seems to be their fierce independence. "McGill students represent the world," says one student. "They are energetic, friendly, and cosmopolitan." Students report little racial hostility, and hot political issues include local politics and university funding. Qualified students are eligible for 1,807 scholarships of $2,000 to $10,000. There is also a work-study program for those in need of financial assistance. There are no athletic scholarships. "Once you have started at McGill, they will do everything they can to help you graduate," says a grad student.

The university's six residence halls house 6 percent of the student population, primarily freshmen from out of town (who are all but guaranteed a room). Dorms run the gamut from "cement box room" to "gorgeous studio flat." Party animals will feel free to crank up the stereo in Molson or McConnell, while bookworms might be better suited for Gardener. Douglas denizens enjoy their hall's quaint charm, and women who want to skip the coed scene can find a room in Royal Victoria College, an all-female dorm. "Almost every building has its own cafeteria and the food is generally good," says a senior. Off-campus apartments are a popular alternative for upperclassmen, who take advantage of Montreal's clean, affordable housing. Despite its urban location, the McGill campus is safe and security is considered more than adequate. "There are student organizations like 'Walksafe' and 'Drivesafe' that will walk or drive students home at night regardless of where they are or where they are going," reports one student.

"There is a thriving social scene at McGill," says one student. Though there are "considerable on-campus social activities, with many clubs and associations," most students venture off campus and into the bars and clubs of Montreal for fun and adventure. "Montreal's rich musical, artistic, and young culture is intoxicating," says a sophomore. A senior adds, "The city of Montreal is absolutely essential to student life. Students live, work, and play [there]." Drinking is a popular pastime, but underage drinkers are few and far between since the legal age in Quebec is 18. "Alcohol is served on campus, but students are asked to show their ID's to prove their age," reports a modern languages major. Well-attended campus events include homecoming, a winter carnival, and Frosh Week activities. Popular roadtrips include New York City, Ottawa, and Toronto. Ski slopes are less than an hour away.

Football, basketball, and ice hockey are the most popular varsity sports. According to one student. hated opponents include "our crosstown rivals at Concordia" and "our arch-enemies at Queen's University, in Kingston, Ontario. Both schools are very old and this is a longstanding traditional rivalry." Intramurals offer would-be jocks an opportunity to blow off steam after classes and on weekends. "As you walk through campus, you are sure to pass by a soccer, flag football, or rugby game on one of the numerous fields," says a student. New athletic facilities are a welcome addition for varsity athletes and "those of us who just like to work out," says a senior.

Overachievers and independent types do best here. "Slackers would be happier elsewhere," quips a senior. Large classes, brutal winters, and mountains of red tape are part of the McGill experience. Nevertheless, most seem happy to be here. "No one is here to hold your hand and make decisions for you," says a student. "But not to worry. You will have a great time—guaranteed!"

Qualified students are eligible for 387 renewable entrance scholarships of $2,000 to $10,000, and 1,400 continuing scholarships of up to $4,000.

Overlaps
N/A

If You Apply To ➤ McGill...Regular admissions and housing: Jan. 15. Does not guarantee to meet demonstrated need. Campus interviews: optional, informational. No alumni interviews. SATs or ACTs: required. SAT IIs: required (three, depending on program). Accepts electronic applications. No essay.

Queen's University

Kingston, Ontario, Canada K7L 3N6

Website: www.queensu.ca
Location: City center
Total Enrollment: 17,510
Undergraduates: 11,886
Male/Female: 44/56
SAT Ranges: N/A †
ACT Range: N/A
Financial Aid: N/A
Expense: Pub $ $ $
Phi Beta Kappa: No
Applicants: 19,012
Accepted: 63%
Enrolled: 25%
Grad in 6 Years: 95%
Returning Freshmen: 96%
Academics: ✍ ✍ ✍ ✍
Social: ☎ ☎ ☎ ☎
Q of L: ★ ★ ★ ★
Admissions: (613) 533-2218
Email Address:
admissn@post.queensu.ca

Strongest Programs:
Engineering
Commerce
Music

Students participating in the Queen's International Study Centre are whisked away to the university's England campus, where they enjoy small classes and integrated field studies while residing in a 15th-century castle.

Students at Queen's University approach work and play with equal zeal and enjoy a potent mix of school spirit and intellectual drive. Success requires energy and a willingness to get into the thick of things. "People who aren't interested in being a part of the school community are better off at a school that isn't such a big family," warns a sophomore. Solid academics, a pervasive school spirit, and longstanding traditions make life at this storied university unique—and demanding. "Getting into Queen's is just the first challenge," says a senior. "Succeeding at Queen's is another battle."

The 161-acre Queen's campus is located on the north shore of Lake Ontario, just minutes from the heart of Kingston, Ontario ("the limestone city") and directly between Montreal and Toronto. "Almost all buildings are constructed using limestone," explains a senior, "a Kingston tradition started by navy stone masons after the War of 1812." Historically significant buildings have been maintained and "there are some modern buildings with a lot of glass to provide a bright and welcoming atmosphere." Ample greenery and open spaces provide students a place to stretch out under the sky and hit the books.

Established in 1841 by Royal Charter of Queen Victoria, Queen's offers undergraduate degrees in a variety of faculties, including arts, science, engineering, commerce, education, music, nursing science, and fine art. Academics are unilaterally solid, but the most demanding are engineering and commerce. The bachelor of commerce program was the first of its kind in Canada, and provides students with an internationally-focused liberal business education, enhanced by new leadership modules and the integration of technology. Future scientists benefit from world-class facilities, including a $56 million biosciences complex featuring classrooms, labs, and the phytotron—a single computer-controlled research-level greenhouse with six separate environmental zones.

General education requirements vary by program, but all students can expect to complete a rigorous series of core and elective courses. Students participating in the Queen's International Study Centre are whisked away to the university's England campus, where they enjoy small classes and integrated field studies while residing in a 15th-century castle. In addition, there are exchange programs with universities around the world.

The academic climate is challenging and competitive, which comes as no surprise to students. "Queen's is very competitive," says a sophomore. "The courses are rigorous but interesting." The general consensus among struggling students is that A's are hard to come by. "After working your butt off and reading stacks of textbooks, your grades pale in comparison to the marks of students at other universities," gripes a biology major. Classes tend to be large for freshmen and sophomores, but dwindle in size as one approaches graduation. The majority of classes are taught by full professors who receive praise for their accessibility and intelligence. "The teachers I have had have been thorough, challenging, and concerned about my success," says a junior. Office hours and special "wine and cheese" functions give students ample opportunity to mingle with faculty. Students report that there is little trouble getting into desired classes, and "there is lots of counseling available for students who need it."

Queen's students are an industrious, intelligent group, and most are used to academic success. Queen's ranks among the top Canadian universities for the overall number of Rhodes Scholars, and consistently admits the most Ontario Scholars into its ranks. Students come from every Canadian province and 80 countries, and a sociology major says that "Queen's is very PC and inclusive, regardless of gender, race, religion, or sexual orientation." A large percentage of the student body is active in extracurriculars, and school spirit is a must. Though there are no athletic scholarships, nearly 800 merit awards of $1,000 to $12,000 are handed out annually. "I have had great help through scholarships and financial aid," relates a senior. "There is quite a lot of money for you...you just have to go after it."

Twenty-five percent of the student body live in one of 11 residence halls, and all freshmen are guaranteed a place to hang their hat. "The residences are very comfortable and the custodial staff is in everyday, becoming your parents away from home," says a junior. Coed and single-sex dorms are available. A mandatory meal plan gives freshmen a wide variety of foods to choose from, including pasta, salad, pizza, and a soup and salad bar. The surrounding city also offers a plethora of dining options. "Kingston is known in our house as the 'city of restaurants'," says a student. "They are everywhere." After freshman year, most students pack their bags and head off campus to the "student village," where comfortable apartments are available. In fact, 80 percent of Queen's students live within a 15 minute walk of campus. Though always a concern, safety is practically a nonissue on campus. Students report that they feel quite safe and that security is more than adequate.

Make no mistake about it, Queen's students know how to have a good time. "Social life is huge at Queen's," says a student. Adds another, "Campus pubs and city pubs have both found their niche." On Thursday nights, students flock to campus bars such as Afic's for a drink or two (or three), while Saturday nights are reserved for city bars and nightclubs. The legal drinking age is 19, and kiddies will have a tough time skirting the law. "The bouncers in Kingston actually have a couple of brain cells and can spot a fake ID from 90 kilometers away," says a senior. Non-alcoholic alternatives include school-sponsored movies and extracurricular clubs (there are over 220!). "Extracurricular activities are a must, not an option!" says one student. Frosh Week is a favorite event with "cheers that even the most blasé of students will be shouting out with pride by the end of the week." The school is steeped in Scottish tradition and its normal to see kilt-wearing bandsmen at important campus events.

Once the capital of Canada, Kingston is described as the "very much a university town." There are several universities in the area (including the Royal Military College), and downtown provides students with places to shop. "Kingston itself has several clubs, three malls, a number of museums, numerous gyms, and three or four movie theaters," says a student. The city's relative isolation makes it the favored stomping ground for students without wheels. Town-gown relations are good and students are very active in the community. Toronto and Montreal (less than three hours away) are popular roadtrips.

With 41 varsity teams, Queen's athletic program is not only the largest in Canada, but also ties with Harvard University for the largest program in North America. Popular sports include men's and women's rugby, women's squash, rowing, golf, and women's lacrosse. The annual "kill McGill" football game against rival McGill University draws pigskin-crazed students from every corner of campus; homecoming is reputed to be a raucous affair featuring "alumni from the 1920's parading around the football field during halftime." Intramural competition is fierce, too, and nearly every student is involved on some level. A student says, "There is so much school spirit, sometimes it makes you sick."

Life at Queen's University is one of extremes. "Students who are able to balance work and pleasure fit in best here," says a junior. The pressure to succeed can be tough and expectations are high. But for those who pull it off, the rewards are well worth the effort. "Queen's has its own culture," says a student. "Don't be afraid to engage it."

If You Apply To ➤

Queens…Regular admissions and financial aid: Mar. 31. Does not guarantee to meet demonstrated need. Campus interviews: optional, informational. No alumni interviews. SATs: required. SAT IIs: required (for engineering candidates only). No essay question.

University of Toronto

Toronto, Ontario, Canada M5S 1A3

Website: www.utoronto.ca
Location: City center
Total Enrollment: 53,428
Undergraduates: 42,546
Male/Female: 43/57
SAT Ranges: N/A
ACT Range: N/A
Financial Aid: 50%
Expense: Pub $ $
Phi Beta Kappa: Yes
Applicants: 43,247
Accepted: 59%
Enrolled: 37%
Grad in 6 Years: 72%
Returning Freshmen: 95%
Academics: 🖎 🖎 🖎 🖎
Social: ☎ ☎ ☎
Q of L: ★ ★ ★
Admissions: (416) 978-2190
Email Address:
   ask@adm.utoronto.ca

Strongest Programs:
   Arts
   Science
   Engineering
   Medicine
   Education

Students at the University of Toronto avoid getting lost in the shuffle by taking part in a unique residential college system that allows them to model their educational experience after their own personalities. Each college has a distinct character and appeal, yet blends seamlessly into the university's overall academic milieu. "Someone who wants to be involved in university life will have great opportunities here," says a student.

Toronto is so large that it spans three campuses. The St. George campus is situated in downtown Toronto and features Gothic architecture and historic buildings, though one students describes the setting as "very much similar to a nuclear power plant." Two suburban campuses—one in Mississauga and one in Scarborough—feature more modern structures. Newer facilities include the Joseph L. Rotman School of Management building and a new residence hall for graduate students.

Students apply directly to one of nine colleges, seven of which are on the St. George campus. Each college has its own set of admissions requirements, but international applicants can expect to submit SAT I and three SAT II scores. Advanced Placement testing is also considered. Strong programs include engineering, medicine, and education. First-Year Seminars are taught by the faculty's leading scholars and provide freshmen with cross-disciplinary discussions in intimate class settings. In addition, there are study abroad programs around the world, internships, co-op programs, and specialized cross-disciplinary courses. Sophomores can choose from nearly 100 research opportunities outside the classroom, where they work side-by-side with the university's most renowned professors. Newer programs include an architectural studies major and programs in forest conservation and health and disease.

"The academic climate is extremely competitive," says a junior. "However, if one puts time and effort into studying and preparing for assignments, they should be fine." Students report that class size can be a problem and it's not uncommon to have more than 100 classmates, even in upper level courses. Still, most large classes break into smaller tutorials, and even freshmen are taught by full professors. "Overall, I have received a very high quality of teaching," says one student. Another adds, "My profs are all very available…most have office hours and email addresses and they respond quickly." With so many students vying for classes, it can be difficult to get desired courses. "Certain courses have restricted numbers and so are hard to get into," says a business major. Academic advising is described as "comprehensive" and "readily accessible to students." U of T's extensive library system hold 12.8 million volumes and "most are open seven days a week," according to one happy bibliophile.

Newer programs include an architectural studies major and a professional program in radiation sciences.

Though Toronto is becoming increasingly popular with outsiders, students from Ontario still make up 89 percent of the student body. International students comprise 5 percent, and students say that the university is "a very inclusive and accepting environment." Perhaps the one trait all U of T students share is a high IQ; students here are smart. "They are the best and brightest students in Canada," says a senior. "Students are generally motivated and there is a very friendly atmosphere," adds a freshman. Hot political debates include homosexual rights and multicultural issues. Top students (and there are many!) vie for 2,400 admission scholarships and 2,000 in-course awards. There are no athletic scholarships.

Twenty-five percent of the student body are residential students, and all are affiliated with one of the nine undergraduate colleges, which act as "local neighborhoods." "Even though 50,000 people attend U of T, all undergraduate Arts and Sciences students choose a college to belong to," explains a junior. "This college has nothing to do with their academic studies, but allows them to meet people from various programs and take part in social events. It breaks the students into smaller communities." Each college has its own residences, which reflect the unique character of its students. St. Michael's College maintains a rich Roman Catholic tradition, while University College has a predominantly Jewish student body. Students of New College enjoy air-conditioned dorm rooms, and Victoria College houses over 750 students. The dorms are "clean, comfortable, and have a great social atmosphere," says a student. There are various dining options (mostly residence-specific), and all are well-regarded. Campus security is adequate, according to most, and students say that they feel safe on campus.

Social life is quite active and takes place both in the city, where nightclubs beckon, and on campus. "There are pub nights and other social events held on campus," says a junior. "Hart House (which is the social and recreational center) has pool tables, an athletic wing, restaurants, and common rooms." The legal drinking age is 19, and students report that "alcohol abuse is not tolerated on campus." For those wishing to party without the aid of chemicals, there are countless university-sponsored events, including movies, guest speakers, and countless extracurricular clubs. Frosh week gives students an excuse to get rowdy and enjoy themselves.

Students find plenty of reasons to love Toronto, their home away from home. "We are near museums, the art gallery, the bar and club district, and Lake Ontario," says one satisfied senior. "There are quite a few shops in the area and the Eaton Centre is just a subway ride away." Shopping is a favorite pastime, as are movies and excursions to the shores of Lake Ontario. Students also support a wide array of volunteer programs.

Toronto fields numerous varsity sports teams; popular sports include hockey, basketball, and soccer. Still, "school spirit is a little low," says a junior. "I believe that this is because so many people commute and only come to school for classes." Rivals include Queen's University and Western Ontario. Intramural competition is popular, and many students can be found cheering the Toronto Raptors, the city's professional basketball team.

Top students (and there are many!) vie for 2,400 admission scholarships and 2,000 in-course awards.

A junior acknowledges that those coming to U of T "must be prepared for a large campus with thousands of students," but goes on to say that "most people are friendly and so relationships are easy to form." Though the mammoth campus can seem daunting at first, those who are willing to take their academic lives

Overlaps

York University, Queen's University, McGill University, University of Western Ontario.

by the reins will be rewarded with an exceptional educational experience and a wealth of friends. "People who enjoy academic activities should come here," asserts a sophomore. "We have everything!"

If You Apply To ➤ **University of Toronto**…Early decision: Feb. 1. Regular admissions: Mar. 1. Guarantees to meet demonstrated need (for Canadian residents). No campus or alumni interviews. SATs or ACTs: required. SAT IIs: required. Accepts the Common Application. No essay question.

Carleton College

100 South College Street, Northfield, MN 55057

Website: www.carleton.edu

Location: Small city

Total Enrollment: 1,882

Undergraduates: 1,882

Male/Female: 47/53

SAT Ranges: V 650–740 M 640–720

ACT Range: 28–32

Financial Aid: 51%

Expense: Pr $ $ $ $

Phi Beta Kappa: Yes

Applicants: 3,457

Accepted: 47%

Enrolled: 32%

Grad in 6 Years: 89%

Returning Freshmen: 95%

Academics: ✏ ✏ ✏ ✏ ✏

Social: ☎ ☎ ☎

Q of L: ★ ★ ★

Admissions: (800) 995-2275

Email Address: admissions@acs.carleton.edu

Strongest Programs:
Mathematics
Computer Science
Chemistry
Physics

Minnesota is many things: the land of 10,000 lakes, home to the massive Mall of America, birthplace of lore from Hiawatha to Paul Bunyan, and proud parent of the Mississippi River. Beyond all that history book stuff, tucked into a small town in the southeastern corner of the state, is Carleton College, possibly the best liberal arts school in the expansive Midwest. Classes are tiny, professors enthusiastic, and students itching to explore academia and the world beyond their doorstep. "I've grown by leaps and bounds as a scholar in this environment," one senior confirms.

Surrounded by rolling farmland, Carleton's 900-acre campus is in the tiny town of Northfield, whose one-time status as the center of the Holstein cattle industry brought it the motto "The City of Cows, Colleges and Contentment." Lakes, woods, and streams abound, and you can traverse them on 12 miles of hiking and cross-country skiing trails. The city boasts of its fragrant lilacs in spring, rich summer greens, red maples in the fall, and glistening blanket of white in winter. There's even a 400-acre arboretum, put to good use by everyone from jogging jocks to bird-watching nature lovers. When it's -8 degrees, the new indoor recreation center provides a rock-climbing wall, gym, putting green, sports courts, track, and dance studio. Carleton's architectural style is somewhat eclectic—everything from Victorian to contemporary, but mostly red brick.

Carleton's top-notch academic programs are no less varied: The sciences—biology, physics, astronomy, chemistry, geology, and computer science—are among the best anywhere, and scores of Carleton graduates go on to earn Ph.D.s in these areas each year. Of all the liberal arts schools in the country, Carleton's undergrads were recently awarded the highest number of National Science Foundation fellowships for graduate studies. English, history, economics, and biology get high marks, too. Engineers can opt for a 3–2 program with Columbia University or Washington University in St. Louis, and for geologists seeking fieldwork—and maybe wanting to thaw out after a long Minnesota winter—Carleton sponsors a program in Death Valley. Closer to home at the "arb," as the arboretum is affectionately known, environmental studies majors have their own wilderness field station, which includes a prairie-restoration site. At the opposite end of the academic spectrum, the arts also flourish. Music and studio art majors routinely get into top graduate programs, even though Carleton lacks a conservatory and doesn't emphasize performance, a music major says.

Distribution requirements ensure that a Carleton education exposes students not only to rigor and depth in their chosen field, but also to "a wide range of subjects and methods of studying them," administrators say. All students must show proficiency in English composition and a foreign language while fulfilling requirements in four broad areas: arts and literature; history, philosophy and religion; social sciences; and math and natural sciences. There's also a Recognition of Affirmation and Difference requirement, under which students must take at least one course dealing with a non-Western culture, and a senior comprehensive project is required in every major field. Carleton offers interdisciplinary programs in Asian, Jewish, urban, African and African American, and women's studies. A new concentration in Cross-Cultural Studies brings in foreign students to discuss global issues and dynamics with their American counterparts. A biochemistry major has been added, while Social Thought has been dropped. Nearly 70 percent of students spend at least one term abroad, and many take advantage of programs available either through numerous organizations, including Carleton and the Associated Colleges of the Midwest.* The school's 799,000-volume library is bright and airy, but students would like to see it stay open past midnight. Students love the four-year-old center for mathematics and computing, which brought together all campus computing functions for the first time.

With highly motivated students and a heavy workload, Carleton isn't your typical mellow Midwestern liberal arts college. The trimester calendar means finals may be just three months apart, and almost everyone feels the pressure. "Carleton is a place where academics come first and foremost," a history major says. Nearly a third of all classes have 10 students or fewer, so Carls are expected to participate actively. Carleton's faculty members are very committed to teaching. "They are very skilled in their areas, and they know how to challenge their students without talking over them," says a senior. "Freshman are always taught by full professors and immediately feel like a vital component of the Carleton environment."

Eighty percent of Carleton's students hail from outside Minnesota, half are from outside the Midwest and most attended public schools. Both coasts are heavily represented, and 15 foreign countries send at least one student. Blacks and Hispanics account for 7 percent of the total student body, and Asian Americans for another 9 percent. But most Carls have a few things in common, such as being intellectually curious yet laid back, individualistic but into building a community feel on campus. Their earthy dress and attitude are very distinguishable from their more traditional crosstown cousins at rival St. Olaf College. The Carleton campus is rather left of center, concerned with issues including the environment, multiculturalism and affirmative action, gay rights, and sexism. One senior notes, however, that incoming classes seem to be getting more conservative. About 80 students receive Carleton-sponsored National Merit and National Achievement scholarships every year, and students call financial aid packages "definitely adequate." Carleton is need-blind for all but 10 percent of applicants, and guarantees to meet the full demonstrated need of all admits.

Campus accommodations range from comfortable old dorms to modern hotel-like residence halls. Everyone is guaranteed a room for four years, although "it can be difficult to get the exact room you want," a wise senior explains. "You have to be flexible." Best of all are the 10 college-owned off-campus "theme"

(Continued)
English
History
Economics
Psychology

A new concentration in Cross-Cultural Studies debuted in the fall of 2000, bringing together diverse students in team-taught seminars to address global issues and dynamics. The first year's theme, "Asia in Comparative Perspective," brought in students from Asia to spend four years at Carleton with their American counterparts.

houses, which focus on special interests such as foreign languages, the outdoors, or nuclear-power issues. With the exception of the Farm House, an environmental studies house sitting on the edge of the arb, all the theme houses (including Women's Awareness House) are situated in an attractive residential section of town close to campus. Dorms are coed by room, but there are two halls with single-sex floors. Davis is the recommended dorm, although Burton enjoys a "fun" reputation. Everyone who stays on campus must be on a meal plan, and dining-room fare is "getting better," a music major says.

Absent a Greek system, Carleton's social life tends to be relaxed and informal and often centers on going out with friends. People go to parties on campus, or if they are of drinking age, bar hop around town. "There are very diverse happenings on any given weekend evening," says a senior. There are activities for those who pass on imbibing; a group called Co-op sponsors dances and Wednesday socials every two weeks, free movies, and special events like Comedy Night. Students agree that Carleton makes little more than token efforts to enforce the drinking age. "A few people are problem drinkers, a few never drink, most drink responsibly and socially," which goes for underage students, too. And a history major adds "there is no pressure to participate in anything you don't want to do." Northfield itself is a quaint, history-filled town with a population of about 17,000. There are old-style shops and a beautiful old hotel. "It's a great place to feel safe and sound," a senior sighs. "It's steeped in tradition and Minnesota friendliness." Students often frequent the St. Olaf College campus and a night spot known as the Reub'n'Stein. Minneapolis–St. Paul, 35 miles to the north, is a popular road-trip destination. Since students aren't allowed to have cars on campus, Carleton charters buses three times daily, seven days a week.

About a third of the students play on varsity teams, but about two-thirds play intramurals. The track, swimming, tennis, and basketball, and baseball teams are competitive, as are the championship cross-country ski teams. Popular events include the fall Reggae Fest, the Spring Concert, and Mai-F'te, a gala celebrated on an island in one of the two lakes on campus. Traditions include the weeklong freshman orientation program, where—during opening convocation—students bombard professors with bubbles as the faculty members process. There's also the annual spring softball game that begins at 5:30 A.M. and runs as many innings as there are years in Carleton's existence. The all-campus 10:00 P.M. scream on the eve of final exams keeps fatigued studiers awake. Notorious outlaw Jesse James failed to rob the Northfield Bank, lo those many years ago, and Carleton still celebrates with a Wild West bank raid reenactment every year. (The robbery was thwarted by brave townsfolk, and the gang broke up immediately afterwards.)

It can be cold in Minnesota, in a face-stinging, bone-chilling kind of way. And the classes are far from easy. But Carleton is a warm campus, and the academics are challenging without being impossible. Carls toe the line between individuality and community, which makes for personal growth and lifelong friendships. "The people you debate with in the dining hall on Friday afternoon are the same people you party with on Friday night," a senior says. It seems Carleton provides all the ingredients for a promising college career.

Overlaps

Williams, Macalester, Brown, Swarthmore, Northwestern.

If You Apply To ➤ **Carleton**…Early decision: Nov. 15, Jan. 15. Regular admissions: Jan. 15. Financial aid: Feb. 1. Guarantees to meet demonstrated need. Campus interviews: recommended, evaluative. Alumni interviews: optional, informational. SATs or ACTs: required. SAT IIs: recommended. Accepts the Common Application and electronic applications. Essay question: turning points in your life; influential people; lunch with anyone; integrating classroom learning into daily life; or your own question.

Carnegie Mellon University

5000 Forbes Avenue, Pittsburgh, PA 15213-3890

The high drama of Shakespeare and the fast-paced dot-com world are both played out on the academic stages of Carnegie Mellon, a university known for its science majors as well as its strong drama and music programs. But students can't get by with a narrow course of study—Carnegie Mellon continues to make every effort to offer both its technical and liberal arts students a well-rounded education that requires a lot of hard work but promises great results.

Carnegie Mellon was formed by the merger of Carnegie Tech and the Mellon Institute, resulting in a self-contained 103-acre campus that is attractively situated in Pittsburgh's affluent Oakland section. Next door is the city's largest park and its major museum, named after—you guessed it—Carnegie. Campus buildings range from early-1900s Beaux Arts style to contemporary eyesores. Construction was recently completed on the Purcell Center for the Arts, and work continues on an addition for the School of Computer Science and an addition to the Graduate School for Industrial Administration.

Carnegie Mellon is divided into six undergraduate colleges: Fine Arts, Humanities and Social Sciences, the Carnegie Institute of Technology, the Mellon College of Science, the School of Computer Science, and the School of Industrial Management. Each has its own distinct character and admission requirements, so applicants may want to contact the admissions office to find out about the varying policies. All the colleges, however, share the university's commitment to what it calls a "liberal-professional" education, which makes the liberal arts extremely relevant while stressing courses that develop technical skills and good job prospects. Humanities and social science types can major in applied history, professional writing, or public policy, for example, instead of traditional disciplinary concentrations. Under the University Choice Program, a select group of students is allowed to design an individualized freshman-year course of study directed toward their particular interest and can defer the selection of a major until sophomore year. In addition, the Fifth-Year Scholars program provides full tuition for outstanding students who want to remain at CMU for an additional year to pursue a course of study that interests them.

Most departments at Carnegie Mellon are strong, but exceptional ones include chemical and electrical engineering. While some humanities courses are praised, most students agree that CMU is definitely more of a science-oriented school. Each college requires core work from freshmen; in the College of Humanities and Social Science, for example, students are introduced to computers in a required first-year philosophy course, using the machines to work on problems of logic. Two majors—logic and computation in the philosophy department, and cognitive science through the psychology department—combine computer science technology with such fields as artificial intelligence and linguistics. The university created a Department of Modern Languages and a Bachelor of Science and Arts degree program was added recently along with a Science and Humanities Scholars Program.

As one English major bluntly puts it, the academic climate at CMU is "very competitive with rigorous courses across all of the majors." The College of Fine Arts' drama department, the first and still one of the best in the country, concentrates on performance, and its faculty is made up of highly regarded working professionals. While the program embraces the art of performance, freshman

Website: www.cmu.edu
Location: City outskirts
Total Enrollment: 8,436
Undergraduates: 5,136
Male/Female: 66/34
SAT Ranges: V 600–700 M 670–760
ACT Range: 27–32
Financial Aid: 80%
Expense: Pr $ $ $
Phi Beta Kappa: Yes
Applicants: 14,114
Accepted: 38%
Enrolled: 24%
Grad in 6 Years: 78%
Returning Freshmen: 92%
Academics: ✑ ✑ ✑ ✑
Social: ☎ ☎ ☎
Q of L: ★ ★ ★
Admissions: (412) 268-2082
Email Address:
undergraduate-admissions@andrew.cmu.edu

Strongest Programs:
Computer Science
Engineering
Drama
Music
Industrial Management
Business
Architecture

must take English and history as well as a basic computer course. After that it's drama all day, every day. Students at CMU work hard, no doubt about it. "There is definitely an emphasis here on students' happiness, as many find the workload overwhelming," says a biology and chemical engineering double major. However, nearly all the classes are small, with fewer than 30 students. Most students agree that the Carnegie Institute of Technology is by far the most difficult college. Professors rate high with most students, who praise their availability and willingness to help. "My professors have always been extremely dedicated to and interested in their students," a senior says.

Carnegie Mellon's professional focus shows through in its internship program. A number of five-year, dual degree options exist, including a joint BS/MS or a co-op program in metallurgical engineering and materials science that places students in the metals industry. Other engineers and scientists vie for a spot in the Junior Year in Switzerland Program. Humanities and social sciences students can spend a semester in England, and political science majors can go to Washington. One innovative program allows students to receive a bachelor's degree, teaching certificate, and master's degree within five years. But to counteract the tendency toward a narrow, preprofessional focus, the university-wide core curriculum requires courses such as fundamentals of the art of communication, fundamentals of computing, and foundations of human thought and values. The idea is to give students with diverse interests a shared intellectual background. As Herbert Simon, the Nobel Prize-winning economist who helped design the core curriculum, puts it, "We want to provide some common topics of conversation besides sports, the weather, and sex."

Nevertheless, Carnegie Mellon remains one of the most fragmented campuses in the nation. Students divide themselves into the actors, dancers, and other artsy types and the engineers, scientists, and architects. In any case, students are united in their quest for a good job after graduation. Still, many complain about the fact that students will give up sleep to study, and that this kind of academic orientation can often hinder social life. There are "too many stressed out people who don't know how to have fun," one junior gripes.

Once a very regional institution, drawing mostly Pennsylvania residents, Carnegie Mellon now counts about 70 percent of its students from out of state. Nearly one-third are from minority groups, including 20 percent Asian-American, 3 percent African-American, 5 percent Hispanic. "We are very diverse and therefore very culturally aware," a biology major says. Censorship of Internet newsgroups, because some provide access to "cyberporn," has garnered national headlines and stirred up student protests. Other students say a big issue is the nearly two-to-one male to female ratio. The university says it remains committed to need-blind admissions, but it provides larger proportions of outright grants in financial aid packages to "academic superstars." CMU has also stopped guaranteeing to meet the financial need of all accepted students, but now offers an early evaluation of financial aid eligibility for interested prospective students. The financial aid office encourages students who have received more generous packages from competing schools to let CMU know so they have an opportunity to match or better them.

Housing, which is guaranteed for all four years, offers old and newer buildings, the most popular being university-owned apartments. Upperclassmen get first pick, with freshman assignments coming from a lottery of the remainder. "The dorms are very comfortable, 80 percent have private bathrooms," a senior says. "Students do opt to live off-campus, usually because it's cheaper." The best dorms for freshmen are Donner, Resnik, and Morewood Gardens. Most halls are coed, but a few are men-only. Students can remain in campus housing as long as they wish, and nearly 70 percent do so each year. Meal plans are said to be restrictive and expensive.

With all the academic pressure at CMU, it's a good thing there are so many opportunities to unwind, especially with the entire city of Pittsburgh close at hand. The Greek system provides the most visible form of on-campus social life, and 22 percent of the students belong. For those who choose not to fraternize, coffeehouses, inexpensive films, dances, and concerts in nearby Oakland, plus downtown Pittsburgh itself (opera, ballet, symphony, concerts, sporting events just 20 minutes away by bus) provide plenty of alternatives. Once every four years the College of Fine Arts sponsors the Beaux Arts Ball, an absolutely amazing all-night masquerade party. The administration is desperately trying to curtail underage drinking, so far with only modest success. Some students say the penalties for being caught are harsh, but others maintain that the rules are "vaguely known."

One event that brings everyone together is the Spring Carnival, when the school shuts down for a day and a big top is constructed in a parking lot. Students set up booths with electronic games, and fraternities race in buggies made of lightweight alloys designed by engineering majors. Students put on original "Scotch and Soda" presentations, two of which—Pippin and Godspell—went on to become Broadway hits. But in a sports-crazed town like Pittsburgh, Carnegie Mellon's Division III varsity teams often have trouble getting attention. "I had to pass out flyers to try to get people to attend the football game Homecoming weekend!" laments a cheerleader. Both the men's and women's soccer teams recently won divisional championships.

CMU appeals to those yearning for the bright lights of Broadway or the glowing computer screens of the scientific and business worlds. "Everyone at CMU is the best at what they do," one student says. "This makes the university very work-oriented as everyone is dedicated and talented." And with a broad range of liberal arts and technical courses available and required, there's no doubt students leave CMU with a well-rounded education as well as an impressive diploma.

A number of five-year, dual degree options exist, including a joint BS/MS or a co-op program in metallurgical engineering and materials science.

Overlaps

MIT, Cornell University, Penn, Stanford, Northwestern.

If You Apply To ➤ **Carnegie Mellon**...Early decision: Nov. 15 (Nov. 1 for fine arts applicants). Regular admissions: Jan. 1. Financial aid: Feb. 15 (priority). Does not guarantee to meet demonstrated need. Campus interviews: recommended, evaluative. Alumni interviews: optional, evaluative. SATs or ACTs: required. SAT IIs: required (varies by college). Essay question: personal statement.

Case Western Reserve University

P.O. Box 128016, Cleveland, OH 44112-8016

Leave the Commodore 64 at home. Case Western Reserve University is a high-tech, computer savvy campus where the arts and sciences meet to create an intellectually stimulating environment. CWRU offers a "good intellectual community and lots of opportunities to be involved in whatever your interests are," says a junior.

Case Western Reserve is located on the eastern edge of Cleveland at University

Website: www.cwru.edu
Location: Urban
Total Enrollment: 9,601
Undergraduates: 3,598
Male/Female: 60/40

(Continued)

SAT Ranges: V 590–710 M 630–730

ACT Range: 26–31

Financial Aid: 58%

Expense: Pr $ $

Phi Beta Kappa: Yes

Applicants: 4,650

Accepted: 71%

Enrolled: 23%

Grad in 6 Years: 73%

Returning Freshmen: 92%

Academics: ✎ ✎ ✎ ✎

Social: ☎ ☎

Q of L: ★ ★ ★

Admissions: (216) 368-4450

Email Address

admission@po.cwru.edu

Strongest Programs:

Engineering

Accounting

Anthropology

Biology

Physics

Music

Psychology

Nursing

All aboard: CWRU students can study abroad in countries including Australia, Denmark, Ghana, Ireland, Israel, Japan, Poland, Spain, and Thailand.

Circle, an artistic 550-acre area of parks and gardens that is home to more than 40 cultural, educational, medical, and research institutions. The buildings represent an eclectic mix of architectural styles, and several are listed on the National Register of Historic Places. Recent construction includes a $20 million project to renovate the residence halls, a new Center for Science Education and Research, and a new building for the School of Management.

Since the marriage between Case Institute of Technology and Western Reserve University in 1967, the university is composed of the College of Arts and Sciences and the Case School of Engineering. Students choose from three cores to fulfill their general education requirements: the Case Core emphasizes mathematics and science; the Western Reserve Core provides a broader base of courses, including the humanities and the arts; and the Arts and Science core includes courses in writing and cultural diversity. Only after students declare their majors are they formally enrolled in either of the colleges.

Among the strongest academic programs in the College of Arts and Sciences are anthropology, art history (conducted with the adjoining Cleveland Museum of Art), management, music (linked with the nearby Cleveland Institute of Music), and psychology. The Case School of Engineering boasts one of the world's first departments in biomedical engineering. Other leading programs include mechanical and aerospace engineering, macromolecular science, mathematics, and physics. As testimony to CWRU's outstanding programs in polymer science and in materials science and engineering, the university received a grant from NASA for the study of materials in space. There are majors in both computer engineering and computer science. Students cite English, philosophy, and the languages as being weak and "often overshadowed by engineering and science." New majors include engineering physics, mathematics, Japanese studies, and women's studies.

Classes tend to be smaller and professors more accessible at the College of Arts and Sciences than at Case School of Engineering. The administration explains that engineering students find their professors more accessible as they move out of the introductory courses and focus on a specialty. The typical advanced class is limited to 20 students, and professors often encourage their students to participate in conducting research.

Students at CWRU work their tails off, even when lake-effect snow dumps a foot of white stuff to blanket the campus. Students stay up late to complete their work, a senior says. An economics major adds, "There's no grade-inflation going on here, and there aren't any blow-off classes." Some even take six or seven courses in one semester. Academic competition exists, but does not rule the campus. And while it would seem that mixing engineering types with liberal arts majors would be chemically and intellectually impossible, all insist that groups mix, especially when students load up with double (and even triple) majors.

Most CWRU students have their eyes on the prize that comes after graduation, which makes pre-professional majors a big hit. The university offers five-year integrated BA/MA degree programs, and the Senior Year in Absentia program lets enterprising students substitute their final undergrad year for their first year of professional school. The best bet of all may be the Preprofessional Scholars program, in which top freshmen who plan careers in law, business, medicine, dentistry, or social work are given conditional acceptance into the CWRU professional schools in their fields. "The opportunity to get involved with faculty, corporations, research, and other career opportunities is a valuable commodity not commonly found at other institutions," explains a biology and psychology double major.

Approximately 70 percent of the freshmen come from the top tenth of their high school class, and 37 percent come from outside Ohio. Asian Americans make up 13 percent of the student body, African Americans make up 5 percent, and Hispanics 2 percent. The school stresses respect for diversity and has developed a university-wide program called Share the Vision, designed to foster respect for different values, ideas, opinions, and ethnic, cultural, and racial differences. Although CWRU students are highly motivated toward their careers, it doesn't prevent them from donating their time to a worthy cause or two. Habitat for Humanity and activities organized through Alpha Phi Omega are popular options.

Case Western Reserve offers students a wide variety of possibilities for meeting costs. The university distributes more than 400 merit scholarships per year, ranging from $500 to full tuition. No athletic scholarships are offered. A four-day orientation gets freshmen up to speed on Case Western Reserve life, and students desiring a longer introduction can attend an optional three-day camp just before the regular program. Students seem generally satisfied with the housing situation at CWRU (73 percent live on campus). "Most of the dorms have recently been renovated and thus are in good condition," a junior says. Upperclassmen seeking more sophisticated living quarters enter a room draw for better choices. Housing is coed, save for one women's dorm and several off-campus men's fraternity houses. Dedicated resident directors, who can even be frazzled law students, help undergraduates with all their needs. Apartments are available but expensive and often a long trek from campus (students say the bus service is inadequate), and financial aid awards are trimmed if students move off campus. Most students living on campus take their meals in one of three cafeterias, and have the option of purchasing snacks at one of the 12 food operations on campus. But the food typically does not draw gastronomic raves.

The city of Cleveland is singled out by most students as a major asset—at least for those who make the time to take advantage of its "cultural cornucopia" of art galleries, theaters, and restaurants. "You have to drive downtown to get anything resembling a 'college town,'" a senior advises. A car is fairly essential, a junior adds. Cleveland is home to the Rock & Roll Hall of Fame, as well as to the Indians professional baseball team. On the downside, crime is a potential problem, but a veritable fleet of police officers, security guards and campus escorts have the campus covered. In warm weather those seeking an escape need not go far: The sandy beaches of a rejuvenated Lake Erie are just a few minutes away, and the university owns a farm that's perfect for picnics and overnighters. Quaint Chagrin Falls, about a half-hour away, has many shops, restaurants and antique stores, not to mention waterfalls.

Socially, CWRU isn't exactly *Animal House*. Students are more likely to share thoughts on technology than kisses over coffee. "You may have trouble finding a date on most weekends, but if your computer crashes on a Friday night, it will be up and running by Saturday morning," says a student. Even after-class activities often have an academic flair. Engineering Week, for instance, features competitions such as the Mousetrap Car Race (all cars must run on a one-mousetrap engine) and the Egg Drop (a foolproof protective package for the tossed egg is key). The Film Society's weekend movies are popular, as are the frequent events sponsored by the University Program Board. Alcohol policies are relatively strict. "If you come here to drink, plan on transferring," one junior says. About one-third of the men and about 16 percent of women are Greek. In describing the social scene at CWRU, one student approaches it scientifically: "CWRU is like an anthill: lots of stuff happening, but you've gotta kick it around to see any of the

The new $31 million Center for Science Education and Research will house state-of-the-art labs in chemistry and biology.

Within walking distance from campus are Severance Hall, where the Cleveland Symphony Orchestra plays, the Cleveland Museum of Art, Western Reserve Historical Society, and the Cleveland Botanical Gardens. Just a few miles away is the Rock & Roll Hall of Fame.

life. If you aren't willing to kick it around, it sucks."

Sports are welcomed at CWRU, though they don't dominate campus. The wrestling team has won the University Athletic Association championship several times in recent years. CWRU also boasts that six swimmers earned All-American honors at the NCAA championships in 2000 and the women's softball team won the University Athletic Association title in 1998-99. The dorm-centered intramural program commands a high level of participation and enthusiasm. And the 26-mile Hudson Relays, held the last week of the spring semester, pit teams of runners from the four classes against one another. There's a spiffy racquetball and squash complex and a field house with an Olympic-size pool.

CWRU is always trying to better itself and enhance its already high-level academic programs. For the engineers and scientists, the university provides a stellar education to propel students to the tops of their fields. The liberal arts program is constantly evolving and CWRU students are down-to-earth and intelligent. "The university is becoming more aware of its prominence and the liberal arts programs are becoming much stronger," notes an economics and English double major. "And it has an amazing amount of smart, creative, talented, fascinating students. The challenge is to meet them."

Overlaps

Carnegie Mellon, Northwestern, Ohio State, Washington, Cornell University.

If You Apply To ➣

CWRU...Early decision: Jan. 1. Regular admissions and financial aid: Feb. 1. Housing: May 1. Does not guarantee to meet demonstrated need. Campus interviews: recommended, informational. Alumni interviews: optional, informational. SATs or ACTs: required. SAT IIs: recommended. Accepts the Common Application and electronic applications. Essay question: writing sample. Audition required for artists and musicians.

The Catholic University of America

Washington, DC 20064

Website: www.cua.edu
Location: City outskirts
Total Enrollment: 5,597
Undergraduates: 2,557
Male/Female: 46/54
SAT Ranges: V 530–640 M 520–630
ACT Range: 22–28
Financial Aid: 71%
Expense: Pr $ $
Phi Beta Kappa: Yes
Applicants: 2,604
Accepted: 88%
Enrolled: 31%
Grad in 6 Years: 70%
Returning Freshmen: 85%
Academics: ✍ ✍ ✍
Social: ☎ ☎ ☎
Q of L: ★ ★ ★

Founded in 1887 with the approval of Pope Leo XIII, The Catholic University of America was the brainchild of United States bishops who wanted to provide a world-class institution where the curriculum was guided by the tenets of Christian thought. Over time, the university has garnered a reputation as a research-oriented school that also provides a strong undergraduate, preprofessional education and an appreciation for the arts.

Catholic's campus comprises 145 tree-lined acres, an impressive layout for an urban university. Buildings range from ivy-covered brownstone and brick to ultra-modern, giving the place a true collegiate feel. Catholic is one of the few colleges in the country that began as a graduate institution, and grad students still outnumber their younger counterparts. Six of its 10 schools (arts and sciences, engineering, architecture, nursing, music, and philosophy) now admit undergrads, while two others (social service and religious studies) provide undergraduate programs through arts and sciences.

Students have excellent options in almost any department at CUA. Apart from politics (which all agree sets the tone on campus), the history, English, drama, psychology, and physics departments are very strong. Philosophy and religious studies are highly regarded and have outstanding faculty members as well. The School of Nursing is one of the best in the nation, and engineering and architecture are also highly regarded. Architecture and physics have outstanding facilities, the latter enjoying a modern vitreous-state lab, a boon for both research and hands-on undergraduate instruction. Also, a high-speed fiber optic network connects the entire campus to the Internet. For students interested in the arts, CUA's School of Music offers excellent vocal and instrumental training, and there's also a program in musical theater. Students cite communications and business as weaker than others.

Students at CUA need at least 40 courses in order to graduate. In the School of Arts and Sciences, approximately 25 of these must be from a core curriculum spread across the humanities, social and behavioral sciences, philosophy, environmental studies, religion, math and natural sciences, and languages and literature. English composition also is required. The brightest students can enroll in a 12-course interdisciplinary honors program that offers sequences in the humanities, philosophy, and social sciences. CUA's library offers approximately 1.47 million volumes.

Standard off-campus opportunities are augmented by internships at the British and Irish parliaments, NASA, the National Institutes of Health, the Pentagon, and the Library of Congress. The School of Architecture and Planning hosts summer classes for seniors and grad students to study in Italy and a host of European and Mediterranean countries. The Rome study abroad program for design students incorporates design studio, field study, history, theory, and the Italian language. Finally, two students are chosen each year to spend a fall semester at the Fondazione Architetto Rancilio (FAAR) in Milan to study themes including architecture, urban studies, and technology. CUA also offers accelerated degree programs in which students can earn bachelor's and master's degrees in five years, or six years for a joint BA-JD. CUA is part of the 11-university Consortium of Universities of the Washington Metropolitan Area and the Oak Ridge Associated Universities consortium. The latter is comprised of 87 U.S. colleges and a contractor for the federal Energy Department. The program gives students access to federal research facilities.

Although Catholic University is research oriented, most classes have less than 25 students. That means special attention from faculty members. It also means that there's no place to hide. "The teachers push us to work hard but at the same time apply the subjects to everyday living," a history major reports. The faculty is given high marks by students. "The quality of teaching is excellent. Professors are usually very willing to help students," praises a veteran. Clergy are at the helm of certain graduate schools, but the School of Arts and Sciences has a primarily lay faculty, with priests occupying less than 15 percent of the teaching posts. Its chancellor is the archbishop of Washington, and Catholic churches across the country donate a fraction of their annual collections to the university.

Catholicism is clearly the tie that binds the student body. Sunday Masses are so well attended that extra services must be offered in the dorms. Says one administrator, "We like students to leave with Catholic values, but most of them come here with those values in the first place." Eighty-eight percent of the students belong to the faith. Most are from the Northeast, and primarily white. Blacks and Hispanics comprise 8 and 5 percent of the student body, respectively. Another 5 percent are Asian-American, and foreign students account for 5 percent. Almost all students are out-of-state, and half of freshmen rank in the top fifth of their high school class. Politically, students are fairly conservative, and the big issues on campus include abortion and gay/lesbian rights. "Everyone is basically the same at Catholic—white, upper-middle-class Catholics," says one student.

The university maintains a need-blind admissions policy. It does not guarantee to meet the full demonstrated need of all admitted, but 64 percent of aid recipients are offered full demonstrated need. Thirty-one lucky students—one

(Continued)
Admissions: (800) 673-2772
Email Address:
cua-admissions@cua.edu

Strongest Programs:
Nursing
Philosophy
Drama
Architecture
Music
Greek and Latin
Physics
Engineering

A 15-minute Metro ride brings students to the center of downtown D.C. and the Capitol. Georgetown, bustling with great shopping, bars, restaurants, and art galleries, is only a half-hour away.

Design students can study in Rome for one semester accompanied by a design studio critic from the School of Architecture and Planning. The program focuses on history, theory, design, and the Italian language.

from each archdiocese in the nation—receive a full-tuition merit scholarship. There are 562 additional merit scholarships available ranging from $1,000 to $19,100, along with various types of financial aid. There are no athletic scholarships.

Sixty-four percent of the students live in the dorms, seven of which are coed by floor. The spacious and ultramodern Centennial Village (eight dorms and 600 beds laid out in suites) is available to all students, many of whom flee CUA's strict visitation (no guests past 2:00 A.M.) and alcohol policies and move into apartments of their own. Best dorms for freshmen are Spellman and Flather (coed), and Conaty (women). Dorm food is fairly tasty, and there's always the Rathskeller, or Rat, the campus bar and grill where students can get a late-night meal or brunch and dinner on weekends. Emergency phones, shuttle buses, and escort services are provided as part of campus security, and students agree that they always feel safe on campus as long as they are careful.

When students want to explore the city, they need only walk to the campus Metro stop and then enjoy the ride. Capitol Hill is 15 minutes away; the stylish Georgetown area, with its chic restaurants and night spots, is only a half-hour away. CUA students do indulge in some serious partying. Some of their favorite locales include the Irish Times, Colonel Brook Tavern, the Tune Inn, and Kitty's. Its no wonder most students agree that the social scene is "off campus at various bars, clubs, and coffeehouses in D.C. Only 1 percent of the men and 1 percent of the women join the Greek system. No one under 21 can drink on campus, and most students agree that this policy is effective in curbing underage drinking. Also, alcohol "abuse" has been added as an offense in addition to use, possession, and distribution. For those eager to repent the weekend's excesses, there are student ministry retreats. Annual festivals on the campus calendar include a weeklong Homecoming celebration, Beaux Arts Ball, Christmas Holly Hop (held in New York City), and Spring Fling. A time-honored winter tradition is sledding down Flather Hill on cafeteria trays.

Sports on campus means varsity and intramural competition. CUA's athletic teams compete in Division III, and the men's swimming team won the CACC championship during the 1998-99 and 1999-00 seasons. The men's football team won the 1999 Old Dominion Athletic Conference championship. Volleyball, field hockey, softball, and swimming are the strongest women's teams. Intramural and varsity athletes alike enjoy the beautiful $10-million sports complex. Many students use their strength for community service, including the Christian-based Habitat for Humanity, in which they build houses for needy families.

When discussions first raised the idea of a Catholic university, the man who would become the university's first Rector, Bishop John Joseph Keane, argued for an institution that would "exercise a dominant influence in the world's future" with a superior intellectual foundation. Now, more than 100 years later, CUA offers students a wealth of preprofessional courses spanning the arts and sciences. The founders' quest for "a higher synthesis of knowledge" is constantly being realized at CUA, a unique university and a capital destination.

Overlaps

American, Villanova, Georgetown, University of Scranton, George Washington.

If You Apply To > Catholic...Early action: Nov. 15. Regular admissions: Feb. 15. Financial aid: Feb. 1. Housing: June 1. Meets demonstrated need of 64%. SATs or ACTs: required. SAT IIs: required (writing and foreign language). Accepts the Common Application and electronic applications. Essay question: local, national, international issue of concern; historical figure to meet. Music applicants must audition.

Centre College

600 West Walnut, Danville, KY 40422

Located in the famed Bluegrass area near the center of Kentucky, Centre College is no doubt a David in a world of academic Goliaths. But what it lacks in size, it more than makes up for with excellent academics, outstanding professors, and top-notch facilities. In fact, Centre is the best of its breed among liberal arts colleges in the Bluegrass State, and one of higher education's best-kept secrets.

Centre's campus is a mix of old Greek Revival and attractive modern buildings, with the surrounding horse country providing a romantic backdrop. The 32,000-square-foot physical science building has helped alleviate overcrowding in the science majors, and the athletic and recreation facilities are undergoing extensive renovations.

Students report that Centre is demanding academically, but its small size gives them one big advantage. "Rarely does a class have more than 30 people in it, so the professors are able to give their students the personal attention they deserve," says a government major. A revised general education curriculum requires students to complete courses in expository writing, math, foreign language, as well as two courses in each context (aesthetic, social, scientific, fundamental questions). In addition, freshmen must participate in a first-year seminar. Professors are very highly regarded here. "Centre professors are extremely personable," says a mathematics major. "Their office doors are always open and they encourage students to visit them." Another student adds, "The teachers here are not only brilliant, but they also go out of their way to help their students succeed."

Biology, English, history, chemistry, economics, government, and art are generally considered Centre's best departments, and consequently are the most popular majors. Glassblowing enthusiasts will find one of the few fully-equipped undergraduate facilities in the nation, which is part of a strong arts program. The computing facilities, including the Unix lab, are on a continuous growth spurt to keep up with a growing demand. Among the weaker departments are the foreign languages, but students say they're improving, citing the addition of Japanese as a language option. But perhaps the biggest academic drawback at Centre is the reality that, with fewer than 1,100 students enrolled, course offerings in many areas are limited.

Nearly half of the students take advantage of the school's study abroad programs, which includes programs in London, Strasbourg, Mexico, and Ecuador. And because of Centre's 4–2–4 calendar, there are also a number of six-week winter term classes that involve group travel and opportunities to study abroad in such places as France, Vietnam, Africa, and the Bahamas. As a member of the Associated Colleges of the South,* Centre also offers its students programs in Central America. A 3–2 liberal arts and engineering program in collaboration with five major universities, including Columbia and Vanderbilt, is also available.

Many students come from middle- to upper-middle-class Kentucky families and are considered to be "preppy" and conservative. While some students claim there is little social or political activism on campus, one junior says that "Centre strives to provide an environment where an open exchange of ideas can take place." The student body is overwhelmingly white (95 percent), with African Americans accounting for 3 percent, Asian Americans 1 percent, and Hispanics less than 1 percent. Sixty-four percent of the students hail from Kentucky, and most attended public high school. Students typically head directly into the work

Website: www.centre.edu
Location: Small town
Total Enrollment: 1,022
Undergraduates: 1,022
Male/Female: 49/51
SAT Ranges: V 570–690 M 580–680
ACT Range: 25-30
Financial Aid: 60%
Expense: Pr $
Phi Beta Kappa: Yes
Applicants: 1,142
Accepted: 86%
Enrolled: 26%
Grad in 6 Years: 73%
Returning Freshmen: 87%
Academics: 🖉 🖉 🖉
Social: ☎ ☎ ☎
Q of L: ★ ★ ★
Admissions: (800)423-6236
Email Address:
admission@centre.edu

Strongest Programs:
Biology
English
Economics
Chemistry
History
Government
Studio Art

The computing facilities, including the Unix lab, are on a continuous growth spurt to keep up with a growing demand.

force after graduating, rather than attend graduate or professional schools.

Students may attend all events at the college's separately endowed Norton Center for the Arts, which brings phenomenal art, music, and drama to campus free of charge. "It's widely acclaimed as one of the best small college arts centers in the nation," boasts one student. The Carnegie Club provides fine dining and offers special theme dinners on weekends and evenings before performances. Centre offers its students academic scholarships ranging from $4,500 to a full ride. Yet because of Centre's relatively small private price tag, even those who have to pay the full price feel they're getting a bargain compared to other liberal arts colleges.

Virtually all of Centre's students live on campus. Freshmen occupy single-sex dorms, while upperclassmen have the option of living in halls that are coed by floor. Hillside is divided into separate six-person units, each with three bedrooms and a living room. Students say the dorms are "big, clean, and kept in very good condition," and are also "close to everything." An apartment was recently purchased and remodeled to provide additional housing and nine new fraternity and sorority houses have created another favored living option for the 60 percent of men and 65 percent of women who belong to the Greek system. Everyone eats together in the main dining hall, Cowan Dining Commons. Though students have complained about the food in the past, improvements made to the facility have brought with them improvements in the cuisine. Meal plans range from 10 meals to 19, meals and a flexible-dollar spending option is available as well. The surrounding community provides several decent restaurants when students really need a break.

Centre's social life is overwhelmingly located on campus. Informal socializing in the dorms is the primary alternative to Greek parties, though "the fraternities have open parties to which everyone is invited." Lexington is a popular draw on weekends for dates and films, as well as shopping. Fortunately, with the addition of a bridge and roadway, the city is now only a 30-minute drive away. And road trips to the countryside are also popular, where there are plenty of places to go camping and fishing. Other quaint traditions include a serenade for the president by the senior women in their bath towels and faculty Christmas caroling for the freshmen. Then there's the long-held tradition of "Running the Flame," which has students running from the fraternity houses, around a sculpture and back— "naked, of course." Although the college is in a dry county and the nearest bar is 30 miles away, the campus has a unique alcohol policy, which students refer to as the "unoriginal container" policy. Basically, students must drink out of cups rather than out of bottles and cans. "If you have your drink in a cup and are acting responsibly, no one will ask you how old you are," reports one student. Men's soccer and women's cross-country and basketball have been the most successful sports in recent years, competing in Division III of the NCAA. Centre's football team has been around for over 100 years but there's one moment in its history that outshines them all. In 1921, Centre beat then-powerhouse Harvard, 6–0, an event that has been called the greatest sports upset in the first half of the 20th century. Although the football team has lost the national spotlight, its still fairly competitive on the Division III level. Students love to brag most about Centre's expansive intramural program.

Centre seems to relish its role as the David among larger schools. With its long and rich history spanning more than 180 years, Centre has put the bigger, more well-known schools on notice that they haven't heard the last from this small college. "Our reputation is growing as well as our student body and the administration is constantly making the improvements needed to keep up," says a biology major. Another student sums it up this way: "Centre is on the move and headed in one direction...up!"

If You Apply To ➤

Centre…Early action: Dec.1. Early decision: Nov. 15. Regular admissions: Feb. 1. Financial aid: Mar. 1. Does not guarantee to meet demonstrated need. Campus interviews: recommended, evaluative for admission; required for scholarships. Alumni interviews: optional, evaluative. SATs or ACTs: required. SAT IIs: optional (writing). Essay question: personal statement.

College of Charleston

Charleston, SC 29424

Charleston, South Carolina: The name itself conjures up images of rich history rooted in deep Southern charm. Founded in 1770 as Colonial South Carolina's first college, this school expects to become, far and above, the finest public liberal arts and sciences institution in South Carolina and among the finest in the Southeast. Walking amid mansions on tree-lined, cobblestone streets, students truly value the beauty of the campus as well as the sense of culture provided by the deep South. And, of course, the education provided by the College of Charleston.

Located in Charleston's famous Historical District, the campus features many of the city's most historic and venerable buildings. Over 80 of its buildings are former private residences ranging from typical Charleston "single" house to the Victorian. The campus has received countless regional, state, and local awards for its design, and has been designated a national arboretum. Although the students complain that the current library is small, construction recently began on a new state-of-the-art library.

C of C has a core curriculum based strongly in the liberal arts and focuses on the development of writing, computing, language acquisition, and thinking skills. Each student is required to complete 6 hours in English, history, mathematics or logic, and social science, 8 hours in natural sciences, and 12 hours in humanities and a modern or classical foreign language. Biology and chemistry are two of the strongest programs; many of the graduates end up at the Medical University of South Carolina a few blocks down the street. Marine biology is also strong, and students use the South Carolina marshes and beaches for a research laboratory. The most popular major is business administration, followed by communication, biology, elementary education, and psychology. Arts management, historic preservation, and international business are among the most recent additions to the curriculum. Many of the new performing arts majors take advantage of internship opportunities with Charleston's annual Spoleto Music Festival. Study-abroad options include the International Student Exchange Program and the Sea Semester.*

The academic climate at C of C is challenging but not cutthroat. The majority of classes at the college are limited to 25 students and students report the quality

Website: www.cofc.edu
Location: Urban
Total Enrollment: 11,624
Undergraduates: 9,713
Male/Female: 37/63
SAT Ranges: V 530–620 M 520–610
ACT Range: 21–26
Financial Aid: 76%
Expense: Pub $ $
Phi Beta Kappa: No
Applicants: 7,313
Accepted: 45%
Enrolled: 43%
Grad in 6 Years: 52%
Returning Freshmen: 81%
Academics: ✑ ✑ ✑
Social: ☎ ☎ ☎
Q of L: ★ ★ ★ ★
Admissions: (843) 953-5670
Email Address: admissions@cofc.edu

Strongest Programs
Business
Communications
Biology
Psychology
Education

of teaching is excellent. "The professors at C of C are not only knowledgeable and caring, they are inspirational," boasts a Spanish major.

Nearly a third of the students hail from out of state, and about half graduated in the top fifth of their high school class. Eighty percent attended public high school. Asian-Americans and Hispanics combine to make up less than 3 percent of the student body, and African Americans make up another 8 percent. Many students report that diversity is greatly valued, while others feel that racism is a concern on campus. In order to enhance diversity, C of C has initiated several new programs and policies dealing with the issues of race, sexual harassment and physical safety along with many others that are already in place. The college offers hundreds of merit scholarships, as well as athletic scholarships in nine sports. A payment plan allows students to spread the cost of tuition over the course of the semester, a handy option some 20 percent of the students take advantage of.

Lack of dorm space is one of C of C's biggest problems. "The dorms are not so great," says a freshman. "They are very hard to get and there's too little room for too many people." To be sure to get a room, students advise you apply early. Late applicants are doomed to scour Charleston for rooms, which are usually expensive. And even if you're lucky enough to get on-campus housing, some students report that many of the dorms need to be renovated.

No matter where they live, students enjoy Charleston, with its festivals, plays, and scenic plantations and gardens. "With so much history and tradition surrounding the campus, there's always something new to discover," says a psychology major. "The social life is great," says one political science major. "The only problem is trying to figure out which activity to choose." There are social events such as movies and plays for students to enjoy on campus as well as all that the town of Charleston has to offer. Students party off campus in local clubs and apartments as well as on campus where 15 percent of the men and 19 percent of the women belong to frats and sororities, respectively. Due to a well-enforced policy on drinking, students report that it is difficult to be served on campus if you are not 21, but off campus is not a problem. Women outnumber men by almost two to one, but females looking to beat the odds can always go to the Medical University of South Carolina or the Citadel Military College, which are both in Charleston. A very old tourist town, "Charleston is not very receptive to the students," complains a senior, and another says that the school's biggest problem is that some people in the historic district are very rude to the students. Based on your tastes, however, you may find the historic quality charming and inspiring. On weekends, students head for "the Grand Strand," Myrtle Beach, which lies 90 miles north, or head south to Savannah and Hilton Head. Others enjoy taking a journey out of state to Georgia or North Carolina.

While by no means a campus obsession, athletics are relatively popular. There is no football team but sailing is gaining popularity with the recent construction of a new sailing center. Soccer and basketball are two of the favorite spectator sports. In 1991 the college moved into the NCAA's tough Division I and it has taken a few years to adjust to the stiffer competition.

"Not only is C of C located on a beautifully historical campus but the professors are challenging and the social life is great," boasts a physical education major. Whether hitting the streets or hitting the books, students at the College of Charleston have a lot to be happy about.

Overlaps

University of South Carolina, Clemson, University of Georgia, Winthrop, Coastal Carolina.

If You Apply To > College of Charleston...Early action: Dec. 1. Regular admissions: June 1. Financial aid: Mar. 15. Does not guarantee to meet demonstrated need. Campus interviews: optional, informational. No alumni interviews. SATs or ACTs: required. SAT IIs: optional. Accepts the Common Application. Essay question: optional, personal statement.

University of Chicago

1116 East 59th Street, Chicago, IL 60637

The University of Chicago attracts a very specific kind of student: one eager to eschew the superficial trappings of Ivy League prestige; one who is much more passionate about physics or Plato than about finding a great party. "This is a place that has always been very proud of its nerdiness," boasts a senior. But this kind of intellectual intensity doesn't come without a price. "People are scared to come here because they think that it's only a place for geeks and dorks, and that we don't have any fun," says a student. "We have a very low application rate and a very high attrition rate, which hurts the school's reputation." UC's administration has responded by launching a controversial campaign to make the school more attractive to high school seniors. The core curriculum has been reduced, and plans include increasing the undergraduate population, building new recreational facilities, and expanding student activities. "The administration has taken many steps to make the college a more fun place to go to school," says a sophomore.

Chicago's 190-acre tree-lined campus is located in the integrated neighborhood of Hyde Park, an eclectic community on the South Side of Chicago surrounded by low-income communities on three sides and Lake Michigan on the fourth. Town-gown relations are said to be calm, and crime is no more a problem than in any other urban setting, but black students complain that they are too often mistaken for trespassers by local police. The campus itself is self-contained and architecturally magnificent. The main quads are steel-gray Gothic—gargoyles and all—and the newer buildings are by Eero Saarinen, Mies van der Rohe, and Frank Lloyd Wright.

Historically, Chicago has been recognized for its graduate programs. But administrators and faculty members alike are beginning to realize that they must concentrate on the holistic experience the school offers undergraduates if Chicago has any hope of remaining competitive with schools like Stanford, Harvard, and Princeton. On the undergraduate level, though, Chicago remains unequivocally committed to the view that a solid foundation in the liberal arts is the best foundation for any walk of life, and that theory is better than practice. Thus, music students study musicology but learn calculus along with everyone else. Indeed, half of a student's 42 courses at Chicago, regardless of major, are taken as part of general education requirements called the common core. Dubbed by one student as the "hallmark of a Chicago education," the core curriculum has undergone a controversial reduction, down from 21 courses to 15 or 18 (depending on the foreign language requirement). What used to account for half of a student's total coursework now takes up only one-third. Requirements include courses in science and math, humanities and civilization, social sciences, and a foreign language. Sound intense? It is, students say, especially because courses are

Website: www.uchicago.edu
Location: Urban
Total Enrollment: 12,327
Undergraduates: 3,917
Male/Female: 59/41
SAT Ranges: V 620–730 M 630–730
ACT Range: 27–31
Financial Aid: 59%
Expense: Pr $ $ $ $
Phi Beta Kappa: Yes
Applicants: 5,361
Accepted: 33%
Enrolled: 57%
Grad in 6 Years: N/A
Returning Freshmen: 95%
Academics: ✑ ✑ ✑ ✑ ✑
Social: ☎ ☎
Q of L: ★ ★ ★
Admissions: (773) 702-8650
Email Address: college-admissions@uchicago.edu

Strongest Programs:
  Economics
  English
  Sociology
  Anthropology
  Political Science
  Geography
  Geophysical Science
  History
  Linguistics
  Mathematics

crammed into 11-week quarters, rather than 13- or 14-week semesters. In addition to the core, seniors are encouraged to undertake final-year projects, which need not be in their area of concentration (although 99 percent of the time they are).

Chicago's brilliant and distinguished faculty is certainly its greatest asset. And although U of C was founded in the tradition of the German research universities, professors here take their teaching role quite seriously. "I have had renowned professors with years of study and experience in their fields," says a student. "In addition, lectures are informative and enjoyable." The university's dedicated professors get more time to teach and do research than they would elsewhere, since Chicago is one of the few schools in the country with full-time advisors to help students with academic and other matters. Most classes have about 25 students, and practically none are larger than 50. A computerized enrollment system makes getting into sought-after classes a little less grueling. And although classes are small, students say graduating in four years is not a problem.

The economics department, a bastion of neo-liberal or New Right thinkers, is Chicago's claim to fame and the most popular major. But biology, English, history, psychology, and political science also draw crowds. Chicago was father to both sociology and political science as scholarly disciplines, and these two programs remain among the best anywhere. The university also prides itself on outstanding interdisciplinary programs and area studies such as East Asian, South Asian, Middle Eastern, and Slavic. The New Collegiate Division of the university offers popular interdisciplinary programs such as Fundamentals: Issues and Texts, and newer majors include computer science and cinema and media studies. Students cite art and design, psychology, and foreign languages as weaker than most.

If Chicago gets too cold and snowy, students may study abroad on one of 17 programs that reach most corners of the globe. A combined-degree program also allows the most motivated premeds to earn a BA and an MD in eight years, with acceptance to Chicago's medical school occurring after the second undergrad year. Other qualified undergrads are able to register for courses in all of the university's graduate and professional schools—law, divinity, social service, public policy, humanities, social sciences, biological and physical sciences, and business. "Those who are ready can accelerate as fast as the faculty and facilities permit," explains an administrator.

Since Chicago is committed to the quarter system it pioneered, the first term starts in late September and is over by Christmas. For practical purposes, this means virtually uninterrupted work straight through the school year, a long summer vacation, and three exam weeks a year. The one concession to the work ethic is a two-day reading period between the end of classes and the beginning of exams. All five of the university's libraries are excellent, containing one of the most extensive collections in the country; "much bigger than an undergrad would ever need."

Chicago has more graduate and professional students than undergraduates, and the climate on campus reflects the lopsided ratio. Some describe it as a high-pressure "grind," but it also translates into an enormous number of research projects and a better-than-even chance that an ambitious undergraduate can get a diploma having coauthored a journal article or two. "Chicago students care about their time here, which means that a lot of students are concerned about grades, curriculum, and the quality of their education," says one student.

Only 21 percent of Chicago's student body come from Illinois; a high percentage hail from the East Coast, and many were raised in academic homes; 87 percent were in the top fifth of their high school class. Fifty-nine percent go on to further study of some kind, which is why the university is known as "teacher of teachers." Asian Americans account for a sizable 27 percent of Chicago's students, while blacks contribute 4 percent and Hispanics represent 5 percent. Both conservatives and liberals are "ably present and vocal," and interests run the gamut from government and politics to music. "Political correctness is pointedly ignored. Students simply treat each other fairly," says one junior. Most students dress in a come-as-you-are style. Freshman orientation, which the administration says was invented at U of C in 1924, is known as O Week, and it's a time when students make lasting friendships.

"We have incredible housing," boasts one student. And he's got a point, considering that one dorm, Shoreland, is a former luxury hotel located on the shore of Lake Michigan. There are 12 dorm complexes on campus, some new and sterile, others old and modeled after Cambridge or Heidelberg, and all coed by room or floor. Shoreland is the largest and most social, but it's also half a mile from campus, a definite hike when the wind is howling off the lake (from November to April). All rooms are connected to a campus-wide computer network, and some are equipped with kitchens. About two-thirds of the students live on campus, and housing is guaranteed for four years. Food is said to be "mediocre but plentiful," and while freshmen and residents of certain dorms are required to be on a full-meal contract, others can buy a meal plan or purchase individual meal coupons.

The nine fraternities and two sororities don't play a very large role in campus life, although frat parties are reasonably well attended. "Social life is very individualistic," says one student. There are two campus bars, both of which are fairly strict about not serving anyone underage, but the administration has never really cracked down on drinking, which "really isn't a social necessity here," says a student. Other weekend entertainment options on campus include low-cost flicks in the 500-seat movie theater, dorm parties, and a plethora of cultural activities. Still, one student asks, "We're in Chicago, where else should we go?" He's referring, of course, to downtown, with its internationally acclaimed symphony, museums, and other cultural facilities. Though everything is accessible by public transportation, cars are a nice luxury if you can find a parking place. With 100-plus extracurricular clubs and programs, everyone should be able to find something of interest on campus.

Robert Maynard Hutchins, the famous president of Chicago from 1929 to 1951, once opined that "having fun is a form of intelligence." As evidence that such views are acceptable, the university belongs to the University Athletic Association, which includes other academically minded schools such as Johns Hopkins and New York University. To everyone's surprise, the recently resurrected football team has already had a couple of winning seasons. Chicago fans often fill Stagg Field to its 1,500-seat capacity to support the school's teams, and the Scholarly Yell they shout out is one of the best cheers around: "Themistocles, Thucydides/The Peloponnesian Wars/X-squared, Y-squared, H2SO4/Who for, what for/Who the hell are we cheering for?/Go Maroons!"

Athletes here are well respected, and—remember, this is the University of Chicago—have a higher overall GPA than the student body as a whole; the wrestling team and women's soccer squad sport all-Americans. Both Chicago's men's and women's soccer teams have been to the Division III Final Four, while the softball team has won the UAA championship in the past. The basketball team, which has been playing since 1896, posted a 22–12 record a couple of years ago, its greatest number of victories in a single season ever. Even weekend warriors get in on the action at Chicago; intramurals attract an enthusiastic three-quarters of the student body. Hans Brinker types flock to the Midway, site of the 1893

World's Fair, which is flooded every winter for skating. In addition, there's Kuviasungnerk (the Eskimo term for happiness), an esoteric winter carnival that features ice sculptures, hockey, poetry readings, and fireside lectures on Arctic food and the meteorology of cold fronts.

U of C students take pride in both their individuality and their intellectual prowess. They come to college to flex their scholarly muscle, not raise their alcohol tolerance. They place a premium on academics, not extracurriculars, and at graduation they are rewarded for their efforts—as one says, "Once this is over, you'll be good enough to tackle anything." Film director Mike Nichols described his own years as an undergraduate here as "wide open," adding that "everybody was strange at the University of Chicago! It was paradise." Current students would likely agree.

Overlaps

Harvard, Cornell University, Stanford, Northwestern, Columbia.

If You Apply To ➤ Chicago...Early action: Nov. 15. Regular admissions: Jan. 1. Financial aid: Feb. 1. Guarantees to meet demonstrated need. Campus interviews: recommended, evaluative. Alumni interviews: optional, evaluative. SATs or ACTs: required. No SAT IIs. Essay question: something that reminds you of your past; why a newspaper story of importance interests you; improvise a story, play, or dialogue; a creative work that's a key to your worldview.

University of Cincinnati

P.O. Box 210091, Cincinnati, OH 45221-0091

Website: www.uc.edu
Location: City outskirts
Total Enrollment: 28,161
Undergraduates: 20,976
Male/Female: 52/48
SAT Ranges: V 480–600 M 480–620
ACT Range: 20–26
Financial Aid: N/A
Expense: Pub $ $ $
Phi Beta Kappa: Yes
Applicants: 7,633
Accepted: 85%
Enrolled: 46%
Grad in 6 Years: 36%
Returning Freshmen: 73%
Academics: ✍ ✍
Social: ☎ ☎ ☎
Q of L: ★ ★ ★
Admissions: (513) 556-1100
Email Address: N/A

Strongest Programs:
  Engineering

Many first-time visitors to Cincinnati are surprised to find it an attractive and most livable city. As they traverse the city's hilly roads, they are in for another surprise—its university. Not only is UC renowned for its extensive research programs, the school's co-op program is also one of the largest of any public college or university in the country.

The compact campus nudges up to the edge of the downtown area and is centered at the top of a hill. Ultramodern buildings rise up next to traditional ivy-covered Georgian halls. A major project is under way at UC to create landscaped green space, complete with an outdoor amphitheater and a 64-foot light tower. Research is a UC specialty. Campus scientists have given the world antiknock gasoline, the electronic organ, antihistamines, and the U.S. Weather Bureau. UC is also the place where, in 1906, cooperative education was born, allowing students to earn while they learn. Across the Cincinnati curriculum, there is an abundance of co-op opportunities available. In all, 42 programs offer the popular five-year professional-practice option. The hands-on experience of the university's strengths—research and co-op—offers students the opportunity to explore learning beyond the traditional classroom setting and to test the concepts that have been presented to them.

The colleges of engineering, business administration, and design, architecture, art, and planning (the schools with the most co-op students) are the best bets at UC. The university's music conservatory, one of the best state-run programs in the field, also offers broadcasting training. The schools of nursing and pharmacy are well known and benefit from UC's health center and graduate medical school. The most popular major is biology. In addition, education is a strong program. The Cincinnati Initiative for Teacher Education requires all education majors to complete a five-year program that ends in an entire year of internships in different education environments. Education students earn two bachelor's degrees: one in education and one in a liberal arts subject. Students say the criminal justice department needs to be improved. The two-year University College is Cincinnati's open-admissions unit, which prepares less-qualified students to transfer into four-year programs and offers a variety of vocational degrees, including paralegal technology and robotics.

The academic grind is determined largely by the major. Fields such as engineering, business, and nursing require a substantially larger academic commitment. "Most classes are laid back until you are admitted to your degree program," says a sophomore. Some courses end up being quite large (in popular design courses, two people to a desk is not unusual), and students say about 20 percent of their classes have up to 100 students. One fine asset is the school's huge library, which has 1.9 million volumes and is completely computerized. The computer facilities are plentiful, and most other facilities, as well as the highly respected counseling services, are more than adequate.

UC has taken steps to improve the quality of the undergraduate education by strengthening its general education requirements and expanding its honors program. Additionally, UC has adopted its Pedagogy Initiative, which allows students to interact with professors and encourages them to develop questions in the classroom. "Most professors at UC are well educated and eager to pass on their knowledge," says an industrial engineering major. Freshmen must take English and math as well as a contemporary issues class; other requirements vary by college. The expanded honors program offers smaller classes to its top students. A third of the faculty members hold outside jobs, bringing fresh practical experience to the classroom

All but 8 percent of the student body come from within the state. Despite this geographical uniformity, the UC student body is fairly diversified. There are art types and business types, liberals and conservatives. African Americans, Asian Americans, and Hispanics comprise 14, 3, and 1 percent of the student body, respectively. Diversity as well as feminine issues are the hot topics on campus. The school offers a variety of merit scholarships ranging from $750 to full tuition. There is also a selection of athletic scholarships doled among all the men's and women's teams. While students say they have noticed the budget squeeze in terms of services being cut and the hiring of new personnel curtailed, the school is growing. "New buildings and parks are going up all over campus," says one student.

Less than 17 percent of UC students live on campus. Noncommuting freshmen and athletes are required to live in the six coed and single-sex dorms, which are described as adequate but crowded. Students say the lack of parking facilities is a much bigger deal than housing conditions. Many upperclassmen, especially the older and married students, consider off-campus living far better than dorm life, and inexpensive apartments can usually be found. Food in the two cafeterias located on opposite ends of the campus is "bland and unappetizing," and many students find stopping at the plastic village of fast-food joints surrounding the campus a tastier, cheaper, and more convenient option. The student union also has extensive snack bar facilities.

Merchants have turned the area surrounding UC, called Clifton, into a mini-college town with plenty to do. A bus line running by the campus takes undergraduates into the heart of the "Queen City" of Cincinnati in minutes. There the students find museums, a ballet, professional sports teams, parks, rivers, hills, and as many large and small shops as anyone could want. Still, the students advise caution, especially at night, when maneuvering through the campus and the

The hands-on experience of the university's strengths—research and co-op—offers students the opportunity to explore learning beyond the traditional classroom setting and to test the concepts that have been presented to them.

The university's music conservatory, one of the best state-run programs in the field, also offers broadcasting training.

"somewhat run-down" urban neighborhood surrounding it. On-campus activities include everything from a mountaineering club to Internat (the international students association) to clubs in various majors. Fraternities and sororities are small but are still the most active places to party on campus, usually opening their functions to everyone. The university sponsors some events, such as the massive but still wacky Springfest, which spotlights local bands playing all day and lots of "crafts and food and beer." The most popular road trips are the city of Cleveland and white-water rafting in West Virginia.

In sports, UC's basketball team is competitive and is giving the school respectability in athletics. Men's and women's soccer are also good, and women's volleyball and swimming aren't bad either. Everyone mentions the football rivalry with Miami (of Ohio) as a game you won't want to miss, and the same holds true when the men's basketball squad takes on Xavier University. Weekend athletes also take advantage of UC's first-rate sports center.

The University of Cincinnati offers a multitude of opportunities for a hands-on education. Students who attend UC not only get a good education at a reasonable price, they also get a chance to put what they've learned into practice while exploring the world outside the university's boundaries.

If You Apply To ➤

UC...Rolling admissions: Dec. 15. Financial aid: Mar. 1. Does not guarantee to meet full demonstrated need. Campus interviews: recommended, informational. No alumni interviews. SATs or ACTs: required. SAT IIs: optional. No essay question. Apply to particular program.

Claremont Colleges

In 1887 James A. Blaisdell had the vision to create a group of colleges patterned after Oxford and Cambridge in England. Over a century later, the five schools that comprise the Claremont Colleges thrive as a consortium of separate and distinct undergraduate colleges with two adjoining graduate institutions, a theological seminary, and botanical gardens. As families can sometimes get, the colleges coexist, interact, and experience their share of both cooperation and tension. Ultimately, however, the Claremont College Consortium forms a mutually beneficial partnership that offers its students the vast resources and facilities one might only expect to find at a large university.

The colleges are located on 317 acres in the Los Angeles suburb of Claremont, a peaceful neighborhood replete with palm trees, Spanish architecture, and the nearby San Gabriel Mountains. The picture-perfect California weather can sometimes be marred by smog, courtesy of the neighbors in nearby L.A., but the administration claims the smog level has declined dramatically in the past few years.

None of the five undergraduate colleges that make up the Claremont Colleges Consortium—Claremont McKenna, Harvey Mudd, Pitzer, Pomona, and Scripps—is larger than a medium-size dorm at a state school. Each school retains its own institutional identity, with its own faculty, administration, admissions, and curriculum, although the boundaries of both academic work and extracurricular activities are somewhat flexible. Each of the schools also tends to specialize in a particular area that complements the offerings of all the others. Claremont McKenna, which caters mainly to students planning careers in economics, business, law, or government, has eight research institutes located on its campus, while Harvey Mudd is the choice for future scientists. Pitzer, the most liberal of the five, excels mainly in the behavioral sciences, and at the all-women Scripps, the best offerings are in art and foreign languages. The oldest of the five colleges, Pomona ranks as one of the top liberal arts colleges anywhere and is the one Claremont school that is strong across the board, with the humanities especially superb.

Collectively, the colleges share many services and facilities including art studios, a student newspaper, laboratories, an extensive biological field station, a health center, auditoriums, a 2,500-seat concert hall, a 350-seat theater, bookstores, a maintenance department, and a business office. The Claremont library system makes more than 1.9 million volumes available to all students, though each campus also has a library of its own. Faculties and administrations are free to arrange joint programs or classes between all or just some of the schools. Courses at any college are open to students from the others (approximately 1,200 courses in all), but each college sets limits on the number of classes that can be taken elsewhere. Perhaps the best example of academic cooperation is the team-taught interdisciplinary courses, which are organized by instructors from the different schools and appeal to a mix of different academic interests.

The Claremont Colleges draw large numbers of students from within California, although their national reputation is growing. These days, about half the students hail from other Western and non-Western states, with a sizable contingent from the East Coast. The tone at Claremont is decidedly intellectual—more so than at Stanford or any other place in the West—and graduate programs in the arts and sciences are more common goals than business or law school. Anyone who is bright and hardworking can find a niche at one of the five schools. Unfortunately, despite their excellence, the Claremonts are also among the most underrated colleges in the nation.

The local community of Claremont is geared more to senior citizens than seniors, juniors, sophomores, and freshmen. "Quiet town of rich white people—boring," yawns an English major. A sophomore says, "Most of the stores have strange granny knickknacks or cosmic aura trinkets." Still, "the Village," a quaint cluster of specialty shops (including truly remarkable candy stores), is an easy skateboard ride from any campus, though the shades come down and the sidewalks roll up well before sunset. Students report that the endless list of social activities offered at the colleges make up for the ho-hum town of Claremont. For hot times, Hollywood's glamour and UCLA-dominated Westwood are within sniffing distance, and a convenient shuttle bus makes them even closer for Claremont students without cars. Nearby mountains and the fabled surfing beaches make this collegiate paradise's backyard complete. Mount Baldy ski lifts, for instance, are only 15 miles away, and you'll reach Laguna Beach before both sides of your favorite tape are played out. For spring break, Mexico is cheap and a great change of pace.

On campus, extracurricular life maintains a balance between cooperation and independence. Claremont McKenna, Harvey Mudd, and Scripps field joint athletic teams, and the men's teams, especially, are Division III powers, due to the exploits of CMC athletes. Pomona and Pitzer also compete together. Each of the five colleges has its own dorms, and since off-campus housing is limited in Claremont proper, the social life of students revolves around their dorms. "Scripps itself is quiet but parties at Harvey Mudd and Claremont McKenna can get pretty wild," admits a Scripps student. There are no fraternities, except at Pomona, where joining one is far from de rigueur. All cafeterias are open to all students, and most big events—films, concerts, etc.—are advertised throughout the campus. Large five-school parties are regular Thursday, Friday, and Saturday night fare. Social interaction among students at different schools, be it for meals or dates, is not what it might be. Pomona is seen as elitist, and its admissions office has been known to try to distance itself from the other colleges. Occasional political squabbles break out between liberal faculty and students at Pitzer and their conservative counterparts at Claremont McKenna. For the most part, students benefit not only from the nurturing and support within their own schools, each of which has its own academic or extracurricular emphasis, but also from the abundant resources the Claremont College Consortium offers as a whole.

Following are profiles of each undergraduate Claremont College.

Claremont McKenna College

890 Columbia Avenue, Claremont, CA 91711

At Claremont McKenna College, the students not only have parties, they study them. Political parties, that is. As a member of the Claremont Colleges consortium, CMC boasts top programs in government, economics, business, and international relations. In addition, Claremont McKenna has eight research institutes located on campus, which offer its undergraduates ample opportunities to

Website:
www.claremontmckenna.edu
Location: Suburban
Total Enrollment: 1,016

(Continued)

Undergraduates: 1,016
Male/Female: 56/44
SAT Ranges: V 640–740 M
640–740
ACT Range: 27–31
Financial Aid: 56%
Expense: Pr $ $ $
Phi Beta Kappa: Yes
Applicants: 2,827
Accepted: 28%
Enrolled: 28%
Grad in 6 Years: 86%
Returning Freshmen: 96%
Academics: ✐ ✐ ✐ ✐
Social: ☎ ☎ ☎
Q of L: ★ ★ ★
Admissions: (909) 621-8088
Email Address:
admission@mckenna.edu

Strongest Programs:
Economics
Government
International Relations
Premed
Prelaw
Business
Accounting
Sciences

The college sponsors an outstanding lecture series at the Marion Minor Cook Athenaeum. Before each lecture, students and faculty can enjoy a formal gourmet dinner together and engage in intellectual debates.

study everything from political demographics to the environment. The arts and humanities are also available, but Claremont McKenna is better suited to those with high ambitions in business leadership and public affairs.

The 50-acre campus, located 35 miles east of Los Angeles, is mostly "California modern" architecture with lots of Spanish tile roofs and picture windows that look out on the San Gabriel Mountains. Described by one student as "more functional than aesthetic," the physical layout fits right in with the school's primarily pragmatic attitude. The most recent addition to campus is Roberts Hall, a state-of-the-art academic center housing classrooms, seminar rooms, a computer laboratory, and faculty offices.

Claremont McKenna offers top programs in economics and government, but the international relations, prelaw, premed, and business programs are also considered strong. The biology, chemistry, and physics departments are greatly enhanced through the use of Keck Science Center, an outstanding facility providing students with hands-on access to a variety of equipment. In addition, the 85-acre Bernard Biological Field Station is located just north of the CMC campus and is available to students for field work. The administration candidly admits that computer science and engineering are not as fully developed as most departments.

CMC's extensive general education requirements include two semesters in the humanities, three in the social sciences, two in the natural sciences, and a semester each in mathematics, English composition and literary analysis, one semester of Questions of Civilization, and a Senior Thesis. The college offers popular 3-2 programs in management engineering and a 4–1 MBA program in conjunction with the Claremont Graduate University. Nearly 40 percent of Claremont McKenna students take advantage of its study abroad programs to countries including Australia, Brazil, Costa Rica, Japan, and numerous others. CMC also offers active campus exchange programs with Haverford, Colby, Spelman, Morehouse, and with universities in Quebec, Canada, and Germany. Another popular program is the Washington Semester program, in which students can intern with E-Span, the State department, the White House, and lobbying groups.

The academic climate is fairly strenuous at Claremont McKenna but not overwhelming. "Courses are definitely rigorous and students study hard," says a senior, "but students also recognize a need for balance." The students at CMC give their professors high marks. "The quality of teaching is phenomenal," says a philosophy major. "The professors encourage you to come to their office for help, to ask questions, or even just to discuss the material." Another student adds, "CMC emphasizes teaching over publishing and uses awards, evaluations, and other merit-based incentives to motivate its faculty." Freshmen are always taught by full professors in classes that rarely exceed 25 students. The school guarantees to meet the demonstrated need of accepted applicants and offers 30 merit scholarships of $5,000 a year.

The CMC student body is 60 percent Californian, with most everyone else from west of the Mississippi. Many attended public high school and 78 percent graduated in the top tenth of their class. The student body is 62 percent white; Asian Americans comprise the largest minority at 17 percent, Hispanics are next at 13 percent while African Americans make up 4 percent. Diversity is a major issue at CMC, which one student describes as "still perceived as very WASPy because of the past and current faculty makeup. It's not hostile, but it's not without conflict." One student says that while the administration and student body traditionally have been conservative, the student body is becoming "more politically balanced." Adds a junior, "We have a very equal split between conservative and liberal students. So, while they are not always politically correct, they are politically active." All freshmen take part in a five-day orientation program that includes a beach trip and a reception with the president and department chairs.

Almost all CMC students (95 percent) live on campus "because of the social life." The maid service probably doesn't hurt. "They dust and vacuum our rooms and clean our bathrooms! We do nothing (except study, of course)!" declares a happy resident. All the residence halls are coed; freshmen are guaranteed a room. Stark Hall, an eight-story residence hall, gives students more living options and a cluster of on-campus apartments equipped with kitchen facilities is a popular option for upperclassmen. Dorm food is said to be adequate, and students can eat in dining halls at any of the other four colleges, though the best bet may be CMC's Collins Dining Hall.

Most students agree that the social life at CMC is more than adequate. "Needless to say, our parties usually center on alcohol," admits one student. Another student adds, "You could easily lead and full and crazy social life without ever leaving campus." In addition to the usual forms of revelry, a calendar full of annual bashes includes Monte Carlo Night, Disco Inferno, Oktoberfest, Chez Hub, and the Christmas Madrigal Feast. Enthuses a junior, "Beer golf is also an interesting tradition. Golf clubs, tennis balls, and BEER...need I say more?" "SYRs—Screw or Set Up Your Roommate dances—are also pretty popular," a government major says. Ponding, another unusual CMC tradition, involves being thrown into one of the two campus fountains on one's birthday. The college sponsors an outstanding lecture series at the Marion Minor Cook Athenaeum on Monday through Thursday nights each week. Before each lecture, students and faculty can enjoy a formal gourmet dinner together and engage in intellectual debates. One enthusiastic fan of the program calls it a "great experience to be able to speak with some of the greatest minds in the world." Recent speakers have included Michael Dukakis and George Plimpton. Road trips to Joshua Tree, San Francisco, Las Vegas, and Mount Baldy are highly recommended by the students.

Athletics are an important part of life at Claremont McKenna. A third of the students play varsity sports and CMC men tend to dominate the teams jointly fielded with Harvey Mudd and Scripps (for women). Recent conference championships have been won by women's cross-country and tennis and men's swimming, track, and water polo. Top rivalries include Pomona, both in athletics and academics, one student claims. "Basketball games rock this campus," another student says.

CMC may be a small college but its mission is to produce great leaders. "Leadership pervades almost everything that goes on here," says a junior. "Claremont McKenna builds character, fosters a sense of ambition among its students, and drives them to set their sights high."

Overlaps

Stanford, UCLA, UC–Berkeley, Pomona, Georgetown.

If You Apply To >

Claremont McKenna...Early decision: Nov. 15. Regular admissions and financial aid: Jan. 15. Housing: May 1. Guarantees to meet demonstrated need. Campus interviews: recommended, evaluative. Alumni interviews: optional, informational. SATs or ACTs: required. SAT IIs: optional. Accepts the Common Application and electronic applications. Essay question: personal statement and issue of importance. Places "strong emphasis on caliber of an applicant's extracurricular activities."

Harvey Mudd College

301 East 12th Street, Kingston Hall, Claremont, CA 91711

Website: www.hmc.edu

Location: Suburban

Total Enrollment: 701

Undergraduates: 695

Male/Female: 75/25

SAT Ranges: V 670–740 M 720–790

Financial Aid: 57%

Expense: Pr $ $ $ $

Phi Beta Kappa: No

Applicants: 1,517

Accepted: 42%

Enrolled: 31%

Grad in 6 Years: 78%

Returning Freshmen: 91%

Academics: ✍ ✍ ✍ ✍

Social: ☎ ☎ ☎

Q of L: ★ ★ ★

Admissions: (909) 621-8011

Email Address:
admission@hmc.edu

Strongest Programs
Engineering
Math
Physics
Chemistry

Students here take a third of their courses in the humanities, the most of any technical college.

A top-ranked technical institution, Harvey Mudd College strives to give its students a sense of balance. Although it's a leading provider of high-quality programs in science and engineering, it also emphasizes a well-rounded education with knowledge in the humanities. Harvey Mudd also encourages balance in work and play and manages to maintain a community feeling in both realms. Although the academic climate is challenging here, the students go out of their way to assist each other, says one engineering major. This desire to help is fostered by the faculty's encouragement of cooperation and team projects.

HMC's mid-'50s vintage campus of cinder-block buildings even "looks like an engineering college; it's very symmetrical and there's no romance." In addition, the buildings have little splotches all over their surfaces that students have dubbed "warts"—not a very attractive picture. While most technical schools tend to have a narrow focus, HMC has come up with the novel idea that even scientists and engineers "need to know and appreciate poetry, philosophy, and non-Western thought," says an administrator.

Students here take a third of their courses in the humanities, the most of any engineering college in the nation. Up to half of them can be taken by walking over to another Claremont school. To ensure breadth in the sciences, students take another third of their work in math, physics, chemistry, biology, engineering design, and computer science. The last third of a student's courses must be in one of six major areas: biology, computer science, chemistry, physics, engineering, or math. And finally, to cap off their HMC experience, all students must complete a research project in their major, as well as a senior thesis in the humanities and social sciences.

Of the six majors, engineering is considered not only the strongest but the most popular by students, with physics not far behind. In the past few years, the number of biology faculty has more than doubled, and with the completion of the Olin Science Center, HMC's program in science is a strong one. Students rave about the engineering clinic program, which plops real-life engineering tasks (sponsored by major corporations and government agencies to the tune of $34,000 per project) into the laps of students. There's also a Freshman Project that allows neophytes to tackle "some real-world engineering problems." The computer science major has been considered weak in the past but students say there have been improvements.

Whatever department students end up in, the workload at HMC is "no cakewalk." As one student emphasizes, "For the sake of students across the U.S., I hope there isn't another college as rigorous as Mudd." Another says the academics are a bit like "drinking from a firehose...this is one tough school." The absence of graduate programs means that undergraduates get uncommon amounts of attention from even top faculty. Students love the small-college atmosphere. "All professors...all Ph.D.s...all the time ," reports a classmate. Another student adds, "The faculty at Harvey Mudd continues to amaze me with their unique blend of brilliance, integrity, and passion." The campus-wide honor code is strongly supported by the student body. These budding technicians are also top achievers: 91 percent graduated in the top 10 percent of their high school class.

"Prospective students should know that it can be temporarily damaging to their egos to come to a school with so many bright students," says a junior. Forty percent of the students are homegrown Californians. African Americans and

Hispanics combine for 6 percent of the student body, while Asian Americans weigh in at over 26 percent. A staggering 42 percent of a recent freshman class was composed of National Merit Scholars. With an endowment that comes to roughly $130,000 per student, HMC's long-term financial future looks bright. The administration advises that prospective applicants should be "passionate" about some aspect of math, science, or engineering. Mudd rolls out the red carpet for freshmen and their parents with a student-directed five-day orientation program.

Five older dorms and two newer, more modern ones are all coed and mix the classes. "They are definitely the engineering school type–functional and efficient," notes a freshman. They range from Atwood ("study hard, party hard") to North ("way cool, so very"). The dorms are also ideal for computer whizzes: all are wired for online access to the HMC mainframe. Campus security is considered ample, especially with the school's recent installations of campus phones, additional lighting, and fences. Workshops in self-defense are also offered for those who are interested.

The college has no fraternities, and most social life takes place in and around the dorms where there are parties every weekend. "Social life is dorm life," says a computer science major. Despite their heavy workload, most HMC students find abundant social outlets, even if it's just joining the parade of unicycles that has overrun the campus. One student complains, "Due to the dominant male population, social life can be rather strained." Another student describes the town of Claremont as "a wonderful place if you're married or about to die." However, most students say there is always fun to be had at one of the five campuses. Down-and-dirty types often frequent the Mudd Hole, a pizza-pinball-Ping-Pong hangout. Underage drinking is "compliments of a peer over 21," as one student puts it. For a school so young, Mudd is rife with tradition, including the annual "pumpkin caroling" trip at Halloween, in which students serenade professors' homes with doctored-up Christmas carols. Another night of screwball fun is the Women's Pizza Party, in which men don dresses and crash a meeting of the Society of Women Engineers. There is also an annual Five Class competition among the four classes and the handful of fifth-year students, complete with amoebae soccer and relay races that include unicycles (backward), peanut butter and jelly, and slide-rule problem solving.

Mudd fields varsity sports teams with Claremont McKenna and Scripps, and mainly because of all the CMC jocks, the teams do extremely well. The men's teams in soccer, track, cross-country, tennis, water polo, and swimming are nationally ranked in NCAA Division III. Women's teams in soccer, basketball, swimming, tennis, and track are perennial high achievers. Not long ago, some enterprising Mudders stole archrival Caltech's cannon, elevating the Mudd-Caltech rivalry to include a soccer game dubbed the Cannon Bowl. Intramurals, also in conjunction with Scripps and CMC, are even more popular. Traditional sporting events include the Black and Blue Bowl, an interdorm game of tackle football, and the Freshman-Sophomore Games, which climax in a massive tug-of-war across a pit of vile stuff.

"Harvey Mudd's problem right now," complains one senior engineering major, "is that it is not well known outside of the western United States." Nevertheless, HMC is right on the heels of Caltech as the best technical school in the West. Mudd doesn't promise you'll end up the owner of your own mining company—or president of anyone else's—within a decade of graduation, but it does offer a gem of a technical education perfectly blended with a dash of humanities and social sciences. HMC's intimate setting also offers something bigger schools can't: a sense of family.

Engineering is the most popular major, and students rave about the engineering clinic program, which plops real-life engineering tasks (sponsored by major corporations and government agencies to the tune of $34,000 per project) into the laps of students.

Overlaps

UC–Berkeley, MIT, Caltech, Stanford, UCLA.

Harvey Mudd…Early decision: Nov. 15. Regular admissions: Jan. 15. Financial aid: Feb. 1. Guarantees to meet demonstrated need. Campus interviews: recommended, informational. Alumni interviews: not available. SATs: required. SAT IIs: required (writing, math II, and one other). Accepts the Common Application. Essay question: compare and contrast relationship between art and science; meaningful moment; describe yourself.

Pitzer College

1050 North Mills Avenue, Claremont, CA 91711

Website: www.pitzer.edu
Location: Suburban
Total Enrollment: 930
Undergraduates: 930
Male/Female: 36/64
SAT Ranges: V 540–650 M 520–640
ACT Range: 21–27
Financial Aid: 60%
Expense: Pr $ $ $ $
Phi Beta Kappa: No
Applicants: 1,716
Accepted: 72%
Enrolled: 20%
Grad in 6 Years: 59%
Returning Freshmen: 86%
Academics: ✍ ✍ ✍
Social: ☎ ☎ ☎
Q of L: ★ ★ ★
Admissions: (909) 621-8129
Email Address:
admission@pitzer.edu

Strongest Programs:
Psychology
Sociology
Film and Television
Media Studies
English
Organizational Studies

"As the most laid-back of the Claremont colleges, Pitzer College is sometimes overlooked as a rigorous academic environment. But this image may be suited for a college that, according to one content alumnus, "doesn't focus on 'rigor' but on interest in learning." In this creative milieu, intellectual exploration and fierce individualism are as plentiful as the random bursts of colorful murals that dot the interior and exterior of the main campus wall. Founded in the '60s, this small school has changed with the times but continues its tradition of progressive thought and open social attitude.

Even the campus is, well, different. The classroom buildings are modernistic octagons, and the grass-covered "mounds" that distinguish the grounds "are perfect for sunbathing and Frisbee," says one student.

In keeping with Pitzer's freewheeling style, each student has the maximum freedom to choose which classes he or she would like to take. A lively freshman seminar program sharpens students' learning skills, especially writing. Students select from 40 majors in sciences, humanities, and social sciences. Almost anything in the social and behavioral sciences is a sure bet, especially psychology (the most popular major), anthropology, sociology, political science, and organizational studies. A psych course, Sexual Deviance, wins the most-popular-class award hands down. The art department also garners praise, while most courses in Pitzer's weaker areas—math and the natural sciences—can be picked up at one of the other Claremont schools.

Interdisciplinary inquiry is encouraged and original research is common. Pitzer students take advantage of Claremont's abundant foreign-study options, including a program in international and intercultural studies combining language proficiency, cultural study, and an off-campus Challenge semester. Class size is generally small, promoting close interaction between students and faculty. "People work together with their professors to create a classroom climate that is supportive and engaging," says a psychology major. "The professors rock!" gushes a senior. "They are all dynamic, brilliant teachers." Academic advising gets the thumbs-up as well. A student says that advisors are "profs in our own majors, so they are knowledgeable."

Individualism is a prized characteristic among Pitzer students, more than half of whom are from California. Pitzer has a substantial minority community: African Americans and Hispanics make up 17 percent of the student body, and Asian Americans 10 percent. "Pitzer students are very active in discussing, protesting, or supporting social and political issues local and worldwide," says a student. Current hot topics include police brutality and workers' rights. Individualism can have its drawbacks, as one student says, "Pitzer has a reputation for being very eccentric and weird. The students have a completely unwarranted reputation for being less intelligent than students at the other Claremont Colleges." Lest anyone get the idea that Pitzer students are too far out in left field, many of them eventually go on to graduate or professional school. Adequate financial aid is guaranteed to those students in need, and Pitzer offers scholarships to outstanding students.

Seventy-three percent of students live on campus. One junior reveals, "As far as housing, umm...well, let's just say an open mind is good." Boarders can choose from a variety of meal plans in the dining hall (which never fails to have a vegetarian plate), join a food co-op, or cook on their own. Campus security is ever-present; a student says, "Pitzer seems to be more safe than other campuses because campus security is so effective." One interesting campus curiosity is Grove House, a structure students saved from the wrecking ball nearly two decades ago and moved to campus. It houses a dining room, study areas, and art exhibits.

Pitzer has no Greek organizations, nor does it want any, and social life tends to be fairly low key. Kohoutek is the big party: "A weeklong art-music fest celebrating the comet that never came," says a senior. Activities include bands, food, and a "whole week of hoopla." The college enforces the 21-year-old drinking age, and all parties that serve alcohol must be registered. Dances, cocktail parties, and cultural events do much to occupy students' leisure time, but without a car things can get claustrophobic. According to one student, Pitzer "doesn't have enough athletic spirit," but the Pomona-Pitzer football team—"The Sagehens"—has had winning seasons and the school fields a variety of teams within the Southern California Intercollegiate Athletic Conference. Students play a large role in Pitzer's community government and sit on all policy committees, including those on curriculum and faculty promotion. Pitzer attracts open-minded students looking for the freedom to go their own way. Notes one student: "Pitzer is the only Claremont school that can claim to be genuinely different, in terms of race, religion, sexual orientation, and political belief. Pitzer is an amalgamation of every color of the spectrum."

Pitzer students take advantage of Claremont's abundant foreign-study options, including a program in international and intercultural studies combining language proficiency, cultural study, and an off-campus Challenge semester.

A lively freshman seminar program sharpens students' learning skills, especially writing.

Overlaps

Occidental, UC–San Diego, University of Southern California, UC–Santa Cruz, UCLA.

If You Apply To ➤ | **Pitzer**...Regular admissions and financial aid: Feb. 1. Guarantees to meet demonstrated need. Campus interviews: recommended, informational and evaluative. No alumni interviews. SATs or ACTs: required. SAT IIs: recommended (English and two others). Accepts the Common Application. Essay question: significant social issue; how do you represent your generation; greatest life lesson.

Pomona College

333 North College Way, Claremont, CA 91711

Pomona College, located just 35 miles east of the glitz and glamour of Hollywood, is the undisputed star of the Claremont College Consortium. This small, elite institution is the best liberal arts college in the West, and its media studies program (film and television) gets top billing. But the school's prestigious reputation doesn't get to the heads of Pomona's friendly students. "Students here are very open about different types of people—[Pomona] prides itself on its diverse community," chirps one Sage Hen (the school's mascot). With stellar liberal arts

Website: www.pomona.edu
Location: Suburban
Total Enrollment: 1,549
Undergraduates: 1,549
Male/Female: 51/49

(Continued)

SAT Ranges: V 670–760 M
670–750

ACT Range: 29–32

Financial Aid: 53%

Expense: Pr $ $ $ $

Phi Beta Kappa: Yes

Applicants: 3,612

Accepted: 30%

Enrolled: 35%

Grad in 6 Years: 89%

Returning Freshmen: 99%

Academics: ✍ ✍ ✍ ✍ ✍

Social: ☎ ☎ ☎

Q of L: ★ ★ ★

Admissions: (909) 621-8134

Email Address:
admissions@pomona.edu

Strongest Programs
English
International Relations
Economics
Neuroscience
Foreign Languages
Media Studies

Students can spend a semester at Colby or Swarthmore, pursue a 3–2 engineering plan with the California Institute of Technology, or spend a semester in Washington, D.C., working for a congressman.

programs and a brilliant atmosphere, Pomona College wins for best supporting role.

The architecture is variously described as Spanish Mediterranean, pseudo-Italian, or, as a sophomore puts it, "a perfect mix of Northeastern Ivy and Southern California Modern." The administration building, Alexander Hall, is described as "postmodern with Mediterranean influences," and one notices more than one stucco building cloaked in ivy and topped with a red-tile roof on campus, as well as eucalyptus trees, canyon live oaks, and an occasional "secretive courtyard lined with flowers." By virtue of its location and beauty, Pomona's campus has served as the quintessential collegiate milieu in various Hollywood movies, including *Beaches*, and appropriately enough, *How I Got into College*. New facilities include the Andrew Building for Sciences and the Smith Campus Center.

Classes at Pomona are challenging. "Most courses are very rigorous," says a student. "Professors expect students to participate actively in class discussions." Another student asserts, "I'm surrounded by so many brilliant students, but students here are not consumed by their academics as they have an uncanny ability to balance the fine line between academics and social life." One undergrad estimates the average student spends 20 to 30 hours a week studying outside the classroom.

Economics, biology, English, psychology, neuroscience, and politics are the most popular majors at Pomona. Newer programs include media studies and cognitive science, and a reorganized self-study curriculum in the history department. One Pomona student reports that the history, chemistry, and politics departments are "rigorous and familial in that students are challenged to their limits by figures (professors) who are somewhat parental but very professional." As for weak spots, students say they tend to avoid a "small number of professors as opposed to entire departments or programs."

A required freshman seminar offers an introduction to critical inquiry through intensive writing on subjects such as Icons of America: The Madonna Factor, Deviance and the Devil, and What is Wrong with Killing People? An Introduction to Ethics. Freshman seminars are designed to "teach students well and early how to use the classroom, foster discussion, step away from destructive competitive behaviors, and push to work collaboratively and supportively." Although no specific course or department is prescribed for graduation, students must take courses that meet the Perception, Analysis, and Communication requirement. Students must also enroll in at least two courses that are writing intensive, one course designated speech intensive, and must demonstrate proficiency in a foreign language. Educational opportunities abound at Pomona. Students can spend a semester at Colby or Swarthmore, pursue a 3–2 engineering plan with the California Institute of Technology, or spend a semester in Washington, D.C., working for a congressman. Nearly one-half of the students take advantage of study abroad programs offered in 22 foreign countries, and many others participate in programs focusing on six cultures and languages at the Oldenborg Center. In addition, the Summer Undergraduate Research Program (SURP) provides students with the opportunity to conduct funded research with a faculty member in their area of study.

Classes are small at Pomona—the average is 14 students—and the faculty makes a point of being accessible. It's not uncommon for professors to hold study sessions at their houses. "My professors have managed to combine their extensive experience and their research with continually inspired teaching and new ideas," a junior waxes. An ever popular take-a-professor-to-lunch program gives students free meals when they arrive with a faculty member in tow, and there is even a prof who leads aerobics classes open to all interested parties. "For the most part, my professors are engaging and intelligent," a senior says. A classmate adds, "I know many of my professors on a personal level and feel that even after graduation, I can call them up for advice, good conversation, and possibly a free lunch!"

Pomona tends to attract "people who produce work of exceptionally high quality, but who also know how to relax and have fun," notes one student. Thirty-seven percent of the students are Californians, and a growing percentage venture from the East Coast. Pomona is proud of its diverse student body: 5 percent are African American, 10 percent are Hispanic, and 18 percent are Asian American. "We want to move beyond debates about statistics and make real integration happen among different ethnic groups," says a politics major. There is a healthy mix of liberals and conservatives on campus, though the leftists, especially the feminist wing, are much more vocal. "There is a high degree of political correctness on campus," claims one student, "though this does not preclude students from speaking their minds." One interesting way students voice their issues is by painting the Walker Wall. Anyone is allowed to paint any message they want on the wall, and four-letter words and descriptions of alternative sexual practices show up on a regular basis. The student government is active, and the administration is credited with respecting students' opinions. Pomona is need-blind in admissions and meets the full demonstrated need of all those who attend. Admissions officers are on the lookout for anyone with special talents and are more than willing to waive the usual grade-and-score standards for such finds. A five-day freshman orientation program divides the new arrivals into groups of 6 to 12 students headed by a sophomore. "We provide a great deal of support in acclimating students to a college environment," says a senior.

The vast majority of Pomona students (96 percent) live on campus all four years. The dorms are coed, student governed, and divided into two distinct groups. Those on South campus are family-like, fairly quiet, and offer spacious rooms and those on the North end have smaller rooms with a livelier social scene. Housing "kicks a** for freshmen," according to one blunt student, while "sophomores kind of get screwed." Freshmen must live on campus and are placed in a "sponsor group" with two guardian upperclassmen, creating a "quasi-family away from home." Upperclassmen generally get single rooms or spacious two-room doubles that sometimes include fireplaces. The open courtyards and gardens are popular study spots. A handful of students isolate themselves in Claremont proper, where apartments are scarce and expensive. Boarders must buy at least partial meal plans. The food is good, with steak dinners on Saturday and ice cream for dessert every day. Students with common interests can occupy one of the large university houses; there is a vegetarian group and a kosher kitchen, both of which serve meals to other undergraduates. Pomona has a well-established language dorm with wings for speakers of French, German, Spanish, Russian, and Chinese, as well as language tables at lunch. Campus security is ever present: "Officers are approachable and easy to find," says a student, "and they create a reassuring presence on campus." Another adds, "The biggest nuisances are occasional incidents of bike theft or theft from dorm rooms."

Students at Pomona often spend Friday afternoons relaxing with friends over a brew at the Greek Theater. Social life begins in the dorms, where barbecues, parties, and study breaks are organized. There are movies five nights a week, and students also enjoy just tossing a Frisbee between kegs of beer set up on the lawn. One student wanted to be sure that incoming freshmen and transfers knew of the Coop's (student union) "best milk shakes west of the Mississippi" and its "game room, with pool, Ping-Pong, pinball, and assorted video games." "With the

Nearly one-half of the students take advantage of study abroad programs offered in 22 foreign countries, and many others participate in programs focusing on six cultures and languages at the Oldenborg Center.

five-college system, there's always something going on somewhere," asserts another Pomona enthusiast. Five-college parties happen nearly every weekend. During midterms and finals, however, the campus is a "social ghost town." Of more concern is the poor air quality, described by a junior as "oppressive on hot days during the fall semester. Most students are willing to live with the smog, but at least one student complains, "I'd prefer to breathe clean air."

Pomona is unique among the Claremont Colleges in that it has six non-national fraternities (four coed; there are no sororities), each with its own party rooms on campus. Seven percent of the men and 2 percent of the women join up. There is "no peer pressure to join frats," and no fraternity rivalry. As for booze, "Kegs are not allowed in dormitories, but there is an 'out of sight, out of mind' policy in which students can have as much alcohol in their rooms as they want," reports one student. Alcohol is not much of a problem, according to another student: "At Pomona no one feels pressured to drink or not drink. I've had a great time at parties completely sober, and no one looks at me like I'm a nerd, and I respect others even if they drink." Harwood dorm throws the five-college costume party every Halloween, and interdorm Jell-O fights keep things lively. Freshman orientation gets interesting, too. "Every freshman participates in a traditional ceremony involving gates and bird noises," reports a student. "I can't say too much because the rest is a secret!"

Time was when Pomona was an athletic powerhouse; the football team even knocked off mighty USC on Thanksgiving Day back in 1899. Currently, women's basketball, tennis, soccer, and swimming, and men's football, baseball, soccer, track, and water polo are strong programs. Intense rivalry exists between the colleges in the Claremont consortium, basketball games between Pomona, Pitzer, and CMS are "particularly heated." Intramurals, including hotly contested inner-tube water polo matches, attract many participants, and Pomona's $14-million athletic complex makes its facilities the best of the Claremonts.

"Pomona offers a unique and desirable juxtaposition of rigorous academics and comfortable social atmosphere," says a student. Another student says, "Once you take advantage of the five-college system, you realize how cool it is." The strongest link in an extremely attractive chain, Pomona continues to symbolize the rising status of the Claremont Colleges—and the West in general—in the world of higher education. There are few regrets about coming to Pomona. Says a senior, "We're in California. The sun is always shining. What's the problem?"

If You Apply To ➤

Pomona…Early decision: Nov. 15. Regular admissions: Jan. 1. Financial aid: Feb. 1. Guarantees to meet demonstrated need. Campus or alumni interviews (students choose one): recommended, evaluative. SATs or ACTs: required. SAT IIs: required (writing and two others). Accepts the Common Application and electronic applications. Essay question: personal statement and choice of most important scientific development; influential character; or how diversity affects college experience.

Scripps College

1030 Columbia Avenue, Claremont, CA 91711

Website:
www.scrippscollege.edu

Scripps College offers its students a solid, well-rounded education with a distinctly female sense of community. Founded in 1926 by newspaper publisher Ellen Browning Scripps, the college continues to pursue the mission of its founder: "to educate women by developing their intellects and talents through active participation in a community of scholars." "Scrippsies," as they are sometimes called, are by and large a moderate to liberal group, with a sprinkling of radical feminists (who will kill you if you call them Scrippsies). All are interested in "proving their worth and combating sexism, stereotypes, and sexual assault."

Scripps's scenic 30-acre campus, listed in the National Register of Historic Places, offers a tranquil, safe, and comfortable environment. The architecture is Spanish and Mediterranean, with Roman roof–tiled buildings and elegant landscaping. "We have more than 20 courtyards and a dozen fountains," says one student. A new student commons is the most recent campus addition.

At the heart of the Scripps academic offerings is the Core Curriculum, a closely integrated sequence of three interdisciplinary courses focusing on ideas about the world and the methods used to generate these ideas. All students are required to take one course in each of the four disciplines: fine arts, letters, natural sciences, and social sciences. In addition, there is a foreign language, mathematics, and multicultural requirement, and all students must complete a senior thesis or project in their chosen field. The academic climate is demanding, but competition among students is rare. "The students are very supportive of one another," says a psychology major. "They are willing to work together in study groups and tutoring sessions."

Anything in the humanities is a good bet at Scripps. The languages (especially French and Spanish) are particularly strong; history and psychology are also good. The strong fine arts program gets an additional boost with the Millard Sheets Art Center, which includes a state-of-the-art studio and a freestanding museum-quality gallery. Psychology tops the list of most heavily enrolled majors, followed by politics and biology. "The math department is weak but you do have the opportunity to take it at one of the other colleges in the consortium," says a physics/premed double major. The Keck Science Center, a joint facility for students studying the sciences at Scripps, Claremont McKenna, and Pitzer, is a prime example of the camaraderie among Claremont schools.

The Women's Collective—Scripps's version of career planning—helps Scripps women integrate elements of their college experience in setting goals relevant to their lives at Scripps and beyond. Computers appear across the curriculum and are located in dorms for convenience. Students usually have no problem getting the courses they want. Inside those courses, students are lavished with attention from professors. "Most of my professors have been...knowledgeable, willing to hear new ideas, available for questions, and excited to teach," says a senior. "The professors are excellent and incredibly accessible," says a linguistics major. "We even run into them in our dining hall and coffee shop."

Forty-two percent of Scripps women are from California. African Americans account for only 3 percent of the student body, Hispanics 6 percent, and Asian Americans make up another 15 percent. As for relations between various ethnic groups on campus, a sophomore notes that "most people seem to mingle without a fuss." Women's issues are always a hot topic, as are gay/lesbian rights and other liberal causes. The college holds several programs on cultural diversity and has adopted "Principles of Community." The college doles out 25 merit scholarships of $7,500 annually to outstanding students. Freshmen take part in a weeklong orientation, and all are assigned to a peer mentor for the whole year.

Practically all the students live in one of the seven small, home-style dorms, which are well maintained, luxurious, and even have "character," according to one chemistry major. "The dorms are beautiful and well-maintained," says a sophomore. Many of the dorms boast their own reflecting pools and inner courtyards;

(Continued)

Location: Suburban
Total Enrollment: 768
Undergraduates: 768
Male/Female: 0/100
SAT Ranges: V 600–690 M 560–670
Financial Aid: 60%
Expense: Pr $ $ $
Phi Beta Kappa: Yes
Applicants: 1,063
Accepted: 70%
Enrolled: 28%
Grad in 6 Years: 73%
Returning Freshmen: 88%
Academics: ✍ ✍ ✍
Social: ☎ ☎ ☎
Q of L: ★ ★ ★ ★
Admissions: (800) 770-1333
Email Address: admission@scrippscollege.edu

Strongest Programs:
English
Studio Art
Biology
Psychology
Foreign Language

At the heart of the Scripps curriculum is the Core Curriculum, a closely integrated sequence of three interdisciplinary courses focusing on ideas about the world and the methods used to generate these ideas.

a number of the rooms have balconies and are furnished with antiques and beautiful rugs. Students praise the dining facilities, which serve vegetarian alternatives at every meal. Students agree that campus security is good. "Scripps is a very safe campus," says a student, "because campus security is good and because we take precautions."

Campus social life centers around the residence halls, which take turns throwing parties. (In December, each puts on a special feast.) Scripps is adamant about stopping underage drinking and the school's alcohol policy is rather strict but it isn't foolproof. One student reports, "Underage students can still get alcohol through their older friends if they want it." Students hang out in the Motley, a coffeehouse, relax at $2 movies on Friday or Saturday nights, or attend the five-college parties that take place nearly every weekend. For male companionship, "Claremont McKenna is just across the street," cheers one sophomore. As far as traditions go, "at the end of orientation week there's Scripps Under the Stars, an exercise in shared humiliation for first-year women," reports a senior. "Everyone does skits or songs on the Wood Steps; it is followed by an ice cream social." Scripps fields joint athletic teams with CMC and Harvey Mudd, and conference championships have been won by the soccer, tennis, swimming, cross-country, and basketball teams.

Scripps has the appeal of being both a women's college, with its supportive environment, and part of the diverse academic and social university environment of Claremont. As a lit major sums up: "I feel supported and encouraged to be outspoken and confident with myself as a student and a woman. Scripps is dedicated not only to education but also to the empowerment and success of women."

Overlaps

UC–San Diego, UCLA, UC–Berkeley, UC–Santa Barbara, Pomona.

If You Apply To ⮞ **Scripps**...Early decision: Nov. 1, Jan. 1. Regular admissions and financial aid: Feb. 1. Housing: Jun. 15. Guarantees to meet demonstrated need. Campus and alumni interviews: recommended, evaluative. SATs or ACTs: required. SAT IIs: recommended. Accepts the Common Application and electronic applications. Essay question: personal statement.

Claremont McKenna College, CA—See CLAREMONT COLLEGES

Clark Atlanta University, GA—See ATLANTA UNIVERSITY CENTER

Clark University

950 Main Street, Worcester, MA 01610-1477

Website: www.clarku.edu
Location: Center city
Total Enrollment: 3,003
Undergraduates: 2,182
Male/Female: 60/40

For nearly a century, Clark as been on the cutting edge of curriculum advances. It was the only American university where Sigmund Freud deigned to give a lecture. Clark also recently became the first school anywhere to offer a doctorate program in Holocaust history. And now, Clark University has made a compelling offer to students: Study hard during your undergraduate years and get an extra year of education free. Students who maintain a B-plus average or better are eligible for a combination bachelor's/master's degree program at no additional cost.

The compact 50-acre urban campus has "enough ivy, tall maples, and collegiate brick buildings to make a traditionalist happy." Buildings range from remodeled Victorian-era residences, former homes of prosperous Worcester merchants, to the architecturally award-winning Robert Hutchings Goddard Library. Clark is always renovating one building or another, and careful restorations have brought a renewed sense of the history of the area. In the past decade, half of the 50 buildings on campus have been either completely renovated or newly built. Jonas Clark Hall, the oldest building on campus, was completely restored, maintaining its prominence as the main academic classroom facility in the center of campus. The recently added Lasry House is home to the Center for Holocaust Studies, and a new visual and performing arts center is slated to open within a few years. A statue of famed psychoanalyst Sigmund Freud stands stoically in the center of the campus, marking the only spot in the nation where Freud ever lectured.

Clark was founded as a research-oriented graduate school, the second such institution after Johns Hopkins. In fact, some majors require research for graduation. "Courses give students exposure to intensive assignments and a rigorous approach toward problem solving, analytical reasoning, and the like," says one senior. Some seminars are limited to 15 students; 80 percent of classes have 25 or fewer. In first-year seminars, which never have more than 15 students, students have isolated strands of DNA, explored the workings of the brain, discussed origins of modern sports, and interned at local elementary schools. The psychology and geography departments have national reputations, the latter having churned out more Ph.D.s than any other school in the nation. The American Psychological Association was founded on campus and preeminent psychologist Carl Jung received an honorary degree at Clark. The departments of government and international relations, history, and chemistry are also strong, while the physics, music, and theater departments receive mixed reviews from students. The school has added two new majors: Urban Development and Social Change, and Environment and Society. In the USDC program, students have helped revitalize Clark's own neighborhood, called Main South, in Worcester.

Emphasis is placed on broad academic exploration during the first two years. Each student must complete a program of liberal studies, which includes two critical thinking courses in two categories—verbal expression and formal analysis—and six perspectives courses in the following areas: aesthetics, comparative analysis, history, science, language and culture, and values. Interdisciplinary programs are also popular—women's studies is especially good—and students may design their own majors. Internships are encouraged in all academic areas, and through the nine-college Worcester Consortium.* Special offerings include taking courses or attending international research conferences at the Clark University Center in Luxembourg. More than 20 percent of all Clark students spend at least one semester studying abroad at one of 14 sites with which the school is affiliated. Clark also offers a special bonus with the Fifth Year Free Program, which allows students with a B-plus average or better to get a combination bachelor's/master's degree with, you guessed it, the last year at no cost.

As for the academic climate, Clark is "rigorous and stimulating, but laid-back and not competitive," according to a government major. Professors get high marks from students. "They are amazing people who bring their life experiences to the classroom," says a business management major.

One-third of Clark's students are from Massachusetts; another large contingent hails from New York and other parts of New England. Students represent nearly 92 foreign countries, but the school is not heavily made up of minority students. About 3 percent of students are African American, 3 percent Hispanic, and 4 percent Asian American. Students tend to support the diversity that does exist

(Continued)
SAT Ranges: V 520–630 M
  520–620
ACT Range: 22–28
Financial Aid: 62%
Expense: Pr $ $ $
Phi Beta Kappa: Yes
Applicants: 3,231
Accepted: 73%
Enrolled: 20%
Grad in 6 Years: 62%
Returning Freshmen: 87%
Academics: ✍ ✍ ✍ ✍
Social: ☎ ☎ ☎
Q of L: ★ ★ ★
Admissions: (508) 793-7431
Email Address:
  admissions@clarku.edu

Strongest Programs:
  Psychology
  Geography
  Government and
  International Relations
  Environmental Studies
  Holocaust and Genocide
  Studies
  History

In first-year seminars, which never have more than 15 students, students have isolated strands of DNA, explored the workings of the brain, discussed origins of modern sports, and interned at local elementary schools.

on campus. "We are open-minded and like to express our freedom of speech and make our opinions known," says one senior. There's even a popular T-shirt that depicts a pea pod filled with different colored peas that reads, "categorizing people isn't something you can do here." The university also has a collaborative educational program with historically black Howard University. Politically, Clark seems to have a reputation for being "extremely liberal" as one student points out, and also socially aware. The environment and gender issues top the list of important causes at Clark, and both social and political debates are frequent. The Multicultural Center provides space for a wealth of groups and has a grant-funded director to host regular programs exploring race relations and diversity.

Clark offers merit-based scholarships that cover part of the tuition, and the school also offers several special tuition-payment plans, including one that locks tuition at the first year's rate, a monthly payment plan that spreads the year's cost over 10 months, and a loan at a fixed rate.

Housing options at Clark are highly regarded by most students. Most live in campus housing that they describe as comfortable and well-maintained. There is free cleaning service, though freshman living space is described as "lacking in aesthetics." Students must play the "room roulette" lottery to get housing, and all dorms, except one, are coed by floor or wing. Freshmen and sophomores are required to live on campus and many juniors and seniors live in cheap apartments close to campus. The on-campus dweller must subscribe to one of several meal plans, which are served in the University Center dining hall with an unusual guarantee: if you don't like the way your entrée is prepared, you can choose another or have it prepared again. There's also a vegetarian option. All students can get a cash card encoded with their student ID number that will allow them to eat anywhere on campus, including the international café.

Worcester boasts 10 colleges, but is hardly what you would call a college town. Nevertheless, the town offers numerous restaurants, dance clubs, concert halls, a resident symphony, theater companies, and good science and art museums. It's also home to the Centrum, a 13,000-seat arena that draws some of the top touring bands in the country. Students seem pretty happy to mix with townspeople and volunteer for community service, especially through the Big Brother–Big Sister program. "Worcester needs a lot of help, and Clark likes to help," a senior says. "Almost everyone does something for the neighborhood." When Clarkies need a change of pace, they travel to Boston, Vermont, New Hampshire, Maine, or Providence.

There are no Greek organizations on campus, but over-21 upperclassmen frequent a few local bars. The campus pub was recently converted into a place called Grind Central, a coffeehouse that offers gourmet coffee, pastries, live entertainment, and various games in a cozy atmosphere. As for booze, "Campus policies are strict in writing, but hard to enforce," says one senior. Be careful, though. No kegs are allowed on campus, and students say this rule is enforced. Other on-campus options include movies, plays, comedy clubs, concerts, and the popular Speakers Forum. One business major explains that Clark is "not a big 'party school.' It's more like a 'hang out with your friends' school."

Coping with the cold New England winters includes quaffing cups of hot chocolate and dreaming about Spree Day—"What every Clarkie lives for," one student says. Spree Day comes as a complete surprise; students awake to canceled classes and a carnival and popular band waiting to entertain them. Completely different is Academic Spree Day, when all undergraduate research is celebrated every year. While Clark has never had a reputation as a jock school, it is respectable in several sports. The women's basketball team has competed in the NCAA Division III tournament. Other top women's teams include cross-country, which participated in the Worcester City Championships, and the field hockey and crew teams. A 4,300-square-foot fitness center houses cardiovascular machines, strength-building machines, and free weights. Clark has also renovated its athletic field and added an extension to the athletic center that houses new basketball and volleyball courts and an indoor track.

The academic mission of Clark has been brought into focus through a new slogan "challenging convention, changing our world." The school envisions itself as a pioneer in the way it teaches, pursues new knowledge, and blends doing and thinking. Clark is willing to challenge old ideas and add to students' awareness of society. Add to that an engaging staff, beautiful campus, and tight-knit community, and Clark has a world to offer.

If You Apply To ➢ | **Clark**…Early decision: Nov. 15. Regular admissions: Feb. 1. Does not guarantee to meet demonstrated need. Campus and alumni interviews: recommended, evaluative. SATs or ACTs: required. SAT IIs: required with writing test. Accepts the Common Application and electronic applications. Essay question: significant experience with meaning; issue of personal, local, national, or internation of concern; person of significance; fiction character, historical figure, creative work and influence on you.

Clarkson University

Holcroft House, Box 5605, Potsdam, NY 13699

At Clarkson University, engineering and ice hockey reign supreme. More than half of the student body is enrolled in the engineering program, and the hockey team is a perennial contender for top honors. Students at this tiny school take advantage of a quality technical education and a small-town environment that offers plenty to do, especially during the dog days of winter. Academically, CU's mission emphasizes a team-oriented experimental focus and partnerships among students, faculty, and businesses. Clarkson is geared toward the individual student and that's what sets it apart from most schools.

The tiny town of Potsdam, New York, is cloistered away between the Adirondacks and the St. Lawrence River. The older part of campus, where red sandstone and brick are the dominant architectural touches, is set in the center of Potsdam and includes most of the academic buildings. The "hill campus," where most freshmen and sophomores live and take classes, relies mainly on modern architecture and lots of woods and wildlife. Personal computers are a must, and countless resources exist on the campus network which can be accessed from dorm rooms. In addition, Clarkson has a large software library where students can copy software easily and cheaply.

Engineering isn't the only thing at Clarkson, but it certainly gets top billing; 61 percent of the students are in the program. The combined programs in electrical/computer engineering and mechanical/aeronautical engineering earn the highest marks from students. Clarkson's School of Management has a strong accounting program, a finance and management information systems program, and another one called Project Arete, which allows students to double major in management and a liberal arts discipline. The school also offers degree programs in computer and aeronautical engineering. Physics and chemistry are the strongest offerings in the sciences, and would-be doctors have the benefit of a

Website: www.clarkson.edu
Location: Small town
Total Enrollment: 2,902
Undergraduates: 2,581
Male/Female: 73/27
SAT Ranges: V 520–620 M 560–660
Financial Aid: 76%
Expense: Pr $ $ $
Phi Beta Kappa: No
Applicants: 2,568
Accepted: 83%
Enrolled: 33%
Grad in 6 Years: 71%
Returning Freshmen: 85%
Academics: ✍ ✍ ✍
Social: ☎ ☎
Q of L: ★ ★ ★
Admissions: (315) 268-6479
Email Address: admission@clarkson.edu

Strongest Programs: Engineering

joint program combining biology and—you guessed it—engineering. The liberal arts and humanities are cited by students as being weaker than other departments.

As part of their Foundation Curriculum requirements, all students at Clarkson are required to take six liberal arts courses, two in mathematics, two in science, and one each in computer programming, engineering, and management. Freshmen are required to take a two-semester Great Ideas course, along with a personal wellness course. A convocation program for new students is designed to introduce them to distinguished speakers and performers whose appearances may broaden their educational horizons. About 30 freshmen are invited to participate in the honors program, which offers specially developed courses and research experiences.

Clarkson prides itself on intimacy and personalized instruction, and the fact that 80 percent of the Foundation courses are taught by full-fledged faculty members proves that it's no idle boast. "The professors here are very intelligent, readily available, and willing to help their students in any way they can," says an environmental science and policy major. Another student adds, "The professors are excited by the subjects they teach and it shows." Clarkson isn't the academic pressure cooker that many technical institutes are, but it really depends on whom you talk to. "The academic climate here is fairly rigorous but not to the point where it's overwhelming," says a business administration and social science double major. A biology major disagrees: "The courses here are extremely tough and sometimes too challenging." The bottom line of a Clarkson education is getting a job after graduation, and students uniformly praise the career counseling office and note with pride Clarkson's high placement rate. One junior says that the career center is "very good at getting students to think about their futures."

At Clarkson the students are friendly, serious-minded, and down to earth; radicals are notably absent. Two-thirds of the students graduated in the top fifth of their class. Twenty-six percent are New Yorkers, and 5 percent are foreign. Clarkson has trouble luring minorities to its remote locale; the combined total of African Americans, Hispanics, and Asian Americans is 7 percent of the student body. "Our campus definitely needs more minority students," says a senior. All accepted applicants demonstrating financial need are offered some aid, but not necessarily enough to meet full need. Clarkson awards a number of merit scholarships each year, ranging from $1,000 to $28,309. Athletic scholarships are offered for ice hockey players only.

Students are required to reside on campus all four years, unless exempted to live in a Greek house. Most dorms are centrally located and are cleaned every day. "The dorms are comfortable and very well maintained," says a student. Four of the dorms are all-men and the rest are coed by floor. All freshman are housed with students in their major areas of study and in some instances in the same department, giving them the chance to study and learn together. Many underclassmen are housed in conventional dorms, but university-owned townhouse apartments offer more gracious living. "The dorm situation is handled by the lottery and housing improves based on your class year," a senior reports.

In keeping with Clarkson's "come as you are" atmosphere, the social scene is low key. "There are activities, such as comedians, picnics, and other types of entertainment on campus," says one senior. "However, a good deal of socializing also takes place off campus." Eighteen percent of the men and 15 percent of the women join the Greek system. Fraternity beer blasts are the staple of weekend life, and those not into the Greek scene (and over 21) can head to the handful of bars in downtown Potsdam. Nearby SUNY–Potsdam is also a source of social life,

Clarkson's School of Management has a strong accounting program, a finance and management information systems program, and another one called Project Arete, which allows students to double major in management and a liberal arts discipline.

The school also offers degree programs in computer and aeronautical engineering.

especially for men frustrated by Clarkson's three-to-one male/female ratio. Drinking is prohibited on campus, and residence life staff are on the watch for violators; however, students report that it's still easy for the underaged to be served off campus. The major social event of the year is the annual Ice Carnival, held midwinter, which includes a parade, an ice sculpture contest, cross-country skiing, and the crowning of a king and queen. For those who crave the bustle of city nightlife, Ottawa and Montreal are each about an hour and a half away by car.

When it comes to sports, men's hockey is first and foremost in the hearts of Clarkson students—the only one in which the university competes in Division I. The team has been ECAC champ in recent years, and contends for the national championship with other blue-chip teams like archrivals Cornell and St. Lawrence. The ski teams, Nordic and Alpine, are among the best in the nation, and men's soccer and golf, and women's soccer and basketball, are also strong. For weekend athletes, an abundance of skiing and other outdoor and winter sports is within easy driving distance.

For those seeking a technical education without having to worry about big-school problems, Clarkson will be like a breath of mountain-fresh air. Come January, you'll feel like an Eskimo, but at least you'll have a high-tech igloo.

A convocation program for new students is designed to introduce them to distinguished speakers and performers whose appearances may broaden their educational horizons.

Overlaps

Rensselaer Polytechnic, Rochester Institute of Technology, University of Rochester, WPI, Lehigh.

If You Apply To ➤ **Clarkson**…Early decision: Dec. 1, Jan. 15. Regular admissions and financial aid: Mar. 1. Does not guarantee to meet demonstrated need. Campus interviews: recommended, informational. Alumni interviews: optional, informational. SATs: required. Accepts the Common Application and electronic applications. Essay question: personal statement.

Clemson University

Sikes Hall, Box 345124, Clemson, SC 29634-5124

Nestled in the foothills of the Blue Ridge Mountains, Clemson University is a place where Southern spirit continues to flourish. The campus occupies terrain that once was walked by John C. Calhoun, former Southern senator and a Civil War–era rabble-rouser of the first degree. Today Clemson features quality academics in technical areas such as engineering and biology, and big-time athletics supported by strong school spirit.

CU's 1,400-acre campus is situated on what was once Fort Hill Plantation, the homestead of Thomas Green Clemson. The campus is surrounded by 17,000 acres of university farms and woodlands, and offers a spectacular view of the nearby lake and mountains. Architectural styles are an eclectic mix of modern and 19th-century collegiate. New additions to the campus include a student center.

Electrical engineering is the university's largest department, and computer engineering is among the nation's best in research on large-scale integrated computer circuitry and robotics. Chemists enjoy the impressive Hunter Laboratory. The College of Architecture, one of the school's most selective programs, offers intensive semesters at the Overseas Center for Building Research and Urban Study in Genoa, Italy. A fantastic resource for science enthusiasts and history buffs is the library's collection of first editions of the scientific work of Galileo and Newton. Because of the prevailing technical emphasis, most students interested in the liberal arts head "down country" to the University of South Carolina. Undergraduate

Website: www.clemson.edu
Location: Small town
Total Enrollment: 16,782
Undergraduates: 13,526
Male/Female: 55/45
SAT Ranges: V 520–620 M 540–640
ACT Range: 23–27
Financial Aid: 11%
Expense: Pub $ $
Phi Beta Kappa: No
Applicants: 9,501
Accepted: 68%
Enrolled: 30%
Grad in 6 Years: 87%
Returning Freshmen: 84%
Academics: ✍ ✍ ✍

(Continued)

Social: ☎ ☎ ☎ ☎

Q of L: ★ ★ ★ ★

Admissions: (864) 656-2287

Email Address: cuadmissions@clemson.edu

Strongest Programs:

Engineering

Architecture

Biological Sciences

Business

The College of Architecture, one of the school's most selective programs, offers intensive semesters at the Overseas Center for Building Research and Urban Study in Genoa, Italy.

Clemson's library is a treasure trove of historic documents, including first editions of scientific work of Galileo and Newton.

teaching has always been one of Clemson's strong points, and for students interested in pursuing a liberal arts curriculum, the school has degrees in fine arts, philosophy, and languages and enjoys a strong regional reputation for its history program. "My favorite academic department has been the political science department," says a senior marketing major. "The professors have challenged me and really helped me to learn while showing me they care." Highly motivated students should consider Calhoun College, Clemson's honors program—the oldest in South Carolina—open to freshmen who scored 1200 or above on their SATs and ranked in the top 10 percent of their high school graduating class. Clemson also offers exchange programs in Mexico, Scotland, Ecuador, Spain, England, Australia, and Italy.

General education requirements include courses in communication and speaking, computer skills, mathematical sciences, physical or biological science, humanities, and social science. Each student is assigned a faculty advisor for help and guidance. "My academic advisors are perfect," says a health science major. Academically, the level of difficulty varies within each department. "Some classes are easier and require little effort," one junior says, "while most others take time and effort to do good." Students report some problems finishing a degree in four years, and class registration can be a hassle.

Clemson's student body has a definite Southern air, as 70 percent of the undergrads hail from South Carolina, with most of the rest from neighboring states. Thirty-four percent were in the top tenth of the high school graduating class. Blacks make up 7 percent of the student body, and Hispanics and Asian Americans account for 2 percent combined. The average Clemson student is friendly and conservative, and though, as a public institution, the school isn't affiliated with any church, there is a strong Southern Baptist presence on campus. The university offers 300 academic and as many athletic scholarships as the NCAA allows. Clemson runs on a need-blind admissions process.

Housing gets positive reviews, and 41 percent of the students live on campus, usually during their first two years. Most of the dorms are single-sex, though coed university-owned apartment complexes are also an option. "It can be competitive to receive a room if you don't send your housing information on time," warns a student. Clemson House and Calhoun Courts, the coed halls, are considered the best places to be. The food is typical dorm fare. Upperclassmen can cook for themselves, and each dorm has kitchen facilities.

After class, many students hop on their bikes and head to nearby Lake Hartwell. The beautiful Blue Ridge mountain range is also close by for hiking and camping, and beaches and ski slopes are both within driving distance. Atlanta and Charlotte are only two hours away by car, and Charleston is four hours away on the coast. Aside from the sports teams, fraternities and sororities provide most of the social life. Twenty-three percent of Clemson students go Greek. Though Clemson empties out a bit on away-game weekends, there are still plenty of off-campus parties where the main activity is drinking beer. The town itself is pretty small, with a few bars and movie theaters, but some students love it. "Clemson is an awesome college town," a marketing major says.

Sports still help make the world go round at Clemson, and on weekends when the Tiger teams are playing, there are pep rallies, cookouts, dances, and parties for the mobs of excited fans. The roads leading to campus are painted with large orange pawprints, an insignia that symbolizes great enthusiasm for Clemson sports. So, too, are half the fans at an athletic event. Football fever starts with the annual First Friday Parade, held before the first home game, and on every game day the campus dissolves into a sea of Tiger orange. Clemson has regained its former gridiron glory under the leadership of Coach Tommy Bowden. Hordes of Tiger fans cram "Death Valley" for every game, and are especially rowdy when the reviled University of South Carolina Gamecocks are in town. Other very competitive athletic teams include basketball, baseball, and men's track.

No haven for carpetbaggers or liberals, Clemson is best at serving those whose interests lie in technical fields. School spirit is contagious, fueled by a love of big-time college sports, and becomes lifelong for many Clemson students. Everyone can become part of the Clemson family, from Southern belle, to Northern Yankee, as long as they're friendly, easygoing, not aggressively intellectual, and enthusiastic about life in general and the Tigers in particular.

Overlaps

University of South Carolina, College of Charleston, UNC–Chapel Hill, University of Georgia, North Carolina State.

If You Apply To ➤   **Clemson**…Rolling admissions: May 1. Financial Aid: Apr. 1. Meets demonstrated need of 75%. Campus interviews: optional, informational. No alumni interviews. SATs or ACTs: required. SAT IIs: required (math II for math placement). No essay question.

Colby College

Lunder House, Waterville, ME 04901

Colby College emphasizes learning on both a global and local level. Its strong programs in international studies and environmental studies ensure that Colby students gain theoretical knowledge about the world around them, and its top study abroad program provides them with practical experience in that world. While Colby students relish their travels, they still cherish this small liberal arts college for its happy, friendly, and oh-so-wholesome qualities.

Secluded from the hustle and bustle of the "real world" in a rustic setting of Waterville, Maine, Colby sits on a high hill with beautiful views of the surrounding countryside. Its 714 acres include a wildlife preserve, miles of cross-country trails, and a pond that is used in winter as an ice-skating rink. Colby's buildings are Georgian in architecture, with a few more modern structures sprinkled in. The oldest buildings are red brick with white trim, ivy, and brass nameplates above their hunter green doors. The more contemporary buildings blend a touch of modernity to the more classic style. As a small college with a history of innovation and educational excellence, Colby boasts a faculty that is devoted to undergraduate teaching. "It is a true teaching college where the professors are equally (if not more) devoted to the academics than students," a senior says. "The quality of teaching I have received has been superb!" One student says the professors are so inspiring that as a freshman it was nearly impossible to pick just one major. Academic standards are high ("good-natured competition"), especially in the most popular programs—biology, English, economics, government, and psychology. The foreign study and languages program also has an excellent reputation. Less traditional programs in creative writing, women's studies, and East Asian studies get rave reviews from students. Not quite up to par are administrative science, math, and computer science, and one senior says the economic department is "very conservative." New programs on the academic roster include minors in Indigenous Peoples of the Americas and Jewish studies.

Ninety-nine percent of the freshmen begin their Colby careers with the COOT program (Colby Outdoor Orientation Trips), four-day excursions by

Website: www.colby.edu
Location: Small town
Total Enrollment: 1,764
Undergraduates: 1,764
Male/Female: 48/52
SAT Ranges: V 610–690 M 610–700
ACT Range: 26–30
Financial Aid: 36%
Expense: Pr $ $ $ $
Phi Beta Kappa: Yes
Applicants: 4,363
Accepted: 32%
Enrolled: 34%
Grad in 6 Years: 88%
Returning Freshmen: 91%
Academics: ✐ ✐ ✐ ✐
Social: ☎ ☎ ☎
Q of L: ★ ★ ★
Admissions: (207) 872-3168
Email Address:
  admissions@colby.edu

Strongest Programs:
  Government
  Environmental *(Continued)*

bicycle, canoe, or foot through Maine's wilderness. Once they are back to civilization, curling up with their books is a popular activity. "Libraries are packed after hours," one senior notes. The library tower is the most noted feature of the college's architecture, and the blue light atop it is viewed with much affection. Every year, students honor the light with a Blue Light Night party, and a key campus saying is "Keep the blue light burning." The library has a decent-size collection—around 925,000 volumes—and boasts several online catalogs and CD-ROM computer reference sources. A new electronic research classroom helps students and faculty mine information from the Internet.

The academic climate at Colby is challenging but not overwhelming, according to students. "Everyone seems to put in their hours at the library, but at the same time there is a very low sense of competition, if any at all," reports an American Studies major. Each student gets a free computer account for unlimited hours of interactive bliss. Faculty advisors help a great deal and show students the value of networking to score a good job. Students also sing the praises of the career services office, which helps students market themselves and brings a multitude of companies up from Boston and New York for interviews.

Colby was the first college to establish a special January program, and students must take three to graduate. During this short term, motivated undergraduates find an internship or study abroad program, or prepare an in-depth report. Other, less serious undergrads might head for the ski slopes or southern beaches and write a quick paper at the end of the month, though they must get a good enough grade to receive credit. Despite the beautiful surroundings, four years on the outskirts of Waterville (population 20,000) is more than many students can take. Incoming freshmen can pack off for Cuernavaca or Dijon to fulfill their language requirement, delaying enrollment until the second semester. There are also Jan-Plan trips to everywhere from Nicaragua to Vietnam, and juniors regularly seek out foreign- or college-exchange opportunities. Popular destinations are Bermuda (for biology), Connecticut's Mystic Seaport, Kyoto, and the great cities of Europe; even China is a possibility. With all of these options, it's no wonder that nearly 75 percent of Colby students spend some time abroad. Still, the administration likes to share the two "big secrets we Mainers like to keep" about Maine winters: the winters are beautiful, and they are a lot harsher and colder in the telling than in the living. For would-be engineers, there are joint 3–2 programs with Case Western Reserve and Dartmouth as well as exchange programs with Pomona and Howard. The Oak Institute organizes symposia on international human rights; most recently an anti-child labor crusader from Pakistan and a rural development advocate from the Congo have been institute fellows.

Social and political issues abound on the Colby campus. "PC is definitely an issue here, but not in a stifling way," says one student. Some complain about the lack of diversity on campus. "Students are very homogenous," one senior says. Minorities make up only 11 percent of the student body (5 percent Asian American and 3 percent each African American and Hispanic). There are several groups on campus that celebrate different cultures, and the college has implemented a program that pairs freshman students of color with upperclassmen mentors. More than 85 percent of Colby freshmen placed in the top quarter of their high school class. Students are admitted without regard to their financial need, and Colby remains committed to meeting the "full calculated eligibility" of all admitted applicants. There are no academic or athletic scholarships.

The campus is divided into three residence hall groups, each with live-in faculty members. Students have a lot of autonomy over their living conditions, even

The library tower is the most noted feature of the college's architecture, and the blue light atop it is viewed with much affection.

to the point of setting dining hall menus. Students can choose a "quiet" residence hall (never "dorm" at Colby), where there are posted hours for making noise, or a "chem-free" house for teetotalers. The dorms are "beautiful," but one student gripes that it's difficult to get rooms other than doubles. Thanks to the new senior apartments, only 2 percent of upperclassmen move off campus to neighboring farmhouses. On-campus dwellers use computerized meal cards for the four dining halls. All the residence and dining halls will renovated by 2003 as part of a $44 million capital project.

The well-entrenched fraternity and sorority system was abolished in 1984, when most Colby students were still learning their ABC's. While one might think that anger among students still lingers, many students say they chose Colby because of the absence of a Greek system. Despite the campus's remote setting, Colby students never seem to be at a loss for things to do—road trips to L.L. Bean and Freeport, Camden, skiing at Sugarloaf, Belgrade Lakes for swimming, Acadia National Park to camp—though drinking is high on many people's lists. It's still pretty easy for underage students to get alcohol on campus, even though the administration has poured a lot of resources into stemming the tide of student drinking. "Kegs can be delivered to dorms for lounge parties on Friday and Saturday nights," one student notes. All-campus parties are given by each of the residential commons, but private parties have become especially popular since they are less likely to attract the attention of the state liquor inspector. The town of Waterville is not exactly thriving: "It is an economically depressed mill town," a senior says.

An enthusiasm for outdoor sports is the major nonacademic credential needed to become a content Colby undergraduate, and the annual winter carnival and snow-sculpture contest are the pinnacle of winter celebration. Athletics have come a long way since the first intercollegiate croquet game here back in 1860, and Colby excels at men's cross-country, soccer, track, and basketball. Women have done very well in lacrosse, skiing, outdoor and indoor track, and swimming. The overwhelming majority of students participate in some 26 intramural sports. Drama and music are popular extracurricular activities, and numerous productions and concerts are mounted each semester.

Students aiming for a well-rounded liberal arts education may find what they want at Colby. "Students enjoy learning and the beauty that surrounds them," a senior says. "They have a lot of school pride." Colby offers a progressive and challenging academic climate, outstanding professors and opportunities abroad while promoting the fun and tradition that makes up so much of the college experience.

Nearly 75 percent of Colby students spend some time abroad, from Cuernavaca, Mexico, or Dijon, France, to Bermuda or Kyoto.

Athletics have come a long way since the first intercollegiate croquet game here back in 1860. Colby students excel at men's and women's cross-country, men's soccer, men's track, and men's basketball.

Overlaps

Bowdoin, Middlebury, Bates, Dartmouth, Williams.

If You Apply To ➤ **Colby**…Early decision: Nov. 15, Jan. 1. Regular admissions: Jan. 15. Financial aid: Feb. 1. Guarantees to meet demonstrated need. Campus interviews: recommended, informational. Alumni interviews: optional, informational. SATs or ACTs: required. SAT IIs: optional. Accepts the Common Application and electronic applications. Essay questions (any one): hopes and fears of the future; describe hometown; global issue of importance; something you've read that has caused you to change your view of the world.

13 Oak Drive, Hamilton, NY 13346

Website: www.colgate.edu
Location: Rural
Total Enrollment: 2,876
Undergraduates: 2,866
Male/Female: 48/52
SAT Ranges: V 600–690 M 610–700
ACT Range: 28–32
Financial Aid: 45%
Expense: Pr $ $ $ $
Phi Beta Kappa: Yes
Applicants: 5,590
Accepted: 42%
Enrolled: 32%
Grad in 6 Years: 89%
Returning Freshmen: 98%
Academics: ✍ ✍ ✍ ✍
Social: ☎ ☎ ☎
Q of L: ★ ★ ★
Admissions: -315) 228-7401
Email Address:
admission@mail.colgate.edu

Strongest Programs:
Political Science
Psychology
Economics
Philosophy/Religion
Geology
History
Foreign Language and
Literature
Biology

All language instruction programs are linked to off-campus study groups led by Colgate professors, and the Lawrence Hall Language Labs and classrooms offer state-of-the-art language studies facilities.

One of the nation's elite liberal arts colleges, Colgate is also the most selective of the "almost-Ivy" group, competing for applicants with Cornell and Dartmouth. With its beautiful campus, fine faculty, and spirited student body, the university, named for the man who founded the famed toothpaste empire, brings pride to the Colgate name. Boasts a psychology major, "Colgate not only academically stimulates it students, it challenges them to think creatively and teaches them the skills they need for every aspect of life."

Back in 1880, William Colgate gave $50,000 to the fledgling university–enough to get its name changed from Madison to Colgate. Though Colgate is called a "university," it is actually a small liberal arts college. Colgate's 515-acre campus is located on a hillside overlooking the village of Hamilton in rural New York. Its ivy-covered limestone buildings are all set amid tree-lined drives and lush green spaces, perfect for rugby, Frisbee, or a host of other outdoor diversions.

Colgate's interdisciplinary first-year seminar program gives freshmen a chance to meet top faculty and congregate in small groups. The faculty first established an interdisciplinary core program in 1928, and, while it has been adapted over the years, the core has been a foundation of the curriculum ever since. The latest revision examines the development of Western and non-Western cultures, and gives students a personal view of science and technology. The school also requires proficiency in a foreign language. Add to that one of 50 majors (or design your own), four physical education classes, and a swim test, and you have the Colgate version of a liberal arts education.

Among the concentrations in the liberal arts curriculum, English/writing, economics, psychology, philosophy/religion, history, and political science stand out. The math department receives some criticism from students. The college offers four concentration programs in environmental studies: environmental biology, geography, geology, and economics. A major in Japanese has recently been added. All language instruction programs are linked to off-campus study groups led by Colgate professors, and the Lawrence Hall Language Labs and classrooms offer state-of-the-art language studies facilities. Colgate's curriculum has an international flavor, and nearly half of all students take advantage of the school's study abroad options. In addition to the Maritime Studies Program* and the Sea Semester,* Colgate offers its students the chance to take part in an impressive array of off-campus study groups, many led by their own professors, in a number of countries including England, Japan, Nigeria, Russia, Poland, Central America, France, Germany, Switzerland, and Spain. One of the newest and most exciting off-campus study programs emphasizes the historical, environmental, and geographical diversity of Australia, and gives the students the opportunity to travel there. "Although there's a lot to learn at Colgate, the university recognizes the fact that there's much to learn elsewhere as well, so they provide the guidance and resources for a student to do so," says an English major. The Center for Ethics and World Studies brings nationally known authorities to campus to focus on different subjects each year.

Colgate works hard to keep its class sizes small; 99 percent of the courses have fewer than 50 students. Perhaps Colgate's greatest asset is a talented and dedicated faculty. "The professors at Colgate are the most committed and engaging groups of people that I've ever had the opportunity to be in contact with," says a political science major. Another student adds, "The professors here are extremely knowledgeable and expect a lot from their students but they are also willing to go the extra mile to help them." Undergraduate research is one of Colgate's greatest strengths, and its faculty receives accolades for involving students in research. Each summer, more than 100 students assist professors in their work. Academic advising is administered through the First-Year Seminar instructor, giving all students a classroom relationship with their advisor. Incoming freshmen get the campus to themselves for orientation, and some go on a weeklong camping trip before that to make friends and see the Adirondacks. For the three-quarters of Colgate grads who go directly to jobs rather than graduate school, the career counseling center is a blessing. Many students credit both the center and Colgate's strong and loyal alumni network with helping them land their first job.

With a combined minority population of only 13 percent, many students lament Colgate's lack of diversity. "One of the biggest issues facing Colgate is its lack of diversity, but the administration is taking great strides to deal with this problem," says a junior. Colgate has implemented an honor code that was developed, written, and passed by the students. "We are especially proud of the honor code because it was a student initiative," says a senior. Though there are no merit or athletic scholarships available, Colgate does meet 95 percent of demonstrated need.

Colgate's housing options range from traditional buildings with fireplaces to new ones that seem more like hotels than dorms. "The dorms are all in good shape because Colgate renovates each one every few years," says an English major. Another student adds, "Whenever friends from other colleges come to visit, they always comment on how nice our living arrangements are." The university offers various special-interest housing, including a substance-free dorm. About 250 upperclassmen are allowed to live off campus each year, and the remaining 74 percent live in university housing.

Despite the renovation of some bars downtown and the addition of a Chinese take-out restaurant, Hamilton is essentially the same place it was two or three generations ago. The town of 3,000 is not a social Mecca by any stretch of the imagination. "Hamilton is not a major metropolitan area, but it does offer a friendly, college town feel that can't be beat," says one senior. There's one very welcome addition to the town's main street, thanks to Colgate. The college recently opened the Barge Canal Coffee Company in a downtown storefront. The informal coffeehouse, open to faculty, students, and townspeople, has been very popular among Colgate students. "Besides serving up some mean java, the atmosphere is terrific, cheap, and there are games, puzzles, magazines, and books to occupy your hours," gushes a sophomore art/theater major.

Forty-two percent of men and 33 percent of women belong to Greek houses, so these still provide many of the social options. The university has increased its funding of student activities fourfold since 1990, and has stepped up its efforts to offer alternatives to frat parties and alcohol. "Colgate has definitely lost its image as a party school," says a sophomore. "The strict alcohol policy and the administration's deterrence of the Greek system are making a big difference." The campus pub and Edge Café offer on-campus social options, and dance parties have recently attracted enthusiastic participation. Spring Party Weekend and Winterfest are popular annual traditions, as is Octoberfest, which features pumpkin carving and a huge bonfire. Under the category of clean fun are the traditional rites of passage that punctuate the Colgate calendar. Among them are torchlight processions in the fall for first-years and the spring for seniors, and, of course, the Colgate vs. Cornell hockey game.

Colgate offers its students the chance to take part in an impressive array of off-campus study groups, many led by their own professors, in a number of countries including England, Japan, Nigeria, Russia, Poland, Central America, France, Germany, Switzerland, and Spain.

One of the newest and most exciting off-campus study programs emphasizes the historical, environmental, and geographical diversity of Australia, and gives the students the opportunity to travel there.

Colgate students love athletics. Period. Colgate's teams play in Division I, and despite being a David among many Goliaths, win more than their share of games. Hockey, football, and baseball are the top varsity spectator sports, and the teams are fierce competitors in the Eastern leagues. Men's and women's soccer also draw great crowds. The men's football team have been league champs, and women's teams have brought home trophies in soccer, field hockey, softball, and volleyball. Colgate also gives its students plenty of space to play and compete, including the Sanford Field House, the Lineberry natatorium, the nationally recognized Seven Oaks golf course, a trap range, a rock quarry for climbing, miles of trails for running and cycling, as well as sailing and crew facilities at scenic Lake Moraine, five minutes north of town.

Colgate is a cozy college with a much larger view of the world. "Colgate is small enough so that a student can really stand out and shine while its outstanding off-campus study programs offer them a chance to broaden their horizon," raves one student. Committed to undergraduate education, the college offers ample opportunities to have diverse and intense academic experiences, either on campus or in a foreign land under the active guidance of dedicated faculty.

Overlaps

Dartmouth, Cornell University, Boston College, Tufts, Middlebury.

If You Apply To ➤

Colgate...Early decision: Nov. 15, Jan. 15. Regular admissions: Jan 15. Financial aid: Feb. 1. Meets demonstrated need of 95%. Campus and alumni interviews: optional, informational. SATs and SAT IIs (English and two others) or ACTs required. Accepts the Common Application and electronic applications. Essay question: Explain how you will contribute to the Colgate community.

Colorado College

14 East Cache La Poudre, Colorado Springs, CO 80903

Website:
    www.ColoradoCollege.edu
Location: Urban
Total Enrollment: 1,964
Undergraduates: 1,941
Male/Female: 44/56
SAT Ranges: V 590–680 M 590–680
ACT Range: 25–30
Financial Aid: 45%
Expense: Pr $ $ $
Phi Beta Kappa: Yes
Applicants: 3,644
Accepted: 55%
Enrolled: 27%
Grad in 6 Years: 77%
Returning Freshmen: 93%

Students who have trouble balancing several academic subjects simultaneously may find solace at Colorado College. Under the Colorado College Plan, a.k.a. the Block Plan, students take their courses one at a time throughout the school year. This program makes for some intensely focused studying. CC is one of only two colleges in the nation offering the Block Plan, and this unusual approach has quickly earned this school a cool reputation among small liberal arts colleges. "CC is getting much more popular," confides a junior. "What better way could there be to learn?"

Founded in 1874, Colorado College is located at the foot of Pikes Peak near downtown Colorado Springs in a neighborhood district recognized by the National Historic Register. Many campus buildings are also part of this register, including Cutler Hall (1879), the college's first building, and Palmer Hall, named after William J. Palmer, founder of Colorado Springs and a major force behind the establishment of the college. Prevailing architectural styles include Romanesque and English Gothic. The school is currently embarking on a 10-year master plan that will feature new buildings and facilities.

Like those at most schools, students take eight courses between early September and mid-May. For three-and-a-half-week periods, students concentrate exclusively on the subject at hand. At the end of each session is a four-and-a-half-day block break during which students relax, head for the hills, or take part in concerts, plays, or other offerings scheduled for such periods. This academic plan defines the school. "Because of our block program, courses can be very rigorous," a senior says. "To miss one day is like missing a week." Yet the advantages of the Block Plan are numerous. Students can immerse themselves in one subject and concentrate on it without having to juggle a complicated schedule or let one course slide in order to get caught up in another. Students and teachers are flexible to odd scheduling needs by offering classes at unique times and in unique places—for instance, astronomy at midnight and anthropology work in Mexico. Class size is limited to 25 (average size is 15), and most students get into the classes they want. The method of securing seats is handled like an academic auction. At the beginning of each year students are given 80 points to "bid" on the classes they want. Those who bid the most for a particular class get a spot. CC students praise their professors. "The professors here are intelligent and caring," says a senior.

There are, of course, trade-offs to the block approach. Students say it is sometimes hard to integrate courses when you are taking them one at a time. There's also the danger of student and faculty burnout because of the amount of material crammed into such a short time and the intensity inherent in keeping a single subject in your mind without diversions.

The ability to take lab classes outside, and a 70,000-square-foot science complex, makes Colorado College's science program a favorite among the students. Classes that focus on fieldwork are particularly popular. "There is something extremely satisfying about going onsite and actually seeing firsthand what you were reading about the night before," says an English major whose introductory geology class featured trips to the Garden of the Gods, a nearby geological wonderland. But not all field trips are so close: students fly to the Caribbean to study coral biology. Additionally, the school sponsors its own programs in Germany, France, and Mexico, and the college offers programs in Chicago, London, India, Japan, Russia, and Hong Kong, as well as several other study abroad opportunities through the Associated Colleges of the Midwest.*

While some students complain that interdisciplinary study is difficult under the Block Plan, an Asian studies major and a women's studies major help to focus interdisciplinary agendas. Some of the social sciences—anthropology and sociology, for instance—are considered the "weaker" offerings by many students. Some also believe that foreign languages fall short in the Block Plan. The college offers a popular program in Southwest studies, which includes spending time at the school's Baca campus, located 175 miles away in the historic San Luis Valley. For more variety, students can design their own majors or take advantage of the International Affairs Option or the American Ethnic Studies program. The Block Plan fosters unique programs such as the Executive in Residence program, which brings senior-level business executives to the economics department for one block of teaching, lecturing, and student interaction.

As part of the general education program, all students are required to take two courses in the Western tradition; three courses in the natural sciences, including lab and field study; and two additional courses in either non-Western or minority cultures. They may also choose what is called a thematic minor, five closely related courses that examine an issue or theme, a cultural group, area of the world, or time period. The library, with 440,000 volumes, is long on hours (open until 2:00 A.M.), but occasionally, students complain, short on books necessary for classwork. Before the school year begins, freshmen are required to participate in New Student Orientation, which includes four days of activities and

(Continued)

Academics: ✏ ✏ ✏ ✏

Social: ☎ ☎ ☎ ☎

Q of L: ★ ★ ★ ★

Admissions: (800) 542-7214

Email Address: admission@ coloradocollege.edu

Strongest Programs:
  Biology
  Geology
  English

The ability to take lab classes outside, and a 70,000-square-foot science complex, makes Colorado College's science program a favorite among the students.

lectures. Colorado College also offers a number of freshman seminars.

Students at Colorado College are a bright and independent lot. Seventy percent are from outside Colorado and 84 percent graduated in the top quarter of their high school class. And while some fear that there has been an influx of right-wingers, students agree that generally social attitudes are rather liberal. The college provides forums for many varied organizations, including the Bisexual, Gay and Lesbian Alliance, the Feminist Collective, the College Republicans, the Jewish Chaverim, and the Black Student Union. But don't worry, the political fervor is not overpowering. "All social and political issues are alive on campus, but not rampantly," a junior psychology major says. Close to 12 percent of the students are minorities—2 percent are African American, 6 percent Hispanic, 1 percent Native American, and 3 percent Asian American—and the school is trying to attract more. Diversity is always difficult at a small school with limited funds. An English major acknowledges, "There is no overall hostility, but some segregation." The admissions office places great weight on the essay, and 10 percent of each year's freshmen begin their work at summer school, take off the fall, and then settle into the regular routine in January. The college guarantees to meet the demonstrated need of most students, and it offers merit scholarships in the natural sciences and mathematics. Thirty-one athletic scholarships are awarded to either male ice hockey players or female soccer stars (the school's only Division I teams).

Sixty-six percent of the students live on campus. Dormitories differ architecturally, from large brick halls to small wooden houses. They also differ by specialty: freshman, same-sex, language, or cultural theme, for example. Language houses cover Spanish, Russian, German, Italian, and French. The college recently spent $10 million to renovate the three primary residence halls. Students are required to live on campus for three years, but housing is guaranteed for all four years. On-campus students usually subscribe to at least 10 meals a week in the dining halls, but one student, citing the food provided, concludes, "I guess we're expected to feed ourselves on thought instead."

The sunny, dry Colorado weather is excellent for outdoor sports. The Freshman Outdoor Orientation Trips (FOOT) help out-of-staters sort out the options: backpacking, skiing, mountain climbing, hiking, rafting, bicycling, even windsurfing. Students frequently camp at a college-owned mountainside cabin. Campus nightlife includes dorm-sponsored and fraternity parties. About 15 percent of the men and women join fraternities and sororities. Despite rather stringent rules for on-campus parties and stricter enforcement of the 21-year-old drinking age, most students agree with a junior who says, "As long as the doors are shut, the students get away with underage drinking." For those who don't want to, the campus center hangout, Benjamin's, serves great milk shakes. The college sponsors a wide variety of activities, and the hockey games entertain many students. The spring festival, Llamapalooza, brings about 10 different bands to play outdoors.

It seems the tie that binds the college together is the Block Plan. This makes or breaks Colorado College, and a decision to go to CC is a decision in favor of the college's academic agenda. Says one student succinctly, "It's why we're here."

Overlaps

University of Colorado, Middlebury, Lewis and Clark, Carleton, Brown.

If You Apply To >

Colorado College…Early action: Nov. 15. Regular admissions: Jan. 15. Financial aid: Feb. 15. Guarantees to meet demonstrated need. Campus interviews: optional, informational. No alumni interviews. SATs or ACTs: required. No SAT IIs. Accepts the Common Application and electronic applications. Essay question: piece of art or literature that is meaningful; experience with a different culture; or important issue of local, national, or international concern. Also, explain educational objectives and why Colorado College.

Colorado School of Mines

1811 Elm Street, Golden, CO 80401-1842

For those seeking a quality technical education, the Colorado School of Mines shines like a gem. This top technical institute, long known for its emphasis on mineral engineering, continues to challenge its bright students with rigorous academic training and exposure to hands-on fieldwork. But life at CSM isn't all about study and work; there's also enough fun for everyone. "The students here work hard during the week so they like to kick back on the weekends," says a chemical engineer major. "And with Denver a mere 15 miles away, the opportunities for entertainment are endless."

Lying in the shadow of the spectacular Rocky Mountains, CSM's 373-acre campus offers a range of architectural styles, from turn-of-the-century gold dome to present-day modern. Lush lawns are punctuated by native trees and greenery. An ambitious campus renewal program is underway at CSM, including renovations on the student center and some of the residence halls. Construction has also been completed on a new $12 classroom building.

Pass/fail grading is unheard of at the Colorado School of mines but failing grades are not. "Academic competitiveness is the hallmark of Mines," notes a sophomore. "If you work and think, you succeed. If you don't, you go to another school." While some teachers may push too hard, most win praise for their accessibility and concern. "The professors at CSM are here to teach, not to do research," says a mechanical engineering major. "They also have a knack for taking complex material and breaking it down so their students can understand it." One program aiming to provide a more well-rounded education is the Engineering Practices Introductory Course Sequence (EPICS), a two-semester sequence that develops communications, teamwork, and problem-solving skills. Another is a program targeted at mineral engineers that offers background on the Third World nations where they will most likely work.

All freshmen take the same first-year program, which includes courses in chemistry, calculus, physical education, physics, and the natural sciences. Another program for freshmen is the Freshmen Success Seminar, an advising and mentoring course designed to increase retention of first-year students. The undergraduate major fields—or "options," as they're called—are quite good, although the humanities and liberal arts programs are cited as lacking substance. Eager students may pick from among such subjects as mining, metallurgy, geophysical, geological, or chemical engineering, or engineering with civil, electrical, or mechanical specialties. There's also a major in economics, the school's first nontechnical degree. Less prominent programs include chemistry and applied mathematics. Courses in a student's option start in the second semester of the sophomore year, and by senior year, courses are generally in one's field. Students say the 145,000-volume library is well stocked with engineering and technical materials,

Website: www.mines.edu

Location: Small town

Total Enrollment: 3,273

Undergraduates: 2,473

Male/Female: 76/24

SAT Ranges: V 530-650 M 600–700

ACT Range: 25–30

Financial Aid: 74%

Expense: Pub $ $ $ $

Phi Beta Kappa: Yes

Applicants: 1,978

Accepted: 75%

Enrolled: 38%

Grad in 6 Years: 65%

Returning Freshmen: 87%

Academics: ✐ ✐ ✐

Social: ☎ ☎ ☎

Q of L: ★ ★

Admissions: (303) 273-3220

Email Address:
admit@mines.edu

Strongest Programs:
Mining Engineering
Petroleum Engineering
Chemical Engineering
Geophysical Engineering
Geological Engineering

but "if you are just looking for a book to read and let your mind wander, you had best go elsewhere," says one future mining engineer.

In addition to the two regular semesters during the school year, students in all options must complete a six-week summer field session to gain hands-on experience in their field. For super-ambitious students, there is the Guy T. McBride Honors Program in the humanities, which consists of 27 credit hours of seminars and off-campus activities. In the summer, the program even takes them to Washington, D.C., for a series of seminars in engineering public affairs. CSM also offers its students a chance to study abroad in Sweden, Austria, Mexico, Australia, France, and several other countries.

CSM is a state school, and 75 percent of its students are from Colorado. Minority enrollment continues to increase: Blacks, Hispanics, Native Americans, and Asian Americans together account for 13 percent of the student body. Everyone agrees that CSM students are conservative. Social issues take a backseat to concern with things like oil gluts and energy development. One student offers this breakdown of the population: "Twenty-five percent squids (those who study 24 hours), and the rest fun-loving and willing to work hard for satisfactory grades." Whatever their study habits, 91 percent of the students ranked in the top quarter of their class. Aside from a handful of athletic scholarships, 400 students receive merit scholarships ranging from $1,000 to $14,716.

The location of CSM at the base of the Rocky Mountains ensures students of gorgeous Colorado weather and easy access to skiing, mountain climbing, and other outdoor sports. "Golden is small and secluded, but it's close to Denver and all of its attractions," says a senior. Denver is home to many governmental agencies and businesses involved in natural resources, computers, and technology, as well as to the regional offices of the U.S. Geological Survey and Bureau of Mines. Golden itself hosts the National Earthquake Center, the National Renewable Energy Laboratory, and of course, the Coors Brewery. (The 3,000-foot pipeline that runs from the Coors plant to the campus is used to convert excess steam from the brewery into heat for the school—not to supply the frats.)

The school's residence halls are comfortable and most are coed, though the preponderance of men results in a few single-sex dorms. The "old" dorms have conventional doubles, but the newer and more popular Weaver Towers house students in five-room suites. "The dorms are cleaned daily and are continuously painted and repaired," says a junior. Many upperclassmen move off campus. The one dining hall offers several meal plans; aside from the salad bar, the food—"a little pricey" for some—receives less than rave reviews.

There is life outside of the library, though at CSM it is well hidden. There are six fraternities and two sororities, which attract 17 percent of the men and women. Rush is dry; nevertheless, it is still possible to hear an occasional chorus of "I drink my whiskey clear. I'm a rambling wreck from Golden Tech and a helluva engineer!" (adapted from Georgia Tech). What about the social life? "The CSM community is close-knit so you make a lot of friends, which makes for a great social life," says a mining engineering major. "A senior agrees but adds, "Mines is 25 percent women, making it a little rough on the guys."

As fate would have it, the biggest social event of the year is known as Engineering Days, a three-day extravaganza with everything from tricycle races to taco-eating contests to what one student describes as "mining events." The M-climb has students climbing up Mount Zion and arranging a giant letter M with white stones. One student notes that "CSM is probably one of the last places where you will find true student athletes. We play for fun." Nevertheless, CSM boasts more varsity sports than any other college in Colorado. The school also won the NCAA II national championship in wrestling, and three of CSM's coaches have received Coach of the Year honors.

"Mines is a school to be endured, not enjoyed," says one student. And yet everyone praises the small size, emphasis on engineering, and the new push to prepare students for more than just their first job. A CSM education equips students for a lifetime in the forefront, and, quite possibly, the boardrooms of resource, technological, and manufacturing companies. As one student explains, "CSM prepares us not just for our careers but for the real world."

If You Apply To ➤ **CSM**…Regular admissions: June 1. Financial aid: Mar. 1. Housing: May 1. Guarantees to meet demonstrated need. Campus and alumni interviews: optional, informational. SATs or ACTs: required. SAT IIs: optional. No essay question.

University of Colorado at Boulder

Campus Box 30, Boulder, CO 80309

At first glance, the University of Colorado seems to have it all. The academic programs are top-notch. There is an active social scene. And the majestic Rocky Mountains provide a breathtaking backdrop and boundless playground for book-weary students. But on closer inspection you'll find that…well, that the school seems to have it all. Says one happy student, "Walking to class after a light dusting of snow overnight, I look at the sparkling Flatirons and am reminded of why I came here."

Tree-shaded walkways, winding bike paths, open spaces, and an incredible view of the Flatirons, a dramatic rock formation, has made the 600-acre Boulder campus a haven for escapees from both the East and West coasts, and even for Coloradans hoping to complete their pursuit of knowledge in a snowy paradise. The campus architecture is fashioned in the style of the Italian Renaissance, and buildings are composed of Colorado sandstone and complemented with red-tile roofs. The campus tends to look and feel a bit like an Ivy League school (CU's architect also worked for Yale and Princeton), and new additions are popping up all the time. The Institute for Behavioral Genetics and a museum collections building are in the planning stages.

The best of the state's public universities, CU–Boulder has also worked hard to shed its longstanding "party school" image. "In general, the atmosphere at CU is one of academic growth rather than partying," says a senior. CU–Boulder offers entering freshmen the choice of five colleges: arts and sciences, business administration, engineering and applied science, environmental design, and music. Each has different entrance standards and requirements; music, for example, requires an audition of all prospective students. The department of molecular and cellular developmental biology, with its state-of-the-art electron microscopes, is one of the best of its kind in the nation. CU can also boast of its space satellite (the only student-run satellite in the country) and of 11 graduates who have made it into space, creating a rather stellar alumni roster. Business, engineering, psychology, and the hard sciences are strong at CU. But despite seemingly limitless course offerings (CU boasts 2,500 courses covering 150 fields of study), students

Website: www.colorado.edu
Location: Suburban
Total Enrollment: 28,373
Undergraduates: 22,660
Male/Female: 52/48
SAT Ranges: V 520–620 M 540–640
ACT Range: 22–27
Financial Aid: 38%
Expense: Pub $ $
Phi Beta Kappa: Yes
Applicants: 14,647
Accepted: 85%
Enrolled: 41%
Grad in 6 Years: 64%
Returning Freshmen: 84%
Academics: 🏛 🏛 🏛 🏛
Social: ☎ ☎ ☎ ☎ ☎
Q of L: ★ ★ ★ ★ ★
Admissions: (303) 492-6301
Email Address:
apply@colorado.edu

Strongest Programs:
Psychology
Biology
Chemistry

CU can also boast of its space satellite (the only student-run satellite in the country) and of 11 graduates who have made it into space, creating a rather stellar alumni roster.

The FallFEST program allows 250 freshmen to register for a set of prepackaged core curriculum classes in an effort to simplify course selection for them.

find most of the foreign languages—with the notable exceptions of Spanish and Chinese—and humanities lagging behind. The set of general education requirements covers two areas of study. The first emphasizes writing, foreign language proficiency, and critical thinking. The second emphasizes learning in several other categories: historical context, cultural and gender diversity, natural sciences, contemporary societies, literature and the arts, and ideals and values.

Counseling and advising at CU–Boulder receive high marks, as does the faculty. "The professors are one of the most valuable resources on campus," says a student. "They are always willing to work with students." Boulder has managed to personalize things further through its residential academic programs: 330 qualified underclassmen take part in the Sewall Hall program, living together and studying in small seminars, while the Farrand Hall program offers 400 other underclassmen a structured academic program, also in a residential setting. Farrand classes are limited to 20 to 25 students each. The FallFEST program allows 250 freshmen to register for a set of prepackaged core curriculum classes in an effort to simplify course selection for them. The President's Leadership Class is a two-year scholarship program of lectures, recitations, and seminars that starts the freshman year. This program exposes the university's most promising students to governors, congresspeople, and business and community leaders, and takes them to sites of Colorado industry, the state capital, community-service agencies, and the like.

Students can't say enough about the weather, the setting, and the beauty of Boulder. Whatever the season, the campus is "the best place on earth," says a journalism major. "Boulder is a great conglomeration of suburbia and a college town," says a molecular and cellular biology major. "There is always something going on." The town does indeed cater to the students: there are three Birkenstock stores and a pedestrian mall with street singers and mimes. The high number of out-of-staters, who make up a nearly a third of the student body, is surprising; students from outside Colorado pay the hefty out-of-state price tag. The CU student body is known for being rather outspoken. CU has such a diversity of students that almost any issue affects a group of students. Similarly, CU has a large selection of student groups that cover almost any interest from ethnic clubs to athletic clubs to volunteer clubs to honor societies. The minority community—African Americans are a mere 2 percent, Hispanics 5 percent, and Asian Americans 6 percent—has been particularly active in pointing out instances of racial prejudice and demanding higher minority enrollments. However, students are quick to point out they are very accepting of those different from them. "We are very open-minded at CU and show respect for others regardless of race, religion, or sexual preference," says a marketing major. Bright students are rewarded with more than 5,000 merit scholarships, which provide up to $26,000 each, and scholarships are available for most sports. The Norlin Scholars Program is a new initiative designed for highly motivated students with excellent academic or creative ability; the program will eventually include 100 Norlin Scholars fellows, who will each receive a $2,000 four-year renewable scholarship.

First-year students are required to live in the dorms. The word from upperclassmen is make reservations early, and make them at Farrand, Sewall, or Kittredge halls. All dorm rooms are equipped with microwaves, refrigerators, cable TV, and Internet hook-ups. After the first year, most students move off campus. The campus is very safe and several students mention the school's Night Walk/Ride program, which provides volunteer escorts after dark. "This campus is very well lit and has an abundance of emergency phones with direct connections to the CU police department," says a math major.

One alternative to the "decent, but not great" school meal plan or the horrid slop at the fraternity houses is the student-run Alferd Packer Grill. This snack shop provides fast food under apparently innocent auspices, but Boulder students and historical trivialists know that Alferd Packer was convicted and sentenced in Colorado for cannibalism in 1883. Still hungry? If so, then the idea of a student-sponsored Alferd Packer Day won't be too hard to swallow, either. This 25-year-old tradition includes rib- and raw-meat-eating contests, a belching contest, and a red onion munch.

Though life at CU still revolves around having fun, as one student puts it, "a new era has begun at CU." CU's Greek system became the first in the nation to vote its houses dry and the ban is taken seriously among the Greeks, who comprise 10 percent of the men and 13 percent of the women. Off campus as well, bars check IDs. "It's not easy for underage students to get served in public venues, but, as is the case with most colleges, they can find booze if they look hard enough," says a molecular biology major. Still, students aren't complaining too much. "There is almost too much to do with so little time," one student reports. In fact, some students have noticed that it is too easy to have a good time at CU. Less than two-thirds of the Boulder students receive degrees within five years.

For the culturally minded, both the university and the town offer all sorts of films and plays, the renowned Colorado Shakespeare Festival, and concerts by top rock bands. On-campus entertainment includes free movies, theater performances, speakers, dances, and barbeques. "There are so many activities here that a student is never bored," says a senior. It's easy to get around by using the free bus service that runs on campus and through town, but many would rather walk, since exercise is the leading extracurricular activity. The student rec center, with its swimming pools, squash and racquetball courts, three weight rooms, and ice-skating rink, is well worth the extra $68 yearly. There's a teeny "practice" ski area just over a half-hour away, but it will take you another half-hour to get to the best resorts. Mountain-climbing enthusiasts have interpreted CU to stand for "Climb with Us." Naturally, the ski team is one of the best in the nation, but the football team has also had its share of success. The Nebraska rivalry always promises to be rowdy, and Ralphie (the CU mascot) is always seen cheering on the team.

While CU offers a smorgasbord of academic courses, extracurricular activities do sometimes tend to get in the way. Some students seem to find it hard to resist the ever present call of the Rockies, a call that tears them away from books and school for an hour, a day, or even a whole semester. Most, however, are in the game to get a well-rounded education and say this university is the perfect place for it. Students in the market for strong academics and abundant recreation will find the best of both worlds at CU.

The President's Leadership Class is a two-year scholarship program of lectures, recitations, and seminars that starts the freshman year.

Overlaps

Colorado State, Arizona State, University of Arizona, UCLA, UC–Santa Barbara.

If You Apply To ➤	**Boulder**…Regular admissions: Feb. 1 for freshmen, Apr. 1 for transfers. Financial aid: Apr. 1. Housing: May 1. Does not guarantee to meet demonstrated need. No campus or alumni interviews. SATs or ACTs: required. SAT IIs: optional. Apply to particular school or program. Accepts electronic applications. Essay question: personal statement.

Columbia College

212 Hamilton Hall, New York, NY 10027

Website: www.columbia.edu

Location: Urban

Total Enrollment: 21,547

Undergraduates: 7,593

Male/Female: 50/50

SAT Ranges: V 650–760 M 650–740

ACT Range: 29–34

Financial Aid: 60%

Expense: Pr $ $ $ $

Phi Beta Kappa: Yes

Applicants: 13,012

Accepted: 14%

Enrolled: 56%

Grad in 6 Years: 90%

Returning Freshmen: 97%

Academics: ✍ ✍ ✍ ✍ ✍

Social: ☎ ☎ ☎

Q of L: ★ ★ ★

Admissions: (212) 854-2522

Email Address:
ugrad-admiss@columbia.edu

Strongest Programs:
English
History
Political Science
Economics
Dance
Drama
Chemistry
Biology

New programs in Asian American Studies, Latino Studies, and American Studies have recently been added to the curriculum.

Though students entering Columbia College will, of course, expect the rigorous academic program they'll encounter at this Ivy League school, there's no room here in the heart of Manhattan for the bookish nerd. Students must be streetwise, urbane, and together enough to handle one of the most cosmopolitan cities in the world. "Columbia College is a small, prestigious Ivy school in the middle of one of the most exciting cities in the nation," says a sophomore. "Anything a student could possibly want is available to him." CC lets its students experience life in the Big Apple, but serves as a refuge when it becomes necessary to escape from New York; ideally, Columbians can easily be part of the "real world" while simultaneously immersing themselves in the best academia has to offer.

Although Columbia is among the smallest colleges in the Ivy League, its atmosphere is far from intimate. With a total university-wide enrollment of 21,000 students, "it's easy to feel lost. "Still, the college is the jewel in the university's crown and the focus is "unquestionably oriented toward undergraduate education," reports a classics major. Columbia's campus has a large central quadrangle in front of Butler Library and at the foot of the steps leading past the statue of Alma Mater to Low Library, which is now the administration building. The red-brick, copper-roofed neoclassical buildings are "stunning," and the layout, says an undergrad, "is well thought out and manages to provide a beautiful setting with an economy of space."

Columbia is an intellectual school, not a preprofessional one, and even though 60 percent of the students aspire to law or medical school (they enjoy a 90 percent acceptance rate), "we are mostly content to be liberal artists for as long as possible," says an English major. Almost all departments that offer undergraduate majors are strong, notably English, history, political science, and psychology. Chemistry and biology are among the best of Columbia's high-quality science offerings. The geology department owns 200 acres in Rockland County, home to many rocks and much seismographic equipment. There are 35 offerings in foreign languages, ranging from Serbo-Croatian to Uzbek to Hausa. The arts are not fabulous, but are improving, thanks to departmental reorganization, new facilities, and joint offerings with schools such as Juilliard. And while the administration admits that the economics and computer science departments are geared too much toward graduate students, at least the comp-sci undergrads benefit from an increase in equipment. Columbia offers many challenging combined majors such as philosophy/economics and biology/psychology. The East Asian languages and cultures department is one of the best anywhere. New programs in Asian American Studies, Latino Studies, and American Studies have recently been added to the curriculum. There is also an African American studies major and a women's studies major that delves into topics from the Asian woman's perspective to the lesbian experience in literature.

The kernel of the undergraduate experience is the college's renowned core curriculum. While these courses occupy most of the first two years and can become laborious, students generally praise them as worthwhile and enriching: "You learn how to read analytically, write sharply, and speak succinctly, and you are exposed to the greatest ideas in Western art, music, literature, and philosophy," exclaims an enlightened sociology major. A junior adds, "The core is the highlight of our education, providing the basis for all other classes and giving you an amazing familiarity with Western civilization...it's been one of the best parts of my experience." The value of the Western emphasis of the core, however, is a subject of much debate. "Why should we study the Western tradition when it represents sexism, racism, imperialism, and exploitation?" asks one incensed student. "The canon is composed almost exclusively of dead European males." Yet, as it has since World War I, the college remains committed to the core, while at the same time expanding the diversity of the canon and requiring core classes on non-Western cultures.

Two of the most demanding introductory courses in the Ivy League—contemporary civilization and literature humanities—form the basis of the core. Both are yearlong, taught in small sections, and generally by full profs. "Nearly everything I'd grown up believing was questioned in one way or another. They forced me to examine my life and to ponder how I fit into the big picture," states an art history major. LitHum (as it is affectionately called) covers about 26 masterpieces of literature from Homer to Dostoyevsky, usually with some Sappho, Jane Austen, and Virginia Woolf thrown in for alternative perspectives. CC examines political and moral philosophy from Plato to Camus, though professors have some leeway in choosing 20th-century selections. One semester each of art and humanities is required, and while not given the same reverence as their literary counterparts, are eye-opening all the same. Foreign language proficiency is required, as are two semesters of science; two semesters of "extended core," classes dealing in cultures not covered in the other core requirements; two semesters of phys ed; and Logic and Rhetoric, a one-semester argumentative writing class that first-year students reportedly "either love or hate."

Columbia is hardly a cakewalk academically, and students always have something to read or write. Student-faculty interaction is largely dependent on student initiative. Additional interaction stems from professorial involvement in campus politics and forums, and from the faculty-in-residence program, which houses professors and their families in spruced-up apartments in several of the residence halls. First-year students are assigned a faculty advisor, and receive a departmental advisor when they declare majors at the end of sophomore year. Columbia students can take classes at Barnard, which maintains its own faculty, reported to be "more caring and involved than Columbia's." As at Barnard, students can also take graduate-level courses in several departments, notably political science, gaining access to the resources of the School of International and Public Affairs and its multitude of regional institutes. For students wishing to spend time away from New York, there are summer, semester, and one-year programs at the Reid Hall campus in Paris; other programs include opportunities with Kyoto University in Japan, Howard University in Washington, D.C., Oxford or Cambridge in England, and The Free University of Berlin.

To call Columbia diverse would be "a gross understatement. We make Noah's Ark look homogeneous," says a sophomore. In fact, Columbia has the largest percentage of students of color in the Ivy League; 10 percent are African American, 8 percent are Hispanic, and 19 percent are Asian American. About 17 percent of the students come from New York City and another 15 percent from elsewhere in the state, especially Long Island. On the whole, the admissions office seeks "an urban type or someone who wants to be." Socially, the campus is also very diverse. "We have Euros, WASPs, jocks, grinds, sorority bunnies, Deadheads, fashion plates, a sizable Jewish population, and plenty of sideburn-sporting, cigarette-smoking, espresso-sipping, angst-ridden folks who own only black clothing," reports an undergrad observer.

Columbia remains one of the nation's most liberal campuses. "Columbia has

Columbia offers many challenging combined majors such as philosophy/economics and biology/psychology.

always been known for its tradition of social and political activism," says a junior. "Students are not afraid to protest to get what they want." No one group dominates campus life. Although 6 percent of the men and 6 percent of the women go Greek, Columbia is hardly a Hellenocentric campus, namely because, as a junior argues, "the frats are chock-full of athletic recruits, the organizations—even the coed ones—are deemed elitist and politically incorrect, and there are too many better things to do in NYC on a Friday night than getting trashed in the basement of some random house." The advent of coed houses has raised interest in Greek life, as has the arrival of sororities open to both Columbia and Barnard women.

With the New York housing market out of control, 95 percent of Columbia students live in university housing, which is guaranteed for four years. Security at the dorms is rated as excellent by students, and every person entering has to flash an ID to the guard on duty at the front door or be signed in by a resident of the building. One exciting aspect of Columbia housing is that many rooms are singles, and it is possible to go all four years without a roommate. Carman Hall is the exclusively first-year dorm and "the fact that you get to meet your classmates compensates for the noise and hideous cinder-block walls," says a music major. First-year students can also live in buildings with students of all years. "Living with upperclasspeople was great. They knew the ins and outs of the university and the neighborhood. It wasn't the blind leading the blind," offers a junior. First-year students are automatically placed on a 19-meal-a-week plan and take most of those meals at John Jay, an all-you-can-eat "binge-a-rama with salad bar, deli, grill, and huge dessert bar." Many soon-bloated students scale down their meal plans or convert to points, a buy-what-you-want arrangement with account information stored electronically on student ID cards. Several dorms have kitchens, allowing students to do much of their own cooking. Some students dine at the kosher dining hall at Barnard.

Social life on campus is best described as mellow. Rarely are there big all-inclusive bashes, the exceptions being fall's '60s throwback, Realityfest, and spring's Columbiafest. "The social scene here is well balanced between school events, concerts and dances, and the variety of activities the city offers," says a senior.

Sports in general are not too bad at Columbia. After a dismal 44-game losing streak in the mid-1980s, the football team is attempting to turn things around. The fencing teams are superlative, placing several members on the 1992 U.S. Olympic team. Men's soccer and basketball are also strong. As an urban school, Columbia lacks team field facilities on campus; however, merely 100 blocks to the north there's the modern Baker Field, home of the football stadium, the soccer fields, an Olympic track, and the crew boathouse. On campus, the Dodge Gymnasium, an underground facility, houses four levels of basketball courts, swimming pools, weight rooms, and exercise equipment. The gym is often crowded and not all the stuff is wonderful. "It does the job, as well as providing for the best pickup basketball this side of Riverside Park," notes a sophomore. Intramural and club sports are popular, with men's and women's Ultimate Frisbee both national competitors.

Columbians are proud that they are going to college in New York City, and most would have it no other way. Explains an art history major: "Choosing to isolate oneself in the middle of nowhere for four years isn't what college is about. It's about taking one's place as an adult in an adult society. Columbia is the perfect place for that."

Overlaps

Harvard, Yale, Brown, Penn, Cornell.

Columbia…Early decision: Nov. 1. Regular admissions: Jan. 1. Financial aid: Jan. 1. Housing: Jan. 1. Meets demonstrated need of 60%. Campus interviews: not available. Alumni interviews: optional, evaluative. SATs or ACTs: required. SAT IIs: required (writing and two others). Essay: personal statement.

Connecticut College

270 Mohegan Avenue, New London, CT 06320-4196

Connecticut College is a small liberal arts school known for its excellent academics, strong study abroad programs, and student-faculty research. This close-knit community is shaped by a student honor code that governs nearly every aspect of a student's life. "The honor code is what makes Conn College unique," says a senior. "It works to build a society on campus that is conducive to the academic and social growth of each student."

Sitting majestically atop a hill, Conn College's lovely campus provides a beautiful view of the Thames River (pronounced the way it looks, not like the "Temz" that Wordsworth so dearly loved) on one side and Long Island Sound on the other. The school is set on a 700-acre arboretum which includes a pond, wetlands, wooded areas, and hiking trails. The granite campus buildings are a mixture of modern and collegiate Gothic, neo-Gothic, and neo-Classical architecture.

Since its founding as a women's school in 1911, Conn College has been dedicated to the liberal arts. Today, students of both sexes must take general education requirements that cover seven broad areas, including philosophical and religious studies, physical and biological sciences, mathematics and logic, historical studies, and a foreign language. In addition, freshmen must complete two courses that are writing intensive or writing enhanced and a freshman tutorial with their advisor.

The dance and drama departments at Conn are superb. Talented dance students often take a few semesters off to study with professional companies, and theater majors have the chance to work with the Eugene O'Neill Theater Institute, named for New London's favorite literary son. Science majors have an observatory, telescope, research labs, and auditorium all at their disposal and students may apply for stipends through special programs to conduct summer research. In what is arguably the best-conceived undergraduate study abroad program anywhere, students can actually study and work in foreign countries like India, Mexico, Morocco, South Africa, China, and Japan. The international studies program allows students to study in another country, learn its language, work there, and then return to reflect upon their experiences in a seminar with other world travelers. The school's arts and technology certificate program—the first of its kind in the nation—examines the connection between the arts and computer technology such as computer animation and virtual reality. In addition, the museum studies program explores "the role of museums in shaping society's knowledge about art, culture, history, and the natural world." Among the school's weaker programs are computer science and math. Conn College is also part of the Twelve-College Exchange* and Venture Program consortiums.*

Students have uniform praise for the college's emphasis on small class size

Website: www.conncoll.edu
Location: Suburban
Total Enrollment: 1,820
Undergraduates: 1,764
Male/Female: 43/57
SAT Ranges: V 600–690 M 590–680
Financial Aid: 51%
Expense: Pr $ $ $ $
Phi Beta Kappa: No
Applicants: 3,700
Accepted: 39%
Enrolled: 33%
Grad in 6 Years: 82%
Returning Freshmen: 91%
Academics: ✍ ✍ ✍ ✍
Social: ☎ ☎ ☎
Q of L: ★ ★ ★ ★
Admissions: (860) 439-2202
Email Address:
admit@conncoll.edu

Strongest Programs:
Psychology
Government
English
Economics
History
Dance

and the quality of their professors. Most classes average only 25 students. "The quality of teaching has been wonderful," says a psychology major. "Professors are passionate about their subjects and committed to imparting that wisdom on to their students." Students also appreciate the feeling of trust embodied in the school's honor code, which allows them to take self-scheduled, unproctored exams anytime during a 10-day exam period. Most agree that competition is mainly within the individual and not so much among students. "The atmosphere is more supportive than competitive," says a sophomore. A senior adds,"Conn has an intellectual climate, students actively engage in discussions in and out of the classroom."

Connecticut College seeks motivated students looking for academic challenges. Fifty-six percent of the student body ranked in the top tenth of their high school class, and average SAT scores are fairly high. However, Conn has now joined the ranks of those making SATs optional, arguing that a transcript is a better indicator of an individual's academic achievement and potential.

The student body at Conn College is 82 percent white and mostly from New England and the Mid-Atlantic states. African Americans and Hispanics each comprise only 3 percent of the student body, while Asian Americans account for 2 percent. In an effort to promote diversity, the administration requires freshmen to attend a student talk where a panel of their peers representing different races, religions, genders, socioeconomic classes, sexual orientations, and physical disabilities addresses today's issues. Unity House continues to be the center for building community relationships across ethnic and racial boundaries. "The students here recognize that everyone has a right to be happy and free," says a chemistry major. "We are a very tolerant community." There are no athletic or academic merit scholarships, and recent budget woes have led to the closure of two dining halls and a dramatic increase in campus health service fees.

The living conditions are among the finest to be found anywhere. Almost everyone (99 percent) lives on campus, and most upperclassmen receive single rooms if they so desire. Freshmen are often put in doubles, triples, or quads in the "beautiful old stone buildings, "which feature living rooms with baby grand pianos and fireplaces." Renovations are under way on six dorms located on the north side of campus called the "plex." All dorms house students from all four classes, which one students says "makes everyone very close." Those with special interests might want to investigate the foreign language or international dorms; others enjoy the Earth House. Monday through Friday, students eat in the small dorm dining rooms, which make some miss Mom's cooking. On weekends, everyone eats at the plex.

Students, rather than the administration, run the dorms, and most activities, including coed intramural sports, revolve around the dorms. There are no fraternities or sororities on campus, but there are weekly keg and all-campus theme parties sponsored by dorms or other student groups. A majority of the social life takes place on campus and is provided by the student-run Student Activities Council. "The social life at Conn College takes place on the campus through a plethora of diverse events including, parties, bands, concerts, dances, and a million other activities," says an English and economics double major. Another student adds, "Conn is not a suitcase school, most people stay on campus for parties." The alcohol policy fits under the honor code, so it is very difficult for minors to get served at campus events, but a student adds, "If underage students want to drink, they will find a way."

The most serious of the school's varsity sports are sailing, men's and women's lacrosse, men's soccer, rowing, field hockey, and ice hockey (the rink heats up like crazy if rival Wesleyan is on the ice). "One of my favorite pictures is of students sitting along 'the bump' that separates the two main playing fields and watching a guy's soccer game one minute, then turning around to see our Lady Camels in action with field hockey the next," remarks one student. Conn students look forward to the annual Floralia celebration, described as "the best time ever". The event takes place on the first Saturday every May, just in time to have some fun before exams set in. For relaxation between classes or at the end of the day, students can even enjoy the natatorium, with its pool and fitness gym, and the field house, which includes rowing tanks and climbing walls.

Connecticut College is notable among the high-quality Eastern colleges for its coastal location. There are gorgeous beaches within 20 minutes of campus, which must make those A's and B's harder to come by as the Connecticut winter finally warms into spring. The town of New London receives mixed reviews from students who appreciate its fine restaurants and "weathered charm," but who feel it lacks many collegiate activities. "New London is not terribly exciting and there's not much to do aside from going to the malls, restaurants, and bars downtown," says a English and economics double major. Many students stay busy doing community service. Volunteering is "huge." "Students are encouraged to volunteer in some way in the community, and the college provides transportation into the city for that purpose," says a psychology major. The Center for Community Challenges offers students with any major a chance to complete a research project and community based internship, which examines social and community issues like inequality and racial/ethnic conflict. Approximately a quarter of Conn students do community service each semester.

All in all, there are plenty of academic and extracurricular reasons for heading to the little college on the hill, though it may be necessary to get some fresh air at times. "Our school is becoming much more global and diverse," notes a senior. "Conn will be an exciting place to be in the next few years."

Talented dance students often take a few semesters off to study with professional companies, and theater majors have the chance to work with the Eugene O'Neill Theater Institute, named for New London's favorite literary son.

Overlaps

Tufts, Skidmore, Brown, Colby, Middlebury.

University of Connecticut

28 North Eagleville Road, Box U-88, Storrs, CT 06269-3088

Founded more than a century ago as an agricultural college—this is where America learned to get more eggs per chicken by leaving the lights on in the coops—the University of Connecticut has emerged as a comprehensive university offering a vast selection of academic programs as well as opportunities to study abroad, participate in research, or join one of the 250 organizations or clubs available. Never mind the herd of cattle grazing near the entrance to the rural campus; this is one Northeastern school that is ready to be taken seriously.

The 4,000-acre campus, about 23 miles northeast of Hartford, is an architectural potpourri consisting of mostly collegiate Gothic and neoclassical architecture and utilitarian modern and half-century-old redbrick structures. The

Website: www.uconn.edu
Location: Rural
Total Enrollment: 15,936
Undergraduates: 12,325
Male/Female: 48/52
SAT Ranges: V 510–610 M 520–620
Financial Aid: 83%

(Continued)

Expense: Pub $ $ $ $
Phi Beta Kappa: Yes
Applicants: 11,781
Accepted: 70%
Enrolled: 36%
Grad in 6 Years: 68%
Returning Freshmen: 86%
Academics: ✐ ✐ ✐ ✐
Social: ☎ ☎ ☎
Q of L: ★ ★ ★

Admissions: (860) 486-3137
Email Address:
beahusky@uconn. edu

Strongest Programs:
Engineering
Physical Therapy
Pharmacy
Nursing
Education
Agriculture
Business
Biology

campus is graced with Swan Lake and Mirror Lake, and is completely surrounded by dense woods. The school is undergoing a remarkable transformation thanks to UConn 2000, a $1-billion, state-financed program to renew, rebuild, and enhance the university that would be the envy of the most heavily-endowed private university. Campus construction and ongoing renovations are the norm, sparking jokes about "University of Construction," but the results are a slew of shiny new state-of-the-art facilities.

At UConn, preprofessional programs, such as engineering, are strong, as are pharmacy, physical therapy, psychology, education, and of course, agriculture. The basic sciences, especially biology, are solid, but the communications department is cited as weak. Engineering is very demanding, and as at many schools the department has a relatively high attrition rate, with many students switching to the less-rigorous Management Information Systems. Four new majors in the school of engineering—environmental engineering, computer science, computer engineering, and metallurgy and materials engineering—now make UConn the only public university in New England to offer these fields of study to undergraduates. A recent financial gift to the university established a unique Visiting Professorship in Human Rights. Students may also now earn minors, either in one discipline or interdisciplinary areas such as criminal justice, American studies, or women's studies. In addition, the university promises to offer instruction in any foreign language provided four students express interest. Core requirements include study in eight areas: expository writing, mathematics, literature and the arts, culture and modern society and non-Western/Latin-American studies, philosophical and ethical analysis, social scientific and comparative analysis, science and technology, and two courses in foreign language (which can be waived if a student has studied three years of a single language in high school).

The university offers advising programs specifically designed for freshmen and sophomores. The First Year Experience program provides a series of special seminars and classes taught by senior faculty to help students with the transition into university life. The Academic Center for Exploratory Students provides advisors to students who are undecided about their majors during their first four semesters at Uconn, though course selection advising receives mixed reviews from students. Faculty here are highly regarded. "Professors are extremely accessible to students, both inside and out of class" says a junior. Full professors teach most lectures, and labs and discussion groups are run by teaching assistants. Many seminar classes are available, though freshmen especially may find themselves in a few enormous lecture classes, depending on the department.

The UConn Honors Program is nationally recognized as a leading program for talented scholars. Residence hall floors are offered to freshman honors students and a newly opened residence hall is specifically reserved for sophomore, junior, and senior level honors students. Uconn is one of only 59 public Research 1 universities in the nation, and approximately 15 percent of the undergraduate population are involved in hands-on research. Engineering, business, pharmacy, and honors students are required to participate in research projects, and each year two teams of finance majors operate the $1-million Student Managed Investment Fund. The university's Eurotech Program places engineering students with interests/studies in a particular language in jobs overseas, and several programs for disadvantaged or underprivileged students are available. In addition, 5 percent of undergraduates participate in the study abroad program, which allows students to travel to more than 30 countries. UConn also has five branch campuses around the state that offer the first two years of the university's undergraduate program as well as selected programs that have a four-year degree. Students who complete their work satisfactorily at these schools are automatically accepted at the Storrs campus for their last two years.

In addition to athletic scholarships, about 20 percent of admitted students are offered merit scholarships for a wide range of skills and abilities, ranging from $1,500 to full tuition. Eighty-two percent of the students are from Connecticut. Nearly half of the entering freshmen were in the top quarter of their high school class, and a majority went to public high schools. Minority enrollment comprises 15 percent of the student body, including 6 percent Asian American, 5 percent African American, and 4 percent Hispanic. The university is continuing its efforts to attract minority students and has brought in many new faculty members who boast culturally and ethnically diverse backgrounds. Opportunities for multi-cultural studies abound, including an African American Cultural Center, Asian American Cultural Center, Latin American and Puerto Rican Cultural Center, and the new Rainbow Center, a gay, lesbian, bisexual, and transgender educational resource. "UConn is a large public university so it's incredibly diverse," says a senior. "And with diversity comes new and challenging experiences, which is what college is all about." Diversity, homophobia, and gender equality are hot campus political issues.

Sixty-nine percent of the students live in university housing, which is available to everyone who wants it. Though a few dorms are single-sex, most are coed by floor. "The new dorms of South Campus are suite style, extremely comfortable, and beautifully designed," boasts an English major. Most older dorms are being renovated and updated with Ethernet access. Students living on campus now have access to "HUSKYvision," a network of data, video, and voice communication services that includes everything from replays of lecture videos to course registration. The trend to live off-campus seems to be growing, and there are several apartment complexes near campus, but most students say that living on campus is much more convenient. Several meal plans are available to dorm residents, but many students would just as soon go out to the snack bar for some ice cream, freshly made with some help from those cows in the front yard.

The school's well-enforced alcohol policy puts a damper on parties in the dorms. "Social life is mostly made up of the bar scene," explains one senior. "People tend to have parties at off campus apartments, or off campus fraternity houses." There are three nearby bars: Ted's, Huskie's, and 4-Play. Although fraternities do provide something of a party scene, only 9 percent of men and 4 percent of women go Greek.

The town of Storrs is small and rural, and students complain about the "boring" surroundings. But, as one student notes, "UConn is a town within itself," with almost everything a student could need available on campus. To make up for the lack of on-campus entertainment, the Student Board of Governors provides a multitude of activities. "SUBOG provides movies, comedy shows, concerts, lectures, and many other events," says a psychology/sociology double major. "There's something here for everyone." UConn's students are also very involved in community service and the Center for Community Outreach provides many opportunities to volunteer. For most big-city needs, Hartford is only 30 minutes away, and Boston, New York City, Cape Cod, and the ski slopes of Vermont are within weekend road-trip range. "Basketball is by far the most popular sport at UConn; the Huskies are a perennial Big East powerhouse and in 1999 won the ultimate prize: the NCAA national championship. The annual UConn vs. UMass basketball game always draws a large crowd. The women, too, have become Big East champions, a level achieved as well by soccer squads of both sexes and men's baseball. Football isn't huge at UConn but a decision to

UConn recently added several courses in entrepreneurship to the Family Business Program, and an environmental sciences program is now offered collaboratively by the College of Liberal Arts and Sciences and the College of Agriculture and Natural Resources.

The First Year Experience program provides a series of special seminars and classes taught by senior faculty to help students with the transition into university life.

upgrade the football program from 1AA to 1A could change that. Intramurals are, in the words of one student, "crucial to students on a personal level because they're the best way to relieve tension." Annual campus events include Homecoming, Winter Weekend, and Midnight Madness—the first official day of basketball practice.

UConn may have started as an agricultural school, but it is zooming into the 21st century as an institution with different opportunities and challenges for everyone. Students here aren't "cowed" by the plethora of offerings, and those seeking greener pastures will be hard-pressed to find a more dynamic public institution.

If You Apply To ➤   **UConn**…Rolling admissions. Early action: Dec. 1. Financial aid and housing: Mar. 1. Campus interviews: optional, informational. No alumni interviews. SATs or ACTs: required. SAT IIs: optional. Accepts the Common Applications. Essay question: what you can contribute to UConn.

Cooper Union

BEST BUY

30 Cooper Square, New York, NY 10003

Website: www.cooper.edu
Location: Urban
Total Enrollment: 907
Undergraduates: 870
Male/Female: 65/35
SAT Ranges: V 510–760 M 510–780
Financial Aid: 40%
Expense: Pr $
Phi Beta Kappa: No
Applicants: 2,216
Accepted: 13%
Enrolled: 69%
Grad in 6 Years: 80%
Returning Freshmen: 90%
Academics: ✍ ✍ ✍
Social: ☎
Q of L: ★ ★ ★
Admissions: (212) 353-4120
Email Address: N/A

Strongest Programs:
    Architecture
    Electrical Engineering
    Art

Some say the best things in life are free. In most cases, they're probably wrong. But not in the case of the Cooper Union for the Advancement of Science and Art. If you manage to get accepted into this top technical institute, you get a full-tuition scholarship and some of the nation's finest academic offerings in architecture, engineering, and art. With cool and funky Greenwich Village in the background and rigorous studying in the forefront, college life at Cooper Union may seem to be faster than a New York minute. Whatever the pace, though, no one can deny that a CU education is one of the best bargains around—probably the best anywhere.

The school was founded in 1859 by entrepreneur Peter Cooper, who believed that education should be "as free as water and air." With hefty contributions from J. P. Morgan, Frederick Vanderbilt, Andrew Carnegie, and various other assorted robber barons, the school was able to stay afloat in order to recruit poor students of "strong moral character." Today, students must pay a few hundred dollars for nonacademic expenses, but tuition is still free.

In place of a traditional collegiate setting are three academic buildings and one dorm plunked down in one of New York's most eclectic and exciting neighborhoods. The stately brick art and architecture building is a beautiful historic landmark. Built of brick and topped by a classic water tower, the dorm blends right in with the neighborhood. The Great Hall was the site of Lincoln's "Right Makes Might" speech and the birthplace of the NAACP, the American Red Cross, and the national women's suffrage movement. Wedged between two busy avenues in the East Village, Cooper Union offers an environment for survivors. One mechanical engineering major describes the climate as "a tropical rain forest. Only the truly dedicated should come here."

The academic climate is intense, yet cooperation is critical, according to students. "The courses are very rigorous depending on your major," says a chemical engineering major. "Sometimes it feels like five years are crammed into four." A junior adds, "You don't know the meaning of stress until you've been through Cooper." The curriculum is highly structured, and all students must take a sequence of required courses in the humanities and social sciences. The first year is devoted to language and literature, and the second to the making of the modern world. In some special circumstances, students are allowed to take courses at nearby New York University and the New School for Social Research. The nationally renowned engineering school, under the tutelage of the nation's first female engineering dean, offers both bachelor's and master's degrees in chemical, electrical, mechanical, and civil engineering, as well as a bachelor of science in general engineering. "Architecture and engineering are the most acclaimed, but then, these occupations are more mainstream, and graduates get big money and success," reflects an art major. "It's harder to measure success in the art school." The art school offers a broad-based generalist curriculum that includes graphic design, painting, sculpture, photography, and video, but is considered weak by some students. The architecture school, in the words of one pleased participant, is "phenomenal—even unparalleled." Requirements for getting into each of these schools vary widely—each looks for different strengths and talents—hence the differences in test score ranges.

The Cooper Union library is small (90,000 volumes), but contains over 100,000 graphic materials. Classes are small and, with a little persistence, are not too difficult to get into. Professors are engaging and accessible. "One of the best aspects of this college is that everyone is taught by full professors," reports a junior. A professional counseling and referral service is available, as is academic counseling, but the school's small size and its rigorously structured academic programs set the classes the students take and eliminate a lot of confusion or decision making. Reactions on career counseling vary between "horrible" from an art major to "excellent" from an engineering major. Students "tend to talk to other students, recommending or insulting various classes and profs around registration time," notes a senior.

Strong moral character is no longer a prerequisite for admission, but an outstanding high school academic average most certainly is. Prospective applicants should note, however, that art and architecture students are picked primarily on the basis of a faculty evaluation of their creative works. For engineering students, admission is based on a formula that gives roughly equal weight to the high school record, SAT scores, and the SAT IIs in mathematics and physics or chemistry.

Sixty-one percent of the students are from New York State, and more than half of those grew up in the city. Most are from public schools, and many are the first in their families to attend college. Forty-four percent of the students are from minority groups, most of them Asian Americans (27 percent); 6 percent are black, and 8 percent are Hispanic. One student attests that diversity is not an issue at CU: "We are a racially mixed student body that stays mixed. There's no overt hostility, and rare self-segregation. One of the officers of the Chinese Student Association is a large black man from Trinidad. Need I say more?" The campus is home to ethnically-based student clubs, but, according to one student, membership is not exclusive: "In other words, you can be white and be a member of Onyx—a student group promoting black awareness." According to one senior, CU is a very liberal place: "If you can't accept different kinds of people, you shouldn't come here." For students who demonstrate financial need, help with living expenses is available.

Students love the dorm, a 15-story residence hall that saves many students from commuting into the Village or cramming themselves into expensive apartments. It is noteworthy that housing here is guaranteed only to freshmen. The facility is composed of furnished apartments with kitchenettes and bathrooms

If you manage to get accepted into this top technical institute, you get a full-tuition scholarship and some of the nation's finest academic offerings in architecture, engineering, and art.

The curriculum is highly structured, and all students must take a sequence of required courses in the humanities and social sciences.

(complete with showers or tubs) and is "in great condition and well maintained," states one resident. A less enraptured dweller notes, "Rooms are barely big enough to fit a bed, a table, and a clothes cabinet." Still, each apartment does have enough space for a stove, microwave, and refrigerator. So, you can cook for yourself or eat at the unexciting but affordable school cafeteria, or at one of the myriad nearby delis and coffee bars.

The combination of intense workload and CU's location means that campus social life is limited, though the administration hopes the dorm will promote more on-campus social activities. "Many students will say that Cooper social life is dead," notes a junior. "In many ways they are right."On the other hand, as one senior puts it, "The East Village is great place to be young, with tons of bars and culture." About 20 percent of the men and 10 percent of the women belong to professional societies. Drinking on campus is allowed during school-sponsored parties for adult students—otherwise, no alcohol on campus. But as one student puts it, "This is New York; one can be served anywhere." The intramural sports program is held in several different facilities in the city, and the games are popular. Students organize clubs and outings around interests such as soccer, basketball, skiing, fencing, Ping-Pong, classical music, religion, and drama. And of course, the colorful neighborhood is ideal for sketching and browsing. McSorley's bar is right around the corner, the Grassroots Tavern is just down the block, and nearby Chinatown and Little Italy are also popular destinations. The heart of the Village, with its abundance of theaters, art galleries, and cafés, is just a few blocks to the west. The Bowery and SoHo's galleries and restaurants are due south; all of midtown Manhattan spreads to the northern horizon.

Getting into Cooper Union is tough, and once admitted, students find that dealing with the onslaught of city and school is plenty tough as well, but most students like the challenge. "The workload, living alone in New York, and the administrative policies force you to act like an adult and take care of yourself," explains a senior. Surviving the school's academic rigors requires talent, self-sufficiency, and a clear sense of one's career objectives. Students who don't have it all can be sure that there are six or seven people in line ready to take their places, and that's quite an incentive to succeed.

Overlaps

NYU, Columbia, Cornell University, MIT, Carnegie-Mellon.

If You Apply To ➤ **Cooper Union**...Rolling admissions (for art applicants, by invitation). Early decision (for art and engineering applicants): Dec. 1. Regular admissions: Jan. 1 (architecture), Jan. 10 (art), Feb. 1 (engineering). Financial aid and housing: May 1. All students receive full-tuition scholarships. No campus or alumni interviews. (Portfolio Day strongly recommended for art applicants.) SATs: required. SAT IIs: required for engineering (math and physics or chemistry). Apply to particular program. Essay question: varies by school.

Cornell College

600 First Street West, Mount Vernon, IA 52314-1098

Website:
www.cornell-iowa.edu
Location: Rural
Total Enrollment: 965
Undergraduates: 965

If you've ever wished that you could fully focus your attention on one course at a time, consider Cornell College. At this small liberal arts college in Iowa (founded 12 years before Cornell University in Ithaca, New York), the school year is divided into nine terms, each separated by a four-and-a-half-day break. Students take one course during eight of the terms. They may elect to use the extra term for a vacation, or take a ninth course at no extra charge.

Cornell is the only college or university in the nation to have its entire campus listed on the National Register of Historic Places. It is perched on a hilltop overlooking the Cedar River valley, and the view from the bell tower of majestic King Chapel is unequaled in the region.

Cornell and Colorado colleges are the only two major schools in the nation to employ the One-Course-at-a-Time (OCAAT) or Block Plan schedule, which definitely has pros and cons. A sophomore philosophy major calls courses "intense," while a senior biology major reminds outsiders that, "one course at a time can be quite demanding." This innovative scheduling means that some students graduate in three and a half years, while others take the full four years; 40 percent recently graduated with a double major. If that sounds intimidating, that's because it is. But a sophomore states, "It allows for total immersion in a subject, as well as a unique opportunity to develop relationships with the professor and classmates." Administrators praise the program, claiming it improves the quality of liberal education and allows students to get accustomed to the pace of the business world, where "what needs to be done needs to be done quickly and done well." A final advantage is academic advising. With a grade every four weeks, trouble can be spotted quickly. The downside of the OCAAT approach is that it can be difficult to pursue cumulative subjects like math and the natural sciences. "Math," says one student, "is very difficult to learn in such an intense and short period of time," and a one- or two-day absence can knock you right out of a term. Homework seems to be just as intensive as the coursework. Students claim to study from 20 to 40 hours a week. However, if you have the right temperament and attention span to deal with a highly concentrated method of learning, Cornell can be an enriching experience.

Cornell stays true to its original liberal arts mission with noteworthy humanities departments, including English and foreign languages (especially Spanish). Economics/business and English are popular majors, as are psychology and secondary education. Weaker areas include theater and communications studies, physics, religion, and computer science. The ethnic studies major addresses issues of ethnic identity and promotes relations among ethnic groups. In addition to need-based financial aid, Cornell awards more than 250 academic and service scholarships of $5,000 to $15,000. Under a work-study program, students are hired by the college as tutors to give free help to those who need it.

In order to walk away with a sheepskin at the end of four years, all students must complete 32 courses, with at least one in each of the following areas: English, fine arts, foreign language, humanities, math, science, and social science. Another route to graduation is provided by the Bachelor of Special Studies (BSS) degree program, in which students and their advisors design a personalized major with no general requirements. Another option for students is the recently added disciplinary and interdisciplinary minors. First-year students must take an English composition and literature class.

Cornell students can take advantage of annual faculty-led courses held in all parts of the world, such as marine science research in the Bahamas, advanced Spanish in Spain, advanced French in Montreal, or social development studies in Latin America, or they can spend a semester in any one of 36 countries through Associated Colleges of the Midwest* programs. Combined degrees and co-op programs are offered in several subjects. And the short breaks between courses include recreational and educational activities such as symposia, Music Mondays, carnivals, and athletic events.

Students praise Cornell's faculty, who make their home telephone numbers standard information on course syllabi. Cornell does not employ graduate

(Continued)

Male/Female: 41/59
SAT Ranges: V 520–650
M 530–630
ACT Range: 22–28
Financial Aid: 83%
Expense: Pr $ $
Phi Beta Kappa: Yes
Applicants: 1,111
Accepted: 81%
Enrolled: 30
Grad in 6 Years: 57%
Returning Freshmen: 80%
Academics: ✍ ✍ ✍
Social: ☎ ☎ ☎
Q of L: ★ ★ ★
Admissions: (319) 895-4477
Email Address:
admissions@
cornell-iowa.edu

Strongest Programs:
Education
Psychology
Geology
Philosophy
Biology

Students don't have to worry about consuming various subjects simultaneously; they take one class at a time in at least eight of the nine three-and-a-half-week terms that comprise the school year.

assistants, and class size seldom exceeds 25 students; more commonly there are 12 to 15 students per class. A biology major says, "One of my profs has invited me out to dinner and sledding with his family!" Freshmen are assigned academic advisors before orientation, and meet with them before classes to begin to plan a program of study. Students select classes through a bidding system rather than traditional registration, and seniors are assured of getting the classes they need. Cornell's library sparkles after its $3.8-million renovation, with improved study space and a fully-automated library collection.

Twenty-six percent of students at the college are Iowans; other Midwestern states are also well represented. Blacks, Hispanics, Native Americans, and Asian Americans make up 11 percent of the student body. Still, students note there isn't a lot of racial diversity on campus, although many say minorities feel accepted. "Diversity appreciation is the buzz phrase here," says a Spanish major. "We have a very visible gay/lesbian/bi/transgender population and strong women's activist groups alongside very conservative groups." The college recently began the Cultural Awareness Program, dedicated to "promoting an open environment in which people feel comfortable asking questions and making comments about cultural concerns."

Most students live on campus, and some of the small but well-maintained dorms have been recently renovated. Two apartment buildings are available to upperclassmen. About half the dorms are coed, and freshmen get their pick of rooms on a first-come, first-served basis. Everyone eats together in the Commons, where the food is not exceptional but usually edible. One student describes Mount Vernon as "a beautiful town with a serene atmosphere." Most students either love it or long for a more active, metropolitan area. There are a few local bars—and a lot of peace, quiet, and safety. Cedar Rapids and Iowa City are less than half an hour away and boast a more collegiate nightlife. One uniting event is the annual May Music Festival, a series that has run for almost 100 years. Parties in the dorms are pretty much a thing of the past; these days, resident advisors patrol the halls with authority to break up parties that get loud. "Campus policy is that you must be 21, with your door shut, in order to drink," explains one student. "Yes, it works, and it is really enforced."

Cornell's football team is usually a contender for its conference title, and wrestling has pinned down a number of conference and national titles. The men's basketball and track teams are also title-winning, and Cornell women have won championships in cross-country and volleyball. In all men's and women's sports, Coe College is Cornell's biggest rival. A $6-million life sports center is helping to make Cornell's varsity and intramural teams even more competitive.

For students who can handle it, Cornell offers an intensive education in a close-knit, naturally beautiful environment. Praises one student, "The one-course-at-a-time program is definitely the draw here, but Cornell also offers a close, supportive atmosphere to its students.

Overlaps

Colorado College, University of Iowa, Iowa State, University of Northern Iowa, Grinnell.

If You Apply To ➤ Cornell College...Early decision: Nov. 15. Early action: Dec. 15. Regular admissions: Feb. 1 for scholars, Mar. 1 for nonscholars. Financial aid: Jan. Meets demonstrated need of 30%. Campus interviews: recommended, informational. No alumni interviews. SATs or ACTs: required. SAT IIs: optional. Accepts the Common Application and electronic applications. Essay question: what you hope to accomplish in college; personal experience; a description of your personal goals.

Cornell University

Ithaca, NY 14850

Cornell has a long tradition for being the lone wolf among the Ivy League universities. So it should come as no surprise that Cornell has taken another huge step away from its Ivy League counterparts by announcing its intention to become the finest research university for undergraduate education in the nation. Cornell's president recently unveiled a $400 million, 10-year plan to improve undergraduate education by combining education and research and having all freshmen live in the same residential area. With rain, drizzle, slush, and snow known as "the four seasons of Ithica," just walking to class across the vast and hilly campus can be challenging. Cornell's highly talented student body and notoriously competitive academics probably make it, in the words of one student, "the only place where you walk up a 45-degree incline in 20-degree weather to get 30 percent on a prelim."

Aside from the great strides in undergraduate education, Cornell also has its stunning campus to lure students to upstate New York. Perched atop a hill that commands a view of both Ithaca and Cayuga lakes, the campus is breathtakingly scenic; or as the saying goes, "Ithaca is gorges." Ravines, waterfalls, and parks border all sides of school's campus. The Cornell Plantation, more than 3,000 acres of woodlands, natural trails, streams, and gorges, provides space for walking, picnicking, or contemplation.

At the undergraduate level, Cornell has four privately endowed colleges: architecture, art and planning; arts and sciences; engineering; and hotel administration. Cornell is also New York State's land-grant university. Therefore, three other colleges are operated by Cornell under contract with New York State: agriculture and life sciences, human ecology, and the school of industrial and labor relations (ILR). Thirty-seven percent of the students in these state-assisted colleges are New York State residents, who pick up their Ivy League degrees at an almost-public price (tuition at these schools are slightly steeper than SUNY rates).

The College of Arts and Sciences boasts considerable strength in history, government, and just about all the natural and physical sciences. The English program has turned out a number of renowned writers, including Toni Morrison, Thomas Pynchon, and Richard Farina. Foreign languages, required for all A&S students, are also strong, and the performing arts, mathematics, and most social science departments are considered good. Among the state-assisted units, the agriculture college is one of the best in the nation and a good bet for anyone hoping to make it into a veterinary school (there's one at Cornell, with state support). The School of Hotel Administration comes as close as anything at Cornell to being an undergraduate business school, and is, along with ILR, world-renowned. Human ecology is among the best in the nation in home- and human-service-related disciplines. The Johnson Museum, designed by I. M. Pei, has been rated as one of the 10 best university museums in America. Students enjoy the $22-million theater arts center, designed specifically for undergraduates. Students say the math department needs improvement.

Student-faculty relations at Cornell are a mixed bag but for the most part students do have a lot of respect for their professors. "The professors here are brilliant and do their best to be accessible," says an industrial labor and relations major. Lower-level courses are generally large lectures, though many are taught by "charismatic profs" who try to remain accessible. The largest course on campus,

Website: www.cornell.edu

Location: Small city

Total Enrollment: 19,284

Undergraduates: 13,442

Male/Female: 53/47

SAT Ranges: V 610–710 M 650–740

Financial Aid: 50%

Expense: Pr $ $ $

Phi Beta Kappa: Yes

Applicants: 19,860

Accepted: 34%

Enrolled: 44%

Grad in 6 Years: 91%

Returning Freshmen: 95%

Academics: ✏ ✏ ✏ ✏ ✏

Social: ☎ ☎ ☎ ☎

Q of L: ★ ★ ★

Admissions: (607) 255-5241

Email Address:
admissions@cornell.edu

Strongest Programs:
Art and Design
Architecture
Hotel Administration
Industrial and Labor
Relations
Engineering
Agriculture
Biology
English

Psych 101, packs in more than 1,000, but students report that scintillating lectures make it a well-loved rite of passage. Some undergrads complain that it is difficult to get into popular courses unless you are a major. The administration, however, is hoping that the decision to make undergraduates a priority will improve most of the problems in the lower-level courses.

For now, first-year students do have access to senior faculty members, including such notables as novelists Alison Lurie and Dan McCall, through mandatory Freshman Seminars. In addition to their thematic focus, most of the seminars stress writing skills.

The Fund for Educational Initiatives gives professors money to implement innovative approaches to undergraduate education, which have included a visual learning laboratory and a course on electronic music. Cornell was early among universities to add women's studies to the curriculum and continues to be a leader with programs in Asian American studies and also by offering its students innovative programs like its Sea Semester.*

Cornell academics are demanding and foster an intensity found on few campuses. "The easiest Ivy to get into; the toughest to get out of," quips one student. "Students spend four to five hours per night on coursework, and at least half the weekend is spent hitting the books." Another student adds, "The courses here are very difficult but can be mastered if the student puts in enough effort." University-wide, 95 percent of Cornell students ranked in the top quarter of their high school class, so those who were the class genius in high school should be prepared for a struggle to rise to the top. To cope with the anxieties the high-powered atmosphere creates, the university has one of the best psychological counseling networks in the nation, including an alcohol awareness program, peer sex counselors, personal growth workshops, and EARS (Empathy, Assistance, and Referral Service).

The library system is superb. Cornell students have access to more than 6.4 million volumes, 63,500 journals, and 1,000 networked resources in the 19 branches around campus. The resources on the Olin Graduate Library's first floor are available to anyone, and a pass from a professor gets you into the graduate stacks. Within the beautiful, underground Carl A. Kroch Library, students study in skylit atriums and reading rooms and move about the renowned Fiske Icelandic Collection and the Echols Collections, the finest Cambodian collection on display.

Academically, Cornell is a veritable plethora of opportunities offering more than 4,000 courses in seven colleges and schools. Co-op programs are available to engineering and human ecology students, and Cornell-in-Washington, with its own dorm, is popular among public policy students. Students looking to study abroad can choose from more than 200 programs and universities throughout the world, including those in Indonesia, Belgium, Ireland, and Nepal. Research opportunities are outstanding at Cornell, and students can take part in some of the most vital research happening in the nation. Recent research findings include solving the mystery of how Jupiter's rings are formed and discovering a new technology to make computer software less vulnerable to bugs.

Prospective students apply to one of the seven colleges or schools through the central admissions office, and admissions standards vary by school. The mixture of state and private, preprofessional and liberal arts at one institution provides a diversity of students rare among America's colleges. City slickers and country folk, engineers and those with an artsy flair, all rub shoulders here. Just over half of Cornell's students are out-of-staters; another 7 percent are foreign. African Americans and Hispanics account for 10 percent of the students, and Asian

Americans 16 percent more. "It's sad but different cultural groups tend not to interact by choice," says one student. Cornell offers many workshops and discussion groups aimed at increasing tolerance. The state-assisted schools draw a large number of in-staters, as well as many students from New Jersey, Pennsylvania, and New England, while arts and sciences and engineering draw from the tristate metropolitan New York City area, Pennsylvania, Massachusetts, and California. Whatever their origin, students seem self-motivated and studious. Upon graduation, 55 percent of Cornell students take jobs, and 31 percent continue to graduate and professional schools.

Cornell is need-blind in admissions and guarantees to meet the demonstrated need of all accepted applicants, but the proportion of outright grants—as opposed to loans that must be repaid—in your financial aid package varies depending on how eager the university is to get you to enroll. The Cornell Installment Plan (CIP) allows students or their parents to pay a year's or semester's tuition in monthly interest-free installments. The university also takes pride in the alumni-developed Cornell Tradition, a unique program of fellowships for students on financial aid who are willing to work extra hours each week. In addition to their salaries, these students receive up to $2,500 to partly replace loans. Another scholarship, called the Cornell Research Scholars, provides paid research opportunities, need-based loan forgiveness, and one summer of funded research for the most academically gifted students who demonstrate an interest in research.

Many changes are in store for Cornell housing as a result of the new plan to transform undergraduate education and the university recently received a $100 million pledge from an anonymous donor to reach this goal. North Campus will receive two new residence halls and a dining room, and will become the home of all freshmen. West Campus will be transformed into a post-freshman-year living, and will have faculty leadership from all the undergraduate schools and colleges at Cornell. A few students are housed in two dorms on the edge of Collegetown, the blocks of apartments and houses within walking distance of the campus. There are dorms devoted to everything from ecology to music, and cultural houses include Chinese, Jewish living, and American Indian (the only facility of its kind in the nation). "Program houses and co-ops are wonderful alternatives to dorm life," says one student. Also available are a small number of highly coveted suites—six large double rooms with kitchens and a common living area. More than half of Cornell students—and most juniors and seniors—live off campus. Many try their luck in Collegetown, where demand keeps the housing market tight and rents high, while others live in fraternity and sorority houses. Cornell's food service is reputedly among the best in the nation. There are seven dining halls that function independently, so, one student enthuses, "there are at least 28 different entrées for each meal." Milk products and some meats come right from the agriculture school, and about twice a semester a cross-country gourmet team—the staff of a famous restaurant—prepares its specialties on campus.

Despite the intense academic atmosphere, Cornell social life beats most of the other Ivies hands down. Once the weekend arrives, local parties and ski slopes are filled with Cornell students who have managed to strike a balance between study and play. Collegetown bars offer good eats and drinks, but those under 21 are barred. However, there is plenty to do at Cornell aside from drinking, students report. "We go to movies, plays, concerts, or just go out to dinner with friends," says a senior. With over 10 percent of men and 10 percent of women pledging, fraternities and sororities also play a significant role in the social scene. Big events include Fun in the Sun, a day of friendly athletic competition, and Springfest, a concert on Libe Slope.

Co-op programs are available to engineering and human ecology students, and Cornell-in-Washington, with its own dorm, is popular among public policy students.

Students celebrate the last day of classes—Slope Day—by hanging out at Libe Slope. There are also innumerable concerts and sporting events. In addition, more than 400 extracurricular clubs ranging from "a tanning society to a society of women engineers."

Hockey is unquestionably the dominant sport on campus (the chief goal being defeating Harvard), and camping out for season tickets is an annual ritual. The Big Red football program has been somewhat revived after years in the Ivy League cellar. Cornell boasts the largest intramural program in the Ivy League; it includes more than 100 hockey teams organized around dorms, fraternities, and other organizations. Rain, drizzle, slush, and snow known as "the four seasons of Ithaca," can make just walking to class across the vast and hilly campus challenging but with the first snow of the winter, "traying" down Libe Slope becomes the sport of choice for hordes of fun-loving Cornellians. Ithaca boasts "wonderful outdoor enthusiast stores," says one student, as well as hosting Greek Peak Mountain for nearby skiing, Cayuga Lake for boating and swimming, and lots of space for hiking and watching the clouds roll by.

Like most other Ivy League universities, Cornell is a premiere research institution with a distinguished faculty and outstanding academics. What sets it apart is the university's willingness to stray from the traditional Ivy League path as it did with the announcement of its plan to make undergraduates its highest priority. Cornell University is a pioneer in the world of education and students unafraid to blaze their own trail will feel at home here.

Overlaps

Penn, Princeton, Harvard, Brown, Yale.

If You Apply To ➤

Cornell…Rolling notification (College of Agriculture and Life Sciences, School of Industrial and Labor Relations, and School of Hotel Administration only). Early decision: Nov. 10. Regular admissions: Jan. 1. Financial aid: Feb. 15. Housing: May 1. Campus interviews: recommended (required for school of Hotel Admin. and College of Architecture, Art, and Planning), evaluative. Alumni interviews: optional, informational (varies by program). SATs or ACTs: required. SAT IIs: required (varies by program). Essay question: applying classroom knowledge; influential person; or ask and answer your own question; and personal statement (optional). Apply to individual programs or schools.

University of Dallas

1845 East Northgate Drive, Irving, TX 75062

Website: www.udallas.edu
Location: Suburban
Total Enrollment: 3,211
Undergraduates: 1,184
Male/Female: 41/59
SAT Ranges: V 575–680 M 540–650
ACT Range: 24–28
Financial Aid: 65%
Expense: Pr $
Phi Beta Kappa: Yes

Texas has never been a state to hew the line set by the other 49, and the University of Dallas is no exception. While many universities around the nation have reexamined their Eurocentric core curriculums, UD remains proudly dedicated to fostering students in "the study of great deeds and works of Western Civilization." "Imagine a party where someone makes a joke about Plato or Dante, and everybody cracks up. That's UD in a nutshell," says one student. And appropriately for a Roman Catholic school, much of the focus is on Rome, where virtually the entire sophomore class treks every year. The unique and intense program focuses on the art and architecture of Rome, the philosophy of man and being, classical literature, Italian, and the development of Western civilization. "The Rome program is the chance of a lifetime," says a senior.

UD's 744-acre campus occupies a pastoral home in a Dallas suburb on top of "the closest thing this region has to a hill." Texas Stadium, home of the Dallas

Cowboys, is right across the street. A major portion of the campus is situated around the Braniff Mall, a landscaped and lighted gathering place near the Braniff Memorial Tower, the school's landmark. The primary tone of the buildings is brown, and the architecture, as described by one student, is "post-1950s, done in brick, typical Catholic-institutional." While it may not be a picture-perfect school, it does have a beautiful chapel and a state-of-the-art science building. Recent construction includes renovations to the Haggar University Center and to the student residence halls. A new four-building Art Village is home to enlarged sculpture, painting, and ceramics creations.

A peek at the curriculum is daunting for those unaccustomed to the rigors of a more traditional liberal arts education. There's even a heavy dose of classics (which leads to those late-night Roman jam sessions). Biology is the most popular major, followed by English, politics, psychology, and history. Political philosophy is also a popular major, although students claim that most courses tend to be slanted toward the conservative side. One junior reports that "philosophy and politics set the tone of the campus." Students say the math and education departments need improvement. The Business Leaders of Tomorrow program can be completed in addition to any undergraduate major. It includes introductory courses in business management, an internship, a mentor who is a business professional, and a choice of electives from the Graduate School of Management—all designed to prepare students to be future leaders. Premed students are well served by the biology and chemistry programs, and about 60 percent of UD graduates go on to grad school.

The Rome semester is considered part of the UD Western Civilization core curriculum, which takes up close to half the requirements for a bachelor's degree. Included in the core are heavy doses of philosophy, history, literature, science, and math, as well as a serious foreign language requirement. In keeping with the church-vessel philosophy, two theology courses (including Scripture and Western Theological Tradition) are required of all students. Those inclined toward the sciences may take advantage of the John B. O'Hara Chemical Science Institute, which offers a hands-on nine-week summer program designed to prepare entering undergraduates for independent research early in their academic careers.

Students report that the academic pressure and the workload can be intense. "The academic climate here is extremely rigorous," says a classics and drama double major. "You can either decide that the work is difficult and strive to accomplish, or get overwhelmed and crumble." The university uses no teaching assistants, and almost all the students take advantage of the low student/faculty ratio by getting to know their professors. "Professors love what they do and it shows in the assignments and class discussions," says a junior psychology major. Getting into the small, personal classes is rarely a problem. Counseling, both academic and career, receives positive reviews.

About 70 percent of UD students are Catholic, and many choose this school because of its religious affiliation. Fifty-seven percent of the students are from Texas, and 13 percent of the student body are Hispanic. Six percent are Asian American and 2 percent are African American. Students say that racial tension is not a problem on campus, although UDers tend to lean to the right politically. "UD is an ultraconservative university," says one senior. "Liberals are not exactly welcomed with open arms, although there are numerous forums for discussion." Rules governing dorms and conduct reflect a traditional religious orientation, with which most students tend to feel comfortable.

UD offers various merit scholarships, ranging from partial to full tuition, but no athletic scholarships. Everyone under 21 who doesn't reside at home with

(Continued)
Applicants: 1,213
Accepted: 76%
Enrolled: 33%
Grad in 6 Years: 60%
Returning Freshmen: 85%
Academics: ✍ ✍ ✍
Social: ☎ ☎
Q of L: ★ ★ ★
Admissions: (972)721-5266
Email Address:
  undadmis@acad.udallas.edu

Strongest Programs:
  Biology
  English
  Politics
  Psychology
  History

Appropriately for a Roman Catholic school, much of the focus is on Rome, where virtually the entire sophomore class treks every year.

their parents must live on campus in single-sex or coed-by-floor dorms, "where visitation regulations are relatively strict," one student reports. As for the dorms, they're "not luxurious, but they are comfortable," one student reports. The most popular dorms are Jerome (all-female) and Madonna (all-male). At Gregory, the dorm reserved for those who like to party, the goings-on are less than saintly. In addition to a spacious and comfortable dining hall with a wonderful view of North Dallas, there is a Rathskeller, which serves snacks and fast food (and great conversation). A car is a must for off-campus life since there is virtually no reliable public transportation in the Dallas/Fort Worth Metroplex.

The University of Dallas is unusual for a Texas school in that its entire population does not salivate at the sight of a football or basketball. Save for the Groundhogs, UD's rugby team, students rarely mention their Division III athletics. "Athletics will always be overshadowed by the academic commitments of the students," says one student. Intramural sports, on the other hand, are well organized and very popular. With no fraternities or sororities at UD, most on-campus entertainment is sponsored by the student government. Three free movies a week, dances, and visiting speakers are usually on the agenda. Church-related and religious activities provide fulfilling social outlets for a goodly number of students. An annual reggae party is complete with "live band, dead pig." Then there's Charity Week in the fall, when the junior class plans a week's worth of fund-raising events. Each year students dread Sadie Hawkins Day and the annual Screw Your Roommate dance—dark nights of the soul, each. The university can be vigorous in enforcing restrictive drinking rules, and as a result, it is difficult for a minor to drink at campus events. "They are fair," says one junior. "They do what they can to cut out alcohol, but to eradicate it is actually quite difficult."

Students describe Irving as "a suburb, just like any other," but the Metroplex offers almost unlimited possibilities, including a full agenda for bar-hopping on Lower Greenville Avenue, about 10 minutes away. The West End and Deep Ellum offer a taste of shopping and Dallas's alternative music scene. And for the more adventurous, New Orleans isn't too far away.

UD is without a doubt the best Catholic-affiliated university south of Washington, D.C. Students pride themselves on being the "Philosopher Kings of the 21st Century," but their roots go back to the Roman thinkers of an earlier era. The mix of religion and liberal arts serves most students well. In the words of one senior, "The best thing about the college is the amazing respect that professors have for their students, especially after Rome. It makes you feel like you can accomplish anything, and after four years at UD, you usually can."

Overlaps

Notre Dame, Texas A&M, University of Texas, Baylor, Austin.

If You Apply To ➤

Dallas…Early action: Dec 1. Regular admissions: Feb. 15. Financial aid and housing: Feb. 15. Does not guarantee to meet demonstrated need. Campus interviews: recommended, evaluative. No alumni interviews. SATs or ACTs: required. SAT IIs: optional. Accepts electronic applications. Essay question: writing sample.

Dartmouth College

McNutt Hall, Hanover, NH 03755

If it is at all possible to make an Ivy League school more academically oriented, Dartmouth College is trying to do just that. Dartmouth continues to place a premium on diversifying the student body, enhancing the out-of-classroom experience, and creating opportunity for present and future students. The Big Green is truly a different species of Ivy; it has the highest graduation rate in the United States; it is one of the safest campuses in the United States; it is a college among universities, and it has the smallest total enrollment in the Ancient Eight. All of this has resulted in a mad rush of high school students lining up for admission.

Dartmouth has turned out lots of businessmen but relatively few academicians, something the administration has been trying to change for some time now. When president James Freedman was hired in the 1980s, he was charged with the task of "leading Dartmouth out of the sandbox" and making it a hospitable place with a more scholarly feeling. He said then that he wanted students "whose greatest pleasures may not come from the camaraderie of classmates but from the lonely acts of writing poetry, or mastering the cello, or solving mathematical riddles, or translating Catullus." (The reference to Catullus may have been the president's little esoteric joke. The Latin poet Catullus wrote erotic, sometimes obscene, verse on topics that included his passion for his mistress Lesbia, a boy named Juventius, and the sexual excesses of Julius Caesar.) Today's Dartmouth hardly resembles the Dartmouth of yesteryear, when liberal elements—mainly women and minorities—squared off against the self-proclaimed heirs of the Dartmouth tradition.

Set in the "small, Norman Rockwell town" of Hanover, New Hampshire, Dartmouth's picturesque campus is arrayed around a quaint New England green with Baker Library at one end and the college-owned Hanover Inn at the other. Although the campus architecture ranges from Romanesque to postmodern, the dominant theme is copper-topped Colonial frame. The nearest significant urban area (Boston) is two hours away, but the Hopkins Center for the Creative and Performing Arts, the Hood Museum of Art, and the Artist in Residence program add a touch of culture to the rural campus. Construction is currently underway on the new $30 million Berry Library.

Much is questioned and considered at Dartmouth, and academic excellence is a given. "Dartmouth holds up its reputation as being a highly rigorous school," says one junior. "Students are challenged in the classroom by the fast-paced nature of our quarter system and by the professors who always demand the best from their students." The Big Green also rates as one of the top in the country for undergraduate teaching. Three professional schools—business, engineering, and medicine—provide additional resources, but Dartmouth's passion still lies in undergraduate liberal arts. Strong programs include government, biology, English, and history. The math department receives lower ratings from students because of its small size. Dartmouth is perhaps best known for foreign languages, including Hebrew and Arabic, which are taught through the Intensive Language Model developed by John Rassias, a nationally renowned language professor. Computer science is also among the best in the nation, thanks in no small part to the late John Kemeny, the former Dartmouth president who coinvented time-sharing and the BASIC language. With the most extensive undergraduate facilities in the nation, computer literacy is a way of life at Dartmouth; indeed, the school has

Website: www.dartmouth.edu

Location: Rural

Total Enrollment: 5,344

Undergraduates: 4,057

Male/Female: 52/48

SAT Ranges: V 670–770 M 680–760

ACT Range: 28–33

Financial Aid: 48%

Expense: Pr $ $ $ $

Phi Beta Kappa: Yes

Applicants: 10,259

Accepted: 21%

Enrolled: 50%

Grad in 5 Years: 94%

Returning Freshmen: 98%

Academics: ✍ ✍ ✍ ✍ ✍

Social: ☎ ☎ ☎ ☎ ☎

Q of L: ★ ★ ★

Admissions: (603) 646-2875

Email Address:
admissions.office@
dartmouth.edu

Strongest Programs:
Biology
Economics
Engineering
English
Foreign Languages
International Studies
History
Dance

Three professional schools—business, engineering, and medicine—provide additional resources, but Dartmouth's passion still lies in undergraduate liberal arts.

gone further than any other college in the nation in extending computing and word processing to every aspect of the curriculum from physics to philosophy. Virtually every academic classroom and all residential dorms are networked.

Dartmouth also offers its students a wide variety of special programs, including the Presidential Scholars Program, which offers one-on-one research assistantships with faculty and the Senior Fellowship Program, which empowers students to undertake interdisciplinary research projects. Another program, the Women in Science Project, encourages women students to pursue their interest in science, mathematics, and engineering, offering mentors, speakers, and even research apprenticeships for first-year students. Another bonus is the Montgomery Fellowships, which bring well-known politicians, writers, and others to the campus for periods ranging from a few days to several months.

Students are generally enthusiastic about their professors. "Although many of the professors at Dartmouth are at the top of their fields and engage in their own research and publication, the main reason they come here is because they want to share their knowledge with their students," says a senior. Another student adds, "The professors here are excellent and always available either by email, open office hours, or discussion sections." Academic and career counseling resources are abundant "as long as students are not shy about taking the first step," says an English major.

Incoming students receive immediate instruction for the use of the written word at the college level: a composition course followed by a mandatory freshman seminar with an emphasis on writing. Students must also take 10 courses distributed across the following areas: arts, literature, philosophy, religion or history, international studies, social analysis, technology or applied science, quantitative reasoning, and natural or physical science. Students are expected to become proficient in at least one foreign language, and must take courses in U.S., Western, and non-Western studies. In addition, Dartmouth has a senior culminating activity—a thesis, public report, exhibition, seminar, production, or demonstration—which allows students to pull together the work of their major and add a creative and intellectual twist of their own.

The school's most important innovation is the Dartmouth Plan, whereby the school operates year-round with four 10-week terms a year, including one during the summer. The D Plan allows students to take classes any of the four seasons they wish, with only the requirement that they be on campus during their entire freshman and senior years and the summer after their sophomore year. "Through the D Plan," one student explains, "students are empowered to schedule their own agenda." Students use their time off for jobs, internships, or travel. About 60 percent of the student body spend at least one term participating in one of Dartmouth's 44 programs of foreign study, either for intensive language training or a departmental study (drama in London or environmental studies in Zimbabwe, for example). The college is also part of the Twelve College Exchange* and the Maritime Studies Program.*

Dartmouth was founded in 1769 to educate Native Americans, and since 1969 the college has made serious efforts to attract them. The formerly all-male school went coed in 1972, and nearly half the current student body is female. Dartmouth has the most outstanding Native American program in the country today. In the early 1970s, the college stopped using the war-painted Indian as a mascot and since then, the school's teams have been known as the Big Green. Blacks account for 5 percent of the student body, Hispanics for 5 percent, and Asian Americans for 10 percent. "Dartmouth is very diverse and the students here have the utmost respect for each other's differences," says a government major. Dartmouth is need-blind in admissions, and guarantees to meet the demonstrated financial need of all accepted students. It was the first of a growing number of privately financed institutions to go into the business of selling tax-exempt bonds through a state authority to underwrite loans to families at low interest rates. Additionally, Dartmouth is trying to lure more middle-class students to campus by offering bigger grants to students whose parents earn less than $60,000 per year. No merit scholarships are awarded, and athletic scholarships are prohibited at all Ivy League institutions.

On the housing front, the 37 dorms have been grouped into eleven clusters that organize activities and programs and provide a sense of community. Separate first-year housing will be provided as an alternative starting with the class of 2005. Rooms are large and homey—some of the older ones have working fireplaces—and the maintenance service even cleans the bathrooms. "There's a large variety of rooms available at Dartmouth," says an engineering major. "All are spacious and kept very clean." Housing is guaranteed only for the first year and some students say that getting a room can be a problem. "There's currently not enough on-campus housing but Dartmouth is building the new residence hall, which should ease the crunch," says a government and international relations double major. And what about food? Students establish a declining balance account at the beginning of each term, the size of which is left up to the individual. First year students, however, are required to a standardized plan for their first term. Eighty-five percent of students live on campus for all four years. Students do live off campus, but generally in larger, rented homes with several other students rather than in apartments.

Dartmouth's Greek system is nationally famous for, among other things, having inspired the movie *Animal House;* fraternities and sororities claim 44 percent of the men and 34 percent of the women, respectively. The college's powerful and intensely loyal Greek alumni are the self-appointed keepers of the flame. This burgeoning family tree began to take root in the days before the interstate highway system, when Dartmouth males had nothing to do on Saturday nights but participate in male-bonding activities of the sort rarely seen outside beer commercials. Almost 20 years ago, the faculty recommended abolishing the fraternities. After an outcry from the alumni, the school compromised by putting the most boisterous on probation. Under the Student Life Initiative, Dartmouth is trying to de-emphasize Greek life, and create more social ad residential alternatives for students. The Big Green also has the most elaborately organized alumni associations in the country—testimony to the loyalty it inspires. It seems as if every other grad has a title like deputy assistant secretary and many return to Hanover when they retire, further cementing their bonds with the college (and driving local real estate prices beyond the reach of most faculty members).

Greeks are no mean contributors to the college's longtime nickname of its surrounding city, "Hangover." In response to the excessive imbibing of some fraternity members, Dartmouth was one of the first to develop a counseling and educational program designed to combat the abuse of alcohol. The administration has set out on a long-range plan to curb fraternity drinking and provide alternative student opportunities. There is, however, a bar on campus called the Lone Pine Tavern, which is described by one student as a place "where students play everything from Scrabble and chess to checkers and Jenga while listening to jazz and acoustic groups."

Of all Dartmouth's traditions, perhaps the best known is Winter Carnival, an annual festival that draws seekers from all over the Eastern seaboard. "Winter Carnival is our festival of the cold, complete with a snow sculpture on the green,

Dartmouth also offers its students a wide variety of special programs, including the Presidential Scholars Program, which offers one-on-one research assistantships with faculty and the Senior Fellowship Program, which empowers students to undertake interdisciplinary research projects.

the traditional winter activities of skiing and skating, and the somewhat unique skills of dining-hall tray sledding," reports a senior. In one popular Homecoming ritual, freshmen build a bonfire 64 railroad tiers high and run around the flames the number of times of their year. During the spring, students celebrate Green Key weekend, which one student calls, "an excuse to drink under the guise of community service." Another unusual tradition, Tubestock, is a day when the entire sophomore class floats down the Connecticut River in rafts.

To the city dweller, Hanover is halfway to the North Pole, but to the outdoors lover it's nearly paradise. "This is a beautiful town with friendly people," says a philosophy major. "It is very much a college town." Another student adds, "Hanover has everything a college student might need yet it maintains the charm of a quaint New England town." Dartmouth's own ski area is 20 minutes distant, the Connecticut River is even closer for canoeing and kayaking, and the great outdoors is literally steps away. More adventurous types take to the wilds of Dartmouth's 27,000-acre land grant in the northeast corner of the state, where cabins can be rented for $5 a night. Most first-year students begin their Dartmouth career with a camping trip led by an upperclass student or faculty member, and the Outing Club is the most popular student organization.

Love of the outdoor life extends to varsity athletics. Recent success stories include the men's cross-country and lightweight rowing teams, and women's basketball, cross-country, soccer, and lacrosse teams. Few Dartmouth students miss the biannual excursion to the Dartmouth–Harvard football game, when thousands of Big Green devotees descend upon Cambridge. Dartmouth's sports center boasts, among other things, a 2,100-seat arena, a 4,000-square-foot fitness center, and the only permanent three-glass-wall squash court in North America. Recent construction includes the $3 million Scully-Fahey Field, an artificial athletic turf facility.

Perhaps the best thing about Dartmouth is its combination of superior academics, a blossoming social life, and a small, community atmosphere. Dartmouth enjoys a tremendous sense of community and tradition, which, while supporting an amazing diversity of talents, interests, and backgrounds, allows one to speak of a common Dartmouth Experience. Students love the "work hard, play hard" ethic, and most cannot imagine themselves attending school anywhere else in the world. "I know that I will leave this place in a few months," says a melancholic senior. "I will take a little piece of Dartmouth with me. I will become one of our thousands of diehard alums, my heart always beating quicker with the memories of 'the College on the Hill.'"

Overlaps

Yale, Harvard, Princeton, Stanford, Brown.

If You Apply To ➢ **Dartmouth**…Early decision: Nov. 1. Regular admissions: Jan. 1. Financial aid: Nov. 1, Feb. 1. Guarantees to meet demonstrated need. Campus and alumni interviews: optional, evaluative. SATs or ACTs: required. SAT IIs: required (any three). Accepts the Common Application and electronic applications. Essay question: academic subject most meaningful to you; meaningful activity; how you spent last summer; and create an essay question and answer it.

Davidson College

P.O. Box 1737, Davidson, NC 28036

When it comes to elite liberal arts schools, Davidson College leads the pack in the South, and is quickly establishing itself as a presence nationwide. Curiously overlooked by many because of its small size and Southern locale, Davidson could be described as an "Ivy wannabe." Strong core requirements and a pervasive honor code distinguish this school from many of its contemporaries and draw cheers from students. "Everyone shares a common belief about what Davidson stands for and we work hard to live up to those standards," says a French major.

Located in a beautiful stretch of North Carolina's Piedmont, Davidson's wooded campus features Georgian and Greek Revival architecture. The central campus is a designated arboretum that develops, maintains, and displays a collection of the woody plants that thrive in the area. It's used as an outdoor laboratory for students, and markers identify the varieties of trees and shrubs. Despite the building boom, Davidson retains its original quadrangle (circa 1837) and two dorms and literary society halls (from the 1850s).

Davidson operates under an honor code that allows students to take exams independently and leave doors unlocked. Every entering freshman agrees in writing to abide by the code, and all work handed in is signed with the word "pledged." "People who don't live it, underrate it—I know I did," says a freshman of the honor code. "It's both a freedom and a responsibility; the campus could not exist without it." Core requirements are extensive here—32 courses in all—and include writing; foreign languages; composition; literature; religion and philosophy; fine arts; history; and four credits in physical education. The academic climate is said to be "strenuous" but not competitive. "The workload at Davidson is strenuous but that keeps us from ever doubting that we're receiving a superb education," says an English major. The most popular majors are biology, English, history, economics, and political science. Areas that do not receive high marks include non-European languages and philosophy. Professors, however, are highly praised. "Professors at Davidson are like housewives," says a sophomore. "They've got a lot to say and you're likely to wind up at their homes eating pastries and watching TV."

Davidson's two-year interdisciplinary humanities program offers an unusual opportunity to study Western civilization in a broad historical context and fulfill many of the core requirements. The Center for Special Studies serves upperclassmen who wish to pursue independent or combined majors. A 3–2 engineering program is available in conjunction with a number of other excellent universities. The college is committed to foreign studies—about 47 percent of the students go abroad—and the Dean Rusk Program for International Studies beefs up offerings in this field. Armed with a Sloan Foundation grant, the college is attempting to integrate technological studies and the liberal arts through courses such as From Petroleum to Penicillin, and Sex, Technology, and Morality. There are also concentrations in applied math, gender studies, international studies, medical humanities, and neuroscience. Students accepted into the School for Field Studies participate in a semester-long program studying environmental issues in other countries. Back home, class size is restricted; you'll have to look hard to find a room other than the cafeteria with more than 50 students in it, so students usually don't have too much trouble registering for classes.

Website: www.davidson.edu

Location: Small town

Total Enrollment: 1,652

Undergraduates: 1,652

Male/Female: 50/50

SAT Ranges: V 610–710 M 610–700

ACT Range: 27–31

Financial Aid: 32%

Expense: Pr $ $ $

Phi Beta Kappa: Yes

Applicants: 2,824

Accepted: 38%

Enrolled: 42%

Grad in 6 Years: 89%

Returning Freshmen: 97%

Academics: ✍ ✍ ✍ ✍

Social: ☎ ☎ ☎

Q of L: ★ ★ ★ ★

Admissions: (704) 892-2230

Email Address:
admission@davidson.edu

Strongest Programs:
International Studies
Math
English
Biology
Political Science
Premed/Medical Humanities
Psychology

The Center for Special Studies serves upperclassmen who wish to pursue independent or combined majors

Most Davidson students come from affluent and otherwise august Southern families, the children of doctors, ministers, and businessmen. Many are Presbyterian, as the school has strong Presbyterian roots. There is an unusually strong national feel here; less than 20 percent of the student body hails from in state. Five percent of the student body are African American, 2 percent Hispanic, and 2 percent Asian American. A project called Tolerance on Campus Establishing New Ground established a summer program for underrepresented students and a minority counselor, among other things. Davidson lures top students with a number of annual merit scholarships ranging from $1,000 to a full ride; athletic scholarships are available for men and women. The five-day orientation program is elaborate and includes such activities as a regatta, scavenger hunt, and Freshman Cake Race. "The school makes a big deal about the 'Freshman Experience,' and everyone makes efforts all year long to integrate them into student life," notes one upperclassman.

Eighty-nine percent of students live on campus in coed or single-sex dorms. Freshmen are housed together in two five-story halls and get to eat in Vail Commons, which gets high marks for food and socializing. Freshmen receive special attention from the Residence-Life Office staff, who devote considerable time to finding the best match for future roomies. Upperclassmen may live either in the dorms, off campus, or in college-owned cottages on the campus perimeter that hold about 10 students each. A freshman notes, "The rooms are nicer with each passing year; the seniors have cottages or apartments that are huge, have appliances, and are wonderful." Most upperclassmen dine in one of 10 eating clubs—7 fraternities and 3 all-women houses—that maintain their own cooks and serve meals family-style.

Social life at Davidson isn't too bad, and the eating clubs are its focal points. All but one are situated in Patterson Court, where freshmen are not allowed for the first three weeks of school. The fees the houses charge go toward not only meals but also parties and other campus-wide events. The fraternities are not much different from the eating clubs, and freshmen simply sign up for the group they want to join, with no "rushing" allowed. Davidson adds to the egalitarianism by requiring that most parties—"at least two per weekend" at the eating clubs—be open to the entire community. Still, a few students feel the need for social outlets other than Patterson Court. The Council of Campus and Religious Life sets campus alcohol policy. "Underage students can't go to the basements of fraternities where beer is served," explains one student. The policy works to the extent that it's a safe environment, but it's always easy for underage students to be served. "No one under 21 is supposed to have alcohol but they can find it if they want it," says one student.

The town of Davidson is described by one student as being "a typical small Southern town—warm, friendly, and conservative." It centers on the college, and so not a whole lot goes on off campus. The town remains uncorrupted by fast-food and convenience stores. However, North Carolina's largest city, Charlotte, and the consequent "civilization" are 20 miles away. But the neighboring town of Cornelius is only a 10-minute drive, so students can catch movies and maybe a drink there. The school's small-town setting is quiet and quaint, and Davidson maintains facilities at nearby Lake Norman for sailing, swimming, and waterskiing. Myrtle Beach and skiing are several hours away, albeit in different directions. Most students spend a lot of time outdoors and participate in intramural sports at some point during their Davidson careers. When forced indoors, they have a titanic athletic complex in which to test their skills. Davidson's varsity athletic teams compete in the Southern Conference. Recent conference championships have been won by the women's swimming and diving teams, men's and women's soccer teams, and men's basketball.

As more and more top students around the nation hear of the opportunities at this little ol' Carolina school, Davidson strengthens its position as one of the nation's top liberal arts institutions. "Davidson is a school with tremendous academic offerings but it is also focused on preparing its students for life in the real world," says a junior. Truly a Southern gem, this school could top a list of "Great Schools You've Only Vaguely Heard Of."

Overlaps

Duke, Wake Forest, UNC–Chapel Hill, University of Virginia, Vanderbilt.

If You Apply To ➢   **Davidson**…Early decision: Nov. 15, Jan 2. Regular admission: Jan. 2. Financial aid: Feb. 15. Does not guarantee to meet demonstrated need. Campus interviews: recommended, informational. No alumni interviews. SATs or ACTs: required. SAT IIs: recommended. Accepts the Common Application. Essay question: significant experience; views on a personal, local, or global issue.

University of Dayton

300 College Park, Dayton, OH 45469-1611

Anyone who thinks that this generation's crop of college students subscribes to post-modern cynicism ought to take a peek at Dayton, where optimism and Catholic charity are alive and well. Dayton students work hard and play hard, and according to one senior English major, "We know when to study, but we know how to have a good time."

Founded by the Society of Mary (Marianists), Dayton continues to emphasize that order's devotion to service. More than 800 students volunteer their time in 25 different public service areas. And like many religiously affiliated schools, Dayton prides itself on the closeness and sense of community among its students and faculty members. "I hate to use a cliché," says one education junior, "but UD is one big happy family."

UD's campus is on the southern boundary of the city, secluded from the traffic and bustle of downtown. The more historic buildings on the parklike campus make up the central core of the campus and blend architectural charm with modern technological conveniences. And the campus is full of wide-open space, recreational areas, and beautiful landscaping. The Jesse Philips Humanities Center features a state-of-the-art multimedia lab and recital hall with the latest sound and recording equipment. The L. William Crotty Center for Enterprise Leadership opened in 1999, allowing enterprising students to jumpstart their own business ventures, and the Ryan C. Harris Learning-Teaching Center—an adaptive computer lab for students with physical or learning disabilities—opened last year.

UD students take full advantage of the strong offerings found in engineering, business, education, and the sciences. The most popular majors are communication, marketing, psychology, mechanical engineering, and biology. Weaker offerings include music, theater, and dance. Most students agree that the academic climate can be either demanding or laid-back, depending on the course and the major. "There are some competitive classes, but you are mostly competing against yourself," several students report.

Website: www.udayton.edu

Location: City outskirts

Total Enrollment: 10,223

Undergraduates: 7,018

Male/Female: 49/51

SAT Ranges: V 510–620 M 520–650

ACT Range: 22–27

Financial Aid: 55%

Expense: Pr $

Phi Beta Kappa: No

Applicants: 7,182

Accepted: 82%

Enrolled: 31%

Grad in 6 Years: 70%

Returning Freshmen: 87%

Academics: ✑ ✑ ✑

Social: ☎ ☎ ☎ ☎ ☎

Q of L: ★ ★ ★

Admissions: (937) 229-4411 or (800) 837-7433

Email Address: admission@udayton.edu

Strongest Programs: Communication

(Continued)
Engineering
Teacher Education
Business
Prephysical Therapy

Dayton's general education requirements include courses in five "domains of knowledge": arts, history, philosophy and religion, physical and life sciences, and social sciences. Faculty members in the College of Arts and Science have developed a 12-course core curriculum that satisfies the general education requirements through an interdisciplinary program that clumps mandatory classes into sequences pertinent to academic disciplines. Programs initiated recently include applied mathematical economics and two new concentrations in management: leadership and entrepreneurship. Students with at least a 1270 combined SAT score or a 29 ACT score who place in the top 10 percent of their graduating class may join the University Scholars Program. This involves taking special courses, including one that hosts a nationally renowned guest author. The administration notes that the majority of the participants who have applied to graduate school have won a full assistantship or fellowship.

The Interdepartmental Summer Study Abroad Program is a popular ticket to Europe's most exciting cities, while the Immersion Program in Third World countries is much praised by participants. Students in engineering, business administration, computer science, and biology can take advantage of the cooperative education opportunities, and everyone can benefit from the information science center, which houses computer classrooms and labs. All students receive a computer upon entering UD, in conjunction with recent computer requirements. Most classes are kept to minimum sizes, between 25 and 50 students, and students speak enthusiastically about contacts with professors outside of the classroom. New students unsure of their majors can take advantage of First Year Experience, a structured program where students are required to meet with their advisors once a week. This enables freshmen to explore majors, set career goals, schedule for upcoming terms, as well as learn about the services, facilities, and opportunities UD has to offer.

Sophomores have an opportunity to live in Virginia Kettering, a residence hall whose amenities evoke luxurious apartments and is also known as "the Hilton on the Hill."

Students, the majority of whom are Roman Catholics, tend to be fun-loving products of middle-American families. Just over half of Dayton's students are native Ohioans. Minorities make up only 6 percent of the student population, with African Americans comprising half of that figure. The Task Force on Women's Issues, an Office for Diverse Student Populations, and an updated sexual harassment policy demonstrate UD's growing sensitivity to campus issues. More than 24 percent of incoming students rank in the top tenth of their high school class, an indication that UD is perhaps more selective than it is given credit for. Dayton's athletic scholarships go to all sports except football. There are also many scholarship and leadership awards that go to those with superior academic credentials.

Seventy-four percent of students are campus residents; those that live off campus generally live adjacent to it. On-campus dwellers can choose from three residence halls, one of which is smoke-free, and housing is readily available for all undergraduate students. Upperclassmen often enter the lottery for coveted university-owned coed apartments and houses located in an adjacent student neighborhood that also contains privately owned homes. Students praise the clean and well-maintained rooms: "UD housing is awesome," exclaims one enthusiast. The best dorm for freshmen, according to many, is Marycrest, with "huge rooms and loads of storage space." Sophomores have an opportunity to live in Virginia Kettering, a residence hall whose amenities evoke luxurious apartments and is also known as "the Hilton on the Hill." The food in the dining halls that dot the campus is generally well received; one dining hall is located in one of the first-year dorms, another in the sophomore complex, and the third is centrally located in the student union.

The L. William Crotty Center for Enterprise Leadership recently opened in 1999, allowing enterprising students to jumpstart their own business ventures.

The student neighborhood (a.k.a., "the Ghetto") serves as a sort of continuous social center. A lit porch light beckons party-seeking students to join the weekend festivities. Because the university owns most of the properties, a 24-hour campus security patrol keeps watch over the area. Block parties are perennial warm-weather favorites, but most smaller affairs are also popular. Much of the social life takes place here or on campus. The more adventurous weekend excursions are trips to Ohio State University, Ohio University, and Cincinnati or Indianapolis. But the best road trip is the Dayton-to-Daytona trip after spring finals, a 17 hour trek which draws loads of students each year. Partying on campus is commonplace and controlled, but parties have sized down due to the university's crackdown on the 21-year-old drinking age. Kegs are allowed only at parties where the legal drinking age of the partyers can be validated. Still, "There is a 'three strikes, you're out' policy regarding drinking, but students at UD, on average, enjoy drinking and have no problem being served at off-campus parties. Greek organizations draw 16 percent of UD men and 20 percent of the women, with all chapters playing an active role in the community service and social life.

More important though are sports, particularly basketball. The football team, which is Division I-AA, plays in the Pioneer Conference and brought home the championship in 1999. UD is in the Atlantic 10 for Division I athletics in all other sports. When students aren't cheering, they can participate in an extensive intramural program. Other activities in the city include an art institute, aviation museum, symphony, and ballet, which are all just minutes away from campus by bus. A large shopping mall is also easily accessible. Those who hunger for a more cosmopolitan atmosphere can frequent Cincinnati and its restaurants, shops, and sports arenas.

The success of Dayton's attempts to provide its students with a high quality of life and a sense of cohesiveness is reflected in many of the students' comments about the terrific social life and family-like atmosphere among both students and faculty. Dayton's Board of Trustees recently established a long-range plan called "Vision 2005," which will build upon Dayton's strengths as a Catholic, Marianist, comprehensive university. As a midsize university where the undergraduates come first, Dayton has managed to maintain an exciting balance of personal attention, academic challenge, and all-American fun.

> *The best road trip is the Dayton-to-Daytona trip after spring finals, a 17 hour trek which draws loads of students each year.*

Overlaps

Miami University (OH), Ohio University, Xavier, Ohio State, University of Cincinnati.

If You Apply To ➤ **Dayton**…Rolling admissions. Financial aid: Mar. 31. Campus interviews: recommended, informational. No alumni interviews. SATs or ACTs: required. No SAT IIs. Accepts electronic applications. Essay question: Personal statement addressing your background.

Deep Springs College

Deep Springs, CA Mailing address: Dyer, NV 89010-9803

At Deep Springs College, all work and no play doesn't makes Jack a dull boy; it makes him one of twenty-five or so male students at this two-year institution that doubles as a working ranch. Bonding is easy here, and students enjoy a demanding and individualized education based on ranch life. Both, it seems, demand the

Website:
www.deepsprings.edu
Location: Rural

same things: hard work, commitment, and pride in a job well done. Deep Springs College students are also rewarded for their efforts in other ways: tuition is free, and so is room and board. Students pay only for books, travel, and personal items; the average cost of one year at Deep Springs is $500.

Many of the men who work, study, and live at this college have shunned acceptance at Ivy League schools to embrace the rigors of a truly unique approach to learning, although many then go on to Ivies once their two years at Deep Springs are over. Deep Springs students tend to be of the academic Renaissance man variety with wide-ranging interests in many fields. Almost all transfer to the most prestigious universities after their two-year program, and 70 percent eventually earn a doctorate.

California's White Mountains provide a stunning backdrop for the Deep Springs campus, set on a barren plain 5,200 feet above sea level near the only water supply for miles around. The campus is an oasis-like cluster of trees and a lawn with eight "somewhat ramshackle" ranch-style buildings that were built from scratch by the class of 1919. Deep Springs is 28 miles from the nearest town, a thriving metropolis known as Big Pine, population 950. The focal point of campus is the Main Building, a venerable ranch house that includes dorm rooms, a computer room, and offices. Faculty houses and the dining facilities are grouped around the circular lawn a few yards away, and the trappings of farm life surround the tiny settlement. The college has 170 acres under cultivation, mostly with alfalfa, and an assortment of barnyard animals. The library is one of the most recent additions to the campus as well as a new student residence.

Founded in 1917 by an industrialist who made a fortune in the electric power industry, Deep Springs today remains true to its charter "to combine taxing practical work, rigorous academics, and genuine self-government." Ideals of self-government, reflectiveness, frugality, and community activity have weathered more than 75 years of a grueling academic climate. "The work here is very rigorous," says one student. "If you don't want to work hard physically, mentally, and emotionally, this isn't the place for you." Explains a freshman, "Our classes are very small—my largest so far had 18 students—so it's hard to hide the fact that you haven't done a reading." Academic learning is the primary activity here, but students are also required to perform 20 hours per week of labor, which can include everything from harvesting alfalfa to cooking dinner. When asked which are the best majors, one wit exclaims, "Dairy is the most popular, but many students swear by irrigation."

The students' input carries a lot of weight at this school. They help choose the college's faculty, and even elect one of their own to be a voting member on the board of trustees. They play a determining role in admissions and curricular decisions. And they abide by a spartan community code that bans all drugs, including alcohol, and forbids anyone from leaving Deep Springs Valley, the 50 square miles of desert surrounding the campus while classes are in session, except for medical visits and college business. Lest these rules sound unnecessarily strict, keep in mind that these are all decided upon and enforced by the student body, not the administration.

Like almost everything else about it, Deep Springs has an unorthodox academic schedule: two summer terms of 7 weeks each, and a fall and spring semester of 14 weeks each. Between 7 and 10 classes are offered every term. The faculty consists of three "permanent" professors (they sign on for five years), plus an average of four others who are hired on a temporary basis to teach for a term or two. The quality of particular academic areas varies as professors come and go. Overall, however, the teaching quality is reported to be "superb." "Professors here

The college has 170 acres under cultivation, mostly with alfalfa, and an assortment of barnyard animals.

eat with students daily," reports one student. "I've often continued discussions over lunch and dinner that started a few hours earlier in class." Although the curriculum is altered yearly, students predict that literary theory and philosophy will always remain superior. The students control the academic program and quickly replace courses—and faculty—that do not work out. Foreign language offerings are still sparse, and lack of high-tech lab equipment puts a damper on chemistry and physics courses. "In eighth grade at least I had a microscope," says a student. Currently, the only required courses are in public speaking and composition.

Deep Springers aren't much for the latest conveniences, but computers have taken the campus by storm; there's one in each student's room, plus several in a common area. With class sizes ranging from 2 to 14, there is ample opportunity for close student-faculty interaction. Close living arrangements have fostered a kind of kinship between faculty and students. Students routinely visit their mentors in their homes, sometimes to confer on academic matters and sometimes to baby-sit.

An average of one student per year decides that Deep Springs is not his cup of tea. Most DS students are from upper-middle-class families and typically rank in the top 3 percent of their high school class. Many Deep Springers are transplanted urbanites; the rest hail from points scattered across the nation or across the seas. Political leanings run the gamut, and there is diversity even among this small population: Seventy-six percent of the student body are white; Asian Americans make up 20 percent; and Hispanics account for 4 percent. "We all enjoy a comfortable level of deep brotherhood," says a student. The college's single-sex status is a source of much discussion, as well as "the extent to which we're justified in removing ourselves so thoroughly from mainstream culture," states a freshman.

Students arrange dorm selection and maintenance is entirely the responsibility of the students. "One cool thing about DS is that you can do anything you want to your room," says a student. "Our walls are painted mauve and there is a pink queen-sized bed hanging from the ceiling called the 'Love Loft.'" Students all pitch in preparing the meals, from butchering the meat to milking the cows to washing the dishes. Given the sequestered location of DS, crime is not an issue. Safety, however, is another matter. "Sometimes we get charged by bulls," admits one student.

Social life can be a challenge. "Socializing takes place on the front porch when people gather and smoke," reports one student. When the moon is full, students go out en masse in the middle of the night to frolic in the 700-foot-high Eureka Sand Dunes with Frisbees and skis. "We slide down the Eureka Valley sand dunes au naturel," says one student. As for "recent technological advancement," they used to have one telephone line for the whole school; now they have six. Perhaps the most popular social activity on campus is conversation over a cup of coffee in the dining hall, where the chatter is usually lively until the wee hours of the morning. Other common activities are road trips to nearby national parks, hikes in the nearby mountains, and horseback riding. The Turkey Bowl, the potato harvest, the two-on-two basketball tourney, and Sludgefest, an annual event involving cleaning out the reservoir, are only some of the time-honored Deep Springs traditions. Critics of Deep Springs charge that DS cultivates arrogance and social backwardness among students who were too intellectual to be in the social mainstream during high school. They argue that students who come here are doomed to be misfits for life, citing a survey that shows many Deep Springers never marry. While that charge is debatable, even supporters of Deep Springs confess to a love-hate relationship with the college.

Perhaps more than any other school in the nation, Deep Springs is a

Tuition is free, and so is room and board. Students pay only for books, travel, and personal items; the average cost of one year at Deep Springs is $500.

Founded in 1917 by an industrialist who made a fortune in the electric power industry, Deep Springs today remains true to its charter "to combine taxing practical work, rigorous academics, and genuine self-government.

community where students and faculty interact day to day on an intensely personal level. Though the financial commitment is small, the school demands an intense level of personal commitment. All must quickly learn how to get along in a community where the actions of each person affect everyone. Urban cowboys who dream of riding into the sunset are in for a rude awakening. For a few, however, the camaraderie and soul-searching fostered in this tight-knit community can be mighty tempting—just stay clear of those bulls.

If You Apply To ⟫

Deep Springs…Regular admissions: Nov. 15. Campus interviews: required, evaluative. No alumni interviews. SATs: required. SAT IIs: required. Essay questions: Describe yourself; critical analysis of book or other work of art; and why Deep Springs?

University of Delaware

Newark, DE 19716

Website: www.udel.edu
Location: Small city
Total Enrollment: 18,574
Undergraduates: 15,443
Male/Female: 42/58
SAT Ranges: V 510–610 M 520–630
Financial Aid: 62%
Expense: Pub $ $ $ $
Phi Beta Kappa: Yes
Applicants: 15,482
Accepted: 64%
Enrolled: 35%
Grad in 6 Years: 72%
Returning Freshmen: 87%
Academics: ✍ ✍ ✍
Social: ☎ ☎ ☎ ☎ ☎
Q of L: ★ ★ ★
Admissions: (302) 831-8123
Email Address:
admissions@udel.edu

Strongest Programs:
Chemical Engineering
Business Administration
Biological Sciences
Psychology
Nursing

If you're looking for an all-American, traditional college experience, take a look at the University of Delaware. This immense public university offers students a private university atmosphere bolstered by solid academics, rowdy athletic traditions, and ample opportunities for research.

Delaware's spacious 1,000-acre campus is an attractive mix of Colonial and modern geometric buildings with a sufficient number of shady and tanning areas. The campus is set among one of the nation's oldest Dutch elm groves, and in the fall "the trees on the mall turn their becoming shades of autumn and set the mood for academia!" one student gushes. The hub of the campus is a grassy green flanked by a distinguished-looking group of classic Georgian buildings. Newer campus attractions include the $3-million Rullo Field Hockey Stadium and Bayard Sharpe Hall, a technologically enhanced gothic cathedral.

Delaware's academic menu includes more than 110 different majors ranging from the usual liberal arts and science departments to vocational programs like fashion merchandising. Boasting one of the largest undergraduate research programs in the country, Delaware recently added Continental European Studies, East Asian Studies, and Latin American Studies. Other new majors include landscape horticulture, exercise and sports science, physical education studies, and figure skating science. Engineering, especially chemical engineering, is generally agreed to be the specialty of the house, with business (most notably accounting, business administration, and economics) not far behind. Psychology, nursing, accounting, English, history and art history, and elementary education departments all claim a fair share of majors as well. The music department is upwardly mobile, with a number of faculty members who have impressive professional performance credits. Meanwhile, students report that the math department could stand improvement.

However, most students find the courses at U of D challenging and rigorous. Students in all programs must take some combination of general education requirements that include courses in four divisions: creative arts and humanities, culture and institutions, human beings and their environment, natural phenomena, and an additional three-hour approved multicultural course. Grading standards and quality of instruction are high. As one student says, "Professors push their students for more and have high expectations." One senior agrees but offers a possible hint: "If you get nervous before an exam due to lack of studying, just stop by the Morris Library and rub your hand on the nose of the bust of Mr. Morris. Rumor has it, a rub on his nose brings good luck!" The outstanding honors program enrolls more than 350 students a year and the undergraduate research and humanities semester programs also attract many of the university's best and brightest. "Your major dictates how rigorous your courses will be," says a civil engineering major. Students report that they have little trouble getting into classes, but on the rare occasions that they are shut out, they can take a couple of classes during the January term to reduce their courseload during the regular semester. Most faculty members are accessible and "outstanding." A criminal justice major confides, "If you show the interest, professors are more than willing to match and exceed your effort. They love to get to know their students." On the other hand, science profs are notorious for finding lower forms of life on their microscope slides more interesting than the higher forms in their classrooms. Academic advising receives mixed reviews, from students who find faculty advisors useless to those who can't stop gushing about them: "My advisor always helps me work out any problem that comes up, and knows and cares about me as a person."

Only 41 percent of the student body are from the First State; many of the rest are from neighboring New Jersey, Pennsylvania, Maryland, New York, and Virginia. Most students are from public schools, and according to a political science major, the students range from "the apathetic to the avant-garde." But the consensus is that "the conservative, suburban, academically successful, socially adept, football-loving kind of student" will do well here. Unfortunately, the outlook isn't as rosy for students of color: African Americans account for a mere 6 percent of the student population, and Hispanics and Asian Americans combine for another 6 percent. Remarks one student, "Racial and ethnic mixing is increasing outside the classroom as a result of 'beefed-up' diversity awareness and education." Others say that the university tries to promote appreciation of cultural differences. Delaware offers more than 165 athletic scholarships, as well as 3,102 merit awards ranging from $1,000 to $18,468. In order to get the academic scholarships into the hands of the most deserving, the university maintains a search program that matches eligible Delaware students with potential scholarships.

Except for those commuting from home, freshmen are required to live on campus. Housing placement is done through lottery but at least it's guaranteed housing for all four years, provided application deadlines are met. U of D provides a wide assortment of accommodations, including coed and single-sex dorms (some with visiting hours and some without), singles, apartments, and suites. The special-interest communities, such as French House, International House, and Martin Luther King, Jr. House, are now all located in three residence halls. All told, about half of the students live in some form of university housing, while the commuters engage in mortal combat for nearby parking spaces. Meal plans must be purchased by students living in traditional residence halls. Other on-campus students and commuters can buy a 30-lunch meal ticket. Dining-hall choices include diet meals, sandwich and salad bars, a taco bar, and vegetarian meals.

"Our school no longer has its party school reputation," observes a junior. This is partly due to the administration-imposed ban on alcohol at campus parties and tighter ID-checking standards in downtown bars. Rumor has it that video cameras

(Continued)
English
History
Political Science

Delaware's academic menu includes more than 110 different majors ranging from the usual liberal arts and science departments to vocational programs like fashion merchandising.

The outstanding honors program enrolls more than 350 students a year, and the undergraduate research and humanities semester programs also attract many of the university's best and brightest.

scan tailgates for errant underage drinkers. A senior elementary education major reflects "I have seen the amount of drinking on campus decline in my years here, but if students really want to drink, they can do it with the risk of being caught." Off-campus house and apartment parties offer more open action, and popular bars such as Stone Balloon draw huge crowds every weekend. There is a nonalcoholic bar on campus, and dry dances are held on Friday nights. Fraternities and sororities claim 12 percent of men and 14 percent of women students. Newark, "a great little city with just about everything you could need," provides an array of fast-food joints, bars, malls, and movies. New York, Washington, Baltimore, and Philadelphia all lie within a few hours' drive. Depending on the season, Rehoboth Beach and ski slopes in Pennsylvania offer diversion. But many students prefer to stay on campus on the weekends. "There's so much to do here, you never want to go home!" exclaims one student. Delaware Day is an annual bacchanal held every spring.

The school's athletic bent emerges on fall Saturdays when Blue Hen football is the big attraction ("Go Hens!"), with tailgate picnics before the game and parties afterward. The women's lacrosse team also attracts a loyal following, and other strong teams include women's volleyball and swimming, and men's basketball, baseball, and golf. Intramural sports are popular, and arena events benefit from the 6,000-seat sports center.

The University of Delaware is a large school for such a small state, and the many programs offer something for everyone. As the university strives to "function and feel like a private college," students in search of a quality education might be wise to give this institution a hard look.

> ### Overlaps
>
> **Penn State, Rutgers, University of Maryland, University of Virginia, Virginia Polytech.**

If You Apply To ➤

Delaware...Early decision: Nov. 1, Dec.1. Regular admissions: Mar. 1 (Feb. 1 for scholarships). Financial aid: Mar. 15. Housing: May 1. Campus interviews: optional, evaluative. Alumni interviews: optional, informational. SATs: required. SAT IIs: optional (recommended for Honors program). Accepts the Common Application. Essay question: what attracts you to U of D; what major interests you; what attracts you to East coast, personal statement.

Denison University

Granville, OH 43023

Website: www.denison.edu
Location: Small town
Total Enrollment: 2,089
Undergraduates: 2,089
Male/Female: 45/55
SAT Ranges: V 560–650 M 560–660
ACT Range: 25–29
Financial Aid: 50%
Expense Pr: $ $ $
Phi Beta Kappa: Yes
Applicants: 2,991

Once affectionately known as Camp Denidoo, Denison is changing its image as a laid-back cousin of the Northeast's elite liberal arts colleges. The university has proven its new commitment to academics by closing the residential fraternity houses and making a concentrated effort to move academics from the backseat to the driver's seat. "Denison has changed from a Greek-dominated preppy school to a much more diverse and academically focused university," says a biology major. "Those who don't take their education seriously will feel out of place here."

Located in the rolling Welsh hills of central Ohio, Denison offers a panoramic view of the surrounding valley. With its huge maples and sloping walkways, the beautifully landscaped campus is reminiscent of a rustic New England hamlet. The buildings, an ensemble of red bricks and white columns, include some of the most attractive Colonial architecture on any campus in the Midwest. Renovations were recently completed on the residential halls of the East and West Quads and the Huffman student dining hall.

For a small liberal arts college, Denison offers a vast array of academic options. Denison also encourages internships and off-campus study through the programs of the Great Lakes Colleges Association* and the Associated Colleges of the Midwest,* and the May Term program offers students over 200 internships around the country in a broad range of careers. The top-notch geology and physics departments enjoy a state-of-the-art facility, complete with a planetarium and laser spectrometer, which was funded by the F. W. Olin Foundation. The college also places a premium on students doing both independent and collaborative research with faculty. The honors program offers over 50 courses each year and is known for its "Chowder Hour," where students and faculty gather for an informal presentation while dining on a faculty member's culinary specialty. Environmental studies is another of Denison's fastest growing programs and has the benefit of a 350-acre biological reserve and a state-of-the-art research station. Biology, economics, and history are among the college's strongest departments. Physical education is a bit flabby but the university is taking steps to whip it into shape. The university library is small, with only about 325,000 volumes, but the computer facilities are excellent and an online network allows students access to collections at other Ohio colleges.

All students must take Words and Ideas, designed to develop reading and writing ability, and they must also choose a second course emphasizing broad themes such as Aesthetic Inquiry and the Human Condition or American Social Perspectives. Other inquiry courses await sophomores and upperclassmen, as do general ed requirements that include life and physical sciences, foreign languages, and American Social Institutions. While this may sound intimidating, students say that some of the courses that count for general education credit are actually quite popular: world cinema, human sexuality, computer science, and creative writing. Students have nothing but praise for their professors. "My relationships with the faculty have been the highlight of my time at Denison," says one student. "The quality of teaching is superior." A classmate adds, "You are not a number, you are an individual whose opinion matters and counts."

Fifty-four percent of Denisonians are from out of state, mostly from the Midwestern or Mid-Atlantic states. New Englanders and Midwesterners mix well on the Denison campus, but the situation with minorities is less than ideal. "Race relations are still tense on campus but progress is being made on this front," says an economics major. African Americans, Hispanics, and Asian Americans combine for 11 percent of the student body. Denison has always had a conservative bent, though students seem far more concerned with "he said/she said" than any national issues. "The faculty on the whole is liberal and I think the student body is shifting in that direction," reports one senior. Part of the reason is the administration's recent effort to give Denison a more intellectual flavor. It has combined a clamp-down on the Greek system with a sustained effort to increase the student body's academic profile.

Community service is an important part of the Denison experience, and the college supports a number of service-learning courses that incorporate community involvement into their subject matter. A biology major sums it up this way: "Getting out into the 'real world' and helping those less fortunate has been an education by itself." One of the most popular service-oriented activities is the Licking River Roundup, where students canoe down the river and pick up all the trash they find.

Denison has been extremely aggressive in wooing excellent (and average) students with a total of 860 merit scholarships. Some of the awards, such as the Wells, Dunbar, and Faculty Achievement awards, are aggressively competitive and

(Continued)
Accepted: 69%
Enrolled: 29%
Grad in 6 Years: 75%
Returning Freshmen: 86%
Academics: ✑ ✑ ✑ ✑
Social: ☎ ☎ ☎ ☎ ☎
Q of L: ★ ★ ★
Admissions: (740) 587–6276 or (800) DENISON
Email Address:
admissions@denison.edu

Strongest Programs:
Environmental Studies
Biology
Chemistry/Biochemistry
Economics
English and Creative Writing
Physics

The honors program offers over 50 courses each year and is known for its "Chowder Hour," where students and faculty gather for an informal presentation while dining on a faculty member's culinary specialty.

cover full tuition. Others (notably the $3,000 to $7,000 Alumni awards) are handed out to virtually anyone who can afford the balance of the bill. All the emphasis on merit scholarships has depleted Denison's reserves for need-based aid, but the university continues to meet at least 93 percent of need for two-thirds of the students who require assistance.

Denison is truly a residential college. Ninety-eight percent of its students live on campus, but Denison offers a wide variety of living situations. Crawford Hall, the freshman dorm, is specially geared to the needs of newcomers, with counseling, entertainment, and information. At Taylor House, academic leaders and scholars live in apartment-style units. The Homesteaders live in student-built solar-paneled cabins on a farm a mile away from campus and raise much of their own food. There are two pleasant dining halls on campus, and the food generally earns praise. Campus security is a nonissue. "My father is the director of corporate security for a Fortune 500 company," says a biology major, "and he sleeps well at night knowing that I am at Denison." A junior adds, "I feel safe on campus, even walking home from the library late at night."

The students are enthusiastic about sports at Denison, and many teams, most notably men's and women's swimming and diving, contend for league and national championships. Other standouts include men's cross-country, lacrosse, and tennis; and women's indoor track and field, soccer, and lacrosse. Enthusiasm reaches a fever pitch during Homecoming Weekend. Friday night features an all-campus gala highlighted by a chocolate volcano, and in the words of a political science major, "Saturday finds people running from sporting event to sporting event. Especially popular is the football game in which the cheering is led by half-naked male cheerleaders." Intramurals are very popular, and Denisonians get especially riled up for any competition against Kenyon and Ohio Wesleyan.

And then there is the Greek life. Roughly a third of the students join, though the demise of "Fraternity Row" has forced many to search off campus for fun, especially if it involves alcohol. "Denison observes state and federal laws regarding underage drinking and campus security, and the residential life staff do enforce the policies," says a history major. Still, most students consider on-campus drinking safe. "It may not be easy for underage students to be served alcohol in the local bars, but at parties the beer flows freely," boasts one student. On campus, social outlets such as plays, concerts, and movies are sponsored by Denison and/or the Student Activities Council. Tiny Granville offers little in the way of nighttime diversions. "Granville is dullsville," says an environmental studies major. "The entire town rolls up by 10:00 P.M." For those with more modest requirements, the nearby city of Newark is "good for late-night fast-food fixes," notes one student. Even with its lack of nightlife, Granville still manages to win the hearts of most students. "I will miss Granville dearly when I graduate," says a biochemistry major. "It is a beautiful town and the residents are very supportive of the students at Denison." The commercial and cultural facilities that Granville lacks can be found in Columbus, the state capital and home to Ohio State University, just 45 minutes away. In response to complaints about a lack of mass transportation to the "real world," the school launched the "Big Red Express," which makes regular runs to the nearby malls and to Columbus for shopping and cultural events. Also, the Central Ohio Transportation Authority now has a commuter bus that runs daily between the campus and Columbus.

Denison has proven itself a scrappy competitor in the battle for students with nearby Miami University and Ohio's many other fine liberal arts colleges. It still attracts mainly the J. Crew crowd, but the emphasis has shifted from alcohol to academics. "We still have a lot of fun at Denison," says a senior. "Now we just study harder before we play."

| If You Apply To ➢ | **Denison**…Early decision: Jan. 1. Regular admissions: Feb. 1. Financial aid: Mar. 1 (Jan. 1 for scholarships). Meets demonstrated need of 60%. Campus and alumni interviews: recommended, evaluative. SATs or ACTs: required. SAT IIs: optional. Accepts the Common Application and electronic applications. Essay question: significant experience or achievement; issue of concern; influential person; most meaningful activity. |

University of Denver

2199 South University Boulevard, Mary Reed Building, Denver, CO 80208

The oldest private university in the Rocky Mountain region, the University of Denver provides plenty of options for students looking to hit the books or hit the slopes. A school with a rich heritage, DU boasts an especially strong business program, and the school's location offers ample opportunities for making job contacts and enjoying the beautiful Colorado landscape.

DU's 125-acre main campus is located in a comfortable residential neighborhood only eight miles from downtown Denver and an hour east of major ski areas. The north campus is home to the law school, the school of music, and several other programs, including the Women's College. Architectural styles vary, and include Collegiate Gothic, brick, limestone, Colorado sandstone, and copper. Special facilities on campus include centers for Judaic studies, Latin American studies, the environment institute, and fine arts. Nearby Mount Evans (14,264 feet) is home to the world's loftiest observatory, a DU facility available to both professors and students.

DU is known for its business school, especially the hotel, restaurant, and tourism management offerings, and for its innovative core curriculum. The school's pre-professional programs are feeders for graduate schools (almost 60% of DU's student body are grad students) and new businesses in the booming West. International studies is another strength, backed by lots of opportunities for study abroad, while chemistry, atmospheric physics, music, psychology, and computer science have solid reputations. Students praise the School of Communications for its numerous internships, its television studios, and computer lab. Outstanding undergrads can get early admittance to DU's graduate schools of business, international studies, and social work, completing both undergraduate and graduate degrees in five years. Despite the inherent pressure of a quarter system, the academic climate is relatively relaxed. Students say that there is little competition with each other, though students at DU routinely push themselves to do their best. Faculty accessibility gets high marks. "All of my classes have been taught by Ph.D.s," boasts one upperclassman. The Partners in Scholarship program pairs students and professors in research projects across the academic spectrum.

The DU core curriculum has received much praise from the National Endowment for the Humanities, and is consistent with the national trend toward structured college curriculums. All undergraduates, poets and engineers alike, must take one year of English, arts and humanities, social sciences, and natural sciences; additional requirements include a quarter of oral communication and two quarters of mathematics. Each student must enroll in the University of Denver Campus Connection, a seminar in which first-year students are introduced to college life and are paired with faculty mentors for advising. The Student Orientation and Registration Program (SOAR) helps smooth the transition to freshman life, with programs in the summer as well as when classes begin.

Website: www.du.edu
Location: City outskirts
Total Enrollment: 9,188
Undergraduates: 3,751
Male/Female: 42/58
SAT Ranges: V 510–610 M 500–610
ACT Range: 21–27
Financial Aid: 43%
Expense: Pr $ $
Phi Beta Kappa: Yes
Applicants: 3,303
Accepted: 84%
Enrolled: N/A
Grad in 6 Years: 69%
Returning Freshmen: 84%
Academics: ✍ ✍ ✍
Social: ☎ ☎ ☎ ☎
Q of L: ★ ★ ★ ★
Admissions: (800) 525-9495
Email Address: admission@du.edu

Strongest Programs:
Biological Sciences
Accountancy
Psychology
Hotel, Restaurant, and Tourism Management
English
Fine Arts
Business
Environmental Science

University rules stipulate that all core courses must be taught by senior faculty. Course titles include the Making of the Modern Mind, Multiple Voices of America, and Understanding Human Conflict. "At first I thought, 'Who wants to take these science, art, and English classes?'" explains a business major. "But now that I've completed the core, I feel better about myself and my world knowledge. Now I can speak of Goya, Berlioz, and define my favorite artists with a knowledge of the period, styles, and works." The average undergraduate class size is 21 students, though introductory courses can be much larger. A rigorous honors program is available, as are numerous study abroad options.

By and large, students come from fairly affluent families. One student jokes that "the stereotypical DU student drives a brand new SUV, wears only Abercrombie and GAP clothing, and skis every weekend." Forty-four percent of the students are from Colorado; minorities account for 15 percent of the student body, and on the whole, race relations are considered good. Because it is one of the few private colleges in the West, DU is also among the most expensive in the region. There are a number of merit and athletic scholarships available to help those who qualify. The financial aid office is notorious for including parent loans in the packages offered to students.

Students are required to live their first two years on campus in the residence halls. "The dorms are comfortable enough," says a sophomore. "They have a beautiful view of the mountains, and at sunset or during lightning storms, students often crowd around lounge windows to watch." The Johnson-McFarlane hall ("J-Mac") is supposed to be the best place for freshmen, though another student says that the Towers are a much quieter on-campus option. Freshman and sophomore dorm residents must sign up for a 15- or 19-meal-a-week plan. Greeks can live and dine together in their houses. Since there are no restrictions concerning off-campus living for upperclassmen, many juniors and seniors opt for the decent quarters found within walking distance of campus.

With consistently beautiful sunny weather and great skiing, hiking, and camping less than an hour away in the Rockies, many DU students head for the hills on weekends. Besides various ski areas, one can explore Estes Park, Mount Evans, and Echo Lake. Additionally, DU is near Moab, Albuquerque, and Las Vegas, the Mecca of all American road trips. Since Denver is not primarily a college town, many students with cars head for Boulder (home of the University of Colorado), about 30 miles away. For those staying home, the transit system makes it easy to get to downtown Denver. Once there, the options are tremendous and include great local restaurants, bars, and stores, many of which cater to students. About 15 percent of the men and 8 percent of the women join fraternities or sororities.

Greeks tend to dominate the social life, and several students mention the Border Bar as a hotspot. Wednesday is pub night at the $10-million student center. Drinking policies abound, and although DU enforces the law, students say it's no harder for an underage student to imbibe at DU than any other school in the country.

When it comes to sports, peace-loving '60s types and partyers unite when the DU hockey team, a national powerhouse, skates out onto the ice, especially against arch-rival Colorado College. Women's gymnastics also competes successfully in Division I, while men's and women's soccer, basketball, tennis, skiing, and swimming, along with men's baseball and women's volleyball have returned to Division I play. Intramural sports, for those with less ability but just as much competitive spirit, also are popular. Every January, all thoughts of academics are put aside for the three-day Winter Carnival. Top administrators, professors, and students all pack off to Steamboat Springs, Crested Butte, or some other ski area to catch some fresh powder and see who can ski the fastest, skate the best, or build the most artistic ice sculptures. In the spring, the whole campus turns out for the annual Chancellors Barbecue.

Students like DU for its modest size and friendly atmosphere. And while there remain some moneyed students with attitude problems, these types are balanced by more down-to-earth kids. As the school pushes for a more diverse student body, and emphasizes teaching and technology, the Denver University is becoming better known. Perhaps in the not to distant future, DU will be better known for its intellectual rigor than its gorgeous setting in the Rocky Mountains.

If You Apply To >

DU...Rolling admissions. Financial aid: Feb. 15. Does not guarantee to meet demonstrated need. Campus interviews: recommended, evaluative. Alumni interviews: optional, informational. ACTs or SATs: required. SAT IIs: optional. Accepts the Common Application and electronic applications. Essay question: What are you thinking, feeling, or laughing about and why?

DePaul University

One East Jackson Boulevard, Chicago, IL 60604

At DePaul University, the basketball team is not the only thing earning big points. The school's reputation, as well as its enrollment, is surging; its student body has almost doubled in the past 15 years. DePaul has also transformed from the "little school under the tracks" to Chicago's version of NYU. This leading Roman Catholic school values diversity, and almost half of the student body are non-Catholic. Located in a city full of opportunities, DePaul students have a world of resources and facilities at their fingertips.

DePaul has two campuses. The Lincoln Park campus is home to the College of Liberal Arts and Sciences, the School of Education, the Theater School, and the School of Music, as well as residence halls, and academic and recreational facilities. The Lincoln Park area is a fashionable Chicago neighborhood with century-old brownstone homes, theaters, cafés, parks, and shops. The state-of-the-art library is among the outstanding facilities on this campus. A $13-million biology and environmental sciences building opened in 1998. The Loop, or "vertical," campus in downtown Chicago houses the Law School, the School for New Learning, and the College of Commerce in four high-rise buildings—56 stories in all. The DePaul Center, a $70-million teaching, learning, and research complex, is the cornerstone of this campus. A 20-minute ride on the elevated train connects the two sites.

DePaul's name is closely associated with Midwestern business and law, and undergraduates are welcomed as interns in local legal and commercial institutions. The School of Accountancy draws many majors and is reported to be the most challenging department in the College of Commerce. The Theater School is renowned, as is the School of Music. The Department of Computer Science and Information Systems remains a national leader. It continually updates its software, and maintains one of the largest Digital Equipment Corporation configurations available to academic institutions. The School of Education and

Website: www.depaul.edu
Location: Urban
Total Enrollment: 19,549
Undergraduates: 11,778
Male/Female: 40/60
SAT Ranges: V 450–570 M 490–630
ACT Range: 22–27
Financial Aid: 70%
Expense: Pr $
Phi Beta Kappa: No
Applicants: 6,100
Accepted: 81%
Enrolled: 36%
Grad in 6 Years: 75%
Returning Freshmen: 82%
Academics: ✐ ✐ ✐
Social: ☎ ☎
Q of L: ★ ★ ★
Admissions: (800) 4-DEPAUL
Email Address:
admitdpu@wppost.depaul.edu

Strongest Programs:
Accounting

several of the science departments (including biology, chemistry, and physics) have been rejuvenated, and the impressive prelaw program balances agreeably with the strong liberal arts and business offerings. Premed, economics, and the life sciences are cited as weaker programs by many DePaul students.

At DePaul courses are small, and senior profs teach on all levels. Student representatives from each school and college are appointed by the administration to sit on faculty promotion and tenure committees. A number of social activities are designed to bring the undergraduates and the faculty together, and students are given a phone book with all the profs' home numbers. "The quality of teaching I have received thus far has been nothing short of phenomenal," a freshman says. The faculty has many real-world practitioners who are praised for savvy advisement. All students take proficiency tests in basic skills at the Student Development Center and are given individual guidance in course selection. The required liberal studies program, which includes world civilization, religion and philosophy, natural sciences, behavioral sciences, fine arts, and writing requirements, takes up about half of all students' workloads. Bachelor of arts recipients are also required to take three courses in a foreign language. Freshmen must take Freshman Seminar and two composition courses. The highly selective honors program includes interdisciplinary courses, a modern language requirement, and a senior thesis. Study abroad options include programs in France, Hungary, Italy, England, Germany, China, Japan, South Africa, Greece, and Mexico.

Founded in 1898 by the Vincentian Fathers, DePaul is run by priests who also teach some of the courses. Almost half of the students are non-Catholic, but Mass is still held every day for those who want it. DePaul has traditionally attracted many students from the state of Illinois (85 percent), but the admissions office has made a concerted effort to attract more out-of-state students and figures are up in that area. Forty-eight percent of the students ranked in the top quarter of their high school class; the administration says DePaul serves "the above-average to very good student who is career oriented." In case you don't have a map, it's easy to tell one campus from the other by looking at its students. "Business classes are all held at the Loop campus, so the College of Commerce sets the tone for the downtown campus. The Lincoln Park campus is more relaxed and laid-back since the music, theater, and liberal arts classes are held there," a business major explains. Hispanics, blacks, and Asian Americans are well represented in the student body—32 percent total—and DePaul wants to boost this figure by reaching out to disadvantaged inner-city inhabitants who show academic potential. Students say race relations are very good. "Everyone is united as one at DePaul. Everyone gets along," says a senior. DePaul offers 550 merit scholarships ranging from $2,000 to a full ride. Athletic scholarships are also available in a wide range of sports, and there are student employment opportunities offered by the administration to help offset college costs.

DePaul has traditionally been a commuter school. Only 33 percent of the students live on campus, but they like their digs. "The residence halls are awesome," says a junior. The university has seven modern coed dorms, and one includes parking, an important issue in this densely populated neighborhood. Another provides apartment living with furniture and built-in cooking facilities. Still, one student complains, "The room reservation system is far too complicated and confusing." Another cites the lack of space as a big issue, "Getting housing here is hell." Campus security is described as "adequate" and "very good", with one senior noting, "We are in a very safe neighborhood, and we have 24-hour escorts on foot and in cars."

On the DePaul sports scene, men's basketball is the headline story. The game

The Loop, or "vertical," campus in downtown Chicago houses the Law School, the School for New Learning, and the College of Commerce in four high-rise buildings—56 stories in all.

A number of social activities are designed to bring the undergraduates and the faculty together, and students are given a phone book with all the profs' home numbers.

against Notre Dame is always played before a packed gym. The Lady Blue Demons are also talented, with an NIT championship trophy among their honors. Men's golf and cross-country, as well as the women's cross-country and softball teams, are also fierce competitors. There is a solid intramural program where, of course, basketball rules. Fraternities and sororities draw minuscule numbers to their ranks, and students agree that most social life is off campus. Still, the Activities Board programs a substantial number of dances and other events. DePaul's alcohol policy forbids beer in the dorms for underage students. "This is difficult to prohibit unless people start to create a disturbance," a senior explains. A classmate confirms that most socializing occurs off campus. "Chicago! It speaks for itself. There are a million things to do." The city offers a multitude of restaurants, both expensive and cheap, plenty of night spots (especially along Rush Street), and all types of shopping. The Lincoln Park area is one of the city's most lively, with many clubs, bars, and theaters. Downtown students also enjoy the beaches of Lake Michigan. For those who like to run, the Chicago Marathon is held every fall. The annual outdoor Blues Festival attracts a major DePaul following from both campuses.

Like that of many other schools, DePaul's student body is growing. The administration credits "increased academic reputation" for enrollment growth, and there's much truth to the statement. Even with increasing numbers of Blue Demons, DePaul offers "small classes that are a little more personalized," a senior says. Another student sums up his view of DePaul, saying, "When you come here you get a big family atmosphere where it is very, very easy to make friends."

The Department of Computer Science and Information Systems remains a national leader. It continually updates its software, and maintains one of the largest Digital Equipment Corporation configurations available to academic institutions.

Overlaps

Loyola (IL), University of Illinois–Urbana-Champaign, University of Illinois–Chicago, Northern Illinois, Northwestern.

If You Apply To > **DePaul**...Rolling admissions. Early action: Dec. 1. Regular admissions: Aug. 15. Financial aid: Mar. 1. Does not guarantee to meet demonstrated need. Campus and alumni interviews: optional, informational. SATs or ACTs: required. SAT IIs: optional. Schools of music and theater require auditions.

DePauw University

313 South Locust Street, Greencastle, IN 46135

DePauw is like a vintage New England liberal arts school plunked down in Middle America and given a flat Midwestern accent. The school has focused, in recent years, on improving its academic standards, developing new spirit among the previously stratified student body, and on trying to live down the fact that it's Dan Quayle's alma mater. "The university has become very academically oriented and more selective," says one freshman. "It's much harder to be accepted into Depauw now than it was five years ago." Several other important changes have also occurred on campus, including a new student judicial code, an enlarged student congress, and integration of technology into the curriculum.

DePauw is set amid the gently rolling hills of west-central Indiana. The lush green campus is dotted with a combination of older buildings and statuesque, modern redbrick structures. At the center of it all is a well-kept park with fountains and a reflecting pool. Among DePauw's more notable facilities are the multimillion-dollar Science and Mathematics Center, with its science library and

Website: www.depauw.edu
Location: Small town
Total Enrollment: 2,216
Undergraduates: 2,216
Male/Female: 44/56
SAT Ranges: V 550–650 M 560–650
ACT Range: 24–28
Financial Aid: 53%
Expense: Pr $ $
Phi Beta Kappa: Yes
Applicants: 2,687
Accepted: 67%

(Continued)

Enrolled: 32%

Grad in 6 Years: 79%

Returning Freshmen: 85%

Academics: ✍ ✍ ✍

Social: ☎ ☎ ☎

Q of L: ★ ★

Admissions: (765) 658-4006

Email Address:
admission@depauw.edu

Strongest Programs:
History
Sociology
Communications
Biology
English
Economics
Computer Science

The Depauw/Wabash rivalry is the oldest west of the Alleghenies and is played for possession of the much-cherished Monon Bell, hence the popular T-shirt that reads, "Beat the bell out of Wabash."

plenty of computer terminals, and the magnificent four-building Performing Arts Center, which holds a music library, practice rooms, theater, auditorium, and recital hall. Depauw also completed a residence hall renovation project and the entire campus has recently been wired for data, phone, and video lines. New additions to the campus will soon include a tennis and track facility for indoor competition, as well as an art building with studios, classrooms, and gallery space.

The student body is as career oriented as they come. The Center for Management and Entrepreneurship and the Center for Contemporary Media are both extremely popular. Depauw offers its students four prominent honors and fellows programs: Honors Scholars, Media Fellows, Management Fellows, and Science Research Fellows. An international business concentration revolves around three majors—political science, economics, or foreign language. Students major in one of these areas while taking selected courses in the other two and participate in an internship abroad. Economics, communications, and computer science are considered to be the strongest among students, while art and education receive a poor grade.

Freshmen are required to remain on campus for the winter term in order to share in an academically focused common experience of exploring an issue such as the environment. For upperclassmen, the January winter term is an ideal time for independent study, exchanges with other schools, mission trips to the Third World, and most popular of all, career-oriented internships. Close to half the students study off campus through programs with the Great Lakes Colleges Association* or in a variety of other study abroad experiences. The administration makes sure that all students receive a healthy dose of liberal arts. Bachelor's degree requirements in the College of Liberal Arts call for courses from six areas: natural sciences and mathematics, social and behavioral sciences, literature and the arts, historical and philosophical understandings, foreign language, and self-expression. In addition, each student must demonstrate competence in writing, quantitative reasoning, and oral communication. First-year seminars are offered in several departments, and students are encouraged but not required to enroll in them. DePauw recently added minors in Japanese and Russian, and dropped the prenursing program.

Students say the academic climate at DePauw is challenging and becoming more so every day. "Courses are competitive and rigorous, but they expand your knowledge and challenge you to think," says one junior. Still, the professors are highly praised. "Professors are dedicated to the success of their students and form close relationships with them," says an English major. "It's not unusual to go to dinner with a professor or even to play a game of golf with them."

In contrast to other liberal arts colleges, DePauw has succeeded in attracting a relatively strong minority population, in part because it has encouraged the formation of black fraternities and sororities. In addition, the growing presence of a new affinity group of dynamic multicultural students recruited by the Posse Foundation in New York City signifies strides toward a comfortably diverse campus. However, whites still comprise 86 percent of the student body, with African Americans accounting for 6 percent, Hispanics for 3 percent, and Asian Americans for 2 percent.

Academic scholarships are awarded, valued from $1,000 to $25,500; there are no athletic scholarships available. Three quarters of DePauw students volunteer their time with area churches and social service agencies, and there are scholarships for those involved with community service. Ninety-four percent of DePauw students live in university housing, and students report that the buildings are well maintained but overcrowded. "The dorms are being renovated and are looking great! Each dorm has a computer lab, a commons area, and a TV lounge," says one junior. Many students recommend Humbert Hall to freshmen because of its hotel-like atmosphere. Men and women joining the Greek system must wait until sophomore year to move into the fraternity or sorority houses. Students report no trouble getting the type of room they desire, and all students are guaranteed some form of housing. Only a few students are allowed to move off campus, which is considered a "privilege" and is decided by lottery.

While a whopping 75 percent of the men and 71 percent of the women go Greek, these organizations have been working hard to change the stereotypical view of Greek social life. They have devised a risk management policy and instituted a community council to review conduct violations that come before the university for action. Rush is delayed until late in the fall so freshmen can at least unpack their bags before setting off in search of a house, and fraternities still maintain the old custom of having "house moms." Students say that it's very easy for underage drinkers to drink, especially at fraternity parties. Another student warns, however, "Fake IDs should not even be attempted here, because they get confiscated quicker than you can take them out." Many upperclassmen prefer smaller group gatherings and the quieter atmosphere of the bars in town.

Well-attended varsity athletic contests tend to turn into social events, especially the annual football game against archrival Wabash College. This rivalry is the oldest west of the Alleghenies and is played for possession of the much-cherished Monon Bell, hence the popular T-shirt that reads, "Beat the bell out of Wabash." Golf, basketball, cross-country, swimming, and soccer teams have all brought home SCA conference championship trophies. In a takeoff of Indiana University's famed Little 500 bike race, DePauw sponsors a Little 500 of its own, with Greeks and independents pitted against each other over a 40-mile course.

Though rural Indiana is hardly a mecca of entertainment opportunities, Greencastle has the basic necessities—such as a movie theater, bowling alley, and several pizza places—and Indianapolis is only 45 minutes away. "Greencastle lacks a college town atmosphere," says a senior. "It is fine for sustaining day-to-day living but doesn't offer many alternatives to the university." Another student adds, "The town is cute but not terribly exciting." Several state parks and a lake for the sailing club are nearby. St. Louis, Chicago, and Cincinnati make for good road trips.

For a small school, DePauw offers a multitude of opportunities including strong academics, abundant extracurricular activities, and a variety of study abroad options. "While education is very important here, so is the chance to grow socially and spiritually," says one student. "DePauw offers its students an excellent opportunity to sample every aspect of college life."

Among DePauw's more notable facilities are the multimillion-dollar Science and Mathematics Center, with its science library and plenty of computer terminals, and the magnificent four-building Performing Arts Center, which holds a music library, practice rooms, theater, auditorium, and recital hall.

Overlaps

Indiana, Denison, Miami University (OH), Northwestern, Butler.

If You Apply To ➤ **DePauw**…Early decision: Nov. 1. Regular admissions: Feb. 1. Financial aid: Mar 1 (in-state), Apr. 1. Guarantees to meet demonstrated need. Campus interviews: recommended, evaluative. No alumni interviews. SATs or ACTs: required. SAT IIs: optional. Accepts the Common Application and electronic applications. Essay question: personal statement.

Dickinson College

P.O. Box 1773, Carlisle, PA 17013

Website: www.dickinson.edu
Location: Small town
Total Enrollment: 2,067
Undergraduates: 2,067
Male/Female: 40/60
SAT Ranges: V 560–650 M
   550–640
Financial Aid: 67%
Expense: Pr $ $ $ $
Phi Beta Kappa: Yes
Applicants: 3,434
Accepted: 64%
Enrolled: 28%
Grad in 6 Years: 80%
Returning Freshmen: 89%
Academics: ✍ ✍ ✍ ✍
Social: ☎ ☎ ☎
Q of L: ★ ★ ★
Admissions: (800)644-1773
Email Address:
   admit@dickinson.edu

Strongest Programs:
   Modern Languages
   English
   History
   International Studies
   Political Science
   Biology
   Psychology

Dickinson graduates more foreign language majors than any other four-year liberal arts college in America, and nearly half of each class will study abroad at some point during their college years.

Dickinson is located in the small picturesque town of Carlisle, but its students are in no way isolated. Students here have the opportunity to roam the world through the college's amazing study abroad program, which boasts offerings in 12 languages, including Chinese, Japanese, Hebrew, Portuguese, and Italian. Dickinson graduates more foreign language majors than any other four-year liberal arts college in America, and half of each class will study abroad at some point during their college years. Students who come to this small liberal arts college find a nurturing, concerned community of students and faculty dedicated to mutual success and achievement. That's why, even after traveling the globe, students still refer to Dickinson as "home."

Almost all the buildings at Dickinson are carved from gray limestone from the college's own quarry, which gives the place a certain continuity. Even the three-foot stone wall that envelops much of the well-wooded 68-acre Dickinson yard is constructed from limestone. The campus is part of the historic district of Carlisle, an economically prosperous central Pennsylvania county seat nestled in a fertile valley. The architectural style of campus buildings is predominantly Georgian, but don't think they're antiquated. Fiber optics and cables that link the dorms and the campus mainframe provide students with foreign programs via satellite, cable television, and full access to the World Wide Web.

Dickinson has strong preprofessional programs in medicine and business. A 3-3 program with the Dickinson School of law of PSU allows students to accelerate into their graduate law program. The international business and management major combines coursework in economics, history, foreign languages, financial and business analysis, and opportunities for internship and overseas education. The biochemistry and molecular biology major requires coursework in four departments and completion of an independent research project. Traditional lectures in math and the sciences are augmented by microcomputer-based labs, and have attracted national attention because of their workshop approach. Physics and political science are also popular, while students say that the education department needs improvement "because there is a high turnover rate among professors."

The academic climate can be rigorous. "Competition among the student body exists, but students are more concerned about how they do individually as opposed to how they rank against other students," says one senior. The professors at Dickinson receive high marks. "I find the faculty to be some of the most fun to know. There's very little pretense around here," says one student. "Professors enjoy the students, learning names and interests quickly." Nearly every class at Dickinson is small, with 50 or fewer students, and students report it's generally not a problem to get the courses they want. "Some classes are more difficult to get into due to popularity, but it is also important to keep class sizes small," notes one senior. However, "just about everyone graduates in four years."

Dickinson's distribution requirements are not to be taken lightly: two courses each in humanities, social sciences, natural and mathematical sciences; courses in foreign language and comparative civilizations; and physical education, as well as requirements appropriate to the student's area of concentration. In addition, all freshmen enroll in seminars with a wide variety of topics including The Myth of Frankenstein and Making Films from Literary Works. Double majors and interdisciplinary studies are quite the fashion at Dickinson. The teaching certification program is likely to become increasingly popular now that Dickinson has created the Teachers for Tomorrow program. This incentive plan gives a $10,000 cash award and $10,000 grant for career advancement to students who teach high school for four years after graduating from Dickinson.

Most Dickinson students are white, upper middle class, and from the Northeast, with 44 percent hailing from the Keystone State. They tend to be principled, competitive, highly motivated to find good-paying jobs, and relatively conservative. "Students here are a bit more concerned with their social standing than those at other institutions," says a senior. Eighty percent were in the top quarter of their high school class. Only six percent of students are minorities, with African Americans accounting for a mere one percent. However, administrators say Dickinson is making ambitious strides toward increasing ethnic diversity by establishing a Visiting Minority Scholars program and employing a director of multicultural affairs to implement various awareness programs. Political correctness seems to be a big issue on campus. "PC is almost stifling with pressure from groups to provide everything from organic vegetables to homophobic education," laments an environmental studies/Russian major.

Dickinson guarantees campus housing to all students, and 92 percent take the school up on its offer of a room. All seniors are now given the option to live off campus, however. Dorms are generally "comfortable and clean." Freshmen have their own dorms (including one for women only). Upperclassman dorms are coed by floor except for a complex of eight-person townhouse suites. A wide variety of special-interest housing, such as Spanish House, Arts House, Multicultural House, Equality House, and Whole Earth House, is available. Campus residents, including Greeks (45 percent of the men and 39 percent of the women), eat at one large dining hall. Breakfast and lunch run together on weekends, an important option since some of Dickinson's social life revolves around weekend late-night dancing and partying at the fraternities.

When it comes to socializing, the fraternities, which throw free parties open to the whole campus, used to give daring students a chance to get around the rigors of Pennsylvania's legal drinking age. (Alcohol isn't allowed in the dorms.) But campus alcohol policies are now more strictly enforced, and as a result activity is shifting away to alternatives like two weekend film societies, live dance bands, and a Thursday night "coffeehouse" with entertainment. "Dickinson has a great social atmosphere," says a sophomore. "From swing dancing on weekends to roadtrips to Washington, D.C., and New York, there truly is something for everyone." Students all over campus flock to the Fall Fest and Spring Fest carnivals, complete with booths, games, and a barbecue. The student-run Public Affairs Symposium, which addresses timely topics, is a favored event. But the most hallowed Dickinson tradition occurs at graduation, when the doors of Old West are thrown open and the seniors walk through them to receive their degrees. (The doors open once more each year, to let the freshman class in.)

Students say Carlisle doesn't qualify as a "college town," but it does offer a performing arts theater and cineplex, a roller-skating rink, bowling alley, and an authentic farmer's market. Students are also active in tutoring and other community service activities in town. In the spring and early fall, Maryland and Delaware beaches beckon; they're just two to three hours by car. Harrisburg, the state capital, is only 20 miles away. Nature lovers will enjoy the nearby mountains and state parks; the Appalachian Trail is 10 minutes from campus, and ski facilities are half an hour distant.

Intramurals are a favorite of the fraternities, but dorms also organize teams,

All freshmen enroll in seminars with a wide variety of topics including The Myth of Frankenstein and Making Films from Literary Works.

The teaching certification program is likely to become increasingly popular now that Dickinson has created the Teachers for Tomorrow program. This incentive plan gives a $10,000 cash award and $10,000 grant for career advancement to students who teach high school for four years after graduating from Dickinson.

and a 19-acre intramural park provides no less than two soccer fields, two softball fields, and lighting for night games. For those interested in headier competition, Dickinson has fielded Centennial Conference–winning varsity teams in golf, men's basketball, women's cross country, women's indoor track, and women's outdoor track. Dickinson also squares off each year with Franklin and Marshall for the coveted Conestoga Wagon trophy, and with Gettysburg College for the Old Oaken Bucket. Club teams organized by students to compete with other schools are popular (especially the ice hockey team), as are a number of less physical campus clubs and organizations.

With all it has to offer, it's no wonder Dickinson College has been around for more than 225 years. Some students say claustrophobia can set in after too many consecutive semesters in Carlisle, but with the college's outstanding study abroad program, no student need confine his or her educational horizons to Pennsylvania, or even the U.S. If you're interested in the well-roundedness of a liberal arts education, it could very well begin here—and end someplace between West Africa, Eastern Europe, and South America. Says a student, "If you want a strong school that will challenge your opinions of yourself and the world, Dickinson is for you."

Drew University

Madison, NJ 07940-4063

Daniel Drew, a nineteenth-century Wall Street wizard, founded Drew University as a Methodist theological seminary in 1867. Since then, the school has maintained a balance between reverence for the past and an exciting race toward the future. This tiny liberal arts university offers students intimate classes and a caring faculty, successfully upholding its original commitment to providing a broad liberal arts-based education.

The school occupies 186 acres of peaceful woodland in the suburban community of Madison, New Jersey, not far from New York City. The 56 campus buildings which peek through splendid oak trees boast classic and contemporary styles, a physical reflection of Drew's respect for both scholarly traditions and progressive education. In attempting to integrate technology with higher education, Drew was the first liberal arts college to provide personal computers to all first-year students.

Political science is Drew's largest, and arguably strongest, undergraduate department. Drew's president, former New Jersey governor Tom Kean, annually teaches a course titled Governing a State. Political science majors can also take advantage of off-campus opportunities in Washington, D.C., London, Brussels, and the United Nations in New York City. Other popular majors include psychology, English, biology, economics, and theater. The Dana Research Institute for Scientists Emeriti offers opportunities for students in biology, chemistry, physics, mathematics, and computer science to do research with distinguished retired industrial scientists. Even more impressive is a program whereby students can earn a BA and MD from Drew and the University of Medicine and Dentistry of New Jersey/New Jersey Medical School in seven years. Future financiers can follow in the footsteps of the school's founder and take advantage of Drew's Wall Street Semester, an on-site study of the national and international finance communities. Other new programs include minors in Holocaust Studies, archeology, and linguistic studies.

Students give low grades to the music department, which is handicapped by a lack of adequate practice and performance facilities, but the study of composition and musical history is enhanced by the latest computers. Drew's commitment to liberal arts education includes a goal of universal computer literacy. In fact, every full-time student is provided with a notebook computer and supporting software, which students take with them when they graduate. The school's campus-wide fiber-optic network links all academic buildings and many residence halls.

General education requirements, which take up a third of each student's total program, involve coursework in eight areas. Students must also show competency in writing, and each first-year student enrolls in seminars limited to 16 people, 80 percent of which are taught by senior faculty. The theater arts department works closely with Playwrights Theater of New Jersey (founded by faculty member Buzz McLaughlin) to produce plays that are written, directed, and designed by students. Drew has long been a proponent of study abroad programs, including the Drew International Seminar program, where students study another culture in depth on campus, then spend three to four weeks in that country. Proposed future sites include Cuba, Puerto Rico, Egypt, Ireland, Chile, Eritrea, Russia, and Tunisia.

Maintaining a rigorous study schedule is key, according to many upperclassmen. "Each person is fighting for their own learning potential, but not competing for this with other students," explains one senior. The industrious grind of hard work is fueled by a cast of highly praised, interactive faculty who generate enthusiasm and ambition. "The professors are completely in touch with the students, and the class size is small enough for the personal attention that is necessary," extols a political science major. Drew's library complex, a cluster of three buildings, contains more than 450,000 titles and offers ample study accommodations, though some students complain that some collections are outdated.

Fifty-six percent of Drew's students are from New Jersey, and 64 percent hail from public high school. Minorities and foreign students account for about 37 percent of the student body. Merit awards for incoming freshman range from $6,000 to full first-year tuition. Students can also win scholarships in the arts of $10,000 each and minority scholarships ranging from $1,000 to $15,000.

Ninety-one percent of the students live in university housing, which includes both single-sex and coed dorms and six theme houses. Current themes include Earth House, Umoja House, Womyn's Concerns, Asia Tree House, and Spirituality Home. All of the freshman dorms have been renovated, and the upperclass dorms are next in line. Several housing options are available to upperclassmen, from dorm rooms of all sizes to suites and townhouses. A lottery gives housing preference to seniors and juniors, and most freshmen reside in dorms situated at the back of campus, which aren't the best. Still, most students live on campus because, as one senior explains, "The area [of Madison] does not accommodate off-campus housing that students can afford." Although the dorms have kitchenettes, everyone must buy the meal plan, which does not receive high ratings from students.

(Continued)
Admissions: (973) 408-DREW
Email Address:
cadm@drew.edu

Strongest Programs:
Political Science
English
Biology
Psychology
Theater

Every full-time student is provided with a notebook computer and supporting software, which students take with them when they graduate. The school's campus-wide fiber-optic network links all academic buildings and many residence halls.

Future financiers can follow in the footsteps of the school's founder and take advantage of Drew's Wall Street Semester, an on-site study of the national and international finance communities.

Social life mostly takes place on campus, most students say. Drew has no Greek system. Officially, nobody under 21 is allowed to drink, but popular sentiment is that alcohol isn't hard to come by on campus. "You make your own fun," says one sophomore. "There are always open parties on the weekends," though students say there is little pressure to drink. Two on-campus coffeehouses, The Other End and The Space, are very popular party alternatives. On-campus social programming is extensive, as one junior reports: "Starting Thursday through Saturday night there are dances, movies, comedians, hypnotists, and there is always some kind of performance. All the activities that take place on campus are free of charge." Many students say that one of the greatest things about Drew is its ready proximity to New York City, Philadelphia, and the New Jersey shore.

The rugby team has been known rouse freshmen to make semiannual midnight pizza runs to Greenwich Village, only 45 minutes away. The First Annual Picnic, held on the last day of classes and numbered like Super Bowls (FAP XVII), gives the students, faculty, parents, and alumni an opportunity to enjoy live music and an assortment of food. Another big event is Multicultural Awareness Day, on which students are excused from one day of classes to celebrate cultural diversity by attending lectures, workshops, and social events. Drew also launched an initiative to give all students and staff opportunities to participate in diversity training.

Madison tends to get discouraging reviews as a college town by students who feel its wealthy residents don't take too kindly to Drewids, as they affectionately call themselves. However, Community Day—designed to bring students and residents together—has become an annual event, and approximately 50 percent of students volunteer in activities such as "Mentors at Drew" and "the Honduras Project," in which a group of Drew students traveled to Honduras to help an orphanage. Madison does provide several shops and restaurants within walking distance of campus, although one student describes it as a "family town" where most businesses are closed by 6:00 P.M. The New Jersey Shakespeare Festival is in residence part of every year, and offers both performances and internships.

Students used to seem more interested in intramural sports than in the school's varsity teams, but interest has grown as the teams have become more successful. In the 1999 season, both men's soccer and women's lacrosse won conference championships. The $15-million athletic center is a 126,000-square-foot state-of-the-art facility that seats 4,000 and is used by varsity sports teams and intramural programs.

Drew University always suffers by comparison to nearby Ivy League Princeton University, a fact many Drewids resent. But at a time when most colleges are gearing their courses more and more toward the job market, Drew remains dedicated to the well-rounded intellect. Armed with an exceptional faculty committed to a solid liberal arts education, Drew University is seeing its stock begin to rise.

If You Apply To ➤

Drew…Early decision: Dec. 1, Jan. 15. Regular admissions and financial aid: Feb. 15. Does not guarantee to meet demonstrated need. Campus interviews: recommended, informational. Alumni interviews: optional, informational. SATs: required. Accepts the Common Application. Essay question: satisfying accomplishments; issues of concern; page 96 of autobiography.

Drexel University

3141 Chestnut Street, Philadelphia, PA 19104

For career-minded students who want to bypass the soul-searching of their liberal arts counterparts, Drexel University offers both solid academics and an innovative co-op education that combines high-tech academics with paying job opportunities. "If you want a good job, you go to Drexel and you do Co-op. Our co-op program was the first in the country, which means we do it the best," says one junior. It's easy to see why Drexel University is nicknamed "the Ultimate Internship." "Drexel's campus is impressive for its downtown Philadelphia location, with gardens and greenery on every block," says a student, "but the campus is woven tightly into the fabric of the city." The buildings are simple and made of brick; most are modern and in good condition. Sitting just west of the city center and right across the street from the University of Pennsylvania, the campus is condensed into about a four-block radius. Students are encouraged to use a shuttle bus between library and dorm at night, and access to dorms, the library, and the physical education center is restricted to students with ID, so most feel safe on campus.

Cooperative education is the hallmark of the curriculum, which alternates periods of full-time study and full-time employment for four or five years, providing students with 6 to 18 months of money-making job experience before they graduate. And the co-op possibilities are unlimited: students can co-op virtually anywhere in this country, or in 11 foreign countries, and 98 percent of undergraduates choose this route. Freshman and senior years of the five-year programs are spent on campus, and the three intervening years (sophomore, prejunior, and junior) usually consist of six months of work and six months of school. A precooperative education course covers such topics as skills assessment, ethics in the workplace, resume writing, interviewing skills, and stress management. Each co-oping student has the opportunity to earn from $7,000 to $30,000 while attending Drexel. And although some students complain that jobs can turn out to be six months of make-work, most enjoy making important contacts in their potential fields and learning while earning. "It starts out laid-back but after a while you begin to feel the competitiveness," mentions one sophomore. "Keep in mind Drexel works on trimesters, so it keeps you on your toes."

To accommodate the co-op students, Drexel operates year-round. Flexibility in requirements varies by college, but in the first year everyone must take freshman seminar, English composition, mathematics, and Cooperative Education 101; engineering majors must also complete the Drexel Engineering Curriculum, which integrates math, physics, chemistry, and engineering to make sure that even techies enter the work force well-rounded and able to write as well as they can compute and design. Students enjoy the 700,000-volume library, which features a computerized card catalog, good hours, and lots of room for studying. Professors receive high praise from most, and are noted for their accessibility and warmth. Says one student, "They take a great interest in the students and are always willing to offer assistance or direction outside of class."

Drexel's greatest strength is its engineering college, which churns out more than 1 percent of all the nation's engineering graduates, BS through Ph.D.. The electrical and architectural engineering programs are particular standouts. The College of Arts and Sciences is well recognized for theoretical and atmospheric physics; chemistry is also recommended. The futuristic Center for Automated

---

Website: www.drexel.edu

Location: City center

Total Enrollment: 12,013

Undergraduates: 9,530

Male/Female: 63/37

SAT Ranges: V 520–620 M 540–640

Financial Aid: 78%

Expense: Pr $ $

Phi Beta Kappa: Yes

Applicants: 9,529

Accepted: 59%

Enrolled: 31%

Grad in 6 Years: 49

Returning Freshmen: 83%

Academics: ✍ ✍ ✍

Social: ☎ ☎

Q of L: ★ ★

Admissions: (215) 895-2400

Email Address: enroll@drexel.edu

Strongest Programs:
   Engineering
   Graphic Design
   Architecture
   Film and Video

Technology complements the strong computer science program. Students mention that the biology and chemistry departments are weak, primarily due to lack of organization and foreign teachers who are hard to comprehend. One film and video major says, "The dramatic writing major is lacking in popularity due to its placement under the College of Design rather than Arts and Sciences."

The performance-oriented student body is 64 percent Pennsylvanian, with another large chunk of students from adjacent New Jersey. The foreign student population is 13 percent, while Asian Americans and African Americans account for 20 percent of the student body. Twenty-three percent of Drexel undergrads graduated in the top tenth of their high school class, and the student body tends to lean right politically. "This is a science and technology school full of conservative students who don't really have the time to worry about liberal issues," says a student. In addition to need-based financial aid, a wide range of athletic and merit scholarships (the latter in amounts up to $10,000 per year) is offered.

Freshmen live in one of four coed residence halls, including a luxurious high-rise, but many upperclassmen reside in nearby apartments or the fraternities, which are frequently cheaper and more private than university housing. Overall, 28 percent of the students live in the dorms; another third commute to campus from home. The cafeteria offers adequate food and plenty of hamburgers and hot dogs, but it's far away from the dorms. While on-campus freshmen are forced to sign up for a meal plan, most upperclassmen make their own meals; the dorms have cooking facilities on each floor. If all else fails, nomadic food trucks park around campus providing quick lunches.

With so many students living off campus and the city of Philadelphia at their disposal, Drexel tends to be a bit deserted on weekends. A student notes, "In a single weekend, I may play paintball in the Poconos, swim at the Jersey shore, see an opera in Philadelphia, and go mountain biking in nearby Wissahickon Park." Friday night flicks are cheap and popular with those who stay around, and dorms sponsor floor parties. The dozen or so fraternities also contribute to the party scene, especially freshman year, but a handful of smaller sororities has little impact. Still, Greek Week is well attended by members of both sexes, as is the spring Block Party, which attracts four or five bands. The Greeks recruit seven percent of the men and women. Drinking is "not a big deal to everyone," and campus policies are strict; dorms require those of age to sign-in alcohol, and limit the quantities they may bring in.

The co-op program often undermines any sense of class unity, and can strain personal relationships. Activities that depend on some continuity of enrollment for success—music, drama, student government, athletics—suffer most. "It's hard to get people involved because of the amount of schoolwork and co-ops," says one woman. There is no football, but men's basketball and soccer are strong. "Our biggest rivalry is our feud with Delaware," admits one frenzied student. "We delight in sacrificing blue, plastic chickens!" Men's and women's swimming and women's volleyball also generate interest. An extensive intramural program serves all students, and joggers can head for the steps of the Philadelphia Art Museum, just like Rocky did in the movies. Students take full advantage of their urban location by frequenting clubs, restaurants, cultural attractions, and shopping malls in Philadelphia, easily accessible by public transportation.

Aspiring poets, musicians, and historians may find Drexel a bit confusing. But for future computer scientists, engineers, and other technically oriented minds, the university's unique approach to learning inside and outside the classroom could give your career a fantastic jump start. As one satisfied customer explains, "The terms are intense, the activities unlimited, but Drexel graduates are surely among the most capable and motivated individuals I have ever met. When I graduate, I will be prepared and proud of it."

If You Apply To ➤ | **Drexel**…Rolling admissions. Financial aid: May. 1. Does not guarantee to meet demonstrated need. Campus interviews: recommended, informational and evaluative. No alumni interviews. SATs: required. SAT IIs: optional. Accepts electronic applications. Apply to particular schools or programs.

Duke University

2138 Campus Drive, Durham, NC 27708

Duke University is one of only a few schools in the country that can stir the desire of the high school valedictorian and the athletic star. Boasting superb academics, gorgeous facilities, and a fistful of national championships, Duke now successfully competes with the nation's oldest and most prestigious schools for students—and wins its share. Add to that a spirited school rivalry with UNC, and Duke is a gem that offers something for almost everyone at the highest levels.

Founded in 1838 as the Union Institute (later Trinity College), Duke University came into being in 1924 when it became the beneficiary of a stack of tobacco-stained dollars called the Duke Endowment. Located in the lush North Carolina forest, Duke's campus includes an adjacent 8,300-acre forest and enough open space to satisfy the most diehard outdoors enthusiast. There are actually two main campuses, West and East. Constructed in the 1930s, West Campus is laid out in spacious quadrangles and is dominated by the impressive Gothic chapel. The hub of the university, it includes residential and classroom quads, the administration building, Perkins Library (boasting 4.2 million volumes, nearly 8.9 million manuscripts, and 2 million public documents), and the student union. East Campus's redbrick Georgian setting, built in the 1920s, has been renovated to house all the freshmen as well as most of the arts facilities. East and West are connected by bus, though many students enjoy the mile-or-so walk along wooded Campus Drive. New facilities include an addition to the Center for Documentary Studies, the Brodie Recreation Center (East Campus), the Center for Jewish Life, and an addition to the Development Office Building.

The university today includes two undergraduate schools, Engineering and Trinity College, the latter a merger of previously separate men's and women's liberal arts colleges. Duke's engineering programs—particularly electrical and biomedical—are national standouts. The natural sciences, most notably biology, chemistry, and physics, are also first-rate. A rite of passage for science hopefuls is Professor James Bonk's chemistry class (Bonkistry), which packs in hundreds of students each year. The proximity of the Medical Center enhances study in areas such as biochemistry, pharmacology, and neurosciences. Lately, literary studies at Duke have received heightened national attention and student interest,

Website: www.duke.edu
Location: Small city
Total Enrollment: 11,011
Undergraduates: 6,368
Male/Female: 52/48
SAT Ranges: V 640–740 M 660–760
ACT Range: 29–33
Financial Aid: 38%
Expense: Pr $ $ $ $
Phi Beta Kappa: Yes
Applicants: 13,407
Accepted: 28%
Enrolled: 43%
Grad in 6 Years: 92%
Returning Freshmen: 97%
Academics: ✍ ✍ ✍ ✍ ✍
Social: ☎ ☎ ☎ ☎
Q of L: ★ ★ ★ ★
Admissions: (919) 684-3214
Email Address:
askduke@admiss.duke.edu

Strongest Programs:
History
Biology
Chemistry
Engineering

particularly literature, English, and Romance studies. However, the English department has fallen on hard times in recent years, with academic superstars like Eve Sedgwick, Stanley Fish, and Michael Moon taking positions at other schools. Duke has recently added a BS in environmental science, and a Hindi concentration in the Asian and African Languages and Literature program.

The highly regarded Sanford Institute of Public Policy offers an interdisciplinary major—unusual at the undergraduate level—with a strong program of internships and apprenticeships for students aspiring to be players in the public sphere. Students are schooled in the machinations of the media, nonprofit organizations, government agencies, and other bodies that deal with the policies that govern our lives. Additionally, Duke offers more than 100 interdisciplinary programs in areas such as genetics, statistics, and decision sciences and hemispheric studies. Programs such as Documentary Studies, Duke in New York Arts, and Duke in Los Angeles Arts and Media offer unique opportunities for learning.

The Trinity College Curriculum 2000 requires students to take courses in arts and literatures, civilizations, social sciences, and natural sciences and mathematics. Faculty advising gets mixed reviews. "If you have questions, they are there to ask, but usually students talk to other students," says an English and history major. All students must fulfill Small Group Learning Experiences, which consist of one seminar-type course during the freshman year and two more as an upperclassman. Students are required to take 34 courses for graduation.

While college hoops fans may think of its main rival as the University of North Carolina, Duke vies for students primarily with Stanford and the upper echelon of the Ivies. The academic atmosphere has become more competitive in recent years, particularly in the sciences. While most students are willing to help each other out, a growing number are placing themselves first. "People seem really concerned about grades and GPA," says a senior history major. "The classes keep you on your toes and demand a lot," adds a political science major. Student-faculty relations are good, and the university's faculty receives high praise from students. "I have had the pleasure of having professors that totally stimulated my mind and made class fun," a sophomore says. The university has focused resources on its undergraduate education, reducing the numbers of non-professors who teach students and having senior professors teach more classes. Interested freshmen can also participate in the highly praised and nationally recognized FOCUS program, groups of seminars clustered around a single, broad theme such as Evolution and Humankind, Health Care and Society, and Origins. Most Duke classes serve fewer than 20 students, and few students report any trouble getting into needed courses.

Career counseling gets high marks nearly all around, allowing students to submit résumés and learn more about prospective careers, and placing many in jobs. Slightly more than half of Duke graduates go on to the work force, while a third head to graduate school or professional programs. "There is a strong pre-professional bent among some, but by no means all, students," one senior says.

Among Duke's student body, the South continues to be the most heavily represented region, but the Northeastern corridor also sends a fair-sized contingent. Only 13 percent of the student body are from North Carolina. Ninety-seven percent of Duke's admits ranked in the top quarter of their high school class. Nine percent are African American, 4 percent Hispanic, and 13 percent Asian American. Students of different ethnicities and races tend to "self-segregate." Therefore, there is little tension, but also little interaction. Overcoming this has been an ongoing quest for students and the administration, which conducts an orientation program focused on diversity. "I think that Duke students are aware of their

The Sanford Institute offers an unusual and highly regarded program in public policy for aspiring players in the public sphere.

intelligence and the privilege of going to one of the world's finest educational institutions," says a student.

Duke admits students without reference to their financial need, and guarantees to meet the full demonstrated need of all accepted applicants. There are also dozens of merit scholarships, ranging from $1,000 to a free ride. A small number of the full-tuition awards include six weeks of summer study at Oxford University. Other merit awards include 20 scholarships a year for outstanding African American students, starting at $1,000, and unlike most other universities of its academic stature, Duke hands out hundreds of athletic scholarships annually.

Eighty-one percent of undergraduates at Duke live on campus, and rooms are large and well maintained. Fraternities and sororities do not have their own houses, but fraternity members live in designated areas of the college dorms. The recent decision to house freshmen on the East Campus was aimed at insulating them from the wilder aspects of the school's social scene and making it easier to introduce them to the life of the mind. The move has also "fostered class unity," according to some students. The West Campus, home to the frat men, boasts the liveliest nightlife. In addition to the East and West campuses, two other satellite campuses offer student housing, one consisting of several dozen university-owned apartments popular with upperclassmen. Theme dorms center on special interests such as women's studies, the arts, languages, and community service. All students who live on campus are affiliated with one of about 60 "living groups" ranging in size from 14 to 250, which is Duke's ad hoc attempt to approximate the living units at Ivy League schools. Student programmers and resident advisors plan lectures and social activities for their groups, and a total of more than 350 faculty members are affiliated with one or another of them. In addition to the living groups, the university operates residential houses shared by a faculty member, his or her family, and 50 to 120 students under its Faculty-in-Residence program, which the administration says is expanding.

No matter what your housing preference, there is a bonanza of eating options on campus, most notably the main dining hall, known as the Pits, as well as a full-serve restaurant, and on-campus pizza delivery. Students use a prepaid meal card to pay for food, and the amount of each purchase is deducted from the total. Full reimbursement for any unused "money" at the end of the semester is an unusual and much-appreciated policy.

As a college town, Durham can't quite measure up to the likes of Ann Arbor, Madison, and Boulder, although there is plenty to do. The Durham area is home to many in the 18 to 35 sector, and there are bars and clubs aplenty to accommodate them, to say nothing of the Durham Bulls, the town's beloved minor league baseball team that coined the term "bullpen." Fraternities and sororities are at the center of campus life, however. Twenty-nine percent of the men and 42 percent of the women pledge, and fraternity parties are open to everyone. Although alcohol is still a part of Duke students' social activities, the university's stricter drinking policies have slowed—but not halted—its flow. "The campus is rich with things to do. Basketball games, movies, and weekend parties are some on-campus attractions, to name a few," a senior public policy major says. When the campus party scene gets stale, students can also take the drive to nearby Chapel Hill or to Raleigh, the state capital and home to North Carolina State University. If they're prepared for a longer drive, Duke students can hit the beach or the ski slopes, depending on the season. North Carolina's broad beaches are two to three hours away, and ski slopes are three to four hours' drive. The popular annual Oktoberfest and Springfest bring in live bands and vendors peddling local crafts and exotic foods.

While college hoops fans may think of its main rival as the University of North Carolina, Duke vies for students primarily with Harvard, Princeton, Stanford, and Yale.

Duke University has epitomized the definition of academic upward mobility in recent years, and is now routinely listed among the nation's top academic institutions.

The contrast between the wealth of Duke and the depressed town of Durham has inspired many students to volunteer in the community, with many tutoring in local schools. Durham is, however, adjacent to the more affluent Research Triangle Park, the largest research center of its kind in the world, about 15 minutes from campus. The park was created by Duke, North Carolina State, and the University of North Carolina at Chapel Hill for nonprofit, scientific, and sociological research, and has helped make the Raleigh/Durham area one of the most booming economic regions in the nation, boasting the highest percentage of Ph.D.s per capita.

Duke's Southern gentility is reflected in students' choice of attire. Here, students appear put together, and their choice of academic apparel is dressier than the rumpled boxers and sweats that dominate some other campuses. Duke is a culturally active campus; theater groups thrive, and the Freewater Film Society shows classic movies each week. During the summer, Duke is home to the American Dance Festival. The school also has a cable-television system that undergraduates use for parodies of game shows and other entertainment.

As for sports? Suffice it to say that Duke's official motto is Eruditio et Religio only to a few straight-laced administrators; everyone else knows it as "Eruditio et Basketballio," which translates more or less as "To hell with Carolina"—the University of North Carolina, that is, Duke's archrival for supremacy in the Atlantic Coast Conference. "As for extracurricular activities," says a student, "there are three: basketball, basketball, basketball." At games, students get the best courtside seats, where they make life miserable for the visiting team. Their efforts paid off this year when the Blue Devils won the NCAA championship—a feat that's becoming almost commonplace here. "By far, basketball season brings out the best of student support," a senior says. "Students camp out weeks ahead to attend the Carolina game." Indeed, a temporary "tent city" is erected as sports-crazed Blue Devils vie for the best seats. Campers will now be able to check their email thanks to lampposts that feature Internet jacks. For part-time jocks, there are two intramural leagues, one for competitive types and one for strictly weekend athletes, which draw heavy participation from the Greeks. Duke even has its own golf course amid the dogwoods and streams behind campus.

Duke University has epitomized the definition of academic upward mobility in recent years. It is the best university in the Southern half of the country and is routinely listed among the nation's top academic institutions. Duke students have found a way to pursue a premier education while also making time to enjoy themselves, whether frolicking in Duke Forest or cheering on the basketball team to another victory. Says one senior, "Students are given a gorgeous campus to spend four years studying with peers who constantly challenge you with their diverse experiences and backgrounds."

Overlaps

Harvard, Princeton, Stanford, Yale, Penn.

If You Apply To >

Duke...Early decision: Nov. 1. Regular admissions: Jan. 2. Financial aid: Nov. 1. Housing: Feb. 1. Guarantees to meet demonstrated need. Campus interviews: optional, evaluative. Alumni interviews: recommended, evaluative. SATs or ACTs: required. SAT IIs: required (vary by program). Accepts the Common Application. Essay question: questioning values; importance of one's home; your own question.

One the nation's academically strongest liberal arts colleges, Earlham is unique in that it prides itself on a strict faithfulness to the Quaker traditions of community and cooperation, both during and after college. The school coddles its students and encourages them to work hard, dream big, and achieve much. "Earlham's Quaker traditions are what distinguishes it from other colleges," says a math and psychology double major. "The school attracts a wide variety of people but most have the same values and principles of living."

The 800-acre campus is seated in the small city of Richmond, yet is only a short distance from the major metropolitan areas of Cincinnati and Indianapolis. Georgian-style buildings dominate the campus, surrounded by mature trees and plantings. The most recent additions to campus include a new equestrian center with indoor riding ring and a $13 million Athletic and Wellness Center. The Japanese gardens on campus are a symbol of the college's long friendship and joint programs with Japan. In fact, there are more than two dozen off-campus programs, including the semester in Japan, as well as programs in Mexico, Kenya, and the American and Canadian wilderness. About 70 percent of the students eventually take advantage of at least one of the off-campus study programs. The school is also affiliated with the Great Lakes Colleges Association.*

Students say the academic climate at Earlham is demanding. "The courses are challenging but a dedicated student can keep up," says a peace and global studies major. Another student adds, "Classes here are fairly rigorous and the faculty expects students to work hard." There are strict distribution requirements, including a two core humanities sequence, two courses in religion and philosophy, four natural sciences, one fine arts, and four courses in athletics, physical education, and wellness. All courses stress the development of library skills, and students praise the library staff and the facilities. Faculty and students have unrestricted access to major online databases from professors' desks.

Cooperative and group learning are vital parts of the academic approach, and class discussion rather than lecture is the predominant learning style. In fact, Earlham created a major called human development and social relations that mixes sociology, anthropology, and psychology and aims to help students understand and work with other people, countries, and institutions. Earlham faculty members are selected for their excellence in teaching and their ability to cross various disciplinary lines. "The professors here are concerned for their students and work hard to make sure they are getting a good education," says a psychology major. Another student adds, "Most professors are willing to spend time in and out of class going over difficult concepts or discussing interesting ones." The close-knit atmosphere of Earlham continues into the classroom, and students find this to be quite an advantage. Notes a politics major, "We are a learning community—a partnership. Professors don't simply dispense knowledge; we work together." Students rate academic advising highly, saying that they may discuss their plans with advisors over dinner. "My faculty advisor is outstanding," says a junior. "I meet with her often to go over classes, to check in, or just to socialize."

Top fields at Earlham are the sciences, especially biology and geology. A special stress is put on Japanese studies, a field in which Earlham is a national leader. (Notes one student: "Richmond, IN, is on all the U.S. maps in Japan because the Earlham presence is so strong there.") Other solid departments are English and

Website: www.earlham.edu

Location: City outskirts

Total Enrollment: 1,191

Undergraduates: 1,123

Male/Female: 43/57

SAT Ranges: V 520–660 M 500–630

ACT Range: 21–27

Financial Aid: 61%

Expense: Pr $ $ $

Phi Beta Kappa: Yes

Applicants: 1,038

Accepted: 84%

Enrolled: 34%

Grad in 6 Years: 70%

Returning Freshmen: 87%

Academics: ✍ ✍ ✍ ✍

Social: ☎ ☎ ☎

Q of L: ★ ★ ★ ★ ★

Admissions: (765) 983-1200

Email Address:
admission@earlham.edu

Strongest Programs:
Psychology
Foreign Languages
International Studies
Natural/Physical Sciences
Japanese Studies
English

Cooperative and group learning are vital parts of the academic approach, and class discussion rather than lecture is the predominant learning style.

PAGS (Peace and Global Studies program). Biology is the most popular major, followed by psychology, English, and human development and social relations. About 14 percent of recent graduates go on to some sort of graduate study, although volunteer and service programs are popular postgraduation choices. In addition, both prelaw and premed students enjoy high acceptance rates at graduate schools. A major in environmental studies has recently been added to the curriculum.

While not particularly diverse racially, Earlham is extremely diverse geographically; barely more than a third of the students are Hoosiers. African Americans make up 8 percent of the student population, and Asian Americans account for 3 percent. "Earlham students are from a wide variety of social, cultural, and economic backgrounds," says a biology major. "You would think that this would cause frequent confrontations, but everyone seems to get along." "EC's Quaker background makes this a very politically active and 'correct' community (though not to the extreme)," says a senior. Rights of all kinds—women's, gay, animal, environmental—are also a big deal at Earlham, and campus organizations exemplify Earlham's commitment to various causes. Groups range from Action Against Rape to BLAC (Black Leadership Action Coalition).

At Earlham, students are strongly encouraged to live on campus, and 90 percent do. Single, double, and triple rooms are comfortable, good-sized, and fairly well maintained, students say. "You can't expect luxury, but many dorms offer personality in return," says one denizen. Examples? "Olvey-Andis is loud and friendly. Earlham Hall and Barrett aren't very spacious. Hoerner has horribly thin walls but is cozy," says one student. "Some college houses are bordering on decrepit, but in general, housing is varied, accessible, and easy to obtain," says a senior. Freshmen have reserved space in each dorm, and upperclassmen divide up the remaining rooms by lottery or petition to live together. Juniors and seniors may move from the dorms into one of 24 college-owned apartments and houses, including a working farm, although demand usually exceeds supply. Most people eat at the college dining hall on one of the three meal plans. A vegetarian main course and a salad and health-food bar are available in the large cafeteria. A coffeehouse, Java Jazz, offers coffee that one student describes as "excellent!"

Quaker beliefs and Indiana's liquor laws prohibit alcohol on campus, but students find the dry campus policy far from intolerable. "The policy creates an environment that doesn't focus on alcohol," one sophomore notes. "If you don't drink, it is very easy to find other options." There are no fraternities or sororities, so fun at Earlham includes movies, bands, hiking in the woods, and time at the Breadbox, a student-run coffeehouse that features student performers. Popular road trips include Cincinnati and Oxford, OH (the latter is home to Miami University), and Indianapolis. An International Festival highlights music and cultural exhibits; Sunsplash, an outdoor reggae festival in the fall, and Umoja, an African American celebration, are also popular. An air guitar and lip-sync contest is a popular winter activity. Almost all students participate in music or theater activities.

Men's and women's varsity athletics (NCAA Division III) receive equal support at Earlham. The men's cross-country and basketball teams are strong, as are women's soccer and basketball.

Earlham functions rather independently of the small city of Richmond and vice versa. "Relations between the college and town haven't always been amazing," reports a sophomore, "but that's beginning to change due to the success of the Earlham Volunteer Exchange." City-oriented people may have to make an adjustment to the slower life, but Richmond, which is not a typical college town,

About 70 percent of the students eventually take advantage of at least one of the off-campus study programs.

does offer a symphony, opera company, and theater and it is big enough to supply part-time jobs and volunteer activities for many students.

Life at Earlham is a collection of paradoxes: it's a very liberal school stuck in a very small, conservative city, and while its physical location is quite isolated, the school is known for its expertise in international studies. Complicating matters further is a favored athletic cheer, diametrically opposed to the proud Quaker tradition of pacifism: "Fight, fight, inner light! Kill, Quakers, kill!" Ah, well. Earlham students work so hard, they've got to relieve their stress somehow, right? Despite the paradoxes, most graduate ready to take on the world, thanks to the school's cooperative, can-do spirit and caring student-faculty community. As one sophomore peace and global studies major puts it, "Earlham will take you around the world, but it'll make sure your feet are planted on the ground when you come home."

> ### Overlaps
> **Grinnell, Oberlin, Guilford, Macalester, Beloit.**

If You Apply To > **Earlham**...Early decision: Dec. 1. Early action: Jan. 15. Regular admissions: Feb. 15. Financial aid: Mar. 1. Does not guarantee to meet demonstrated need. Campus interviews: recommended, evaluative. Alumni interviews: optional, evaluative. SATs: required. SAT IIs: optional. Accepts the Common Application and electronic applications. Essay question: choose one from five options: important issue, significant experience, or valued relationship; significant book, piece of writing, or research article; analysis of H. L. Mencken's critique of Christianity; the balance of freedom and responsibility; the importance of creativity.

Eckerd College

4200 54th Avenue South, St. Petersburg, FL 33711

Eckerd College offers its students a demanding curriculum in a laid-back setting. Although marine science attracts much student attention and praise here, there's also a slew of other distinctive programs for those with less aquatic interests. In addition to its unique programs, Eckerd pioneered the 4–1–4 academic year schedule, in which students spend the month of January working on a single project for credit. "Eckerd continues to improve and expand on every front," says an economics major.

Founded in 1960 as Florida Presbyterian College and renamed a decade later after a generous benefactor of drugstore fame, Eckerd College is a church-affiliated undergraduate institution. The campus, lush with grass, flowering bushes, trees, and small ponds is located on the tip of a peninsula and bounded by the Gulf of Mexico and Tampa Bay. It's not unusual to spot dolphins frolicking in the adjacent waters. The architectural style of the buildings is modern and there's no building taller than three stories on campus. Construction is underway on a new Information Technology Center.

Student-faculty relationships at Eckerd are close and informal, and every student has a faculty mentor. "Professors push each student to their academic limits, yet they are always readily available to help students if they are having trouble with the material," says a political science major. "Beefing with professors" and "pizza with professors" are popular events sponsored by the campus snack bar and student government to bring the students and faculty together. All classes are taught by regular professors.

One of the unique programs open to Eckerd students is the Academy of Senior

Website: www.eckerd.edu
Location: City outskirts
Total Enrollment: 1,530
Undergraduates: 1,530
Male/Female: 45/55
SAT Ranges: V 520–630 M 520–640
ACT Range: 22–28
Financial Aid: 60%
Expense: Pr $ $
Phi Beta Kappa: No
Applicants: 1,783
Accepted: 76%
Enrolled: 30%
Grad in 6 Years: 62%
Returning Freshmen: 79%
Academics: ✍ ✍ ✍
Social: ☎ ☎ ☎
Q of L: ★ ★ ★ ★ ★
Admissions: (727) 864-8331

(Continued)
Email Address:
   admissions@eckerd.edu

Strongest Programs:
   Biology/Premed
   Creative Writing
   Environmental Studies
   International Relations
   International Business
   Marine Science

One of the unique programs open to Eckerd students is the Academy of Senior Professionals, a subcommunity of senior citizens who serve as mentors for students.

Marine science programs include a Sea Semester* and the Eckerd College Search and Rescue, which performs over 300 marine rescues annually.

Professionals, a subcommunity of senior citizens who serve as mentors for students. Academy members come from all walks of life and become part of a shared learning process by taking classes with students, working with professors on curriculum development, helping students with career development, and leading workshops in their area of expertise. Eckerd's study abroad program is strong with approximately half its students taking advantage of the opportunity to study in such countries as Austria, Bermuda, China, and France. The school also has its own campus in London, England. Marine science programs include a Sea Semester* and the Eckerd College Search and Rescue, which performs over 300 marine rescues annually.

Freshmen arrive on campus three weeks early for orientation, during which each student earns one credit for a seminar that introduces him or her to the reading, writing, speaking, and study skills required for college-level work. Freshmen also take an interdisciplinary two-course sequence called Western Heritage in a Global Context, which focuses on influential books. First-year students must meet a writing proficiency requirement as well as a quantitative methods requirement in mathematics or computer science. One year of foreign language study is also mandatory. Sophomores and juniors take four courses from a list of options in broad perspectives on human existence: aesthetic, environmental, global, scientific, and social relations. Popular departments other than marine science include environmental studies, international business, and biology. Music, non-Western languages, and some offerings in the math department are on the weak side. Seniors take a capstone seminar called the Quest for Meaning, in which they draw on what they've learned throughout college to find solutions to important issues.

Eckerd considers itself Christian nonsectarian but maintains a formal "covenant" relationship with the major Presbyterian denomination, from which it receives some funds. However, only a minority of the students are Presbyterian, and the campus political climate is very open. "The students here are very open-minded," says a senior. "They will not criticize your beliefs but they will probably offer their own." Seventy percent of Eckerd students are from out of state and 13 percent are international. Eighty-nine percent of the student body is white, and African Americans, Hispanics, and Asian Americans combine for the another 7 percent. Overall, "students are focused on achieving their educational goals," says a sophomore—sometimes to the detriment of other aspects of campus life.

Eckerd usually works out viable financial packages for those who require monetary help; 89 percent of students get some kind of financial assistance. Need-based and merit scholarship awards are often combined; 50 Presbyterian students, for example, are nominated each year by pastors for scholarships worth up to $7,000. Fifteen incoming freshmen are awarded up to $1,500 to complete significant research with a faculty member. Seventy-five athletic scholarships are available.

Seventy-one percent of students live in one of eight housing quads separated from the rest of the campus by Dorm Drive. Both single-sex and coed-by-floor dorms are available, with mostly double rooms. Freshmen live on floors with upperclassmen and are assigned rooms with an eye toward compatible personal habits—pets or no pets, smoking or nonsmoking, etc. It's a system that many claim does not work. "It appears the administration doesn't care about who they place with whom," says a student, "since there are several people placed in pet dorms who are allergic to animals." Rooms are fairly large and air-conditioned, and waterfront views are provided at no extra charge. The trendy townhouse-style residence hall provides suite living above and beyond the standards of other dorms, and other dorm lounges have been renovated to make space for computer labs and common kitchens. Students complain that campus security is "one of the bigger laughs" because patrols focus more on breaking up parties than curtailing crime.

There are no Greek organizations at Eckerd, and a strict campus drinking policy (no kegs on campus, no alcohol at university events) includes wristbands for those over 21 at campus parties. Still, says a junior, "It is fairly easy for minors to get 'connections' to alcohol." Though the administration implemented a taxi service last year, "students leave the campus in flocks only to return obliterated," says a student. As for St. Petersburg, "although the tourist board and chamber of commerce will do their best to persuade you that it's not just an urban nursing home, except for a few weeks around Spring Break, the prominent hair color is blue," sighs one student. However, the city does offer restaurants, shops, and theaters, and the Tampa Bay area provides professional baseball, football, hockey, and soccer.

Eckerd doesn't have a football team, but intramural athletic options pit dorms against each other and range from flag football to the assassin game, in which students try to shoot their peers with dart guns. Men's basketball and, not surprisingly, water skiing and sailing are also top-notch. Weekend warriors and varsity team members alike have benefited from a new athletic complex with baseball, soccer, and softball fields. Other fun events include monthly dorm-sponsored parties like Delta Flashback, Epsilon Shipwrecked, and Zeta Halloween. Eckerd's Distinguished Speaker Series draws the community to the campus to hear speakers, which in the past have included Jimmy Carter, Coretta Scott King, Ken Burns, and Elie Wiesel.

Eckerd is enticing for many reasons: its beach locale, small student body, and emphasis on having fun outside the classroom. But just as important are the school's innovative programs, knowledgeable and caring faculty members, and academic excellence. One student sums it up this way: "I have thought-provoking classes, dedicated teachers, and all the sun I can handle. It just doesn't get any better than this."

> *Seniors take a capstone seminar called the Quest for Meaning, in which they draw on what they've learned throughout college to find solutions to important issues.*

Overlaps
University of Florida, University of South Florida, Rollins, Stetson, Florida Tech.

If You Apply To ➤ **Eckerd**...Regular admissions: Apr. 1. Housing: May 1. Financial aid: Apr. 15. Housing: May 1. Meets demonstrated need of 70 percent. Campus interviews: recommended, evaluative. Alumni interviews: optional, informational. SATs or ACTs: required. SAT IIs: recommended. Accepts the Common Application and electronic applications. Essay questions: significant experience; important book or author; or a main concern.

Emory University

Jones Center, Atlanta, GA 30322

There is a real sense of anticipation in the halls of Emory University these days. Students see new buildings sprouting up on the grounds and watch as quality professors are lured to their campus from other top-rated schools. They notice the constant development of new programs funded by large donations from companies like Atlanta-based Coca-Cola. Despite these infusions of financial resources, though, leaders of Emory, including an overly cautious and unimaginative board of trustees, have yet to figure out how to invest their newfound riches—and articulate a vision—that would help it realize its potential as another Vanderbilt or Duke in the South and as a major player on the national scene.

Website: www.emory.edu
Location: Suburban
Total Enrollment: 11,000
Undergraduates: 5,800
Male/Female: 48/52
SAT Ranges: V 640–720 M 640–740

(Continued)

ACT Range: 28–32
Financial Aid: 57%
Expense: Pr $ $ $ $
Phi Beta Kappa: Yes
Applicants: 9,444
Accepted: 44%
Enrolled: 30%
Grad in 6 Years: 90%
Returning Freshmen: 94%
Academics: ✍ ✍ ✍ ✍
Social: ☎ ☎ ☎
Q of L: ★ ★ ★ ★
Admissions: (404) 727-6036
Email Address:
  admiss@emory.edu

Strongest Programs:
  History
  Political Science
  English
  Psychology
  Business
  Art History
  Natural Sciences

Political science benefits from well-known professors who regularly appear on CNN and have ties to the Carter Center.

Set on 631 acres of woods and rolling hills, the campus is centered on an academic quad of marble-covered, red-roofed buildings, with more contemporary structures dotting the periphery of the lush, green grounds. Recent additions to the ever-changing campus include a chemistry building and new facilities for science research and the nursing school.

Emory's edifice complex has been complemented by an aggressive faculty recruitment campaign that has added both star quality and teaching and research competence to key departments. "The professors here are excellent and really care about their students," says a senior. Over the past decade, for instance, the chemistry and biology departments have been beefed up dramatically. More recently, Archbishop Desmond Tutu became a member of the faculty of the school of theology. Former president Jimmy Carter also teaches on campus. The history department earns high marks, as do English, psychology, and business. New majors were recently added in dance, environmental studies, and neurology and behavior. Political science benefits from well-known professors who regularly appear on CNN and have ties to the Carter Center. The natural sciences benefit from Emory's proximity to the Centers for Disease Control and other highly reputed national research centers. The math department, however, is cited as lacking substance.

More than a third of every student's total coursework goes toward fulfilling rigorous and comprehensive distribution requirements in the liberal arts. This core program is divided into six categories with names like Tools of Learning, the Individual and Society, and Aesthetics and Values. Foreign language proficiency was also added as a general education requirement. Only a third of these required courses are taught by senior faculty members; many of the courses taught by the academic heavyweights are reserved for upperclassmen and graduate students. Freshmen must take an Emory College Seminar to gain a structured introduction to the school, become part of a small social group, and establish contact with a faculty mentor. Another option for entering freshmen is enrollment in Emory's two-year Oxford College, where 600 students live and study in a "small-town" atmosphere while earning an associate's degree. The school also offers courses and additional resources as a member of the Atlanta Regional Consortium for Higher Education.* Students who wish to enrich their education in foreign countries will soon have more options, as Emory is developing 30 university-operated study abroad programs. Serious instruction in an intimate learning environment has always been the hallmark of an Emory education. Emory's grant funding, via the Woodruffs and Candlers of the Coca-Cola soft-drink empire, has made more student scholarships and research grants available.

Twenty percent of the students are Georgians, and a little over half are from the Southeast. New York, New Jersey, California, and Florida are all well represented, and the university has a large Jewish contingent that dwarfs that of any other Southern university. The typical student is from an upper-middle-class family, is dedicated to preparing for a career, and can be seen dressed "from rags to Rolexes. One downside of the student mix is that it includes a significant number of Northerners who did not get into other schools and never really bond with Emory. "Minorities constitute more than one-quarter of the student population: African Americans, Hispanics, and Asian Americans account for 10, 4, and 14 percent, respectively. Students cite race relations and gay rights as strong campus issues. The Multicultural Office and RAPP (Racism Awareness Pilot Project) work to improve relations on campus, as does the Office of Gay and Lesbian Life.

Outstanding freshmen will find the school most accommodating with financial aid, which is described by students as "quite good for those who are in need."

While it does not guarantee to meet the full demonstrated financial need of every admit, it tries to accommodate everyone, and 95 to 97 percent of those who apply for aid receive a substantial package. A variety of scholarships of up to full tuition plus fees, room, and board, are offered on the basis of personal and academic achievement, regardless of need. There are no athletic scholarships.

Seventy percent of the students live on campus. Campus housing is guaranteed all four years, and dorms, which were spruced up for the 1996 Olympics, are lavish by college student standards. "They are all air-conditioned and carpeted, and most have sinks in the room," a senior English and history major says. "They also all have cable and are hard-wired with the Ethernet system. Our smallest rooms tend to be larger than most big rooms at other schools." Newcomers are housed together their freshman year, a time viewed with nostalgia by upperclassmen. The spacious dining hall inside the student center serves palatable meals with a variety of options. Students who live on campus are required to get a variation of the meal plan, which includes options in the dining hall, campus restaurant, kosher deli, snack bar, even the ice cream and frozen yogurt shop.

Thirty percent of men and women join a fraternity or sorority, and most acknowledge that Greek life is the dominant social force on campus. The frats and sororities tend to attract the preppier members of the student body, while a flourishing off-campus community, composed mainly of upperclassmen, and a variety of special-interest dormitories provide options for independents. While the campus is now BYOB, most underage students find creative ways to get alcohol if they want it. Participation in student government is high among Emory students, and the student center has spawned the development of more all-campus events. Dooley's Week, a spring festival in honor of Emory's enigmatic skeleton mascot, William M. Dooley, who is reputed to have escaped from the bio lab almost 100 years ago, is the most popular campus tradition. "Presidents may come, presidents may go. Professors may come, professors may go. Students may come, students may go. But Dooley lives on forever," says a senior. Part of the weeklong celebration dictates that if Dooley enters a classroom and soaks a professor with a watergun, class is dismissed. If that's not enough, there's always Atlanta for entertainment—hands down the most exciting city in the Southeast. "Atlanta is a fantastic city. With a young population and booming economy, I can't think of a place I would rather be," a senior says. Students take occasional drives to the Carolinas or the coast, and New Orleans for Mardi Gras is a popular road trip.

Although school spirit may suffer because Emory does not field a varsity football team, students can enjoy the thrills of competition through the extensive intramural program and other successful Division III programs. The school has built a huge gymnasium, and organized a men's basketball team to compete in the University Athletic Association along with other top academic institutions, including the University of Chicago, the Johns Hopkins University, and Carnegie Mellon University. The sports department has traditionally taken pride in its men's and women's tennis and swimming varsity teams and its men's soccer squad, but sports are being strengthened all across the board.

While most schools in the region suffer from an endemic provincialism, Emory has cultivated a national reputation and a student body that comes from near and far. Because Emory has profited from Coca-Cola's cash, many refer to the school simply as Coca-Cola University. Despite all of its cola money, though, the school is still struggling to find identity as a first-class university. But students aren't concerned. "The school and its students have an aggressive and optimistic attitude toward the future," says a senior. It's no doubt that Emory has become "the real thing."

Freshmen must take an Emory College Seminar to gain a structured introduction to the school, become part of a small social group, and establish contact with a faculty mentor.

Overlaps

Duke, Washington University (MO), Georgetown, Penn, Vanderbilt.

The Evergreen State College

BEST BUY

Olympia, WA 98505

Website: www.evergreen.edu
Location: City outskirts
Total Enrollment: 4,102
Undergraduates: 3,855
Male/Female: 41/59
SAT Ranges: V 530–660 M 490–610
Financial Aid: 50%
Expense: Pub $
Phi Beta Kappa: No
Applicants: 1,526
Accepted: 86%
Enrolled: 33%
Grad in 6 Years: 49%
Returning Freshmen: 65%
Academics: ✍ ✍ ✍
Social: ☎ ☎ ☎
Q of L: ★ ★ ★ ★
Admissions: (360) 866-6000
Email Address:
admissions@evergreen.edu

Strongest Programs:
Environmental Studies
Media Arts
Native American Studies
Political Science

When it comes to bucking the mainstream, few schools are so insistent—and successful—as this school at the edge of Puget Sound. The school's unofficial motto? *"Omnia extares,"* Latin for "Let it all hang out." Founded in 1971 as Washington state's experimental college, Evergreen is a school without grades, majors, or departments, where students have almost unlimited control over their academic destinies. While this may sound strange, it works: among its alumni, Evergreen counts Matt Groening, creator of *The Simpsons* and *Life In Hell*.

True to its name, Evergreen lies in a fir forest, within walking distance of the Washington coast. The 1,000-acre campus includes a 13-acre organic farm for both plants and animals; on the waterfront, 3,300 feet of undeveloped beach beckon nature lovers.

Most of the campus buildings are angular concrete-and-steel creations; though the Longhouse Education and Culture Center is designed in the traditional style of the Northwest Native Americans. The communications lab has been remodeled to accommodate animation studios.

At first glance, Evergreen's wide-open curriculum looks like a first-rate excuse to party: There are no required classes and few traditional exams to slog through at the end of each 10-week quarter. And instead of signing up for a set of unrelated courses to fulfill requirements, students enroll in one coordinated "program," which can last as long as a year. Each program is team-taught by three or four professors; a recent program, Problems Without Solutions, looked at topics such as AIDS or homelessness from the perspective of political science, philosophy, anthropology, economics, statistics, and writing. Motion and Matter incorporated physics, calculus, and chemistry. This integrated approach draws raves from students—"Evergreen is an interactive college, courses are as hard as you make them," says a sophomore, but a classmate warns that it also requires self-motivation. "There are no grades, only narrative evals, so the competition is only against one's self," the student says. Freshmen select one interdisciplinary core program, while upperclassmen concentrate in more specialized areas, often capping the experience with a thesis or an Individual Learning Contract devised with their faculty sponsor.

Since there are no traditional departments at Evergreen, it's more difficult to assess the quality of various programs. But even without rankings and ratings, there are some definite winners, including media arts and political economy. The highly praised environmental science program invariably fills up fast, and includes offerings in ornithology, marine biology, and wetlands studies. Students can also explore Puget Sound on one of two 40-foot boats that serve as floating classrooms, or spend seven weeks at a bird sanctuary in Oregon. These programs, along with the general penchant for activism, set the tone on campus. The animation program is a big draw, too, and graduates are quickly snapped up by Hollywood studios like Disney. However, students consider the math and business departments weak.

Administrators have begun working to ease the transition problems that Evergreen's many nontraditional freshmen experience. Academic affairs personnel have become "adjunct faculty, to help students to be effective participants in seminars," the administration says. The faculty has also been asked to make a greater effort to help students adjust to Evergreen's uniquely challenging environment, and most students agree that faculty members care. "The professors who teach here are outstanding and communicate with their students on a first name basis," says an environmental studies major. Another students adds, "The professors who come here usually do so because of our unique approach to learning." There is no tenure at Evergreen, and thus much less pressure for professors to conduct research and publish findings. Faculty members focus on teaching, and most classes have 25 or fewer students. Still, individual interest and motivation are the keys to taking advantage of Evergreen's system. According to one student, "If you take the initiative and find out where the career center is, and ask for help, then it can be a good resource."

In general, "Greeners" are an environmentally conscious, nonconformist lot, and not surprisingly, open-minded and liberal. A high proportion are community college transfers. "Political correctness is a constant problem," complains an English literature concentrator. "Sensitivity and diversity issues are discussed to the point of obsession. We are not a diverse college, but we pretend to be." Currently, minorities make up 13 percent of the student body, with Asian Americans accounting for 5 percent and African Americans and Hispanics accounting for almost 4 percent each. Other hot topics include campus response to sexual assault, freshman retention (only 65 percent return for their sophomore year, but that's partly because their average age is 24 and many have already finished community college), and safety and security. A majority of students come from Washington and Oregon. Ideologically, this is still one of the best schools for students who think they were born 30 years too late, and if the '60s was your decade, take heart: admissions preference is given to students older than 25, as well as Vietnam veterans and physically challenged applicants. There are 104 merit scholarships of up to $3,000 apiece, but athletic awards have been eliminated as Evergreen prepares to join Division III of the NCAA.

Less than a third of the college's students, mostly underclass folk, live on campus and are happy to be there. "Campus housing is good, especially if you don't have a car," says one student. Rooms are divided into single and double studios, apartments, and modular units with kitchens for three to six students. Other students find affordable housing in the surrounding community, and take advantage of the efficient bus system. Evergreen's cafeteria offers rather "routine and repetitive" meals as well as a traditional board plan and a deli.

Nearby Olympia (the state capital) doesn't really qualify as a college town, but most students find it pretty cool anyway. Situated at the southernmost point of the Puget Sound, it naturally offers a lot of water-related activities. Seattle (an hour away) and the rugged Oregon coast (three to four hours) are great changes of scenery for students with cars. But most free time focuses on the breathtaking scenery kept green by Washington's infamous rain. "It rains too much here," says a senior. "I used to enjoy rainy weather before I came here but now I realize what it's like not seeing the sun all winter." The college rents all types of outdoor equipment, from backpacks and skis to kayaks and sailboats. Evergreen also boasts a

Each program is team-taught by three or four professors; a recent program, Problems Without Solutions, looked at topics such as AIDS or homelessness from the perspective of political science, philosophy, anthropology, economics, statistics, and writing.

The highly praised environmental science program invariably fills up fast, and includes offerings in ornithology, marine biology, and wetlands studies.

large College Activities Building (CAB for short), which houses a radio station, the student newspaper, and space for student gatherings.

As Evergreen's mascot (an eight-foot clam named "Gooeyduck" after the large geoduck clams found in the Sound) suggests, organized sports aren't a big deal among Greeners. The school still manages to field competent Division III teams in men's and women's soccer, though, and basketball and tennis debuted in 1997–98. Many students also enjoy intramural Frisbee, volleyball, skiing, and sailing. As might be expected at this nonconformist mecca, fraternities and sororities are nowhere to be seen. Instead, organized social life revolves around movies, dances, and parties. The biggest event of the year is Super Saturday, a huge community fair the day before graduation, featuring bands, arts and crafts, and ethnic foods.

Evergreen invites—and demands—an active effort from its students in shaping their own education. And while this lack of structure might be frustrating, some students will find the experience of charting their own college course exhilarating. "Evergreen is not for everyone, but it is a good nontraditional school," says a sophomore. "Academics and atmosphere are the strong points. It's things like money and political correctness that need work."

If You Apply To ➤ | **Evergreen**…Regular admissions: Mar. 1. Financial aid: Feb. 15. Meets demonstrated need of 35%. Campus and alumni interviews: optional, informational. SATs or ACTs: required. SAT IIs: optional. Essay question: currently under development.

Fairfield University

1073 North Benson Road, Fairfield, CT 06430-5195

A comprehensive Jesuit university, Fairfield's mission is to "prepare students for lives of leadership and service in a constantly changing world." To provide its students with a well-rounded education, the school combines solid academics, real-world opportunities in and outside of the classroom, and an abundance of community service projects. No doubt about it, Fairfield is making a case for mention in the same breath as older, more revered East Coast Jesuit institutions.

The university's physical beauty, a scenic, tree-lined campus just 90 minutes from Manhattan, is a source of pride. The administration takes pains to preserve a lush atmosphere of sprawling lawns, ponds, and natural woodlands. Buildings are a mix of collegiate Gothic, Norman chateau, English manor, and modern. The library, Campus Center, and Science center have all undergone recent expansion, and the business school recently relocated to a new building with state-of-the-art teaching facilities, seminar rooms, and group study areas. A new 51,000-square-foot Athletic Center offers improved locker facilities for varsity players and an aerobics and free-weight area for weekend warriors.

Despite the beautiful facilities, students may find it difficult to squeeze a workout into their demanding class schedules. Everyone must complete the liberal arts core curriculum during the first two years, with two to five courses from each of five areas: math and sciences, history and social science, philosophy and religious studies, English and fine arts, and modern and classical languages. The core constitutes almost half of a student's total courseload.

Fairfield's main academic strengths are business (accounting, finance, and economics), the social sciences (sociology and psychology), and the natural sciences (biology and physics). Students also rave about the nursing program and the English faculty. Weaker offerings reportedly include chemistry, communications, and studio art.

Fairfield's academic climate is far from cutthroat. "The academic climate here is challenging but not overly competitive," says a sophomore. "Students tend to help each other out." Recent additions to the curriculum include minors in legal studies, classical studies, Irish studies, and Italian studies, which maintains strong ties to the Lorenzo de'Medici Institute in Florence. Engineering students may enroll in joint five-year programs with the Rensselaer Polytechnic Institute, Columbia University, or the University of Connecticut. Approximately 150 students study abroad each year, through their choice of more than 100 programs in 50 nations. Six students from Fairfield's class of 2000 were awarded Fulbright Scholarships for post-graduate studies abroad.

Back on campus, Fairfield's advanced fiber-optic network brings email, Internet, and video capabilities to classrooms, offices, and dorm rooms. All classes are taught by full professors, and one senior biology major notes that, "In general, I've found that teachers are usually very dedicated to the students and provide numerous opportunities for assistance." Most classes have fewer than 35 students.

About 80 percent of Fairfield's students come from Roman Catholic families, and approximately one-quarter are Connecticut natives. Minority enrollment is small, with African Americans constituting 3 percent of the student body, Hispanics 4 percent, and Asian Americans another 3 percent. Students are somewhat self-conscious about their conservative, preppy image, referring jokingly to themselves as "J. Crew U." Volunteerism abounds, and issues of diversity and prejudice are at the top of the campus political agenda; the T.E.A.M. peer group helps Fairfield deal with race relations and sexual harassment. Minority recruiting efforts include programs in Latin American, Asian, Women's, Judaic, and Black studies. Campus diversity celebrations now encompass Hispanic heritage month, black history month, and women's studies month.

Aid for students struggling with Fairfield's steep sticker price has increased steadily in recent years, and the school now offers 160 merit scholarships annually, ranging from $7,000 to $12,500. In addition, the university awards many full athletic grants-in-aid. One senior confides: "I worked in financial aid and the program is so-so." A junior sighs, "I guess they try their best, but it's still expensive here." Once they've figured out how to pay the bills, freshmen are introduced to Fairfield with a thorough orientation program. Two days of academic orientation occur in June so that freshmen can meet faculty advisors, experience classes, register, and meet roommates. An extensive parents' program is also conducted at that time; another two-day student orientation occurs in September, just before classes begin. After settling in, all first-semester freshmen must complete the noncredit, nongraded First Year Experience Program.

Fairfield's "comfortable and well-maintained" residence halls house three-fourths of the student body. Freshmen and sophomores usually live in one of the quad's five coed dorms. Juniors and seniors opt for the university townhouses or enter a lottery to move off campus, preferably to nearby beach houses, which they can rent at off-season rates. Meal plan options are available to all students.

Fairfield's proximity to the beaches of the Long Island Sound, a quick 5-minute drive from campus, provides students with a scenic social space for

All freshmen complete the noncredit, nongraded First Year Experience program during their first semester, and all students must take a course with a diversity component.

(Continued)

Q of L: ★ ★ ★ ★

Admissions: (203) 254-4100

Email Address:
admis@fair1.Fairfield.edu

Strongest Programs:
Accounting and Finance
Psychology
Economics
Sociology
Philosophy
Biology
Marketing and International
Studies

everything from romantic retreats to rowdy parties like the annual Luau and Clam Jam. Still, students say most of the social life takes place on campus, where sponsored events range from concerts and dances to hanging out at the coffeehouse and on-campus pub. Harvest Weekend at the end of October, and Dogwoods Weekend at the end of April, provide relief from the stress of studying. Road trips to New York (only an hour by train) and Boston are also popular. The alcohol policy is fairly strict where underage drinking is concerned. One junior says simply, "If you don't get caught, you don't get punished. But if you do, be prepared to pay the price. Still, if you want alcohol, you can find it." Although Jesuits are very much in evidence, and often live in the dorms, students say they do not hinder the social scene. The Campus Ministry draws a large following, with daily Masses, retreats about three times a semester, and regular community service work including two weeks of programs in the Caribbean and Latin America. As for the surrounding area, one senior says, "Fairfield is generally a wealthy town with beaches on the Long Island Sound and a cute, New England-type downtown strip area. Nice restaurants and shops are all around." Unfortunately, relations with residents of the quiet, wealthy town could be better. Community service work in the less advantaged community of nearby Bridgeport is a common pastime for Fairfield students eager to do their part, and perhaps improve their image at the same time.

Athletics have finally come of age at Fairfield, with men's and women's tennis, men's lacrosse and golf, and women's soccer, volleyball, and basketball winning recent Metro Atlantic Athletic Conference championships. Men's and women's basketball both draw crowds, and the boisterous home-court fans, who come to games in full Fairfield regalia, have been dubbed the "Red Sea." In 1996, nonscholarship varsity football came to Fairfield, another source of athletic excitement. Living up to the Jesuit motto of sound mind and sound body, many students play on intramural teams, whose exploits are copiously chronicled in the campus newspaper. The school also takes pride in its 92 percent graduation rate for scholarship athletes, one of the highest rates in the country.

Like the graduation rates of its student athletes, Fairfield University is a school on the rise. Fairfield "is growing exponentially in facilities, student quality, and academic integrity," a student notes. With efforts in place to preserve the natural beauty of Fairfield's charming campus and the modernization of key facilities to meet the needs of tomorrow's students, Fairfield is hoping to attract more students dedicated to its motto: "It's not the destination, but the journey that counts."

Florida Institute of Technology

150 West University Boulevard, Melbourne, FL 32901-6975

Florida Institute of Technology invites its students to explore the endless depths of the ocean or to shoot for the stars. With Cape Canaveral only 40 minutes from campus and the ocean literally next door, it's not surprising that some of the most cutting-edge work in space and water-related sciences is under way at Florida Tech. Combine academic excellence with a bustling Central Florida location—just an hour from the bright lights of Disney World—and it's easy to see why students are flocking to this innovative school.

Founded in 1958 to meet the needs of engineers and scientists working at what is now Kennedy Space Center, Florida Tech's contemporary 130-acre campus features more than 200 species of palm trees and the botanical gardens in a tropical setting. Campus architecture ranges from modern to Georgian Gothic. Construction was recently completed on an engineering complex and several buildings for life sciences.

If you're considering Florida Tech, you need a strong background in math and science (especially chemistry and physics). Few students choose to major in the less practical sciences. Though many students grouse that Florida Tech is too expensive for their tastes, students who plan their education well are able to get high-paying technical jobs immediately following graduation. Prospective aviation students can major in aviation management, aviation meteorology, aviation computer science as well as aeronautics with or without flight option. The flight school has a modern fleet of 35 airplanes and a flight simulator, and the precision flying team regularly wins titles. Florida Tech, the only independent technological university in the Southeast, garners some of the best young minds in the country. The computer and mechanical engineering majors have gained popularity recently, although marine biology is still a popular major. And where else in the country could you get a BS in aquaculture? (Answer: nowhere.) Weaker areas are the humanities, due to the institute's technical orientation. The Applied Research Lab and Skurla Hall are impressive facilities, as is the Claude Pepper Institute for Aging.

The academic climate at FIT is challenging. "The courses here are no walk in the park," says a space science major. "They require an enormous amount of time and dedication." Classes, especially labs, have strict ceilings, but it's usually possible to graduate in four years with the help of academic advisors who can open "closed" sections. Graduate teaching assistants are not overused. "The professors are passionate about the subjects they teach at Florida Tech," says an ecology major. "They go out of their way to help their students understand the material." Another student adds, "We have knowledgeable, caring professors from all over the world." All majors offer co-op programs and senior independent research at the Indian River Lagoon or on the *RV Delphinus*, a 60-foot research boat the school owns. Recent marine research includes manatee preservation, beach erosion, and sea turtle studies. Most students, however, are job-minded; the majority of graduates go to work after getting their degrees; nearly a quarter go straight to graduate school. Regardless of major, everyone must take communication, a physical or life science course, one math course, one humanities, and a social sciences class.

Forty-five percent of Florida Tech students are out-of-staters, and another 28 percent arrive from out of the country. Still, the student body is 57 percent white.

Website: www.fit.edu

Location: Small city

Total Enrollment: 4,178

Undergraduates: 1,933

Male/Female: 69/31

SAT Ranges: V 500-610 M 530-630

ACT Range: 22-27

Financial Aid: 55%

Expense: Pr $

Phi Beta Kappa: Yes

Applicants: 1,939

Accepted: 80%

Enrolled: 26%

Grad in 6 Years: 52%

Returning Freshmen: 76%

Academics: ✐ ✐ ✐

Social: ☎ ☎ ☎

Q of L: ★ ★ ★

Admissions: (321) 674-8030

Email Address: admissions@fit.edu

Strongest Programs:
Aeronautics/Aviation
Computer Engineering
Mechanical Engineering
Marine Biology

The Applied Research Lab and Skurla Hall are impressive facilities, as is the Claude Pepper Institute for Aging.

All majors offer co-op programs and senior independent research at the Indian River Lagoon or on the RV Delphinus, a 60-foot research boat the school owns.

Political correctness and diversity-related issues seem to be taken in stride because of the preponderance of international students, and the students here tend to feel more concern for the environment than anything else. "There are many cultures and lifestyles," notes a freshman, "Everyone is friendly and seems interested in their fellow students." Florida Tech offers almost 200 merit scholarships, ranging from $2,000 to $12,000, and 127 athletic scholarships in six sports (though there are few women's teams). Incoming freshmen are welcomed with a weeklong orientation program highlighted by trips to Disney World and the beach, just three miles away. On campus, freshmen may take part in the University Experience Program, which helps first-years adapt to college life.

Dorms at Florida Tech are modern, air-conditioned (whew!), and well-maintained. "The rooms here are comfortable and convenient and much larger than in most college dorms," says a marine biology major. Freshmen are required to live on campus in single-sex halls whose double rooms are fairly large. The rooms may not have much privacy, but they do have Internet access and a microwave-refrigerator unit for concocting late-night snacks. Six-student apartments are available to a small percentage of qualifying upperclassmen, with graduate students given first priority. Fifty-one percent of students live off campus, drawn by cheap rent and not much else, because "Melbourne, Florida, is a small but close-knit community," reports a senior. The meal plan is an open, unlimited arrangement, and students report that the food is survivable.

Most Florida Tech students who don't have cars choose bikes as their favorite mode of transportation. Diversions can be found in Orlando (with Epcot and MGM Studios abutting Disney World) or at the Kennedy Space Center, only 40 miles away. Watching space shots from campus with a trained eye (and a cold brew) is a treasured pastime. The campus bar, the Rat, is a popular hangout. Otherwise, though, campus social life is predictably hampered by the low male/female ratio. "There's a greater influx of females to the school that will dramatically improve the social scene," says a molecular biology major. Another student adds, "The social life at Florida Tech is what you make of it, which means sometimes you have to create your own fun."

Fraternities and sororities are becoming more popular at Florida Tech, claiming 17 percent of the men and 13 percent of the women but not dominating the social life. "The Greek organizations offer excellent extracurricular activities that help you both socially and academically," says a freshman. And while the campus is officially dry, every frat party has beer that the underage eagerly guzzle, students say. Besides partying, students spend their off time surfing, fishing, hanging out at the beach, shopping, or going for a "Sunday drive" (in the sky) with a flight school student. Every April, students brace for the invasion of other collegians on spring break. Techies also look forward to Greek Week and intramural sports competitions. With so much water around, it's not surprising that the crew team is awesome.

Students eager to get their hands dirty studying marine life or building rockets should consider Florida Tech, a young school with a growing reputation, relatively low costs for its specialized, high-quality course offerings, and an enviable beachside location. Here, most everyone is serious about studying, having some fun, and eventually graduating with marketable skills.

Overlaps

University of Florida, Embry-Riddle, Florida State, University of Central Florida, MIT.

Florida State University

A2500 University Center A, Tallahassee, FL 32306-2400

For many, Florida State University means one thing: football. But the Seminoles on the gridiron aren't the only thing making headlines at this Sunshine State institution. Here, you could have a Nobel laureate for a professor, study in one of the finest science facilities in the Southeast, or get your feet wet in state government through an internship at the state capitol. The choices are plentiful at FSU, and the pace of life makes it possible to taste a little of everything: study hard, relax in the Florida sunshine, and enjoy some rowdy football while you're at it

FSU is located in Tallahassee, a land described as the "Other Florida," with rolling hills, flowering dogwoods and azaleas, and a canopy of moss-draped oaks 30 minutes from the Gulf of Mexico. The main campus features collegiate Gothic-style structures surrounded by plenty of shade trees, with some modern facilities sprinkled in. Situated on 400 compact acres, the campus is the smallest in the state university system—it's just a 10-minute walk from the main gate on the east side to the science complex on the west side. The University Center, which wraps around the football stadium, offers centralized services, including counseling, financial aid offices, undergraduate studies, and an active career center. Bicycling and skating are popular forms of transportation, though the parking garage provides spaces for more than 1,000 cars and a free shuttle bus circles campus for those without wheels.

FSU has outstanding programs in music, drama, art, and dance; it's moving up fast in the natural sciences with improved equipment and facilities in physics, chemistry, and biology. In fact, FSU has 25 programs rated exemplary by the state university system, more than any of the other nine system schools. Five hundred interactive terminals support the growing computer science program, and communications, statistics, and business (especially accounting) have strong reputations in the Southeast. The School of Motion Picture, TV, and Recording Arts, the school's newest, has consistently won an impressive array of national and international awards. For gifted students, the honors program offers smaller classes and closer faculty contact, as well as 40 special seminars each year. And Directed Individual Study courses offer undergraduates the chance to participate in independent research projects with faculty direction; over 900 students and 200 faculty members participated last year. Internships and political jobs abound for tomorrow's politicians, since the state capitol and Supreme Court are nearby. A number of programs give students the opportunity for real-life experience in positions related to the running of the Sunshine State.

Recently, liberal studies requirements were reduced from 49 to 36 hours, common prerequisites were established, and the total hours for a bachelor's degree were dropped to 120 (with a few exceptions). The general education requirements—courses in math, English, history and social sciences, humanities and fine

Website: www.fsu.edu
Location: City outskirts
Total Enrollment: 32,878
Undergraduates: 25,965
Male/Female: 45/55
SAT Ranges: V 520–620 M 530–630
ACT Range: 22–27
Financial Aid: 31%
Expense: Pub $
Phi Beta Kappa: Yes
Applicants: 21,159
Accepted: 64%
Enrolled: 38%
Grad in 6 Years: 63%
Returning Freshmen: 86%
Academics: ✍ ✍ ✍
Social: ☎ ☎ ☎
Q of L: ★ ★ ★
Admissions: (850) 644-6200
Email Address:
admissions@admin.fsu.edu

Strongest Programs:
Biology
Business
Chemistry
Dance
Meteorology
Motion Picture

Overlaps

University of Florida, University of Central Florida, University of South Florida, University of Miami (FL), Florida International.

arts, and natural sciences—are reported to be among the easier classes at FSU. Within FSU's liberal studies program, students must also complete six hours of multicultural understanding coursework—three focusing on diversity within the Western experience, and three focusing on cross-cultural studies. Freshmen must take math and English, and may find a TA at the helm in these courses. But overall, faculty members do teach, and they get kudos for their efforts in the classroom and as advisors. "The professors really care about what they're teaching," says an English major. Registration, made easier through a phone system, is still somewhat of a hassle. For those aching for a break from the large-university scene, FSU offers foreign-study centers in Florence and London, and summer programs in Costa Rica, France, Spain, Russia, Switzerland, the Czech Republic, Vietnam, and Italy.

Perhaps not surprisingly, FSU's student body has a distinctly Floridian flavor: in-staters comprise 77 percent of the group. The majority of students, 76 percent, are Caucasian; 12 percent are African American and 8 percent are Hispanic. There's little evidence of racial tension: "Cultural diversity is a big issue," says one student. "Individuality is encouraged here." Seminoles are a mixture of friendly small-towners and city dwellers, and political tastes tend toward the conservative. While tuition is a hot topic of campus conversation, so are issues like voter registration, the environment, and student government concerns. Sixteen percent of FSU's students live in the university dorms. Students may opt for older halls, typically spacious but not air-conditioned, or newer ones with air that tend to be more cramped. For the most part, students say the dorms are clean and well maintained. "I live in the nicest dorm on campus, which is nicknamed the hotel," says a junior. "It's a good example of how FSU strives to meet every expectation of the students who live on campus." The number of students who can live in the dorms is limited, however, and rooms are assigned on a first-come, first-served basis. Upperclassmen generally forsake the housing rat race and move into nearby apartments, houses, or trailers, where they take advantage of the city and campus bus systems (substantially cheaper and infinitely easier than driving and parking a car in FSU's crowded lots) to get to school. The dorms are equipped with kitchens; meal plans that offer "good but expensive" food are also available.

When they're not studying, dorm parties, plays, concerts, and films keep FSU students busy. Those with wanderlust and a good ID can head for one of Tallahassee's bars or restaurants, which fall somewhere between "college hangout" and "real world." Generally, though, students give the area a thumbs-up: "Tallahassee is definitely a college town," says an English major. "For every home football game, the entire town decks out in garnet and gold." As for Greek life, 7 percent of the men and 8 percent of the women join fraternities and sororities, which constitute another important segment of the social scene. In sports, the big-time Seminole football team won two national titles in the '90s and was runner-up in 2000. Going to games is an integral part of the FSU social scene, especially when games are against FSU's two most hated rivals: the University of Florida and the University of Miami. FSU's baseball team also draws an enthusiastic following, as do the Lady 'Noles volleyball and softball teams.

While Florida State has all the elements of a party school, the merrymaking here never seems to reach the riotous excesses for which some universities are known. FSU students would rather go to the beach with friends when they need to let off steam. Diversity and friendliness go hand in hand at this Southern school, which offers a lot more than just sunshine and championship football.

University of Florida

Gainesville, FL 32611

Set on 2,000 acres of rolling, heavily forested terrain in north-central Florida, the University of Florida is an athletic powerhouse, an academic dynamo, and a bastion of diversity. But most of all, it is gigantic. Enrollment is on the increase, and students have mixed feelings concerning the size of their school. The university continues to see a boost in applications, bolstering the school's selectivity and causing one student to report that the climate on campus is "becoming more academically oriented, but not too stuffy!"

The central campus, which is listed as a National Historic Area, has 21 buildings from the early 20th century on the National Register of Historic Places. Buildings are designed in the collegiate Gothic architectural style, featuring red brick with white trim. New facilities include a 233,000-square-foot physics building and a $60-million brain institute.

Academically, UF is strongest in preprofessional areas, and is known for its programs in engineering, tax law, and pharmacy. Business administration is the most popular major, followed by finance and psychology. Other popular majors are accounting, electrical engineering, elementary education, and advertising. The schools of engineering, medicine, law, business, education, and journalism are winners, according to student critics. The well-known College of Journalism and Communications was the first to offer students an electronic newsroom, and broadcasting students run their own radio and television stations. UF's honors program is reserved for students with 3.6 GPAs and SAT scores of at least 1280 overall. Students mention foreign languages and math (too many TAs) as weaker areas, along with fine arts and music. Some summer courses have been cut due to budget cutbacks. Regardless of a student's main interests, he or she has a good chance of finding a major program, since only two universities, Ohio State and Minnesota, offer more degree programs on one campus than UF.

To complement the preprofessional leanings of its students, UF has a general education program through which students must fulfill credits in composition, literature and arts, historical and philosophical studies, international studies and cultural diversity, social sciences, mathematical sciences, and the physical and biological sciences, to be taken over the four-year BA program. UF has reduced its required general education credit hours by six in an attempt to graduate more of its students in four years. Students feel it is generally not difficult to graduate in four years unless, says one student, "you decide to switch majors or take an internship." Volunteer work in Gainesville and cooperative-education options are growing in popularity. Those who want to flee the Sunshine State can study through exchange programs in Brazil, Israel, Colombia, Japan, China, or more than a dozen cities in Eastern and Western Europe. New programs include digital arts and an interdisciplinary studies major in quantitative sciences.

Website: www.ufl.edu
Location: Center city
Total Enrollment: 43,382
Undergraduates: 31,633
Male/Female: 49/51
SAT Ranges: V 570–670 M 600–690
ACT Range: 26–29
Financial Aid: 64%
Expense: Pub $
Phi Beta Kappa: Yes
Applicants: 13,967
Accepted: 60%
Enrolled: 44%
Grad in 6 Years: 67%
Returning Freshmen: 91%
Academics: ✑ ✑ ✑ ✑
Social: ☎ ☎ ☎ ☎
Q of L: ★ ★ ★ ★
Admissions: (352) 392-1365
Email Address: N/A

Strongest Programs:
Engineering
Counselor Education
Tax Law
Latin American Studies
Journalism/Communications
Chemistry
Anthropology
Citrus Science

Like many supersized universities, UF suffers from an impersonal environment and a mountain of bureaucracy. Occasionally, lectures in the College of Business Administration have to be videotaped (and also offered through cable TV) so everyone can see them. Although course registration has been frustrating for some in the past, all first-year students are now guaranteed seats through the university's telephone registration system. One satisfied veteran claims, "With our new phone registration system, Tele-Gator, there has been no difficulty whatsoever with getting classes." One student says that the quality of teaching is outstanding. "Professors are very helpful and most have an open door policy," says one senior. Academic pressure varies with each major and each student. "Classes can be challenging," one student says. "The academic qualifications of our students are steadily increasing; thus, studying is of growing importance."

Faculty advisement is said to be fair, and is bolstered by the Academic Advising Center. Experiences differ among students, with one junior reporting that advising is "atrocious" and that advisors often lack a genuine interest in student's needs. To improve academic counseling, UF instituted a program to monitor undergraduates' progress toward upper-division classification. Students receive personalized letters as they reach 30, 45, and 60 hours, telling them of specific grade and course requirements in their programs. A similar program is being developed to track freshmen and transfers in engineering and political science. An "incredible" career resource center has many students singing its praises: here students can seek advice, conduct research, and interview for jobs.

Florida has a largely homegrown student body: more than 90 percent of the young scholars on campus are Floridians, and 86 percent finished in the top fifth of their class in high school. Despite the geographical homogeneity, students claim they're a diverse bunch. A veteran says that diversity "is a highly emphasized subject" at UF. "There is a wide variety of people, all with different views and ideas. I am constantly bombarded with literature and information regarding them." People Awareness Week, a multicultural celebration, has grown into a popular campus event, and UF recently established a Latino-Hispanic Cultural Center to serve the majority minority on campus. Many of the black student body belong to their own set of fraternities, and notes one student, "There's no hostility between ethnic groups, but not very much mixing." Hispanics make up 10 percent, Asian Americans 7 percent, and blacks another 9 percent of the students. UF offers more than 200 athletic scholarships, as well as 3,100 merit scholarships, ranging from $500 to $3,000. National Merit Scholars automatically qualify if they list UF as their first choice.

Housing is iffy in terms of getting a room if you're not a first-year student. Selection is governed by a Social Security number lottery, and there are just not enough rooms for everybody. Freshmen are guaranteed space, but after that the unlucky must fend for themselves in the off-campus housing market. Only about a quarter of the undergraduates get campus housing, available in doubles, triples, or suites. Most of the dorms are coed by floor. Fraternity and sorority houses provide another housing alternative. For most meals, students on campus eat on the university's meal plan, which is "pretty bad," or use the dorm kitchens. There are also several student pubs on campus, as well as a food court that offers KFC, Taco Bell, and Dunkin' Donuts. The Gator Corner Dining Center provides another on-campus eating option, presumably with more balanced dietary offerings.

Students love their home-away-from-home—Gainesville—described by one agriculture economics student as "a great college town." A city of about 125,000 midway between the Atlantic Ocean and the Gulf of Mexico, Gainesville offers plenty of stores, restaurants, and bars as well as a sports arena. Campus security is excellent. There's even a voluntary apartment safety program whereby students can get the names of apartment complexes that have been inspected by police for safety.

The university owns a nearby lake, which is "great for lazy Sundays" as well as more vigorous water sports, and there are more than enough parks, forests, rivers, and streams close by for backpacking, camping, and canoeing. "The social life is awesome," one student reports. Fifteen percent of the men and women join fraternities and sororities, making Florida's Greek system one of the nation's largest. Most of the Greek parties, which must comply with strict guidelines for serving alcohol, are closed to outsiders, but independents needn't fret; there's always a party going on somewhere. The best road trips are to UF away football games and to the beach.

Sports are a year-round obsession at Florida. The university has one of the top intercollegiate programs in the nation, with varsity competition for men and women in 16 sports, including nationally ranked teams in football, baseball, track, golf, tennis, gymnastics, volleyball, and swimming and diving. In the fall, Gator football sets the campus on its ear with a flurry of "big weekend" social events, most notably the annual Homecoming extravaganza—"Gator Growl"—which boasts a half-million-dollar budget and attendance averaging 78,000 people each year. Basketball is the biggest winter spectator sport, and both the men's and women's swimming teams are powerhouses. Women's sports are generously funded and also get a fair amount of fan support; a new women's softball stadium now highlights that program. After men's football and basketball, women's gymnastics and volleyball are the next most popular, and women's tennis has enjoyed national prominence, as has men's golf. Intramural sports are also big, and a 60,000-square-foot fitness park offers aerobics, martial arts, basketball, racquetball, softball, squash, strength conditioning, tennis, and volleyball for self-motivated athletes. Gator sports fans can often be seen wearing a favorite UF T-shirt that states, "If you're not a Gator, you're Gator bait!"

For some students, the sheer size of UF is overwhelming. For others, that's a drawing card. Whether standing in line at registration or for kickoff at the football stadium known as "the Swamp," loyal Gators certainly have spirit. And they aren't afraid to talk about it. As one student comments, at UF she has found "top-notch academics with unparalleled athletics: the best of both worlds!"

Overlaps

Florida State, University of Central Florida, University of Miami (FL), University of Georgia, UNC–Chapel Hill.

If You Apply To ➤

Florida...Early decision: Oct. 15. Rolling admissions: Jan. 29. Financial aid: Apr. 15. Campus interviews: optional, evaluative. No alumni interviews. SATs or ACTs: required. SAT IIs: required for some programs. No essay question.

Fordham University

Rose Hill Campus: 441 East Fordham Road, Bronx, NY 10458
Lincoln Center Campus: 113 West 60th Street, New York, NY 10023

Website: www.fordham.edu
Location: Urban
Total Enrollment: 13,551
Undergraduates: 6,578
Male/Female: 41/59
SAT Ranges: V 550–640 M 528–620
ACT Range: 23–28
Financial Aid: 68%
Expense: Pr $ $
Phi Beta Kappa: Yes
Applicants: 8,600
Accepted: 62%
Enrolled: 30%
Grad in 6 Years: 69%
Returning Freshmen: 88%
Academics: ✍ ✍ ✍
Social: ☎ ☎ ☎
Q of L: ★ ★ ★
Admissions: (800) FORDHAM
Email Address: enroll@fordham.edu

Strongest Programs:
Business
Theater and Drama
Psychology
English
Philosophy
Theology
History

A BFA in dance is offered in conjunction with Alvin Ailey; students must be accepted both by Fordham's admissions committee and Alvin Ailey's audition panel.

Any New Yorker could tell you that the Bronx and Manhattan simply do not have the same feel. So students must choose wisely when deciding between Fordham University's two distinct campuses. The Rose Hill campus in the Bronx is an oasis of trees, green grass, and Gothic architecture within the hectic and fast-paced Big Apple. But head to the university's Lincoln Center campus in Manhattan and feel the metropolitan, industrial setting of a fast-paced, no-nonsense city. The Jesuit philosophy and motto of Fordham University, "Wisdom and learning," is maintained by the emphasis on a liberal arts education spread over these two campuses in New York City. And this philosophy is further enhanced by the rich sense of diversity that Fordham offers its students.

Although the university is an independent institution, its Jesuit heritage rings loudly through its concern for liberal values on both campuses. For most students, the Roman Catholic influence is positive, and many students say that the Jesuit tradition is the school's best feature. If nothing else, the Catholic influence and the politics of the '90s keep the campus lively. "Because of the amount of Catholics here there are differences in opinions concerning religious beliefs," says a junior theater major. "Yet I find the student body very liberal and free-thinking."

The 85-acre Rose Hill campus (a.k.a. the countryside in the city) seats Fordham College as well as undergraduate schools of business administration and general studies. Fordham College at Rose Hill, the largest liberal arts school, is full-scale back to basics in the broadest sense. The imaginative core curriculum, which takes up almost half of a student's courseload, concentrates on developing a liberal arts foundation in three distinct but interlocking stages: the history of the Western world, study of the contemporary world, and an introduction to the various disciplines scholars choose in studying both the past and the present. The business program is especially strong in marketing, accounting, and finance, and it provides hundreds of internships in all areas of Manhattan's business community, many leading to jobs. Freshmen are required to take courses in literature, English composition (which students cite as weak), foreign languages, history, philosophy, and theology.

The Manhattan campus at Lincoln Center has its own college as well as the law school and other graduate programs. Started as an alternative-style urban institution with no grades, it has become more traditional over the years and now shares the common core curriculum with Rose Hill. The university recently agreed to take over Marymount College, a small women's college in Tarrytown, New York, where Fordham has already leased space for graduate programs. Under the merger agreement, Fordham will continue to operate Marymount as a women's college while looking for ways to integrate the two institutions.

Both colleges have strong humanities departments: Rose Hill's strengths include history, philosophy, psychology, and economics, while Lincoln Center's forte is, appropriately enough, theater. A BFA in dance is offered in conjunction with Alvin Ailey; students must be accepted both by Fordham's admissions committee and Alvin Ailey's audition panel. Communications/media studies is praised at both schools, but some students cite the lack of an on-campus television studio as a major fault. Both colleges offer interdisciplinary majors, including black and Puerto Rican studies, and preprofessionals may enter 3–2 engineering programs at Columbia or Case Western Reserve. Rose Hill offers an innovative set of seminars, taught by the philosophy and theology departments, to help upperclassmen involved in community service analyze their experiences. Classes are assigned to freshmen during their fall semester, but they have the option to change their given schedule. Overall, students say faculty members are accessible and knowledgeable. "Fordham is definitely top-notch teaching," a sophomore says. Faculty advising leaves something to be desired but the career counseling center is said to have an abundance of material and information on jobs and internships.

Sixty percent of the students are from New York, and nearly two-thirds are from private or parochial high school. Seventeen percent of Fordham's undergraduates are African American or Hispanic, and the minority community is vocal. Opinions vary as to how well races mix at Fordham. According to one student, there is no hostility evident on campus, but others feel a slight tension. Another student says, "In New York City, many people value diversity. Otherwise, they wouldn't be here." The atmosphere at both campuses is less intellectual than at nearby Columbia and New York universities, and Fordham students must motivate themselves.

A large number of students (68 percent) receive financial aid. There are 650 merit scholarships, with stipends ranging from $7,500 to full tuition plus room. Athletic scholarships in nine sports are available as well. Students say they haven't noticed many budget cuts as far as services are concerned, though they have noticed the effects of cuts on financial aid and tuition. Responding to a declining commuter population and an increasing housing crunch, the university offers a $4,000 tuition discount for entering freshmen who continue to live at home and commute to the college.

Responding to a declining commuter population and an increasing housing crunch, the university offers a $4,000 tuition discount for entering freshmen who continue to live at home and commute to the college.

The college has been seeking to build its national appeal and residential character. Sixty-three percent of the students now live on campus. All dorm residents are guaranteed rooms for the next year, but housing space is still tight. Lincoln Center students gladly welcome the 20-story, 850-bed dorm, so they don't have to deal with pricey rents in nearby apartments or in two specially priced hotels. Still, others live at home. One student says the dorms are "roomy and well structured."

And what's there to say about the social life? "New York has so much to offer and it's right outside the gates," says a sophomore. The school sponsors some extracurricular activities, including an intramurals program in Central Park, but they pale against the city's vast cultural smorgasbord. Students say there's much happening on campus, too, including parties, movies, social events, bands, and plays, and there's a pub and coffeehouse. The university's cultural affairs program brings the Bronx campus students into the Big Apple for a little high life; Manhattan is, after all, just half an hour away by train, subway, or college shuttle bus. Two of the most enjoyable events of the year are Spring Weekend and Homecoming. "The ten o'clock scream," a ritual every Thursday night in which everyone leans out their window and screams for one minute, is a favorite stress reliever.

Both Rose Hill and Lincoln Center students agree that theirs is not a typical college town. But the Bronx community does play a large role in the Rose Hill students' lives, including volunteering. The Rose Hill campus is backed up against the Bronx Zoo, the beautiful botanical gardens, and Belmont, the "Little Italy" of the Bronx. Of course, since we are talking about New York City, students must constantly be aware of their surroundings. But guards at each entrance to the campus and roving security give Rose Hill a safe feeling within the city.

The marvelous Lombardi Athletic Center (named for that famed alumnus) inspires an active program of club sports and intramurals, while "grandstand athletes" especially enjoy rooting for the varsity basketball team, not to mention the rapidly improving football and baseball teams. The basketball team is competitive nationally, and one student says it is a source of pride on campus. "Opponents named the Fordham Gym one of the most feared in the whole nation. They view our loyalty to our team and having to come to the Bronx and face a Fordham home crowd as intimidating," a former student says. Fordham is a member of the Atlantic 10 Division and has recently produced championship men's baseball and women's rowing teams. Says one sports-minded student, "Winning draws big crowds and gives the campus a new level of energy."

And it's that high level of energy that continues to propel Fordham University into the future. This school, like its home city, is built on the idea that diversity and a strong sense of community need not be mutually exclusive.

Overlaps

NYU, Boston University, St. John's University, Boston College, Manhattan College.

If You Apply To ➤

Fordham...Early decision: Nov. 1. Regular admissions and financial aid: Feb. 1. Does not guarantee to meet demonstrated need. Campus and alumni interviews: recommended, evaluative. SATs or ACTs: required. SAT IIs: recommended. Apply to particular school or program. Accepts the Common Application and electronic applications. Essay question: earliest memory; personal identification with a literary character; college goals.

Franklin and Marshall College

637 College Avenue, Lancaster, PA 17604-3003

Website: www.fandm.edu
Location: Small city
Total Enrollment: 1,862
Undergraduates: 1,862
Male/Female: 50/50
SAT Ranges: V 570–670 M 590–680
ACT Range: 24–31
Financial Aid: 65%
Expense: Pr $ $ $
Phi Beta Kappa: Yes
Applicants: 3,926
Accepted: 49%
Enrolled: 25%
Grad in 6 Years: 79%
Returning Freshmen: 95%
Academics: ✑ ✑ ✑ ✑
Social: ☎ ☎ ☎
Q of L: ★ ★ ★
Admissions: (717) 291-3951

At Franklin and Marshall College, set in the serene hills of Pennsylvania's Amish country, you have to be extra careful when driving. You never know when your Saturn may come nose to nose with a horse and buggy—and they don't have antilock brakes. While the city has modernized beautifully, parts of this historic town and many of its residents look much the same as they did when President James Buchanan insisted in 1853 that Marshall College merge with Franklin College in his hometown of Lancaster.

F&M's 125-acre campus is surrounded by a quiet residential neighborhood shaded by majestic maple and oak trees. The campus itself is an arboretum and boasts 47 buildings of Gothic and Colonial architecture. The College Square complex, which offers a Laundromat, printing service, two restaurants for student dining, and bookstore, appeals to students seeking a study respite. Recent construction projects include the renovation of the physical science laboratories and renovations to transform Hensel Hall, the former assembly hall, into a first-class music recital hall with seating for more than 500.

Although there are no required courses freshman year, four out of five students enroll in First-Year Residential Seminars. Participating students live together in groups of 16 on coed freshman floors and study a major theme or concept within a discipline. Some recent examples include the Gothic Novel, American Landscape, and Environment and Human Values. Recently, the college curriculum was significantly revised. The general education requirements include a writing and language requirement, scientific inquiry, arts, foreign culture, historical studies, literature, social analysis, and systems of knowledge and belief. Collaborations are optional opportunities to get course credit for an experience that includes working with others.

The chemistry, English, government, and earth science departments are highly praised, while foreign languages are weaker. Course offerings in modern languages have been expanded, with majors only in French, German, and Spanish and minors in Italian, Greek and Russian. However, faculty members have been added in Russian, Hebrew, and Japanese, and the entire program has been enhanced by the addition of a $250,000 high-tech Language Resource Center. A program in biological foundations of behavior offers students an interdisciplinary major with a focus on either animal behavior or neuroscience. In addition, many students engage in independent study or research with faculty during the academic year or have internships or independent studies on campus during the summer. A preprofessional college in line with Lafayette and Bucknell, F&M has an excellent reputation for preparing undergrads for medical school and other careers. Students praise career services for its innovative approach to placing students in jobs—staff send out emails to keep students apprised of opportunities.

Approximately 50 Marshall and 75 Presidential scholars are named each year. Marshalls receive a tuition grant, a Macintosh computer, and the chance to apply for up to $3,000 in research travel funds. Presidential scholars receive a $7,500 tuition grant. F&M also offers 150 merit scholarships, ranging from $5,000 to $18,000, and two Rouse scholarships worth full tuition, books, and fees. There are no athletic scholarships.

The academic climate is rigorous. "The atmosphere is demanding and cutthroat," says a senior. "Many students elect to focus solely on their studies during their time at F&M." Students rate the quality of teaching as outstanding, and the relatively small number of students fosters a strong sense of community between themselves and faculty members. "All faculty are involved in their courses and do so much work for the class, it's amazing," a sophomore says. Another student adds, "The professors here have a deep respect for teaching and it shows." F&M offers cross-registration with two other small Pennsylvania colleges—Dickinson and Gettysburg—and several domestic-exchange and cooperative-degree programs. In the summer, Franklin and Marshall sends students to countries such as Japan and Russia, and nearly 25 percent study in locations around the world during the junior year. Others participate in the Sea Semester.*

Seventy-eight percent of the student body ranked in the top tenth of their graduating high school class, and students hail from 40 states and 62 countries. Merely one-third are from Pennsylvania. Asian American students comprise 5 percent of the student body; African Americans and Hispanics represent 3 percent each. Students praise the school for its handling of diversity. "The college has become more diverse in the past five years, and thankfully so." Although an occasional political debate may waft through the murmurs of light social exchanges during dinner, according to one student the big issue on campus is the lack of issues on campus. Fummers do, however, take an interest when it comes to activities and social opportunities. The 115 clubs on campus will attest to that.

Student housing, all coed, ranges from campus dorms to theme houses, a co-op, and private apartments near the campus. While all students are guaranteed housing, freshmen and sophomores are required to live on campus. All of the residence halls are new or recently renovated. The newest, Weis Hall, was likened by one student to a beautiful hotel. Students say the dorms are very well maintained. All have heating, air-conditioning, carpet, hard wiring, and cable. "The dorms here are clean and comfortable," says a sophomore. Although on-campus hous-

(Continued)
Email Address:
admission@fandm.edu

Strongest Programs:
Business
Biology
Chemistry
Physics
Government
Political Science
Classics
Philosophy

Faculty members have been added in Russian, Hebrew, and Japanese, and the entire program has been enhanced by the addition of a $250,000 high-tech Language Resource Center.

ing is widely available, many juniors and seniors live off campus in houses and apartments. Boarders eat most of their meals in the campus cafeteria under a flexible meal plan, but students are issued debit cards that they may use at a number of different food stops on campus. Regarded by the college as independent social organizations, nine frats and three sororities are integral to much of the nightlife, although the residence halls and special-interest groups offer a range of alternatives, including concerts, comedians, and Ben's Underground, a popular student-run nightclub. Hildy's, a tiny local bar, is a favorite campus meeting place. In recent years, the student-run and college-funded College Entertainment Committee has brought the Gin Blossoms, Rusted Root, Live, Ben Folds Five, Indigo Girls, and Vertical Horizon to the campus.

Lancaster is a historical and well-to-do city of 60,000 people located in a larger metro area of 300,000. The town offers about a dozen movie theaters, scores of shops, a farmer's market, brick-and-cobblestone streets (with hitching posts for the Amish horses and buggies), and a plethora of quaint restaurants and cafés. Students have a measured, realistic appreciation of its urban amenities and rural ambiance. The Amish culture draws the interest of some students, and many frequent the charming farmer's market to shop for handmade quilts. "People who complain that there is nothing to do just aren't looking hard enough," says one senior. Those with a hankering for contemporary action take road trips to Philly, Baltimore, Washington, D.C., and New York City. The biggest annual event is Spring Arts, which is held the weekend before the last week of classes and includes student air-band contests, real bands, and booths. Other highlights include the freshman Pajama Parade, the Sophomore Sensation and the Senior Surprise, International Day, and Black Cultural Arts Weekend.

The college has a good selection of intramural sports, which include popular coed competitions. In addition to a wrestling powerhouse, F&M boasts recent victories in baseball, basketball, women's tennis, and volleyball. Varsity squads are called the Diplomats, a name that is irresistibly abbreviated to "the Dips." But after years of yelling "Go Dips," some F&M football fans have resorted to calling their team the Fighting Amish—a name that some members of the local community might not find too amusing. The annual football game against Dickinson is always a crowd-pleaser.

Franklin and Marshall's small size and peaceful location don't leave students feeling bored or isolated. In fact, many students say on-campus activities have improved lately, and they don't have to go far to find action. While some students complain of being overworked or stressed, most tell tales revealing a college experience that blends rigorous academics with a healthy dose of fun.

Overlaps

Bucknell, Lafayette, Colgate, Penn, Lehigh.

If You Apply To ➢

F&M…Early decision: Nov. 15, Jan. 15. Regular admissions and financial aid: Feb. 1. Guarantees to meet demonstrated need. Campus interviews: recommended (required for early decision), evaluative. Alumni interviews: optional, informational. SATs or ACTs: required (optional for applicants in top 10% of their class or who have a 3.6 out of 4.0 at schools with no ranking). SAT IIs: optional. Accepts the Common Application and electronic application. Essay question: important academic achievement; literary or artistic work; travel or life in foreign country; or significant person.

Furman University

3300 Poinsett Highway, Greenville, SC 29613

Some call it the "Country Club of the South." Others refer to it as the "Furman Bubble." But beyond the lush lawns and tight-knit student body, Furman University has made a name for itself as a leading liberal arts institution. A core emphasis on undergraduate research and traditional values give this school its distinct atmosphere. "The students at Furman are not just involved with their studies but also take part in sports, social activities, community service, and the world in general," says a psychology major.

The campus is so beautiful that townspeople treat it as a city park. On weekends, people wander the campus's 750 acres of lush countryside featuring a formal rose garden, an outdoor amphitheater, fountains, and flowering trees and shrubs; others picnic beside its man-made lake full of swans and ducks. The architectural style of the campus, designed specifically for Furman, features elements of Greek Revival and Colonial Williamsburg, with porches and pediments and distinctly Southern touches. One senior rhapsodizes, "On pretty days you can walk around the lake, feed the swans, [or] play golf or tennis on wonderful facilities." The most recent additions to the campus include a multipurpose arena for athletics, concerts, and other school and community events, and a state-of-the-art academic building for the political science, psychology, and sociology departments.

The rather hefty general education requirements include freshman composition, four humanities courses, one course in math, two courses each in natural sciences and social sciences, one course in fine arts, one course in health and exercise science, one course from the Asian-African program, and a foreign language proficiency. Freshmen must take a special course to fill the composition requirement. According to students, the political science department has some of the most desirable faculty and courses, along with numerous opportunities for internships and international study. Chemistry, political science, music, and psychology are the school's strongest departments, while communications is said to be somewhat under-resourced. Recent additions to the curriculum include a concentration in environmental studies and new interdisciplinary courses in the sciences and humanities. Furman students take three courses during the fall and spring terms, and two courses during the shorter eight-week winter term.

"Students say the academic climate at Furman is intense. "It is very competitive, and most of the classes are rigorous," says one political science/communications double major. "Because of our unusual academic schedule, professors really expect a lot out of their students." The low student/faculty ratio results in small class size and excellent student-faculty relations. One student double-majoring in history and health and exercise science describes Furman professors as "well-prepared, interested, involved, available, and demanding." The prized Furman Advantage and other special programs fund a legion of upperclassmen who hold research fellowships, internships, and teaching assistantships in their fields of study. Furman also traditionally sends one of the largest student delegations to the annual National Conference of Undergraduate Research. Study abroad options include a special exchange program with Kansai-Gaidai University in Japan and study in the Middle East, England, France, Spain, Germany, Central and South America, and Africa. Furman is also a member of the Associated Colleges of the South* consortium.

Diversity, both cultural and religious, is a hot issue on campus. Most Furman

Website: www.furman.edu

Location: City outskirts

Total Enrollment: 3,453

Undergraduates: 2,840

Male/Female: 45/55

SAT Ranges: V 570–670 M 580–670

ACT Range: 25–30

Financial Aid: 50%

Expense: Pr $ $

Phi Beta Kappa: Yes

Applicants: 3,200

Accepted: 65%

Enrolled: 33%

Grad in 6 Years: 73%

Returning Freshmen: 92%

Academics: ✍ ✍ ✍

Social: ☎ ☎ ☎

Q of L: ★ ★ ★

Admissions: (864) 294-2034

Email Address: admissions@furman.edu

Strongest Programs:
  Chemistry
  Psychology
  Political Science
  Music
  Biology
  Art and Design

A core emphasis on undergraduate research and traditional values give this school its distinct atmosphere.

Recent additions to the curriculum include an academic concentration in classical studies and new interdisciplinary courses in the sciences and humanities.

undergrads are white Southerners from middle- to upper-class families with politically conservative backgrounds, though less than a third are actually from South Carolina. Although many denominations are represented at Furman, the Baptist influence has been the tradition on campus. In 1992, Furman broke its ties with the South Carolina Baptist Convention after a 166-year affiliation, and the school continues to struggle with issues concerning its heritage. "Spending four years surrounded by white, upper-class Christians probably isn't good preparation for life in the 'real world,' "says a senior. Blacks make up 6 percent of the student body, and Hispanics and Asian Americans make up 3 percent combined. Over 50 percent of Furman graduates go straight into the work force after college; 35 percent go on to professional and graduate schools. Each year, Furman awards a variety of merit scholarships, which range from $2,500 to a full ride, as well as 140 athletic scholarships.

Furman is somewhat unique among universities of its ilk in that it maintains a dry campus. One senior explains, "Freshman and sophomore dorms are fairly strict, with Resident Advisors on each hall, although plenty of drinking still occurs. North Village [new university-owned apartment building] is much more relaxed. If there are no noise violations or outright violations, what goes on in your apartment is private." North Village, completed in 1998, contains four-bedroom apartments that one senior describes as "amazing!" as well as five different language houses. All dorms are equipped with telephone, cable TV, and Internet access. Only seniors may elect to live off campus, and dorms at Furman have created long-lasting friendships for many. "Most of the students are required to live on campus and this promotes friendship as well as a sense of community," says an urban studies and political science double major. All students have a choice of several different meal plans. The dining hall is organized into food courts, and options include a breakfast bar, salad bar, Chinese food, grilled items, Italian pastas, and a section for yogurt and baked goods. Students refer to the campus as the Furman Bubble because of the high level of safety and security that surrounds them. "My biggest worry is parking tickets, if that tells you anything," says one student.

The Student Activities Board sponsors movies, dances, coffeehouses, and bowling and skating parties. According to students, most parties and Greek functions take place off campus. "Furman is a dry campus but the students here still know how to have fun, with or without alcohol" says a communications studies major. Greenville has also become a popular spot, with a wide variety of coffee shops, bars, and clubs. And the Peace Center for the Performing Arts attracts many students to downtown Greenville, where they can attend Broadway shows and see first-rate performing artists. "Greenville is a great city with a revitalized downtown and a good population," says a senior. "There are fantastic restaurants to choose from, popular bars and clubs, and an impressive music scene." Atlanta is a two-and-a-half-hour drive away; skiers can hit the slopes after a two-hour drive; and for dedicated sojourners, the great South Carolina beaches are about four hours from campus.

Thirty percent of men and 35 percent of women belong to one of the eight fraternities and seven sororities on Furman's campus. And while fraternities and clubs are popular, there are several other organizations available. A large number of students also choose to devote spare time to the Collegiate Educational Service Corps, which organizes community social-service projects such as the annual May Day-Play Day carnival, which converts the Furman campus into a student-sponsored playground for underprivileged children. Football and soccer games are spectator favorites on campus, but Furman's powerhouses lie in other sports.

During the past few years, women's tennis and golf and men's soccer have won the Southern Conference Championships. Almost 70 percent of the students compete for the coveted All Sports Trophy by participating in the well-organized intramural games, which range from flag football to horseshoes.

While "The Country Club of the South" may be falling out of favor as concern for political correctness grows, four years in such a beautiful and challenging environment sounds like a pretty attractive deal to many college applicants. The opportunities that Furman offers have attracted a student body that is, in the words of one senior, "a very confident, amiable, and intelligent group of individuals."

If You Apply To ➤ **Furman**…Early decision: Dec. 1. Regular admissions and financial aid: Feb. 1. Meets demonstrated need of 88%. Campus and alumni interviews: optional, informational. SATs or ACTs: required. SAT IIs: optional, required for home-schooled students. Accepts the Common Application and electronic applications. Essay question: personal statement.

Overlaps

Wake Forest, Vanderbilt, UNC–Chapel Hill, Clemson, University of South Carolina.

George Mason University

4400 University Drive, Fairfax, VA 22030-4444

Just 40 minutes from the White House and the Smithsonian, smack in the middle of greater Washington, D.C.'s budding high-tech corridor, stands a fledgling university aiming to capitalize on its proximity to the nation's power center. George Mason University's urban campus and symbiotic relationship with the surrounding region contrast starkly with Virginia's two other major universities, which have held classes for a hundred years in the relative isolation of Charlottesville and Blacksburg. With just 30 years on its Fairfax campus—and only 45 years of life experience—GMU is clearly the new kid on the block. But thanks to cutting-edge ideas and a hunger for success, the school is poised to leap into the big leagues.

Founded as a sleepy outpost of the University of Virginia, GMU sits on a 583-acre wooded campus in the Washington, D.C., suburb of Fairfax, Virginia. Campus architecture is modern and nondescript; most structures were erected after the mid-'70s. GMU's 10,000-seat arena, the Patriot Center, hosts both sporting and entertainment events. In addition, a new aquatic and fitness center, featuring two pools, a whirlpool, and coed saunas was recently completed. And although GMU's campus doesn't have the Colonial ambiance or tradition of William and Mary or UVA, its namesake does have the same Old Virginia credentials. George Mason drafted Virginia's influential Declaration of Rights in 1776, though he later opposed ratification of the federal Constitution because there was no Bill of Rights attached.

Mason's general education requirements stipulate that all students take the equivalent of two courses in English composition, humanities, social sciences, and math and sciences. Students who prefer to find their own way can design a major under the Bachelor of Individualized Study program. The academic climate is intense but manageable. The courses here are rigorous but not to the point of consuming your life," says a premed major. Another student adds, "The academic climate is challenging but not overly competitive." If they do fall behind or need some guidance, academic counseling is likely to set them back on course. Advisors

Website: www.gmu.edu

Location: Suburban

Total Enrollment: 24,010

Undergraduates: 14,234

Male/Female: 44/56

SAT Ranges: V 460–570 M 470–580

ACT Range: 17–23

Financial Aid: 40%

Expense: Pub $ $

Phi Beta Kappa: No

Applicants: 6,035

Accepted: 63%

Enrolled: 55%

Grad in 6 Years: 51%

Returning Freshmen: 71%

Academics: ✍ ✍ ✍

Social: ☎ ☎

Q of L: ★ ★

Admissions: (703) 993-2400

Email Address:
admissions@gmu.edu

Strongest Programs:
Economics
Engineering

"have been so helpful and really supportive," says a marketing major.

Mason has grown by leaps and bounds for most of the past two decades; recent additions to the curriculum include degree programs in classical studies, international transactions, computational sciences, public policy, and urban systems engineering. Another option is the Century College degree program, which teams small groups of faculty and undergraduates on projects that can be easily connected to the world outside GMU. However, though it is growing up fast, Mason's youth shows in a number of ways. First, programs taken for granted at more established universities are just hitting their stride here. Next, GMU's relatively small endowment of $18 million means almost constant tuition increases: "Tuition has got to stop going up for us to continue with our growth," gripes a student. Last, some of the school's facilities are just plain inadequate for its more than 20,000 students. The library, for example, has fewer than 700,000 volumes, though it now subscribes to more than 300 online databases and allows students to borrow books from all eight members of the Washington Research Library Consortium.

The lack of resources in the library may present less of a problem for GMU's career-focused students, who seem to like learning on the job: 70 percent enter the working world after graduation, and just 20 percent proceed to graduate and professional schools. Psychology tops the list of popular majors, and economics—which boasts its own Nobel laureate—is probably the strongest department. Other well-regarded majors include computer science, nursing, engineering, and English; not surprisingly, given the school's location, the public policy department also receives accolades. The drama department, once a weak sister, is now part of the Institute of the Arts, created to make arts an intrinsic part of every student's GMU experience. The institute includes a professional theater company, which hosts actors and playwrights in residence.

Another new option is the Century College degree program, which teams small groups of faculty and undergraduates on projects that can be easily connected to the world outside GMU.

Foreigners account for only 3 percent of Mason's student body, but the campus is fairly diverse, likely due to the diversity of the surrounding area. Minorities make up 32 percent of the student population—9 percent African American, 7 percent Hispanic, and 16 percent Asian American. Students are politically aware and tend to lean rightward. That said, racial tensions haven't been a problem, perhaps thanks to the four-year-old Stop, Look, and Learn program. The program attempts to increase campus discussion on prejudice, discrimination, and harassment.

George Mason has been a commuter school for much of its short existence, but there is on-campus housing, and 14 percent of undergrads choose this option. Another several thousand live around campus in university-sponsored housing. The administration admits that room-and-board costs are inflated because the university's entire housing stock dates from 1978 or later, which means the buildings are modern and air-conditioned—but still being paid for. And though the dorms are comfortable and well maintained, there's still a lot of building to do. "The dorms are nice enough but most students still prefer to live off-campus," says a junior. Freshmen live together in Presidents Park, while other students get rooms on a first-come, first-served basis, based on class status. Those looking for an active social life should definitely consider a stint in the dorms, particularly in Presidents Park or the Freshman Center. But freshman dorms are dry, and you can get the boot if you're caught having a party with alcohol.

Business tops the list of popular majors, and economics—which boasts its own Nobel laureate—is probably the strongest department.

GMU's University Center, with its food court, movie theater, classrooms, computer labs, and study areas, has become the center of on-campus social life. The center is a convenience and a lure for students who commute to school and have gaps between classes. On the weekends, students find a predictable assortment of malls and shopping centers in Fairfax, just southwest of D.C., but off-campus parties and the sights and sounds of downtown Washington, Georgetown, and Old Town Alexandria beckon when the sun goes down. Best of all, these are only a short commute away via a free shuttle bus to the subway. Those searching for a more lively collegiate scene take road trip other local schools, including James Madison and UVA.

With barely a generation under its belt, Mason is notably lacking in traditions and annual events: "Come here and invent one!" a student urges. Patriots Day and Mason Day are the two major bashes, in addition to Homecoming, Greek Week, and International Week. GMU competes in Division I, and basketball dominates the sports scene since there's no football team. Any game against James Madison University draws a big crowd. Other successful teams include women's soccer, men's and women's track, and women's volleyball. Intramurals are catching on, now that many games are held in the Patriot Center.

The name of George Mason may not have the cachet of George Washington, James Madison, or the other luminaries of Virginia history who have had universities named for them. But with improving academics, a growing and improving physical campus, and the rich cultural and economic resources of Washington, D.C., Mason's namesake looks like it's set to follow in those other schools' fine footsteps.

> ## Overlaps
>
> **Virginia Tech, James Madison, Mary Washington, University of Virginia, University of Maryland.**

If You Apply To ➢   **Mason**...Early action: Dec. 1. Regular admissions: Feb. 1. Financial aid: Mar. 1. Meets demonstrated need of 40%. Campus interviews: required, informational. Alumni interviews: optional, informational. SATs: required. SAT IIs: optional. Accepts the Common Application and electronic applications. Essay question: personal statement.

George Washington University

2121 I Street NW, Washington, DC 20052

George Washington University offers it students an intellectually stimulating education and cultural enlightenment in the midst of the countless business, technological, scientific, and political opportunities of Washington, D.C. GW allows its students tremendous access to the bigwigs of D.C. Prominent figures such as President Clinton, Madeleine Albright, Andrew Young, Janet Reno, and the Dalai Lama have all addressed GW students. In addition, the campus also serves as host site for CNN's *Crossfire* and other political television programs.

GW now has two campuses in Washington. Its main campus is located only three blocks down Pennsylvania Avenue from the West Wing and the Oval Office. Known as "the school without a campus," GW inhabits an interesting mix of renovated federal row houses and modern urban structures that are barely distinguishable from the urban milieu that surrounds them. This non-campus is also near the historical Foggy Bottom district, where the State Department is located. GW's new Mount Vernon campus, located only three miles from Foggy Bottom, is set on 26 wooded acres and has five residence halls. All GW students can take classes and attend the activities at the Mount Vernon campus, but the residential facilities are restricted to women. Recent additions to the Foggy Bottom campus include research labs, a new center for Judaic Studies, and the Mid-Campus

Website: www.gwu.edu/
Location: Urban
Total Enrollment: 20,346
Undergraduates: 8,695
Male/Female: 42/58
SAT Ranges: V 570–670 M 570–660
ACT Range: 24–28
Financial Aid: 45%
Expense: Pr $ $ $ $
Phi Beta Kappa: Yes
Applicants: 14,326
Accepted: 50%
Enrolled: 30%
Grad in 6 Years: 70%
Returning Freshmen: 92%

(Continued)

Academics: ✍ ✍ ✍

Social: ☎ ☎ ☎

Q of L: ★ ★ ★

Admissions: (202) 994-6040

Email Address:

gwadm@gwu.edu

Strongest Programs:

Political Communications

Economics

International Affairs

Political Science

Electronic Media

International Business

English

Psychology

The campus also serves as host site for CNN's Crossfire and other political television programs.

The student center is currently being renovated, and construction is underway for a Media and Public Affairs Center that will provide classrooms, electronic media studios, teleconferencing, and a 350-seat auditorium.

Quadrangle, featuring a clocktower, fountain, and food vending arcade. The student center is currently being renovated, and construction in underway for a Media and Public Affairs Center that will provide classrooms, electronic media studios, teleconferencing, and a 350 seat auditorium.

Students cite political science, international affairs, psychology, English, and biology as the school's strongest programs. As for weaker programs, students say math and sociology need improvement. During the freshman year, English composition is the only requirement that all undergraduates must fulfill. All schools have general curriculum requirements varying from 17 to 51 credit hours. Students starting in the school of arts and sciences must complete core requirements that cover literacy, quantitative and logical reasoning, natural sciences, social and behavioral sciences, creative and performing arts, humanities, and foreign languages and cultures.

George Washington University's honors program offers honors seminars, independent honors studies, and a University Symposium for the entire school. The School of Engineering and Applied Science also offers an honors program that allows students to work one-on-one with a professor on a research project of mutual interest. An Integrated Engineering/MD program joined the Arts and Sciences/MD program for honors students in the medical preparation options. Students who meet stated conditions in these programs are guaranteed admission to the MD program at GW at a fixed tuition rate upon completion of their baccalaureate work. The Presidential Science and Arts Scholar Programs allow students to work with nationally known faculty in renowned facilities in the Washington metropolitan area and beyond.

The political communications major at GW, which combines political science, journalism, and electronic media courses, is one of the few undergraduate programs of its kind in the country. The George Washington University at Mount Vernon College experience is available to undergraduate women and provides special programs and academic initiatives for women students. The School of Business and Public Management offers combined five-year BBA/Master of Public Administration, BBA/Master of Information Systems Technology, and BBA/Master of Tourism Administration Programs. A five-year BA/BS program in Physics and Engineering and a BBA/MSIST program in Business Administration and Information Systems Technology have also recently been added. Two newly approved undergraduate degrees, a BA in computer science and a BA in applied science and technology, became effective in the 1999–2000 academic year. The climate is described as "cooperative but competitive." One sophomore says, "Initiative and intellectual development are encouraged, but overall students are willing to help each other out with classes."

The faculty at GW is universally praised. For two consecutive years, GW professors have been recognized by the Carnegie Foundation for the Advancement of Teaching. "Professors who have a full first hand comprehension about the subject they are teaching, instead of just textbook teachers have taught all my classes," says a computer science major. Almost half the professors divide their time between the halls of academia and the corridors of power, many holding high-level government positions. This ensures that their teaching is state-of-the-art, but also means their loyalties are somewhat divided. But then, so are their students,' many of whom get a head start on their careers with internships and part-time summer jobs in Congress and along the business corridor of K Street. For those in an even bigger hurry, there is an accelerated program that allows students to graduate in three normal academic years. The library, a member of the Association of Research Libraries, features card catalogs on CD-ROM, a one-stop periodical and research area, interlibrary catalog access, and a 65-seat reading room offering 24-hour study space for students. The online catalog can be accessed through a personal computer in the library or from the student's home or dormitory room. The library's membership in the Washington Research Library Consortium enables online access to a shared catalog of the seven member institutions and rapid interlibrary loans. As additional backup, there's always the Library of Congress, only a 10-minute subway ride away.

Like Washington itself, GW draws people from all over America and around the world. There is strong minority representation—6 percent of the students are African American, 4 percent Hispanic, and 10 percent Asian American—and a generous 7 percent of the students come from foreign countries. Some have remarked that GW students are "trendy and urban," and many hail from wealthy, upper-class families. The large international population, however, "adds a flavor of culture and diversity not found at other universities."

As for financial aid, 2,906 merit scholarships ranging from $5,000 to $20,000 are awarded to finalists in the National Merit Scholarship, National Achievement, and National Hispanic Programs and to other outstanding applicants. Another program offers honors scholarships of $5,000 to continuing students with a minimum of a 3.7 GPA. GW meets the demonstrated need of 88 percent of its accepted applicants and offers half-tuition discounts to siblings of undergraduates.

About half the students live off campus—many live in nearby D.C., within a nine-block radius of campus. Others choose to live in Maryland and Virginia suburbs, only a short subway ride away. On-campus housing in converted apartments or hotels is well-maintained and relatively spacious. "The dorms are incredible! Most rooms have a private kitchen, and all are furnished, with a private bathroom," raves one upperclassman. Most freshmen are booked into suites with up to four roommates in Thurston Hall, which is the biggest and rowdiest dorm on campus. Freshmen are guaranteed a room; upperclassmen and transfers take their chances in a lottery that awards students a chance at rooms in apartment-style buildings. The students describe the campus as "fairly secure." The excellent meal plan, mandatory for resident freshmen and sophomores, offers a variety of options, including cash credit for everything from cappuccino to Taco Bell at the food court, in addition to standard dining-hall fare.

Student athletes have become competitive in the Atlantic 10 Conference as well as NCAA Division I tournament play. Not only have the men's and women's basketball teams both made the NCAA "Sweet 16" in the past, but the women's team has also made the "Elite Eight." Midnight Madness launches spirit week activities as part of Family Weekend and the beginning of basketball season. Intramurals also enjoy wide popularity. Major festivals include Fall Fest, Spring Fling, and Freshman Block party. Fraternities and sororities attract 14 percent of the men and 10 percent of the women, and are growing in popularity. "Greek life is the best here," says one student. "They definitely know how to have a good time."

After 12 years of implementing new initiatives under the leadership of president Stephen Joel Trachtenberg, the university has developed a true sense of community and a strong vital spirit that attracts students from all over the country and the world. In addition, GW offers a sound academics program, the opportunity to mingle with the Washington's elite, and a chance to be a part of the bustle and excitement of the nation's capital city.

The political communications major at GW, which combines political science, journalism, and electronic media courses, is one of the few undergraduate programs of its kind in the country.

Overlaps

Boston University, Georgetown, NYU, American, University of Maryland.

Georgetown University

Washington, DC 20057

Website: www.georgetown.edu

Location: Center city

Total Enrollment: 12,498

Undergraduates: 6,361

Male/Female: 46/54

SAT Ranges: V 620–730 M 630–720

ACT Range: 27–31

Financial Aid: 55%

Expense: Pr $ $ $ $

Phi Beta Kappa: Yes

Applicants: 13,244

Accepted: 23%

Enrolled: 50%

Grad in 6 Years: 90%

Returning Freshmen: 97%

Academics: ✍ ✍ ✍ ✍

Social: ☎ ☎ ☎ ☎

Q of L: ★ ★ ★ ★

Admissions: (202) 687-3600

Email Address: N/A

Strongest Programs:

Government

Chemistry

Philosophy

Business

International Relations

Diplomatic History

International Economics

As the most selective of the nation's Roman Catholic schools, Georgetown University offers students an intellectual milieu that is among the nation's best. With unparalleled access to Washington, D.C.'s corridors of power, aspiring politicos benefit from the university's emphasis on public policy, international business, and foreign service. For avid sports fans, there is the perennially powerful basketball team. The national spotlight shines brightly on this elite institution, drawing dynamic students and athletes from around the world.

From its imposing, hilly location blocks from the Potomac River, Georgetown affords its students an excellent vantage point from which to survey the world. The 104-acre campus reflects the history and growth of the nation's oldest Jesuit university: the Federal style of Old North, home of the school of business administration, once housed guests such as George Washington and Lafayette. It contrasts with the towers of the Flemish Renaissance-style Healy Hall, a post–Civil War landmark on the National Register of Historic Places. A $750-million capital campaign is designed to address problems associated with the university's older buildings. Although Georgetown is a Roman Catholic university, founded in 1789 by the Society of Jesus, the religious atmosphere is by no means oppressive. Just over half of the undergraduates are Catholic, but all major faiths are respected and practiced on campus.

That's partially due to the pronounced international influence here. International relations, diplomatic history, and international economics are among the hottest programs. Through its broad liberal arts curriculum, GU focuses on developing the intellectual prowess and moral rigor its students will need in future national and international leadership roles. The curriculum has a strong multidisciplinary and intercultural slant, and students can choose from several programs abroad to round out their classroom experiences.

Would-be Hoyas may apply to one of four undergraduate schools: Georgetown College, Nursing, McDonough School of Business, and the Walsh School of Foreign Service, which gives future diplomats, journalists, and others a strong grounding in the social sciences. Prospective freshmen must declare intended majors on their applications, and their secondary school records are judged accordingly. This means, among other things, intense competition within the college for the limited number of spaces in Georgetown's popular premed program.

Georgetown's liberal arts program is also very strong: American studies gets favorable reviews, as do history, government, English, and, of course, theology. The School of Foreign Service stands out for its international economics, regional and comparative studies, and diplomatic history offerings; recent changes introduced a freshman proseminar and decreased requirements in history and political science. SFS also offers several five-year undergraduate and graduate degree programs in conjunction with the Graduate School of Arts and Sciences. The business school balances liberal arts with professional training, which translates into strong offerings in international and intercultural business as well as an emphasis on ethical and public policy issues. The School of Nursing runs an integrated program combining the liberal arts and humanities with professional nursing theory and practice, and offers a new major in Health Studies. The Faculty of Languages and Linguistics, the only undergraduate program of its kind nationwide, offers excellent instruction in 15 languages and grants degrees in nine. The computer science department has been bolstered by the recruitment of a chair with a national reputation, but students continue to cite it and the anthropology department as weak.

Georgetown's general education requirements are of two types: applicable to all students (literature, philosophy, and theology), and specific to certain divisions (chemistry, biology, physiology, math, philosophy, and sociology for nursing students, for example). The library holds 2.3 million volumes and features quiet study areas, audiovisual equipment, and access to special collections. That GU views most subjects through an international lens is evidenced by the 35 percent of students who study abroad. More than 80 university-sponsored study programs—in Asia, Latin America, Poland, Israel, France, Germany, and at the university's villas in Florence, Italy, and Alanya, Turkey—attract the culturally curious. The freshman orientation program, which includes trips, dances, dinners, and lectures, draws cheers. There are no special academic requirements for the freshman year, but about 30 Georgetown College freshmen are accepted annually into the liberal arts colloquium.

Georgetown likes to boast about its faculty, and well it should; former Secretary of State Madeline Albright will return to the School of Foreign Service in Fall 2001. "The quality of teaching at Georgetown is amazing," says an international politics major. "The professors are interesting and encourage their students to discuss the subjects being taught." Academically, the environment is tough but manageable. Says a finance and accounting major: "Two hours of studying for every one hour spent in class. While courses are challenging, anyone capable of getting into GU should not have any major problems succeeding."

The GU community includes students from all over the United States and abroad. About ninety-nine percent are from outside the District of Columbia, and 9 percent are foreign. African Americans and Hispanics make up 12 percent of the undergraduate group, and Asian Americans add 8 percent. A student committee works with the dean of student affairs to improve race relations and develop strategies for improving inclusiveness and sensitivity to issues of multiculturalism.

Students take studying seriously; they also say that each faculty member likes to think you're majoring in his or her subject. Surveys of the past two years' graduates reveal 80 percent moving directly into the job market after graduation, helped by the more than 120 résumé-building clubs, organizations, and student government activities available at this incubator for aspiring public leaders. Georgetown offers no academic merit scholarships, but it does guarantee to meet the full demonstrated need of every admit, and some 160 athletic scholarships draw male and female athletes of all stripes.

University-owned dorms, townhouses, and apartments accommodate two-thirds of students, and the university guarantees housing for three out of four years. All dorms are coed, and some have more activities and community than

The School of Foreign Service stands out for its international economics, regional and comparative studies, and diplomatic history offerings; recent changes introduced a freshman proseminar and decreased requirements in history and political science.

others. "The newer dorms are great but some of the older ones need to be renovated," says a student. Two dining halls serve "passable" food, but the popular student-run café offers more palatable options. Although D.C. has a high crime rate, GU students feel relatively safe on campus thanks to the school's ever-present Department of Public Safety and its walking and riding after-dark escort services. "To enter a residence hall, your student ID must be flashed," says a senior. "I've never felt threatened on campus or in the vicinity," a sophomore claims.

Jesuits, who know all about secret societies, frown upon fraternities or sororities at their colleges, and so there are none at Georgetown. The university's strict enforcement of the 21-year-old drinking age has led to a somewhat decentralized social life, not necessarily a bad thing. Alcohol is forbidden in undergrad dorms, and all parties must be registered. The dozens of bars, nightclubs, and restaurants in Georgetown—Martin's Tavern and the Tombs are always popular—are a big draw for students who are legal, but they can get pricey. The Hoyas, a campus pub in the spectacular student activities center, is a more affordable alternative. Popular annual formals such as the Diplomatic and the Blue/Gray Ball force students to dress up and pair off.

Washington offers unsurpassed cultural resources, ranging from the museums of the Smithsonian to the Kennedy Center. "Washington, D.C., is an ideal place to go to school," says one student. "It is a vibrant, cosmopolitan city with many opportunities for cultural enrichment, employment, and community service." And given the city's excellent public transit system and the absence of on-campus parking, a car is probably more trouble than it's worth. "Some of the best road trips," a student says, "are the organized and cheap bus trips to away basketball games."

And speaking of Hoya basketball, should you notice the hills begin to tremble with a deep, resounding, primitive chant—"Hoya…Saxa…Hoya…Saxa"—don't worry; it's just another Georgetown basketball game. Their mascot, the Hoya, is derived from the Greek and Latin phrase, "*hoya saxa*" which means, "what rocks!" Some say it originated in a cheer referring to the stones that comprised the school's outer walls. The Hoya team is always tough, especially when Syracuse, Villanova, or UConn come to town, and GU usually figures prominently in the NCAA postseason tournament in March. The thrill of victory in intramural competition at the superb underground Yates Memorial Field House is not to be missed, either.

For anyone interested in discovering the world, Georgetown offers an outstanding menu of choices. Professors truly pay attention to their undergrads and the diverse student body represents a variety of "interests, aspirations, backgrounds, and perspectives," a senior says. "A combination of excellent location, diverse student body, and passionate people make it a great place to go to school," claims a marketing and management major. The internationally oriented curriculum is unparalleled, and there's always plenty to do on the weekends.

Overlaps

Harvard, Duke, Penn, Boston College, University of Virginia.

If You Apply To ➤ **Georgetown**…Early action: Nov. 1. Regular admissions: Jan. 10. Financial aid: Feb. 1. No campus interviews. Alumni interviews: required, evaluative. SATs or ACTs: required. SAT IIs: recommended (English and any other two). Apply to particular schools or programs. Essay question: personal statement plus one additional question for each school.

If your college daydreams feature parties, bars, and dates rather than lecture halls, libraries, and exams, Georgia Institute of Technology may not be the school for you. On the other hand, if you see college as a stepping stone to a high-paying, prestigious career, a place to work hard for four or five years, have a great time on the weekends, and graduate with a solid professional direction, then you may want to think about "Tech." Georgia Tech students take their studies and future careers—mainly engineering—very seriously. But when the whistle blows, they let down their crew cuts, stash their pocket protectors, and get crazy at basketball and football games, fraternity parties, and in downtown Atlanta.

Located just off the interstate in Georgia's capital city, Georgia Tech's 330-acre campus consists mainly of modern buildings. In 1996, the physical plant was completely transformed by the construction of the Olympic Village on Tech's campus. Its glorious remnants include seven new residence halls, an aquatic center, a coliseum, a sports performance complex, and an amphitheater.

Tech academics are as rigorous as they come, but "that's why a degree from Georgia Tech means so much," claims a senior chemical engineering major. "The courses are challenging and the workload requires an great deal of self discipline," says an electrical engineering major. Before your heart starts missing beats at the thought of this grind, take heed: "Tech students are not dull. We take school seriously but also make time for social activities," says a senior. The institute is a national leader in most engineering fields, notably electrical, computer, civil, industrial and systems, as well as mechanical and aerospace. Materials, ceramic, chemical, and nuclear engineering programs are also part of the curriculum. Degree programs in international affairs and public policy combined with the institute's engineering and science offerings prepare students to make policy in the increasingly technological and global markets of the 21st century. Aside from the technical fare, there is an increasingly popular management college, and a strong school of architecture, which is known for its work in historic preservation and energy conservation. The liberal arts are somewhat weaker, but the general education requirements ensure that all students receive some schooling in the humanities and social sciences. Also weak are the building construction and physics departments. Since most coursework requires computers, students are faced with long lines at the 375 computer labs. Soon, students will be required to bring their own computers; the school hopes to provide each admit with $2,000 to help defray the cost. Another big change has come to Tech: the university recently shifted from quarters to a semester system.

Five years of college is standard at Georgia Tech because of the rigorous academic requirements for engineering students and the popularity of the co-op program. More than 3,000 students finance their education and gain on-the-job experience by working half a school year and going to classes the other half through the school's co-op program. Tech offers a number of five-year combination programs with sections taken at the University of Georgia, 10 historically black colleges, and 20 women's colleges. Special travel programs include a year in Paris for architects, a summer in London for chemical engineers, and a graduate-level degree from Metz, France; others participate in the study abroad programs run jointly with the University of Georgia. After Tech, 70 percent of the students get jobs, while 20 percent go to graduate and professional schools. The school also

Website: www.gatech.edu

Location: City center

Total Enrollment: 12,985

Undergraduates: 9,469

Male/Female: 72/28

SAT Ranges: V 620–630 M 680–690

Financial Aid: 45%

Expense: Pub $ $

Phi Beta Kappa: No

Applicants: 7,676

Accepted: 61%

Enrolled: 39%

Grad in 6 Years: 62%

Returning Freshmen: 85%

Academics: ✍ ✍ ✍ ✍

Social: ☎ ☎

Q of L: ★ ★

Admissions: (404) 894-4154

Email Address:
admissions@
success.gatech.edu

Strongest Programs:
Engineering
Architecture

offers courses and additional resources as a member of the Atlanta Regional Consortium for Higher Education.*

The faculty at Georgia Tech is renowned for its research. They have turned out volumes of learned tracts over the years and have aided in the development of Star Wars defense technology and the space shuttle. Some argue that undergraduate teaching has suffered in the process. "Most of our professors conduct impressive research and some are more interested in the research than in teaching their students," says an international affairs major. Still, Georgia Tech does have many stellar professors. "The professors here are knowledgeable and well respected in their fields," says one student. Don't seek too many cozy seminars at Tech: many classes are large—often more than 100 students. Stringent grading is the rule at Tech: "The biggest problem is trying not to get 'shafted' by professors who must have a certain percentage of their students get low grades in order to 'even out the class average,'" complains a sophomore computer science major.

Nearly two-thirds of Georgia Tech's largely male student body come from Georgia—the vast majority went to public school, and 9 out of 10 ranked in the top fifth of their high school class. Political conservatism is the norm, though most students are too busy studying to pay attention to politics. "Being pro-Republican doesn't hurt at this school," says a senior, but "people are more likely to be arguing about computers or sports than politics," remarks another. One in four Tech students is a racial minority, with African Americans accounting for 10 percent of the student body, Hispanics, 4 percent, and Asian Americans, 12 percent. The Office of Minority Educational Development helps minority students adjust to life at Tech. Technology rules, even in the admissions office, where a complex, computerized formula based on academic average and SAT scores (in varying fractions, set each year by the State Board of Regents) is used to determine clear-cut acceptances and rejections. Human judgment intervenes in borderline cases. To limit burgeoning enrollment, out-of-state applicants must meet slightly higher criteria than their Georgia counterparts. The university does not guarantee to meet the demonstrated financial need of every accepted applicant, but a variety of merit scholarships are awarded each year. In addition, 183 students get full athletic scholarships each year.

The 1996 summer Olympics left more than just memories of Kerri Strug's courageous vault and Michael Johnson's golden dash. Georgia Tech was briefly transformed into the Olympic Village, and when the Olympiads departed, they left Tech with brand-spanking-new dormitories and "refurbished" old ones. "The housing at Tech is awesome," says a junior. "Many of the dorms have full kitchen facilities and individual bedrooms." More than half of Techies live in dorms, and freshmen are guaranteed a room. Most halls are single-sex, though visitation rules are lenient. Students who go Greek often live in their chapter houses; housing off campus is generally comfortable, but parts of the surrounding neighborhood are unsavory. While some students feel infallible despite the urban area, others are more cautious: "I don't go out by myself at night, but during the day the campus is fine. There are campus police and student escort services until 4:00 A.M.," says a senior. Tech has two large dining halls on campus, where the food is said to be "adequate and somewhat overpriced."

Tech's hometown is "Hot-Lanta," as the students refer to it, and it offers an endless supply of social and dining opportunities. As one student puts it, "Atlanta is one of the most exciting cities in the nation. The people are friendly, there are a lot of young adults, a great social atmosphere, good cultural activities, beautiful (and green) spaces, and a booming economy." Another student adds, "Atlanta has more to do than would be possible in a lifetime." Tech students can be found at restaurants or movies in midtown Atlanta, or at teeming bars in Atlanta's Buckhead district. The city also offers plenty of community service opportunities. More than a quarter of the students belong to one of the dozens of fraternities and sororities, which are responsible for a good deal of the on-campus social scene. Greek or not, however, students study much of the weekend (often in groups), although just about everyone takes time out for a sporting event or evening entertainment. "The basketball season at Georgia Tech is awesome and students generally camp out for tickets to the big games," says one student.

Tech's varsity sports have become as big-time as any in the South. During the past few years, Georgia Tech teams have taken home trophies in tennis and track, and women's volleyball and track, and men's basketball. Techies look forward to Homecoming Week, which culminates in the Rambling Wreck Parade of student-owned cars. There's also a traditional "rivalry with the neighboring University of Georgia that escalates each Thanksgiving at the annual 'Georgia game,'" a student explains. Among its many other traditions are some that may seem odd to the uninitiated: "Stealing the T is the most famous prank." Students try to remove the huge yellow letter T from the tower on the administration building and then return it to the school by presenting it to a member of the faculty or administration. The recent addition of alarms, motion sensors, and heat sensors on the T has made the task more difficult but "certainly not impossible for a Georgia Tech engineer," says an electrical engineering major. Another is the Mini 500, a 15-lap tricycle race around a parking garage with three pit stops, a tire change, and a driver rotation.

Georgia Tech students like to say, "We don't fit the mold, we make it." They are proud of their self-direction and promising futures. As one senior puts it, "The students here are intelligent, independent, and driven by very high expectations for the future." Georgia Tech supports their drive by recruiting faculty who are leaders in their fields and by making the campus an enjoyable place to spend four to six years studying. Lively school traditions and the thriving city of Atlanta are waiting for Techies when they're finally ready to take a break.

In 1996, the physical plant was completely transformed by the construction of the Olympic Village on Tech's campus.

Overlaps
University of Georgia, MIT, Duke, Georgia State, Emory.

If You Apply To ➣ **Georgia Tech**…Regular admissions: Feb. 1. Financial aid: Mar. 1. Housing: May 1. Meets demonstrated need of 45%. No campus or alumni interviews. SATs or ACTs: required. SAT IIs: optional. No essay question. Looks for high math and science aptitude.

University of Georgia

212 Terrell Hall, Athens, GA 30602-1633

The University of Georgia is arguably the fastest-rising public university in the country. As recently as a decade ago it was known primarily for its dynamite football team—a sleepy party school that would readily accept virtually anyone with a high school diploma and a 98.6-degree body temperature. Now fast forward to the present. With a big boost from Georgia's Hope Scholarship program, which pays the tuition and fees at any state college or university for Georgia residents with at least a B average, UGA has turned into a highly selective flagship public university that is able to pick and choose from among the region's best high

Website: www.uga.edu
Location: Small city
Total Enrollment: 30,912
Undergraduates: 24,040
Male/Female: 46/54
SAT Ranges: V 550–640 M 550–650

(Continued)

ACT Range: 24–28
Financial Aid: 66%
Expense: Pub $ $
Phi Beta Kappa: Yes
Applicants: 13,791
Accepted: 63%
Enrolled: 51%
Grad in 6 Years: 63%
Returning Freshmen: 89%
Academics: ✍ ✍ ✍
Social: ☎ ☎ ☎ ☎ ☎
Q of L: ★ ★ ★
Admissions: (706) 542-8776
Email Address:
undergrad@admissions.uga.
edu

Strongest Programs:
Business
Journalism
Education
Ecology
Genetics
Studio Art

Selected freshmen can participate in the BIG (Busily Involved at Georgia) Event, a three-day retreat the summer before enrollment designed to introduce students to UGA history and resources, improve leadership skills, and help them adapt to new academic and social challenges of college.

school seniors. The average SAT score and grade point average for entering freshmen has soared, and the university has moved aggressively to provide programs to challenge its new and brainier breed of students. "The quality of professors has improved, and the level of respect given to UGA as a research institution has skyrocketed," says a senior. Enthusiasm for "dem Dawgs" has taken on a new meaning.

Situated on an attractive 605-acre campus, Georgia is speckled with greenery and wooded walks. The older north campus, which houses the administrative offices and law school, features 19th-century architecture and landscaping while more modern buildings and residence halls are found on the southern end of campus. A striking feature is the university's lush botanical garden. Founded in 1785, Georgia was the nation's second chartered state university, and spent most of its first two centuries expanding. New facilities include the $18.5-million Animal Science Complex and the $19.6-million Animal Health Research Center. Planned facilities include the 60,000-square-foot Applied Genomics Technology Center.

Despite great strides toward improving the quality of education and the campus, some UGA undergraduates still take a low-key approach to the academic program. Many of the toughest academic requirements are found in premedical, preveterinary, and other preprofessional concentrations, as well as in the highly regarded honors program. UGA's strongest programs include business (especially accounting and management), journalism, ecology, and genetics, but students rate the math department as weak due to its small size. Broadcast news, wildlife and wetlands management, digital media, science illustration, and sport studies are just a few of the newest additions to UGA's undergraduate program. The core curriculum requires students to complete a total of 42 semester hours in humanities and fine arts, English, natural sciences, mathematics, social sciences, environmental concerns, and cultural diversity. Selected freshmen can participate in the BIG (Busily Involved at Georgia) Event, a three-day retreat the summer before enrollment designed to introduce students to UGA history and resources, improve leadership skills, and help them adapt to new academic and social challenges of college.

Professors at the University of Georgia receive high marks from the students. "The professors here are excellent," says an international business major. "All professors are accessible, cooperative, and encouraging for the most part," adds another. Registration for classes, previously a formidable process at UGA, has been significantly simplified by a computerized registration system that allows students to enroll electronically. First pick for all courses usually goes to honors students and varsity athletes, and the rest follow by seniority. Gut courses can be found for those intent upon attending Camp Georgia, but serious students may partake of several special programs, such as a five-year business/engineering degree offered in conjunction with Georgia Tech. In addition, UGA offers study abroad programs in France, Germany, Greece, Italy, and five other foreign countries. Summer courses, night classes, and free tutorial sessions are also available as well as high-quality services for the student with learning disabilities. The school also offers courses and additional resources as a member of the Atlanta Regional Consortium for Higher Education.*

The university's student body is overwhelmingly Georgian and 82 percent are public school graduates. Many belong to one of more than a dozen religious organizations on campus (the Wesley Foundation is the largest) or become members of one the other 400-odd campus organizations. African Americans account for 6 percent of the students, and Hispanics and Asian Americans combine for 4 percent. "Race and diversity are big issues on campus," says a senior. Georgia makes its admissions decisions without regard to student financial need. The school does not guarantee to meet the demonstrated need of every admit, but 39 percent of admitted students are offered complete financial aid packages. Aid is awarded on a first-come, first-served basis. There are hundreds of merit scholarships and 97 percent of in-state freshmen receive the Georgia Hope Scholarship, which covers full tuition and is renewable for students who maintain at least a B average.

Tales of miscreant air-conditioning and elevators in some regular dorms often lure freshmen to the high-rise variety, where they find the smallest rooms on campus. Most upperclassmen prefer the roomier low-rise dorms, if they haven't already moved off campus. The residence halls are described as "pretty decent and livable." One student says, "Housing on campus takes some adjusting, but the dorms are well kept and secure." Students aren't required to buy one of the two meal plans (for five or seven days a week), but most do. There are three dining halls plus the student union's snack bar. On-campus activities are numerous. "At a school this size, there is always something going on that everyone can enjoy, whether it be sports or a cultural event," says one senior. Downtown Athens—a well-known spot on the national rock map, having spawned such hit groups as R.E.M. and the B-52's—borders the university and provides free bus service and an abundance of diversions. "Athens gets a '10' for being a college town," says a psychology major. "It's a very artsy place and the people are extremely friendly." One nightclub enthusiast notes that many of the clubs in Athens cater to UGA students and admit those who are under 21 as long as they get a stamp saying they can't drink. It is difficult but not impossible to obtain alcohol on campus. "Underage students can easily obtain alcohol but usually get caught trying to do so," says one student.

"How 'bout dem Dawgs?" is the question that's likely to roll off the lips of Athens residents, who worship UGA's fierce football team. But other sports have been impressive lately as well. UGA's gymnastics team is strong. Men's and women's golf teams, women's basketball and swimming and diving teams regularly capture conference and national titles as well. The university has everything the weekend jock could want, including indoor and outdoor tennis and swimming; handball, racquetball, and tennis courts; and a jogging and exercise trail. Athletic rivalries with Auburn, Florida, and Georgia Tech make the hairs stand up on the Bulldogs' necks. A speech communications major jokes that Georgia has a tremendous disgust for the color orange, since it reminds them of Florida and Tennessee.

Georgia's 30 fraternities and 21 sororities provide most of the social activity, though a campus policy banning open parties has put a damper on things. Only 15 percent of the men and 19 percent of the women pledge, but almost everyone attends at least a couple of Greek bashes each year. Atlanta is only an hour away, and Savannah and Myrtle Beach are other popular getaways. Students descend on Florida en masse twice a year: first for the Florida football game and then for spring break.

With more than 24,000 undergraduates, UGA is not a school where students are coddled. But outstanding educational opportunities—like scientific research and the honors program—await serious students, just as football games and live music await those who want to coast. Says one satisfied Dawg: "UGA offers so many incredible opportunities and programs that everyone can find a niche here."

Broadcast news, wildlife and wetlands management, digital media, science illustration, and sport studies are just a few of the newest additions to UGA's undergraduate program.

Overlaps

Georgia State, Georgia Tech, Georgia Southern, Florida State, Emory.

Gettysburg College

Gettysburg, PA 17325-1484

Website: www.gettysburg.edu

Location: Small town

Total Enrollment: 2,182

Undergraduates: 2,182

Male/Female: 48/52

SAT Ranges: V 540–630 M 550–630

Financial Aid: 57%

Expense: Pr $ $ $ $

Phi Beta Kappa: Yes

Applicants: 3,871

Accepted: 68%

Enrolled: 26%

Grad in 6 Years: 75%

Returning Freshmen: 90%

Academics: ✍ ✍ ✍

Social: ☎ ☎ ☎

Q of L: ★ ★ ★

Admissions: (717) 337-6100 or (800) 431-0803

Email Address: admiss@gettysburg.edu

Strongest Programs:
History
Psychology
Natural Sciences
Business
Political Science

Mention the word "Gettysburg," and patriotic heart palpitations and echoes of the "Battle Hymn of the Republic" are likely to occur. Whether the reference is to the Pennsylvania town steeped in Civil War history or the small, high-caliber college located in the famed battlefield's backyard, a certain pride and reverence become immediately evident. This feeling is not lost on students at Gettysburg College, who come to southeastern Pennsylvania looking not only to acquaint themselves with the American past but also to gear themselves up for the future.

Situated in the midst of gently rolling hills, Gettysburg's 200-acre campus is "a historical treasure," an eclectic assemblage of Georgian, Greek, Romanesque, Gothic Revival, and modern architecture, plus several styles not easily categorized. One campus building—Penn Hall—was actually used as a hospital during the Battle of Gettysburg. Rumor has it that ghostly soldiers can still be seen walking the grounds.

Indoors, the English department, home of the *Gettysburg Review*, is among the strongest at Gettysburg, as are the natural sciences, which are well endowed with state-of-the-art equipment. The fine psychology department offers opportunities for students to participate in faculty research. The management major is the most popular. Also popular, of course, is the excellent history department, which is bolstered by the school's nationally recognized and prestigious Civil War Institute. The library system boasts more than 345,000 volumes, a library/learning resource center, and an online computer catalog search. Students agree that there are hardly any "weak" departments. "I don't think there are any weak departments," says a student, "just some that are smaller." These include physics and classics.

The small class sizes make for close student-faculty relationships. "All the professors are quite knowledgeable and passionate about their subjects and are always available for extra help," says a sophomore. Advising is often described as "excellent" by students. "[My advisor] is always there for me, professionally, academically, and personally," says one happy undergrad. The college-wide honor system contributes to the atmosphere of community and mutual trust. About a third of each student's coursework is spent on distribution requirements covering many fields, including religion (a remnant of the days when the school's Lutheran affiliation really meant something). The freshman seminar in liberal learning, also required, aims at strengthening reasoning, writing, and speaking skills using a multidisciplinary theme. Another popular program is the Area Studies Symposium, which focuses each year on a different region of the world and offers lectures and films for the whole campus in addition to academic credit for participating students. There are disciplinary programs such as biochemistry, environmental studies, and Latin American studies.

Gettysburg sponsors a Washington semester with American University, a United Nations semester through Drew University in New Jersey, and cooperative dual degree programs in engineering and forestry. The management, biology, and physics departments offer structured internships, and the chemistry department offers a summer cooperative research program between students and professors in which most chemistry majors participate and work on a joint publication. Through the Central Pennsylvania Consortium, students may take courses at two nearby colleges, Dickinson and Franklin and Marshall. Outstanding seniors may participate in the Senior Scholar's Seminar, with independent study on a major contemporary issue, but all students have a chance to do independent work and/or design their own majors. Study abroad programs are approved on a case-by-case basis. There are programs in affiliation with the Center for Cross-Cultural Study in Seville, Spain, and the Université de Haute Bretagne in Rennes, France.

Conservative, white, and middle to upper middle class describes about 95 percent of Gettysburg's students. "As opposed to our rivals, I would say our students are more attractive and pretty ambitious," quips a senior. Though the administration is trying to lure more minorities with activities sponsored by the Intercultural Advancement Division, black, Asian American, and Hispanic enrollment each constitute 1 percent. Students are so interested in public service that the school set up a Center for Public Service to direct their community activities. "Gettysburg has a continuous concern for the connection between the classroom and life off and beyond the campus," reports a veteran. Three-quarters of the students come from public high school, and the majority were in the top quarter of their high school class. No athletic scholarships are available, and the number of offerings based on academic merit varies by year.

"The residence life staff is excellent," enthuses one denizen. "Freshman year they match you up very well and are conscientious about making sure you are happy in your residence." Campus housing is guaranteed all four years, and students can choose from coed residence halls or single-sex halls with three visitation options. The top scholars in each class get first crack at the best rooms. Student rooms have been added in renovated historical properties on campus, and there are more options for interest housing and suite living. About a fifth of the men live in fraternity houses; the sororities are nonresidential. Off-campus apartments lure 10 to 15 percent of the upperclassmen, but freshmen are required to remain in the residence halls and take three meals a day in the renovated dining hall. There are a variety of dining options, including the ever popular Bullet Hole, the campus snack bar and grill room where many students take their regular meals. Kitchens are also available in the residences for upperclassmen.

Social life at the 'Burg involves the Greek system and other activities. Thirty-eight percent of the men belong to the dozen fraternities; the seven sororities draw 42 percent of the women. Greek parties are open and attract crowds eager to dance the night away, although students insist that "they definitely aren't the only source of fun on campus." A Student Activities Committee provides alternative social events, including concerts, comedians, bus trips to Georgetown, movies, and campus coffeehouses. Favorable reviews have come in for the campus nightclub. Those who get the munchies can make the short walk to the Lincoln Diner or take a brief road trip to Stavros, a locally famous pizza parlor. Officially the campus is dry, but like many such campuses, drinking can be done, albeit carefully, students report. The orchards and rolling countryside surrounding the campus are peaceful and scenic, and there is a small ski slope nearby. Students also get free passes to the historic attractions in town. Many participate in the November 19 Fortenbaugh Lecture by noted historians commemorating

The English department, home of the Gettysburg Review, is among the strongest at Gettysburg, as are the natural sciences, which are well endowed with state-of-the-art equipment.

the Gettysburg Address and in the yearly wreath-laying ceremony in front of the Eisenhower Admissions Office to commemorate the general's birthday. Geared toward the tourist trade because of its historical legacy, Gettysburg occupies a spot "in the middle of nowhere but not far from anywhere," within an hour and a half of Washington, D.C., and considerably closer to Baltimore, where students enjoy the scenic Inner Harbor area.

About a quarter of Gettysburg's students earn varsity letters, and the college has upgraded the women's athletic program. Women's field hockey and swimming are traditionally strong, while men's baseball and lacrosse have also won conference titles. Both the men's and women's soccer teams have competed in the Division III playoffs. The annual football game against Dickinson draws a good turnout, and the "little brown bucket" is passed to the team that wins. Both track and swimming frequently produce all-Americans.

"This college recognizes that its job is to prepare students for the future," says a veteran, and does "an excellent job of achieving that." Students here appreciate the school's approach to preparing them for their future in a world that is in dire need of those who can think and learn for themselves. And what a fine backdrop the town of Gettysburg and its grand history make, where men and women put their beliefs into action!

Overlaps

Bucknell, Dickinson, Franklin and Marshall, Lafayette, Richmond.

If You Apply To >

Gettysburg…Early decision: Feb. 1. Regular admissions and financial aid: Feb. 15. Meets demonstrated need of 95%. Campus interviews: strongly recommended, evaluative. No alumni interviews. SATs or ACTs: required. SAT IIs: optional. Essay question: significant experience; important issue or person.

Gordon College

255 Grapevine Road, Wenham, MA 01984

Website: www.gordon.edu
Location: Suburban
Total Enrollment: 1,548
Undergraduates: 1,487
Male/Female: 47/53
SAT Ranges: V 540–660 M 540–640
Financial Aid: 74%
Expense: Pr $
Phi Beta Kappa: No
Applicants: 963
Accepted: 76%
Enrolled: 58%
Grad in 6 Years: 61%
Returning Freshmen: 87%
Academics: ✐ ✐ ✐
Social: ☎ ☎

At Gordon College, students receive an education that not only feeds the mind but the soul as well. In an ever changing world, the mission of Gordon has remained the same: "To graduate men and women distinguished by intellectual maturity and Christian character." Students praise the school's ability to "incorporate a Christian perspective into the academics" and enjoy the company of "friendly people who are committed to God and committed to learning." For these students, Gordon's integration of solid academics, traditional values, and a caring faculty is truly a blessing.

Gordon is located on the scenic North Shore in Massachusetts, 3 miles from the Atlantic Coast and 25 miles from Boston. The beautiful campus lies in the midst of hundreds of acres of forest land and five lakes, one of which students use for swimming in the warmer months. The academic buildings and dorms are clustered in one small area so it doesn't take more than two or three minutes to walk anywhere on campus. Most of the buildings are Georgian influenced, traditional red brick, except for the old stone mansion that houses the administration and faculty offices. Recent additions to the campus include the Phillips Music Center and Barrington Center for the arts.

Religious commitment is seen as an enhancement rather than a threat to free and rigorous academic inquiry at Gordon. "We are different from other similar institutions in that Gordon is committed to a traditional liberal arts education along with the historic Christian faith," explains one administrator. Psychology, English, and education are the most popular majors, and not surprisingly, the programs in biblical and theological studies are strong. Music, English, and sociology are also good offerings. Computer science receives weaker ratings due to inadequate facilities.

Gordon's core curriculum of interdisciplinary studies includes courses in biblical studies, computer sciences, math, humanities, social and behavioral sciences, natural sciences, and fine arts. Freshmen are also required to take a first-year seminar as well as New and Old Testament history, literature and theology, and writing. Fitting all this into a schedule is a challenge, and many students find they have to set up their four-year study plan as soon as they arrive. The faculty receives high marks for being knowledgeable and concerned. "My professors are amazing," says an elementary education and psychology double major. "Their lives are dedicated to the students and they all strive to enrich not only our intellectual life but our entire being as well." Another student adds, "The professors here are very accessible and ready to talk about anything, including those things not related to class work."

Gordon offers an interesting array of off-campus programs. Those interested in politics may go to Washington, D.C., with the American Studies program, or go international as part of the Council for Christian Colleges and Universities. About 45 students each year are placed in cooperative-education jobs that give them experience in area high-tech firms, Boston publishing houses, and local service organizations. About 240 of the best students get merit scholarships ranging from $500 to $15,000. Students come to Gordon from all over the United States in search of a college that integrates faith and learning, although this regional diversity doesn't result in ethnic diversity as well. Most students are white, middle class, and socially conservative, and about one-third are from Massachusetts. African Americans constitute only 1 percent of the student body, while Hispanics and Asian Americans each represent 2 percent. Gordon students face the same campus issues as most college students—homosexuality and abortion, for example—yet most "look at the social and political issues from a Christian point of view," says a student.

"Coed dorms" at Gordon mean that men and women live in separate wings of the same building separated by a lobby, a lounge, and a laundry room. Persons of the opposite sex are allowed to traverse these barriers only at specified times. The dorms are modern and comfortable, and freshmen can count on getting the nicest rooms. The other three classes enter a lottery for the remainder. Only 16 percent of students live off campus, with permission to move out granted only after all the dorms are filled. As drinking and smoking are forbidden on campus (and can result in suspension or expulsion), the dining hall is a main focus of campus social life. The food offerings and services have vastly improved with the addition of the food court. Gordon has been rated the third safest school in the nation, and many students feel secure leaving dorms and bikes unlocked.

In between chapel services and Bible classes, students also find time for sports. Of particular note, the men's and women's soccer teams are rated among the top 10 best in New England. For outdoorsy types, Gordon's setting on Cape Ann is ideal, though others might describe it as a bit isolated. The campus offers cross-country ski trails and ponds for swimming, sailing, and skating. The ocean is a quick bike ride away, and students frequently ski New Hampshire's nearby White Mountains. For social activities, most students are content with weekend excursions to Boston, church-related functions, movies, and an occasional square

(Continued)

Q of L: ★ ★ ★ ★

Admissions: (978) 927-2300 or (800) 343-1379

Email Address: admissions@gordon.edu

Strongest Programs:
Biblical Studies
Biology
Education
English
Music
Psychology
Social Sciences

At Gordon, religious commitment is seen as an enhancement rather than a threat to free and rigorous academic inquiry.

Gordon has been rated the third safest school in the nation, and many students feel secure leaving dorms and bikes unlocked.

dance; all look forward to the Castle Hill Christmas formal (held in a real castle) and the Last Blast spring party. "The social life here is great," says a student. "There's always something to do."

At Gordon, ancient biblical dictates have a huge impact on campus life, regulating the very boundaries of what's acceptable in speech and conduct. Though many modern-day students would chafe at such restrictions, the rules are an integral part of why students here chose Gordon. They appreciate the shared sense of purpose and spirit fostered when all members of the community adhere to the gospel of Christ. They pray for the reconciliation of the "God Squad" and the "Alternative Crew," two campus groups with opposing beliefs, for example. And when they leave, they do so happily, equipped with lasting friendships, imbued with optimism, grounded in faith, and prepared to work as servant-leaders in the global community.

If You Apply To ➤ Gordon…Rolling admissions. Early decision: Dec. 1. Financial aid: Mar. 1. Does not guarantee to meet demonstrated need. Campus interviews: required, evaluative. No alumni interviews. SATs: required. SAT IIs: optional. Accepts electronic applications. Essay question: Do you consider yourself a Christian; and why a college like Gordon?

Goucher College

1021 Dulaney Valley Road, Towson, MD 21204

Website: www.goucher.edu
Location: Suburban
Total Enrollment: 1,700
Undergraduates: 1,131
Male/Female: 28/72
SAT Ranges: V 550–660 M 520–630
ACT Range: 21–28
Financial Aid: 58%
Expense: Pr $ $ $
Phi Beta Kappa: Yes
Applicants: 2,121
Accepted: 83%
Enrolled: 18%
Grad in 6 Years: 64%
Returning Freshmen: 80%
Academics: ✍ ✍ ✍
Social: ☎ ☎ ☎
Q of L: ★ ★ ★
Admissions: (410) 337-6100
Email Address:
admissions@goucher.edu

Goucher, a private, liberal arts and sciences college, has a strong reputation for quality academics, and for combining classroom study with extensive off-campus and international experiences. Once a women's college, Goucher is now committed to empowering men and women of all ages and backgrounds, educating and representing them equally in an intimate setting. "The best thing about Goucher is its size," says a dance major. "It's a small community that allows us to feel more connected, not only with other students but with the faculty as well."

Indeed, Goucher has a long-standing history of excellence. Phi Beta Kappa established a chapter on campus only 20 years after the college was founded, and the college ranks among the nation's top 50 liberal arts colleges in turning out students destined for Ph.D.s in the sciences. Set on 287 landscaped acres in the suburbs of Baltimore, Goucher's wooded campus features lush lawns, stately fieldstone buildings, and rare trees and shrubs from all corners of the globe. Yet despite the pastoral ambiance, the campus is a short walk from the suburban community of Towson.

A rigorous general education program forms the foundation of every Goucher student's education. The core curriculum requires a first-year colloquium (Frontiers), one course in each of the humanities, social sciences, and mathematics, a lecture/lab course in the natural sciences, computer proficiency, and four physical education courses (including first-semester Transitions). Of Goucher's offerings, the science department's are arguably the strongest, with a nuclear magnetic resonance spectrometer and scientific visualization lab available for student use. Other facilities include dedicated research space, a greenhouse, and an observatory with a six-inch refractor telescope. The dance and education departments are also strong. Physics, once cited as weak, has been strengthened and is now offered as a major. An honors program offers special team-taught interdisciplinary seminars for participants from freshman through senior years. Interdisciplinary programs include international studies, peace studies, American studies, Judaic studies (in cooperation with Baltimore Hebrew University), and a program in theory, culture, and interpretation. There's also a German minor offered through Loyola College (MD), and a 4–1 program in international business ending with a Goucher BA and an MA with California's Monterey Institute of International Studies. Future engineers can take advantage of the 3–2 program offered in conjunction with the Whiting School of Engineering at Johns Hopkins University.

For those with wanderlust, Goucher sponsors working trips to numerous countries, including Israel, France, Spain, Ghana, and Germany, as well as an exchange program with a Ukrainian university. In addition, Goucher students may take courses at nearby Johns Hopkins and seven smaller area colleges. The campus library houses 280,000 volumes and draws complaints from some students, mainly because it closes at 6:00 P.M. on Saturdays. However, Goucher students have free access to the libraries at Hopkins and other nearby schools.

Faculty members here devote most of their time and energy to undergraduate teaching and have a good rapport with students. "I have had wonderful professors at Goucher who are more than willing to go out of their way to help their students," says a political science major. Each freshman has a faculty advisor to assist with the academic and overall adjustment to college life, which are made easier by Goucher's trademark small classes and individual instruction. A sophomore adds, "Even if I hated everything else here, I would stay for the close interaction with engaging teachers." The top students strive for better, and many hold leadership roles." Another student says, "There is pressure to do well but more often than not it's the students who place it on themselves." In addition to their academic work, all Goucher students are required to do a three-credit internship or off-campus experience related to their major. Popular choices include congressional offices, museums, law firms, and newspapers. Another option is the three-week-long Public Policy Seminar in Washington, D.C., where students meet informally with political luminaries.

Thirty-five percent of Goucher's students are homegrown, and most of the rest hail from Pennsylvania, Virginia, New York, and New Jersey. African Americans, Hispanics, and Asian Americans together make up about 15 percent of the student body. Diversity, one student says, "is discussed easily in the small Goucher community," and students agree that multiculturalism is an important campus issue. Goucher offers unlimited merit scholarships for those who are qualified, some providing full tuition, room, and board each year. And coeducation seems to be working well; applications for recent classes have increased substantially, and enrollment is up.

Goucher has four coed dormitories, divided into 13 residential units of about 50 students each. Freshmen double up in spacious rooms, while upperclassmen select housing through lotteries; the available singles usually go to juniors and seniors, though a lucky sophomore may occasionally get one. "At present, there are only six triples," says a sophomore who lives in one. "The rest are apartments, singles or doubles, but we enjoy our room. We have great cable and Internet/voice-mail hookups." The administration has been offering incentives to upperclassmen, encouraging them to move off campus to avoid a housing crunch; women who want an apartment closer to male-dominated Johns Hopkins can usually get one.

And what about the social life? "It stinks," says a junior, citing a "significant

Of Goucher's offerings, the science department's are arguably the strongest, with a nuclear magnetic resonance spectrometer and scientific visualization lab available for student use.

Interdisciplinary programs include international studies, peace studies, American studies, Judaic studies (in cooperation with Baltimore Hebrew University), and a program in theory, culture, and interpretation.

Future engineers can take advantage of the 3–2 program offered in conjunction with the Whiting School of Engineering at Johns Hopkins University.

lack of planned events." The 3:1 female-to-male ratio doesn't help matters, either. Access to a car is a virtual necessity, for many students travel to nearby universities (Loyola and Towson State) or Baltimore's Inner Harbor for entertainment. Students who are of age frequent restaurants and bars in Towson, the small but bustling college town a five-minute walk away. Goucher has no sororities or fraternities, but the close-knit housing units hold periodic events, and the college hosts plenty of weekend movies, concerts, and lectures. Major annual social events include Rocktoberfest, Spring Fling, and the Blind Date Ball each fall ("It can be great, or your roommate can be dead at sunup," a sophomore quips). Biggest of all is GIG, Get-into-Goucher Day, when classes are unexpectedly canceled and the whole campus celebrates. Popular road trips include Ocean City, New York, Philadelphia, and Washington, D.C.

Since Goucher was a women's college for so many years, women's athletics are more highly developed than those at many coed schools. Successful teams include field hockey, tennis, swimming, volleyball, lacrosse, soccer, and cross-country. The genteel sport of horseback riding is popular, thanks to the indoor equestrian ring, stables, and beautiful wooded campus trails. Goucher also has several tennis courts, a driving range, practice fields, a swimming pool, and saunas.

Nostalgic alumnae no doubt shed some tears at the passing of the old Goucher, but the switch to coeducation seems to have worked well. The school's traditional Southern stance has slowly evolved into a more Northern-looking slant. And more recently, its bucolic location, large investment in technology, strong academic reputation, and "all those girls" have helped bring more guys to Goucher. Every year that the percentage of men at Goucher creeps toward 50, this quaint school comes closer to becoming truly coed—and to proving that the genders can succeed in tandem.

Overlaps

Towson State, University of Maryland, University of Maryland–Baltimore County, Loyola (MD), NYU.

If You Apply To ➤ **Goucher**...Early Decision: Nov. 15. Early action: Dec. 1. Regular admissions: Feb. 1. Financial aid: Feb. 15. Guarantees to meet demonstrated need. Campus interviews: recommended, informational. Alumni interviews: optional, informational. SATs or ACTs: required. SAT IIs: optional. Accepts the Common Application. Essay questions: significant experience or achievement; personal, local, national or international issue and why it is important to you; significant person; topic of own choosing. Interview, essay, and recommendations stressed.

Grinnell College

Box 805, Grinnell, IA 50112

Website: www.grinnell.edu
Location: Small town
Total Enrollment: 1,335
Undergraduates: 1,335
Male/Female: 45/55
SAT Ranges: V 620–730 M 610–710
ACT Range: 27–31
Financial Aid: 66%
Expense: Pr $ $

Josiah Grinnell was the young man to whom Horace Greeley addressed his famous admonition in 1846 to "Go West, young man, go West." The result of Grinnell's wanderings into the rural Iowa cornfields, 55 miles from Des Moines and 60 from Iowa City, is the remarkable college that bears his name. The school's location is better known for the movie *Field of Dreams* than for its academic prowess. But despite its physical remoteness, Grinnell is a powerhouse on the national scene. Ever progressive, it was the first college west of the Mississippi to admit African Americans and women, and the first in the country to establish an undergraduate department of political science. It was once a stop on the Underground Railroad, and its graduates include Harry Hopkins, architect of the New Deal, and Robert Noyce, inventor of the integrated circuit, two people who did as much as any pair to change the face of American society in the 20th century. Grinnell is now second only to Carleton as the best liberal arts college in the Midwest.

The school's 95-acre campus is an attractive blend of collegiate Gothic and modern Bauhaus academic buildings and Prairie-style houses. (Architecture buffs should take note of the dazzling Louis Sullivan bank facade right off campus.) The Noyce Science Center, a technological showpiece, recently underwent a $15.3-million renovation, and a 75,000-square-foot addition to the Fine Arts Center—including gallery, studio, performing and rehearsal space—has been completed.

True to its liberal arts focus, Grinnell maintains an open academic style without a structured set of requirements. As one student says, the school is "very liberal, academically and socially." Students determine their own course of study with the aid of a faculty member. The only requirement outside the major field is the first-year tutorial, modeled after Oxford University's program. The more than 30 tutorials, limited to 13 students each, are designed to enhance critical thinking, research, writing, and discussion skills, and to allow first-year students to work individually with professors. Study abroad is offered in London and more than 100 other locations. Co-op programs in architecture, business, law, and medicine and 3–2 engineering programs are additional options.

Strong departments are those in the natural sciences and foreign languages, boosted by a major influx of research grants, including one from the National Science Foundation. The chemistry department (including the new biological chemistry major) draws its majors into independent research projects, and biology, English, and philosophy are popular, too. Russian majors can take a semester in Moscow, St. Petersburg, or Krasnodar. Anthropology and Chinese studies also draw raves. Programs earning negative reviews include American Studies, art, and music.

The Afro-American studies interdisciplinary concentration has been changed to Africana studies, to emphasize history, literature, and traditions in Africa and the African diaspora. Students can take advantage of more than 100 study abroad options, including those offered through the Associated Colleges of the Midwest* consortium and the Grinnell-in-London program.

Grinnell's standards are high, and nearly a quarter of alums move on to graduate and professional schools. Students who don't mind studying, even on weekends, will be happiest here. "During midterms and finals, Grinnell is known as Grin-Hell," a senior says. Another adds, "The courses are very rigorous and we have a very heavy courseload, but there is a great spirit of cooperative learning." Teaching is the top priority for Grinnell faculty members, since the college awards no graduate degrees, and "the profs are generally really good," says a sophomore. "They are all virtual geniuses in their fields, although they are not always great teachers." A side benefit of Grinnell's lack of graduate students is no TAs; all courses are taught by professors, whose main job is to do just that. Academic advising also receives near-universal praise: "You pick your advisor, so you know what you're getting," an English major reasons. It's rare to find classes with more than 50 students, and the great majority of classes have 25 or fewer.

The Burling Library is plush, close to the dorms, and well stocked with periodicals and over 390,000 volumes, an impressive collection for a small college. Grinnell is a national leader in the use of computers in arts and science education, and over 280 computer terminals are available for student use in several locations around the campus, including the library and residence halls.

Grinnell is a bit of Greenwich Village in corn country. Despite the rural environment, the college attracts an urban clientele, especially from the Chicago area.

(Continued)

Phi Beta Kappa: Yes
Applicants: 1,816
Accepted: 65%
Enrolled: 28%
Grad in 6 Years: 82%
Returning Freshmen: 92%
Academics: ✍ ✍ ✍ ✍
Social: ☎ ☎
Q of L: ★ ★ ★
Admissions: (800) 247-0113
Email Address: askgrin@ grinnell.edu

Strongest Programs:
Foreign Languages
Biology
Chemistry

The Afro-American studies interdisciplinary concentration has been changed to Africana studies, to emphasize history, literature, and traditions in Africa and the African diaspora.

Students range "from practical and sporty to artsy and philosophical," but most are liberal and progressive: "Everyone is intelligent and individual," says an anthropology and Latin American studies major. "It's nice to come here after being taught to conform for four years of high school." The campus is very socially and politically aware, and groups like PAFA (the Politically Active Feminist Alliance), GEAR (Grinnell Escalating AIDS Response), and Fearless (formed to combat gender-based violence) set the tone. Community service is also a big draw. A popular T-shirt points to "150 years of anarchy and revolution at Grinnell College."

The financial aid office works overtime to guarantee to meet the full demonstrated financial need of every admit, and that extends to funding study abroad. There are a number of merit scholarships for first-year students, and National Merit Scholars who list Grinnell as their first choice are automatic recipients. Grinnell's portfolio managers have been among the best in the country in recent years, posting the highest return in the country and boosting its healthy endowment to $1 billion. Budget cuts are not a problem at Grinnell, and a junior says the grant portion of her financial aid package actually increased after her first year.

The college guarantees four years of campus housing and 86 percent of students take advantage of the dorms, which they describe as well-maintained. "All dorms have kitchens on each floor, cable, and a computer room," a happy denizen explains. All but two dorms are coed, and after freshman year students participate in a room draw. Two dining halls, one on each side of the campus, serve food that is rumored to be the best college cuisine in America. Meal plans range from full board to just dinner, and special dinners are served family-style every other Wednesday night.

Student opinion of the town of Grinnell (pop. 8,900) ranges from "dumpy" to "charming." "The town is very small," deadpans a junior. "The stereotypical small Iowa town." Community service helps bridge the town-gown gap. Outdoor recreation is popular, and the area near Rock Creek State Park lends itself to biking, running, and cross-country skiing. There are a few bars and pizza joints downtown, but for those craving bright lights, Iowa City and Des Moines are within an hour's drive of campus, and Chicago and Minneapolis are each about four hours distant.

With no fraternities or sororities, intramurals and all-campus parties revolve mainly around the dorms. Each dorm periodically sponsors a party using wordplay from its name in the title. For instance, Mary B. James Hall puts on the Mary-Be-James party, in which everyone comes in drag. As for alcohol, a philosophy major reports, "Campus policy is very lenient. Basically, we do whatever we want with the understanding that we'll be responsible for our actions." A classmate adds, "If you want alcohol, it's about as hard to get as a candy bar...and while not every Grinellian drinks, if you don't, you'll eventually grow bored of the scene."

Nondrinkers need not fear, however. Grinnell offers a wide variety of social groups and activities, such as the Society for Creative Anachronism, the Black Cultural Center, improvisational workshops, poetry readings, and GORP (Grinnell Outdoor Recreational Program), which sponsors outdoor trips and provides the necessary tents, canoes, backpacks, cross-country skis, and kayaks. The student union, known as the Forum, is a popular hangout, as is the Harris Social Center, which offers movies, parties, and concerts on weekends. Highlights of the campus calendar include semiformal Winter and Spring Waltzes ("Yes, we really waltz"), where "most people wear formals and look very nice, not a common occurrence at a school where comfort is the usual standard and women rarely wear makeup," notes one student. Another dance party is Disco, where "everyone dresses up in clothes from the '70s and dances all night." Other social events are a band/tie-dying fest called Alice in Wonderland, a student-made film festival, Pipe Cleaner Day ("May 5 generally brings upwards of 20,000 of the sculptable wires to campus"), and the Zirkle Circle, described by a senior as "a spontaneous dance around a famous campus sculpture, usually after imbibing intoxicating liquids." Grinnell competes in Division III, and the men's cross-country, basketball, swimming, and soccer teams have garnered conference championships in recent years. The football team finished the 1998-1999 season with a championship. On the women's side, both the basketball and soccer teams have won conference titles.

Grinnell wouldn't put a grin on every prospective college student's face. Its "students are its biggest assets as well as its largest turn-off," admits an anthropology major. "They are active, interesting, and unique. Unfortunately, this can lead to self-righteousness and an exaggerated sense of self-importance." Still, for those seeking the combination of small-town friendliness and safety with the bend toward social and political activism more common in big cities, Grinnell could be a great place to spend four years. The school's openness and flexibility make it easy for students to wring the most from their college experiences; all majors leave with the ability to "think, analyze, interpret, and communicate," and few leave disappointed.

If You Apply To ➤ Grinnell...Early decision: Nov. 1. Regular admissions: Jan. 20. Financial aid: Feb. 1. Guarantees to meet demonstrated need. Campus interviews: recommended, evaluative. Alumni interviews: optional, informational. SATs or ACTs: required. SAT IIs: optional. Essay question: changed opinion; or original essay (expository, fictional, or poetic, but descriptive of applicant's style and abilities).

Guilford College

5800 West Friendly Avenue, Greensboro, NC 27410

Founded in 1837 by the Religious Society of Friends (Quakers), Guilford College is one of the nation's best-kept secrets. Consistent with its heritage, students and teachers here are on a first-name basis. "The Quaker heritage and liberal social consciousness of Guilford has changed the lives of many students," says a senior. "You learn to value the sense of community that thrives here." Students at Guilford are also offered a seriously good education, based on Quaker principles of inclusiveness and equality but with an up-to-date emphasis on interdisciplinary and service learning.

Located on 340 wooded acres in northwest Greensboro, Guilford is the only liberal arts college in the Southeast with Quaker roots. Guilford is also the oldest coeducational institution in the South and the third oldest in the nation. It was one of a few Southern colleges to remain open throughout the Civil War and was an embarkation point on the Underground Railroad. The buildings are Georgian in style and feature redbrick construction. Beyond the campus gates students can find all of the essentials—restaurants, grocery stores, movie theaters, and numerous specialty shops. Downtown Greensboro is only ten minutes away,

Website: www.guilford.edu
Location: City outskirts
Total Enrollment: 1,245
Undergraduates: 1,245
Male/Female: 47/53
SAT Ranges: V 530–660 M 510–620
ACT Range: 22–27
Financial Aid: 55%
Expense: Pr $
Phi Beta Kappa: No
Applicants: 1,227
Accepted: 76%
Enrolled: 25%

(Continued)

Grad in 6 Years: 59%

Returning Freshmen: 78%

Academics: ✍ ✍ ✍

Social: ☎ ☎

Q of L: ★ ★ ★

Admissions: (800) 992-7759

Email Address:
admission@guilford.edu

Strongest Programs:
English
Geology
Management
Justice and Policy Studies
Psychology
Education

The physics department gives students hands-on experience with the technical tools professional scientists use, including a seismograph, an observatory, and equipment for research in optics, robotics, and laser technology.

Guilford also believes in experiential learning and offers the option of studying geology in the Rocky Mountains, marine biology on the East Coast, art in New York City, or political science in Washington, D.C.

while the riches of Raleigh, Durham, and Chapel Hill are within easy driving distance. The Frank Family Science Center, complete with a computer-driven, sixteen-inch telescope, opened its doors recently and construction is underway on a new fitness and recreational facility.

In the academic realm, management and justice and policy studies come highly recommended at Guilford, as do most sciences, especially geology and physics. Geology students spent one recent winter break in Puerto Rico conducting field studies. The physics department gives students hands-on experience with the technical tools professional scientists use, including a seismograph, an observatory, and equipment for research in optics, robotics, and laser technology. Guilford boasts a Science Computer Visualization Library for geology, chemistry, and physics projects, and publishes both the *Journal of Undergraduate Mathematics* and the *Journal of Undergraduate Research in Physics*.

The college offers several innovative interdisciplinary and intercultural programs, including conflict resolution within the sociology/anthropology department. New additions to the curriculum include majors in environmental studies, African American studies, and Peace and Conflict studies. Students say the music and math departments need improvement.

Guilford also believes in experiential learning and offers the option of studying geology in the Rocky Mountains, marine biology on the East Coast, art in New York City, or political science in Washington, D.C. Students interested in really getting away can study abroad anywhere from Germany to Ghana through the Council on International Educational Exchange; about 40 percent take advantage of this option. Guilford also offers it students new opportunities for information-based decision modeling and quantitative research in the 24-hour telecommunications/computer center. In total, over 400 computer terminals are available for use, and students get Internet access the day they arrive.

Guilford's general education curriculum consists of five tiers, each designed to support the school's Quaker and liberal arts traditions. Each learning tier builds upon the last, and focuses on developing competencies in writing, oral communication, research, information technology, and quantitative reasoning. Guilford's general education requirements were also recently reduced from 13 to 9 and a quantitative competency expectation was added. The academic climate is described as intense. "Most of the courses are intellectually stimulating," says an English major. "In fact, students at Guilford are encouraged to engage in critical thinking and to develop their own voice and opinions." Despite the occasional "yawner," professors are generally described as "engaging," "intelligent," and "demanding." "The quality of teaching is Guilford's number one priority for tenure and it shows," says a junior. "We have an incredible faculty here." Another student adds, "The professors are truly concerned about the students' welfare and take the time to get to know them on a personal level." Faculty advisors are praised for their accessibility, and the career counseling center is improving.

Ask a Guilfordian to describe his or her classmates, and the answer will invariably be "diverse." Students come from 40 states, 30 countries, and a wide range of socioeconomic backgrounds, although most are liberal. Hot issues include animal rights, women's rights, the role of government, and community service. "Homophobia and racism are not compatible with Quaker beliefs, and receive a hostile reception here," an English major adds. Minority enrollment at Guilford is modest but expanding: African Americans make up 7 percent of the student population, and Hispanic and Asian-American enrollment is 4 percent combined. Only 10 percent of current Guilford students are Quakers, but the faith makes its presence felt nonetheless. One sophomore sums it up this way: "We do things by consensus, we have respect for differences, we have a strong belief in community, and, yet, we are casual and laid-back."

Despite its small size, Guilford sponsors 42 clubs, including the Entrepreneur's Network, Strategic Games Society, Hillel, and the African American Cultural Society. It's estimated that Guilford students give more than 40,000 hours of community service each year. Guilford also has social and scholarship programs that attract service-oriented students. No athletic scholarships are available, but there are 40 merit-based scholarships ranging from $7,500 to $24,600.

When it comes to housing, rooms here get high marks. They tend to be spacious and easily available in the "cooperative dorms, coed dorms, female dorms, male dorms, and more-social dorms." Upperclass students can choose apartment-style residences with single rooms in four-person suites, but many would rather live off campus. Because getting permission to move is difficult, however, only 5 percent of the students—most of them seniors—move off campus each year. Many of the three single-sex dorms are quite popular; students in one women's dorm engage in communal cleaning and get reduced rent in return. Campus security is said to be tight. Improved lighting and locked residence halls have added to dorm-dwellers' feelings of safety.

Social life at Guilford is low key but enjoyable, with restaurants, bars, and even a bowling alley nearby. And with so many colleges in the area, you can still find drinking luaus, toga parties, formals, coffeehouses, and the like. "There's so much happening at Guilford and at the other colleges nearby that there's never a problem finding something to do" says a senior. No alcohol is allowed at official college functions, but students who are of drinking age may have alcohol in their rooms. Serendipity, "a four-day festival of games, music and fun, usually a drunk-fest," is "the big thing here." Popular road trips include the Appalachian Mountains for hiking (two hours away) or Myrtle Beach for fun in the sun (three hours).

Guilford believes in the development of the whole person, both mentally and physically, and the school fields 12 NCAA Division III teams. Men's football and golf have won conference championships, and the women's rugby team even plays in prom dresses once a year! Students are also encouraged to take advantage of school-sponsored outdoor adventure events such as a ropes course, sailing, and white-water rafting.

Guilford has evolved from its humble beginnings as a lone Southern outpost of liberalism, but is still devoted to the traditional Quaker goal of "educating individuals not only to live, but to live well, with animation, conviction, and creative purpose." Sighs an already-nostalgic sophomore, "The Quakers call themselves Friends, and this college is a friend for anyone who needs it."

Guilford boasts a Science Computer Visualization Library for geology, chemistry, and physics projects, and publishes both the Journal of Undergraduate Mathematics and the Journal of Undergraduate Research in Physics.

Overlaps

UNC–Chapel Hill, UNC–Greensboro, Appalachian State.

If You Apply To ➤

Guilford...Early decision: Nov. 15. Regular admissions: Feb. 15. Financial aid: Mar. 1. Meets demonstrated need of 85%. Campus interviews: recommended, evaluative. Alumni interviews: optional, evaluative. SATs or ACTs: required; personal portfolio or presentation may be substituted. SAT IIs: optional, but recommended. Accepts the Common Application and electronic applications. Essay question: personal or societal issue and its importance to you; most significant person. Graded writing sample also required.

Gustavus Adolphus College

800 West College Avenue, St. Peter, MN 56082

Website: www.gac.edu
Location: Small city
Total Enrollment: 2,492
Undergraduates: 2,492
Male/Female: 44/56
SAT Ranges: V 560–670 M
  560–670
ACT Range: 23–29
Financial Aid: 68%
Expense: Pr $ $
Phi Beta Kappa: Yes
Applicants: 1,895
Accepted: 82%
Enrolled: 42%
Grad in 6 Years: 80%
Returning Freshmen: 91%
Academics: 🖋 🖋 🖋
Social: ☎ ☎ ☎
Q of L: ★ ★ ★
Admissions: (507) 933-7676
Email Address:
  admission@gustavus.edu

Strongest Programs:
  Physics
  Psychology
  English
  Biology
  Music
  Chemistry
  Communications Studies

The sidewalk running through the middle of the spacious Gustavus Adolphus campus is nicknamed the "Hello Walk," because students venturing down the path always greet each other—whether or not they've met. "This is a close-knit community and the people are so friendly here that you feel welcome from day one," says a communications major. Cozy Gustavus Adolphus College may be just the place for students looking for a college experience centered on friendship and community.

GAC is named for Sweden's King Gustav II Adolph (1594–1632), who is credited with making Sweden a major European power. While the king's battle victories earned him the title "Lion of the North," he was also a brave advocate of education and culture. Save for the women now attending classes, King Gustav would probably feel at home at the college that bears his name, where a not-so-subtle Swedish influence pervades everything from the buildings to the curriculum.

The 330-acre Gustavus Adolphus campus is perched on a hill overlooking the Minnesota River valley, about 65 miles southwest of the Twin Cities. The campus architectural theme is, not surprisingly, Scandinavian, with subdued, semimodern to modern brown brick buildings dominating. Highlights include the 113-year-old Victorian Old Main Building and the centrally located Christ Chapel, with spires and shafts that resemble a crown. The campus also hosts 30 bronze works by sculptor-in-residence Paul Granlund, and the 130-acre Linnaeus Arboretum and Interpretive Center provides space for plant study and retreats. The campus boasts 1,000 new trees and many new windows, carpets, computers, and roofs—all reminders of the 1.5-mile-wide tornado that blew through St. Peter in March 1998, causing more than $60 million in damage. Fortunately, students were on spring break; there were no injuries or deaths. Unfortunately, the college's oldest residence hall had to be destroyed but it has since been replaced by two new apartment-style dorms. New additions to the campus include a residence hall and an outdoor 400-meter track, which encircles an Olympic-sized soccer field.

In the classroom, GAC offers an academic smorgasbord to students seeking excellence in the liberal arts. Innovative offerings include Scandinavian studies and athletic training; students may also choose interdisciplinary programs in peace studies, environmental studies or materials science—or they may design their own major. Students sing the praises of the music and natural science departments (especially physics and biology). Psychology, classics, and political science are also popular and highly rated programs; communications and management attract students in droves. In addition, the college hosts several internationally renowned conferences each year, including the Mayday Conference in Peace Studies and the Nobel Conference, an annual meeting of eminent scientists. Students mention women's studies as weaker because of its small size, and administrators note that sociology has been improved with the addition of new faculty.

Gustavus students have two options for fulfilling core requirements. The standard Curriculum I includes 12 courses from seven areas of knowledge, plus a first-term seminar covering liberal arts skills such as critical thinking, writing, speaking, and recognizing and exploring values. Curriculum II is an integrated 12-course sequence focused on related classic works from various disciplines—"an intense liberal arts study." These students must take the first four courses in the liberal arts core: Historical Perspective I and II, the Biblical Tradition, and the Individual and Morality. Although students report that Curriculum II is more rigorous, it's not exclusive; 60 students enroll each year on a first-come, first-served basis. In addition to these required core courses, there's a "writing across the curriculum" component, in which students take three courses requiring a substantial amount of writing, and Values in Writing, the required first-term seminar.

Overall, academics at GAC are challenging but not overly competitive, students say. "The academic climate is competitive but only on an individual level," says a business management major. "Most students work very hard and strive to do their best in their classes." There are plenty of opportunities to do just that at GAC, especially for the 35 freshmen selected for the Partners in Scholarship program, which matches undergraduates with faculty research mentors and gives them $7,500 grants.

In fact, undergraduate research is a hallmark of the college's program—despite the library's paltry 250,000 volumes—and Gustavus Adolphus students recently presented 42 papers at the National Conference on Undergraduate Research, the third-highest total in the nation. For the professionally minded, Gustavus offers 3–2 engineering programs with Washington University in St. Louis, the University of Minnesota, and Mankato State University.

When winter winds force almost everyone indoors during the January term, Gustavus students (known as Gusties) may take concentrated study on campus, or enjoy travel and co-op opportunities. Gustavus sponsors study abroad programs at five colleges and universities in Sweden, as well in Japan, India, Malaysia, Australia, Russia, the Netherlands, and Scotland. Back on campus, students find their professors knowledgeable and friendly. "Every professor I've had has been very unique in their teaching style, which makes the classes much more entertaining," says a biology major. Another student adds, "The faculty is very involved with the students so it's not unusual to see them at sporting events or other activities outside the classroom."

For all its good points, though, this liberal arts college is hardly a model of diversity, and is more reminiscent of the population of Garrison Keillor's Lake Wobegon. Over 90 percent of students are white, 70 percent are Minnesotan, and about two-thirds are Lutheran. Some students lament the lack of diversity, and the school has expanded minority recruitment efforts. "Political correctness is an issue in that we all try to respect each other's beliefs," says a sophomore. The school offers 200 merit scholarships ranging from $1,000 to $10,000 for budding researchers, talented musicians, and volunteer leaders, as well as for outstanding academic achievement.

Eighty percent of Gusties live in the dorms, which have 24-hour computer labs and most of which are "comfortable and in good repair," says a junior. Norelius is the only dorm exclusively for freshmen and sophomores; upperclassmen have exclusive access to two dorms as well as to college-owned houses, and also get priority at room draw. Twenty-six percent of the men and 20 percent of the women go Greek, but socialization is not centered around fraternities and sororities. The Dive is a popular on-campus dry bar, and "musical groups, comedians, etc. are brought to campus by the student-run campus activities board," one student explains. Those searching for alcohol find it at frat parties or in upperclass friends' rooms. The town of St. Peter "has a great coffee shop, a few places to eat, and a five-screen theater just went up," reports a history major. Mankato, with more restaurants, movie theaters, and shops, is only 10 miles away; the Twin Cities are within an hour's drive.

The college hosts several internationally renowned conferences each year, including the Mayday Conference in Peace Studies and the Nobel Conference, an annual meeting of eminent scientists.

GAC's football team draws a loyal following, particularly in its annual match-up against "St. Zero" (St. Olaf). And the school's overall success in Division III competition has kept its teams among the top 20 finishers for the Sears Director's Cup for three consecutive years. Men's and women's tennis (third and fifth nationally, respectively), men's basketball (final eight nationally), and men's golf (eighth nationally) are among the teams that have recently brought home conference championships. About 80 percent of students participate in intramural programs, and the Festival of St. Lucia is an annual cause for celebration.

After four years in their close-knit haven, Gustavus Adolphus students develop a solid foundation in the arts and sciences—as well as a certain levels of skill steering toboggans and cross-country skis. Proud to be "Gusties for life," they face their biggest challenge upon leaving the friendly and supportive college cocoon, even if they're exiting with citations in significant scientific journals. As these young adults continue marching toward new frontiers, eager to share their knowledge, King Gustav would no doubt be pleased.

Overlaps

St. Olaf, University of Minnesota, Luther, University of Wisconsin, University of St. Thomas.

If You Apply To ➤ **Gustavus Adolpus**…Early decision: Nov. 15. Early action: Jan. 15. Rolling admissions and financial aid: Apr. 1. Housing: June 1. Does not guarantee to meet demonstrated need. Campus interviews: recommended, informational. No alumni interviews. SATs or ACTs: required. SAT IIs: optional. Accepts the Common Application and electronic applications. Essay question: significant experience; what you hope to gain from college; or personal goals.

Hamilton College

198 College Hill Road, Clinton, NY 13323

Website: www.hamilton.edu
Location: Rural
Total Enrollment: 1,765
Undergraduates: 1,765
Male/Female: 48/52
SAT Ranges: V 580–670 M 580–670
Financial Aid: 60%
Expense: Pr $ $ $ $
Phi Beta Kappa: Yes
Applicants: 3,811
Accepted: 39%
Enrolled: 31%
Grad in 6 Years: 82%
Returning Freshmen: 93%
Academics: ✍ ✍ ✍ ✍
Social: ☎ ☎ ☎ ☎
Q of L: ★ ★ ★
Admissions: (800) 843-2655

Back in 1978, Hamilton was a traditional men's college that seemed to have everything: money, prestige, and academic excellence. But after 166 years of bachelorhood, Hamilton decided to walk down the aisle with Kirkland College, the artsy women's college next door that was founded under Hamilton's auspices a decade before. The marriage was rocky at first, but the gender wars eventually gave way to cooperation. Today, Hamilton is much the richer for its diverse heritage, combining old school traditionalism with a touch of right-brain flair. Women may be from Venus and men from Mars, but at Hamilton both sexes have found common ground.

Set on a picturesque hilltop overlooking the tiny town of Clinton and crafted of rich, warm brownstone, the old Hamilton campus features a glorious array of collegiate Victorian architecture. By contrast, the adjacent Kirkland campus consists of boxy concrete structures of a 1960s "brutalist" vintage. Straddling the ravine that divides the two campuses, and joining them literally and figuratively, is a Student Activities Building that features a diner, lounges, and areas where students and faculty can relax. In all, Hamilton owns more than 1,200 acres of woodlands, open fields, and glens with many lovely trails for hiking or cross-country skiing within the grounds. Construction was recently completed on residence halls for 60 students.

In the classroom, Hamilton is pure liberal arts. English, economics, and government top the list of most popular majors, the latter enjoying a national reputation in public policy. In fact, the Arthur Levitt Public Affairs Center is emerging as a model public policy think tank where students can actively engage in research for local, regional, and state social service organizations and government agencies. The natural sciences are also strong, with up-to-date equipment and small labs. Under a grant from the National Science Foundation, the geology department sends students to Antarctica for research each year, and Hamilton's rocky terrain provides fertile research territory for those who remain. The economics and psychology departments are unusually productive in terms of research and publication, often giving undergrads a piece of the action. Over the past 12 years Hamilton's physics department has had three finalists for the American Physical Society's Apkar Award, which recognizes the best undergraduate research project in physics. The administration admits that the rhetoric and communication department needs to be strengthened.

A major curriculum reform goes into effect for the class of 2005 and features a series of proseminars—classes of no more than 16 that require intensive interaction—that emphasize writing, speaking, and discussion. There will also be a required sophomore program that stresses interdisciplinary learning and culminates in an integrative project with public presentation. Hamilton is among the few colleges that requires all seniors to produce an independent project in their area of concentration. Up to seven outstanding seniors—designated as Senior fellows—replace their normal courseload with a fellowship project that culminates in written theses and a public lecture to the college community. Another interesting opportunity is the Adler Conference, where students, faculty, administration, and staff discuss issues for a weekend, come up with ideas for change, and file a report for the rest of the campus to read. Hamilton offers yearlong or semester-long programs in France, Spain, and China, study in Sweden, and terms in Washington, D.C., and Mystic Seaport with the Maritime Studies Program.* In an intensive six-year program, students can earn both a BA degree from Hamilton and a law degree from Columbia University. Aspiring doctors with superior grades can take advantage of the Medical School Early Assurance Plan.

Hamilton students take pride in their school's dedication to quality instruction. "In the past two years we've had a professor recognized as 'New York Professor of the Year' by the Carnegie Foundation for the Advancement of Teaching and another as 'National Professor of the Year,'" boasts a senior English major. Students report that the courses here are challenging. "The academic climate is competitive," says an economics major. "The library is almost as popular as some of the parties." Small classes add to the experience; most have 20 students or fewer. Faculty members make sure they are available outside of class, and often give out their home phone numbers and invite students to lunch or their homes. "The classes are very small, so if you're looking for a place to hide and be a number in the crowd, this isn't it," says a sociology major.

The student body is composed of 41 percent New York residents (most from downstate), and 63 percent public high school graduates. The majority are socially conservative and "live their lives out of L.L. Bean and J. Crew catalogs," in the words of a psych major. Minority enrollment makes up 12 percent, with African Americans comprising 4 percent. A bigger issue than race relations on campus is gay and lesbian rights, and there are three gay/lesbian/bisexual support groups.

Hamilton offers about 10 merit scholarships, ranging from $5,000 to $10,000 each, but no athletic scholarships. Housing at Hamilton can vary, as described by one senior: "Just as there are some absolutely beautiful and unique places to live (especially the north side of campus), there are also some fairly conventional, boring, cell-like dorm rooms (mostly on the south side of campus)." The Hamilton

(Continued)
Email Address:
admission@hamilton.edu

Strongest Programs:
Public Policy
Physics
Chemistry
Geology
English
Computer Science
Government

The Arthur Levitt Public Affairs Center is emerging as a model public policy think tank where students can actively engage in research for local, regional, and state social service organizations and government agencies.

Under a grant from the National Science Foundation, the geology department sends students to Antarctica for research each year, and Hamilton's rocky terrain provides fertile research territory for those who remain.

side of campus is reputed to be the place for party animals, while the Kirkland dorms have a more mellow, individualistic reputation. On the Hamilton side, students have likened Dunham to a "dungeon," but note that its problems are outweighed by its social draw for freshmen. Both sexes and all four classes are mixed together in most of the halls, a number of which have been renovated to create small-group living units. Rooms are assigned to first-year students; upper-classmen rely on a lottery system. At the top of the list are several stately mansions that offer posh amenities. Students have the option of living in a coed cooperative house, and several substance-free, smoke-free, and quiet houses. A student food co-op offers opportunities for experimental cooking which can make up for the rather unpopular food services.

Twenty-nine percent of the men and 12 percent of the women join fraternities and sororities, despite housing rules that ban frat houses from campus. Most students stay on campus to socialize, but options are limited. The college is scrambling to beef up on-campus social options, since "the declining activity of the fraternities and sororities has left the college's social life in a weird state of limbo and staleness," reports a senior. An old barn was recently reopened as a campus pub, and the campus activities board sponsors concerts with some popular college acts like the Goo Goo Dolls, Blues Traveler, Indigo Girls, and Barenaked Ladies.

For those interested in other forms of leisure, Clinton has good cross-country skiing, and there's plenty of room for walking or jogging on campus. Clinton is described by a freshman as "a quaint little town with small gift and specialty shops." Adds a senior, "There isn't much to Clinton—if students do go downtown, it's usually to drink at one of the two bars." The nearest small city, Utica, is only 10 minutes away by car and offers a few more attractions. Culture seekers with time on their hands can hop a bus or drive to Boston, New York, Toronto, or Montreal, all about five hours away. Students always anticipate the last day of class in the spring for Class and Charter Day, a campus-wide picnic with games and bands and other related activities.

In athletics, Hamilton finished in the top 25 of nearly 400 colleges eligible for the Sears Cup, which recognizes overall athletic excellence. Men's soccer scored the UCAA championship and advanced to the NCAA Division III tournament, while men's basketball won capped an undefeated season by winning the UCAA championship. Students' school spirit, which often seems dormant, is on display at the annual Citrus Bowl, where Hamilton students pelt the opposing goalie with oranges after the first goal of the first home hockey game is scored. In football, a major event is the annual Rocking Chair Classic against Middlebury (the winner keeps the chair). Intramurals also are popular.

Hamilton students are, by necessity, hearty. According to a junior, "It gets freezing here, and it snows a lot. If you get seasonally depressed in the winter, Hamilton may not be the school for you." Perhaps to counter the cold, Hamilton has shown knack for community building, evident not only in its thriving marriage with former neighbor Kirkland and its warm relationship with the town of Clinton, but also in its successful use of cozy seminars, labs, and co-ops in the education and socialization of its small student body.

Overlaps

Colgate, Colby, Middlebury, Bowdoin, Williams.

If You Apply To ➤ **Hamilton**...Early decision: Nov. 15. Regular admissions: Jan. 15. Financial aid: Feb. 1. Guarantees to meet demonstrated need. Campus interviews: recommended, evaluative. Alumni interviews: optional, evaluative. SATs or ACTs: required. SAT IIs: recommended. Accepts the Common Application. Essay question: special interest, experience, achievement; issue of concern; or person who has had significant influence on you. Also submit an example of expository prose.

This small liberal arts college takes pride in its all-male status and its reputation for turning awkward boys into "gentlemen." Change comes slowly to the Hampden-Sydney campus, nestled in the heart of Virginia's rolling hill country. But that's just fine with H-SC students. In fact, most of them proudly identify the college's Code of Honor—more than a century old—as its best feature. Students are proud that they may keep their doors open, leave their bicycles unlocked, and take their exams unproctored, all without fear of mischief. One sophomore proudly relays the H-SC's mission, "Educating good men and good citizens in an atmosphere of sound learning."

Located on 660 acres nestled in the rolling hills of south-central Virginia, Hampden-Sydney's campus of redbrick, Federal-style buildings is completely surrounded by farmland and woods. The town of Farmville, home of Longwood College, is about five miles away and offers restaurants, stores, and a movie theater, although one junior says it is "not really a good college town." Farmville also provides opportunities for community service and outreach work, especially Good Men, Good Citizens, a strong volunteer group on campus, in addition to tutoring, highway clean-up, and Habitat for Humanity projects. Construction is underway to renovate all of the fraternity houses in the next five years.

Hampden-Sydney's most popular major is economics; in fact, over half of the school's alumni have gone on to careers in business. History, political science, biology, psychology, and English hold their own in terms of strength and popularity, and classics is also notable. The public-service program prepares graduates for "significant roles in government. Because of the school's small size, there are some academic drawbacks, including few computer courses, limited offerings in the applied sciences and a total of only 27 majors.

The students say the academic climate is very challenging. "The academic climate at Hampden-Sydney epitomizes that desired of a liberal arts college," says a history major. "The emphasis is on increasing your knowledge, not just providing enough information to pass the courses." To graduate, students must demonstrate proficiency in rhetoric and a foreign language in addition to completing seven courses in the humanities, three in the social sciences, and four in the natural sciences and mathematics. Classes are small; a course with more than 25 students is rare, but those who register on time seem to have little trouble getting needed classes. Most of the college's faculty lives on campus, and not only do they all encourage their students to drop by their offices, they may occasionally make house calls to find out why a student missed class. "You live near, and even eat meals, with professors, so they are also your friends. Professors here press you to the limit, and help you learn in any way they can," describes an economics and philosophy double major. Another students adds, "The professors here want you to do well and are extremely accessible."

Prospective students who are white, upper middle class, conservative, and Southern should have no problem fitting in at Hampden-Sydney. Others? Well...there are few minorities: African American enrollment is 4 percent, Asian Americans account for 1 percent, and Hispanics add another 1 percent. In spite of, or perhaps because of, this low minority enrollment, race relations are not really an issue—preserving the college's all-male status seems to take top priority. Thirty-five percent of H-SC's students went to private or parochial high school,

Website: www.hsc.edu

Location: Rural

Total Enrollment: 996

Undergraduates: 996

Male/Female: 100/0

SAT Ranges: V 500–600 M 510–610

ACT Range: 19–25

Financial Aid: 54%

Expense: Pr $

Phi Beta Kappa: Yes

Applicants: 991

Accepted: 74%

Enrolled: 42%

Grad in 6 Years: 64%

Returning Freshmen: 80%

Academics: ✍ ✍ ✍

Social: ☎ ☎ ☎ ☎

Q of L: ★ ★ ★

Admissions: (804) 223-6120

Email Address:
hsapp@hsc.edu

Strongest Programs:
Economics
History
Political Science
Biology
English
Psychology

Hampden–Sydney's most popular major is economics; in fact, over half of the school's alumni have gone on to careers in business.

and 14 percent ranked in the top tenth of their class. While athletic scholarships are not offered, since Hampden-Sydney is a Division III school, the college gives out merit scholarships to nearly one-third of the freshman class each year, ranging from $5,000 to $16,000.

As far as dorm life, H-SC students rarely complain. Ninety-seven percent of the students live on campus and housing is guaranteed for four years. "The dorms are distributed by grades, and if you work hard it pays off," advises one resident. All rooms also have Internet connections, cable television, and private phone lines. Venable Hall is said to be comfortable, while Cushing Hall is the dorm of choice for first-year students. Built in 1824, Cushing boasts "big rooms, excellent parties, and at least three ghosts." Says one student, "Cushing can be a bit noisy, but it's still the best dorm for freshmen because it lends itself to a special kind of bonding."

When they're not engaging in male bonding, what do Hampden-Sydney students do out there in the woods all by themselves? Remember, the closest town is Farmville (population 6,600), which means it must be time to welcome the guests! Most of the women guests come from four conveniently located all-female schools: Sweet Briar, Hollins, Mary Baldwin, and Randolph-Macon Woman's College. (Yes, all of Hampden-Sydney's dorms have a 24-hour visitation policy.) And when guests don't come knocking, H-SC men venture out: "The best road trips are to the women's colleges, D.C., or to the beach." Others may travel to surrounding cities (Richmond, Lynchburg, or Charlottesville) and ski slopes (Wintergreen) that are all within three hours of campus.

Hampden-Sydney's social nexus is the Circle, the site of 11 of the school's 12 fraternities, which claim 37 percent of the students. As for drinking, "Campus policies are in accordance with Virginia law. However, students may unofficially drink with secondary containers." Many students reveal that underage drinkers who want to imbibe will find alcohol if they want it. Greek Week is an annual springtime event, during which Hampden-Sydney students forget that they're supposed to be gentlemen. Another unique tradition is the bell run, where naked H-SC boys sprint to the bell tower at midnight.

Hampden-Sydney men are competitive, and that spells excellence in athletics. Football is big; students go to games in coat and tie, and H-SC's football rivalry with Randolph-Macon (not the famed women's college!) is the oldest in the South. At the annual bonfire before the game, the college rallies to sing songs and hear student and faculty leaders vilify the enemy and extol "the garnet and gray." The basketball team won their conference championship and participated in the NCAA Division III play-offs as recently as 2000. The lacrosse team participated in NCAA Division play-offs in 1998 and 1999. In 1999, the golf team had one player that was named to the NCAA tournament. Intramurals (lacrosse and rugby) are popular, too.

Hampden-Sydney really is a place where everybody knows your name. The school's small size and traditional mindset, starting with its revered honor code, lead to a family feeling on campus, which envelops both faculty and students. No one gets misty-eyed about H-SC and its long heritage of single-sex education; after all, these are macho Southern men we're talking about. Students who value tradition above all else, who don't mind having to hop in a car to get a date, could be very happy here.

Overlaps

James Madison, Randolph-Macon, Virginia Tech, University of Virginia, William and Mary.

<table>
<tr><td>**If You Apply To** ></td><td>**Hampden-Sydney**...Early decision: Nov. 15. Regular admissions and financial aid: Mar. 1. Housing: May 1. Meets demonstrated need of 23%. Campus interviews: recommended, informational. No alumni interviews. SATs or ACTs: required. SAT IIs: recommended. Accepts the Common Application and electronic applications. Essay question: who would you interview; significant experience; significant personal belonging; experience with those of different race, background, or culture.</td></tr>
</table>

Hampshire College

P.O. Box 5001, Amherst, MA 01002-5001

Legend has it that the famous Five Colleges—Hampshire, the University of Massachusetts at Amherst, Smith, Mount Holyoke, and Amherst College—are each represented by one of the five members of the hapless *Adventures of Scooby Doo* crew. In the show, Hampshire College came to life as the free-wheeling Shaggy, who always seemed to have the most fun. Indeed, Hampshire College is easily one of the most freewheeling—and intellectually strenuous—colleges in the country. There are no tests and no grades; students here have to take on the responsibilities of developing their own programs of study.

Located in the Pioneer Valley of western Massachusetts, Hampshire's 800-acre campus is situated amid former orchards, farmland, and forest. The campus's buildings are eclectic and contemporary, and the school is most proud of its bio-shelter, arts village, multisports center, and multimedia center. The newest facilities to pop up on campus include the Lemelson Machine and Fabrication Shop and the Student Affairs Center.

The academic structure at Hampshire is different from that of most other schools. Instead of grades, professors hand out "meaningful assessments," which consist of written evaluations and critiques. Degrees are obtained not by accumulating course credits, but by passing a series of examinations and independent studies. The first hurdle, known as Division I, consists of courses or independent projects in each of the four multidisciplinary schools of study: natural science, social science, cultural studies and cognitive science, and humanities and arts. A typical exam in Division I is a single project or paper, two courses, or an experiment presented to one or two professors.

The second hurdle, Division II, is each student's "concentration"—the rough equivalent of a major elsewhere. The concentration consists of individually designed programs of courses, independent work, and often fieldwork or internships. In Division III, or "advanced study," students are asked to complete a major independent study project centered on a specific topic, question, or idea, much like a senior thesis. As a result of the division system, there are as many curriculums at Hampshire as there are students; the burden is on each individual to come up with a viable, coherent program, specific to themselves. "The fact that so many people are doing their own thing makes competition irrelevant," says a sophomore, "but the fact that so many people are doing what they love makes it pretty intense." The common denominator is a heavy workload, an emphasis on self-initiated study, close contact with faculty advisors, and the assumption that first-year students can function like graduate students at other schools.

The importance of qualified, attentive faculty is extraordinary, as the emphasis at Hampshire is placed on professor evaluations rather than letter grades.

Website: www.hampshire.edu

Location: City outskirts

Total Enrollment: 1,160

Undergraduates: 1,160

Male/Female: 44/56

SAT Ranges: V 590–710 M 530–650

ACT Range: 25–30

Financial Aid: 60%

Expense: Pr $ $ $ $

Phi Beta Kappa: No

Applicants: 2,066

Accepted: 64%

Enrolled: 27%

Grad in 6 Years: 54%

Returning Freshmen: 77%

Academics: ✎ ✎ ✎ ✎

Social: ☎ ☎ ☎

Q of L: ★ ★ ★

Admissions: (413) 559-5471

Email Address:
admissions@hampshire.edu

Strongest Programs:
Film and Television
Photography
Video
Communication
Cognitive Science
Creative Writing

Students at Hampshire tend to have nothing but praise for their professors—not just their pedagogical abilities, but their personalities as well. "They strive to be engaging," says one student. The Hampshire academic year is made up of a fall and spring semester, each with four months, and an optional January term, and internships are encouraged during all three. Despite the somewhat unstructured nature of the school, nearly 100 percent of graduates go on to graduate school, and many Hampshire students begin their own businesses in fields such as computer programming, construction, or film production.

Hampshire's flexibility is ideal for artists, and the departments of film and photography are dazzling, which is also the reason they are overcrowded. Hampshire is strong in the social and natural sciences, as well as communications, creative writing, and environmental studies. The Science Center's bio-shelter is used for carefully controlled experiments. A popular program called Invention, Innovation, and Creativity exposes students to the independent reasoning and thinking that is essential to the process of inventing. Another academic innovation is cultural studies, a multidisciplinary program in the arts, cultural history, and critical theory.

For quality courses in modern and classical languages, students must travel to another school in the Five College Consortium,* as foreign language classes are not available at Hampshire. And although Hampshire's library is a quiet and pleasant place to study, it has a limited collection of only 114,000 volumes. Still, if you count the library resources at all five institutions, students in effect have ready access to more than 3 million volumes. There is no extra cost for use of the other schools' facilities or the buses to get to them.

Hampshire draws students from all over the country, and only 17 percent are state residents. They tend to be bright, self-assured, intellectually aggressive, and uniformly leftist—political correctness is the norm. Undergrads are extremely concerned with on-campus issues that will affect them, such as new administrative policies and the restructuring of student affairs. But student concern doesn't stop at the campus gate. Students say that big issues on campus include Kosovar refugees, Tibetan independence, and racial justice in the US.

The minority community at Hampshire is relatively small at 11 percent (4 percent black, 3 percent Hispanic, and 4 percent Asian American), and most students would like to see that figure rise significantly. With the school's hefty price tag, financial aid is a constant concern. Financial aid, including 34 merit awards, is available, but Hampshire does not guarantee to meet the demonstrated need of all students who are admitted.

First-year students live in coed dorms, about two-thirds of them in double rooms. The dorm residents eat at the dining hall, where the food is OK by college standards. The alternative living situation includes more than 100 different "mods"—apartments in which groups of 4 to 10 students share the responsibility for cleaning and cooking. Special quarters are arranged for nonsmokers, vegetarians, and others with special preferences. Campus security is adequate according to most.

Hampshire is no place for competitive jocks, since many sports are coed and primarily for entertainment only. There are paid instructors in a handful of sports, but most students organize their own clubs (men's and women's soccer and basketball are the biggies) and intramural teams (including Ultimate Frisbee, equestrian, volleyball, and softball). There's a nice multisports center, and there is an outstanding outdoors program that offers frequent opportunities for mountaineering, cross-country skiing, and kayaking; all equipment can be borrowed at no cost. Other sports amenities include a jogging/exercise trail, a superb gym with solar-heated pool, and a well-populated coed sauna.

On weekends, many students head for Boston, New York, Hartford, or, in season, the ski trails of Vermont and New Hampshire. But there are plenty of cultural resources within the Five College area, and the free 20-minute bus rides to Amherst (the ultimate college town), Northampton, and South Hadley are much used. The annual Spring Jam brings live bands to campus, and throughout the year there's almost always a party going on, including the much-anticipated Halloween bash, an intense, all-campus blowout complete with fireworks.

The lack of grades and other standard forms of evaluation and competition at Hampshire reduces the stress in one sense but also throws a lot of the responsibility back on the students. Still, Hampshire's drive for academic freedom and experimentation gives students the opportunity to explore their own interests under the guidance of qualified advisors and professors.

Overlaps

Bard, Sarah Lawrence, Oberlin, NYU, Brown.

If You Apply To >   **Hampshire**…Early decision: Nov. 15. Early action: Jan. 1. Regular admissions and financial aid: Feb. 1. Does not guarantee to meet demonstrated need. Campus and alumni interviews: recommended, evaluative. SATs or ACTs: optional. SAT IIs: optional. Essay questions: personal statement, and sample of academic work or persuasive critical essay on a complex issue.

Hartwick College

Oneonta, NY 13820

Hartwick has been working very hard to change its reputation from party school to a quality liberal arts college. Judging from the innovations of the last few years, it is on the way. Upon entering, each student receives a notebook computer to keep through college and beyond, to use in class, at the library, or in the room to surf the Internet. Hartwick's dedication to forging a new path through computers has set it apart from other liberal arts colleges slower to jump on the bandwagon.

Hartwick's campus has a New England feel with its ivy-covered, redbrick buildings and white cupolas, gables, and trim. The campus setting on the Oyaron Hill, overlooking the city and the Susquehanna Valley beyond, provides a breathtaking view that may be lost on some students during the uphill trek they must make to get to class. Colorful autumns pave the way for long, cold winters, and it helps to have a bit of mountain goat in your gene pool.

Hartwick's liberal arts and sciences framework ensures that its academic mountain goats are exposed to what one administrator terms "a broad swath of human knowledge." The most popular major is management, followed by psychology and nursing. Students are enthusiastic about political science and English, as well as life sciences, which one student accurately terms an "up-and-coming" program. Science facilities are currently being renovated and expanded so that science can be taught as a hands-on experience. Art and music also are praised, while the languages and sociology courses are said to be weak.

Hartwick's general education program is divided into five areas: continuity (Western tradition), interdependence, science and technology, critical thinking and effective communication, and choices. Among the voluminous requirements are two Great Books courses, a course in Western and non-Western culture,

Website: www.hartwick.edu
Location: Small city
Total Enrollment: 1,450
Undergraduates: 1,450
Male/Female: 48/52
SAT Ranges: V 500–610 M 500–600
Financial Aid: 75%
Expense: Pr $ $ $ $
Phi Beta Kappa: No
Applicants: 2,164
Accepted: 89%
Enrolled: 24%
Grad in 6 Years: 55%
Returning Freshmen: 77%
Academics: ✍ ✍ ✍
Social: ☎ ☎ ☎ ☎
Q of L: ★ ★ ★
Admissions: (607) 431-4150 or 888-HARTWICK
Email Address: admissions@hartwick.edu

Awakening, an Outward Bound type program, completed by freshmen as part of orientation, is also an option for management majors who want to test their leadership skills.

In addition to offering trips to Chiang Mai, Thailand, for first-year students, there is a field station used by the biology department on an island in the Bahamas, and Hartwick owns a closer, lakeside environmental studies field station.

foreign language, two decision-making seminars, a course in the creative or performing arts, and a senior research thesis. Another example of Hartwick's academic enrichment is the honors program that provides students with the opportunity to design and carry out a coherent program of study characterized by challenges exceeding those offered in typical course work required for graduation. The course offerings are necessarily limited by Hartwick's small size, but the Individual Student Program (ISP) enables students to create their own major dealing with a particular interest, and students may take courses at the nearby State University College at Oneonta (SUCO). "The college is competitive and rewarding at the same time for students who work hard," says one senior. Hartwick offers other unconventional learning options, many of them in off-campus locations. Students have traveled to all parts of the world while pursuing their Hartwick education. In addition to offering trips to Chiang Mai, Thailand, for first-year students, there is a field station used by the biology department on an island in the Bahamas, and Hartwick owns a closer, lakeside environmental studies field station. Awakening, an Outward Bound type program, completed by freshmen as part of orientation, is also an option for management majors who want to test their leadership skills. The four-week January term is also a favorite time to explore the world beyond Oneonta.

The faculty wins universal praise from the students. "You get to know a great many of your professors on a personal level, so failure to do your best is like disappointing a friend and mentor," says a biology senior. Private tutoring and help sessions are offered, along with an innovative freshman Early Warning program that identifies struggling students early and offers counseling.

Hartwick has traditionally attracted a somewhat less academically-oriented student body than most of the colleges with which it competes, but has been working to alter this image. Seventeen percent of students come from the top fifth of their class. Sixty-two percent of students are from New York State, especially upstate, and most of the rest come from New England or the Mid-Atlantic states. The student body is 89 percent white; 5 percent are black, 4 percent Hispanic, and 1 percent Asian American. As far as social and political issues are concerned, one senior reports, "Lack of interest or apathy and drinking are about it. Political correctness is important among staff and students alike, but not psychotically." Students at the Wick are generally from "fairly well-to-do" families and tend to be relaxed, sociable, and politically sedate. Hartwick college awards merit scholarships that range from $4,000 to $18,000, and there are a handful of athletic scholarships for Division I men's soccer and women's water polo.

Life "on the hill" was improved with the completion of two new residence halls, which were designed by a joint student-faculty team. In general, the dorms receive mixed reviews. Newly renovated halls are applauded, referred to as "Hotel Hartwick," by some, but others complain that the older dorms "could stand a little cleaning." Upperclassmen covet a place in one of the four townhouses described by one as "the yuppie version of on-campus living." Freshmen, sophomores, and juniors are required to live on campus, though the latter may move into one of the fraternity or special-interest houses. Each dorm has designated quiet hours, though they may not always be observed. Hartwick's environmental campus, Pine Lake, has cabins that are heated by pellet stoves and a lodge where environmentally-inclined students can live in rustic style. One student says that it is "very selective, but well worth the application process." On-campus students eat at a single dining commons, where the food has been dubbed "not so bad." Well, there's always the view.

From campus, it's only a short walk, bike ride, or bus ride downhill into the small city of Oneonta, with its tantalizing profusion of bars. But the underage Hartwick students usually don't get past the front doors of these taverns, and the administration is tough about enforcement on campus. No alcohol is allowed in dorm rooms. "The alcohol rules work as well as on any campus, but alcohol is not hard to come by and people find ways around all rules," admits one senior. Tamer entertainment includes Saturday movies as well as occasional lecturers and comedians, and just hanging out at the student union. The Greek system attracts 15 percent of the men and 17 percent of the women. Popular campus-wide bashes include a Last Day of Classes party, the Holiday Ball, and Winter and Spring Weekends, the latter of which features the notorious "Wick Wars," a school-wide sports competition. Walking to class each day provides great hill workouts for your ski legs, and skiing is popular throughout the region. Another nice diversion is Pine Lake, which offers cross-country trails, swimming, boating, and fishing. Nearby Cooperstown offers entertainment for baseball and history buffs.

Football is new at Hartwick; this is traditionally a soccer school. The 10 or so athletic scholarships awarded at Hartwick go to soccer and water polo, and the entire county gathers when the Hawks play at home. The Mayor's Cup Soccer Tournament weekend is a big event. Hartwick is nationally ranked at the Division I level in soccer; the remainder of the teams compete in Division III. The women's field hockey team reached the NCAA semifinals, and conference championships have been won by men's basketball, swimming, and baseball, and by the women's basketball, soccer, and lacrosse teams. Intramurals are popular as well.

Hartwick is developing into an academically competitive, liberal arts college from its partying past. Students recognize that Hartwick's reputation is changing for the better. "Over the past five years, Hartwick has adjusted with the times and undergone some major changes," says a student. It's these changes that have allowed Hartwick to forge a path into the new millennium. They are on their way up—both figuratively and literally.

Hartwick's environmental campus, Pine Lake, has cabins that are heated by pellet stoves and a lodge where environmentally-inclined students can live in rustic style.

Overlaps

Ithaca, SUNY–Geneseo, Elmira, Hobart, St. Lawrence.

If You Apply To >   **Hartwick**…Early decision: Jan. 15. Regular admissions: Feb. 15. Financial aid: Feb. 1. Campus interviews: recommended, informational. Alumni interviews: optional, informational. SATs or ACTs: optional. SAT IIs: optional. Accepts the Common Application and electronic applications. Essay question: writing sample.

Harvard University

Byerly Hall, 8 Garden Street, Cambridge, MA 02138

Over the past 350-plus years, the name Harvard has become synonymous with excellence, prestige, and achievement. At this point, Harvard University is the benchmark against which all other colleges are compared. It attracts the best students, the most academically accomplished faculty, and the most lavish donors of any institution of higher education nationwide. Sure, some academic departments at Hah-vahd are smaller than others. But all have faculty members who have made a name for themselves, and many of whom have written the standard texts in their fields. Olympic athletes, concert pianists, and Rhodes Scholars blend in nicely here, ready to embrace the challenges and rewards only Harvard's quintessential Ivy League milieu can offer.

Website: www.fas.harvard.edu
Location: City outskirts
Total Enrollment: 18,036
Undergraduates: 6,684
Male/Female: 54/46
SAT Ranges: V 700–800 M 700–790
ACT Range: 30–34

(Continued)

Financial Aid: 70%

Expense: Pr $ $ $ $

Phi Beta Kappa: Yes

Applicants: 18,161

Accepted: 11%

Enrolled: 79%

Grad in 6 Years: 97%

Returning Freshmen: 96%

Academics: ✍ ✍ ✍ ✍ ✍

Social: ☎ ☎ ☎

Q of L: ★ ★ ★ ★

Admissions: (617) 495-1551

Email Address:
college@fas.harvard.edu

Strongest Programs:
Economics
Biology
Social Studies
Government
English
African American Studies
East Asian Studies
Anthropology
Music
History of Science

*Students can also petition
for individualized majors,
typically during the
sophomore year.*

Spiritually as well as geographically, the campus centers on the famed Harvard Yard, a classic quadrangle of Georgian brick buildings whose walls seem to echo with the voices of William James, Henry Adams, and other intellectual greats who trod its shaded paths in centuries past. Beyond the yard's wrought-iron gates, the campus is an architectural mix, ranging from the modern ziggurat of the science center to the white towers of college-owned houses along the Charles River. Loker Commons, a student center beneath the new Annenberg freshman dining hall, provides a place for students to meet and philosophize over gourmet coffee or burritos of epic proportions. The Barker Center for humanities has emerged from the shell of the Union, the old freshman dining hall, and the Maxwell Dworkin building, which houses the computer science and engineering departments, has also been completed.

Harvard's state-of-the-art physical facilities are surpassed only by the unparalleled brilliance of its faculty. Under its "star" system, Harvard grants tenure only to scholars who have already made it—usually someplace else—and then gives them free rein for research. It seems like every time you turn around, a Harvard professor is winning a Nobel Prize or being interviewed on CNN; every four years half the government and econ departments move to Washington to hash out national policy. But one of Harvard's finest qualities is also one of its biggest problems. "You can have unlimited contact with professors, but it must be on your initiative," notes a biology major. "But, this is not a small liberal arts college where people will reach out to you." That's not to say profs are completely uncaring. Most teach at least one undergraduate course per semester, and even the luminaries occasionally conduct small undergraduate seminars (including those reserved for freshmen, which can be taken pass/fail). Harvard also sponsors a faculty dining program, encouraging professors to eat at the various residential houses and chew over ideas as well as lamb chops.

Harvard's best-known departments tend to be its largest; economics, government, biology, English, and biochemistry account for a large chunk of majors. But many smaller departments are gems as well: East Asian studies is easily tops in the nation. And under the leadership of Henry Louis Gates, the African-American Studies department has assembled the most high-powered group of black intellectuals in American higher education. Smaller, interdisciplinary honors majors, to which students apply for admission, boast solid instruction and happy undergraduates, too. These programs—social studies, history and science, history and literature, and folklore and mythology—are the only majors that require a senior thesis, although many students elect to do one in other departments.

Harvard's visual and environmental studies major serves filmmakers, studio artists, and urban planners, and concentrations in women's studies and environmental sciences have been well received. Students can also petition for individualized majors, typically during the sophomore year. All students must choose some sort of major at the end of their freshman year, a year earlier than most schools. The field of concentration can be changed later, but Harvard expects its students to hit the ground running. Regardless of the department, students uniformly complain about the overuse of teaching fellows (graduate students) for introductory courses in mathematics and the languages. TFs aren't all bad, though, says a junior: "They can give good advice, having just been in our position." Besides, it's easier to ask "dumb questions" of mere mortals than of the demigod-like professors.

Back in the mid-1970s, Harvard helped launch the current curriculum reform movement. The core curriculum that emerged ranks as perhaps the most exciting collection of academic offerings in all of American higher education. Now students crowd into Stephen J. Gould's lectures on the history of life or listen to Michael Sandel apply the philosophy of Aristotle, Locke, and Kant to current debates over pornography, affirmative action, and creationism. The best and brightest freshmen can apply for advanced standing if they have enough Advanced Placement credits. And should you not find a class you are looking for, admittedly highly unlikely, Harvard offers cross-registration with several of its graduate schools and the Massachusetts Institute of Technology.

In formal terms, the core requires students to select eight courses, or a quarter of their program, from a list of offerings in six different "modes of inquiry": foreign cultures, historical studies, literature and arts, moral reasoning, sciences, and social analysis. For the three or four most popular courses, enrollment is limited by the number of seats in the various large auditoriums on campus; sometimes places in these lectures are determined by lottery. Freshmen also face quantitative reasoning and foreign language requirements, as well as a semester of Expository Writing (Expos), taught mainly by preceptors.

For many students, the most rewarding form of instruction is the sophomore and junior tutorial, a small-group-directed study in a student's field of concentration that is required in most departments within the humanities and social sciences. Teaching of the tutorials is split between professors and graduate students, and the weight of each party's responsibility varies with the subject and the professor. Juniors and seniors seek out professors with whom they want to work.

The oft-made claim that "the hardest thing about Harvard is getting in" is right on target. Failing out takes real effort. Once on campus, the possibilities are endless for those who are motivated. Then again, Harvard can feel uncaring and antisocial. While it offers unparalleled resources—including fellow students—brilliant overachievers who desire the occasional ego-stroke might be better off at a small liberal arts college. Although most students feel little competition, the academic climate is still intense. "The courses at Harvard are very demanding," says a social studies major. "If you choose to be competitive, you'll find the competition can be cutthroat." Sooner or later, all roads lead to Widener Library, where incredible facilities lie in wait (and where snow-covered steps make prime sledding runs in the winter).

Harvard does have one thing its $19 billion endowment can't buy: a diverse, high-powered, ambitious, and exciting student body. You will meet smooth-talking government majors who appear to have begun their senatorial campaigns in kindergarten. You will meet flamboyant fine arts majors who have cultivated an affected accent all their own. You will sample the intensity of Harvard's extracurricular scene, where more than 6,600 of the world's sharpest undergrads compete for leadership positions in a luminous galaxy of extracurricular opportunities. "Most of the social life takes place on campus and there is a million things to do," says a history/government double major. "Yes, despite what you may think, Harvard people have parties and Harvard people date!" Stressed-out students can count on help from a variety of quarters, including the various deans' offices, the Bureau of Study Counsel, the Office of Career Services ("dedicated to working with Harvard students and alums for the rest of their lives," claims a senior), and counselors associated with each residential house. All students participate in weeklong orientation, and the First-Year Urban and Outdoor Programs help students acquaint themselves with one another and the Boston area.

No one can tell you exactly what it takes to gain admission to Harvard (and if anyone tries, apply a large grain of salt), but here's a hint: 90 percent of the current student body ranked in the top tenth of their high school class and two-thirds went to public high school. Though there are a few old-money types who

It seems like every time you turn around, a Harvard professor is winning a Nobel Prize or being interviewed on CNN; every four years half the government and econ departments move to Washington to hash out national policy.

Harvard's visual and environmental studies major serves filmmakers, studio artists, and urban planners, and concentrations in women's studies and environmental sciences have been well received.

For many students, the most rewarding form of instruction is the sophomore and junior tutorial, a small-group-directed study in a student's field of concentration that is required in most departments within the humanities and social sciences.

probably spit up their baby food on a Harvard sweatshirt, their numbers are smaller than one might imagine on this liberal campus. (They enter as sophomores.) Undergrads come from all 50 states and scores of foreign countries, although the student body is weighted toward the Northeast. Minority groups account for nearly a third of the enrollment. There are no merit or athletic scholarships to ease the pain of Harvard's hefty tuition, but a generous financial aid policy recently added $2,000 annually to every student aid package.

In the past, women students benefited from "dual citizenship" in both Harvard and Radcliffe colleges, receiving degrees ratified by the presidents of both colleges. However, Radcliffe has been phased out as a separate institution; everyone is now considered a Harvard student, though students can still take advantage of Radcliffe's network of professional women, researchers, and alumnae.

Every first-year class lives and eats as a single unit in Harvard Yard, a privilege made more enticing by recent renovation of all the freshman dorms. Freshmen now eat in Annenberg Hall, the new name for beautifully renovated Memorial Hall. For their last three years, students live in one of 12 residential houses, built around their own courtyards with their own dining halls and libraries. All the houses are coed, and each holds between 300 and 500 students. Designed as learning communities, the upperclass houses come equipped with a complement of resident tutors, affiliated faculty members, and special facilities, from art studios to squash courts. Each house has a student council, which plans programs and parties and arranges the fielding of intramural teams. Students are now randomly assigned (with up to 15 friends) to one of the houses, but some houses still retain a personality from the days of old when each stood for a particular ideology, interest, or economic class. "Harvard housing is beautiful," says a history of science major. "Freshmen have amazing rooms and upperclass houses are great."

The nine houses along the Charles River feature suites of rooms, while the three houses at the Radcliffe Quad, a half-mile away, offer a mixture of suites and single rooms. Some students value the greater privacy of the Quad houses' singles; others consider it equivalent to a Siberian exile, especially during harsh Cambridge winters. The older dorms provide spacious wood-paneled rooms, working fireplaces, and the gentle reminders of Harvard's rich traditions. Most rooms are also wired for direct Internet access. With all these features and amenities, it's no wonder few students move off campus.

What socializing there is at Harvard tends to occur on campus and in small groups. "It's certainly normal to spend Friday and Saturday nights studying," says a philosophy major. With the exception of the annual all-school Freshman Mixer and the annual theme festivals each house throws, parties tend to be private affairs in individual dorm rooms. Though Harvard does enforce the drinking age at university events, in individual houses, it's up to the resident tutors. For some, the key to happiness in Harvard's high-powered environment is finding a niche, a comfortable academic or extracurricular circle around which to build your life. Outside activities include about 80 plays performed annually, two newspapers and several journals, and plenty of community service projects.

The possibilities of Harvard's social life are increased tenfold by Cambridge and Boston, where there are many places to have fun. Harvard Square itself is a legendary gathering place for tourists, shoppers, bearded intellectuals, and coffeehouse denizens. Robert Brustein's American Repertory Theater, transplanted from Yale in the mid-1980s, offers a season of professional productions and nearly as professional student shows. Cambridge also enjoys an exceptional selection of new and used bookstores, including the Starr Bookshop (behind the Lampoon building), McIntyre & Moore, Grolier Books, and, of course, the Harvard Bookstore and the mammoth Harvard Co-op, known universally as "the Coop." Boston itself features Faneuil Hall, the Red Sox, the Celtics, and 52 other colleges. "Cambridge/Boston is the ultimate college town," says an English major. "Everything is geared toward the students."

Harvard's athletic facilities are across the river from the campus, and their incredible offerings often go unnoticed by students buried in the books. Both the men's and women's squash and crew teams are perennial national powers, and the men's ice hockey team draws a crowd of few, but dedicated fans. The women's lacrosse team is strong, as are tennis, swimming, and sailing. As for football, the team has been doing better in recent years, but the season always boils down to the Yale game, memorable as much for the antics of the spectators and marching band as for the fumbles of the players. Intramural sports teams are divided up by house, and each fall, league champs play teams from Yale the weekend of the Game. Another fall highlight is the annual Head of the Charles crew race, the largest event of its kind in the world, where as many as 200,000 people gather to watch the racing shells glide by.

Nowhere but Harvard does the identity of a school—its history, its presence, its pretense—intrude so much into the details of undergraduate life. Admission here opens the door to a world of intellectual wonder, academic challenges, and faculty minds unmatched in the United States—but then drops students on the threshold. "I have quickly gained exposure to major theories in literature, psychology, anthropology, social sciences, and evolutionary biology," says a junior. "I gauge myself by how many allusions in The *New Yorker* I understand." That's the way Harvard is; what other kind of place could produce statesmen John Quincy Adams and John F. Kennedy, pioneers W.E.B. DuBois and Helen Keller, and artists T.S. Eliot and Leonard Bernstein? But beware: It is only the most motivated and dedicated student who can take full advantage of the Harvard experience. Others who attempt to drink from the school's perennially overflowing cup of knowledge may find themselves drowning in its depths.

Overlaps

Princeton, Yale, Stanford, MIT, Brown.

If You Apply To ➤ **Harvard**...Early action: Nov. 1. Regular admissions: Jan. 1. Financial aid: Feb. 1. Housing: May 1. Guarantees to meet demonstrated need. Campus interviews: optional, informational. Alumni interviews: optional, evaluative. SATs or ACTs: required. SAT IIs: required (any three). Accepts the Common Application. Essay question: uses Common Application questions.

Haverford College

Haverford, PA 19041-1392

Students at Haverford College are steeped in a tradition of honor and trust. They schedule their own final exams, take unproctored tests, and develop a strong sense of trust with their professors. Socially, they adhere to the concepts of respect, concern, and responsibility. "The honor code encourages Haverford students to be morally and socially conscious beings, and is based on the mutual respect of every person," says a junior. While Haverford is smaller and less well known than many of its peer institutions, it is unquestionably one of the finest in the country. In response to an often-heard comment of "I've never heard of Haverford," one student says he and his peers have adopted a slogan from

Website: www.haverford.edu
Location: Suburban
Total Enrollment: 1,118
Undergraduates: 1,118
Male/Female: 47/53
SAT Ranges: V 640–740 M 630–720

(Continued)

Financial Aid: 44%

Expense: Pr $ $ $ $

Phi Beta Kappa: Yes

Applicants: 2,650

Accepted: 33%

Enrolled: 35%

Grad in 6 Years: 91%

Returning Freshmen: 97%

Academics: 🖎 🖎 🖎 🖎 🖎

Social: ☎ ☎ ☎

Q of L: ★ ★ ★ ★ ★

Admissions: (610) 896-1350

Email Address:
admitme@haverford.edu

Strongest Programs:
Natural Sciences
English
History
Political Science
Economics
Philosophy

The advising system is also well regarded: from the moment freshmen arrive on campus for their Customs Week orientation, they are surrounded by advisors.

humorist and Haverford alumnus Dave Barry: "We haven't heard of you either!"

Founded under Quaker auspices in 1833, Haverford functions as much like a family as a conventional academic institution. The campus is on 216 acres just off Philadelphia's Main Line railroad, and it looks plenty peaceful, like a well-ordered summer camp. Complete with pond, nature trails, and more than 400 species of shrubs and trees, it is as densely wooded and self-contained as a college campus can be. The architecture consists mainly of 19th- and early 20th-century stone buildings, with a sprinkling of modern structures added here and there. The combination enhances the sense of a balanced community, bringing together two traditional Quaker philosophies: development of the intellect and appreciation of nature. The campus itself is designed as an arboretum and includes an observatory and a duck pond. The new Integrated Natural Science Center is under construction, and will bring together many departments in a setting designed to facilitate interdisciplinary collaboration.

Haverford's curriculum reflects its commitment to providing what is truly a liberal arts education. Starting with the unusually strong physical and biological sciences and continuing through economics, English, history, and political science, Haverford's host of offerings is almost uniformly impressive. Languages, weak in the past, have improved, thanks to the addition of a state-of-the-art language learning center. Anthropology and sociology receive negative reviews from students, but academic complaints in general are few and far between. Haverford's participation in a tricollege system that includes Bryn Mawr and Swarthmore allows students to major in subjects that would otherwise be off-limits. Those include engineering, art history, growth and structure of cities, and environmental studies. "We are fortunate to be able to take advantage of our relationship with Bryn Mawr College, enabling us to major over there," says an English major. Since there are no graduate students, undergraduates often get to assist professors in their research, and several produce one or two publishable papers each year. Perhaps Haverford's biggest selling point is its faculty, praised for being teachers and scholars, in that order. Described as both "brilliant" and "personal," professors at Haverford are routinely close with their students, thanks to small classes, after-school study sessions, and even dinners at the professors' homes. "The professors here take an interest in their students and are a part of the community," one senior says. In fact, sixty-five percent of professors live on campus. The courseload is considered by most to be intense. "Most courses demand a lot of reading and a fair amount of writing," says a sociology major. The advising system is also well regarded: from the moment freshmen arrive on campus for their Customs Week orientation, they are surrounded by advisors. The class is divided into groups of 10, with two upperclass advisors each. During the academic year, students are also assigned individually to an upperclass advisor and faculty advisor.

Haverford's general education requirements call for three courses in each of three divisions: social sciences, natural sciences, and humanities. One of these nine courses must fulfill a quantitative reasoning requirement. In addition, students must demonstrate proficiency in a foreign language and must complete freshman English plus one course that fulfills the social justice requirement.

One of Haverford's most distinctive features is its honor code, which governs all facets of life. The code, administered entirely by students and ratified each year, helps instill the values of "integrity, honesty, and concern for others." But few have found it to stifle free speech. "We all have strong opinions here, and we like to share them and learn from others," a senior says. "The social honor code, while broadly maintaining certain community standards, encourages students to voice virtually any opinion so long as it is expressed rationally." In good Quaker tradition, the faculty makes decisions by consensus rather than formal voting, and students also play a large role in formulating college policy, through the Honor Council, Student's Council, and membership on various college committees.

What students can't get at Haverford can usually be found a mile down the road at Bryn Mawr. The two schools have a unique relationship stemming from the days, almost two decades ago, when Haverford was all-male. Students at each institution can take courses, use the facilities, eat, and even live in the dormitories of the other. Haverford and Bryn Mawr students cooperate on a weekly newspaper, radio station, orchestra, and other clubs and sports, and a free shuttle bus runs between the campuses. Cross-registration is also available at Swarthmore and the University of Pennsylvania. Under a 3–2 engineering program, students can transfer to Penn after their junior year to complete an engineering major after two more years. Also, by combining resources with Bryn Mawr and Swarthmore, Haverford offers students an extensive language program: Japanese, Chinese, Italian, and Russian, in addition to the traditional languages. Haverford also permits students to take time off during their college careers; some work at a job, while others travel or enroll at other colleges for a semester or two. Many students participate in the Eighth Dimension program, which coordinates campus- and community-based student volunteer opportunities.

Only 17 percent of the student body hail from Pennsylvania, but a large percentage are East Coasters nonetheless. Forty-six percent come from private and parochial schools, and 76 percent ranked in the top tenth of their high school class. Approximately 10 percent of the campus are Asian American, 5 percent are Hispanic, and 6 percent are African American. One student says discussions about hot social issues spill over outside of class. "Conversation about issues of race, sexuality, gender, and many other topics occurs not only at club meetings or special forums, but also in the dorms and around dinner tables." Though the college is nonsectarian, the continuing Quaker influence lives on in the form of an optional Quaker meeting each week.

The residence halls, spacious and well maintained, are in harmony with most students' privileged backgrounds. Ninety-eight percent of all students live on campus, and approximately 70 percent of those live in singles. One student describes the residence halls as "riot-proof"—a vestige of '60s architecture—with "single rooms, mazelike hallways, and winding staircases." All the dorms are coed, but students can request single-sex floors. Freshmen are guaranteed housing, and even the sophomores, who draw last in the lottery, can usually get a decent room. The college-owned Haverford College Apartments, located on the edge of campus, are an extremely popular option. They include one- and two-bedroom apartments, each with a living room, kitchen, and bathroom. Upperclassmen living in the apartments can cook for themselves, but all others living on campus (and all freshmen regardless of where they live) must participate in a complete meal plan that covers weekends. Campus security is broad and crime virtually nonexistent. "A crime here is a duck meandering from the pond and being found in the dining center," muses a senior.

Life in this close-knit, introspective environment can get stifling at times, but students can easily ditch Haverford with a train trip to downtown Philadelphia, 20 minutes away, where they can take advantage of bargain orchestra tickets and Flyers, Eagles, and Phillies games. New York City, Washington, the New Jersey beaches, Pocono ski areas, and Atlantic City are only a couple of hours away by car.

While the community spirit at Haverford works well for academics and

One of Haverford's most distinctive features is its honor code, which governs all facets of life. The code, administered entirely by students and ratified each year, helps instill the values of "integrity, honesty, and concern for others."

Haverford's participation in a tricollege system that includes Bryn Mawr and Swarthmore allows students to major in subjects that would otherwise be off-limits.

personal development, it doesn't always carry over into the social scene. In the absence of fraternities and sororities, Haverford and Bryn Mawr hold joint campus parties. One senior admits that Haverford is "not the place to come if a really dynamic social life is your priority." The alcohol policy abides by the law of the commonwealth of Pennsylvania, but is connected, as well, to the honor code. "A lot of student responsibility is granted and respected. Underage students can drink easily but in an amazingly safe and healthy environment," explains one student. There are frequently movies, concerts, and other activities, usually for free. Traditional events include Haverfest—Haverford's closest approximation to Woodstock—and a winter Snowball dance. Perhaps Haverford's most interesting rite is the annual Suitcase Party, in which everyone enters a lottery for a trip to someplace warm.

There is no longer a football team at the Ford, and soccer, a sport in which Haverford played in the first intercollegiate game more than 80 years ago, has become the most popular among fans. Track and cross-country are also strong, with both the men's and women's teams winning regional conference championships in the last few years. Every year, Haverford competes with archrival Swarthmore for the coveted Hood Trophy, which falls to the school that wins the most varsity contests between the two. Haverford also boasts the number-one varsity college cricket team in the country because, well, it's the only school that has one! Intramural sports are popular, especially because participation counts toward the six quarters of athletic credit Haverford requires during the freshman and sophomore years. In spite of all the teams and athletics, the mascot for these Quakers has been an eclectic mix of animals and emotions: the Fighting Quakers didn't fit quite right, but then, neither did the Aardvarks or the Angry Skullbashing Quakers. For now, it's the Black Squirrels.

Just about the only problem Haverford students have with their school stems from the same source that provides them with the quality education they so cherish: the small size. "I miss the big football games and proms of my high school years," admits one student. But alas, Haverford students have no regrets. "It was a trade I was willing to make for small classes, great ties with professors, and a small, friendly community."

Overlaps

Swarthmore, Brown, Amherst, Penn, Williams.

If You Apply To ➤   **Haverford**...Early decision: Nov. 15. Regular admissions: Jan. 15. Financial aid: Jan. 31. Guarantees to meet demonstrated need. Campus interviews: recommended (required for those living within 150 miles of the school), informational. Alumni interviews: recommended, informational. SATs: required. SAT IIs: required (writing and two others). Essay question: personal statement, acceptance of honor code.

University of Hawaii at Manoa

2530 Dole Street, Room C200, Honolulu, HI 96822

Website: www.hawaii.edu
Location: Center city
Total Enrollment: 17,004
Undergraduates: 11,785

One of the goals of the University of Hawaii at Manoa is to "serve as a bridge between East and West." This multiculturalism is evident in everything from course offerings to the student body. And while you may be thinking about surfing as much as studying, don't be fooled: it will take more than a great tan to earn your degree here. Says a senior, "The usual assumption is that a student must go to the mainland (continental U.S.) to obtain a quality education. UH provides a quality education at a very affordable price." And if you can catch a few waves in the process, so much the better.

The UH campus occupies 300 acres in the Manoa Valley, a residential Honolulu neighborhood. The architecture is regionally eclectic, mirroring historical and modern Asian Pacific motifs, and is enhanced by extensive subtropical landscaping. "There are many plants and trees that make our campus more environmentally friendly," says a sophomore. UH offers bachelor's degrees in 88 fields. Among the best are astronomy, Asian and Pacific area studies, languages and the arts, ethnomusicology, and tropical agriculture. It should come as no surprise that marine and ocean-related programs are also first-rate. The university also takes pride in its programs in engineering, geology and geophysics, international business, political science, and travel industry management. Both medical and law schools are gaining reputations for excellence. UH has also recently added a BA degree in information and computer science. Beyond these few specialties, programs are adequate but hardly worth four years of trans-Pacific flights. The math department is cited by several students as the school's biggest problem. Students describe the academic climate as "fairly competitive" and somewhat laid-back.

Despite the relaxed atmosphere, core requirements are extensive. All students must take a semester in expository writing and math, two courses in world civilization, two years of a foreign language or Hawaiian, and three courses each in the humanities, social sciences, and natural sciences. There are freshman seminar classes that offer small-group learning in a variety of subjects. Desirable classes and times are said to be difficult to get into for freshmen and sophomores. You may need to talk to profs, one student advises. Another problem seems to be that certain classes are only offered one semester a year. The academic advising is described as "good" if you know the professor and know what you want to study. Nonacademic counseling rates "an 8 out of 10," for one student. "They will help you with everything from career planning to a marital dispute."

Hawaii is unique among major American universities in that 78 percent of the students are of Asian descent. Caucasians account for 20 percent, and African Americans and Hispanics 1 percent each. The different groups seem to get along well, according to students. Mainland Americans account for about 7 percent of the students, and another 3 percent are foreign. "Hawaii is a unique place where diversity is recognized and accepted. There are many mixed-race students and many interracial couples," a senior says. Hot campus issues include gay rights, campus parking, and Hawaiian sovereignty. Especially promising students can compete for more than 108 merit scholarships, and a total of 310 athletes get grants-in-aid.

Only 21 percent of the student body live in campus housing, which is parceled out by a priority system that gives preference to those who are from across the sea. Students recommend the four towers, Ilima, Lehua, Lokelani, and Mokihana; the rooms are small, and the hallways are happening. "Students never know what to expect," one student explains. If you're thinking about off-campus housing, take note: the administration warns that housing in Honolulu is scarce and expensive. Once you are accepted into housing, continuous residency is not that difficult to obtain. Cafeterias are located throughout the campus and serve "edible" fare.

Because of all the commuters, UH is pretty sedate after dark. "On the whole, UH seems to be an academically-focused campus, meaning that school is for on campus and socializing is for off campus," a psychology major says. Many students hit nearby dance clubs or movies, or else head for home. Four percent of the men and two percent of the women join the tiny Greek system. Drinking is

(Continued)

Male/Female: 46/54
SAT Ranges: V 480–580 M 510–630
Financial Aid: 30%
Expense Pub: $ $
Phi Beta Kappa: Yes
Applicants: 8,714
Accepted: 76%
Enrolled: 44%
Grad in 6 Years: 55%
Returning Freshmen: 82%
Academics: ✍ ✍
Social: ☎ ☎
Q of L: ★ ★ ★
Admissions: (808)956–8975
Email Address:
 ar-info@hawaii.edu

Strongest Programs:
 Astronomy
 Asian and Pacific Area Studies
 Languages
 Travel Industry Management
 English as a Second Language
 Ethnomusicology
 Tropical Agriculture
 Geosciences

It should come as no surprise that marine and ocean-related programs are also first-rate.

not allowed in the dorms. A couple of local hangouts provide an escape and the campus pub, Manoa Garden, is also an option. Lest anyone forget, some of the world's most beautiful resorts—Diamond Head, and all the rest—are less than a 20-minute drive away. Waikiki Beach? Within two miles' reach. And round-trip airfare to the neighboring islands—including Maui, Kauai, and the Big Island—is not unreasonable.

About the only thing that generates excitement on campus are the athletic teams, the Rainbow Warriors, with football, volleyball, basketball, baseball, and swimming among the top draws. The Rainbow women's teams are also well supported, especially the championship volleyball team. The Homecoming Dance is one of the most popular events of the year. But what students really look forward to is Kanikapila, a festival of Hawaiian music, dance, and culture. Don Ho, eat your heart out.

Students seeking warm weather and great surfing won't be disappointed at UH, but mainlanders should think twice about it unless they are set on one of the university's specialized programs. It's up to you, one student says, to get the best out of UH. "Many do not recognize the high quality of education possible through choosing challenging courses and instructors who urge achievement and high-quality work."

Overlaps

Hawaii Pacific, UH–Hilo, University of Washington, UCLA, University of Southern California.

If You Apply To >

UH…Rolling admissions: May 1. Financial aid: Mar. 1. Housing: May 1. Guarantees to meet demonstrated need. Campus interviews: optional, informational. No alumni interviews. SATs or ACTs: required. Achievement tests: optional. No essay question.

Hendrix College

1600 Washington Avenue, Conway, AR 72032

Website: www.hendrix.edu
Location: Small town
Total Enrollment: 1,147
Undergraduates: 1,143
Male/Female: 46/54
SAT Ranges: V 590–690 M 560–670
ACT Range: 25–31
Financial Aid: 42%
Expense: Pr $
Phi Beta Kappa: No
Applicants: 962
Accepted: 88%
Enrolled: 39%
Grad in 6 Years: 62%
Returning Freshmen: 86%
Academics:

Hendrix College is a surprisingly liberal school plunked down in the heart of America's Bible Belt, offering rigorous academics in an intimate setting. "Most students here are able to maintain their own unique values and interests while simultaneously accepting and honoring those different from their own," says a psychology major. Graduating students leave Hendrix with more than a degree; they also come away with good friends, a solid education, and a healthy dose of nonconformism.

Hendrix's compact and comfortable campus is nestled between the Ouachita and the Ozark mountains. The college owns about 160 acres with more than 80 varieties of trees and shrubs, and more than 10,000 budding flowers each spring. The main campus—with its own lily pool, fountain, and a gazebo—occupies about one-fourth of the total acreage. The redbrick buildings are a mix of old and new, and a pedestrian overpass connects the main campus to the college's athletic facilities and a wooded fitness trail. Soon-to-be-completed construction includes the Center for Life Sciences.

Hendrix is strong in many areas, but the natural sciences are definitely its forte. Politics, psychology, history, and English are also well-respected, and future entrepreneurs flock to economics and business. In the past, students say the anthropology department was weak but is now improving with the addition of an anthropologist to the faculty. For would-be engineers, Hendrix has five-year programs with Columbia, Vanderbilt, and Washington University in St. Louis. Undergraduate research is a distinctive feature at the school and students are given the chance to present their research at regional and national symposia. Hendrix also offers several study abroad opportunities including exchange programs in Austria and England, Hendrix-in-London and Hendrix-in-Oxford, and the study of ecology in Costa Rica. In addition, Hendrix is a member of the Associated Colleges of the South* consortium.

To graduate from Hendrix, all students are required to take three courses in each of three areas: the humanities, natural sciences, and social sciences. Freshmen must also take a two-term Western Intellectual Traditions sequence, which is aimed at introducing the major issues, problems, and achievements of Western culture and two courses in Other Cultural or Linguistic Traditions. Finding something that appeals to you should be relatively easy since Hendrix is constantly adding new programs. Recent additions include a master's degree in accounting, a major in computer science and mathematics, a major in international relations and global studies, and a minor in cultural anthropology.

Students say that doing well at Hendrix means keeping up with the workload. "The academic climate is competitive," says an economics/business double major. "The work load is heavy and preparing for class also takes a lot of time and effort." This means plenty of time in the $10-million library, which features a 40-station computer laboratory, access to online databases, CD-ROM bibliographic facilities, carrels for 24-hour individual and group study, and an extensive audiovisual center. Students describe their professors as dedicated and caring. "The professors at Hendrix are awesome," says a chemistry major. "Not only are they passionate about the subject they teach, they care about the students and their opinions too."

Sixty-seven percent of the students at Hendrix are from Arkansas. African Americans constitute 5 percent of students, while Asian Americans and Hispanics contribute another 6 percent. The school attracts an interesting cross-section of students, and this diversity is valued. "This is a very open-minded campus but there is always room for growth and improvement," says a junior.

All but one of Hendrix's dorms are single-sex, and freshmen are required to live on campus, which students say adds to the sense of community. "The dorms are great and provide a sense of belonging," says a biology major. Each has a personality all its own: Galloway (women's) is most beautiful; Raney is likened to a perpetual summer camp; Veasey and Martin are party dorms; and Couch houses 90 percent of the school's vegetarians. Seventy-eight percent of students live on campus, but some seniors get permission to move into nearby college-owned apartments. In the past, housing was a bit scarce but the construction of six new dorms solved that problem. Each of the dorms has a kitchen for general use, and there's now a "port for every pillow," providing students with direct connection to the Internet.

The two F's that dominate social life at most Southern schools—football and fraternities—can't be found at Hendrix. Students are proud of their independence; the annual Hendrix Olympics allows them to celebrate the absence of Alphas, Betas, and Gammas from their campus. Major affairs include the Toga Party, Oktoberfest, and Beach Bash, as well as the annual Toad Suck Daze, a rollicking carnival that features bluegrass music. Last but not least is the Shirttail Serenade, in which first-year men from each dorm croon out a song-and-dance routine in their shirts, ties, shoes, socks—and underwear—for the benefit of freshman women. The latter rate each performance on the basis of singing, creativity, legs,

(Continued)

Social: ☎ ☎ ☎ ☎

Q of L: ★ ★ ★ ★

Admissions: (501) 450-1362
  or (800) 277-9017

Email Address:
  adm@hendrix.edu

Strongest Programs:
  Biology
  Business
  Premed
  English
  History
  Psychology
  Politics
  Religion

Hendrix is strong in many areas but the natural sciences are definitely its forte.

Recent additions include a master's degree in accounting, a major in computer science and mathematics, a major in international relations and global studies, and a minor in cultural anthropology.

and so on, and respond two days later with their own Long Shirts/Short Skirts Serenade.

On the subject of booze, "the college does not abridge the personal decision of any student to drink, but no alcohol may be displayed in its original container," says one student. Kegs, however, are prohibited, so it's not surprising that Hendrix is one of the nation's leading schools for good clean fun.

When students go off campus looking for fun, Little Rock is the most common destination, about half an hour's drive away. Conway is home to two other colleges but it's in a dry county, so trips to places as far-flung as Dallas and Oklahoma City (each five hours' drive) are not unusual for concerts and the like. For those who stay in town, "there is a Volunteer Activities Center that has activities planned just about every weekend," notes a student. An innovative orientation program sends all incoming freshman classes on one of 20 three-day excursions with upperclassmen and faculty for everything from windsurfing to tours of Memphis, Tennessee.

With no football team to cheer for, basketball and soccer are the hottest sports on campus, and Rhodes College is the chief rival. For outdoor buffs, the college sponsors a number of trips around Arkansas for canoeing, biking, rock climbing, spelunking, and whatever else strikes one's fancy.

At first glance, Hendrix may seem too good to be true. But it isn't and the students claim it is only getting better. "Hendrix is on the move," says a molecular biology major. "The college has voted to change to a semester system, many new state-of-the-art facilities are being constructed, and the academic programs are constantly expanding." Those seeking a liberal dose of academics in a Southern setting may do well to trade the bright lights of the big city for four years of Conway's folksy charm.

Overlaps

University of Arkansas, University of Central Arkansas, Rhodes, Washington University (MO).

If You Apply To ➤ **Hendrix**...Rolling admissions. Financial aid: Feb. 15. Housing: May 1. Meets demonstrated need of 89%. Campus interviews: recommended, evaluative. Alumni interviews: optional, informational. SATs or ACTs: required. SAT IIs: optional. Accepts the Common Application and electronic applications. Essay question: meaningful experience; why Hendrix is a good match for you; strong influence of an individual.

Hiram College

P.O. Box 96, Hiram, OH 44234

Website: www.hiram.edu
Location: Rural
Enrollment: 895
Undergraduates: 895
Male/Female: 48/52
SAT Ranges: V 500–650 M 490–610
ACT Range: 21–27
Financial Aid: 87%
Expense: Pr $ $
Phi Beta Kappa: Yes

At Hiram College, the feeling of community is highly cherished. "I like the fact that some professors I've never had and never will have shown concern for me," says a sophomore. But for all their emphasis on closeness, Hiram students are hardly homebodies—more than 50 percent study abroad in locales ranging from Europe to Australia to Costa Rica. The school's flexible schedule makes it even easier to split campus for a while. Clearly, these Hiram Dawgs are loyal to their school but always willing to learn new tricks.

Set on a charming hilltop campus that occupies the second-highest spot in Ohio, Hiram is blessed with an abundance of flowers and trees as well as a nice view of the valley below. The prevailing architectural motif is New England brick, and many Hiram buildings are restored 19th-century homes. The college just renovated Bowler Hall, the oldest standing structure on campus, investing $1.5 million to transform it into a modern, air-conditioned, Ethernet-ready dorm while retaining its 11-foot ceilings and Victorian charm. A $6.2 million science facility opened its doors in January of 2000, providing ample space for the biology majors who are tops by sheer numbers at Hiram, followed by education and management devotees.

Future tycoons don't get the same fieldwork opportunities as budding doctors and researchers, though. Hiram's bio majors work at a 260-acre college-owned ecology field study station a mile away, with a specialized lab, a 70-acre beech and maple forest, artificial river, and numerous plant and animal species. Other sciences, especially chemistry, are also strong at Hiram. The German language program (as well as several other foreign languages) is weaker because of its small size. Recent additions to the curriculum include a major in biomedical humanities, very popular with incoming students, and a minor in international studies.

Hiram offers several unusual summer opportunities, most notably the Northwoods Station in northern Michigan, where students choose courses ranging from photography to botany and geology to writing. And Hiram is the only affiliate college of the Shoals Marine Lab, run by Cornell University and the University of New Hampshire, which offers summer study in marine science, ecology, coastal and oceanic law, and underwater archeology.

Hiram's core curriculum is extensive. All students must complete two courses from each of the college's four divisions (fine arts, humanities, natural sciences, and social sciences), plus the Freshman Colloquium, a writing and speaking skills seminar, and an upper-division interdisciplinary requirement. First year students are also enrolled in a seminar with a focus on western intellectual traditions with an emphasis on writing. "The atmosphere is not entirely laid-back, but the stress level is not abnormally high," a political science major says. A classmate adds, "If you are planning to pursue graduate or professional school, the courses you need to properly prepare can become very overwhelming." Teamwork is emphasized and grade-grubbing is rare.

The Hiram Plan allows students to cover a breadth of material in three courses during each semester's longer 12-week session, and to focus on a seminar-style class during the additional 3-week term. Even nonseminars are small, though; 85 percent of Hiram's courses have 25 or fewer students, which leads to impressive faculty accessibility. "If you want to really master a subject, the professors will answer every question and work with you until your brain is literally full," says one student.

While intramurals are popular elsewhere, at Hiram the buzzword is "Extra Murals," Hiram-speak for study abroad. Hiram offers an array of professor-led trips to all corners of the globe, and all participating students get academic credit. Students can also study at Hiram's Rome affiliate, John Cabot International University, and transfer their credits. Hiram's unique academic calendar allows ample opportunity for off-campus endeavors of all types, including the Washington Semester* at American University, which Hiram helped found.

Seventy-nine percent of Hiram students are in-staters, and many of the rest hail from New York and Pennsylvania, though the administration is working to broaden the college's geographic base. Minority students are present, too, with African Americans constituting 9 percent and Asian Americans and Hispanics comprising another 3 percent. Hiram heads off race-related conflict with a dorm program called Dialogue in Black and White that encourages open discussion on multicultural issues. There's also a one-credit course that has as its final project the creation of a plan of action on campus race relations. In addition to need-based financial aid, Hiram awards an impressive 466 merit scholarships, ranging from $1,250 to $12,000.

(Continued)

Applicants: 853
Accepted: 86%
Enrolled: 41%
Grad in 6 Years: 66%
Returning Freshmen: 81%
Academics: ✑ ✑ ✑
Social: ☎ ☎ ☎
Q of L: ★ ★ ★
Admissions: (800) 362-5280
Email Address:
  admission@hiram.edu

Strongest Programs:
  Biology
  Chemistry
  Computer Science
  Education
  English
  History
  International Economics and
  Management
  Mathematics

The college just renovated Bowler Hall, the oldest standing structure on campus, investing $1.5 million to transform it into a modern, air-conditioned, Internet-ready dorm while retaining its 11-foot ceilings and Victorian porches.

Almost all Hiram students live on campus, and everyone who wants a room gets one. Community lounges in each hall boast big-screen TVs and computer labs. Most halls are coed, and students choose between 24-hour quiet, 24-hour noise, and a happy medium. Upperclassmen who like their location can stay in the same room year after year. "Occasionally, the windows are hard to shut or the closet doors stick, but the rooms are pretty big," observes a history and Spanish double major. Most students live in two-person suites; the popular (and larger) triples and quads are scarcer and thus harder to get. Dorm dwellers are required to buy the meal plan, but two gourmet dinners each term liven up the menu with delicacies like swordfish and prime rib.

When the weekend rolls around, don't expect to find Hiram students hunched over a keg. There's one totally dry dorm, Henry Hall, and even middle-of-the-roaders should remember that "it is not easy to get alcohol if you are underage, at least enough to drink to excess." The town revolves around the college. If you've seen one countryside, you've seen them all, so students must make their own fun. Typically, that means hanging out in each other's rooms, or if they're 21, at CJ's Down Under, an on-campus pub that serves pizza (and karaoke on Tuesdays). The Student Programming Board plans concerts, comedians, speakers, movies, and both formal and informal dances. Road trips to Cleveland's Jacobs Field or the Rock and Roll Hall of Fame, as well as the Sea World, Geauga Lake or Cedar Point amusement parks, beckon in good weather, and sometimes the college offers free tickets to concerts, plays, and ballets in town. Every semester also brings a surprise Campus Day, when classes are cancelled and a slew of activities planned. Other diversions include an excellent golf course three miles away, a college-owned cross-country ski trail, and good downhill slopes about an hour distant.

Hiram is hardly a mecca for budding all-Americans, but it does have a decent Division III sports program. Football, baseball, and soccer are among the most popular men's teams, while soccer, volleyball, and softball attract women. A fitness center is open to all.

Those looking for a school where anonymity will be ensured need not apply to Hiram. People here are so close that they share an equivalent of the secret handshake. "Everyone smiles at you as you walk by, even if they don't know you," says a freshman. "Hiram takes great pride in its ability to make sweeping technological improvements while retaining its old-world values."

Overlaps

Wooster, John Carroll, Mount Union, Miami University (OH), Wittenberg.

If You Apply To ➤

Hiram...Rolling admissions: Mar. 15. Financial aid: Mar. 1. Does not guarantee to meet demonstrated need. Campus interviews: recommended (required for scholarship consideration), evaluative. Alumni interviews: optional, informational. SATs or ACTs: required. Accepts the Common Application and electronic applications. Essay question: what you look forward to in college; biggest misconception about yourself; significant experience or achievement; or influential person.

Hobart and William Smith Colleges

Geneva, NY 14456

Students at Hobart College for men and William Smith College for women benefit from the schools' unique "coordinate" relationship. Each has its own dean, admissions office, and student government, but students eat together, study together, and even live together in co-ed residence halls. "Neither women's issues nor men's issues are ignored," explains a senior anthropology major. "If you weren't very involved on campus, you probably wouldn't notice that we were two separate schools."

H-WS's tree-lined campus on a 200-acre stretch of ground above the shores of Seneca Lake is the kind of place made for crisp fall afternoons. Architectural styles range from Colonial to postmodern, and feature stately Greek Revival mansions and ivy-clad brick residences and classrooms. The Thomas A. Melly Academic Center, or "Big Mac," provides students with a vast array of resources, including computer workstations, Internet access, CD-ROM indices, and a multimedia classroom. "The only academic institutions with better libraries than ours are universities with the word 'Technology' in their names," boasts the college librarian.

The colleges' innovative curriculum begins with an interdisciplinary first-year seminar with a heavy emphasis on writing and critical thinking. Instead of traditional distribution requirements, students are required to complete a major and either a minor or second major, one from a traditional department and one from an interdisciplinary program. Some of the newest majors include international relations, European Studies, and media and society. The academic climate is "competitive," but not overly so. "It's a competitive environment but we are also well supported by our professors," says a biology major. Classes are small; two-thirds have fewer than 25 students, and most students report little trouble getting into courses they want and need. Academic advising is highly praised, as is the Career Development Center. "It is not unusual to meet with an advisor for lunch, to catch up on how everything is coming along, or to have dinner at his or her house with a group of advisees," says a senior.

The colleges have traditionally been strong in the humanities and premed, and creating individualized majors is highly encouraged. In fact, the latter are the most popular program on campus, followed by English, psychology, history, and economics. The colleges encourage students to take a term abroad through one of a number of programs across the globe, and over 65 percent of students participate in some type of off-campus study. Qualified students may also take part in the honors program, the Venture Program,* and undergraduate research. Students say that the theater department needs improvement.

New Yorkers make up half of H-WS's student body, which is 86 percent white, 6 percent African American, 4 percent Hispanic, and 2 percent Asian American. Though hardly diverse, the campus abounds in progressive good intentions, as indicated by small but flourishing women's, African American, and Third World cultural studies departments. Major social and political issues include racial and gender concerns. "Everyone is very careful not to offend anyone else," says an economics major.

Ninety percent of H-WS students live on campus and most seem happy there. "The housing here is excellent," says an international relations major. "The rooms are very large and the furniture is well-maintained." First-year students, who may opt for single-sex or coed dorms, usually get their first choice. Geneva (Hobart)

Website: www.hws.edu

Location: Small city

Total Enrollment: 1,830

Undergraduates: 1,830

Male/Female: 48/52

SAT Ranges: V 530–620 M 530–620

Financial Aid: 68%

Expense: Pr $ $ $ $

Phi Beta Kappa: Yes

Applicants: 2,762

Accepted: 72%

Enrolled: 28%

Grad in 6 Years: 82%

Returning Freshmen: 88%

Academics: ✍ ✍ ✍

Social: ☎ ☎ ☎

Q of L: ★ ★ ★

Admissions: (315) 781-3472

Email Address:
admissions@hws.edu

Strongest Programs:
Creative Writing
Teacher Certification
Economics
Environmental Studies
Biology
English
Political Science
Psychology

The colleges encourage students to take a term abroad through one of a number of programs across the globe, and over 65 percent of students participate in some type of off-campus study.

Qualified students may also take part in the honors program, the Venture Program,* and undergraduate research.

and Hirshon (William Smith) are favorites, while Durfee, Bartlett, and Hale halls, known as "Miniquad" and formerly the most avoided living spaces on campus, have undergone a renaissance in popularity among Hobart men. Most sophomores live in a large coed complex known as J-P-R (Jackson, Potter, and Rees halls). The new "Village at Odell's Pond" offers upperclass students townhouses, each with four to five bedrooms and two bathrooms. "I live in a big college-owned house right on the lake," an anthropology major gloats. "I have my own porch with great views."

While six Hobart fraternities claim 20 percent of the college's men, who aren't permitted to pledge until sophomore year, there are no sororities at William Smith (so much for the Socratic mean). Hence, Greek life is an option, not an imperative. For men who'd rather not join fraternities, Bampton House (the men's honors house) and McDaniel's House are good bets. Women prefer smaller residence halls, like Blackwell and Miller houses, which contribute to a feeling of community without rigid structure. William Smith has also retained a number of traditions typical of women's colleges, most notably Moving Up Day, in which the seniors symbolically hand over their leadership role to the juniors.

Geneva is "not like being in a big city," a political science major says. Bars, movie theaters, a Blockbuster, and Wegmans, an upscale grocery chain, are within walking distance of campus, and student groups sponsor lectures, concerts, and readings. Still, students do like to get away, and the best road trips are to Ithaca, Elmira, Syracuse, Buffalo and Rochester, New York and Toronto, Canada, they say. Underage drinking goes on at frat parties, but appears to be a more difficult undertaking at downtown bars. The annual Celebrate Service, Celebrate Geneva Day attracts over 500 students and faculty for community service projects. Favorite events include Winter Carnival, Snowball, and Folkfest, a two-day music- and craft-filled party. "The third weekend in May, out on the Quad from Friday until Sunday night, is filled with bands, food vendors, and illegal substances—so much fun!" says a senior.

Some of the newest majors include international relations, European Studies, and media and society.

Campus organizations range from Young Entrepreneurs to the Clown Club, but sports are unquestionably the most popular. In the spring, the campus comes alive with mania for men's lacrosse. The team won 16 straight NCAA Division III championships before joining Division I in 1995. For the annual Hobart-Syracuse game, practically the whole campus travels to Syracuse as a cheering squad. The women's field hockey, soccer, and lacrosse teams are perennial powerhouses in Division III. The colleges' sailing was ranked third nationally in 1999, while the William Smith crew team is the only Division III school invited to NCAA post-season competition in each year since the competition began. Intramurals are also extensive, helped by a $6.5-million indoor recreation center.

Hobart and William Smith Colleges provide an amalgam of autonomy and community that's hard to come by these days. Though their name may not be as well known as some other northeastern schools'—a popular campus T-shirt reasons, "Not Williams...Not Smith...William Smith!"—students at these ruggedly beautiful colleges are unabashedly loyal to the special type of education they receive. "Our coordinate system which provides an environment where we as men learn how to interact with other men as well as women, and vice-versa," says a biochemistry major. Another student agrees: "The students at Hobart and William Smith Colleges truly do get a well-balanced education."

Overlaps

Skidmore, Hamilton, Union, University of Vermont, SUNY at Geneseo.

If You Apply To ➤	Hobart and William Smith...Early decision: Nov. 15, Jan. 1. Regular admissions: Feb. 1. Financial aid: Feb. 15. Meets demonstrated need of 94%. Campus and alumni interviews: recommended, evaluative. SATs or ACTs: required. SAT IIs: optional. Accepts the Common Application and electronic applications. Essay question: personal statement. Examples of creative work invited.

Hollins University (formerly Hollins College)

Roanoke, VA 24020

Don't tell the students at this small liberal arts institution—newly christened a university—that the time for single-sex education has passed. They know that "women who are going places start at Hollins." Founded in 1842, Hollins is one of the nation's oldest women's colleges, and it still offers a quality education and a sense of community that affirms the equal worth of women and men. "Hollins really fuels determination in ambitious students and gives them the will to do anything," says a junior.

Described by *The New York Times* as "achingly picturesque," the neoclassical redbrick buildings at Hollins date back to the mid-19th century. Hollins's campus is in the midst of a building boom. Funds are being raised for a $10.5 million visual arts center for art history, studio art, film, and photography. The state-of-the-art Wyndham Robertson Library has been completed, and Pleasants Hall, the main social science building, has been renovated thanks to the generosity of a loyal alumna.

Whether it's the award-winning writing program, the state-of-the-art computer facilities, the highly prized honor system, or student-administered Independent Exam System, which allows students to take exams whenever they choose (within limits) without faculty supervision, Hollins has much to offer. The academic program is rigorous, but many students agree that the environment is encouraging and nurturing. "It's only competitive in the sense that you're expected to work to your maximum potential," says an international studies major. The best departments are English, particularly creative writing, and psychology, each with nationally known faculty and coed master's degree programs. Art is also a popular choice; a link to Christie's in London gives students a yearlong opportunity to learn about galleries and auction houses, with strong emphasis on writing and research. Ironically, women's studies draws jeers; a junior majoring in the discipline complains that it's "still under construction."

Standard distribution requirements include competencies in written and oral communication, quantitative reasoning, computer literacy, and two courses in each of four divisions: fine arts, humanities, natural sciences and mathematics, and social sciences.

Two terms of phys ed are required, too. Strongly self-motivated students are encouraged to design individualized major programs. New additions to the academic menu include majors in business and computer science, and a new summer graduate program in screenwriting and film studies. Although it does emphasize liberal arts, Hollins offers a combined-degree program in engineering and architecture. As a member of the Seven-College Exchange* consortium, Hollins also allows its students cross-registration options with other participating institutions.

Website: www.hollins.edu

Location: City outskirts

Total Enrollment: 1,084

Undergraduates: 826

Male/Female: 0/100

SAT Ranges: V 530–650 M 500–580

ACT Range: 23–27

Financial Aid: 59%

Expense: Pr $

Phi Beta Kappa: Yes

Applicants: 722

Accepted: 86%

Enrolled: 38%

Grad in 6 Years: 71%

Returning Freshmen: 79%

Academics: ✍ ✍ ✍

Social: ☎ ☎ ☎

Q of L: ★ ★ ★ ★

Admissions: (540) 362-6401

Email Address: huadm@hollins.edu

Strongest Programs:
English/Creative Writing
Psychology
Art
Dance

Those with wanderlust can spend semesters at Hollins's extended campuses in England, France, Mexico, Spain, or Japan. They can also study in Ireland, Austria, Greece, or Italy, and a service-learning program takes students to Jamaica every year. The popular January term offers a break for on-campus projects, travel, or internships; alumnae help arrange housing in Washington and other cities. "These internships create contacts and references that will get us the jobs we want," says a senior.

Back on campus, classes are small; the vast majority have 25 or fewer students. "I have been able to form close relationships with all of my professors due to the small environment," one student says. "The professors here are amazing," says another senior. "They tend to be very supportive and accessible." The college also garners praise for its strong counseling program—whether for academic, psychological, career, or financial concerns. "My advisor has been so helpful in making sure I graduate on time," says a senior communications major. The new library lures students with its collection of over 400,000 items, two-story periodical reading room, and multimedia production facilities.

The typical Hollins woman—once disparaged as a "Hollie Collie"—might well fit the antebellum image: white and traditional. But she is also intelligent; some 25 percent of students here graduated in the top tenth of their high school class. Twenty-nine percent of the students come from private schools, and 42 percent are homegrown Virginians. The student body is 80 percent white, with African Americans the largest minority at 5 percent. Of course, women's issues get top billing, and there is conflict between "traditional nonfeminists and modern, nontraditional feminists". A creative writing major says, "We still have the pearl and bow girls, but now there's just a little variety to go along with them." But a junior adds, "We're mostly tolerant and understanding, and in a place where we almost all know one another, political correctness isn't necessary." Hollins's administration remains proud of its financial aid policy and is need-blind in 97 percent of admissions decisions. The school awards 339 merit scholarships, ranging from $3,000 to $15,000, but no athletic scholarships. Several tuition payment plans are offered.

"Dorms are nice, large, and airy with plenty of windows, closet space, and lots of room to decorate," one woman enthuses. Styles vary, from the modern Tinker and Randolph buildings to the Front Quad, where students are almost guaranteed single rooms with wood floors, brass doorknobs, cathedral ceilings, walk-in closets, and for some, even fireplaces. "The beds are so comfortable that I often find it difficult to get up and go to class!" jokes a junior. University-owned apartments across the street cost the same as the dorms and are popular among seniors. Dorm rooms are connected to the computer network, which gives students access to all computer labs and software, as well as links to major university libraries and computer systems nationwide, which may explain why just 2 percent of students live off campus.

Outside of class, the Hollins Outdoor Program offers hiking or spelunking in the beautiful Shenandoah Valley and Blue Ridge Mountains. Hollins's large on-campus stable complements the school's extensive equestrian program, which has frequently produced national champion riders. Swimming also has won national Division III championships. The city of Roanoke has much to offer culturally, and students give back through volunteer work at the free clinic, homeless shelter, and women's shelter.

Hollins shuns sororities but does organize school-wide mixers and maintains several traditions. At the annual Tinker Day festivities, sometime after the first frost, classes are canceled, everyone eats breakfast in her PJs, and the whole school dresses up in "wacky costumes" and hikes to the top of Tinker Mountain for songs, skits, and a picnic lunch. On Ring Night, juniors receive their class rings from senior ring sisters, and on Hundredth Night seniors put on skits to celebrate the 100th night before graduation. Socially, drinks are available in the on-campus snack bar, but students say it's almost impossible for underage students to be served at college events. And road-tripping remains the preferred social option for women in search of "the frat environment." Favorite destinations include Hampden-Sydney College, the University of Virginia, and Washington and Lee, where there are, of course, men.

Hollins students continue to cry "Better dead than coed!" and the Board of Trustees recently fired the president for suggesting that they reconsider this policy as a way to bolster enrollment. Students here realize that stellar faculty, updated facilities, a noncompetitive environment, and "the chance to form friendships that will no doubt last a lifetime" prepare a woman well for whatever her future may hold, even if they temporarily impair her social life. According to one woman, Hollins produces "open-minded individuals and teaches you to be a leader."

<aside>

Overlaps

University of Virginia, James Madison, Sweet Briar, Virginia Tech, Mary Washington.

</aside>

If You Apply To ➤

Hollins...Rolling admissions: after Feb. 15. Early decision: Dec. 1. Regular admissions: Feb. 15. Financial aid: Feb. 15. Meets demonstrated need of 57%. Campus interviews: recommended, informational. Alumni interviews: optional, informational. SAT or ACT: required. SAI IIs: recommended (writing and two others). Accepts the Common Application. Essay question: a personal career goal; a volunteer community service you performed; how you express your creativity or use it to solve problems; a woman you admire outside your family.

College of the Holy Cross

Worcester, MA 01610

Community is more than just a buzzword at this deeply Jesuit and academically stout New England college. A warm, friendly feeling truly pervades the place, and students can always find support or spiritual guidance. "People walking around campus are not just random students," insists a senior history major. "Instead, they are friends, neighbors, study partners, or teammates." Bonds forged in the lab or on the field are strengthened through participation in activities like SPUD (Student Programs for Urban Development), which helps students follow the Jesuit tradition of becoming "men and women for others." Professors genuinely concerned with their students' well-being—"academically and otherwise"—are one more point of pride at Holy Cross. The school's relatively urban location and proximity to nine other colleges are added bonuses.

Located on one of the seven hills overlooking the industrial city of Worcester, the 174-acre Holy Cross campus is a registered arboretum, mixing classical and modern architectural styles within a picturesque and well-planted area. In fact, the campus's landscaping has won some half-dozen national awards, among them two first-place prizes as the best landscaped campus in the nation. Recent additions include a greenhouse for the biology building, a new theater "pit," a two-story wellness center, and new chemistry classrooms and research labs. The biology building and campus center have also been completely renovated.

Other Holy Cross award winners are its small classes, which help faculty members keep in touch with undergraduates. "The quality of teaching is really

<aside>

Website: www.holycross.edu

Location: City outskirts

Total Enrollment: 2,801

Undergraduates: 2,801

Male/Female: 47/53

SAT Ranges: V 550–670 M 550–670

ACT Range: N/A

Financial Aid: 50%

Expense: Pr $ $ $

Phi Beta Kappa: Yes

Applicants: 4,836

Accepted: 44%

Enrolled: 35%

Grad in 6 Years: 93%

Returning Freshmen: 95%

Academics: ✍ ✍ ✍ ✍

Social: ☎ ☎ ☎ ☎

Q of L: ★ ★ ★ ★

</aside>

(Continued)

Admissions: (508) 793-2443 or
(800) 442-2421

Email Address:
admissions@holycross.edu

Strongest Programs:
Classics
Biology/Premed
History
Economics

Recent additions include a greenhouse for the biology building, a new theater "pit," a two-story wellness center, and new chemistry classrooms and research labs. The biology building and campus center have also been completely renovated.

Twenty-five percent of Holy Cross's first-year students enroll in the living/learning First Year Program, which attempts to answer Tolstoy's critical human question, "How then shall we live?"

the reason I transferred to HC," says a junior English major. "Here, the relationship between the professor and the student is a close one. Freshmen are always taught by full professors who genuinely want to help them." Although courses are rigorous, the overall academic climate is laid-back; students don't compete with each other because professors encourage "working together in order to make the learning process most effective," says a junior. They still study plenty, though: "For each hour inside the classroom, the student is expected to put in roughly four hours of work outside," a senior notes.

The English program at Holy Cross is highly rated, as are religious studies, economics, biology/premed, and history. Psychology is popular, and the college has a regional reputation for excellence in classics and economics/accounting. New additions to the curriculum include a major in Italian and a minor in economics/accounting. Music, theater, and fine arts are reportedly weaker because of their small size, but as the student/faculty ratio in these departments is about two to one and tutorials are encouraged, carefully chosen seminars can be excellent. Generally, students report no trouble getting needed classes, and the school guarantees entry into at least one major course each semester.

Nearly one-quarter of Holy Cross's first-year students enroll in the living/learning First Year Program, which attempts to answer Tolstoy's critical human question, "How then shall we live?" Students take specially designed classes that aim to "bring different disciplines into common focus and to examine ethical dimensions of different disciplines." General requirements encompass 10 courses in six categories: arts and literature, cross-cultural studies, religious and philosophical studies, historical studies, social science and natural science, and math. Students must also demonstrate competence in a classical language, a modern foreign language, or American Sign Language. Still, in all majors, the emphasis is on ideas and thinking, rather than preparation for a specific vocation.

Holy Cross is part of the Worcester Consortium,* which offers students privileges at the region's most prestigious colleges and universities. An interdisciplinary humanities program provides a chance to study a particular topic with three or four different professors. Education courses and internships at local primary and secondary schools are offered, and the teacher certification program was recently accredited by the Massachusetts Department of Education. Would-be engineers can choose Holy Cross's 3–2 program with Columbia, Dartmouth, or Washington University (MO). The Center for Experimental Studies offers a wide range of alternatives, including local internships, the Washington Semester* program, and international, gerontology, and peace studies.

The selective honors program gives special attention to top students, and the Fenwick Scholars program allows students to design and carry out an independent project. Through the Venture Program* and direct partnerships with foreign universities, students may spend their junior year in one of 11 countries across Europe, Asia, and Africa. About one-fifth do so.

The religious influence at Holy Cross is somewhat greater than at some other Jesuit schools; most students are Roman Catholics, 33 percent are in-staters, and about the same fraction attended parochial school. Yet the religious atmosphere beckons without scolding. Daily attendance at Mass is not required, but the chaplain's office offers a five-day silent retreat four times annually, in which student volunteers follow the spiritual exercises of Jesuit founder St. Ignatius Loyola. Perhaps not surprisingly, then, Holy Cross's campus lacks racial and ethnic diversity; African Americans and Asian Americans each make up 3 percent of the student body, while Hispanics account for 5 percent. Still, students say the school is dedicated to raising awareness of multicultural issues—and "a task force composed of students has been assembled to aid the administration in increasing the diversity here on campus," a senior reports. Indeed, in recent years, the college has seen the growth of student groups such the Black Student Union, the Multicultural Awareness Club, Asian Students for International Awareness, Latin American Students Organization, and the Social Concerns Committee.

The college's dorms have mostly double rooms, are coed by floor, and are professionally cleaned on a regular basis. "The dorms for freshmen and sophomores are pretty substandard—very basic," reports a junior, though they are wired for Internet access. "After that, however, they are all new suites," two- and three-bedroom units that include a living room, a bathroom, and sometimes a study. Nonetheless, 20 percent of undergrads, mostly seniors, move off campus, where housing is cheap and plentiful. Most first-year students live on "Easy Street," the row of five dorms (Healy, Leahy, Hanselman, Clark, and Mulledy) located on the college's central hill, next to the Hogan Campus Center. In the past few years, overcrowding has forced some freshmen to triple up, leaving them understandably longing for the roomier upperclass dorms. Students are rather unenthusiastic about the meal plan, but special vegetarian fare is an option.

When dorm food is totally inedible, students head into Worcester, New England's second-largest city. The community boasts museums, movie theaters, an orchestra, restaurants, and the Worcester Centrum's world-class athletic events and rock concerts. "Worcester is big and has everything one would need, but it is not the most visually pleasing," says a junior. Boston is about an hour away, and the Cape Cod beaches and White Mountain ski slopes aren't much farther. Socially, since students are discouraged from having cars, most take advantage of activities planned by the Campus Activities Board, such as live-band concerts and dances.

Holy Cross is increasingly conscientious about enforcing Massachusetts drinking laws. Campus parties are closely monitored, and only students over 21 are permitted to have beer in their rooms. The campus pub carefully scrutinizes IDs; according to a freshman, "Campus is definitely not like *Animal House*, and known violators are subjected to punishment." Off-campus parties are another story, though. Students look forward to a series of campus-wide festivals throughout the year, capped by the 100 Days weekend, marking the time seniors have left until graduation, and HC by the Sea (a week in Cape Cod at the end of the year). Semiformal dances, Spring Weekend, and Fall Classic inspire camaraderie and cohesiveness. And given the high percentage of Irish Catholic students, St. Patrick's Day is honored with much pomp and mirth. On ordinary weekends, students attend varsity football and basketball games en masse, and have made an art of tailgating. The football stadium holds 23,500 screaming Crusaders fans, who cheer with religious zeal, although a sophomore sadly notes that "With many of our sports teams rebuilding, athletic rivalries and other traditions are not what they used to be."

Catholicism and the Jesuit tradition are squarely at the center of the Holy Cross experience. With a comprehensive academic planning initiative focused on these issues currently under way, and with plans for four new tenure-track faculty to teach and study them, this commitment is sure to evolve and deepen in the coming years. Still, as always, students as concerned with preserving their faith as they are with having serious collegiate fun will find happiness in becoming Crusaders.

Through direct partnerships with foreign universities, students may spend their junior year in one of 11 countries across Europe, Asia, and Africa. About one-fifth do so.

The football stadium holds 23,500 screaming Crusaders fans, who cheer with religious zeal.

Overlaps

Boston College, Georgetown, Dartmouth, Notre Dame, Fairfield.

Hood College

401 Rosemont Avenue, Frederick, MD 21701

Website: www.hood.edu

Location: Small city

Total Enrollment: 1,776

Undergraduates: 894

Male/Female: 11/89

SAT Ranges: V 500–630 M 490–590

ACT Range: 19–25

Financial Aid: 61%

Expense: Pr $ $

Phi Beta Kappa: No

Applicants: 533

Accepted: 77%

Enrolled: 34%

Grad in 6 Years: 67%

Returning Freshmen: 84%

Academics: ✍ ✍ ✍

Social: ☎ ☎ ☎

Q of L: ★ ★ ★

Admissions: (301) 696-3400 or (800) 922-1599

Email Address: admissions@hood.edu

Strongest Programs:
  Biology
  Economics/Management
  Humanities
  Social Work/Sociology
  Education
  Psychology

At Hood College, where the president, 55 percent of the faculty, and 89 percent of the student body are women, the goal is to prepare Hood women, and a few men, to face challenges in the professional environment. Hood College encourages excellence in the study of business, science, politics, and education. The school also builds leadership skills, friendship, and confidence to prepare students for the challenges that lie ahead.

Hood was founded in 1893. Its strikingly beautiful 50-acre campus features red-brick buildings and lush, tree-shaded lawns in the historic Civil War town of Frederick. Hood is within an hour and a half of nearly 30 colleges, within minutes of a major National Cancer Institute research complex, plus high-tech firms, small and large businesses, and both Washington, D.C., and Baltimore. On campus, technology programs are considered important, with the recent groundbreaking of a new science and technology center which will house all of the natural and quantitative sciences.

Students see their school's biggest strength as its people: students, staff, and faculty. "As soon as you step on campus you feel at home," says a junior English major. All incoming students participate in the Freshman Colloquium, a series of intellectual, social, and cultural events that focus on a different topic each year. Sophomore Experience helps students pick a major and plan a career. The student-run honor system also is an important part of a Hood education. The academic honor code permits unproctored exams and self-scheduled finals; the social code allows for self-governed residence halls, where students call the shots in place of resident assistants.

Hood's required core curriculum is divided into three parts. Foundation courses include English, foreign language, computation, physical education, and fitness. Methods of Inquiry offers courses that acquaint students with scientific thought, historical and social/behavioral analysis, and philosophy. The Civilization section requires coursework in modern technology and Western and non-Western civilization at the junior-senior level. Even with these comprehensive requirements, there is still a great deal of flexibility; creative interdepartmental majors are often approved. Hood's major strength lies in the sciences, especially the biology department, with its special focus on molecular biology, marine biology, and environmental science and policy. Management is the most popular major. Education is also a program of note, as is English; math classes draw criticism for being difficult and hard to follow. Hood has added graduate programs in Information Technology Management and Regulatory Compliance. The college also established a Center for Public Policy and Ethics that focuses on preparing students to take a larger role in addressing issues once they graduate.

Hood students, sometimes called "Hood-lums," praise the competence and accessibility of the faculty. "I would rate the quality of teaching as exceptional," says a junior. "Professors go above and beyond what I expected." Almost everyone is taught by full-time professors in classes of about 15 students (25 in intro courses). A computer network links every dorm room and academic building to the campus-wide information system, and students have 24-hour Internet access.

If you really want to work, the four-year honors program features team-taught courses and a sophomore-year seminar on the ethics of social and individual responsibility, with student involvement in a community service project. Many students (over 100 yearly) will complete internships that include overseas jobs for language and business majors and legislative and cultural positions in Washington, D.C. With the outstanding resources of the Catherine Filene Shouse Career Center (including a national electronic listing for resumes), students have a leg up on their next step in life—sixty-six percent of graduates go straight into jobs after graduation; 23 percent enroll in grad school. A three-week May term offers study tours, to countries including France and Mexico, that meet core requirements.

The Hood student body is mostly white and middle to upper middle class. Twelve percent of the student body are African American, 3 percent Hispanic, 2 percent Asian American, and 5 percent international. Twenty-one percent of Hood students are from out of state, with a large contingent from the Northeast. There is a minority recruitment plan for students, faculty, and staff. Of the important social issues on campus, one student says, "Hood walks that fine line between living and practicing diversity and pushing it down your throat. Hood attracts her share of liberals, and we have some pretty exciting discussions, both inside and out." Another contentious issue is cost-cutting. "I feel that we should put more money towards hiring quality teachers," says a senior.

Students recognize early on that the school demands they be committed to their studies. Seventy-one percent ranked in the top quarter of their high school class. Students believe they have support, more than competition, from their peers. "I was shocked to hear from friends at other women's colleges that their schools have a sort of 'catty' competition. Hood's academic base is a very supportive one," says one woman. Still, Hood women describe themselves as studious and grade-oriented. Hood provides numerous merit scholarships, which can range to full tuition.

Hood's dorms are for women only (as men can only be day students), and are well liked. "Mine was built in 1922, and while there are newer residence halls, ours always has fresh paint and has incredibly beautiful woodwork and stairways," says one happy camper. Another says, "The halls are comfortable compared to their age. There is always a need for more laundry machines." The lottery system is based on seniority. Freshmen can expect to be assigned to doubles (seniors and juniors can compete for singles), and three small language dorms house students who choose to speak French, Spanish, or German exclusively.

Social life among the students is centered around the dorms, as each has its own personality as well as its own house council, rules, and social activities. Students report that there are parties every weekend, along with movies, dances, or other forms of entertainment. The Whitaker Campus Center, with its pool tables, snackbar, bookstore, and meeting rooms, offers a great gathering place 24 hours a day. "Seniors go downtown and stay on campus—bars, movies, the mall, Baker Park, walking, and the Naval Academy all are popular," says one woman. Campus alcohol policies follow state law and the honor code, but in general drinking is not a big deal at Hood. "If you want to drink, you can probably get

The academic honor code permits unproctored exams and self-scheduled finals; the social code allows for self-governed residence halls, where students call the shots in place of resident assistants.

Hood's major strength lies in the sciences, especially the biology department, with its special focus on molecular biology, marine biology, and environmental science and policy.

Many students (over 100 yearly) will complete internships that include overseas jobs for language and business majors and legislative and cultural positions in Washington, D.C.

away with it, but most people don't drink" says one biochemistry major. Students also frequent scenic Frederick, which is described as small, safe, and beautiful, but without too much in the way of entertainment.

With a 100-year history, Hood is rife with traditions. Some of the most important ones include Class Ring dinner and formal, Senior Prank, and Strawberry Breakfast, a fall semester midnight breakfast served by faculty and staff on the eve of finals. In sports, lacrosse, field hockey, basketball, volleyball, soccer, and tennis are tops.

Small, private women's colleges are often characterized as insulated from the real world, but at Hood, the emphasis is on preparing intelligent, well-educated women to take their places in fast-paced fields like politics and science. While still remaining true to its deep roots and traditions, Hood has managed to maintain a vision that looks forward with confidence to the 21st century.

If You Apply To ➤ **Hood**…Early action: Nov. 1. Regular admissions and financial aid: Feb. 15. Meets demonstrated need of 56%. Campus interviews: recommended, evaluative. Alumni interviews: optional, informational. SATs or ACTs: required. SAT IIs: recommended. Accepts the Common Application and electronic applications. Essay question: significant experience; important issue; and interview of historical figure.

Hope College

P.O. Box 9000, Holland, MI 49422-9000

Every fall since 1897, Hope College freshmen have spent three grueling hours engaged in "the Pull." This unusual event is an epic tug-of-war against the sophomore class, which stands assembled on the opposite end of a 650-pound rope—across the 15-foot-wide Black River. Perhaps this annual tradition symbolizes the struggle Hope students face as they strive to maintain their faith in a world that seems to challenge it at every turn. This liberal arts college aims to provide its 2,900 students a solid education and a deeper understanding of their purpose in life. The heritage of Hope's Dutch founders remains strong and visible on campus; still, you don't have to be Dutch to appreciate this conservative Christian school known for its programs in the natural sciences, arts, and business.

Hope College, which dates to 1866, is situated on six blocks near downtown Holland (population 60,000), a short bike ride from the shores of Lake Michigan. The campus sports a luscious pine grove in its center, and features an eclectic array of buildings in architectural styles ranging from 19th-century Flemish to modern. A new science building is in the works.

Among Hope's academic offerings, the sciences (especially biology, physics, and chemistry) stand out, with excellent laboratory facilities and faculty who frequently receive grants from the National Science Foundation and include students in their research projects. During the school year, undergraduates can conduct advanced experiments and may even get their names on published papers; in the summer, more than 75 biology, chemistry, mathematics, computer science, and physics students are involved in full-time research. Not surprisingly, many science majors go on to medical and engineering schools and Ph.D. programs. But for those otherwise inclined, Hope's offerings in history, political science, classics, and business and economics are strong, too. The Speech Communication Association has named Hope's Department of Communication one of two nationwide Programs of Excellence. And Hope is one of only 14 colleges and universities in the United States with accredited programs in art, dance, music, and theater. English majors are enjoying an expanded creative writing program, though the more journalistically inclined may find offerings in that field limited. Recently, the college gained special accreditation for its athletic training major, added majors in engineering and engineering sciences, and replaced business administration with a new management program.

Most Hope students select a major from one of the college's 39 fields, but the truly adventurous can design their own composite major. Hope's general education curriculum is designed "to demonstrate to students the interrelatedness of knowledge, and to prepare them for adaptation to change in the workplace and in society." The curriculum provides more room for exploration by exposing students to everything from cultural heritage and language to health dynamics and expository writing. All freshmen also take the First Year Seminar. Students say the academic climate is competitive but not cutthroat. "Courses are challenging but you get out of it what you put into it," says a French major. Then again, there's lots of faculty support; a senior notes that "The professors love to teach and they enjoy getting to know their students." Advisors get high marks, too. "My advisor has been wonderful in helping me plan courses. There are so many career help opportunities, one just needs to take advantage of them," says a senior.

As a member of the Great Lakes Colleges Association,* Hope offers a variety of off-campus programs, including semesters at other U.S. colleges combining classes and internships. Students can also study abroad in places such as Austria, England, Greece, Japan, or Jerusalem. The modern and classical language departments offers opportunities for majors proficient in a second language to use their skills in community volunteer work and research with faculty members. The Visiting Writers Series gives students an opportunity to interact with noteworthy authors.

Less than a fourth of Hope's students belong to the Reformed Church in America, but the student body is overwhelmingly Christian, white, and conservative. Seventy-seven percent are Michigan natives. African Americans, Hispanics, and Asian Americans make up just 5 percent of the student body, but students don't mention race relations among hot-button campus issues. Still, there is friction, "between those who affirm Christianity as taught by the Bible and those who don't," says a business administration major.

Other ongoing debates include gay and lesbian rights and whether chapel should be voluntary or mandatory. "Our campus ministry has been dealing with sticky issues, and it is hard for some to accept religious recommendations," ventures a special education major.

Hope has a variety of housing options, including on-campus apartments, small houses called cottages, and traditional dorms (single-sex and coed). Freshmen are assigned dorms and roommates; thereafter, rooms are doled out by lottery, with upperclassmen getting first dibs. The dorms are "well-maintained and kept very clean," says a religion and economics double major. On-campus students eat in two large dining halls, and few complain about the food, especially the homemade bread and desserts. Shuttle vans and campus police help off-campus dwellers feel safe.

For most students, social life is a mix of on- and off-campus happenings. Hope's seven fraternities and six sororities, all local organizations, claim about 26 percent of the men and 28 percent of the women. The Social Activities Committee

(Continued)
Strongest Programs:
 Biology
 Chemistry
 Dance
 English
 Music
 Political Science
 Psychology
 Religion

Among Hope's academic offerings, the sciences (especially biology, physics, and chemistry) stand out, with excellent laboratory facilities and faculty who frequently receive grants from the National Science Foundation and include students in their research projects.

plans concerts, talent shows, formal and semiformal dances, the Spring Festival, and films. Alcohol is banned on campus, and offenders perform community service. One student reports, "Alcohol is rarely brought into dorms, but cottages are less monitored. Off-campus houses can and do have alcohol." At Hope, however, social options lean more toward sports games and coffeehouses than keg parties.

When the Hope campus gets a little too friendly, students head to the beaches of Lake Michigan or drive half an hour to Grand Rapids, which offers some larger-city amenities and good weekend rental deals at the ski slopes. Chicago is also a draw. Holland is described as a "mid-sized town with a small-town atmosphere," and is the site of Tulip Time, one of the largest flowers festivals in the U.S., every spring. Many Hope students are involved in community outreach and volunteering programs, and activities such as charity walks bring the community together.

On the field and on the court, the Flying Dutchmen and Flying Dutch (Hope's varsity teams) are fearless and talented. The men's football team has been conference champion two of the last three years, and the women's swim team recently finished sixth in the nation. Last year, Hope won the Michigan Intercollegiate Athletic Association All-Sports Championship for the fifth time in the past six years; the trophy recognizes the school with the conference's best cumulative sports program for men and women. The best rivalries are any competition against Calvin (a century-old rivalry) and football versus Albion. More than half of Hope's students are involved in intramural sports.

Hope, says a senior, "is a Christian college that seeks to balance excellent education with deepening spirituality." That's a difficult balance to achieve, and it is beginning to cause tension on campus; not all students agree with the increased emphasis on Christianity in all facets of college life. For now, though, students cherish Hope's conservative Christian atmosphere, and enjoy the luxury of a campus small enough for everyone to know their names.

Overlaps

Michigan State, Western Michigan, University of Michigan, Grand Valley, Calvin.

If You Apply To ➤ **Hope**…Rolling admissions. Meets demonstrated need of 85%. Campus interviews: optional, informational. No alumni interviews. SATs or ACTs: required. SAT IIs: optional. Accepts the Common Application and electronic applications. Essay question: what you have gained from and contributed to activities or employment; something important to you; and thoughts on careers and career preparation.

Houghton College

Houghton, NY 14744

Website: www.houghton.edu
Location: Rural
Total Enrollment: 1,217
Undergraduates: 1,217
Male/Female: 36/64
SAT Ranges: V 530–660 M 520–630
ACT Range: 22–26
Financial Aid: 85%

Houghton College proclaims its calling from the mountaintops above New York's Genesee Valley: in administrators' words, "The integration of faith and learning is central to the mission." This liberal arts institution, run by the Wesleyan Church of America, celebrates its Christian heritage and tries to ensure that its students do the same. Applicants must explain in their essays why they want to go to a Christian college, for example, and thrice-weekly attendance at chapel is a must. But these mandates help create true community on campus. "I love the fact that so many people share the same belief that I do, and that we are Christians who encourage and support one another," says an accounting major. "I love how much we learn about and grow in our relationship with God here."

Perched on a hill, Houghton's scenic campus spans 1,300 acres of rural beauty, surrounded by vast expanses of western New York countryside. The academic buildings are a mix of area fieldstone and brick, with ivy-covered walls. The newest addition to the campus is a 44,000-square-foot music and fine arts center.

Students say the academic climate is challenging. "Houghton's admission standards are high so that part of the college is competitive," says a Bible major, "but the on-campus climate is much more collaborative than competitive." Houghton's most popular majors are education and psychology, but business and music also draw crowds. Physics is a weaker department, but administrators say improvements are being made. Unusual minors such as equestrian studies—which takes advantage of Houghton's 386-acre riding facility—and linguistics have been joined by newer programs, such as a prephysical therapy track for students interested in pursuing graduate study in that discipline. Across departments, however, the school's faculty gets high marks for teaching and accessibility. "I've been impressed with the high levels of personal involvement demonstrated by the faculty," says a communication major. Getting into needed classes can be tough, though, since Houghton is small and registration goes by last name, with letters scrambled each semester.

Once they've enrolled, Houghton students face broad general education requirements known as Integrative Studies, designed to provide a context and framework for the entire educational program. IS includes courses in writing, literature, communications, a foreign language, social science, history, physical education, math, natural science, religion, philosophy, and fine arts. A research requirement cuts across the curriculum, and the Educational Technology Initiative provides all students with laptops. Freshmen must take biblical literature, principles of writing, and a course titled FYI (First-Year Introduction), designed to ease the transition to college. The First-Year Honors Program allows about 30 students to spend the spring semester of their freshman year in London, studying under two Houghton professors.

Houghton has really begun to emphasize off-campus study recently, and students who want to get away can spend a semester at any Christian College Consortium* member school. They may also participate in an American Studies program in Washington, D.C., sponsored by the Coalition for Christian Colleges and Universities.* The Oregon Extension program allows 30 Houghton students to spend the fall studying in the Cascade Mountains, while Houghton's own extension campus in Buffalo offers internships in various fields, and provides living quarters for students completing their student teaching. A 3–2 engineering program with Clarkson University (NY) is available, too.

Students seeking admission to Houghton must submit five personal statements to evaluate their interest in a Christian college, and 55 percent of those who eventually enroll are from New York. The minority community is tiny, accounting for only 4 percent of the student body. Hot-button issues include "whether or not to have nudes in the art classes," a chemistry major says. "Political correctness is not in the forefront, but you feel it when women insist on being ordained ministers." Houghton's increasing use of technology sparked a campus debate when the school's board decided to block access to some Internet sites that contained sexually explicit materials or references. "There were students on both sides of the censorship issue, and eventually some of the restrictions were loosened," says a sophomore.

Houghton's single-sex dorms and 16 townhouses are "roomy and well maintained," and students are required to live in them as freshmen and sophomores. Kitchens are available on each floor. In-room visitation is only allowed at weekly

(Continued)

Expense: Pr $
Phi Beta Kappa: No
Applicants: 960
Accepted: 86%
Enrolled: 37%
Grad in 6 Years: 64%
Returning Freshmen: 86%
Academics: ✐ ✐ ✐
Social: ☎ ☎ ☎
Q of L: ★ ★ ★
Admissions: (800) 777-2556
Email Address:
   admission@houghton.edu

Strongest Programs:
   Biology/Premed
   Business
   Music
   Chemistry
   Education
   Psychology

Unusual minors such as equestrian studies—which takes advantage of Houghton's 386-acre riding facility—and linguistics have been joined by newer programs, such as a prephysical therapy track for students interested in pursuing graduate study in that discipline.

"open houses," but dorm lounges are open daily to members of the opposite sex. After their first two years, almost half the students move off campus, but many opt for college-approved townhouses where regulations are self-imposed. This isn't exactly surprising, considering the other rules voluntarily obeyed by students here, including chapel attendance on Monday, Wednesday, and Friday mornings, abstaining from vices such as tobacco, alcohol, drugs, and swearing, and optional Sunday church and Tuesday prayer meetings.

Houghton's boondocks village has only a country store, bank, doctor's office, Laundromat, gas station, pizza shop, and post office. "In a car, it takes about three minutes from the time you enter Houghton, NY, until the time you leave," agrees a sophomore. Social life consists of on-campus movies, coffeehouses, concerts, and picnics. The student body is two-thirds female, so dating can be a challenge. Drinking occurs, but because it's officially taboo, "you are in the out-crowd here if you drink," a senior says. Students often make the hour-and-a-half drive to Buffalo, Niagara Falls, or Rochester or to nearby parks and ski areas; the college even has its own ski trails. Since the surrounding area is one of the poorest regions in New York State, there are many volunteer opportunities, such as Big Brothers/Big Sisters and nursing home visitation programs. A major annual event, Christian Life Emphasis Week, offers programs with a spiritual bent.

Soccer is the spectator sport of choice at Houghton, especially since there is no football team; the team won conference championships in 1996 and 1997. Women's powerhouse teams include cross-country, field hockey, basketball, and volleyball. The school's sports facilities have undergone extensive renovation and now include new tennis courts, an all-weather track, and lighted soccer and field hockey fields. Intramurals, including pool and Ultimate Frisbee, provide fun competition for all.

With the nearest mall a half-hour away, Houghton students are in the middle of nowhere. Their rural environment can get boring. But many choose to look at the flip side: with little to distract them from their studies, their campus's natural beauty and their connection to God, Houghton can be a fulfilling place to spend four years.

Overlaps

Messiah, Grove City, Gordon, Wheaton (IL), Roberts Wesleyan.

If You Apply To ➤

Houghton...Early action: Nov. 16. Regular admissions: Begin Jan. 1 and continue as space allows. Financial aid: Mar. 15. Housing: June 15. Meets demonstrated need of 25%. Campus interviews: recommended, evaluative. No alumni interviews. SATs or ACTs: required. SAT IIs: optional. Music majors apply directly to music program. Essay question: five personal statements used to evaluate writing skills and interest in a Christian college.

Howard University

2400 Sixth Street NW, Washington, DC 20059

Website: www.howard.edu
Location: Center city
Total Enrollment: 10,211
Undergraduates: 6,541
Male/Female: 42/58

Perhaps it's no surprise that Howard University is located in the nation's capital, near the monuments and memorials erected to honor this country's history and heritage. This historically black university strives to educate its students about the great achievements of African Americans, and to honor the African American perspective in the context of a traditional curriculum. Buoyed by the arrival of president (and alumnus) H. Patrick Swygert, Howard has strengthened its financial position and has begun implementation of a new strategic plan structured around "Leadership for America." The four-part plan focuses on strengthening academic programs and services, promoting excellence in teaching and research, increasing private support, and enhancing national and community service.

Founded in 1866 by Gen. Oliver Howard, primarily to educate freed slaves, the university now operates four campuses and serves about 10,000 students. The 89-acre main campus houses most classrooms, dorms, and administrative offices, as well as the university center, the Founders Library, and the undergraduate library. The Howard Law Center is located on the west campus near Rock Creek Park; the Divinity School is located on a 22-acre site in northeast Washington; and there's also a 108-acre campus in suburban Beltsville, Maryland. Architecturally, the main campus is a blend of old and new, with numerous sculptures and murals created by Jacob Lawrence, Richard Hunt, Elizabeth Catlett, and the late Romare Bearden. The campus is an easy bus ride from the attractions of the nation's capital, all the more visible now thanks to a campus-wide window-replacement initiative. Auditoriums, office spaces, classrooms, galleries, and computer labs across campus have undergone large-scale renovation in recent years; the physics, chemistry, and fine arts facilities have also been completely redone.

Contrary to the advice of early black leaders such as Booker T. Washington, who argued in favor of technical training, Howard since its inception has promoted the liberal arts. This focus has served the school well; Howard's law school counts former Supreme Court Justice Thurgood Marshall among its alumni, and Nobel Prize–winning author Toni Morrison went here, too. The school also has excellent programs in African studies, music, art, and theater arts. Other intriguing academic options are accelerated programs for a BS on the way to a medical or dental degree, coursework in the institute of jazz studies, programs in zoology and engineering (especially electrical engineering), and programs in communication science and disorders. And despite Howard's historical focus on the liberal arts, preprofessional programs are among the most heavily enrolled here. The most popular major is nursing, followed by radio/TV/film and accounting. Programs in ancient Mediterranean and international studies are being developed. Weaker departments include classics and physics.

All students must complete general education requirements, which vary by school or college, but uniformly encompass 18 credits in social sciences and humanities and one Afro-American studies course. Freshman seminars and various other special programs for first-year students are available in the schools of communication, engineering, and arts and sciences. And seniors in arts and sciences must weather a comprehensive exam to graduate. In general, students say that the workload at Howard is demanding. "You must treat homework as a very important part of your life," admonishes a junior. "If you do not, it will be hard to get by in a majority of classes. Seek help and keep on top of all your subjects!" Another student adds, "Come to Howard ready to study." Most students agree that professors are ready and willing to help when asked, though academic advising is not Howard's strength. "Sometimes, you may get professors who do not know how to break down anything," explains a psychology major. "Then, it is your job to talk up and ask questions. You must ask questions because a closed mouth does not get fed!" Students who need a break from the academic scene seek out internships in town or across the country. Many also study abroad at one of the more than 200 institutions in 36 countries where Howard grants credit.

Eighty-three percent of Howard students are African American, and 12

(Continued)

SAT Ranges: V 430–640 M 410–680

ACT Range: 16–27

Financial Aid: 74%

Expense: Pr $

Phi Beta Kappa: Yes

Applicants: 5,964

Accepted: 53%

Enrolled: 42%

Grad in 6 Years: N/A

Returning Freshmen: 85%

Academics: ✐ ✐

Social: ☎ ☎ ☎

Q of L: ★ ★ ★

Admissions: (202) 806-2700

Email Address: admission@howard.edu

Strongest Programs:
African Studies
Music
Art
Architecture
Business
Psychology
Electrical Engineering

Howard's law school counts former Supreme Court Justice Thurgood Marshall among its alumni, and Nobel Prize–winning author Toni Morrison went here, too.

percent hail from foreign countries. Most come from decidedly middle-class backgrounds. Although Howard seems to be a very cohesive community, career-minded and highly motivated men and women fit in best, students say, and most are politically liberal. Hot issues include women's empowerment, student government, fraternities and sororities. Howard is the home of the nation's first black fraternities and sororities, but these groups do not have their own housing or dining facilities, and only 2 percent of the men and women now go Greek. Howard awards a wide variety of athletic scholarships, and merit scholarships are also available to students who maintain a 3.5 GPA. A deferred-payment plan also allows families to pay each semester's tuition in three installments. But even with financial aid, costs are steep; President Swygert hopes that will change as he encourages more alumni to give back to their alma mater.

Interestingly, Howard is one of a handful of universities in the nation supported partly by federal subsidies; these days, the school gets about 55 percent of its budget from Congress. Bethune Hall, a $14-million housing complex, has helped ease the space crunch, but only about half of Howard's students can be accommodated on campus. "Housing at Howard is average in regards to availability, maintenance and comfort," says one student. Freshmen get room assignments, while upperclassmen take their chances in a lottery. The halls are coed, and the 11 residential computer labs have more than 200 state-of-the-art machines for student use. But many students live off campus purely to avoid the mandatory meal plan. Still, the administration is doing its best to bring students back, and Drew, Meridian Hill, Baldwin, Carver, Truth, and Crandall halls have recently gotten facelifts.

Weekends bring an assortment of social happenings to campus, many of which take place in the student center. On-campus parties and sports events are always big draws, but the bars of Georgetown and Adams Morgan, the restaurants and clubs in the "New U" Street corridor, and the MCI Center arena (home to the NBA's Wizards and NHL's Capitals)—most accessible by public transit—also beckon. Though small in numbers, the Greeks are "an integral part of the university." Athletics are also an important presence on campus, particularly varsity basketball, soccer, football, and track, and the highlight of the season is always the grudge match with Hampton University, to decide which school is the "true HU." Students list Howard's Homecoming as one of the best annual events, along with various Greekfests, concerts, and talent shows that alumni, current students, and members of the community enjoy together.

Among America's historically black colleges and universities, Howard stands out as the standard-bearer, a longtime center of excellence and leadership. Its scholarship and collections of artworks, rare books, manuscripts, and photographs are a repository of the African American experience. The current generation of students is writing a new chapter of that very experience. "The future appears very bright for Howard University," says a senior electrical engineering major. The future's not only bright for the university, but for those students who receive their education at Howard, too.

Overlaps

Hampton, Clark Atlanta, Spelman, Morgan State, Florida A&M.

If You Apply To ➤

Howard…Early action: Nov. 30. Regular admissions and financial aid: Apr. 1. Meets demonstrated need of 39%. Campus and alumni interviews: not available. SATs or ACTs: required. SAT IIs: required, (writing only). Audition, tape or portfolio required for fine arts applicants. No essay question unless applying for scholarship consideration by Early Action deadline.

Students at the Illinois Institute of Technology are here for one reason, and one reason only: to get one of the best engineering degrees money can buy. With strong offerings in electrical, mechanical, computer, and aerospace engineering, it's understandable why IIT is one of the top technical institutes in the nation. The lopsided male/female ratio is not exactly conducive to finding a lifetime mate, but that doesn't stop students from having fun. After all, they've got to relieve the stress somehow.

IIT's home is an urban, 120-acre campus designed by Ludwig Mies van der Rohe, the influential 20th-century architect who directed the architecture school for 20 years. Founded in 1890, the school is just three miles south of Chicago's Loop, one mile west of Lake Michigan. Meisian-style buildings are adorned by trees and grassy open parks. Comiskey Park, home of the White Sox, is located directly across from the campus. The S. R. Crown Hall, home of IIT's College of Architecture, is considered a landmark, and fundraising for the restoration of the building is underway. In fact, a major campus renewal is currently in progress, including the construction of a campus center and plenty of landscaping.

Students agree that engineering sets the tone at IIT. All engineering departments are outstanding. Computer engineering is the most popular major, followed by architecture, computer science, chemical engineering, and aerospace engineering. The sciences, physics in particular, are first-rate; high energy physicist and Nobel laureate Leon Lederman teaches freshman—yes, freshman—physics. Computer literacy is demanded of all students. In addition, all freshmen take an introduction to the professions seminar, which includes discussion of innovation, ethics, teamwork, communication, and leadership, and all students must participate in two interprofession projects. Newer academic options include a major in technical communications and an honors research program in molecular biochemistry and biophysics. Weaker offerings include the social sciences and, not surprisingly, the humanities.

The architecture curriculum emphasizes a team approach that mixes third- through fifth-year students together under the supervision of a master professor. Guided by an academic reorganization, the physical sciences have been bolstered, grouped together with career-oriented fields like psychology, political science, and computer information systems.

Along with humanities and social science courses, students must fulfill general education requirements that include mathematics, computer science, natural science and engineering; writing is emphasized across the curriculum. IIT's academic climate is pretty unforgiving, students say. Both the workload and the competition is fierce. "Sometimes it is hard to ask your peers, even your friends, for help because then it looks like you can't handle the work," says a chemical engineer major. Professors always teach their own classes at IIT, while TAs are available for labs and extra help. Both groups are praised for their accessibility. "Professors are knowledgeable and practiced in theory and industry," asserts a civil engineering major. Another student adds, "The professors want you to learn and are easy to contact and even easier to talk to."

In addition to meeting outside of class to go over problem sets or for career direction, IIT students and professors often work side-by-side on research projects. Engineering students have the use of sophisticated labs, and independent

Website: www.iit.edu
Location: Urban
Total Enrollment: 6,062
Undergraduates: 1,706
Male/Female: 74/26
SAT Ranges: V 580–680 M 640–730
ACT Range: 25–30
Financial Aid: 100%
Expense: Pr $ $
Phi Beta Kappa: No
Applicants: 2,866
Accepted: 60%
Enrolled: 16%
Grad in 6 Years: 47%
Returning Freshmen: 84%
Academics: ✎ ✎ ✎ ✎
Social: ☎ ☎
Q of L: ★ ★
Admissions: (312) 567-3025
Email Address: admission@iit.edu

Strongest Programs:
Electrical
Chemical
Mechanical
Aerospace Engineering
Architecture

research labs in Chicago are also available. The five-year co-op program, another possibility for hands-on experience, helps lead IIT grads into high-paying jobs after graduation. Combined BS/MS degrees in engineering, food safety and technology, and business administration and public administration are available, as is a BS/JD program in law, in addition to a variety of newly designed master's tracks. To round out the combined program offerings, a BS/MS in medical physics and an honors program for students seeking a BS in engineering along with an MD are offered in conjunction with the Chicago Medical School. There are study abroad programs that include France, Spain, Scotland, and Germany.

A majority of IIT students graduated from public high school in the top fifth of their class. Out-of-state students account for 26 percent of the undergraduate population. Sixteen percent are from foreign countries. African Americans and Hispanics constitute 16 percent of the student body, Asian American students 14 percent. "Since IIT is so diverse, you have to be careful not to offend someone or some group," says a veteran. But classmates say International Fest is one of the year's most popular events, and IIT offers a multitude of cultural awareness workshops to help avert potential problems. Politics are also important on campus; a senior says, "The institution itself and the administration are pretty laid-back, but the students that come here are pretty conservative."

Knowing their political leanings, then, it's not surprising that most IIT students spend time thinking about classwork and future jobs, without much energy or enthusiasm for late-night debates. The campus bar—called the Bog—is said to be a hotspot on Thursday nights. "Faculty and students sometimes drink together!" says a senior. IIT offers 343 merit scholarships, ranging from $250 to a full ride, and a number of athletic scholarships. There are plenty of opportunities for non-need scholarships as well. IIT's ROTC program has grown and matured into one of the finest in the nation, even hosting a popular annual formal ball.

As befits the school's urban location, many students commute. The 55 percent of students who live in residence halls report that rooms are "kind of small" but comfortable. Six of the seven dorms are coed, with one hall for women only. The McCormick Student Village is popular, and South and North are said to be the nicest dorms. Fowler has the biggest rooms, but no air-conditioning; the rest of the dorms have A/C. Some students live in apartments in the area or on Chicago's North Side; others inhabit one of the eight fraternities, which claim 17 percent of the men. (Sororities nab 13 percent of the women, proving that Greek letters aren't only found in formulas a prof slaps on the board during lecture.) The dining hall has several meal plans, with a special vegetarian menu. Breakfast and lunch can also be eaten in the cafeteria at the student union, while the campus pub serves lunch and dinner. Engineers and architects—notorious late-night studiers—have to hit the library early, since it closes at 10:00 P.M. Though students tend to feel safe on campus, the surrounding area is a different story. "It is difficult to get to a doctor, pharmacy, or grocery store and feel safe, unless you have a car," says a student.

IIT's six-block campus is contiguous to Chicago's "Gap" community, where historic but rundown homes are being rehabilitated to form one of the city's hottest new urban residential areas. Most students love exploring Chicago; the city skyline is beautiful, and is a veritable museum, with buildings designed by the likes of Frank Lloyd Wright, Louis Sullivan, and, of course, van der Rohe. The university provides free shuttle bus service to downtown on weekends, where students take in some culture or hit the town's hip bars and restaurants, including one owned by former Chicago Bulls superstar Michael Jordan. Lake Michigan is within jogging distance, and Chinatown is a walk away for lunch or dinner.

Because IIT has such a large commuter population, many students head home on weekends. For those who stick around, the Union Board offers movies, concerts and comedians, and the Bog brings in bands on Thursdays and Saturdays. Students can also plan events like a formal on the *Odyssey*, a sightseeing boat, or an outing to the Chicago Symphony. The eight-day Winter Festival and the Spring Formal are other popular annual events. As for alcohol, the school follows the 21-year-old age law and students say it works. In sports-crazy Chicago, IIT athletic teams are not much of a draw. Students praise the men's baseball and swimming teams, along with women's volleyball, which compete in the NAIA. The intramural program is strong, but students hate the fact that the facilities close at 5:00 p.m. on weekends. The Olympics occur every year at IIT when Greek Week and Sports Fest kick off, featuring Olympic-type competition for all students.

The workload at IIT is tremendous, and students endure more than their fair share of all-nighters as a result. But many believe today's struggle is worth tomorrow's success. And they haven't forgotten that college is supposed to be an experience, with some fun and frolic interrupting hours of studying and research. In fact, students say they play a big part in their education. "Students can make a big difference on campus," reflects one a senior. "Anyone can get involved."

Overlaps

University of Illinois, University of Illinois at Chicago, Northwestern, MIT, Depaul.

If You Apply To ➤ IIT...Rolling admissions. Housing: May 1. Financial need: Mar. 15. Guarantees to meet demonstrated need. Campus interviews: recommended, evaluative. Alumni interviews: optional, evaluative. SATs or ACTs: required. SAT IIs: optional. Accepts the Common Application and electronic applications. No essay question.

University of Illinois at Urbana–Champaign

901 West Illinois, Urbana, IL 61801

Like many of its Midwestern neighbors, the University of Illinois has its roots in agriculture. The Morrow Plots, the oldest experimental fields in the nation, still stand in the middle of campus—and when the wind blows the wrong way, students are not-so-subtly reminded of their heritage as a farm school. But these days, students describe the U of I as having "an atmosphere like no other." Whether it's cheering for the Illini or participating in one of the hundreds of extracurricular clubs and activities that are always recruiting new members, students here are a happy, sociable bunch. This is, after all, the school that invented Homecoming. Students enjoy the benefits of their oh-so-big school while taking the detriments of size in stride. "Students can get lost here if they don't have personal initiative," frets a food industry and business major. But there's plenty of "opportunity, reliability, and availability of resources for self-motivated students to fly with."

The Illinois campus is located between the twin cities of Champaign and Urbana, equidistant from Chicago, Indianapolis, and St. Louis. The university's airport, with flights to and from these cities, is 10 minutes away. Designed along a mile-long, north-south axis, the campus has many trees and walkways—a park-like environment with a few stately brownstone Gothic and white-columned brick Georgian buildings. Physically challenged students tend to appreciate the

Website: www.uiuc.edu
Location: Small city
Total Enrollment: 36,684
Undergraduates: 27,492
Male/Female: 53/47
SAT Ranges: V 550–650 M 590–710
ACT Range: 25–28
Financial Aid: 49%
Expense: Pub $ $ $
Phi Beta Kappa: Yes
Applicants: 17,867
Accepted: 71%
Enrolled: 51%
Grad in 6 Years: 77%
Returning Freshmen: 92%
Academics: ✏ ✏ ✏ ✏ ✏

(Continued)

Social: ☎ ☎ ☎
Q of L: ★ ★ ★
Admissions: (217) 333-0302
Email Address:
admissions@oar.uiuc.edu

Strongest Programs:
Accounting
Engineering
Biology
Psychology
Architecture
Business Administration

Illinois has eight undergraduate colleges and more than 150 undergraduate programs, but if nothing strikes your fancy, you can design your own.

The National Center for Supercomputing Applications at U of I developed Mosaic, the predecessor to Netscape's Navigator World Wide Web browser.

campus because it is flat and well-equipped with ramps and widened doorways.

Illinois has eight undergraduate colleges and more than 150 undergraduate programs, but if nothing strikes your fancy, you can design your own. Distribution requirements vary, but all students must complete six semester hours in each of three major distribution areas: humanities and the arts, social and behavioral sciences, and natural sciences and technology. In addition, all students fulfill a two-part English composition requirement, a quantitative reasoning requirement, a six-hour cultural studies requirement, and a new foreign language requirement. Engineering, architecture, business, and the sciences—especially agriculture and veterinary medicine—get high marks from students and lots of resources from administrators, but the art and humanities departments suffer by comparison, students say. Academics at Illinois are far from laid-back. "The University of Illinois offers its students a very competitive environment," says a history/political science double major. "People are very focused on schoolwork, and academics is of key importance."

Partially because of its size, Illinois can afford to support excellent programs across the university, including the expansion of undergraduate minors campuswide and the constant revision of curriculums (most recently forestry, computer science, and German). Yet even with all those people, the registration process is relatively painless, thanks to an online registration system that allows students to choose courses by "sitting down at your own computer for 10 minutes." Nevertheless, freshmen may still have trouble getting into certain general education classes, like foreign languages, that sophomores also need. And engineering majors say their programs are difficult to finish in just four years anyway. Once you've chosen your classes, keeping up with the work becomes easier when you remember that Illinois houses the largest public university library in the world.

Other notable academic endeavors at Illinois are the Beckman Institute for Advanced Science and Technology, an interdisciplinary center designed to bring biological and physical sciences together in pursuit of new insights into human and artificial intelligence, and the Grainger Library and Information Center. The National Center for Supercomputing Applications at U of I developed Mosaic, the predecessor to Netscape's Navigator World Wide Web browser. The undergraduate honors program includes a faculty mentor program, intensive seminars, advanced sections of regular courses, and access to special resources. More than 850 undergraduates travel and study abroad each year, roaming 100 countries around the globe. Another program, the Ronald E. McNair Scholars Program, is designed to foster undergraduate research opportunities, and is available for minority, low-income, and first generation college students completing a baccalaureate degree.

Back on campus, Illinois has its share of stellar faculty, including four National Medal of Science winners and 29 members of the National Academy of the Sciences. "Even though this is a large school, the professors care about their students," says a sophomore. Even freshmen stuck in large lectures (think 2,000 seats) will find more personal attention in the discussion sections that follow, led by teaching assistants. In general, however, students get more faculty attention as they advance in their academic programs. Freshmen who take the initiative—or enroll in the Discovery program, which offers seminars taught by full professors and capped at 20 members—will be pleased.

Just over 91 percent of UIUC's undergrads are homegrown. They tend to be competitive, career-oriented, and upper middle class. While only 12 percent of total enrollment, the number of African Americans and Hispanic students has almost doubled since the mid-'80s. There's an equal number of Asian Americans, due in large part to the administration's effort to attract high-achieving students through the President's Award of financial support for state residents. But even this moderate amount of student body diversity hasn't dampened the controversy over Chief Illiniwek, the school's mascot. "The division is between 'racial stereotypes that dehumanize' and 'honored tradition,'" sighs one student.

Illinois has 22 undergraduate residence halls, both coed and single-sex, ranging in size from 51 to 660 beds and set in large clusters across campus. However, some are a hike from classrooms—on the order of 14 blocks, veterans warn. All student rooms have a direct fiber-optic connection to the Internet, and many residence halls have living/learning programs, such as WISE (Women in Math, Science, and Engineering) and Unit One (academic support and educationally focused programming). Each quad is a mini-neighborhood, with dining halls, darkrooms, libraries, music practice rooms, computers, and lounges creating a sense of community. The dorms have unique personalities, a senior says, so it's important to choose the right one: "Champaign dorms are loud, party places, while Urbana is more focused on school. ISR has engineers, Allen is alternative, LAR is quiet, PAR is relaxed and fun, and FAR has air-conditioning in the rooms." Private certified housing is not as good as the dorms, students say. One-quarter of students live in the traditional dorms (it's required during your first 30 credit hours), another 15 percent bunk in Greek houses, and many upperclassmen move to on- or off-campus apartments and houses. (The university claims to have the largest Greek system anywhere—more than 75 fraternities and sororities—and it attracts 17 percent of men and 22 percent of women.)

Illinois attracts a socially oriented student body, which may be why the influence of the Greeks is particularly strong; parties and intramural sports are the most important parts of their domain. Independents needn't fret, as there are more than 850 non-Greek student organizations here as well. The Illini Union showcases bands, comedians, and hypnotists most weekends, while the impressive Krannert Center for the Performing Arts, with four theaters and more than 350 annual performances, serves as the area's cultural center. Assembly Hall hosts gigs of the stature of Phish, Smashing Pumpkins, Garth Brooks, and Bill Cosby—and students get a discount at both facilities. Chicago and the shores of Lake Michigan beckon when the weather warms up. Though drinking is prohibited in the dorms, 19-year-olds can get into bars—and can also get alcohol fairly easily. "Once you're in, it's not hard to find someone to buy for you," an accounting major explains.

The Illini compete in the Big 10, and count as their biggest rivals nearby Iowa (both sports), Northwestern (football), and Indiana (basketball). Hockey is also big. Although football draws the crowds and media attention, the women's basketball team, which won the Big 10 championship in 1997, also deserves attention. The intramural program is extensive, mainly because of the university's excellent sports facilities: 16 full-length basketball courts, 5 pools, 19 handball/racquetball courts, a skating rink, a baseball stadium, and the $5.1-million Atkins Tennis Center, with 6 indoor and 8 outdoor courts.

Don't be scared off by the enormity of the University of Illinois. Its size is probably its greatest asset—drawing students from all over the world, and offering them a multitude of opportunities not available elsewhere, so long as they seek them out. Though state budget cuts have pushed tuition up and meant the loss of some programs, students still leave Urbana–Champaign with a great education and equally great memories of good times shared with friends outside the classroom. "There an unlimited opportunity for growth at the University of Illinois for those who accept the challenge," says a psychology major. Agrees an accounting major: "There is something here for everyone."

The Ronald E. McNair Scholars Program, is designed to foster undergraduate research opportunities, and is available for minority, low-income, and first generation college students completing a baccalaureate degree.

Overlaps

University of Wisconsin, Northwestern, Purdue, University of Michigan, Washington University.

Illinois Wesleyan University

210 East University, Bloomington, IL 61702-2900

Website: www.iwu.edu

Location: Small town

Total Enrollment: 2,091

Undergraduates: 2,091

Male/Female: 44/56

SAT Ranges: V 560–660 M 580–680

ACT Range: 25–29

Financial Aid: 65%

Expense: Pr $ $

Phi Beta Kappa: No

Applicants: 2,565

Accepted: 64%

Enrolled: 35%

Grad in 6 Years: 77%

Returning Freshmen: 91%

Academics: ✍ ✍ ✍

Social: ☎ ☎ ☎

Q of L: ★ ★ ★ ★

Admissions: (309) 556-3031

Email Address:
iwuadmit@titan.iwu.edu

Strongest Programs:
Biology/Premed
History/Prelaw
English
Psychology
Mathematics
Music

Illinois Wesleyan University has set its sights on a special breed of student. "At Illinois Wesleyan, students do not have to sacrifice one interest to pursue another," a school publication says. "Students aren't nudged into either-or choices. Instead, they are encouraged to pursue multiple interests simultaneously—a philosophy in keeping with the spirit of a broad liberal arts education." In fact, 14 percent of the student body has two or more majors.

Founded in 1850, IWU occupies a 72-acre campus sits in a northside residential district of Bloomington. The heart of the campus is the central quadrangle, and tree-lined walkways connect buildings that range in style from gray stone Gothic to ultramodern steel and glass. A recent $5.1-million renovation transformed an old science building into the new Center for Liberal Arts, which features classrooms, faculty offices, and seminar rooms. In addition, a $23 million library is in the works.

IWU is a mecca for students with preprofessional interests, especially those with unusual interest pairings like management and music. The College of Fine Arts houses the three separate schools of music, art, and drama; music is the standout, having turned out opera star Dawn Upshaw. Among the top-notch programs in the College of Liberal Arts are biology, English, chemistry—where faculty members have received a National Science Foundation grant to develop a new curriculum that will merge organic and inorganic topics—and math. Students say the computer science and foreign language departments need improvement.

In addition to the usual fall and spring semesters, IWU has an optional, three-week May term. The courses during this term must have one of five features—curricular experimentation, nontraditional approaches to traditional subject matter, student-faculty collaboration, crossing of disciplinary boundaries, or experimental learning through travel, service, or internships. The university's study abroad program offers students the opportunity to travel to a variety of countries around the world including England, Denmark, and Japan. IWU hosts an annual student research conference that attracts students from all disciplines.

The school's general education requirements emphasize critical thinking, imagination, intellectual independence, social awareness, and sensitivity to others. All first-year students must take a Gateway Colloquium, a topic-based, seminar-style class of 15 students, that stresses the critical reading, writing, discussion, and analytical skills, and introduces students to the intellectual life of the university. Recent topics include, Science and Society: Visions of Discovery, Disabilities: Fact and Fiction, and The Business of Business. Classes are challenging, and students jockey for high grades, especially since the institution of a plus/minus grading system. "I would say that the courses are competitive and rigorous, but professors are more focused on creating an environment where everyone is allowed to learn," says a senior. Students describe the faculty members as "knowledgeable" and "caring." "The professors don't stop teaching when class is over," a junior says. "They are always accessible and eager to assist students." While career counseling is praised, academic advising can be frustrating.

Students at IWU are mostly the homegrown variety, with 88 percent hailing from Illinois. Although IWU began admitting African American students back in 1867, the campus is still predominantly white. African Americans only account for 3 percent of the student body, Hispanics 2 percent, and Asian Americans 4 percent. The hottest issue on campus is diversity. "Most students would like to see more minority and international students attend the school," says one student. Still, participation in groups like Circle K, the Alpha Phi Omega service fraternity, and Habitat for Humanity provides evidence for the social consciousness of the IWU campus.

Housing is guaranteed for four years, and 82 percent of the students live in the modern, "well-maintained" dorms. The students report few problems getting a room, especially since the new residence hall was built. "New House Residence Hall looks like a luxury hotel inside," says a senior. "I'll be lucky to find a place this nice when I'm making six figures." About three-fourths of the dorms are single-sex, and students must be 21 to live off campus. Campus security is described as "pretty good" and most students acknowledge that they feel safe on campus, though common sense is a must.

Thirty-three percent of the men and 30 percent of the women go Greek, because fraternities and sororities are the focus of IWU's social life. "The majority of students use the Greek system as a social outlet, whether they're members or not," says a public accounting major. How much you drink depends upon the crowd you hang out with. A new alcohol policy allows of-age students to have beer and wine in their dorms; underage drinkers must trek off campus to be served. Each fall during Homecoming, the fraternities and residence halls compete in the Titan Games to get appropriately psyched. Other annual festivities include the Far Left Carnival, the Gospel Festival, and Earthapalooza (on Earth Day). The Student Senate also sponsors guest speakers; Spike Lee, Bonnie Blair, and Maya Angelou have addressed the students in recent years.

Thanks to the proximity of Illinois State University in nearby Normal, IWU offers more than the typical small-college-town atmosphere. The total school population of about 25,000 helps to offer students at tiny IWU "the best of both worlds," says a senior. "There's always something happening on campus, from concerts to sporting events and theatrical productions to movies," says a junior. The best road trips are to Peoria or Urbana–Champaign (home of the University of Illinois), both 45 minutes away, or to Chicago or St. Louis, each two and a half hours away.

In the IWU arena, baseball and football are well and good, but basketball really gets students going; the men's team progressed to round 16 in the 1998 NCAA Championship Tournament. "Our basketball team is a small-college powerhouse and attendance rate for students and non-students is the highest in the country for NCAA Division III," says a junior. "The games are very exciting, and because we are so good, every team is our rival." Although you wouldn't think of IWU as a jock factory, it was the launching pad for many a professional athlete, including longtime basketball star Jack Sikma and Doug Rader, former manager of the California Angels. Women's volleyball and softball also rouse the fans, as does women's basketball. The Fort Natatorium houses a whopping 14-lane swimming pool. Intramural sports include volleyball, badminton, and coed inner-tube water polo.

Chemistry faculty members have received a National Science Foundation grant to develop a new curriculum that will merge organic and inorganic topics.

All first-year students must take a Gateway Colloquium, a topic-based, seminar-style class of 15 students, that stresses the critical reading, writing, discussion, and analytical skills, and introduces students to the intellectual life of the university.

With its diverse academics, caring faculty, and cozy atmosphere, Illinois Wesleyan University is the perfect place for the multitalented student to thrive and one of the nation's best-kept secrets. One junior sums it up this way: "It is such a great community with so many amazing opportunities. You can get involved in anything."

If You Apply To ➤ Illinois Wesleyan…Regular admissions and financial aid: Mar. 1. Guarantees to meet demonstrated need. Campus interviews: recommended, evaluative. No alumni interviews. SATs or ACTs: required. SAT IIs: recommended. Accepts the Common Application and electronic applications. Essay question: significant event; talents and abilities; or topic of your choice.

Indiana University

300 North Jordan Avenue, Bloomington, IN 47405

Website: www.indiana.edu
Location: Small city
Total Enrollment:: 36,201
Undergraduates: 28,511
Male/Female: 46/54
SAT Ranges: V 490–600 M 490–610
ACT Range: 22–27
Financial Aid: 65%
Expense: Pub $ $ $
Phi Beta Kappa: Yes
Applicants: 20,095
Accepted: 81%
Enrolled: 41%
Grad in 6 Years: 68%
Returning Freshmen: 87%
Academics: ✑ ✑ ✑ ✑
Social: ☎ ☎ ☎ ☎
Q of L: ★ ★ ★ ★
Admissions: (812) 855-0661
Email Address: iuadmit@indiana.edu

Strongest Programs:
  Business
  Dance
  Journalism/Communications

With more than 35,000 students on its enormous campus, Indiana University is the prototype of the large Midwestern school. Indeed, President Myles Brand has boldly pledged that the school will become "America's New Public University." With strong academics, a thriving social scene, and some of the best sports teams around—but no more Bobby Knight—this top-notch public institution is a testament to Hoosier determination.

Located in southern Indiana's gently rolling hills, the 1,800-acre campus boasts architecture from Italianate brick to collegiate Gothic limestone to the distinctive style of world-famous architect I. M. Pei. Other unique campus features include fountains, gargoyles, an arboretum of more than 450 trees and shrubs surrounding two reflecting pools, a limestone gazebo, and the Jordan River, a pretty creek that runs alongside a shaded path.

IU's 10 schools offer many majors and minors, cross-disciplinary study, an individually designed curriculum, intense honors and research programs, and yearlong study in 27 countries (and 16 languages). The highly touted business school, with its respected international studies component, is second only to arts and sciences in popularity. The internationally known Kinsey Institute for the Study of Human Sexual Behavior is housed on IU's campus, and the music school is tops in its field, setting the tone for much of the campus. Many of the communications programs have been merged into the new Communications and Culture department, and the university has also added a gender studies program and a new degree program in Environmental Science. Students don't complain about many departmental weaknesses, but note that large introductory lectures, especially in the sciences, are a hazard of IU's size. The GradPact program guarantees that Indiana will pay all fees if a qualifying student has to stay on campus for more than four years. "IU is a four-year institution," says one economics major. "If a student takes longer than that, they probably have three majors, changed their majors, or are bad planners." Despite its size, Indiana prides itself on its liberal arts education—freshman are admitted not to preprofessional schools but to the "university division." Majors are declared after one or two years, and the university discourages premature specialization. IU's Communications and Culture department advances the study of communication as a cultural practice, while the Environmental Science Joint Program is an under-graduate degree program that specifically considers the environment as a scientific entity.

(Continued)
Languages
Music
Optometry
Fine Arts

General education requirements vary from school to school, but usually include math, science, arts and humanities, social and behavioral sciences, English and writing, culture, and a foreign language. Students describe the aca-demic climate as rigorous but not cutthroat. "With 4,000 different courses per semester, a variety of intensity levels exist," says a marketing major. "There is a balance, with room for both competitive overachievers and laid-back carefree individuals." Students say they regularly share ideas with each other and group projects are commonplace. Faculty members bring their research results directly to students, and some profs bring undergrads into their labs to assist with ongo-ing projects. Students say the quality of teaching is excellent. "The professors here are remarkable," says an art history/telecommunications major. "They not only care about their field of study, they care about their students." As for advising, many students seem surprised by the personal attention they receive at such a large university, but they warn that many available resources are helpful to those students who seek them out. Some students complain of confusing bureaucracies and problems parking.

Seventy-two percent of IU students are from in-state, while the remainder hail from every state and more than 100 foreign countries. Out-of-staters face much more rigorous minimum admissions standards, including rank in the top quarter of their high school class and SAT scores in the 1050 to 1100 range. African Americans comprise 4 percent of the student body, Hispanics 2 percent, and Asian Americans 3 percent. By and large, students do not seem particularity concerned with social and political issues.

The school's rolling admissions system enables students to know their fate only a month after their application is in. And while IU does not guarantee to meet the full demonstrated need of every admit, it admits on a need-blind basis and offers the Early Approximate Student Eligibility (EASE) program to help prospective freshmen gauge how much financial aid they will get. Merit scholar-ships are awarded to qualified students; applicants must be in the top 10 percent of their graduating class and have a minimum combined SAT score of 1200. There is also an "NCAA maximum" program of roughly 225 full athletic scholarships, encompassing 10 men's sports and 9 women's.

Housing ranges from Gothic quads (coed by building) to 13-floor high-rises (coed by floor or unit, except for one all-women dorm), and halls are considered "clean and comfortable." One student explains the housing situation this way: "All dorms have laundry facilities, cafeterias, computer clusters, and undergradu-ate advisors, and some even have special amenities like language-speaking floors." A junior adds, "There is no trouble getting a room, but preference of dorm may be harder." Academic floors (requiring a GPA of 3.1 or better) are popular with more serious students who are not interested in the intense nightlife in the high rises. Housing is guaranteed to all incoming freshmen, and those who stay in the university housing system won't ever face rent increases. Based on results from a student survey, some dining halls have been modernized to resemble mall food courts, with outlets offering international and healthful menus sprinkled among the fast-food options. Alcohol is prohibited in the dorms, which may explain why 61 percent of the student body live off campus. Most off-campus residents choose

With low costs, across the board excellence, one of the most active social scenes in the Midwest, and some of the best sports teams in the Big 10, Indiana is well on its way to being America's New Public University.

apartments or small wooden houses with big front porches, within walking distance of the campus or of the IU bus system.

Although campus organizations host numerous events, the most active on-campus groups, in terms of social life, seem to be the Greeks. About 7 percent of IU men and women are in the Greek system, and membership is a status symbol. Some complain of a polarized atmosphere, "There is a large separation between the Greek community and the rest of the social body," says a senior. Every fall there is a 36-hour Dance Marathon to raise money for Riley's Children's Hospital in Indianapolis. The Little 500 bike race, which was modeled after the Indianapolis 500, is one of the most highly attended events of the year at Indiana. With concerts, ballets, recitals, and festivals right on campus, students are not lacking for things to keep them busy. The IU student union is the largest in the nation, and the range of extracurricular organizations is also impressive. "Bloomington is a great, small college town," says one senior. "There are opportunities to get involved in the community if you seek them out." There are many excellent bars, shops, and restaurants, including one of the few Tibetan restaurants in the country. Locally, the area offers some impressive rock quarries (often used as illegal but refreshing swimming pools), miles of public forests, and three nearby lakes. Spelunkers will find heaven underground in the many nearby caves. Chicago, Cincinnati, Indianapolis, St. Louis, and even New Orleans are popular road trips.

Intramurals pale in comparison with varsity athletics here; basketball is an established religion in the state of Indiana. The Hoosiers basketball program is entering a new era now that the combative and controversial coach Bobby Knight has finally been fired for roughing up players and other sins. Although students and faculty are all eligible for tickets, they've got to get requests in early—and even those lucky enough to get tickets don't count on going to more than a quarter of home games. In recent years, men's and women's soccer, women's golf, and women's tennis have all claimed at least a share of the Big 10 championship, and even the football team is beginning to draw red and white crowds. Recently, women's water polo has attained varsity status. Purdue is IU's traditional athletic rival, and teams play for the Old Oaken Bucket, found on a farm in southern Indiana in 1925 and alleged to have been used during the Civil War.

Most students feel the education they get at IU is worth every penny. They come away from Bloomington with knowledge, lifelong friends, and a new world view. "Indiana University offers so much more than just academics," says an accounting major. "You really can do it all here."

Overlaps

Purdue, Ball State, Miami University (OH), University of Illinois, University of Michigan.

If You Apply To ➤

Indiana…Admissions deadlines: Feb. 1, fall; Nov. 1, spring. Campus interviews: recommended, informational. No alumni interviews. SATs or ACTs: required. SAT IIs: recommended. No essay question.

Iowa State University

100 Alumni Hall, Ames, IA 50011

Love for Iowa State University runs deep and genuine. Although there are over 25,000 students at this big state university, the atmosphere is not overwhelming. "I love how small ISU has become to me in the past two years," says a sophomore. Strong programs in engineering, business, and agriculture attract students from around the globe. The close-knit family atmosphere keeps them here.

The university has lavished attention on its parklike campus, located on a 1,984-acre tract in the middle of Ames, population 50,000. The campus, which boasts a combination of dignified old buildings and award-winning new ones, is a landmark of landscape design, with numerous shady quadrangles with floral plantings and artwork that create a gardenlike quality. History and tradition prevail, from the campanile, which serenades the campus with its carillon bells, to the huge public art collection, including sculptures by Danish artist Christian Petersen. New additions, such as a national swine research center, a student health facility, and an athletic office and training facility, along with renovations to Memorial Union, add a contemporary feel to the campus. An intensive livestock research facility and teaching and research complex for the engineering department have also recently been completed. Much of the campus is closed to cars, largely for the benefit of walking, bicycling, and in-line skating students as well as the swans (named Sir Lancelot and Lady Elaine) and the ducks who reside on Lake LaVerne.

When Iowa State opened in 1869 as a land-grant university, agriculture and engineering ruled the academic roost. These days, though, the liberal arts are at least as popular, and the College of Liberal Arts and Sciences is the largest of ISU's nine colleges. Among the university's 100-plus majors, the College of Agriculture still fields outstanding programs in animal science, agriculture technology, agribusiness, and agronomy. Other colleges include business, design, education, education, veterinary medicine, family and consumer sciences (formerly home economics), and the graduate college.

All undergraduates must take two semesters of English composition freshman year and demonstrate proficiency in English prior to graduation. Other general education requirements vary by college and focus on gaining breadth in the natural and social sciences, but everyone takes a half-credit course on the use of the library. A modem network allows students to link their personal computers with the university system, and hundreds of Iowa State pages now inhabit the World Wide Web.

Students can also use the AccessPlus system of electronic kiosks sprinkled around campus to check the status of their university bill or financial aid package, print an unofficial transcript, or get their current schedules. An honors program enrolls nearly 300 outstanding freshmen each year, many of whom live in honors housing. A summer language program in France, Germany, and Spain is one of 50 programs that students can choose from for work or study in 35 countries worldwide. Newest additions to the curriculum include majors in applied physics, communication studies, international business, materials engineering, production/operations management, and sustainable agriculture. ISU has discontinued majors in geography and social work.

Despite the university's size, professors teach most classes, with the exception of some freshman English options. Students learn from faculty stars like Pulitzer

Website: www.iastate.edu
Location: Small city
Total Enrollment:: 26,110
Undergraduates: 21,503
Male/Female: 55/45
SAT Ranges: V 520–660 M 550–690
ACT Range: 21–27
Financial Aid: 48%
Expense: Pub $ $
Phi Beta Kappa: Yes
Applicants: 9,284
Accepted: 91%
Enrolled: 48%
Grad in 6 Years: 60%
Returning Freshmen: 84%
Academics: ✐ ✐ ✐
Social: ☎ ☎ ☎
Q of L: ★ ★ ★
Admissions: (800) 262-3810
Email Address:
admissions@iastate.edu

Strongest Programs:
Engineering
Agriculture
Design
Family and Consumer Sciences
Veterinary Medicine
Natural and Physical Sciences
Business

Prize–winning author Jane Smiley. "My professors have worked hard to integrate technology into classes and are always available to speak with me," says a sophomore. Academic and career counseling draw praise, too, and advisors are known to "go that extra mile" to help students. In 1995, the university announced a "guarantee" program for students who want to ensure they will graduate in four years.

Seventy-eight percent of ISU's students are Iowans, though all 50 states and 116 countries are represented in the student body. A healthy contingent of out-of-state students comes from Illinois, and foreign students comprise another 5 percent of the student body. Iowa State was the first coed land-grant institution, but attracting minorities has proven more difficult: minority students account for only 6 percent of the student body. To help remedy this situation, ISU launched a $25-million campaign aimed at increasing the number of scholarships available for minority students, student athletes, and student leaders. Freshman orientation has come to include the topics of race relations and cultural diversity, and entering frosh participate in learning teams, through which groups of students with similar interests and career goals take courses together and live in the same dorms during their first year.

In addition to need-based financial aid and a variety of athletic scholarships, many merit awards are available, ranging from $500 to a full ride. Thirty-three percent of undergrads live in on-campus residence halls and apartments. Freshmen seeking a room submit questionnaires outlining their preferences, which are processed on a first-come, first-served basis. Single-sex and coed dorms are available. Rooms are said to be comfortable and well maintained, and one student indicates that the janitors throw a picnic every spring. Special floors are available for international students, teetotalers, and particularly studious undergraduates; separate housing is available for married students. Each year, the food service sponsors a Favorites from Home contest, in which recipes entered by students are selected and adapted to feed thousands. Many upperclassmen live off campus, and Greek life claims 16 percent of ISU men and women.

Iowa State is not simply located in Ames—in many respects it is Ames. Des Moines, the state capital, is about 30 minutes away, and Iowa City, Minneapolis, and Chicago are other easy and enjoyable road trips. Socializing tends to stay on campus, with big-name bands playing Hilton Coliseum and parties always rocking. The campus is supposedly dry, but according to one junior, "It is very easy to get someone who is 21 to 'buy' for you." The big event every spring is a two-day campus festival called VEISHEA (an acronym for ISU's original five colleges), which features parades, exhibitions, food, and a fun-run. Another tradition is campaniling, where students must kiss under the campanile at the stroke of midnight to be considered "true" coeds.

And students have learned not to walk over the Zodiac sign in the Memorial Union–it brings bad luck. In sports, basketball is king; the men's team is a usual invitee to the NCAA tournament. The men's cross-country team is perennially strong and both the men's squads along with the men's track team have garnered Big Eight titles. Football remains popular despite a string of unsuccessful seasons; a new coach and promotional campaign are bringing fans back to Cyclone Stadium/Jack Trice Field. An astounding 80 percent of the students participate in one of the largest intramural sports programs in the nation.

Students agree that Iowa State has something for just about everyone. Says a child and family services major, "What makes ISU so special is its challenging academics, incredibly friendly students, beautiful campus, and the wealth of student activities available." Cows and computers seem to coexist happily at Iowa State, an institute founded to train future farmers that now turns out top-notch engineers experienced in the latest virtual reality and Internet-related technologies, too.

If You Apply To ➤

Iowa State…Rolling admissions and housing: Aug. 21. Guarantees to meet demonstrated need. Campus interviews: optional, evaluative and informational. No alumni interviews. SATs or ACTs: required. No SAT IIs. No essay question.

University of Iowa

BEST BUY

107 Calvin Hall, Iowa City, IA 52242-1396

At first glance, Iowa might seem to be a standard-issue Midwestern school. But beneath the bland exterior of flat fields and corn lies one of the most dynamic schools in the country—and one of the best buys to boot. Iowa has long been a potent force in the creative worlds, particularly writing, and its small-town atmosphere is just one more reason students nationwide flock to this "budget Ivy League."

The 1,880-acre campus, located in the rolling hills of the Iowa River valley, is bisected by the Iowa River and merges with downtown Iowa City. Among the 90 primary buildings is Old Capitol, the first capitol of Iowa, a national historic landmark, and the symbol of the university. The primary architectural style of the campus buildings is Greek Revival and Modern. Renovations to Schaeffer Hall, home to the College of Liberal Arts, were recently completed and the $21-million Levitz Center for Advancement, which houses the University of Iowa Foundation and the Alumni Association, opened in 1998. The newly renovated Seamens Center for the Engineering Arts and Sciences opened in the summer of 2000.

Iowa has a long tradition in creative arts. It was one of the first universities to award graduate degrees for creative work, and is also the home of the first Writer's Workshop. The school also prides itself on its International Writing Program, which brings a wide array of prominent authors to the campus. "The English department is stellar," raves one English major. "It's possibly the best in the country—at least for creative writing." Iowa's on-campus hospital is one of the largest teaching hospitals in the United States. The Health Sciences Center, affiliated with the hospital, encompasses four colleges: medicine, dentistry, pharmacy, and nursing. Undergraduates benefit from the strong Health Center course offerings in related health professions, such as physician's assistant or medical technician. Combined degree programs, which permit students to earn degrees across colleges, exist between liberal arts and a choice of the following: business administration, engineering, nursing, and the College of Medicine. The University Honors Program provides special academic, cultural, and social opportunities to

Website: www.uiowa.edu

Location: Small city

Total Enrollment: 28,846

Undergraduates: 19,537

Male/Female: 46/54

SAT Ranges: V 520–660 M 540–660

ACT Range: 22–27

Financial Aid: 50%

Expense: Pub $

Phi Beta Kappa: Yes

Applicants: 11,358

Accepted: 83%

Enrolled: 40%

Grad in 6 Years: 62%

Returning Freshmen: 82%

Academics: 🖎 🖎 🖎 🖎

Social: ☎ ☎ ☎

Q of L: ★ ★ ★

Admissions: (319) 335-3847

Email Address: admissions@uiowa.edu

Strongest Programs:
Creative Writing
Theater Arts
Dance

outstanding students in the Colleges of Business, Administration, Education, Engineering, Liberal Arts, Nursing, and Pharmacy. Honor students may also participate in the Research Scholars Program, which allows them to collaborate with faculty members on research projects. Iowa's Study Abroad program gives students a chance to travel to 29 different countries. Recent additions to the academic program include a MFA in nonfiction writing and a certificate in sexuality studies. Speech pathology, psychology, and fine arts programs are popular, while students report that the foreign language department is weak due to limited majors and low enrollment. Agriculture, veterinary medicine, forestry, architecture, and animal science are not offered at Iowa, but are taught at its sister institution, Iowa State.

Each of the undergraduate colleges has its own general education requirements. Liberal arts students must take courses in rhetoric, natural science, social sciences, foreign language, interpretation of literature, historical perspectives, humanities, and quantitative or formal reasoning. Distributed general education, including courses in cultural diversity, foreign civilization and culture, and physical education, are also required. Iowa's academic climate is described by the students as moderately competitive. "There is always a pack of students gunning for the number one spot in the class," says one chemistry major. "The only way to get on top and stay on top is to do your work and not slack off." Most classes have up to 50 students and some introductory courses have more. Registration is done by computer, so the process is fairly easy. The University of Iowa's Four-Year Graduation Plan guarantees that students who fulfill certain requirements will not have their graduation delayed by unavailability of a needed course. Students give their professors high marks. "Overall, the quality of the teaching has been terrific," says one biology major. "Full professors have taught nearly every course I have taken, from freshman year up." There are often smaller sessions led by graduate students as a way to make the classroom experience more accessible. Academic advising gets some hot and cold remarks, but according to one senior, "the career development program is great."

Seventy percent of the undergraduates hail from Iowa, with most of the rest coming from contiguous states, especially Illinois. African Americans, Hispanics, and Asian Americans account for about 8 percent of the student body; but, as the administration points out, the state of Iowa has only 4 percent minority population. Yet, students say the campus is extremely tolerant and that almost anyone can find their niche at Iowa. Besides the 200 athletic scholarships available in all sports, there are 880 other scholarships available with stipends ranging from $200 to $7,000. The Roy J. Carver Scholarships are awarded to 82 students who have overcome social or psychological barriers; it is one of the first awards was bestowed on a former homeless man. Some students say they have been able to fund their entire education through scholarships. However, the school does not guarantee to meet the demonstrated financial need of every admit.

Students say that campus residence halls are clean but very sociable and therefore not very quiet. All are coed by floor or wing. Some students say that "campus housing is great, and very popular," while others think the dorms are "as satisfactory as dorms can be." A few students get sloughed off to temporary housing, so it is important to apply early. There are many praises for the custodial staff that keeps the buildings clean. Don't get too excited, though; your own room is up to you! Only 28 percent of the students live in university housing, and more than half live in apartments or houses that are adjacent to the campus. "Off-campus housing is popular but the high rents are often an issue," says one student. Each dorm has its own dining hall, and the food is described as "predictable and

The school also prides itself on its International Writing Program, which brings a wide array of prominent authors to the campus.

uninspired." The student union, improved by a $10-million renovation, includes a pastry and coffee shop, two cafeterias, and the State Room Restaurant.

Eleven percent of the men and 12 percent of women belong to fraternities and sororities, and these groups tend to play less of a role in the social life than they do elsewhere. "Social life at the University of Iowa is a very big part of the draw for many students," says one theater arts major. "Downtown Iowa City, which is practically in the center of campus, is bursting with nightlife, even during the week." There are two university theaters right on campus and many affordable cultural events take place at Hancher Auditorium. "The social life revolves around bars and movie theaters in town," says a sophomore. The Union Bar and Grill, Mickey's, Sports Column, and George's are all popular hangouts with students. The school officially follows the state policy regarding alcohol; the legal drinking age is 21.

Although Iowa City is located in a semirural area, it still has a vast array of bars, dance clubs, restaurants, and other social activities. Yet for those who tire of the local scene, Chicago, Kansas City, or St. Louis are all within six hours by car, a short road trip by Midwestern standards. Skiing is another hour away in Minnesota. Riverfest, held at the Iowa Memorial Union and on the banks of the Iowa River, is a weeklong, all-campus event celebrating the long-awaited spring. Another annual event the students look forward to is the Iowa City Jazz Festival.

As for sports, there's that big football stadium, which now has the team it deserves. Iowa has become a national power and is a regular on New Year's Day bowl games. Hawkeye fans are serious about their team. But if you want a real powerhouse, look no further than the Hawkeye wrestling team, a perennial national champion. Basketball draws lots of fan support, and the women's field hockey team is also a crowd pleaser.

The University of Iowa not only boasts a beautiful campus, it offers its students a broad range of academic programs, an abundance of social activities, and a sense of belonging. With its combination of quality academics, mammoth resources, renowned specialty programs, and extensive research opportunities, this Midwest school is anything but featureless.

Overlaps
University of Illinois, Iowa State, University of Wisconsin, Northwestern University, Indiana University.

If You Apply To ➤

Iowa...Rolling admissions and housing: May 15. Does not guarantee to meet demonstrated need. No campus or alumni interviews. SATs or ACTs: required. SAT IIs: optional. Accepts electronic applications. No essay question. Apply to particular schools or programs.

Ithaca College

953 Danby Road, Ithaca, NY 14850-7020

Founded as a conservatory of music in 1892, this small college in upstate New York has more to brag about than its Division III athletic teams. Strong programs in the arts—including drama, television and film, and music—are the cornerstone of an educational experience that emphasizes quality over quantity. The drive to innovate results partly from Ithaca's desire to shine beyond the shadow of its much larger Ivy League neighbor, Cornell University. But it's the school's dedication to small classes and "hands-on" learning that have students here singing its praises.

Website: www.ithaca.edu
Location: Small town
Total Enrollment: 5,960
Undergraduates: 5,702
Male/Female: 44/56
SAT Ranges: V 530–630 M 520–630

(Continued)

Financial Aid: 67%

Expense: Pr $ $

Phi Beta Kappa: No

Applicants: 8,302

Accepted: 74%

Enrolled: 26%

Grad in 6 Years: 71%

Returning Freshmen: 85%

Academics: ✍ ✍ ✍

Social: ☎ ☎ ☎ ☎ ☎

Q of L: ★ ★ ★

Admissions: (800) 429-4274

Email Address:
admission@ithaca.edu

Strongest Programs:
Music
Theater Arts
TV/Radio
Physical Therapy
Natural Sciences
Psychology

Ithaca College is located in the center of the Finger Lakes region, on a 600-acre plot with spectacular views overlooking the city of Ithaca. None of the streamlined, modern campus buildings are more than a few decades old, since the college moved to its present location in the 1960s. Many believe the campus is one of the country's most beautiful, including author Tom Wolfe, who dubbed the school "the emerald eminence at the fingertip of Lake Cayuga." Newest campus additions include the Center for Health Sciences, a 7,000-square-foot fitness center, and the Clinton B. Ford Observatory.

Through its five schools—music, communications, business, health sciences and human performance, and humanities and sciences—Ithaca offers 92 undergraduate degree programs. With its prominent faculty and many opportunities for student performance, the college's reputation for music education and performance are almost unparalleled. The Park School of Communications has its own elaborate $12-million facility. The school has grown up alongside the broadcast industry and is known for programs in radio and TV production (the most popular major) and cinema and photography. Students say Ithaca's business school is weaker, though it has grown rapidly over the past decade; all students now matriculate into the business administration major, and declare one of seven concentrations after the first or second year.

In the School of Health Sciences and Human Performance, the physical therapy program is a national drawing card, and boasts nearly a 100 percent placement rate; five-year BS/MS programs in physical and occupational therapy are available in conjunction with the University of Rochester. Ithaca also offers a dual teacher certification program in health and physical education, majors in therapeutic recreation and environmental studies, and a 24-credit, nondegree certificate in gerontology. In addition, Ithaca boasts one of the nation's most complete sports studies programs, with majors including exercise science, rehabilitation, athletic training, sports management, and sports communication.

Though not the most well known, with more than 2,000 students, Humanities and Sciences is the largest school on Ithaca's campus. The school has refocused its general education program around human communities, and students now explore how communities form, function, and express meaning. The program emphasizes global and historical perspectives through courses in self and society; science, mathematics and formal reasoning; and human expression. Among the strongest of 19 humanities and sciences departments are the natural sciences, which offer research and even publishing opportunities for undergraduates. The $23-million science building boasts state-of-the-art teaching and research facilities for biology, chemistry, and physics. To enhance student-faculty interaction, Ithaca redesigned Williams Hall, adding new computers and lab facilities for the departments of mathematics, computer science, and psychology. Theater arts offers solid acting and technical production programs, but the English and foreign language programs need work, students say.

All Humanities and Science students are required to take writing and statistical analysis courses; H&S also offers a freshman seminar combining rigorous study of a selected subject with transition-to-college topics such as personal, social, and academic responsibility. Applied psychology and telecommunications management are popular majors that cross disciplinary lines. Ithaca students can go to Cornell to take courses not offered on their campus, and vice versa. Other off-campus opportunities include numerous internships and foreign-study programs, including the Ithaca College London Center and the new Ithaca-in-Madrid program for upperclassmen.

The majority of Ithaca's classes are small, and praise for professors abounds.

In the School of Health Sciences and Human Performance, the physical therapy program is a national drawing card, and boasts nearly a 100 percent placement rate.

Students appear especially impressed by the fact that all classes—even labs—are taught by full professors, not TAs. "It was unheard of to call a professor by his or her first name, meet a professor for coffee or lunch at the snack bar—let alone talk to them on the phone at their home at 9:30 P.M.—until I came to Ithaca!" says a speech communication major.

"A blend of preppies and tree-huggers," is how a senior describes the Ithaca population. Students generally hail from the Northeast, with nearly half from New York, and most from middle- to upper-middle-class backgrounds. The school has a large, well-organized Jewish community, but the black, Hispanic, and Asian American populations are small, with each about 2 percent of the student body. Students lament the homogeneity of their campus, but the administration's focus of late has been unity, with Unity Relays and Unity Day bringing together students and faculty from all walks of campus life. And the self-motivated thrive here. More than 1,700 merit scholarships are awarded each year, ranging from $3,000 to a full ride. Athletes, however, get no such aid.

While there may be a figurative place for everyone at Ithaca, only 70 percent find a physical place to hang their hat in campus residence halls. Though they are guaranteed space in the residence halls, arriving freshmen can find themselves squeezed into triples that used to be doubles or packed into a common-room lounge. But don't despair: many lounges have TVs, fireplaces, and terraces, and overcrowding is usually remedied by Thanksgiving, students report. Dorm rooms are comfortable and well-maintained. "Compared to other schools I have seen, ours are in wonderful shape," notes a student. "Only upperclassmen are permitted to live off-campus," adds a junior.

Since "Ithaca is gorges," there are plenty of opportunities to get out of those dorm rooms for hiking, biking, sledding, and skiing. Officially, Ithaca is a dry campus. On weekends, Ithaca students take advantage of an array of college-oriented activities, both on campus, in the town of Ithaca, and at next-door neighbor Cornell. They frequent restaurants, movies, clubs, and festivals downtown, or may road-trip to Cortland, Syracuse, and Binghamton, New York (each an hour away, with plenty of malls) or Philadelphia, Washington, D.C., New York City, or Canada, less than six hours' drive. Ithaca's Greek scene is low key, with three professional music frats and one social service sorority; only about 2 percent of men and women each join the organizations. Homecoming is an occasion for revelry, as is the not-too-esoteric tradition of Terrace mudslides. All Ithacans also look forward to the annual Rocktoberfest, which features games, dunking booths, and Jell-O wrestling. The quirky Fountain Day is a much-anticipated pregraduation event, when seniors jump into a campus fountain to celebrate the completion of their degrees.

Almost all 23 of Ithaca's men's and women's varsity teams—the Bombers—regularly turn in winning seasons. Women's volleyball is a national Division III powerhouse, often making the NCAA semifinals. The men's wrestling team is competitive nationally, football and baseball are competitive, and the men's swimming team had an unbeaten dual-meet season in 1996. Students really get into Ithaca's football rivalry against Cortland State, known as the "Cortaca Jug" match (or the Division III Superbowl). Sailing is a favorite warm-weather activity, and horseback riding is also available.

Though Ithaca College students are segregated by academic interest from day one, due to the existence of five separate professional schools, so many IC students excel across fields that there are cellists on the crew team and physicists singing in the fall opera. And overall, students at Ithaca are a satisfied bunch, almost smug about their school's smallness and setting. "The warm reception and

Through its five schools—music, communications, business, health sciences and human performance, and humanities and sciences—Ithaca offers 92 undergraduate degree programs.

All students in Ithaca's business school now matriculate into the business administration major, and declare one of seven concentrations after the first or second year.

Overlaps

Syracuse, Boston University, NYU, University of Massachusetts, Penn State.

accepting community of Ithaca College has allowed me to grow academically, emotionally, and personally," says a senior. "My interaction with faculty and students has taught me to take positive risks and challenge myself. I've been able to explore new places (abroad), and developed a much more open mind."

If You Apply To ➤ **Ithaca**...Early decision: Nov. 1. Regular admissions: Mar. 1 (Nov. 1 for Physical Therapy). Financial aid: Feb. 1. Meets demonstrated need of 28%. Campus interviews: recommended, informational. Alumni interviews: optional, informational. SATs or ACTs: required. SAT IIs: optional. Apply to particular school or program. Accepts the Common Application and electronic applications. Essay question: important personal, local, national, or international issue.

James Madison University

Harrisonburg, VA 22807

Website: www.jmu.edu
Location: Small town
Total Enrollment: 15,223
Undergraduates: 13,668
Male/Female: 43/57
SAT Ranges: V 540–620 M 540–640
Financial Aid: 74%
Expense: Pub $ $
Phi Beta Kappa: No
Applicants: 12,980
Accepted: 65%
Enrolled: 36%
Grad in 6 Years: 79%
Returning Freshmen: 90%
Academics: ✍ ✍ ✍
Social: ☎ ☎ ☎ ☎
Q of L: ★ ★ ★ ★
Admissions: (540) 568-6147
Email Address: gotojmu@jmu.edu

Strongest Programs:
Music
Media Arts and Design
Chemistry
Speech and Communication

Make no mistake: James Madison University means business. Programs in the business major continue to garner national attention as the university grows at a phenomenal rate. But the school's real strength, according to one student, is its ability to "develop the student completely."

JMU is situated in the heart of the Shenandoah Valley, some two hours from Washington, D.C., and Richmond, Virginia. Two distinct types of architecture make up the campus. The buildings on Front campus have red-tile roofs and are constructed of a distinctive limestone block known as bluestone. Newer buildings on the back campus are more modern and made of red brick. Despite JMU's scenic surroundings, Madison isn't as isolated as one might expect. The university straddles Interstate 81, an outlet to several major East Coast cities. Recent construction includes a new eastern campus for the university, which houses the already well-acclaimed College of Integrated Science and Technology.

James Madison University is recognized nationally for programs in the business major; social sciences and education are also strong. The most popular programs are psychology, communications, and English. The sciences are also strong bets at JMU, and undergraduates in the biology department have even employed recombinant DNA technology to help develop organisms that produce biodegradable plastics. Also worth noting is the geology and geography departments' summer geology field camp for undergraduates. Although the math department is cited as weak, its development of a mathematical modeling laboratory is used by select undergrads to solve real-world applied math problems. "The academic climate at JMU is pretty competitive, especially as you progress," a senior psychology major warns. Recent curriculum changes include new majors in recreation and special education, as well as a minor in biochemistry.

The General Education Program requires each student to take courses in several clusters, including Skills for the 21st Century, Arts and Humanities, the Natural World, Social and Cultural Processes, and Individuals in the Human Community. The idea is to offer students a basis for lifelong learning by challenging them to become active in their own education and to explore the foundations of knowledge. If you're worried about budget cuts hampering your academic prowess, take notice: James Madison is doing more with less. JMU president Linwood H. Rose admission continues to increase the school's selectivity, while coeducation has become a reality, and seemingly everything from total enrollment to the size of the faculty has doubled.

As Madison's enrollment has now exceeded 15,000, the school is suffering some growing pains, and parking—or rather the lack of space for parking—is a constant complaint, although a new 500-vehicle parking deck should ease the situation. With undergraduates far outnumbering grad students, JMU's main mission is undergraduate teaching. "I think that the teachers here are excellent," says one student. "They are very cooperative and are willing to work with you." Students say that faculty advising can be hit or miss. But if you are willing to find the time, some students say that even weekly meetings with these gurus are possible. "I received excellent counseling from my academic advisors," notes one student, "but I am one of the very, very few." Students do say, though, that faculty members are helpful and friendly. This friendliness helps color the entire academic climate, which students describe as "quite warm." Those looking for a more intense intellectual experience can check out the honors program, which offers small classes and opportunities for independent study. Many upper-level programs encourage undergraduate participation with faculty research, another plus of this school. If JMU gets a little confining, students may opt for a semester in London, Paris, Florence, or Salamanca.

One interesting quality about JMU is the student body homogeneity. Ninety-five percent of the students attended public high school, and 70 percent are from Virginia. In fact, there's a 30 percent cap on out-of-state enrollment at JMU. African Americans account for just 5 percent of the student body, and Hispanics and Asian Americans combine for another 6 percent. "Students from different backgrounds don't seem to have trouble mixing, but I think overall, we just choose not to," notes one sociology major. JMU offers 350 merit scholarships, ranging from $100 to $4,000 and 370 athletic scholarships for men and women in a variety of sports.

Many students find the JMU campus a perfect place to call home for four years. Forty-three percent of the students live in the dorms, which run the gamut from the old high-ceiling variety to newer, air-conditioned models that come complete with carpet and a fitness center in the building. While most upperclassmen opt to move off campus to nearby apartments or houses, they still feel like part of the campus community. And "anyone with 12 or more credit hours is guaranteed housing," one student notes. Students rave about the meal plan, which has a handful of options every day, including a salad bar and low-calorie meals, Top Dog (hot dogs), Spaghetti Western (spaghetti and Mexican), and even a steak house.

And what do students do for a good time? In the words of one student, "Life at JMU is always exciting. When students have free time, there is always a play, concert, sporting event, or party to attend." A classmate agrees: "Many Greeks hold parties on JMU's Greek row, but you do not have to be Greek to have fun!" Although the school does not allow underage drinking on campus, "minors can find ways to drink." The Greek system attracts 14 percent of the men and 17 percent of the women, though most agree that going Greek is by no means mandatory. Greeks and independents alike participate in JMU's many annual rites, including Homecoming and Christmas on the Quad. As for road trips, the favorite destination seems to be the University of Virginia, almost an hour's drive

The sciences are also strong bets at JMU, and undergraduates in the biology department have even employed recombinant DNA technology to help develop organisms that produce biodegradable plastics.

Recent curriculum changes include new programs in health, computer sciences and information security, and a new doctoral program in assessment.

to the south. Equally enticing, however, are the many natural delights of the Shenandoah Valley, including hiking, camping, and even skiing, all nearby. Other scenic getaways include the Blue Ridge Mountains. Most students find local Harrisonburg a friendly Southern town. Says one senior media arts and design major, "Harrisonburg is a small town, but has an incredible array of restaurants and shopping spots."

Sherman Dillard was named the new coach of the JMU Dukes basketball team in 1997 and replaced famed coach Lefty Driesell. The fans here are known as the Electric Zoo and are enthusiastic about their teams. Conference, state, and regional championships have been won in recent years by the men's archery, soccer, and swimming and diving teams, while the women have captured crowns in gymnastics, swimming and diving, fencing, field hockey, and golf. The football team has made the national quarterfinals twice in the '90s, and the program has produced several current NFL players. Intramural sports are very popular.

Though JMU still has a ways to go before establishing itself as a front-rank national university, it has made considerable progress in the past two decades. "While it's still pretty small, it's nice here because of the coziness, because no one becomes just a number. Yet, there's a huge variety of cultures to meet people's interests," a senior says. And with the whole East Coast just a few hours away, JMU's location is certainly another plus.

Overlaps

Virginia Tech, University of Virginia, William and Mary, George Mason, Mary Washington.

If You Apply To ➤ | **JMU**...Early action: Nov. 1. Regular admissions: Jan. 15. Financial aid: Feb. 15. Housing: May 1. No campus or alumni interviews. SATs: required. SAT IIs: required (writing and foreign languages for placement). Accepts electronic applications. Essay question: personal statement.

The Johns Hopkins University

3400 North Charles Street, Baltimore, MD 21218

Website: www.jhu.edu
Location: Urban
Total Enrollment: 5,294
Undergraduates: 3,925
Male/Female: 54/46
SAT Ranges: V 630–730 M 660–750
ACT Range: 27–34
Financial Aid: 43%
Expense: Pr $ $ $ $
Phi Beta Kappa: Yes
Applicants: 9,496
Accepted: 33%
Enrolled: 32%
Grad in 6 Years: 89%

With one of the world's premier medical and scientific programs, as well as first-rate programs in areas as diverse as writing, international studies, and art history, Johns Hopkins is clearly among the elite schools in the country. Long revered as one of the nation's top breeding grounds for future doctors and scientists, Johns Hopkins University has spent more money than any other academic institution on research and development in science and engineering. It is now trying to take the lead in integrating technology into the classroom, including the creation of virtual labs on the Internet. With so much to offer, it's curious as to why Hopkins is often overlooked when the finest universities are listed.

The arts and sciences and engineering schools are located on the picturesque 140-acre Homewood campus, located just three miles north of Baltimore's revitalized Inner Harbor. Tree-lined quadrangles, open lawns, and playing fields make for an idyllic setting on the edge of a major urban center. The architecture on this woody urban campus is mainly Georgian red brick, with several recently built, more modern structures scattered throughout. A new biomedical engineering building is currently under construction, as are a new student arts center and recreation center.

As much as some try to deny it, premeds dominate the campus. Nearly 30 percent of entering freshmen say they are premed, and biomedical engineering tops the list of most popular majors (followed by biology, international studies, public health, and psychology). The university's hospital provides excellent research opportunities, and the Graduate School of Hygiene and Public Health offers a popular undergraduate major. Medicine at JHU plays such a major role in campus life that students sometimes fear it overshadows other aspects of the school. "The medical campus is the school's biggest problem," says one student majoring in biomedical engineering and classics. "Most students resent having it, although we also love it. It provides research opportunities for scientists like myself, but it also overshadows the vibrant undergrad life that exists at Homewood." Biomedical engineers also enjoy a strong department—a popular T-shirt notes "Biomedical engineers do more after 1:00 A.M. than most people do all day." The only departments that really receive any criticism from students are math and classics. Hopkins now offers BA degrees in biology and physics, and a special BS/MS in biology and biophysics. A major in film and media studies meets the needs of students who have technical talent but are oriented toward the arts and humanities. Whether it's science or the humanities, undergraduates have enormous praise for the outstanding faculty members at Johns Hopkins. "The quality of teaching at Hopkins is magnificent," raves one junior. "Most professors possess an extreme understanding and passion for their field and pass their knowledge and love on to their pupils." Graduate students teach some, but not many classes; often they lead small sections to compliment a large lecture taught by a professor.

Although Johns Hopkins is a firm supporter of traditional scholarship, there are no university-wide requirements other than a four-course writing component. Each major has its own distribution requirements, and there are several creative seminar offerings for freshmen. Students can receive a BA in creative writing through the Writing Seminars program, where they study with authors and playwrights such as John Barth. But students warn that these writing courses are quite popular, and getting into them can be difficult. The Humanities Center espouses a casual, interdisciplinary approach, and with maximum curriculum flexibility allowed them, undergraduates are free to range as broadly or focus as specifically as they want. Students can also take a broad "area majors," such as social sciences or quantitative studies, and choose from a cluster of related disciplines to design their own program. Even the strictly structured engineering course plan stresses the importance of interdisciplinary and interdepartmental exposure. An arts and sciences faculty committee on excellence periodically reviews the curriculum and promises perennial vigor in undergraduate teaching. All students must take at least 30 credits outside their major area.

Students also benefit from the well-developed graduate side of Johns Hopkins. The International Studies Program, for example, is enriched by its offerings at the university's Bologna Center in Italy and at its School of Advanced International Studies in nearby Washington, D.C. Undergraduate research is also a hallmark of a Hopkins experience. The university probably offers more opportunities than just about any other place, with 70 percent of students having at least one research experience. The provost awards 60 grants of up to $2,500 each for undergraduates to do summer research. And those who are interested should start thinking about those grants early—one of Hopkins admissions essays asks what sort of research a prospective student might want to do.

Overall, students find the academic climate competitive but not overwhelming. "It's extremely competitive in the engineering and natural sciences classes,"

(Continued)
Returning Freshmen: 97%
Academics: ✍ ✍ ✍ ✍ ✍
Social: ☎ ☎ ☎
Q of L: ★ ★ ★
Admissions: (410) 516-8171
Email Address:
 gotojhu@jhu.edu

Strongest Programs:
 English/Writing
 History
 International Studies
 Biomedical Engineering
 Art History
 Biology
 French

Medicine at JHU plays such a major role in campus life that students sometimes fear it overshadows other aspects of the school.

says one history major. "The climate is a little more laid-back in the social sciences, though the courses are very hard." The curved grading system encourages intense competition, and the absence of plus or minus grades can make life especially harsh. Hopkins is one of the strongest schools in the country, and the workload reflects that—many students say they work constantly. Academic advising receives mixed reviews from students. With faculty, residential, multicultural, student, and first-year advisors, some students have said they wish they could get a little less advice. Others, however, are downright rapturous about their experience. "My college advisor was wonderful," said one student. "He helped me [decide] not only what classes to take but in how I should organize my time, pursue extracurricular activities, and apply for research positions." There is a pre-major faculty advisor for freshmen, and students are required to wait until at least their sophomore year to declare a major. Johns Hopkins also generously allows freshmen to take an entire semester on a pass/fail basis to ease them into the academic rigor of the place. After this "honeymoon" period, students buckle down to a Herculean workload. Some relief is offered, however—the optional January intersession—during which students can take courses or pursue independent study for one or two credits.

Hopkins students are remarkably talented, with 73 percent from the top tenth of their high school class. Politically, Johns Hopkins is usually considered rather conservative, but that might be changing. "We're hip on diversity," says one sophomore. "Southern Society lives peacefully with the Black Student Union, the Jewish Students Association and the Muslim Students Association co-sponsor events, frat guys tolerate the Gay, Bisexual Lesbian and Transgender Alliance and vice versa." Indeed, gay and lesbian issues as well as the involvement of ROTC on campus head the list of hot debate topics. Seventy-two percent of the school is white, and Asian Americans make up 19 percent of the population. Blacks comprise 6 percent, and 2 percent of the school is Hispanic. Geographically, most students come from the Mid-Atlantic states and New England—only 12 percent come from Maryland.

Hopkins's endowment is among the top 20 in the country at nearly $1.4 billion, and it strives to meet the full demonstrated financial need of virtually every admit. Prepayment and monthly payment plans and long-term parent loans help middle-income families, and Hopkins generously rewards the extraordinarily talented with 15 hefty merit scholarships worth $18,500 per year, regardless of need, and renewable annually for those who keep a 3.0 GPA. A new scholarship, based on need, replaces the loans in the aid packages of selected students from underrepresented minority groups. Twenty athletic scholarships are also awarded in women's and men's lacrosse, where Hopkins is a perennial national powerhouse. Word is that non-premeds are looked on with particular favor by the financial aid office. Finally, Hopkins offers a free online scholarship search service for all of its students.

Freshmen and sophomores are required to live on campus in either single-sex or coed-by-floor dormitories. Twenty-five percent of the upperclassmen, once left to fend for themselves, are now guaranteed housing in one of six residence halls or university-owned apartments. "The dorms are well maintained and fairly comfortable," says one student. "But they are very expensive for the room you get." Upperclassmen live in dorms that are regarded as very nice, and they now have the option of new "luxury" apartments. All in all, 65 percent of Hopkins undergrads live in university housing.

According to students, the social scene at Hopkins is improving. "Social life has been on a continual rise since the early '90s," says one junior. "Events

Though students know how to unwind under the bright lights of Baltimore's Inner Harbor or cheering on the lacrosse team, the light that burns the brightest at Hopkins is the midnight oil.

continue happening off campus, and are slowly re-centering on the campus itself." With one-third of the students dispersed among the city's apartment buildings, rowdy dorm parties and all-campus events are few and far between. But fraternity parties can be found on the weekends, though only 25 percent of the men and women belong, and the E-level bar on campus is also popular. The 21 age limit is officially enforced, but students say it's easy for minors to get served at nearby bars or in Baltimore. "There are many strict policies," says one underclassman. "And there's not a chance of them working. Students will drink anyway." Students also tend to hang out in groups that center on a particular interest, usually academic, and get together at someone's apartment. Though the student activities office sponsors' movies, dance and theater performances, and a Friday afternoon "Hoppy Hour," students bemoan the lack of campus spirit.

But the biggest and most popular undergraduate social event of the year is the annual student-organized Spring Fair, which draws crowds from the surrounding communities as well. The school recently partially renovated the student union with a new social club for undergrads and vastly expanded space for student offices and meeting rooms. Downtown Baltimore and the famed Inner Harbor are not too distant, and some of the city's best—albeit expensive—attractions, such as the art museum and Wyman Park, are right near campus. Students also head to Baltimore for plays, the symphony, films, clubs, restaurants, the zoo or the aquarium and major league sports—Camden Yards, home of baseball's Orioles, is the most commodious park in the country. When things become tiresome there, Annapolis and Washington, D.C., are less than an hour from campus, and Philadelphia and New York are just a train ride away.

When the stellar lacrosse team takes the road against opponents, students often take advantage of the opportunity to road trip with them. Undergrads come together—even leaving the library at times—to cheer on their nationally acclaimed Blue Jays and release some study tension. Women's and men's basketball, and men's soccer have each brought home conference trophies recently. Always a welcome alternative to the books, Hopkins's intramural sports program provides some playing time for other students.

Though students know how to unwind under the bright lights of Baltimore's Inner Harbor or cheering on the lacrosse team, the light that burns the brightest at Hopkins is the midnight oil. Most students at this elite school were admitted because of their pursuit of academic excellence, and drive like that doesn't end with high school graduation. For those looking for top-notch professors, incredible resources, and unparalleled research opportunities, Hopkins is hard to beat. At this prestigious school, students truly take pride in the fact that they belong to the cream of the academic crop.

Overlaps

Cornell University, Penn, Duke, Harvard, Yale.

If You Apply To ➤

Johns Hopkins…Early decision: Nov. 15. Regular admissions: Jan. 1. Financial aid: Feb. 1. Does not guarantee to meet demonstrated need. Campus interviews: recommended, evaluative. Alumni interviews: optional, informational. SATs or ACTs: required. SAT IIs: required (writing and two others or ACT). Accepts the Common Application and electronic applications. Essay question: choose a metaphor to describe the body; design a course around your favorite music, art, film, or book; create an invention with several given objects; describe potential independent research topics; or choose important person and give significance. Seeks highly motivated students interested in doing "creative research" in their chosen fields.

Kalamazoo College

1200 Academy Street, Kalamazoo, MI 49006-3295

Website: www.kzoo.edu

Location: City outskirts

Total Enrollment: 1,367

Undergraduates: 1,367

Male/Female: 44/56

SAT Ranges: V 590–690 M 570–670

ACT Range: 26–29

Financial Aid: 52%

Expense: Pr $ $

Phi Beta Kappa: Yes

Applicants: 1,410

Accepted: 77%

Enrolled: 34%

Grad in 6 Years: 71%

Returning Freshmen: 89%

Academics: ✍ ✍ ✍

Social: ☎ ☎ ☎

Q of L: ☎ ☎ ☎ ☎

Admissions: 800-253-3602

Email Address:
admission@kzoo.edu

Strongest Programs:
Biology
Chemistry
International Studies
Languages
English
Economics
Health Science

While Kalamazoo College is a small school in a small town in the heartland of America, for most of its students, it is also a launching pad to the world. The college urges students to take part in its "K" Plan, which emphasizes teaching, internships, independent research, and subsidized study abroad. And the 85 percent of students who embrace the program and traverse the globe, like weary travelers, are relieved to return to the warm and supportive environment that awaits them on campus.

Life on Kalamazoo's wooded, 60-acre campus centers on the Quad, a green lawn where students ponder their destiny and play Ultimate Frisbee with equal ease. With its rolling hills, Georgian architecture, and cobblestone streets, the campus has a quaint and historic New England look that belies its proximity to the city of Kalamazoo and its 80,000 residents. This tranquil setting provides a four-year home for the small number of students who choose not to explore the world on the numerous study abroad programs, and a restorative home base for those who do.

Kalamazoo operates on the quarter system and students are required to spend their entire first year on campus. Before they become temporarily landlocked, many freshmen choose to begin the year with a "land-sea adventure," three weeks of canoeing and climbing in the mountain wilds of Canada, followed by sailing a brigantine ship down Lake Huron to Windsor, Ontario. By the end, they're convinced they can survive anything, including the rigors of a Kalamazoo education (and the bitter Michigan winters). Safely ashore on campus, they begin to explore possible majors and fulfill distribution requirements, including three courses each in literature and fine arts, social sciences, and cultures, and two courses in math/sciences and religion/philosophy. Students also must demonstrate proficiency in a foreign language, take a course in quantitative reasoning, and participate in physical education.

After the freshman year, most of K-zoo's undergrads meet life's challenges with suitcase in hand, studying wherever their heart takes them, for the regular tuition price (thanks to a special endowment). Students can participate in off-campus studies in a variety of programs, including those offered through the Great Lakes College Association.* The final year brings the Senior Independent Project, pursued in either summer or fall term and sometimes both. This can be an internship, directed research, an art project, student teaching, or a traditional thesis, anything that will cap off each student's education in some meaningful way. The new Center for Experiential Education is another resource for information on careers, internships, and study abroad.

The synthesis of travel and an on-campus liberal arts education was designed to guide students through academic and career planning, and to prepare them for real-life choices. The atmosphere inside the classroom is both competitive and supportive. "Everybody is in the same boat, and everyone is rooting for everyone else. At the same time, each individual is trying to do better than the next," one sophomore explains. The natural sciences are exceptionally good and students heap praise on the psychology and languages departments, but economics wins the popularity contest. As for weaker programs, music and theater are panned by many; religion and philosophy are also given mixed reviews. Most professors give students individual attention and are rewarded by some of Michigan's highest faculty salaries. "The teachers at 'K' love to teach and are always willing to meet with you outside of class," a psychology/sociology major says.

Formerly associated with the American Baptist Churches and founded in 1833, Kalamazoo is the oldest college in Michigan. State residents make up about two-thirds of the student body, with Midwesterners and a sprinkling of Easterners and foreign students accounting for the rest. Three percent of the students are black, 2 percent Hispanic, and 5 percent are Asian American. Many K-zoo students crave more diversity; they cite this and multiculturalism as important campus issues. One student comments that there is "a division between PC groups and laid back college students. Protests are common, although small and quiet." Kalamazoo awards merit scholarships, worth $3,500 to $10,000 a year.

With so many students away from campus because of the K Plan (200 to 300 students each quarter), a certain instability pervades all activities, from athletics to student government. "The 'K' Plan students are always coming and going. This makes it hard for relationships and sometimes you don't see your friend for six to nine months," laments a senior. All resident halls are coed and none are divided by class standing. And unlike the situation at most colleges, K-residents don't need to lug rolls of quarters to the laundry—washers and dryers are free for students in each dorm. Trowbridge is said to be the dorm of preference for most freshmen. The dorm rooms come in suites for six, four, two, or one. There are no sororities or frats, but theme houses offer a more community-oriented atmosphere that includes family-style dinners. The dining facilities have been completely redesigned and renovated. The central dining-hall's food is good, but it's no match for the decor: the six "motif" rooms are each done up to fit a nationality—the English pub has wood panels and stained-glass windows.

"Yes, there really is a Kalamazoo!" proclaims a T-shirt donned by some students, and they appreciate the small city for its restaurants, theaters, bars, and concerts, and its proximity to Lake Michigan's beaches and Chicago's urban playground. With four schools in Kalamazoo, "the city creates a typical 'college town,'" says a political science major. The facilities and functions of other colleges in town are open to Kalamazoo students, who particularly take advantage of the library and gym at large Western Michigan University, right across the street. Many K-zoo students build houses for Habitat for Humanity and volunteer for other local organizations. On campus, K-zoo students appreciate traditions such as a pseudo-casino and dance event called Monte Carlo Night, Homecoming, a party and trip give-away called Bahama Boogie, and Quadstock, an all-day music fest on the much-loved Quad. In the spring, students and faculty also participate in the Day of Gracious Living, where, without prior warning, classes are canceled and students can take day trips or help beautify the campus. Politically, Kalamazoo is liberal and students are socially and politically active.

For those who equate college with big-time varsity athletics, Kalamazoo has something to offer—even if it's not nationally televised games or tens of thousands of screaming fans. The Kalamazoo Hornets have a long-standing rivalry with Hope College which culminates in the football teams' annual competition for the "infamous wooden shoes," says a sophomore. At athletic events, K-zoo fans are known as "the stingers," and they "are the most loyal, knowledgeable, and greatest fans ever," gushes a sports-crazed senior. Kalamazoo also has a respectable men's tennis team. However, an economics and business major reports that "Frisbee golf is the thing to play, and K's golf course is used by Kalamazoo students, some faculty, and some townies."

Well-traveled, well-grounded, and well-prepared for their careers, students at Kalamazoo College say they get the best of all worlds. Kalamazoo students are

Many freshmen choose to begin the year with a "land-sea adventure," three weeks of canoeing and climbing in the mountain wilds of Canada followed by sailing a brigantine ship down Lake Huron to Windsor, Ontario. By the end, they're convinced they can survive anything, including the rigors of a Kalamazoo education.

Unlike the situation at most colleges, K-residents don't need to lug rolls of quarters to the laundry—washers and dryers are free for students in each dorm.

proud of their studiousness and their worldliness, and say it's this "mix of academic and real-life experiences," that makes them say "whoop-dee-doo for Kalamazoo." And they do it with a straight face.

If You Apply To ➤

Kalamazoo…Rolling admissions: Feb. 1. Financial aid: Feb. 15. Does not guarantee to meet demonstrated need. Campus interviews: recommended, evaluative. No alumni interviews. SATs or ACTs: required. SAT IIs: optional. Accepts the Common Application and electronic applications. Essay question: a situation where you've made a difference, or significance of multicultural education, or someone or something that had a lasting impact on you.

University of Kansas

126 Strong Hall, Lawrence, Kansas 66045

Website: www.ukans.edu
Location: Small city
Total Enrollment: 27,838
Undergraduates: 19,477
Male/Female: 47/53
ACT Range: 21–27
Financial Aid: 33%
Expense: Pub $
Phi Beta Kappa: Yes
Applicants: 8,409
Accepted: 69%
Enrolled: 67%
Grad in 6 Years: 53%
Returning Freshmen: 78%
Academics: ✑ ✑ ✑ ✑
Social: ☎ ☎ ☎ ☎
Q of L: ★ ★ ★ ★
Admissions: (785) 864-3911
Email Address:
  adm@ukans.edu

Strongest Programs:
  Architecture and Urban Design
  Education
  Environmental Studies
  Journalism
  Nursing/Pharmacy

The rest of the country is finally learning what folks in Kansas knew all along: the University of Kansas is one of the nation's best buys in higher education. With solid academics, outstanding extracurricular programs, winning athletics, and a stellar social life, it's easy to see why thousands of students call KU home.

The 1,000-acre campus is set atop Mount Oread ridge—once a lookout point for pioneer wagon trains—and spread out on rolling green hills overlooking valleys. The wooded and hilly Lawrence campus is one of the most beautiful in the United States. Many of the buildings are made of indigenous Kansas limestone. But the real beauty of the campus lies in its landscape, particularly the breathtaking foliage that appears each autumn. There are nearly as many trees on campus—19,000 at last count—as there are undergrads. But make sure you bring a good pair of walking shoes, because as one physically fit senior says, "At KU, we have a lot of stairs and hills. Oh, what a workout!" Recent construction includes renovations to the football stadium and a new parking garage. Murphy Hall, part of the School of Fine Arts, has been renovated to include rehearsal rooms, recording studios, a computing technology lab, and a comprehensive music and dance library.

KU applicants apply to the individual school of their choice. Those not admitted to one of the professional schools will automatically be considered for admission to the College of Liberal Arts and Sciences, where 70 percent of the undergraduate population is enrolled. Students in most of the professional schools, with the exception of engineering, architecture, and fine arts, spend their first two years completing the liberal arts requirements. The general education curriculum is intended to expose students to the foundations of the humanities, sciences, and social sciences. It also includes math, English, and oral communication, and requires courses in both Western and non-Western civilization. Foreign language and laboratory science courses are required as well for all BA candidates.

Of the 14 graduate and professional schools, those most noted for undergraduate programs are architecture and urban design, allied health, fine arts, social welfare, pharmacy, nursing, education, business, and engineering. The journalism, architecture, and business programs receive rave reviews from students. The lower-rated programs include math, Western civilization, and the oft-maligned physical education. Those with outstanding high school records should definitely look into the honors program, which offers small classes with top professors. The Mount Oread Scholars program allows students who graduated in the top 20 percent of their high school class access to special advising and networking with outstanding professors. About 80 freshmen participate in a yearlong orientation program called Excellence in Ellsworth. Residing in Ellsworth Hall, the students take sociology together and participate in a variety of social, educational, cultural, and recreational activities designed to enhance their transition to university life. Freshmen can also opt to take University Seminars, a two-credit course that helps students learn problem-solving, decision-making, and communication skills.

Students describe the academic atmosphere as fairly competitive but a new Kansas law ends open admissions, which should improve the academic standards for all students. Professors earn high marks for their teaching ability and dedication, and while some students complain about the number of graduate students teaching courses, others say the TAs at Kansas are quite good. There is a great range in class size; introductory chemistry takes the prize as the largest, with more than 800 students, but most classes range from 20 to 50 students. "The teaching quality is strong, but in an effort to have more professors teach freshmen, many classes have become 500-student lecture formats," a senior political science and journalism double major laments.

Aside from the usual coursework, options include independent study or the more than 75 study abroad programs in 52 countries, including Brazil, France, Germany, and Ghana. Kansas provides several area study programs supported by language instruction in more than 20 languages. The top-ranked Latin American, Spanish, and Portuguese studies programs, which benefit from an exchange with the University of Costa Rica, are three good examples. Undergraduates at KU may receive research awards to work with faculty members in publishing papers and poetry. And students are pleased with their library system, which includes a 3.5-million-volume main library, a research library, and science and engineering libraries.

Sixty-eight percent of the students are from Kansas, and most of the rest are fellow Midwesterners (with lots from Chicago). The most vocal groups on campus are African Americans, gays, and lesbians. Vocal yes, highly represented, no: African Americans, Hispanics, and Asian Americans combined account for only 9 percent of the students. Gay rights, diversity, alcohol policies, and political correctness are the hottest topics discussed by students; one senior Journalism major describes KU as "a liberal oasis in the middle of conservative Kansas." KU is known less than affectionately as "Snob Hill" by students at other Kansas schools, who tend to come from humbler origins. Out-of-staters must have a 3.0 high school GPA or a 24 on the ACT to get in. KU gives out about 5,000 academic merit awards and 435 more benefit from a wide variety of athletic scholarships. Freshman orientation begins with a series of one- or two-day summer sessions. And the seven days before classes are officially called Hawk Week, but are more commonly known as Country Club Week because of all the partying that goes on—though it's been less in recent years due to tougher liquor laws.

Only 21 percent of the students live in university housing, and both coed and single-sex dorms are available. Overall, students describe the housing as "ugly" and in great need of repair, though renovations are under way to correct the

(Continued)
Social Welfare
Business

Undergraduates at KU may receive research awards to work with faculty members in publishing papers and poetry.

problem. Students with 2.5 GPAs can live in one of the 11 scholarship halls—"the best of all possible living situations"—where 50 men or women live in a cooperative-type arrangement. These scholars do their own chores, such as cooking and cleaning, and in turn enjoy an academic style of fraternizing and reduced board rates. A vast majority of KU students live off campus in Lawrence apartments, which are considered expensive only by Kansas standards. Scholarship dormers claim their menu offers less variety than the cafeteria, but they do enjoy the "more home-cooked taste." A dining complex called Mrs. E's provides extended-hour access to food court-style meals for 2,500 residence hall occupants.

The university's bus system is run entirely by students and much appreciated by tenderfeet, especially during the cold, windy winters. Lawrence with its myriad boutiques, restaurants, and bars, receives rave reviews from students. Students describe the town as "kind of artsy, kind of alternative," and volunteerism in the community among students seems to be on the rise. The university is supplying more activities than ever.

For example, Lied Center offers a wide variety of acts, ranging from Johnny Cash to the St. Petersburg Ballet, to a showing of *Tommy*. City slickers can trek off to Topeka, the state capital, or to Kansas City, each less than an hour's drive. The KC airport makes for easy long-distance transportation, and the area is also served by Amtrak.

The Greek system, which attracts 19 percent of the men and 21 percent of the women, tends to be a major force in the on-campus social life, though tension does exist between Greeks and independents. Sorority rush is completely dry, but rumor has it that the frats are a little more lenient when it comes to alcohol. Overall the social life is described as "incredible" and "very active," with lots of choices and alternatives. Scholarship halls, dorms, and other student groups sponsor large campus parties and events, but students agree that most of the social life takes place off campus. There is little boredom to be had, with more than 400 organized groups and other extracurricular activities including movies, poetry readings, and concerts by local or visiting performers.

KU varsity teams—the only ones in the nation that carry the name Jayhawks—compete in the tough Big 12 Conference. The basketball team, which won the Big 12 Championship for the third consecutive year in 1999, is legendary and James Naismith, who invented basketball, was KU's first coach—and the only one with a losing record.

The traditional "Rock Chalk Jayhawk" KU cheer is enough to bring a pang of nostalgia to the heart of even the most grizzled Kansas alumnus. To demonstrate their loyalty to the Jayhawks, thousands of students show up for the first basketball practice of the season at 12:01 A.M. on October 15. This nocturnal tradition is lovingly labeled "Late Night with Roy Williams," the coach, or "Midnight Madness." KU's most-hated rival is Missouri, and the winner of the annual football game takes possession of an Indian War Drum. Favorite road trips are determined by where the basketball team is playing. The women's basketball team is also worth watching, as are the men's and women's tennis teams and the women's swimming and diving team.

With KU's huge number of high-ranking academic programs, its national reputation (the nonbasketball one) has certainly improved. "KU is a special place because it exudes a certain character that speaks of tradition yet pushes into the future at the same time," says one sophomore, "KU is a great place to be." It's true: Kansas is a heck of a deal.

Overlaps

Kansas State, University of Missouri, Washington University (MO), University of Nebraska, University of Illinois.

University of Kentucky

100 Funkhouser Building, Lexington, KY 40506-0032

You probably know that the University of Kentucky Wildcats are perennial attendees at the NCAA postseason basketball tournament, dribbling and shooting their way to a national championship in 1998. What you may not know is that the University of Kentucky's excellence stretches beyond its winning athletic teams—into outstanding medical and premedical programs, scientific research involving both professors and students, and a social calendar packed so full of Southern tradition that it would make even the most composed debutante's head spin. The school's aim is a Top 20 ranking among public universities nationwide by 2020, and building on its bevy of well-regarded graduate programs, that goal may just be attainable.

The University of Kentucky campus, home to a major public research university as well as a community college, contains a mixture of old and new, modern and traditional buildings that date back to the late 1890s. The campus buildings indicate a transition beginning with the original red brick structures to designs using contemporary glass and concrete as one moves south following the path of development. Most visitors would agree that the grounds are well-maintained, organized around the comfortable park-like spaces influenced by Frederick Law Olmsted's design. The campus contains a vast amount of mature trees and lawns set in a natural arrangement of open spaces, typical of the great land-grant universities. Of course, UK's location in the heart of one of the finest horse-breeding areas in the world makes it a natural place for the Gluck Equine Research Center, a headquarters for research into horse diseases. The new William T. Young Library is ranked 30th among public research libraries by the Association of Research Libraries.

Students sing the praises of many departments at UK, but several unique programs stand out. The Lexington campus is home to the Gaines Center of the Humanities, which is unusual in its study of public higher education. Lexington also hosts the Patterson School of International Diplomacy, one of the smallest yet most respected schools of its type in the country. The chemistry department turned out three National Science Foundation fellowship winners in 1998-99, a feat matched only by Harvard, Cornell, Rice, Princeton, and the Massachusetts Institute of Technology. Weaker areas include lower-level "monster" science classes, which one student describes as "extremely large and not at all personalized." All but 10 percent of classes at UK have 50 or fewer students, unusual for a state university, but undergraduates still complain about trouble getting into courses they need, especially entry-level offerings. According to a marketing major, students "have difficulty if they are freshmen, because most of them have to take the same classes, and sometimes they don't get the right times—or the

Website: www.uky.edu
Location: Center city
Total Enrollment: 23,060
Undergraduates: 16,841
Male/Female: 48/52
ACT Range: 22–27
Financial Aid: N/A
Expense: Pub $ $
Phi Beta Kappa: Yes
Applicants: 8,320
Accepted: 73%
Enrolled: 32%
Grad in 6 Years: 53%
Returning Freshmen: 79%
Academics: ✍ ✍ ✍
Social: ☎ ☎ ☎ ☎
Q of L: ★ ★ ★
Admissions: (859) 257-2000
Email Address:
admissio@pop.uky.edu

Strongest Programs:
Business
Premed
Predentistry
Nursing
Engineering
Chemistry

Kentucky's aim is a Top 20 ranking among public universities nationwide by 2020.

classes at all." It's hard to complete the engineering, health, business, and architecture programs in four years, students say. Term-time internships, known as co-ops, also complicate, but enliven the picture.

Students praise UK's professors. "With very few exceptions, I have been very pleased with the quality of teaching," says a mathematics major. TAs and full professors teach about the same number of freshman classes. "The Central Advising Service, or CAS, is helping to improve the quality of academic guidance.

To graduate, all students must take mathematics and a foreign language, as well as written and oral communication classes and a statistics, calculus or logic course. The core program, called University Studies, also requires exposure to natural and social sciences, humanities, an introduction to cross-disciplinary education, and experience with non-Western ways of thinking. Additionally, all freshmen are encouraged to take an academic orientation class called UK101, designed to help them adjust to college life. The academic climate is laid-back, but students shouldn't expect easy As. "When it comes to study time and classwork, the students are always competing with themselves to earn the best grades they can," explains a junior.

For upperclassmen, UK offers a number of joint programs with other colleges and universities, including Transylvania, Centre, and Georgetown (in Kentucky). There's also a cooperative program with the Army and Air Force ROTC. Students studying prevet at UK will find coveted slots reserved for them at Auburn and Tuskegee in the advanced veterinary medicine program, at in-state tuition rates. UK is a member of the Academic Common Market, which provides students in 15 states the opportunity to pay in-state tuition at any of these states' schools if they want to enroll in a program not offered in their home state.

The UK student body hails from all fifty counties in Kentucky, with 13 percent from out of state and 4 percent from foreign countries. The student body is predominantly white; blacks account for 6 percent of students, and Hispanics and Asian Americans combine for a little more than 3 percent. Despite these small numbers, students say diversity is valued. "Respectfulness is an issue," says one student. "But Southern hospitality abounds." The university aims to be an "inclusive learning community," achieving academic excellence by working toward "social responsibility and community building, with particular focus on equity, fairness, and safety for each person," among other initiatives. Merit scholarships, ranging from $500 to a full ride, are offered to qualified students.

Kentucky's dorms are clean and convenient, as well as a great way to meet people, students say, though there's quite a range of what amenities you may get. Dorms are located on three parts of the campus—north, central, and south. North campus housing is old, but the halls are small, so they afford a chance to form close relationships. They're also within a short walking distance of classrooms, the student center, and the bookstore. South campus offers newer dorms with small rooms and air-conditioning, while Central campus offers the biggest rooms. Recommended for freshmen: Kirwan-Blanding Complex, since "everything seems to happen there." Getting a room is not a problem as long as you apply by the deadline. Also, since students are not required to live on campus, only 25 percent do.

Students say that while Lexington is a great place to go to school, it's not a typical college town. "Lexington is almost 250,000 people strong," an upperclassman explains. "It's small enough to drive across town easily, but large enough not to see everyone you know when you go to Wal-Mart." Despite the lack of diversity on campus, Lexington abounds with a multitude of ethnic eateries, as well as theaters, shopping malls, and nightspots. On campus, students enjoy movies, presentations, seminars and athletic events, the most popular being basketball games at the legendary Rupp Arena. Other campus activities include the Little Kentucky Derby, a weeklong student-run festival that features a balloon race and concerts. Among the highlights of any student's career at UK are two one-month periods—one in the fall, one in the spring—when students spend afternoons at Keeneland Race Track enjoying the tradition of Kentucky horse racing

About 15 percent of the men and 17 percent of the women go Greek, but fraternities and sororities offer the great majority of on-campus activities, as well as opportunities for volunteer work in the community. The university has a strict no-alcohol-on-campus policy that is enforced, but it doesn't tend to impact students with fake IDs. When it's time for a road trip, UK students head to Cincinnati and Louisville (one hour away), or to Atlanta and Chicago (six hours)—that is, if they're not taking leisurely Sunday drives through nearby Blue Grass country. And the best road-trip destinations are anywhere there's a steamy, noisy gym and a basketball team ready to play UK's always-strong Wildcats. Home games at Lexington's Rupp Arena—what one student calls "a magical experience"—are consistently packed.

"In Kentucky, basketball is like a second religion," agrees another true-Blue Wildcat fan. Although screaming yourself hoarse for five guys hitting the hardwood may not be as genteel as cheering while sipping a mint julep at the track, for many students, the mix of collegiate craziness and old-world Southern hospitality found in Lexington is just about perfect.

<aside>
Overlaps

University of Louisville, Miami University (OH), Indiana, Ohio State, University of Tennessee.
</aside>

If You Apply To ➤ **Kentucky**…Rolling admissions: February 15. Financial aid: Feb. 15. Does not guarantee to meet demonstrated need. Campus and alumni interviews: optional, informational. SATs or ACTs: required. SAT IIs: optional. No essay question.

Kenyon College

Ransom Hall, Gambier, OH 43022-9623

Let's clear up one thing right off: while Kenyon College is located in the tiny hamlet of Gambier, Ohio, and while this hamlet is undoubtedly rural, it should not be confused with the African country of Kenya, which is a lot bigger. True, the school is small, with just over 1,500 students, and it retains a pure liberal arts and sciences emphasis that's less and less common. But don't describe that approach as anachronistic. "I chose Kenyon over Harvard because Kenyon has what I feel Harvard does not—an academic environment conducive to self-development," says a senior. "You get to know people pretty quickly. And getting to care about them is something that follows, usually not long after."

Set on a wooded hillside (the "Magic Mountain") overlooking a river, woods, and fields, Kenyon's 800-acre campus is scenic and soothing. The college's oldest building, Old Kenyon, dates from 1826 and is considered the first collegiate Gothic building in America. The Brown Family Environmental Center includes a butterfly garden and extensive perennial gardens planted with community donations. Construction is nearly completed on new facilities for the math, physics,

<aside>
Website: www.kenyon.edu
Location: Rural
Total Enrollment: 1,574
Undergraduates: 1,574
Male/Female: 44/56
SAT Ranges: V 610–710 M 580–690
ACT Range: 27–31
Financial Aid: 42%
Expense: Pr $ $ $ $
Phi Beta Kappa: Yes
Applicants: 2,420
Accepted: 68%
Enrolled: 20%
</aside>

(Continued)
Grad in 6 Years: 83%
Returning Freshmen: 93%
Academics: ✍ ✍ ✍ ✍
Social: ☎ ☎ ☎
Q of L: ★ ★ ★
Admissions: (800) 848-2468
Email Address:
admissions@kenyon.edu

Strongest Programs:
English
Art and Design
Dance
Drama
History
Political Science
Modern Languages and
Literatures
Biology

neuroscience, and chemistry departments, a new greenhouse, and additions for the molecular and biochemistry departments.

Kenyon's focus on the liberal arts makes for a challenging, but largely non-competitive, learning environment. "The academic climate at Kenyon is challenging, but in ways probably different from other colleges," says one political science major. "The course material requires students to be attentive to their work as well as thoughtful when doing it. But, the real difference at Kenyon is the close relationship you have with the faculty." In fact, at Kenyon, it's hard to find a weak department. "Courses can be rigorous, easy, fun or a mixture of all three," says an English and premed student.

English, a nationally renowned subject at Kenyon since the 1930s, is the most popular major, and it, along with the drama department, set the tone of campus life. This is, after all, home to *The Kenyon Review*, a prestigious literary quarterly, and a school about which alum E. L. Doctorow has said, "Poetry is what we did at Kenyon, the way at Ohio State they played football." Political science is said to be solid, drawing undecided majors with its introductory class, "Quest for Justice," because it "introduces the material in such a way that you're left hungry for a greater understanding of it!" says one devotee. The Integrated Program in Humane Studies, which incorporates English, history, political science and art history, is also popular. One junior describes the biology department as "all-consuming," but many students choose that major precisely for its academic rigor.

The hallmark of Kenyon's academic philosophy is an almost fanatical devotion to the liberal arts and sciences. "Academic life at Kenyon is rooted in three strong tenets," an administrator explains. "That students thrive when they can work closely with their professors; that they can best explore their own potential when they have enough flexibility to experiment; and that they learn most productively in an atmosphere of cooperation." Vocational programs are taboo; other than a 3–2 engineering program with several universities, there aren't any. But with high acceptance rates to graduate programs in law, business, and medicine, Kenyon's emphasis on arts and sciences is clearly yielding positive results. In fact, three out of four recent Kenyon grads took jobs when they finished, rather than continuing on to graduate or professional schools. "The Career Development Center is very good with helping with grad schools and employment opportunities, both summer and after graduation. Probably their strongest asset though is the active support of Kenyon alumni," says one junior.

While there is no core curriculum at Kenyon, all students must complete at least one unit of credit in the college's four divisions: humanities, fine arts, social sciences, and natural sciences. In 2000, the faculty voted to require quantitative reasoning and foreign language study of new students as well. A bevy of academic counselors, including upperclassmen and professors, help ensure that freshmen stay on the right track. About 20 percent of juniors are invited by their departments to read for honors, and about 15 percent graduate with departmental honors. The culmination of each student's coursework at Kenyon is the senior exercise, which may take the form of a comprehensive examination, an integrative paper, a research project, or some combination of these.

Classes are small at Kenyon—the great majority have 25 or fewer students—and even the larger introductory courses use a two-part format in which students meet for lectures one week and split up for discussion sections with the professor the next. "It is not uncommon to be invited to professors' homes and to have classes conducted there at times," asserts one student. A classmate adds that, "Professors are usually open and willing to meet and talk with you about both your academic work and your personal life. It is a comfort to know that they are

Vocational programs are taboo; other than a 3–2 engineering program with several universities, there aren't any.

eager to be involved in our academic and personal lives."

Twenty percent of Kenyon students are Ohioans, and together, African Americans, Hispanics, and Asian Americans make up just 10 percent of the student body. "We are constantly trying to get more minorities to come to Kenyon, to make it more diverse, although—even as a minority myself—I feel that Kenyon is diverse as it is," says a senior. The anti-sweatshop and Free Tibet movements that have been sweeping the nation's campuses have found their homes at Kenyon as well; on-campus political issues include the formulation of a new sexual harassment policy and underage drinking. "Racial diversity has been a big issue for many years because Kenyon students are mostly Caucasian," says a student. Gay and lesbian issues have also been on the front burner recently, and Kenyon students and staff alike have been moving towards greater acceptance of people's differences, says one senior.

All Kenyon students live on campus, with housing guaranteed for four years. Freshmen in five dorms at the north end of campus, and most move south to recently remodeled housing the next year. Although renovations and expansions are always in the works, they are currently having some trouble keeping up with demand. "Because of the large influx of students, there is now a bit of a housing crunch," explains one senior. "The College has had to ask some students (between 15 and 30 every year) to live off campus in nearby apartments. The housing crunch makes students grumble a bit, and these grumblings get louder every year." Rooms are selected via a harrowing housing lottery, and typically upperclassmen "opt for one of the historic dorms—Old Kenyon, Hannah or Leonard, or one of the campus-owned apartments—the Aclands, Bexleys or New Apartments." Most dorms are coed. Rather than their own houses, fraternities occupy sections of the south-campus dorms, making that area the center of the party scene. Students live on campus all four years, because as one puts it, "to live off-campus would be to live in another town." Everyone, including those in the apartments with kitchens, must eat college chow; dining halls operate on each end of the campus, though only one is open on weekends.

The school's Greek system draws 23 percent of the men but only 2 percent of the women, and the frats throw lively parties that are open to all. Like most campuses, Kenyon is slowly moving away from the animal-house paradigm of social life. "The social scene is evolving," says one senior. "It used to be that students had the option of going to a frat party or going to Columbus. Now, thanks to a strong student sentiment that there must be an on-campus alternative to drinking, there are fun activities, bonfires, coffeehouses, concerts, and movies that run every Friday and Saturday night between 10:00 P.M. and 2:00 A.M." While Kenyon's rural location makes for a safe environment ("Security here is mostly the target of jokes during student comedy sketches," confides one student), it does not offer much in the way of off-campus entertainment. Gambier is a small town, with a couple of bars and no movie theaters, but there are a few more options 15 minutes away in Mount Vernon, to which the college runs a daytime shuttle bus. On-campus events and college-sponsored activities are growing more popular to help keep boredom at bay. With its deli, market, inn, restaurant, bank, and post office, Gambier is at least quaint. Students enjoy buying real maple syrup, fresh bread, and cheese from Amish farmers with stands on its main street on Saturdays.

Kenyon remains defined by its traditions, the most hallowed of which is renewed each year as incoming freshmen sing college songs to the rest of the community from the steps of Rosse Hall. Departing seniors sing the same songs at graduation. On Matriculation Day each October, after a formal ceremony,

Kenyon remains defined by its traditions, the most hallowed of which is renewed each year as incoming freshmen sing college songs to the rest of the community from the steps of Rosse Hall. Departing seniors sing the same songs at graduation.

freshmen sign the very book that contains the signatures of virtually every Kenyon student since the early 1800s. Other major events include Spring Riot, Homecoming, the Summer Send-Off, and the annual Gambier Folk Festival. To break February's icy cold, the school holds a formal ball called Philander's Phling, remembering founder Philander Chase; an alum donates money for the dance. There are two small ski areas near campus, but for those feeling really trapped, Columbus and Ohio State University are a 45-minute drive south. The adventurous sometimes road-trip to Cleveland (home of the Rock and Roll Hall of Fame), Cincinnati, Chicago or Ann Arbor.

In addition to its emphasis on academics, Kenyon was instrumental in establishing the North Coast Athletic Conference, which includes a number of academically strong Midwestern schools, including longtime rival Denison. A junior cites the annual hockey game versus Denison, when "both teams have to drive to Newark and a surprising number of fans from both colleges attend." The women's tennis and basketball teams are reigning conference champs, while Kenyon's swimming and diving teams dominate Division III competition. Soccer games against Ohio Wesleyan draw large crowds. Clubs sponsor everything from Frisbee to water polo.

Kenyon introduces the upper crust of the Eastern seaboard to rural Ohio, and often makes it hard for them to tear themselves away. "It doesn't sound all that attractive, but once you visit, you feel differently!" exults one. For the many young artists, writers, and budding intellectuals here, it's hard to face the end of their four years. "The feeling of a close community in conjunction with the beautiful environment is what makes Kenyon a special place," says one junior, "as well as the fact that education is highly valued and encouraged."

Overlaps

Oberlin, Denison, Carleton, Middlebury, Washington University (MO).

If You Apply To ➢ **Kenyon**...Early decision: Dec. 1, Feb. 1. Regular admissions, financial aid, housing: Feb. 15. Meets demonstrated need of 95%. Campus interviews: recommended, evaluative. Alumni interviews: optional, evaluative. SATs or ACTs: required. SAT IIs: optional. Essay question: special interests, experience, or achievement. Accepts the Common Application.

Knox College

2 East South Street, Galesburg, IL 61401

Website: www.knox.edu
Location: Small city
Total Enrollment: 1,220
Undergraduates: 1,220
Male/Female: 45/55
SAT Ranges: V 550–680 M 550–650
ACT Range: 24–29
Financial Aid: 80%
Expense: Pr $ $
Phi Beta Kappa: Yes

The Prairie Fire might not be the most conventional choice for a college mascot, but Knox College seems to have established a name for itself by breaking away from the conventions of the day. Founded in 1837 as the Knox Manual Labor College in Galesburg, Illinois, this liberal arts college was the first in the state to graduate an African American student and among the first in the nation to admit women. The warm and supportive academic community is tight-knit but also encourages a strong sense of individualism.

Located in the heart of the Midwest—almost midway between Chicago and St. Louis—the 82-acre campus has spacious, tree-lined lawns and a dynamic mixture of architecture that reflects the 140-year span of construction dates of existing buildings. Old Main, constructed in 1857, is a National Historic Landmark and the only building remaining from the 1858 Lincoln-Douglas debates.

Students say the academic relationships at Knox are infused with a spirit of cooperation and equality. Beyond the classroom, students, faculty, and administrators make decisions on boards together, each with identical voting power. First-year students confront the core issues of liberal education in Preceptorial, a one-term seminar examining questions of ethics and truth through multidisciplinary reading and critical writing. But while many schools have small, intense classes for first year students, Knox takes things a bit further by mandating an advanced preceptorial for seniors. This class connects their expertise in their major to a broad topic. Other graduation requirements incumbent on all students must demonstrate proficiency in math and a foreign language, and take two classes in each of the following: math and science, humanities and fine arts, and social science. Knox also boasts of the Ford Foundation Research Fellowship Program, which was created in the mid 1980s to encourage students to consider careers in college teaching and research. Ford Fellows work with selected faculty mentors to design and carry out a research project in an area of interest. Through this permanently endowed foundation, Knox is able to offer stipends for summer research to a full one-fifth of the junior class. Moves like these have helped Knox earned a national reputation for its independent undergraduate research.

Strong departments include creative writing, education, theater, and the natural sciences, with biology attracting lots of research grant money. The school's literary journal, *Catch*, has won national awards. Students can take part in the Chicago Semester in the Arts, and dramatists also benefit from several theaters, including one with a revolving stage. Students cite the modern languages and philosophy as weak. Study abroad options include programs in more than 30 countries, and the college is a member of the Associated Colleges of the Midwest consortium.* Environmental studies has been added to Knox's list of majors.

Knox operates on an honor system that allows students to take tests in any public area unproctored, but few students would even think of cheating. "Knox is very rigorous and challenging, but the students are supportive of their peers more than anything else," says one sophomore. Where faculty is concerned, students offer uniformly glowing reviews. "The quality of teaching has been outstanding," says one biochemistry major. Another student notes, "however close you wish to become to a professor is up to you—the office is always open." The vast majority of classes have fewer than 25 students. Knox's trimester system packs a great deal of studying into a short period, but students are only required to take three courses per term. Before each school year begins, all students, faculty, and staff gather in the middle of campus to shake hands in a ceremony known as Pumphandle.

Knox's student advising system is praised by students. "On one of your first days on campus as a first year, your Faculty Advisor takes his or her advisees out to dinner," says one sophomore. "They are always able to make time to discuss planning and are very helpful."

An early identification of premed freshmen guarantees 10 students admission to Rush Medical College in Chicago if they maintain a four-year B average. Knox also offers 3–2 or 3–4 programs in engineering, nursing, medical technology, law, and architecture.

The bulk of students (50 percent) are from Illinois, and 11 percent of students come from foreign countries. American minorities make up 11 percent of the student body (3 percent African American, 5 percent Asian American, and 3 percent Hispanic), and maintain an active profile on campus. While Knox does not seem to be a terribly politically active school, there appears to be a commitment to diversity across campus. One of the most popular forms of activism is "chalking,"

(Continued)
Applicants: 1,357
Accepted: 75%
Enrolled: 30%
Grad in 6 Years: 74%
Returning Freshmen: 88%
Academics: ✍ ✍ ✍
Social: ☎ ☎ ☎
Q of L: ★ ★ ★
Admissions: (309) 341-7123
Email Address:
  admission@knox.edu

Strongest Programs:
  Biology
  Education Studies
  Theater
  Creative Writing
  Premed

First-year students confront the core issues of liberal education in Preceptorial, a one-term seminar examining questions of ethics and truth through multidisciplinary reading and critical writing.

where students write messages in chalk on campus walkways. Most students went to public high school, and 73 percent graduated in the top quarter of their class. More than 140 merit scholarships are available from $5,000 to more than full tuition. There are no athletic scholarships.

Housing is not a problem on the Knox campus; recent renovations have improved housing for most students, though some students complain that most rooms are not air conditioned. "Our suite system is particularly nice because people have common living space," says one junior. Coed living arrangements are available, although freshmen must live in single-sex suites with one or two upperclassmen as residential advisors. Students suggest that freshman women would be happiest in Post Hall, while men should try to live anywhere in Old Quad. Older students may band together with friends or form a special-interest or theme suite. The five fraternities are residential; the two sororities are not. It takes a minor miracle for students to obtain permission to move off campus, which has become a common complaint among juniors and seniors. Food service, as at many colleges, gets a thumbs down, with some students lamenting that it is difficult to get off the board plan. Security is "very visible on campus, driving around in their 'chariots of justice' or golf carts," says a student.

Galesburg is a small Midwestern railroad town, and some students say they had trouble adjusting to the sounds of locomotives. At one time this city of about 35,000 was a center of abolitionism, and the honorary degree that the college bestowed on then-presidential candidate Abraham Lincoln was his first formal title. Nearby Lake Storey offers boating, water slides, and nature trails, and students looking for more excitement can travel to Peoria, about 40 miles away. Slightly further away, Chicago is about 140 miles to the northeast. Weekends are filled with dance and fraternity parties, but you don't have to be Greek to join the fun. The alcohol policy is liberal, and as one sophomore notes, "Personal responsibility is valued above all." One of the best all-time traditions is Flunk Day. At 5:30 on a spring morning, Old Main's bell rings and classes are canceled to make way for dunk tanks and Jell-O pits. One sophomore proudly notes that "the newest tradition on campus is to steal a cafeteria tray during the first snow of the year and go sledding down the Knox Bowl."

Athletics generate a reasonable degree of enthusiasm. Both the men's and women's golf teams won conference championships in 1998, and the men repeated in 1999. Every fall the football team risks life and limb against archrival Monmouth to bring home the highly prized Bronze Turkey Award, a throwback to the time when the game was played on Thanksgiving Day.

Though Knox school is not well known, students here have the privilege of living their college years with honor and self-respect. Academics take priority, but it is the connections that students forge with faculty and other students that makes Knox so unique.

Overlaps

University of Illinois, Grinnell, Beloit, Northwestern, Washington University (MO).

If You Apply To ➤

Knox...Early action: Nov. 15. Regular admissions: Feb. 1. Financial aid: Mar. 1. Guarantees to meet demonstrated need. Campus interview: recommended, informational. No alumni interviews. SATs or ACTs: required. SAT IIs: optional. Accepts the Common Application and electronic applications. Essay question: significant experience; issue of concern; discuss work of art, literature, music; or high school paper you wrote.

Lafayette College

118 Markle Hall, Easton, PA 18042

Lafayette College, long considered a haven for preppy partyers, is taking major steps towards academic excellence with curricular changes, increases to financial aid, and a multi-million dollar building boom. One of the few liberal arts colleges of its size to offer engineering, Lafayette has also won considerable respect for its technical and science programs. Indeed, this small college offers competitive academics and a traditional college environment.

Lafayette is located upon a stately hill in Easton, Pennsylvania, just one and a half hours west of New York City. Its campus represents an eclectic blend of architecture and a landscape that supports more than 125 species of trees. The main library holds 490,000 volumes, offers a 24-hour study room, and students can access its card catalog online at any time from the comfort of their own rooms. In recent years, the school has completed an $8.5-million renovation of the Kirby Hall of Civil Rights, an $8 million Residence Hall, a $26 million Kirby Sports Center, a $13 million science building. On top of that, the bricks and mortar crazed Lafayette administration is still in the midst of a $100 million building campaign. "Hardhats nearly outnumber baseball caps as the preferred headgear on campus," quips one administrator.

The school's engineering, technical, and science programs have long been highly-esteemed at Lafayette, and economics/business is also a popular major. Others include psychology, English, government and law, and history. Weaker programs include foreign languages, sociology, and music. The standard student class load is four courses per semester instead of five, with a 32-course graduation requirement. All first-year students participate in an interdisciplinary seminar, which is often grouped by theme, designed to introduce them to intellectual inquiry by engaging them as thinkers, speakers, and writers in a tightly focused course. The students also share special co-curricular activities during the seminars. All students must take an intensive writing course, as well as Values in Science/Technology and four units in both math/natural sciences and humanities/social sciences. Students working for a BA must meet a foreign culture requirement through foreign language studies or study abroad, or complete a group of courses providing intensive exposure to a specific foreign culture. Engineering students, too, are offered the opportunity to explore a foreign culture.

An unusual arrangement with the Free University of Brussels makes it possible for engineering majors to study there while maintaining normal progress toward their degree. Another course, dubbed Technology Clinic, allows an interdisciplinary group of students to tackle a real-world problem. One recent clinic developed and implemented a comprehensive marketing plan for a nearby community that was struggling economically to survive. In addition, joint research with faculty is highly encouraged, and the undergraduates here are able to perform the kind of research that only graduate students are allowed to do at big universities. Cross-registration is available with other participating colleges through the Lehigh Valley Association of Independent Colleges.*

Classes at Lafayette are small (nearly all with fewer than 25 students) and are fairly easy to get into. Students enjoy frequent interaction with professors, especially those who are accepted into the McKelvy Scholars program, which allows selected honors students to live in a special living-learning atmosphere. Students

Website: www.lafayette.edu

Location: City outskirts

Total Enrollment: 2,283

Undergraduates: 2,283

Male/Female: 50/50

SAT Ranges: V 560–650 M 600–690

ACT Range: 24–29

Financial Aid: 60%

Expense: Pr $ $ $

Phi Beta Kappa: Yes

Applicants: 4,429

Accepted: 48%

Enrolled: 24%

Grad in 6 Years: 83%

Returning Freshmen: 96%

Academics: ✏ ✏ ✏ ✏

Social: ☎ ☎ ☎ ☎ ☎

Q of L: ★ ★ ★

Admissions: (610) 330-5100

Email Address: admissions@lafayette.edu

Strongest Programs:
   Engineering
   Economics/Business
   Chemistry
   Art
   Biology
   Psychology
   English

An unusual arrangement with the Free University of Brussels makes it possible for engineering majors to study there while maintaining normal progress toward their degree.

claim that the small size is Lafayette's best asset. "The faculty is well-qualified and they are more than willing to spend time one-on-one with their students," says government/art double major. Another student adds, "The professors are the most valuable component at Lafayette and their number one commitment is to the students."

Lafayette is taking steps to diversify its student body. Many students come from conventional suburban backgrounds, and 66 percent attended public high school. "Lafayette has a good mix of students but they tend to come from upper middle and upper class families," says one electrical engineering major. African Americans and Hispanics constitute only 7 percent of the student body. Several student organizations such as CLASS (Campus League Against Sexual Stereotyping) have been formed in recent years, and other campus-wide seminars and meetings have been devoted to topics such as homosexuality awareness, race relations, and sexual harassment. Lafayette does not offer athletic scholarships, but is boosting its academic scholarships. The Marquis Scholarship program offers 60 incoming students merit-based awards of at least $12,500. The school has also launched the Trustee Scholars program, for 32 students who will receive at least $7,500 per year.

Virtually the entire student body lives on campus, and housing is guaranteed for all four years. Possibilities include Greek houses, as well as independent dormitories and college-owned apartments that offer a variety of living and eating arrangements.

A 60-person residence hall devotes each floor to a special interest such as science and technology. Most students can get into the dorm of their choice, but there is a competitive lottery system. Ruef and South College are considered social, while Watson Hall and Kirby House are quieter and more exclusive. Dorms are "clean and well maintained. "The dorms are very comfortable with spacious rooms," one student says. Most upperclassmen, including women and non-Greek males, join meal plans at fraternities or the social dorms. Thirty-one percent of the men and 45 percent of the women are Greek, and that number has been shrinking in recent years. Students feel safe on campus, thanks to a comprehensive security program and good location. Safety measures include escorts, regular security patrols, and passes that are required for entry into the dorms.

Greek houses are the prime site for social life, but there are other options. "If you're not into the party scene, you have to be a bit inventive, but the Lafayette Activities Forum does a lot to provide an alternative to the Greek scene," says one senior. Students over the age of 21 may be served on campus, providing they have identification. The college is undergoing a major change in alcohol policy, students say. One proposal would ban alcohol at all social gatherings. "It has become more difficult in the last year for underage students to get served," admits one student, "although it is still pretty easy." The student center sponsors activities on campus including movies, comedians, speakers, and other forms of entertainment. The arts program offers performers ranging from Wynton Marsalis and the American Indian Dance Company to the Orpheus Chamber Orchestra and the Juilliard Quartet at the new Williams Center for the Arts. And for students who are committed to community service, volunteer work is encouraged. Volunteers work with preschoolers, Habitat for Humanity, Adopt-a-Grandparent, soup kitchens, or they tutor prisoners in the county jail on equivalency exams, all under the auspices of Lafayette's Community Outreach Center.

Easton, resting where the Lehigh and Delaware rivers meet, is a industrial city in the midst of some urban renewal. But it has a proud history—it is one of three cities where the Declaration of Independence was publicly read. The city is

Another course, dubbed Technology Clinic, allows an interdisciplinary group of students to tackle a real-world problem.

geographically divided into three sectors: College Hill, Downtown, and the South Side. Students who are willing to venture off the hill and visit the city's downtown will find headline acts at the State Theatre, art exhibitions, a variety of small museums and archives, and a plethora of boutiques and coffeehouses. The Crayola Factory and the largest Crayola store in the world "draw" big crowds. Atlantic City, New York City, and Philadelphia are close enough to make spicy weekend or day trips.

The Lafayette Leopards football and soccer teams play in the Patriot League. The annual football game with nearby Lehigh is intense and students claim it's the oldest rivalry in the U.S. When the two teams play, extra bleachers must be installed to accommodate the crowd. Men's basketball and soccer have won championships in recent years. In other sports, women's field hockey and cross-country are strong, as is men's lacrosse. All Leopard varsity teams compete in Division I except for football, which is I-AA. Due to budget cuts, the athletic department is considering eliminating some sports. For those not up to varsity level, there is an extensive intramural program. "Intramurals are a huge part of campus life and most students are involved in them in one way or another," says one student. The most important nonathletic campus event of the year is All-College Day, a springtime festival with beach balls, bathing suits, bands, and the like.

Lafayette is a small school where students work hard and play hard, and in recent years, there has been an increased emphasis on the former. With a growing focus on academics, Lafayette is making its mark.

If You Apply To ➤

Lafayette...Early decision: Feb. 15. Regular admissions and financial aid: Apr. 1. Housing: June 1. Does not guarantee to meet demonstrated need. Campus interviews: recommended, evaluative. Alumni interviews: optional, informational. SATs: optional. SAT IIs: recommended. Accepts the Common Application and electronic applications. Essay question: describe decision you made and would like to make again; ask and answer one question you wished Lafayette had asked; or relate an anecdote about yourself that reveals your character and personal values.

Lake Forest College

555 Sheridan Road, Lake Forest, IL 60045

With Lake Forest College situated on a beautiful stretch of land in a posh suburb of Chicago, it's no wonder that students call their school the Enchanted Forest—even if the Forest may seem barren in the middle of those Windy City winters. The school's true bounty is most apparent in its academics, with small classes, dedicated professors, and a familiar atmosphere among the close-knit student body. Professors "are your friends and look out for your best interests," says a physics and biology major. "I don't know of another place where you can hang out at a bar with your professor before a mid-term exam."

With its mixture of century-old Gothic and modern glass structures, Lake Forest's 107-acre campus is storybook beautiful. Located on Chicago's North Shore, about an hour from the heart of downtown, the campus has three parts—North, Middle, and South. Each has a mix of residence halls and academic facilities. The college recently opened the Cleveland-Young International Student

Website: www.lfc.edu
Location: Suburban
Total Enrollment: 1,254
Undergraduates: 1,241
Male/Female: 43/57
SAT Ranges: V 510–620 M 510–630
ACT Range: 22–28
Financial Aid: 74%
Expense: Pr $ $ $
Phi Beta Kappa: Yes

(Continued)

Applicants: 1,296
Accepted: 77%
Enrolled: 34%
Grad in 6 Years: 66%
Returning Freshmen: 78%
Academics: ✐ ✐ ✐
Social: ☎ ☎ ☎ ☎
Q of L: ★ ★ ★
Admissions: (847) 735-5000
Email Address:
  admissions@lfc.edu

Strongest Programs:
  Business
  Economics
  Biology
  Art and Design
  English
  Political Science
  Education

*The Richter Apprentice
Scholars program
encourages freshmen to
join faculty members in
conducting scholarly
research—and then to
consider careers in research
and teaching.*

Center, to provide seminar and library space in addition to living quarters for all incoming foreign students. In addition, a new varsity locker room has opened in Halas Hall, formerly the home of the Chicago Bears, which the College shares with the Chicago Fire professional soccer team. The wealth and seclusion of Lake Forest make the College a real dreamland—but also feed the insularity that many students come with or begin to feel once on campus. Nature lovers can explore the wooded ravines on the many undeveloped acres leading to Lake Michigan. Still, without Chicago nearby, "Lake Forest College would be quite dull," says an economics major.

Students are expected to fulfill a variety of course requirements at this small liberal arts school. A general education curriculum requires two credits of natural and mathematical sciences, two credits of humanities, two credits of social sciences, and two classes in cultural diversity. In addition, freshmen must take a Freshman Studies course and seniors must complete a senior seminar or senior thesis. "If you don't wish to go to class and just want to drink, you can," says a senior. "If you wish to excel and be challenged academically, you also can." The Independent Scholar program, which allows undergrads to create their own majors across traditional disciplines, is valued by students who seek more academic autonomy. There's also the Richter Apprentice Scholars program, which encourages freshmen to join faculty members in conducting scholarly research— and then to consider careers in research and teaching.

Students say LFC's best departments are politics, education, English, and economics. The $4-million Student/Faculty Science Research Center provides plenty of lab and office space for students and faculty alike. The theater and music departments are said to weaker, owing to limited faculty and facilities. The "Information Revolution" has inspired LFC to create a new program in Communications, and students can benefit from the new Latin American Studies major as well, although comparative literature has been dropped. Students who don't like what's offered at Lake Forest can create their own classes, provided they find professors to teach them.

Lake Forest believes deeply in the value of study abroad and many students participate in programs such as the Greece and Turkey Program, where archeological sites and museums provide cultural classrooms, or the marine biology program, which includes work at a tropical field station. Unlike part-time internships at other schools, Lake Forest interns work full-time in business, education, social and political activities, and at nonprofit agencies. The International Internship program has placed students in organizations including the Paris Cultural Affairs Department, UNESCO, UNICEF, and Eurospace. Lake Forest students also can be found in secondary schools and multinational corporations in both Paris and Santiago, Chile. The school is a member of the Associated Colleges of the Midwest too, which offers programs in Russia, Zimbabwe, Japan, India, and central Europe, among other locales.

While Foresters like the small class sizes, flexible academic guidelines, and large doses of individual attention, nothing seems to compare to the quality of the faculty. Professors "are well-versed in the subjects they teach and come from outstanding educational backgrounds," raves an international relations and Spanish major. Adds a physics and biology major: "The quality of teaching is unparalleled...What are TAs?" Students praise the Career Development Center for its symposia, workshops, and résumé clinics, though an economics major says Lake Forest "does a poor job of recruiting major companies to the college for job placement."

When it comes to recruiting, Lake Forest prides itself on its interstate appeal.

Forty-five percent of students come from outside the Land of Lincoln, with about one-quarter of these from either New England or the Mid-Atlantic states. Another 43 percent of Foresters come from Illinois, and international students account for the remaining 12 percent. Blacks comprise 6 percent of the student body, Hispanics 3 percent, and Asian Americans 5 percent, though this doesn't seem to bother anyone much. "For the most part, the majority of the student body doesn't care what's going on other than weekend plans," one student says.

Few students have the megabucks to live off campus in affluent Lake Forest, so 84 percent live in the dorms, where housing is coed by floor or quad unit except for one single-sex dorm. "North campus is nice, but no parties," says an in-the-know senior. "Middle is great if you like to study on a Saturday night, and South campus is in rough shape but a lot of fun." Each residence hall has a computer room and a television lounge; some rooms even have fireplaces. Freshmen are assigned rooms by the dean of students, while upperclassmen fend for themselves through a lottery based on seniority. Deerpath, an all-freshmen dorm, is by all accounts the top spot, and a recently completed $7 million renovation added air-conditioning, an aerobics and fitness center, and a state-of-the-art computer network. An honors dorm is home to the brainy crowd. Everybody eats in a pleasant central dining hall, the social beehive of the campus, where unlimited helpings are served except on Thursday, which is steak and shrimp night.

The party scene on LFC's campus has picked up with the arrival of fraternities and sororities, which attract 18 percent of men and 14 percent of women, though parties are open to all. Students report that the campus alcohol policy is "don't ask, don't tell." "As long as you are in a room with the door closed, you can drink, no matter what age," says a junior. "At parties, IDs are checked, but once inside it is easy for anyone to get a beer." For students not interested in the frat scene, LFC offers movies, speakers, and coffeehouses with musical and comedy acts. Major events on the campus social calendar include the Festival of Ra, the Egyptian god of the sun, held every spring with a week of games, parties, talent shows, pie-throwing contests, and Jell-O wrestling. Other festivities celebrate ethnic and cultural diversity, such as Semana Latina (Hispanic culture) and CelebrAsian. Since the movie *Class* was filmed at Lake Forest, each entering freshman class gets an encore presentation. The Big Chill in February is something akin to a winter carnival, and for diehard traditionalists, there's always Homecoming weekend in the fall. Borderline made *Playboy* magazine's list of the Top 10 college parties in the nation.

Though Chicago is only an hour away by train, it helps to have a car for maximum freedom to get downtown and to other suburbs. "Lake Forest is possibly the richest town in America," says a junior. "The houses around the college are all fantastically huge and beautiful, and not a day goes by without seeing a Range Rover." The town is full of quaint restaurants and cafés—though many close by 6 p.m., to students' chagrin—and several high-priced boutiques. Neighboring communities like Highwood have bars—most notably Rainbows and the Wooden Nickel—frequented by students. The recent construction of a coffeehouse now provides Foresters with a setting for informal, nonalcoholic mixing. Aside from pure socializing, a few students take part in volunteer programs with low-income students in Chicago-area high schools. Another program sends students to the Appalachian Mountains in Virginia and Tennessee every spring break to help local townspeople repair substandard housing.

Lake Forest isn't exactly what you'd call a football factory, but the school does field a number of competitive athletic teams. Hockey is undoubtedly the biggest sport on campus, but men's handball is a perennial international collegiate

Since the movie **Class** *was filmed at Lake Forest, each entering freshman class gets an encore presentation.*

champion and men's tennis claimed its first Midwest Conference Championship in 20 years in 1999. Men's and women's swimming and diving are often tops in the Division III Midwest Athletic Conference as well. More than 65 percent of LFC students participate in athletics at some level, from club to varsity sports.

Lake Forest is a campus in flux. While there's still a substantial contingent of spoiled rich kids who are happy to drink their college years away, LFC is also working hard to attract sharp minds who are searching for a safe, cloistered environment and professors who know all of their students by name. "The college is looking to increase both the size and quality of the student body," a senior says. "I believe they will have to sacrifice one for the other." Only time will tell if he's right.

If You Apply To ➤   **Lake Forest**…Early action: Dec. 1. Early decision: Jan. 1. Regular admissions, housing and financial aid: Mar. 1. Campus interviews: recommended, evaluative. No alumni interviews. SATs or ACTs: required. SAT IIs: optional. Accepts the Common Application and electronic applications. Essay question: anything you haven't already shared on application and graded paper from junior or senior year of high school.

Lawrence University

706 East College Avenue, Appleton, WI 54912

Website: www.lawrence.edu
Location: Center city
Total Enrollment: 1,246
Undergraduates: 1,246
Male/Female: 46/54
SAT Ranges: V 590–690 M 580–690
ACT Range: 25–30
Financial Aid: 72%
Expense: Pr $ $ $
Phi Beta Kappa: Yes
Applicants: 1,348
Accepted: 81%
Enrolled: 30%
Grad in 6 Years: 72%
Returning Freshmen: 85%
Academics: ✑ ✑ ✑ ✑
Social: ☎ ☎ ☎
Q of L: ★ ★ ★
Admissions: (920) 832-6500
Email Address:
  excel@lawrence.edu

In quiet Appleton, Wisconsin, sits Lawrence University, an unpretentious school that appeals to both the left and right side of students' brains. For those with a more analytical bend, there is Lawrence's uncommon laser physics program, while more creative types can take advantage of the school's Conservatory of Music, one of only two to reside at a small liberal arts college (the other is at Oberlin).

Lawrence's campus is on a wooded bluff above the Fox River, perfect for long walks, jogging, or simply meditating underneath the trees. It was chosen in 1847 by one of Appleton, Wisconsin's, earliest settlers. The pristine 84-acre campus reflects several architectural styles of the past 150 years, including classical revival, 1920s Georgian-inspired, and 1950s and 1960s institutional, unified by their limestone color. The award-winning Wriston Art Center and the Conservatory's Ruth Harwood Shattuck Hall of Music (both designed by Lawrence graduates) bring contemporary architectural touches to the campus. Recently, a 41-stop mechanical-action organ was installed in the Lawrence Chapel. Its $18 million science facility opened in the fall of 2000, and houses the chemistry, biology, and physics programs.

The second coeducational college established in the nation, Lawrence was founded to educate German immigrants and Native Americans. While coeducation was shocking, innovators at Lawrence didn't stop there. More than 50 years ago, administrators introduced the Freshman Studies program, a required two-term course focusing primarily on the great works of art, music, and literature of primarily the Western tradition. These days, general education requirements at Lawrence include Freshman Studies, and focus on two other areas: Language and Civilization (humanities and fine or performing arts, with at least one English course and one intermediate or advanced foreign language course) and Logic and

Observation (the natural and social sciences, with at least one math course and one laboratory science course). New majors on the academic menu include environmental science and gender studies.

At the school's Conservatory of Music, first-year music students are offered courses including theory and analysis, keyboard skills, sight-reading, ear training, and applied study in music. The Conservatory's instrument collection includes an 1815 Broadwood piano identical to Beethoven's Broadwood, and a Guarneri violin. There is also a first-rate jazz group along with classical and world music programs; it offers a bachelor's degree in music within its liberal arts environment, plus a unique five-year bachelor's and master's program that receives regular national acclaim. "Music is the unifying theme at Lawrence," says one student. "Almost everybody plays it or studies it or likes to listen to it and talk about it." Overall, however, the most popular major is biology, followed by music performance and psychology. Students say that they tend to avoid the government department because "the professors are old and dry." Lawrence is known for its London Study Center, which allows students to take classes "across the pond" while taking advantage of the city's many cultural activities. Other off-campus programs involve the Kurgan Technical Pedagogical Institute in Russia, Waseda University in Japan, and the Ecoles des Beaux Arts in France. Programs in marine biology research are held in the Cayman Islands. In all, more than two dozen off-campus programs are available, including those through the Associated Colleges of the Midwest consortium.*

Back on campus, Lawrence students appreciate their professors' expertise and experience. They say faculty members are accessible and highly encouraging of intellectual curiosity while still showing compassion for students social, spiritual, psychological, and emotional needs. The academic climate is intimate and intense, because of the three-term calendar. Still, a biology major says, "The academic climate is self-competitive; students try to better their own academic performance, but are supportive of one another." And the school certainly attracts a range of students: "Students run the gamut from intellectual/creative geniuses to total idiots," says one frank senior. Students choose their own advisors from among the faculty ranks, and meet with these professors at least once a term.

Most of Lawrence's 1,200 students hail from Wisconsin or the Midwest. Most attended public high school, and 78 percent graduated in the top quarter of their class. Minority enrollment is only about 5 percent, with Asian Americans the largest group at 3 percent. International students account for 9 percent of the student body, representing more than 40 countries. The political climate on campus is somewhat liberal but "for the most part, students seem to stay in a 'Lawrence bubble' and are rather apathetic to outside events," says one student.

The dorms at Lawrence are fairly popular; all but 3 percent of students live on campus. That's because you have to get permission to move off, which is no mean feat. A full 30 percent of men and 22 percent of women go Greek at Lawrence, and that gives the men the opportunity to live in their houses. However, sorority sisters don't have that option since they don't have houses. Two dorms are reserved for upperclassmen, and six small university-owned houses handle overflow. However, students complain that on-campus mail delivery is not reliable. All halls are coed, by room or by floor, and all have laundry facilities, kitchens, televisions, Internet links, and lounges. Students report that the older halls are more elegant, but the newer ones are more practical, with extra storage space and other amenities. On-campus students have a choice of meal plans and eat in one of the two dining halls, where meals are reportedly monotonous. But following the nutritional guidance of college students everywhere, culinary salvation is found

(Continued)
Strongest Programs:
Music
Drama
Biology
Physics
Psychology
English

For those with a more analytical bent, there is Lawrence's uncommon laser physics program, while more creative types can take advantage of the school's Conservatory of Music, one of only two to reside at a small liberal arts college.

The Conservatory's instrument collection includes an 1815 Broadwood piano identical to Beethoven's Broadwood, and a Guarneri violin.

in microwave ovens and soft-serve ice cream machines.

Social life at Lawrence stays almost entirely on campus, although some say it's beginning to move off campus because of stricter alcohol policies. It's almost impossible for underage students to be served at the on-campus bar, but the story is different at private parties. A senior concedes that "alcohol is formally banned from parties, but students have no trouble drinking in their rooms." Fraternity parties, room parties, and the on-campus bar provide most of the entertainment, especially for underage students. Conservatory concerts, film series, coffeehouses, and art openings also keep students busy. Those over 21 frequent Pat's Tap and the Wooden Nickel in town. But on the whole, students are not generally very enthusiastic about the town. The school radio station also broadcasts a 50-hour trivia contest in January, in which each hall has its own team, and students stay up for the entire weekend answering offbeat questions. Once spring finally arrives, students look forward to a popular arts festival aptly called Celebrate! Octoberfest is also a big event, held in conjunction with the city of Appleton.

And what would a Midwest fall Saturday be without football? The Lawrence team draws good crowds almost every weekend. Women's basketball and softball have brought home recent Midwest Conference championships. Men's basketball is notable, too. The sparkling recreation center helps students fend off midwinter blues, sometimes in very strange ways: five years ago, 187 "Larries" set a Guinness world record by traveling 220 feet on a 120-foot toboggan in Appleton's Memorial Park. Participating in a rousing game of intramural broomball, which is ice hockey played on shoes with brooms as sticks and kickballs as pucks, is a must for students, even if all you do is watch.

Students rarely venture into Appleton for fun; although the campus can seem suffocatingly small, there's not much to do in the town. "Appleton is great if you like restaurants and novelty shops, but any normal college student would hate it," gripes one biology major. The nearest grocery store is a five-minute drive away, as is the nearest theater, and many students see a car as a necessity. A music student says that most students don't go off campus often to do things, though administrators insist that townspeople frequently visit for theater, concerts, art exhibits and lectures. Volunteerism is popular, however, and students regularly take part in activities such as tutoring at local schools. The best road trips are Milwaukee (two hours), Green Bay (half an hour), and Chicago (four hours). There are also weekend seminars at Bjorklunden, the college's 400-acre estate on the shores of Lake Michigan.

With its outstanding liberal arts curriculum, knowledgeable and caring faculty, and an administration that treats students like adults, all tucked into a charming country setting, Lawrence University is easily one of the best unknown schools in the country. And of course, if you have a musical ear, Lawrence's symphony of offerings sounds pleasant indeed.

Overlaps

University of Wisconsin, Macalester, Northwestern, Oberlin, Grinnell.

If You Apply To ➤

Lawrence...Early decision: Nov. 15. Regular admissions: Jan. 15. Financial aid: Mar. 15. Guarantees to meet demonstrated need. Campus interviews: recommended, informational. Alumni interviews: optional, informational. SATs or ACTs: required. SAT IIs: Optional. music applicants must audition. Accepts the Common Application and electronic applications. Essay question: movie, play, book or piece of music that has challenged your thinking; significant invention or scientific breakthrough; or what you would do with a year of funding.

Lehigh University

27 Memorial Drive West, Bethlehem, PA 18015

Although Lehigh University has a solid reputation for engineering, this multifaceted university offers something for every intellectual interest. Between the College of Arts and Sciences (the school with the highest enrollment), the College of Engineering and Applied Science, and the College of Business and Economics, Lehigh students can choose from a near limitless selection of courses, regardless of major. Lehigh students enjoy the balance of a large research university and the atmosphere of a small college. As one administrator observed, "Lehigh is large enough to be powerful, yet small enough to be personal."

When picturing a college campus, some think of ivy-covered Gothic style buildings, others may imagine sweeping modern brick-and-glass buildings. Lehigh has both. This combination of old and new is complemented by tall oaks, shaded walkways, and green lawns with Adirondack chairs grouped for casual conversation. In recent years, construction has been completed on two student apartment buildings, and there have been serious renovations to the school's athletic facilities. Lehigh's lovely campus contrasts somewhat with the worn state of the south side of Bethlehem, a once-great steel town that fallen on rough times, as has much of the Rust Belt. However, Lehigh has joined with the town in a $400 million redevelopment effort that will include a Smithsonian Institute Museum of Industry, a multiplex theater, and a large new hotel and conference center. And though the university's immediate neighborhood may leave something to be desired, Bethlehem's active downtown and beautiful historical district offer entertainment as well as aesthetic charm.

As always, a large part of Lehigh's good reputation rests on its consistently strong engineering program. In keeping up with the fast pace and increased importance of new technology as well, Lehigh recently announced that it will invest $75 million over the next five to seven years to enhance academic programs "critical to its future," including optoelectronics, bioscience, and biotechnology. For those interested in the bottom line, students say business administration, accounting, finance, economics, management, and marketing departments are strong as well. The College of Arts and Sciences boasts strong departments in a slew of fields, including psychology, political science, architecture, and biology. Students do have some criticisms of the fine arts and foreign languages programs, although they are popular choices to round out an otherwise science-heavy curriculum.

The workload at Lehigh is heavy, especially in engineering and business. As at many schools there is a pretty wide range in the rigor of the courses. Professors get high marks for quality of teaching and personal attention. About 75 percent of the classes at Lehigh have 25 or fewer students, but students say they never have problems getting into the courses they want. "For required classes, everyone who registers gets in," says one chemical engineering major. "In certain cases, student demand has caused the school to offer classes they were not going to originally." Faculty advisors get fair-to-good ratings, with career advising faring better. "The career services department is very helpful when it comes to on-campus interviews or just plain advice and tips," remarks one satisfied engineer.

Distribution and other requirements vary by academic area, with engineers the most limited in their choices. All freshmen must take two semesters of English, and the second semester is says to be an improvement over the first. A

Website: www.lehigh.edu
Location: City
Total Enrollment: 6,359
Undergraduates: 4,605
Male/Female: 60/40
SAT Ranges: V 558–654 M 598–687
Financial Aid: 51%
Expense: Pr $ $ $ $
Phi Beta Kappa: Yes
Applicants: 8,853
Accepted: 48%
Enrolled: 26%
Grad in 6 Years: 80%
Returning Freshmen: 93%
Academics: ✑ ✑ ✑ ✑
Social: ☎ ☎ ☎ ☎
Q of L: ★ ★
Admissions: (610) 758-3000
Email Address:
   admissions@lehigh.edu

Strongest Programs:
   Engineering
   Accounting
   Finance
   Business
   Social Sciences
   Sciences
   Architecture

variety of special degree options are offered: a combined BA/MD can be earned in six years, or a BA/DDS in seven years through programs with two Pennsylvania medical schools; a five-year arts/engineering programs is also available. A new scholarship program rewards students who graduate with a 3.5 GPA in four years with a fifth year of study tuition-free. A new honors program leads to a BS in Integrated Business and Engineering. Students are encouraged to spend their summers obtaining field-related work experience; extensive internship and career-shadowing opportunities can be obtained, and for engineers a co-op program is available that provides paid work experience while still enabling students to graduate in four years. Lehigh also offers students interested in studying abroad a choice of over 100 programs in 30 countries. The Lehigh Clipper Project allows high school students accepted for early admission to take Web-based freshman courses at no cost, thus getting a jump on those graduation requirements.

The two main libraries at Lehigh receive universally high marks from students, and the newer one is especially well equipped. Both include a computerized card catalog system that can be accessed by students who have personal computers in their rooms, or through centrally located computer labs. Virtually all rooms in the campus buildings, including residences, have a high speed Ethernet connection to the Internet. Also noteworthy are the International Multimedia Resource Center, which receives news broadcasts from more than 25 countries via satellite, and a recently completed wireless laptop lab in the College of Engineering and Applied Science.

Thirty percent of Lehigh's students come from Pennsylvania, and most of the rest hail from other areas of the Northeast. Some students lament the student body's conservatism and general lack of diversity. The school is gradually becoming more diverse, however, with 16 percent of recent classes made up of minority students. Strong career goals are common among the mostly upper-middle-class student body. One sophomore laments "I haven't found many people interested in politics. In fact, I know straight 'A' students who know nothing about current events." Another senior characterizes his classmates this way: "People are well-off, but they are still laid-back...They're not snobby. Overall, students are conservative and love to party."

Lehigh offers nearly 100 merit scholarships of up to $7,000 and 23 athletic scholarships per class for wrestling and men's and women's basketball. It does not guarantee to meet the full demonstrated financial need of every admit, but students report that aid packages are generally generous and consistent.

Most students praise Lehigh's friendly atmosphere, and reportedly one in every four Lehigh students volunteers in the community, often with children at the local Boys and Girls Club or through the America Reads program. Special-interest housing, including the Umoja House for interested African Americans and Hispanics, adds cultural enrichment to residential life. Residential colleges, in which faculty masters, resident assistants (known as "gryphons"), freshmen, and upperclassmen live together, are a newer (and more popular) option. Freshmen and sophomores are guaranteed housing, but only freshmen are required to live on campus. One student explains, "There are two types of freshman dorms: Lower Cents, small halls that are more close-knit at the end of a year, and the Freshman Quad buildings, which are large and introduce a lot of people in one year. "The dorms are nice, but since they all have different setups, the apartment-style ones are in highest demand," says another. The majority of upperclassmen live off campus, or in on-campus Greek houses. Parking is a major problem. The dining halls have been refurbished, and the food is considered above average.

Social life at Lehigh revolves around "the Hill," where the vast majority of fraternities and a new sorority are situated. The annual Greek Week/Springfest is one of Lehigh's major events and includes toga races, pie-eating contests, and reasonably continuous partying that concludes with a huge, free picnic and live concert. Like most universities these days, Lehigh is struggling to deal with an entrenched drinking culture. The university is one of ten schools receiving a grant from the Robert Wood Johnson Foundation to curb abusive drinking. New policies aim to make the campus a "healthier, safer living and learning environment" by changing the drinking culture. The changes so far boil down to stricter rules about parties and tailgating, as well as expanded alcohol-free programming. Students naturally grumble at the changes, but administrators point to a decrease in crime and emergency-room visits as proof of progress.

While the Greek scene is definitely popular, one junior adds, "Great improvements have been made with respect to the social aspect during my years at Lehigh—University Productions comes up with many interesting social alternatives, as does Global Union, with many cultural events. There's always something going on at Zoellner Arts Center!" Few students leave campus on the weekends, though Philadelphia, New York, the Poconos, and the Jersey shore are mentioned as popular road trips. For those who are health-minded, there is the Taylor Fitness Center, which features a weight room, two pools, and racquetball and squash courts. The on-campus 16,000-seat Goodman Stadium hosts athletic events, and performers and concerts are regularly scheduled at the 6,000-seat Stabler Arena.

Center-city Bethlehem is only five minutes from campus. In late August, just before classes begin, the town offers Musikfest, a celebration complete with oompah bands, "chicken dancing" (that's a polka), and free concerts featuring well-known artists. Shortly thereafter, CelticFest is under way. Back on campus, the intramural program is very strong and highly competitive. The varsity wrestling team has been a powerhouse for years, but the biggest deal is still the annual sell-out football game against Lafayette. "I hate football," says one Mountain Hawk (the school mascot), "but I go to this game; a lot of alumni come back and most of the students get involved." Volleyball and women's lacrosse have won league championships in recent years.

An ambitious bunch, Lehigh students enjoy the balance of a large research university and the atmosphere of a small college. Though parties may still reign on the weekend, these students are also focused on educational and career success. All of this, in a setting one sophomore describes as "the most beautiful and peaceful campus I've ever been to!"

Overlaps

Penn State, Penn, Cornell, Bucknell, Boston College.

If You Apply To ➤ Lehigh...Early decision: Nov. 15. Regular admissions: Jan. 1. Financial aid: Feb. 1. Meets demonstrated need of 49%. Campus interviews: recommended, informational. No alumni interviews. ACTs or SATs: required. Three SAT IIs: required. Apply to particular program. Accepts the Common Application and electronic applications. Essay question: Why is Lehigh a good match for you, greatest accomplishment in high school, what can you contribute to Lehigh.

0615 Southwest Palatine Hill Road, Portland, OR 97219-7899

Website: www.lclark.edu

Location: Suburban

Total Enrollment: 3,203

Undergraduates: 1,742

Male/Female: 41/59

SAT Ranges: V 580–680 M 570–660

ACT Range: 25–29

Financial Aid: 55%

Expense: Pr $ $ $

Phi Beta Kappa: Yes

Applicants: 3,013

Accepted: 69%

Enrolled: 25%

Grad in 6 Years: 59%

Returning Freshmen: 82%

Academics: ✍ ✍ ✍

Social: ☎ ☎ ☎

Q of L: ★ ★ ★

Admissions: (503) 768-7040

Email Address:
admissions@lclark.edu

Strongest Programs:
International Affairs
Sociology/Anthropology
Psychology
Biology
English
History

Lewis and Clark requires that all students achieve competency in a foreign language and international study, and most students fulfill these requirements by studying overseas for a semester or more.

Almost 200 years ago, the Oregon Coast was the destination for American pioneers Lewis and Clark. Today, the college that bears their names is a launching pad for students who want to explore the world. Billing itself as "one of the nation's most international liberal arts colleges," Lewis and Clark has sent more than 7,500 students out to explore the world since 1962. Back at home, the school's broad spectrum of academic programs and outstanding professors have earned the school a reputation as one of the best liberal arts colleges in the Pacific Northwest.

Lest students become too enchanted when overseas, Lewis and Clark lures them back with what must be one of the most gorgeous campuses in America. The college is perched atop fir-covered bluffs that overlook the Willamette River. The campus is an old estate, complete with elaborate gardens, fountains, and pools. Cement is almost nonexistent; instead, the roads are paved with cobblestones. Newer structures, intermittently added to the traditional Tudor buildings, were designed to reflect the Northwest Indian architecture. Lucky dorm residents have views of Mount St. Helens, Mount Hood, or the Portland skyline. The natural beauty is complemented by substantial facilities that recently got a $22-million face-lift, including a library addition, which doubled its size, and new buildings for the humanities and the fine arts. New residence halls are currently under construction.

Lewis and Clark requires that all students achieve competency in a foreign language and international study, and most students fulfill these requirements by studying overseas for a semester or more. Students have the opportunity to study abroad in an incredible number of countries, including Australia, China, Colombia, Ecuador, Japan, Kenya, Germany, France, and Scotland. Students can also study in a number of American cities. The cost of participation in the study abroad programs is roughly equivalent to that of on-campus study. Over 60 percent of Lewis and Clark students take advantage of the programs, and some study in two or three countries. In addition to the international requirement, freshmen must take a class called Inventing America, where they analyze the formation of the United States. Students are also required to complete courses in the creative arts, international studies, mathematics and natural sciences, quantitative reasoning, and physical education.

Not surprisingly, one of the most popular departments at Lewis and Clark is international affairs, though the sociology/anthropology major is also strong. As one International Affairs major explains it, "International affairs is a major mover and shaker on campus, although it is always countered by its bitter rivals, the sociology/anthropology departments. There is always feuding between these majors and it polarizes the campus." While the titans clash, however, the gender studies minor and majors in political science, history, English, psychology, and biology are earning respect both on and off campus. Less impressive, according to students, are drama, philosophy, and economics. The environmental studies major, added in 1998, is becoming increasingly popular. Honors programs are available in all majors, and 3–2 programs in engineering are also offered.

Lewis and Clark offers a Portfolio Path to admissions, which allows students to present a package representing their talents and interests and thereby forgo the SAT/ACT requirement. In addition to meeting regular admissions requirements,

PP students must supply three teacher recommendations and graded samples of their high school work, such as essays, lab reports, or samples of art or music. Some students who use this approach feel standardized tests don't do them justice, while others have "incredible test scores." The key to a good portfolio is a "well-rounded approach. The more creative, the better, but be sure it's not solely artwork or writing samples."

Students say they rarely openly compete with each other, but the internal pressure can be brutal. "Students are laid-back in that they don't compete with each other," explains one international affairs major. "Rather, they are likely to put pressure on themselves to do their best for the professors they like so much." Freshmen and graduating seniors are given priority in the registration process, but most agree that classes are accessible. Students say that those who want to can usually graduate in four years, and those classes listed as "full" often open up to motivated students who show some enterprise. Grad students don't teach classes, and professors get high marks from students. "The teaching is exceptional," says one freshman. "It's like taking the one best teacher I had in high school, making 20 of him, increasing his ability, and voila! You have L&C profs." Every year, students and faculty members organize three major symposia—one on international affairs, one on environmental affairs, and the other on gender studies.

The students that Lewis and Clark attracts from the West Coast tend to be the types seeking a small liberal arts college education. It's also a haven for easterners who do not readily fit into the typical prep school or fancy suburban high school scene and like L&C's open and outdoorsy feel. Lewis and Clark students tend to be independent, outgoing, and interesting. The campus is racially homogeneous (83 percent white), but diverse for Oregon. Students say that the school is "more liberal than conservative" and that students are very aware of political insensitivity. "This is a very socially active campus," says one senior. "Environmental issues, human rights, and our own campus policies bring out protestors and outraged students."

A residency requirement keeps students on campus for their first two years, and 58 percent of the student body live on campus. There are six different coed residence halls and one that's all women, as well as theme floors exclusively for students in performing arts, foreign languages, and other programs. The rooms are adequate and maintenance is fast, students say. "It's a real community," says one communications major. Safety is a priority on campus. Residence halls are equipped with card swipe entry systems and door alarms, and campus security, which has officers on duty 24 hours a day, provides escorts for students after dark. In addition to the Fields Dining Room (a.k.a. the Airplane Hangar because of its high ceilings and width) students can eat at two student-run restaurants that serve as gathering spots for study breaks, movie nights, and musical performances.

Fun-seeking Lewis and Clark students rely primarily on SOFA (Students Organized for Activities) for on-campus movies, contests, study breaks, and talent shows. For the more adventurous student, College Outdoors sponsors weekend trips to locations like Mount Hood (for skiing) or the coastal beaches. Seattle and Vancouver, B.C., are favorite road-trip destinations. Despite the famous rains of the Pacific Northwest, the campus is officially dry. "Students under 21 do get alcohol sometimes; they get in trouble sometimes; they get judicial sanctions sometimes," says a junior.

The neighborhood immediately surrounding the college is pleasant, affluent suburbia, which provides a sense of security but few activities. The excitement of downtown Portland is only 15 minutes away on the city's public transit system or

The excitement of downtown Portland is only 15 minutes away on the city's public transit system or the campus shuttle service called the "Pioneer Express."

the campus shuttle service called the "Pioneer Express."

The school has excellent athletic facilities and a well-organized intramural program. The men's basketball team won the Northwest Conference in 2000 and has advanced to the NAIA national championship twice recently, winning the championship in 1997–98. Women are making waves in track, tennis, and volleyball.

Lewis and Clark College's greatest strength lies in its sense of independence and the tremendous opportunities it offers its students to travel abroad. The school attracts students with diverse interests and adventuresome spirits with a desire to explore the world. Precisely the traits that would have made Lewis and Clark, the explorers, proud.

Overlaps

Puget Sound, Whitman, Colorado College, Willamette, University of Oregon.

If You Apply To ➤ | **Lewis and Clark**…Early action: Dec. 1. Regular admissions: Feb. 1. Financial aid: Mar. 1. Does not guarantee to meet demonstrated need. Campus interviews: recommended, evaluative. Alumni interviews: optional, informational. SATs or ACTs: required (except Portfolio Path). SAT IIs: optional. Accepts the Common Application and electronic applications. Essay question: significant person or experience; important issue; who you'd invite to dinner; recently read book.

Louisiana State University

110 Thomas Boyd Hall, Baton Rouge, LA 70803

Website: www.lsu.edu
Location: Urban
Total Enrollment: 30,966
Undergraduates: 25,911
Male/Female: 47/53
ACT Range: 21–26
Financial Aid: 29%
Expense: Pub $
Phi Beta Kappa: Yes
Applicants: 9,661
Accepted: 82%
Enrolled: 65%
Grad in 6 Years: 52%
Returning Freshmen: 83%
Academics: ✍ ✍
Social: ☎ ☎ ☎ ☎
Q of L: ★ ★ ★
Admissions: (225) 388-1175
Email Address:
lsuadmit@lsu.edu

Strongest Programs:
Accounting
Engineering

Whether it's the abundance of azaleas and Japanese magnolias, the smell of Cajun cuisine, the antebellum mansions that are home to sorority women, or the diehard football rivalry with Ole Miss, few schools say "Southern" like Louisiana State. Students here enjoy tailgate parties, road trips to New Orleans, festivals such as Groovin' on the Grounds—and somehow squeeze in classes, too. "One enjoys all the perks and benefits of a large university, with the closeness and security of a small college," says a senior.

LSU's campus includes more than 250 principal buildings on the main 650-acre plateau—most in the Italian Renaissance style, with tan stucco walls and red-tile roofs. They sit along the banks of the Mississippi River on the grounds of a former plantation. Lakes and huge oak trees diffuse the strong sun and help temper Louisiana's legendary humidity. New student apartments and an athletic medical center at Tiger Stadium have been completed recently.

The historic emphasis on *"Laissez les bons temps roulez!"* (letting the good times roll) at LSU is shifting as administrators work overtime to make the school competitive. Formerly an open-admissions university for state residents, LSU has been tightening its standards, requiring all freshmen to have successfully completed 17.5 high school units in designated academic areas, including a foreign language and computer studies. For out-of-state applicants, grades and test scores are weighed equally. Students encounter a rigorous core curriculum, including 39 semester hours in six areas: English composition, analytical reasoning, arts, humanities, and the natural and social sciences.

Student give high marks to LSU's French, design, theater, history and geology departments, and note that while the sciences are solid, they're tough. Engineering and accounting are also highly regarded. And, as one of the nation's 25 sea-grant colleges (as well as a land-grant college), LSU's offerings in coastal studies and coastal ecology are notable as well. Across the board, students praise the faculty, and say graduate students mainly teach lab sections in the sciences. "The professors are very knowledgeable and willing to help," says a mechanical engineering major.

Although some faculty members' preoccupation with research can be annoying, most are accessible to undergraduates. Indeed, contact with professors here is said to be better than average, perhaps because 84 percent of freshman classes have fewer than 50 students. The career counseling program "provides excellent help for those about to graduate and those seeking employment," says one senior. Taking initiative seems good advice at this 30,000 student hub of activity, where a junior reports that "general advisors are not readily available, but department advisors are very accessible and willing to help" if asked.

Eighty-nine percent of LSU Tigers are Louisiana residents, but don't try to tar them with the stereotypical Southern conservative brush. "Students are always voicing opinions on every issue from A to Z," says a junior. "Our campus is very diverse. We consider ourselves the melting pot of the South" says a horticulture major. Still, just a few years ago, students were proudly calling LSU "the deepest of the Deep South universities." Whites comprise 79 percent of the student body, African Americans 10 percent, Hispanics 2 percent, and Asian Americans 4 percent. "Although LSU is a large and diverse university, there are enough groups around the campus and community that any student can easily find his or her niche," says a public relations major.

Housing is available to all students who apply, and 23 percent of students live in campus residences. "I recommend that everyone live on campus at least once" says a senior, adding that upperclassmen tend to prefer off-campus housing. The best dorms for freshman women are said to be Herget or Miller, and for men it's Kirby Smith. All dorms are single-sex with visiting hours, and students report that rooms fill up quickly, so it's important to apply early. The meal plans that come with dorm dwelling are reportedly inexpensive. Campus security is "good and improving," says one student. "The campus is well-lit and well-patrolled," adds another. The school has a nighttime transit system so students don't have to walk alone.

Though the administration is working hard to improve academic standards, make no mistake about it: LSU offers one of the wildest party atmospheres around. One way to ensure a nonstop campus social life and a more formal dating scene at LSU is to join one of the Greek organizations that draw 10 percent of the men and 15 percent of the women. Although strong, the Greek scene came under fire recently for hazing practices that led to a student's death. The campus is now theoretically dry, a junior says, "LSU has cracked down heavily on underage drinking." Still, students admit that a determined underclassman can still get a drink. For teetotalers, or the underage, the student union offers a wide variety of events, including movies, plays, concerts, fashion shows, lectures, and banquets. Homecoming is one of the year's biggest events, and Mardi Gras is always a popular draw. Road trips to Elvis Presley's Memphis birthplace and to the Florida beaches are also popular.

While Tiger football is king in Baton Rouge, LSU athletes have also earned their laurels (and championship trophies) in sports including men's baseball and women's track and field. When the Tigers are on the road, the campus tends to empty out as students follow the team or find their fun elsewhere, often to Oxford, Mississippi (home of Ole Miss) or South Bend, Indiana (Notre Dame). Students are pleased with life in Baton Rouge, and one junior says, "I love it so much, I plan to stay here after graduation!" As the state capital, the city offers

(Continued)
Economics
Political Science
Physics
English
Animal Science
Plant Biology

Although some faculty members' preoccupation with research can be annoying, most are accessible to undergraduates.

The trees and traditions may date back over a hundred years, but up-to-date technology is an integral part of the academic culture.

**University of
Southwestern
Louisiana, Tulane,
Loyola (LA),
Southeastern Louisiana,
Louisiana Tech.**

numerous chances to get involved in politics or volunteer programs. "The Greek system does community work all the time," says a senior.

LSU offers traditional Southern charm and a plethora of academic opportunities. No one is forced to spend their years at LSU shuttling between keg parties and the stadium, but few can resist the temptations of the Big Easy. Still, one student notes, "The administration is emphasizing technology, and better teachers." The trees and traditions may date back over a hundred years, but the future is the focus.

If You Apply To ➤ **LSU**…Rolling admissions: May 1. Financial aid: Dec. 15 (for priority consideration). Does not guarantee to meet demonstrated need. Campus interviews: optional, informational. No alumni interviews. ACTs: required. No SAT IIs. Accepts electronic applications. No essay question.

Loyola University New Orleans

6363 St. Charles Avenue, Box 89, New Orleans, LA 70118

Website: www.loyno.edu
Location: Urban
Total Enrollment: 5,008
Undergraduates: 3,478
Male/Female: 38/62
SAT Ranges: V 540–660 M
520–630
ACT Range: 23–28
Financial Aid: 47%
Expense: Pr $
Phi Beta Kappa: No
Applicants: 2,190
Accepted: 83%
Enrolled: 37%
Grad in 6 Years: 53%
Returning Freshmen: 80%
Academics: ✍ ✍ ✍
Social: ☎ ☎
Q of L: ★ ★ ★
Admissions: (800) 4-LOYOLA
Email Address:
admit@loyno.edu

The Big Easy may be a big party town, but for the students at Loyola University New Orleans, their main goal is getting a solid education and developing close friendships with a diverse group of peers. If that process is hastened by frozen daiquiris and some famously crazy costumed parades a few times a year, then what's the harm? Classes are small at the South's largest Catholic university, offering plenty of opportunity to interact with challenging, influential faculty members who really know their stuff, according to students. What's more, professors care about getting to know their students—both inside and outside of the classroom. "When you walk across campus, you don't feel like one more," says a senior. "Instead, you are aware of who the other people are, and chances are that you know most of them."

Loyola's attractive and well-kept 20-acre main campus overlooks acres of Audubon Park and beyond that, the mighty Mississippi River. The compact main campus mixes Tudor, Gothic, and modern structures, and is nestled in the University section of Uptown New Orleans. Two blocks up St. Charles Avenue, Loyola's Broadway campus offers an additional 4 acres, which is home to the Loyola School of Law, the Twomey Center for Peace through Justice, the visual arts department, and a residence hall.

Loyola offers comprehensive undergraduate degree programs in College of Arts and Sciences. Majors in communications, biology, psychology, and international business are the most popular with students. Also in demand is the College of Business Administration and the nationally renowned College of Music, which has recently established a Music Business program. The administration admits that a national trend in Greek and Latin studies has them seeing a decline and fall in the number of majors of the classical empire. Two popular courses that fill up quickly are American Hero: Harrison Ford and Zen Buddhism. One senior says, "The professors here really try to be available and plan a lot of hands-on experience." All students must fulfill an extensive 120-hour general education requirement which includes courses in writing, math, social science, natural science, philosophy, religious studies, and the arts.

Students say Loyola is competitive, depending on the program of study you choose. A history major says the courseload is demanding because "teachers expect a lot out of the students. They really are not going to tolerate mediocre effort." First-year students are required to take two world civilization classes, a religion course, argumentative writing, and math models (or calculus for science majors). Loyola students benefit from the university's involvement in the New Orleans Consortium with cross-registration and library usage at Tulane, Xavier, the University of New Orleans, and other schools in the New Orleans area. Loyola offers opportunities to study abroad in Mexico, England, Ireland, Belgium, and Spain. For those looking to have a varied educational experience in this country, there is a formal 3–2 liberal arts/engineering arrangement with Tulane. The J. Edgar and Louise S. Monroe Library houses 500,000 volumes and "is nothing short of awesome," says one student.

Fifty-four percent of Loyola students are Louisiana natives, and many of the remaining students are from Florida, Texas, and Georgia. Religion has a significant influence on the tone of the campus, with about 63 percent of the students Roman Catholic. "The Jesuit tradition here also encourages community service and character development, says a senior English major. Daily mass is voluntary, and many students attend regularly. Hispanics constitute 9 percent of the student body at Loyola; African Americans make up 12 percent; and Asian Americans comprise 4 percent. One student says that racism and political correctness are big issues on campus, but "people don't get obsessive about it." Loyola awards 10 Ignatian scholarships covering full tuition and room, and there are a number of academic merit scholarships ranging from $2,000 to $18,638 annually, but there are no athletic scholarships. Loyola does not guarantee to meet the demonstrated need of all admits.

Most of the student body commutes from home or their own apartments; 33 percent live on campus. As for the residence halls, the last five years have been ones of brick and mortar, which the construction of a new residence hall and renovations of existing ones, as well as a parking garage and courtyard. Though the city of New Orleans is a hotbed for crime, students say that they feel safe on campus, thanks to "excellent" and "very visible" security measures that include 24-hour patrols, escorts, and tight restrictions for dorm access.

Intercollegiate varsity sports returned to Loyola in 1991, with baseball and basketball the first two sports competing again under the school's name in the Gulf Coast Athletic Conference, NAIA Division I. "The increase in athletic programs has improved school spirit and attracted well-rounded students," a senior chemistry major says. For those who want to participate, there is a fine sports complex with racquetball, basketball, an Olympic-size pool, and steam and sauna rooms. A huge intramural program draws plenty of participants every year.

Many students are also involved in the Loyola University Community Action Program, a volunteer organization that places students in community service work. Fraternities and sororities are rarities at Jesuit schools, but they are popular at Loyola. About 17 percent of the men join fraternities, with an equal number of women choosing to belong to sororities. Major campus-wide social events include the annual Riverboat Dance, Swamp Stomp, Loyolapalooza, Murder Mystery Dinner, and the Leadership Banquet. Perhaps best of all, Loyola is only a streetcar ride away from the French Quarter. And there is always Mardi Gras, of course. Students agree that this is both a good and bad thing, for "the many temptations can academically distract students without a sense of discipline," says a senior.

<aside>
(Continued)
Strongest Programs:
Creative Writing
Visual Arts
Voice/Opera
Drama
Religious Studies
Premed
Economics
Music Business
</aside>

Perhaps best of all, Loyola is only a streetcar ride away from the French Quarter. And there is always Mardi Gras, of course.

With the combination of a Jesuit education in a town like New Orleans, they have the best of both worlds.

And as for underage drinking, Louisiana law requires that you be at least 21 to buy alcohol, but only 18 to consume it in private residence. Interestingly enough, Loyola maintains that dorms are private residences.

Students agree that New Orleans is the ultimate college town, with the atmosphere of Bourbon Street, the riverfront, restaurants, big bands, and even bigger parties. But despite these diversions, they know why they've chosen this small, community focused liberal arts university: "Small classes, personal attention, warm weather, [and] plenty of things happening in New Orleans," says a senior. It seems students here have the best of all worlds.

If You Apply To ➤ **Loyola**...Rolling admissions. Financial aid and housing: May 1. Does not guarantee to meet demonstrated need. Campus interviews: recommended, informational. No alumni interviews. An audition is required for admission to the College of Music and the Department of Drama and Speech. A portfolio is required for admission into the Visual Arts Program. SATs or ACTs: required. SAT IIs: optional (writing recommended). Accepts the Common Application and electronic applications. Essay question: personal accomplishments, favorite course in high school.

Macalester College

1600 Grand Avenue, St. Paul, MN 55105

Website: www.macalester.edu
Location: City outskirts
Total Enrollment: 1,835
Undergraduates: 1,835
Male/Female: 42/58
SAT Ranges: V 610–720 M 610–690
ACT Range: 27–31
Financial Aid: 69%
Expense: Pr $ $ $
Phi Beta Kappa: Yes
Applicants: 3,161
Accepted: 53%
Enrolled: 27%
Grad in 6 Years: 78%
Returning Freshmen: 90%
Academics: ✍ ✍ ✍ ✍
Social: ☎ ☎ ☎
Q of L: ★ ★ ★ ★
Admissions: (651) 696-6357
Email Address:
admissions@macalester.edu

Strongest Programs:
International Studies
Physics and Astronomy

Haven't had your fill of bagpipes lately? Macalester College, smack in the middle of the Twin Cities' hustle and bustle, annually entertains its students with kilt-clad bagpipers, men throwing telephone poles, and highland sword dancers. As one of the nation's top liberal arts colleges, Macalester prides itself on both its Scottish roots and dedication to diversity. A healthy endowment (the largest of any small liberal arts college in the country), friendly students, and outstanding professors contribute to Macalester's growing national reputation. Overlook the frigid winter weather, and pleasant surprises await you at Mac. "There is a more cosmopolitan feel to the campus than schools like Grinnell, Carleton, and Oberlin," a sophomore explains. "People come to Mac because they are socially aware *and* socially adept."

Macalester is located in a friendly, family-oriented neighborhood on the outskirts of St. Paul, Minnesota, one block from a tree-lined avenue featuring some of the state's most beautiful historic homes. The self-contained, 53-acre campus hosts a mix of architectural styles, with buildings arranged around the 110-year-old Old Main, a splendid Victorian structure listed on the National Register of Historic Places. Campus buildings are united by their redbrick exteriors, and are punctuated by the black-glass, octagonal Weyerhaeuser Chapel.

The academic atmosphere at Macalester is challenging but not overwhelming. "Mac is academically rigorous, but you'd never guess it from the student body. There's a real sense of cooperation and camaraderie," says a political science and geography major. Academic strengths include drama, economics, international studies, communication studies, anthropology, and geography, according to students. Natural sciences, especially chemistry and biology, are also notable. Mac's impressive science facilities include an observatory, a fully equipped animal operant chamber, an electronic instrumentation laboratory, computer modeling facilities, and a laser spectroscopy laboratory. Recently, the university added a core concentration in astronomy. Students say weaker spots are English, sociology, French, and music.

(Continued)
Biology
Economics
History

While a Mac degree is flexible, a few courses are required. Students must take social sciences (8 hours), natural sciences and math (8 hours), humanities and fine arts (12 hours), along with 4 hours each in designated international and domestic diversity courses. Students also must show proficiency in a foreign language. All students begin at Macalester with one of more than 30 first-year courses, capped at 16 students and taught by a professor who becomes their advisor. Advisors at Mac are "an invaluable mentor and advocate" for students, says one nostalgic senior. The senior year includes a required capstone experience involving original work, a seminar, or performance. Teaching is paramount. "What I love is going out with my advisor for a beer at the local bar on Friday afternoon, or going over to a prof's house for dinner," says a senior. More than 60 students do stipend-supported collaborative research with Mac professors each summer, and since a number of faculty members play intramurals, students may find professors dishing off passes on the basketball court.

Macalester draws students from every state and from 83 other nations. In addition, nearly 50 percent of students spend part of their academic careers studying abroad, either through approved independent programs or through the Associated Colleges of the Midwest.* Mac undergraduates who get claustrophobic on campus may cross-register at five other Twin Cities colleges or enroll in cooperative-degree programs in engineering, occupational therapy, nursing, and architecture with larger Midwestern schools.

Despite Mac's small size, students are surrounded by a wealth of different backgrounds. "All perspectives are represented—rich, poor, radical, reactionary, Somalian, Norwegian Lutheran," reports a sophomore. Minorities and foreign students comprise just over one-quarter of the Mac student body. According to its president, Macalester welcomes students who "want an academic challenge, to encounter new ideas and cultures, and to make an impact in their communities." Mac is a big protest school—even for the sake of protesting, it seems," advises a political science and geography major.

Students say Mac's dorms are "traditional," with doubles for the first two years, when they're required to live on campus, and suites for upperclassmen. Many rooms include sinks, which students say is key. In all, 69 percent of students live on campus, and while "getting a room is no problem; getting the room you want is another game," a recent grad notes. Still, single-sex floors are guaranteed to those who want them. Many students have singles, and some live in language houses; a sophomore crows that "my room looks like a treehouse—we have three levels, it's amazing." There's a kosher residence, where residents prepare their own meals. Other students cope with the food service, which offers several meal options, or by buying hot plates, cheap noodles, and frequently calling out for pizza. An outside vendor, Bon Appetit, has increased satisfaction with campus dining due to quality, choices of entrées, and a vegetarian selection at each meal.

Students rave about the nearby metropolis. "I saw *Les Miserables* for $10. *Rent's* been here multiple times. Clean, great food, geared to college kids," says an anthropology major. "It's an amazing city, very cosmopolitan and progressive." Coffee shops and bookstores are close to campus, and Mac is only a 10-minute walk from the Mississippi River. For shopping, there is, of course, the Mall of America nearby (though Mac students tend to tire of it quickly).

Without Greek organizations and with the proximity of a major metropolitan area, Macalester's on-campus social life suffers to some extent. Cheap movies are an option, along with dance parties and jazz concerts. Far more popular are the Twin Cities' bars, clubs, and professional sports teams. "Road trips to the local casinos or to see Babe the Blue Ox in Brainerd are not uncommon," reports a

More than 60 students do stipend-supported collaborative research with Mac professors each summer, and since a number of faculty members play intramurals, students may find professors dishing off passes on the basketball court.

The senior year includes a required capstone experience involving original work, a seminar, or performance. Teaching is paramount.

senior. During the first weekend in May, Macalester hosts the annual Scottish Fair: "Imagine 100-plus bagpipers on the lawn starting at 8:00 A.M. and ending at 3:00 P.M.; it's an experience," says a sociology and religious studies major. Other popular events include SpringFest and the Queer Union Dance.

Historically, Mac hasn't been "much on sports." But men's and women's soccer recently joined the debate team as Mac's nationally ranked squads. The annual Brain Bowl pits Mac against in-state rival Carleton in football and gives students a chance to be irreverent. "Our school cheer is 'Drink blood, smoke crack, worship Satan, go Mac!' even though we don't partake in those activities," quips a sophomore.

Macalester students are an independent bunch who enjoy the chance to do things just a bit differently during their undergraduate years—to work hard, play hard and stay mellow while trying to keep warm through the freezing Minnesota winters. Perhaps a political science major says it best: "It's nice to be a top liberal arts school without the elitist atmosphere of comparable East Coast colleges."

Overlaps

Carleton, Oberlin, Brown, Northwestern, Grinnell.

If You Apply To ➢

Macalester...Early decision: Nov. 15, Jan. 13. Regular admissions: Jan. 13. Financial aid: Feb. 9. Guarantees to meet demonstrated need. Campus interviews: recommended, evaluative. Alumni interviews: optional, evaluative. SATs or ACTs: required. SAT IIs: optional. Accepts the Common Application and electronic applications. Essay question: Why Macalester; an original piece of written work.

University of Maine–Orono

Orono, ME 04469

Website: www.umaine.edu
Location: Rural
Total Enrollment: 9,945
Undergraduates: 7,882
Male/Female: 49/51
SAT Ranges: V 480–590 M 480–600
ACT Range: 20–26
Financial Aid: 86%
Expense: Pub $ $ $
Phi Beta Kappa: Yes
Applicants: 4,568
Accepted: 85%
Enrolled: 42%
Grad in 6 Years: 53%
Returning Freshmen: 80%
Academics: ✍ ✍
Social: ☎ ☎ ☎ ☎
Q of L: ★ ★ ★
Admissions: (207) 581-1561

Maine is known for its unspoiled wilderness, its seacoast hiking trails, and ski slopes, which beckon visitors from far and wide. Students, however, come to this small state for another reason: to help themselves to UMaine's range of strong academic programs, from traditional fields like business and engineering to nontraditional choices such as forestry and wildlife management. Best of all, the cost of a UMaine diploma is reasonable, even for out-of-staters. Where else will you find the whole campus taking a break from classes just to keep the place pristine, as UMainers do on Maine Day?

Situated on an island between the Stillwater and Penobscot rivers, UMaine's 660-acre campus encompasses a large grass mall with lots of trees. The architectural theme at this flagship of the state university system ranges from English academic to contemporary. In the past few years, the school has completed a global sciences building, a new sports stadium and field, and a new hall for the performing arts.

UMaine's seven undergraduate colleges have been restructured into five schools with greater interdisciplinary emphasis: education and human development; business, public policy and health; engineering; liberal arts and sciences; and natural sciences, forestry, and agriculture. Despite the restructuring, transferring from one college to another is expected to remain relatively easy. Specific requirements vary from college to college, though all students are required to meet general education requirements in physical or biological sciences, human values and social context, math, writing and ethics; a capstone experience within the major is also mandatory.

UMaine's engineering programs are widely viewed as the most demanding on campus. Other claim-to-fame programs include forestry and agriculture, Canadian studies, and marine science. Forest ecosystem science builds on a strong natural sciences foundation with specialized classes exploring the complexities of forests from the cellular to the ecosystem levels. Newer undergraduate degree programs include marine science (with concentrations in physical sciences and marine biology), interdisciplinary studies, and women's studies. The forest engineering program has been dropped. The interdisciplinary Institute for Quaternary Studies collaborates with other research entities around the world in focusing on the Quaternary period, a time of numerous glacial and interglacial cycles leading up to the present.

UMaine's library, one of the state's finest, is the regional depository for American and Canadian government documents and houses several of alumnus Stephen King's papers. Former U.S. Senator William S. Cohen, a UMaine faculty member before he became defense secretary, donated his personal papers to the university as well. The papers, which chronicle Cohen's 24-year congressional career, will be used to develop a nonpartisan center on international policy and commerce focused on teaching, research, and public service and named in Cohen's honor. They are also available to scholars interested in researching Cohen's career.

UMaine students don't expect long lines at registration, and report that graduating in four years is virtually certain, unless you pursue a double major. It can sometimes be difficult to get your first-choice classes, but as one business major explains, "If you decide on a major at the beginning of your enrollment, you should be all set." The Academic and Career Exploration program allows students to work with professionals in different areas before declaring their degree choices. Although the academic climate is laid-back, students still have to make an effort to learn. "Since this is a fairly large school, self-motivation is key to getting the most of your education," says a sophomore. To graduate, students must have at least 120 credit hours and a 2.0 GPA; 72 hours must be completed in the student's major.

At UMaine, approximately 200 students with a minimum combined SAT score of 1200 are admitted to the honors program, the oldest in the nation. Internships and co-ops are available in most fields, and there's a Semester-by-the-Sea and a Lobster Institute for nautical types. Juniors who want a reprieve from Maine's often brutal winters can head for Brazil, while the heartier types study in Canada, Scandinavia, and Ireland. Most students, however, are immune to the weather, since 83 percent are from Maine and many of the rest hail from other parts of New England. In fact, the student body is almost entirely white—93 percent—but it is relatively oblivious to social and political controversy. "We are pretty mellow when it comes to the issues," says one senior. "Discussions are held, but not shouted over." There are 450 merit scholarships for qualified students.

Fifty-six percent of UMaine students live off campus, in Orono, nearby Bangor, or the sparsely populated area in between. Dorms are coed, single-sex or co-op; some have gyms, computer labs, or apartment-style suites. "Dorms are constantly being renovated to improve quality and space," says one student, adding, "The university always has room for a student." Some housing or wings are set aside for specific majors. Dining-hall food is average, but Greeks—14 percent of men and six percent of women go Greek at UMaine—may eat in their chapter houses.

Despite UMaine's relatively isolated location, the campus pulses with social life. The party scene is largely off-campus, in bars, clubs, and house parties. On

(Continued)

Email Address:
um-admit@umaine.edu

Strongest Programs:
Forestry and Agriculture
Natural Resources
Engineering
Marine Sciences
Business

Where else will you find the whole campus taking a break from classes just to keep the place pristine, as UMainers do on Maine Day?

Internships and co-ops are available in most fields, and there's a Semester-by-the-Sea and a Lobster Institute for nautical types.

campus, there are constant programming options, including concerts, comedians, sports, movies, and dances. "If you're bored, it's because you choose to be," says a sophomore. Over 150 student organizations, including flying and scuba diving clubs, exist on campus. Concerts and dances are planned every weekend. Big winter events are the "bed sled" race, in which students race beds down a campus hill, and the annual carnival, featuring a school-wide snow-sculpting competition. Come spring, students go all out for Bumstock Weekend, a huge event featuring bands playing outdoors from dawn 'til dusk.

The medium-sized town of Orono offers a few bars, a dollar theater, and a few other hangouts. Buses to Bangor, a fair-sized city 10 minutes away, run every 15 to 20 minutes. A car is helpful, although there are gripes about parking on campus. UMaine students tend to be outdoor enthusiasts, and popular road trips include Bar Harbor, Boston, Acadia National Park, skiing at Sugarloaf USA, L.L. Bean's 24-hour store in Freeport, and the real-life Mt. Katahdin, which appears on Bean's logo. Hockey reigns here, especially when played against Boston University or Boston College, and UMaine is a perennial NCAA champion. Intramurals cover a range of sports from swimming and wrestling to hoopball (golf with a basketball) and broomball (ice hockey with a dodgeball and a broom, played with shoes instead of skates).

While UMaine's natural beauty has been attracting summer vacationers—including at least one former U.S. president—for years, students are also drawn by the laid-back academics, active social life, and dedicated faculty. UMaine offers a mix to satisfy outdoor enthusiasts, serious students, and those who just want to have fun.

Overlaps

University of Southern Maine, University of New Hampshire, University of Vermont, University of Massachusetts, University of Maine–Farmington.

If You Apply To ➤

Maine…Rolling admissions. Financial aid: Mar. 1. Does not guarantee to meet demonstrated need. Campus interviews: recommended, informational. No alumni interviews. SATs or ACTs: required. Essay question: academic goals and objectives or essay of student's choice.

Manhattanville College

2900 Purchase Street, Purchase, NY 10577

Website: www.mville.edu
Location: Suburban
Total Enrollment: 2,370
Undergraduates: 1,483
Male/Female: 31/69
SAT Ranges: V 520–780 M 520–710
ACT Range: 20–24
Financial Aid: 68%
Expense: Pr $ $
Phi Beta Kappa: No

Manhattanville College is increasing both its national profile and the size of its student population. During the 1999–2000 school year, Manhattanville refined its mission statement to reflect its desire "to educate students to become ethically and socially responsible leaders for the global community." Although it's experienced growing pains—crowded dorms, too few parking spaces—what hasn't changed is the school's emphasis on individuality. The Portfolio System, Manhattanville's distinct approach to undergraduate education, requires students to create a body of work reflecting their entire college career. Students must craft a freshman assessment essay, a study plan and program evaluation, specific examples of work in writing and research, and a resume. The Portfolio Program, however, is only one way Manhattanville encourages individuality and personal growth. "Manhattanville is a special place because the administration and faculty truly love and care about each student," says a junior. "They hope that

Manhattanville graduates leave here well-rounded and better than when they came."

Manhattanville College, which began as a Roman Catholic academy for girls on Houston Street in New York City, pulled up stakes in the 1950s for a 125-acre estate in Purchase, New York. Today, the campus is located in wealthy Westchester County, near the town of White Plains—home to several major corporations but just 28 miles from the excitement of the Big Apple. The focal point of the campus, which was designed by Central Park architect Frederick Law Olmsted, is Reid Hall, a 19th-century replica of a Norman castle.

Manhattanville's distribution requirements include courses in five areas: humanities, social sciences, fine arts, mathematics and sciences, and languages. Students must demonstrate English writing competency as well. Freshmen complete the Preceptorial, a two-semester introduction to college-level work, as well as a library and information studies course. Manhattanville's strongest offerings include art and design (enhanced by the proximity of New York City's many museums and galleries), music, and education, while economics and psychology are also popular. More than 95 percent of M-ville's School of Education graduates have passed the New York State Teaching Exam every year for the past five years. The languages—French, Spanish, Asian Studies, and Classics—attract the fewest majors, and students say they avoid math and science because of the difficulty of the classes and the age of some labs. English also gets low marks; it's described as "boring" and "archaic." There's a new finance major, along with a new minor in social justice and communication, and a new credit option in community service. The physics and classics programs have been reactivated. Students may also opt to design their own major. Career Services, which offers internship opportunities at over 350 locations in the New York metro area and beyond, is "phenomenal," securing placements at companies such as Fox News, Dedicated Records, PepsiCo, and the Westchester County Board of Legislators.

The academic climate at Manhattanville is fairly laid back, but "professors always know what you're up to," says a senior, owing to the low student-faculty ratio. "Don't expect to not do work and pass without a struggle," agrees a sophomore. The Presidential and Honors Scholarships offer qualified students an Honors Preceptorial, Honors Seminar, and honors program within their major, while five-year combined degree programs in business administration and in prenursing are offered with NYU. Pre-professional programs are available in law, medicine, dentistry, physical therapy, and computer science. The college has exchange programs with Mills College and with American University's World Capitals Program, plus study abroad options in England, France, Germany, Ireland, Italy, Japan, Mexico, and Spain. Students have nothing but praise for their professors. "The quality of teaching is the highest," says an English and history major.

Manhattanville's student body is becoming more diverse as larger numbers of out-of-state students apply. However, females outnumber males by a ratio of two to one. Thirty-nine percent of undergraduates come from outside of New York, while 7 percent come from overseas. Hispanics comprise the largest minority group at 14 percent, followed by African Americans at 6 percent and Asian Americans at 3 percent. Students may apply to live in the Intercultural Center, where all backgrounds live together. "The campus is not racist, but sometimes racially divided," sighs a romance languages major. Students recovering from alcohol or drug addiction can live in "Choices," a section of the dorms with weekly group counseling and student-developed guidelines that govern the living quarters.

(Continued)

Applicants: 1,800

Accepted: 66%

Enrolled: 32%

Grad in 6 Years: 67%

Returning Freshmen: 85%

Academics: ✍ ✍ ✍

Social: ☎ ☎ ☎

Q of L: ★ ★ ★

Admissions: (914) 323-5464

Email Address:
admissions@mville.edu

Strongest Programs:
Music
Art and Design
Economics and
Management
Education
Sociology
Psychology

The focal point of the campus, designed by Central Park architect Frederick Law Olmsted, is Reid Hall, a 19th-century replica of a Norman castle.

Eighty-five percent of Manhattanville's students live on campus in one of four dorms, which have lounges, communal kitchens, laundry rooms, cable TV, and Internet access. Freshmen are assigned rooms which are "quite comfortable" according to a first-year art major, while upperclassmen enter a lottery—and complain they never get what they want. Campus dwellers can choose 15- or 19-meal-a-week plans, and can also use their meal cards at Café de Ville, a deli-type eatery. The dining hall has been renovated, and offers fresh-baked goods and a well-stocked salad bar.

Manhattanville's hometown, Purchase, "is not a college town at all," says a junior. With increasing numbers of male students enrolling, things seem to be picking up, and with no fraternities or sororities, off-campus parties are usually open to all. The student programming board is working to improve the social life, with weekend events such as dinners, formals in the castle, parties, comedy and talent shows, plays, and concerts. The student center has a movie theater. Thirty student-run organizations help to fulfill the cultural, intellectual, and social interests of the student body, but off-campus bars still draw many students—whether of age or not. Parties in the freshman dorm are dry, but M-ville's alcohol policies are said to be lax. "It's really easy to obtain alcohol, either from a store or a bar," says a sophomore. Road trips include Rye Beach in the warmer months and upstate New York or Vermont for skiing in the winter. Many students take the 30-minute train ride into Manhattan to shop, see plays, or try and get into nightclubs, and the college has started a van route that makes New York City and White Plains even more accessible. Every spring, students look forward to Quad Jam, "an all-day, all-night concert and carnival and party," a junior says. There's a Fall Jam as well, and "our Castle Classics in athletics are always well-attended, too," says a junior.

Speaking of sports, Manhattanville's women's teams are just as competitive as the men's. Women's tennis won conference championships in 1998 and 1999, as did women's volleyball in 1998 and softball in 1999. Men's soccer, ice hockey, lacrosse, golf, basketball, and baseball are also popular. In 2000, the men's tennis team won the Skyline Conference championship. Intramurals sometimes draw flak because of organizational problems, but overall, students enjoy them. Weekend warriors and letter-winners alike applaud the college's gym, fitness center, swimming pool, tennis courts, and athletic fields.

Manhattanville is a "true community," says a sociology major. "As a bicoastal student, Manhattanville makes me feel like I'm at home, whenever I get homesick." The closeness can get old, though, says a junior: "We are 'Rumorville,' a drawback to a small school where everyone knows everyone else." The familial atmosphere can get claustrophobic at times, but for those wishing to be part of a close community, Manhattanville may be worth a look.

If You Apply To ➤

Manhattanville...Early decision: Dec. 1. Rolling admissions, financial aid: Mar. 1. Housing: July 2. Meets demonstrated need of 35%. Campus interviews: optional, evaluative. No alumni interviews. SATs: required. SAT IIs: optional. Accepts the Common Application. No essay question

Marlboro College

Marlboro, VT 05344

Marlboro College is only a half-century old, but already the college is known far and wide as an innovator in liberal arts education. It was founded on the principles of independent and in-depth study just after World War II, when returning GIs renovated an old barn as the college's first building while they lived in Quonset huts. And today's Marlboro students are just as trail-blazing; they prepare for the next century by digging into self-developed Plans of Concentration, including one-on-one tutorials and a thesis or project judged by outside examiners from "the best Eastern colleges and universities." With 300 students and 38 faculty members, Marlboro is its own little world, where students enter as novices and leave as pros.

Positioned atop a small mountain, surrounded by maples and pines, and with a gorgeous view of southern Vermont, Marlboro's physical beauty is striking. Buildings are adapted from barns, sheds, and houses that stood on three old farms that today make up the 350-acre campus. Among the renovated buildings, many with passive solar heating, are nine dormitories, a library, a science building, art studios and music practice rooms, a 350-seat theater, and a campus center. Above the athletic field is the college's astronomical observatory. The school recently completed a new art gallery and studio, photography lab, sculpture studio, and it is working with a professor of architecture from Yale to develop a campus planning model.

While some schools see growth as a sign of their success, Marlboro intends to remain one of the nation's smallest liberal arts institutions. Administrators believe that the size stimulates dynamic relationships between students and faculty, making learning happen both inside and outside the classroom. This isn't a place where students can fade into the background: the institution relies on everyone to share their talents and skills. The same philosophy will apply to the college's new Graduate Center; its first programs—a master of arts in teaching with Internet technologies and a master of science in Internet strategy management—are as innovative as the college's heritage.

The cornerstone of an undergraduate Marlboro education is the Plan of Concentration, which each student develops independently. Juniors and seniors "on plan" take most coursework in one-on-one tutorials with the faculty sponsors. Seniors present their thesis or project to their sponsors, who are backed up by outside examiners, experts in the student's field unaffiliated with the college. The administration boasts that by bringing in these outsiders for two- to three-hour oral examinations of its seniors, Marlboro has created its own accountability system, ensuring that neither students nor faculty at this isolated institution are cut off from the most current academic thinking. Faculty members often find the exams as stressful as the students, as it means their teaching is being judged by outsiders. The only other requirement is the Clear Writing course, usually completed freshman year. Marlboro's flexibility should not be confused with academic flabbiness, though. Grades are an integral part of the evaluation process, professors are stingy with As, and most students work hard.

Marlboro offers solid instruction in literature, writing, environmental science, sociology, psychology, and theater. Administrators and students alike praise the World Studies program, which provides an eight-month professional internship and or study experience abroad. Music and math are said to be weaker, and since

Website: www.marlboro.edu

Location: Rural

Total Enrollment: 380

Undergraduates: 290

Male/Female: 41/59

SAT Ranges: V 580–680 M 500–620

Financial Aid: 95%

Expense: Pr $ $

Phi Beta Kappa: No

Applicants: 308

Accepted: 80%

Enrolled: 40%

Grad in 6 Years: 40%

Returning Freshmen: 78%

Academics: ✍ ✍ ✍

Social: ☎ ☎ ☎

Q of L: ★ ★ ★ ★

Admissions: (800) 343-0049

Email Address:
admissions@marlboro.edu

Strongest Programs:
World Studies
Writing and Literature
Environmental
Studies/Biology
Sociology
History

Seniors present their thesis or project to their sponsors, who are backed up by outside examiners, experts in the student's field unaffiliated with the college.

one professor can constitute an entire discipline at Marlboro because of the college's small size, a personality conflict may mean problems with a whole department. Even that can be remedied, though; in most years, students can choose among 250 courses and more than 600 tutorials. Only six had more than 20 students. Students give most profs high marks and appreciate the low student/teacher ratio: "Everything at Marlboro screams 'interactive learning,'" says one student.

In the old independent Yankee spirit, Marlboro's library operates on the honor system, where students sign out their own books 24 hours a day. Ditto for the computer center, science, and humanities buildings. The school has only one security guard. "I feel really safe here," says one freshman. "Everyone is out at night and nobody's worried about assault—except maybe by bears." Indeed, the college operates on a New England town-meeting style of government involving students, faculty, staff, and their spouses in every aspect of policymaking. Students can veto the faculty members on hiring and retention decisions, and it takes a two-thirds vote of the faculty to override them.

Clearly, 1960s-era liberalism is still the dominant political tone on this campus. A big issue these days is parking: "Should students be able to park on campus, or are cars too hideously ugly to be seen at Marlboro?" asks a psychology major. Minority enrollment continues to be low (4 percent), in spite of the administration's program to recruit and support poor rural Vermonters. The college offers 50 merit scholarships of up to $5,000 every year, but no athletic scholarships for the single reason that there are no varsity sports.

The dorms are mostly coed, and students say they have a "rustic" appeal. "The rooms are huge, something I took for granted until I visited friends at other schools," says one dorm-dweller. Housing is based on credits, so freshmen have triples, sophomores have doubles, and upperclassmen have singles. Twenty-two percent of students live off campus in Brattleboro, 20 minutes away, and shuttle to and from campus in a school van.

Students agree that the town of Marlboro, highlighted by a post office and general store, isn't much to write home about. Most head to Brattleboro for its restaurants, bookstores, and coffee shops. As might be expected, Marlboro has no Greek organizations; a new staff member was recently hired to coordinate the planning of student activities like poetry readings, trips to Boston and New York City, vans to local movie theaters, and pumpkin-carving contests. Snowball fights by the library are a big draw in winter. On Community Work Day, students and faculty skip class and work together to improve the campus through various manual labor projects. The annual Cabaret and Halloween parties are unofficial costume contests showcasing student creativity.

The school mascot, the Fighting Dead Trees is emblazoned on the shirts of the ever popular co-ed soccer team, and broomball, a variation of ice hockey played on shoes with brooms instead of sticks and a kickball instead a puck—is also always popular for athletes and spectators. The "incredibly dynamic" outing club ensures plenty of opportunities to enjoy the local wilderness, including hiking and cross-country skiing on runs that radiate from the center of campus. Excellent downhill skiing is only a few minutes' drive away.

This iconoclastic school continues to push the academic envelope and remains proud of doing and being the unexpected. And that suits students here just fine. Says a student, "Basically, we're a bunch of crazy, dedicated, love-struck, joyful, cynical, conscious freaks who go blasting around campus in a frenzy of creative and destructive energy." Could anywhere be more appropriate?

Overlaps

Hampshire, Bennington, Bard, Earlham, Evergreen State.

Marquette University

1217 West Wisconsin Avenue, Milwaukee, WI 53233

At Marquette University, students practice what they preach. Rooted in traditional Jesuit doctrines, the educational experience at this university has not left its Catholic origins behind, and includes emphasis on civic responsibility, community service, and personal growth. Innovative programs combine classroom theory with volunteer opportunities in Milwaukee and beyond.

Eighty acres of "concrete with interludes of grass and trees," Marquette University is located just a few blocks away from the heart of downtown Milwaukee. While offering the advantages of an urban setting, its campus does have plenty of open spaces suitable for everything from throwing a Frisbee to throwing a barbecue. Although most of the buildings are relatively modern, the campus is the site of the oldest building in the Western Hemisphere, the St. Joan of Arc Chapel, which was built in France in 1400 and later transported to Wisconsin. Planning is currently underway for a new 259,000-square-foot library and an athletic facility.

Marquette has undergraduate colleges of nursing, arts and sciences, engineering, business administration, and communication, along with a school of education. Medical technology is one of a host of health-related undergraduate options. Physical therapy wins much praise from students, and the College of Arts and Sciences is applauded for its political science, biology, and psychology programs. Through an affiliation with the Milwaukee Institute of Art and Design, two art minors, studio art and art history, are available. Marquette has its own art museum and an active theater program. The university has recently stopped admitting students to the struggling physics, social work, and dental hygiene majors, and some students complain that the university is notorious for dropping majors without warning.

Depending on the field of study, undergraduates complete approximately 128 credit hours in general education requirements distributed among various academic areas, including English composition, history, mathematics, foreign languages, natural sciences, philosophy, theology, and the fine arts. The curriculum is, however, slated for changes, as the administration wants the program to "reflect a common academic experience" for all undergraduates. In addition to myriad study abroad programs, the university is the proud owner of the Les Aspin Center for Government located in Washington, D.C., which allows students to take courses in philosophy, political science, and theology, while simultaneously participating in an internship with a federal government agency.

Many classes are limited to 50 students, but students usually manage to get into the ones they want. The administration encourages students to "put our beliefs into practice" through volunteer activity, which serves the elderly, the sick,

Website: www.marquette.edu

Location: Urban

Total Enrollment: 10,780

Undergraduates: 7,437

Male/Female: 46/54

SAT Ranges: V 520–620 M 520–640

ACT Range: 23–28

Financial Aid: 55%

Expense: Pr $

Phi Beta Kappa: Yes

Applicants: 6,925

Accepted: 84%

Enrolled: 30%

Grad in 6 Years: 72%

Returning Freshmen: 89%

Academics: ✍ ✍ ✍

Social: ☎ ☎ ☎

Q of L: ★ ★ ★

Admissions: (414) 288-7302

Email Address: admissions@marquette.edu

Strongest Programs:
 Dentistry
 Law
 Biomedical Engineering
 Biology
 Nursing
 Philosophy/Theology

and the poor in the Milwaukee area and elsewhere. "The Jesuit emphasis on service is one of the parts of our university I'm most proud of," a junior says. Student religious organizations are active, and weekly Masses are held in the dorms by the resident priest. Roman Catholics understandably predominate in the student body, but religious practice is left to the individual. The academic climate is described as "fairly competitive," rather than cutthroat. A junior says, "Many people realize that we are all here for the same purpose." Students praise the counseling program with words like "awesome," and "helpful."

An honors program with small classes is available for 65 highly motivated students in each year, while the Freshman Frontier program offers admission and intensive assistance to students "who did not reach full academic potential in high school." Students praise the orientation program as one of the best in the nation. "It is a four-day program of educational seminars and social events that helps new students feel comfortable," a veteran explains.

Although the university actively recruits in 35 or so states and several U.S. territories, most of the student body is from the Midwest, 47 percent from Wisconsin itself. In general, Marquette boasts a friendly collection of middle-class students who did well enough to graduate in the top quarter of their high school class. Like their curriculum, Marquette students are vocationally oriented; 63 percent of them go straight into the job market on graduation. Blacks and Hispanics combine to make up 9 percent of the student body, while Asian Americans make up another 4 percent. "The student body is mostly white," a senior says. "The African Americans and the Caucasians don't seem to mix unless it's just on an individual basis." Marquette offers a very successful Educational Opportunity Program, which enables low-income, disadvantaged students, most of whom are minorities, to have the advantage of a college education.

The university accepts students without regard to their financial need, and assembles aid packages on a first-come, first-served basis, so apply early. There are a variety of merit scholarships, ranging from $4,000 to full tuition. In fact, 40 percent of the student body receives merit-based aid of one form or another.

As for on-campus life, all but two residence halls are coed. Residency is required for freshmen and sophomores, but by junior year an overwhelming majority of students choose to move off campus, though housing is guaranteed for all undergraduate students through a lottery. A student's ID card validated for food service ensures entrance into any of the halls' cafeterias. The university works hard to keep the campus safe, though some liken the atmosphere of on-campus dorms to a "prison ward." In addition to residence hall guards, the school has blue-light emergency phones throughout the campus, and operates a safety patrol escort program (to provide safe travel between the campus and surrounding residential areas) and an intracampus shuttle service complete with vans known as "limos."

Students are less than enthusiastic about the city beyond the campus, characterizing Milwaukee as "filthy and gloomy." An old advertising slogan once claimed that "Milwaukee Means Beer," and few Marquette students would disagree. The city has more bars on a single block than are found in some entire cities. Marquette is stricter than most universities in enforcing the drinking age, but getting served off campus is not as difficult, and most students happily declare their school a "party school" by any standard. Another well-loved tradition is the Miracle on Central Mall, the annual lighting of the campus Christmas tree and accompanying Mass. There are fraternities and sororities, and they attract about 9 percent of the students. Their impact on student life is "minuscule," notes one student. Sports fans will be impressed with Milwaukee's Bradley Center, close to campus and home to Marquette basketball and the NBA's Milwaukee Bucks. Nature lovers can head to Lake Michigan, a 40-minute walk from campus, or to Kettle Moraine, a glaciated region ideal for hiking and cross-country skiing. Chicago is only 95 miles away. As the school grows, varsity sports are gaining a higher profile, and men's and women's track, men's soccer, and women's tennis are strong, while the women's cross-country and soccer teams won conference championships in 2000.

Still, no matter how dynamic the basketball team or how impressive the facilities, it's the students and school together that make Marquette a fine experience. The location forces students to become "more aware of the numbers of people in our own neighborhoods who need help." The classes challenge, and the instructors lead the way. "I am learning more and more," says a junior. "I love this community more each day, and they continue to meet my needs."

If You Apply To ➤ **Marquette**...Rolling admissions (priority deadline March 1). Does not guarantee to meet demonstrated need. Campus and alumni interviews: optional, informational. SATs or ACTs: required. SAT IIs: optional. Accepts the Common Application and electronic applications. Essay question: What is most important about you?, What in the last four years makes you proud?, Choose four objects that represent the modern human experience, (physical therapy only) Why are you interested in physical therapy?. Apply to particular school or program.

Mary Washington College

BEST BUY

1301 College Avenue, Fredericksburg, VA 22401

Strolling among Mary Washington's elegant buildings of red brick and white columns has led more than one pleased parent to declare, "Now this is what a college should look like." Indeed, for an aura of history and tradition, few schools stack up to this small college in Fredericksburg, a site of Civil War action and the boyhood town of George Washington. If the campus architecture puts some people in mind of the University of Virginia, it's no accident: MWC was the all-female branch of that august institution before going coed and cutting its ties in 1970. Three decades later, the college has made a name for itself as one of the premium public liberal arts colleges, and continues to attract bright students from around the globe.

Located in historic Fredericksburg, Mary Washington College is the classic college campus prototype, featuring classical Jeffersonian buildings, sweeping lawns, brick walkways, and breathtaking foliage. It's practically mandatory to spend time outside on this gorgeous campus. Newer buildings include a $13 million science center.

Mary Washington's core curriculum emphasizes its strong liberal bent. Students select courses to meet specific goals in the arts, literature, natural and social sciences, and critical thinking. English composition, five writing-intensive courses, and foreign language competency are also required. Students also must complete across-the-curriculum general education requirements in five areas: written communication, oral communication, race and gender, global awareness, and the environment. For majors, business and English are the two most popular programs, and two of the best. Political science and international affairs are very strong, as is a unique program in historic preservation. The dance and Russian departments are criticized as being weaker than the rest. "The courses are

Website: www.mwc.edu
Location: Small city
Total Enrollment: 4,000
Undergraduates: 3,965
Male/Female: 30/70
SAT Ranges: V 570–650 M 550–640
Financial Aid: 50%
Expense: Pub $ $
Phi Beta Kappa: Yes
Applicants: 4,405
Accepted: 55%
Enrolled: 34%
Grad in 6 Years: 74%
Returning Freshmen: 85%
Academics: ✍ ✍ ✍ ✍
Social: ☎ ☎ ☎
Q of L: ★ ★ ★ ★
Admissions: (800) 468-5614
Email Address: admit@mwc.edu

challenging and interactive," reports a psychology major. "There is no cutthroat competition, but the standard of work is pretty high."

Students are encouraged to take on research projects of their own design, and several departments offer grants for work abroad or in the U.S. Many students study abroad during their junior or senior year. The college's location, roughly an hour from both Washington, D.C., and the state capital, Richmond, is a handy asset for approximately 350 budding politicos who seek internships every year. Because of the rise in Mary Washington's popularity, some students are concerned about potential overcrowding. As enrollment increases, so grow the lines to registration, which might be tough for underclassmen since classes are purposely kept small. "It is hard to finish the teaching program in four years," says one senior. "But on the whole, graduating on time is definitely possible." Most profs will use the force-add system to let people into full classes; but this doesn't always work, especially in the psychology department, which is notoriously strict.

The close ties between students and faculty are a great source of pride at Mary Washington, where classes usually have fewer than 25 students and rarely more than 50. "The quality of teaching I have received has been phenomenal," says one historic preservation major. "I am constantly amazed by the backgrounds and expertise of my professors and have really benefited from it."

In general, Mary Washington students are a "friendly and unpretentious" bunch, fairly hardworking and generally conservative, if not apolitical. Multicultural issues are hot, as was an issue that was finally resolved last year: the ability to have visitors in the dorms 24 hours a day, seven days a week. Blacks make up 5 percent of the student population, Hispanics 3 percent, and Asian Americans 3 percent. Sixty-five percent of the student body is from Virginia, and a large majority continues on to jobs after graduation, rather than graduate school. The college offers a number of merit scholarships ranging from $500 to $8,500, but no athletic scholarships.

Students have great affection for MWC housing. "Each building is a community, not simply a place to live," reports a junior. "The rooms are a good size—comparable to a room at home." There is a residence advisor within each dorm, although some students complain that the rules they set would be "better suited for high school students." Freshmen are housed together in four residence halls that are equipped with TVs and VCRs, while upperclassmen enter a lottery for placement in coed dorms. Housing is guaranteed for all four years. Once they find a room that suits them, students can "homestead," or retain that room for their remaining years. In addition to standard cafeteria service, students can use their meal cards to eat at a campus snack bar or the Steak House, a restaurant-style dining hall.

Small and friendly, nearby Fredericksburg is a "quaint, historic town." While it lacks some of the nightlife of a larger community, it has enough museums to satiate even the most avid history buff. Students tired of prowling the monuments find themselves within striking distance of dance clubs and bars in both Richmond and D.C. Likewise, women frustrated by the disadvantageous gender ratio can reach UVA in an hour and a half, and Georgetown in even less. Both the scenery of the Chesapeake Bay and hiking in the Blue Ridge Mountains are roughly an hour away, due east and west, respectively. On campus, plenty of events are held by various student organizations. Although there are parties both on and off campus on any given weekend, alcohol does not dominate the social scene, and there are no frats or sororities. A band plays the campus snack bar most Thursday nights, and the student council often sponsors dances. "There is always something to do, but it won't come looking for you," says one history major.

(Continued)
Strongest Programs:
Historic Preservation
Psychology
English
Biology
International Affairs

Although the school is fully co-educational, Mary Washington was a women's school as recently as 1970. That legacy lives on in the school's demographics—approximately two-thirds of the student body is female.

The close ties between students and faculty are a great source of pride at Mary Washington, where classes usually have fewer than 25 students and rarely more than 50.

Even though Mary Washington doesn't have a football team, other sports are alive and well. MWC has captured the Capital Athletic Conference All Sports Award for each of the past eight years, and men's and women's cross-country and tennis, and men's soccer have all been championship winners in recent years, with men's tennis recently taking home the state Division III crown. Non-varsity types also use the 76-acre sports and field complex, complete with an Olympic-size pool, for a variety of intramural and club sports, including rugby and crew.

Mary Washington students take an uncommon interest in college traditions. Several annual outdoor parties, including Grill on the Hill and Weststock, never fail to attract a large crowd. All third-year students brace themselves for Junior Ring Week, during which they are the victims of practical jokes prior to receiving their rings from the school's president. Another tradition is Devil-Goat Day, an all-day competition pitting odd- and even-yeared classes against each other in events such as sumo wrestling, jousting, and the Velcro wall. Homecoming is observed with the usual round of sporting events (particularly soccer), dances, and dinners. The multicultural festival is also popular.

With a first-rate liberal arts education in an intimate environment, Mary Washington College is a smart choice for anyone seeking the most bang for their buck. It offers a pleasing blend of beautiful architecture, engaging people, and first rate faculty, all those good things that colleges are supposed to have.

Overlaps

James Madison, University of Virginia, William and Mary, Virginia Tech, University of Richmond.

If You Apply To ➤ Mary Washington...Early decision: Nov. 1. Regular admissions: Feb. 1. Financial aid: Mar. 1. Does not guarantee to meet demonstrated need. Campus interviews: optional, informational. No alumni interviews. SATs or ACTs: required. SAT IIs: recommended. Accepts electronic applications. Essay question: personal statement and your sense of honor.

University of Maryland–College Park

College Park, MD 20742

To bring good luck on their exams, students at the University of Maryland rub the nose of Testudo, the school's terrapin mascot. But even without touching the revered statue, many students feel lucky just to be attending a school with so many course offerings, such a diverse student body, numerous state-of-the-art research programs and institutes—and the kind of parties that bring life to those old college legends. (And that's not even counting the excellent basketball team!) "This what college should feel like," says one impressed student. "A big, beautiful campus, tons of students, a wide variety of classes, and tons of ways to get involved on and off campus. I love it all."

College Park's redbrick and white-pillared Georgian buildings are arranged in graceful quadrangles that punctuate the grassy knolls and valleys of the 1,350-acre campus. Recent additions to campus include a campus recreation center and a 318,000-square-foot performing arts center. As enormous as the campus itself is the range of academic programs—everything from soil conservation to business law. Students choose a major from one of the 14 schools and colleges; Maryland has earned a strong reputation for its engineering, physics, and computer science departments, as well as its Robert H. Smith School of Business and College of

Website: www.umd.edu
Location: Suburban
Total Enrollment: 32,864
Undergraduates: 24,717
Male/Female: 51/49
SAT Ranges: V 560–660 M 580–680
Financial Aid: 42%
Expense: Pub $ $ $
Phi Beta Kappa: Yes
Applicants: 18,731
Accepted: 54%
Enrolled: 39%
Grad in 6 Years: 64%
Returning Freshmen: 90%

Journalism. Students cite the arts and humanities as below par.

Maryland's general education requirements comprise one-third of every undergrad's total courseload, and mandate mastery of basic English and mathematics skills, as well as exposure to human cultural diversity. The requirements also offer a broad-based sampling of courses in all the major academic divisions, and culminate in two interdisciplinary advanced studies courses. For students at the extremes of the academic spectrum, the university provides an honors program and an intensive educational development and tutoring program. College Park Scholars can focus on subjects of particular interest, such as American cultures, environmental studies, and international studies. An individual studies program allows students to combine established majors and create their own programs; other options for those going stir-crazy on campus include internships in Washington and Baltimore and study abroad in Israel, London, and Sri Lanka. The Terrapin Reading Society hosts year-round discussions, movies, lectures, and courses that revolve around one book. More than 2 million other books can be found in the university's seven-branch library system, which also serves as a regional depository for federal documents.

Students say Maryland's academic climate is somewhat competitive and the curriculum is challenging. Lower-level classes tend to be large and impersonal ("easy to hide in, even easier to skip"), but they are broken up into weekly discussion sections led by teaching assistants. The situation improves by junior year, however, when classes of 20 to 40 students become the norm. However, access to professors remains constrained, and many students note that teacher-pupil contact must be student-initiated. Attempts to alleviate this problem include Faculty Appreciation Week and Take-a-Professor-to-Lunch Day. Still, there are exceptions; at least one student says, "Professors are totally accessible—willing to speak with you from their homes and help you get ahead after graduation." Academic advising is hit-or-miss, though.

Seventy-two percent of the students here are from Maryland; New York and New Jersey are also well represented. Middle-class backgrounds predominate, and while many insist it's impossible to stereotype Maryland students, strength and independence are required characteristics for every undergrad at this enormous institution. Admission for in-state residents from the top third of their high school class is easy; out-of-staters face stiffer competition. Just under a third of the students are minorities; 14 percent are African American, 5 percent are Hispanic, and another 14 percent are Asian American. Still, PC isn't an issue, students say; concerns focus on equal rights for all. Decisions on financial aid and housing are affected by acceptance date, so the earlier you apply, the better off you'll be. The school also offers 9,738 merit-based scholarships, ranging from $200 to $17,314, while outstanding male and female athletes vie for 417 additional awards.

Campus housing accommodates 39 percent of students, mainly freshmen and sophomores. Choices include single-sex or coed dorms, described by one student as "fairly basic, nothing special." Housing is guaranteed to all freshmen who return their contracts on time, and assigned to other students by seniority. Freshmen generally live in the high-rises or the low-rises; South Campus features air-conditioning, carpeting, and new furniture. It is often cheaper to live off campus, and many students commute from nearby apartments or home. The university also offers on-campus apartments, and suites on campus usually taken by juniors and seniors. Standard dining hall fare is "adequate, often great, and offered in a wide variety." And there is an endless variety of snack bars and restaurants on campus, including McDonald's and Taco Bell.

Maryland's reputation as a party school is slowly changing, but one student

Maryland has earned a strong reputation for its engineering, physics, and computer science departments, as well as its Robert H. Smith School of Business and College of Journalism.

says the biggest problem remains "students who care more about partying than studying." In the frats, in the dorms, at local pubs, or in nearby D.C., there's always something happening. Campus diversions include a movie theater, bowling alley, and pool—and if that's not enough, a host of beaches and other colleges lurk nearby. The administration's attempts to enforce a "dry campus" policy have posed little problem; students are merely more careful about what they do. For those who want to party sober, the campus sponsors nonalcoholic events every Thursday, Friday, and Saturday evening. Nine percent of the men and 10 percent of the women go Greek, but students contend that no one group sets the tone of campus life. Extracurricular activities and their participants come in every shape and size.

Despite the highly social atmosphere, College Park can sometimes feel too small. Not to worry, though; a few bucks and a few minutes on the Metro brings Terps into downtown D.C. lickety-split. Back on campus, favorite annual events include Art Attack (in which local artists share their crafts), Homecoming, and men's basketball games, for which students turn out en masse. Terrapin fans are unsinkable, despite some of the troubles the athletic program experienced in years past. The men's varsity lacrosse, football, and soccer teams also draw crowds these days, as do women's lacrosse (national champions for the last five years), soccer, and volleyball. Thousands of students claim their moments of glory on the intramural fields, where "participation is high among all types of campus populations."

The undergraduate experience at the University of Maryland is defined by the school's overwhelming size. Largeness can translate into long lines at computer terminals, large classes, parking problems, and hassles everywhere. But it can also be exciting, offering unparalleled learning and friendship-forming opportunities for those who come prepared.

> The Terrapin Reading Society hosts year-round discussions, movies, lectures, and courses that revolve around one book.

Overlaps

Penn State, University of Maryland–Baltimore County, Towson State, Virginia Tech, University of Delaware.

If You Apply To ➤ **Maryland**...Early action: Dec. 1. Regular admissions and financial aid: Feb. 15. Campus interviews: optional, informational. No alumni interviews. SATs: required. SAT IIs: optional. Accepts electronic applications. Essay question: personal values; important academic experience. Students who do not meet academic standards may submit additional information for consideration.

Massachusetts Institute of Technology

Room 3-108, 77 Massachusetts Avenue, Cambridge, MA 02139

MIT is, in a word, excellence. With a student body that averaged near-perfect scores on the math portion of their SATs, and verbal scores not far behind, this is a place that restores faith in the American educational system. Engineering, science, and math are MIT's specialties, but students come here to learn about everything—and learn they certainly do.

MIT is located on 154 acres that extend more than a mile along the Cambridge side of the Charles River basin facing historic Beacon Hill and the central sections of Boston. The main campus of neoclassical architecture carved from limestone was designed by Welles Bosworth and constructed between 1913 and 1920. Since then, more modern designs in brick and glass have been added. The buildings give off a utilitarian aura; most are even known by number instead of

Website: web.mit.edu
Location: Urban
Total Enrollment: 9,885
Undergraduates: 4,372
Male/Female: 59/41
SAT Ranges: V 670–760 M 730–800
ACT Range: 30–33
Financial Aid: 59%

(Continued)

Expense: Pr $ $ $ $
Phi Beta Kappa: Yes
Applicants: 8,250
Accepted: 23%
Enrolled: 55%
Grad in 6 Years: 92%
Returning Freshmen: 97%
Academics: ✍ ✍ ✍ ✍ ✍
Social: ☎ ☎ ☎
Q of L: ★ ★ ★
Admissions: (617) 258-4791
Email Address:
admissions@mit.edu

Strongest Programs:
Engineering
Science
Architecture
Economics
Management

Though students often wonder what life at a so-called typical college would have been like, chances of survival and even satisfaction at MIT are excellent.

by name. Athletic playing fields, recreational buildings, dorms, and dining halls are closely arranged on the campus and provide a sense of unity. Sculptures and murals, including the works of Alexander Calder, Henry Moore, and Louise Nevelson, are found throughout the campus.

Originally called Boston Tech and now frequently referred to as "the Tute," MIT stresses science and engineering studies with a "concern for human values and social goals." Every science and engineering department is superb. The biology department is a leader in medical technology and the search for designer genes. Nevertheless, pure sciences tend to play second fiddle to the engineering fields that, along with computer science, draw the bulk of the majors. Electrical engineering and computer science are almost universally credited as tops in the nation. Students in these two areas may now pursue a five-year-degree option, where they can obtain a professional master's degree upon completion of their studies. Biomedical, chemical, and mechanical engineering, physics, and the tiny aeronautics department are also highly praised programs. The most popular majors include biology, mechanical engineering, chemical engineering, and management. The humanities are strong here as well, though not on par with more technical programs.

MIT has always attracted top nontechnical professors, including such luminaries as linguist Noam Chomsky. Economics, political science, management, urban studies, linguistics, graphics for modern art, and holography—plus anything that can be linked to a computer—are strong, and the tiny minority who major in these subjects receive enough personal attention to make any college student envious. "Some professors really know how to engage the interest of the student," says a senior.

The administration worries that engineers of the future will need to possess not only first-rate technical skills but also a better understanding of the social system in which they will be operating. As one dean put it, "Too many MIT graduates end up working for too many Princeton and Harvard graduates." The general education program does require undergraduates to take at least eight courses that stress such fundamental academic themes as literary traditions and the origins of political institutions. Perhaps to ensure that they will be able to make their future discoveries known, students must also complete a two-phase writing requirement. Technical types are also able to choose a minor in a nontechnical field, in subjects ranging from philosophy to women in society. There's also a four-class physical education requirement as well as a mandatory swimming test to be passed by the end of freshman year.

One of MIT's most successful innovations is the Undergraduate Research Opportunities Program (UROP), a year-round program that facilitates student-faculty research projects. Considered one of the best programs of its kind in the nation, it allows students to earn course credit or stipends for doing research. The Experimental Study Group allows freshmen and sophomores to set a self-paced course of study as they learn through tutorials instead of in the traditional lecture format. Many students have access to even the world-renowned professors and the Nobel Prize winners, who carry lighter teaching loads to allow them time for students and research. Faculty advising is "pretty good for freshmen," one student says, but after that, "it's as good as you make it." The library system, which includes a recently expanded architecture facility, is vast and contains more than 2 million volumes, including some one-of-a-kind manuscripts on the history of science and technology. One library is even open 24 hours a day, and "some students spend the majority of their time (awake or asleep) there," one student reports.

A mandatory pass/fail grading system helps freshmen adjust to "MIT brain-stretching": freshmen receive grades of P, D, or F in all subjects they take. P means C or better performance; Ds or Fs do not receive credit or appear on the permanent record. Grades or not, most MIT students set themselves a breathtaking pace. "MIT is intense and will take you for quite a ride," a biology/premed student says. "The courses demand your full attention and a lot of extra work," another says. Some relief from "tooling" (that is, studying) is found through the optional January period of independent activities offering noncredit seminars, workshops, and activities in fields outside the regular curriculum as well as for-credit subjects. Participation in the engineering co-op program, junior year abroad, or cross-registration at all-female Wellesley College are other helpful ways to get young noses away from the grindstone. Academic and psychological counseling are well thought of by students. A student-run hotline provides all-night peer counseling. Many upperclassmen return to school at least two weeks before classes start, "to help integrate the freshmen."

While MIT somewhat justly earned an image as a "conservative, rich white boys' school" in the past, there is certainly enough racial if not gender variety to beat the rap today. African Americans account for 6 percent of the student body, Hispanics 10 percent, and Asian Americans a hefty 28 percent. If anything, women may feel "a different tone, as the campus is three-fifths male." Almost 100 percent of students come from the top fifth of their high school class, and average SAT and ACT scores are simply mind-boggling. "The average MIT student can be characterized as having a passion and singular drive for what they really want in life," offers a chemical engineering major. MIT helps financially needy students pay the superhefty tuition bill, and it also guarantees to meet demonstrated need. It does not give purely merit or athletic scholarships, but it has its own parent loan fund with favorable interest rates to augment the federal loan programs.

Freshmen decide on their housing arrangements during orientation week, a seven-day ordeal that some claim is the most pressure-packed part of the whole MIT experience. Assigned temporary housing when they first arrive, the confused tenderfeet must, during the first week, be successfully rushed by a fraternity or sorority, join an "independent living group" (sort of like special-interest coed fraternities), or choose a dorm. But there is some relief: all freshmen are now required to live in dorms, eliminating the harried housing gauntlet. Cat lovers will be glad to learn that the MIT administration, which recently cracked down on surreptitiously harbored kitties in dorm rooms, has now backed off its no-pets-except-fish policy and permitted students to bring their beloved cats with them. Cats, however, face one admissions requirement not yet extended to undergraduates: they must be spayed or neutered. Guaranteed housing is either single-sex or coed; the dorms are in the middle of campus, and most of the fraternities and living groups are a mile or less away across the Charles. Ninety-five percent of the undergraduates live on campus, and mandatory meal plans exist, depending on the living group. Some dorms have kitchens, and the meal plan is optional. Dorms without kitchens have a required meal plan. Frat-types feast on spreads prepared by their full-time cooks, and the Kosher Kitchen, run by Hillel, provides some refuge for others.

MIT's social scene is varied. There's Greek life, to which 45 percent of the men and 25 percent of the women belong. Then there are campus movies and lectures. There's the ubiquitous workload, worming its way into the uneasy consciousness of a techie's every waking hour. And there's the great city of Boston, with its many restaurants, clubs, parks, shopping opportunities, and nearly 50 other colleges. On-campus dances, parties, and dorm activities keep other students busy. Most

Almost 100 percent of students come from the top fifth of their high school class, and average SAT and ACT scores are simply mind-boggling.

Supposedly, there are more clubs and organizations at MIT than at any other school in the country, and a sampling of the offerings explains why. The Rocket Society, the Guild of Bell Ringers, a singing group called the Corollaries, and the Exotic Fish Society are only a sampling of the diverse interests on this campus.

on-campus drinking for over-21 students is relaxed and accepted, "as long as the alcohol does not result in unlawful behavior or cause any problems," a student explains. For those with the urge to roam, the multifaceted greater Boston metropolis lies only a few subway stops away.

When the MIT megabrains take a break, practical jokes, or "hacks" (described by one student as "practical jokes with technical merit"), are sure to follow. In past years, popular hacks have included disguising the dome of the main academic building as a giant breast, unscrewing and reversing all the chairs in a 500-seat lecture hall, and, of course, welding shut Harvard's gates. Hacking can also involve late-night explorations by students in the tunnels and shafts that run through restricted parts of the campus, a practice that's definitely frowned upon by the school.

When not studying or hacking, these engineering jocks often turn into real jocks: MIT fields the second-highest number of intercollegiate varsity sports in the country with 39 (Harvard has 42). Athletic accomplishments in the past three years include Constitution Athletic Conference championships in men's cross-country; the New England Women's 8 title in crew; and national championships for the air pistol and women's sports pistol teams. Hockey is popular, and even more popular is the extensive, well-organized intramural program, with sports ranging from Ping-Pong, billiards, and bowling to the more traditional basketball and volleyball. Everyone has access to MIT's extensive athletic facilities. Supposedly, there are more clubs and organizations at MIT than at any other school in the country, and a sampling of the offerings explains why. The Rocket Society, the Guild of Bell Ringers, a singing group called the Corollaries, and the Exotic Fish Society are only a sampling of the diverse interests on this campus.

Though students often wonder what life at a so-called typical college would have been like, chances of survival and even satisfaction at MIT are excellent. Students are able to comprehend the incredible experience of attending one of the nation's leading academic powerhouses. A biology major puts it bluntly: "It will take you right up to what you think your limits are, and then MIT will shatter them and make you realize how great your potential is."

Overlaps

Harvard, Stanford, Princeton, Yale, Cornell University.

If You Apply To ≫   **MIT**…Early action: Nov. 1. Regular admissions: Jan. 1. Financial aid: Jan. 11. Guarantees to meet demonstrated need. Campus interviews: optional, informational. Alumni interviews: required, evaluative. SATs or ACTs: required. SAT IIs: required (writing, history, or science and math). Essay question: create your own question; or explain an opinion you had to defend. Looks for aptitude in math and science.

University of Massachusetts–Amherst

Amherst, MA 01003

Website: www.umass.edu
Location: Small town
Total Enrollment: 25,301
Undergraduates: 19,372
Male/Female: 50/50

The University of Massachusetts at Amherst, a leading land-grant university with more than a century of tradition, offers students a dizzying array of majors and extracurricular options. The school is located in the heart of one of the nation's top college towns, and boasts an extensive research program, a strong honors program, and an endless supply of social opportunities—all at an affordable price. What makes the school special? Try to pick just one aspect from this happy senior's list: "A wide variety of cultures and people from all descents, a wide variety of majors to choose from, a good marching band, a big library, a beautiful campus, and the freedom to do what you want."

UMass's sprawling 1,463-acre campus is centered around a pond full of ducks and swans, while architectural styles range from Colonial to modern. The school is located on the outskirts of Amherst, a city that combines the energy of a bustling cosmopolitan center with the quaintness of an old New England town. Students agree that Amherst caters to college life. New additions on campus include the Animal Care Facility and the first phase of the Engineering and Computer Science Complex, with a second phase on the way.

Of UMass's 10 undergraduate colleges and schools, offerings in management and engineering are top-ranked. Polymer science is notable, as is the English department, which features such names as 1992 Pulitzer Prize-winning poet James Tate, and John Edgar Wideman, a two-time PEN/Faulkner Award winner and MacArthur "Genius Grant" Award recipient. Political science, creative writing and international studies also draw praise. New to the menu are bachelor of arts programs in Earth systems and linguistics, while biology, math, computer science, and the natural sciences are regarded as especially tough. Students report little difficulty getting into courses they want or are required to take. Engineering students may face a bit of a challenge in finishing in four years; they are required to take 130 credit hours while most programs require 120 credit hours.

All undergraduates must complete two courses in writing, six Social World courses including literature, arts/liberal arts, historical studies, social and behavioral sciences, and an interdisciplinary elective, three courses in biological and physical science, one basic math skills course, and a course in analytic reasoning. Freshmen must also complete the College Writing Program, taught in sections of 24 or fewer. The school's honors program, Commonwealth College, offers qualified students special courses and sponsors interdisciplinary seminars, student gatherings, service projects, a newsletter, and a housing option. Students seeking to stand out from the masses (pun intended) might consider the interdisciplinary major in Social Thought and Political Economy or the bachelor's degree in the Individual Concentration program, a design-it-yourself major. The study abroad program offers options in 30 different countries, including Japan, the Netherlands, and Australia. The Center for Student Business offers one of the most unique programs at UMass, allowing students to staff and manage nine campus businesses. Students learn not only how to run the business but also how to work with others and resolve conflicts professionally.

UMass's intellectual and political climate is extraordinarily fertile for a state university, perhaps in part because of its membership in the Five College Consortium. This special alliance allows students to attend UMass and take courses at the other four consortium schools—Amherst College, Smith, Hampshire, and Mount Holyoke. Students say that generally, the quality of teaching at UMass is excellent. Most courses are taught by full professors, and some of the larger ones are broken down into smaller sections with graduate-level teaching assistants. Academic and career counseling is a "helpful resource which is not used enough," according to one junior. A communications major points out that "it is very important that you are assertive and stay in touch with your counselor."

The majority of UMass students are white public school graduates from Massachusetts who make a beeline for the job market after graduation, especially since out-of-state enrollment is capped at 25 percent of students. African Americans and Hispanics make up 10 percent of the student body, while Asian Americans constitute 7 percent. The university has established cultural centers on

(Continued)

SAT Ranges: V 510–620 M
  520–620
Financial Aid: 49%
Expense: Pub $ $ $ $
Phi Beta Kappa: Yes
Applicants: 19,915
Accepted: 69%
Enrolled: 30%
Grad in 6 Years: 60%
Returning Freshmen: 81%
Academics: ✍ ✍ ✍
Social: ☎ ☎ ☎ ☎
Q of L: ★ ★ ★
Admissions: (413) 545-0222
Email Address:
  mail@admissions.umass.edu

Strongest Programs:
  Chemical Engineering
  Computer Science
  Electrical and Computer
  Engineering
  English/Creative Writing
  Linguistics
  Philosophy
  Psychology

Polymer science is notable, as is the English department, which features such names as 1992 Pulitzer Prize-winning poet James Tate, and John Edgar Wideman, a two-time PEN/Faulkner Award winner and MacArthur "Genius Grant" Award recipient.

Engineering students may face a bit of a challenge in finishing in four years; they are required to take 130 credit hours while most programs require 120 credit hours.

campus providing activities and support for students from different backgrounds, but affirmative action is still an issue, students report. "There are always rallies about better programs and aid for minorities," says a senior. Students from other New England states are treated as Massachusetts residents for admission purposes if their own state schools don't offer the programs they want.

UMass has the sixth-largest residence hall system in the country. Forty-two dorms, organized in five residential areas, house 58 percent of students. Freshmen can choose single-sex or coed living and also submit a list of their preferred living areas, and they're required to live on campus through sophomore year. About half of the freshmen end up in the Southwest Area, a "huge, citylike complex" with five high-rise towers and 11 low-rise residence halls. The university is expanding its Residential Academic Programs that allow first-year students with similar interests to live and study together in specialized interdisciplinary courses to ease their transition into campus life. Approximately 40 percent of freshmen participate. "The dorms are fun at times, but bathroom cleanliness is horrible," says a finance major.

UMass offers an abundant social life, marked by "noisy dorms, overflowing fraternities, off-campus parties," says a freshman. Both on campus and off, alcohol policies are strict and well-enforced. First-time underage offenders are sent to alcohol education programs. Those 21 and over can patronize one of Amherst's dozen bars or drink at two on-campus spots. About two dozen fraternities and sororities occupy the time of 5 percent of the men and 4 percent of the women, but they are somewhat out of the mainstream. A free public transportation system allows maximum mobility not only among the Five Colleges but also to nearby towns, which are graced with a number of exceptional bookshops. The annual Spring Concert around the pond is a daylong event where musicians such as U2, Bob Dylan, and the Beastie Boys perform.

Settled in the Pioneer Valley and surrounded by the Berkshire foothills, Amherst is close to good skiing, hiking, and canoeing areas. It's also 90 miles west of Boston, 150 miles north of New York City, and 25 miles south of Vermont and New Hampshire, making a car very useful (and very expensive if you get too many tickets from overzealous campus cops, students say). Varsity sports are popular and UMass has been a model for achieving gender equity in athletics. Men's basketball is a national powerhouse; "Midnight Madness," the first men's basketball practice of the season, held annually at midnight with everyone invited, is a hot campus ticket. The football team recently won a conference championship, as have men's baseball and swimming and women's basketball, crew, cross-country, field hockey, softball, soccer, and track. Two on-campus gyms offer excellent facilities for the recreational athlete, and two Olympic-size skating rinks mark the recent reintroduction of intercollegiate hockey to the university.

UMass is big enough to offer a vast number of academic and extracurricular opportunities, but also big enough to feel impersonal and overwhelming. "It is such a typical university rat race!" grumps a freshman. While this is tempered by its participation in the Five College Consortium, which gives students access to four leading New England private colleges, UMass might be best for students assured of what they want to do after graduation—and not shy about demanding guidance to get there. "There is a good atmosphere here," confirms a sophomore. "The students are friendly, and the town is very accommodating."

Overlaps

Northeastern, Boston University, Boston College, University of Connecticut, University of Rhode Island.

McGill University, Canada—See CANADIAN UNIVERSITIES

Miami University (OH)

301 S. Campus Avenue, Oxford, OH 45056

Some people might mistake Miami University for its similarly named counterpart in Florida, but the students here know the school has a well-respected reputation of its own. Its name comes from the Miami Indian tribe. After nearly 70 years, Miami University has changed the name of its sports teams from the Redskins to the Redhawks, out of respect for Native Americans. The university will, however, keep using the portrait of an Indian chief as its logo since the Miami Tribe urged them to do so. One of the premier public institutions in the nation, Miami University offers an outstanding academics program, an excellent faculty, active social life, and a beautiful campus all in one location.

The university is staked out on 2,000 wooded acres in the center of an urban triangle of approximately 3 million people, encompassing Cincinnati and Dayton, Ohio, and Richmond, Indiana. The campus is dressed in the modified Georgian style of the Colonial American period and it remains as impeccably groomed as its students. Ground has been broken on a new academic center and a training facility for athletes.

Miami University was founded in 1809 to provide a classical liberal education, and has never strayed from its central commitment to liberal arts. Still, many of the university's strongest offerings are in the School of Business Administration. Other popular programs include accounting, architecture, international studies, education, and zoology. For those with an inclination toward forestry or the paper industry, the university's unique pulp and paper science technology degree is in a league of its own. Miami also offers a 3–2 program in engineering, and a new biochemistry major has recently been added. Students say the theater and history departments could use improvement.

The academic atmosphere at Miami is fairly competitive but not cutthroat. "The classes are challenging, and a great majority of students put academic performance first, making peer interaction a big plus," says one English major. University requirements, or foundation courses, provide for a broad education, and all undergraduates must complete foundation courses in English composition, fine arts, humanities, social sciences and world cultures, biological and physical sciences, and mathematics, formal reasoning, or technology. Additional requirements include 12 credits of advanced liberal education focus consisting of

Website: www.muohio.edu

Location: Rural

Total Enrollment: 16,575

Undergraduates: 15,288

Male/Female: 45/55

SAT Ranges: V 540–630 M 550–660

ACT Range: 24–28

Financial Aid: N/A

Expense: Pub $ $

Phi Beta Kappa: Yes

Applicants: 11,993

Accepted: 79%

Enrolled: 38%

Grad in 6 Years: 79%

Returning Freshmen: 90%

Academics: ✐ ✐ ✐

Social: ☎ ☎ ☎

Q of L: ★ ★ ★

Admissions: (513)529-2531

Email Address:
admission@muohio.edu

Strongest Programs:
Paper Science Engineering
Accountancy
Business Economics
Music
Zoology

(Continued)
Education
International Studies
Architecture

For those with an inclination toward forestry or the paper industry, the university's unique pulp and paper science technology degree is in a league of its own.

Miami also offers a 3–2 program in engineering and a new biochemistry major has recently been added.

The John E. Dolibois European Center in Luxembourg offers a semester or yearlong program in the liberal arts, and an opportunity to live with a foreign family.

9 credits of thematic and sequential study in-depth outside of the student's major, and 3 credits of the Senior Capstone Experience, which ties in liberal education with the specialized knowledge of their major.

The professors at Miami are described as "exceptional." "Teaching is [Miami's] biggest strength," raves one senior. "The personal attention and concern I got was not what I expected at a university this size." Fifty percent of classes have less than 25 students, and most are taught by full professors. While getting into required classes can sometimes be a problem, especially with foundation classes, students report that the professors will usually let you into the class if you plead your case. Approximately 40 percent of students take advantage of a wide array of study abroad opportunities. The John E. Dolibois European Center in Luxembourg offers a semester or yearlong program in the liberal arts, and an opportunity to live with a foreign family. Exchange programs with universities in Denmark, Japan, Brazil, Mexico, Austria, and England are available as well as summer programs in France, Italy, Germany, and Scotland. Majors in biochemistry and engineering technology have been added to the curriculum.

Ninety percent of the student body are white, and mostly from middle- or upper-middle-class families. Seventy-three percent of students are from Ohio, and the campus has a reputation for conservatism. In recent years, Miami has begun an effort to attract more students of color, but for the moment, African Americans account for only 4 percent of the students, Asian Americans 2 percent, and Hispanics 2 percent. "Miami's students are harder to characterize than some would believe," insists a senior. "There are liberals and conservatives, and dozens of ethnic cultures on campus." Through a community forum model developed by the Kettering Foundation, the university holds a series of problem-solving forums addressing issues facing African American students on campus. Miami also holds a series of workshops for faculty, staff, and students on creating a safe environment for gay, lesbian, and bisexual students on campus.

Miami has a lively on- and off-campus social life, although students complain that social restrictions on campus are on the rise. "Many get busted for underage drinking. If you get caught you have to take a substance abuse class and do 100 hours of community service," explains one senior. A lot of socializing takes place in the restaurants, bars, and clubs of Oxford. Despite changing priorities, however, since the Greek life is alive and well at Miami, with 24 percent of the men and 27 percent of the women involved in fraternities or sororities. In fact, Miami is known for the fact that several fraternities started here. "Greeks are very active and provide a lot of on-campus activities," says a marketing major. Dorm rooms are reported to be very nice and well-kept, if "a little small." A few of the dorms remain single-sex and are accompanied by visitation rules. Most upperclassmen find good, cheap off-campus housing by their senior year, but remain very involved on campus.

The town of Oxford also inspires loyalty, as one students explains: "The students comprise two-thirds of its population, and most of its shops cater to the students. It is a wonderful and distinct 'college town.'" Those seeking urban action and romantic dining may have to travel to Cincinnati, which is about 35 miles away. Much of the recreational activity on campus revolves around athletics. The well-organized intramural program provides teams for just about every sport (including the ever-popular korfball and broomball), and the Student Recreational Sports Facility offers a complete range of fitness opportunities. Swimming, tennis, and volleyball are among Miami's best varsity sports, but football, which in recent years has regularly defeated highly ranked opponents, and men's basketball reign as the most popular spectator sports. The men's baseball team brought home the 2000 MAC conference trophy. Ice hockey, which is one of the top 10 programs in the country, is also extremely popular, and the women's precision ice skating team is the only one at collegiate level in the nation. For cycling enthusiasts, the annual 20/20 Bike Race is one of the largest collegiate events of its kind in the U.S. Other annual events include Green Beer Day in March, Make a Difference Day in cooperation with Oxford, Homecoming, and continued rivalries with Ohio University.

Although Miami University of Ohio's academic reputation has been largely regional in the past, it is now gaining national recognition as an excellent state university. The administration is always striving for improvement, with a current goal to be in the top 25 of national schools by 2009, and students seem ready to help lift their school into the upper echelons. T-shirts around campus fiercely proclaim students' pride: "Miami University was a college before Florida was a state!"

> ## Overlaps
> **Ohio University, Ohio State, Indiana University, Dayton, Notre Dame.**

If You Apply To ➤ | **Miami**…Early decision: Nov. 1. Regular admissions: Jan. 31. Financial aid: Feb. 15. Housing: May 1. Does not guarantee to meet demonstrated need. Campus interviews: optional, informational. No alumni interviews. SATs or ACTs: required. SAT IIs: optional. Accepts electronic applications. Essay question: what would you change about your school or community, or topic of student's choice.

University of Miami

P.O. Box 248025, Coral Gables, FL 33124-4616

Year-round sunshine and the colorful Miami culture could tempt even the most dedicated students to leave their desks behind. But at the University of Miami, students can have their fun and get a solid education at the same time. "The first thing I noticed about UM that made me fall in love with it, was its complete balance of academic and social atmosphere," says a junior physical therapy major. "Students at UM like to hang out, but they also know they are here to study." Miami is steadily growing and improving in many academic areas, while reining in the legacy of past excesses.

Twenty minutes from Key Biscayne and Miami's beaches, and 10 minutes from downtown Miami, the university's 260-acre campus is located in tranquil suburbia. With its own lake in the middle of the campus (and on the cover of most brochures), the campus is architecturally varied from postwar international style structures to modern buildings, most with open-air breezeways to let in the warm, salty winds. Recent construction includes the Cobb Stadium for soccer and track and field, and the Ryder Convocation Center, a multipurpose facility.

Miami has one of the nation's top programs in marine biology, and was the first university to offer a degree in music engineering. Miami's main strengths are in the preprofessional and professional areas. The school also boasts an unusual program in jazz, and students recommend any of the strong premed offerings. Chemistry majors have access to a nuclear magnetic resonance spectrometer, an essential tool for modern chemistry. The school's six-year medical program for outstanding students, and dual degree (grad/undergrad) programs in law, marine science, business, physical therapy, biomedical engineering, and medicine receive high marks. Women's studies and philosophy are said to be weaker. The newest

Website: www.miami.edu
Location: Suburban
Total Enrollment: 13,715
Undergraduates: 8,628
Male/Female: 45/55
SAT Ranges: V 520–630 M 530–640
ACT Range: 22–27
Financial Aid: 58%
Expense: Pr $ $ $
Phi Beta Kappa: Yes
Applicants: 12,264
Accepted: 55%
Enrolled: 28%
Grad in 6 Years: 61%
Returning Freshmen: 83%
Academics: ✑ ✑ ✑
Social: ☎ ☎ ☎ ☎
Q of L: ★ ★ ★
Admissions: (305) 284-4323

(Continued)

Email Address:
admission@admiss.msmail.
miami.edu

Strongest Programs:
Marine Science
Music
Business
Political Science
Biology/Premed

Though hurricane season hits most of the Southeast coast in late summer, in Miami, 'Cane season lasts straight through New Year's, when the football team is typically found battling it out in a prestigious postseason bowl game.

major is media business, while the real estate and sports management programs have been dropped.

Students report that most classes at this "laid-back" school have 25 or fewer students, and give professors high marks for knowledge and accessibility. Most courses are taught by full professors. Though many have a pre-professional bent, students at Miami receive a broad liberal arts education. Distribution requirements vary from school to school, but general education requirements include proficiency in English composition, mathematics, and writing across the curriculum (courses that involve a substantial amount of writing). In addition, a certain number of credits must be earned in each of three areas of knowledge: natural sciences, social sciences, and arts and humanities. Students looking for a change of pace can take advantage of Miami's summer semester program in the Caribbean. In addition, the study abroad program offers options at 50 schools in countries such as Australia, Israel, France, Japan, the Netherlands, and Argentina.

Highly motivated students in any field can apply to the school's comprehensive honors program, which enrolls students who were in the top tenth of their high school class and have a combined SAT score of at least 1360. UM still attracts its share—though it's declining—of beach bums who drop by for a couple of classes in the morning, spend the rest of the day at the shore, and almost never see the inside of the library. That's a shame, though; the facility is one of the best in the region, with more than 2 million bound volumes and another 3-million-plus on microform.

Thirty-seven percent of UM's students come from out of state, mostly from the Northeast, Ohio, and the Chicago area. UM is unique among universities of its caliber in the incredible diversity of its student body; Hispanics account for a substantial 30 percent of the total, African Americans 12 percent, and Asian Americans 5 percent. Students say that diversity is one of UM's best assets. "Everyone here has a place, and it's very rare that someone feels unwelcome," says one student. The school's large number of Hispanics is traceable to the influx of Cuban and other Caribbean refugees into southern Florida, and at times it seems that Spanish is the mother tongue on campus. The Latin influence mixes colorfully with that of the wealthier New Yorkers, many of whom view their time at "Sunshine U" as an extended vacation. The one characteristic everyone seems to share is the hope of getting high-paying jobs after graduation. Nearly 3,500 merit scholarships and 203 athletic awards ease the school's hefty price tag for qualified students.

Miami offers a distinctive system of five coed residential colleges, modeled after those at Yale University. Each college is directed by a Master, a senior faculty member who organizes seminars, concerts, lectures, social events, and the monthly community dinner. Faculty members often host study breaks in their homes and provide guest speakers from all walks of life to discuss current issues. Generally, students give the dorms low marks. "Housing on campus is not great," says one junior. "Much of it is not up-to-date." Maybe that's why slightly less than half of undergrads live on campus; others bunk in off-campus apartments or Greek houses. Still, all dorm housing at Miami is coed, and students can choose apartment-style housing when they tire of the residential colleges' closeness. Scrounging up grub on campus is easy; the residential colleges have their own cafeterias with a variety of plans, from 5 to 20 meals, and there is a kosher alternative.

On the weekends, Miami students frequent nearby bars or the Campus Rat, home also to the popular Fifth Quarter post-football-game parties. On-campus alcohol policies are relatively strict for underage students, sometimes including parental notification for offenses. Fraternities still manage to thrive, accounting for 12 percent of the men and providing a space for most of the underage drinking at UM (although not during rush, which is dry). The sororities, with no housing of their own, attract 12 percent of the women. Many of the frats and sororities are small (averaging about 30 members), but they often join forces in throwing parties.

If keg parties aren't your scene, though, UM offers a plethora of other social opportunities. Those who shun sand between their toes bike down to the boutiques in Coconut Grove, Bayside, or South Beach, or attend on-campus events, such as International Week, Sportsfest, and the Cardboard Boat Races. "The majority of students at Miami fit into the trendy, clubbing profile," explains a psychology major. "They like trendy up-to-date clothes, and going to clubs in order to see and be seen." Public transportation runs in front of the residential colleges, but most students recommend a car in order to get "the full Florida effect." Parking can be a problem, though, says a senior: "If you want a parking space, you need to get to school by 8:00 A.M., and parking decals are way too expensive." The best road trips are Key West, Key Largo, and, of course, UM football games, especially those against Florida State.

Though hurricane season hits most of the Southeast coast in late summer, in Miami, 'Cane season lasts straight through New Year's, when the football team is typically found battling it out in a prestigious postseason bowl game. Although football is undisputed king of the hill on campus, the baseball squad has won a College World Series and represented the U.S. in the World Baseball Tournament for Peace in Russia. Several individual titles were won in diving and the men's tennis recently won the Big East Championship. A $11 million rec center, with juice bar and spa, and the annual intramural Sportsfest, also draw crowds.

It's hard to imagine a school in the perpetual sunshine of Florida without a generous allotment of fun, and UM is no exception. Life really is a beach for students at the University of Miami, although its days as a beach bum hideout are long over. These days, UM students are just as likely to search long and hard for the perfect instrumental phrase or mathematical proof as they are to scope out the perfect wave. Perhaps that's why so many students head for UM. It offers the best of both worlds—academics and fun!

Students say that diversity is one of UM's best assets. "Everyone here has a place, and it's very rare that someone feels unwelcome," says one student.

Overlaps

University of Florida, Florida State, Florida International University, NYU, Boston University.

If You Apply To ➤ | **Miami**…Early decision and early action: Nov. 15. Regular admissions: Mar. 1. Financial aid: Feb. 15. Does not guarantee to meet demonstrated need. No alumni or campus interviews. SATs or ACTs: required. SAT IIs: optional. Apply to particular schools or programs. Accepts the Common Application and electronic applications. Essay question: experience or achievement that is special to you; personal, local, or national concern important to you; person who has had significant influence on you; role of academic integrity.

Michigan State University

250 Administration Building, East Lansing, MI 48824

Michigan State began as an agricultural school, and like most seeds planted in well-tended fields, the school's "cash crop"—a solid education in a friendly and fun-loving atmosphere—grows stronger each year. "Coming from a small town, MSU was perfect for me," says a prelaw student. "It offers all the positive aspects of a large city and the safety of a town." The school's focus has broadened to

Website: www.msu.edu
Location: City outskirts
Total Enrollment: 43,381

(Continued)

Undergraduates: 33,571

Male/Female: 47/53

SAT Ranges: V 480–610 M
500–630

ACT Range: 21–26

Financial Aid: 42%

Expense: Pub $ $ $ $

Phi Beta Kappa: Yes

Applicants: 22,751

Accepted: 66%

Enrolled: 67%

Grad in 6 Years: 69%

Returning Freshmen: 87%

Academics: ✍ ✍ ✍

Social: ☎ ☎ ☎ ☎

Q of L: ★ ★ ★

Admissions: (517) 355-8332

Email Address:
admis@pilot.msu.edu

Strongest Programs:
Hotel, Restaurant, and
Institutional Management
Packaging
Veterinary Medicine
Engineering
Accounting
Education

*With 80 study abroad
programs located in over 40
countries around the world,
it's not surprising that MSU
sent more than 1,300
students to terms away last
year, more than any other
U.S. research university.*

include would-be engineers, entrepreneurs, hoteliers, and doctors of the veterinary, traditional, and osteopathic persuasions, in addition to future farmers. But the more than 40,000 students who populate East Lansing have one thing in common: "Everyone has a smile for you here," says a communications major. "I noticed it from the first day."

MSU's parklike campus is a unique blend of the traditional and the innovative. The older heart of the campus, north of the Red Cedar River, boasts ivy-covered brick buildings, some built before the Civil War and listed on the National Register of Historic Places. This area houses five colleges, and includes the MSU Union and 10 residence halls. Across the Red Cedar is the medical complex, the modern residence hall complexes, and not one but two 18-hole golf courses. On the southernmost part of campus are University Farms, where researchers keep up MSU's reputation as a premier land-grant university through work in agricultural and animal production. Newest campus additions include the Detroit College of Law building, the Pavilion for Agriculture and Livestock Education, and a major addition to the engineering building.

The academic climate at MSU can be as daunting as its size. "Most classes are fairly difficult, and require a fair amount of reading," says a chemistry major. "But because most classes are graded on a sliding scale, rather than a hard curve, cooperative learning plays a major role." The computerized enrollment system has done away with long registration lines, and advisors can help with overrides for classes that are technically full. Most lectures are given by professors, who students describe as caring and "very approachable." Reports a microbiology major, "Most professors seem to enjoy teaching but, of course, not all can do it well." Labs and smaller recitation sections are led by less-skilled TAs, students say. "Math classes are hard enough, but add a foreign TA and it can be impossible," one laments. Also controversial among students is the technique of teaching some classes via cassettes or videotapes, followed by 20-minute discussion sessions with graduate assistants and one writing session per week. But in general, students praise the teaching, especially in smaller, upper-level courses, which garner more personal attention from the top professors. Academic advising also gets high marks: "I have had as much help as I was willing to take advantage of," says a junior.

As a land-grant university, MSU traditionally has been strong in agriculture and preveterinary science. However, psychology, accounting, finance, engineering, education, and criminal justice are also among the school's top drawing cards. Math is cited as weaker than most. Recent curricular additions include environmental biology and zoo and aquarium science. MSU boasts the nation's first school of packaging, and student trainees from the Hotel, Restaurant, and Institutional Management program staff the university hotel.

To graduate, all students must complete 26 credits of integrative studies in four areas: arts and humanities; general science; social, behavioral, and economic science; and transcollegiate courses. There is a strong international component, too. With 80 study abroad programs located in over 40 countries around the world, it's not surprising that MSU sent more than 1,300 students to terms away last year, more than any other U.S. research university.

Despite MSU's farm-school heritage, most students are urban types from the state of Michigan. They're not all the same, though. Indeed, blacks and Hispanics account for 11 percent of students, and Asian Americans make up 4 percent. Relationships across ethnic and racial lines are calm, a communications major says: "Sharing of views, and respect for others' views, is encouraged." Each year hundreds of students win scholarships for outstanding academic performance;

athletic scholarships lure devotees of many different sports.

With a capacity of nearly 18,000, MSU's residence system is the largest of any university in the nation. Almost half of all undergrads live on campus. MSU has divided its massive college into two smaller residential colleges, James Madison (organized around the social sciences) and Lyman Briggs (emphasizing the natural sciences and math). Each houses fewer than 1,000 students, and aims to create the feeling of a small undergraduate institution. Three much bigger living-learning complexes, each with about four residence halls, are also available, giving residents access to libraries, faculty offices, classrooms, counseling, cafeterias, and recreation areas. An honors college brings the brightest freshmen together, houses them separately if they wish, and assigns them a special advisor. Other living-learning programs, known by their catchy acronyms, include RISE (focus on the environment), ROIAL (arts and letters), ROSES (science and engineering), and STAR (Support-Teamwork-Achievement-Resources).

Freshmen and sophomores usually live in "clean and well-maintained" residence halls with populations from 250 to more than 1,200. The halls offer various living options, including single-sex or coed, high-rise or low-rise, smoking or nonsmoking, and extra quiet or alcohol-free. Room and board includes various meal plans at any of the cafeterias sprinkled throughout the residence halls, all of which receive good reviews. For juniors and seniors, apartment living often becomes the thing, in college-owned facilities or in East Lansing. But parking places are in chronically short supply. Fraternity and sorority members mostly live in their own off-campus houses. And despite its bucolic surroundings, campus safety is as much of an issue here as anywhere: State has its own police force, green light emergency phone system, and riding and walking escort services for those who need to travel at night. "All of this, plus common sense, makes students feel safe," a sophomore says.

With so many people concentrated in one spot, it's no wonder the residence halls and active Greek system (9 percent of the student population) sponsor popular MSU social events. As at most schools, the rule on alcohol is "no one under 21 is served," but a zero-tolerance policy—meaning that police can breathalyze any student suspected of being under the influence—gives the rule teeth here. Other popular leisure-time fare includes picnics, pizza-eating contests, hall Olympics, hayrides, and ice-skating outings. The annual Michigan Festival brings big-name performers such as R.E.M., Elton John, and the Red Hot Chili Peppers to campus. The town of East Lansing, where the Land Shark and Rick's are popular hangouts, is a short walk from campus and many students do volunteer work in the community.

Weekends are dominated by Big 10 athletic competitions, with the Michigan-MSU rivalry especially fierce. A sophomore proudly describes the pregame ritual: "During the week before the U of M-MSU football game, students guard our mascot Sparty, the largest free-standing ceramic statue in the world, and protect him from sneaky Wolverines." More than a few times, the Spartans have upset their archrivals in football and basketball; the latter team even won last year's NCAA championship. The marching band is also a national award winner.

With so many stand-out programs in such a pretty, friendly place, it's easier to see why students here are so incredibly content. Once they get recover from the initial shock caused by State's large size, most thrive on the opportunities offered at such a large school.

Despite its bucolic surroundings, campus safety is as much of an issue here as anywhere: State has its own police force, green light emergency phone system, and riding and walking escort services for those who need to travel at night.

The annual Michigan Festival brings big-name performers such as R.E.M., Elton John, and the Red Hot Chili Peppers to campus.

Overlaps

University of Michigan, Western Michigan, Central Michigan, Oakland University, University of Illinois.

University of Michigan

1220 Student Activities Building, Ann Arbor, MI 48109-1316

Website: www.umich.edu
Location: Urban
Total Enrollment: 37,846
Undergraduates: 24,493
Male/Female: 50/50
SAT Ranges: V 570–670 M 600–710
ACT Range: 26–30
Financial Aid: 47%
Expense: Pub $ $ $ $
Phi Beta Kappa: Yes
Applicants: 21,132
Accepted: 64%
Enrolled: 41%
Grad in 6 Years: 83%
Returning Freshmen: 97%
Academics: ᎗ ᎗ ᎗ ᎗ ᎗
Social: ☎ ☎ ☎
Q of L: ★ ★ ★
Admissions: (734) 764-7433
Email Address:
  ugadmiss@umich.edu

Strongest Programs:
  Premed
  Engineering
  Art and Design
  Architecture
  Music
  Film and Television
  Journalism/Communications
  Business

One of the nation's elite public universities, Michigan offers its students an excellent faculty, dynamite athletics, an endless number of special programs—all the other benefits of a world-class American university. "Michigan is a special place because it has a deep history and reputation," says a senior. "It is an excellent school and no matter what degree you have, it is respected."

Situated on 3,129 acres, Michigan's campus is so extensive that newcomers may want to come equipped with maps and a compass to find their way to class. The university is divided into two main campuses. Central Campus, the heart of the university, houses most of Michigan's 19 schools and colleges. North Campus, which is two miles northeast of Central, is home to the College of Engineering, School of Music, School of Art and Design, College of Architecture and Urban Planning, and the new Media Union. Other campus areas include the Medical Center complex containing 7 hospitals and 15 outpatient facilities, and South Campus, featuring state-of-the art athletic facilities. Architecturally, the main drag of campus features a wide range of styles, from the classical Angell Hall to the Gothic Law Quad. Recent renovations include a new parking deck, stadium expansion, and refurbished residence halls, with more projects on the way.

Academically, students describe the courses as challenging and rigorous but not cutthroat competitive. "Although some students are overly ambitious, most are willing to share their notes and study together," says a senior. The university ranks among the best in the nation in so many fields of study, mainly because it attracts some of the biggest names in academia to teach and research in Ann Arbor. The College of Literature, Science, and the Arts is the largest school at Michigan. The College of Engineering and School of Business Administration are well respected, and the university's programs in health-related fields are also top-notch. Students report that professors are "knowledgeable." One student says, "The professors here are intelligent and seem to enjoy teaching." Students claim excellent academic and career advising is available but only for those who seek it. The administration, however, notes the advising office, which registers nearly 12,000 clients each year, offers individually tailored services like counseling appointments, programs, and workshops. The Career Planning and Placement Office processes about 120,000 transactions each year, provides individual and group career counseling/planning and individual job placement, and works with 950 companies annually in recruiting UM graduating students.

One of Michigan's most distinct characteristics is its special academic programs, which seek to offer the best of both worlds—personalized attention and a large university setting. Approximately 627 active degree programs, including about 226 undergraduate majors as well as individualized concentrations are offered, mainly through the College of Literature, Science, and the Arts. Some of these special programs include double majors, accelerated programs, independent study, field study, and internships. In addition, students can choose from several small interdisciplinary programs. The instructors live and teach in the residential hall in the Residential College and the Lloyd's Scholar Programs. The Comprehensive Studies Program allows students to become part of a community of scholars to work in programs designed to best realize an individual student's potential.

The University of Michigan's Honors Program, considered to be one of the best in the nation, offers qualified students special honors courses, opportunities to participate in individual research or collaborative research, seminars, and special academic advisors. A preferred admissions program guarantees 150 top high school students admission to Michigan's professional programs in business, engineering, architecture, or pharmacy, provided they make satisfactory progress during their first years. The Undergraduate Research Opportunities Program enables students to work outside the classroom with a small group of students and a faculty member of their choice. The most popular majors at University of Michigan are business administration, mechanical engineering, psychology, English, and political science, but students say the statistics department needs improvement. Michigan also offers a number of foreign language majors not found many other places, including Arabic, Armenian, Persian, Turkish, and Islamic Studies. The newest addition to the undergraduate program is the athletic training major.

No courses are required of all freshmen at Michigan, but all students are required to complete some coursework in English (including composition), foreign languages, natural sciences, social sciences, and humanities. Students in the College of Literature, Science, and the Arts must also take courses in quantitative reasoning and race or ethnicity. In addition, the university offers a series of seminars designed specifically for freshmen and sophomores, which are taught by tenured and tenure-track faculty.

Off-campus opportunities abound at the UM. Students have the chance to visit and study abroad in more than 30 different countries, including Australia, China, Costa Rica, Finland, France, Greece, India, Ireland, Japan, Russia, Sweden, and Turkey. Some specific programs include a year abroad in a French or German university, a business program in Paris, summer internships in selected majors, and special trips organized by individual departments.

The University of Michigan's admissions office sifts through some of the best students in the country, with 63 percent of the students in the top tenth of their high school class. Two-thirds of the undergraduates are from Michigan. The student body is remarkably diverse for a state university. In fact, Michigan's Program on Intergroup Relations, Conflict, and Community has been recognized by former President Clinton's Initiative on Race as one of 14 "promising practices" that successfully bridge racial divides in communities across America. Minorities now comprise one-fourth of UM's total enrollment, an all-time high. African Americans and Hispanics combined make up 13 percent of the student body, and Asian Americans make up another 12 percent. There is a large and well-organized Jewish community at Michigan, and gays and lesbians are also organized and prominent. While the student body is more conservative today than it was a decade ago, it is still "most noticeably liberal," says a history major, and political issues flare up from time to time on campus.

Michigan really socks it to out-of-staters with a $13,000-plus surcharge. However, the university guarantees to meet the demonstrated financial need of all admitted Michigan residents. Students can also vie for merit scholarships of up to $25,000, as well as 408 athletic scholarships for men and women. Dormitories at

The University of Michigan's Honors Program, considered to be one of the best in the nation, offers qualified students special honors courses, opportunities to participate in individual or collaborative research, seminars, and special academic advisors.

One of the University of Michigan's most distinctive characteristics is its special academic programs, which seek to offer the best of both worlds—personalized attention and a large university setting.

University of Michigan traditionally have well-defined personalities. Sixties-inspired types and "eccentrics" find the East Quad the "most open-minded dorms" (the residential college is here). The Hill dorms are "more sedate." For those seeking alternative housing arrangements, a plethora of special-interest housing is available, including substance-free residence halls. On-campus housing is comfortable and well maintained. "The dorms are a tad small but livable with a little bit of work," says a history major. Overcrowding is a thing of the past thanks to a major renewal and improvement project; residence halls were actually under capacity last fall. Housing is guaranteed for all incoming freshmen, leaving many upperclassmen to play the lottery. For the student who wants to live off campus, the UM housing office provides information, listings, and advice for finding suitable accommodations. Other alternatives include fraternity and sorority houses, and a large number of college- and privately owned co-ops.

Detroit is a little less than an hour away, but most students become quite fond of the picturesque town of Ann Arbor. "It's a great city with something for everyone," says a political science major. "There are coffeehouses, bars, sporting events, movie theaters, and a lot more." A surprising variety of visual and performing arts are offered in town and on campus. Underage drinking is not allowed, and a senior has a stern warning for any potential schemers: "Your fake ID will be taken. Plan on it. Do not be surprised, no matter how good it is." An annual art fair held in Ann Arbor draws craftspeople from throughout the nation and Canada, and the annual Hash Bash appeals to students' bohemian sides. Many lakes and swimming holes lie only a short drive away and seem to keep the large summer-term population happy. As one junior says, "we are ranked high enough to be known for our academic success, but we still have a reputation for having a good time." Michigan winters, though, are known for being cold and brutal. Eighteen percent of the undergraduates go Greek, though these groups are the bane of campus liberals. Many students also volunteer in the community. One senior explains, "Most students get involved, especially if it has something to do with helping kids."

Football overshadows nearly everything each fall as students gather to cheer, "Go Blue." In 1999, the Wolverines football team won the Big Ten Conference championship, as did the baseball, men's cross-country, men's and women's gymnastics, women's indoor track, and the women's softball teams. Attending football games is an integral part of the UM experience, students say, and "you shouldn't be allowed to graduate if you haven't gone to a hockey game," quips a sophomore. Intramurals, which were invented at the University of Michigan, provide students with a more casual form of athletics.

The University of Michigan strives to offer its students a delicate balance between academics, athletics, and social activities. On one hand, this is American college as it's characterized in movies like *Animal House*—football and fraternities. But it's also a college with a fine faculty and top-rated programs, intent upon making America competitive in the 21st century. For assertive students who crave spirit and action as well as outstanding academics, Michigan is an excellent choice.

Overlaps

Michigan State, Northwestern, Cornell University, Duke, Penn.

If You Apply To > **Michigan**...Rolling admissions. Regular admissions: Feb. 1. Financial aid: Mar. 15. Guarantees to meet demonstrated need of in-state students. Campus and alumni interviews: optional, informational. SATs or ACTs: required. SAT IIs: optional. Essay question: personal statement. Apply to particular school or program. Policies and deadlines vary by school.

One of New England's top liberal arts colleges, Middlebury College is home to many proud "Midd Kids," a group that students say is defined by its intelligent, competitive nature. The school's picturesque campus and rural Vermont charm have fostered the nickname "Club Midd," yet this highly selective and academically demanding school is anything but a vacation. It is renowned for outstanding, immersion-based summer foreign language programs, paired with exciting opportunities in areas ranging from international studies to environmental science.

The college's 350-acre main campus is situated on a hill overlooking the village of Middlebury, Vermont which one junior describes as "very much a college town." Community members support the school's activities and sporting events. The 1,800-acre mountain campus, site of the Bread Loaf School of English, the Bread Loaf Writers' Conference, and the college's Ski Bowl, is nearby. Walking across the campus on historic Old Stone Row, one is taken back to the college's founding in 1800 and reminded of the simple lines and rectangular shapes of the mills of early New England. The campus buildings of marble and limestone are aligned in quadrangles that afford vistas of the Adirondacks and Green Mountains. Middlebury has undergone many recent facility additions including a new science building with over 100,000 square feet of lab, library, and observatory space.

Despite the recent building boom, Middlebury's priorities are academic. And within its hallowed halls, Middlebury leaves little doubt precisely where these priorities lie: one-fourth of the faculty teaches languages and literature. Every summer, Middlebury banishes English from its campus and teaches hundreds of "linguiphiles" a foreign language through its distinctive "immersion" method—students live, learn, and, hopefully, think only in their chosen language. The language departments continue their excellent instruction during the school year; especially notable are Russian, Chinese, and Japanese. Although there is no foreign language requirement, just about every student studies another tongue, if only to prepare for going abroad; any student, regardless of major, can take advantage of Middlebury's campuses in France, Germany, Italy, Spain, and Russia—about two-thirds of students study abroad prior to graduation. The school is also a member of the Maritime Studies Program.

Other highly touted Middlebury departments include English (the most popular major, bolstered by its connections to Bread Loaf), biology, and theater/dance. Regardless of major, "the classes are challenging, rigorous, and interesting," says a French and Spanish major. "Profs expect high-quality work, and there are no 'easy majors' or 'blow-off' classes." Still, a geology major notes that "teamwork is emphasized." While administrators claim there's no way to measure which Middlebury departments are weak, some students feel visual arts could be improved, and others warn against taking organic chemistry or geographic information systems.

Middlebury's academic rigor is reflected in its curriculum. During their first semester, students enroll in a writing-intensive First-Year Seminar capped at 15 people and taught by their academic advisor. By the end of sophomore year, students complete a second writing-intensive course. In addition to fulfilling their major requirements, students must satisfy distribution requirements in seven of

Website: www.middlebury.edu

Location: Small town

Total Enrollment: 2,270

Undergraduates: 2,265

Male/Female: 49/51

SAT Ranges: V 690–760 M 680–750

ACT Range: 28–31

Financial Aid: 36%

Expense: Pr $ $ $ $

Phi Beta Kappa: Yes

Applicants: 5,156

Accepted: 25%

Enrolled: 45%

Grad in 6 Years: 90%

Returning Freshmen: 96%

Academics: ✍ ✍ ✍ ✍

Social: ☎ ☎ ☎

Q of L: ★ ★ ★

Admissions: (802) 443-3000

Email Address:
admissions@middlebury.edu

Strongest Programs:
Political Science
Language Study
Environmental Studies
Biology
Economics
English
International Studies
Dance and Theater

eight academic areas, including literature, the arts, philosophical and religious studies, history, physical and life sciences, deductive reasoning and analytical processes, social analysis, and foreign language. Students also take three courses focused on cultures and civilizations, and two non-credit courses in physical education. With all of these requirements, it's no wonder students and faculty develop close relationships. "I've had dinner at my professors' houses and played golf with them, and find them to be my friends as well as my teachers," says a senior.

About three-quarters of Middlebury's students graduated in the top tenth of their high school class, and students of color constitute 11 percent of the student body. Middlebury recently created a partnership with New York City's Posse Foundation that will bring 10 inner-city students to the school each year, beginning with the class of 2003. Other than diversity, students get riled up about racism, homophobia, and the president's plans for the campus (a proposal to restructure the dorm groupings and decentralize dining has drawn jeers). Political correctness is present, too, sighs a sophomore, but "thankfully, someone always speaks up and rocks the boat soon enough, and we have real discussions."

Few Middlebury students live off campus (5 percent), since their comprehensive tuition fee includes housing, which is guaranteed for four years. Students choose from a variety of coed dorms, and may live in suites, college-owned houses, the Environmental House (where residents cook all of their own food), academic interest houses, and more "standard" situations. Newer options are the Substance-Free Social House (Xenia), which provides gathering space for interested students, and the Gender Studies Academic Interest House, which may become a residential house in the future. Rooms for upperclassmen are distributed via lottery, based on seniority. Students on the meal plan eat at one of five dining halls.

Students note a division between Midd's academic and social life; a hard week of classes and then a fun weekend of play is typical. Socially, most students stay on campus and attend college-sponsored movies, dances, parties, discussions, special dinners, sports, and arts functions. Kegs are outlawed in the dorms, and all parties must be registered. Still, one student says, "I'm not familiar with campus alcohol policies—it appears as if they're pretty determined to keep Middlebury an alcohol-, fun-, and student-friendly environment." For those who tire of Greek-like affairs at the social houses, the college's Gamut Room provides a mellow weeknight alternative and dance music every Thursday.

Many describe Middlebury's campus as "quaint and welcoming" and "cute, rural, and smallish." The town itself, according to a senior, is "sometimes claustrophobic," but it includes necessities such as fast food, a grocery store, drug store, hardware store, and clothing shops. Still, the administration airlifts or buses in culture and entertainment on a regular basis. February can get a little grim, and road trips are popular for a brief change of scenery. The progressive city of Burlington is 45 minutes away, Montreal is barely three hours, Boston four, and New York City five. Middlebury's own Ski Bowl ($75 for the season) and proximity to most Vermont ski slopes make this a paradise for ski fanatics, a breed Middlebury attracts in predictably large numbers.

Middlebury athletics draw rabid fans, especially when cheering the powerful ski and ice hockey teams. The cross-country and women's lacrosse teams are also popular and successful (1999 NCAA champs). The administration shows its support, too, by favoring student-athletes in admissions. Perhaps the biggest outdoor activity of all is the three-day Winter Carnival, an annual extravaganza of fun in the snow including parties, cultural events, sporting competitions, and ice-skating at an outdoor rink.

Students have noticed changes at Middlebury over the past few years—expanded and renovated facilities, improved educational technology, additional study-abroad opportunities. But "a combination of hard-working students who also know how to have fun, help others, and perform in the arts" are helping Middlebury retain the personality and feel that's endeared it to so many over the years, says a senior. Indeed, Middlebury students are an enthusiastic bunch, busy enjoying college to its fullest by combining a quality education with a dose of the north woods—and the wider world.

If You Apply To ➤

Middlebury...Early decision: Nov. 15 (preapplication and application); Dec. 15 (preapplication) and Dec. 31 (application). Regular admissions: Dec. 15 (preapplication) and Dec. 31 (application). Financial aid: Nov. 15 , Dec. 31. Guarantees to meet demonstrated need. Campus and alumni interviews: optional, evaluative. Three SAT IIs or ACTs or three AP exams or three IB exams required; must include English with writing, a quantitative test and one of the student's choosing. Accepts the Common Application and electronic applications. Essay question: one Common Application essay; and what is important about you.

Mills College

5000 MacArthur Boulevard, Oakland, CA 94613

"Strong Women, Proud Women, All Women, Mills Women!" proclaim the students of Mills College, the premier women's college west of the Rockies. Mills women feel that it is their destiny to "educate and empower all women." Convinced of these virtues, Mills students went on strike in 1990, and turned back the plans of the board of trustees to admit men in order to solve the institution's budget crisis. Today, Mills is the home of students who feel that the college is "Better dead than coed."

Mills was founded in 1852 as a young ladies' seminary. Then, most of the students were the children of California gold rush adventurers who were determined to see their daughters raised in an atmosphere of gentility rather than among the rowdiness of mining camps. Today, the combination of student diversity and educational opportunity guarantees that no one can graduate without having her horizons well extended. It is a place where issues are debated and analyzed, and many students are politically active in such groups as NOW, Young Women's Political Caucus, and League of Women Voters; campus issues include racism, sexism, and homophobia.

The park-like 135-acre campus, located just below the Oakland hills, boasts both historic and modern architecture set among rolling meadows, woods, and a meandering creek. Residence halls and classrooms are located within easy walking distance of one another. In an effort to make itself more attractive to prospective students, the college developed a series of interdisciplinary lower-division seminars including Science and Pseudoscience, Music and the Written Word, and Tribal Cultures in Fact and Fiction. At least half of each student's work must be taken outside of her major field, and students must take two courses in each of the following areas: natural sciences and math, social sciences, fine arts, and humanities. In addition, every Mills student must take at least two writing courses. Classes range from small to smaller; 87 percent of the classes taken by freshmen have fewer than 25 students. "For the most part, a vast majority of the

Website: www.mills.edu
Location: City outskirts
Total Enrollment: 1,180
Undergraduates: 870
Male/Female: 0/100
SAT Ranges: V 540–650 M 500–600
ACT Range: 22–26
Financial Aid: 78%
Expense: Pr $ $
Phi Beta Kappa: Yes
Applicants: 530
Accepted: 83%
Enrolled: 35%
Grad in 6 Years: N/A
Returning Freshmen: 78%
Academics: ✍ ✍ ✍
Social: ☎ ☎ ☎
Q of L: ★ ★ ★
Admissions: (510) 430-2135 or (800) 87-MILLS
Email Address: admission@mills.edu

Strongest Programs: English

professors are very good, but there are a few that need to change their curriculum," a sophomore English major states. Professors are friendly and accessible, and with a remarkable 60 percent of them women, there's no shortage of excellent female role models. "Career counseling has lots of resources, says a liberal studies major, "helpfulness and relevance depend on you." Students consider classes rigorous and grading strict, but emphasize the supportive academic atmosphere. "It's slightly competitive, mostly supportive, and definitely NOT laid-back," says a junior.

English, history, psychology, art, and dance are all praised by Mills students. But most agree the natural sciences are the most improved; premed students enjoy a 75 percent acceptance rate at med schools. Popular among prelaw students is the interdisciplinary program in administration and legal studies. The fine arts department is Mills's traditional stronghold, and electronic and computer music specializations within the music program are worthy of note, as is the fact that Mills was the first women's college to offer a major in computer science. Students and the administration consider that pioneering move to have been a good investment in what is now among the best mathematics and computer science programs around. With the exception of philosophy, very few departments are considered out-and-out weak, but foreign languages are somewhat limited. Only French, German, and Spanish are offered, though others can be taken through cross-registration at Berkeley. A major in business economics prepares students for business careers immediately after graduation, within a liberal arts context.

Mills students are encouraged to explore beyond the Oakland campus, and many take advantage of the excellent programs abroad and exchanges with other American schools. A year at a women's or coed college in the East is especially popular. Mills has concurrent cross-registration agreements with UC–Berkeley and most Bay Area universities, with five-year engineering programs with several of the same schools. Opportunities for internships abound. Students take advantage of the fully automated $6-million F. W. Olin Library, with access to the huge facilities at Berkeley.

Over three-quarters of Mills women are from California. One-third of them are from minority groups (12 percent Asian American, 8 percent African American, and 7 percent Hispanic), with 6 percent from foreign nations. According to a junior, "there are great racial divides," yet others feel that students are slowly "bridging racial walls." Three-quarters of the students are graduates of public high school, with one-half ranking in the top 5 percent of their graduating class. An influential subgroup of the student body are "resumers," women returning to college after a break of several years.

Four Mediterranean-style old dorms and three California-modern hill dorms offer a plethora of spacious single rooms. "You must fight to get a double," says a junior. Student cooperative housing, college-owned apartments, and French- and Spanish-language wings are also available. Older dorms are more homey, with high ceilings and long windows. According to many students, each dorm has its own specific "personality." Each of the older dorms has its own dining room, in which traditions are very important.

Each Wednesday night a sit-down candlelight dinner is served, and each year students feast on a Christmas dinner of Cornish game hens and flaming plum pudding. Another old-dorm dining tradition is the Candle Passing ceremony: a candle is passed around the table until the honored woman blows it out. Students living in the three newer dorms eat together at the commons. And there isn't a place on campus where the food is not excellent.

At least half of each student's work must be taken outside of her major field, and students must take two courses in each of the following areas: natural sciences and math, social sciences, fine arts, and humanities.

Older dorms are more homey, with high ceilings and long windows, and some even have their own porches.

Fears about a stunted social life on this tiny campus quietly linger throughout. Says a junior, "If you want to party, don't come to Mills!" Another student adds, "Social activities are best off campus." While many students agree that the social options on campus are lacking, others enjoy activities such as going to a movie or dance on campus, having a party in their rooms, or going into Berkeley or San Francisco. Adds one junior, "There is a social life on campus, but it's usually not about alcohol." Frat hops are popular around Berkeley, and many a man is let into Mills functions. Of course, friendships and romances among women are understandably strong.

With a bus stop on campus, it is easy to get around Oakland and into San Francisco to take advantage of the dining, dancing, and cultural resources of both cities. Farther away, there's the college ski lodge in the Sierra Nevadas and gambling in scenic Reno. The NCAA Division III varsity teams in tennis and basketball have been successful, as well as a championship crew team in all divisions. Participation in student government and other campus organizations is strong. Other activities include Amnesty International and environmental activism.

There's clearly no doubt that the students at Mills are strongly committed to keeping Mills a women's college. "Because we are an all women's college, made up of people from diverse backgrounds, we offer the opportunity to be stimulated by strong, wise women," coos a senior. Now that Mills, as yet another campus T-shirt says, is "For women again," all they have to do is convince a couple hundred more women that that's a good idea.

Overlaps
UC–Berkeley, UC–Santa Cruz, Scripps, Smith, UC–Davis.

If You Apply To ➤ | **Mills**…Rolling admissions. Financial aid: Feb. 15. Does not guarantee to meet demonstrated need. Campus and alumnae interviews: recommended, evaluative. SATs or ACTs: required. SAT IIs: optional. Essay question: submit sample of academic work; college expectations; and special circumstances.

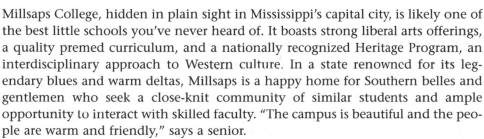

Millsaps College

1701 North State Street, Jackson, MS 39210

Millsaps College, hidden in plain sight in Mississippi's capital city, is likely one of the best little schools you've never heard of. It boasts strong liberal arts offerings, a quality premed curriculum, and a nationally recognized Heritage Program, an interdisciplinary approach to Western culture. In a state renowned for its legendary blues and warm deltas, Millsaps is a happy home for Southern belles and gentlemen who seek a close-knit community of similar students and ample opportunity to interact with skilled faculty. "The campus is beautiful and the people are warm and friendly," says a senior.

Millsaps is situated in the center of Jackson, but owing to the city's smaller size, it offers the ivory-tower serenity of a less urban environment. Surrounded by an eight-foot wrought-iron fence, the campus is centered around the Bowl, which, according to legend, is the crater of an extinct volcano. The architecture is a mix of modern and traditional early 19th-century buildings. The 122-foot-tall, copper-sheathed Millsaps Tower, at the east entrance to campus, is the school's focal point. Several new tennis courts were recently finished, as were renovations

Website: www.millsaps.edu
Location: Center city
Total Enrollment: 1,314
Undergraduates: 1,191
Male/Female: 45/55
SAT Ranges: V 550–650 M 530–620
ACT Range: 24–29
Financial Aid: 58%
Expense: Pr $
Phi Beta Kappa: Yes
Applicants: 912
Accepted: 87%

(Continued)

Enrolled: 36%

Grad in 6 Years: 72%

Returning Freshmen: 85%

Academics: ✍ ✍ ✍

Social: ☎ ☎ ☎

Q of L: ★ ★ ★

Admissions: (601) 974-1050

Email Address:
admissions@millsaps.edu

Strongest Programs:
Accounting
Business Administration
Economics
Biology/Premed
History

A new Campus Life Complex, with a renovated student center and expanded physical activities complex, was recently completed.

to two dorms. A new Campus Life Complex, with a renovated student center and expanded physical activities complex, was also completed recently.

All Millsaps freshmen take a one-hour Perspectives class, led by an academic advisor, to aid the adjustment to college life and prepare for the rigorous core curriculum, which ensures a breadth of study (and substantial work) for every undergrad. All new students also must take an Introduction to Liberal Studies seminar, which emphasizes the development of critical thinking and writing skills in the context of a liberal education, and begin the humanities sequence of the core with either Heritage or Topics of the Ancient World. In addition, all students must complete 10 courses designed to develop their abilities in reasoning, communication, quantitative thinking, valuing, and decision-making. Four of these courses are humanities, while four are science and mathematics; the group is capped with freshman and senior seminars.

Students and the graduate schools that welcome them after their years at Millsaps hold in high regard anything prelaw or premed, though biology classes are reputed to be very difficult. The college has also received national recognition for its Heritage Program, an interdisciplinary study of Western culture, designed primarily for freshmen. The Else School of Management, one of the best in the Sunbelt, offers solid bachelor's degree programs in accounting, administration, and economics. There's a new German major, and administrators say computer studies is gaining strength with the addition of 70 new PCs and two additional computer labs. Foreign languages and philosophy could be improved, students say.

When campus feels too small, students may escape to the Oak Ridge Science Semester, complete research in marine sciences at the Gulf Coast Research Laboratory, or gain academic credit for internships in business, government, and health. Other options include study abroad in London, Paris, Munich, Prague, Costa Rica, Rome, or Athens, among other locations, and cooperative programs through the Associated Colleges of the South* consortium, of which Millsaps is a founding member. It's unclear why anyone would leave at all, however, given the raves Millsaps' faculty members draw for teaching skill and accessibility. "I love my classes and feel that the professors are always willing to talk—either about school problems or other problems," says a senior. "That, combined with a sense of academic rigor, makes our profs valuable."

Millsaps has broadened its recruiting efforts in recent years, and 43 percent of students now come from out of state. They're also getting smarter; 44 percent of a recent freshman class graduated in the top tenth of their high school class. Millsaps was the first college in Mississippi to voluntarily adopt a policy of open admissions for minority students, but, like many colleges, it still has a way to go to achieve racial diversity. African Americans account for 9 percent of the student body; Asian Americans 3 percent and Hispanics 1 percent. Still, students are conscious of the need to create an inclusive community.

Most Mississippians view Millsaps as a hotbed of liberalism, and their worst fears have been realized: Millsaps has coed dorms. Freshmen, however, are still required to live in single-sex halls. Coed or not, the dorms draw cheers. They're "comfortable, well-maintained, spacious, and conducive to studying," says a sociology and history major. There's competition for certain dorms, a senior says, "but we work on a lottery system, so it works out fairly in the end." Junior and senior men can live in one of four fraternity houses, as the Greek system claims 55 percent of men and 56 percent of women, but there's no sorority housing. About a quarter of students opt to live off campus. Security includes 24-hour patrols, emergency call boxes, and locked residence halls. "The city of Jackson, especially in the Millsaps area of town, has a lot of crime," says a senior. "Millsaps security does its best to keep us safe, but unfortunately, we are not immune."

Socially speaking, Greeks dominate Millsaps life. Recent efforts to diversify campus social life have met with some success, and Greek rush is now held after fall midterms instead of during the first hectic week of school. Frat houses remain popular hangouts, though the underage shouldn't expect to imbibe there. "It is not very easy for the underage to get served," says a former fraternity president. Much grumbling has met the recent administration edict banning Thursday night parties on campus. Students report that a fair amount of social life takes place off campus at bars such as Hal and Mal's, Cherokee, and The Rez. Ten miles to the north is a huge reservoir, popular for weekend water sports; New Orleans and Memphis are popular road trips. On campus, the annual Major Madness festival draws a big crowd for bands and activities in the Bowl, and prospective freshmen are often invited to join in on the fun. Homecoming draws parents and alumni to campus, and if the game is against arch-rival Rhodes, watch out!

Millsaps belongs to the Southern Collegiate Athletic Conference (SCAC), but it isn't nearly as sports-crazy as most Southern campuses, as it competes in Division III. For the men, football, basketball, baseball, and soccer draw the largest crowds; basketball, soccer, and volleyball are the most popular among women's teams.

Millsaps College is "an academic community where men and women pursue a life of scholarly inquiry and intellectual growth," according to the Honor Code prospective students sign when submitting their applications and re-sign when registering for classes. "The foundation of this community is a spirit of personal honesty and mutual trust." Add a heaping helping of Southern hospitality, accessible faculty and strong liberal arts and pre-professional preparation, and it's no wonder Millsaps remains one of higher education's better-kept secrets.

Computer studies is gaining strength with the addition of 70 new PCs and two additional computer labs. Foreign languages and philosophy could be improved, students say.

Overlaps

University of Mississippi, Mississippi State, Rhodes, Mississippi College, University of the South.

If You Apply To ➤ **Millsaps**…Early action: Dec. 1. Regular admissions: Feb. 1. Financial aid: Mar. 1. Does not guarantee to meet demonstrated need. Campus interviews: recommended, informational. No alumni interviews. SATs or ACTs: required. SAT IIs: optional. Accepts the Common Application and electronic applications. Essay question: community, state, national, or world issue in which you've gotten involved; what fictional character would you be and why; describe a significant hour from your life.

University of Minnesota–Morris

600 East 4th Street, Morris, MN 56267-2199

The University of Minnesota–Morris is far more comprehensive than its small size might indicate. Founded by a Roman Catholic nun as a school for Native Americans, Morris has since grown into a full-fledged university with solid academics, a dedicated faculty, opportunities for collaborative research, and options for study abroad. One of the four University of Minnesota campuses, Morris has become a quality public liberal arts college where personal attention is commonplace.

The school lies on 130 acres in west-central Minnesota, which for some students means "mootown." The campus is composed of 26 traditional brick-and-mortar buildings loosely arranged around a central mall. Plans are underway for

Website: www.mrs.umn.edu
Location: Small town
Total Enrollment: 1,959
Undergraduates: 1,959
Male/Female: 40/60
SAT Ranges: V 500–630 M 540–630
ACT Range: 22–28
Financial Aid: 79%

(Continued)

Expense: Pub $ $ $ $
Phi Beta Kappa: No
Applicants: 1,345
Accepted: 80%
Enrolled: 55%
Grad in 6 Years: 65%
Returning Freshmen: 85%
Academics: ✍ ✍ ✍
Social: ☎ ☎
Q of L: ★ ★ ★
Admissions: (800) 992-8863
Email Address:
admissions@mrs.umn.edu

Strongest Programs:
Premed
Predentistry
Preveterinary
Engineering
Natural Sciences
Math

One of the college's innovations is Morris Academic Partners, in which select students receive a stipend to conduct their own research with a faculty member.

Among major fields, the sciences and math are highly regarded, as is Morris's psychology department, which is known for breakthrough studies of daydreams.

In 1996, the school began a partnership with the Anti-Defamation League's World of Difference Institute, to decrease prejudice and increase intergroup understanding and communication.

a $28-million addition to the science building, which will double the size of the science and math facility, and a regional fitness center that will serve the entire community.

In the classroom, Morris students must complete at least 90 credits of general education coursework outside their major, in subjects ranging from writing, foreign language, mathematical and symbolic reasoning, and artistic performance to historical perspectives, human behavior, communication, fine arts, physical and biological sciences, and the global village. Freshmen are also required to take a diversity seminar. Among major fields, the sciences and math are highly regarded, as is Morris's psychology department, which is known for breakthrough studies of daydreams. Pre-professional programs for wanna-be doctors, lawyers, veterinarians, pharmacists, and physical therapists are recognized, too.

One of the college's innovations is Morris Academic Partners, in which select students receive a stipend to conduct their own research with a faculty member. The merit-based Undergraduate Research Opportunities Program offers financial rewards to students for research, scholarly, or creative projects undertaken in collaboration with a faculty member. Students in the English Language Teaching Assistant Program travel to schools in foreign countries to assist English teachers. The study abroad program at Morris allows students to live and learn in Africa, the Middle East, Asia, the South Pacific, and Europe.

Class sizes at Morris are generally small by public university standards; 90 percent have 50 or fewer students. The quality of teaching is "outstanding," says a management major. "Professors are always more than willing to sit down with you and discuss things," adds a freshman. Faculty also receives high marks from students for their individualized approach and willingness to get to know students as people, not just numbers on a class list. Every freshman is assigned an academic advisor who must approve his or her schedule. "I can always get the help I need from academic or career counseling," says a sophomore.

Morris draws 82 percent of its students from Minnesota, but these are no local yokels: 76 percent of last year's freshmen graduated in the top quarter of their high school class. Most are proud of their academic standing, as illustrated by a popular cheer against archrival Duluth: "It's better to fail at Morris than graduate from Duluth!" Minorities comprise 17 percent of the student body at UMM, with Native Americans topping the list at 7 percent. In 1996, the school began a partnership with the Anti-Defamation League's World of Difference Institute, to decrease prejudice and increase intergroup understanding and communication. Once each quarter, Morris also sponsors a Diversity Jam in which all ethnic groups are celebrated. E-Quality hosts activities for lesbian, gay, bisexual, and transgendered students during "Hearing All the Voices" week. Even though it's already a bargain, Morris provides financial aid to 90 percent of those who apply for it. And in keeping with its heritage, Morris also automatically grants free tuition to Native Americans.

Forty-eight percent of Morris freshmen live on campus in one of five residence halls. Upperclassmen either move off campus or enter a lottery for space in a campus apartment complex. The dorms feature a 24-hour visitation policy with kitchenettes on every floor and a TV lounge on the ground level. "I found living in the freshman dorms to be a pleasurable experience," says student. "It was a quick and easy way to meet people." Students find campus safe, and say even the dining halls aren't a danger zone: "There are salad bars for lunch and dinner, and food service is more than willing to fix a special lunch," says a math major.

The phrase "Make your own fun" might well have been invented here, since students are left to their own devices when it's time to relax. "There are always activities taking place on campus," says one student. "Activities occurring off campus usually involve close friends getting together." That's because the drinking age is strictly enforced on campus and in local bars. Some students use weekends to participate in community service. Others head for home with laundry bags in tow.

For those who stick around campus, more than 90 clubs and student organizations are available, focusing on everything from juggling to geology. Morris sponsors several outstanding music groups, including a jazz ensemble that was selected to play at the 1994 Jazz Festival in Amsterdam. Intramural sports are also a big hit, especially basketball, volleyball, wrestling, and football. Morris competes in Division II, and crowds gather to cheer on the basketball, football, baseball and women's wrestling teams, among others.

A home on the range at UMM isn't for everyone; some might chafe at the school's low-key social life and relative isolation. But for those looking to test their academic stamina for four years, Morris offers a way to leave distractions behind. "The small size allows you to get more help from professors," says one happy student. And the affordable price tag sure doesn't hurt.

If You Apply To ➢

Morris...Early action: Dec. 1, Feb. 1. Regular admissions: Mar. 15. Financial aid: Apr. 1. Housing: May 1. Meets demonstrated need of 90%. Campus and alumni interviews: optional, informational. SATs or ACTs: required. SAT IIs: optional. Essay question: how UMM will contribute to your intellectual development and overall growth. Accepts electronic applications.

University of Minnesota–Twin Cities

240 Williamson, 231 Pillsbury Drive SE, Minneapolis, MN 55455

Like the nearby Mall of America, the University of Minnesota is overwhelming in its seemingly endless variety of offerings and its gargantuan size. With more than 150 professional programs, UM offers an abundance of academic choices. "There are so many opportunities here," says a journalism major. "Whether it be academic, social, or cultural, students have many options to choose from."

The vast Twin Cities campus actually consists of two campuses with three main sections, and within each the architecture is highly diverse. The St. Paul campus encompasses the colleges of agriculture, food, and environmental science, natural resources, human ecology, veterinary medicine, and biological sciences. The Minneapolis campus is divided by the Mississippi River into an East Bank and a West Bank that are home to the other colleges and most of the dormitories, as well as most of the fraternities and sororities. Both campuses offer a blend of traditional and modern architecture, with columned buildings seated next to sleek geometric structures. The two campuses are five miles apart and linked by a free bus service. Academic facilities are excellent, beginning with the 5-million-volume library system, which is the 15th largest in North America. Every one of the colleges has its own library, many of which are good places to study. There is also a 695-acre arboretum that is used for research and teaching.

Minnesota offers more than 150 undergraduate majors in 28 separate schools. The Institute of Technology is notable for the options it offers for tutorials and

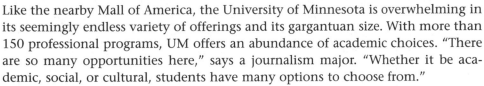

Website: www.umn.edu
Location: Urban
Total Enrollment: 39,595
Undergraduates: 25,903
Male/Female: 49/51
SAT Ranges: V 530–650 M 540–670
ACT Range: 22–27
Financial Aid: 48%
Expense: Pub $ $ $
Phi Beta Kappa: Yes
Applicants: 14,480
Accepted: 77%
Enrolled: 46%
Grad in 6 Years: 44%
Returning Freshmen: 85%
Academics: 🖊 🖊 🖊 🖊
Social: ☎ ☎ ☎

(Continued)

Q of L: ★ ★ ★

Admissions: (800) 752-1000

Email Address:

admissions@tc.umn.edu

Strongest Programs:

Chemical Engineering

Psychology

Management

Geography

Health Care

Mathematics

Education

internships; its electrical and mechanical engineering programs are particularly strong and well subscribed. Psychology, the most popular major on campus, has a good reputation, as do political science, management, economics, law, and journalism. Undergraduates also have access to more esoteric fields, from aging studies and biometry to therapeutic recreation and mortuary science. Anthropology, foreign languages, and math could be better, students say. The university recently revised its distribution requirements.

While efforts to limit class size have been stepped up, classes still top out at 300-plus, with introductory classes typically the largest. While Minnesota is a large school, the thoughtful student can find ways of rising out of the sea of anonymity. "You have to work hard and be willing to compete if you want to make yourself known at such a large school," says one junior. The place is crawling with potentially helpful teaching assistants, and the excellent honors program in the liberal arts college allows close contact with faculty members as well as leeway to enroll in certain graduate courses and seminars. Students say the academic climate varies with the school. "The University of Minnesota is extremely competitive," reports a junior. "Courses are rigorous and challenging, but well worth the effort."

While undergraduates have had a difficult time enrolling in all the courses they want at registration, the use of computer registration has made life a lot easier. One junior reveals, "If a class is closed and somebody really needs it, they can usually get a magic number from the department to be able to register for it." The administration explains the school's low six-year graduation rate on the fact that that students are more likely to center their lives in spheres outside the university—in work and off-campus homes. However, the four-year plan guarantees graduation in four years provided students follow program requirements, including frequent academic counseling and specific coursework.

Professors receive high marks from most students as being approachable and knowledgeable. "Many professors are currently practicing in their fields, which allows students to learn about current ideas and issues," says a senior architecture major. Students find plenty of internship opportunities at the many corporations and government agencies in the Twin Cities area. The university recently converted to the semester system, and almost all classes have a pass/fail option (limited to no more than a quarter of a student's courses).

Academic facilities are excellent, beginning with the 5-million-volume library system, which is the 15th largest in North America.

Sixty percent of students at the university come from the top quarter of their high school class, and three-quarters of them are from Minnesota. Half the students commute to school. Minorities constitute 14 percent of the students, with 4 percent African American, 2 percent Hispanic, and 8 percent Asian American. One student hails the school for its diversity. "You can find anything/everything, anyone/everyone at the University of Minnesota." In addition to need-based financial aid, hundreds of merit scholarships are awarded every year. National Merit Scholars who specify Minnesota as their first choice qualify automatically. The athletic department hands out 391 awards in a multitude of sports. There are also plenty of student employment opportunities on campus.

In the spring and summer, Minnesota's famed 10,000 lakes offer swimming, boating, and fishing.

Dorm life at Minnesota follows the big school, wait-in-line theme. Nearly 15 percent of all undergraduates live in residence halls, as there are now eight traditional halls and one new apartment-style facility, with at least one more on the way. Dorm rooms are hard to obtain, and parking spaces for all those commuters are almost as scarce. Students who have rooms get the chance to keep them for the next year. Freshmen, at one time, got the leftover dorm rooms, but the administration ensures that first-year students who apply for housing by May 1 are guaranteed residence hall space. Students recommend that freshmen live in the dorms.

"It's a wonderful place to meet friends and get involved," one says. Once you're there, you're required to join a meal plan. Campus security is adequate, although bike thefts are common. "You don't need to be scared, just smart," one junior says.

Since so many students live off campus, on-campus social life is described as low key but not the only diversion available. The downtown areas of the Twin Cities are easy to get to by bus, and there are scores of good bars, restaurants, night spots, and movie theaters. This is an athletically inclined bunch of students, as both intramural and varsity sports are popular. The men's basketball team went to the 1997 NCAA Final Four and won the 1998 National Invitational Tournament championship, but the pennants in the gym have been taken down due to an academic fraud scandal prompted by the revelations that, among other things, staff members had completed tests and papers for basketball players. Students are always hoping that the current season will be one in which the gridiron Gophers take home the roses in a bowl victory, but short of that, a victory over Michigan for custody of the Little Brown Jug is cause for celebration. The extent of the University of Minnesota's rivalry with the University of Wisconsin is considerable, especially since U of M has a large Wisconsin population. Intramural competition can go on well past midnight.

Minnesota can get brutally cold in the winter, but for those who enjoy skiing or skating, that's no hardship. For students who want to avoid the winter winds, many of the campus buildings are linked by underground tunnels. In the spring and summer, Minnesota's famed 10,000 lakes offer swimming, boating, and fishing. More than 400 extracurricular organizations offer respite from the books. The Carnival Weekend put on by the Greeks each April to raise funds for charity is the biggest such event on campus. Spring Jam, featuring regional and local bands, and Campus Kick-off Days in the beginning of the fall quarter are much-anticipated activities.

Although it's easy to feel somewhat overlooked at the University of Minnesota, it's also possible to take advantage of a plethora of campus resources. Says one veteran, "The large size scares a lot of people, but it's really not that big. The steely blue Minnesota sky's the limit if you're willing to get involved."

Students are always hoping that the current season will be one in which the gridiron Gophers take home the roses in a bowl victory, but short of that, a victory over Michigan for custody of the Little Brown Jug is cause for celebration.

Overlaps

University of Wisconsin–Madison, University of Minnesota–Duluth, University of Wisconsin–Eau Claire, St. Thomas, Marquette.

If You Apply To	Twin Cities…Rolling admissions: Dec. 15 (priority). Financial aid: Feb. 15. Housing: May 1. Campus and alumni interviews: optional, informational. SATs or ACTs: required; ACTs preferred. SAT IIs: optional. No essay question.

University of Missouri–Columbia

130 Jesse Hall, Columbia, MO 65211

Tradition reigns supreme at the University of Missouri, the oldest public university west of the Mississippi. Indeed, the tradition of Homecoming was born here in 1911 and it's celebrated grandly to this day—though now there's an emphasis on community service (students have helped collect more than 30,000 boxes of macaroni and cheese ("Mizzou-roni") for the hungry and 4,500 units of blood for the sick in recent years). While its roots remain firmly planted, Mizzou continues

Website: www.missouri.edu
Location: Small city
Total Enrollment: 22,930
Undergraduates: 17,827
Male/Female: 47/53

(Continued)

ACT Range: 24–29

Financial Aid: 67%

Expense: Pub $ $ $

Phi Beta Kappa: Yes

Applicants: 9,091

Accepted: 90%

Enrolled: 48%

Grad in 6 Years: 60%

Returning Freshmen: 84%

Academics: 🖎 🖎 🖎

Social: ☎ ☎ ☎ ☎

Q of L: ★ ★ ★

Admissions: (573) 882-7786

Email Address:

mu4u@missouri.edu

Strongest Programs:

History

Journalism/Communications

Business

Accounting

Engineering

Agriculture

Education

Students helped collect more than 30,000 boxes of macaroni and cheese ("Mizzou-roni") for the hungry and 4,451 units of blood for the sick in recent years.

to forge ahead by updating technology, improving facilities, and engaging in a comprehensive strategic planning process.

Mizzou's spacious, tree-filled campus is flanked by mansionlike fraternity and sorority houses. The Francis Quadrangle Historical District, with 19 National Historic Landmark buildings, is the core of the Red Campus (so named for the predominant color of brick). Central to this area are the 60-foot granite columns of the original Academic Hall—the building was destroyed by fire in 1892. To the east of the columns is the original tombstone of Thomas Jefferson. The White Campus consists of vine-covered limestone buildings, symbolized by the Memorial Union Tower. A $46-million critical care facility for the University Hospital, a transgenic greenhouse facility, and a two-story addition for the College of Agriculture, Food, and Natural Resources have been completed. Plans are in the works for a $27-million building for the College of Business and a $49-million Center for Life Sciences Research.

With 255 degree programs and 18 schools and colleges, Mizzou offers a comprehensive set of choices for basic and advanced study. A sophomore says, "Many students I've talked to from other schools say that their school is geared one particular way. MU is a place where students can find what they want." Young writers can get intensive training at the brand new Center for the Literary Arts, and then hands-on experience with the *Columbia Missourian*, the 6,000-circulation local daily paper edited by J-school faculty members. KBIA, MU's National Public Radio station, is popular among students and has the second-highest number of listeners of any public radio station in the nation. In addition, seven Missouri journalism alumni won Pulitzer Prizes in 1999; not surprisingly, newspapers like the *Washington Post* and *New York Times* send recruiters to campus. Agriculture is also nationally ranked, especially in the areas of agricultural economics and applied research for farm communities, and there's a new major in agribusiness management. The College of Engineering maintains several notable undergraduate segments, including biological and civil engineering. The College of Business is highly competitive and features a five-year bachelor's/master's accounting program, while the College of Education has added a degree in middle school education and made recent strides to integrate more technological experiences into its courses.

Committed preprofessionals will be glad to know that MU offers highly able and directed freshmen guaranteed admission to its graduate-level programs in medicine, law, veterinary medicine, nursing, and health-related professions. Mizzou is also one of the leading public research institutions in the country for the number and range of lab and scholarly opportunities it offers undergraduates. The school has received more than $3.5 million over recent years from the National Science Foundation and others to continue expanding research opportunities. MU is also committed to making study abroad opportunities affordable for all students and currently 10 percent—more than 1,700 students—study overseas each year.

MU's general education program has been revamped to facilitate a strong "distribution of knowledge" requirement, in addition to two writing-intensive courses, math/reasoning and computer proficiency, and a capstone experience. In addition, students must take 18 hours of courses in areas outside their major. Full professors teach the lecture courses at Mizzou, supplemented by a weekly discussion session led by a teaching assistant to go over material presented in class. An international studies major describes Mizzou professors as "accessible, helpful, and knowledgeable."

Students say the courses at Mizzou are challenging but not impossible if you are willing to work hard. "I am continually challenged and pushed to new levels by professors, instructors, and fellow students," says an education major. Owing to MU's size, classes can fill up quickly, but professors do give overrides for students who must take certain credits at specific times. Missouri guarantees the availability of coursework to complete a degree in four years. The study-conscious will find plenty of room and resources in the MU library system. Mizzou's libraries are the 47th-largest collection in North America, with more than 2.6 million books, 5 million microfilms, and 16,000 periodicals. (Thank goodness there's a course on how to use it all.)

The Mizzou campus is home mostly to Missourians (83 percent), though every state in the union and 114 foreign countries are represented, too. African Americans account for only 6 percent of the student body, while Asian Americans and Hispanics combine for 3 percent. To boost its minority population, MU has established several scholarship programs designed especially for them. It's also opened a state-of-the-art, $2.4-million home for the Black Culture Center and an Asian Affairs Center.

Forty-seven percent of MU students live on campus, and freshman under age 20 are required to do so. Residence halls have double rooms and are often crowded and noisy—and thus are incredibly fun places to be, though single-sex halls, a few single rooms, and round-the-clock quiet floors are also available. Dorm choice is first come, first serve, and half of the halls offer coed living by floor or wing. Students can also choose to live in one of 22 "learning communities," where residents share a common interest, such as engineering, arts, or nursing. More than 90 different Freshman Interest Groups, where 15 to 20 students with shared academic interests live in the same residence hall and enroll in three classes together, also draw raves. The programs are "very conducive to learning," says a junior. Dorm dwellers are required to purchase meal plans, but credits can be used at all-you-can-eat dining halls, coffee bars, and take-out stands, among many options. Most upperclass students move into one of Columbia's many apartment complexes, primarily in search of single rooms. The fraternity and sorority houses are livable (the frat houses less so), although not all members can fit; 23 percent of Mizzou men and 25 percent of women go Greek.

Mizzou, a champion of tough alcohol policies, works hard to maintain a dry campus and has won national awards for its alcohol prevention program. MU will require fraternities to become substance-free by the year 2000 if they choose to allow freshmen to live in their houses. "Of course, not everyone abides by the policy; sometimes successfully, frequently not," a sophomore says. Despite the strict alcohol policies, students say MU's social life is packed with options, including movies, shopping, eating out, the usual Greek parties, and great parks and hiking areas on the outskirts of town. "Columbia is the ideal college town," says one student. "It's safe, it's not too big, it has many things to do for people of all ages, and it's easy to get around in." Columbia offers the benefits of a large city—a versatile bar scene, lots of pizza joints, coffee shops, and expensive boutiques—and the friendly atmosphere of a small town. Students support the town by engaging in community service and the community caters to them in return; their concern even goes beyond the borders of campus to the plight of the wild tiger and the preservation of its habitat. At Mizzou, service goes hand-in-hand with learning; in partnership with the Office of Service Learning, the university offered 65 courses designated as service-learning in 2000-2001. Road trips to St. Louis or Kansas City offer a change of scenery.

Mizzou's Tigers compete in the Big 12, and basketball and football games draw big crowds. In fact, the entire town turns out in black and gold for any

Despite the strict alcohol policies, students say MU's social life is packed with options, including movies, shopping, eating out, the usual Greek parties, and parks and hiking areas on the outskirts of town.

football game. The heated rivalry with Kansas dates back to 1891 in football, but can be traced back to the Civil War, when Kansas abolitionists sparred violently with pro-slavery Missouri farmers. An indoor practice facility for football, baseball, softball, and soccer and a track/soccer complex offers seating for 2,000 fans. MU's popular intramural program has nearly two dozen sports and two skill divisions, so bloodthirsty competitors and weekend warriors alike can get what they want.

The University of Missouri continues to pay tribute to the past, and traditions like Homecoming remain strong, but students say MU's real treasure is its people."It's a big campus with a very personal feeling," explains one junior. Adds a fellow Tiger, "You really have to experience what 'Mizzou Pride' is for yourself!"

If You Apply To ➤ **Mizzou**…Rolling admissions. Financial aid: Mar. 1. Guarantees to meet demonstrated need. Campus and alumni interviews: not available. SATs or ACTs required; ACTs preferred. No SAT IIs. Accepts electronic applications. No essay question. Physical therapy program applicants must be state residents.

Montana Tech of the University of Montana

1300 West Park Street, Butte, MT 59701-8997

Website: www.mtech.edu
Location: City outskirts
Total Enrollment: 2,460
Undergraduates: 2,365
Male/Female: 52/48
SAT Ranges: V 480–590 M 490–630
ACT Range: 19–25
Financial Aid: 75%
Expense: Pub $
Phi Beta Kappa: No
Applicants: 563
Accepted: 97%
Enrolled: 70%
Grad in 6 Years: 44%
Returning Freshmen: 70%
Academics: ✍ ✍ ✍
Social: ☎ ☎
Q of L: ★ ★ ★
Admissions: (406) 496-4178
Email Address:
admissions@mtech.edu

Strongest Programs:
General Engineering

Plunked down in the midst of western mining country, Montana Tech, as you might expect, shines in land-related engineering fields, like petroleum, mining, and geophysics. Students get a hands-on education geared toward "things metallic" (as the school's motto loosely translates). In fact, the school's mascot is Charlie Oredigger, and students are affectionately dubbed "diggers."

Situated on a shoulder of "the richest hill on earth" (some of the greatest copper, molybdenum, zinc, and manganese deposits in the world), Montana Tech's 50-acre campus is composed of 16 buildings of Classical college brick architecture. This is exemplified by Main Hall, constructed in 1900, and the Engineering, Laboratory, and Classroom building (the ELC), built in 1987 and modernized to the tune of $850,000. Other unique features on campus include the Museum Building, which houses one of the country's largest mineral collections; an Earthquake Studies Office, which records tremors throughout southwestern Montana; and the Montana Bureau of Mines and Geology, a research arm of the college that produces geological and mineralogical maps and publications. Recent campus additions include a residence hall and renovations to the student union and several classrooms.

Tech's degree programs emphasize the study of minerals, energy, and the environment, but students graduate with a well-rounded education. Strong degree programs include environmental engineering, business information and technology, and general engineering (formerly engineering science). Efforts have been made in recent years to strengthen the basic sciences underlying the engineering programs. The school also works to place upperclassmen in summer jobs in their fields. Everyone faces general education requirements including communications, humanities, social sciences, mathematical sciences, and life sciences, although students say the nonscience offerings are weak. For those who want more than just a straight-science experience, Tech has a major in science and technology that attempts to relate liberal arts to today's increasingly technological society. New additions to the curriculum include an ASRN program and a BS in general science and general engineering. Montana Tech also continues to add degree programs in software engineering, nursing, and biological sciences.

(Continued)
Mining
Environmental Engineering
Business Information and Technology
Petroleum Engineering

Academic work at Tech is rigorous, with gym the only subject that can be taken pass/fail. "Montana Tech is competitive in a good way," says a business information and technology major. "It's rigorous enough to be challenging and motivating but it's not cutthroat." Faculty members have a genuine interest in teaching and work hard to accommodate students. In addition, most engineering faculty has spent an average of eight years on the job. "I know all my professors on a first-name basis as do most students at Tech," a student reports. Freshmen are always taught by full professors, and students must sit down with their academic advisors each term to discuss their schedules. One student claims, however, that counselors are hardly involved. Eighty-three percent of Tech's students are from Montana. Residents and nonresidents alike must be in the top half of their high school class or maintain a 2.5 GPA and score at least 22 on ACT composite or 920 on the combined SAT to gain admission.

Student diversity stems from the 3 percent foreign enrollment. Only 2 percent of the students are Hispanic or Asian American. The student body is conservative, and "political correctness is nonexistent," a petroleum engineering major says. Students vie for 100 merit scholarships, ranging from $200 to $2,000. And while there are 100 athletic scholarships distributed among football, basketball, volleyball, and golf, a petroleum engineering major says, "We suck at sports. The reasons for coming here are academic." Registration and incidental fees are waived for some Montana state residents, including war orphans and those of at least one-fourth Native American blood.

New additions to the curriculum include an ASRN program and a BS in general science and general engineering.

Twelve percent of the students live in Prospector Hall, which is "comfortable and spacious," but those who can't fit are often forced to live in married student housing. Prospector includes modern baths, carpeting, exercise rooms, and kitchens, and it is "in the middle of everything." Each room is wired with a microcomputer connected to the campus mainframe. The school likes freshmen to live on campus, but the vast majority of upperclassmen live either in the many nearby apartments or in houses with reasonable rents. The campus is said to be safe, without a major crime in the past two years. "If someone were to attack me, there's a good chance I'd know exactly who they were because we have such a small campus," quips a junior. For students without cars, there's a bus service that runs into town.

Butte (population 40,000) gets a fair enough rating as a college town, although it is suffering from a collapse of the mining industry. "It's a friendly town for the most part," says an environmental engineering major, adding that townspeople are proud of Tech and like to help students whenever possible. Students give back through participation in programs like Big Brothers/Big Sisters and Habitat for Humanity. Although the ratio of men to women is about three to two, little dating occurs among Tech students, who usually seek entertainment with hometown friends. On weekends, students who don't go home attend music or comedy shows on campus, see movies, go to a game, or frequent the bars in town. Butte's setting—nestled in the slopes of the Continental Divide—is magnificent for skiing, fishing, hiking, and camping. Yellowstone Park is a favored road trip.

Montana Tech's Earthquake Studies Office records tremors throughout southwestern Montana.

Athletics at Tech, which competes in the NAIA, are up-and-coming, and jocks are generally considered "cool." The most popular varsity sports are football and men's and women's basketball; one T-shirt reads, "Tech football: a miner miracle."

But other varsity teams, including men's and women's cross-country teams and women's volleyball, are also strong. Tech students take advantage of the excellent intramural program and the facilities of the modern physical education complex. Tech's biggest rival is Western Montana College, and freshman football players from WMC face off with those from Tech in an annual boxing match known as the "Smoker." The student union features a dining area, game room, bookstore, student-owned FM radio station, and a television where students are known to tune in to cartoons in the afternoon. St. Patrick's Day is widely celebrated on and off campus, and on M-Day, part of a three-day festival before spring finals, students whitewash the large stone "M" on a hill above campus and host the largest bonfire in the state.

Montana Tech's students know why they've chosen their school; they want a solid grounding in earth-related engineering disciplines at a reasonable cost. Though state budget cuts have reduced the number of credits required to graduate, the school still boasts an impressive 95 percent job placement rate for graduates. Tech doesn't offer your typical college experience, but for would-be miners and geophysicists, its programs can't be beat.

Overlaps

University of Montana, Montana State-Bozeman, Carroll College, Western Montana, Montana State-Billings.

If You Apply To ➤

Montana Tech...Rolling admissions. Meets demonstrated need of 59%. Campus and Alumni interviews: optional, informational. SATs or ACTs: required; ACTs preferred. SAT IIs: optional. Accepts electronic applications. No essay question.

Morehouse College, GA—See ATLANTA UNIVERSITY CENTER

Morris Brown College, GA—See ATLANTA UNIVERSITY CENTER

Mount Holyoke College

50 College Street, South Hadley, MA 01075-1488

Website: www.mtholyoke.edu
Location: Small town
Total Enrollment: 1,982
Undergraduates: 1,979
Male/Female: 0/100
SAT Ranges: V 600–660 M 570–650
ACT Range: 25–29
Financial Aid: 72%

There may be flowers blooming around the Mount Holyoke campus, but there are no shrinking violets among its student body. The women of Mount Holyoke, the nation's first all-female college, are vocal about their opinions, eager to bond, and hungry for the well-rounded liberal arts education they receive at MHC. Students rave about the quality of teaching and the small classes. The environment cultivates independent, intellectual women who aim to become leaders in their chosen professions. "Everyone I know has an opinion," a first-year says. "MHC is an institution that helps create an atmosphere for students to think on their own and be supported for doing so."

The school is located in the heart of New England on 800 acres of rolling hills, lakes, and waterfalls. Modern glass-and-stone buildings stand alongside the more traditional ivy-covered sandstone structures that make up the majority of the campus. Notable features include the Japanese Meditation Garden and Teahouse, an art building with studios and bronze-casting foundry, an 18-hole championship golf course, and an equestrian center. Major renovations are underway in facilities for the sciences, art, and music.

Despite a few modernizations, the curriculum at this 162-year-old institution remains traditional. Requirements are fairly standard, including courses in foreign language and physical education, three courses in humanities, two in science and math (with at least one lab), and two in social science. All students must fulfill a multicultural requirement, visible proof of the school's commitment to "break away from the strictly Eurocentric focus" of U.S. liberal arts education. In addition, students must complete a minor or a concentration in addition to their major. A small number of exceptional students are invited to participate in the First-Year Honors Tutorial Program, which provides an opportunity to work closely with a faculty member on a topic of mutual interest. Small seminars intensive in writing, speaking, or both are offered to first-year students, and a common reading is required. The 2000 selection was *Refuge* by Terry Tempest Williams, who then visited the campus to speak about her work. Students take their work seriously, and so, it seems, do professors. According to one account, a German professor made tracks through a New England blizzard on cross-country skis to deliver a scheduled exam on time.

Mount Holyoke is decidedly strongest in the sciences, boasting top-of-the-line undergraduate chemistry labs and a science library. A solar greenhouse, a scanning electron microscope, several nuclear magnetic resonance spectrometers, and a linear accelerator are available for student use. Also well-equipped are the students who emerge from these labs; Mount Holyoke produces more female Ph.D.s in chemistry and biology than any other liberal arts college. In addition, Mount Holyoke is a center of women's studies research, and politics and international relations are increasingly popular. Every year the college hosts the oldest forum for presenting undergraduate psychology papers. Students praise English (the most popular major), politics, women's studies, biology, and the arts, but astronomy, medieval studies, and classics draw fewer enrollees. Computer science is said to be extremely tough. The new Weissman Center for Leadership has merged the Center for Leadership and Public Advocacy with the college's Speaking, Arguing, and Writing program. Courses incorporate oral presentation and feedback aimed at developing students' powers of persuasion. The college also recently announced that SAT scores are now optional for applicants.

Although some intro courses can have as many as 100 students, most upper-level courses are small and intimate—some as tiny as three students. (Don't fret about not graduating in four years; the only class consistently over-subscribed is ballroom dancing, a junior says.) With a 10–to–1 student/faculty ratio, students easily develop close relationships with faculty members—relationships even a first-semester freshman can enjoy. "Most of my profs have been full professors, and all I have taken are intro classes!" a first-year raves. "The professors seem to honestly care about their students' well-being as well as their academic progress." Also, students adhere to an honor code that includes self-scheduled, self-proctored final exams.

The January winter term is optional at Mount Holyoke; students often opt to take a two-credit, nontraditional course or participate in an off-campus internship instead of returning to school. The Washington Internship program is the most popular of these experiences. About 25 percent of students pack their bags junior

(Continued)

Expense: Pr $ $ $ $
Phi Beta Kappa: Yes
Applicants: 2,435
Accepted: 60%
Enrolled: 39%
Graduate in 6 Years: 79%
Returning Freshmen: 90%
Academics: ✍ ✍ ✍ ✍
Social: ☎ ☎ ☎
Q of L: ★ ★ ★
Admissions: (413) 538-2023
Email Address:
  admission@mtholyoke.edu

Strongest Programs:
  English
  Biological sciences
  Economics
  International Relations
  Psychology
  Politics

More than 70 foreign nations are represented in Mount Holyoke's diverse student body.

year and leave Massachusetts for a semester or a year abroad. These sojourners are able to study in more than 25 countries either through the Twelve-College Exchange Program* or one of the college's own programs. Those interested in the sea can opt to take part in the Maritime Studies Program.*

Mount Holyoke attracts students from all over the nation and the world, and students value this diversity, as well as what they have in common. They call their peers "ambitious, great leaders, friendly, liberal, activists, and laid-back," but note that the campus can be overbearingly P.C. "It's hard to have an opinion and not have someone disagree," one student says. "But those disagreements usually end up in a discussion." African Americans make up 5 percent of the student body, Asian Americans 9 percent, and Hispanics 5 percent.

Ninety percent of students live in the 19 residence halls, and most give the rooms rave reviews. Students say the dorms are homey and spotlessly clean, noting that the older dorms are all antique-like with fireplaces and high ceilings. The dorms range from 65 to 130 students each, and all maintain proportional representation of the classes. Freshmen are included in every dorm and even have a choice of which one they prefer. After the first year, students endure both a dorm and a room lottery. The older dorms, with their large, odd-shaped rooms and huge bay windows, are the coveted prizes. Upperclassmen usually win singles; freshmen and sophomores have large, one-room doubles. Dinner is served in the dorms or in cafeterias. And anyone who finds studying at night leads to the munchies need not go hungry at Mt. Holyoke, because milk and cookies—or healthier fare like hummus and vegetables—are served at 10:00 each night. "Not many students live off-campus, as the college encourages the development of community," a sport science major says.

Students find the Five College Consortium* one of Mount Holyoke's greatest assets. A free bus service runs every 20 minutes between UMass, Amherst, Smith, and Hampshire, multiplying a Holyoke student's access to academic, social, and cultural opportunities. The South Hadley Center includes eateries, a pub, shops, and apartments. The key to social life here is willingness to make your own fun. "I know people who stay in every weekend and do homework," a first-year says. "But if you go out and look for a party, you will find one." Some of the best road trip includes Boston, Montreal, and New York City. The campus is constantly abuzz with multicultural festivals, musical performances, and theater productions. "Every week is an awareness week of some type," one student says. As for safety on campus, security guards patrol constantly, dorms are locked, and receptionists monitor activity. Administrators have tightened the regulations governing alcohol, but students still find ways to score liquor even if they're underage.

Mount Holyoke women, perhaps more than their counterparts at Smith and Wellesley, have made a virtue out of their school's most visible "vice": the lack of men. Students enjoy the fact that all leadership positions are filled by women, and there's a strong and supportive community spirit (but boys are not far away at nearby schools.) As expected, feminism and women's rights are focal points of debate, as is homophobia and lesbianism. And like most happy families, Mount Holyoke students relish the rich traditions of the school. A first-year student faces a bevy of rituals: upon arriving at MHC, she is endowed with a secret elf (a sophomore), a big sister (a junior), a disorientation leader (a senior), and plenty of activities and traditions. Mountain Day occurs every fall when students awake to ringing bells, classes are canceled (even the library is closed), and the entire student body treks up Mount Holyoke for picnicking and foliage viewing. Also, Pangynaskeia, a festival dating to 1979 that celebrates the diversity of women, has quickly become one of the school's most popular traditions.

The college encourages athletic participation for everyone and tempts laggards with a demanding 18-hole golf course, jogging trails, and two lakes. The 20-acre equestrian center includes a 57-stall barn, two riding areas, a training and show area, and seating for 300. Varsity teams are strong on the whole, especially track and field and riding, which produced national champions in 1999. Crew regattas and softball take the place of football games; nearly everyone comes out to cheer.

Situated just far enough from cities within a beautiful natural setting, MHC provides its students with the space and encouragement to be their own women. Opinions are expressed and celebrated, while the multicultural texture of the campus is ever-apparent and enjoyed. "There is every type of person here and each one is accepted," a senior says. The rich fabric of tradition underscores the college's proud history and make for wonderful memories. One student sums it up this way: "The traditions create a family atmosphere that you are part of forever."

If You Apply To ➤ **Mount Holyoke**...Early decision: Dec. 1, Jan. 1. Regular admissions and financial aid: Jan. 15. Guarantees to meet demonstrated need. Campus interviews: recommended, evaluative. Alumni interviews: optional, evaluative. ACTs or SATs: optional. SAT IIs: optional. Accepts the Common Application and electronic applications. Writing sample with teacher's comments required. Essay question: what draws you to Mount Holyoke, most meaningful activities; one of the following: which charity you would support, wisest advice you've received, influence of other cultures on sense of self, important person, experience or achievement.

Muhlenberg College

2400 Chew Street, Allentown, PA 18104-5586

Forget the vision of a stodgy professor blandly lecturing to masses of glassy-eyed students. Professors at Muhlenberg College are more than just teachers—they become friends and confidantes. "Professors treat students as colleagues, and the result is a mutual respect that often develops into a scholarly friendship," says an economics major. "This ease of communication makes for a hell of a strong college." While that type of language might not befit a college that began with Lutheran roots, Muhlenberg has grown up and evolved into a strong liberal arts college. Students are openly encouraged to explore a range of academics and extra-curricular activities to help them wend their way toward a fulfilling career.

Set on 75 park-like acres, the Muhlenberg campus is a combination of older Gothic stone structures and newer buildings in a variety of architectural styles. Prominent facilities include a lovely chapel, the high-tech Trexler Library, a 40-acre biological field station and wildlife sanctuary, and a 48-acre arboretum with more than 300 species of wildflowers, broadleaf evergreens, and conifer trees. The campus also boasts a football stadium and all-weather track, the 50,000 square-foot Trexler Pavilion for the Performing Arts that features a dramatic 45-foot glass outer shell and houses a variety of performing spaces, and the new Moyer Hall, a high-tech academic center that houses state-of-the-art space for the psychology, education, religion, and philosophy departments.

Muhlenberg's regional reputation rests on its premedical program, which continues to attract a large proportion of students. An agreement with Philadelphia's

Website: www.muhlenberg.edu
Location: City outskirts
Total Enrollment: 2,400
Undergraduates: 2,035
Male/Female: 43/57
SAT Ranges: V 540–620 M 541–621
Financial Aid: 65%
Expense: Pr $ $ $
Phi Beta Kappa: Yes
Applicants: 3,274
Accepted: 55%
Enrolled: 31%
Grad in 6 Years: 82%
Returning Freshmen: 92%
Academics: ✏ ✏ ✏
Social: ☎ ☎ ☎
Q of L: ★ ★ ★ ★
Admissions: (484) 664-3200

(Continued)

Email Address:
admissions@muhlenberg.edu

Strongest Programs:
Premed/Biology
Prelaw
Business
Psychology
Theater Arts
English

Hahnemann University Medical School guarantees seats for up to six Muhlenberg students per year. The college's theater arts program is also a national draw and a few alumni have even gone on to star on Broadway. Science lab equipment at Muhlenberg is cutting edge, and a comprehensive natural science major allows for a sampling of it all. The "Living Writers at Muhlenberg" series has brought a number of noted authors to campus, including Maya Angelou, Joyce Carol Oates, and Studs Terkel. Muhlenberg sends study groups to Washington, D.C., and students may spend semesters abroad in England, France, Spain, Germany, Argentina, the Czech Republic, and the Netherlands—or any program sponsored by the International Student Exchange. Muhlenberg is also a member of the Lehigh Valley Association of Independent Colleges* consortium.

The school offers two honors programs, the Muhlenberg Scholars Program and the Dana Associates Program, each of which are limited to 15 students per entering class. They carry an annual $3,000 stipend and culminate in an in-depth mentored senior research project. Psychology is Muhlenberg's most popular major; classics and social work have been dropped; and a women's studies minor has been added. General education requirements are organized into two major groups: Skills (writing, oral expression, reasoning, and foreign language) and Perspectives (literature and the arts, meaning and values, human behavior and social institutions, historical studies, physical and life sciences, and other cultures). One semester of physical education is required. Each freshman is assigned a First-Year Advising Team, usually consisting of four students (a student mentor, a student advisor, and two academic advisors) and a faculty member. "They encourage us to fulfill college requirements as early as possible so we have plenty of time for classes for ourselves," one freshman reports.

The fun-filled, three-day freshman orientation program carries one requirement: learning the alma mater and then hightailing it to the president's house to serenade him. All freshmen also take a writing-intensive, discussion-intensive First-Year Seminar, with enrollment capped at 15. Except for introductory science lectures, about half of the classes have fewer than 25 students. "Small classes and personal involvement with professors foster an intellectual environment," says a freshman. The close working relationships means students are "treated as more than social security numbers," according to an English/theater major. Professors expect a lot from students, but they're also known for distributing their home phone numbers, offering extra office hours, and even inviting students out to dinner.

Muhlenberg draws about 32 percent of its students from Pennsylvania. While the campus is 90 percent white, other kinds of diversity exist. "Muhlenberg's population has its Ambercrombians, Phish-lovers, jocks, geniuses, and artisans," says one senior. "People sometimes have trouble looking over the glaze of a 'country club' college. There is diversity economically, politically, and culturally." Appreciation of other cultures is emphasized as Muhlenberg strives for a more ethnically and religiously varied campus. But the Berg is "not very activist, and is less liberal than many of its counterparts," says an economics major.

Muhlenberg encourages on-campus living and guarantees housing to all undergraduates except transfers. About 95 percent of the student body live in on-campus housing. All dorms have computer labs, study lounges, and vending machines. Prosser is recommended for freshmen because of its coed wing, while upperclassmen praise the Muhlenberg Independent Living Experience, or MILE, townhouses. New West, a 113-bed dorm with central air and private bathrooms, is also popular. Freshmen choose from a seven- or five-day meal plan. The food is decent, with a salad bar, pasta machine, soup-and-bread line, brown-bag lunches,

Gotta dance? The 50,000 square-foot Trexler Pavilion for the Performing Arts features a dramatic 45-foot glass outer shell. It opened with a performance by Broadway dancer/actor Gregory Hines, and features a black-box experimental stage and set shop.

"wellness" entrées, and the ever-popular ice cream machine. Also, Starbucks opened a coffee bar in the student union.

Most social life at Muhlenberg takes place on campus. The Muhlenberg Activities Council (MAC) provides comedians every Thursday evening, current movies in the Red Door Café, live band concerts (Smashmouth was a recent visitor), and new movies on the lawn. City buses stop five minutes from campus for trips to Allentown proper and area malls, though many students say the townies are not especially friendly. But Muhlenberg students are very active in community service, and over 200 participate in the Big Buddy Program, which pairs them with elementary school kids. For those who want to really get away, there are daily bus runs to New York City (for clubbing and theater), Philadelphia (for nightlife and cheesesteaks), and Baltimore and Washington, D.C. Outdoorsy students also can pick up the Appalachian Trail for a little hiking.

Thirty-five percent of the men and 36 percent of the women pledge their undergraduate years to fraternities and sororities, but Greek life does not dominate the social scene. Alcohol is available, but forbidden if you're underage, per Pennsylvania law. The drinking that does occur rarely gets to the *Animal House* stage. "To be sure, Muhlenberg is not the poster child for the temperance movement," a freshman says, "but the drinking that is done takes place with reason and restraint." Big social events include Spring Fling Weekend, East Fest, Benfer Bash, and the Celtic Games, held at midnight every St. Patrick's Day. There's also a candlelight ceremony where freshmen write down their college goals, and then re-examine them four years later, the day before graduation.

For the athletically inclined, intramural sports arouse a great deal of passion. Men's and women's basketball are strong, winning Centennial Conference championships and NCAA Tournament bids. Other sports, including men's golf, women's soccer and softball, have garnered regional awards. The school's Life Sports Center offers a pool, basketball court and other all-purpose courts, and a jogging track. Also popular is Frisbee golf; there's an 18-hole course on campus, where play goes on during all seasons and all hours of the day and night.

It's no mean feat for a college to provide so many interesting, compelling courses that students regularly want to wake up on time to catch classes. "At least two per semester will be 'don't miss' classes," says a biology/English major. For example, "literature comes alive with the passion each professor exudes. Some professors inspire and make you delve into the subject." Outside of the classroom, the Berg provides a close-knit, family-esque atmosphere that really helps students shine. "Muhlenberg gives me the feeling of home that is so important for a student to enjoy their years in college," explains a biology major. Simply put, it's just a pleasant place to be. "It amazes people that random individuals will smile and say hello as you walk on campus," says a theater major. "We are an extremely friendly school. I think that's the big difference.

An agreement with Philadelphia's Hahnemann University Medical School guarantees seats for up to six Muhlenberg students per year.

Overlaps

Lafayette, Gettysburg, Franklin and Marshall, Dickinson, Lehigh.

If You Apply To ➤ **Muhlenberg**…Early decision: Jan. 15. Regular admissions and financial aid: Feb. 15. Meets demonstrated need of 92%. Campus interviews: recommended, evaluative (required, along with a graded paper, if students choose not to submit SAT scores). Alumni interviews: optional, informational. SATs or ACTs: optional. SAT IIs: optional. Accepts the Common Application and electronic applications. Essay question: significant experience or achievement; issue of personal, local, national or international concern; or influential person.

Website: www.unl.edu

Location: Center city

Total Enrollment: 22,142

Undergraduates: 17,804

Male/Female: 53/47

SAT Ranges: V 500–635 M 515–660

ACT Range: 21–27

Financial Aid: 42%

Expense: Pub $ $

Phi Beta Kappa: Yes

Applicants: 6,997

Accepted: 74%

Enrolled: 71%

Grad in 6 Years: 47%

Returning Freshmen: 79%

Academics: 🎓 🎓 🎓

Social: ☎ ☎ ☎ ☎

Q of L: ★ ★ ★

Admissions: (800) 742-8800

Email Address:

nuhusker@unl.edu

Strongest Programs:

Agribusiness and Agronomy

Animal Science

Audiology and Speech Pathology

Music

Chemistry

Entrepreneurship

Food Sciences

Journalism

Nestled in the capital of the Cornhusker State is the University of Nebraska at Lincoln, a school aiming high and striving to become known for its ever improving range of majors and courses. More than 20,000 students call UNL home, and their school pride is contagious. On crisp fall weekends, when spirits are high and the Big Red football arcs through the air, Huskers cheer and paint the town of Lincoln red and white in show of appreciation for their alma mater. In fact, on home-game Saturdays, the stadium is the third largest city in the state, holding 5 percent of the population. Away from the stadium, in the classrooms, UNL has more reason to cheer with top programs ranging from music to agriculture to journalism.

UNL spreads across two campuses. The East Campus is home to the colleges of agricultural sciences and natural resources, human resources and family sciences, law and dentistry. Most entering students end up on the larger City Campus, where the architectural style ranges from the modern Sheldon Art Gallery designed by Philip Johnson to the architecture building, which is on the National Register of Historic Places. There are also several malls, an arboretum, and a sculpture garden. This is the home of six of the eight undergraduate colleges: architecture, arts and sciences, journalism and mass communications, business administration, fine and performing arts, engineering and technology, and the teachers college. In the past two years, the UNL has completed a major addition to and renovation of the student union, added more university-owned apartments, and constructed a much-needed 600-car parking garage. More than $93 million dollars of new construction and renovations are underway across the campus.

Nebraska's College of Agricultural Sciences and Natural Resources is known for its outstanding programs in food science and technology, agribusiness, and animal science, housed in a $19-million complex. The school of music's opera program has received national attention, and the performing arts programs benefit from the $18-million Lied Center for the Performing Arts, which seats 2,300. Education, business administration, and psychology are some of the most popular majors. New programs include majors in engineering, film studies, architectural engineering, natural resource, and environmental economics, and even grazing livestock systems. UNL can be academically challenging—by choice. "It's possible to pursue only honors classes and research, but there are also those who just 'get by'," says one premed student.

Nebraska's Comprehensive Education Program provides students with a common set of educational experiences across the majors and colleges. It has four components: Information Discovery and Retrieval (1 course), Essential Studies (9 courses), Integrative Studies (10 courses), and Co-Curricular Experience. To help novice freshmen get oriented, a one-semester University Foundations class covers the inner and outer workings of the campus, organized around academic subjects. Big Red Welcome combines entertainment and food in a carnival setting to welcome new students, and the SIPS program (Summer Institute for Promising Scholars) is a six-week pre-orientation session for incoming minority students. The J. D. Edwards Honors Program gives computer science and management students internships to complement their coursework.

Getting into courses in the most popular areas, especially education, business, and engineering, can be a problem, students say; preregistration is a must. Though many top profs teach introductory courses, freshmen and sophomores should expect to spend much of their time with graduate teaching assistants. "There are many graduate students teaching freshman courses, and they grade extremely difficult," says a biochemistry major. But one junior had a different experience. "I've been fortunate to have had great professors. Many have been recognized by students or the university for their incredible dedication to students and their fields." Students also can study abroad in places like Costa Rica, Germany, Mexico, and Japan.

The UNL student body is mostly conservative, mostly white, and mostly from the Cornhusker State. Asian Americans make up 2 percent of the student body, with blacks and Hispanics at 4 percent combined. "Diversity is hard to find on campus," a senior says. "There are not many minority students on campus [which] creates tension." Other hot-button issues include underage drinking, homosexuality, and abortion.

Still, UNL is big and there's a group or activity for everyone; fraternity and house parties, roller skating, the movies, eating out, visiting coffee shops and bars (for those of age), and road trips to Omaha or Kansas City are just some of the activities that keep students busy. For some, the fall semester revolves around football weekends and postseason bowl games. Anyone within 100 miles can hear the triumphant refrain gleefully floating from the football stadium. "There is no place like Nebraska/where we're all true blue/We'll all stick together/in all kinds of weather/for dear old Nebraska U!"

About 25 percent of students live in the university's single-sex or coed dorms, and there's usually no trouble getting a room. Dorm lotteries favor those wanting to stay in the same room or on the same floor. Students say the dorms are clean and well-maintained, though the freshman dwellings can be a bit cramped. Each room also is wired for the Internet. Freshmen, who must live on campus, are welcomed to the residence halls through the FINK program, which is friendlier than it sounds (the acronym stands for Freshman Indoctrination of New Kids).

Fraternities draw 16 percent of UNL men and sororities attract 17 percent of the women. They offer both social events and a chance to get involved in the Lincoln community. Homecoming, Greek Week, and Ivy Day are among the most-anticipated campus events, as is The End, new alcohol-free programming at the end of each semester, during "dead week" and finals week. For those who want to indulge, plenty of bars are within walking distance of UNL, providing relief to students dissatisfied with the dry campus. It's difficult to be served on campus, and one student says the ban on alcohol has made some on-campus parties as exciting as bingo night. Lincoln itself is a great college town, with shopping, theaters, restaurants, and movies. If you need more action, Omaha is only 45 minutes away. Pachyderm enthusiasts will be delighted by the Nebraska Museum of Natural History's outstanding collection of prehistoric elephant skeletons. Beyond the sidewalks are miles of flat road and plains ideal for biking, cross-country skiing, and snowmobiling.

In addition to football, UNL is a men's gymnastic powerhouse, and is gaining a reputation in women's volleyball and basketball, and men's baseball. In all, Husker teams finished in the top 10 nationally in more than 10 sports in the past two years, and won numerous Big 12 championships. The biggest football rivalries are with Colorado and Oklahoma. Husker fans proclaim that if forced to choose between going to Oklahoma and going to hell after death—well, it would be a tough choice.

At Nebraska, future farmers mingle with techno-whizzes, while teachers-in-training brush elbows with architecture mavens. "The kindness and sincerity of the students and professors make this university special," explains an exercise science major. "The opportunities outside the classroom are truly unique at UNL." Whether studying overseas, immersing themselves in an internship, or going wild on Saturday afternoon, students here know how to make the most of their time as Cornhuskers.

If You Apply To ➢

Nebraska...Rolling admissions: June 30. Housing: March 24. Campus and alumni interviews: optional, informational. SATs or ACTs: required. SAT IIs: optional. No essay question.

New College of the University of South Florida

BEST BUY

5700 North Tamiami Trail, Sarasota, FL 34243-2197

New College was new about 35 years ago, and though the rest of the country may be marching into the new millennium, the school is eagerly preserving the 1960s-style radicalism that suggested its rather unimaginative name in the first place. New College has no grades, no GPAs, and no required courses, nor does it boast Greek groups or powerhouse athletic teams like some other members of the Florida state university system. But students don't miss these typical trappings of college life. They're more interested in "the freedom to learn in an environment that encourages students to take charge of their lives and minds," says a senior. The bargain-basement price tag doesn't hurt, either.

New College is part of the University of South Florida system, which leads to a number of contradictions. It started in 1960 as a private college, but when inflation threatened its existence in the 1970s, it offered its campus to the University of South Florida. It's now a state school that receives public funding, but has its own endowment (legislators tend to be stingy). New College also serves as the honors college of the state university system of Florida, but is an academically independent entity. Clearly, the school still has a mind of its own, as do its students, who are "extremely motivated and know how to balance work and play," says a psychology major. This student also says his peers are more laid-back than students at places like Amherst and Williams and more social than students at Reed.

New College's campus is adjacent to Sarasota Bay and consists of historic mansions from the former estate of circus magnate Charles Ringling, abutting modern dorms designed by I. M. Pei. The central quad is filled with palm trees, and sunsets over the bay are spectacular. New College shares its campus with the Sarasota branch of USF, which offers upper-level courses in business, education, and engineering. New facilities include two 70-bed apartment-style residence halls, a building with library, office, and classroom space for the natural sciences, and a marine biology research center that was completed in 2000.

The administration says that at New College, "rather than impose arbitrary school-wide curriculum or distribution requirements, the faculty guides students' academic choices with the double purpose of individual growth and solid grounding in their areas of specialty. Self-motivation and self-discipline are expected, encouraged, and rewarded with a highly individualized and rigorous education." This "revolutionary" attitude is reflected in the calendar: the two 14-week semesters are separated by a month-long January Interterm, during which students devise and carry out their own research or conduct group projects. Students work out a "contract" with their advisor each semester and receive written evaluations instead of grades. Seven semester-long contracts and three independent study projects lead to an area of concentration, capped by a senior thesis and an oral baccalaureate examination. Due to the highly individualized nature of the curriculum, getting into some classes can be a challenge, especially for science majors looking to fulfill requirements for grad school admission, says a senior. The shape of any student's program depends heavily on the outlook of his or her faculty sponsor, and students say advising—both academic and career-oriented—is readily available.

New College doesn't offer the specialized courses of a large university, but there's still plenty to choose from, especially for students interested in the social sciences, the humanities, and the physical sciences, where a 1,100-gallon sea water system is available for lab experiments in animal behavior and physiology. Anthropology wins raves, but at least one student warns against wandering into the physical sciences if they're not your forte or area of concentration, as professors tend to treat non-majors and majors differently. Fine arts suffers from a lack of core faculty, and it remains to be seen whether the interdisciplinary international studies program will really pull professors together from various departments, administrators say. Regardless of discipline, the Jane Bancroft Cook Library makes up for its small—less than 300,000 volumes—size with a language lab, videotape viewing area, an interlibrary loan program with the entire state university system of Florida, and a classroom equipped for teleconferences.

Students praise the personalized attention they receive from New College professors, since graduate students and teaching assistants don't lead classes here. During a typical semester, about half of the students are engaged in one-on-one tutorials, and most other classes are seminars. All disciplines provide the opportunity for original research and students also may conduct field research around the globe, including the study of coral reefs in Central America, Buddhism in India, and history in Europe. "Professors are open to students' suggestions, sometimes creating new courses when there is enough interest," says one student. The academic climate at New College is rigorous, though without grades, competition is "more about motivation and responsibility."

In keeping with the revolution theme, students on this relatively cosmopolitan campus tend to be creative liberal types with '60s nuances. About 63 percent of students hail from Florida, perhaps because New College has yet to make a national name for itself. Minorities account for 14 percent of the student body. Social and political issues receive much attention, "There are groups that work on issues ranging from international trade agreements to environmentalism to Native American movements," says a history major.

Two-thirds of students and 98 percent of freshmen live in campus housing. Rooms in the Pei dorms "are gigantic and have their own bathrooms," says a senior. The Dart dorms, two new apartment-style halls, accommodate 140 students in two-bedroom, two-bath suites with a kitchen, living area, and—of course—air-conditioning (as essential as food and water in these parts). Rooms are chosen by lottery; though in the past older students were encouraged to move off campus to make room for new students, the new dorms are drawing them back, students report.

Seven semester-long contracts and three independent study projects lead to an area of concentration, capped by a senior thesis and an oral baccalaureate examination.

The Dart dorms, two new apartment-style halls, accommodate 140 students in two bedroom, two bath suites with a kitchen, living area, and—of course—air-conditioning (as essential as food and water in these parts).

On campus, social life is T-shirts-and-shorts relaxed. "Walls," free-form parties every Friday and Saturday night, can last until 4:00 or 5:00 A.M. the following morning. Alcohol policies follow state law; no one under 21 can drink, but "it is fairly simple for underage students to access any type of alcohol" if they pour it from the bottle into a cup and don't alert friendly campus cops to what they're sipping, says a senior. While Sarasota isn't a college town, it offers plenty of cultural enrichment in the form of theater, dance, and live music. The Ringling Museum of Art and the Asolo State Theater adjoin the campus. Many New College instrumentalists perform with the Florida West Coast Symphony, Sarasota's professionally led symphony orchestra. Other students are active in the community and volunteer in learning centers, local schools, and programs like Best Buddies. In the past, students have raised their own fees to fund plays, films, and programs like AIDS awareness; all kinds of clubs are active and vocal, including groups focusing on feminism, vegetarianism, animal rights, the environment, and gay/lesbian/bisexual issues. The open road to Tampa, Gainesville, Key West, New Orleans, Atlanta, and even Washington, D.C. ("to protest stuff"), beckons when Sarasota becomes too quiet.

New College is definitely not a haven for jocks, since it fields no varsity teams, somewhat of an oddity in football-crazy Florida. The yearly faculty-student softball game is popular, and anyone can play. Students also look forward to the Crucial Barbecue in January with music and mud wrestling, the Male Chauvinist Pig Roast, the SemiNormal, a semiformal event on the bay, and the Bowling Ball, a formal-dress occasion at a bowling alley. Palm Court Parties, held on Halloween, Valentine's Day, and Graduation, are not to be missed, as according to the student government constitution, the Palm Court is the center of the universe. While the school has a 25-meter swimming pool, students complain than it closes at 10:00 P.M. The nearby ocean (which does not close) is a bigger draw.

New College is a largely undiscovered gem that receives far fewer applicants than it deserves. If it were located in the Northeast or Midwest, students would be breaking down the doors to get in. But that makes it all the better for students who have figured out that New College offers a quality liberal arts program at a bargain price.

Overlaps

University of Florida, Florida State, Oberlin, Eckerd, Brown.

If You Apply To ➤   **New College**…Rolling admissions: May 1 (priority consideration Mar. 1). Financial aid: Mar. 1. Housing: May 1. Campus interviews: optional, evaluative. No alumni interviews. SATs or ACTs: required. SAT IIs: optional. Accepts the Common Application. Essay question: a book that has influenced you; extracurricular interest you might pursue in college; why New College; views on an issue important to you.

University of New Hampshire

Grant House, 4 Garrison Avenue, Durham, NH 03824-3510

Website: www.unh.edu
Location: Small town
Total Enrollment: 13,591
Undergraduates: 10,877

Although it weighs in at a hefty 13,500 students, the University of New Hampshire has an intimate feel, bolstered by quaint surroundings, strong faculty-student interaction, cozy classes, and other benefits usually absent at large state institutions. Students say that despite the size, there is always a way to connect with other members of the UNH community.

The university's wide-open grassy campus hosts a blend of modern facilities and ivy-covered brick buildings. The sprawling lawns are surrounded by 3,000 acres of farms, fields, and woods. During the past few years, UNH has invested in large-scale construction and renovation projects, including a recent $19-million expansion and renovation of Diamond Library. The project resulted in a 207,000-square-foot building with three grand reading rooms and state-of-the-art technology. The Donald M. Murray Journalism Laboratory, featuring over $100,000 of computer and projection equipment, was also completed recently, and renovation of the student union made space for two theaters, a food court, and the university bookstore. The new $8.5-million environmental technology building will be a multi-disciplinary science and engineering facility.

UNH's traditional emphasis on technical education is enriched by interdisciplinary programs and the many research opportunities offered by its five undergraduate schools. Business and engineering are the most respected programs, and the English department has a fine creative writing program. Marine biology is also considered stellar, due to UNH's proximity to the water. "I like being able to study something in class, and then go out into the state and see it as it exists in nature," raves a microbiology student, who adds that a chance to work in a research lab as a freshman was a terrific experience. Environmental studies, chemistry, occupational therapy, and nursing all are strong as well. UNH's programs in Classics, French, German, Italian, Japanese, Russian, and Spanish recently merged into a new Department of Languages, Literatures, and Cultures.

The university's general education requirements apply across the board, and mandate completion of 10 courses from eight categories: writing skills; quantitative reasoning; biological, physical, and technological sciences; historical perspectives; foreign cultures; fine arts; social science; and works of philosophy, literature, and ideas. Freshman composition is mandatory as part of a four-course "Writing Intensive" requirement. Classes are relatively small, almost always 50 students or fewer, and TAs only facilitate discussion sections or labs. "I feel lucky to have been taught by people who are world-renowned for their publications, teaching, or contribution to major projects," says an environmental conservation major. The academic climate is as competitive or laid-back as individual students desire, one senior says.

UNH prides itself on producing undergraduates with research experience. The Undergraduate Research Opportunities Program provides about 100 research awards each year for undergraduates to work closely with faculty on original projects. Budding scientists and sociologists have opportunities to work at research centers for space science and family violence; other students can take advantage of the Institute for Policy and Social Science Research, the Center for Humanities, and the Institute for the Study of Earth, Oceans, and Space. The Interoperability Lab enables students to work with professors and businesses on cutting-edge problems of computing equipment compatibility. The Isle of Shoals Marine Laboratory, which operates several research projects with Cornell University, is just seven miles off the coast. And then there's UNH's Technology, Society, and Values Program, designed to address the ethical implications of the computer age. UNH's study abroad program offers exchange programs with more than 140 U.S. colleges via the Center for International Education. Students can even earn a dual major by combining foreign study and classes in international affairs with those of any other program.

While UNH is New Hampshire's major public institution, it has long been popular with out-of-staters, who make up a full 43 percent of its students. The school is working on becoming more diverse; only 3 percent of the student body are minorities, which students mention as an area of concern. Another big issue

(Continued)

Male/Female: 41/59

SAT Ranges: V 510–600 M 510–610

Financial Aid: 55%

Expense: Pub $ $ $ $

Phi Beta Kappa: Yes

Applicants: 8,833

Accepted: 81%

Enrolled: 36%

Grad in 6 Years: 70%

Returning Freshmen: 84%

Academics: ✍ ✍ ✍

Social: ☎ ☎ ☎ ☎ ☎

Q of L: ★ ★ ★ ★

Admissions: (603) 862-1360

Email Address:
admissions@unh.edu

Strongest Programs:
Biological Sciences
Environmental Studies
History
English
Performing Arts
Occupational Therapy
Engineering
Nursing

The University Honors Program puts selected freshmen in small classes and seminars, and they continue honors work throughout their undergraduate education and must complete a senior thesis.

is state funding, which has decreased so dramatically in recent years that tuition went up 14 percent in 1997 and another 12 percent in 1998, making UNH one of the priciest public institutions anywhere. Social issues at UNH include alcohol awareness and—as might be expected in a place with such lush natural beauty—the environment. "UNH is becoming more environmentally conscious, especially with its recycling program and attempt to cut down on paper waste," remarks an international affairs major. The school offers more than 1,000 merit scholarships ranging from $100 to $7,500.

Fifty-five percent of UNHers live in the school's 30 single-sex and coed dorms, where "housing is reasonable," a senior says. The dorms offer special-interest groupings, lounges, fireplaces, TV lounges, study rooms, kitchenettes, and high-speed connections to the campus network. But there's more to dorm life than the tangible. "The atmosphere is great," says a student. "I got support when I needed it from hall staff." Freshmen and sophomores are guaranteed dorm rooms; most upperclassmen live off campus or in Gables and Woodside, on-campus apartment complexes, though one senior recommends staying on campus as long as possible to avoid "missing too much fun." Students also gripe that parking is difficult on campus.

Less than a five-minute walk from campus is the beautiful little town of Durham, which caters to the student clientele. Along Main Street, Durham has many restaurants, coffeehouses, a grocery store, an ice cream parlor, and a few bars, which have been divided into separate sections (for legal consumers of alcohol and everyone else). Greek groups, which claim 10 percent of UNH men and 7 percent of the women, are among those volunteering for walk-a-thons, clean-up, and playground restoration projects in town. The Greeks also throw parties, which are subject to the university's no-tolerance alcohol policy that evicts from on-campus housing underage students caught with alcohol more than once. One science major reports that violations also entail "protective custody for the night and a letter sent to your parents." For nondrinkers, the university offers weekend social events including concerts, dances, movies, and coffeehouses. Popular road trips include Boston and the White Mountains, or apple picking at a nearby farm. Late nights at L.L. Bean have also become commonplace, and Homecoming, Greek Week, Winter Carnival, Casino Night, and Spring Fling draw crowds every year. And every four years, New Hampshire takes the spotlight when the state holds the nation's earliest presidential primaries.

UNH teams that regularly enjoy national rankings and generate strong spectator interest include men's and women's ice hockey, which recently won the NCAA Championship, and students celebrate the first UNH goal of each game by inexplicably throwing a large fish onto the ice. Women's gymnastics, men's and women's basketball, and football, which recently won the New England Division Championship, are also impressive. However, students complain that athletics has felt more of the pinch from state budget cuts than any other department. Many students are unhappy that the men's baseball, lacrosse, and golf teams have been cut. Still, the university has a strong intramural sports program, through which more than 8,500 students played more than 900 teams last year.

When there's no game to watch or postgame revelry to indulge in, nature provides UNH students with more than enough to do—if they can find time off. (The school's nickname is the University of No Holidays, since an exceptionally generous winter break limits the number of days off during other seasons.) Skiing, camping, fishing, and hiking in nearby forests are favorite seasonal pastimes, and the Outing Club is among the most popular student activities. "The majority of campus is very outdoorsy and active," a senior says. And when students put away their skis and hit the books, they know they are enjoying a solid, well-rounded education. "A large number of my professors have motivated and inspired me to go after what I want in the world," says an environmental conservation major. "My education here at UNH has prepared me to do it."

If You Apply To ➤ New Hampshire…Early action: Dec. 1. Regular admissions: Feb. 1. Financial aid: Mar. 1. Housing: Feb 1. Campus interviews: optional, informational. No alumni interviews. SATs or ACTs: required. SAT II: optional. Does not guarantee to meet demonstrated need. Accepts the Common and electronic application. Apply to particular school or program. Essay question: best piece of advice you have received, challenge you have faced, or topic of your choice.

The College of New Jersey (formerly Trenton State College)

P.O. Box 7718, Ewing, NJ 08628-0718

The College of New Jersey is a public institution with an emphasis on undergraduates more commonly found at a private school. TCNJ offers professors focused on teaching and a campus physically similar to one found down the road at Princeton University—without the Ivy League price tag. Formerly a teachers' college, TCNJ strives to offer students a solid education and to prepare them for life after college. "The small size develops a closeness among all the students and faculty," says a senior.

TCNJ is set on 289 wooded and landscaped acres in suburban Ewing Township, six miles from Trenton. The picturesque Georgian Colonial architecture centers on Quimby's Prairie surrounded by the original academic buildings of the 1930s. A flock of Canada geese makes their home in one of the two campus lakes. The year 2000 saw the opening of a brand new $50 million science complex, as well as a new School of Business.

To graduate, students must earn 120 credits for all BS programs in the School of Business, BA programs except for teacher preparation, and the Bachelor of Science in Nursing. In addition, the list of majors and study abroad opportunities continues to grow. The First Year Experience program, a required two-semester sequence consisting of From Athens to New York and Society, Ethics, and Technology, is designed to ease students into the demanding reality of college life with an approach that integrates academics, individual development, and social understanding, including 10 hours of community service. Says an alum who's returned to work in admissions: "Every student is expected to get involved and leave The College a better place for having been here." Also required of incoming freshmen: Expectations, a one-day program to help students and parents understand what they can expect from the college and what the college expects of them; the 10-week College Seminar, to smooth the transition to college; Welcome Week, which gives freshmen a chance to meet their classmates and become acquainted with the campus; and Summer Readings, which exposes students to the kind of scholarship and dialogue they can expect at The College of New Jersey.

Website: www.tcnj.edu
Location: Suburban
Total Enrollment: 6,747
Undergraduates: 5,930
Male/Female: 40/60
SAT Ranges: V 560–650 M 580–670
Financial Aid: 50%
Expense: Pub $ $ $ $
Phi Beta Kappa: No
Applicants: 5,755
Accepted: 55%
Enrolled: 38%
Grad in 6 Years: 78%
Returning Freshmen: 93%
Academics: ✍ ✍ ✍
Social: ☎ ☎ ☎
Q of L: ★ ★ ★
Admissions: (609) 771-2131
Email Address: admiss@vm.tcnj.edu

Strongest Programs:
  Biology
  Chemistry
  History
  Elementary Education

Recent choices include *Race Matters* by Cornel West and Ralph Ellison's *Invisible Man*. Other requirements include two semesters each of rhetoric and mathematics, 26 credits of "perspectives on the world," and three semesters of foreign language (arts and sciences students only).

TCNJ's origins as a teachers' college are reflected in the fact that elementary education is the second most-popular major. The business school is strong, as are the natural sciences, while sociology and health and physical education are considered weak. Academically, "the environment is quite competitive, but not impossible," says an information systems management major. The college offers a combined, four-and-one-half-year BS/MA in law and justice, taught jointly by TCNJ and Rutgers; a seven-year BS/MD degree program with the University of Medicine and Dentistry of New Jersey; and a seven-year BS/OD degree with SUNY College of Optometry. TCNJ also offers foreign study in 11 countries, and is a member of the International Student Exchange Program, giving students access to 131 colleges and universities across the U.S., including Alaska, the Virgin Islands, Puerto Rico, and Guam. The college has no teaching assistants, and faculty members get high marks for accessibility. "I don't think I would have pursued an internship like this, or even the field of geophysics, without the guidance of professors I've come to know," says a physics major who spent a recent summer doing field work in Alaska.

The year 2000 saw the opening of a brand new $50 million science complex, as well as a new School of Business.

The school has no cap on out-of-state admissions, but only six percent of TCNJ's students are non-Jerseyans; 57 percent of the freshmen graduated in the top tenth of their high school class, and 65 percent attended public high school. The college has aggressively pursued minority students, and today, African American, Hispanic, and Asian American students account for 16 percent of the student body. "Diversity programming—bringing talent to serve all campus student needs—is a big social and political issue," says a finance major. The college offers merit scholarships ranging from $1,500 to full tuition (including room and board) a year, depending on SAT scores and class rank. "TCNJ brings in many of the best New Jersey students who are accepted to Ivy League schools but cannot afford them," says a senior.

Dorm housing, which is described as "very good" and "well-maintained," is only guaranteed for freshmen and sophomores, though 60 percent of all students (and 95 percent of first-years) live on campus. Freshman hang their hats in either Travers-Wolfe, a two-building, 10-story hall, or Lakeside, a four-building complex. After that, students can enter the lottery for about 2,100 upperclass spaces in the apartment-style Townhouses, Community Commons, or New Residence Hall or try one of several local apartment complexes. Although suburban Ewing doesn't really cater to students, funky New Hope, PA, and preppy Princeton, NJ, are just up the road; restaurants, bars, movie theaters—and this being New Jersey, many malls—are within a short drive. State alcohol policies are strictly enforced, and the underage shouldn't hope to imbibe at the campus bar, the Rathskeller. Seventeen percent of both men and women belong to fraternities and sororities, which provide many of the off-campus parties. Campus programming includes dances, concerts (Billy Joel, Fiona Apple), and movies. "You must join clubs," says a senior. "It is the best way to meet people." Road trips to Philadelphia and New York, each about an hour distant and accessible by train, are also highly recommended.

TCNJ's origins as a teachers' college are reflected in the fact that elementary education is the second most-popular major.

The College of New Jersey's 21 varsity teams are big fish in the small pond of NCAA Division III; since 1979, they've won 35 Division III crowns in six different sports and 28 runner-up titles. Students rally around the football and basketball squads, especially when archrival Rowan comes to town, and the women's field hockey, lacrosse, and soccer teams have a faithful following. TCNJers also look forward to several annual events, including Homecoming, a Family Fest Day, and—the springtime favorite—Senior Week.

The College of New Jersey is one of the nation's "budget Ivies", with reasonable tuition and a location that offers media types, artists, and budding scientists a relaxed suburban haven within shouting distance of the editors, producers, directors, curators, and pharmaceutical companies that will be clamoring for their skills after graduation. The small size means that "the friends that I have met here will last," says one senior. Graduates take not only fond memories, says an administrator, but a well-rounded education and a foundation for their future.

If You Apply To ➤

The College of New Jersey...Early decision: Nov. 15. Rolling admissions: Feb. 15. Does not guarantee to meet demonstrated need. Campus interviews: optional, informational. No alumni interviews. SATs or ACTs: required, SATs preferred. SAT IIs: required (writing). Accepts electronic applications. Essay question: what your reflections on college will be on the day before graduation; how a societal event from the past four years has affected your life; a challenge you overcame; your career goal and how a biology degree from TCNJ will help in achieving it (biology majors only; in addition to one of the other three topics).

New Jersey Institute of Technology

University Heights, Newark, NJ 07102

It's cheap. It's close to home. And it offers students a respectable preprofessional education. The New Jersey Institute of Technology provides a no-frills technological education that prepares them for a future in an ever-changing global workplace. NJIT's challenging programs emphasize education, research, service, and—not surprisingly—economic development. It's an enticing combination for students seeking a high-tech, low-cost education.

NJIT's urban 45-acre campus is dotted with 24 buildings of diverse architectural styles, ranging from Elizabethan Gothic to contemporary design. Some of New Jersey's greatest cultural institutions are just blocks away, including the Newark Museum, Symphony Hall, and the new New Jersey Center for the Performing Arts. Construction is nearly constant on campus, and newer construction includes a student services mall, renovation of labs, and a new Building Sciences Complex.

NJIT is composed of the Newark College of Engineering, the School of Architecture (the only state-supported one in New Jersey), the School of Management, the College of Science and Liberal Arts, and the Albert Dorman Honors College. More than 100 entering freshmen made up the Dorman class in 1998, and enrollment in the college is almost 500 students. Top applicants are offered a spot in Dorman as NJIT freshmen, and keep these places as long as they continue to do well academically. Perks of Dorman membership include guaranteed dorm rooms, research opportunities, and acceptance into the BS/MS program after completion of five courses for the undergraduate major. Engineering and computer science garner the most student praise, while mechanical engineering is especially challenging. Not surprisingly, students say humanities are weak. Every incoming student gets a personal computer, which can be purchased after graduation at a reduced rate. Computers are integrated into almost every subject. To graduate, students must fulfill general education requirements in areas ranging

Website: www.njit.edu

Location: Urban

Total Enrollment: 8,191

Undergraduates: 5,177

Male/Female: 79/21

SAT Ranges: V 490–600 M 540–640

Financial Aid: 47%

Expense: Pub $ $ $ $

Phi Beta Kappa: No

Applicants: 2,196

Accepted: 63%

Enrolled: 45%

Grad in 6 Years: 40%

Returning Freshmen: 80%

Academics: ✍ ✍ ✍

Social: ☎

Q of L: ★ ★

Admissions: (201) 596-3300

Email Address: admissions@admin.njit.edu

Strongest Programs:
  Architecture
  Computer Science

from English to management. All freshmen take calculus I and II, English composition, computer science, physical education, and Freshman Seminar, a course that introduces students to university life.

Nine new degrees have been added to the curriculum recently, including an MS program in power engineering and a Ph.D. in biomedical informatics. NJIT has also worked with Rutgers to create a number of joint-degree programs, from biology to history.

Most NJIT courses have 50 students or fewer, "small enough so you can't hide if you don't do the work," warns one undergrad. But most students say the atmosphere is surprisingly laid-back. A sophomore explains, "A student working regularly will always get a B." The administration assists students who are having a difficult time, arranging for leaves of absence or extra semesters with a lighter courseload. "Graduating in four years would be miraculous at NJIT," especially for some engineering students. Coeds say they sometimes have problems getting into classes offered once a year and capped at relatively low enrollments. But one student confides that if a freshman has all of the prerequisite courses, it shouldn't be too tough to graduate on time.

Students give teaching quality average to high marks. Since most profs have worked in industry, they can offer job information along with academic assistance. "The professors enjoy what they are doing and put a lot of work into their teaching," says a freshman. However, some complain that understanding the coursework is easier than understanding the professors. "Many professors have strong accents, which makes it very hard for students to understand the lecture," says a future civil engineer. Academic advising is spotty, students say, but career counseling is helpful in preparing students for the job hunt. NJIT's most-favored academic option is the co-op program, which enables juniors to get paid for two six-month periods of work at technical companies.

As New Jersey's comprehensive technological university, NJIT attracts a wide range of students with different interests. But, one sophomore warns, "We need women." African American and Hispanic students together make up a substantial 25 percent of the student body, and Asian Americans account for 20 percent. Only 9 percent of the students hail from out of state or from foreign lands, but World Week—with cultural performances and ethnic foods—is a popular spring event. "We are very diverse and we try hard to get along," says a future electrical engineer. "And you know what—it works."

NJIT has a chapter of Tau Beta Pi, the national engineering honor society. The university does not guarantee to meet the financial aid of all admits, but offers about 1,200 merit scholarships, ranging from $500 to tuition and room and board. The college works with local businesses to recruit qualified minority scholars, offering them scholarships and summer jobs.

NJIT's four residence halls can accommodate one-third of the students. Freshmen and students living farthest away get first crack at the rooms, and those who get in are guaranteed space the next year. Consensus has it that the best freshman dorms are Redwood Hall and Cypress. NJIT is still primarily a commuter school, with students living at home to cut costs, so getting a room is no problem. Upperclassmen move into fraternity houses or nearby off-campus apartments. The dorms and frats both have kitchen facilities. Because of its urban location, safety is always a consideration at NJIT. Students praise the public safety efforts the school has undertaken; in the words of a junior, "Students feel physically safe on campus, but once you step off campus, you have to be extremely careful."

All that commuting (and the five-to-one male/female student ratio) definitely

All freshmen take calculus I and II, English composition, computer science, physical education, and Freshman Seminar, a course that introduces students to university life.

puts a crimp in the social life. "Social life needs tremendous improvement," says a student, "especially for residents on weekends." Most students agree that the administration's strict alcohol policies work, but one says that it's "all too easy" for underage students to get served. About 12 percent of the men and 10 percent of the women join the Greek system. One of the best annual campus events is Spring Week, which includes bands, novelties, and a semiformal. Diwali, the Indian festival of lights, and Chinese New Year also give undergrads pause to party. Another option is the beach, an hour away, with windsurfing and sailing equipment courtesy of NJIT. For those who stay in Newark, the city offers a museum, Symphony Hall, the New Jersey Performing Arts Center, and the art deco Pennsylvania Railroad Station, minutes from campus.

NJIT students take pride in their athletic prowess. Men's varsity volleyball was a recent champion, and popular sports include basketball, swimming, and tennis. The outstanding athletic facilities are open to all, and include an indoor running track, fitness center, racquetball and squash courts, a six-lane pool, and areas for weight training, archery, or aerobics. Outdoor facilities include lighted tennis courts, a sand volleyball court, and a multiuse soccer stadium seating 1,000. A proud (and sweaty) tradition is the Hi-Tech Soccer Classic, which pits NJIT athletes against rivals from MIT, RPI, and Stevens Institute of Technology.

NJIT students are motivated and goal-directed; they've chosen their school because they want a top-notch technical education without the topflight price tag. Academics are the priority here, with social life a distant second, but no one seems to mind. After all, these students know highly skilled jobs will beckon after graduation. Getting through is a challenge, but there's ample compensation available for NJIT alums in the technologically dependent workplaces of today—and tomorrow.

NJIT's most-favored academic option is the co-op program, which enables juniors to get paid for two six-month periods of work at technical companies.

Overlaps

Rutgers, Stevens Institute of Technology, College of New Jersey, Montclair State, Penn State.

If You Apply To ➤ **NJIT**…Rolling admissions. Financial aid: Mar. 15. Housing: Apr. 15. Does not guarantee to meet full demonstrated need. Campus and alumni interviews: requirements vary by program. SATs: required. SAT IIs: required (math I or II). Essay question: Why NJIT? Architecture applicants must submit portfolio of work.

New Mexico Institute of Mining and Technology

Campus Station, Socorro, NM 87801

When they say the climate at New Mexico Tech is perennially sunny, they could be talking about the weather or the academics. An average of 172 days per year of clear sunshine provides a perfect backdrop for this top-notch technical institute's rigorous training, which is no day at the beach. NMT's educational program emphasizes creative approaches to complex issues, solving technical and scientific problems through coursework, research, and public service.

Tech's tree-lined campus, 76 miles south of Albuquerque, is dotted with picturesque, white adobe and red-tiled buildings and plenty of grassy open spaces that "capture the spirit of the Southwest." NMT owns 20,000 acres adjacent to the town of Socorro (population 9,000), including Socorro Peak, which provides a mother lode of research and testing facilities. A thunderstorm lab sits on another

Website: www.nmt.edu
Location: Rural
Total Enrollment: 1,513
Undergraduates: 1,218
Male/Female: 64/36
ACT Range: 23–29
Financial Aid: 54%
Expense: Pub $
Phi Beta Kappa: No
Applicants: 1,168

(Continued)

Accepted: 70%

Enrolled: 21%

Grad in 6 Years: 32%

Returning Freshmen: 75%

Academics: ✍ ✍ ✍

Social: ☎ ☎

Q of L: ★ ★

Admissions: (505) 835-5424

Email Address:

admission@admin.nmt.edu

Strongest Programs:

Earth Science

Electrical Engineering

The departments of earth and environmental science, petroleum, and environmental engineering are among Tech's best, as is the program in hydrology.

mountaintop 20 miles away. Not surprisingly, mountain bikers, runners, astronomers, hikers, bikers, campers, rock climbers, geologists and rock hounds, and scenery enthusiasts will be at home here.

NMT offers a number of excellent programs in three main areas: science, engineering, and natural resources. The departments of earth and environmental science, petroleum, and environmental engineering are among Tech's best, as is the program in hydrology, but administrators admit that the mineral engineering department could be bolstered. The mining programs are also a dying breed. Humanities and fine arts at Tech are as barren as the surrounding countryside. In fact, the closest thing to a well-regarded program in the soft sciences is technical communication—and at least one student says that program suffers from a lack of funding.

Regardless of major, "Everybody here is at least a closet nerd," one student says. As might be expected, then, students are drawn to Tech's spacious library, which holds 255,000 books. Computer facilities on this very technically oriented campus are also quite good. And teaching gets high marks, though because of Tech's relatively small size, most courses in the technical fields are offered sequentially, and students who don't take a cluster all the way through may wait several semesters before the necessary course is offered again. To graduate, students must take courses in seven areas, including calculus, physics, chemistry, written English, humanities, social sciences and biology, geology, or engineering. Though a technical communications major says the academic climate is supportive, with "more than enough outlets to help if you want or need it," another student says, "the pressure to succeed and do well causes some students to crack."

Tech's student/faculty ratio is quite low for a technical school, and though professors are research-oriented, they do take teaching seriously. Class sizes vary, though 95 percent have 50 or fewer students. Still, one student says, "The early classes are taught by full professors but are so crowded that little personal interaction is possible." Jobs with mineral industries, research laboratories, and government agencies are available through the five-year cooperative work-study program. Undergraduates can also work part-time at any of the three research divisions on campus: the New Mexico Bureau of Mines and Mineral Resources, the Petroleum Recovery Research Center, and the Energy Materials Testing and Research Center. As 99 percent of the faculty does research and most hire undergraduates, opportunities for scientific investigation and independent study are plentiful. Quality advising, on the other hand, is not: "Some advisors really care about their students and try to help, while others sign your forms and can't wait to get back to their research," gripes a biology major.

Only 20 percent of Tech's undergraduates are from out of state, and 2 percent are foreign nationals. Hispanics account for 17 percent of the student body, blacks 1 percent, and Asian Americans 3 percent. Thirty-six percent of students are female—high for technical schools, but not enough to normalize the social life. Racial tension and political correctness are pretty much nonexistent, says a senior, noting that "the only issue here is Macs versus PCs." Tech's housing facilities have improved and expanded since the days when women resided in the school's trailer park. Forty-five percent of students live in the six coed and single-sex dorms on campus, which one resident describes as "comfortable but a little crowded." Upperclassmen favor the newly completed apartment-style suites, although a little legwork can turn up decent and "incredibly cheap" housing off campus. Plus, dorm-dwellers are required to buy the meal plan, and the food is said to be less than appealing. Luckily, students say, there is "more Mexican food in town than you can shake your tail feathers at."

The town, Socorro, is a tiny mining-turned-farming area in one of the most sparsely populated areas in the Southwest, but the nearby desert and spectacular mountains provide a wealth of outdoor opportunities. According to one Techie, "This is a small Western town with a deep Hispanic and Indian culture—it's very relaxed." Still, even those who enjoy the scenery and their classmates' company see a direct correlation between sanity and access to a car, which can take them to Albuquerque and El Paso, or the Taos ski slopes. Socorro "is a college town only because the college is keeping the town alive," sighs a biology major. "They need to put in more hangouts, maybe a bowling alley or skating rink. There really isn't anything for the under-21 crowd around here."

With no Greek system and little of interest in Socorro, it's no wonder students at Tech have always had to work to make their own fun. The alcohol policy—"in your room only, over 21 only"—works in residence halls with active resident advisors, but a senior says that alcohol "is easy to get if you look for it." There are no varsity sports at Tech, but the men's and women's rugby and soccer teams do travel to challenge other schools. Many students also enjoy an extensive intramural program and the school's 18-hole golf course. And in the absence of teams to cheer for, Tech's most popular annual events are 49ers Weekend, a Homecoming tribute to the miners of yore with gunfighters and a bordello/casino, and Spring Fling, a mini-Homecoming. Fall Fest, a new event, welcomes new and old students back to campus.

With just over 1,200 undergraduates, New Mexico Tech boasts one of the most intimate technical educations—and certainly some of the best weather—in the nation. NMT is an island of intensity in the otherwise calm New Mexico desert, but those who make it through four years leave with a top notch technical education at a rock-bottom price.

Humanities and fine arts at Tech are as barren as the surrounding countryside. In fact, the closest thing to a well-regarded program in the soft sciences is technical communication.

Overlaps

New Mexico State, University of New Mexico, Colorado School of Mines, MIT.

If You Apply To ➢ **New Mexico Tech**...Rolling admissions: Aug. 1. Financial aid: Mar. 1. Meets demonstrated need of 90%. Campus interviews: recommended, informational. No alumni interviews. SATs or ACTs: required. SAT IIs: optional. Accepts electronic applications. No essay question.

University of New Mexico

P.O. Box 4895, Albuquerque, NM 87196-4895

Though UNM's heritage goes back to 1889, when New Mexico was still a territory, the university's current curriculum and strengths—especially in Latin American affairs and Southwest Hispanic studies—reflect the rich history of the American Southwest. The University of New Mexico is not a typical state school; many students are commuters or of nontraditional age. UNM also boasts New Mexico's only law, medical, and architecture and urban planning schools, as well as its only doctor of pharmacy program.

Seated at the foot of the gorgeous Sandia Mountains, in the lap of Albuquerque, the beautifully landscaped campus sports both Spanish and Pueblo Indian architectural influences, with lots of patios and balconies. The duck pond is a favorite spot for sunbathing, and the mountains, which rise majestically to

Website: www.unm.edu
Location: Urban
Total Enrollment: 24,374
Undergraduates: 16,874
Male/Female: 42/58
SAT Ranges: V 480–600 M 470–590
ACT Range: 19–25
Financial Aid: 35%
Expense: Pub $

(Continued)

Phi Beta Kappa: Yes

Applicants: 4,346

Accepted: 92%

Enrolled: 62%

Grad in 6 Years: 37%

Returning Freshmen: 69%

Academics: ✑ ✑

Social: ☎ ☎ ☎

Q of L: ★ ★ ★

Admissions: (505) 277-2446

Email Address:

apply@unm.edu

Strongest Programs:

Southwest Hispanic Studies

Photography

Lithography

Geology

Environmental Studies

Laser Optics

Latin American Affairs

The Tamarind Institute, a nationally recognized center housed at UNM's School of Fine Arts, offers training, study, and research in fine-art lithography.

Anthropologists may root around one of New Mexico's many archeological sites, and engineers may join in major solar-energy projects.

the east, are visible from virtually any point on campus. The relatively new Dane Smith Hall provides classrooms and a fully networked teaching facility.

UNM offers more than 4,000 courses in 11 colleges and 2 independent divisions, running the gamut from arts and sciences, education, and engineering to management, fine arts, and the allied health fields. Academic and general education requirements vary, but the core curriculum mandates three English courses focused on writing and speaking, two courses in each of the humanities, social and behavioral sciences, and physical and natural sciences, and one course in each of the fine arts, a second language and math. Those reluctant to specialize can spend a few semesters in the broad University College, which also offers the most popular degree, a bachelor of university studies. Freshmen are encouraged to participate in the Freshman Forum and Core Legacy Courses. The Tamarind Institute, a nationally recognized center housed at UNM's School of Fine Arts, offers training, study, and research in fine-art lithography. Anthropologists may root around one of New Mexico's many archeological sites, and engineers may join in major solar-energy projects. Other popular majors include biology, education, psychology, and nursing. Bachelor's degrees in radiologic studies, African American studies, and women's studies are now available. Despite the school's large size, a computerized registration system keeps track of course requests, notifying students who register early when additional sections of courses they need are created.

By virtue of its location, UNM enjoys a diverse mix of cultures, even though 84 percent of students are state residents. A large minority student enrollment—31 percent Hispanic, 3 percent African American, and 3 percent Asian American—reflects this cultural diversity. A cultural awareness task force and student diversity council work to keep race relations from becoming rancorous, while the new student orientation program includes a cultural awareness component, and a full-time human awareness coordinator develops diversity-related programs for the residence halls. UNM also hosts the Arts of the Americas, a broad cross-cultural program that involves U.S. and Latin American artists in festivals, classes, and exhibits. Many classes, and several complete degree programs, are offered in late afternoon and evening sessions, and about half of the student body take advantage of these after-hours options.

Many UNM students commute, and students say finding parking spots continues to be difficult as a result. With only 10 percent of students living on campus, the dorms are "mostly a stopover before finding off-campus housing." One fairly new apartment complex offers students a reprieve from the older "shoddy and high-rent" units across the street from the campus. An escort service, emergency phones, good lighting, and police who patrol around the clock help students feel safer. And although students say campus food is not worth the wait in line, more edible fare is available from campus delis and on nearby "junk-food row."

Albuquerque is New Mexico's largest city, and it offers a variety of cultural attractions, including the nation's largest hot-air balloon fiesta, a growing artists' colony, and concert tours to charm the ears. Santa Fe is an hour away. Those with cars or pickup trucks take advantage of the state's natural attractions: superb skiing in Taos, the Carlsbad Caverns, the Sandias, as well as excellent hiking and camping opportunities. For the historically inclined, numerous Spanish and Indian ruins are within an easy drive. And for those who yearn for more exotic locales, study abroad programs beckon from Mexico, Brazil, Venezuela, Costa Rica, and Scotland.

Alcohol, while supposedly banned on campus, is readily available, according to most students. Though only 3 percent of the men and 2 percent of the women go Greek, fraternity and sorority parties keep the campus police busy on weekend nights. Most students enjoy partying at home or at nearby campsites, "watching the sunset, starting at about 9:00 P.M., with a cooler of beer stocked to last the day." Annual social events include Welcome Back Days in the fall and Nizhoni Days, a celebration of Native American culture. Each spring the whole campus turns out for a four-day fiesta with food and live music.

The men's basketball and football squads and the women's basketball and volleyball teams usually draw crowds. Each year, UNM parcels more than 300 athletic scholarships for male and female athletes, in sports ranging from gymnastics and swimming to soccer and wrestling.

UNM's campus and educational emphases consciously recall the Indian pueblos that dot the New Mexico landscape. For those who are unconcerned about having a "complete" college experience, or for those planning to balance college classes with a part-time job, UNM offers a sun-drenched location that's satisfactory for most of its homegrown constituents—precisely because its academic climate is as relaxed as the rolling desert dunes.

UNM also hosts the Arts of the Americas, a broad cross-cultural program that involves U.S. and Latin American artists in festivals, classes, and exhibits.

Overlaps

New Mexico State, Eastern New Mexico University, University of Colorado, Arizona State.

If You Apply To ➤ **UNM**…Regular admissions: June 15. Financial aid: Mar. 1. Does not guarantee to meet demonstrated. Campus interviews: optional, informational. No alumni interviews. ACTs or SATs: required, ACTs preferred. SAT IIs: optional (home-schooled students and those from non-accredited high schools). Accepts electronic applications.

New School University–Eugene Lang College

(formerly New School for Social Research)

65 West 11th Street, New York, NY 10011

Students seeking a typical college experience—large classes, rowdy football games, and rigid academic requirements—need not apply to Eugene Lang College. That's because Lang College has no majors, no departments, and not a single varsity sport. Instead, this small, urban liberal arts college offers individualized academic programs, small classes, and a campus that reflects the quirky and kinetic atmosphere of Greenwich Village. Students control their destiny at this school. Says a student, "Our unique tradition of innovative intellectualism is what makes the New School so special to students and valuable to the public as an institution."

Lang fits right in amid the brownstones and trendy boutiques of one of New York's most vibrant neighborhoods. The majority of Lang's classrooms and facilities are located in a single five-story building between Fifth Avenue and Avenue of the Americas on West 11th Street, although New School University occupies 15 buildings in the Village. NYU and the excitement of Washington Square Park are only about three blocks to the south.

The New School was founded in 1919 by a band of progressive scholars that included John Dewey, Charles Beard, and Thorstein Veblen. A decade and a half later, it became a haven for European intellectuals fleeing Nazi persecution, and over the years it has been the teaching home of many notable thinkers, including Buckminster Fuller and Hannah Arendt. Created in 1978, the undergraduate college was renamed in the late '80s for Eugene Lang, a philanthropist who (surprise,

Website: www.newschool.edu
Location: Urban
Total Enrollment: 408
Undergraduates: 408
Male/Female: 32/68
SAT Ranges: V 570–673 M 470–633
Financial Aid: N/A
Expense: Pr $ $ $
Phi Beta Kappa: No
Applicants: 403
Accepted: 80%
Enrolled: 32%
Grad in 6 Years: 85%
Returning Freshmen: 85%
Academics: ✍ ✍ ✍
Social: ☎
Q of L: ★ ★ ★

(Continued)

Admissions: (212) 229-5665

Email Address:
  lang@newschool.edu

Strongest Programs:
  Writing
  Fine Arts
  Education Studies
  Cultural Studies

The New School was founded in 1919 by a band of progressive scholars that included John Dewey, Charles Beard, and Thorstein Veblen. A decade and a half later, it became a haven for European intellectuals fleeing Nazi persecution.

surprise!) made a significant donation to the school.

The two most distinctive features of Lang College are the small classes—fewer than 16 students—and the practice of having undergraduates design their own program of study with no required majors or distribution of courses. As freshmen, students choose from a broad-based menu of seminars, and as sophomores they select from five overarching areas of concentration—writing, literature, and the arts; social and historical inquiry; mind, nature, and values; cultural studies; and urban studies. In their final year at Lang, students take on advanced "senior work" through a seminar or independent project in order to return to a broad plane of thought for a new perspective on the more specialized work of their middle years. The standard courseload is at least four seminars a semester, with topics such as From Standup to Shakespeare, and the History of Jazz. All first-year students must take one year of writing and a series of workshops focusing on nonacademic concerns and library research skills. Because each student pursues an individualized educational program, cooperation, not competition, is the norm. "Teachers and students have a lot of freedom to shape the nature, pace, and expectations of courses," says a student. "The general atmosphere is more communal than competitive."

Lang's top offerings include political and social theory, anthropology, history, literature, and literary theory. Its city location lends strength to the urban studies and education programs. Writing is highly praised, especially poetry, and theater is strong. The natural sciences and math are weak areas, though courses are offered through an arrangement with nearby Cooper Union. While introductory language courses are plentiful, upper-level language offerings are limited. And the college has beefed up its offerings on the history and literature of Third World and minority peoples, which were already better than those at most colleges. The professors at Lang are well versed and engaging, according to many students. "We get an exceptional degree of personal attention from highly-trained and involved professors who are prominent and respected in their fields."

The main academic complaint is that the range of seminars is somewhat limited by the small size of the school, but outside programs offer more variety. After their first year, students may enroll in courses outside Lang from a limited number of approved classes in other divisions of New School University. A joint BA/BFA with Parsons School of Design has proven very popular. There's also a BA/BFA program in jazz and a BA/MA in media studies with the New School's communications department. A newer addition is the exchange program with Sarah Lawrence College, established to provide motivated students with additional academic opportunities. Advanced students also have the option of taking courses in the Milano Graduate School of Management and Urban Professions and the graduate faculty offerings in the social sciences. The New School's library is small, but students have access to the massive Bobst Library at nearby New York University.

Lang College attracts a disparate group of undergraduates, but most of them can be described as idealistic and independent. Some students are slightly older than conventional college age (sometimes they are transfers from other schools) and are used to looking after themselves. Twenty-one percent of the students are black or Hispanic, another 3 percent are Asian American, and 4 percent are foreign. A junior says that most of his classmates "want the freedom of an interdisciplinary education at a small school in a big city." Forty-two percent of Lang's students are from New York City, and many cite the school's location as one of its best features. "Whatever is desired can be found somewhere in New York City," says a junior. "It's a nice place to be if you want to party or be a stone-cold intellectual." Lang College admits students regardless of their finances, and strives to meet the demonstrated need of those enrolled. However, the school does not guarantee to meet the demonstrated financial need of all admits. A deferred-payment plan allows students to pay tuition in 10 installments, and there are various loan programs available. There are no academic merit or athletic scholarships.

Dorm life at Lang engages only about half of the student body, though the rooms are in good shape. One student offers this assessment: "Union Square is comfortable and fun to live in. "Loeb Hall is the newest and is mostly for freshman. Marlton Hall is in sort of a drab location...and is just old and generally uncomfortable." Off-campus dwellers live in apartments, in the Village if they can afford it, or in Brooklyn or elsewhere in the New York City area. Eighty percent of freshmen live on campus. A meal plan is available, but most students opt for the hundreds of delis, coffee shops, and restaurants that line the Avenue of the Americas.

The social network at Lang is quite small, and like many things, is left up to the student. "Since we generally live off campus, our lives are off campus as well," says one student. The social activities found on campus generally involve intellectual pursuits such as poetry readings and open-mike nights, as well as typical college activities like the student newspaper and the literary magazine. A popular annual festival allows students to write, cast, design, direct, rehearse, and perform plays—all in one 24-hour period. Occasionally, students organize dances and parties, like the Spring Prom, a catered affair with live music that is "a satirical offshoot of the high school tradition." Students generally avoid drinking on campus, and when they do imbibe, alcohol is "far from the central focus of activity," asserts a junior.

Students relish the freedom they are given at Eugene Lang College. For a student who yearns for four years of "traditional" college experiences, Lang would be a disappointment. But for those desiring an intimate, seminar-style education in America's cultural center, with an emphasis on reading, analytical writing, and critical discussion, Lang offers all of the stimulation of the city it calls home—a unique version of "Auld Lang Syne."

A popular annual festival allows students to write, cast, design, direct, rehearse, and perform plays—all in one 24-hour period.

Overlaps

Sarah Lawrence, NYU, Bard, Hampshire, Fordham.

If You Apply To ➤ **Eugene Lang**...Early decision: Nov. 15. Regular admissions: Feb.1. Meets demonstrated need of 80% Campus interviews (or by telephone): required, evaluative. No alumni interviews. SATs or ACTs: required. SATIIs: optional. Essay question: explain how your community has affected your thinking; or discuss a social, economic, or political issue of personal importance; and personal statement. Seeks "independent" students.

New York University

22 Washington Square, New York, NY 10011

New York University is a top-notch research institution that caters to an eclectic liberal arts crowd. Situated in artsy Greenwich Village, NYU gives students a world-class chance to live in the city that never sleeps. Rigorous courses and the pulsing nightlife of the city offers students a blend of opportunities that is hard to beat. "Many students are deeply entwined in the New York City social life, with concerts, parks, dancehalls, theater," says an acting major. "Most people

Website: www.nyu.edu
Location: Urban
Total Enrollment: 37,132
Undergraduates: 18,204
Male/Female: 41/59

(Continued)

SAT Ranges: V 620–710 M
  610–710

Financial Aid: 60%

Expense: Pr $ $ $ $

Phi Beta Kappa: Yes

Applicants: 28,794

Accepted: 31%

Enrolled: 39%

Grad in 6 Years: 72%

Returning Freshmen: 88%

Academics: ✎ ✎ ✎ ✎

Social: ☎ ☎ ☎

Q of L: ★ ★ ★

Admissions: (212) 998-4500

Email Address: N/A

Strongest Programs:
  Drama
  Dance
  Business
  Art and Design
  Film and Television
  Music

So you want to direct? NYU's Tisch School of the Arts trained the likes of Spike Lee, Martin Scorcese, and Oliver Stone.

specifically attend NYU so that they can be in New York City." Students here feed their minds while taking a bite out of the Big Apple.

New York University is centered at Washington Square. Trendy shops, galleries, clubs, bars, and eateries lace the Village and nearby SoHo, and the aromas tell you Little Italy and Chinatown are just blocks away. The modern and historic NYU academic buildings mix with 19th-century brick townhouses surrounding Washington Square Park (the closest thing NYU has to a quad), where parades of rappers, punks, Deadheads, junkies, and dealers are common. There's a new University Health Center in case too much partying—or studying—knocks you out.

The city scene is only one part of the NYU education. More important to students are the wide range of distinctive academic programs. The renowned Tisch School of the Arts trained directors including Martin Scorcese, Spike Lee, and Oliver Stone, so it's no wonder Tisch is besieged each year with thousands of applicants. Today's undergrads continue to win the lion's share of national student filmmaker awards. Tisch also boasts excellent drama, dance, photography, and television departments.

For a glimpse of the bulls and the bears of Wall Street, try the Leonard N. Stern business school where undergrads benefit from its center for Japanese and American business and economic studies. A favorite department among students (and New York corporations who recruit them after graduation) is accounting, known for its high job placement rate. The arts and sciences, slightly less stellar than the preprofessional programs, boast strong English, journalism, history, and political science offerings. NYU is also the place for applied math. The international studies program is on the rise, and there's an increased emphasis on foreign exchange and study abroad, with new campuses in London and Buenos Aires. There are also university-sponsored programs in Paris, Madrid, Florence, and Prague, and exchange programs with universities in Chile, Mexico, Sweden, Denmark, and Germany. The innovative Gallatin Division provides flexible schedules, course freedom, and independent study for those wishing to develop their own majors. There are new concentrations in sports and entertainment marketing and hotel catering management. Students wishing to study Greek culture can take advantage of the Onassis Center for Hellenic Studies, while the Casa Italiana Zerilli-Marimo adds spice to the Italian studies program. A new extracurricular program titled "Speaking Freely" encourages undergraduates to learn conversational language in residence halls.

The academic climate at NYU varies from program to program, and students can find themselves with tough schedules or lots of spare time. The growing number of students aiming for medical, law, and business school may find the academics particularly grueling and competitive. At least the NYU library is accommodating—it's one of the largest open-stack facilities in the country (over 3 million volumes).

Under the Morse Academic Plan, freshmen and sophomores take a broad distribution of courses, including foreign language, expository writing, foundations of contemporary culture, and foundations of scientific inquiry. Like other large universities, NYU inflicts "gargantuan" introductory courses on freshmen, and graduate students lead foreign language courses, writing workshops, and the recitations that accompany lectures. Still, students say the quality of teaching is top-notch. "Many of the educators are very skilled with a vast array of knowledge," a senior says, "but they are also workers in their fields and are able to bring their everyday life experiences into the classroom." Honors seminars for freshmen are designed to give students more one-on-one attention. Students interested in information technology can take classes at the new Center for Advanced Digital Applications (CADA) in Manhattan, a facility with which NYU has a partnership.

The variety of degree options here may tempt students to hang around the Village for more than four years. There are five-year programs to receive a BA and a master's in science, and a seven-year dental program. NYU also has a five-year joint engineering program with the Stevens Institute of Technology, and a BA/MD program in which a student is admitted to NYU Medical School at the time of college acceptance. Freshmen selected as University Scholars travel abroad each year; on campus, a wide range of cultural centers provide students the opportunity to explore international studies and language. Because of the school's New York location, internships are easy to come by, ranging from jobs on Wall Street to assignments with film industry giants. The career counselors are pretty terrific, says an education major. "I got to know them so well that they weren't just my counselors, they were also my friends," the student says. "I could always stop in and talk to them about anything." The career center has thousands of listings for on-campus jobs, full-time jobs, and internships.

Forty-seven percent of NYU freshmen are from New York State, primarily the city and nearby 'burbs. African Americans make up 7 percent of the student body, Asian Americans 16 percent, and Hispanics 8 percent. "There is no way to classify or describe a typical NYU student," a dance major says. "You really are encouraged to be yourself and not have to fit some kind of mold." The diversity of opinion on campus means a variety of issues are constantly debated, including animal rights, women's rights, gay and lesbian rights, and policy brutality. Merit scholarships provide qualified students with up to $20,000.

An unusual psychological counseling program run by students, Peers Ears, tries to ensure that students don't go off the deep end under the pressures of city living. New students are urged to attend an all-campus freshman orientation program, one specifically designed for their school, or both. Academic advising is also highly regarded, and students must meet with their advisors once a semester to review their plans before they're permitted to register for courses.

For concerned parents and students, the Office of Student Life, Protection, and Residence Halls hosts a series of workshops on keeping safe at NYU. There are also programs like the NYU Trolley and Escort Van Service, which provides door-to-door service for students from 8:00 P.M. to 3:00 A.M. on weekdays and from 7:00 P.M. to 3:00 A.M. on the weekends. All of the residence halls have two people on duty 24 hours a day, and visitors, including parents, must sign in and leave proper identification.

NYU's greatest strides during the past decade have been on the housing front. Where once students had to fend for themselves in New York's outrageous housing market, the university now guarantees four years of housing to all freshmen (and most transfers) who seek it. About a dozen dorms, ranging from old hotels to a converted monastery, provide a wide range of accommodations. Most rooms have private baths and are larger than many city apartments, enticing 50 percent of students to stay on campus. "Dorms are incredible," one junior gushes. "Unbelievable location, facilities, and space. Often, you won't get your dream dorm until junior or senior year, but all the dorms are cool." There are no "freshman halls," and rooms are assigned by a lottery held each spring. The Third Avenue North Residence Hall boasts amenities such as a computer center, practice rooms, kitchens, and even a small theater. The school also owns an apartment complex off Union Square. Some NYU housing is quite far from campus, reports one student, but the university provides free shuttle buses for all students. For those on the meal plan, three of the dorms have cafeterias, but most students

Students wishing to study Greek culture can take advantage of the Onassis Center for Hellenic Studies, while the Casa Italiana Zerilli-Marimo adds spice to the Italian studies program. The "Speaking Freely" program encourages undergraduates to learn conversational language in residence halls.

Students can take a break from the books with free movie screenings in Washington Square Park or the clubs and funky shops that populate the Village.

prefer to take advantage of the profusion of nearby delis.

Students can't say enough about NYU's social life, particularly because the campus and the city are so intertwined. On campus, there are concerts, movies, fraternity and sorority events (seven percent of the men and six percent of the women go Greek). The springtime Strawberry Festival provides a good time for all, with free berries, cotton candy, bands playing outside, and carnival amusements like a jumping bubble. Many students march in the Halloween Parade, New York's answer to Mardi Gras. The Violet Ball, a dinner/dance held each fall in the atrium of Bobst Library, is also a celebrated occasion. As for alcohol, getting carded happens, but students take their chances.

While sports have not historically been NYU's strength, the men's basketball team recently played in the Division III finals. Fencing is successful, and both the men's and women's divisions have also earned titles in recent years. More than 7,000 students participate in intramural sports, offering the usual standbys as well as quickball, in-line hockey, and arm wrestling. The university also has an athletic center with a rooftop running track. Road trips to Boston or D.C. are only occasional, with many students finding plenty to occupy themselves in the Big Apple.

Like Boston University and George Washington University, NYU's identity is inseparable from the city with which it shares its name. Students here enjoy a dizzying environment and solid academics. World-class arts courses, as well as nose-to-the-grindstone business classes, help churn out NYU grads to the tops of their fields. And while there, the students discover a little something extra. Says one student: "It's a wonderful place to really find yourself...and help you prepare for life past your degree."

Overlaps

Boston University, Penn, Cornell University, Columbia University, UC–Berkeley.

If You Apply To ➤

NYU...Early decision: Nov. 15. Regular admissions and housing: Jan. 15. Financial aid: Feb. 15. Meets demonstrated need of 75%. No campus or alumni interviews. SATs or ACTs: required. SAT IIs: recommended (writing and two others). Accepts the Common Application (with NYU supplement) and electronic applications. Essay question: your own cultural experience; situation when values or beliefs were challenged; international issues and cultures; influential creative work.

North Carolina State University

Box 7103, Raleigh, NC 27695-7103

Website: www.ncsu.edu
Location: City suburbs
Total Enrollment: 28,011
Undergraduates: 19,337
Male/Female: 60/40
SAT Ranges: V 530–620 M 550–650
ACT Range: 22–27
Financial Aid: 43%
Expense: Pub $
Phi Beta Kappa: Yes

Whether you're looking for a stellar education in engineering and textiles or a top-rated national basketball program, North Carolina State is one of the bright leaves of the Tobacco Belt. NCSU offers students the benefits of a large school—reputable professors, a diverse student body, and plenty to do on weekends—while making sure that no one feels left out. Says one junior, "No matter how weird or crazy you are, there is someone just like you on campus."

The 107-year-old, 1,900-acre campus consists of redbrick buildings, brick-lined walks, and cozy courtyards dotted with pine trees. There is no dominant style, but more of an architectural stream-of-consciousness that reveals a campus that grew and changed with time. New facilities include a student health center and marine sciences research lab.

NCSU excels in the professional areas of engineering, pulp and paper science, statistics, design, agriculture, and forestry, which are the largest and the most demanding divisions. Not surprisingly, given its location in the heart of textile country, the school also boasts a first-rate textile school, the largest and one of the best such programs in the country. Business tops the list of most popular majors, followed by engineering and accounting. Even the most technical of majors requires students to take a broad range of liberal arts courses, although the humanities are far from the biggest game on campus. English and sociology get poor marks from students. University-wide general education requirements include two semesters each of English composition, math, and science, as well as foreign language proficiency and electives in the humanities and social sciences. Freshmen are required to take English and math, and there are numerous seminars and orientation courses in each area of academic interest.

An important feature of NC State's approach to education is the cooperative-education program, through which students in all schools can alternate semesters of on-site work with traditional classroom time. There are also domestic and international exchanges with over 97 countries and a Residential Scholars program in which academic standouts live together and participate in weekly activities such as guest lectures. A First Year College program provides guidance and counseling for incoming students to introduce them to all possible majors. Many classes at State are large, but the faculty gets high grades for being accessible, interested in teaching, and friendly. Says a junior, "On a scale of 1 to 10, I would rate the quality of teaching here as an 8. I was taught by full professors as a freshman." Aside from regular hassles that come with attending a large school, the academic atmosphere is relatively relaxed. Free tutoring in most subjects is made possible by grants from state industries. The library contains 6 million volumes and is considered a good place to do research, but it's also a hot social spot.

The university benefits greatly from its relationships with Duke, the University of North Carolina at Chapel Hill, and private industry through the state's high-tech Research Triangle Park. The students at NC State are largely hardworking, bright North Carolinians. Some 91 percent are in-state students. Seventy-eight percent graduated in the top quarter of their high school class, and 91 percent attended public high school. Ten percent of the student body are black, while Hispanics and Asian Americans make up another 7 percent. Amid the public school diversity, conservatism abounds, the largest political organization is the College Republicans. Jocks and sports fans are visible, and the university offers 387 scholarships for men and women in 22 sports. Those with outstanding academic qualifications can compete for one of 108 merit scholarships that range from $2,500 to $19,000 per year. To be considered for merit awards, students must file a separate application in the early fall of their senior year in high school.

As for housing, 34 percent choose to stay on campus in one of 20 dorms. All students are guaranteed rooms for all four years. Sullivan and Lee are recommended for freshmen because they provide a mixture of academic and social activities. Most of the older dorms lack air-conditioning, and are described as "well maintained" though students admit that some of the dorms are ancient and need major reconstruction. Rooms range in size from spacious to cramped. Students report that dorm dwelling is actually more expensive than several off-campus units. Two big issues, students report, are parking and financial aid. One students says, "The financial aid packets have caused me nothing but stress." About 35 percent of the students commute. If you don't mind such minor annoyances, off-campus housing and social activities are plentiful. A small percentage of students are housed in fraternities and sororities, and the international house is also an option. The dining hall feeds all freshmen and anyone else who cares to join the meal plan. It's an all-you-can-eat deal, and students can use their meal

(Continued)
Applicants: 12,227
Accepted: 62%
Enrolled: 47%
Grad in 6 Years: 65%
Returning Freshmen: 88%
Academics: ✎ ✎ ✎
Social: ☎ ☎ ☎
Q of L: ★ ★ ★
Admissions: (919) 515-2434
Email Address:
undergrad_admissions@
ncsu.edu

Strongest Programs:
Design
Statistics
Engineering
Pulp and Paper Science
Agriculture
Forestry
Textiles

An important feature of NC State's approach to education is the cooperative-education program, through which students in all schools can alternate semesters of on-site work with traditional classroom time.

The library contains 6 million volumes and is considered a good place to do research, but it's also a noisy social center.

cards at numerous campus snack bars and sandwich shops.

As with many other schools, alcohol policies are not strictly enforced. The 21 fraternities and 5 sororities attract about 10 percent of the men and 9 percent of the women. The Greek scene provides much of the entertainment but dorm and suite parties are also popular, and public transportation affords easy access to downtown, with its shops, restaurants, theaters, and night spots. The university is well integrated into Raleigh, and its proximity to three all-women's colleges helps alleviate the imbalance of the three-to-two male/female ratio. Annual events include Wolfstock, a band party, and an All-Nighter in the student center. Many students also like to head to the beach, which is less than two hours away, or to the ski mountains, which are about a three-and-a-half-hour trip.

With home close by for so many students, the campus does tend to thin out on weekends. Those who stay can cheer on the home teams, which do well in men's tennis, swimming, soccer, football, and men's and women's cross-country and track and field. But needless to say, basketball reigns supreme. The Wolfpack plays in the high-powered Atlantic Coast Conference. "We have an ongoing rivalry with the University of North Carolina," says a junior. Some crazy NSCU fans have stormed nearby Hillsborough Street following game-day victories. The annual State versus Carolina football game usually packs the stadium, and the never-ending fight to "Beat Carolina!" permeates the campus year-round. Intramurals also thrive, and a particularly popular event is Big Four Day, when NC State's intramural teams compete against their neighbors at Duke, Wake Forest, and UNC–Chapel Hill.

North Carolina State seems to have overcome many of the obstacles associated with large land-grant universities. It has attracted a dedicated and friendly student body: independent enough to deal with the inevitable anonymity of a state school, but spirited enough to cheer the Wolfpack to victory. NC State works well for both those who can shoot hoops and those who can calculate the trajectory of the same three-point shot.

Overlaps

UNC–Chapel Hill, Appalachian State, UNC–Charlotte, Virginia Polytech, UNC–Wilmington.

If You Apply To >

NC State…Rolling admissions: Feb. 1. Early action: Nov. 15. Financial aid: Mar. 1. Housing: May 1. Does not guarantee to meet full demonstrated need. No campus or alumni interviews: SATs or ACTs: required. SAT IIs: recommended (math) for placement only. Accepts electronic applications. Essay question: optional, benefits of a college education and how NC State fits into your plans.

University of North Carolina at Asheville

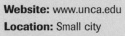

1 University Heights, Asheville, NC 28804-3299

Website: www.unca.edu
Location: Small city
Total Enrollment: 3,164
Undergraduates: 3,125
Male/Female: 4/58
SAT Ranges: V 530–640 M 520–620
ACT Range: 21–26

Whether it's the lush environment or the money you're saving, the University of North Carolina at Asheville will have you seeing green. This public liberal arts university offers all of the perks that are generally associated with pricier private institutions: rigorous academics, small classes, and a beautiful setting. And it does it for a fraction of the cost. Natural sciences are strong here, too, and students praise the close interaction between themselves and faculty. Any way you look at it, UNAC is a bargain that may have your friends turning green with envy.

Located in the heart of North Carolina's gorgeous Blue Ridge Mountains, the 265-acre campus lies in the middle of 1-million acres of federal and state forest near the tallest mountain in the East and in the most heavily visited national park in the country. The campus was built in the 1960s, and much of the brick architecture reflects the style of that decade, although half of the buildings were added within the past few years. The University Botanical Gardens, adjacent to the main campus, features thousands of labeled plants and trees, and serves as a wildlife refuge and study center for botany students. Newer additions to the campus include a teleconference center, facilities for the Mass Communication Department, and a 150-bed residence hall.

The university is dedicated to providing a liberal arts education that "teaches students to become their own best and lifelong teachers." The demanding core curriculum, among the nation's oldest, discourages channeling into disciplines too soon and focuses on uncovering diverse worldviews and cultural values. Each student takes a nationally recognized, four-course humanities sequence: the first three are historical surveys and the fourth a senior-level class that addresses modern society in light of its traditions. It may be tough, but it's also popular. There are also smaller requirements in English composition, math, social science, natural science, arts and ideas, and a foreign language.

The academic climate is demanding and students admit that it can be competitive at times. "Classes are rigorous," says a senior, "but with the small class sizes and amount of personal attention you receive, you are well prepared to succeed." Political science, humanities, and literature receive near-unanimous praise, and one student says the once-struggling math department "is undoubtedly the strongest on campus." The most popular majors are management, psychology, environmental science, sociology, and biology. Students cite chemistry and physics as being weaker than other offerings.

Asheville also offers 2–2 programs with NC State in engineering, forestry, and textile chemistry; study abroad is already an option in Europe, Asia, and South America. The UNCA Honors program offers special courses—as well as cultural and social opportunities—to motivated students who can make the grade. There are also ample opportunities for undergraduate research; in fact, nearly half of all students will have had an undergraduate research experience by graduation. Professors are given high marks and noted for their passion and experience. "I don't think I can voice how awesome the teaching has been [during] my four years here," says a senior. "They make class interesting and are always helping students outside of class." Newer programs at UNCA include a major in multimedia arts and sciences, and a joint degree-related extension program in mechatronics.

The head count at Asheville has risen dramatically over the past decade, but only 10 percent of the student body come from out of state. (The school limits its out-of-state admits to 18 percent.) As one student points out, "The school is located in the Bible Belt but all political attitudes thrive here." Environmental causes, gay and lesbian issues, various campus issues, such as parking, and multiculturalism are a few of the buzzwords on campus. "The big subject right now is diversity in the student population," says a student. Currently, the college is 3 percent African American, 1 percent Hispanic, and 1 percent Asian American, but Asheville is making special efforts to bring more students who are "underrepresented" to the campus. Asheville offers 131 athletic scholarships in basketball, baseball, volleyball, tennis, soccer, track, and cross-country, as well as 363 merit scholarships ranging from $50 to full tuition.

The majority of the students commute from nearby communities, while nearly one-third reside on campus. Students can choose from air-conditioned suites in Mills Hall, double occupancy in the Highrise Residence Hall, or singles in the wooded Governor's Village complex. There is no lottery and freshmen are

(Continued)

Financial Aid: 36%

Expense: Pub $

Phi Beta Kappa: No

Applicants: 1,866

Accepted: 61%

Enrolled: 41%

Grad in 6 Years: 55%

Returning Freshmen: 78%

Academics: ✍ ✍ ✍

Social: ☎ ☎ ☎

Q of L: ★ ★ ★ ★

Admissions: (828) 251-6481

Email Address:
    admissions@unca.edu

Strongest Programs:
    Accounting
    Environmental Studies
    Education
    Premed
    Engineering

There are ample opportunities for undergraduate research; in fact, nearly half of all students will have had an undergraduate research experience by graduation.

Asheville also offers 2–2 programs with NC State in engineering, forestry, and textile chemistry; study abroad is already an option in Europe, Asia, and South America.

mixed in with upperclassmen. "Dorms at UNCA are wonderful. The rooms are spacious and there are no hall bathrooms," notes a political science major. For meals, students have three options: the dining hall, Dante's (a snack bar), and a café in the library. Vegetarian entrées are available at most meals, in addition to a salad and sandwich bar. Crime is nearly nonexistent on campus, but many feel it's because of the school's rural location rather than effective security measures. "Campus security could be a lot better," says a senior. "There is no escort service and the only emergency phone is right outside the public safety office."

After class, there's lots to do, especially for the many Asheville students with a hankering for the great outdoors. The college is surrounded by the Blue Ridge Mountains and the Smokies, where students can hike and rock climb; water buffs can go rafting on the nearby French Broad River. For students with cars, the Blue Ridge Parkway is a short drive away, while Spartanburg and Charlotte are one and two hours away, respectively. Real big-city action takes extra effort, though, since Atlanta is a four-hour trek. Asheville offers a tame but inviting nightlife, with popular hangouts like Boston Pizza and MacGuffy's. "Social life is where Asheville struggles," says a student. Most parties take place off campus, especially since RAs stalk underage drinkers in the dorms and no alcohol is sold on campus. Ten percent of the men and 6 percent of the women belong to fraternities and sororities, but their presence is not influential. There are more than 70 campus organizations, including a large student newspaper, *The Banner*.

Involvement is no problem for the athletic teams. The Bulldogs boast Big South conference championship teams in volleyball and men's basketball. Women's tennis has captured the league crown three times, and the soccer team has imported recruits from Germany and England. Most recently, women's cross-country has brought home conference trophies. Intramurals are at least as popular as the varsity sports. The Justice Center Sports Complex houses a pool, weight room, and dance studio. Apart from athletics, several campus-wide events bring the school together each year, including Homecoming, a spring fling, and a mock casino night with an auction. Greenfest, a semesterly environment and beautification project, is also very popular. "There are lots of annual events but the one I feel makes our campus unique is the annual Greenfest," says a student. "All groups on campus—faculty, staff, and students—come together for two or three days to help make a designated section of campus more beautiful."

All the ingredients for a superior college experience lie in wait at Asheville: strong academics, dedicated professors, and an administration that continues to push for excellence. "The people make [Asheville] special," notes a senior. "From the chancellor to the custodians, [Asheville's] people are committed every day to making this college a warm and inviting place." It's a place to get the kind of liberal arts education usually associated with private colleges—but for a lot fewer greenbacks!

Overlaps

Appalachian State, UNC–Chapel Hill, North Carolina State, UNC–Greensboro, UNC–Wilmington.

If You Apply To ➤ UNC–Asheville...Early action: Oct. 15. Regular admissions: Mar.15. Financial aid: Mar. 1. Meets demonstrated need of 64%. Campus interviews: optional, evaluative. No alumni interviews. SATs or ACTs: required. SAT IIs: optional. Accepts the Common Application and electronic applications. No essay question.

University of North Carolina at Chapel Hill

CB 2200, Jackson Hall, Chapel Hill, NC 27599-2200

Welcome to "the Southern part of heaven," a place where the sky is Carolina Blue and the academics are red hot. As the flagship campus of the state university system and the oldest public university in the United States, UNC–Chapel Hill has earned its place among the South's most prestigious universities. The atmosphere here is uniquely Southern, a rowdy mixture of hard work, sports fanaticism, and tradition that seems to attract bright, fun-loving students from everywhere.

UNC's campus occupies 730 acres dotted with trees, lawns, and 30 miles of brick-paved walkways. The architecture ranges from Palladian, Federal, and Georgian to postmodern, but red brick is the prevailing motif. The original administration building is a replica of the central section of Princeton's gorgeous Nassau Hall. The university is currently in the designing stage of a master plan for the extensive renovation of the campus.

Chapel Hill offers 86 undergraduate degree programs. Strong programs include sociology, chemistry, business, political science, journalism and mass communications, classics, and biology. One of the most popular on-campus offerings is the small honors seminars open to all undergraduates. UNC's honors program is nationally recognized as being one of the best in the country. A sophomore feels that the Carolina Leadership Development Office deserves recognition. "It administers programs, including the North Carolina Fellows Program (a highly selective four-year leadership development program), the Emerging Leaders Program, and the Womentoring Program, which matches female students with female faculty members who serve as mentors." The drama department runs a repertory company with professional actors, as well as sponsoring 10 or more student productions a season. On the flip side, the administration admits that the geology department is not rock solid. The new Carolina Computing initiative mandates that, beginning in 2000, all incoming freshman own laptop computers. To this end, the university has allocated substantial funds for computer training, free email, and generous payment options.

General requirements, which must be completed in the first two years, include multiple semesters of English composition, foreign languages, physical education, natural and social sciences, aesthetics, and history as well as single courses in mathematical science, philosophy, and (just added recently) cultural diversity. The low-pressure, low-tension academic atmosphere, unusual at a school of UNC's caliber, lets students set their own scholarly pace. "We motivate ourselves to study late, cram for exams, and write the best research papers, but we wouldn't have it any other way," says one student. Another adds, "I find there are stimulating academic opportunities both inside and outside the classroom if students are looking to be challenged." Academic and social life are governed by a student-run honor system.

Registration is by web or telephone, and students register according to seniority. For those tired of the classroom rush, Research Triangle Park, a nearby research and corporate community, and home of the National Humanities Center, employs many students as research assistants. Foreign study is available in France, England, Germany, Italy, Spain, Latin America, Australia, and Japan during the academic year and in more exotic places over the summer. In addition, WUNC-FM, a National Public Radio affiliate licensed to Carolina, serves more than 175,000 listeners in 16 central counties in North Carolina 24 hours a day.

Website: www.unc.edu
Location: Suburban
Total Enrollment: 24,653
Undergraduates: 15,434
Male/Female: 44/56
SAT Ranges: V 550–680 M 560–670
ACT Range: 24–30
Financial Aid: 40%
Expense: Pub $
Phi Beta Kappa: Yes
Applicants: 16,022
Accepted: 39%
Enrolled: 55%
Grad in 6 Years: 80%
Returning Freshmen: 94%
Academics: ✍ ✍ ✍ ✍ ✍
Social: ☎ ☎ ☎ ☎
Q of L: ★ ★ ★ ★
Admissions: (919) 966-3621
Email Address:
uadm@email.unc.edu

Strongest Programs:
Journalism
Information and Library Science
Business
Sociology
Political Science
Classics
Drama

WUNC-FM, a National Public Radio affiliate licensed to Carolina, serves more than 175,000 listeners in 16 central counties in North Carolina 24 hours a day.

The Carolina faculty is, for the most part, top-notch. Professors keep regular office hours and welcome those students who seek them out. "I have been more than satisfied with my teachers' knowledge, lecturing skills, and willingness to address questions," reports a sophomore. "The quality of teaching is incredible for a public university of this size," adds a senior. While career counseling is a bright spot, academic counseling is reportedly less than stellar. "Some departments are overloaded and there are not enough advisors to effectively assist students," says a senior.

Under statewide guidelines, 82 percent of UNC's freshman class must be state residents, and the admissions office has no problem filling this quota with the cream of the North Carolinian crop. Thus, unless you're an athlete, out-of-state admission is extremely tough. Some Carolinians spend their childhoods talking about "when I get to Chapel Hill." A good number of them can't afford or don't want to pay for an Ivy League or private school education. Big social and political issues on campus include multiculturalism, gender roles, local and national elections, and religious issues. African Americans account for 11 percent of the student body, Asian Americans 5 percent, and Hispanics 1 percent. The Sonja Haynes Stone Black Cultural Center is currently housed in the student union, but this Spring the university has broken ground on a $9-million permanent facility. The facility will house classrooms, a library/reading room, theater/multimedia room, art gallery, dance studio, a suite for the Upward Bound program, and multipurpose areas for performances, lectures, and meetings. This heavily sports-minded school awards 400 athletic scholarships in all of the major sports. Students also can vie for 150 merit scholarships, ranging from $2,500 to $10,000. The university also offers a need-based loan program with low interest and repayment periods running as long as 10 years after a student leaves school—quite a deal when you consider that UNC's tuition is already a bargain. The Student Government carries on a part-time employment service, which provides about 500 student jobs.

Spring at Carolina brings a glorious flowering of azaleas and dogwoods, and, to the delight of returning students, no more housing lottery, which once made them scramble for rooms. Freshmen and returning students are guaranteed university housing, and returning students may reserve their rooms for the upcoming academic year. Housing on the north side of campus offers old but comfortable dorms; the south side offers high-rise cell blocks of cramped four-room suites, which are a good hike from classroom buildings (not to worry—there's a free campus shuttle). "Living in a dorm is one of the best experiences of college!" says one excited junior biology major. Students may opt to be part of a living/learning community; house themes include foreign languages, substance-free, wellness, and women's issues. Campus security is said to be good, and students feel relatively safe at UNC. "As a female, I try not to walk alone at night," says a senior, "but the university provides countless services to ensure that I generally don't have to ever walk alone." These services include free bus and shuttle rides, emergency call boxes, and a fully accredited campus police department.

Chapel Hill, as one student puts it, is "the quintessential college town." "Depending on your tastes, anything is possible," notes another. One student notes that while campus alcohol policies have tightened recently, "no plan is foolproof." Anyone wanting a secure handle on a social life should head straight for the fraternities or sororities, some of which date to the 1880s. The Greeks exert an influence far beyond their numbers (19 percent of undergraduates).

"'College town' in the dictionary should show a picture of Chapel Hill," boasts one senior. Franklin Street, the main drag in town that runs across the northern boundary of campus, offers Mexican and Chinese restaurants, ice cream parlors, coffeehouses, a Greek restaurant, vegetarian eateries, bakeries, a disco, and a generous supply of bars. Students look forward to several annual festivals: Apple Chill, Festifall, and the North Carolina Literary Festival, which recently featured performances by numerous authors including best-seller John Grisham. Students are involved in the community, many through a unique service learning program for which they receive academic credit.

The Tar Heel varsity teams are extremely popular, especially football and, well, basketball, which is virtually always in the top 20. A game with NC State makes any Carolina fan's heart beat faster, but Duke takes the prize as the most hated rival of all. "Everyone follows these games," says a student. "People go insane!" The slam-dunking Tar Heels play in the 21,750-seat Smith Center, named for retired coach Dean Smith, who just happens to be the winningest college basketball coach of all time. The school has taken more than 175 ACC championships since the league was founded in 1953. The baseball, tennis, and lacrosse teams are also strong, but the team with one of the best records (besides men's basketball of course) is the women's soccer team, which has claimed 17 of the 20 NCAA championships awarded in their sport. Women also sport national championships in field hockey and women's basketball and conference championships in volleyball and track. A strong intramural program draws heavy participation. Those not quite so competition-minded can enjoy the $4.9-million student recreation center, which includes a weight-training facility, a place for aerobic dance, and the student wellness center. Those who crave fresh air can take advantage of the Outdoor Education Center, which offers mountain-bike trails, an 18-hole Frisbee golf course, rope courses, and the longest zipline in the U.S.

Often touted as one of the best college buys in the country, the University of North Carolina at Chapel Hill gives students everything they want, both academically and socially. The 200-year history of this school creates an atmosphere of extreme pride, monumental school spirit, and a love for tradition. A student says, "I came to the University of North Carolina in hopes of finding a strong academic environment, outside-of-class opportunities, and a university peopled with students from diverse socioeconomic backgrounds who come together to educate one another, and I have not been disappointed."

The Student Government carries on a part-time employment service, which provides about 500 student jobs.

Overlaps

North Carolina State, Duke, University of Virginia, Appalachian State, Wake Forest.

If You Apply To ➤   **UNC–Chapel Hill**…Early action: Nov. 15. Regular admissions: Jan. 15. Does not guarantee to meet demonstrated need. No campus or alumni interviews. SATs or ACTs: required. SAT IIs: required (math II). Optional essay question.

University of North Carolina at Greensboro

1000 Spring Garden Street, Greensboro, NC 27412

At the University of North Carolina at Greensboro an aggressive campaign is under way to make the school more "student-centered." Living Learning Communities have been developed to help meet the needs of freshmen and make the matriculation experience less daunting. The administration is also taking steps to make all students feel at home. "Being a student at UNCG is so much

Website: www.uncg.edu
Location: Center city
Total Enrollment: 12,998
Undergraduates: 10,286

(Continued)

Male/Female: 34/66

SAT Ranges: V 460–570 M
  460–570

Financial Aid: 35%

Expense: Pub $

Phi Beta Kappa: Yes

Applicants: 6,650

Accepted: 77%

Enrolled: 38%

Grad in 6 Years: 47%

Returning Freshmen: 74%

Academics: ✐ ✐

Social: ☎ ☎

Q of L: ★ ★ ★

Admissions: (336) 334-5243

Email Address:
  undergrad_admissions@
  uncg.edu

Strongest Programs:
  Literature
  Biology
  Psychology
  Biology
  Environmental Studies
  Art and Design

Outstanding students can vie for 500 merit scholarships, which range from $250 to $12,000; 140 athletic scholarships are also offered.

more than going to class, studying, and getting a degree," says a senior. "There's so much opportunity to get involved here and many ways to make your total college experience valuable and lots of fun."

Set on 200 acres sprinkled with magnolia and dogwood trees, Greensboro's well-landscaped campus features a mix of Colonial, Georgian, brick, and modern architecture. Still standing is the original university building, the Victorian-style Julius Foust Building; built in 1892 and now on the National Register of Historic Places, it is located on a knoll in the center of the campus's original 10 acres.

Within the College of Arts and Sciences, psychology, fine arts, and literature are strong. The university's program in human environmental sciences is also highly regarded, and business and nursing are the most popular majors. Under Plan II, industrious students can design their own major and program of study. The School of Music has three ensembles, a symphony orchestra, and three choral groups, and has won the National Opera Association's production competition three of the past four years. There are some unusual interdisciplinary programs, such as therapy training, which combines classes from the dance, education, fine arts, and theater departments. Greensboro's program in human environmental sciences is North Carolina's largest. New majors include special education and hospitality management.

New general education requirements allow students to complete core requirements in as few as 36 semester hours, provided they have met requirements in global perspectives, writing across the curriculum, and speaking across the curriculum.

The academic climate is rigorous and "very competitive," says a sophomore. Students take their education seriously, and so do the professors. "They are concerned about the students and eager to get to know them and help them," says a senior. Enrollments in introductory courses sometimes swell to over 100, but preregistration is done through an online computer system. Those who make it into the residential-college program enjoy the atmosphere of an intimate "academic community" with class sizes usually ranging from 15 to 20 students. The school's Residential College is among the nation's oldest living/learning programs. The honors program allows talented students the opportunity to tackle a broad interdisciplinary program through small seminars, while undergraduate research assistantships allow 65 students to work with faculty in all fields. To emphasize the importance of writing both as an essential skill and as a tool for learning, majors in the College of Arts and Sciences must take writing-intensive courses.

Ten percent of freshmen come from outside North Carolina, mostly from the South. African Americans account for 18 percent of the student body, and the Neo-Black Society is very active on campus. Hispanics and Asian Americans combine to make up 4 percent of the student body. According to a senior, "Diverse religions, ethnic makeups, sexual preferences, and educational backgrounds all converge on one campus—from extreme faddish clothing, tattoos, body-piercing, and hair-dyeing to the ultraconservative."

Outstanding students can vie for 90 merit scholarships, which range from $1,000 to $12,000; 110 athletic scholarships are also offered. A summer orientation program allows freshmen to get their feet wet before classes begin. Each academic year starts off with the Fall Kickoff, when campus organizations line College Avenue with the trappings of their activities, creating a festival atmosphere. UNCG has more than 140 student organizations, including club sports, religious groups, service organizations, media groups, national societies, and professional organizations.

Twenty-seven percent of the undergraduates live in Greensboro's 23 residence halls, but students note that getting a room can be a challenge. "The past few years have been cramped and we have been experiencing a housing shortage," says a student. "But the rooms are okay." The Tower Village Apartments provide suite-style living on campus for 300 lucky students who get private bedrooms. Rooms in the older buildings are spacious, those in the quad are more attractive, and the most modern, high-rise dorms offer cramped quarters. One-third of the dorms are single-sex, and at the beginning of the year, each residence hall votes on guidelines establishing the visitation policy for members of the opposite sex. For those who still want to avoid institutionalized living, off-campus housing is plentiful and cheap. Students who live on campus choose from a variety of meal plan options in the university dining hall or in specialty shops.

Eight fraternities and eight sororities are a relatively recent addition to campus life, attracting about 9 percent of the men and 5 percent of the women. For others, dances, coffeehouses, concerts, movies, and other social activities pick up some of the social slack. "Greensboro is a wonderful, old Southern town," reports one student. Bars, restaurants, and stores are within walking distance, and the 23,000-seat Greensboro Coliseum, a scant two miles away, regularly plays host to rock bands and athletic events. Weekend trips are to the beach (three hours) or the mountains (two hours).

Greensboro never used to have a reputation as a sports powerhouse, but that is changing. UNCG moved to Division I in 1991 and now offers a comprehensive athletic program as part of the Southern Conference. Both the men's and women's soccer teams are powers within the conference, and the men's and women's basketball teams are strong. Intramurals are also popular.

Some students complain that Greensboro, living in the shadow of its big sister at Chapel Hill, lacks the reputation it deserves for providing a first-rate education in such diverse fields as liberal arts, nursing, and education. Others say it is becoming somewhat of a commuter school, but it may be too early to tell. With its strong academic offerings, tight-knit community, and low cost, Greensboro is easily one of North Carolina's best values in higher education.

Each academic year starts off with the Fall Kickoff, when campus organizations line College Avenue with the trappings of their activities, creating a festival atmosphere.

Overlaps

UNC–Chapel Hill, North Carolina State, UNC–Charlotte, Appalachian State, East Carolina.

If You Apply To ➢ | **UNC–Greensboro**...Rolling admissions. Financial aid: Mar. 1. Meets demonstrated need of 60%. Campus interviews: optional, informational. No alumni interviews. SATs or ACTs: required. SAT IIs: optional. Accepts the Common Application. No essay question.

Northeastern University

360 Huntington Avenue, 150 Richards Hall, Boston, MA 02115

Northeastern University's mission is to "provide individuals with the opportunity for upward mobility through excellence in education." And provide they do: Students get the benefit of classroom schooling, workplace experience, and real-life exposure to Boston's hustle and bustle. Northeastern students, besides being refreshingly "straightforward and open-minded," learn big-city savvy when it comes to school, work, and even play. How could they not when they're situated in the ultimate college town?

Northeastern's campus is an urban oasis located in the heart of Boston, just

Website: www.neu.edu
Location: Urban
Total Enrollment: 16,628
Undergraduates: 12,300
Male/Female: 50/50
SAT Ranges: V 510–600 M 520–620

ACT Range: 22–26

Financial Aid: 70%

Expense: Pr $ $

Phi Beta Kappa: No

Applicants: 16,418

Accepted: 62%

Enrolled: 24%

Grad in 6 Years: 51%

Returning Freshmen: 80%

Academics: ✍ ✍

Social: ☎ ☎

Q of L: ★ ★

Admissions: (617) 373-2200

Email Address:
admissions@neu.edu

Strongest Programs:
Business
Health Professions
Engineering
Protective Services
Communications
Criminology

Northeastern, which was founded as a YMCA educational program, has traditionally served many local students from diverse socioeconomic backgrounds.

minutes away from Fenway Park, shopping centers, nightclubs, cafés, Symphony Hall, and the Museum of Fine Arts. The campus's green spaces are interspersed with brick walkways, outdoor art, and a sculpture garden. Older buildings sport utilitarian gray-brick architecture while newer structures are of modern glass and brick design. During inclement weather, students can be found traversing the underground tunnel system that connects many campus buildings. A new health sciences building is scheduled for completion in 2002.

The academic year, including the summer, is divided into four quarters. Freshmen spend their first year, and seniors their last term, on campus. In between, students alternate eight quarters of study with either seven or eight on the job. For each quarter spent on the job, students earn a co-op/experiential-learning credit; it takes five years to earn a bachelor's degree. For students in the College of Arts and Sciences, there are many alternatives to the co-op, such as internships, study abroad, and undergraduate research opportunities. Each of the six colleges presents its own core curriculum, but all freshmen must complete two quarters of English and a diversity requirement. Freshmen are also required to attend the summer orientation program, where they are introduced to their classmates and the university itself; placement testing, advising, and registration are also administered.

For six months' worth of work, students average $10,803, which generally is used to defray college-related costs. Most of the jobs are in the Boston area and related to the student's major, and about half of Northeastern's grads, especially those in the more technical fields, end up taking jobs with one of their co-op employers. Although this sounds promising, students warn against becoming overly reliant on co-op advisors for good jobs or good advice. Besides the money they can earn in co-op programs, outstanding students can compete for 143 merit scholarships that range from $7,500 to $28,995. And there are 277 athletic scholarships for a wide range of sports. New programs include an MS in physician assistant studies, and BS degrees in architecture, information sciences, and computer engineering.

Undergrads say that most of their teachers are concerned with their needs, and most of Northeastern's classes have 35 or fewer students. A senior says, "Most professors avoid straight lecturing and use more interactive teaching methods." Scheduling can be difficult, as students sometimes find that courses they want are offered only when they're scheduled to be away on a job. Beware of what one junior calls the "NU shuffle", a syndrome of having to go to eight different offices before getting the answers they need.

Northeastern, which was founded as a YMCA educational program, has traditionally served many local students from diverse socioeconomic backgrounds. Forty-three percent of the students are from Massachusetts, and most of the rest are from other parts of New England in addition to New York, New Jersey, and other Mid-Atlantic states. African Americans comprise 6 percent of the population; Hispanics and Asian Americans combine for 12 percent. In order to improve race relations on campus, the Faculty Senate recently approved a resolution to establish a diversity course requirement.

"Northeastern has traditionally been a commuter school, but that is changing and housing is becoming tight," warns a political science major. For the 65 percent of the students who live in school dorms and apartments, there is a mixed reaction among students. As one physics major simply states, "The dorms are typical of any college: small but cozy." NU has recently completed the West Village residence hall, a 13-story apartment megaplex that houses up to 600 students, and was applauded by local media for alleviating neighborhood rental shortages.

Off-campus options include privately owned apartments or suites located adjacent to the residence halls. Campus safety is a priority, and students speak highly of NU Public Safety.

The co-op program puts a strain on campus social life. There are many clubs and activities, but the continuous flow of students on and off the campus tends to be disruptive. "I may see a friend one quarter in class and then not again for six months. It's hard to stay connected," a student explains. Fraternities and sororities are small (1 percent of students) and mostly overlooked as a part of Northeastern's social life. Boston, with its huge student population and wealth of bars, restaurants, museums, theaters, shops, and parks, serves as a fully acceptable substitute.

In the winter, students head to the ski slopes of Vermont, and in balmier weather they're off to the beaches of Cape Cod and the North Shore. Not surprisingly in the city the Celtics made famous, the basketball team attracts adoring fans, especially after having produced the late Celtic star Reggie Lewis. But the biggest sports series of the year is the Beanpot Hockey Tournament, which pits Northeastern against rival teams from Harvard, Boston College, and Boston University. Northeastern's female pucksters have frequently prevailed as champs. And the fleet-footed men's and women's track and cross-country teams, who work out in the newly renovated Bernard Solomon Indoor Track Facility, regularly leave their opponents blinking in the dust. The competitive nature of the sports teams, especially toward those also in the Boston area, is epitomized by one T-shirt that reads, "No—we don't want to B.U."

Northeastern is not the place for a student looking for the traditional collegiate experience. It is a place for those who have a good idea of what they want to do in life, or at least a strong desire to find out. If their co-op experience does not turn into a permanent job, it certainly gives them a jump on the job market over graduates who receive a traditional education.

If You Apply To ➢   **Northeastern**…Rolling admissions and financial aid: Feb. 15. Housing: May 1. Does not guarantee to meet demonstrated need. Campus and alumni interviews: optional, informational. SATs or ACTs: required. SAT IIs: optional. Essay question: personal statement.

Northwestern University

1801 Hinman Avenue, P.O. Box 3060, Evanston, IL 60204-3060

Northwestern University may have finally proved to the rest of the world what its students and faculty have known all along: NU is a school of winners. The university was briefly thrust into the national spotlight in 1995, when the long-suffering football team placed first in the Big Ten conference and went to the Rose Bowl. The hard work, pride, and dedication that were evident on the football field are also present in the academic halls of this challenging university. Northwestern has become a "hot" school seen on a par with the Ivies even though it lacks the strong liberal arts core of the great Eastern schools. The Midwest's answer to Penn, Northwestern is, along with Chicago, tops in the region.

Website: www.nwu.edu
Location: Suburban
Total Enrollment: 15,406
Undergraduates: 7,842
Male/Female: 48/52
SAT Ranges: V 640–730 M 660–740

(Continued)

ACT Range: 28–32

Financial Aid: 60%

Expense: Pr $ $ $ $

Phi Beta Kappa: Yes

Applicants: 15,460

Accepted: 32%

Enrolled: 39%

Grad in 5 Years: 92%

Returning Freshmen: 95%

Academics: ✍ ✍ ✍ ✍ ✍

Social: ☎ ☎ ☎

Q of L: ★ ★ ★

Admissions: (847) 491-7271

Email Address:
ug-admission@nwu.edu

Strongest Programs:

Engineering

Economics

Journalism

Communications Studies

Psychology

Drama

Northwestern is situated on 231 acres along the shore of Lake Michigan, about a dozen miles north of the Chicago Loop. The newer buildings are located adjacent to a 14-acre lagoon, part of an 85-acre lakefill addition built in the '60s. This area provides students with a prime location for picnicking, fishing, running, cycling, rollerblading, or just daydreaming. Newest additions to the picturesque campus include a 184-bed apartment-style dorm and a $125-million renovation to the Technological Institute.

As for the academic climate, Northwestern offers a choice of some widely known programs; among the six undergraduate schools, the School of Speech, the Medill School of Journalism, the School of Music, and the McCormick School of Engineering and Applied Science have national reputations. The School of Speech has excellent departments across the board, from theater and radio/TV/film to communicative disorders. The School of Journalism offers invaluable experience and the opportunity to make important job contacts through 10-week internships at about 50 newspapers, 15 magazines, and 13 television stations across the nation. There's also a four-year accelerated BSJ/MSJ program. A dazzling electronic studio centralizes Medill's state-of-the-art broadcast newsroom and the speech school's radio/TV/film department. The McCormick School of Engineering and Applied Science is particularly strong in all aspects of engineering, and five-year co-op options are available. The physical and social sciences are the strongest of the liberal arts. The Asian Studies program is newest on the academic roster.

Fine arts programs in the music school, particularly in the brass and wind departments, enhance the university's offerings, and a new major in dance has already drawn attention from students. Says a student in the Medill School of Journalism: "I've never had a class here that didn't open my mind up to new ideas and viewpoints." There are many accelerated and combined-degree programs. Special academics programs like the Center for the Writing Arts, who sponsor one or more professional writers of national prominence to teach undergraduate courses, conduct seminars and present readings and discussions of their own work, are highly praised. Interdisciplinary programs, ranging from American culture, integrated arts, mathematical methods in the social sciences, and integrated sciences, are offered in 18 fields. In addition, the university has a Junior Tutorial Program, in which small groups of undergrads in a variety of fields work with senior faculty members on advanced topics.

Each of the undergraduate schools determines its own general education requirements, but the distribution requirements are similar. Each school requires a graduate to have coursework in "the major domains of knowledge"—science, mathematics and technology, individual and social behavior, historical studies, values, the humanities, and the fine arts. Unlike most schools on a 10-week quarter system, Northwesterners take four (not three) courses each quarter, except in engineering, where five are permitted. A senior says, "The quarter system makes the academic climate at NU intense. It feels like people are constantly studying for midterms or finals." The Primal Scream before each finals period (at the appointed time, everyone opens their window and screams) does help to relieve a small bit of the tension. Students can also take a break from the campus through any of 20 field study programs and 11 programs abroad. Perhaps one reason students study so hard is the motivation provided by their professors. Most seem in awe of NU faculty members. "The quality of teaching is out of this world," says one senior. "I am friends now with so many of my teachers because they cared about my work and my ideas and my growth." Virtually all undergraduate courses, including required freshman seminars (of 10 to 15 students) in arts and sciences, are taught by regular faculty members. Introductory courses are larger than most, but the

A dazzling electronic studio centralizes Medill's state-of-the-art broadcast newsroom and the speech school's radio/TV/film department.

average 100-level class size is about 30 students. Faculty advising on academic matters is somewhat tenuous; one student notes that "for work in the arts, your best connections are your profs."

The library is, of course, a popular location on campus, and you won't be disappointed pursuing information among its 4.8 million volumes. All 150 buildings are connected to the campus's fiber-optic system, so students can access the library and Internet from their rooms. They are supported by student consultants that live in each residence hall who are on call 24/7 to provide computer support. The library resources online include the catalog, over 700 journals and more than 200 databases and indexes.

Seventy-five percent of the ethnically and religiously diverse student body come from outside Illinois borders, and 83 percent graduated in the top tenth of their high school class. Students claim the diversity among majors is one of Northwestern's finest qualities. "Theater majors are very different from those students who go to Medill School of Journalism, who are very different from those in tech (engineering)." Minorities represent 26 percent of the student body, with Asian Americans accounting for 16 percent, African Americans 6 percent, and Hispanics 4 percent. But the size of the minority population does not mean that groups intermingle extensively. "Ethnic groups tend to polarize out of genuine interest in each other and common life experiences. There is little tension here, because I think most students value diversity," a junior says. The abundance of preprofessionals has added to Northwestern's image as "young corporate America," and the acceptance rate for medical school applicants is 63 percent while that of graduates at schools of business and law hovers around 90 percent. There are no academic merit scholarships, but NU does guarantee to meet the full demonstrated need of every admit, and it provides 320 scholarships for its athletes. Loans for middle-income families are available through the university.

With the recently completed Kemper residence hall, there is now ample on-campus housing. "Rooms are spacious compared to other schools," says a junior. "My friends are always in awe of how big they are." Housing is guaranteed to freshmen; upperclassmen must try their luck in a lottery. Dorms range from small single-sex houses to large coed buildings, the most popular of which are organized in suites of eight students around a common living room. Students may join thematic or nonthematic residential colleges, which bring students and faculty members together during faculty "firesides" or simply over meals. Themes for the residential colleges include communications, international studies, commerce and industry, performing arts, public affairs, and engineering. Fraternity and sorority housing is another option, but fraternity rooms reportedly have a decidedly lived-in look. Students can choose to eat at the coffeehouse or any one of the many dining halls on campus. A variety of meal plans are available, including one that provides Sunday brunch. Evanston offers some comfortable apartments to the 28 percent who live off campus, but rents are high and zoning laws prohibit occupancy of a house or apartment by more than three unrelated people. Students have no qualms about campus security. One student says, "Even though the campus is located so close to Chicago, I feel extremely safe."

Students agree that Evanston is not a great college town, and in fact there has traditionally been hostility between townspeople and students. "It's kind of a 'we're both here so we'll put up with each other' attitude," a sophomore says. Another student feels the tension is lessening, and says, "One mayoral candidate ran on an 'anti-NU' platform and was soundly defeated." The town is currently constructing a complex that will include a cineplex, hotel, and shopping mall. Of course, there's always the option of catching the El, which runs 24 hours a day,

Fine arts programs in the music school, particularly in the brass and wind departments, enhance the university's offerings, and a new major in dance has already drawn attention from students.

The Primal Scream before each finals period (at an appointed time, everyone opens their windows and screams) does help to relieve a small bit of tension.

to downtown Chicago where opportunities are limitless for good restaurants, movies, cultural events, shopping, or just walking around.

Although social life is circumscribed by the academic pressure, "anyone who says he can't find anything to do just isn't looking," declares a student. Much of the social life on campus is centered around the Greek system and 32 percent of the men and 36 percent of the women go Greek. For those not interested in Greek life, on-campus entertainment opportunities are numerous, including theater productions, concerts, and movies. The school's alcohol policy is tough, but not always effective. "Minors will not be served, but it's usually not hard to find someone who will buy for you," says a journalism major. The student government and Activities and Organizations Board sponsor an array of campus-wide events, such as the very popular 30-hour Dance Marathon and Dillo Day, an end of the year party with numerous bands and other activities. Another tradition is upheld when representatives of student organizations slip out in the dead of night to paint their colors and slogans on a centrally located rock. As a bonus to the social atmosphere as well as to educational hands-on experience, the campus has its own radio station, television studio, and award-winning newspaper, and, says one administrator, "Certainly any student who wishes to act, produce, direct, conduct, build scenery, or play in a musical ensemble has ample opportunity to do so."

Dubbed the "Cinderella story" of college football by many, the Wildcats overcame a long history of losing seasons to win the 1995 Big 10 championship and an historic trip to the Rose Bowl. The men's golf team brought home consecutive Big Ten championships in 1999 and 2000, as did the women's tennis team. Other competitive women's teams include volleyball, softball, field hockey, and swimming. As far as facilities, NU is on par with many schools its size and larger, with the beautiful Norris Aquatics Center/Henry Crown Sports Pavilion and the Nicolet Football and Conference Center, used for conditioning of varsity athletes. The student-sponsored intramural program provides vigorous competition among teams from dorms and rival fraternities.

For a school with so much to offer, Northwestern's biggest challenge may be to garner the recognition it deserves. "Administration and students seem to be constantly trying to prove that we are as good as the Ivy schools," says one student. "Northwestern needs to start feeling comfortable with its own identity." Demanding academics, a caring faculty, and a sizzling athletic program are all part of that identity, and all reasons why anyone looking for a top-notch education might give Northwestern a good look.

Overlaps

Michigan, Penn, Washington University (MO), Duke, Cornell University.

If You Apply To ➤ **Northwestern**…Early decision: Nov. 1. Regular admissions: Jan. 1. Financial aid: Feb. 1. Guarantees to meet full demonstrated need. Campus and alumni interviews: optional, informational. SATs or ACTs: required. SAT IIs: required for Integrated Science Program and Honors Program in Medical Education. Apply to particular school or program. Accepts electronic applications. Essay question: required, choice of four.

University of Notre Dame

Room 113, Notre Dame, IN 46556-5602

Among the best-known universities in the nation, Notre Dame takes almost as much pride in its renowned football team as it does its solid academic reputation. Founded 155 years ago by the French priest Edward Sorin, Notre Dame has come a long way from its fledgling days in a rustic log cabin. While it is described as "a Catholic academic community of higher learning," students need not be affiliated with the Roman Catholic church. According to the administration, "What the university asks of all its scholars is not a particular creedal affiliation, but a respect for the objectives of Notre Dame and a willingness to enter into the conversation that gives it life and character." And, of course, an interest in sports doesn't hurt.

With a total of 1,250 acres of rolling hills, twin lakes, and woods, the university offers a peaceful setting for studying. The lofty Golden Dome that rises above the ivy-covered Gothic and modern buildings and the old brick stadium where in the 1920s Knute Rockne made "the Fighting Irish" almost synonymous with college football are national symbols. Newest additions to campus include a visitor's center, bookstore, sports and recreation center, and a golf course.

Liberal education is more than just a catchphrase at Notre Dame. No matter what their major, students must take the First Year of Studies, one of the most extensive academic and counseling programs of any university in the nation. The core of the program is a one-semester university seminar that is limited to 20 students and is writing-intensive. The remainder of each freshman's schedule is reserved for the first of a comprehensive list of general education requirements: one semester each in writing and mathematics and two semesters in natural science, as well as one semester chosen from theology, philosophy, history, social science, and fine arts. The First Year of Studies program also includes a strong counseling component in which peer advisors are assigned to each student, as are academic advisors and tutors, if necessary. Administrators are quick to point out that, due in part to the success of the first-year support program, a whopping 97 percent of the freshmen make it through and return for sophomore year.

In the College of Arts and Letters, highly regarded departments include English, theology, and philosophy, while physics and chemistry are tops in the College of Science. Within the engineering school, chemical engineering rules. The College of Business Administration's accountancy program is ranked among the nation's best, and the chemistry labs in the Nieuwland Science Hall have first-rate equipment. While weak departments are hard to come by at Notre Dame, some students complain about the creative arts programs. The academic climate at Notre Dame is said to be fairly rigorous. "The workload is very demanding," says a senior. "It requires the student to have very good time-management skills." And while the atmosphere is competitive, students agree that it is not cutthroat by any measure. Faculty members are praised for being dynamic, personable, knowledgeable, and accessible. "The professors here care a great deal about their students and it shows," says a biology major. Students report that it is sometimes hard to get all the classes you want during a particular semester, but that it's not difficult to graduate in four years.

Notre Dame offers a variety of special academic programs and options. One of the most popular is the Program of Liberal Studies (PLS), in which students study art, philosophy, literature, and the history of Western thought within their Great Books seminars. The Kaneb Center for Teaching and Learning, the

Website: www.nd.edu
Location: City outskirts
Total Enrollment: 10,654
Undergraduates: 8,014
Male/Female: 55/45
SAT Ranges: V 620–710 M 640–720
ACT Range: 29–32
Financial Aid: 39%
Expense: Pr $ $ $
Phi Beta Kappa: Yes
Applicants: 10,010
Accepted: 35%
Enrolled: 20%
Grad in 6 Years: 95%
Returning Freshmen: 97%
Academics: ✍ ✍ ✍ ✍
Social: ☎ ☎ ☎
Q of L: ★ ★ ★
Admissions: (219) 631-7505
Email Address:
admissions@admissio.1@nd.edu

Strongest Programs:
Theology
English
Philosophy
Chemical Engineering
Program of Liberal Studies
Business
Chemistry
Accounting

university's most recent commitment to teaching, is based in DeBartolo Hall, an 84-classroom complex with state-of-the-art computer and audiovisual equipment. The Arts and Letters Program for Administrators combines a second business major with liberal learning, and the College of Science also allows students the option of pursuing majors in two departments. In addition, Notre Dame offers programs in military and naval science, aerospace studies, and an international study programs that allows students to travel to Australia, France, Spain, Mexico, Japan, Italy, Israel, and England.

With a predominantly lay board of trustees and faculty, Notre Dame remains committed to "the preservation of a distinctly Catholic community." The president and several other top administrators are priests of the Congregation of the Holy Cross, and each dorm has its own chapel with daily Masses. Nearly 85 percent of the students are Catholic, leaving some skepticism about the comfort level of those who are not. Students feel Notre Dame nurtures their faith as well as their minds. The main social issues discussed on campus include abortion, gender and racial issues, homosexuality, and faith. Diversity is also a concern, and some students feel that it is a big problem. In an attempt to alleviate the problem, the administration has created the Diversity Exchange Program, inviting several students from predominantly black and Hispanic universities to study for a semester at Notre Dame. Minority enrollment is growing. African Americans and Hispanics make up 10 percent of the student body, and Asian Americans another 4 percent. Despite its relative cultural homogeneity, Notre Dame recruits from all over the country; 90 percent of the students are from outside Indiana. The university offers competitive academic scholarships to students with outstanding high school records and financial need, and 350 athletic scholarships are available.

Dorm life at Notre Dame appeals to 78 percent of the students. "Notre Dame dorm life is extraordinary," says a junior. "The dorm rooms are all very well kept and very comfortable." Once assigned to a dorm during their freshman year, students are encouraged to stay in the same one until graduation. Fraternities are banned, and freshmen are spread out among all campus dorms. The single-sex dorms really become surrogate fraternities and sororities that breed a similar spirit of community and family. Parietal rules (midnight on weekdays, 2:00 A.M. on weekends) are strictly enforced. Boarders eat in either the North Quad or South Quad cafeterias, and must buy a 19-meal plan. For those who tire of institutional cuisine, the Huddle offers plenty of fast-food options as well as a pay-as-you-go snack bar. Students can also reserve the kitchen to cook their own meals.

Notre Dame has been open to female applicants since 1972, and with a 55 to 45 breakdown in the freshman class, the ratio is now comparable to many other formerly all-male schools. ND's social life isn't as rambunctious as it once was, thanks to the policy that forbids alcohol at campus social events. The rules relating to alcohol in the dorms are a bit more relaxed, though kegs and drinking in the hallways are prohibited. For those who choose not to indulge, there are several groups dedicated to good times without alcohol. Most activities take place on campus and include parties, concerts, and movies. Each dorm holds theme dances about twice a month, and there's always the annual Screw Your Roommate weekend, where students are paired with the blind dates selected by their roomies. Another popular event is the An Tostal Festival, which comes the week before spring finals and guarantees to temporarily relieve academic anxiety with its "childish" games such as pie-eating contests and Jell-O wrestling. The annual Sophomore Literary Festival is entirely student-run and draws prominent writers and poets from across the country. Students are involved in the community through volunteer work. "Notre Dame students are very active in the community through a variety of service organizations," says a junior. The best outlet for culture is nearby Chicago, about 90 minutes away.

The talk of the fall semester at ND typically is football. With its proud gridiron heritage, there's nothing like the Fighting Irish spirit. From Knute Rockne and the Gipper right on down to modern-day greats like Joe Montana, the spirit of Notre Dame football reigns supreme. It wasn't intentional—at least that's what they say—but the giant mosaic of Jesus Christ on the library lifts his hands toward the heavens as if to signal yet another Irish touchdown. Tailgate parties are also celebrated events, occurring before and after the game.

Aside from football, Notre Dame offers one of the strongest all-around athletic programs in the country with nationally ranked teams in women's soccer, volleyball, basketball, tennis, softball, and fencing, and men's tennis, lacrosse, fencing, baseball, and cross-country. Diehard jocks who can't make the varsity will find plenty of company in ND's very competitive intramural leagues. The Bookstore Basketball Tournament, which is the largest five-on-five, single-elimination hoops tournament in the world, with over 700 teams competing, lasts for a month.

Everyone at the university, from administrators to students, is considered part of the "Notre Dame family." Traditions are held in high esteem. For those looking for high-quality academics, a friendly, caring environment, and an excellent athletics program, ND could be just the place.

The Kaneb Center for Teaching and Learning, the university's most recent commitment to teaching, is based in DeBartolo Hall, an 84-classroom complex with state-of-the-art computer and audiovisual equipment.

Overlaps
Boston College, Northwestern, Duke, Georgetown, Princeton.

If You Apply To ➤	ND…Early action: Nov. 1. Regular admissions: Jan. 7. Financial aid: Feb. 15. Guarantees to meet demonstrated need. Campus interview: optional, informational. No alumni interviews. SATs or ACTs: required. SAT IIs: optional. Essay question: influence of particular work of art or literature; comments on the works of Dorothy Day, Martin Luther King, Jr., or National Conference of Catholic Bishops.

Oberlin College

101 North Professor Street, Carnegie Building, Oberlin, OH 44074-1075

At Oberlin College, founded in 1833, they put the "liberal" in liberal arts. The small, iconoclastic Ohio school has long been a bastion of independent thinking and uncommon ideas; it was the first American college to accept women and minorities. Though the political slant of the student body is anything but, Oberlin's curriculum reflects its long-standing appreciation of diversity. Bright spots range from an outstanding conservatory of music to strong offerings in the natural sciences. And despite their reputation as long-haired slackers, students are focused, bright, and determined. What differentiates an Oberlin education? "The community feeling, the intellectual atmosphere, and the quality of the students— not just as students, but as people," says a senior.

Oberlin's attractive campus features a mix of Italian Renaissance buildings (four designed by Cass Gilbert), late 19th- and early-20th century organic stone structures, and some less interesting 1950s barracks-type dorms. The buildings rise over flat lands typical of the Midwest, which do little to stop brutal winter winds. The art museum, sometimes mentioned in the same breath as Harvard's and Yale's, is one of the loveliest buildings on campus, with a brick-paved,

Website: www.oberlin.edu
Location: Small town
Total Enrollment: 2,873
Undergraduates: 2,873
Male/Female: 43/57
SAT Ranges: V 630–740 M 600–700
ACT Range: 26–31
Financial Aid: 65%
Expense: Pr $ $ $ $
Phi Beta Kappa: Yes
Applicants: 5,267
Accepted: 44%
Enrolled: 35%
Grad in 6 Years: 98%

(Continued)

Returning Freshmen: 92%

Academics: ✑ ✑ ✑ ✑ ✑

Social: ☎ ☎ ☎ ☎

Q of L: ★ ★ ★ ★

Admissions: (440) 775-8411

Email Address:

admissions@oberlin.edu

Strongest Programs:

Neuroscience

Creative Writing

Environmental Studies

Art History

Music

Students share class notes and study for tests together in hopes that everyone can do well; they measure progress on an individual basis, not in comparison to how their friends are doing.

Students are required to take one-quarter of the semester hours needed to graduate outside their major's division, and to participate in three January terms, during which they pursue monthlong projects, traditional or unique, on or off campus.

flower-laden courtyard and a fountain. Currently, an environmental studies building is under construction.

The architectural mishmash couldn't be more different from Oberlin's academic menu, where offerings are uniformly excellent. In fact, Oberlin has been a leader among liberal arts colleges seeking to promote their science offerings; biology and chemistry are two of the college's strongest departments, and undergraduates may major in interdisciplinary programs like neuroscience and biopsychology. Oberlin's conservatory of music holds a well-deserved spot among the nation's most prominent performance schools; the voice, violin, and TIMARA (Technology in Music and Related Arts) programs are especially praised. English is also lauded, and—not surprisingly at such a liberal school—interdisciplinary and self-created majors, such as black, Latin American, environmental, Russian, Third World, and women's studies, are popular. East Asian studies have long been outstanding at Oberlin as well; a study abroad program at China's Yunnan University is available, and the two-year Shansi fellowship in an Asian country is a popular and sought-after post-graduate goal. Studio art and creative writing "are really impressive in reputation, but nobody ever gets into the classes, so it isn't really important," a sociology major says.

Oberlin's students are as serious about their schoolwork as they are about politics, justice, and other social causes. Courses are rigorous; heavy workloads and the occasional Saturday morning class are the norm. Still, a sociology major says, "The academics are competitive, but taken more as a recreational event. This is a place where most people are really excited about academics, which is great." Students share class notes and study for tests together in hopes that everyone can do well; they measure progress on an individual basis, not in comparison to how their friends are doing. The intense pressure is somewhat minimized by the credit/no-entry policy, which allows students to take an unlimited number of grade-free courses (if they can get in). Plus, anything below a C-minus is scratched from a student's transcript. Generally, however, students at Oberlin are gifted and want to challenge themselves. Recognizing that, most departments offer group and individual independent study opportunities and invite selected students to pursue demanding honors programs, especially during their senior year. Professors are "as excited about teaching as students are about learning," says a biology and dance major.

There are no requirements for freshmen at Oberlin, but general education requirements include proficiency in writing and math, and nine credit hours in each of the three divisions—arts and humanities, math/natural sciences, and social sciences—plus another nine credit hours in cultural diversity courses. Students are also required to take one-quarter of the semester hours needed to graduate outside their major's division, and to participate in three January terms, during which they pursue monthlong projects, traditional or unique, on or off campus. About 25 different freshman/sophomore colloquia are available, with enrollment limited to 15 students each, and though the majority of other classes are limited to 25 students, the computerized registration system makes it easy to get in.

One of Oberlin's most unusual offerings is EXCO, an experimental college that offers students and interested townsfolk the chance to teach one another. "EXCO classes range from beer-making to sexual information, to martial arts, to the Beatles discography," notes one student. "Oberlin is a place that values almost any form of knowledge." Many learning opportunities are available beyond the town of Oberlin as well, including a semester at the Oberlin Center of European Studies in Strasbourg, France, or programs in China, London, France, Germany, and Dublin through the Great Lakes Colleges Association.* Sea lovers can travel to Mystic Seaport.* In fact, so many students leave Oberlin for a semester or two, seeking a break from the Ohio monotony, that a break is practically part of the curriculum. Back on campus, the Mudd Library has more than a million volumes and is a superb facility for research and studying or socializing; the famous A-level is the place to be on weeknights. Even more special is the music conservatory, with its 153 practice rooms, substantial music library, and more Steinway pianos under one roof (168 grands, 18 uprights) than anywhere else in the world. Qualified students can earn both a BM and a BA in a five-year dual degree program.

Aside from their similar political leanings, "Obie-Dobies" are a fairly homogeneous lot: two-thirds come from public school and 80 percent are white. Still, more than 85 percent of students are from out of state. African Americans account for 8 percent of the student body, Asian Americans 7 percent, and Hispanics 4 percent. Initiatives to increase diversity at Oberlin include advisors from various ethnic and racial backgrounds and a multicultural resource center with a full-time director. The campus is politically active, with issues of sexuality, race, and gender coming to the fore. Everyone's correct, incorrect, and debating. A popular annual event is the Drag Ball, sponsored by the Lesbian Gay Bisexual Union, in which half the student body shows up in full drag. The event includes a runway competition and a disco string orchestra, and brought MTV's cameras to campus a few years ago. "Safer Sex Night is also quite an event,' says a sophomore. According to one senior, "Student participation on campus is extremely high, it's only choosing between all the activities and organizations that is difficult."

Eighty percent of Oberlin's students live on campus. They choose from among 25 dorms, ranging in size from 15 to 235 people, several of which center on foreign languages. Dorms vary dramatically in shape, size, mood, and feel. "All of the housing is well-maintained, and there's really no vandalism," a senior says. "Students are guaranteed housing, just maybe not their first choice." Only two dorms are single-sex; all dorms are four-class except Barrows, which is reserved for freshmen. The best dorms are said to be the program houses, including French House, African Heritage House, Russian House, and Third World House. Seniors and lucky juniors can land the preferred singles (thanks to their upperclass standing or good lottery numbers), but many move into cheaper off-campus apartments, although only a fraction are allowed off the college's meal plan. Oberlin's dining hall system includes six dining rooms in four buildings, chosen through another lottery. An appetizing alternative to institutional fare can be found at one of the six co-ops that comprise the Oberlin Student Cooperative Association (OSCA), a $1-million-a-year corporation run entirely by students. Co-opers plan and prepare their own meals, and though only 12 percent of the student body actually live in these houses, almost 25 percent take their meals there, enjoying everything from homemade bread to whatever's left in the pantry before the next food shipment arrives.

Social life, like so much of the Oberlin experience, is what you make of it, students report. One student describes it as "tremendous," saying "We're in the middle of farmland, yet I'm rarely bored." Another agrees, "It becomes a question of what can be fit into one's schedule." House parties, plays, movies, and conservatory performances are planned every other night. And since there's no Greek system, nothing is exclusive. As for drinking, "I don't know what the policy is, but it certainly doesn't have any bearing on real life," says a sociology major. The "tiny but complete" town of Oberlin offers the essentials, students say: "a small-town movie theater, two bookstores, pizza places, banks, grocery stores, and a

Oberlin's dining hall system includes six dining rooms in four buildings, chosen through another lottery.

Oberlin is a charter member of the North Coast Athletic Conference, which emphasizes scholarship and considers women's sports on par with men's.

bakery with great doughnuts." Town-gown relations are good; "Tons of students get involved in community service," according to a senior. Volunteer options include hospitals and a mentoring program for college-bound kids. If all else fails, Cleveland—including the Rock and Roll Hall of Fame and major league baseball—is 30 miles away. "Trips to Cleveland for a nice dinner or a performance or protest are common," says a senior. Other good road trips are Chicago (6 hours) and Washington, D.C. (six-and-a-half hours).

Oberlin competes in the Division III athletics, but the varsity sports have lukewarm followings. That may be because Oberlin is a charter member of the North Coast Athletic Conference, which emphasizes scholarship and considers women's sports on par with men's. Women's lacrosse and tennis have both captured the NCAC championship in recent years; other decent teams include men's swimming, men's and women's soccer and track and field, and women's basketball. Participation in club sports, particularly rugby and Ultimate Frisbee, is on the rise.

An Oberlin education is a study in contrasts. A junior says other students are both her biggest complaint about the school—and its "biggest bonus." Classmates lament their rural Ohio location, but note that there's often so much going on that they can't fit everything in. All students appreciate the opportunity to push themselves in a supportive atmosphere. Oberlin is special because of the emphasis on "student participation and scrutiny about every facet of life here," says a women's studies and music education major.

Overlaps

Wesleyan, Brown, Vassar, Carleton, Northwestern.

If You Apply To ➤ **Oberlin**…Early decision: Nov. 15, Jan. 1. Regular admissions: Jan. 15. Financial aid: Feb. 1. Housing: May 1. Guarantees to meet demonstrated need. Campus and alumni interviews: recommended, evaluative. SATs or ACTs: required. SAT IIs: recommended. Accepts the Common Application and electronic applications. Essay question.

Occidental College

1600 Campus Road, Los Angeles, CA 90041

Website: www.oxy.edu
Location: Urban
Total Enrollment: 1,603
Undergraduates: 1,570
Male/Female: 44/56
SAT Ranges: V 550–660 M 550–660
Financial Aid: 60%
Expense: Pr $ $ $
Phi Beta Kappa: Yes
Applicants: 3,015
Accepted: 59%
Enrolled: 22%
Grad in 6 Years: 78%

The administration at Occidental College aims to create a "community in which students may, in some small measure, experience a world that could be." If "what could be" includes "an academically challenging, incredibly tight-knit and diverse community, on a peaceful, gorgeous campus, in the middle of an exciting city"—in the words of a sophomore—those in charge appear to have succeeded. While some might feel stifled at a school with 1,600 students—"We're like a big family, and big families sometimes really suck," a classmate sighs—remember that Oxy is spitting distance from the glitz of Beverly Hills and the goofiness of Disneyland, so there's plenty to do outside of class.

Set against the backdrop of the San Gabriel Mountains, Occidental's self-contained Mediterranean-style campus is a secluded enclave of flowers and trees between Pasadena and Glendale, minutes from downtown Los Angeles. Inside this urban oasis resides a thriving community of high achievers who don't for a moment believe that the liberal arts are dead, or even wounded. Required first-year cultural studies seminars include topics in human history and culture, emphasizing learning skills, critical thought, and a wide range of human activities, including art, philosophy, politics, and literature. Students must also complete one year each of English writing, foreign language, and science (with lab), one semester each of fine arts, math, and pre-industrial-era coursework, and three semesters of world cultures courses. Most students consider the core program, with its small classes and intimate labs, worthwhile. Upper-level classes often enroll fewer than a dozen students, and if students can't graduate in four years because classes were closed or were not offered, Oxy will pay for any necessary extra semesters. All this makes for lots of hard work. A sophomore says, "Students are competitive, but generally with themselves and not with other students." One student wryly says, "Transfer students make me nervous. Jeez, take a chill pill. It's only college."

As rigorous as its requirements are, Occidental encourages diverse learning experiences through internships, independent study, and study abroad. Students also can propose an Independent Pattern of Study to avoid a fixed distribution of courses. Independent study on special projects is possible under an honors program for outstanding students, and all departments offer honors courses. For aspiring techies, there is a computer science "emphasis," but no major. There is, however, a cognitive science major that combines math, philosophy, computers, and psychology. As for quality, many of Occidental's academic departments are excellent, with biology, psychology, politics, and an innovative diplomacy and world affairs program among the strongest, and economics the most popular. The college even has its own marine biology research vessel, the *Vantuna*. Perhaps because of Oxy's small size, the American studies, classics, and women's studies departments have less prowess, and there are no communications or foreign language majors. However, owing to Oxy's location, the television and film program is said to be strong.

Faculty members are readily available in and out of the classroom, and teaching is one of Occidental's strong points. "These folks are irreplaceable," says a senior. Plus, the emphasis is on ideas and their application, not memorization of meaningless facts. The great majority of classes have 25 or fewer students, and the university will not cancel classes because of small enrollment. And, since academic advisors are responsible for about four students per class (16 total), personal relationships develop quickly. "Professors are not only brilliant researchers, but truly committed educators," says a kinesiology major. "They seem to really care about students' best interests." For those going stir-crazy on campus, Oxy has study abroad programs in Western Europe, Japan, China, Mexico, Nepal, Zimbabwe, Hungary, Costa Rica, and Russia. For politicos, there's Oxy-in-Washington and Oxy-at-the-U.N. There are also 3–2 engineering programs with Cal Tech and Columbia University, exchange programs with Spelman and Morehouse colleges in Atlanta, and cross-registration privileges with Cal Tech and Pasadena's Art Center College of Design. Oxy's library is linked by computer to other area institutions,' and college-owned vans take students to UCLA to get needed materials.

Over half of Occidental's students are from California, and minorities constitute 40 percent of the student body, arguably tops in the nation. Perhaps not surprisingly, students tend to be liberal. Says one senior history major, "We are very conscious of political issues on campus. Gay rights, police brutality, globalization, discrimination, international politics, feminism—you name it." Multiculturalism and how it can be best achieved is a constant source of debate. Administrators say "excellence and equity in education" is Oxy's top priority, though admission is not need-blind. Still, the college does offer a varying number of merit scholarships each year, ranging from $10,000 to $17,500. There are no athletic scholarships.

(Continued)
Returning Freshmen: 87%
Academics: ✍ ✍ ✍ ✍
Social: ☎ ☎ ☎
Q of L: ★ ★ ★ ★
Admissions: (323) 259-2700
Email Address:
    admission@oxy.edu

Strongest Programs:
    English
    Biology
    Theater
    Politics
    Economics
    Psychology
    Diplomacy and World Affairs

Occidental's core program provides the foundation for "total education," emphasizing personal, ethical, social, and political growth with an interdisciplinary, intercultural focus.

For politicos, there's Oxy-in-Washington and Oxy-at-the-U.N. There are also 3–2 engineering programs with Cal Tech and Columbia University, exchange programs with Spelman and Morehouse colleges in Atlanta, and cross-registration privileges with Cal Tech and Pasadena's Art Center College of Design.

Students rave about Oxy's friendly and supportive environment, but also complain that the school's smallness can lead to gossip and cliques. Upperclassmen on the "O-team" plan freshman orientation, the week before school starts. Housing is guaranteed; freshmen are required to live on campus and eat in the dining hall, though there are plenty of hole-in-the-wall eateries nearby, including Burger Continental (BC's), Auntie Em's, and the Big O. The 11 residence halls are small—fewer than 100 students each—and coed by floor or room. Seventy percent of students live on campus, in dorms ranging from "'five-star hotel' to 'this isn't too bad.'"" What you get depends on your luck in the housing lottery, but everything is at least clean and well maintained. In fact, university housekeeping will clean your room for you three times a week. Students from all four classes live together, many in special-interest houses like the Multicultural Hall, the Environmental Quad, the Women's Center, or the Substance-Free Quad. A few students live off campus, although students characterize the surrounding neighborhood of Eagle Rock as "unsafe and declining economically and socially." Student escorts, shuttles, and a 24-hour campus security system contributing to the feeling of safety.

While the bright lights of L.A. often beckon on weekends, on-campus social life can still be satisfying, students say, with Greek and other parties always an option and free tickets to the theater usually available. Fraternities and sororities, though declining on the Oxy social ladder, attract 8 percent of men and women, but they are neither selective nor exclusive; students choose which to join, rather than being chosen, and the frats must invite everyone to their functions. Alcohol policies "seem liberal," says a sophomore. The annual Founders Day dinner-dance brings the campus together, and the Senior Smack offers graduates-to-be the chance to smooch whomever they've wanted to during the past four years. Other big events include parties such as Sex on the Beach and Da Getaway, a Roaring Twenties bash where students gamble with fake money and Charleston 'til they drop. Here's a tip: Keep your birthday a secret, or on that unhappy day, a roaring pack of your more sadistic classmates will carry you out to the middle of campus and mercilessly toss you in the Gilman Fountain. It's a tradition, after all.

When students weary of the incestuous social life in the "Oxy fishbowl," they head for the bars, restaurants, museums, and theaters of downtown Los Angeles, where, one student notes, "you can find almost anything except snow." What! No snow? Never fear, the ski slopes of the San Gabriel Mountains are not far away. Neither is Hollywood nor the beautiful beaches of Southern California. When they tire of California, students try their luck in Las Vegas—or trek south of the border, into Tijuana. A car—your own or someone else's—is practically a necessity, though the college runs a weekend shuttle service to Old Town Pasadena. The weather is warm and sunny, but the air (cough! cough!) is often thick with that infamous L.A. smog.

Oxy's sports teams compete in Division III and draw a modest following. Football is the most popular, followed by men's basketball and soccer. Men's track and field is strong, and any match against rivals Pomona, Pitzer, Claremont McKenna, Scripps, and Harvey Mudd draws a crowd. The most popular intercollegiate sport of all, according to one student, is studying, but beach volleyball has fans, too. And don't forget that L.A. is home to the NBA's Lakers, the NHL's Kings, and baseball's Dodgers.

Occidental's creative, motivated—and diverse—students are not here for the bright lights and beautiful people of Los Angeles; those are just fringe benefits. Instead, students are drawn to this intimate oasis of learning by professors who hate to see anyone waste one whit of intellectual potential.

Overlaps

Pomona, Claremont McKenna, University of Southern California, UCLA, Stanford.

Oglethorpe University

4484 Peachtree Road NE, Atlanta, GA 30319

Situated in the rolling hills of northern Atlanta, Oglethorpe University offers an educational experience that "invites students to be thoughtful, inquisitive, and reflective about the human condition and the world around them." That world includes a city that bustles with endless social opportunities, yet does not intrude on the school's intimate campus community. Oglethorpe's small size encourages the kind of meaningful student-faculty interaction that many larger schools can't provide. "Not only do most of the students know each other," says an English major, "but the professors and the students are close."

Founded in 1835, the school is named for the founder of the state of Georgia. Its 118-acre campus is located near suburban Buckhead, a ritzy area about 10 miles north of downtown Atlanta. The heavily wooded, slightly rolling terrain is perfect territory for walks or long runs, and the beautiful campus has served as the backdrop for several movies and TV shows. Oglethorpe's academic buildings and some residence halls are in the English Gothic style; every year the campus plays host to the Georgia Shakespeare Festival.

Oglethorpe's strengths are business administration, English, biology, accounting, and psychology. Weaker bets are the fine arts and foreign language departments, though the latter does offer courses in Japanese, German, French, and Spanish. However, the university is working on its language programs, with the help of a Japan Foundation grant, the formation of the Japanese Studies Advisory Council, and the hiring of additional faculty. And whatever isn't offered at Oglethorpe can usually be taken through cross-registration at other schools in the Atlanta area.

Aspiring engineers may take advantage of 3–2 dual degree programs with Georgia Tech, the University of Southern California, Auburn, and the University of Florida. The school also offers courses and additional resources as a member of the Atlanta Regional Consortium for Higher Education.* Oglethorpe also offers a wide variety of study abroad programs, including a semester at Seigakuin University in Japan and sister-school exchanges in Argentina, the Netherlands, Germany, France, Russia, and Monaco. According to administrators, Oglethorpe "emphasizes the preparation of the humane generalist" and "rejects rigid specialization." That doesn't mean the curriculum's a cakewalk, though. "Classes are always challenging," says an English major. "I have never breezed through a class."

The university's guiding principle is the "Oglethorpe Idea," which says students should develop academically and as citizens. This philosophy is based on the conviction that education should help students make both a life and a living. To achieve this goal, the school has redesigned its core curriculum. All students

Website: www.oglethorpe.edu

Location: City outskirts

Total Enrollment: 1,288

Undergraduates: 1,178

Male/Female: 36/64

SAT Ranges: V 550–670 M 550–640

Financial Aid: 57%

Expense: Pr $ $

Phi Beta Kappa: No

Applicants: 744

Accepted: 71%

Enrolled: 27%

Grad in 6 Years: 70%

Returning Freshmen: 81%

Academics: 🖉 🖉 🖉

Social: ☎ ☎ ☎

Q of L: ★ ★ ★

Admissions: (404) 364-8307 or (800) 428-4484

Email Address: admission@oglethorpe.edu

Strongest Programs:
Biology
Accounting
Business Administration
English
Psychology

now take the sequenced, interdisciplinary program at the same point in their college careers, providing them with a model for integrating information and gaining knowledge. In addition to the ability to reason, read, and speak effectively, the core asks students to reflect upon and discuss matters fundamental to understanding who we are and what we ought to be. The core requires Narratives of the Self (freshmen), Human Nature and the Social Order (sophomores), Historical Perspectives on the Social Order (juniors), and Science and Human Nature (seniors), plus a fine arts core course in music and culture or art and culture, and coursework in modern mathematics or advanced foreign language.

Oglethorpe's faculty may be tough, but they're also friendly and helpful. "I would rate the teaching quality as an A. Freshmen are always taught by professors," a senior says. Another student adds, "The personal contact with each professor is what helped me learn more than anything I could have found in any book." Classes are generally small, and most students notice few problems at registration. Advising services are said to be helpful. The library's holdings are minuscule, though—just over 131,000 volumes.

What's an Oglethorpian like? The vast majority are smart, semiconservative offspring of middle- and upper-middle-class Southern families. Three-quarters ranked in the top quarter of their high school class; most come from public schools and over half are native Georgians. "Piercings, BMWs, poor, rich, jocks, and nerds—we harbor them all," says a senior. Oglethorpe prides itself on being one of the first Georgia colleges to admit black students, and today 22 percent of the students are members of minority groups: roughly 12 percent are black, 3 percent are Asian American, 2 percent are Hispanic, and 4 percent hail from abroad. There's a level of comfort with racial differences, students report. "I have never noticed any tension between different groups. People seem to be, as a whole, very accepting and open to all sorts of people," one student reports. Some students complain that their peers can be rather cliquish, but says that all in all, everyone gets along well.

Seventy percent of Oglethorpe's students choose to live on campus—and love it. "The dorms rock!," gushes an English major. Most rooms are suites with private bathrooms, and some singles are available. Some students commute to campus; a quarter live in Atlanta—not a college town, but where the wild life is. "The social life on campus is secondary to most things at OU," one student explains. Fraternities and sororities, which claim 33 percent of the men and 28 percent of the women, throw parties that draw big numbers. Officially, the campus is dry, but underage students can find alcohol if they try, students agree. One sums up the policy by saying, "'Put it in a cup' is the usual thing." It's rumored that Oglethorpe barflies do more hopping than Georgia bullfrogs, and bars, clubs, and cafés abound within 10 minutes of campus.

Those who tire of the Oglethorpe scene can find excitement on the campuses of the dozen or so other colleges in the area ("Georgia Tech boys can be spotted from a mile away with their skinny, pale legs and baseball caps," says a student), or in downtown Atlanta, which at least one student considers "a great place to come to college." Atlanta proper offers everything you can imagine—arts, professional sports (including basketball's Hawks, football's Falcons, and baseball's Braves), and entertainment (ride the Great American Scream Machine at Six Flags). Facilities built for the 1996 Olympics also provide a diversion. Oglethorpe always has a big contingent going to Savannah for St. Patrick's Day and to New Orleans for Mardi Gras. The campus celebrates its origins once a year during Oglethorpe Day. And the unusual Boar's Head Ceremony, held every Christmas, celebrates a student who years ago halted a stampeding wild boar by ramming his copy of Aristotle down the animal's throat.

Intramurals are important at Oglethorpe, sometimes more so than varsity sports. Perhaps Atlanta's diversions or the relatively small number of students on campus cause varsity sports to be a weak draw. Still, the Stormy Petrels men's basketball team has brought home a Southern Collegiate Athletic Conference title, and games against cross-city rival Emory are popular. The Georgia landscape makes possible a plethora of outdoor activities, including hiking at nearby Stone Mountain and boating or swimming in Lake Lanier (named for Georgia poet Sidney Lanier—Oglethorpe class of 1860).

Though Oglethorpe may lack widespread name recognition, its students get all the attention they need from a caring faculty on a close-knit campus. And being in a large city like Atlanta provides anything else that might be lacking, ranging from great nightlife to internships and postgraduate employment with big-name corporations. In a sea of large Southern state schools, Oglethorpe stands out as a place where "students come first."

> **Overlaps**
>
> **University of Georgia, Emory, Georgia State, Georgia Tech, Mercer.**

If You Apply To > **Oglethorpe**…Rolling admissions. Early decision: Nov. 30. Early action: Dec. 30. Financial aid: Mar. 1. Housing: May 1. Meets demonstrated need of 34%. Campus interviews: recommended, evaluative. Alumni interviews: optional, informational. SATs or ACTs: required. SAT IIs: optional. Accepts the Common Application. Essay question: more about you.

Ohio State University

3rd floor, Lincoln Tower, 1800 Cannon Drive, Columbus, OH 43210

Think big. Think very big. Think very, very big. Envision a school with almost 50,000 students and too many opportunities to count. What should come to mind is Ohio State University, located in the heart of the state's capital, offering 19 colleges and over 10,444 courses in 175 undergraduate majors. If those numbers aren't staggering enough, consider the fact that OSU has 34 varsity teams, 44 intramural sports, and 51 sports clubs. While students cite the school's size as both a blessing and a curse, all seem to agree that at OSU, the sky is the limit for those with a desire to learn.

This mega-university stands on 3,200 wooded acres, rubbing the edge of downtown Columbus on one side. On the other side, across the Olentangy River, is farmland associated with the College of Agriculture. OSU's architectural style is anything but consistent, yet it's all tied together in one huge redbrick package. "One part of the campus maintains a nostalgic air, while another is relatively modern," observes a student. The grounds are nicely landscaped, and a centrally located lake provides a peaceful setting for contemplation.

Business, education, geography, industrial design, and engineering are among the school's most celebrated departments. OSU bills itself as the place to go for computer graphics and has a supercomputer center to back up its claim. It also boasts the largest and most comprehensive black studies program anywhere, and turns out more black Ph.D.s than any other university in the nation. Furthermore, the university has the nation's only programs in welding engineering and geodetic science, and the state's only program in medical communications. Although

Website: www.osu.edu
Location: Center city
Total Enrollment: 48,003
Undergraduates: 36,092
Male/Female: 52/48
SAT Ranges: V 500–620 M 520–640
ACT Range: 22–27
Financial Aid: 66%
Expense: Pub $ $
Phi Beta Kappa: Yes
Applicants: 19,805
Accepted: 74%
Enrolled: 41%
Grad in 6 Years: 56%
Returning Freshmen: 83%
Academics: ✍ ✍ ✍
Social: ☎ ☎ ☎ ☎
Q of L: ★ ★ ★
Admissions: (614) 292-3980

OSU has the nation's only programs in welding engineering and geodetic science, and the state's only program in medical communications.

It also boasts the largest and most comprehensive black studies program anywhere, and turns out more black Ph.D.s than any other university in the nation.

immensely popular, students report that the English program needs improvement.

The university's fundamental commitment to liberal arts learning means all undergrads must satisfy rigorous general education requirements that include at least one course in math, two each in writing and a foreign language, three in social science, four in natural science, and five in arts and humanities. To top it all off, students must complete a capstone requirement that includes a course on Issues of the Contemporary World. A quarterly selective admissions program has replaced OSU's old open-door policy, but a conditional-unconditional admissions policy allows some poorly prepared students to play catch-up in their designated insufficient areas. Some 10,500 students receive merit-based scholarships ranging from $300 to $12,600, while 418 athletes receive scholarships in 16 sports.

Freshmen, who are grouped together in the University College before entering one of the degree-granting programs, find most introductory lectures huge. Teaching assistants, not professors, hold smaller recitation sections and deal on a personal level with students. "If you decide to attend OSU, come prepared to take responsibility for your education," says an animal science major. "The classes are large and the professors are very busy so you will not be pampered." Students find that class sizes are whittled down as they continue in their fields of study. OSU's honors program allows 2,500 students to take classes that are taught by top professors and limited to 25 students each. Internships are required in some programs and optional in others, and possibilities for study abroad include Japan and the People's Republic of China. A personalized study program enables students to create their own majors.

Inside OSU's ivy-covered halls and modern additions is some of the best in up-to-date equipment and facilities, including a "phenomenal" library system with two dozen branches and nearly 4 million volumes—all coordinated by computer. Complaints about long registration lines have been answered by BRUTUS, Ohio State's Touch-Tone telephone registration system, which saves on time but does little to ease class overcrowding. It's becoming increasingly difficult to graduate within four years, according to many students.

Eighty-nine percent of Ohio State's students come from Ohio, and the other 11 percent come largely from adjacent states. Every type of background is represented, most in huge numbers. Paradoxically, this school, with its nationally recognized black studies program, has a student body that is 8 percent African American; Hispanics and Asian Americans make up another 7 percent. One student bemoans the lack of integration between the black and white social groups. A psychology major, however, disagrees: "Ohio State has such a diverse population that its easy for anyone to fit in." Several programs are aimed specifically at "enhancing" efforts to attract and retain minority students, including a statewide Young Scholars Program that yearly guarantees admission and financial aid to seventh graders following high school.

The residence halls that house 24 percent of the Ohio State masses are located in three areas: North, South, and Olentangy (that is, those closest to the Olentangy River). Freshmen—required to live either at home or in the dorms—are scattered among each of OSU's 27 residence halls. Upperclassmen, when they don't head for off-campus life in Columbus, find the South campus section among the most desirable (it's more sociable, louder, and full of single rooms). The Towers in the Olentangy section have gained more popularity since their conversion to eight-person suites. All in all, students have a choice of single-sex, coed (by floor or by room), or married-couples apartments if they want to live in campus housing. Computer labs are located in each residence area. A system of variable

A personalized study
program enables students
to create their own majors.

room rates based on frills (i.e., air-conditioning, private bath, number of room-mates, etc.), as well as a choice of four meal-plan options, give students flexibility in determining their housing costs. Dormitory students have a choice of five dining halls, but others cook for themselves or eat in fraternity houses.

Such a large student market has, of course, produced a strip of bars, fast-food joints, convenience stores, bookstores, vegetarian restaurants, and you-name-it along the edge of the campus on High Street, and downtown Columbus is just a few minutes away. The fine public transportation system carries students not only throughout this capital city but also around the sprawling campus. In addition to the usual shopping centers, restaurants, golf courses, and movie theaters, Columbus boasts a symphony orchestra and ballet, and its central location in the state makes it easily accessible to Cleveland and Cincinnati. Outdoor enthusiasts can ski in nearby Mansfield, canoe and sail on the Olentangy and Scioto rivers, hike around adjacent quarries, or camp in the nearby woods.

Ohio State is a bustling place on weekends. "Student involvement is over-whelming," says one student. Various social events are planned by on-campus housing groups—floors, dorms, or sections of the campus. The Michigan–Ohio State football game inspires the best partying of the year, and other annual events include a Renaissance Festival and River Rat Day. Two student unions run eateries as well as movies on Friday and Saturday nights, and High Street's zillion bars, saloons, restaurants, and discos come to life. Campus policies prohibit underage drinking in dorms, but one socializer discloses, "I can get served in almost any bar on campus." Just 6 percent of men and 7 percent of women on this vast campus belong to one of the 61 fraternities and sororities. By one account, these students make the Greek system "a way of life and isolate themselves from the rest of the student population."

The school's vast resources aren't limited to academics. "You name the sport, and OSU offers it," boasts an agriculture major. There are 26 courts for handball, squash, or racquetball, and 12 courts for basketball. "It rained one day and 200 softball games were rained out," one student reports. Basketball now rivals football as a focus of school spirit. For some diehard fans, the first official day for practice as dictated by the NCAA, dubbed Midnight Basketball, is considered a kind of annual celebration.

OSU's sheer size is sometimes overwhelming to be sure, but students say they "thrive on the challenge and excitement of a big university." They enjoy "the freedom to pick and choose courses, programs, activities, and friends to fit their needs." For those who really want to be a Buckeye, jump in with both feet and heed the old campus saying: "Welcome to the Nut House."

Overlaps

**Ohio University,
Bowling Green State,
University of Cincinnati,
Miami University (OH),
Kent State.**

If You Apply To ➤ | **OSU**...Rolling admissions and financial aid: Feb. 15. Meets demonstrated need of 66%. Campus interviews: recommended, informational. No alumni interviews. SATs or ACTs: required. SAT IIs: optional. Accepts the Common Application and electronic applications. No essay question.

Website: www.ohiou.edu
Location: Rural
Total Enrollment: 19,638
Undergraduates: 16,554
Male/Female: 46/54
SAT Ranges: V 500–600 M 490–600
ACT Range: 21–26
Financial Aid: 79%
Expense: Pub $ $ $
Phi Beta Kappa: Yes
Applicants: 11,785
Accepted: 80%
Enrolled: 37%
Grad in 6 Years: 70%
Returning Freshmen: 84%
Academics: 🖎 🖎 🖎
Social: ☎ ☎ ☎ ☎
Q of L: ★ ★ ★
Admissions: (740) 593-4100
Email Address:
frshinfo@ohiou.edu

Strongest Programs:
Engineering
Journalism
Business
Communications
Dance

One of the newest additions to the curriculum is the Global Learning Community Certificate, an innovative program that prepares students for leadership opportunities in a rapidly changing world.

Once known as the prototypical party school, Ohio University is shedding that image for that of competitive public institution with a classical touch. Students and faculty members are still forced to chide well-meaning outsiders who confuse the school with its rival Ohio State. The locals call Ohio University "Harvard on the Hocking," the Hocking being the local river. While some would care to argue the comparison, students of Ohio University fiercely defend their beloved institution. Established in 1804 as the first institution of higher learning in the old Northwest Territory, Ohio University is located in Athens, about 75 miles from Columbus, the state capital. Encircled by winding hills, the campus features neo-Georgian architecture, tree-lined redbrick walkways, and white-columned buildings all clustered on "greens," which are like small neighborhoods. Long walks are especially nice during the fall foliage season. Current campus beautification includes a $25 million renovation of Grover Center, an athletic mall, and two new research facilities.

One of the focal points of an Ohio education, and something that sets the school apart from run-of-the-mill state institutions, is the honors tutorial college. This unique program is modeled on the tutorial method used in British universities, notably Oxford and Cambridge. Students in the honors program take an individualized curriculum in a major field, including weekly tutorials with profs on a one-to-one basis. Most participants finish their degrees in three years and then go on to attend leading graduate programs with close to a 100 percent acceptance rate. Students are eligible for special privileges as paid research apprenticeships, priority class registration, special library policies, and exemption from most university general education requirements. Other top areas are the College of Communication and its three offspring: the schools of telecommunications, visual communication, and journalism, which feature the latest graphics and microcomputer equipment. One of the newest additions to the curriculum is the Global Learning Community Certificate, an innovative program that prepares students for leadership opportunities in a rapidly changing world.

General education requirements involve a minimum of one course in math or quantitative skills, two courses in English composition, one senior-level interdisciplinary course, plus 30 quarter hours in applied sciences and technology, social sciences, natural sciences, humanities, and cross-cultural perspectives. To lighten the load, you can take electives such as Humor Writing or the Language of Rock Music, which Mom and Dad are sure to love. Study abroad offers worldwide destinations for anywhere from two weeks to one year. They include media studies in Dominica and theater in London. But despite the vast array of options, only 2 percent of students study abroad. Co-op programs are available for engineering students, and nearly anyone can earn credit for an internship. The Extern program, offered through the alumni association, provides weeklong internships in which students stay at the homes of alums and work with them on a daily basis.

Regarding their profs, students are generally pleased with what they've found. "The professors at OU are qualified, approachable, and willing to help their students in any way possible," says a business administration major. Freshmen usually are taught by full professors, with TAs handling study sessions. Classes of 100-plus students do exist, but the average class size for freshmen is about 25.

Older students advise their younger counterparts to plan carefully the classes they'll need to take, since younger students often have problems getting into courses. Faculty advisement is generally hit or miss. The academic climate at OU is debatable, depending on the classes and major you choose. One student explains, "The professors reinforce the concept that as long as we help each other, we can learn and master the material effectively. This camaraderie is needed to endure the academically rigorous classes."

You'll find many classmates from the Buckeye State; 84 percent are Ohioans. Almost everyone attended public high school and 18 percent graduated in the top tenth of their class. The student body is 94 percent white, with African Americans the largest minority group at 4 percent. Hispanics and Asian Americans combine for 2 percent of the population. The university has established an Office of Multicultural Programs and, despite its apparent homogeneity, one student says, "This campus is diverse and accepting of different types of people." Ohio offers about numerous merit scholarships and 237 athletic scholarships.

Campus housing is plentiful (40 dorms) and well liked. Most everyone lives on campus for two years, then moves off. Freshmen and sophomores live in one of three residential neighborhoods, or greens. Campus housing comes with a variety of options: coed, single-sex, quiet-study, academic-interest, and even an international dorm. At the "mods," six men and six women occupy separate wings but share a living room and study room. Upperclassmen usually move to fraternity or sorority houses, nearby apartments, or rental houses. Four different meal plans are available at four cafeterias and include fast-food counters next to regular dorm-food fare. Fraternities and sororities have their own private cooks.

The social life is vibrant, as you'd expect at a state school. "Students here keep busy by going to parties and bars and attending the many social events available on campus," says a senior. Uptown features over 20 bars, and besides campus activities such as plays, speakers, and performers (Jay Leno, Spike Lee, and Steven Wright to name a few), the Greeks take up the slack. Twelve percent of men and 16 percent of women join their ranks. The administration and some students have tried to downplay OU's party-school image by strictly enforcing the alcohol policy. But despite their efforts, one student reports, "the campus is full of underage drinkers. They can also be served in almost all the bars, except when the 'Feds' are in town." Two students mention drinking on campus as the school's biggest problem, but also say, "What college doesn't have problems with underage consumption?" Each year, students look forward to Spring Fest, when each residential green hosts a "green weekend," culminating with a free, all-campus outdoor party at the Hocking River. Athens's fabled Halloween celebration, "a huge block party with people from all around Ohio, Pennsylvania, Virginia, Indiana, and the Midwest," wouldn't be missed by many students. The International Street Fair features food and music from the different cultures on campus. Besides activities in Athens, which one student calls "the perfect college town," many students love to hike and camp at the nearby state parks or trek to Columbus. Volunteer opportunities, such as Habitat for Humanity and a local homeless shelter, are available through the Center for Community Service.

Sports are a big draw at Ohio, whether men's or women's basketball, cross-country, football, or baseball. Any competition pitting the Bobcats against "hated" Miami of Ohio draws a rowdy crowd. In addition, the Athens Criterium bicycle race draws competitors from throughout the nation.

It seems that almost everyone can be happy at Ohio, which is neither too big nor too small. While it's not overwhelmingly difficult academically, there's plenty of interaction with professors, especially in the honors program. "The friendliness

Other top areas are the College of Communication and its three offspring: the schools of telecommunications, visual communication, and journalism, which feature the latest graphics and microcomputer equipment.

The Extern program, offered through the alumni association, provides weeklong internships in which students stay at the homes of alums and work with them on a daily basis.

Overlaps

Ohio State, Miami University (OH), Bowling Green, Kent State, University of Cincinnati.

and easygoing attitude of the students make OU a great place," a senior says. Add to that a jumping social life and a beautiful campus, and Ohio University proves to be a quality institution with a reasonable price tag.

If You Apply To ➤

OU…Regular admissions: Feb. 1. Housing: May 1. Does not guarantee to meet demonstrated need. Campus and alumni interviews: optional, informational. SATs or ACTs: required. SAT IIs: optional. Essay question, optional personal essay.

Ohio Wesleyan University

South Sandusky Street, Delaware, OH 43015

Website: www.owu.edu

Location: Small town

Total Enrollment: 1,930

Undergraduates: 1,930

Male/Female: 49/51

SAT Ranges: V 550–660 M 570–660

ACT Range: 24–28

Financial Aid: 58%

Expense: Pr $ $ $

Phi Beta Kappa: Yes

Applicants: 2,057

Accepted: 83%

Enrolled: 30%

Grad in 6 Years: 69%

Returning Freshmen: 77%

Academics: ✍ ✍ ✍

Social: ☎ ☎ ☎ ☎ ☎

Q of L: ★ ★ ★

Admissions: (740) 368-3314

Email Address:

owuadmit@cc.owu.edu

Strongest Programs:

Psychology

Zoology

Though you may associate the Buckeye State with its immense public universities, there's another option: private Ohio Wesleyan University, tucked away in the hamlet of Delaware, where just under 2,000 students are eagerly pursuing a well-rounded education. Hallmarks at OWU are strong preparation for graduate and professional school, a solid grounding in the liberal arts, and an emphasis on having fun outside the classroom. "The strength of this university lies in the variety of learning options made available to its students," says a psychology major. That's why OWU is attracting many of Ohio's most promising young minds.

Situated smack in the center of the state, OWU's spacious 200-acre campus is peaceful and quaint, with 11 buildings on the National Register of Historic Places. The architecture ranges from Greek Revival to Colonial to modern, with ivy-covered brick academic buildings on one side of a busy thoroughfare, and dormitories and fraternities on the other side of the highway. Stately Stuyvesant Hall, with its majestic bell tower, is the main campus landmark. The R.W. Corns Center, which houses the economics department, information systems, and the writing center, has recently been renovated.

Preprofessional education has always been OWU's forte, and in 1998, the school placed all of its pre-health graduates in medical, dental, or veterinary schools. New additions to the curriculum are majors in neuroscience and East Asian studies, and the highly popular zoology and microbiology departments are interesting alternatives to the traditional premed route. The Woltemade Center for Economics, Business, and Entrepreneurship caters to budding entrepreneurs, and the music and fine arts programs offer both professional and liberal arts degrees. Students say the French department lacks "pizzazz," while administrators insist "there are no 'gut' majors here!"

A member of the Great Lakes College Association* consortium, Ohio Wesleyan offers numerous innovative curricular programs. The most prominent is the National Colloquium, a yearlong series of lectures on a timely issue. Recent speakers have included David Wetherell, president and CEO of CMGI, and novelist Gloria Naylor. The Honors Program offers qualified students one-on-one tutorials and a chance to conduct research with faculty members in areas of mutual interest. The Special Languages program offers the opportunity for self-directed study and tutoring by native speakers in languages such as Arabic, Chinese, Japanese, and modern Greek. Students can travel to Mexico for a community service experience during spring break, while fine arts, theater, and music majors can spend a semester in New York City to study with professionals.

To graduate, OWU students must take a year of foreign language, three courses in each of the social sciences, natural sciences, and humanities, and one course in the arts. Students must also pass three mandatory writing classes to sharpen their written communication skills, but these aren't burdensome; students universally laud OWU's faculty for ability and accessibility. Says one, "The enthusiasm of our faculty is related and relayed to the students not only in the classroom but during calls at home and over home-cooked dinners." The school highly values opportunities for students to interact closely with its thoughtful and dedicated faculty. "The quality of teaching here is excellent," says a botany and environmental science major. "Our small classes make it easy for students to interact with the faculty."

Still, there is a lingering rift between the remaining party animals, generally from Eastern prep schools, and the more studious Midwestern public school types. Forty percent of students come from Ohio; another big contingent consists of students from Mid-Atlantic and New England states, while recruits from Chicago and California are increasing. Students agree that diversity is valued on campus, but African Americans make up only 4 percent of the student body, Hispanics 2 percent, and Asian Americans 2 percent. "This campus is very diverse and everyone is tolerant of those who are different from themselves," says a student. Fifty-eight percent of students receive some type of financial aid, and merit scholarships recognizing academic or artistic ability, ranging from $4,000 to $21,880 are available.

All but one dorm is coed, and rooms are mostly apartment-style, four-person suites or doubles. Fraternities, unlike sororities, offer a residential option. Special-interest houses, such as Creative Arts House, House of Black Culture, House of Spirituality, and Women's House, are available, as is Welch Hall, which is for students with GPAs over 3.20. "The dorms are comfortable and the rooms are fairly large," says a genetics major. Seniors are now permitted to live off campus, a policy change that has drawn raves. Each meal eaten on the college plan subtracts a certain number of points (far too many in the opinion of most students) from students' accounts, but there are numerous culinary choices, from all-you-can-eat in the three dining halls to pizza and snacks from the college grocery store.

Does the button-down seriousness of recent years mean that OWU has forsaken its heritage of raucous partying? Administrators certainly hope so. Trying to stamp out drunken binges, OWU slaps fines of up to $150 on all underage students caught drinking and puts them on probation after the fourth offense. Nevertheless, one student says, "You can still get alcohol at fraternity parties even if you are underage." Part of OWU's commitment to mend its partying ways includes dry rush for all fraternities and an armband policy at parties. Greek membership, however, still attracts 44 percent of men and 37 percent of women. Among OWU's best-loved traditions are Fallfest and Monnett Weekend in the spring—campus-wide bashes for students, parents, and alumni that include bonfires, a Fun Run, and open houses for the Greeks. Romantics will enjoy the President's Ball the weekend before finals in the winter, and the famous Little Brown Jug harness race provides offbeat fun.

The Special Languages program offers the opportunity for self-directed study and tutoring by native speakers in languages such as Arabic, Chinese, Japanese, and modern Greek.

Recent speakers have included David Wetherell, president and CEO of CMGI, and novelist Gloria Naylor.

Delaware, a town of 25,000, is "not much of a college town," reports one senior. Another student disagrees: "This town is big enough to be interesting and convenient but small enough not be overwhelming." Approximately 85 percent of the students volunteer in the community for Habitat for Humanity and other charitable organizations. Ohio's capital and largest city, Columbus, is only 30 minutes away by car and offers many job and internship opportunities. Lakes, farms, and even ski slopes are within a few hours' drive.

The women's Battling Bishops basketball team won the NCAC Championship and a bid to the NCAA tournament in 1999, while men's indoor and outdoor track won the NCAC Championship. Sports fever carries over into single-sex and coed intramurals, and a massive annual game of Capture the Flag begins at 11:00 one night and lasts until the wee hours.

OWU's academic offerings span the gamut from anthropology to zoology, while its extracurricular offerings have expanded from raucous frat parties to National Colloquium lectures with renowned speakers. Cap these off with a dedicated, caring faculty and a student body small enough to make everyone much more than a number, and it becomes clear that Ohio Wesleyan University is an exciting option in higher education.

Overlaps

Denison, Wooster, Miami University (OH), Ohio State, Wittenberg.

If You Apply To ➤ **Ohio Wesleyan**…Early decision: Dec. 1. Early action: Dec. 15. Regular admissions: Mar. 1. Financial aid: March 15. Does not guarantee to meet demonstrated need. Campus interviews: recommended, evaluative. Alumni interviews: optional, informational. SATs or ACTs: required. SAT IIs: recommended. Accepts the Common Application and electronic applications. Essay question: significant experience; influential person; or value of community service to society. Places less reliance on standardized test scores than do similar colleges.

University of Oklahoma

1000 Asp Avenue, Room 127, Norman, OK 73019

Website: www.ou.edu
Location: Suburban
Total Enrollment: 21,339
Undergraduates: 17,264
Male/Female: 52/48
ACT Range: 21–27
Financial Aid: 89%
Expense: Pub $
Phi Beta Kappa: Yes
Applicants: 6,384
Accepted: 89%
Enrolled: 58%
Grad in 6 Years: 48%
Returning Freshmen: 81%
Academics: ✍ ✍ ✍
Social: ☎ ☎ ☎
Q of L: ★ ★ ★

Thanks to an aggressive self-improvement kick and a new national championship, Sooner Pride is at an all-time high. The campus is alive once more—building new facilities, hiring new faculty and placing a major emphasis on improvement. "Our college is a new place in the last five years," says a senior English education major. "The administration's goal is for OU to be just as prestigious and stimulating as any Ivy League or private institution." Not bad for a school where a former president once said, "We want a university the football team can be proud of."

Located about 18 miles south of Oklahoma City, OU's 2,000-acre Norman campus features tree-lined streets and predominantly redbrick buildings. Many are historic buildings in the Cherokee or Prairie Gothic style. The campus houses 12 colleges; 6 medical and health-related colleges are located on the OU Health Sciences Center campuses in Oklahoma City and Tulsa. Newer facilities on the Norman campus include the $16-million Catlett Music Hall, the Charlie Coe Golf Learning Center, and upgraded facilities for the softball and baseball teams. The Sam Noble Museum of Natural History, which opened in mid-2000, is the largest university-based museum of natural history in the nation, with more than 5 million artifacts.

All Oklahoma freshmen start out in the university college before choosing among several degree-granting institutions, including the colleges of architecture, arts and sciences, education, business administration, and fine arts. The engineering school offers specializations in geological, aerospace, petroleum, and environmental engineering; the petroleum program ranks among the best in the nation, and is home to numerous recent national Black Engineers of the Year. OU has the state's only comprehensive fine arts college, with one of the nation's oldest collegiate ballet programs. In the College of Arts and Sciences, the natural sciences, notably chemistry, are strong. The state-of-the-art $50-million Energy Center houses some of the brightest energy-related programs under the sun. The College of Geosciences brings together Oklahoma's strong programs in meteorology, geology and geophysics, and geography. OU offers majors in both Native American and African American studies, and newer programs in energy management, Chinese, and public administration. Interestingly, the OU Native American Studies program teaches more American Indian languages than any other institution in the US. Future forecasters can stay on to get their masters degrees in professional meteorology, while the College of Education's rigorous, nationally accredited five-year teacher certification program, Teacher Education Plus (TE-PLUS), incorporates field experience, mentoring, and instruction from 30 full-time professors. Students cite women's studies and film studies as among OU's weaker offerings.

Each college has its own set of general requirements, but nearly half the student body is enrolled in degree programs requiring at least one computing course. Other general education requirements consist of three to five courses in symbolic and oral communication, including English composition, two courses in natural science, two courses in social science, four humanities courses, an upper-division General Education course outside the major, and a one-course Senior Capstone Experience. OU also offers optional "Gateway to Learning" classes for freshmen, which provide a survey of the university's academic opportunities, services and resources; a participant described the course as "a ticket to ensured success." Another rich opportunity is the Presidential Travel and Study Abroad Scholarships, which provides $75,000 for students and faculty to study and conduct research around the globe.

For the academically ambitious, the Honors College offers small classes with outstanding faculty members, independent reading and research for credit, and interdisciplinary studies. It also has its own dorm which houses 200 of the program's 1200 students. Along with the Honors College, top students can apply for admission to the Scholarship-Leadership Enrichment Program, through which well-known lecturers from outside the university give seminars for academic credit. With all of these opportunities for the bright and highly motivated, plus its reasonable price tag, it's no wonder OU attracts one of the highest concentrations of National Merit Scholars of any school in the nation. At the other end of the scale, however, special guidance counseling and a concerned tutorial staff are available for students who need remedial help.

Though OU is one of the smaller Big 12 schools, it can still overwhelm. A freshman orientation program, involving both students and faculty, tries to ease the transition to college, and when it's time to hit the books, students can check out wireless laptops from the library if they don't yet have their own. Class size is not generally a problem; advisors and professors can usually get students into most courses, even if they're officially closed, and with a little upfront planning and dedication to the coursework required for your major, students report little trouble graduating in four years. Students also give the faculty high marks, and note that even freshmen encounter full profs, though a whopping 38 percent of

(Continued)
Admissions: (800) 234-6868
Email Address:
   admrec@ouwww.ucs.ou.edu

Strongest Programs:
   Meteorology
   Finance and Accounting
   History of Science
   Chemistry and Biochemistry
   Counseling Psychology
   Petroleum and Geological
   Engineering
   Chemical Engineering and
   Materials Science
   Music

The engineering school offers specializations in geological, aerospace, petroleum, and environmental engineering.

The petroleum program ranks among the best in the nation, and is home to numerous recent national Black Engineers of the Year.

undergraduate courses are led by graduate students. An English education major notes that students should utilize both faculty and departmental advisors; the former can offer perspective on their academic field, while the latter know OU's bureaucracy and logistics. Each college also offers advisors and support organizations, such as Project Threshold and the Minority Engineering Program.

OU's student body is primarily homegrown, with only 16 percent from outside the Sooner state. Minorities account for 23 percent of the student body; blacks and Native Americans make up 7 percent each, Asian Americans 5 percent, and Hispanics almost 4 percent. Foreign students comprise almost 8 percent. The Center for Student Life has hosted programs such as "A Day of Dialogue on Race," but political correctness, acceptance of alternative lifestyles and the power of the Greek system appear to be more pressing issues these days. OU awards 12,681 merit scholarships, ranging from $100 to $10,000, and 243 athletic scholarships in a variety of sports.

The university's residence halls provide a happy, if unremarkable, home to only 20 percent of the undergraduate students. Says one English major, "All dorms are well-maintained; some rooms are more comfortable than others." Most halls have been renovated; some feature air-conditioned buildings with color TV lounges and recreation rooms. (Of course, there are also basic box accommodations with no frills attached.) Most halls are coed by floor, and many of the lounge areas on the halls have been refurbished. Off-campus housing is affordable (most students choose this option); though fraternities draw 19 percent of the men and sororities 20 percent of the women, only 10 percent of students live in Greek housing.

Students love the town of Norman, Oklahoma's third-largest city, which provides restaurants and shops plus numerous volunteer opportunities. "Students can get anywhere in 20 minutes, which helps a lot," notes one student. Frat parties are the highlight of weekends at OU, as are annual events such as the road trip to Dallas for the OU-Texas game, the first-of-the-football-season Big Red Rally, the Medieval Festival, and the University Sing, a talent show.

OU sports big-time athletics as part of the Big 12 conference. The football team went undefeated in 2000-2001, and brought home a national championship under second-year coach Bob Stoops.

There's a dedication and spirit of family evident in Norman, Oklahoma, these days, and not just among fans of Sooner football, says a senior. "A remarkable faculty, staff, and president are working to make OU a top-notch university, and help students do the same," she explains. Indeed, there's much to cheer about as OU heads into the new millennium, including 12 additional endowed faculty positions, 48 presidential professorships, an Adopt-a-Prof program to encourage faculty mentoring, and roundtables, lectures, and dinner discussions at the president's house, open to all. OU students have a favorite saying: "Sooner born and Sooner bred, when I die, I'll be Sooner dead!"

If You Apply To ➤

OU...Rolling admissions: July 15. Financial aid: March 1. Meets demonstrated financial need of 91%. Campus interviews: optional, evaluative. No alumni interviews. SATs or ACTs: required. No SAT IIs. No essay question.

Oregon State University

Corvallis, OR 97331-2106

With a wide range of academic programs, Oregon State University could very well be the setting of its own movie, entitled *Planes, Trains, and Submarines*. You see, Oregon State is one of just a handful of universities in the country with land-, sea-, and space-grant designations. Though the school might be happy to forget its many years of being called Moo U, that doesn't mean its agriculture department should go unnoticed. In fact, many of the contributions made by Oregon State researchers center on the field of agriculture. Still, there's more to OSU than fruits and vegetables. The school is strong in many departments, including biotechnology, forestry, and engineering.

Located in the pristine but rainy Willamette Valley, OSU's campus is a mix of older, ivy-covered buildings and more modern structures. In addition to the 500-acre main campus, OSU owns 13,000 acres of forestland near campus and numerous agricultural tracts throughout Oregon. Thousands of azalea and rhododendron bushes welcome springtime on campus with their colorful blooms, and summers are unfailingly sunny. (All that rain during the rest of the year has to be good for something, right?) Recent additions to the campus map include a forest resource lab, a residence hall, and a baseball field.

OSU's College of Liberal Arts ranks with Business and Engineering as the largest on campus, but there are many more preprofessionals than poets. With the exception of history and English, the liberal arts—including such standard fare as sociology, psychology, economics, and philosophy—play second fiddle to more practical, technical fields. The departments of engineering (with their up-to-date electrical and computer engineering building) and forestry are major drawing cards, and even though agriculture doesn't lure as many students as it used to, those who do come find excellent programs. Business administration is the most popular major, followed by exercise and sport science, liberal studies, general science, and psychology. The business school offers some of the finest business-related programs in the state, while the health and human performance program—a euphemism for home economics—has expanded its offerings recently. Newer degree programs include ethnic studies and environmental engineering; also relatively new is the Honors College. Freshmen become familiar with the college environment through OSU Odyssey.

OSU's extensive Baccalaureate Core requires courses in a variety of areas, including skills; perspectives; and difference, power, and discrimination. One writing-intensive course is required as well. Perhaps the core's most innovative facet is its "synthesis" requirement, in which upperclassmen take two interdisciplinary courses on global issues in the modern world. The campus's global awareness is also evident in the new International Degree, which can be coupled with any other course of study. Thus, students can earn a BS in forestry and a BA in international studies in forestry simultaneously. The level of academic pressure varies by major, but even those in the various honors programs say they don't feel overworked. "The academic climate here fosters learning," says a business major. "The courses are challenging but manageable." Students have good access to professors, but classes tend to be crowded, and one student notes that "many business and engineering people are bumped from their courses." (In fairness, that may be because of the major's immense popularity.)

Of particular note is OSU's Experimental College, where undergraduates spice

Website: www.osu.orst.edu
Location: Small city
Total Enrollment: 16,091
Undergraduates: 13,167
Male/Female: 53/47
SAT Ranges: V 480–590 M 490–610
ACT Range: 20–26
Financial Aid: N/A
Expense: Pub $ $
Phi Beta Kappa: No
Applicants: 6,494
Accepted: 91%
Enrolled: 42%
Grad in 6 Years: 56%
Returning Freshmen: 80%
Academics: ✍ ✍ ✍
Social: ☎ ☎ ☎
Q of L: ★ ★ ★
Admissions: (541) 737-4411
Email Address:
osuadmit@orst.edu

Strongest Programs:
Agriculture
Biotechnology
Forestry
Engineering
Business

up their semesters with noncredit courses in a range of imaginative subjects—everything from wine tasting to the art of bashing, a medieval war technique. Those who can afford a semester abroad may study at universities in England, France, Australia, Mexico, New Zealand, China, and Japan—or participate in individual exchange programs in still more countries. (Oregon State returns the favor, playing host to about 1,500 foreign students from more than 90 nations each year.) The university's small-town location (population 45,000) makes it difficult to find much career-oriented part-time employment, and term-time internships are hard to come by. (OSU operates on a quarter system.) Students in almost all majors, however, can participate in the cooperative-education program, which allows them to alternate terms of study with several months of work in a relevant job.

Statistically, Oregon State certainly doesn't offer the most diverse student body. Seventy-eight percent of the students are from Oregon, and the 13 percent minority population is mostly Asian American. Foreign students account for another 10 percent of the total. Communication between different racial and ethnic groups is poor, students report, despite a new ethnic studies program. Other big issues are underage drinking and tuition increases. Most Oregon Staters are conservative and "very all-American—not cowboys and not city slickers, but very middle of the road in all respects," a business major observes. Says an engineering major, "The college has its intelligentsia, its social butterflies, its determined athletes, and any combination of those."

Freshmen are expected to live in college housing, though fraternity pledges have the option of living in their houses. Coed and single-sex options are available in the comfortable and well-maintained dorms, which house about a third of the students. "The residence halls are comfortable and well maintained, for the most part," says a forestry major. "They also offer many opportunities to get involved and meet new people." In addition to standard rooming situations, a new "wellness" hall offers an exercise room and low-calorie meals. Students can also choose life in one of eight cooperatives or the plentiful off-campus apartments. Foraging for food on your own generally beats so-so dorm grub; the better chow at frat and sorority houses is one motivation for students to go Greek, which about 14 percent of the men and 12 percent of the women do. Alcohol still flows freely at Greek affairs, but recent crackdowns by the administration and local police have begun to curb the most wanton debauchery.

Cheering for the Beavers' nationally ranked wrestling team, which has had four Top 10 national finishes in the last five years, demands a lot of students' time and energy here, as does participation in the well-rounded intramural program. Other talented varsity squads include women's gymnastics, basketball, and volleyball, and men's football and baseball; the basketball team has the eighth-winningest program of all time among NCAA Division I schools. As for rivalries, one student says, "Civil War games between OSU and U of Oregon are a big part of every season."

Another popular student activity is complaining about the Willamette Valley weather: "People in the valley don't tan, they rust," warns one native. One reward for this sogginess, however, is the abundance of flowers that bloom in every color and shape each May. Many students consider Corvallis a good-size town; a number of bars and cheap theaters cater to their entertainment needs. Beautifully rugged beaches are less than an hour away, and some of the best skiing in the country can be found in the Cascade Mountains, two hours east. Hiking and rafting are nearby, too, and trips to powwows in the area and camping on the coast provide other good times. Popular campus traditions include the annual Fall

Festival ("crafts and good ol' greasy food") at the beginning of the school year, Dad's Weekend in February, and Mom's in May.

Oregon State University continues to build on its solid reputation as an agricultural institution, marching into the millennium as an old and faithful part of the state's university system. OSU doesn't scream for attention. Instead, it's content to be a "nice" college, in "a safe and pleasant little town," where professors are "helpful" and even if everyone doesn't know your name, they'll lend you an umbrella whenever the skies open up.

If You Apply To ➢

Oregon State…Early action: Nov. 1. Regular admissions: Mar. 1. Financial aid: Feb. 1. Does not guarantee to meet demonstrated need. Campus interviews: optional, informational. No alumni interviews. SATs or ACTs: optional. No SAT IIs. Accepts the Common Application and electronic applications. No essay question.

University of Oregon

Box 1226, Eugene, OR 97403-1226

Students at the University of Oregon say their school boasts "the world's coolest Web site." But they're not referring to the university's virtual presence on the Internet: They mean Autzen Stadium, home of their football team, the (mighty) Ducks. Sure, the joke's a little hokey, but its offbeat humor is typical of the laid-back, slightly eccentric attitude that prevails here in Eugene, where bicycles are the main form of transportation, recycling is a requirement, and littering is passé.

UO's buildings date from as early as 1876 to as late as 1999; they're surrounded by the university's lush 280-acre arboretum-like campus, which boasts 2,000 varieties of dew-kissed trees. Most academic buildings were built before World War II and represent a blend of classical styles, including Georgian, Second Empire, Jacobin, and Lombardic. Residential facilities range from 19th-century Colonials to modern high-rises.

While a liberal arts emphasis underlies Oregon's entire curriculum, general education requirements are not highly structured. The calendar is composed of quarters, and students must take two terms of English composition, two years of foreign language (for a BA), one year of math (for a BS), and one term of a race- or gender-sensitive course, plus six courses in each of three areas: arts and letters, social sciences, and natural sciences. The academic climate is "relatively low on stress," a sophomore psychology major reports. Freshman seminars introduce students to top professors in small-group settings and profs have to apply to teach them, a process students applaud. Freshman Interest Groups help new students acclimate to campus life through informal meetings and activities with upperclassmen.

Oregon's professional schools—journalism, architecture and allied arts, education, law, business, and music—are highly regarded, with journalism and business drawing the most student praise. Of the more than 35 departments in the College of Arts and Sciences, students give high marks (and high enrollments) to psychology and biology, and the science departments within this particular college offer many opportunities for research. Newer majors include Judaic Studies,

Website: www.uoregon.edu
Location: Small city
Total Enrollment: 16,716
Undergraduates: 13,426
Male/Female: 47/53
SAT Ranges: V 498–617 M 496–607
Financial Aid: 45%
Expense: Pub $ $
Phi Beta Kappa: Yes
Applicants: 9,499
Accepted: 89%
Enrolled: 37%
Grad in 6 Years: 57%
Returning Freshmen: 82%
Academics: 🖉 🖉 🖉
Social: ☎ ☎ ☎
Q of L: ★ ★ ★ ★
Admissions: (541) 346-3201 or (800) BE A DUCK
Email Address:
uoadmit@oregon.uoregon.edu

Strongest Programs:
Architecture
Music

biochemistry, mathematics and computer science, and environmental studies, which drew over 400 students in its first year of existence. Marriage and Family Studies has recently been added to the College of Education.

Highly motivated undergraduates may join the Honors College, a small liberal arts college with its own courses, and outstanding liberal arts majors may spend five years on campus to earn their master's degree in the Graduate School of Management. The student-run ESCAPE (Every Student Caring About Personalized Education) program provides credit for community volunteer work, while on-campus internships allow students to earn credit for work with university organizations and academic departments.

Like many state schools, UO has experienced a bit of a budget crunch. The speech program was cut entirely as a result (although the education program was resurrected on the undergraduate level), and students complain about overcrowding in popular courses, especially during their first semester or two. A telephone and Web registration program has improved the registration process so that it is no longer "like battling in an arena." One student notes that Advanced Placement credits help new students register earlier than their peers, since students get priority for the classes they request based on accumulated credits. The UO library system remains the best in the state, and students say the career center is "first-rate." "My counselors have been more than happy to help me with whatever I needed," says a senior.

Some students say UO is one of the last collegiate strongholds for people who "are open-minded and liberal politically." Another, however, warns, "You really have to watch what you say. Some people here take things very seriously and can be offended or get defensive about certain issues." In general, every part of the white Anglo-Saxon spectrum is well represented, with an especially heavy dose of the athletically inclined. There is a noticeable contingent of international students, who account for 7 percent of the student body. Asian Americans account for another 6 percent, African Americans 2 percent, and Hispanics 3 percent. The 20 percent of students who come from out of state are mostly from California.

Since there are no residence requirements and few dorms, 80 percent of the students live off campus in nearby apartments (although 64 percent of freshmen choose to live on campus). There are a number of thematic living arrangements— a cross-cultural dorm, an academic-pursuit residence hall, a music dorm; students recommend Walton, Carson, and University Inn. Rooms in the residence halls tend to be small but clean and comfortable, and they have Internet connections. Any student can sign up for the meal plan in the two main dining halls; restaurants in the student union and off-campus fast food round out the menu.

Eugene, the second-largest city in Oregon, is "where all the hippies went when the '60s were over," a sophomore says. "The town of Eugene is a college town in that it caters to the students," says an environmental studies major. Popular hangouts include Old Taylor's and Rennies, and community and public service projects also draw crowds. The one drawback to all this fun is Oregon's weather: it rains and rains. "Eugene gets some sunny days in early fall, late spring, and summer," reports a veteran. "The winter rain is occasionally depressing, but it keeps the city green." Still, the moist climate rarely dampens enthusiasm for the many expeditions available through the university's well-coordinated outdoor program, from rock climbing to skiing. An hour to the west, the rain turns to mist on the Pacific Coast; an hour to the east it turns to snow in the Cascade Mountains. Students can also escape the weather year-round in the new recreation center, complete with rock-climbing wall and juice bar.

Eleven percent of UO men and women join Greek organizations, which

The student-run ESCAPE (Every Student Caring About Personalized Education) program provides credit for community volunteer work, while on-campus internships allow students to earn credit for work with university organizations and academic departments.

Freshman Interest Groups help new students acclimate to campus life through informal meetings and activities with upperclassmen.

provide living space along with some interesting social activities (the movie *Animal House* was filmed in one of the fraternity houses on campus). Oregon's 21-year-old drinking age means that alcohol is theoretically banned from college-owned dorms, but students claim this rule can be broken. "If they look hard enough, there's always a way for minors to get alcohol," says a junior. Major events include the Eugene Celebration, the Oregon Country Fair, the Martin Luther King, Jr. Festival, and weekly street fairs attended by local vendors. University Day, which happens twice a year, offers students an opportunity to clean up their campus. The Willamette Valley Wine Festival is a fun road trip.

Second only to parties, athletic activities head the list of favorite free-time activities. The Ducks' biggest athletic rival is the Oregon State Beavers, and each year the Civil War game in football is huge. When students aren't on the tracks and fields themselves, they're trooping down to the stadium to join the Quacker Backers in cheering on the successful basketball and football teams. Track is also prominent; Nike is headquartered in nearby Beaverton.

A recent University of Oregon Orientation Week T-shirt sported a picture of a duck and the simple exhortation "Let your future take flight." UO certainly offers many ways for those with lofty ambitions to succeed. With UO's caring faculty, excellent academics, and abundance of social activities, UO is all it's quacked up to be.

Freshman seminars introduce students to top professors in small-group settings and profs have to apply to teach them, a process students applaud.

Overlaps

University of Washington, University of Colorado, Oregon State, UC–Santa Barbara, UC–Davis.

If You Apply To ➤ **UO**…Rolling admissions: Feb. 1. Financial aid and housing: Mar 1. Meets demonstrated need of those who meet eligibility and priority deadline of Mar. 1. Campus interviews: optional, informational. No alumni interviews. SATs or ACTs: required. SAT IIs: required if home schooled or graduate of nonstandard high school (English, math, one of choice). Accepts the Common Application and electronic applications. No essay question.

University of the Pacific

3601 Pacific Avenue, Stockton, CA 95211

University of the Pacific looks like several hundred acres of New England plunked down in the midst of California wine country. With its stately combination of red brick and ivy, it looks for all the world like an East Coast liberal arts college. But instead of a blanket of snow, UOP is surrounded by the lush greenery of the San Joaquin Valley.

With majestic evergreens and flowering trees, UOP is home to six undergraduate professional schools and the College of the Pacific, the university's liberal arts and sciences division. There is also a school of law in Sacramento and a superlative school of dentistry in San Francisco. Strong departments are any in the schools of engineering, pharmacy, and business (with special programs in the arts/entertainment management and entrepreneurship) as well as education, psychology, and the sciences. The school of international studies is gaining a national recognition. The university-wide general education program is divided into two main components: the liberal learning program (interdisciplinary courses spread across three categories of learning) and fundamental learning skills classes, which students can avoid by scoring high on writing and quantitative tests. A number of internship and co-op programs are available, as are several accelerated programs in which students may earn a joint degree between liberal

Website: www.uop.edu
Location: Suburban
Total Enrollment: 5,640
Undergraduates: 2,944
Male/Female: 42/58
SAT Ranges: V 480–600 M 500–620
ACT Range: 20–26
Financial Aid: 78%
Expenses: Pr $ $
Phi Beta Kappa: No
Applicants: 2,831
Accepted: 82%
Enrolled: 32%
Grad in 6 Years: 64%
Returning Freshmen: 87%

(Continued)

Academics: ✍ ✍ ✍
Social: ☎ ☎ ☎
Q of L: ★ ★ ★ ★
Admissions: (209) 946-2211
Email Address:
  admissions@uop.edu

Strongest Programs:
  Biology
  Computer Science
  Music
  Predental
  Pharmacy and Health
  Sciences
  Business
  Education
  Engineering

studies and a professional program over five or six years. Students may also design their own majors with faculty approval. An extensive study abroad program offers 200 choices in 70 countries. All freshmen are required to take Mentor Seminars I (Timeless Issues, including: What is appearance/What is reality? What do we come to think, to know? and Why be good?) and II (Today's Decisions, focusing on selected public policy decisions that students may face during their lifetimes). Another seminar (Ethical Application of Knowledge) is required during the junior or senior year.

Although the academic climate varies, each major has its own "hell courses." "You may work hard and still not get an A," warns a sophomore. Studying accounts for anywhere from 10 to 40 hours a week. The university guarantees graduation in four years (assuming the student follows all university guidelines), or it will pay for the extra schooling. Professors at UOP get raves for accessibility and personal attention. "The professors understand their first and foremost priority is to educate and teach students," one junior says. "Research comes secondary to the quality and care given to teaching. Classes generally average 25 students, and the TAs teach only the labs. The Student-to-Student Advising Center and the Education Resource Center are very strong, as is the Career and Internship Center.

The campus air has been a little less tranquil in recent years because of a series of budget cuts. In 1997, after a yearlong review of its programs, the university decided to cut out 10 undergraduate majors that had not been attracting many students, including cultural anthropology, linguistics, and preministerial studies. With the arrival of a new administration and some intensive reviews, however, the university claims to have regained its footing. Enrollment has grown, and many facilities are being built or renovated.

Eighty percent of UOP students are Californians. Hawaii and Colorado are also strongly represented, while foreign students make up 5 percent of the student body. Asian Americans account for nearly a third, while blacks and Hispanics make up 12 percent. Students come from a mix of economic backgrounds (78 percent receive financial aid), and 84 percent graduated from public high school. The school is middle of the road to conservative, though politics in general play a small role on campus. One junior notes, "This campus is not known for major political activity; most of the issues that get attention involve purely campus matters."

Though not unusually expensive by national standards, the university seems expensive when compared to the University of California system. The UOP has stepped up efforts to compete using merit scholarships, which range from $6,500 to $10,000, as well as full and partial scholarships to athletes in a variety of sports. With its high costs compared to the other schools with which it shares applicants, students sometimes jokingly refer to UOP as U. Owe Plenty; however, the financial aid packages generally get good reviews, and make it possible for most students at UOP to pay the bills.

Freshmen and sophomores are required to live on campus, and the few complaints mostly center around aging facilities, some of which are undergoing much-needed renovations. In terms of quality of life, however, residential life is praised for plentiful social programming and a fun atmosphere where "people are very friendly and fun to hang out with," as one junior commented. Grace Covell Hall, with 350 people, is the largest residence. Rooms and roommates are assigned by the Residential Life staff according to cards filled out by students. With three meal plans, three dining halls, and one fast-food-type facility, residents are well provided for. In addition to the regular entrées and a salad bar, special theme dinners add flair.

Social activities are offered on campus by ASUOP (Associated Students of UOP, the main student governing body), the Residence Hall Association, intramural and club sports, conservatory and drama/dance productions, Division I athletics, campus movies, sororities and fraternities, and more than 100 student clubs.

For weekend excitement, UOP students love to hit the road: within about two hours, they can be skiing, shopping in San Francisco, or surfing in Monterey. Stockton itself (population 250,000) offers shopping and plenty of fast-food joints, as well as numerous volunteer opportunities. Social opportunities on campus are offered by ASUOP (Associated Students of UOP), the Residence Hall Association, intramural and club sports, conservatory and drama/dance programs, Division I athletics, campus movies, sororities and fraternities, and more than 100 student clubs. Twenty percent of the men and twenty percent of the women join the Greek organizations. However, one senior says, "It's a false perception that you must be a Greek to have a social life. There are lots of social activities on campus." Dorm social programming provides a popular option, and the school occasionally hosts big-name concerts and other campus-wide events. As for alcohol, the campus policy prohibits alcohol in common areas of residence halls (but not in individual dorm rooms), and by August 2001 the majority of Greek houses will be substance-free, following a national trend enforced by their national organizations. One junior explains, "Generally, underage students can get alcohol at any time if they want to and consume it in small groups, but the days of large parties with alcohol being served are over." Annual campus festivities include Diversity Week, International Spring Festival, and the popular Fall Festival and Greek Week. In sports, women's volleyball is always high ranking nationally, and men's water polo also has received national attention.

Pitted against the state's immense public university system, UOP offers major university opportunities in a small-college setting. For those who seek individual attention and tough but supportive faculty in a picture-perfect setting, becoming a Tiger may be the perfect choice. "It may be expensive," a senior says, "but it's worth every penny. After four years, I can say it's the best decision I ever made."

If You Apply To ➤ **UOP**...Early action: Dec. 15. Rolling admissions and financial aid: Feb. 15. Meets demonstrated need of 70%. Campus interviews: recommended, evaluative. No alumni interviews. SATs or ACTs: required. SAT IIs: optional. Essay question: significant experience; what will make your college experience a success.

Pennsylvania State University

201 Old Main, University Park, PA 16802

Penn State offers a vast array of quality programs, knowledgeable professors, and an academic reputation that is matched only by its renowned social environment. They don't call it Happy Valley for nothing.

Sporting an eclectic architectural mix, including white-columned brick, stone, and some modern apartments, this land-grant university continues to experience growth as major renovation and expansion projects continue. The university has also provided each student and professor with email accounts for faster communication. The system has been rewarded by handling over 1 million email messages daily.

Penn State maintains strong programs in the scientific and technical fields such as earth sciences, engineering, agricultural sciences, and life sciences, as well as nutrition and family studies. The meteorology program boasts alumni

Website: www.psu.edu
Location: Small city
Total Enrollment: 40,658
Undergraduates: 34,505
Male/Female: 54/46
SAT Ranges: V 540–640 M 560–670
Financial Aid: 50%
Expense: Pub $ $
Phi Beta Kappa: Yes
Applicants: 26,079

(Continued)

Accepted: 49%

Enrolled: 39%

Grad in 6 Years: 80%

Returning Freshmen: 93%

Academics: ✍ ✍ ✍

Social: ☎ ☎ ☎ ☎ ☎

Q of L: ★ ★ ★

Admissions: (814) 865-5471

Email Address:
admissions@psu.edu

Strongest Programs:
Agricultural Sciences
Business Logistics
Engineering
Human Development/Family
Studies
Astronomy
Chemistry
Film and Television
Architecture

The Penn State library contains approximately 3.8 million volumes, and a branch library is open 24 hours every day for the after-hours crowd.

worldwide, including the founder of Accu-Weather, an internationally renowned private forecasting firm that is headquartered here. Newer majors include Industrial Health and Safety and electrical engineering. Engineering is good in all areas, while the Agriculture College has extensive facilities that include huge live-stock barns. Dairy products from the school's cows are sold at an on-campus store, and courses are offered in the production of its famous ice cream. Students can choose from 225 baccalaureate programs and 155 graduate fields, and the Dickinson School of Law, located near the state capital. At a school of Penn State's size there are bound to be some weaknesses. Students say cultural and ethnic studies—courses that focus on Asian and Latin American history—need help, while the administration continues to concentrate on improving the humanities in general. Increased funds are being allocated for program requests in the arts and liberal arts, but chronic underfunding by the state is an unwieldy obstacle. According to the administration, the university's appropriation is $72 million lower than the average for flagship public universities across the nation.

General education requirements include several communications and quantification courses as well as humanities, arts, natural sciences, social and behavioral sciences, and health and physical education courses. The incorporation of critical thinking skills has been a priority in redesigning the general curriculum; Penn State's Schreyer Institute for Innovation in Learning is playing a central role in developing an academic culture of active and collaborative learning that helps graduates become critical problem solvers and lifelong learners. In addition, undergrads must enroll in "diversity-focused" courses that encourage awareness of minority concerns. But all this education can be put to good use with the helpful career counselors. "They have a ton of resources to take advantage of," says a biology major. Academic counselors get somewhat lower marks, with students having to take the initiative to seek them out. About 1,500 of the university's best and brightest are invited to participate in the University Scholars Program, which offers opportunities for independent study and graduate work as well as honors options in regular courses.

Those binoculars you use when sitting in the bleachers may come in handy in some of Penn State's intro level lecture courses, which sometimes draw up to 400 students. Though such enormous classes can feel impersonal, students rate the quality of teaching very high, one student gives faculty an A-. For cramming outside of class, the Penn State library contains approximately 3.8 million volumes, and a branch library is open 24 hours every day for the after-hours crowd. Not every major is a pressure-cooker, though science and engineering are generally tough. "No one will take your hand and make you do your work," a senior says. "You have to be proactive in your own education." A large number of students study abroad, and combined undergraduate/graduate degree options are available, as are co-op programs in engineering, distance learning, and student-designed majors.

Most undergraduates are residents of Pennsylvania, with 20 percent hailing from out of state and a 1 percent sprinkling of foreign students. Nearly 90 percent ranked in the top quarter of their high school class. Asian Americans make up 5 percent of the undergrad population, and blacks and Hispanics combine for another 7 percent. Penn State's president has made diversifying Happy Valley one of his top priorities, but students say ethnocentric attitudes are still prevalent on campus. A whopping 609 athletic scholarships are available, covering all NCAA-approved sports, as are 500 merit awards ranging from $100 to $12, 000. Freshmen must live in the dorms, which, by all accounts, are comfortable and well maintained. Recent housing crunches seem to have subsided for the most part. Still, more than half of upperclassmen forgo the annual lottery for off-campus living. The meal plan operates on a point system where you pay for what you eat. Nearly two-thirds of Penn State's undergraduates spend their first two years at one of the university's 17 campuses across the state, or at Penn State's Behrend College in Erie, which offers four-year programs, too.

Penn State's students take advantage of the picturesque and peaceful locale by engaging in outdoorsy activities including skiing at a close-by slope, and sailing, canoeing, hiking, and renting cabins in Stone Valley. The town of State College is the "quintessential American college town...that completely revolves around Penn State and completely caters to the students," one senior explains. The town offers some cultural events, such as symphonies, theatrical shows, and ballets, while the Bryce Jordan Convocation Center hosts top-notch performers, including Elton John, Rod Stewart, the Eagles, Smashing Pumpkins, Bush, and Alan Jackson.

Partying at Penn State is almost as legendary as the football team, which registered two national championships in the '80s. "There is something to do socially all the time!" raves a biology major. Students mostly go to bars and parties off-campus in State College. The administration "tries to be strict about enforcing the alcohol policy" of keeping booze out of underage hands. It doesn't always work, but the bars usually have enough dancing and music that scamming a beer becomes less important. The HUB, the campus union building, is open 24 hours, so students seeking nonalcoholic entertainment are encouraged to attend. The prospect of legal action has forced Greeks—which includes 14 percent of Penn State men and 11 percent of women—to have BYOB parties.

Even more exciting than casual parties are football weekends, when legendary coach Joe Paterno's Nittany Lions take to the gridiron. With thousands of "insanely loyal" alumni converging on State College for each game, the festivities include tailgate parties replete with marshmallow throwing, pregame parties, and postgame revelry. As a member of the Big 10, Penn State's foes include Michigan and Ohio State, both of which make great road trips. Other popular events include the mid-July art festival, the Dance Marathon, and of course, Homecoming.

While the football team captures its share of Big 10 titles, it's just one of 29 varsity teams in town. In fact, Penn State teams have won more than 40 national titles in a wide variety of sports, including men's and women's volleyball, field hockey, and fencing. There are three large gyms, a competitive-size pool, an indoor ice rink, and an extensive intramural program for the recreational athlete.

Living it up with more than 40,000 classmates in Happy Valley is the perfect college experience for some, though it might not fit everyone's idea of a good time. But those who muster the energy to take advantage of the roaring social life and diverse academic offerings find they are well rewarded. "From educational interests to extra-curricular activities, Penn Staters cover the spread," says an electrical engineering major. "All Penn Staters feel a strong, undescribable bond to PSU."

Study all the time? Good luck, especially when the nearby Bryce Jordan Convocation Center hosts top-notch performers such as Elton John, Rod Stewart, the Eagles, Smashing Pumpkins, Bush, and Alan Jackson.

Overlaps

University of Pittsburgh, Temple, University of Maryland, Indiana University of Pennsylvania, University of Delaware.

If You Apply To ➤

PSU...Rolling admissions: priority consideration given if sent by Nov. 30. Financial aid: Feb. 15. Meets demonstrated need of 1%. Campus interviews: optional, informational. No alumni interviews. SATs or ACTs: required. No SAT IIs. Accepts electronic applications. Essay question optional. Apply to particular school or program.

I College Hall, Philadelphia, PA 19104-6376

Website: www.upenn.edu
Location: Urban
Total Enrollment: 21,729
Undergraduates: 9,133
Male/Female: 51/49
SAT Ranges: V 640–730 M
  660–750
ACT Range: N/A
Financial Aid: 48%
Expense: Pr $ $ $ $
Phi Beta Kappa: Yes
Applicants: 16,658
Accepted: 29%
Enrolled: 49%
Grad in 6 Years: 90%
Returning Freshmen: 96%
Academics: ✑ ✑ ✑ ✑ ✑
Social: ☎ ☎ ☎
Q of L: ★ ★ ★
Admissions: (215) 898-7507
Email Address:
  info@admissions.ugad.upenn
  .edu

Strongest Programs:
  Business
  History
  English
  Economics
  Anthropology
  American Studies
  Cognitive and Computer
  Science
  Nursing
  Art and Design

Though best known for dangerous experiments with kites and keys, Founding Father Benjamin Franklin pulled off a number of other remarkable stunts in the mid-18th century, not the least of which was founding the University of Pennsylvania.

Frustrated with the philosophizing and intellectual dithering of the earliest New England colleges, Franklin wanted Penn to provide a practical education for citizens and merchants, and over the next 250-odd years the school did just that. Penn established the nation's first medical school, the first business school, the first journalism curriculum, and the first psychology clinic. In her inaugural address Penn's president, Judith Rodin, paid tribute to Franklin as "the ultimate visionary and pragmatist." "Franklin thought education should be for the body as well as for the soul—that it should enable a graduate to be a breadwinner as well as a thinker, that it should produce socially conscious citizens as well as conscientious bankers and traders," she said. "Franklin saw far more clearly than any of his contemporaries that the classical inheritance of knowledge divorced from civic betterment or practical application was unsuited to the modern temper." Unfortunately, while Penn developed a series of first-rate graduate and professional schools, it virtually ignored both the liberal arts and its undergraduate population until World War II, and thus began late to build the "core" of the university. But the school has worked hard to bolster these areas, and the undergraduate School of Arts and Sciences is now central not only to its undergraduates but also to the remaining three undergraduate schools that tap into its programs and course offerings.

Penn is situated in a tree-shaded, totally self-contained 260-acre nest called University City, which is adjacent to downtown Philadelphia. Its 116 buildings range from Victorian Gothic to postmodern. There are very old structures, such as College Hall, with red and green foliage creeping up its facade, and newer ones, such as Wharton's Steinberg-Dietrich Hall, which stretches out just west of the Schuylkill River. While many students thrive on Philadelphia's cultural abundance, the school is located in the west part of town, considered to be the most dangerous. The area is slowly gentrifying, but it's still an area of major concern for many. "Penn's biggest problem is probably its close surroundings of West Philadelphia and the security issues this poses," said a sophomore.

Still, Penn's reputation is primarily wrapped up with its 12 graduate schools, especially the prestigious Wharton School for business administration, the Annenberg School of Communication, and the well-known law, medical, and veterinary schools. Three of four undergraduate schools—engineering, nursing, and the undergraduate division of Wharton—are also professionally oriented and offer an education that's hard to beat anywhere. The undergraduate College of Arts and Sciences (a.k.a. "The College") has come into its own in the past decade or so and provides students with high-quality instruction as well as the chance to run into a Nobel laureate here and there.

Finance is the most popular undergrad major, followed by history and communications. Economics is also a strong department, and even the natural sciences draw praise from students. Penn's anthropology department ranks with Chicago's as perhaps the best in the country, while programs in management and technology are outstanding. Penn has earned applause in the field of cognitive and computer sciences because of its special program linking psychology, linguistics, and computers with philosophy. Another popular créme de la créme interdisciplinary major, Biological Basis of Behavior, combines psychology, economics, and anthropology. Undergrads also single out folklore and the legal studies concentration as good A&S bets. Students are allowed to design their own individualized majors, and they can hop from school to school—undergraduate or graduate—in doing so. In addition to the self-designed majors, Penn has constructed its own innovative and marketable joint majors. Design and structural technology or management and technology, for example, lead to dual arts and engineering or business and engineering degrees in four years.

At the Wharton School, officials have introduced the Joseph Wharton Scholars program, which emphasizes breadth in the arts and sciences and includes a language requirement. In fact, all undergraduates must attain proficiency in one of the 45 foreign languages taught at Penn. Another added plus that comes with a Penn undergraduate education is the opportunity for early entry (submatriculation) into the university's graduate programs. Juniors may apply to any master's program (continuing into the Wharton MBA program is especially popular) and begin completing graduate requirements during their senior year. Penn offers no co-op programs and discourages full-time internships for credit, remaining true to the Ivy League belief that learning is best done in the classroom. Those who want to explore more exotic classrooms may study abroad at Penn's programs in Italy, Scotland, Japan, France, England, China, Nigeria, Spain, Germany, and Russia, among others. Freshmen are encouraged (but not required) to participate in a seminar program that explores various areas of academic interest, and also in the Penn Reading Project, which involves student and faculty discussion of a common text.

Freshmen are encouraged (but not required) to participate in a seminar program that explores various areas of academic interest, and also in the Penn Reading Project, which involves student and faculty discussion of a common text.

Professors at Penn take their research responsibilities seriously, leaving graduate teaching assistants to manage all but the lectures and office hours for some lower-level classes. Freshman seminars and general honors courses (usually more demanding versions of introductory courses) provide exceptions to the rule. "The quality of teaching has been really good and as a freshman, I had several full professors," says a sophomore. "I have found the teachers to be very accessible and willing to help." The academic program at Penn is well supplemented by its huge and busy library, which houses more than 3 million volumes.

Despite all the preprofessional programs, Penn never lets its undergraduates stray too far from the liberal arts. All Penn students fulfill distribution requirements, which vary by school. All Wharton undergraduate students take a core curriculum that consists of courses in Social Structures, Language, Arts and Culture, and Science and Analysis. Engineering requires students to take 7 humanities courses, and the College of Arts and Sciences requires 10 courses from seven sectors. There also is a writing requirement, and all freshmen are encouraged to take at least one course in the Freshman Seminar Program, designed to give students an opportunity to work closely with a faculty member. Strict academic policies and demanding professors exacerbate the academic pressure. But while students find the school competitive, not all are complaining. "Personally, I have found it to be a good competition," says one sophomore. "It keeps me on my toes." But unlike some other schools, Penn strikes a good balance between academics and social life. A senior adds, "Penn students seem to find a way to balance out the competitive atmosphere. We definitely strive to do well and this involves a serious commitment to coursework. But we don't let this inhibit our Penn experience by keeping us in the library nonstop." Each year students evaluate every class themselves and publish their findings in a guide. Thousands of faculty and students give expression to Benjamin Franklin's adage that service to humanity is "the great aim and end of all learning." They work with local public school students as part of academic coursework in disciplines as diverse as history, anthropology, and mathematics. There are tons of opportunities to volunteer—from tutoring to Big Brother/Big Sister to the Ronald McDonald House. Back in the classroom, one classics professor uses modern Philadelphia and 5th-century Athens to explore the interrelationships among community, neighborhood, and family.

Penn is a diverse campus; 20 percent of the population is Asian American, and African Americans and Hispanics combine for 10 percent. But students are not diverse in their brainpower—they're all smart. Ninety percent of the students rank in the top tenth of their high school class. Nearly 60 percent come from public high school. Penn's Diversity Awareness Program for freshmen helps students from various backgrounds blend more harmoniously. Freshman orientation includes skits that depict students in various situations of possible conflict and include discussions about each situation.

Penn admits students regardless of need but does not offer any merit scholarships, athletic or academic. Through its innovative Penn Plan, the university strives to ensure that virtually every family with a college-bound son or daughter, no matter what its income, can benefit from financial assistance. For some this means subsidized loans and other traditional forms of aid. Other possibilities under the Penn Plan, however, include prepayment and borrowing options designed with the rate of inflation in mind and aimed at families in the higher-income brackets. In all, Penn students have six payment plan options.

Nearly all freshmen and 55 percent of all undergraduates live on campus and enjoy a wide range of living options. Dorms are coed. The Quad seems to be the hot spot, described as "beautiful, self-enclosed, and social" and "the greatest place in the world for freshmen." Upperclassmen reluctantly move to the high-rises across campus that look like "prefabricated 24-story monsters" but do offer more space as well as kitchens. Students may also apply for a number of small College Houses, which provide a greater community experience. There are living-learning programs for those who are interested in the arts, Asian studies, and so on, and want to be surrounded by others with the same interests. Rather than compete in the lottery for rooms, many juniors and seniors simply head off campus—"for the freedom, plus it's a lot cheaper," a junior says. Some end up in nearby renovated three-story houses in the neighborhood. "Off-campus living is just an extension of student neighborhoods, as we tend to stay in large groups," explains a senior. Like housing, the meal plans are optional (though strongly recommended in the freshman year as an important source of social life), and the food isn't all that bad for institutional fare, though there is no food served on weekends.

Undergraduates may work hard during the week, but in contrast to most Ivy League achievers, they leave it behind them on weekends. "Penn has a vibrant social scene," a junior says. "A lot of the social life takes place on campus because of the Greek system and the many student-run clubs, such as a capella singing groups and comedy and theater groups," says a sophomore. After an underage student suffered from alcohol poisoning, the university stiffened its alcohol policy, but with only limited effectiveness say students. More than two dozen fraternities attract 30 percent of the men and provide "your basic meat-market scene." Similarly, sororities claim 30 percent of the women. The frats' exclusive claim to the houses along Locust Walk, the main artery on campus, has been undone: after some controversy, it was determined that non-Greeks, too, must be able to live at the social nexus of the campus.

Two big annual events at Penn are Spring Fling, a three-day weekend "nothing short of absolutely incredible fun," and Hey Day, when juniors, donning Styrofoam hats and bearing the president of the university on their shoulders, march down Locust Walk to officially become seniors, taking chomps out of each other's hats as they go. A less formal tradition is the Quad Streak, when uninhibited undergraduates run through the crowd naked. Road trips include New York City, Washington, D.C., Atlantic City, even Maine and Florida. Downtown Philadelphia, only a few minutes away by foot, cab, or public transportation, offers enough social and cultural activities to make up for the less attractive aspects of city living. "Students constantly take advantage of all the social and academic opportunities the city has to offer," a senior says. "I don't know if I would call it a college town, because there is so much else going on here, but there is plenty for students to do!" Students frequent sporting events, malls, South Street ("a miniature Greenwich Village"), and of course, myriad bars and dancing joints.

Penn is more sports-minded than most Ivy schools, and football is the biggie. The team has grown accustomed to sitting on the top of the Ivy League and has sparked a widespread revival of school spirit. Tickets are free for those with a student ID. The Penn-Princeton rivalry is always a crowd pleaser. At the end of the third quarter of each home game, everyone in the stands begins belting out the lyrics of the Penn fight song, and when they get to "Here's a toast to dear old Penn," the students shower the field with burnt toast, "a moment that makes all Penn students proud," gushes a senior. Aside from football, recent Ivy championship teams include men's basketball and wrestling, and women's field hockey, basketball, and fencing. Nearly two dozen intramural sports bring thousands of less-seasoned athletes out to play each year, and all types of athletes benefit from the swanky track and weight-lifting facilities. Each spring, Penn hosts the prestigious Penn Relays, a track-and-field extravaganza that attracts the nation's best track athletes.

While its students work hard, Penn lacks the intellectual intensity of some of the top Ivies, and you can even detect some undercurrents of anti-intellectualism. Some undergraduates still carry a chip on their shoulder about not getting into Harvard or Yale, and many more are quick to note that Penn is a member of the Ivy League. But most accept it for what it is: a first-rate university where you can live a relatively normal life. Penn is one Ivy League university where no one apologizes for having fun!

Overlaps

Harvard, Princeton, Yale, Cornell, Brown.

If You Apply To ➤ **Penn**...Early decision: Nov. 1. Regular admissions: Jan. 1. Financial aid: Feb. 15. Guarantees to meet full demonstrated need. No campus interviews. Alumni interviews: optional, informational. SATs or ACTs: required. SAT IIs: required (writing and two others). Essay question: how you and Penn are a good match and how you envision your freshman year; an influential person, a page of your autobiography, or influential quotation.

Pepperdine University

24255 Pacific Coast Highway, Malibu, CA 90263-4392

Website: www.pepperdine.edu

Location: Suburban

Total Enrollment: 7,885

Undergraduates: 3,230

Male/Female: 45/55

SAT Ranges: V 570–670 M
580–680

ACT Range: 25–29

Financial Aid: 75%

Expense: Pr $ $ $ $

Phi Beta Kappa: No

Applicants: 4,602

Accepted: 33%

Enrolled: 36%

Grad in 6 Years: 71%

Returning Freshmen: 89%

Academics: 🖉 🖉 🖉

Social: ☎ ☎

Q of L: ★ ★ ★ ★

Admissions: (310) 456-4392

Email Address: admission-
seaver@pepperdine.edu

Strongest Programs:
Business
Accounting
Communications
Natural Science

With picturesque surroundings, it's easy to confuse Pepperdine University with its nicknames—Pepperdine Resort and Club Med. Surrounded by the beautiful Southern California seashore, Pepperdine University might seem paradise found for students seeking sunshine rather than studies at this conservative, Christian-affiliated university, though students take their work and their worship seriously. "The philosophy of the school is that God and the academic experience must be married," says a senior telecommunications major. "This creates an intimate learning environment that prides itself on moral integrity and a high academic standard." Business and communications are the blessed programs, though other departments deserve recognition, too. Undergrads praise their educational opportunities, the strength of their school's spiritual community, and God's good grace in creating cute little bikinis for the vast sandy beaches beckoning below their hilltop campus.

There's no denying that Pepperdine's location—high in the Santa Monica Mountains, about 25 miles northwest of Los Angeles—is a strong selling point. The 830-acre Malibu campus, to which the school moved in 1972, overlooks the Pacific Ocean and features fountains, hillside gardens, mountain trails, and a 20-minute-walk to the beach. Cream-colored, Mediterranean-style buildings topped with red terra-cotta roofs dot the landscape. A 125-foot-tall white stucco cross stands near the center of campus, reminding students and faculty of the school's affiliation with the Churches of Christ.

Pepperdine was founded in 1937 by George Pepperdine, a devout Christian who had amassed a fortune through his mail-order auto-parts supply company. The church's continued influence on the school pervades many aspects of campus life, from the prohibition of overnight dorm-room visits by members of the opposite sex to the requirement that students attend convocation—similar to chapel—14 times each semester. Students at Seaver College, Pepp's undergraduate school, must also take three religion courses. While drinking is officially prohibited on campus, the administration has lifted the ban on dancing, and now allows students to choose their own seats at convocation. Though restrictions like this would drive the average kid up a wall, most at Pepperdine like the "highly moral" atmosphere. Says one student: "In comparison to other schools, Pepperdine students generally have a more religious foundation and thus have high standards of moral integrity."

Seaver's academic programs aim to provide students "with a liberal arts education in a Christian environment, and relate it to the dynamic qualities of life in the 20th century." Individual classes are demanding, as is the required General Studies program, which includes a freshman seminar, a physical education course, three courses in Western heritage, two courses each in American heritage, and English composition, and one class each in a foreign language and non-Western culture. However, faculty members are said to be accessible and responsive—not surprising when the average class has 17 students. "The quality of teaching is very personal and exceptional," says an art major. Another student adds: "Because it is a small school, professors don't accept excuses or laziness. They demand a lot from their students and expect a high standard and quality of work."

The Business Administration Division is unequivocally the strongest and most popular department at Pepperdine, and it tends to set the tone on campus.

The Communications Division, with majors including advertising, public relations, and journalism, is also highly touted, especially now that it boasts radio and television broadcasting studios. Biology and computer science are said to be strong, and sports medicine, rare at the undergraduate level, is both popular and well respected. Although music studios and a $10-million humanities and visual arts center have been built to enhance the Fine Arts Division, students still rate art and music as relatively weak. The languages major has been dropped, although instruction in individual languages is still available, and a Great Books Colloquium for those interested in literature is available to 80 freshmen each year. Juniors interested in European culture may spend a year at Pepperdine's own facilities near Heidelberg Castle, or in London or Florence. Other study abroad programs are available in Japan and Australia; locations for summer study include France, Spain, Israel, Asia, and Russia.

Back on campus, students trying to complete term papers can use one of the 292 public computer terminals and the collections of Pepp's eight-facility library system, which boast more than 515,000 volumes and 375,000 titles on microfilm. The well-organized campus Career Center allows students sign up for job fairs, interviews, and individual and group career-counseling sessions.

One might expect students at this religiously oriented school to be conservative, and politically, they most definitely are. Many come from well-to-do Republican, California families; there is also a relatively high percentage of wealthy international students. Students joke that there's never a shortage of Porsches and BMWs on campus, but there is a shortage of places to park them. Hispanics account for 7 percent of the students, Asian Americans 6 percent, and African Americans just 4 percent. The Republican influence is felt far and wide. Pepperdine has received millions of dollars from conservative Pittsburgh financier Richard Mellon Scaife. And forget about political correctness here; in 1997, vandals defaced posters announcing a meeting of a new feminist group by scrawling "kitchen" in the space meant to list their meeting location. One student summed up the climate gently: "Pepperdine tends to shy away from political activism."

Some say flashy student vehicles fit into the small, very wealthy community of Malibu better than the students themselves; the city sees the university as a catalyst for development, and that hurts town-gown relations. Because the social scene in Malibu is pretty slack, with a 10:00 P.M. noise curfew and high price tags for everything, students typically head to L.A., Hollywood, Westwood, and Santa Monica for fun. "For a large proportion of students, academics and their social lives take priority over religious matters," says a public relations major. "Parties on weekends are well attended, and probably draw a larger portion of students than church on Sunday." About 25 percent of both men and women join one of six national fraternities or eight national sororities, which are playing a larger role in social life. Along with student government, they sponsor dances, movies, and other typical college activities, including the occasional illicit drink. "Pepperdine enforces a 'dry' campus, but 'damp' would be a better way of describing the residential community," says one student. "I think most of us would like to see Pepperdine get out of the dark ages in these matters."

Except for commuters, students are required to live on campus if they are single and under 21. That's a good thing, says one senior, who declares that Pepperdine's dorms are "comfortable, convenient and really quite nice." The single-sex dorms and apartments are connected to the campus computer network. Rooms are assigned on a first-come, first-served basis, and the housing stock consists of 22 dorms with 26 rooms each, a 135-room tower, and a 75-unit apartment complex for juniors and seniors. Freshmen are typically assigned to suites with

Juniors interested in European culture may spend a year at Pepperdine's own facilities near Heidelberg Castle, or in London or Florence.

The church's continued influence on the school pervades many aspects of campus life, from the prohibition of overnight dorm-room visits by members of the opposite sex to the requirement that students attend convocation—similar to chapel—14 times each semester.

bathrooms, living rooms, and four double bedrooms. Some consider these arrangements crowded, but a junior says they "connect freshmen instantly to seven suitemates and friends." Despite the above-average cost of living in the Malibu area, many upperclassmen choose to live off campus. The relatively new student union serves as the main campus social center, and annual events including Songfest, Family Weekend, and Midnight Madness draw crowds.

Sports receive a lot of attention at Pepperdine, with athletic scholarships offered in multiple sports and a tennis pavilion and recreation center drawing varsity jocks and weekend warriors alike. The men's golf team and men's water polo team have recently won NCAA championships. Men's volleyball is always a contender for the national championship, and a Pepperdine men's tennis singles player has won the national title. Eleven club and intramural sports, including lacrosse, rugby, cycling, surfing, and soccer, keep students busy, as does the physical education department, with classes in everything from surfing to horseback riding.

Students here love to tease their well-manicured university with T-shirts proclaiming, "Pepperdine. 8 month party. 20K cover charge." But most seem to think the solid, values-oriented education they receive is worth the stiff price tag. Pepperdine faces a unique challenge in trying to marry the Christian focus of a Bible college with the academic rigor of a purely secular university—all in a location not known for the strength of its moral fiber. "Pepperdine is a bit contrarian," the president admits. "We stand for what we believe in, and we don't care all that much whether the establishment is heading in that direction or not."

Overlaps

University of Southern California, UCLA, Stanford, UC–San Diego.

If You Apply To ➤

Pepperdine...Early action: Nov. 15. Regular admissions: Jan. 15. Financial aid: Feb. 15. Housing: May 1. Does not guarantee to meet demonstrated need. Campus interviews: recommended, informational. No alumni interviews. SATs or ACTs: required. SAT IIs: optional. Accepts the Common Application and electronic applications. Essay question: current topics; ethical dilemma; or most embarrassing moment.

University of Pittsburgh

Bruce Hall, 2nd floor, Pittsburgh, PA 15260

Website: www.pitt.edu
Location: City
Total Enrollment: 26,162
Undergraduates: 17,168
Male/Female: 47/53
SAT Ranges: V 520–620 M 520–620
ACT Range: 22–28
Financial Aid: 70%
Expense: Pub $ $ $
Phi Beta Kappa: Yes

Pittsburgh has shaken off its idled steel factory stigma and joined the ranks of the most livable cities in the U.S. The University of Pittsburgh has matured, too, becoming one of the most formidable research institutions in the country. The school offers top-tier opportunities for students pursuing technical, medical, and engineering careers, but leaves a great deal of room for exploration in the liberal arts. Students are encouraged to be individuals and carve out their own academic niche, either with multiple majors or certificate programs. Combine this with a satisfying social life, and Pitt has discovered the formula for a great college experience.

Pitt began as a tiny educational academy in the Allegheny Mountains in 1787. Oh how times have changed. The university is now part of the landscape of shops, parks, museums, galleries, and apartment complexes that make up Oakland, the heart of Pittsburgh's cultural center. Spacious, light-filled, contemporary buildings and generic, modern office buildings make up the Pitt campus, but the architectural delight is a 42-story, neo-Gothic academic building, appropriately called the Cathedral of Learning, a National Historic Landmark. The Cathedral, with its unique Nationality Rooms, attracts 100,000 visitors annually. And contrary to images you may hold of inner city Pittsburgh, the campus borders a 456-acre city park. The state has granted Pitt nearly $140 million for renovations and new construction. In the works are garden-style residence halls, practice fields, 12,500-seat basketball arena, and many buildings at satellite campuses.

With 10 undergraduate schools and more than 280 degree programs, Pitt rightfully claims to accommodate students with diverse needs. The academically motivated can take advantage of the excellent University Honors College, which an one sophomore gushes is "the best thing at Pitt. It can do so much for any students taking a serious interest in their education." It offers "small, intensive classes so students can work with professors and do independent research." Honors students publish the *Pittsburgh Undergraduate Review*, which receives submissions from students nationwide. Pitt's extensive research programs are its finest asset. The University of Pittsburgh is one of the top 20 institutions in the nation in terms of the federal research dollars that it attracts. And for good reason. Pitt astronomers discovered what appear to be two new planets orbiting a nearby star, and its physicians were the first to utilize gene therapy on a person with rheumatoid arthritis. The Schools of Engineering and Nursing are excellent and attract high-caliber students. Premed students can even watch transplants at the famed University of Pittsburgh Medical Center, which is one of the world's leading organ transplant centers. On the arts side, faculty and students in the music department consistently rake in more awards and fellowships than their counterparts at other U.S. universities.

Pitt now offers guaranteed admission into graduate programs in communication science, public and international affairs, dental medicine, law, medical school, and physical therapy, for outstanding freshman applicants. In two national studies, Pitt had four programs—philosophy, information science, history, and philosophy of science, and nursing—ranked in the top six of their fields, and several others rated very high on the list. The College of Arts and Sciences (CAS) has academic requirements that include skill requirements in writing, quantitative and formal reasoning, foreign languages, and distribution requirements in the humanities, social and natural sciences, and foreign cultures. Psychology ranks among the most popular majors, and a heavily subscribed option permits students to combine a business major with a CAS degree. The university has a new Center for International Studies and has added a BS in scientific computing. Qualified freshmen may enter the School of Engineering, the College of Business Administration, or the School of Nursing, as well as the College of Arts and Sciences. For undergraduates who want to travel, the university cosponsors a Semester at Sea Program, where students visit ports around the world and take classes at the same time. Closer to home, Pitt is a partner in the Pittsburgh Supercomputer Center, one of five such centers nationwide established by the National Science Foundation. The center houses the fastest computer in the world, performing one trillion calculations per second. There is also the Engineering Co-op, a program in which students alternate terms of study with work experience. Students in the co-op may take more than four years to graduate.

Pitt students take advantage of the school's flexible scheduling, which includes a strong evening program and summer sessions, and take on double and even triple majors, ensuring themselves of plenty of education and a degree that's

(Continued)
Applicants: 12,863
Accepted: 66%
Enrolled: 36%
Grad in 6 Years: 62%
Returning Freshmen: 85%
Academics: ✎ ✎ ✎
Social: ☎ ☎
Q of L: ★ ★
Admissions: (412) 624-PITT
Email Address:
  oafa+@pitt.edu

Strongest Programs:
  Nursing
  Business
  Engineering
  Philosophy
  International Studies
  History and Philosophy of
  Science
  Information Science
  History of Art and
  Architecture

Students can tackle the most pressing scientific issues of the day at the Center for Biotechnology and Bioengineering, which offers about 80 interns the chance to work with faculty in fields ranging from musculoskeletal research to tissue engineering.

well worth the money.

First-year students undergo an extensive orientation that includes three days in the summer focused on academics, another three days before the term starts, and a one-credit orientation seminar. Class sizes are not out of control. Out of 1,917 courses, 61 percent have fewer than 29 students enrolled, and only 6 percent have 100 or more. Most students agree that professors are very approachable. "I have never met a professor who is not willing to help a student outside of the classroom," says a biology major.

Eighty-six percent of all undergraduates are from Pennsylvania, including a substantial number from the Pittsburgh area. African American students account for 10 percent of the student body, Asian Americans 4 percent, and Hispanics 1 percent. Incoming freshmen discuss diversity during orientation, and a cultural diversity fair is held at the beginning of the school year. To top that off, every student must take a pledge to promote civility on campus. The university admits students without reference to financial need, and 70 percent of undergraduates receive need-based financial aid. Pitt also offers 600 merit awards of $1,000 to a full scholarship to qualified students. Athletic scholarships are also offered in 19 varsity sports.

While student housing may have been scarce in the past, Pitt is working to increase the amount of on-campus living space. Forty percent of full-time undergraduates live in on-campus university housing, which features 11 coed and single-sex dorms with liberal visitation hours and all kinds of rooming situations, from singles to seven-person suites. The new Bouquet Gardens apartments have been expanded, and more student housing will open as part of the new north campus. Sutherland Hall boasts a view of Oakland and the rest of the city, and offers its own computing lab. Suites in McCormick and Brackenridge halls have two-story windows in the living rooms. Lothrop Hall tends to attract the quieter students, and features attractive singles. Many students opt to live off campus "because it can be less expensive and students can have more freedom," says a biology major.

Pitt's urban location provides a wide variety of social activities. Within minutes of campus are shops, parks, museums, and sporting events. "I would say Pittsburgh is a great college town in which students can always find something to do," a sophomore. Though only 11 percent of the men and 7 percent of the women belong to the Greek system, the fraternities and sororities play a vital role on campus. Many students say alcohol policies on campus are pretty tough for underage students. "Students somehow find a way to bring alcohol to campus," one student confides. "However, the penalties are severe when students get caught." A senior notes that under-21 students caught drinking are referred to the Pittsburgh police department. Students feel safe on campus, considering the extensive network of campus lighting, emergency phones, the shuttle bus route and on-demand van system. In addition, Pitt students can ride the city PAT bus system for free to nearby neighborhoods to shop, go to coffeehouses, bookstores, or movie theaters. Adjacent Schenley Park offers ice-skating, golfing, a pool, jogging trails, and tennis courts. Ski slopes and mountain trails are not far away, and road trips to Penn State and Philadelphia, Boston, and New York City are popular. Although the Pitt Panther football team has endured some unhappy (read: losing) seasons of late, the university is striving to change that by bringing in new coaches. Men's basketball is also popular, and competition is heated in Big East hoops.

Pitt boasts innumerable resources and opportunities for its students in the sciences and the arts, and is improving not only in its academics but in the caliber of its student body. Pitt is raising its sights, and in many cases, breaking records. The university is molding its offerings to fit in with the new fields, such as bioengineering, that are dominating headlines. Students who opt to attend this progressive school will find themselves riding a wave to a promising future.

If You Apply To ➢

Pitt...Rolling admissions. Financial aid: Mar. 1. Housing: May. 1. Meets demonstrated need of 70%. Campus interviews: recommended, informational. Alumni interviews: optional, informational. SATs or ACTs: required. SAT IIs: optional. Accepts the Common Application and electronic applications. Essay question: optional.

Presbyterian College

503 Broad Street, Clinton, SC 29325

The mission of Presbyterian College is embodied in the slogan, "While we live, we serve." Though this small liberal arts school offers its students a well-rounded education, equally important to those who attend is its philosophy of community service. In 1880, founder William Plumer Jacobs wanted "education at a higher level" for students at a local orphanage, and so the college was born. Today's Presbyterian student is intelligent and focused, but not driven by the almighty dollar. Although it is a small college, it is big on academic honor and integrity, and helping those less fortunate.

PC is located on 225 acres in the South Carolina Piedmont and its campus is a blend of oak trees, red bricks, and columns. All the buildings share a common Georgian architecture and several are listed in the National Register of Historic Places. The campus is designed to resemble Jefferson's University of Virginia, with structures grouped around a series of three plazas that are great for reading, studying, or throwing a football. The library only holds 156,000 volumes but it is reportedly adequate and houses the Online Computer Library. New additions to the campus include an academic house, an alumni and admissions center, and an international house.

"Presbyterian's mission to develop students' mental, physical, moral, and spiritual capacities has not changed during its 120 years," according to the administration. Approximately 50 percent of PC students volunteer each year for some type of community service. "We are a very service-oriented campus and are very involved in many areas of the community," says a junior early childhood and elementary education major. All students must complete a core curriculum that includes studies in English, math, history, social sciences, science, physical education, and foreign language. In addition, students must attend ten Cultural Enrichment Programs a year, which range from drama, film, and musical performances to lectures and panel discussions. These "CEPs" are very popular among students and are always well attended. PC's most popular majors are business, political science, education, biology, and English. During the month of May or "Maymester," the biology department takes trips with its students. Some of the most recent trips have been to the Galapagos and Hawaiian Islands. The four-year

Website: www.presby.edu
Location: Small town
Total Enrollment: 1,119
Undergraduates: 1,119
Male/Female: 47/52
SAT Ranges: V 500–600 M 500–610
ACT Range: 23–27
Financial Aid: 80%
Expense: Pr $
Phi Beta Kappa: No
Applicants: 994
Accepted: 81%
Enrolled: 33%
Grad in 6 Years: 78%
Returning Freshmen: 91%
Academics: ✍ ✍ ✍
Social: ☎ ☎ ☎
Q of L: ★ ★ ★ ★
Admissions: (864) 833-8230
Email Address: admissions@presby.edu

Strongest Programs:
Biology
Business
Education
English
Political Science

honors program, open to any sophomore, junior, or senior with sufficient grades, includes special meetings with deans and dignitaries, a series of honors seminar classes in great issues, thinkers, and literary works, and opportunities for independent research. Internships may also be arranged. Some students feel that the foreign languages and visual arts are weaker departments, due to few resources and little interest.

Presbyterian College's academic climate is competitive, students say. "Studying is certainly a part of our daily schedules," confirms a sophomore. "The courses are quite rigorous." Students agree that the professors are the most valuable asset at PC. "Not only are they thorough, but also they can explain something so clearly that I am rarely ever confused," says a freshman. "They are such good teachers that their students can't help but do well." Assistants are nonexistent, and the classes are small. Faculty members also invite students to their homes for dinner sometimes. The career counseling program at Presbyterian receives high marks, but academic advising could be improved. "Although many are good teachers, they are not good advisors and are not in tune with the requirements," says a freshman. The Winter Conference, held in January of each year, is a retreat for faculty, students, and staff, and provides them an opportunity to interact with the Thomas F. Staley Distinguished Christian Scholar.

Presbyterian follows a need-blind admissions policy. Each year the school offers merit scholarships, ranging from $1,500 to full tuition. Also, gifted athletes qualify for scholarships in eight sports.

Slightly more than half of the PC student body hails from South Carolina herself. The great majority of incoming students attended public high school, and 36 percent graduated in the top tenth of their high school class. Being Presbyterian is not a requirement to attend PC, though around a third of the students are active in a Presbyterian church. Ninety-three percent of the student body are white. The administration admits that the lack of cultural diversity on campus is a weakness, and aggressively recruits a multicultural group of students, faculty, and staff. But students don't see the lack of diversity as a problem. The biggest campus issues are underage drinking, the Greek system, and the meal plan, which students dislike. Most students describe their school as a genuinely friendly environment, and many attribute it to the caring faculty. "The professors know their students and care about them. They have an open door policy and even have us over for dinner at their house occasionally," a junior says. "I love the personal atmosphere here." The student body is bound by an 80-year-old honor code, which is taken quite seriously.

With 85 percent of the students living on campus, there's a "nice community feel" to dorm life. "The dorms are comfortable," says a freshman. "If there are any problems, maintenance answers quickly and usually fixes the problem on the first try." But the student cautions: "The lobbies need to be redone—the furniture is straight out of the 1970s." Only seniors are allowed to live off campus. PC does not use an institutionalized food service, but has its own cooking staff. Students continue to complain of a less than wonderful dining hall.

Clinton is a town of 10,000 inhabitants, and while it doesn't offer much for entertainment, students report many volunteer opportunities and a warm relationship between the college and townspeople. "It's not a college town, but the town rallies around the college," a freshman reports. PC students volunteer through the Student Volunteer Services program, the largest organization on campus. Road trips include Columbia and Greenville. Most social life involves activities on campus, at fraternity court, or in the dorms. About 44 percent of the men and 41 percent of the women belong to one of the six fraternities and three sororities. PC has taken a firm stand against underage drinking, but students agree with a junior who says, "Drinking goes on at all schools, and PC is no exception. While many students drink, many choose not to and there is no pressure to drink." Some of the campus traditions include the Blue Sox Festival at Homecoming, a candlelight Christmas service, and a beautiful graduation ceremony under the oaks with bagpipes and trumpets heralding students and faculty in full academic regalia.

The ten varsity sports teams compete in Division II of the NCAA and call themselves the Blue Hose, a reference to the stockings of their Scottish ancestors. In fact, some of the students wear kilts during athletic events. "The Blue Hose show school spirit by showing off some very unsightly legs," jokes a junior. Men's basketball and golf, and men's and women's soccer and tennis are strong programs. The 31-acre recreational facility, with lighted softball, football, and soccer fields, volleyball and horseshoe pits, a driving range, a basketball court, a track, and an amphitheater, keeps everyone active.

PC students are proud of their school's history, which includes its own tartan and a bagpipe processional at opening convocation and graduation that "bring chills if not tears every time." Students say they feel fortunate to be a part of an up-and-coming college that encourages not only academic excellence but spiritual growth as well. And it's these enduring qualities that make Presbyterian one of higher education's better-kept secrets.

Overlaps

Furman, Wofford, Clemson, University of South Carolina, College of Charleston.

If You Apply To >

Presbyterian...Rolling admissions. Early action: Dec. 5. Does not guarantee to meet demonstrated need. Campus interviews: recommended, informational. No alumni interviews. SAT or ACT: required. SAT IIs: optional. Accepts the Common Application and electronic applications. Essay question: what would people be surprised to learn about you; Presbyterian College's motto; ethics of lying, cheating, and stealing.

Prescott College

220 Grove Avenue, Prescott, AZ 86301

Future *Survivor* contestants take note: This tiny outpost of environmentalism in the wilderness of central Arizona is a perfect spot for the nature lover who seeks adventure, wants to learn survival skills, and likes studying outdoors. Where else but Prescott College could you major in Adventure Education or take courses like Mountain Search and Rescue, Ecopsychology, and Wilderness Rites of Passage? Before any Prescott student sets foot in a classroom, the college sends him or her to the outback for three weeks of hiking and camping. Wilderness Orientation is an introduction to everything Prescott stands for: hands-on experience, personal responsibility, cooperative living, and stewardship of the environment.

Founded in 1966, Prescott retains the air of a 1960s commune. The student body has an abundance of shaggy mountain men and beaded daughters of the Earth, three-quarters of whom transferred from traditional four-year colleges. "Most Prescott students (like myself) have had negative experiences with large universities," says a senior environmental science/creative writing major. "We come here because we want to learn, not to have a fancy piece of paper hanging in our office." Another student describes her peers this way: "They have a clear

Website: www.prescott.edu
Location: Small city center
Total Enrollment: 663
Undergraduates: 500
Male/Female: 50/50
SAT Ranges: N/A
ACT Range: 18–32
Financial Aid: 47%
Expense: Pr $
Phi Beta Kappa: No
Applicants: 334
Accepted: 84%
Enrolled: 54%
Grad in 6 Years: 54%
Returning Freshmen: 83%

Prescott bills itself as a college "for the liberal arts and for the environment," and most students envision themselves becoming teachers, researchers, park rangers, or wilderness guides.

vision and are committed to making a difference on the planet. They are each unique and talented in their own way and they have come to PC because they know it is the only college they can study their particular passion."

Surrounded by national forest, the college's "campus" consists of a two-block-long handful of buildings in the small town of Prescott. The largest of the college's buildings was once a convent; its chapel is now used for meetings, art shows, and performances. Behind the chapel, a student center houses the Butte Creek Café and community garden, which was once a volleyball court. The architectural style of the campus ranges from the historic (and recently renovated) 220 Grove to the Sam Hill Warehouse, a multipurpose classroom, rehearsal, and performance space, and the small cottages of the admissions and registrar's offices. A new student computer lab is three times the size of the lab it replaced. A recent library expansion doubled the space available for book storage and study; though the facility holds just 19,000 volumes, students praise the helpful staff, and electronic systems offer online access to 17 nearby municipal libraries. Other new additions include labs for students in the biology, geology, agroecology, and GIS (geographical information science) programs.

Prescott bills itself as a college "for the liberal arts and for the environment," and most students envision themselves becoming teachers, researchers, park rangers, or wilderness guides. Adventure Education, a major including everything from alpine mountaineering to sea kayaking, is a specialty. Also popular is Environmental Studies, which provides offerings of impressive breadth and depth for such a small school. The major in Social and Human Development, a hodgepodge of sociology, psychology, and new age mysticism including unorthodox courses such as Dreamwork Intensive, has been reconceptualized into Integrative Studies. IS is a "home" for core Humanities and Liberal Arts areas such as religion, philosophy, and social sciences, as well as an "incubator" for new programs such as Peace Studies. Among the college's few concessions to practicality is the Teacher Education Program, which offers all students teaching credentials in elementary, secondary, special and bilingual education, and English as a Second Language. Prescott does not offer a comprehensive program in advanced math, chemistry, physics, and foreign languages other than Spanish. The school also lacks a developed sociology curriculum, which, given the state of sociology on most campuses, is not a major problem.

Prescott's requirements for graduation are characteristically unorthodox. "There are no formal tests at Prescott College, with the exception of classes that award first-aid certification," explains one student. Instead of grades, faculty members give narrative evaluations. And rather than accruing credits, students design individualized "degree plans" that outline the competence (major) and breadth (minor) areas they will pursue, and the Senior Project (thesis) they will complete to demonstrate competence (graduate). Students must also obtain two levels of writing certification (college level and thesis level), and math certification, showing knowledge of college-level algebra.

Prescott's calendar is divided into three periods, each with one 10-week quarter and one 4-week block. During the quarters, students follow a traditional schedule, studying liberal arts and spending time doing fieldwork and student teaching. During the blocks, students pursue intense immersion in one course, most likely in the field, perhaps the backcountry of Baja, California, the alpine meadows of Wyoming, or even a local service clinic. Students can even take a one-month rafting trip down the Colorado River for credit! Summers may be spent studying field methods in agroecology at Prescott's 30-acre Wolfberry Farm. Though Prescott does not offer a traditional study abroad program, it encourages students to take courses at the Kino Bay Center for Cultural and Ecological Studies in Mexico.

While Prescott carefully studies the global problems of the environment, it does so in an intimate localized setting. Each class is limited to 12 to 14 students, so "it is difficult to teach in this sort of environment if you are not dedicated," a senior says. There's no tenure track at Prescott, so publishing and research take a backseat to teaching. "The nature of PC courses (often in the field) help them create intimate relations with their students," says a senior holistic health and spirituality major. "Teachers become lifelong friends."

Prescott is sometimes known as PC, an apt description in more ways than one. Liberal politics predominate, though one student declares that "ecological correctness is more of an issue than political correctness." The school is in the mist of converting itself into a "sustainable campus," which would use alternative fuels and solar technologies, along with eco-friendly architecture and landscape. Prescott's unconventional approach entices many well beyond Arizona. Indeed, 35 percent of students come from the Northeast; only 6 percent are in-staters. The minority population is small, with blacks, Hispanics, and Asian Americans making up only 4 percent of the total. Part of the problem is the college's meager supply of financial aid. Since the school's endowment is just $160,000, needy students rely on government loans and grants.

Because the college has no housing, students fend for themselves in the town of Prescott, a rapidly growing community of approximately 35,000 where almost everything is accessible by bicycle. The college assists with the apartment hunt by providing lists of available properties and by cosigning leases when necessary. "Housing is a hassle, but it always works out," one senior says. As for the townsfolk, students describe them as retirees who are extremely conservative. Prescott recently set up a meal plan, though many students still eat at home or in town.

Prescott social life is informal and spontaneous. Aside from environmental activities, Prescott offers a nationally recognized literary magazine, Alligator Juniper, and a chapter of Amnesty International. The college also operates a turn-of-the-century opera house that is a local hotspot for dance and drama. Those looking for nightlife can hit Whiskey Row, the town bar scene, or drive to Flagstaff (90 minutes) or Phoenix (2 hours). Though the college offers no athletics, students often participate in city sports leagues. Prescott's personal touch extends to graduation, a unique experience where each student is spoken about personally for one minute by a faculty member and then speaks on their own behalf for a minute.

Though Prescott lacks the financial resources and academic breadth of more established schools, it more than compensates with small classes, innovative programs taking full advantage of the nearby Southwestern wilderness, and a student body with '90s-style ambition and '60s-style social consciousness.

If Grizzly Adams had gone to college, he probably would have chosen Prescott, where a popular T-shirt attests that "Education is a journey, not a destination."

Overlaps

Evergreen State, Hampshire, Marlboro, Warren Wilson, Antioch.

If You Apply To > **Prescott**…Regular admissions: Feb. 1, Sep. 1. Financial aid: Apr. 15. Does not guarantee to meet demonstrated need. Campus interviews: optional, evaluative. No alumni interviews. SATs or ACTs: optional. SAT IIs: optional. Apply to particular school or program. Essay question: personal statement, past academic experiences and reasons for attending Prescott.

110 West College, Princeton, NJ 08540

Website: www.princeton.edu
Location: Small town
Total Enrollment: 6,324
Undergraduates: 4,556
Male/Female: 53/47
SAT Ranges: V 680–770 M 680–770
Financial Aid: 40%
Expense: Pr $ $ $ $
Phi Beta Kappa: Yes
Applicants: 14,875
Accepted: 11%
Enrolled: 68%
Grad in 6 Years: 96%
Returning Freshmen: 99%
Academics: ✍ ✍ ✍ ✍ ✍
Social: ☎ ☎ ☎
Q of L: ★ ★ ★
Admissions: (609) 258-3060
Email Address: N/A

Strongest Programs:

Physics
Molecular Biology
Public Policy
Economics
Philosophy
Romance Languages
Computer Science
Math

At Princeton, exclusivity is endemic. Admissions officers brush off countless valedictorians, athletes, and legacies with the contents of one thin envelope—sans mercy. A mere 11 percent of applicants are accepted, and those who get in find other entrances barred. Only graduating seniors may pass through a northern campus gate, such a sacred tradition that no uniformed sentries are needed to enforce it—no upstart undergraduates would dare step through it. But the wait is well worth it. Undergraduates at Princeton are surrounded by intellect and intensity and 250 years of finely honed educational tradition, delivered today by some of the nation's most brilliant, scholarly stars. And now that Princeton has decided to replace all loans in its financial aid packages with grants, a lot more of those stars will be able to afford the place.

Cloistered in the secluded but upscale New Jersey town, Princeton's architectural trademark is Gothic, from the cavernous and ornate university chapel to the four-pronged Cleveland Tower rising majestically above the treetops. Interspersed among the Gothic are examples of Colonial architecture, most notably historic Nassau Hall, which served as the temporary home of the Continental Congress in 1783 and has defined elegance in academic architecture ever since. A host of modern structures, some by leading American architects Robert Venturi and I. M. Pei, add variety and distinction to the campus, but the ambiance is still quintessential Ivy League at its best. Among the newest additions are an athletic stadium and new student housing.

Princeton is unique in its scale (among the Ivies, only Dartmouth has a lower total enrollment) and its emphasis on undergraduates. For a major research institution, the university offers its students unparalleled faculty contact. With fewer graduate students to siphon off resources or consume faculty time than at large research universities, undergraduates get the lion's share of both; at last count, 70 percent of Princeton's department heads taught introductory undergraduate courses. Freshmen explore various texts and ideas that have shaped Western culture in interdisciplinary seminars taught by senior faculty members. Lovers of literature can study with Joyce Carol Oates or Toni Morrison, and nearly every other department has a few stars of its own. At least one or two of the small discussion groups that accompany each lecture course are led by senior professors, and the seminar program for freshmen based in the residential colleges further enhances student-faculty interaction. Every liberal arts student must fill distribution requirements in epistemology and cognition, ethical thought and moral values, historical analysis, literature and the arts, quantitative reasoning, social analysis, and science and technology. Students must also take writing courses. During their junior year, liberal arts students work closely with a faculty member of his or her choice in completing two Junior Papers—about 30 pages of independent work each semester in addition to the normal courseload. Princeton is also one of the few colleges in the country to require every graduate to complete a senior thesis—an enterprise that serves as a culmination of their work in their field of concentration.

As one might expect, Princeton's small size means the number of courses offered is smaller than at other Ivies, but lack of quantity does not beget lack of quality. Princeton's math and philosophy departments are among the best in the nation, and English, physics, economics, molecular biology, public policy, and romance languages are right on their heels. Princeton is one of the few top liberal arts universities with equally strong engineering programs, most notably chemical, mechanical, electrical, and aerospace engineering, and computer sciences (which has its own facilities). In fact, the Department of Civil Engineering and Operations Research has split into two departments: Civil and Environmental Engineering and Operations Research and Financial Engineering. One of Princeton's best-known programs is the prestigious Woodrow Wilson School of Public and International Affairs ("Woody Woo" to the students), which admits undergraduates on a selective basis. The university has undertaken a major effort to become a national center in the field of molecular biology, with a laboratory for teaching and research staffed by 28 faculty members, including one who shared the Nobel Prize in medicine in 1995.

Princeton's semester system gives students a two-week reading period before exams in which to catch up, with first-term exams postponed until after New Year's, much to the dismay of many ski buffs and tropical sun worshipers. The university honor code, unique among the Ivies, allows for unproctored exams. The outstanding library facilities embrace 5 million volumes and provide 500 private study carrels for seniors working on their theses; there are another 700 enclosed carrels in other parts of the campus.

About 10 percent of the student body take advantage of the opportunity to study abroad. Except for students with sufficient advanced standing to complete their degree requirements in three and a half years, leaves of absence must be taken by the year, not the semester, an impediment to "stopping out." The university does offer an intriguing five-year program that includes intense language in an Asian country and a joint bachelor's of law degree program. A limited number of courses can be taken on the pass/fail option and the University Scholars program provides especially qualified students with what the administration calls "maximum freedom in planning programs of study to fulfill individual needs and interests." Although the faculty gets high ratings for its academic advising, students are rather cool on the university's nonacademic counseling programs.

The majority of Princeton undergraduates are "highly organized, highly competitive, goal-oriented" students, both in terms of academics—high school valedictorians make up 30 percent of each class—and extracurricular activities. Black and Hispanic enrollment combined now stands at 13 percent, Asian American at 12 percent. While diversity is present, mixing is often not. "As an African-American I can say that even the African Americans are subdivided based on economics, place of origin, and whether you went to public or private school," explains one senior. And the campus remains socially conservative, with tweed and penny loafers adorning many students. Artists aren't a dominant social force on campus, but the administration hopes that renovations of the arts facilities, coupled with a $5.9-million expansion of the art gallery, will make the university more appealing to future Picassos and Baryshnikovs. As the southernmost of the Big Three, Princeton has traditionally attracted a sizable Southern contingent. This contributes to the atmosphere of social conservatism and strong sense of tradition that pervade the campus. African Americans and women tend to feel less comfortable here than at comparable institutions.

Princeton undergraduates are admitted to the university without regard to their financial need, and those who qualify for aid get an appropriate package of benefits. There are no merit or athletic scholarships, but Princeton's reconfigured financial aid package is generous to middle-class families: the average student will receive about $1,400 in extra grants. Each student's Princeton experience begins with a week of orientation; 500 each year participate in Outdoor Action, a few

With fewer graduate students to siphon off resources or consume faculty time than at large research universities, undergraduates get the lion's share of both; at last count, about 70 percent of Princeton's department heads taught introductory undergraduate courses.

days of wilderness activities immediately preceding orientation.

In an attempt to improve the quality of life for freshmen and sophomores, Princeton has grouped many of its dorms into residential colleges, each with its own dining hall, faculty residents, and an active social calendar. Under this system, nearly all the freshmen and sophomores live and dine with their residential college unit, alleviating the formerly fragmented social situation. However, by providing a separate social sphere for these students, the system "creates a gulf between underclassmen and upperclassmen." And all too often the upper-level eating clubs steal the thunder from the college's social events. As a result, "the underclassmen spend too much time pining for the day when they, too, can join the closest thing Princeton has to cliques," says one student.

The university's turn-of-the-century Gothic dorms may look like crosses between cathedrals and castles, but conditions on the inside are often less glamorous. Some halls have amenities, including living rooms and bay windows. Several new dorms have helped ease the space crunch somewhat, and more dorms are planned as part of the school's 250th anniversary fund-raising campaign. Only 3 percent of the students live off campus. The modern and roomy Spelman dorms, which come complete with kitchens, are the best on campus and fill up quickly every year with seniors who do not belong to eating clubs.

Ah, yes, the eating clubs: Princeton's most firmly entrenched bastions of tradition. Run by students and unaffiliated with the school, they line Prospect Avenue, and have, for over a century, assumed the dual role of weekend fraternity and weekday dining hall. Of the 12, seven admit members through an open lottery, but the other five still use a controversial selective admissions process called bicker (because of the wrangling over whom to admit), to the embarrassment of the administration and most of the students. While many of the clubs opened their doors to women back when Princeton went coed, two of the oldest and most exclusive—the Ivy Club and the Tiger Inn—remained all-male until 1991, when a court decision compelled them to admit women. Now all clubs are coed.

Catering exclusively to upperclassmen, the clubs provide a secure sense of community for their members. More than half of all sophomores join one of the clubs at the end of the year, becoming full-fledged members by the fall of their junior year. Annual dues vary; the most expensive is the Ivy Club, which charges its members almost $5,000 a year. Unfortunately, the social options for those who choose not to join are limited. Some opt for life in independent dormitories or join the handful of Greek fraternities and sororities (not sanctioned by the administration) that have sprung up on campus over the past few years.

Princeton's campus is self-contained, but those who venture outside its walls will find the surroundings quite pleasing. "There are no factories, toxic waste dumps, or smokestacks, contrary to popular belief," states one student. One side of the campus abuts quaint Nassau Street, which is dominated by chic (and pricey) boutiques and restaurants, most out of the range of student budgets, although coffee shops and affordable restaurants are becoming more prevalent. The other side of campus ends with a huge man-made lake that was financed by Andrew Carnegie so that Princetonians would not have to forgo crew. Students rarely venture much farther than New York or Philadelphia, each one hour away (in opposite directions) on the train. Few students complain about boredom, and many praise the affluent town of Princeton for the parks, woods, bike trails, and, most important, the quiet and safety it offers students. McCarter Theatre, adjacent to campus, is the nation's seventh-busiest performing arts center and houses Princeton's Triangle Club, which counted Jimmy Stewart and Brooke Shields as members. The roundup of annual campus events includes Communiversity Day, an international festival, and the P Party in the spring, which features a big-name band. Each year about 2,000 students engage in volunteer activities such as tutoring, working in soup kitchens, or helping the elderly.

Princeton has the oldest licensed college radio station in the nation, plenty of journalistic opportunities, a prestigious debating and politics society (Whig-Clio) whose ranks included James Madison and Aaron Burr, and a plethora of arts offerings. The sports program includes several national championship teams, including men's lacrosse, men's heavyweight crew, and men's lightweight crew. The women's rugby club is also outstanding, having won its second straight national title as part of a 59-match winning streak. The men's basketball team is a phenomenal success and was rated in the top 10 this year for the first time in decades. It has appeared in numerous NCAA championships and has done rather well. Well-attended events are found on the intramural fields, where teams from the eating clubs and residential colleges compete. Every fall, the freshman and sophomore classes square off in Cane Spree, an intramural Olympics that has been a tradition since 1869.

It's easy to be humbled at Princeton. Even the most jaded students must be awed and inspired when they think of those who've traversed the campus paths before them: former U.S. presidents James Madison and Woodrow Wilson attended the university, as did writer F. Scott Fitzgerald, to name just a few luminaries. While some may find the ambiance too insular, not many turn down membership in this very exclusive—and rewarding—club.

If You Apply To ➤ | **Princeton**…Early decision: Nov. 1. Regular admissions: Jan. 1. Financial aid: Feb. 1. Guarantees to meet demonstrated need. Campus interviews: recommended, evaluative. Alumni interviews: optional, informational. SATs: required. SAT IIs: recommended (engineering applicants required to take either physics or chemistry and math I or II). Essay question: changes every year.

Principia College

Elsah, IL 62028

Let's face it: the college student who abstains from alcohol, drugs, tobacco, and premarital sex is a rarity indeed. At Principia, that rarity is the norm. That's because Principia students are all Christian Scientists. What makes them different? "We hold people at a higher moral standard," remarks one sophomore. "Students have a high sense of right and wrong." Principia's main objective is to allow each student to grow both "academically and spiritually." Hence the college maintains a curriculum that emphasizes the "Whole Man" concept, calling for academic, athletic, social, moral, and spiritual growth with a focus on character education.

Principia students have always enjoyed the natural beauty of their 2,600-acre campus, which is reminiscent of an English village, and were overjoyed when the campus attained its National Historic Landmark designation in 1993. Many of the buildings, including most dormitories, were designed by Bernard Maybeck, a contemporary of Frank Lloyd Wright. Maybeck urged Principia trustees to locate the college on bluffs overlooking the Mississippi River when it was relocated from St.

Website: www.prin.edu

Location: Rural

Total Enrollment: 542

Undergraduates: 542

Male/Female: 46/54

SAT Ranges: V 530–640 M 520–660

ACT Range: 22–28

Financial Aid: 75%

Expense: Pr $

Phi Beta Kappa: No

Applicants: 300

Accepted: 84%

Enrolled: 64%

(Continued)

Grad in 6 Years: 74%

Returning Freshmen: 85%

Academics: ✍ ✍ ✍

Social: ☎ ☎ ☎

Q of L: ★ ★ ★ ★

Admissions: (800) 277-4648

Email Address:

  collegeadmissions@prin.edu

Strongest Programs:

  Biology

  English

  Environmental Science

  Political Science

  Studio Art

  Education

Principia holds the oldest student run public affairs conference in the nation and every year it draws students and speakers from all over the world.

Distinguished guests speakers have included Margaret Thatcher and George Bush.

Louis, Missouri, in 1935. His advice was accepted, and his vision paid off. The campus draws on Colonial American, medieval, and American vernacular stone building traditions. Newest additions to the campus include a 200-seat multipurpose hall, and computer mini-labs were installed in each of the residence halls. Plans are pending for the construction of a performing arts theater and renovation of the athletic facilities.

As for academics, the school is particularly strong in biology, English, environmental science, political science, and studio art. Mass communication majors have the added advantage of a television studio, FM radio station, and editing rooms at their disposal. Prin's science center provides students with an aviary, greenhouse, 13 laboratories, and a computer weather center. Foreign languages and sports management are considered the school's weaker departments, although many students comment that Education is currently being restructured and is unsettled at the present time. Although the academic climate is fairly competitive, the students say the emphasis is more on learning than on grade averages. "Courses can be rigorous but the atmosphere here is one of encouragement and support," says one senior.

Prin's professors are given high marks by their students. "I've found the teachers here to be demanding, creative, accomplished in their fields, and passionate about their subject material," says a political science major. The small class size provides intimate forums for discussing ideas and the opportunity for individualized attention. Beginning in the fall of 2000, Principia will be implementing new general education requirements, which include proficiency in at least one foreign language as well as courses in literature, history, the arts, religion or philosophy, social science, math, and lab science. Students also must fulfill requirements in moral reasoning, writing proficiency, and physical education as well as a survival swim test.

Approximately 65 percent of Prin's students take advantage of the excellent Prin Abroad as well as the Mini-Abroad programs. Students are also able to connect with administrators and entrepreneurs in the San Francisco Field Program, as well as other organizations and businesses in independent internships. Another interdisciplinary program, Diakonia, allows students to integrate academic study with off-campus community service activity.

Despite their common faith, Principia students are geographically quite diverse. Most are from either the East or West coasts, and 77 percent are from out of state. Minorities constitute 6 percent of the student body. The school awards merit scholarships each year, ranging from $2,500 to full tuition. About 15 percent of each year's new students have transferred from other colleges, and there is a small but growing contingent of "nontrads," or students over the age of 23, returning to school or beginning college.

Everyone lives on campus and seems to love it. One student describes the dorms as "beautiful houses that feel like castles." After their first year, most students elect to become "house" members and stay in the same building—similar to a sorority or a fraternity—for the duration of their stay at Prin. But as part of Prin's character education goal, students change rooms and roommates every quarter. Students pick up their meals in the "scramble room" and then eat together in the plush dining hall.

Settled in the 1800s, Elsah, Illinois, is small and quaint, and "not exactly hopping with weekend activity," says a studio arts major. Another student laments, "College town? We are the town." The social committee is good about providing activities on campus, but it is clear that those who have cars make friends fast. Nearby St. Louis is a quick one-hour getaway. Students are very active in the community, and many helped with restoration efforts after Elsah was hit by the Mississippi River flood of 1993. Religious services are run by the Christian Science Organization (a.k.a. "the Org").

Principia's athletic teams have met much success in NCAA Division III competition. Cross-country, tennis, and soccer are all strong sports for both Prin men and women. Principia has great athletic facilities, including a four-court indoor tennis center, and Hay Field House, with its large gym and a pool, a weight room, and squash and racquetball courts. There also are many outdoor courts and a network of running trails. Intramurals are popular, with competition usually organized by the houses. One of the most popular festivals is the springtime Whole World Festival, where international students have food, clothing, and display booths representing their home countries. Principia holds the oldest student run public affairs conference in the nation and every year it draws students and speakers from all over the world. Distinguished guests speakers have included Margaret Thatcher and George Bush.

Prin's guiding principles and Christian Science base may seem overwhelming to some, but they definitely are not to the students who attend the school. And they are not without a sense of humor: a popular T-shirt advertising the "Surf Elsah" surfing competition has students drying pointing out that "it's tough to surf on the Mississippi River." Prin is truly unique in that despite its small size and lack of traditional partying methods, the students still seem happy here. Principia's commitment to not only the intellectual side of an individual, but to the whole person, sets it apart from other colleges.

Mass communication majors have the added advantage of a television studio, FM radio station, and editing rooms at their disposal.

Overlaps

Purdue, Indiana, Ball State, UCLA, UC–Berkeley.

If You Apply To ➤ | **Principia**…Regular admissions: March 1. Financial aid: June 1. Meets demonstrated need of 90%. Campus interviews: recommended, informational. No alumni interviews. SATs: required. SAT IIs: required (foreign language for placement purposes). Essay question: significant book or creative endeavor; defend personal or political issue; or choose your own creative topic. Only college in the world that admits only Christian Scientists.

University of Puget Sound

1500 North Warner, Tacoma, WA 98416

In earlier years, students affectionately referred to the University of Puget Sound as the "University of Parties and Sex" and "University of Pound-it-Down." But much has changed on this campus, located just two hours from the Pacific Ocean. UPS has developed a reputation as a jumping off point—both literally and figuratively—to Asia. Its curriculum stresses two of the fastest growing fields in the region: Asian studies and Pacific Rim economics. Nearly one-third of Puget Sounders take at least one Asian studies course, and 35 lucky students spend nine months traveling through Japan, Thailand, Korea, India, and Nepal, studying native art, architecture, politics, population, and philosophy. Like the package-delivery company with the big brown trucks, "UPS delivers"—but in the case of the school, the package is a quality liberal arts education with a strong focus on the Far East.

The university is cradled between the Cascade Range and the rugged Olympics, with easy access to the city life of Seattle and the natural beauty of

Website: www.ups.edu
Location: Suburban
Total Enrollment: 2,973
Undergraduates: 2,695
Male/Female: 39/61
SAT Ranges: V 570–670 M 580–660
ACT Range: 25–29
Financial Aid: 59%
Expense: Pr $ $ $
Phi Beta Kappa: Yes
Applicants: 4,138

(Continued)

Accepted: 74%

Enrolled: 22%

Grad in 6 Years: 73%

Returning Freshmen: 83%

Academics: ✍ ✍ ✍

Social: ☎ ☎ ☎

Q of L: ★ ★ ★ ★

Admissions: (253) 879-3211

Email Address:

admission@ups.edu

Strongest Programs:

Asian Studies

Biology

Chemistry

Economics

History

International Political

Economy

English

Mount Rainier. Puget Sound's 97-acre campus boasts beautifully maintained lawns, native fir trees, and tons of other plants, trees, and greenery, thanks to the omnipresent rain. Most of the school's buildings, with their distinctive arches and porticos, were built in the 1950s and 1960s, but the university has also experienced a building boom over the past few years. Recently, the Wheelock Student Center was renovated, resulting in expanded seating capacity and additional meal options in the main dining facility, and a new espresso bar was opened. A 10-year cycle of renovations, touching all of the residence halls and University-owned Greek houses, was completed, too. Wyatt Hall, a new state-of-the-art academic building was also opened last fall.

Along with the physical facilities, academics at Puget Sound have been improved in recent years. Students must complete a 12-course core curriculum, which includes classes in written communication, oral communication (or foreign language), mathematical reasoning, historical perspective, humanistic perspective, international studies, natural world, science in context, fine arts, society and comparative values. They also satisfy additional writing requirements within their major field and enroll in a freshman advising course during their first year. Additionally, first-years may participate in writing seminars, a highly selective honors program, or the selective Business Leadership Program. A $250,000 grant enabled Puget Sound to create a set of interdisciplinary business-related majors grounded in liberal arts.

After navigating through the requirements, students find a wealth of majors to choose from in Puget Sound's five undergraduate schools. The most popular majors are English and biology, thanks to the school's proximity to both mountains and bodies of water. Psychology is popular, too, as are business, natural science, and politics and government. "In the sciences, it is quite rigorous. Non-scientific courses are much less competitive," says a junior politics and government major. "What surprised me the most was the amount of reading day in and day out. There is also a lot of paper writing," adds a classmate. Puget Sound recently added a classics major and minors in African American studies, Latin American studies, and environmental studies.

Regardless of the department or program, positive interaction with professors is a big selling point at Puget Sound. "Freshmen are almost always taught by full professors—we don't have graduate students that teach," a junior says. "Teachers really care and spend a lot of time with students." The president holds monthly Fireside Dinners at her home, with a standing invitation to all. Classes generally have 50 students; the majority have 25 or less. For students interested in traveling abroad, Puget Sound offers a yearlong Pacific Rim/Asia studies program. It also offers an honors program, a business mentoring program, and a summer research program. Perhaps because of its small size, diversity—or rather the lack thereof—is a problem at Puget Sound. Blacks and Hispanics combined make up just 4 percent of the student body. Asian Americans, who constitute 11 percent, appear to be more integrated, and an active Hawaiian student organization sponsors a number of events, including a massive luau. Other student organizations exist for various minorities and special-interest groups. A senior biology major observes: "Diversity is always an issue, but people fail to compare us to other comparable institutions. At this level, we are doing well and improving." The new Student Diversity Center is an attempt to foster cooperation among ethnic, religious, gender, and sexual minorities. Administrators have also implemented a "theme year" program to encourage diversity awareness; the most recent theme was Asian and Pacific Americans. Finally, the admissions office recently hired a professional to solely focus on minority recruiting and retention. Puget Sound offers 650 merit

Puget Sound professors have taken a lead in interdisciplinary fields such as International Political Economy, a relatively new undergraduate field in which the professors are authoring the texts.

scholarships, ranging from $1,000 to $10,635, for achievement and promise in general academics and specific talent areas, such as music, art, and debate.

At Puget Sound, freshmen are guaranteed on-campus housing. Of the nine dorms, one is all-female; the others are coed by floor or room. Spaces are reserved for freshmen in all dorms except University Hall; Phibbs Hall and Todd Hall are the best choices, according to students. All rooms are connected to ethernet and have voice mail. After their first year, students may move to one of many university-owned houses, possibly creating their own theme houses along the lines of the current "women in science," "outhaus" (outdoor adventure), and "multicultural" houses. Other options include four foreign-language houses, which offer immersion in other cultures. Forty-six percent of students live off campus. Meals can be taken in the Wheelock Student Center, which has a dining area, game room, television lounge, and the student-run Pizza Cellar and Diversions Café.

"Social life is what you make of it here," says a biology major. Twenty-five percent of men join fraternities, and 24 percent of women belong to sororities, providing ready opportunities to mix and mingle. But off-campus independent parties and school-sponsored activities such as the Mistletoast winter formal and Casino Night are also popular. Foolish Pleasures, a festival of short student-produced films, is another favorite. With the mountains and beaches so close by—Seattle is 30 minutes away by car, Portland is two hours south, and Vancouver, British Columbia, is three hours north—road trips are de rigueur. That's especially true during ski season, because the university rents out all the equipment necessary for a variety of weekend outings. Seventy-five percent of the undergraduates participate in community volunteer programs. While Tacoma is a nice place to live and offers plenty of opportunities for volunteer work, Seattle is where it's at. Back on campus, the alcohol policy—if you live in the dorms and are under 21, you can't drink—is "enforced fairly strictly," a senior says. The Greek houses have banned kegs. "Students get away with it, of course," another student admits.

Among Puget Sound's varsity teams, the Loggers, women's cross-country, swimming, and volleyball and men's swimming have won national championships, and men's cross-country is also strong. The annual football game with local rival Pacific Lutheran University unfailingly draws a crowd. As part of its move to Division III athletics, Puget Sound stopped offering athletic scholarships.

The University of Puget Sound stands ready to welcome students who appreciate the natural beauty of the outdoors, the unique challenge presented by the liberal arts, and the special bond that can be forged with professors in classes of only a few dozen students. It's especially appealing for students who want to participate in the growing Asian economy. "You get a quality education, make good friends, and virtually every opportunity is there if you go looking for it," a junior says.

For students interested in traveling abroad, Puget Sound offers a yearlong Pacific Rim/Asia studies program. It also offers an honors program, a business mentoring program, and a summer research program.

Overlaps

University of Washington, Lewis and Clark, Whitman, Willamette, Colorado College.

If You Apply To ➤ **Puget Sound**…Early decision: Nov. 15 and Dec. 15. Regular admissions and financial aid: Feb. 1. Housing: May 1. Meets demonstrated need of 42%. Campus interviews: recommended, evaluative. Alumni interviews: optional, informational. SATs or ACTs: required. SAT IIs: optional. Accepts the Common Application and electronic applications. Essay question: topic of your choice or one of the following: hometown's impact on your life, original work's effect on your thinking, experiences with diversity, time when humor has helped diffuse a difficult situation, responsibilities of an educated person, plan for accomplishing lifetime goal.

Website: www.purdue.edu

Location: Small city

Total Enrollment: 37,762

Undergraduates: 30,835

Male/Female: 57/43

SAT Ranges: V 480–590 M 500–630

ACT Range: 22–27

Financial Aid: 60%

Expense: Pub $ $

Phi Beta Kappa: Yes

Applicants: 19,625

Accepted: 84%

Enrolled: 42%

Grad in 6 Years: 64%

Returning Freshmen: 86%

Academics: ✍ ✍ ✍

Social: ☎ ☎ ☎

Q of L: ★ ★ ★

Admissions: (765) 494-1776

Email Address:
admissions@purdue.edu

Strongest Programs:
Engineering
Flight Technology
Computer Science and Technology
Nursing
Restaurant and Hotel Management
Pharmacy
Veterinary Medicine and Technology

For a college to be successful in Indiana, it helps to have three characteristics: a strong agricultural program, a powerhouse basketball team, and a conservative student body. At Purdue University, all of these characteristics are present in abundance; the school has gained a reputation for offering a balanced collegiate experience. "Purdue is a very friendly place with an excellent academic reputation," says a health promotion major. Befitting its students' practicality, pre-professionalism rules, with top-notch engineering, aeronautics, agriculture, and management programs especially good—and liberal arts all but non-existent. Purdue is the main attraction in the small industrial town of West Lafayette. The campus architecture is traditional: a combination of redbrick and limestone buildings and lush shaded courtyards. The new food sciences building, complete with extensive research labs, is the most recent addition. Among Purdue's most famous graduates are astronauts Neil Armstrong and Gus Grissom; Amelia Earhart was once a career counselor here. Who says you can't dream big on the endlessly non-descript plains of the Great Midwest?

The Purdue mission freely states that the school "does not offer comprehensive programs in some of the liberal and fine arts and some of the social sciences." That said, what it does, it does well. In fact, the university has awarded more bachelor's degrees in engineering than any other institution. And students flock to the five-year engineering co-op program, one of the most competitive on campus because it marries classroom study with real-world work. Purdue also offers a strong undergraduate program in flight technology, which includes hands-on training at the university's own airport. Generally, according to students, the pharmacy and management departments are likewise excellent, and the restaurant, hotel, institutional, and tourism management program has gained a following. Not surprisingly, the creative arts do not exist save the required writing requirements.

Each of the university's 10 schools establishes its own, usually extensive, set of curriculum requirements, but all require English, math, and science at various levels, and some require a foreign language. All but 16 percent of courses have 50 or fewer students, and it's usually not a problem to get everything you want unless you wait until the last minute to register. Graduation requirements can be fulfilled in four years unless students change their major or elect a co-op. Research is a must for the science and social science faculties, but it doesn't appear to take away from their time with students. "The quality of teaching is excellent," crows a senior. "Students have professors beginning their first year." Still, about half of freshman classes are taught by graduate students and academic advisors, who are available to answer questions and provide career advice.

Although Purdue offers rolling admissions, prospective students should apply early in their senior year of high school to beat the cutoff date for certain programs. The student body is fairly homogeneous, with most from Indiana and only 8 percent minorities: 3 percent African American, 3 percent Asian American, and 2 percent Hispanic. Although some complain that the campus looks like the world's biggest Abercrombie and Fitch catalog, Boilermaker pride is said to stretch across boundaries of race, gender, and background.

Forty-three percent of students live in Purdue's dorms, where attendants enforce visitation hours between men and women; the notion of a "coed dorm" here means that both sexes share a dining hall and a lobby. Almost all freshmen live on campus, though they aren't required to, and Harrison Hall wins the Best Freshman Dorm Award. Dorms are clean and well maintained, and "offer amenities and services like recreational activities, laundry facilities, clubs, and cafeterias," says a hotel/restaurant management major. Most upperclassmen hunt down inexpensive and accessible off-campus housing options, including group houses, Greek houses, apartments, and co-op houses. With more than 40 officers on patrol, walking and riding escorts, and emergency call boxes, students feel safe.

Officially, Purdue is as dry as Death Valley, but according to a senior, "It is very easy for underage students to get alcohol." Forget the local bars, where you must show an I.D.; fraternity and off-campus house parties are accessible to those underage. Greek life, though declining in popularity, is still described as "huge" by more than a few students. Most students stay close to campus to party, where the residence halls plan bowling, movies, and day trips, and where Purdue's more than 621 campus organizations provide students with a plethora of diversions. "With student organizations ranging from the BBQ society to professional development clubs, students can easily find somewhere to fit in," says an industrial management major. Community service, with organizations like Habitat for Humanity and Big Brothers/Big Sisters, is also a popular pastime. The annual Grand Prix, where a week of fun and parties leads up to Saturday's go-cart races, takes place each spring. Students also look forward to the Slater Slammer, a free Labor Day weekend concert. And while the drive to Indianapolis or Chicago is not unbearable, most students use the weekends for forgetting the books, sleeping in, catching a flick, or frequenting Harry's Chocolate Shop—a bar, not a candy store. Some even call Purdue "the only sign of life between Chicago and Indianapolis."

This is a big sports school with an extensive, all-purpose athletic facility, and the mammoth intramural program fosters animosity almost as intense as that felt for the Indiana Hoosiers on the varsity level. Boilermaker pride manifests itself at varsity games of all types, especially when the opposing team is "that school down south," in the annual struggle for possession of the Old Oaken Bucket. Every year, the winner adds a link to a chain on the bucket, with each in the shape of either an "I" or "P." The men's football team is strong, and the women's basketball team took home the 2000 Big Ten championship. Women's golf and softball are also popular, as are men's basketball and baseball.

Whether it's screaming themselves hoarse for their beloved Boilermakers on the gridiron or the hardwood, or hitting the books to learn to fly or synthesize a new agricultural protein, Purdue students get a healthy dose of academics and athletics, in a relaxed, almost rural environment. Like the saying goes, "Hoosier by birth, Boilermaker by the grace of God." For those planning to stay true to their Midwestern roots or shoot for the moon, Purdue just might be worth a look.

All but 16 percent of courses have 50 or fewer students, and it's usually not a problem to get everything you want unless you wait until the last minute to register.

Overlaps

Indiana, Valparaiso, University of Illinois, Rose-Hulman Institute of Technology.

If You Apply To ➤

Purdue…Rolling admissions. Financial aid and housing: Mar. 1. Meets demonstrated need of 35%. Campus interviews: optional, informational. No alumni interviews. SATs or ACTs: required. SAT IIs: optional (English composition, math and lab science for home-schooled students). Accepts electronic applications. No essay question.

Queens University, Kingston, Ontario—See CANADIAN COLLEGES AND UNIVERSITIES

Randolph–Macon Woman's College

2500 Rivermont Avenue, Lynchburg, VA 24503

Website: www.rmwc.edu

Location: Residential

Total Enrollment: 709

Undergraduates: 709

Male/Female: 0/100

SAT Ranges: V 543–670 M 500–610

ACT Range: 24–29

Financial Aid: 51%

Expense: Pr $

Phi Beta Kappa: Yes

Applicants: 719

Accepted: 84%

Enrolled: 33%

Grad in 6 Years: 63%

Returning Freshmen: 77%

Academics: ✍ ✍ ✍

Social: ☎ ☎

Q of L: ★ ★ ★ ★

Admissions: (800) 745-7692

Email Address:

admissions@rmwc.edu

Strongest Programs:

Psychology

Biology

English Literature

Fine Arts

Classics

Though Randolph-Macon Women's College is steeped in Southern tradition, it refuses to be bound by the past. Instead, the college is constantly updating academic programs to meet students' keen interests and critical needs for personal and professional growth. The college's comprehensive plan provides each student with an integrated series of classes, extra-curricular activities, internships, and career planning customized to meet each student's goals. The college's 100-acre campus is located in a gracious residential area of Lynchburg, a city of almost 80,000 on the James River at the foot of the Blue Ridge Mountains. The old and majestic buildings, arrayed in a semicircle, are strewn with purple wisteria vines and surrounded by grand trees that burst into bloom in the spring and melt into colors in the fall. Glass corridors called trolleys link nearly all campus buildings. Main Hall, built in 1893, houses student rooms, classrooms, and faculty and administrative offices. But the campus is not stuck in the past—the college features well-equipped computer labs hooked up to the campus network and set off with scanners, printers, and good Internet access. The college's Maier Museum of Art houses one of the country's most extensive collections of 19th-and 20th-century American art and features paintings by Bellows, O'Keeffe, Homer, Stuart, and Cassatt, among others. The college's 100-acre equestrian center is in the nearby Blue Ridge foothills.

At Randolph-Macon, adherence to the honor code inspires trust among students and faculty. While each student develops a tailor-made program designed with a faculty advisor, there are general education requirements in three areas: skills (composition, math, and a foreign language), distribution (courses in literature, artistic expression, history, philosophy or religion, and the social sciences), and dimensions (a women's studies course and three cultural diversity courses). Students can major in traditional departments or interdisciplinary programs, or they may create their own course of study. The college offers many unusual studies, including the American Culture Program, a semester-long study that takes students on the road to key locations in Virginia and the Mid-Atlantic states. Students are gaining hands-on investment experience with the Peggy Penn Weitnauer Student Foundation, which donates money to help students learn about finances, allocation, and development. And the proceeds go to a good cause—special student activities. Students and faculty have also studied in such exotic locales as South Africa, Senegal, Indonesia, Japan, Tunisia, and the rain forests of Central America; the college has established a Visiting International Professorship and an annual travel-study trip.

Psychology is the most popular major, followed by English, politics, biology, and communication. English, biology, and psychology are the strongest programs, students say. Smaller departments, such as music and physics, are cited as weaker, primarily due to their size. The college has recently added bachelor of science degrees in biology, chemistry, math, and physics. First-year students share common readings linked thematically to the college's annual symposium; a recent topic was Body Politics: Women, Culture, and Experiences of the Physical Self.

R-WMC's library is limited, offering students only 167,900 volumes. The collection is supplemented by the local library and interlibrary loans, and online information systems offer access to area colleges' holdings. Randolph-Macon's participation in the Seven-College Exchange* gives women opportunities to experience other campuses, including a year or semester abroad at the University of Reading in England, the Universidad de las Americas in Mexico, or the University of Economics in Prague. There's also a 3-2 nursing program with Johns Hopkins and Vanderbilt. And the college participates in American University's Washington Semester program, and the Tri-College Exchange. About 65 percent of R-MWC students intern in Lynchburg or elsewhere. Students recently worked for the Chicago Lyric Opera, the Democratic party, the American Council for International Education, and the White House.

On campus, students find small classes and attentive professors. "The quality of teaching is excellent," a political science major says. "I chose to come here because of the profs." Classes are challenging, but grade-grubbing is not an issue. "The courses are very rigorous; there is no such thing as a 'basket weaving' course here," a senior biology major explains. Academic advising gets rave reviews, and every year the school hosts a dinner for juniors and their advisors, called Smorgasbord, to strengthen the relationship in a less academic setting.

Thirty-six percent of Randolph-Macon women hail from Virginia. Nearly 40 percent graduated in the top tenth of their high school class. African Americans and Hispanics together make up 11 percent of the student body, Asian Americans 3 percent, and international students 9 percent. The college sponsors workshops on multicultural awareness and is a member of the International 50, a group of colleges committed to global awareness. Hot topics on campus include ending domestic abuse and abusive relationships, homosexuality, and women's rights. An organization called BIONIC—Believe It Or Not I Care—organizes volunteer events, and more than half of R-WMC's students volunteer in the community or elsewhere.

The college admits students regardless of financial need, but the best scholars get aid packages with proportionately more grant money, and about half are offered packages meeting their full demonstrated need. Merit scholarships of $4,000 to full tuition are offered to 190 deserving students, but there are no athletic scholarships.

Eighty-three percent of the students live in the college's residence halls, three of which were recently renovated with new paint, hardwood floors, and carpeting in fresh colors. Main Hall, once nicknamed "the Hilton," is the largest dorm, and its central location makes it most convenient. "The dorm rooms are really big and nice," explains one student. "They are very comfortable and are provided with good furniture, plenty of electrical outlets, heat, and they have real walls, not cinder block, " adds a biology major. Seniors are guaranteed single rooms and first-years live alongside upperclass students, which speeds their integration into the college community. Speaking of integration, all rooms have video, voice, and data capabilities. Students say they feel very safe on campus, thanks to security phones and an escort service, and most even know the security staff by name.

However, those security officers don't hesitate to crack down on drinking, which is barred for underage students. Campus life is spiced a little by the school's secret societies and long-standing traditions, including the annual Tacky Party (tasteless attire required), Pumpkin Parade, and rivalry between "Odds" and "Evens" (those who graduate in odd- or even-numbered years). Senior Dinner Dance, Ring Night, and Daisy Chain Day number among the other annual events. R-MWC hosts mixers with other schools, and the programming board sponsors movies, concerts, and other entertainment every weekend. But many students get their kicks on Route 66 and hit the highways for fun and excitement. "Students travel to other colleges and cities for entertainment," says a senior. "Students need cars here."

Art-lovers revel in Randolph-Macon's Maier Museum of Art with its extensive collection of 19th- and 20th-century paintings by the likes of Cassatt, Bellows, O'Keeffe, Homer, and Stuart.

Psychology majors present their research at the Virginia Psychological Association where they have garnered honors time and again in recent years.

Lynchburg, while host to a number of colleges, is not really a college town. "There are now a few clubs, a couple of good coffee shops, and a few movie theaters, but almost everything in town closes at 10:00 P.M.," gripes a senior. Those in need of caffeine for late-night studying will find a coffee bar at the campus's upscale bookstore. For those who want to get out, but don't want to make the long haul, the area just beyond Lynchburg offers plenty of natural attractions, with ski slopes, camping, and hiking close by. Lynchburg is one hour from the University of Virginia and three hours from Washington, D.C. Still, some students say that the lack of recreation options is the school's biggest problem. "Social life needs to be spiced up to entertain the students," says one biology major. "You can't work all the time."

Most Randolph-Macon athletic teams post respectable results in Division III competition, and with almost 20 percent of students playing intercollegiate sports, athletics set the tone of campus life, some students say. The college boasts an award-winning riding team, a WNBA draftee, and top-notch swimmers and field hockey players.

R-MWC students dispel the myth that women are the weaker sex and forge ahead intellectually, athletically, and professionally. They despise the stereotypes accorded to women's colleges, and instead are grateful for the diversity and opportunity the college provides. Just glimpse a popular T-shirt worn unapologetically around campus to get the whole picture: "Randolph-Macon Women's College: Not a girl's school without men, but a women's college without boys."

Overlaps

Sweet Briar, Agnes Scott, Mount Holyoke, William and Mary, University of Virginia.

If You Apply To ➤ **R-MWC**...Early decision: Nov. 15. Financial aid: Jan. 1 (early decision), Mar. 1. Regular admissions: March 1. Meets demonstrated need of 51%. Campus interviews: recommended, informational. Alumni interviews: optional, informational. SATs or ACTs: required. SAT IIs: optional. Accepts the Common Application. Essay question: inspirational work of art, dance, music, theatre, literature; does anyone speak for your generation; discuss statement: "the primary need in the world...is a mutual knowledge between people about one another." Looks at high school record over test scores.

University of Redlands

1200 East Colton, P.O. Box 3080, Redlands, CA 92373-0999

Website: www.redlands.edu
Location: City outskirts
Total Enrollment: 1,800
Undergraduates: 1,600
Male/Female: 47/53
SAT Ranges: V 490–610 M 500–610
ACT Range: 21–27
Financial Aid: N/A
Expense: Pr $ $
Phi Beta Kappa: Yes
Applicants: 1,848

Amid the dozens of gigantic and well-known universities in the state of California exists the University of Redlands. With its innovative living/learning college and strong preprofessional emphasis, this versatile school is one of higher education's better-kept secrets, and a place where students receive all the personal attention they could want. One student describes it as a "small liberal arts college in sunny Southern California with great financial aid packages."

The University of Redlands' 140-acre campus, covered in majestic oak trees, is designed around "The Quad," a group of dorms which face one another. The two main landmarks are the Memorial Chapel and the Administrative building. Redlands' facilities are a mixture of older, more historical columned buildings and more modern, renovated ones. The view from the college can only be described as breathtaking. Mountain ranges form the backdrop, and neighboring Big Bear Lake and Arrowhead ski resorts give endless getaway opportunities. Also nearby are the San Gorgonio Wilderness and Joshua Tree National Park. For those looking for big city adventures, Los Angeles is only an hour away.

One of Redlands' most distinctive attributes is its experimental living/learning college where students create their own course of study and are judged by self- and professor evaluations, rather than grades. The Johnston Center for Integrative Studies was established in 1969 to function as an "alternative" college within a traditional setting; about 10 percent of the students here take advantage of this opportunity. The program offers unusual academic freedom; there are no departments, majors, or distribution requirements. Instead, students "contract" with professors for their entire plan of study. At the beginning of each course, students make up the syllabus by consensus and then set their own research and writing goals. Each student develops four-year goals—which are reviewed by a student-faculty board for direction and breadth—within one or more broad areas: the social sciences, behavioral sciences, humanities, and fine and performing arts.

Compared with other Redlands students, Johnston undergrads are better qualified academically, with average SATs that are 50 to 75 points above the Redlands median. One student explains, "Johnston center students tend to be independent thinkers, self-motivated, and [don't] take classes just because they have to." Johnston's enrollment declined in the late '70s and '80s as students became very career oriented and found that alternative education no longer fit their needs. Fortunately, student interests and needs have once again changed, and Johnston is seeing its highest enrollment in nearly two decades.

Aside from Johnston, Redlands is unusual among liberal arts institutions mainly in that it also offers professional programs. The schools of education and music provide strong career training, as does the excellent program in communicative disorders. Business is the most popular major, followed by Integrative Studies, psychology, government and political science, and English. The environmental studies program consists of courses in natural science, humanities, and social science focusing on values-based environmental problem solving. Students can receive degrees in environmental studies, environmental science, and environmental management. Redlands has also emerged as a national leader in science curriculum reform. An example is the introduction of "Calculus in Context," which focuses on discovery-based learning principles. It has been so successful that in a recent year the percentage of students taking second-semester calculus nearly doubled from 45 to 85 percent.

The liberal arts foundation gives students the fundamental skills essential to effective learning and scholarship by challenging them to examine their own values and the values of society. With its 4–1–4 calendar, Redlands has students take one intensive course each January. Students may also choose among 60 study abroad options, mainly in Europe, Asia, Africa, and Latin America. The highly acclaimed freshman seminar program places small groups of first-year students with some of the school's best professors, while the selective honors program enables outstanding students to work individually with professors, who are very accessible outside of class and occasionally even come by the dorms for "fireside chats. "Freshmen are always taught by full professors," says one sophomore, and a writing major declares that at Redlands, "the professors are the school's biggest asset." Most students agree that Redlands's laid-back academic atmosphere is much appreciated.

Fifty-seven percent of the student body comes from within the state, creating a mellow, Southern California atmosphere on campus. The climate is a definite plus, with temperatures rarely below 50 degrees. The typical Redlands student tends to be fairly conservative, although one student reports that the minority of liberals are quite vocal. The racial makeup of the school is fairly diverse, with

(Continued)
Accepted: 83%
Enrolled: 24%
Grad in 6 Years: 63%
Returning Freshmen: 78%
Academics: ✍ ✍ ✍
Social: ☎ ☎ ☎
Q of L: ★ ★ ★
Admissions: (800) 455-5064
Email Address:
  admissions@uor.edu

Strongest Programs:
  Government
  English
  Creative Writing
  Biology
  Chemistry
  Engineering

About 10 percent of the students here opt for one of the most unorthodox educations on the West Coast: an experimental living/learning college where students create their own course of study and are judged by self- and professor evaluations, rather than grades.

Hispanics representing a solid 8 percent, Asian Americans 7 percent, and blacks 4 percent. About half of the graduating class each year move on to graduate schools, while the other half head into the work force. Redlands annually awards a variety of merit scholarships, ranging from $1500 to full tuition. There are talent awards in art, writing, music, and debate, but there are no athletic scholarships.

Students have nothing but rave reviews for the dormitories in which 89 percent of the campus live all four years. "Each dorm has a personality of its own," exclaims one student. "The dorms are comfortable and complete with ping-pong and pool tables," raves a sophomore. Most of the dorms are coed, though there is an all-women dorm. Students agree that freshmen should check out Merriam Hall first. Other housing options include on-campus apartments and student-run co-ops. Students enjoy their food in the new dining hall, part of the $9-million Hunsaker University Center. Students can mingle in the "town square" atmosphere of the center's bookstore, café, and student life offices.

The Southern California heat and smog can become unpleasant, and students with wheels often flee Redlands on weekends for healthier pleasure spots along the California coast or in the mountains. But overall, social life is centered around campus activities. Local fraternities and sororities claim 26 percent of men and 21 percent of women as members, and their parties are open to all, but even these parties are rarely raucous. Road trips to Hollywood and Palm Springs, San Francisco, the beach, and even Mexico are common. Despite the school's enforcement efforts, alcohol is fairly accessible. "It is very easy. Students operate bars out of their rooms," reports one student.

The sports program injects a measure of excitement into the social scene, and about 7 out of every 10 students join at least one intramural team. The swimming and water polo teams are enjoying a brand-new facility, and Redlands has won two recent national championships in women's water polo. But the team that has long been a national power in Division III is men's tennis. Football has made a resurgence, with the team winning the conference three times and advancing to the NCAA championships twice in the last seven years. Also very competitive are men's basketball and Frisbee, and women's basketball, softball, and volleyball. But the team to watch is, to no one's surprise, the debate team—a perennial powerhouse.

The University of Redlands is a lot of different things to a lot of different people. With hardly more than 100 faculty members, it manages to be a preprofessional institute, a liberal arts college, and an alternative school all in one. The Johnston Center is clearly the path to travel for the innovative individualist, but even those who don't join Johnston will likely find what they want and need at Redlands.

If You Apply To ➢   **Redlands**…Regular admissions: Dec. 15. Financial aid: Feb. 15 (for merit scholarship), Mar. 2 (need-based aid). Does not guarantee to meet demonstrated need. Campus interviews: recommended, evaluative. Alumni interviews: optional, informational. SATs or ACTs: required. SAT IIs: optional. Essay question: personal statement.

Reed College

3203 S.E. Woodstock Boulevard, Portland, OR 97202

Reed College, a haven for nonconformists and individualists, has been home to 31 Rhodes Scholars, 43 Fulbright Scholars, and two Pulitzer Prize winners. Reed is one of a handful of colleges that requires all students to write a senior thesis to graduate. On the thesis due date, seniors march from the library steps to the registrar's office in a Thesis Parade, inscribe their names on a giant thermometer known as the Thesis Meter, and then throw the Renn Fayre, an affair described by one student as "an all-blowout party lasting three days." One of the nation's top colleges, Reed is home to, as one student puts it, "the eccentric, brilliant, and work-obsessed."

Located in a handsome residential area, Reed is just five miles from downtown Portland and its 100-acre campus consists of wide lawns, trees, and a pond in a fern-banked canyon that has been designated as protected wetlands. The architectural style of the main buildings is Tudor Gothic in brick, carved limestone, and concrete. Planned additions to the campus include a $12-million educational technology center and a $2-million expansion of the current studio art facilities.

The school offers unsurpassed intellectual opportunities for its size, including a loan program that allows students to buy personal computers through small monthly payments to the school. In addition, all dormitory rooms are connected to a network providing 24-hour access to hundreds of computers distributed throughout the campus. The Triga Research Nuclear Reactor is run by students and staff who have passed an eight-hour Atomic Energy Commission examination. Although the college works within a structure of personal freedom, the curriculum is—contrary to what one might expect—highly traditional. The administration takes pride in the fact that it hasn't changed for over fifty years. All undergraduates must complete a full-year course or the equivalent in semester courses in each of the following areas: literature, philosophy, and the arts; history and the social sciences; natural sciences; mathematics, logic, linguistics, or foreign languages. First-year students are required to pass a year-long humanities course taught by prestigious faculty. Juniors must pass a qualifying examination.

Interdisciplinary programs and opportunities to design an individual major abound, and several 3–2 engineering, business, forestry and environmental science, visual arts, and computer science programs are also offered at Reed. Many students take a leave of absence to participate in Reed's study abroad programs, available in 19 overseas countries, including Germany, Russia, China, France, and Costa Rica. Most students spend all four years at Reed in classes with 25 people or less.

Studying is a way of life at Reed, and students say they have neither time nor inclination to do much else. Most take full advantage of the library's late hours. "Academic advising is seen as adequate while career advising has received mixed reviews. "The career center has a ton of information, but it's not disseminated in a useful manner," says one student. The professors are willing to put as much energy into teaching as they demand from their students in class. Students rarely attend class unprepared for what is sure to be lively intellectual banter between inquiring and active minds. One student says, "These profs are some of the most intelligent people I have ever come into contact with—it's one of the best things about Reed." Faculty members must regularly write evaluations of students' work

Website: www.reed.edu

Location: City outskirts

Total Enrollment: 1,373

Undergraduates: 1,353

Male/Female: 46/54

SAT Ranges: V 640–730 M 610–700

ACT Range: 28–30

Financial Aid: 48%

Expense: Pr $ $ $ $

Phi Beta Kappa: Yes

Applicants: 2,018

Accepted: 68%

Enrolled: 24%

Grad in 6 Years: 68%

Returning Freshmen: 88%

Academics: ✍ ✍ ✍ ✍ ✍

Social: ☎ ☎ ☎

Q of L: ★ ★ ★ ★

Admissions: (503) 777-7511

Email Address: admission@reed.edu

Strongest Programs:
Biology
Chemistry
Psychology
English
Philosophy
History
Physics

Over the years, a quarter of Reed's grads have gone on for Ph.D.s, the highest percentage of any liberal arts college in the country.

and are known for their brutal honesty. Most courses are run as seminars or "conferences" with enrollments of 20 or fewer. Over the years, a quarter of Reed's grads have gone on for Ph.D.s, the highest percentage of any liberal arts college in the country.

Reed has been around for more than 80 years, and its offerings currently attract students from all over the nation. Fifteen percent come from Oregon, and most come from upper-middle-class backgrounds. "Freshpeople"—orientation Reed-style—includes a four-day backpacking trip and community service trips. Despite the conservatism found on many of the nation's campuses, Reed seems committed to remaining an island of intellectual independence, diversity, and free thinking. "Reedies tend to be very liberal and accepting of alternative lifestyles," says one senior, and another points out that you would be hard-pressed to find conservatives ambling about Reed's campus. Despite its wide-open attitude, minorities are poorly represented on campus; 1 percent are African American, 2 percent Hispanic, and 7 percent are Asian Americans, a situation many students lament. "Far too many Reedies are oblivious to the outside world," says an English major. "Its frustrating to people like me who work off campus and spend most of their lives in the 'real world' that so many Reedies stick their heads in the academic sand and refuse to look up." But students claim this is changing. "Reedies have a genuine curiosity about the world around them," states this senior. A percentage of students with demonstrated need are routinely waitlisted for aid, but no merit or athletic scholarships are available.

Sixty-eight percent of the students live on campus in small, homey coed or single-sex dorms that usually house fewer than 30 people, and some of the rooms feature such niceties as fireplaces or balconies. "There is a lot of variety when it comes to housing at Reed," says one student. First-year students are guaranteed housing, while the rest must endure the lottery. Singles usually go to on-campus seniors, but there is sufficient privacy for all; even most doubles have two rooms. "There is enough difference in preference among the students that basically everyone gets to live where they want to live," shares one student. Many upperclassmen prefer to live off campus, and houses to share are cheap and plentiful. On-campus students must join the meal plan and eat in the Commons. A salad bar adds some alimentary diversity, but students are most appreciative of the student-run coffee shop.

Just about everyone goes to the campus socials, which feature a wide variety of Northwestern alternative bands. Movies, coffeehouses, television, and dinner out take up the rest of weekend time. "We do, contrary to common belief, have a lot of fun," a senior assures. Another student notes, "There are a lot of speakers that come to campus every week and these tend to be real popular among the students." The Halloween social is noted for its "utter zaniness" and "uninhibited bodily movements," and the end of every academic year brings the Renn Fayre, "a big party complete with live chess, a naked Slip 'n Slide, and any number of bizarre activities," says a junior. One way Reedies avoid the January blahs is to divide into teams that use recycled home-building materials to build catapults on the campus lawn and see whose contraption can propel an object the farthest. The only rule is that students have to fire something that won't put holes in buildings, the lawn or, of course, people). Paideia, two weeks between semesters when students take "fun" classes, including breadmaking and wool spinning, is also a popular tradition among the usually stressed-out students.

Underage drinking occurs, but is forbidden per the Reed Honor Principle. But that doesn't mean alcohol isn't around. "Reed is a very liberal institution and things like alcohol and drugs aren't as taboo here as they are at other schools," says a senior. Quieter escapes include the beautiful Oregon coast, an hour away. Plus Portland has lots to offer. One sophomore comments, "Portland is unique in that it possesses a distinct urban, cosmopolitan atmosphere, but is not threatening to the individual inexperienced to city life."

The school maintains its own ski cabin on nearby Mount Hood with sleeping space for 30. There are no varsity athletics, although some clubs, such as basketball, soccer, and rugby, compete with clubs from other colleges in the area. One student reports that the lack of organized sports is the school's best quality. The closest thing Reed has to an official school mascot is the Doyle Owl, a 300-pound concrete structure that is regularly stolen from one dorm to the next. There is wide interest in sports on a casual basis, and the sports center offers beautiful squash and paddleball courts, a swimming pool, and other facilities.

One thing is for sure—Reedies are an entirely different breed of student. When asked whether or not his school had a slogan, one sophomore offered a unique reply, saying that "the fact that Reed doesn't have a slogan is its strongest point. In a community so diverse, our slogan would be pages long. With footnotes. And a bibliography."

Overlaps

Brown, Oberlin, UC–Berkley, Stanford, Swarthmore.

If You Apply To ➤ Reed...Early decision: Nov. 15, Jan. 2. Regular admissions: Jan. 15. Does not guarantee to meet demonstrated need. Campus and alumni interviews: recommended, evaluative. SATs or ACTs: required. SAT IIs: recommended (English and writing). Accepts the Common Application and electronic applications. Essay question: significant educational experience; fictional character with whom you would spend the day; which possession reveals the most about your character; or the biggest risk you have ever taken. Graded writing sample also required.

Rensselaer Polytechnic Institute

Troy, NY 12180-3590

In world driven by rapidly developing technology, Rensselaer Polytechnic Institute has forged a unique niche for itself by combining the newest possibilities of the Information Age with tried-and-true values of hard work, experiential learning, and a firm grounding in "the application of science to the common purposes of life." Small seminars, which RPI professors favor over large lectures, allow students to exploit technology and their own imagination to explore, experiment, create, simulate, and synthesize. Rensselaer is one of the first research universities to figure out what millions of students have known for decades: Students with hands-on control of their learning retain much more than passive listeners.

High on a bluff overlooking Troy, New York, Rensselaer's 260-acre campus is a mix of modern research facilities and Classical-style, ivy-covered brick buildings that date back to the turn of the century. Recently, the school has completed renovations to the Troy Building and the School of Management's Pittsburgh Building, now featuring a virtual trading floor for a hands-on education in stock trading. Despite the glamour of high finance, RPI made its reputation as one of the nation's premier engineering schools, and it continues to excel in traditional favorites such as chemical and electrical as well as newer entries such as environmental and computer systems engineering. The nuclear engineering department has its own linear accelerator, and both graduate and undergraduate students take part in research projects at the Center for Industrial Innovation. A

Website:
  http://admissions.rpi.edu
Location: City outskirts
Total Enrollment: 7,650
Undergraduates: 4,926
Male/Female: 76/24
SAT Ranges: V 560–660 M 620–710
ACT Range: 24–29
Financial Aid: 85%
Expense: Pr $ $ $ $
Phi Beta Kappa: No
Applicants: 5,264
Accepted: 78%
Enrolled: 32%
Grad in 6 Years: 73%
Returning Freshmen: 90%

(Continued)

Academics: ✍ ✍ ✍ ✍

Social: ☎ ☎ ☎

Q of L: ★ ★ ★

Admissions: (518) 276-6216

Email Address:

admissions@rpi.edu

Strongest Programs:

Engineering

Sciences

Management and

Technology

Electronic Media, Arts, and

Communications

Architecture

Computer Science

Information Technology

RPI, as the school is known, has forged itself into one of the nation's premier technical schools by harnessing brute intellectual and technological strength to the blue-collar industriousness of Upstate New York.

$7-million computer center contains one of the largest computer graphics laboratories in the nation, and RPI is a national leader in the study and application of electronic media.

It would be an exaggeration to say that technology is "god" at RPI, though the school's conversion of an erstwhile Gothic chapel into a computer lab does hint in that direction. RPI pioneered the teaching of calculus via computer in the early '90s, and now it is using technology to redefine its curriculum. Studio courses allow students to interact with professors in small groups and then go back to their workstations for hands-on problem-solving and collaborative projects.

One of RPI's hottest programs is the Lally School of Management and Technology, which combines elements of a business school with exposure to the latest technical applications. Entrepreneurship is one of its specialties, and students get the unique opportunity to participate in the Lally School's "Business Incubator," a support system for hundreds of start-up companies run by Rensselaer students and alumni. Beginning with this fall's incoming freshmen, all students will be required to take courses in entrepreneurship or have an "entrepreneurial experience" before they graduate. A BS program in Information Technology was introduced in the spring of 1998, and has quickly become one of the hottest majors. Students explore a second discipline as well, with IT/e-commerce and IT/Arts being among the popular combinations. Majors in the humanities and social sciences are limited, and their quality is directly related to applicability to technical fields. All students must sample the offerings via the First-Year Studies program, which features interdisciplinary and collaborative work. Dorm rooms have an Ethernet port for every bed, and all freshmen are required to have laptop computers. Short courses are offered to bring freshmen quickly up to speed on the finer points of mobile computing.

Over two-thirds of the students at Rensselaer are undergraduates, a high percentage for a top engineering school, and RPI has worked hard in recent years to ensure smaller classes and more attention to individual needs. Students say the quality of the teaching ranges from superb to unengaging. "Some teachers talk over the heads of the students, but are always available for extra help with mandatory office hours," says a sophomore biomedical engineering major. Juniors and seniors enjoy small classes, self-paced course options, and occasionally paid assistantships in faculty research. Academic advising gets fair reviews from students who use it. But even with the best of help, the average workload at the school is Herculean. "If you take the time to learn the material, the semester could go smoothly. Cut throat? Not at all," says a biomedical engineering major. "The courses here are pretty hard, so in order to do well, you gotta study," chimes in another study. But it all pays off in the end: RPI survivors are an extremely marketable commodity; the school's preprofessional students enjoy a 90 to 95 percent acceptance rate in graduate programs.

For students who can't wait to get their feet wet in the job market, popular co-op programs in over a dozen fields help them earn both money and credit. There are seven-year dual degree options in medicine and dentistry, a six-year degree program in law and four- and five-year master's programs in biology, geology, mathematical science, and architecture. Whereas most engineering schools discourage study abroad, Rensselaer offers exchange programs in several European countries, most notably at Switzerland's renowned Federal Institute of Technology.

More than half of the students graduated in the top 10 percent of their high school class, and nearly all in the top half. Asian Americans comprise 11 of the student body; blacks and Hispanics combine for only 8 percent. RPI students tend to be bright, studious, and technically savvy. "Honestly, this campus is full of dorks," says one sophomore. "Friendly and helpful dorks, though, and even some attractive ones, too!" RPI is far from a center of political activism, although students report that the campus is concerned with protecting the environment. With an acceptance rate of 78 percent, RPI is less selective than other marquee schools such as MIT and Carnegie Mellon. But it's a self-selecting group that applies and almost everyone who does so is highly qualified. Rensselaer does not guarantee to meet the full financial need of all students, but help is available. There are 705 academic merit scholarships averaging $10,700 each, and 18 full rides offered each year to players on the Division I hockey team.

Fifty-seven percent of students live in university residence halls, including 98 percent of all freshmen. Freshmen are required to live on campus and, for the fall semester, must buy the meal plan. The dorms are both coed and single-sex and vary in quality, though recent renovations have improved the older ones. A brand new freshman dorm was recently completed. Upperclassmen can exercise squatter's rights, enter the campus room lottery, or live in college-owned apartments off campus (widely considered the nicest option). About half of the upperclassmen live in fraternity and sorority houses, where they eat meals family-style.

Free shuttle buses run regularly from campus to downtown Troy, but there aren't a lot of good reasons for college students to make the trip. "Troy, N.Y.—what a horrible place. Definitely not a college town, but students and many fraternities do get involved with the town," says one freshman. A six-screen movie theater is also within easy reach, and for a taste of nightlife in a somewhat larger city, Albany is within a half-hour drive. For scenic excursions, the Berkshires, Catskills, Adirondacks, Lake George, Lake Placid, the Saranac Lakes, and the New England countryside are also within spitting distance.

When it comes to social life, everyone agrees that the ratio—three times as many males as females—is a major hassle. Thirty percent of men and 20 percent of women go Greek as a way to round out the social offerings. On weekends, many lovelorn male engineers haunt Russell Sage (next door) or Skidmore (40 minutes away). Campus social life revolves around sporting events, live entertainment, concerts, movies, the half-dozen local pubs, and Greek parties. Extracurricular clubs, organized around such interests as chess, dance, judo, and skiing, are all chartered and funded through the student union, which doles out several million dollars annually and is managed and controlled by the students themselves. Professors are forbidden from giving tests during Grand Marshal Week, a boisterous weeklong carnival and party that celebrates campus elections.

The sports scene at Rensselaer can be summarized in three words: hockey, hockey, hockey. One of the biggest weekends of the year is Big Red Freakout, when festivities all center around cheering on the beloved Big Red. "Hockey at RPI equals insanity," a freshman says. "If you go to one hockey game all season, go to the men's hockey season opener. The place is packed with rowdy RPI students that scream and chant in unison." Though less celebrated, other varsity teams do exist. (All besides men's hockey play in Division III.) The men's and women's tennis and women's basketball teams are especially strong. Rensselaer's football players vie with Union College every year for the coveted Dutchman's Shoes.

Students at RPI enjoy a rare combination of cutting-edge technological instruction in an atmosphere carefully designed to foster both individual and cooperative learning. Though lacking some of the social accouterments that students at other schools enjoy, Rensselaer students know that their hard work will probably be rewarded with job offers at graduation. After four years immersed in some of the best educational technology in the nation, students leave RPI poised to influence the technical destiny of the nation.

The nuclear engineering department has its own linear accelerator, and both graduate and undergraduate students take part in research projects at the Center for Industrial Innovation.

Overlaps

Cornell University, MIT, Worcester Polytechnic, Carnegie Mellon, Rochester Institute of Technology.

| If You Apply To ➢ | Rensselaer…Early decision: Nov. 15. Regular admissions: Jan. 1. Financial aid: Feb. 15. Does not guarantee to meet demonstrated need. Campus and alumni interviews: optional, informational. SATs or ACTs: required. SAT IIs: optional (writing, math, and chemistry or physics required for applicants to accelerated programs). Accepts the Common Application and electronic applications. Essay question: significant experience; issue of importance; or influential person; others, depending on program. Apply to particular programs. |

Rhode Island School of Design

2 College Street, Providence, RI 02903

Website: www.risd.edu

Location: City center

Total Enrollment: 2,001

Undergraduates: 1,786

Male/Female: 40/60

SAT Ranges: N/A

Financial Aid: 45%

Expense: Pr $ $ $

Phi Beta Kappa: No

Applicants: 2,007

Accepted: 43%

Enrolled: 44%

Grad in 6 Years: 87%

Returning Freshmen: 96%

Academics: ✍ ✍ ✍

Social: ☎ ☎

Q of L: ★ ★ ★ ★

Admissions: (401) 454-6300

Email Address:

admissions@risd.edu

Strongest Programs:

Architecture

Illustration

Graphic Design

Industrial Design

Founded in the late 19th century to address this country's need for more artisans and craftsmen, the Rhode Island School of Design has grown into the ultimate creative incubator. It's a place where today's artists and designers gather to share ideas and create tomorrow's masterpieces and architectural icons. RISD grants degrees in virtually every design-related topic, and like the varied curriculum, the students and their creations are as diverse as the colors on an artist's palette. "We're on a first-name basis with renowned artists who will bend over backward to give us whatever help we need," says a senior. "Being surrounded by so many talented students is intense, as well—sometimes it's scary and discouraging, usually it's inspiring."

Though you might expect an art school like RISD to occupy funky, futuristic buildings, the predominant look here is Colonial New England. Set on the upgrade of College Hill, RISD sits at the edge of Providence's beautifully preserved historic district across the street from Brown University. Many campus buildings date from the 1700s and early 1800s; the mostly redbrick-and-white-trim group includes converted homes, a bank, and even an old church with the campus pub in what used to be its attic. The six-story Industrial Design building, designed by faculty member Jim Barnes, occupies the old Roitman furniture company warehouse. Its 50,000 square feet are designed for wood- and metal-working and prototype making. About the only thing RISD's campus doesn't offer is a lot of open space. Those wanting to toss a football or a Frisbee would be well advised to take up a sport better suited to the streets of Providence, like hopscotch or people-watching.

While RISD looks traditionally New England on the outside, behind its historic walls lies something else entirely. Students give the architecture, graphic design, and industrial design programs top marks, while liberal arts are considered more of a "joke." As a graphic design major explains, "Liberals arts is pretty limited, and it is hard to relate courses back to our majors." That said, bachelor's and master's programs in art history are available, complementing offerings in furniture design (for undergrads) and architecture and interior architecture (for grad students). RISD also offers cross-registration at adjacent Brown University for students seeking more diverse courses. The institute's highly specialized library contains 450,000 nonbook items (prints, etc.) and 80,000 volumes, and students are likely to be found at their personally assigned studio carrels. Perhaps RISD's most prized facility is its 100,000-piece art museum, a superlative collection that includes everything from Roman and Egyptian art to works by Monet, Matisse, and Picasso. A new wing has allowed more of these wonderful works to be viewed.

To graduate, students must be in residence for at least two years, and must complete a final-year project. They must also finish 126 credit hours—54 in their major, 18 in the Freshman Foundation program (an integrated year of "functional and conceptual experiences" that leads to "an understanding of visual language"), 42 in the liberal arts (art and architectural history, English, history/philosophy/social sciences, some electives), and 12 in nonmajor electives. Hands-on studio courses abound, and classes typically have fewer than 20 students. Still, an illustration major says, "Getting the courses you need is no problem. Getting the ones you want isn't hard, either—you can always petition the teacher." During RISD's winter session, six weeks between the first and second semesters, students are encouraged to take courses outside their major. And each year about 30 juniors and seniors venture to Rome for the European Honors Program, which offers independent study, projects with critics, and immersion in Italian culture.

While students at RISD don't "hit the books" in the traditional sense, the in-studio workload is tremendous. "Often the freshman year is said to be the most demanding in the nation," reports a senior. But "liberal arts classes are almost the opposite, very lax," notes a classmate. Students praise faculty members' knowledge and accessibility. "The quality of teachers is excellent—most are practicing, successful artists who teach because they like teaching, not because they need the money," an illustration major says. Career counseling offers lots of resources, but "it is not organized in an easy-to-understand way," notes a sculpture major.

RISD students (referred to as "RISDoids" or "Rizdees") come to Providence to form a largely urban mix of styles and personalities. In a word, the school is diverse, and that can create tension. "There's some resentment toward students, in particular some from overseas, who were accepted because they could pay full tuition, and now their lack of talent and/or effort brings down the level of our classes," a senior gripes. Indeed, only 8 percent of students are native Rhode Islanders, not surprising given the state's small size. Many of the rest are from the vicinity of other East Coast cities, notably New York and Boston. Though highly selective, RISD will often take a chance on students who did not perform well in high school (by the usual academic criteria), but make up for that with special artistic talent. The racial makeup of the campus is fairly mixed, with Asian-Americans making up 11 percent of the student body, blacks 2 percent, and Hispanics 3 percent. Issues of ethnicity and sexuality top the campus agenda, though a senior says that "generally, students are too wrapped up in their own little worlds to get organized and fight for anything." Tuition and fees here are steep, with the annual tab nearing $30,000. Though RISD offers some merit scholarships, athletic scholarships are nonexistent, and the school does not guarantee to meet financial need.

All noncommuting freshmen are required to live in coed dorms that one student says "can be a little beaten up by the artists who've lived there." The dorms are comfortable and feature common studio areas and connections to the campus computer network, but a graphic design major says "it is hard to get repairs done." The vast majority of upperclassmen move off campus to nearby apartments, many of which occupy floors of restored homes; RISD also owns an apartment building and some renovated Colonial and Victorian houses. All boarders buy the meal plan, which students say has improved of late.

Despite a student body that looks like it could have been plucked from the streets of New York's Greenwich Village, RISD is not the place to come for wild and funky nightlife. "Social life?" asks a senior. With three eight-hour studios each week, plus two other classes (and that's just freshman year), "typical social activity is running out for a cup of coffee. If you're desperate, there's always Brown University." The Taproom shown on the campus map went dry years ago,

The six-story Industrial Design building, designed by faculty member Jim Barnes, occupies the old Roitman furniture company warehouse. Its 50,000 square feet are designed for wood- and metal-working and prototype making.

The vast majority of upperclassmen move off campus to nearby apartments, many of which occupy floors of restored homes; RISD also owns an apartment building and some renovated Colonial and Victorian houses.

Though RISD isn't much for traditions, one big annual event is the Artist's Ball, a November formal where dress is "formal or festive, which has been interpreted as everything from chain mail to buck naked."

and each year, those 21 and over vote on whether to allow drinking in their residences. But underage students can swill "as long as they're responsible and don't draw attention to themselves," an illustration major says. Though RISD isn't much for traditions, one big annual event is the Artist's Ball, a November formal where dress is "formal or festive, which has been interpreted as everything from chain mail to buck naked," says a senior. "The only other event we're known for is graduation, which can be a real circus." When claustrophobia sets in, students can flee to the RISD farm, a 33-acre recreation area on the shores of nearby Narragansett Bay. Boston and New York are one and four hours away by train, respectively.

Though jocks are an endangered species at RISD, recreation opportunities abound. There is no intercollegiate sports program in the ordinary sense, though there is a hockey team, called the Nads (which, of course, leads to RISDoids hollering "Go Nads!").

Students do get involved in intramural sports, ranging from football and baseball to sailing and cycling. There's also a weight room for those who thrive on pumping iron.

Students come to RISD committed to their crafts, and most march to the beat of their own drummer as they rush from studio courses to gallery openings to exhibitions. But this professional preoccupation is not a problem. "We're very focused," says a senior. "We're in a specialized school because we know exactly what we want to do." RISD knows how to help them do it.

Overlaps

Pratt Institute, Parsons School of Design, Massachusetts College of Art, Cooper Union, Syracuse.

If You Apply To ➤

RISD…Early action: Dec. 15. Regular admissions and financial aid: Jan. 21 (priority), Feb. 15 (final). Does not guarantee to meet demonstrated need. Campus interviews: optional, informational. No alumni interviews. SATs or ACTs: required. SAT IIs: optional. Essay question: your educational goals and interests.

University of Rhode Island

Green Hall, Kingston, RI 02881

Website: www.uri.edu
Location: Small town
Total Enrollment: 14,577
Undergraduates: 10,639
Male/Female: 44/56
SAT Ranges: V 490–590 M 500–600
ACT Range: 21-27
Financial Aid: 62%
Expense: Pub $ $ $
Phi Beta Kappa: Yes
Applicants: 10,034
Accepted: 79%

Once known as a great party school, the University of Rhode Island is building a new reputation for challenging academics and friendly associations. In the years since President Robert Carothers cracked down on the wild drinking scene, the school has become more focused on Monday morning than Saturday night. "The students at URI are far more interested in studying than partying," says a biology major. "But that doesn't mean we don't let loose now and then."

URI's 2,000-acre campus is located in the small town of Kingston. Surrounded by farmland and only six miles from the coast, it is also within driving distance of cities such as Providence, Boston, and New York. The main academic buildings, a mixture of modern and "old New England granite," surround a central quad on Kingston Hill. At the foot of Kingston Hill lies the athletic buildings and agricultural fields. Plans are in the works for a new convocation center and a five-year renovation of the residence halls is also underway.

For their first two years, students here pursue a general education program in University College, which includes communication skills, fine arts and literature, natural and social sciences, letters, mathematics, foreign language, and culture requirements. All students also take a freshmen seminar titled Traditions and Transformations, designed to help ease the transition into college. Students then choose more specialized colleges, such as the nationally-ranked College of Pharmacy or the well-regarded marine or environmental sciences programs (housed within four different colleges). Newest additions to the curriculum include programs in public relations, international business, African and African American Studies, and marine biology. Weaker programs include studio art, communications, and education.

By and large, students here balance academic demands with a more laid-back atmosphere. "Though during the school hours it is pretty competitive, the majority of the time it is not that bad," says a sophomore. "It depends on the student." For most students, graduating in four years is not a problem, though getting the first-year classes they want can be challenging. Students are generally pleased with their professors and the overall quality of instruction; freshmen are usually taught by full professors, except in lab. "The quality of teaching at URI has been excellent," says a communicative disorders major. "The professors are very dedicated and put a lot of effort into making their classes interesting." Another student adds, "You won't find a more devoted group of professors than the ones who teach at URI." Outside of class, there are plenty of options, too, including the public-service-oriented University Year for Action, study abroad, independent study, and field placement. An honors program offers students the chance to work on individualized senior projects.

Though URI is becoming more popular with outsiders, Rhode Islanders still make up 63 percent of the student body. Twenty-three percent of the students are African American, Hispanic, Asian American, or a member of another minority group, and a junior says the school is "politically correct" and "strives for unity on campus." Students take an active role in encouraging diversity with groups such as URI Students for Social Change. Top students can vie for the 2,395 academic scholarships offered annually, which range from $200 to $11,286. About 240 athletic scholarships are offered in a variety of sports.

Only 36 percent of students live on campus, and while housing is guaranteed for those who get their money in on time, the dorms don't get rave reviews from students. "The tower-style dorms are not as well-maintained as the others, but are okay," says one student. "Many seniors live down by the beaches in the summer housing. Those are great houses." Many dorms are traditional—long hallways with bathrooms at the end—although some dorms have saunas, balconies, or weight rooms. A women's dorm and first-year student dorm complement the mostly coed, mixed-class halls. URI is in the process of renovating its dorms, with the goal of finishing the process by 2004. There is ample public transit, which is helpful since there's a chronic shortage of parking near campus. "The parking places always seem to be far away from everything!" grumbles a student. There are seven meal plans; options range from a cooked-to-order wok station to a pasta kiosk. In addition, students may participate in the All-Campus Card program, which can be used for services at campus restaurants, vending machines, movie theaters, and retail shops. Six percent of the men and 7 percent of the women belong to Greek organizations, and a sizable percentage of the student body commutes from home. While the hearty New England winters are invigorating for some, many students wind up catching colds, earning URI the unflattering nickname Upper Respiratory Infection.

Kingston is a sleepy New England college town, say most students. "We pretty much are the town," says a sophomore. Town-gown relations are good; the

(Continued)

Enrolled: 30%
Grad in 6 Years: 55%
Returning Freshmen: 79%
Academics: ✍ ✍
Social: ☎ ☎ ☎
Q of L: ★ ★ ★
Admissions: (401) 874-7000
Email Address:
  uriadmit@uri.edu

Strongest Programs:
  Pharmacy
  Engineering
  Marine and Environmental
  Sciences
  Communicative Disorders

All students also take a freshmen seminar titled Traditions and Transformations, designed to help ease the transition into college.

university mandates volunteer work as a segment of the required freshman seminar, and clothing drives, food drives, and work with children are common, says a finance and accounting major. URI is also within striking distance of both Rhode Island's famous beaches and the major New England ski slopes. Newport, with its heady social scene, is just 20 minutes away, and those feeling lucky can get to the Foxwoods Resort and Casino in 45 minutes. Other fun road trips include Providence (30 minutes), Boston (90 minutes), and New York City (4 hours).

Many natives find going home on weekends a pleasant diversion, but on campus there are always movies and guest speakers, plus the usual Greek parties. The campus coffeehouse hosts open mike nights, and movie theaters, clubs, and malls beckon just off campus. The student newspaper that covers it all has one of the most original names anywhere: *The Good 5¢ Cigar.*

Sports are big at Rhode Island, and basketball games are especially exciting. Midnight Madness (the team's first sanctioned practice of the year) is always well attended, and URI fans love it when the team defeats archrival Providence College. URI's men's basketball made a big splash at the NCAA Tournament in 1998 by making all the way to the Elite 8, beating out powerhouses Kansas and Valparaiso on the way. As befits the school's locale, sailing draws much interest, and the team regularly produces all-Americans. Oozeball, volleyball played in deep mud, is a favorite among weekend warriors.

Centrally located in dense New England, URI students are close to the beaches and ski slopes, and within easy reach of some major cities. The administration works hard and the students feel at home. "This is a place where lifelong friends and great memories are made," says a biology major.

If You Apply To ➤ URI…Early action: Dec. 15. Rolling admissions and financial aid: Mar. 1. Meets demonstrated need of 71%. Campus interviews: recommended, evaluative. Alumni interviews: optional, evaluative. SATs or ACTs: required. Essay question: personal statement (optional).

Rhodes College

2000 North Parkway, Memphis, TN 38112-1690

Website: www.rhodes.edu
Location: City residential
Total Enrollment: 1,510
Undergraduates: 1,499
Male/Female: 45/55
SAT Ranges: V 590–700 M 600–690
ACT Range: 26–30
Financial Aid: 46%
Expense: Pr $ $
Phi Beta Kappa: Yes
Applicants: 2,273
Accepted: 77%

The Rhodents of Rhodes College are some of the most trusted students in the nation. Students at this leading Southern liberal arts school are part of an honor system that expects—and requires—students not to cheat, lie, or steal. The Honor Code and Council are two of the oldest traditions at Rhodes College. "The honor system creates a special spirit of trust and respect on campus." Professors leave the classroom during exams, and there are no meal cards to prove who's on the meal plan. Students are assumed to be honest and capable of policing themselves. This high level of trust along with a caring faculty and small classes provides the students here with a gratifying college experience.

Rhodes was founded as a Presbyterian school in 1848 in Clarksville, Tennessee, and moved to Memphis in 1925. The 100-acre campus is located in a residential section of midtown Memphis, across the street from a 175-acre park housing the city's largest art museum, a golf course, and the Memphis Zoo. The original Gothic structures of brownish orange stone, leaded-glass windows, and slate roofs have served as models for all forthcoming buildings. With the exception of its underground science center, Rhodes's elegant, old-fashioned tonality remains intact. Thirteen of the original buildings are listed on the National Register of Historic Places. The newest addition to the campus is the $22.5-million Bryan Campus Life Center, which provides extensive facilities for sports and fitness (squash and racquetball courts, a suspended indoor track, and a sports arena) and extracurricular activities. It is the largest gothic structure built in America in 40 years.

Rhodes offers a wide array of traditional and interdisciplinary programs. The natural sciences are Rhodes's forte (biology is the most popular major), and labs are equipped with state-of-the-art equipment. Strong programs also exist in business administration, economics, and English (Renaissance literature is especially strong). The political science department has produced four national championship teams at the National Intercollegiate Mock Trial Tournament. The respected international studies program offers summer internships abroad in exciting locales such as Madrid, Hong Kong, and Johannesburg through the Buckman International Fellows program. And the burgeoning Greek and Roman Studies program offers a travel-study option that includes a 24-day excursion to Greece and sizable scholarships. Rhodes is also a member of the Associated Colleges of the South consortium.*

In addition to standard distribution requirements and a foreign language mandate, all students must fulfill a humanities requirement that includes taking a four-course sequence from the following: Search for Values in the Light of Western History and Religion (SEARCH for short) or Life: Then and Now. The SEARCH course (previously called MAN) has been a staple of the school's curriculum for almost 50 years. It takes students through the whole history and culture of Western civilization, with a special emphasis on the Bible. With lectures, seminars, honors programs, one-on-one tutorials, studies at Oxford, supervised internships, bridge (multiple) majors, and independent Directed Inquiry, there are dozens of ways to get an education at Rhodes. In addition, Rhodes now has exchange programs in countries including France, Japan, Scotland, and Belgium. Also popular is the Dual Degree Program with Washington University, which has defined tracks for engineering students.

The workload and curriculum are demanding but not unreasonable. "Students here value academics and so they place their studies high on their priority list," says a political science major. Rhodes's small size and the professors' attention keep the learning process informal and intimate. "I am constantly amazed by the amount of time and enthusiasm professors put into class lectures and discussion," a religious studies major says. Even though classes are small, most students say they've had few problems at registration. "We have a high-tech computer program that successfully matches students with their courses based on the student's need or demand for a course," explains a political science major. Both academic and career counseling programs receive high marks.

Rhodents come from a fairly homogeneous background. Students are drawn from both public and private schools, with 56 percent from the top tenth of their high school class. The flavor of Rhodes's student body is definitely Southern, and about a third of the undergraduates come from both rural and urban areas of Tennessee. The student body is 91 percent Caucasian, 3 percent Asian American, 4 percent African American, and 1 percent Hispanic. "It is a very conservative, mostly white school," observes one sophomore. "We want more diversity." The college has a healthy endowment, and while financial aid has been cut recently, the school still offers merit-based scholarships.

(Continued)

Enrolled: 25%

Grad in 6 Years: 71%

Returning Freshmen: 83%

Academics: ✍ ✍ ✍

Social: ☎ ☎ ☎

Q of L: ★ ★ ★

Admissions: (901) 843-3700 or (800) 844-5969

Email Address:
adminfo@rhodes.edu

Strongest Programs:
Biology
Chemistry
Physics
International Studies
English
Economics
Political Science
Business Administration

The natural sciences are Rhodes's forte (biology is the most popular major), and labs are equipped with state-of-the-art equipment.

The political science department has produced four national championship teams at the National Intercollegiate Mock Trial Tournament.

All dorms are single-sex, air-conditioned, and clean; some attract students with a special "academic interest" like French or art. "The dorms are old but still comfortable," says a senior. Freshmen occupy their own single-sex residence halls (the best are said to be Glassell for men and Williford for women) while upperclassmen fend for the rooms they want in the yearly lottery. Thirty percent of the students live off campus, where room and board can be cheaper, but few recommend the move. "Residence halls have the most convenient parking and are a short walk from computer labs, the library, campus, dining...and most important, their friends on campus," says one happy resident. Regarding meals, more than one student admits the food is "pretty bad."

Campus security is tight: an ironwork fence encircles the whole 100 acres and residence halls remain locked at all times. Rhodes also has a 24-hour escort policy and 60 emergency phones across campus. "Although Memphis can be frightening, the campus is extremely safe," states a biology major. "I have never felt unsafe walking across the campus at night alone."

Much of social life takes place on campus. Activities include bands, movies, and amphitheater parties such as the Rites of Spring (three days of nonstop music, picnics, and a mud-slinging contest). "We have a new campus life center and a lot of people hang out there during the week," says a biology major. The Greek scene draws quite a few Rhodents: 57 percent of the men join fraternities, 55 percent of the women pledge to sororities. Since Greeks do not live in their houses, the tension between "Greeks and Freaks" is kept within reasonable bounds. The school's alcohol policy allows on-campus parties where those 21 or older can drink in the presence of underage students. One senior warns, "Twenty-one-year-olds are required to wear bracelets when drinking [each bracelet has a number on it that is registered to the student]." As for sports, there's not much sweat here but rivals include Sewanee and Trinity. The women do well in tennis, and the women's track team recently won a title as did the men's soccer and cross-country teams.

Rhodes now has exchange programs in countries including France, Japan, Scotland, and Belgium.

With all of Memphis just outside the gate, who cares about sports anyway? Memphis is famous for being the hometown of the King (a.k.a. Elvis) but that's not all—it's the stomping ground of W. C. Handy, "the Father of the Blues," and Beale Street is also a main attraction. In May, the city sponsors a cultural festival, including everything from barbecue-cooking contests to the Sunset Symphony. Aside from enjoying the city's leisure activities, Rhodes College maintains a strong tradition of community service. "Approximately 70 percent of our student body participate in a volunteer program on a regular basis," declares a senior. "Service is promoted and is a very large part of Rhodes."

The Rhodents of Rhodes College receive an enriching education while enjoying the freedom of trust and honesty. Like a mouse to cheese, they are lured to their Memphis home away from home.

Overlaps

Vanderbilt, Tulane, University of the South, Trinity College, Davidson.

If You Apply To ➤   **Rhodes**...Early decision: Dec. 1. Does not guarantee to meet demonstrated need. Campus interviews: recommended, evaluative and informational. No alumni interviews. SATs or ACTs: required. SAT IIs: optional. Essay question: significant person or experience; issue of concern; illustrated biography.

Rice University

6100 Main Street MS-17, Houston, TX 77005-1892

The phrase "big things come in small packages" is more than just a cliché when considering Rice University in Houston, Texas. With top-notch programs in the liberal arts and sciences, a huge endowment ($2 billion), and a below-average tuition, Rice is one of the best buys around. It is the dominant university in the Southwest, and second only to Duke in the entire South. Add to that a strong football team, a spirited student body, and an impressive success rate for graduates, and you've got yourself an incredible deal.

Created under the will of legendary Texas cotton mogul William Marsh Rice nearly 100 years ago, Rice was modeled after such disparate institutions as progressive, tuition-free Cooper Union and the more traditional Princeton University. Despite its resemblance to other institutions, Rice maintains distinctive characteristics of its own. The predominant architectural theme of the campus, situated three miles from downtown Houston, is Spanish Mediterranean, and it's surrounded by a row of hedges—the singular buffer between the quiet campus and the sounds of the city. Two recent campus additions are the Baker Institute for Public Policy and a center for nanoscale science and technology.

The students tend to put a lot of pressure on themselves to succeed. "Most classes are graded on a curve," reports a managerial studies student. "So students are not just competing to get an A, but also competing with each other to define what an A is."

And no matter how much coursework is assigned, "you can always be assured that someone else will have more." Science and engineering are the strongest programs here; competition in the engineering and premed programs is especially intense, and each year a good number of students who start in these fields retreat to the humanities, which in general are less demanding. In fact, Rice has a long tradition of encouraging double, and even triple, majors in such seemingly opposite fields as electrical engineering and art history. Engineering is the most popular major, followed by English, managerial studies, biology, and economics.

Architecture is one of the finest undergraduate programs in the nation, and the space physics program works closely with NASA. The university excels in the sciences and engineering, and the SEs (as these students are called) still dominate the student body. Rice has a fairly new department of biochemistry and cell biology, housed in the up-to-date bioscience/bioengineering building. Under a Mellon Foundation grant, humanities majors can spend the spring and summer of their senior year in "responsible" positions, mainly with local corporations. Some students give less than favorable reviews to social and computer science offerings; foreign languages (especially German) aren't recommended either.

Under the area-major program, students can draw up proposals for independent interdisciplinary majors. An additional option is the "coherent minor" program, which can replace distribution requirements. All students are required to take foundation courses in areas outside of their major fields. Hence, science and engineering majors must take their foundation courses in humanities; social science and humanities majors must take them in science; and music and architecture students must take them all. Class size rarely presents a problem: "One of my classes has four students, and another one has about one hundred," reports a student, "and all the others are somewhere in between." Faculty members for the most part are friendly and accessible, sometimes providing upperclassmen with

Sidebar

Website: www.rice.edu

Location: Urban

Total Enrollment: 4,285

Undergraduates: 2,714

Male/Female: 56/44

SAT Ranges: V 650–760 M 680–770

ACT Ranges: 30–34

Financial Aid: 85%

Expense: Pr $

Phi Beta Kappa: Yes

Applicants: 6,375

Accepted: 27%

Enrolled: 40%

Grad in 6 Years: 86%

Returning Freshmen: 95%

Academics: 🖊 🖊 🖊 🖊 🖊

Social: ☎ ☎ ☎

Q of L: ★ ★ ♠ ♠

Admissions: (713) 527-4036 or (800) 527-OWLS

Email Address: admi@rice.edu

Strongest Programs:
Architecture
Space Physics
Engineering
History
Music

Because much of the university's $2-billion endowment is dedicated to keeping tuition low, Rice costs thousands of dollars less than most other selective, private universities.

research opportunities. "The professors eat with students, attend parties, and even coach intramural teams," one student reports. Under an extensive advising system, incoming students are assigned two or three student counselors and two professors during the first two years. Everyone operates under the honor system, and most exams go unsupervised.

Those who want to take their education on the road can visit Swarthmore, and there are internships for engineering and architecture students. The library is stocked with most needed materials and, thanks to a renovation, has become more inviting. The career counseling program is a disappointment to many. "They essentially cater to engineering majors and pretty much forget about seniors in the humanities and social sciences," says one biology/anthropology major. But the administration reorganized the Career Services Center and now notes "limited data" as the only drawback.

Rice was founded to serve "residents of Houston and the state of Texas," but Texans no longer dominate the student body. Today, 51 percent of Rice students come from out of state, with high percentages transplanted from California, Florida, the Northeast, and other Southern states. Sixteen percent of the student body are Asian-American, 10 percent are Hispanic, and 7 percent are African-American. Many students claim that, by Texas standards anyway, they are liberal. Others report an intense amount of political apathy. Because much of the university's $2-billion endowment is dedicated to keeping tuition low, Rice costs thousands of dollars less than most other selective, private universities. Still, for all its riches, Rice is still fairly provincial Texas. Rice guarantees to meet the full demonstrated need of every admit, and there are a variety of merit scholarships available every year, ranging from $1,000 to full tuition. There are also a number of athletic scholarships awarded to both men and women.

Fraternities and sororities are forbidden on campus—Rice's founder did not approve of elitist organizations—but their functions are largely assumed by the eight residential colleges, Rice's version of dorms. Each college houses about 225 students, who remain affiliated with it for all four years and develop a strong sense of community, even for those who later move off campus. Freshmen are assigned a college depending on their preference for one of the eight coed dorms. Many freshmen enjoy rooms as spacious as their older colleagues, and a dormer contends that "no college is better than another, they're just different." Air-conditioning is a standard weapon against Houston's muggy climate. Everyone is guaranteed a room for at least three of the four years, though students sit through a lottery system. About 25 percent of the students go packing, many seeking quieter surroundings and cheaper rents. Students can eat at any of the college dining halls, and cafeteria-hopping can be a "great way to meet people." Though the food receives average marks for college cafeteria food, students report that it's getting better with each year. Apparently the salad bar and frozen yogurt machines have won converts.

Houston has plenty of nightlife, but to enjoy it bring a car; mass transit is virtually nonexistent. Luckily, parking on campus is easy. Galveston's beaches on the Gulf of Mexico are only 45 minutes away, and heading for New Orleans, especially in February, can make a great weekend trip. In fact, there's only one problem with the school's location: It attracts blackbirds—every year, during the rainy winter, about a million of these squawking creatures roost at Rice. So far even the campus ornithologists have not come up with an explanation for the birds.

Ardent football fans are positively glowing about Rice's resurgence on the gridiron. With a conference title in 1995, the Owls are a talented bunch with a bright future in football. Tearing down the goalposts after home victories remains a happy Rice tradition. A familiar chant echoes, "Two, four, six, eight, our players graduate." Other strong programs include baseball, women's cross-country, men's indoor track, and both men's and women's tennis. Rice students go really wild for intramurals—the most popular pits the colleges against each other in a Beer-Bike Race in which coed teams of 20 chug cans of beer and speed around a bicycle track—which gives them a chance to let off academic steam.

Students don't have time to plan anything more formal on weekends than the traditional TGIF lawn parties on Friday afternoons, but campus-wide parties sponsored by one of the residential colleges spring up from time to time. Night of Decadence is Rice's Halloween party, where it is reported that the students appear in "lingerie or less." Drinking age or no, students are expected to unwind on the weekends. "People who study constantly are considered dullards, and people who are negligent about academics aren't taken seriously," a history and English major explains. If nothing else, there's always the campus movie.

Rice has a reputation for doing better in academics rather than in athletics. But the students don't mind too much. Instead they yell, "That's all right, that's OK, you're gonna work for us someday." In fact, 53 percent of them head straight to jobs after graduation, wasting no time in climbing those corporate ladders or hitching themselves to a dot-com. But most don't like to leave. They've had a terrific academic experience and a decent social life for four years, and their wallets are still thick thanks to a pint-sized tuition.

Overlaps

Stanford, Harvard, MIT, Princeton, Duke.

If You Apply To > | **Rice**...Early decision: Nov. 1. Early action: Dec. 1. Regular admissions: Jan. 1. Housing: Jan. 1, May 1. Guarantees to meet demonstrated need. Campus or alumni interviews: recommended, evaluative. SATs or ACTs required. SAT IIs: required (varies by program). Essay question: important experience, achievement, or interest; issue of concern; or influential person or event.

University of Richmond

28 Westhampton Way, Richmond, VA 23173

Travel to the University of Richmond and you won't find too many students sitting on their porches sipping mint juleps. That's because students are hard at work trying to make a name for themselves in business, science, and the arts. Small classes and terrific faculty interaction are just a few of the perks of being a Richmond Spider—and they even make up for having an arachnid for a school mascot. "Aside from having one of the most beautiful campuses in the country, the students have healthy attitudes toward their education," one freshman says. "We know when to study and when to party, and we do both of them really well."

The school's 350-acre campus is situated amid rolling hills, stately pines, and a 10-acre lake. Located about 15 minutes from downtown, the university's academic buildings, residence halls, and athletic and student-life facilities are designed in traditional collegiate Gothic architecture. Students are housed in two single-sex residential colleges: Richmond College for men and Westhampton College for women. While this system emphasizes a single-gender residential and student government experience, 25 percent of the students, mostly upperclassmen, live in coed apartments available on campus, and all study within a fully coeducational academic program.

Website: www.richmond.edu
Location: Suburban
Total Enrollment: 3,777
Undergraduates: 3,034
Male/Female: 50/50
SAT Ranges: V 600–680 M 620–690
ACT Range: 27–30
Financial Aid: 31%
Expense: Pr $ $
Phi Beta Kappa: Yes
Applicants: 6,234
Accepted: 44%
Enrolled: 32%
Grad in 6 Years: 84%

(Continued)

Returning Freshmen: 92%

Academics: ✍ ✍ ✍

Social: ☎ ☎ ☎

Q of L: ★ ★ ★

Admissions: (804) 289-8640

Email Address: N/A

Strongest Programs:
Biology
Business
International Studies
English
History
Psychology
Leadership Studies

Business is the most popular major, followed by biology, political science, international studies, and English, all of which are considered strong programs. The business school enrolls students who have completed two years in the School of Arts and Sciences, and it's exceptionally popular among eager, financially ambitious students. The International Studies major has been gaining in popularity recently, and the E. Claiborne School of Business has instated an International Business Major to accommodate for this trend. As most Richmond students are considered pre-professional, the arts, theater, and hard science majors garner low ratings from students. The Jepson School of Leadership Studies is, according to the administration, the nation's first school of its type and is dedicated to leadership in service to society. Majors in this school must complete an internship in a social service organization.

One of Richmond's most valuable assets is its small class size and accessible faculty. First-year students are guaranteed classes with full professors, all of whom have completed a Ph.D. in their field. With the exception of a handful of courses, Richmond classes generally have twenty-five students or fewer. "Nothing beats the quality of the professors," raves one student. "They know their areas well and are very dedicated to giving the students the best education possible." Students have a love/hate relationship with the university's general ed requirements, which include courses in expository writing, foreign language to the intermediate level (now including Chinese and Japanese), dimensions of wellness and phys ed (though this is being phased out in an effort to redirect resources toward other programs), and two semesters of core courses, including "Exploring the Human Experience," a required course for first-year students. Students describe their Richmond education as academically rigorous, but not overly competitive. "There is a certain amount of competitiveness between students, but students also offer a lot of help to each other," says one student.

Most of the Richmond student body hails from out-of-state, only 17 percent are Virginia residents. Richmond students are overwhelmingly white (86 percent), with only 6 percent African American, 3 percent Asian American, and 3 percent Hispanic. The university does, however, draw a small, but growing percentage of international students. Students admit the lack of diversity, but are quick to point out that "while in terms of skin color the student population may be largely similar, students do enjoy diversity of thought, activity, and background." The university sponsors a host of workshops and programs, including a White House Unity Program, aimed at discussing race relations on campus. Richmond offers 55 merit scholarships, ranging from half to full tuition, including benefits, and 168 athletic scholarships.

Programs such as WILL (Women Involved in Living and Learning) and Spinning Your Web, an orientation program for first-year men, are two approaches the university has tried to educate students on gender. The university also sponsors Richmond Quest, a "biennial campus-wide investigation of a single issue, put in the form of a question." Every department and organization on campus participates in Richmond Quest, and every two years the student who poses the winning question wins a full-tuition scholarship which can be directed towards university tuition or graduate school.

A whopping 92 percent of students live on campus all four years, a testament to the high quality of residential life at Richmond. Most residence halls and student apartments are newly built or recently remodeled, and blend in tastefully with the older, more typically collegiate Gothic buildings. Campus housing also includes townhouses—University Forest Apartments—but these options are open only to upperclassmen. Men's and women's residence halls are a 15-minute walk

First-year students who are invited into the Honors Law Program and maintain a 3.4 GPA while at Richmond are guaranteed admission into the U of Richmond's law school without taking the LSAT.

apart, an outmoded arrangement that draws more than its share of grumbles.

Richmond students mirror the administration's dual focus on keeping in line with tradition while simultaneously pushing forward with new initiatives. Most Richmond students say that the university's traditions, though tedious at times with women and men living on separate sides of the lake, make it unique among its liberal arts school peers. On Proclamation Night, women write letters to themselves on their goals for college during a candlelight service, which they will read when they are seniors. During the Ring Dance, junior women don white gowns while they are presented with their class ring. Richmond College freshman males have Investiture Night, when they officially are inducted into the university. At the end of the school year, Richmond students celebrate with a campus-wide Pig Roast, where every fraternity opens itself and serves "cheap beer and great barbeque." While some of these traditions may fuel the perception of the University of Richmond as the "University of Rich Kids," students attempt to combat the stereotype by engaging in community service throughout the city. While most say that Richmond isn't a huge college town, many students travel into the city to do some kind of volunteer work, or just to hang out at bars downtown on a Thursday night.

The weekend begins on Thursday at Richmond, with many upperclassmen caravaning downtown to hit the throng of bars and restaurants at Shockoe Bottom. On campus, Fraternity Row is the place to see and be seen, but there are also comedians, movies, bands, and even hypnotists each weekend on The Pier, a coffeehouse-type atmosphere that was established in the wake of allegations of sexism against fraternities. While most Richmond students prefer to stick around on weekends, popular road trip destinations include Daytona Beach for Spring Break and Nags Head or Myrtle Beach for the end-of-the-year Beach Week.

Richmond competes in Division I athletics, and the men's baseball and basketball teams have brought home Colonial Athletic Association titles in the past. Women's tennis is also strong. The synchronized swimming team also placed third at the collegiate championships. Basketball is the most popular varsity sport, followed by football (the school's only Division I-AA team). Games that draw the biggest crowds feature rivals such as William and Mary and UNC-Wilmington. For those interested in actually playing a sport, intramurals are a popular option. The recently renovated Spider Sports Center also provides a state-of-the-art facility in which students are free to work out on their own time.

Richmond is a great choice for students looking for a full, fast-paced academic, extracurricular, and social life. One student describes a day in the life of a Richmond student as a harried affair, and "somewhere along the way [students] go to class, intern, volunteer, attend Student Government meetings, take step aerobics, feed the homeless, and give blood. Sleep? Who needs sleep?"

Programs such as WILL (Women Involved in Living and Learning) and Spinning Your Web, an orientation program for first-year men, are two approaches the university has tried to educate students on gender.

Overlaps

University of Virginia, William and Mary, Wake Forest, Boston College, Vanderbilt.

If You Apply To ➤

Richmond...Early decision: Nov. 15, Jan. 15. Regular admissions: Jan. 15. Financial aid: Feb. 25. Housing: May 1. Does not guarantee to meet demonstrated need. No campus or alumni interviews. ACTs or SATs: required. SAT IIs: required without ACT only (writing and math). Accepts the Common Application and electronic applications. Essay question: describe an independent study project; influential public figure; pressing social issue; personal statement.

300 Seward Street, P.O. Box 248, Ripon, WI 54971

Website: www.ripon.edu

Location: Small town

Total Enrollment: 746

Undergraduates: 746

Male/Female: 48/52

SAT Ranges: V 580–650 M
   580–630

ACT Range: 20–29

Financial Aid: 80%

Expense: Pr $ $

Phi Beta Kappa: Yes

Applicants: 824

Accepted: 87%

Enrolled: 39%

Grad in 6 Years: 56%

Returning Freshmen: 85%

Academics: 🖉 🖉 🖉

Social: ☎ ☎ ☎

Q of L: ★ ★ ★

Admissions: (920) 748-8337

Email Address:
   adminfo@ripon.edu

Strongest Programs:
   Biology
   English
   History

The chemistry and biology (especially premed) programs at Ripon are particularly strong and well known, and are enjoying the benefits of an ongoing $4.5-million renovation of the science center.

Ripon College, affectionately known as "The Cookie College," gets its nickname from a local sweetspot. But the cookie factory is not the only source of sweetness around these parts. "Everyone looks out for everyone and cares," coos one delighted Red Hawk. It's a good thing Ripon students like each other so much, because the school enrolls less than 700 of them. And when it gets cold, students depend on each other and residents of their small town for just about everything. "Because we are so small in size, we are like a close-knit family," boasts one freshman.

Set on a hill in a tiny east-central Wisconsin town, just a block from Main Street, Ripon's 250-acre campus features tree-lined walks, wetlands, prairie, and woods, and a mixture of 19th- and 20th-century architecture that gives the campus a "majestic" atmosphere. Founded as a coed school in 1851, Ripon is a place where the curriculum is rooted in tradition, and there is little room for dabbling in trendy educational fashions. Academic work does take a high priority among Ripon students, and while the quiet, rural setting has both cultural and down-home Midwestern activities for those who seek them out, there isn't much danger of twinkling neon lights distracting anyone from his or her studies. Students spend anywhere from 10 to 25 hours a week studying. The courses are rigorous but not unusually so, and just as anywhere else, there are competitive people. "Not a large sense of competitiveness, but rather students helping students," a French/elementary education double major says.

The chemistry and biology (especially premed) programs at Ripon are particularly strong and well known, and enjoy the benefits of the science center. Other departments that get high marks include English, history, physics, politics and government, economics, and psychology. Religion is a one-person department, and is said to be weaker than other majors. Latin American studies could also use some improvement. The most popular majors are biology, history, English, business, and theater. Recently, an Environmental Studies major was added. Students eager to finish college in three years should investigate Ripon's accelerated-degree program.

Distribution requirements cover natural sciences and mathematics, foreign language, writing skills, behavioral and social sciences, fine arts, humanities, global studies, and physical education. In addition, freshmen are required to take Introduction to the Liberal Arts. Ripon students delight in their small classes; if the student/faculty ratio wasn't the reason they applied here, it's one reason they stay. "These are the most concerned and dedicated professors that I have ever encountered," says a junior. Students and professors are regularly on a first-name basis, and critiques of the academic advising range from superb to just plain excellent. Students agree that the school's smallness is its best quality, and they report no problems getting the classes they need. For temporary changes of scenery, study abroad is available through the college's own programs in Chicago and overseas (German majors may study in Bonn), in addition to programs sponsored by the Associated Colleges of the Midwest.* The Fisk Exchange program with Fisk University has improved diversity and race relations between Ripon and the predominately black Southern university.

Seventy-one percent of the Ripon student body hails from Wisconsin. Overall, students come from 41 different states and 19 different countries. The vast majority are white, upper-middle-class conservatives, with Asian Americans, African Americans, and Hispanics accounting for 6 percent of the population. Twenty-eight percent come from the top tenth of their high school graduating class. With enrollment down more than 300 from the early 1970s, officials are hoping for more widespread recognition of the school. The college offers a variety of renewable merit awards ranging from $1,000 to full tuition. No athletic scholarships are available, although the school does promote an athletic program.

Freshmen are housed together and are given a choice between coed and single-sex halls, as are the upperclassmen. Ninety-four percent of the students live on campus. For most dorms, those students who want singles will have to pay a premium each term. One student comments on some dorm perks, "great facilities like exercise rooms and free laundry rooms, and entertainers are brought into the halls and union weekly." All students eat in one large dining hall, and food is described as good and plentiful. Campus security measures include regular foot patrols and key cards for access to residence halls.

The small Midwestern town of Ripon (about 7,500 residents) is well known to history buffs as the birthplace of the Republican party—at a meeting on the college campus on February 28, 1854, to be exact. One student describes the town as "very supportive of the college." Where else do you find a community that holds a welcome-back picnic for students at the beginning of the year? Students pay back in the form of volunteer work. Ripon officials boast that their little town is so safe that many people don't bother to lock their doors or chain their bicycles. For students who want to get away on weekends, Chicago is a three-hour drive; Milwaukee is just 80 miles away. For those staying in town, local bars offer a break from boredom for those 21 and older. The school's new BYOB policy allows of-age students to imbibe on campus, while those under 21 must skirt school rules to drink. Other social activities include an array of concerts, plays, and cultural activities including free Wednesday night movies. A weekend of dancing and music in the spring attracts alumni back to the campus enclave. "Most of the social life happens on campus. There are always fun activities to do," cheers one student. Fifty-nine percent of the men enroll in fraternities and 33 percent of the women opt to join sororities, and with all Greeks living in dorms and eating in the dining hall, there is little tension between them and nonmembers. Fraternity parties are the main form of campus social life, and Ripon is so darned friendly that independents are included in just about all Greek events.

Ripon is located in the wonderful North Woods territory, a spot in the state where the scattered trees begin to grow thicker and then give way to rugged pine forests. Frozen lakes and a blanket of snow are a natural part of the winter landscape, and students can cross-country and downhill ski, toboggan, skate, and attend dogsled and iceboat races. Nearby Green Lake boasts facilities for skiing and, when it's not winter ("for one month during the year," warns one student), facilities for water sports. Athletic matches against the rival team from Lawrence University usually draw excited crowds. Strong teams include men's and women's basketball. Other attractions in terms of athletic facilities include a women's softball field, intramurals field, baseball field, and six tennis courts—all new.

The small-town atmosphere is both the greatest asset and the greatest liability of this liberal arts college. Students appreciate the intimacy of their classes and the attention they get from their professors, but the lack of privacy can be a high price to pay. As one student admits, "the school is too small and word gets around fast." At the same time a student says, "It is so special because everyone cares about each other and looks out for others."

The college offers a variety of renewable merit awards ranging from $1,000 to full tuition. No athletic scholarships are available, although the school does promote an athletic program.

Frozen lakes and a blanket of snow are a natural part of the winter landscape, and students can cross-country and downhill ski, toboggan, skate, and attend dogsled and iceboat races.

Overlaps

University of Wisconsin–Madison, St. Norbert, Carroll College, University of Wisconsin–Stevens Point, Lawrence.

Rochester Institute of Technology

60 Lomb Memorial Drive, Rochester, NY 14623-5604

Website: www.rit.edu

Location: Suburban

Total Enrollment: 12,775

Undergraduates: 10,746

Male/Female: 65/35

SAT Ranges: V 520–620 M 560–660

ACT Range: 22–28

Financial Aid: 75%

Expense: Pr $ $

Phi Beta Kappa: No

Applicants: 7,497

Accepted: 77%

Enrolled: 38%

Grad in 6 Years: 60%

Returning Freshmen: 85%

Academics: ✍ ✍ ✍

Social: ☎ ☎ ☎

Q of L: ★ ★ ★

Admissions: (716) 475-6631

Email Address:
admissions@rit.edu

Strongest Programs:
Photography
Computer Science
Engineering
Business

The first undergraduate school to offer programs in software engineering, imaging science, and microelectronics, the Rochester Institute of Technology is as career-oriented as they come. Students looking for challenging, up to date technological training will be at home at RIT, and those who are geared up and ready to go professional will be happy to know that the school places 2,700 juniors and seniors in full-time paid positions in business and industry. At RIT, the focus is on career-oriented and technology-based academic programs. Be warned: If you're still trying to figure out how to set the clock on your VCR, or you only use computers to play solitaire, then the Rochester Institute of Technology is probably not the place for you.

The main campus is located on 1,300 suburban acres, six miles from downtown Rochester. RIT shares the city with six nearby colleges, making Rochester "quite a college town." The campus was built in 1968, when the institute moved from its original location downtown. The redbrick buildings have sharp, contemporary lines. A major $8-million addition to the College of Science opened last year, providing new laboratory facilities and classrooms fully equipped with the latest technology for multimedia-based instruction.

The institute specializes in carving out niches for itself with unusual programs, and majors are offered in more than 200 fields, from basic electrical and mechanical engineering to packaging science and nuclear medicine technology. Fortunately, applicants narrow the range of choices to a manageable size by applying to one of seven undergraduate colleges: applied science and technology, business, engineering, imaging arts and sciences, liberal arts, science, and the National Technical Institute for the Deaf (NTID). Created for the hearing-impaired, NTID offers students technical and professional training in more than 30 programs, including business, science and engineering, and visual communications. NTID students and faculty use a combination of communication methods including sign language, fingerspelling, and visual aids, and the college boasts a placement rate of 95 percent. New programs include the nation's first undergraduate program in New Media. This program combines graphic design, printing, publishing, and information technology courses to help students prepare for jobs in digital-based media such as the World Wide Web.

Predictably, engineering is the most popular major, but one might be surprised to know that the third-most popular major is art and design. Engineering technology, business, and photography (Rochester is home to Eastman Kodak) also grace the top of the list. Academic programs include aerospace engineering, environmental management, food marketing and distribution, information technology, and a physician assistant program. The RIT School for American Crafts offers excellent programs in ceramics, woodworking, glass, metalcraft, and jewelry making, and students have the run of Brevier Gallery, where visiting artists provide firsthand instruction. The small College of Liberal Arts, which offers only five degree programs, is cited as weaker than the other colleges.

All students take liberal arts requirements, which total a third of their undergraduate work and include a senior seminar and project. These requirements are offered through the college of liberal arts and include courses in humanities, social science, and English composition. Students also must take three physical education courses, but the emphasis is more on health and wellness than competitive sports. Unlike many universities, RIT allows freshmen to schedule significant coursework in their major early on, and spreads out liberal arts requirements over a more extended period. RIT's academic pressure is fairly high, although it is not a competitive pressure. "The coursework is very, very tough, but not impossible," says a mechanical engineering major. "I feel that it is pretty competitive. The courses are challenging but well worth the work required," states another student. Many faculty members lead a double life with some kind of commitment to the professional world. "The professors have all been in the 'real world,' and can relate the theoretical to the applied," says one student. Career counseling is a "great system" according to students, but it is up to each individual to utilize the resources.

Forty percent of undergraduates come from outside New York State, and most of those are from New Jersey, Pennsylvania, and Connecticut. Minorities make up 14 percent of the student body: 5 percent are African American, 3 percent are Hispanic, and 6 percent are Asian American. Preprofessionalism is a common bond, but beyond that interests vary. The unique mix of art, engineering, business, and science students, along with the large number of deaf students, creates a diverse atmosphere on campus. "It seems like everyone has a different attitude towards school, and looks at it differently," explains one junior. RIT admits without regard to student financial need, and it meets the demonstrated need of 90 percent of the students for as long as the funds allow. RIT offers over 1,800 renewable merit scholarships to each freshman class, ranging from $500 to $17,934, made without reference to need. Most of the time students are oblivious to the issues going on in the outside world because "we are too busy with our own work," a student says.

Seventy percent of the students live in college dorms and apartments, and students report that getting a room is not that difficult. Freshmen are required to live in the dorms, while upperclassmen can vie for campus apartments through a lottery, but that shouldn't be too tough since, according to the administration, RIT has the largest number of on-campus apartments in the country. Recently 700 new campus apartment units were added. Dorms are well maintained and offer a variety of living styles: single-sex, coed by room, or coed by floor. Special-interest floors range from nonsmoking to "mainstream" (with hearing-impaired students). Campus residents choose among several meal plans, all of which provide good food from the campus-run food service. Those who choose to live off campus take advantage of areas serviced by the school shuttle bus. Then there are the 8 percent of men and women who choose to go Greek and live and eat in RIT's 15 fraternity and 8 sorority houses. Campus safety is largely a nonissue; most students feel secure.

Though the competition among peers at RIT probably won't drive students to drink, many indulge anyway. "It is for the most part a wet campus," says one observer. "There is no alcohol allowed on the dorm side of campus, and it is allowed in the apartments," explains a junior. The only facilities within walking distance of this sedate suburban campus are a variety of shopping plazas,

The institute specializes in carving out niches for itself with unusual programs, and majors are offered in more than 200 fields, from basic electrical and mechanical engineering to packaging science and nuclear medicine technology.

Created for the hearing-impaired, the National Technical Institute for the Deaf offers students technical and professional training in more than 30 programs, including business, science and engineering, and visual communications.

including the largest one between New York and Cleveland. Students take road trips to Buffalo, Syracuse, Rochester, and Canada. For those without transportation, there's always something to do on campus. Drama and other creative arts are less common than parties and movies, but a fine jazz ensemble and a chorus perform regularly. RIT also livens things up with several major weekend bashes throughout the year. EMANON festival is a favorite carnival among some students. Intramurals attract the more active students, as do the 23 varsity sports. Men's hockey is the overwhelming favorite, a real winter crowd pleaser that draws even the campus commuters and local residents to the rink. Other sports such as cross-country, men's basketball and lacrosse, and women's volleyball are strong but not followed.

For those seeking a competitive, high-tech education, RIT may be just the ticket. For all its other amenities, one of the best things about the school, says one student, "is that you get a good job when you graduate."

If You Apply To ➤ **RIT**...Early decision: Dec. 15. Regular admissions: Feb. 15 (priority). Financial aid: Mar. 1. Meets demonstrated need of 90%. Campus interviews: recommended, informational. No alumni interviews. SATs or ACTs: required. SAT IIs: optional. Accepts the Common Application and electronic applications. Essay question: career goals; why RIT; or significant experience.

University of Rochester

Rochester, NY 14627

Website: www.rochester.edu
Location: Small city
Total Enrollment: 7,681
Undergraduates: 4,452
Male/Female: 51/49
SAT Ranges: V 590–690 M 620–710
ACT Range: 26–30
Financial Aid: 70%
Expense: Pr $ $ $
Phi Beta Kappa: Yes
Applicants: 8,880
Accepted: 62%
Enrolled: 17%
Grad in 6 Years: 77%
Returning Freshmen: 95%
Academics: ✍ ✍ ✍ ✍
Social: ☎ ☎ ☎
Q of L: ★ ★ ★
Admissions: (716) 275-3221

The University of Rochester is not afraid of change. In 1996, this distinguished private university implemented its unique Rochester Renaissance Plan, and it has never looked back. The five-year plan, which includes a 20 percent reduction in the size of the freshman class, more merit scholarships, a refocusing of the curriculum, and new investments in library and computer/networking resources and campus facilities, has been the major catalyst in a new, improved, user-friendly University of Rochester.

Cold weather and snow are a given at the University of Rochester, but anyone who visits will find a flourishing community thriving on a clandestinely snug little 90-acre campus, which nestles up to a bend in the Genesee River. One student acknowledges that the university has "perpetually gray [read winter] skies," but finds comfort that "it's great for winter sports or studying or even sleeping late on a snowy Saturday." Another student adds, "The nippy winter days are perfect for sitting inside and hitting the books." Although a few buildings are modern—the Wilson Commons student center designed by I. M. Pei, for example—most of the older structures come in Greek Revival and Georgian Colonial styles. There is an aesthetically pleasing contrast between old and new, and the Eastman Quadrangle, with the library and original academic buildings, adds to Rochester's stately look. Recent construction projects include a 240,000-square foot building to house the Institute of Biomedical Sciences.

Degree requirements vary slightly from college to college, but all are designed to ensure that students are exposed to the full range of liberal arts. The curriculum—known as the Rochester Curriculum—focuses on three classic divisions of learning: humanities and arts; social science; and natural science, mathematics, and engineering. Students choose a major from one of these areas and also complete a cluster of three courses in each of the remaining two divisions. These clusters give students the opportunity for integrated study in diverse fields and the chance to participate in three very different types of learning. Freshmen have the option of taking seminar-style Quest courses, which teach them how to learn and how to make learning a lifetime habit. Quest courses can involve extensive work with original materials, existing and experimental data, and primary texts. Orientation Rochester-style includes a weeklong fall festival called Yellow Jacket Days, designed to help new students "become fully integrated in the university community."

The university's 175 degree programs span the standard fields of study, but Rochester takes special pride in its famed Eastman School of Music. It also excels in the engineering and scientific fields—competition is keen to "beat the mean" among science majors. A cognitive science program—a cooperative venture among faculty in computer science, psychology, and philosophy—is innovative and popular. The Institute of Optics, the nation's first center devoted exclusively to optics, is a leader in basic optical research and theory. The most popular majors include psychology, political science, economics, and biology. Students cite math and anthropology as being weak.

The academic climate at Rochester is challenging, owing much of that to its energetic professors, although large classes can interfere with the student-teacher relationship at times. No matter what their field of interest, students who are sufficiently advanced may combine undergraduate with graduate study. The Rochester Early Medical Scholars program offers highly qualified first-year students guaranteed admission to the med school after four years. In addition, Rochester offers a tuition-free fifth year that allows students to explore interests outside their major. The Center for Work and Career Development receives praise for its vigorous preparation of seniors for the job market. Students may also study abroad, and the university sponsors programs in a variety of places ranging from Russia to Singapore, not to mention what one student calls a "chance of a lifetime" British Parliament internship program. In an effort to attract scholars, the university offers in-state applicants and children of alumni a $5,000 annual grant. Its strongest applicants are awarded a Rush Rhees Scholarship, which ranges from $5,000 to $10,000 per year. A work-study program called Reach for Rochester provides students with on- or off-campus jobs, summer employment options, and individually tailored "experienceships."

Fifty-one percent of the students hail from New York State. Many also come from New England, and there's been a large jump in the numbers from Florida, the Midwest, California, and overseas. Asian Americans make up 11 percent of the student body, while African Americans account for 6 percent, and Hispanics another 5 percent. "We could use more students of color on campus," says one senior. Another student adds, "People here are very accepting of others who are different from themselves."

As far as housing is concerned, there's virtually nothing but praise from the 78 percent of students who live on campus. "Dorms are comfortable, modern, high tech, very generously sized, well maintained," a senior says. Some of the housing units offer such benefits as computer terminals, telephones with voice mail features, oak floors, and marble trim. All housing offers Internet access. New students are assigned to rooms—usually doubles—and upperclass students can usually get singles or suites through the lottery. Susan B. Anthony comes highly recommended. Single-sex, coed-by-floor, and coed-by-room dormitories are

(Continued)

Email Address: admit@ admissions.rochester.edu

Strongest Programs:
Premedicine
Engineering
Music
Optics
Biology
Psychology
Economics
Political Science

The Institute of Optics, the nation's first center devoted exclusively to optics, is a leader in basic optical research and theory.

The university's 175 degree programs span the standard fields of study, but Rochester takes special pride in its famed Eastman School of Music.

available. Though few students choose to live off campus, a new shuttle bus runs to and from the major off-campus living areas. Dormitory students may eat meals in the cafeteria, where a credit system ensures they pay per meal instead of in one lump sum. The fare served in the dining halls receives high ratings from students, especially the á la carte options such as tacos and burritos and the deli bar. Other meal options available include a kosher deli, the Common Ground Coffee House, and a submarine sandwich shop.

Twenty percent of the men and 14 percent of the women go Greek. "The Greek scene plays a large factor in social life here, but it is by no means the only social outlet," says one student. Yet, fraternities still contribute heavily to the social life of Greeks and independents alike by sponsoring parties and concerts. UR does have its own set of movie theaters that charge $3 or less per ticket and campus concerts always draw a crowd. Despite the university's best efforts to enforce a stricter alcohol policy, underage drinking still occurs. "This school's policy in no way curtails underage drinking unless students take it upon themselves to obey," one student says. Many students take the free campus shuttle into "Rochchacha," where they may entertain themselves on the beaches of Lake Ontario, in the International Photography Museum at the George Eastman House, or at the Rochester Philharmonic Orchestra. Favored out-of-town ventures are Niagara Falls, about 70 miles westward, and, for the more venturesome, Toronto, 125 miles farther westward. Other favorite activities include cappuccino at the student union, frequent ski trips, Yellow Jacket Days, and a spring fling known as Dandelion Day. The Viennese Ball and the Boar's Head Dinner are also popular events, as is the unforgettable Screw Your Roommate Dance. A less official Rochester tradition calls for each student to eat a "garbage plate" at the infamous dive called Nick's before graduating. Students are involved in the community through projects on and off campus, and Rochester was recently recognized nationally for its high percentage of student volunteers.

The varsity sports teams are coming of age at the Rochester, which competes in the University Athletic Association. For those who want something to cheer about, the golf team, the basketball teams, men's and women's soccer, tennis, and cross-country are all quite successful. Intramurals are a popular outlet for "ex-jocks from high school who miss their glory days gone by." Even if intramurals aren't your bag, Rochester has an $8-million sport complex, complete with basketball tennis, squash, and volleyball courts, lighted rooftop tennis courts, a Nautilus fitness center, the Speegle-Wilbraham Aquatic Center with an eight-lane pool, and an indoor track.

In the past, students bemoaned the fact that the school didn't have a wider academic reputation but that's changing due, in part, to the Rochester Renaissance Plan. Improvements have been made in the curriculum, the facilities, and just about anywhere you look on campus. Rochester seems to be winning its battle for a spot among the nation's leading private universities. Now if they could only do something about all that snow.

Overlaps

Cornell University,
Brown,
SUNY–Binghamton,
Northwestern,
Washington University.

If You Apply To ➤ **Rochester**…Early decision: Nov. 1. Regular admissions: Jan. 15. Financial aid: Feb. 1. Housing: June 1. Guarantees to meet demonstrated need. No campus interviews. Alumni interviews: optional, informational. SATs or ACTs: required. SAT IIs: recommended. Musicians apply directly to the Eastman School of Music. Essay question: life in a different era; personal diversity. Looks closely at recommendations, activities, and "indications of intellectual curiosity and a zest for college life."

Rollins College

1000 Holt Avenue, Box 2720, Winter Park, FL 32789-4499

It's no secret that Orlando is home to many of the world's greatest attractions. There's Walt Disney World, Sea World, and Universal Studios, to name a few. And for those seeking a quality education, Central Florida offers an attraction of another sort: Rollins College. Here you can dig your toes in the sand while studying theater or biology, and enjoy making waves while making grades. But don't let the natural beauty distract you; students here must be disciplined if they're to keep up with the rigorous curriculum.

Although founded in 1885, Rollins's commitment to Spanish Mediterranean style architecture was established in the 1930's by then President Hamilton Holt. Capitalizing on its location on beautiful Lake Virginia, campus planners have succeeded in combining the natural beauty of the lakeside with consistent architecture. Recent additions include the Cornell Campus Center, with meeting rooms, dining facilities, and new space for the bookstore complete with a coffee bar, as well as an electronic research and information center, and a $10.1 million sports center that helps students keep their bodies as well-exercised as their minds.

The path to a bachelor's degree at Rollins leads all students through three areas of general education requirements: skills (writing, foreign language, public speaking, mathematical methods, decision-making); cognitive (Western and non-Western culture, natural world); and affective (expressive arts and literature). For freshmen acclimating to college, the fall-semester Rollins Conference eases the transition by placing them into groups of 17 or fewer to discuss themes such as banned books, the economy, or the environment. Each group has a professor-advisor and two upperclass peer mentors. Students also have the opportunity to pursue independent research, and during a recent summer, 17 chemistry majors did just that.

Students give the philosophy department their highest marks, and also praise history, English, theater, psychology, environmental studies, international studies, and economics. The chemistry department turned out the winner of the 1987 Nobel Prize. Students say they avoid the sciences, but only because instructors are so tough and science majors so competitive. The Annie Russell Theatre hosts productions staged by the active theater department, which takes pride in having set the stage for such stellar actors as alumni Buddy Ebsen and Tony Perkins. A major in International Business was added recently, and future *Fortune* 500 types can take, an eight-course minor in business studies combined with a major selected from the 28 liberal arts offerings. An Accelerated Management Program allows qualified freshmen to gain guaranteed admission to the Roy E. Crummer Graduate School of Business when they enter Rollins, leading to BA and MBA degrees in five rather than six years.

While the workload at Rollins varies by major, academics are important. "You can't come here and expect to party and not study," says an international relations major. "To get decent grades, you have to work for them." That's made easier by the fact that there aren't any TA's here; teaching is the responsibility of professors. "It's probably the best part of Rollins, the individual attention of extraordinary professors," raves a sophomore. Many students take advantage of Rollins' study-abroad program, which offers programs in Sydney, Australia and Merida, Mexico for regular tuition costs, as well as internships in London.

Rollins draws about half of its students from outside Florida and has more

Website: www.rollins.edu

Location: Suburban

Total Enrollment: 3,483

Undergraduates: 1,519

Male/Female: 40/60

SAT Ranges: V 540–630 M 540–630

ACT Range: 24–28

Financial Aid: 40%

Expense: Pr $ $ $

Phi Beta Kappa: No

Applicants: 1,748

Accepted: 73%

Enrolled: 35%

Grad in 6 Years: 64%

Returning Freshmen: 80%

Academics: ✐ ✐ ✐

Social: ☎ ☎ ☎ ☎

Q of L: ★ ★ ★

Admissions: (407) 646-2161

Email Address: admission@rollins.edu

Strongest Programs:
  English
  Theater/Drama
  Latin American Studies
  Chemistry
  Psychology
  Politics
  Philosophy
  Biology
  Economics

A $10.1 million sports center helps students keep their bodies as well-exercised as their minds.

than its share of rich kids, hence the nickname, "Rollins College Country Club." Adequate financial aid, however, is available, with merit scholarships for qualified students and athletic scholarships given to male and female standouts in eight sports. Fourteen percent of the students are members of minority groups and 5 percent are international, and each fall there's a week of programming aimed at celebrating diversity. Still, the school's homogeneity is a concern for some. "For the most part, the minority population at Rollins feels isolated," says one student.

Sixty-eight percent of the college's students live on campus in comfortable coed dorms. "The dorms are better than most hotel rooms," says a sophomore, though a senior warns "it's getting harder to get a room because of increasing enrollment." Freshmen who want to study should choose Ward, students say, while McKean is the social center. Some students live in special-interest houses or move off campus. Dining facilities are located in the campus center and food is charged on a credit card system, so students eat when they want and pay only when they eat.

The high-powered Greek scene claims 27 percent of the women and men at Rollins, so there's almost always a party somewhere. Still, "with downtown Orlando 15 minutes away everybody has something to do," says a sophomore. Also, the administration has clamped down on the social scene, with party monitors checking IDs and a student activity director attending each on-campus party. No open containers of alcohol may be carried on the campus grounds, and if you're caught with one, campus safety "will make you pour it out," says a history major. "The college tries hard to catch us, but sometimes we slip through." With beaches close by, students add sailing, sunbathing, and windsurfing to their daily activities, and the Florida Keys are a popular roadtrip destination. Fox Day is "a sacred tradition"—the president cancels classes for the day by placing a fox statue on the front lawn. Students look forward to the tradition every spring and, though they never know exactly which day the president will choose, almost everyone heads for the beach once the day arrives. Many students volunteer with programs such as Habitat for Humanity and tutoring at local schools. Orlando's offerings include entertainment complexes like Church Street Station and the Cheyenne Saloon, and amusement parks like Disney World, Epcot Center, and Universal Studios, complete with giant mechanical sharks.

Sports are also important and Rollins rules in water-skiing. Recently, teams have struggled because Rollins is more academically competitive than many Division II opponents. However, the women's tennis team recently placed fourth in the NCAA national championships; the women's golf team captured second place in their own sport.

Students at Rollins may not realize how lucky they are. They have gorgeous new facilities to complement the natural beauty of Florida's sun and surf, plus a lake in their own backyard. Their biggest gripes are a lack of on-campus parking and a campus safety force too eager to hand out citations for expired meters or underage drinking. It's true that high tuition costs and a lack of diversity have some students concerned. But for those who want to put off entry into the "real world" just a bit longer, Rollins could be an ideal oasis in which to spend four years.

If You Apply To ➤

Rollins…Early decision: Nov. 15, Jan. 15. Regular admissions: Feb. 15. Meets demonstrated need of 13%. Campus interviews: recommended, evaluative. No alumni interviews. SATs or ACTs: required. SAT IIs: recommended. Accepts the Common Application and electronic applications. Essay question: significant experience or achievement; issue of personal, local or national concern and its importance; significant person.

Rose–Hulman Institute of Technology

5500 Wabash Avenue, Terre Haute, IN 47803

Engineers rule at Rose-Hulman Institute of Technology. Four of the five most popular majors involve the study of engineering (mechanical, electrical, computer, and chemical). And as you might expect, with an emphasis on technology and engineering, the school has far more men than women. Though not as prominent as its peers on the coasts (MIT and Caltech), Rose-Hulman churns out graduates who are near the top of their field. With only 1,600 students and 11 majors, the Rose-Hulman Institute of Technology doesn't have much room to lose its focus.

Established in 1874, Rose-Hulman is the oldest private engineering school west of the Allegheny Mountains. Its 138-acre campus boasts an idyllic setting of trees and two small lakes. Among the most recent additions are a senior-level projects building, a new academic building, an athletic facility, and a new residence hall. The university isn't stopping there, though. It has plans to build a new fine arts center, as well as an on-campus chapel within the next few years.

The common bond for all Rose students is the immense work load, which garners both applause and criticism from the student body. But all seem to agree that the "education is second to none," with full professors teaching every class offered at Rose. In addition to gems such as a major in applied optics—the only undergraduate program of its kind in the country—Rose-Hulman also offers students a rare technical translator's certificate program in either Russian or German, as well as double majors and humanities minors. Programs such as Fast Track Calculus enable students to accelerate in areas where they demonstrate special aptitude. There is also an integrated curriculum available to a quarter of the freshman class, in which all required academic disciplines are combined into one team-taught course. And given the technical focus of the school, the campus is awash with high-tech gadgets such as a 60-MHz nuclear magnetic resonance spectrometer, neutron howitzers and generators, electron accelerators, and holography tables. The technical resources are indicative of a greater effort on the part of the administration to provide its undergraduates with a complete technical education, from the most basic general ed requirements all the way through job placement.

Rose-Hulman offers 11 degree programs in engineering, chemistry, computer science, math, and physics. It was the first private college to offer a bachelor's degree in chemical engineering, and this department remains among its strongest. Electrical and mechanical engineering are also popular with students, but for every student, a fifth of their academic program will consist of classes in the humanities and social sciences. Rose-Hulman's library system is excellent in technical fields, but for anything else, students must trek to nearby Indiana State University, where they have free access. For the most part, though, students seem happy with the school's tech-oriented outlook. The humanities are named as some of the "most avoided" departments.

Nearly all the students at Rose are white (95 percent) and used to academic success (95 percent of them were in the top quarter of their high school class). Though the administration is attempting to recruit more minorities, African Americans and Asian Americans account for only 4 percent of the student body combined, and there are virtually no Hispanics. Racial tension is said to be nonexistent, but many students are quick to point out that this is directly related to the school's extreme lack of diversity. One major change in the makeup of the

Website: www.rose-hulman.edu

Location: City outskirts

Total Enrollment: 1,680

Undergraduates: 1,600

Male/Female: 84/16

SAT Ranges: V 580end700 M 650–750

ACT Range: 28–31

Financial Aid: 75%

Expense: Pr $ $

Phi Beta Kappa: No

Applicants: 3,085

Accepted: 65%

Enrolled: 20%

Grad in 6 Years: 80%

Returning Freshmen: 93%

Academics: ✑ ✑ ✑

Social: ☎

Q of L: ★ ★

Admissions: (812) 877-8213

Email Address: admissions@rose-hulman.edu

Strongest Programs:
　Applied Optics
　Chemical Engineering
　Mechanical Engineering
　Electrical Engineering

Though not as prominent as its peers on the coasts (MIT and Caltech), Rose Hulman churns out graduates who are near the top of their field.

student body in the past five years has been the addition of women. Rose became coed in 1995, and already has a significant enough female population to warrant the existence of sororities and women's sports teams, including the ever-popular volleyball and soccer. Rose-Hulman also offers a varying number of merit scholarships each year, worth $2,500 to $10,000. None of these scholarships cover full tuition, but students consistently praise the administration's efforts to make Rose affordable for those prepared to take on its challenging curriculum.

While the work is hard, the resources are many and life is comfortable. Students consistently rave about the new dorm, which has considerably eased the undergraduate housing crunch. Students enjoy daily housekeeping service. "They even make our beds!" exclaims one student. Seventy-five percent of upperclassmen choose to live off-campus, and although Terre Haute receives low reviews from Rose students, many find trips to Indianapolis, Bloomington, and Cincinnati a fun way to spend the weekends. Most social life at Rose takes place off campus in fraternity houses where it is easier to find alcohol than Rose's dry campus. Greek participation is on the rise, with 40 percent of males in fraternities and 50 percent of females in sororities.

The town of Terre Haute gets about the same review from students as the cafeteria food. It is home to three colleges (St. Mary's in the Woods and Indiana State are close by), which means lots of co-eds and plenty of malls and eateries in the area. Despite playing host to three colleges, Terre Haute has failed to evolve into a real "college town." But some say that the town's best asset is its proximity to Indianapolis, Chicago, and St. Louis. While students at some schools say their college town stinks, Rose-Hulman students are in the rare and unfortunate situation of contending with truly odious odors. "Terre Haute is a great town, but it's smelly because of the paper mill."

Feelings about Terre Haute aside, Rose students live a happy, active life. Lest anyone envision Rose-Hulman students as pale lab dwellers, be aware that athletics are very popular. Over 90 percent of the students are involved in intramurals, and even faculty members get into the act. Varsity teams play in Division III of the NCAA with football, basketball, baseball, and cross-country among the strongest teams. The Indianapolis Colts even use the facilities as a training camp. Homecoming brings a major class conflict: The freshmen build a bonfire and a wooden mascot elephant, and the sophomores do their best to destroy both. The bonfire is the largest in the country, so big, a senior reports, that the "Indianapolis airport reroutes airplanes around the area."

For the serious, focused student, Rose provides an incredible technical education that ranks among the best in the country. Life in Terre Haute may not be that exciting, but a world of possibility awaits any student that can engineer their way to a Rose-Hulman degree.

If You Apply To ➢

Rose-Hulman…Rolling admissions: Mar. 1. Meets demonstrated need of 80%. Campus interviews: recommended, informational. Alumni interviews: optional, informational. SATs or ACTs: required. SAT IIs: optional. Accepts electronic applications. No essay question.

Rutgers–The State University of New Jersey

65 Davidson Road, Piscataway, NJ 08854-8097

Life at Rutgers University is all about choice. Choices between the more than 100 undergraduate majors and 4,000 courses offered between its campuses in New Brunswick, Newark, and Camden. Choices about which of the more than 400 student organizations to join. Even choices about which library to visit since there are 18 branches with holdings of more than 3 million volumes university-wide. "Rutgers's best quality is its wide variety of majors, classes, and social activities," says one junior.

Rutgers University has three regional campuses in Camden, Newark, and New Brunswick. Rutgers–New Brunswick, which has the largest concentration of students, is composed of five smaller campuses located along the Raritan River. The campuses are connected by a free university bus system and students travel among campuses to take classes. Rutgers–Newark is in a downtown section of Newark, giving the campus neighborhood a collegiate feel. The smallest campus in the Rutgers system is in Camden, located one stop away from the shopping and cultural offerings of downtown Philadelphia. The RUNet 2000 project, a $100-million infrastructure initiative in progress, promises to transform student-faculty interaction through access to voice, video, and data from just about any location on campus.

Among the nearly 100 majors, the three most popular are psychology, biological sciences, and accounting. Especially strong academic programs include accounting, history, political science, and chemistry. The workload is steady for most students; science majors and pharmacy students can expect the heaviest load. "The courses here require a great deal of thought and outside preparation if you want to be successful," says a political science major. Recently added majors include cell biology and neuroscience; genetics and microbiology; biomedical engineering; evolutionary anthropology; and allied health technology. As at any big state university, registration can sometimes be a headache. But Rutgers now has telephone registration at its New Brunswick campus, and students say the situation has improved.

In an effort to reverse the traditional exodus of New Jersey high school superstars from the state, Rutgers offers a variety of honors programs, including special seminars, internships, independent projects, and research opportunities with the faculty. Rutgers also provides its undergraduates with a chance to study abroad in Britain, Costa Rica, France, Germany, India, Ireland, Israel, Italy, Mexico, Switzerland, and Spain. Biology students have the run of the 370-acre Rutgers Ecological Preserve and Natural Teaching Area. In addition, Rutgers is also home to more than 100 specialized research centers and institutes dedicated to the study of topics ranging from ancient Roman art to mountain gorillas. Professors generally get high marks. "I completely revere most of my professors," says a junior. "They are intelligent, well respected in their fields, and present dynamic lectures."

Though the administration has been trying to increase the number of out-of-staters, in recent years more than 90 percent of Rutgers students have been from New Jersey. Nevertheless, the student population is as diverse as that of the state, with a good proportion of students from cities, suburbs, farms, and seaside communities. Minorities account for 37 percent of the students: 11 percent are African American, 9 percent Hispanic, and 17 percent Asian American. "I feel I've grown

Website: www.rutgers.edu
Location: Small city
Total Enrollment: 49,465
Undergraduates: 37,112
Male/Female: 45/55
SAT Ranges: V 510–620 M 520–650
Financial Aid: 55%
Expense: Pub $ $ $ $
Phi Beta Kappa: Yes
Applicants: 26,593
Accepted: 67%
Enrolled: 36%
Grad in 6 Years: 69%
Returning Freshmen: 88%
Academics: ✍ ✍ ✍ ✍
Social: ☎ ☎ ☎
Q of L: ★ ★ ★
Admission: (732) 445-3777
Email Address: admissions@asb-ugadm.rutgers.edu

Strongest Programs:
Accounting
History
Pharmacy
Biological Sciences
Political Science
Psychology
Engineering

so much here and learned so much about being a member of a rich and diverse community," explains one senior. The school's administration takes pride in their Committee to Advance Our Common Purpose, for students who want to reduce prejudice and promote diversity on campus. In the past, the committee developed a World Wide Web page for multicultural resources and submitted a proposal for the creation of an Intercultural Relations Study Group.

The university has eight liberal arts schools spread out among its campuses, for those seeking a broad-based education. Seven colleges cater to the needs of students wanting a preprofessional school (business, nursing, life and environmental studies, fine and performing arts, engineering, and pharmacy). The school does not guarantee to meet the full demonstrated need of every admit, but 24 percent of the applicants are offered full demonstrated need. About 400 students receive athletic scholarships in a wide range of sports, and more than 6,500 receive merit awards. Students say they have noticed budget cuts in terms of tuition increases, fewer course offerings, shorter hours at buildings around campus, and fewer administrators.

On-campus housing in New Brunswick accommodates 47 percent of full-time students. "There has been a big push recently to renovate the dorms so most of them are really nice," says a history major. "Another student says, "With the exception of a few mediocre dorms for freshmen, most are extremely large and have air-conditioning; some have free cable TV; and a good number are directly hard-wired with fiber-optic cables into the Internet." Current on-campus options range from conventional dorms to special-interest areas to apartment complexes with kitchens and living rooms. The university also offers a special dormitory for students who are trying to overcome addictions to drugs and alcohol.

The city of New Brunswick is an attractive place to go for a drink or dinner on the town. Just don't stray *too* far from the campus. True, Rutgers has its own police department that possesses the same training and powers as the N.J. state police. "I personally don't feel safe in New Brunswick so I restrict my outings to on-campus locations," one student admits. For those who want to hit the road for fun, New York City and Philadelphia are each only about an hour distant, and students flood the Jersey shore in springtime. The Rutgers College Program Council offers trips ranging from white-water rafting to mountain climbing to skiing. "The variety of activities at Rutgers provides you with the opportunity to have fun any way you desire," says one student. "There are lots of on-campus social activities," a senior explains. "Movies, coffeehouses, local and bigger bands, lectures, parties. Off-campus activity includes frat parties and bars." In the past five years, students enrolled in the Citizenship and Service Education Program at Rutgers contributed over 90,000 hours of service to communities across New Jersey. "Students definitely get involved in the surrounding community and do a lot of volunteer work," says a senior.

The Greek system, which attracts 2 percent of the men and women, is entirely off campus. While the school neither owns nor administers any of the Greek organizations, it does have a university office for Greek affairs, which oversees the welfare of those belonging to fraternities and sororities. Students say a lot of the nightlife for the New Brunswick campuses take place at the Greek houses. Reportedly, it is "difficult to drink in dorms," but underage students drink if they really want to. Each college has its own student center with pinball machines, pool tables, bowling alleys, and a snack bar. Major social events include Reggae Day at Livingston, Agricultural Field Day at Cook, and Oktoberfest for the campus as a whole. Pioneer Pride Night is Camden's big party. During Homecoming, tailgate parties are held in the stadium parking lot, featuring tons of food—including roast pigs and whole sides of beef—continuous music, and thousands of revelers.

Varsity, intramural, and club sports fill whatever gap is left by the social scene. The Rutgers's baseball team is competitive, as are many other sports including football, basketball, tennis, lacrosse, soccer, cross-country, and track. Women's basketball, fencing, soccer, softball, field hockey, tennis, and track teams are also strong. A member of the Big East in football, Rutgers faces a tough schedule that includes Boston College, Miami, Syracuse, and West Virginia. Big East Conference competition makes up for not getting to play Princeton, which in 1980 bowed out of what was then the oldest football rivalry in the nation.

Rutgers has a plethora of people and programs characteristic of large state universities. It also has a lot more, including loyal support from the state's legislature and private sector, and tuition at an affordable price. Says one satisfied student: "From the diversity of its majors and courses to the hundreds of student organizations on campus, Rutgers gives me a chance to explore a world of options."

Overlaps

College of New Jersey, Montclair State, NYU, Penn State, Rowan University.

If You Apply To ➤

Rutgers...Rolling admissions: Dec. 15. Financial aid: Mar. 15. Housing: June 15. Meets demonstrated need of 24%. No campus or alumni interviews. SATs or ACTs: required. No SAT IIs. No essay. Apply to particular school.

St. John's College

Annapolis campus: P.O. Box 2800, Annapolis, MD 21404-2800

Santa Fe campus: 1160 Camino Cruz Blanca, Santa Fe, NM 87501-4599

Although the two campuses of St. John's College are separated by more than 1,000 miles and boast two very different climates, they share one very important characteristic—a consuming quest for knowledge. There are no lectures, no grades, and no professors. But an incredible amount of learning goes on at both St. John's campuses. Students learn from each other and from the great philosophers and thinkers of our time and generations past. The truth is, St. John's is the most intellectual college in the country; it makes Chicago look like a party school. "We deal with some of the essential questions which have plagued men for centuries," says a junior. "Anything other than devoting yourself entirely to your studies is unacceptable."

Physically, the two St. John's campuses are more than just time zones away. The Colonial brick buildings of the one in Annapolis, with its historic 1742 central classroom building, are a tight fit on this small urban campus. Located in the midst of the historic district of Annapolis, with the Maryland state capitol and the U.S. Naval Academy both in the neighborhood, St. John's exudes an old-world prestige. The Annapolis campus has a new library and student activities center, which includes a computer lab and reading rooms. The other campus, meanwhile, occupies 250 acres on the outskirts of sun-drenched Santa Fe, against a backdrop of the Sangre de Cristo Mountains. The campus consists of adobe-style buildings, and has beautiful views of both the city below and the mountains above. Though it's not near any public transportation, students are close to the wilderness via a nearby national forest. Recent construction on the Santa Fe campus includes a new student activities center. Students may attend both campuses during their programs of study.

Annapolis Website:
www.sjca.edu
Location: Center city
Total Enrollment: 516
Undergraduates: 452
Male/Female: 55/45
SAT Ranges: V 660–750 M 580–680
Financial Aid: 62%
Expense: Pr $ $ $ $
Phi Beta Kappa: No
Applicants: 446
Accepted: 78%
Enrolled: 38%
Grad in 6 Years: 77%
Returning Freshmen: 80%
Academics: 🖉 🖉 🖉 🖉 🖉
Social: ☎ ☎ ☎
Q of L: ★ ★ ★ ★
Admissions: (800) 727-9238
Email Address:
admissions@sjca.edu

(Continued)

Santa Fe Website:
   www.sjcsf.edu
Location: City outskirts
Total Enrollment: 534
Undergraduates: 431
Male/Female: 57/43
SAT Ranges: V 650–710 M
   590–670
ACT Range: 26–30
Financial Aid: 75%
Expense: Pr $ $ $ $
Phi Beta Kappa: No
Applicants: 355
Accepted: 84%
Enrolled: 42%
Grad in 6 Years: 65%
Returning Freshmen: 85%
Academics: 🖉 🖉 🖉 🖉 🖉
Social: ☎ ☎ ☎
Q of L: ★ ★ ★ ★
Admissions: (800) 331-5232
Email Address:
   admissions@mail.sjcsf.edu

Strongest Programs:
   The Great Books Program

The reason there are no professors at St. John's is that the Great Books—about 150 of the most influential works of Western civilization—are the teachers. Students read the books, discuss them in seminars, and write about them in papers. In between, they ponder, debate, and philosophize about the riddles of human existence that have captivated intellectuals for centuries. "Our school has a focus on education that I believe is unmatchable," says one student. "The structure and content of the program give students no end of subjects for inquiry and investigation." A senior adds, "Every student is here to learn the profound philosophical and moral thoughts that have shaped mankind, and the political theories that have moved nations."

With a history that goes back more than 275 years, both campuses follow a curriculum that would have delighted the poet and educator Matthew Arnold, who argued in an 1882 essay that the goal of education is "to know the best which has been thought and said in the world" and that the best way to meet it is to immerse students in the greatest classical texts. The curriculum, known as the Program, follows that model to a T, with every student reading the Great Books in roughly chronological order. There are no registration or scheduling hassles: the daily course of study for all four years is mapped out before a student sets foot on campus. The breakdown is four years of mathematics, two years of ancient Greek and French, three years of laboratory science, a year of music, and, of course, four years of Great Books seminars. Freshmen study the Greeks and Romans, sophomores advance to the Renaissance, juniors cover the 17th and 18th centuries, and seniors do the 19th and 20th centuries. Readings are from primary sources only: you learn math from Euclid and Ptolemy, physics from Einstein, psychology from Freud, and so on for all fields. Preceptorials introduce an elective element into the otherwise all-required program. For about seven weeks in the junior and senior years, the seminar is suspended, and the students select a book or topic to study in depth with a tutor. The assumption is that the Great Books can stand on their own, representing the highest achievements of human intellect. Overall, students say the junior year, with its advanced curriculum in math and the natural sciences, is the most challenging.

Though the Great Books curriculum is the only reason anyone enrolls here, students mix hearty praise for the program with some criticism. "There is no extra time to read other material," says one sophomore. A junior complains about the occasional arrogance in the classroom: "Students need to be intelligent and humble in order to survive this school, without warrants for their death issued." Students uniformly praise the teaching of math, but say the teaching of music is weak compared to other fields, "because music is tough to philosophize about." Rote language learning (Greek and French) is also not looked upon too highly. Still, the format of learning is what is most appreciated here, and the campus atmosphere is affected largely by what is read. "When freshman are reading Homer, members of all classes will reminisce....When juniors are reading Kant, there's often a more glum sense on campus (likely because these juniors cease to chat in the dining hall, but rather sit with knitted brows, poring over the Critique of Pure Reason while they eat)," reports one student.

Though the formidable curriculum is far more structured and classical than any other college's, the method of presenting it is as radical as that of any alternative school. The tutors would be professors at any other institution, but at St. John's they are considered only the most advanced students in class. Like true Renaissance men, tutors must be able to teach any subject in the curriculum, and in a few years' time they do. Many never publish at all, and they put teaching above all else. Instruction is entirely by small discussion groups, where the tutor's responsibility is to lead discussion rather than lecture. Not surprisingly, the tutors are highly praised and student-faculty relations are excellent. "Our tutors are brilliant," says one student. "They impart a wisdom that comes with age." Another student adds, "Tutors who guide the dialectic process at St. John's want to be here because they desire to participate in the process of being set free by a liberal arts program in the truest sense."

Many St. John's students find they need a year off between sophomore and junior year. Some decide simply to switch from the Annapolis campus to Santa Fe or vice versa, not only for a change of scenery but also for a change of atmosphere. Santa Fe, founded in 1964 to increase St. John's size without sacrificing the virtues of a small campus, is definitely more relaxed than the comparatively uptight Annapolis campus. As dutiful as the cadets at the naval academy across the street, Annapolis Johnnies come as close as students possibly can to learning every waking hour of the day.

Though the reasons students choose the St. John's program are never simple, the common thread among students is a fierce love of learning. A quarter of the students have transferred to St. John's from more conventional colleges—an act of devotion, since St. John's accepts no transfer credits and requires all students to begin as freshmen. But devotion is a must to do well here and keep up with the reading overload. At St. John's, the books always come first, as a prospective student noticed on a visit to campus: "Students at most schools put their books over their heads when it rains, but at St. John's they put them under their shirts." Most students are bright, opinionated, and have no use for the status quo. Politically, liberalism prevails. "'Johnnies' are the students from high school that always stuck out a little. They 'though too much' or would ask a question that no one in the class would understand. We all have this in common," asserts a senior. Minorities represent 11 percent of students at the Annapolis campus and 10 percent at the Santa Fe campus. Racial tension is virtually nonexistent, as students are judged by their intelligence only.

Qualified students are admitted on a first-come, first-served basis. After all spaces fill up (the school keeps a strict cap on enrollment), admissions begin for the following semester. About half the students on both campuses ranked in the top fifth of their high school class. Operating on a need-blind basis, St. John's attempts to meet the full demonstrated financial need of all accepted applicants, but there are no merit or athletic scholarships.

Dorms on the Annapolis campus are coed, small, and some well worn (dating to the mid-19th century). Freshmen usually live on campus, but 29 percent of the student body have found housing elsewhere in what one student calls "a pleasant small town." Juniors and seniors not off campus usually receive singles. The Santa Fe campus boasts a luxurious collection of small two-story dorms housing 20 students each. The rooms are spacious and, with the campus located at 7,000 feet on the edge of mountains that turn blood red at sunset, provide a more scenic view than most luxury hotel rooms.

Santa Fe undergraduates plunge into the outdoor life encouraged by their location, while Annapolis students limit their adventures to well-organized intramural teams ("a bunch of intellectuals getting exercise") with such names as the Druids, the Spartans, and the Furies. And then there's the annual croquet tourney with the U.S. Naval Academy, which is across the street from the Annapolis campus. Trips to Washington, Baltimore, Chesapeake Bay, or West Virginia are not infrequent. In Santa Fe, blues and jazz clubs are popular, as are coffee shops, movies, and malls. An Annapolis student says, "With such a small campus, there is not really such a thing as an isolated Johnnie." Drinking provides the favored

The truth is, St. John's is the most intellectual college in the country; it makes Chicago look like a party school.

The tutors would be professors at any other institution, but at St. John's they are considered only the most advanced students in class.

release for Johnnies, who have of course read Plato's Symposium and are familiar with the likes of Rabelais. Although no one under 21 can be served under strict campus rules that include expulsion if caught, students admit that underage undergrads can easily tip their share of the brew. "Our school's alcohol policy is basically, 'If we don't see you drinking, it's not a problem,'" says one student. The academics, however, even seem to overshadow the student's social life. "Due to the unique academic program, the social and academic life often blend," says a senior.

Aside from parties, other popular events include monthly semiformal waltz and swing parties, discussion sessions, and the annual Seducers and Corrupters parties for incoming freshmen. Two favorite all-campus events on the Annapolis campus are Senior Prank, a 24-hour-long surprise party for the whole college community, and Reality, a weekend-long party that includes a mock Olympics (which features such events as Ptolemy's epicycle races and Spartan madball).

There is an almost mystical reverence for learning at St. John's. Students will tell you they're looking for truth, beauty, and other lofty ideals in their education instead of seeking a thorough grounding in something as pedestrian as political science.

The nearly cultlike atmosphere keeps everyone in place, and seemingly happy. For those who want to enroll here: You probably already know who you are. Says a senior, "St. John's is a way of thinking."

Overlaps

Chicago, Reed, Bard, Oberlin, Sarah Lawrence.

If You Apply To ➤ **St. Johns**…Rolling admissions: Mar. 1. Financial aid: Feb. 15. Campus interviews: recommended, evaluative. Alumni interviews: recommended, informational (Annapolis) or optional, evaluative (Santa Fe). SATs and ACTs: optional. SAT IIs: optional. Essay questions: evaluate the strengths and weaknesses of your formal education to date; describe reading habits, choose significant book; and describe important experience. Special attention given to essays.

St. John's University and College of St. Benedict

BEST BUY

St. John's campus: P.O. Box 7155, Collegeville, MN 56321-7155

St. Benedict campus: 37 South College Avenue, St. Joseph, MN 56374-2099

Website: www.csbsju.edu
Location: Rural
Total Enrollment: 3,932
Undergraduates: 3,803
Male/Female: 47/53
SAT Ranges: V 520–630 M 520–640
ACT Range: 22–27
Financial Aid: 73%
Expense: Pr $
Phi Beta Kappa: No
Applicants: 2,278
Accepted: 87%
Enrolled: 50%

St. John's University and the College of St. Benedict are two single-sex campuses, three miles apart, with a common heritage and mission: providing an educational and spiritual atmosphere where professors and students work in concert to tackle the issues of the day. There's a true closeness here, a feeling that encourages neighbors to look out for one another—and for those they don"t yet know. "The environment, setting, and interaction with the monastery makes this place a great community," says a St. John's senior. "The college has a very comfortable atmosphere."

Owned and operated by the largest Benedictine monastery in the world, St. John's occupies 2,400 pristine acres in rural Minnesota. With its forests, lakes, and wide-open spaces, the campus is an ideal stomping ground for the roughly 1,700 men who constitute the student body. Alongside an ancient quadrangle erected by monks is a strikingly modern church designed by Marcel Breuer, with a towering bell banner and three-story stained-glass window. Along with fine academics and an abiding sense of Christian purpose, the campus itself is one of the main reasons many choose this school. St. Benedict, down the road in St. Joseph, is connected to St. John's by free shuttle service. That campus is an impressive combination of contemporary and carefully restored and maintained turn-of-the-century buildings. St. John's has invested $18.3 million in facilities in recent years, including a football-stadium overhaul, new outdoor and indoor tracks, renovation of Warner Palaestra, construction of an all-purpose field house and the building of a 48,000-square-foot science center.

Comprising one of the few joint universities in the country, St. John's and St. Benedict emphasize their Roman Catholic roots while providing the academic rigor students need to prepare for numerous professions. The most popular major is management, followed by biology and elementary education. Nursing and theology also get high marks. Students say communications and English could use some work, but that's more because they aren't strictly pre-professional in nature. The forests on and around the campus are a boon to the field biology offerings. An innovative management program places majors in control of computer-simulated corporations and lets them try their hand at free-market enterprise. The strong medieval studies program benefits from the Hill Monastic Manuscript Library, one of the foremost microfilm collections of handwritten manuscripts.

St. Benedict shares extensive cross-registration programs and joint departments with St. John's, so students mix easily and comfortably. Owing to the schools' small size, every class has fewer than 50 students, and classes can fill up fast. Still, only education majors typically spend more than four years getting their degrees, because of student-teaching requirements. "Classes may sometimes be tough to get into, but the school makes sure you take what you need," says a St. John's communication major. The small classes also encourage strong student-faculty ties. "The professors I've had have defined my education," says an environmental studies major. "The focus here is on teaching, so professors want to interact with students." The schools help keep instruction quality high by asking students to evaluate their courses at the end of each semester. "Tenure here is based on teaching skill before anything else," a student says. Monastery brothers make up 20 percent of the St. John's faculty, and sisters make up a contingent of the St. Benedict professors. "I would rate the teaching staff as excellent, because they take as much pride in our success and this school as the students do," says a senior economics major.

Exploring the Human Condition, the schools' core curriculum, encompasses all four years, starting with a first-year symposium and finishing with a senior seminar. Proficiency in a foreign language and math is required, in addition to classes in fine arts, humanities, natural sciences, and social sciences. Students also take courses that examine issues from a gender or global perspective, and courses that emphasize discussion, quantitative reasoning and writing. Each January, students take a break from their regular schedules for J-term, a month-long, for-credit opportunity to study a subject in depth or partake in study abroad (also available during the semester). Programs are offered in Austria, China, Costa Rica, England, France, Greece, Italy, Ireland, Japan, South Africa, or Spain; each is limited to about 30 participants, and about 40 percent of St. John's and St. Benedict students go abroad during their undergraduate years. Closer to home, there's also an honors program for exceptional freshmen, and sophomores can apply, too.

Though 80 percent of students are Roman Catholic, few resemble priests in training. In fact, almost three-fourths climb the corporate ladder after graduation. Eighty-four percent are from Minnesota, and most are white, public school alumni from middle-class backgrounds. While the administration is trying to increase minority enrollment, minorities only make up 4 percent of the student body. "Lack of diversity is now a big complaint among students," admits a

(Continued)
Grad in 6 Years: 71%
Returning Freshmen: 90%
Academics: ✍ ✍ ✍
Social: ☎ ☎ ☎
Q of L: ★ ★ ★
Admissions: (320) 363-2196 (St. John's)(320) 363-5308 or (800) 544-1489 (St. Benedict)
Email Address: admissions@csbsju.edu

Strongest Programs:
  Biology
  Chemistry
  Computer Science
  English
  Music
  Political Science
  Math

Comprising one of the few joint universities in the country, St. John's and St. Benedict emphasize their Roman Catholic roots while providing the academic rigor students need to prepare for numerous professions.

sophomore. Social action and justice are important here; during the spring 1999 conflict in Kosovo, students held rallies and open-mike assemblies to debate how peace should be achieved.

Seventy-six percent of students here live on campus, and a committed residence staff, including the monks at St. John's and sisters at St. Benedict, oversees homey dormitory life. Incoming students are assigned to doubles on freshman floors in one of the six dorms. Other options include small houses off campus for half a dozen students each, an experimental Christian community housing project of five units for 110 students, and college-owned apartments, including an earth-sheltered complex on the shore of a lake. Upperclassmen who live off campus in a nearby town commute by car or college bus. "We have the big city nearby, and we live in the country," says a freshman. "It has the perfect atmosphere."

Since there are no social fraternities or sororities, the social scene tends toward private or college-sponsored parties, as well as bar-hopping in St. Joseph and nearby St. Cloud, a city of 50,000 that is 15 minutes away by car. For more refined tastes, the Stephen B. Humphrey Fine Arts Theater at SJU and the Benedicta Arts Center on the CSB campus host a wide variety of cultural events. For those seeking typical college fun, "the Joint Events Council put on many different activities throughout the week—dances, movies," says a St. Benedict junior. "The best road trips are to Duluth or Minneapolis." Among the most popular annual happenings are the fall Watab Island party, Christmas tree lighting, formal dances each semester, the year-end spring Pinestock Folk Festival (named for the school's Pine Curtain setting), and the St. John's–St. Thomas football game, otherwise known as the Tommy-Johnnie.

Religion may be the most dominant program on campus, but football is a close second. The team is a perennial Division III powerhouse, and its fanatical following rivals the likes of Notre Dame with their devotion. Curiously enough, a team of guys functions as a cheerleading squad: "Instead of cheerleaders we have 'The Rat Pack' who cheer for our football team," says a sophomore. "This team riles up the crowd like nothing you've seen." Soccer and ice hockey are popular among both men and women. SJU cross-country, baseball, and track and field and CSB volleyball and swimming and diving are among the teams that have brought home conference championships in the past two years. The St. Benedict basketball team reached the NCAA finals. Non-varsity students can use the college's modern athletic facilities and participate in an extensive intramural program, the ultimate goal of which is a chance at the coveted "red cotton," T-shirts that proclaim championship status.

With their emphasis on Benedictine precepts and rugged but beautiful location in the rural Minnesota boondocks, St. John's and St. Benedict mainly attract committed Catholics who are willing to sacrifice big-city conveniences for solid pre-professional training. Students eager for a true community with their peers and professors are seldom disappointed. "Too much school work, too many activities—there's not enough time in the day!" laments a St. Benedict junior. "Time goes by way too fast."

If You Apply To > St. Johns and St. Benedict…Rolling admissions. Financial aid: Feb. 1. Housing: May 15. Meets demonstrated need of 90%. Campus interviews: recommended, evaluative. Alumni interviews: optional, informational. SATs or ACTs: required. SAT IIs: optional. Accepts the Common Application and electronic applications. Essay question: personal statement.

St. Lawrence University

Canton, NY 13617

Boasting a conventional student body with a streak of outdoorsy nonconformity, St. Lawrence University draws those seeking an education that exercises body and mind. Located deep in upstate New York, this school's excellent liberal arts curriculum is complemented by a close-knit community—and one of the best environmental studies programs in the nation. Students take full advantage of their pristine and rugged surroundings, and are equally fond of their peers and faculty members. "Everyone's so friendly," gushes a junior. "It's easy to get to know people, make friends, and just be happy."

The St. Lawrence campus—which has undergone $80 million in construction and renovation over the past few years—is just 90 minutes away from Ottawa, the Canadian capital. Hiking trails, a river, and a golf course surround 30 buildings, which sit centered on 1,000-acres. Many buildings date from the late 19th century, and though their exteriors have been preserved, their interiors are fully modernized and up-to-date. To combat winter temperatures, which average between 20 and 30 degrees, it's only a 10-minute walk between the two most distant buildings. There's been a bit of a building boom recently, with extensive remodeling of the library and student center, renovation of the main dining hall, and construction of a new bookstore and playing field. A new, nine-lane track, team facilities, and stadium grandstand were also recently completed.

St. Lawrence offers a classical liberal arts education, emphasizing quality over quantity. Enrollment has been reduced to improve the student/faculty ratio (11 to 1), keep classes small, and allow for more team teaching. New majors include computer science and global studies. St. Lawrence is well-known for their environmental studies. Among the unique offerings are outdoor education courses in music and writing, and a student-run, self-sustainable residence. The faculty is also reviewing general education requirements, which can now be satisfied through one of two tracks. The "standard track" requires one course in the natural sciences, one in social sciences, one in humanities and one in any non-Western topic, plus two courses in "classical liberal arts" (math or symbolic logic, arts, and language). The "alternative track" is based on St. Lawrence's Cultural Encounters program, which includes core courses, foreign language study, science and mathematics, one semester of study abroad, and a senior seminar.

The university's First-Year Program—small, interdisciplinary, two-semester courses taught by professors from all departments, who then become academic advisors—is "a good stepping stone, to get you into the college environment," says a junior. Biology is the most popular major, followed by psychology, economics, government, and English, but many students prefer less conventional programs, such as Renaissance music. Administrators say the music department is small but growing steadily with the recent addition of an instrumental music faculty position.

Striving "to make the world our classroom," St. Lawrence augments its on-campus offerings with numerous study abroad programs. More than half of the students head overseas to such places as Kenya, Japan, Russia, or India. Students may also take advantage of group-sponsored exchange programs in Denmark, Canada, Costa Rica, or Washington, D.C. Frequent trips to Ottawa for cultural and political events are part of the academic and extracurricular agendas. There are also five-year programs with other universities in engineering, nursing, and

Website: www.stlawu.edu
Location: Village
Total Enrollment: 1,978
Undergraduates: 1,875
Male/Female: 48/52
SAT Ranges: V 510–610 M 520–600
Financial Aid: 71%
Expense: Pr $ $ $ $
Phi Beta Kappa: Yes
Applicants: 2,235
Accepted: 74%
Enrolled: 35%
Grad in 6 Years: 74%
Returning Freshmen: 83%
Academics: ✍ ✍ ✍
Social: ☎ ☎ ☎
Q of L: ★ ★ ★
Admissions: (315) 229-5261
Email Address: admiss@stlawu.edu

Strongest Programs:
Psychology
Sociology
Environmental Studies
Math
Speech and Theater
English

To combat winter temperatures, which average between 20 and 30 degrees, it's only a 10-minute walk between the two most distant buildings.

management. Some lucky students will have the opportunity of participating in the St. Lawrence University Fellows Program, which supports faculty-student research done in the summer before the student's senior year.

St. Lawrence students speak highly of their professors, and say administrators have worked hard to increase the school's academic rigor over the past few years. That results in some disconnects: "The academic climate is mixed, split between those who are excited by their academics and those who don't care," says a senior. "But the coursework is pretty demanding." Small classes make for a lot of attention and assistance from professors. "I have had the opportunity to study with exceptional instructors who motivate me, interest me, and care about my future," an English and government major reports. Still, most "Larries" agree that there is no cutthroat competition here. The emphasis on shared learning is furthered by the school's "residential college system," through which students living in the same dorm take a common interdisciplinary course team-taught by professors from multiple disciplines. To complement their yearlong common course, first-year students live together in one of 12 residential "communities" with 40 to 50 students each.

St. Lawrence is a fairly homogeneous place; the student body is 84 percent white, with African Americans, Hispanics and Asian students adding another 5 percent combined. One student says, "a small percentage of minorities feel exposed," but St. Lawrence has La Casa Latina, the Louis Ray House of Brotherhood, and the International House as choices and resource centers for these students. There is a director of multicultural affairs and a full-time minority affairs office on campus. "Overall, though, everyone's laid-back and pretty happy in 'Larryland,'" says a junior.

Dorm life at St. Lawrence is your standard bed, dresser, chest of drawers, and desk-with-a-light. Most rooms are well maintained, though students complain it sometimes takes a while for repair requests to be addressed. Most dorms also have coed wings, and students generally live in doubles. Freshmen are placed in their residential colleges, while everyone else gets rooms by lottery with priority given to upperclassmen (they get all the singles). Seniors occasionally gain permission to live off campus; 95 percent of the student body live on campus. "That's part of what makes our campus close-knit," one student comments. Campus living also has its rewards: The food served in the dining hall frequently features student recipes. Twenty-eight percent of the women and 19 percent of the men live and eat in fraternity and sorority houses. Other options for grub include the campus pub in the Student Center, a café in the physical education building, and a convenience store.

The social life at SLU centers on campus, since—thanks to the school's small size—most students know each other. The university provides activities, such as a nonalcoholic campus nightclub, a new pool hall, four different current movies each week, and the campus coffeehouse—a great place to hear a band, acoustic guitarist, or comedian. Still, students say, "most of the social life revolves around Greek houses," where independent students are welcome, too. No hard liquor or kegs are allowed on campus. Wristbands are required at frat parties for those of legal drinking age (21 or over), though a junior says "they won't give you much trouble [if you're underage] as long as you don't cause trouble." At St. Lawrence, to "make a run for the border" doesn't mean heading for Mexican fast food; the purchasing age for liquor in Ontario is a mere 19.

Canton is a charming town of restored Victorian buildings and storefronts offering everything from bagels to handmade jewelry to bars and restaurants. As a college town, however, it rates "nonexistent," says a sociology major.

"Potsdam, 10 minutes away, has more stuff and we go there." On campus, the university's Winterfest is an annual two-week celebration of the season, planned with local community members as an effort to improve town-gown relations. On "Peak Weekend" the SLU Outing Club tries to "put St. Lawrence students on every peak in the Adirondacks." Most St. Lawrence students enjoy sports; the school's fine athletic facilities, including an indoor field house, eight squash courts, indoor tennis, a pool, and ropes course, cater to varsity athletes and weekend warriors alike.

St. Lawrence's on-campus golf course doubles as a running route and a cross-country skiing trail during the winter. Hiking and rock climbing are other outdoor exercise options, as is canoeing the St. Lawrence River. In varsity sports, men's hockey is the top draw—especially when played against archrival Clarkson. The men's soccer team is strong, recently capturing the NCAA Division III title. Other championship teams include women's hockey and lacrosse and men's cross-country, field hockey, and track. About 90 percent of the student body participate in intramurals, with competition ranging from softball to hockey to volleyball.

With administrators raising the academic bar and a lengthy round of renovation and construction about to conclude, St. Lawrence is a school on the rise. It could be the perfect school for those seeking a small, caring environment—and wanting to get back to nature.

> ### Overlaps
> **University of Vermont, Hamilton, Hobart and William Smith, Skidmore, Colgate.**

If You Apply To > **St. Lawrence**...Early decision: Nov. 15, Jan. 15. Regular admissions and financial aid: Feb. 15. Does not guarantee to meet demonstrated need. Campus interviews: recommended, evaluative. Alumni interviews: optional, informational. SATs or ACTs: required. SAT IIs: optional. Essay question: how to rate the best small town in America; how would jealousy be guaranteed.

Saint Louis University

221 North Grand Boulevard, St. Louis, MO 63103-2097

Within sight of Saint Louis's famed Gateway Arch, the historical gateway to the American West, sits Saint Louis University, the first university established west of the Mississippi River. SLU (pronounced "slew") is true to its name in offering students a slew of programs from which to choose, from aviation and engineering to public service, social work, and meteorology. The school's academic atmosphere is shaped by its Jesuit tradition; administrators ensure each student receives personal care and attention, and expect graduates to contribute to society and lead efforts for social change.

The SLU campus is structurally diverse and continually in flux. Cupples House, a beautiful old mansion in the middle of campus, houses 19th-century furniture and an art gallery—and is just steps from the futuristic glass structure of the law school. The most impressive of the vision and revisions is the Pius XII Library, with bright and comfortable study areas. SLU likes to boast about Kiel Center, a state-of-the-art 20,000-seat arena where its men's basketball team regularly plays to a sold-out house. Parks College's McDonnell Douglas Building houses a flight simulator and computer labs, while the Allied Health building contains state-of-the-art labs and facilities for aspiring doctors, nurses, and physical therapists.

Website: www.slu.edu
Location: Urban
Total Enrollment: 11,069
Undergraduates: 6,889
Male/Female: 45/56
SAT Ranges: V 530–630 M 520–640
ACT Range: 23–28
Financial Aid: 85%
Expense: Pr $ $
Phi Beta Kappa: Yes
Applicants: 4,990
Accepted: 69%
Enrolled: 37%
Grad in 6 Years: 65%

(Continued)

Returning Freshmen: 87%

Academics: ✍ ✍ ✍

Social: ☎ ☎

Q of L: ★ ★ ★

Admissions: (314) 977-2500

Email Address:
admitme@slu.edu

Strongest Programs:
Biology
Communications
Science
Mathematics
Theological Studies
Allied Health
Psychology
Aviation and Engineering

The new College of Public Service offers majors in communication disorders, educational studies, and urban affairs, which encourage students to put research into action.

In keeping with its strong Jesuit commitment to education in the broader sense, all SLU undergrads must complete distribution requirements in international cultures, fine arts, English, literature, science, social/behavioral science, mathematics, and history. Additionally, students must take philosophy and theology courses, such as SLUVision, which integrates community service with the philosophy and theology component. The most popular majors are biology, physical therapy and psychology, while pre-med also gets high marks from students. As might be expected, philosophy and theology are outstanding. Weaker spots are hard to find; a junior insists that "students don't seem to avoid any academic departments." SLU attracts scholars from around the globe with one of the world's most complete microfilm collections of Vatican documents. Parks College of Aviation and Engineering, America's first certified college of aviation, offers degree programs in Aviation Science where students can become professional pilots. The College of Arts and Sciences's meteorology program provides students with an opportunity to study with specialists in satellite, radar, and mesoscale meteorology. The new College of Public Service offers majors in communication disorders, educational studies, and urban affairs, which encourage students to put research into action.

Sixty-five percent of a recent SLU freshman class came from the top quarter of their high school class, and a physical therapy major reports, "Course difficulty level is highly dependent on the field of study. As a whole, though, students are here to achieve academic success." Students praise the faculty for their accessibility. "I have had teachers print their home phone numbers on their syllabi so we could reach them after hours," says a marketing major. "They make a point to relate class material to real-life situations." Students report few problems getting into classes, despite the fact that most enroll less than 50, and say that graduating in four years is the norm. Study abroad is an option, too; SLU has one of the most charming and largest European campuses of an American university in Madrid, Spain.

More than 60 percent of SLU students hail from the Show-Me State, and most of the rest are from other parts of the Midwest. The student body is moderately diverse, however, with blacks making up 10 percent, Asian Americans 5 percent, and Hispanics 2 percent. Race relations tend to be nonconfrontational, and political correctness is not a big deal—issues such as church doctrine and the just-increased parking fees spark more debate. The Residential Life department also trains diversity advocates who serve as programmers and facilitators for the dorms; they get more in-depth training about diversity, racism, and oppression. Generally, students come from private, religiously affiliated high schools, and are a friendly bunch dedicated to community service. The school offers 11 athletic scholarships, along with merit scholarships worth up to $23,168.

Speaking of residential life, 46 percent of students choose from single-sex, coed by floor, coed by suite, and scholarship dorms. However, housing is not guaranteed, and "is becoming a concern for incoming freshmen," according to a sophomore, "many students turn to off-campus housing." Upperclass members can move into courtyard-style apartments, which are newly furnished because they opened last year, reports a junior. SLU has all the advantages and problems usually associated with being in the middle of a city. But most students feel safe on campus, since the school has officers on 24-hour patrol ("bicycles, cars, and walking," says a junior) and ID checks at dorm doors. "Streets that run through campus have been closed to make walkways, making campus ever safer," one student reports. "SLU is always buying new land and buildings to expand parking, recreation, and classroom space."

Social life at SLU includes campus events, such as movies in the Quad, dances, and Greek parties, and options in downtown St. Louis, such as comedy clubs and sporting events. Road trips to Kansas City, Chicago, and nearby schools like the University of Illinois and Indiana University are also popular. Greek life at SLU—highly unusual for a Jesuit institution—claims 17 percent of the men and 13 percent of the women. Alcohol doesn't play a big role; "open containers" aren't allowed on campus, and only students who are of age can drink, in their own rooms, without underage roommates present. Spring Fever and Fall Festival, both annual events, feature bands, club-sponsored booths, and vendors. True to tradition, Sunday evening mass is usually packed, and "community service and outreach work are some of the most valued student activities," a marketing major says.

SLU has no varsity football team, but other Billiken squads more than compensate for this deficit. What's a Billiken? A history major says, "It was a common good-luck charm in the early 1900s." A popular sportswriter of the time said the charm resembled the then-football coach, and the name stuck. SLU men's soccer is among the top five winningest programs of the '90s. Men's basketball brought home the Conference USA championship in 200 and annually contends for an NCAA Tournament berth; games against Marquette or Cincinnati draw crowds. For weekend warriors, the Simon Recreation Center boasts a 40-meter pool, six racquetball courts, and loads of equipment.

St. Louis University may not have the marquee name or reputation of some of its larger Jesuit peers, but it's winning students' devotion and increasing its national visibility by combining a caring faculty with athletic excellence and friendly and diverse undergraduates. "Simply put, students come to SLU because they want to learn, and teachers come to SLU to teach," sighs a junior. No wonder students are proud to "Just SLU it!"

> *Men's basketball has emerged as a top 50 program that annually contends for an NCAA Tournament berth, and games against Marquette or Cincinnati draw crowds.*

Overlaps

University of Missouri, Truman State, Marquette, Washington University (MO), Creighton.

If You Apply To ➢

SLU…Rolling admissions (scholarship deadline Dec. 1, physical therapy program deadline Dec. 15). Meets demonstrated need of 78%. Campus interviews: recommended, informational. Alumni interviews: optional, informational. SATs or ACTs: required. SAT IIs: optional. Apply to particular programs. Accepts the Common Application and electronic applications for some programs.

St. Mary's College of Maryland

St. Mary's City, MD 20686

St. Mary's is one of the best deals on the East Coast. Despite its religious-sounding name, the school is a public institution that has been designated the state's "honors college." Ten years ago, St. Mary's was just another complacent public college with a dazzling waterfront. But now, with test scores on the rise, increased state support, and growing numbers of applications, suffice it to say that St. Mary's is out to make waves. It also has the advantage of being one of the East Coast's prettiest schools, with its own beautiful marina located right on the St. Mary's River and plenty of opportunities to stroll along the shore and watch gorgeous sunsets.

St. Mary's got its start in 1840 as a women's seminary intended to educate the "mothers of Maryland." The campus, built on a peninsula in southern Maryland where the Potomac River meets the Chesapeake Bay, is a mix of Colonial and modern architecture clustered directly on the waterfront. The college has taken

Website: www.smcm.edu
Location: Rural
Total Enrollment: 1,682
Undergraduates: 1,682
Male/Female: 41/59
SAT Ranges: V 590–690 M 570–660
Financial Aid: 48%
Expense: Pub $ $ $ $
Phi Beta Kappa: No
Applicants: 1,721

(Continued)

Accepted: 61%

Enrolled: 33%

Grad in 6 Years: N/A

Returning Freshmen: 90%

Academics: ✍ ✍ ✍ ✍

Social: ☎ ☎ ☎

Q of L: ★ ★ ★

Admissions: (800) 492-7181

Email Address:
admissions@
honors.smcm.edu

Strongest Programs:
Biology
Psychology
Economics
Music

The strong music department includes prize-winning pianist Brian Ganz as head of the piano faculty.

Campus organizations, including a film society, sponsor several events a week. In nice weather, students spend time enjoying the waterfront or nearby bike trails.

advantage of its setting by establishing an outstanding center for marine research along the river. It's also part of a 1,200-acre national historic landmark commemorating Maryland's first settlement; archeological digs dot the campus and provide inspiration for a strong program in Colonial history. Crescent-shaped townhouses add a distinctly creative flavor to the campus.

Students may sail through the bay, but not the academics; the curriculum is continuously improved and the courseload is getting tougher. "The courses can be quite rigorous at times," reports a sophomore. "There is a tinge of competitiveness in the air, but most students encourage one another." Students have excellent departments to choose from, especially biology, which places many of its grads into jobs at Johns Hopkins Hospital and Research Labs. It is also the most popular major, followed by psychology, economics, English, and history. The strong music department includes prize-winning pianist Brian Ganz as head of the piano faculty. St. Mary's has also created an independent-student-designed major for more free-thinking types. Education is said to be one of the weaker departments. A state-of-the-art science center, with 55,000 square feet of classrooms, labs, and research space benefits the already strong science departments. In the designing stages are plans for both a new student center and a modern physical education/recreation building.

All entering freshmen must take a course in English composition in addition to a math course, a foreign language, and Legacy I and II, a two-semester history sequence. The ambitious general studies curriculum emphasizes Western heritage, writing, and math, but also includes art history, literature, science, and a philosophy course for juniors and seniors. The school offers study abroad programs at Oxford's Center for Medieval and Renaissance Studies, and exchange programs in Germany and China. Closer to home, biology students can cruise the bay on the college's 40-foot research boat. The honors program, both highly respected and very selective, has further boosted St. Mary's academic standards. "Overall, the quality of teaching I have received has been excellent," an enthusiastic junior reports. "My teachers have all been very knowledgeable of the subjects and were enthusiastic in attempting to spark my interests," a fellow classmate adds. All classes are taught by faculty, and most have 25 people or fewer.

Eighty-three percent of the student body hail from Maryland, and 80 percent are from public schools. More minority students are also finding their way to the peninsula; 8 percent of the school are African American, and 9 percent of the student body are Hispanics and Asian Americans combined. The big social issue on campus, according to students, is the environment. The political atmosphere on campus is described as fairly liberal and laid-back. "There is a very sensitive and openly accepting student body," reports a senior. St. Mary's offers 70 scholarships for academic merit that range from $500 to $6,000, but there are no athletic scholarships.

Students tend to enjoy living on campus, as three-quarters of the students remain there at any given time. Options include five residence halls, three of which are coed. Best of all are the 81 two-story townhouses that allow upperclassmen with sufficient credits to do their own cooking. "Everyone looks forward to having enough credits to get into a townhouse," remarks an anxious sophomore. Older students get preference if they decide to retain a room or want one nearby, and students select rooms based on the number of academic credits they have acquired. Those who do live off campus have enticing options, including old farmhouses and riverside cottages available for rent. The cafeteria food is bland, but students who tire of it can join the vegetarian co-op or just go catch their own fish and crabs.

St. Mary's secluded location—about an hour and a half from either Washington, D.C., or Baltimore—means there's little nightlife off campus. The seclusion gets mixed responses from students: "St. Mary's is a pretty close community. Weekend social life is usually centered around a few parties that everyone attends," one student comments. Given the isolation of the campus, St. Mary's is a "make your own fun" kind of place. When students become tired of relaxing in the upperclassman townhouses and dorm rooms, they take it upon themselves to create their own activities. Campus organizations, including a film society, sponsor several events a week. In nice weather, students spend time enjoying the waterfront or nearby bike trails. The main source of fun, of course, is the surrounding water and its sporty offerings. "It's virtually impossible to graduate without knowing how to sail," says one student. The waterfront also becomes the focus of campus-wide activities, including an Earth Day celebration and an all-day Riverfest each September, when students race cardboard and wooden boats of their own design. One-third of students become involved in community service.

Although certainly not known for its athletics, Division III St. Mary's has recently taken off. The coed and women's sailing teams, coached by a former member of the U.S Olympic team, have been nationally ranked, and the women won the Sloop National Championship several years back. Women's sailing and men's lacrosse are also strong. The Frisbee golf club team has a heated rivalry with Navy, and even attracts considerable alumni interest. A popular T-shirt reads, "St. Mary's college football—undefeated," but of course, there is no football team.

St. Mary's is bent on establishing itself as one of the country's premier public liberal arts colleges. While it lacks the traditions—academic and otherwise—of more established institutions, it is gaining stature and attracting more and more students for whom it is the first choice. With its unique blend of learning and life on the waterfront, says one student, "It's like your parents are paying for you to live at a vacation resort for eight months of the year."

Those who do live off campus have enticing options, including old farmhouses and riverside cottages available for rent.

Overlaps

University of Maryland, Loyola College (MD), James Madison, Mary Washington, William and Mary.

If You Apply To ➤ | **St. Mary's**...Early decision: Dec. 1 and Jan. 15. Regular admissions: Jan. 15. Financial aid: Mar. 1. Guarantees to meet demonstrated need. Campus interviews: recommended, informational. No alumni interviews. SATs or ACTs: required. SAT IIs: optional.

St. Olaf College

1520 St. Olaf Avenue, Northfield, MN 55057-1098

Northfield, Minn., home of St. Olaf College, calls itself the home of "Cows, Colleges, and Contentment." And students at St. Olaf generally agree with that statement. They are drawn to this small Minnesota school, founded by Norwegian Lutheran immigrants and named for the country's patron saint, because it aims to be "an excellent liberal arts college of the church," according to the administration. One student describes her peers at St. Olaf as "Minnesota nice." She elaborates: "You can't go anywhere without saying 'hi' to people. Even if you don't know a person, there is still a feeling of belonging to the same community. We are friendly, outgoing, hardworking, and we love to have fun."

St. Olaf's meticulously landscaped 350-acre campus, featured in several

Website: www.stolaf.edu
Location: Small town
Total Enrollment: 2,879
Undergraduates: 2,879
Male/Female: 43/57
SAT Ranges: V 580–680 M 570–680
ACT Range: 24–29

(Continued)

Financial Aid: 61%

Expense: Pr $ $

Phi Beta Kappa: Yes

Applicants: 2,359

Accepted: 76%

Enrolled: 42%

Grad in 6 Years: 77%

Returning Freshmen: 92%

Academics: ✍ ✍ ✍ ✍

Social: ☎ ☎ ☎

Q of L: ★ ★ ★ ★

Admissions: (507) 646-3025 or
(800) 800-3025

Email Address:
admissions@stolaf.edu

Strongest Programs:
Biology
Psychology
Economics
English
Mathematics

Since the program in international studies is an important part of the school's curriculum, more than 60 percent of students take advantage of study abroad opportunities.

architectural journals, is located on Manitou Heights, overlooking the Cannon River valley and the city of Northfield. More than 10,000 trees, native prairie, and a wetlands wildlife area surround the 34 native limestone buildings that form the campus. The student union, the Buntrock Commons, offers dining and food services, a bookstore, post office, conference and banquet facilities, movie theater, and game room. It lays claim to being the largest commons area at a small private college in the country.

All students at St. Olaf complete a general education requirement that covers three areas: foundation studies, core studies, and integrative study. A first-year seminar emphasizing writing, a foreign language, math, oral communication, and physical education fulfill the first area. Two courses in each of six disciplines—Western culture, multicultural studies, art, literary studies, biblical studies, and theological studies—with two courses in natural sciences and two in social sciences complete the second requirement. A course in ethical issues and perspectives fulfills the third area. Typically, 14 to 16 courses satisfy the general education requirements; some courses may fulfill requirements in more than one area.

Students give the nod to biology and chemistry at St. Olaf, which boasts a solid premed program; economics, psychology, and English literature are also popular majors. The music department draws high praise, too, because it offers many performance opportunities with five school choirs, a band, and an orchestra. The choirs are often featured at church services and other religious events, and can regularly be heard singing with the Minnesota Orchestra. In the last quarter-century the college has cultivated an international agenda for its students and faculty, and has created the largest international studies program in the country among liberal arts colleges. The Finstad Center conveys knowledge about the challenges, risks, rewards, opportunities, and responsibilities of being an entrepreneur. Weaker academic departments include family resources, sociology, and physical education. Still, all students get faculty advisors, and the vast majority of students graduate in four years. Students who participate in the intensive, nontraditional program—the two-year Great Conversation course in classic works—live together in one dorm to facilitate late-night study sessions. Additionally, since the program in international studies is an important part of the school's curriculum, more than 60 percent of students take advantage of study abroad opportunities, including those offered through membership in the Associated Colleges of the Midwest consortium.*

Faculty members at St. Olaf are highly praised by students. "My writing has improved dramatically while my thinking skills have been honed and strengthened," a junior philosophy major says. Instructors participate in and out of the classroom, reportedly having as many as 10 hours of open office time a week. Still, just because professors want to see them succeed doesn't mean students can coast. "The courses are challenging and the climate is competitive, but not cutthroat. Students here definitely want to achieve but there is not some overwhelming pressure to sabotage the work of others," a sophomore social work and multicultural studies major says. There's also an annual study break where professors serve their stressed-out pupils ice cream.

Diversity is the hot topic at St. Olaf. The student body is extremely homogeneous, with 90 percent white, meaning there are only about 250 minority students in the whole school—a situation the administration says it is working to change through workshops and other awareness programs. Students also recognize that while there is no overt hostility among white and minority students, there is a degree of separatism. "Any celebrations of diversity or forums on multicultural issues are mostly attended by students of color," says one sophomore. Most students at St. Olaf are high achievers from Midwestern public schools, drawn in part by 629 merit scholarships ranging from $2,000 to $6,000. Despite their similar backgrounds, students say they have their differences. "Unfortunately, there is a typical or stereotypical Ole. They are typically blond, well-off, and very attractive. At the same time, two people who may look like they are similar may have very different views," a sophomore says.

Ninety-six percent of students live in on-campus housing, with college-owned houses available off campus, and freshmen are assigned double rooms in 20-student "corridors," each with two junior counselors. Dorms are coed by floor, and each has its own personality. Rooms are selected by lottery, which students consider very fair. Students eat in a large modern cafeteria, where the food is considered above average for college fare. Every December the dining hall serves a special meal of traditional Norwegian cuisine, including lutefisk, which "tastes awful," according to one junior philosophy major.

Opinions diverge on St. Olaf's social life. Some students blame peer apathy for the lack of things to do, noting that "it's what you make of it." Others grouse about the dry campus or students' efforts to circumvent it. One sophomore complains that this official policy "only seems to encourage students to drink in secret." Most weekend activities are on campus, including a nightclub called Lion's Pause and a coffeehouse, the Alley. The fine arts department provides many music, theater, and dance performances. And because there are no fraternities or sororities at St. Olaf, any large-scale weekend partying usually occurs off campus—at the few bars in town, or even better, at cross-town rival Carleton College. The Student Activities Committee sponsors occasional dances, speakers, and cultural events, covered by student fees and at-the-door ticket sales. Daily chapel services, though not mandatory, are heavily attended, and studying is always another weekend option

In the city of Northfield, there is little of social interest for St. Olaf students aside from Carleton, Olaf's liberal neighbor and chief rival. The most talked-about annual event, running more than 75 years, is the four-day Christmas Festival during which choirs, orchestras, and bands combine in televised concerts celebrating the birth of Jesus. Many students volunteer in Northfield and report a friendly rapport with the community. "It's small but has a nice Minnesota charm. We're far enough away from the city not to be bothered by noise and pollution." Nonetheless, for those with wanderlust, buses leave regularly for the twin cities of Minneapolis and St. Paul, which are less than an hour's drive, where one can experience a shopper's paradise at the huge Mall of America. Chicago is also a popular road trip.

St. Olaf has outstanding athletic programs. Volleyball, tennis, and men's and women's swimming regularly win conference titles. The men's ski team are reigning national champions, while the women's team ranked second in nationals. There is also an extensive intramural program, and broomball—ice hockey played with brooms instead of sticks, and shoes rather than skates—is the sport of choice in the winter. The St. Olaf football team competes against Carleton for the honor of having the statue in the town's square face the winning campus. The chorus of the school's fight song is "Um Ya Ya," which has become a popular chant on campus.

Those yearning for a school where spirituality and scholarship exist on the same exalted plane will find St. Olaf is a good bet. It's a place where students work hard, are encouraged by good teachers, toughened by Minnesota winters, and nourished by strong moral values, in addition to hearty Scandinavian food. "Oles," don't have much of the boisterous social life common to other small

Daily chapel services, though not mandatory, are heavily attended, and studying is always another weekend option.

Students eat in a large modern cafeteria, where the food is considered above average for college fare. Every December the dining hall serves a special meal of traditional Norwegian cuisine.

Overlaps

Gustavus Adolphus,
Carleton, Luther, St.
Thomas, University of
Minnesota.

colles. But for most, the challenging, character-building atmosphere of concern and friendship they experience here is well worth the sacrifice.

If You Apply To ➤ **St. Olaf**…Modified rolling admissions. Early decision: Nov. 15. Financial aid: Mar. 1 (priority). Guarantees to meet demonstrated need. Campus interviews: recommended, informational. No alumni interviews. SATs or ACTs: required. SAT IIs: optional. Accepts the Common Application. Essay question: how your actions affected the life of someone else; situation in which your values or beliefs were challenged by someone you respect; significant experience or achievement; how email has changed the way we communicate.

University of San Francisco

2130 Fulton Street, San Francisco, CA 94117-1080

Website: www.usfca.edu
Location: Urban
Total Enrollment: 7,990
Undergraduates: 4,690
Male/Female: 37/63
SAT Ranges: V 480–580 M 480–590
ACT Range: 20–25
Financial Aid: 54%
Expense: Pr $ $
Phi Beta Kappa: No
Applicants: 3,064
Accepted: 77%
Enrolled: 27%
Grad in 6 Years: 65%
Returning Freshmen: 83%
Academics: ✑ ✑ ✑
Social: ☎ ☎ ☎
Q of L: ★ ★ ★ ★
Admissions: (415) 422-6563
Email Address: N/A

Strongest Programs:
　Nursing
　Business
　Communications
　Biology

Housing is so scarce right now in red-hot San Francisco that you might expect some students to apply to the University of San Francisco just to secure prime real estate in town. But there are even more compelling reasons to choose USF, especially for those enrolling in the highly regarded nursing or business schools. Founded in 1855, the university maintains its fervent commitment to high standards of learning and scholarship in the Jesuit tradition. Despite the school's religious affiliation, the student body comes from diverse backgrounds and cultures, including students from 70 foreign nations.

USF's 55 well-kept acres spotted with beautiful basilica-type buildings and modern facilities are, as one student puts it, "wedged into the heart of San Francisco." The campus stands atop one of San Francisco's seven hills, adjacent to Golden Gate Park, overlooking San Francisco Bay and the city skyline. The university has lately undertaken some major construction and building renovations, including a revamped education building and an expanded library.

Liberal arts are the centerpiece of USF, both in terms of numbers of students and academic quality. There is also a strong emphasis on preprofessional programs, especially nursing, premed, communications, and business. The Center for the Pacific Rim allows students to do interdisciplinary majors with an Asian focus, as does the Asian Studies program. The 51-unit general education curriculum requires students to take courses in six major categories: foundation skills (writing, oral communication, analytical skills), natural sciences, history and social sciences, cultural perspectives, literature and arts, and philosophy and theology. One way to avoid the general-education blues is through enrollment in the St. Ignatius Institute program, which offers an integrated four-year curriculum based on the Great Books of Western civilization presented in an unusual seminar/lecture combination. The St. Ignatius program is not restricted to only the top students, and its participants are able to study in Oxford and Innsbruck.

Some of the preprofessional majors are demanding, and students say that competition is common but not cutthroat. "I find myself in constant competition with all the students in my class," says a freshman. Another student says that difficulty "varies from class to class and depends on the professor." Extensive and mandatory academic advising ensures that students' courseloads are manageable, and is praised as one of USF's highest virtues. Also highly regarded is the teaching staff. As one student puts it, "I had professors who really cared and wanted to see the students pass the courses."

The university operates on the basis of fall and spring semesters, with five weeks off at Christmastime. Students interested in speeding up their education can enroll in optional three-week courses in January at extra cost. The average class size is about 25, so "the instructor isn't a faint vision at the bottom of the lecture hall," reports one student. Two computer labs make sure USF's computing capabilities are up to speed, and every residence hall will be linked to the campus mainframe. A BFA program has been added that provides a joint degree with the California College of Arts.

"Although the school is located in a liberal city, I would classify most of the students as ultraconservative," an economics major says. But a classmate contends, "The wide variety of views don't lend themselves to one particular group affecting the tone of the campus." While 77 percent of the students are from California, half are Roman Catholic, and 39 percent went to parochial high school. The student body is far from homogeneous. More than half are from minority groups, with Asian Americans the largest contingent at 22 percent, African Americans accounting for 5 percent, and Hispanics comprising 10 percent. One of the university's missions is to "prepare men and women to shape a multicultural world with creativity, generosity, and compassion." A student remarks, "As a black student I feel very comfortable at the University of San Francisco. Students from different backgrounds mix." The only definite faction on campus seems to be the St. Ignatius students, "who kind of condescend to everyone else, but everyone else thinks they are geeks," says an English major.

Admissions are need-blind, and the university makes an effort to provide financial aid to accepted students, although it's not guaranteed. About 80 athletic scholarships for men and women are awarded, as well as 131 merit scholarships.

Thirty-five percent of the students live in university housing, and most of these campus dwellers are freshmen, sophomores, and any other students under 21, who are required to live on campus. Those upperclassmen who don't live at home often leave campus to brave the city's high rents and tight rental market. Students who do want dorm rooms (some with views of San Francisco Bay) have four choices: an all-women dorm, a coed-by-floor dorm that "caters to a younger population," a coed hall that is said to foster "a more liberal lifestyle," or the quiet and renovated coed Lone Mountain Hall for upperclassmen. "Dorms are livable but I wouldn't consider them comfortable," notes a sophomore environmental science major. On-campus students eat in a commons, where various meal plans are offered (though some grumble about the cost).

USF's greatest asset is undoubtedly its location. San Francisco is a cosmopolitan city. "It is definitely a busy city with a great, diverse community," says a student. Students can take advantage of the city's reliable public transportation, including the famous cable cars, to get to a variety of cultural attractions, ranging from Chinatown to the symphony. Nightlife is great for those who want to dance at the clubs or meet in the bars. "Haight Street is a definite attraction. Anything and everything is found on that strip," says one student. Campus activities include the Hawaiian Club's annual luau and the Barrio Festival held by the Filipino-American Club. The freshmen and sophomores are the only loyal fraternity fraternizers, but with the more stringent alcohol policies on campus, even

(Continued)
Computer Science
Pacific Rim Studies

The Center for the Pacific Rim allows students to do interdisciplinary majors with an Asian focus, as does the Asian Studies program.

USF's greatest asset is undoubtedly its location. Students can take advantage of the city's reliable public transportation, including the famous cable cars, to get to a variety of cultural attractions, ranging from Chinatown to the symphony.

they are not as "fraternal as once observed," notes one student. The academic fraternities—the accounting frat, the honors frat, etc.—add social options to the mix. There are no black fraternities or sororities at USF. The campus pub, known affectionately as the Fog and Grog, still serves alcohol—but, of course, only to those 21 or older. There are frequent forays to the California beaches and Lake Tahoe.

Varsity athletics provide a popular diversion, and USF touts a conference-winning national powerhouse in soccer. The women's basketball team recently brought home two conference championships. The traditional basketball rivalries with Berkeley, Stanford, and Notre Dame continue to be part of campus life. Other successful teams include men's golf and women's volleyball. Varsity as well as nonvarsity athletes are pleased with their health and recreation center, which touts an Olympic-size swimming pool, exercise rooms, courts, and snack bar.

While the city pulsates around it, "There's always a sense of peace and tranquillity on campus," claims one student. Perhaps USF's religious roots deserve credit. Or maybe it's the frenzied city surroundings that allow USF to maintain an inner calm. But for many students, the school is a hallowed place of learning and a sanctuary from the fast-paced world.

Santa Clara University

500 El Camino Real, Santa Clara, CA 95053

Website: www.scu.edu
Location: Suburban
Total Enrollment: 7,707
Undergraduates: 4,332
Male/Female: 46/54
SAT Ranges: V 530–630 M 550–640
Financial Aid: 68%
Expense: Pr $ $
Phi Beta Kappa: Yes
Applicants: 5,940
Accepted: 67%
Enrolled: 27%
Grad in 6 Years: 80%
Returning Freshmen: 92%
Academics:
Social: ☎ ☎ ☎ ☎

As California's oldest institution of higher learning, Santa Clara University is doing everything possible to stay current and prepare today's students to be tomorrow's leaders. What else would you expect from a school that sits in the heart of Silicon Valley, the center of high-tech innovation? As a Jesuit school, SCU blends a sense of history and tradition with a progressive vision that emphasizes a deep commitment to social justice. Classes remain small and intimate, while the revised curriculum focuses on an expanding global society. SCU is solidifying its position as one of the best regional universities in the West.

SCU's Old World charm includes 104 acres complete with lush green lawns, palm trees, and luscious rose gardens, accented by authentic Spanish architecture. The Mission Gardens, with many olive trees, are a beautiful escape from the pressures of school. The famous 18th-century classic mission church stands as a reminder of the school's Jesuit tradition, and campus renovations continue to improve facilities. A $68-million expansion project, which got under way in 1997, includes 11 buildings (new and renovated). A new performing arts center offers offices, studios, and recital halls. A new ethics and communications building offers modern classrooms, a TV facility, editing suites, and faculty offices. Newly opened in 2000 were the renovated Leavey Event Center, and a new apartment-style residence hall.

While there is a solid emphasis on professional programs, the engineering school in particular focuses on a well-rounded curriculum uniting humanities and technological subjects. The Leavey School of Business is renowned along the West Coast, with accounting, agribusiness, and retail management being particularly strong. The school recently received an award from the Kemper Foundation for its efforts to serve as a model for other regional business schools. Santa Clara also has an excellent interdisciplinary communication department, integrating theory and practice in the study of myriad media. The Eastside Project offers students the unique opportunity to apply theoretical knowledge to real-life situations by working with underserved populations. The School of Engineering's senior design capstone uses volunteer consultants from Silicon Valley. One of the design groups recently built an Earth satellite that was expected to be launched into orbit. Despite integration into the core curriculum, students say art, ethnic studies, and women's studies are weaker programs. In the College of Arts and Sciences, psychology remains popular, as do biology, communications, and English. The Combined Sciences program allows students who desire a broad curriculum to include courses from both the natural and social sciences.

The core curriculum, whose theme is "Community and Leadership for a Global Society," is presented as an integrated whole with three stages of development: community, global societies, and leadership. Courses include composition, Western culture, world culture, the United States, ethics, religious studies, mathematics and the natural sciences, technology, social sciences, and foreign language. An honors program places 45 selected freshmen in special honors classes, and endowed scholarship sponsors one student for his or her junior year at Mansfield College, Oxford University. In conjunction with other institutions, study abroad programs are offered at more than 100 sites in Europe, Central and South America, Africa, and Asia. In addition, Santa Clara offers its own summer programs in Cuba, England, Italy, Trinidad and Tobago, and Vienna.

As at any small school, resources and facilities are limited. Students report that the library is not always adequate for research needs, forcing many to go to nearby Stanford to get the materials they need. But one benefit of being small: Students generally have no problems getting into SCU's cozy classes and enjoy a unique rapport with their professors. "The quality of teaching is exceptional—especially when compared to perspectives of students at other institutions. [Professors] are very interested and invested in students' success," says a senior business management major. The academic climate is described by students as being "competitive yet friendly." A senior explains, "People will get stressed out over tests or papers, but there's no cut-throat competition, and most people are eager to help others or fill you in if you miss a class." Academic and career counseling receive favorable nods from students, too.

More than half the students are Roman Catholic, and religion, while not intrusive, is a factor in many aspects of campus life. Campus ministry provides counseling and opportunities for spiritual development, and many students are active in local volunteer organizations. The Jesuit presence is also a contributor to the family atmosphere that most students say is their favorite aspect of SCU.

Sixty-six percent of the undergraduates are from California and most of the rest are from the West Coast or at least the West—Oregon, Hawaii, Washington, and Arizona. The student body is equally divided between graduates of public and parochial or other private schools, and over two-thirds of the students come from the top quarter of their high school class. People of color make up 38 percent of the student body—3 percent African American, 14 percent Hispanic, and 21 percent Asian American—and racial issues seem to be getting a lot of attention from

(Continued)

Q of L: ★ ★ ★ ★
Admissions: (408) 554-4700
Email Address:
ugadmissions@scu.edu

Strongest Programs:
Accounting
Biology
Chemistry
Classics
Economics
Finance
Sociology

A $68-million expansion project, which got under way in 1997, includes 11 buildings (new and renovated).

The School of Engineering's senior design capstone uses volunteer consultants from Silicon Valley. One of the design groups recently built an Earth satellite that was expected to be launched into orbit.

students, faculty, and administrators. The Santa Clara Community Action Program, a student volunteer outreach program, provides community service opportunities for the entire campus. One not-so-nice slogan for the school is "Spoiled Children's University." Explains a senior, "Most students come from good families that have enough money to send their children here."

Santa Clara admits students regardless of their financial need and uses a variety of means to help all students pay the bills. Though the school does not guarantee to meet the full demonstrated financial need of every accepted applicant, it does meet an average of 76 percent of each student's need. Besides 141 athletic scholarships, Santa Clara awards about 250 merit scholarships. There are also talent awards in debate, music, and theater. Santa Clara also has an excellent freshman and transfer orientation program, according to the students, that includes academic advising and social events introducing student activities and services. Mom and Pop are also invited.

Housing is guaranteed to almost all who apply, except for seniors. Nearly 90 percent of freshmen live on campus, but after their first year, 58 percent pack their bags and fend for themselves off campus. Most residence halls are coed by floor. The halls are well-maintained, and many students make them the focus of their social lives. The Freshman Residential Community program gives incoming students the opportunity to room with others pursuing the same course of study. Participating students are housed at the Graham residence complex and not only study the core curriculum, but virtually eat, sleep, and breathe it. Casa Italiana provides about 60 students with the opportunity to develop an in-depth understanding of Italian language, culture, and cuisine. A substance-free living program houses 70 students at Campisi Hall.

Perhaps somewhat surprising is the amount of partying that goes on at the university. One reason may be the weather. The California sun encourages excursions to the beach at Santa Cruz, 20 miles away. San Francisco is 45 miles away. The campus is "technically" dry, and beer and wine are served on campus only to those 21 and older. This translates into an amazing amount of ingenuity on the part of underage students, as well as active alcohol education programs aimed at addressing the problems of alcohol abuse found on most U.S. campuses. What used to be a modest Greek presence on campus has blossomed into four fraternities and three sororities, which now enroll 14 percent of the men and 12 percent of the women.

Santa Clara fields 16 Division I teams, many of which in recent years have been nationally ranked. For two consecutive years, the women's basketball team won the West Coast Conference championship, a fact that has not gone unnoticed on campus. Men's soccer and golf, and women's soccer also brought home WCC championship trophies for their school. For those not up to intercollegiate sports, club sports and intramurals are quite popular. "The biggest complaint is probably school spirit," says a senior electrical engineering major. "We have great sports teams, but we could use a lot more spirit and support."

Santa Clara University is an institution on the move. SCU students seem to consider their school's friendly and supportive community spirit one of its biggest assets. "The Jesuit tradition is felt everywhere—the importance of forming strong virtues and being intellectually strong," says one student. It's this comfortable blend of traditional values and progressive academics that leaves students here charmed and asking for more.

Sarah Lawrence College

1 Mead Way, Bronxville, NY 10708-5999

The students and faculty of Sarah Lawrence College believe that there aren't any rules, except that, if they do exist, they are made to be broken. Nowhere is individualism and self-expression encouraged more than at this elite liberal arts school. "We produce students who are unafraid to be different, think differently," brags a sophomore. Freedom and exploration are valued more highly than any tradition, and it's this commitment to the individual and the mind that makes Sarah Lawrence College such a creative place to learn.

Founded in 1926, the college sits on a quaint, 40-acre campus. English Tudor buildings and mansions of converted estates intermingle with more modern structures. The landscape is hilly and green, with more than 100 types of trees and abundant rock outcroppings. The school's founders believed that there should be as little physical separation as possible between life and work, so classrooms, dormitory suites, and faculty offices are all housed in the same ivy-covered buildings. The expanded Siegel Student Center gives students twice as much space for meeting and socializing.

It's tough to find two Sarah Lawrence students studying the same thing, because every student has an individually designed program of study and almost no subject is out of bounds. Instead, you'll find uniquely combined concentrations, such as French and dance, or literature and philosophy. Grades are recorded for transcript purposes only; more emphasis is placed on written faculty evaluations. Some students become overwhelmed here, but those who stay find that the combination of close faculty supervision and an endless slate of choices provide an experience unavailable elsewhere. "The structure of education here requires a great deal of independence and innovation," says a senior.

Students will become intimately acquainted with the written word at Sarah Lawrence—one of the few things that everyone does here. Writing begins in the first year and continues relentlessly "across the curriculum" for the next three years. All first-year students take a First-Year Studies Seminar in one of more than 30 subjects. Each student meets with the professor individually each week to discuss his or her independent projects, academic plans, and transition to college. Other than that, undergraduates write their own academic ticket, with the help of their first-year seminar leader, who serves as an academic guru (called a "don" from the Latin for "gift"). "My don rocks!" boasts a studio arts major.

At Sarah Lawrence, students take three courses each semester. Courses can last a semester or the full year, depending on the nature of the course. Students also work on independent projects with faculty members in individual, one-to-one conferences every two weeks for each of these classes. Perhaps because of the close personal contact with professors, the registration process is rigorous: students

Website: www.slc.edu

Location: Suburban

Total Enrollment: 1,495

Undergraduates: 1,178

Male/Female: 28/72

SAT Ranges: V 590–700 M 520–610

ACT Range: 23–28

Financial Aid: 62%

Expense: Pr $ $ $ $

Phi Beta Kappa: No

Applicants: 2,070

Accepted: 43%

Enrolled: 31%

Grad in 6 Years: 63%

Returning Freshmen: 92%

Academics: ✍ ✍ ✍ ✍

Social: ☎ ☎

Q of L: ★ ★ ★

Admissions: (914) 395-2510

Email Address:
slcadmit@slc.edu

Strongest Programs:
Music
Dance
Drama
Creative Writing
Psychology
Theater
Political Science
Biology
Literature

interview their prospective teachers to determine whether the course fits their academic plan, and to make sure the instructor is someone they respect and want to study with. Students get very involved with the individual projects that result from the seminar/conference system, which is modeled after Oxford University's and said to be intense. "The campus isn't that competitive because everyone is working on different things, and grades aren't that important to the students," says a junior. "However, the academic year is extremely vigorous." Seminar enrollment is strictly limited, and even the largest lecture courses have only around 60 students. Getting into popular classes can be a problem, but the administration guarantees students at least two of their first three course choices each semester.

The Sarah Lawrence writing program is arguably one of the strongest in the country. And, says an education administration major, "The theater department is huge! It swallows up the campus." Other highly rated fields include literature, visual arts, and psychology. The psychology department offers fieldwork at the college's Early Childhood Center. The premed program, more structured than other offerings, places nearly all of its eligible graduates into medical schools while science students have the opportunity to use the state-of-the-art Science Center, with 22,500 square feet of classrooms, labs, and computer workspaces. The film department has been upgraded with expanded offerings in filmmaking and film history, and environmental studies and computer science has expanded offerings as well. Students report that the math department is the weak link.

Since individual attention is the cornerstone of the Sarah Lawrence educational philosophy, even grading is done personally. Teachers give students written evaluations twice a year, though conventional grades also go on record. The library, though small (224,000 volumes and more than 1,000 periodicals), is a delight, with an area for eating and a pillow room for cozy studying and occasional dozing. For the travelers, there are academic years in Oxford, Paris, Florence, and a London theater program for study at the British American Drama Academy.

Sarah Lawrence students are not your run-of-the-mill young American men and women; a campus T-shirt says that "Here at Sarah Lawrence, even the squirrels wear black." While one student describes Sarah Lawrence as "a predominantly female-oriented school," there appears to be very little tension between the sexes. And what about campus issues? They center on diversity and identity: gay rights, minority rights, labor rights, sexism, ageism.... "Most people lean toward radical politics, or else they keep quiet," says a sophomore.

Twenty-five percent of SLC's students come from New York State—the bulk from nearby New York City—and most of the rest are from somewhere along either the East or West Coast. African Americans make up 6 percent of the student body, Asian Americans 5 percent, Hispanics 5 percent, and foreign students 5 percent.

Eighty-five percent of Sarah Lawrence students live on campus, where freshmen usually get doubles in the newer dorms and upperclassmen are guaranteed singles in the prettier, older dorms or college-owned houses. One popular dorm contains four townhouses, each with seven single rooms. In fact, accommodations are so good that there's been a bit of a housing crunch lately. And since Bronxville is a staid, super-rich suburb, off-campus students often commute from Westchester County's lower-rent districts or from New York City. The cafeteria cooking is good, and the health food bar and student center's greasy spoon fill in the gaps. Most dorms also have their own kitchens.

Weekend life often revolves around New York City (half an hour away by train after a 10-minute walk to the station), where SLC's large theatrical contingent takes advantage of the art and culture of the Big Apple. For those who stick around over the weekend, there are free dances and movies, plays, poetry readings, guest lectures, and several tea and coffeehouses. There's also the end-of-the-year megaparty Bacchanalia, and the oldest college AIDS benefit in the country, the Deb Ball. Other traditions include Coming Out Week and May Fair, which brings community children to campus for games and food. Still, says a political science major, "There aren't many all-campus social events to attend, so you have to find a group that you enjoy being in." Drinkers, largely ignored in the past, are now subject to rules regarding on-campus consumption, but one student says it isn't an issue. And although the relationship between the school and surrounding community is improving, Bronxville is still described as "too expensive," and one student notes that "the people generally seem to be wary of SLC students."

Sports are not a high priority among Sarah Lawrence's bookish undergrads. "There's virtually no athletics here," one student ventures. While the school does field several intercollegiate clubs (the Sarah Lawrence riders do well in equestrian competitions, and the women's tennis team is strong), nary a "Go get 'em" is heard from these students.

The Sarah Lawrence community is, in a word, small, and students say this is both a challenge and a blessing. The social life is "a bit claustrophobic at times," but Sarah Lawrence students will gladly exchange a little excitement for extra time with their professors. In this academically intense community where disdain for blatant preprofessionalism is still fashionable, the distance between the academic and the extracurricular is negligible. For students willing to put up with a bit of unfriendliness from fellow students too buried in their books, Sarah Lawrence offers a nearly extinct kind of liberal arts education. "People learn best what they want to learn, and Sarah Lawrence takes each student's ideas and goals very, very seriously," says a junior.

Overlaps
NYU, Oberlin, Smith, Bard, Vassar.

If You Apply To ➤   **Sarah Lawrence**…Early decision: Nov. 15, Jan. 1. Regular admissions: Mar. 1 Financial aid: Feb. 1. Meets full demonstrated need of all admitted students who file on time. Campus interviews: recommended, evaluative. Alumni interviews optional, evaluative. SATs or ACTs: required. SAT IIs: recommended. Accepts the Common Application and electronic applications. Essay question: explain something about who you are that isn't obvious: issue of importance; recent scientific advancement; or work of art; photocopy of a graded academic paper.

Scripps College, CA–See CLAREMONT COLLEGES

Skidmore College

815 North Broadway, Saratoga Springs, NY 12866

Artists and nature lovers, future business leaders and jetsetters unite: Skidmore College offers a refreshing mix of old and new, artistic and scientific, business and

Website: www.skidmore.edu

(Continued)

Location: City outskirts

Total Enrollment: 2,573

Undergraduates: 2,511

Male/Female: 40/60

SAT Ranges: V 560–640 M
540–640

ACT Range: 24–26

Financial Aid: 40%

Expense: Pr $ $ $ $

Phi Beta Kappa: No

Applicants: 5,444

Accepted: 48%

Enrolled: 23%

Grad in 6 Years: 77%

Returning Freshmen: 91%

Academics: ✍ ✍ ✍ ✍

Social: ☎ ☎ ☎

Q of L: ★ ★ ★

Admissions: (800) 867-6007

Email Address:
admissions@scott.skidmore.edu

Strongest Programs:
Drama
Studio Art
English
Biology
Government
Psychology
Business
Music

fine arts in a very liberal atmosphere. Founded in 1903 as a women's arts school, Skidmore still excels in the fine and performing arts, but little else remains the same. In the 1960s, the college traded its quaint Victorian campus in the heart of Saratoga Springs for a modern 48-building complex on 800 acres on the outskirts of this town of 30,000, and went coed soon after.

The Skidmore campus integrates modern architecture with a woodland setting for a secluded, peaceful atmosphere. The Tang Teaching Museum and Art Gallery, opened its doors in the fall of 2000 as scheduled. Skidmore's academic approach is based on a tradition of strong liberal arts, yet its facilities are quite modern. That makes for a particularly strong combination of music, theater, art, and dance majors, as well as those interested in science and athletics.

Skidmore's students describe their mandatory core program as an "imaginative way" to explore the liberal arts. Implemented in 1985, Skidmore's Liberal Studies curriculum attempts to give students strong foundations in both the arts and preprofessional worlds. This begins with a course called Liberal Studies I: The Human Experience, a team-taught course with professors from all departments combining lectures, performances, readings, and discussions examining the issues and dilemmas of our lives as human beings. In addition, before the end of their junior year, students must complete one course in each of the following: Liberal Studies II-Cultural Traditions and Social Change, Liberal Studies III-Artistic Forms and Critical Concepts, and Liberal Studies IV-Science and Society. They must also fill requirements in lab science, visual and performing arts, foreign language, and non-Western culture before diving into their major.

Business, English, psychology, government, and studio art rank as the school's most popular departments, and students say that there are no "weak" departments, just small ones. But there is an advantage to smaller classes. "Classes are small, creating a less formal environment where one feels comfortable participating and playing an active role in discussions," says a government major. Also popular are art and design, performing arts, biology, and preprofessional majors. Skidmore students can obtain a bachelor's degree and a law degree in six years through a cooperative program with the Cardozo Law School. The school also offers 3–2 programs in engineering with Clarkson University and with the Thayer School of Engineering at Dartmouth College.

The school has matched its liberal arts offerings with preprofessional training both in the classroom and in the "real world." For instance, students majoring in studio art and art history are frequently found in business classes, where students work in groups and make presentations for real-life business execs. Skidmore also has an aggressive internship program, and students often move from a spring internship into a summer job. Another much-praised option is the junior year abroad spent in a Skidmore-run program in France, England, Spain, India, or one of several other countries available through other colleges. Students who just can't get enough may compete to spend their summer at Skidmore collaborating with a professor on a research project or attending one of the school's many incredible summer programs. Biology majors also have the opportunity to conduct fieldwork in the marsh at the northern end of the campus. Another program called PASS allows high school students to take two courses for college credit during a six-week academic summer program. In addition, the University Without Walls Program offers older students an unusually flexible and inexpensive route to a bachelor's degree via coursework, tutorials, and internships. "Skidmore allows students to mold and shape their college experience through its vast opportunities and special programs," says a senior.

The academic climate at Skidmore is competitive but not cutthroat.

"Skidmore is a laid-back school," says one English major. "Students compete merely with themselves to do better and there is no active competition among students to achieve the highest grade." The school likes to keep class sizes down to fewer than 25 students. But in general, students on the waiting list can usually get into even the most popular courses. Year after year students describe the faculty as "deeply committed" to the welfare of the undergrads. "The professors are outstanding," says a premed major. "They know their material and are very accessible to their students." Another student adds, "Many professors even set up study sessions before exams with themselves as facilitators, clearly demonstrating how far they will go to help their students succeed." Given the school's hefty price tag, it's not surprising that the students at Skidmore are typically well-off and from the Eastern seaboard, especially New York State and the Boston area. Forty percent, however, are not well enough off to go without need-based financial aid. Skidmore doesn't offer merit or athletic scholarships, but does offer low-cost, flexible loan programs.

Students here are rather restrained and the school's biggest problem seems to be overcoming stereotypes. "We are not a rich kids' school. We do not dress in designer clothes, and we do not wear sweats to class," says one senior. Minority enrollment has been increasing due to the administration's efforts to recruit them. African Americans constitute 2 percent of the students, Hispanics 5 percent, and Asian Americans 4 percent. Skidmore has an assistant to the dean of Student Affairs for Multicultural Student Affairs, which is the '90s way of saying someone is responsible for integrating multicultural student affairs into the mainstream. "Diversity is Skidmore's best asset," says an American Studies/English major. "It's refreshing to be able to walk from one end of the campus to the other and see a variety of different cultures represented, especially at such a small school." More than two decades of effort to recruit men has paid off for this former women's college, and prospects seem good for a 50/50 ratio not too far down the road.

Anyone who might try to nickname the school Skid Row should check out the dorms first. Skidmore has some of the most luxurious living accommodations in the East, and 80 percent of the students take advantage of them. The majority of the dorms boast carpeted rooms, air-conditioning, and cozy window seats. All dorms are integrated by class and are coed by floor or suite, with kitchenettes and lounges on every floor. The rooms in South Quad tend to be livelier than those in North Quad, where students are assured of doubles. Juniors and seniors routinely enjoy singles. With the exception of the 13 percent of the students who live in Scribner Village, who prepare their own meals, everyone on campus eats in one of three dining halls, which serve exceptionally good college fare. Falstaff's, the student-run pub, is a popular eatery and place to hold parties.

With no frats or sororities, Skidmore students flock to dorm parties, especially if there's live music. There's an ample supply of activities available on campus including, lectures, movies, theater productions, and concerts. "The social life on campus is certainly healthy," says a sophomore. "Students work hard during the week and blow off steam on the weekends." Skidmore has also hosted three annual Campus Comedy Festivals. A campus event card is distributed to of-age students who plan to drink on school grounds. The campus is dry, but according to at least one senior, "if underage students want to drink, they'll find a way." The nearby Adirondacks make the school a haven for backpackers and skiers. Saratoga, an old resort town, offers plenty of civilization, including the Saratoga Performing Arts Center and the country's oldest thoroughbred racetrack. It's also the summer home for the New York City Ballet, the New York City Opera, and the

Implemented in 1985, Skidmore's Liberal Studies curriculum attempts to give students strong foundations in both the arts and preprofessional worlds.

The school also offers 3–2 programs in engineering with Clarkson University and with the Thayer School of Engineering at Dartmouth College.

Philadelphia Orchestra, and there are numerous shops, restaurants, and clubs as well. Students reach out to the Saratoga community through Benefaction, a large student volunteer group connected to several local aid agencies. "Both Skidmore and Saratoga work hand-in-hand to enhance the entire community," says one student.

The sports program and facilities at Skidmore have been drastically improved in recent years, and men's and women's tennis and the equestrian team have claimed several conference championships. Surprisingly, the usual Skidmore enthusiasm does not extend to watching spectator sports. Perhaps that's because a sizable proportion of students are busy playing in the intramural sports program, which boasts over 20 teams, a student commissioner, and 250 acres of new playing fields. Division athletes and intramuralists alike enjoy the all-weather 400-meter track and the athletic center, which includes a gym, fitness center, and locker rooms. Skidmore's more traditional activities, which have lingered even after years of coeducation, include Junior Ring Week, when juniors receive their class rings and a dance is held in honor of their initiation; "It's somewhat old-fashioned but still extremely well-liked and attended," attests one sentimental student. More decadent traditions include the annual OktoberFest, Spring Fling, and Winter Carnival celebrations, and an unofficial event called the Senior Week Pub Crawl.

Twenty-five years after coeducation began there, Skidmore continues to win the hearts of its on-the-move students with flexibility, openness, and receptivity to change and growth. "Skidmore offers an abundance of opportunities to challenge yourself both inside and outside of the classroom," says a business/social work major. "Every student can find their niche here regardless of their interests."

Overlaps

Vassar, Colgate, Oberlin, Smith, Hamilton.

If You Apply To ➤ Skidmore…Early decision: Dec. 1, Jan. 15. Regular admissions and financial aid: Feb. 1. Housing: May 1. Campus interviews: recommended, evaluative. Alumni interviews: optional, evaluative. SATs or ACTs: required. SAT IIs: recommended. Essay question: significant experience; important issue of personal, local, or national concern; or important person.

Smith College

College Lane, Northampton, MA 01063

Website: www.smith.edu
Location: Small city
Total Enrollment: 3,168
Undergraduates: 2,665
Male/Female: 0/100
SAT Ranges: V 600–710 M 580–670
ACT Range: 25–39
Financial Aid: 58%
Expense: Pr $ $ $
Phi Beta Kappa: Yes

Only heaven knows what Sophia Smith would think of the college she founded with a bequest in 1871. Working closely with her minister, she intended Smith to be "pervaded by the Spirit of Evangelical Christian Religion." There are still evangelicals at Smith, but today they crusade against societal injustices such as racism, classism, sexism, and heterosexism. Though the school remains strongly committed to its liberal arts mission, it continues to educate women for careers in the sciences. With the addition of the Picker Program in Engineering and Technology, students here have an opportunity to become leaders in a predominantly male-dominated field. Smith President Ruth Simmons agrees, calling the program "a bold venture but an important one for a forward-looking women's college."

Founded in 1871, Smith is located in the small city of Northampton, an artsy oasis in the foothills of the Berkshire Mountains. The 125-acre campus resembles a medieval fortress from the front gate, but inside it sparkles with many gardens, Paradise Pond, and a plant house. Buildings cover a range of styles from late 18th century to modern, and the college has successfully retained its historic atmosphere while keeping facilities up to date. Plans for a new student center and renovations to the Fine Arts Center are under way, both expected to be complete by the year 2002, and a new exercise classroom will host a variety of sports and feature a climbing wall.

Be ready to hit the books with your new-found sisters at Smith. "The academic climate at Smith is quite competitive, but it's mostly a competition with oneself," says a psychology and French double major. "Most people are 'strivers' and big go-getters." Smith's student-run honor system, which covers everything from exams to library checkout, is widely praised and enforced. Students usually do not discuss their grades.

Government is the favorite major on campus, followed closely by psychology, English, economics, and art. One in four Smith women majors in science and thereby enjoys numerous opportunities to assist professors with their research. They also benefit from a spacious science center that is state of the art. Two electron microscopes are available for student use, and, through the Five College Consortium,* students have access to one of the best radio astronomy facilities in the world. Smith's art history department is among the best in the nation and enjoys access to the college's superb museum. Interdisciplinary majors in American studies, women's studies, and Latin American studies are strong, as are minors that range from marine sciences to urban studies.

With the exception of a mandatory writing course, Smith women have unusual freedom to plan a course of study. Faculty advisors take that cue and do not pressure students. Their laissez faire attitude has its ups and downs. "I would have liked a little more guidance from them," says a French studies major, "but I have always been pushed to think for myself." Qualified students may enter the Smith Scholars program and embark on one or two years of independent or extra college research for full credit. About 250 older students are enrolled in the Ada Comstock Scholars program for women going back to college. The Picker Program for Engineering and Technology offers students the opportunity to pursue an ambitious engineering program that will focus on computer engineering, electrical engineering, and environmental engineering. The program is the first of its kind at a women's college, and administrators hope the curriculum will lead to greater gender parity in the field of engineering.

The quality of teaching is generally "superb," and one student says professors who may not have been great teachers were at least enthusiastic about their subjects. "Profs expect a lot and get a lot in return," a sophomore says. "They are also very available," usually at teas and departmental gatherings. Smith's four libraries have almost 2 million holdings among them, making it one of the largest collections of any liberal arts college in the country. Students can study for a semester or two at one of 12 well-known New England colleges through the Twelve-College Exchange Program,* or take advantage of the innovative Maritime Studies Program.* Students are also enthusiastic about the opportunity to take part in Smith's well-known study abroad program, which includes opportunities for study in France, Germany, Switzerland, Italy, India, China, Spain, Russia, and Japan.

With an endowment of over half a billion dollars, Smith has deeper pockets than many of its competitors. And though it's got a hefty price tag, the school manages to recruit a diverse group of women. An astrophysics major says her classmates are "very vocal and interested in discovering who they are. They are

(Continued)
Applicants: 2,998
Accepted: 56%
Enrolled: 40%
Grad in 6 Years: 82%
Returning Freshmen: 89%
Academics: ✍ ✍ ✍ ✍
Social: ☎ ☎ ☎
Q of L: ★ ★ ★ ★
Admissions: (413) 585-2500
Email Address:
admission@smith.edu

Strongest Programs:
Economics
Art
Biological Sciences
American Studies
Psychology
English
Government
Music

Every Smith student is guaranteed at least one paid summer internship during her undergraduate career through the Praxis program.

ready to debate any topic." Nobody argues that Smith is a liberal place with the social issues of the day dominating conversations. "I was called a 'feminazi' in high school, and here I practically feel conservative!" a sophomore exclaims. "It's an eye-opening experience." On this politically correct campus, students debate the finer points of women's rights, racism, sexual freedom, politics, and police brutality. Nearly 90 percent of the students ranked in the top quarter of their high school class. Seventy-eight percent of Smithies are from out of state, African Americans account for 4 percent of the student body, Asian Americans 9 percent, and Hispanics 4 percent.

Housing at Smith is unashamedly adored. "The houses are the best part of Smith," a senior says. "They foster a family atmosphere, with individual dining rooms, Friday tea, and public spaces," another student raves. Others note that they often eat breakfast in their pjs and that the bathrooms are probably much cleaner than if there were boys around. Each of the 35 houses, accommodating from 13 to 100 students, is a self-governing unit, responsible for everything from visiting hours to weekend parties and concerts. Accouterments in each house include a living room, a TV room, and a study room, many with a fireplace and a grand piano. The head resident, selected by the administration, is the leader of the house, but day-to-day affairs are run by the elected house council.

The atmosphere is almost unremittingly homey, less that of a sorority than of an extended family. Except for one senior house, classes are mixed in each house, and first-year students easily mingle with seniors. Incoming students can indicate a preference for size and location of their first house, and changes are possible by entering a lottery. All undergraduates except for Ada Comstock Scholars must live on campus—a bone of contention among some juniors and seniors. Two alternatives offered are a vegetarian cooperative and an apartment complex. Meals are a variation on the same community theme, though budget cuts have forced consolidation of dining facilities, causing much grief on campus. The food is highly praised. Professors are often invited to Thursday dinners, which are served family-style, by candlelight, to add a touch of graciousness midweek.

You will not be greeted with a rocking social scene at Smith, but there are plenty of parties to be had and great places to visit. "You have to work to have fun—it doesn't fall in your lap," a sophomore says. Meeting men is made easier by the five-college system. In addition, each house throws an average of two parties a semester. For special weekends a whole fraternity may be invited from Dartmouth or another nearby college, an arrangement that is only slightly more civilized than the typical college bar scene. Students must be 21 to drink alcohol at campus parties; IDs are checked and hands stamped. If mixers don't suit a student's fancy, there is free bus service to the other four members of the consortium, which among them offer a broad range of social and cultural opportunities.

Northampton, known as NoHo after New York City's SoHo neighborhood, is a college town of about 30,000 that is known for funky bohemianism. The town is home to multiple subcultures, and is generally tolerant of everyone. "Northampton is great—small, but happening," one student says. Downtown is home to lots of shops and moderately priced restaurants. Smith also offers time-honored traditions like Mountain Day, when the president cancels class for a day of hiking and female bonding, complete with brown-bag lunches. The New England countryside has numerous special charms, including ski slopes only 10 minutes away. The best road trips are to Boston (two hours) or New York (three hours).

Smith has a long tradition of success in athletics; the college was the first women's college to join the NCAA, and still places a premium on recruiting scholar-athletes. Top teams include cross-country, track and field, crew, softball, and tennis. Smith's multimillion-dollar sports complex includes indoor tennis and track facilities, a six-lane swimming pool, and a riding ring. Interhouse competitions include everything from kickball to inner-tube water polo. For nonathletic types, the student government plays an important role in the life of the college, with the president serving as a trustee of the college for two years after graduation. Service Organizations of Smith (SOS) arranges for students to volunteer in about 600 placements in Northampton, the surrounding communities, and on campus.

So the strict evangelism is gone, and maybe today's women aren't exactly Sophia Smith wannabes. But her namesake lives on at this eclectic, open-minded institution where women don lab coats and power suits and combat boots and even white dresses at graduation. There's no way to pigeon-hole this rising star, or its students. "Everyone can find their niche," a senior says. "I receive support from everyone."

If You Apply To ➤ **Smith**…Early decision: Nov. 15. Regular admissions, financial aid and housing: Jan. 15. Guarantees to meet demonstrated need. Campus interviews: recommended, evaluative. Alumni interviews: optional, evaluative. SATs or ACTs: required. SAT IIs: strongly recommended (writing and two others). Accepts the Common Application and electronic applications. Essay question: significant person; a situation in which your beliefs were challenged; significant academic or intellectual experience.

University of the South (Sewanee)

735 University Avenue, Sewanee, TN 37383-1000

Two elements separate the University of the South from other liberal arts schools: Southern traditions and the generosity of Tennessee Williams. The school, known as Sewanee after the city in which it is located, has a storied tradition dating back more than 140 years. Episcopal bishop Leonidas Polk founded the university in 1857 and envisioned it as a distinguished center of learning in the South. Through the years, a host of customs have emerged: students wear gowns to class, dress up for football games, and adhere to an honor code. With proceeds from Williams' estate, the university holds an annual conference to promote the art of writing and recently unveiled a $3.3 million theater complex bearing his name.

Sewanee is located atop Tennessee's Cumberland Plateau between Chattanooga and Nashville. The university's stately English collegiate Gothic buildings of native mountain beige-and-pink sandstone are home to both a college of arts and sciences and a seminary. The 10,000-acre campus is fondly known as "the Domain." Noteworthy structures include the St. Luke's and All Saints Chapel, and Convocation Hall, built in 1886. Owned by 28 dioceses of the Episcopal Church, the university calls its semesters Advent and Easter. The student body is overwhelmingly Christian, and students report that religion is often a big part of their life. Under construction is a new dining hall with a 450-seat formal eating room, a 250-seat informal room, and a 150-seat outdoor dining area.

Sewanee's undergraduate curriculum is broad in the classical sense. All students must complete 32 full courses, including 21 courses outside the major field, and must attain an overall grade point average of at least 2.0 on all academic

Website: www.sewanee.edu
Location: Village
Total Enrollment:: 1,378
Undergraduates: 1,326
Male/Female: 49/51
SAT Ranges: V 570–670 M 580–660
ACT Range: 25–29
Financial Aid: 39%
Expense: Pr $ $
Phi Beta Kappa: Yes
Applicants: 1,792
Accepted: 68%
Enrolled: 31%
Grad in 6 Years: 77%
Returning Freshmen: 89%
Academics: ✑ ✑ ✑ ✑
Social: ☎ ☎ ☎
Q of L: ★ ★ ★
Admissions: (800) 522-2234

(Continued)

Email Address:
admiss@sewanee.edu

Strongest Programs:
English
History
Mathematics
Chemistry
Geology

Owned by 28 dioceses of the Episcopal Church, the university calls its semesters Advent and Easter. The student body is overwhelmingly Christian, and students report that religion is often a big part of their life.

In keeping with the European tradition, Sewanee seniors take comprehensive exams in their majors as part of their graduation requirements. While students take the test, their friends decorate their cars and prepare for parties when they are finished.

work. Students also must spend at least four semesters in residence, including their final year. Core curriculum requirements include English and one other course in literature or English and a writing-intensive course, foreign language at the third-year level, math, a lab science, history, religion or philosophy, fine arts, and physical education. In keeping with the European tradition, Sewanee seniors take comprehensive exams in their majors as part of their graduation requirements. While students take the test, their friends decorate their cars and prepare for parties when they are finished.

The English department is unquestionably the top program on campus. The university publishes *Sewanee Review*, the nation's oldest continuously published literary quarterly, and sponsors the Sewanee Writers' Conference through the gift of Tennessee Williams' estate. History and mathematics are also strong. Several of the science programs are top-notch, including chemistry and geology, and about a third of new graduates continue their schooling after receiving their diploma. Of course, every school has weaker departments, and Sewanee is no exception: Italian and Japanese need some improvement. For students who wish to specialize in engineering or forestry, joint five-year programs are offered with several universities. Of the study abroad opportunities, the summer British studies program at Oxford is especially popular. The school is also a member of the Associated Colleges of the South* consortium. Sewanee recently added a major in art history.

Sewanee maintains many old customs and standards that add a quaint veneer to campus life. A voluntary dress code calls for women to wear dresses or skirts and men to wear jackets and ties to class. Professors as well as the numerous honors students (members of the Order of Gownsmen) wear black academic gowns to class. An honor code is strictly observed, and lying, cheating, or stealing usually results in expulsion. Students take the code so seriously that "professors are not present when we take exams," says a student.

Sewanee faculty members receive high praise from students. "The quality of teaching is exceptional," said a senior Spanish major. "Professors demand quality, effort, and thinking." Professors routinely give out their home numbers and even teach classes in their homes. This feeling of cordiality is bolstered by small class sizes; upper-level courses may contain as few as six people. Most Sewanee students understand what is expected of them academically. "In true Southern style, no one would admit to being competitive, but we are," said a junior anthropology major.

Tradition carries over into other aspects of life at Sewanee. Many students hail from Southern families, while "some proud Yankees" represent New York, New Jersey, Pennsylvania, and New England. The student population is 95 percent white, with African Americans the largest minority group at just 3 percent. "Alternative lifestyles or minority students really stand out on campus compared to the general population," a junior warned. The university's board of regents recently passed a resolution to strengthen the institution's efforts to increase diversity among faculty and the student body. Sewanee also offers several minority scholarships, including the Tutu Scholars program for students from South Africa. Sewanee awards 34 merit scholarships, ranging from $9,085 to a free ride, but there are no athletic scholarships. A financing plan enables families to pay tuition in 10 monthly installments. Students who maintain a 3.0 cumulative GPA may have the loan portion of their award replaced by a grant.

Chances are you've probably never heard of the town of Sewanee. The town has a population of only about 3,500, not including students. "The university is the town, period," a junior said. "It is beautiful and quaint and I would not change it, but the closest Walmart is 30 minutes away." Students are very involved in the community and often run into their professors in town. A whopping 98 percent of students live on campus, mostly because of the requirement. Most of the dorms are single-sex, but two newly renovated halls are now coed, and there are three coed language houses. "Dorms are either better than hotels or worse than Motel 6," a student said. The few seniors who move off campus must live in university-approved housing. Many students complain about the quality of the food.

An honor code is strictly observed, and lying, cheating, or stealing usually results in expulsion. Students take the code so seriously that professors are not present when they give exams.

Although Sewanee is not known for student activism, the school's one concession to populist thinking is its policy that virtually no one gets cut from varsity sports squads. The most popular sport on campus is probably football—not so much because of the sport, but because games are social events where everyone shows up in coats and ties and dresses. There is also some serious competition going on; conference championships have been won by the men's tennis and basketball teams, and the women's field hockey and tennis squads. The university recently added equestrian competition as a varsity sport. Their facilities include a dressage area, jumps, over 30 acres of pasture, individual paddocks, and miles of trails. The cheer here is: "Sewanee, Sewanee, leave 'em in a lurch. Down with the heathens and up with the Church. Yea, Sewanee's right."

The social life occurs, of course, on campus. Greeks provide an important social outlet, and 65 percent of the men and 55 percent of the women join up. "If you don't drink, don't come here," a student said. "This school is all about alcohol." A popular T-shirt talks about how much fun students have at the annual Fall and Spring Party Weekends: "Spring party weekend: they tell me I was there." The party scene is changing, however, as the university has revised its policy concerning alcohol to ban all common sources, such as kegs, on campus. Homecoming weekend, the Shakespeare Festival, and a blues fest are popular campus happenings. For students who want to bug out of town, the beautiful rural setting, complete with lakes, waterfalls, and even caves and caverns, makes outdoor activities popular. The Sewanee Outing Program provides endless opportunities for students to hike, rappel, kayak, or canoe together. Students who occasionally feel a need for the "real world" can go to nearby Chattanooga, Memphis, or Nashville. A favorite trip is to the Jack Daniel's Distillery in Lynchburg, Tenn., population 361.

For the most part, though, students are in no rush to get away. They seem content with their school's way of life, its rich past, beautiful location, and caring people. As a student puts it, "You're not a number here, you're a person. Teachers talk to you if you bump into them. They remember your name. There are some downsides to Sewanee, but when you walk through the quad on a warm, beautiful day, it more than makes up for it."

Overlaps

Vanderbilt, Rhodes, Wake Forest, Washington and Lee, Davidson.

If You Apply To ➤ Sewanee…Early decision: Nov. 15. Regular admissions: Feb. 1. Financial aid: Mar. 1. Campus interviews: recommended, informational. No alumni interviews. SATs or ACTs: required. SAT IIs: optional. Accepts the Common Application. Essay question: An issue of great concern and importance; or personal statement.

University of South Carolina

Columbia, SC 29208

Website: www.sc.edu
Location: Center city
Total Enrollment: 23,430
Undergraduates: 15,551
Male/Female: 45/55
SAT Ranges: V 490–610 M 490–610
ACT Range: 20–27
Financial Aid: 45%
Expense: Pub $ $
Phi Beta Kappa: Yes
Applicants: 10,162
Accepted: 67%
Enrolled: 39%
Grad in 6 Years: 60%
Returning Freshmen: 81%
Academics: ✍ ✍ ✍
Social: ☎ ☎ ☎
Q of L: ★ ★ ★
Admissions: (803) 777-7700
Email Address:
admissions-ugrad@sc.edu

Strongest Programs:
Biology
English
International Business
Psychology
Criminal Justice
Nursing
Business

The University has a top-notch library, with numerous special collections, including the world's most comprehensive collection of F. Scott Fitzgerald research materials.

Whether it's football or international business, the students at the University of South Carolina are game—they're the Gamecocks and they've got plenty of fighting spirit. Sure, South Carolina's a somewhat crowded state university, but students here rarely feel cooped up. The bevy of courses offered and plenty of interesting academic programs to explore make for a campus that seems to have a lot more space than it actually does. Which is not to say that South Carolina's an impersonal school—this is the South, after all. Gamecocks may lay claim to their school, but old-fashioned Southern charm still rules the roost.

Carolina's large modern campus is located right in the heart of Columbia, a city of more than 450,000 and capital of the state. Government buildings and downtown businesses are all within walking distance of the campus and serve as fertile hunting grounds for internship opportunities. Mild winters are typical. Snow—even a few flurries—is a traffic-stopping event. The old section of the campus, which dates back to the school's founding in 1801, includes the glorious oak-lined Horseshoe, composed of numerous 19th-century buildings, 10 of which are now listed in the National Register of Historic Places. New additions include a library annex and a graduate science research center.

The University of South Carolina offers 79 professional, liberal, and technical bachelor's degrees to its undergrads. Biology is the most popular major, but the school is also known for its psychology, nursing, English, and criminal justice programs.

Students in the huge marine science program enjoy a splendid 17,000-acre facility located about three hours from the main campus. The university is also the beneficiary of an excellent film library. Much of the economy of South Carolina is tied to foreign trade, and, fittingly, the university has developed a top-notch international business program. Art students have access to the latest cameras, editing stations, and computers, as well as kilns and other equipment necessary for their studies.

Among the liberal arts, English is one of the best departments in the region, and the natural sciences are strong. The four-level, 1,000-square-foot music building features studios, classrooms, a music and performance library, chamber and music rooms, recording studios, and a 250-seat lecture hall. A unique minor called Medical Humanities is designed for future med students; it provides an understanding of the ethical, sociocultural, legal, economic, and political factors that affect medical practice.

Many classes are predictably large, and freshmen should not be surprised to find themselves taught by graduate students in "microphone classes" where they are known only by their Social Security numbers. In the past, registration has been a hassle, but students now have the option of using the phone or Internet to register, making the task less troublesome. Required courses vary by college, but degree-seeking students must take a comprehensive two-year core curriculum, which generally forces freshmen to take English, numerical and analytical reasoning (math or philosophy), humanities and social sciences (history and fine arts), natural sciences (lab science), and a foreign language. Also required for freshmen is University 101, a three-hour seminar designed to help freshmen adjust to the university. The University has a top-notch library, with numerous special collections, including the world's most comprehensive collection of F.

Scott Fitzgerald research materials. While responsibility for faculty contact rests squarely on the students, the student-teacher relationship seems good here. "I have had excellent advisors and they are very interested in my academic career," says a student.

The student body is 87 percent South Carolinian, and most come from public school. Thirty-four percent are from the top tenth of their high school class. Nineteen percent are African American, and Asian Americans and Hispanics account for 4 percent combined. "Relations are good, but the integration could be better," reports a journalism major. Groups like SEED (Students Educating and Empowering for Diversity) tend to be popular. USC offers thousands of merit scholarships, ranging from $500 to $3,000, and 622 athletic scholarships.

The advice to prospective students: Apply immediately or at least before Christmas if you want a room on campus. Forty-eight percent of the students live on campus, and everything here works on a first-come, first-served basis—freshmen as well as upperclassmen must compete for space. The best rooms in the stately old Horseshoe section of campus cost considerably more than one-room, two-bed arrangements in dorms with bathrooms in the hall. Nearly every choice of living space is available, and the surest way to beat the housing system is to get into the Honors College, which entitles you to some of the best rooms. On-campus dining options are numerous, including a sub shop, baked potato bar, Mexican food bar, frozen yogurt, and a pizza delivery service. USC employs both all-you-can-eat meal plans and cash cards of various denominations.

Fall football weekends are a big deal, and fans have reason to cheer now that Coach Lou Holtz has given the program new life and much respect. The USC-Clemson rivalry is one of the oldest and most colorful in college sports. The festivities begin weeks in advance and include a blood drive where the two schools compete for the most blood, the annual Tigerburn parade and bonfire, and lengthy all-night tailgating parties. Winter weekends bring basketball, and when warm weather hits, Myrtle Beach is three hours away. For hiking, skiing, camping, or just getting away, the mountains are located just four hours to the north; but those interested in watching top-ranked swimming and tennis teams should stick around the campus. Club sports have been eclipsed by the varsity teams, but intramurals are still strong.

Athletic victories and losses are equally good excuses for setting up weekend-long parties on campus, but stricter campus policies regarding alcohol have cramped the traditional Carolina style. As one undergrad notes, "It's easy for underage students to get alcohol from older students, but real hard to get served in bars." However, another student claims, "If you have any kind of ID you can get served." In South Carolina, drunkenness can be punished by the city police and the university. About 13 percent of the men and 14 percent of the women join the fraternities and sororities, but these organizations orchestrate much of the nightlife. On campus, university-sponsored events include movies, dances, theater, orchestra, and comedy shows. And with more than 200 political, religious, social, and service clubs on campus, everyone can find something to get involved in. For those inclined to stray off campus, Columbia offers theaters, a comedy club, a performing arts center, and Five Points, which includes a strip of six different bars.

Of course, with such a large school, the potential of becoming a "little fish in a big pond" is great. Students who aren't ready to take initiative would be wise to look elsewhere. But students who enjoy a lively, sports-oriented collegiate life and are ready to take responsibility for their academic involvement may find that no place could be finer.

With more than 200 political, religious, social, and service clubs on campus, everyone can find something to get involved in.

The USC–Clemson rivalry is one of the oldest and most colorful in college sports. The festivities begin weeks in advance and include a blood drive where the two schools compete for the most blood, the annual Tigerburn parade and bonfire, and lengthy all-night tailgating parties.

Overlaps

Clemson, College of Charleston, Winthrop, UNC–Chapel Hill, University of Georgia.

University of Southern California

University Park, Los Angeles, CA 90089-0911

Website: www.usc.edu

Location: Center city

Total Enrollment: 29,194

Undergraduates: 15,571

Male/Female: 50/50

SAT Ranges: V 590–690 M 620–710

ACT Range: 28–31

Financial Aid: 60%

Expense: Pr $ $ $

Phi Beta Kappa: Yes

Applicants: 26,351

Accepted: 34%

Enrolled: 33%

Grad in 6 Years: 73%

Returning Freshmen: 94%

Academics: ✍ ✍ ✍

Social: ☎ ☎ ☎ ☎

Q of L: ★ ★ ★

Admissions: (213) 740-1111

Email Address:
admapp@enroll1.usc.edu

Strongest Programs:
Cinema/Television
Business
Communications
Drama
Accounting
Music Industry

Students go into USC with a few connections and come out four years later with more connections than they know what to do with. USC has many fine programs, but if the entertainment or communications business is one's desired destination, USC's ticket is guaranteed to take a graduate there. Programs in journalism/communications, drama, and music are top-notch. And with a little help from its friends Steven Spielberg, George Lucas, and Johnny Carson, who made possible the addition of a high-tech, state-of-the-art cinema/TV complex, USC is able to boast a stellar cinema/television department. Let's not overlook how many employers (male or female) might get the warm fuzzies at the mention of USC's superstar sports teams. Whatever one's major, a USC diploma is like money in the bank.

Try as they might, USC cannot hide its South Central Los Angeles address. Despite the rotten location, the campus itself is a veritable urban oasis, and security is tight compared to most other college campuses, as USC police patrol several blocks around the school in addition to USC-owned grounds. The campus occupies 150 parklike acres but is a mere 10-minute drive from the heart of Los Angeles. An immaculate mix of traditional ivy-covered and modern structures, the campus provides a richly foliated and well-shaded refuge from city asphalt and the Southern California sun. A new track stadium, internationally-themed residential college, and neurogenetics research center are slated for ribbon-cutting ceremonies soon.

The campus isn't the only thing that's changing. Curriculum restructuring of the last three years has transformed USC into an interdisciplinary smorgasbord. The school is now home to several unique programs for freshmen, including Learning Communities, a seminar-sized group of students interested in the same broad topic who study and take classes together. The group meets up to six times throughout the semester and is guided by a faculty advisor responsible for advising and mentoring the students during their first year at the school. The year 2000 saw 17 different Learning Communities groups arranged around such topics as Image and Culture: From the Trojan Wars to Star Wars and Medicine and Technology. The Thematic Option or "Traumatic Option" as it's commonly called by students, is USC's version of a freshman honors program. Admission is tough, requiring a near-perfect GPA and 1360 SAT score. Participating students have smaller classes and are exposed to a more cohesive group of core courses than most freshmen.

For upperclassmen, simplification of the general ed requirements during the last two years has allowed many to major and minor in a variety of disparate subjects, something that was previously impossible to do without sticking around for a fifth year. In fact, the administration touts the high numbers of students with interdisciplinary academic records, and it's not uncommon to meet an art history major with a biomedical sciences minor. The school recently created the Renaissance Scholars program which recognizes students excelling in academic breadth. To be eligible for the prize, you must major or minor in two or more disparate fields of study and graduate with a 3.5 or higher GPA. Last year, the school awarded 79 prizes.

USC is a California school through and through, as most of its alumni go on to lucrative jobs in L.A.'s private sector. If you want to make connections in the film and music industry, this is the place to do it. To say that USC loyalty among alumni is strong is an understatement. The "once a Trojan, always a Trojan" mantra seems to hold water with many USC alums, and many students find that their continued school spirit has paid off in their job search after college.

USC is composed of a predominantly upper-middle class student body, making it an easy target for the oft-repeated "University of Spoiled Children" moniker. USC students are quick to point out that despite their cushy upbringing, they are dedicated to diversity; an overwhelming majority of students are actively involved in community service in L.A. The campus itself is extremely diverse: 48 percent are Caucasian, 23 percent Asian American, 14 percent Hispanic, and 6 percent African American. Sixty-five percent hail from California, though the out-of-state and international percentages are increasing each year. Tuition isn't cheap, but the university offers a need-blind admissions policy and guarantees to meet demonstrated financial need for all students for all four years. The school also offers 750 academic scholarships, ranging from $1,000 to full tuition.

Students complain little about university-sponsored housing, which is available both on and off campus. Students say that finding housing is a fairly painless process, and freshman housing is all but guaranteed. Dorms, both coed and single-sex, are large, comfortable, well-maintained, even luxurious by most standards. Swimming pools, tennis courts, carpeting, air-conditioning, dishwashers; you name the convenience and you can find it in a USC dorm. But you pay for what you get, and housing—on or off campus—is expensive. About 31 percent of undergraduates live on campus. Dining halls serve croissants and gourmet coffee among other delicacies. Safety both on and off campus is a big concern, as the area around campus is questionable at best. Most students agree that campus security patrols are excellent, though long waits for campus cruiser escorts are common.

Though L.A. can hardly be described as a "college town" in the traditional sense, no one complains about a lack of social options. In addition to community service, downtown L.A. offers a vast array of internships and a hopping social scene for budding professionals. Although only a small percentage of students go Greek, the scene tends to dominate the social landscape at USC. Jaded upperclassmen say that the frat parties are easily avoided by taking trips into Hollywood or Santa Monica.

On campus, sports are pretty much the biggest thing going. USC water sports teams are solid, with winning teams in men's and women's water polo and crew, and swimming. Still, it's football that's truly king. Two of USC's biggest school-wide traditions revolve around the ol' pigskin. The first is Troy Week—the week leading up to the UCLA game—which culminates with a huge bonfire and pep rally in the middle of campus where the UCLA Bruin is burned in effigy. Ask any USC student what the best road trip of the year is, and they'll tell you that the massive Trojan migration to San Francisco for the Stanford or Berkeley game is where it's at. Throngs of USC undergrads, alumni, and fans gather together in

Curriculum restructuring of the last three years has turned USC into an interdisciplinary smorgasbord.

Union Square for a huge pep rally, featuring the band, cheerleaders, and university personalities.

USC is a place where everything seems large and prosperous, and getting to be more so all the time. It's keeping academics on the upswing, and has an energetic student body that works hard, concentrating simultaneously on studies, careers, parties, and athletics in equally substantial portions. For those planning on remaining in L.A., the connections you'll forge could possibly be your ticket to success.

If You Apply To ➤ **USC**...Regular admissions: Jan. 10. Financial aid: Feb. 1. (Dec. 15 for scholarship applicants). Guarantees to meet demonstrated need. Campus and alumni interviews: optional, informational. SATs or ACTs: required. SAT IIs: recommended. Accepts electronic applications. Essay question: story about yourself; important experience (or why USC, for transfer and foreign students). Also requires a résumé.

Southern Methodist University

P.O. Box 750296, Dallas, TX 75275-0296

Website: www.smu.edu

Location: Suburban

Total Enrollment: 10,361

Undergraduates: 5,552

Male/Female: 46/54

SAT Ranges: V 520–620 M 520–630

ACT Range: 22–27

Financial Aid: 72%

Expense: Pr $ $

Phi Beta Kappa: Yes

Applicants: 3,280

Accepted: 89%

Enrolled: 31%

Grad in 6 Years: 71%

Returning Freshmen: 84%

Academics: 🖉 🖉 🖉

Social: ☎ ☎ ☎ ☎

Q of L: ★ ★ ★ ★

Admissions: (214) 768-2058

Email Address:
ugadmission@smu.edu

Strongest Programs:
Drama
Dance
Natural Sciences/Premed

Southern Methodist University, located near Dallas, is anxious to be your home away from home. Once known as "Southern Millionaires' University," SMU is working towards becoming a place for intellectuals who take advantage of the strong programs in business and the performing arts. The school still holds conservative views but that does not stop students from getting "a well-rounded education," says one student.

The SMU campus is located 10 minutes from downtown Dallas. It boasts a beautiful suburban campus rich with flower beds, fountains, stately buildings, and neatly trimmed lawns. The architecture is traditional brick collegiate Georgian. Dallas Hall, with its four-story rotunda, is the campus centerpiece, and fittingly, one of the largest Methodist churches in North America is nearby. Although it was founded by what is now the United Methodist Church, SMU is nondenominational and welcomes students of all faiths. The associate chaplain is a female rabbi. Ground was broken in 1999 for a new library center, life sciences building, stadium, and all-sports center.

SMU's administrators believe that "the liberal arts are central to the goals of higher education." In fact, a new General Education Curriculum replaced the required liberal arts minor in 1997. It includes courses in Cultural Formations (interdisciplinary humanities and social sciences options, emphasizing writing), Perspectives (one course in each of arts; literature; religious and philosophical thought; history; politics and economics; and behavioral sciences), Information Technology (understanding technology and its social, legal, and ethical implications), Human Diversity, and a Foreign Language.

While SMU is known nationally for the Cox School of Business, the Meadows School of the Arts shines just as brightly, with two theaters—the Bob Hope Theater and the Greer Garson Theater—provided by the performers. The Garson, a 50,000-square-foot facility, includes a thrust stage for the study and performance of classical theater. SMU's humanities offerings are notable, too; English especially stands out. The school's acclaimed literary festival brings well-known poets and authors (such as Adrienne Rich and Edward Albee) to campus to give readings, participate in classes, and interact with aspiring writers. SMU also publishes *Southwest Review*, one of the four oldest continuously published literary quarterlies in the nation. SMU's history program has been enhanced by a $10-million endowment that began funding a Ph.D. program and the interdisciplinary Center for Southwest Studies; the center's programs are available to undergraduates as well. Other undergraduate majors include public policy, medieval studies, and telecommunications systems.

The Cox School offers SMU's most popular major, business administration. The Business Associates Program pairs students with corporate mentors in Dallas for term-time internships and postgraduation jobs. Similarly, engineers have access to an extensive co-op program, thanks to Dallas's proximity to more than 800 high-tech companies. The John Goodwin Tower Center for Political Studies, named for the former U.S. senator, focuses on international relations and comparative politics. A weaker spot is the Center for Communication Arts, popular because its programs are considered easy, says a journalism major.

Outstanding students can qualify for an accelerated three-year program at SMU, and the honors program has been revamped to emphasize internationalism and intellectual community. Additionally, 13 study abroad programs are available in places ranging from Austria to Australia; about 400 students participate each year. SMU also operates a second campus near Taos, New Mexico, at historic Fort Burgwin, a mid-19th century army outpost. The re-created adobe buildings house classrooms and labs for study in anthropology, archeology, and the arts.

SMU prides itself on small classes; most courses have 50 or fewer students. Students find professors at the lectern, as teaching assistants conduct labs only. "I would give the quality of teaching I have received a 100," says a junior. "I have been in classes with engaging, brilliant faculty," one student claims. The career center benefits from SMU's strong alumni network, but business and engineering students generally find more help here than liberal and fine arts majors do, students say.

There is money on this campus, where "political issues are not debated very often, largely because most students are conservative," says a junior. As one student describes, "the stereotypical SMU student is white, upper class/upper middle class who could not get into Emory, Vanderbilt, Rice, etc." Another student informs, "don't be surprised to see Chanel book bags, Khakis instead of jeans, BMWs, and Rolexes." "SMU has long been known for being socially and politically apathetic," recalls the senior. This attitude does seem to be changing, albeit slowly.

More than 90 percent of students have received some sort of financial aid in recent years, and SMU is proud of its student-loan program, designed for middle-income families that do not meet federal guidelines for need-based loans. "Financial aid is given abundantly to high quality students who normally cannot afford SMU." SMU also provides merit scholarships, ranging from $1,000 to $14,000, as well as 254 athletic scholarships.

Texans make up about 60 percent of the SMU student body, which includes students from all 50 states and more than 90 foreign countries. Of the minority population, Hispanics account for 9 percent, African Americans 7 percent, and Asian Americans about another 6 percent. While campus diversity has increased over the past few years, ethnic groups tend to band together. "Racial tension is the big social issue," reports a political science major. Social issues might be "mixed couples or interracial dating" notes another student. Some attribute this division to the Greek system. But the administration is working to increase understanding

(Continued)
History
Geological Sciences
Business
Political Science
Ethics

SMU is nondenominational and welcomes students of all faiths. The associate chaplain is a female rabbi.

The Business Associates Program pairs students with corporate mentors, and close ties to the Dallas business community often lead to internships and jobs after graduation.

among races, with activities such as Intercultural Student Orientation. And perhaps most important, SMU students have begun to emerge from the "bubble" of their posh Park Cities location: administrators say community involvement is at an all-time high, with about 1,000 students volunteering regularly for service projects.

About 30 percent of the students live on campus, and freshmen are required to; most upperclassmen find off-campus apartments or dwell in Greek houses (37 percent of the women and 36 percent of the men go Greek). All 13 residence halls are coed by floor, and a variety of options, such as an honors floor and an "expressive living" floor, are available. Large-scale renovations began last year, and students say they are producing attractive results. "SMU-owned apartments are cheap but almost impossible to obtain" says a senior." Adds a classmate: "All the first-years live in the South Quad together. One thousand students living, eating, sleeping, and playing together cannot help but bond."

The extracurricular life at SMU is quite active, with 152 student organizations. "Most of the campus's social life revolves around the Greek life," says a self-identified sorority girl. "We hold most of the formals and theme parties. However, plenty of partying is done by non-Greeks." Dallas offers plenty of additional options in funky areas like the West End and Deep Ellum. Since SMU is a dry campus, the city's bars and clubs hold even greater allure for those old enough to get in, or clever enough to sneak in with a fake ID. "It is a fun college town although it is difficult to navigate without a car," remarks a student. Road trips include South Padre Island (for sunning on the Gulf Coast) and New Orleans (for Mardi Gras). "Many students bet their allowances in Shreveport," adds a mechanical engineering major. "Others go to Austin and party along Sixth Street, or down to San Antonio's beautiful Riverwalk."

SMU also offers outstanding cultural options. Each year, for example, the Meadows School sponsors more then 400 theatrical performances, concerts, and exhibits. The on-campus Tate Forums provide informal question-and-answer sessions with national and international figures. Highlights of the campus calendar include Peruna's Birthday, a day honoring the mustang mascot, and the Celebration of Lights, when students gather to admire Christmas lights at Dallas Hall.

Sports have taken a backseat at SMU ever since a late-1980s football scandal and resulting NCAA sanctions, but the team still gets fired up to play archrivals Texas and Texas Christian. SMU competes in the Western Athletic Conference, and women's and men's swimming and diving, soccer (the soccer field was upgraded as a World Cup practice site), and track are among programs garnering national recognition. Nineteen SMU students competed in the 1996 Olympics, including a gold medal swimmer.

If y'all are looking for a superb faculty that cares about undergraduates, at a school dedicated to serving up education with a healthy dose of Southern hospitality and athletic boosterism, then Southern Methodist fits the bill. "I feel like I can be myself here," gushes a junior. "Everyone is so friendly and caring, I can actually call SMU my home."

Overlaps

Texas, Texas Christian, Vanderbilt, Texas A&M, Tulane.

If You Apply To > **SMU**…Rolling admissions: Jan. 15 (priority), Apr. 1 (final). Early action: Nov. 1. Financial aid: Feb. 1. Housing: May 1. Does not guarantee to meet demonstrated need. Campus and alumni interviews: optional, informational. SATs or ACTs: required. SAT IIs: optional. Accepts the Common Application. Essay question: create a family, community, or school tradition; what sets you apart; or a topic of your choosing.

Southwestern University

1001 E. University Avenue, Georgetown, TX 78626

Southwestern University demonstrates that not everything in Texas has to be big to be the best. This small school is academically strong, and the combination of highly qualified professors, diverse student body, and an abundance of extracurricular activities has allowed the university to build a solid reputation for itself.

Southwestern is situated on 500 acres at the edge of the rolling Texas Hill Country. The campus boasts turn-of-the-century Texas limestone buildings in a Romanesque architectural style. There are plenty of wide-open spaces, including a nine-hole golf course and outdoor tennis courts. Construction of a new campus center and an addition to the science hall were recently completed, as was an expansion the fine arts building.

"Students at Southwestern are competitive academically, but it's not a knockdown, drag-out situation," says a communications major. "It's more of an internal competition, meaning students compete to be the best they can personally be." Biology, communications, and psychology are considered the school's finest programs and are quite popular with students. Weaker departments include computer science and non-Western languages; however, the latter is improving due to the addition of the Language Learning Center. Each spring, classes are suspended for two days for the Brown Symposium, an annual series of discussions and seminars organized around a single topic such as genetic engineering, computers in everyday life, or the achievements of a single scholar or artist.

Graduation requirements include three Foundation Courses, including a First-Year Colloquium, 10 courses from a larger group identified as Perspectives on Knowledge sequence, and English Composition. There's also a stipulation that students take a foreign language through sophomore year and two hours of a fitness or recreational activity are mandatory. Southwestern also introduced first-year seminars in the fall of 1999, which allow students to explore a variety of topics while introducing them to college life. The study abroad program is very strong, and as many as one-third of the students here take advantage of opportunities in London, Jamaica, Mexico, and Germany. Several student exchange programs are offered as well. Internships are available, including one to study art in New York and another to study politics, foreign policy, journalism, and architecture in Washington, D.C. Undergraduate research is encouraged in all majors. The biology department offers a summer research program to students interested in working with a faculty member, which also provides a $3,000 student stipend. In addition, Southwestern has been a member of the prestigious Associated Colleges of the South* consortium since 1991.

Students report that 80 percent of their classes have had 25 or fewer students enrolled, and as a result, they've gotten to know professors very well. Professors even occasionally invite students to their homes. "The quality of teaching here is like none other and worth every penny of tuition expense," says a senior. Another student adds, "Professors seek to cultivate and open up perspectives rather than imposing their views and shutting down options." Perhaps because of their respect for their profs, Southwesterners take their academics seriously, and staying in to study is a legitimate excuse for not going out.

The student body is fairly diverse: 84 percent are Caucasian, 9 percent Hispanic, 3 percent Asian American, and 3 percent African American. And despite the administration's vigorous recruitment efforts, 90 percent of the students are

Website:
www.southwestern.edu
Location: Suburban
Total Enrollment: 1,256
Undergraduates: 1,256
Male/Female: 42/58
SAT Ranges: V 570–670 M 570–670
ACT Range: 24–29
Financial Aid: 57%
Expense: Pr $ $
Phi Beta Kappa: Yes
Applicants: 1,495
Accepted: 67%
Enrolled: 36%
Grad in 6 Years: 70%
Returning Freshmen: 88%
Academics: ✍ ✍ ✍
Social: ☎ ☎ ☎
Q of L: ★ ★ ★
Admissions: (512) 863-1200
Email Address: admission@southwestern.edu

Strongest Programs:
Music
Psychology
Economics and Business
Biology/Premed
Communications
Women's Studies
International Studies
History

Texans, with large numbers from the metropolitan areas of Houston, Dallas, and San Antonio. Still, insists a junior biology major, "There are people from all over the world on this campus. Those students who aren't aware of the way of life of students in other countries will be able to broaden their horizons." SU's tuition is markedly less than at institutions of similar quality in other parts of the nation, and the university has several special tuition payment plans, including a new loan program for all families. The school also offers merit scholarships to each class, ranging from $1,000 to a full ride.

Over the past few years, Southwestern has changed a number of programs to keep up with the times. It developed a sexual harassment policy involving students, faculty, and staff as advisors, and created a Gender Awareness Resource Center on campus to offer programs on gender communication and acquaintance rape. An alcohol coalition was also created to help deal with alcohol issues on campus. All new students go through an afternoon diversity workshop called Facing Differences, which focuses on relating in spite of racial, ethnic, cultural, and other differences. Still, one senior laments, "Political correctness is a huge issue on our campus. I often feel that people are hypersensitive when it come to diversity, sexual preference, and gender issues." Another student adds, "You have to be careful of what you say because there is always someone who will take offense to something!"

Since Georgetown is on the small side (pop. 26,000), there is not an overabundance of off-campus housing. Eighty-seven percent of students live on campus. Some students say it's becoming more difficult to get a room, but those who do seem quite content living in the school's coed and single-sex European-style residence halls. "The dorms are comfortable and well-maintained by an amiable staff of housekeepers and maintenance workers," says a history major. Another student adds, "The dorms are spacious and clean, and each one offers a different social environment." Different meal plans are available and students can also eat in the student union snack bar.

Most social life on campus is centered around the Greek system, to which 36 percent of the men and 34 percent of the women belong. The frats host house parties open to everyone most weekends. For those who don't pledge or dislike that scene, the fine arts department sponsors dances and plays, and there are campus-wide picnics with carnival-style entertainment, plus an annual Block Party on the Square. During Homecoming, students look forward to Sing, an event where students produce short musical skits about Southwestern. Georgetown, once a stop on the famed Chisholm Trail, also has some of its own treasures. "The Blue Hole is a beautiful swimming hole with a small waterfall where we spend our afternoons when it gets warm," says a history major. For the real action, many students travel 30 minutes south to Austin's great restaurants, concerts, and live music shows on Sixth Street. Another popular campus activity is "rolling," where students pack as many people in a car as they can and drive very slowly on the back roads with blaring music. The official school policy on drinking is consistent with the law: no underage drinking. "Students who want to drink will find a way, but Southwestern does its best to control the amount on campus and always takes appropriate actions to any situation that involves alcohol," says a chemistry major.

Intramural sports are popular and Southwestern is a member of the Southern Collegiate Athletic Conference in the NCAA's Division III. Baseball, women's basketball, volleyball, and golf have all won conference championships, and soccer is gaining in popularity. Crowds gather anytime SU plays San Antonio's Trinity University because of a strong rivalry between the two schools.

Southwestern is a strong academic institution with a heart. "I really like the small atmosphere at SU because it lends itself to becoming friends with other students and with professors," says one biology major. "There's a definite sense of community found here." Southwestern may not be a large university by Texas standards, but it's big in its own unique way.

If You Apply To ➤ | **SU**…Rolling admissions: Feb. 15. Early decision: Nov. 1, Jan. 1. Financial aid: Mar. 1. Meets demonstrated need of 90%. Campus interviews: recommended, evaluative. Alumni interviews: optional, evaluative. SATs or ACTs: required. SAT IIs: optional. Accepts the Common Application and electronic applications. Essay question: a personal experience or achievement that has changed you.

Spelman College, GA—See ATLANTA UNIVERSITY CENTER

Stanford University

Stanford, CA 94305-3005

Many Easterners think that the only difference between Stanford and the Ivy League is a couple of hundred extra sunny days each year. Think again. From the red-tiled roofs to the lush greenery and laid-back California aura, Stanford is a world away from the Gothic intellectual culture of the Ivies. Virtually all the great universities of the East began as places to ponder human existence and the meaning of life using the great European universities as their models. Stanford built its academic reputation around science and engineering—only later cultivating excellence in the humanities and social sciences. Let there be no doubt: Stanford is the country's first great "American" university.

The difference between Stanford and the older institutions with whom it competes every year for the country's top high school seniors is evident in everything from the architecture to the curriculum. Its California mission-style buildings look outward rather than inward to ivy-covered courtyards. Founded in 1891 by Leland and Jane Stanford, the university has been coed from the beginning. During its centennial, the school became the first university in the United States to successfully launch a billion-dollar capital campaign, and now the endowment coffers expand at an annual rate of 32 percent, the highest in the nation. Although some architectural critics say the campus looks like the world's biggest Mexican restaurant, central buildings were planned by Frederick Law Olmstead, designer of New York City's Central Park. The campus stretches from the foothills of the Santa Cruz Mountains to the edge of Palo Alto in the heart of Silicon Valley, and resides smack in the middle of earthquake country. The university has spent billions over the past ten years in the "seismic strengthening" program, and 1999 saw the reopening of the Cantor Center for Visual Arts, the Green Library, and Hanna House (first built by Frank Lloyd Wright). Current construction includes the new Global Learning Center and the Center for Clinical Research.

In keeping with the Stanfords's legacy, a preprofessional attitude pervades much of the student body. Human biology (i.e., premed) is an especially popular major, though not as popular with seniors as it is with freshmen. One junior says

Website: www.stanford.edu
Location: Suburban
Total Enrollment: 18,083
Undergraduates: 7,784
Male/Female: 51/49
SAT Ranges: V 670–770 M 690–780
ACT Range: 28–33
Financial Aid: 70%
Expense: Pr $ $ $ $
Phi Beta Kappa: Yes
Applicants: 17,919
Accepted: 15%
Enrolled: 56%
Grad in 6 Years: 90%
Returning Freshmen: 99%
Academics: ✍ ✍ ✍ ✍ ✍
Social: ☎ ☎ ☎ ☎
Q of L: ★ ★ ★ ★ ★
Admissions: (650) 723-2091
Email Address:
undergrad.admission@ forsythe.stanford.edu

Strongest Programs:
English
Communications/Journalism
Engineering

that everyone seems to arrive at Stanford premed, and by the time graduation rolls around, about 10 percent of them are left. There are also strengths to be found in Stanford's programs in the humanities, social sciences, and arts. In recent years, Stanford has developed a particularly interesting set of interdisciplinary majors, which allow students to cull courses from a number of departments and fashion one major track. A junior symbolic systems major describes his program of study as a combination of computer science, psychology, philosophy, and linguistics. One student describes Stanford as the "center of the physics universe," a statement that might not be far off. The department boasts nine Nobel laureates, and the campus is home a half-mile long linear accelerator, as well as the second largest astronomical radio-dish telescope in the United States.

General education requirements are extensive. All students take a three-quarter Introduction to the Humanities sequence, designed to hone skills in humanistic disciplines through close reading and critical investigation of a limited number of works, as well as three courses in the humanities and social sciences. The Science, Mathematics, and Engineering Core allows students another option for fulfilling requirements in natural sciences, applied science and technology, and mathematics. One course in at least two of three areas of world culture, American culture, and gender studies is also required. The new Stanford Introductory Studies programs are designed to "enrich the first two years of college studies" by offering a series of innovative learning experiences for freshmen and sophomores. Freshman Seminars give students the chance to work one-on-one with faculty in small-group settings. Stanford manages the "sophomore slump" through programs like Sophomore College, a three-week summer program that puts incoming sophomores together under one roof for faculty-led projects designed to foster mentoring relationships, while Sophomore Dialogues are small seminar-size courses for second-year students only.

Stanford's laid-back California location might be a misleading. Make no mistake—studying is a full-time job here. "On average, students spend between 25 and 40 hours a week studying, depending on the major and course level," a senior explains. Another student adds, "I'd categorize [the climate] as academically rigorous and very cooperative—not competitive." Stanford's faculty ranks among the best in the nation, with most departments boasting a nationally known name or two. Academic advising is described as first-rate. Classes are generally small and students report that registration is relatively painless and hassle-free.

For students who want a break from "the Farm," Stanford's overseas campuses offer a blend of luxury and leisure that few colleges can match. Described as "excellent" by students, semesters abroad are available in Japan, Mexico, Chile, England, Russia, Germany, Italy, and France. Closer to home, there's a Stanford-in-Washington program that allows 60 students to live, study, and serve internships in the nation's capital each year. The Haas Center for Public Service gives students the opportunity to pursue service-learning courses spanning a wide range of disciplines. The communications department also sponsors the Rebele internship, which allows students to land a paid internship with a host of California newspapers. The President's office also offers 200 Intellectual Exploration Grants of $3,000 to select incoming freshmen to pursue extracurricular research interests. One student even studied microentrepreneurship in Tunisia.

Despite its upscale image, Stanford tends to have the same demographic profile as its state-supported neighbor in Berkeley. Sixty-five percent of the students attended public high school, and 88 percent graduated in the top tenth of their class. Fifty-one percent of the student body are from out of state, and foreigners

The new Science, Mathematics, and Engineering Core allows students another option for fulfilling requirements in natural sciences, applied science and technology, and mathematics.

from 64 countries account for 5 percent of the incoming freshmen. Minority enrollment is above average, with Asian Americans accounting for 24 percent of the student body, Hispanics 11 percent, and blacks 8 percent. "Diversity is a big student concern right now," explains a senior. " Another student divides his classmates into "techies" (engineering, math, computer science majors) or "fuzzies" (humanities types), and assures that there are plenty of fuzzies to balance the more prevalent techies.

About 20 percent of Stanford's students take advantage of the university's liberal stop-out policy, which allows students to take some time out along the way rather than stay in school for four straight years. Stanford is need-blind in its admissions, and there are 280 athletic scholarships awarded annually in everything from football and basketball to gymnastics and diving. The university guarantees to meet the full demonstrated financial need of every admit. An impressive 70 percent of the students receive some form of financial aid. A week-long freshman orientation program includes a square dance, field day, and the obligatory dunking in the pool.

Freshmen are required to live on campus, and Stanford guarantees housing to all. More than 90 percent of the students accept the offer each year, in part because of the lack of affordable options in the extraordinarily expensive Silicon Valley. For those who stay on campus, the annual lottery system decides one's fate. But sticking around campus isn't so bad, as one student notes that Stanford housing is "utopian." " The multimillion-dollar Governor's Corner dorm complex is luxurious, with its all-oak fixtures, homey rooms with views into the foothills, microwave ovens in the kitchenettes, and Italian leather sofas in the lounges. "The dorms are comfortable and most have been renovated or are scheduled to be soon," a senior says. Those living in residence halls must sign up for a meal plan, but the food comes highly rated. Students describe the campus as "ridiculously safe" and, according to a sophomore, "Our only real problem is bicycle theft."

When academic pressures become too great, students have much to enjoy in the outdoors. The nearby hills are perfect for jogging and biking, and a small lake is great for sailing and windsurfing (the most popular P.E. class in the spring). Trips to the Sierra Nevada mountains (four hours away) or to the Pacific coast (45 minutes) are popular. As one student explains, "The social life is very campus oriented, from athletic events to social events."

"Palo Alto is a rich yuppie haven that closes at 11:00 P.M.," says a student, voicing exasperation with the early closing times of local establishments. Another adds, "Palo Alto is not a college town. It's a pricey suburb with about one sushi restaurant per person." For those not into raw fish, San Francisco offers plenty of diversions, and many students do volunteer work in nearby East Palo Alto, which is less affluent than Palo Alto proper.

Like most things at Stanford, activities and social life vary a great deal. As tradition goes, incoming women aren't "true Stanford women" until they've been kissed at midnight in the quad by a senior. Full Moon on the Quad occurs at the first full moon and features a bevy of giggling first-year women eager to receive their initiation (courtesy of a well-timed entrance by fraternity brothers). Several students note, however, that first-year male students now receive similar initiation rites from senior women. Greek organizations claim 17 percent of the men and 12 percent of the women, and provide their share of parties. Staple Greek events, open to all, include Thursday night happy hours and weekend beer bashes. Another Stanford tradition is the Viennese Ball, a February event that makes you wish you'd taken ballroom dancing lessons. Halloween finds students partying at the Mausoleum—the final resting place of Jane and Leland Stanford.

The new Stanford Introductory Studies programs are designed to "enrich the first two years of college studies" by offering a series of innovative learning experiences for freshmen and sophomores.

About 20 percent of Stanford's students take advantage of the university's liberal stop-out policy, which allows students to take some time out along the way rather than stay in school for four straight years.

Though the university has cracked down on beer at all campus parties, most students agree that you can drink anyway.

Stanford has a proud tradition in athletics. The Cardinals recently won the Sears Director's Cup for the best overall college athletics program for the sixth consecutive year. Stanford had fourteen national championships from 1994 to 1997, and Cardinal athletes carried home sixteen gold medals during the Atlanta Olympics. The football team has pulled off its share of upsets, and the annual game against Cal (Berkeley) is the "Big Game." "UCB is our rival—they're weenies!" gloats one student. Stanford also offers a full slate of intramurals. The vast sports complex includes 26 tennis courts, 2 gymnasiums, a stadium, an "athletic pavilion," an 18-hole golf course, and 4 swimming pools.

By any standard, Stanford is one of the nation's preeminent universities. Its sunny demeanor and infectious West Coast optimism offer students an alternative to the gloom that seems to hang over some Ivies, without sacrificing the academics and resources that have made them great. Says a junior: "Stanford is such a wonderful group of unique, talented, and upbeat people that the community here on campus makes this a wonderful place to go to school."

Overlaps

Harvard, Yale, Princeton, Brown, MIT.

If You Apply To ➤

Stanford...Early decision: Nov. 1. Regular admissions: Dec. 15. Guarantees to meet demonstrated need. No campus or alumni interviews. SATs: required. SAT IIs: strongly recommended. Essay question: How has the place in which you live affected your life? Tell us about a tradition that is important to you.

State University of New York

As the largest university system in the world, the State University of New York provides over 400,000 students with a vast landscape of educational opportunities—both figuratively and literally. Encompassing 66 campuses and 21,000 acres of property, SUNY's staggering physical presence is exceeded only by the scope of its academic offerings.

The statistics of SUNY (pronounced "SOOney") are awesome. The university has an annual operating budget of billions, greater than the gross national product of many countries and larger than the budget of more than a dozen American states.

It has more than 4,000 academic programs and 24,500 faculty members and maintains more than 2,200 buildings. Every year it awards approximately 65,000 degrees, from associate to Ph.D., in thousands of different academic fields. And—you're not going to believe this one—it has more than a million living graduates.

Such figures are all the more remarkable because until 1948 New York had no state university at all. That year, the legislature created State University around a cluster of 32 existing public institutions, the best of which focused on the training of teachers, to handle the flow of returning World War II veterans. But a "gentleman's agreement" not to compete with the state's private colleges (which for generations had enjoyed a monopoly on higher education in New York) hindered SUNY's movement into the liberal arts. Not until Nelson A. Rockefeller became governor in 1960 and made the building up of the university his major priority did SUNY begin its dramatic growth.

SUNY has now ripened into a network of 4 research-oriented "university centers," 13 arts and sciences colleges, 6 agricultural and technical colleges, 5 "statutory" colleges, 4 specialized colleges, 30 locally sponsored community colleges, and 4 health science centers. The fruits of the labor, though practiced in as high-cost a state as there is, have become legitimately advertised as among the best bargains in the nation, particularly at the undergraduate level. Annual costs at institutions like SUNY–Albany are still barely more than half of what it costs to attend such hoary and prestigious publicly supported flagship campuses as California at Berkeley and the University of Michigan. Nevertheless, the SUNY system faces continuing budget cuts, and New York State's investment per capita in higher education as a whole is 47th in the country.

Prospective students apply directly to the SUNY unit they seek to attend. Forty-six of the colleges, though, use a "common form" application that enables a prospective student to apply to as many as four SUNY campuses at the same time. The central administration runs a SUNY Admissions Assistance Service that helps students who are not admitted to colleges where they applied find places at other campuses. Students who earn associate degrees at community or other two-year colleges are guaranteed the chance to continue their education at a four-year institution, though not necessarily at their first choice. The level of selectivity varies widely. Most community colleges guarantee admission to any local high school student, but the university centers, as well as some specialized colleges, are among the most competitive public institutions in the nation. As part of a recent "standards revolution," SUNY trustees voted to adopt a new budgeting model designed to financially reward campuses that increase enrollment. Undergraduates at all liberal arts colleges and university centers pay the same tuition, but the rates at community colleges vary (and are lower). Out-of-state students, who make up only 4 percent of SUNY students, pay about double the amount of in-state tuition.

Mainly for political reasons, the State University of New York chose not to follow the model of other states and build a single flagship campus the likes of an Ann Arbor, Madison, or Chapel Hill. Instead, it created the four university centers with undergraduate, graduate, and professional schools and research facilities in each corner of the state. When they were created in the 1960s, each one hoped to become fully comprehensive, but there has been a certain degree of specialization from the beginning.

Albany is strongest in education and public policy, Binghamton is best known for undergraduate arts and sciences, and Stony Brook is noted for its hard sciences. Buffalo, formerly a private university, maintains a strong reputation in the life sciences and geography but comes the closest of any of the four to being a fully comprehensive university. Critics of the system say that the decision to forgo a flagship campus guarantees a lack of national prominence, and the lack of big-time football or other sports programs has affected SUNY's reputation as well. Still, many insist that somewhere in the labs and libraries of these four university centers are lurking the Nobel Prize winners of this century. To these supporters, it's only a matter of time before SUNY achieves excellence in depth as well as breadth.

The 13 colleges of arts and sciences likewise vary widely in size and character. They range from the 26,000-student College at Buffalo, whose 125-acre campus reflects the urban flavor of the state's second-largest city, to the rural and highly selective College at Geneseo, where half as many students nearly outnumber the year-round residents of the small local village. Still others are suburban campuses, such as Purchase, which specializes in the performing arts, and Old Westbury, which was started as an experimental institution to serve minority students, older women, and others who have been "bypassed" by more traditional institutions.

With the exception of Purchase and Old Westbury, which were started from scratch, the four-year colleges are all former teachers' colleges that have, for the most part, successfully made the transition into liberal arts colleges on the small, private New England model. Now they face a new problem: the growing desire of students to study business, computer science, and other more technically oriented subjects. Some have adjusted to these demands well; others are trying to resist the trend.

SUNY's technical and specialized colleges, while not enjoying the prominence of the colleges of arts and sciences, serve the demand for vocational training in a variety of two- and four-year programs. Five of the six agricultural and technical colleges—Alfred, Canton, Cobleskill, Delhi, and Morrisville—are concerned primarily with agriculture, but also have programs in engineering, nursing, medical technology, data processing, and business administration. The sixth, Farmingdale, offers the widest range of programs, from ornamental horticulture to aerospace technology. A new upper-division technical campus at Utica-Rome now provides graduates of these two-year institutions with an opportunity to finish their education in SUNY instead of having to head for Penn State University, Ohio State, the University of Massachusetts, or destinations in other directions.

Four of the five statutory schools are at Cornell University—agriculture and life sciences, human ecology, industrial and labor relations, and veterinary medicine—while the internationally known College of Ceramics is housed at Alfred University, another private university. In addition to Utica-Rome, the specialized colleges consist of the College of Environmental Sciences and Forestry at Syracuse, the Maritime College at Fort Schuyler in the

Bronx, the College of Optometry in New York City, and the Fashion Institute of Technology, whose graduates are gobbled up as fast as they emerge by employers in the Manhattan Garment District.

The 29 community colleges have traditionally been the stepchildren of the system, but the combination of rampant vocationalism and the rising cost of education elsewhere is rapidly turning them into the most robust members of the family. Students once looked to the community colleges for terminal degrees that could be readily applied in the marketplace. Now, with the cost of college soaring, a growing number of students who otherwise would have been packed off to a four-year college are saving money by staying home for the first two years and then transferring to a four-year college—or even a university center—to get their bachelor's degree.

Following are full-length descriptions of SUNY–Purchase, which is the liberal arts institution best known beyond New York's borders, SUNY–Geneseo, and the four university centers.

SUNY–Albany

1400 Washington Avenue, Albany, NY 12222

Website: www.albany.edu
Location: Suburban
Total Enrollment: 16,901
Undergraduates: 11,737
Male/Female: 51/49
SAT Ranges: V 500–600 M 520–610
Financial Aid: 55%
Expense: Pub $ $ $
Phi Beta Kappa: Yes
Applicants: 15,312
Accepted: 61%
Enrolled: 24%
Grad in 6 Years: 62%
Returning Freshmen: 83%
Academics: ✍ ✍ ✍ ✍
Social: ☎ ☎ ☎
Q of L: ★ ★ ★
Admissions: (518) 442-5435
Email Address:
ugadmissions@albany.edu

Strongest Programs:
Criminal Justice
Atmospheric Science
Biology
Physics
Sociology
Psychology
Business
Political Science

Located in the state's capital and founded in 1844 as the first institution in New York to train teachers, SUNY–Albany is set up primarily for graduate research, but the school's outstanding education and public policy programs attract undergrads from around the nation who are eager to take advantage of the vast resources. "I love the fact that it is so big and has so many opportunities," says a senior. "There is always something going on on campus."

Designed by Edward Durrell Stone, who also designed the Kennedy Center and Lincoln Center, SUNY–Albany's campus is modern and suburban. Almost all the academic buildings are clustered in the center of the campus, while students are housed in five symmetrically situated quads so similar in appearance that it usually takes a semester to figure out which one is yours. (Hint: The quads are named for periods in New York history—Indian, Dutch, Colonial, State, and Freedom—and progress clockwise around the campus.) Last year saw the opening of the new, $16-million Center for Environmental Sciences and Technology Management.

Most of the science departments and preprofessional programs are among the finest of any SUNY branch. Students in the public administration and social welfare programs may take advantage of their proximity to the state government to participate in internships. Biology, physics, sociology, and psychology are other notable majors, and undergrads are clamoring for admittance to the university's business administration program, which is especially strong in accounting. The New York State Writers' Institute is the newest and least traditional of Albany's offerings, and with William Kennedy as head of the institute, the university's dream of becoming distinguished for its creative writing has nearly come true.

All undergraduates must fulfill Albany's 24-credit general education program, which includes courses in natural sciences, social sciences, humanities and the arts, cultural and historical perspectives, and two writing-intensive courses. If this liberal arts exposure whets your appetite for interdisciplinary study, try your hand at human biology, information science, or urban studies. The more career-minded can sign up for one of 40 BA/MA programs or opt for a law degree with the bachelor's in only six years. Many students take advantage of SUNY–Albany's superior offerings in foreign study. Don't be surprised if you find yourself sitting in class next to someone named Ivan; the university was one of the first in the nation to develop exchange programs with Russia (and China, for that matter). Undergraduates may also study in several European countries as well as in Brazil,

Costa Rica, Israel, Japan, and Singapore. Project Renaissance brings together groups of 100 freshmen with a team of senior faculty, librarians, computer specialists, and assistants in a shared academic and living community. Participants engage in a yearlong, unified course of study covering 12 hours of the university's general education requirements, and have access to special perks including housing and faculty mentors.

The student body comprises "bits and pieces of every Long Island high school and a dash of upstate, topped off with a Big Apple or two." All but 4 percent of the students are native New Yorkers, about one-third from Long Island and more than half from upstate New York. African American and Hispanic enrollment now stands at 15 percent combined, while Asian Americans make up another 8 percent. Racial issues are hot, but a senior says, "No problems, just a lot of diversity." SUNY–Albany is one of the more selective public universities in the nation, and 45 percent of the students are from the top quarter of their high school class. One undergraduate describes his peers as "intelligent, assertive, hardworking, urban—generally pretty fast company." Albany students tend to spend a lot of time thinking about their future. But, lest you get the wrong impression, another adds, "They're also highly motivated to party at every available moment." SUNY–Albany makes available 500 merit scholarships of $1,000 to $6,000 each.

Housing at Albany is described as "average." Freshmen are required to live in dorms, and the administration makes no promises to upperclassmen looking for rooms. The coed quads are exceptionally friendly, surprisingly quiet, and comfortable. "They are compact and force unity and friendship," says one undergrad. Each floor of these dorms is divided into four- to six-person suites. But the word from most students is that the best dorms are in the Alumni Quad on the downtown campus. "Alumni has much more attractive rooms and ambiance overall," says a business major. Many students move off campus because "the transportation system to and from campus is convenient and the cost of apartments is as cheap (or cheaper) than living on campus," says a junior. Students on the main campus take their meals at any of the four dorms or at the campus center that includes a popular food court and bookstore, while downtowners haunt the cheap local eateries as well as their own cafeterias.

While most people are serious about their work, a SUNY–Albany weekend starts on Thursday night for many. Students go to parties or go bar-hopping about town. Students warn that alcohol policies forbidding underage drinking are strict and well enforced. "It is easy for underage residents to drink on campus, but if you're caught there are severe penalties," says a student. The Greek life is experiencing something of a renaissance at Albany. Fraternities and sororities now attract 15 percent of the male and female students, and have become the main party-throwers on campus. Albany students tend to be traditional, but rites-of-spring festivals, mandatory after enduring the miserable upstate winters, have produced Guinness records for the largest games of Simon Says, Twister, and musical chairs. Fountain Day brings thousands of students together for the spring turn-on of the infamous podium fountain. Mayfest is a huge all-school concert party that brings in well-known as well as up-and-coming bands.

The natural resources of the upstate region keep students busy skiing and hiking. Treks to Montreal and Saratoga are popular. Plus, the student association owns and operates Dippikill, a private camp in the Adirondacks. Men's basketball, tennis, wrestling, and football and women's softball, volleyball, and basketball advanced to the NCAA Division II in 1995, and the school has made a recent move to Division I. Meanwhile, intramurals engender a great deal of student enthusiasm, and participation numbers in the thousands.

The more career-minded can sign up for one of 40 BA/MA programs or opt for a law degree with the bachelor's in only six years.

Students in the public administration and social welfare programs may take advantage of their proximity to the state government to participate in internships.

SUNY–Albany is not the concrete, sterile diploma mill it may appear to be. It's a place of opportunity for those willing to put in the hours and hard work. As one veteran warns, "You can find an outlet here for even the most obscure interest, but this is not a school that will educate you when you're not looking."

If You Apply To ➤ **SUNY–Albany**...Early action: Dec. 1. Regular admissions: Mar. 1. Financial aid: Mar. 15. Meets demonstrated need of 18%. Campus interviews: optional, informational. No alumni interviews. SATs: required. SAT IIs: optional. Accepts electronic applications. Optional essay question: personal statement.

SUNY–Binghamton University

P.O. Box 6001, Binghamton, NY 13902-6000

Website: www.binghamton.edu
Location: Suburban
Total Enrollment: 12,564
Undergraduates: 9,872
Male/Female: 47/53
SAT Ranges: V 540–640 M 570–660
Financial Aid: 65%
Expense: Pub $ $ $
Phi Beta Kappa: Yes
Applicants: 16,386
Accepted: 42%
Enrolled: 30%
Grad in 6 Years: 81%
Returning Freshmen: 91%
Academics: ✑ ✑ ✑ ✑
Social: ☎ ☎ ☎
Q of L: ★ ★
Admissions: (607) 777-2171
Email Address: admit@binghamton.edu

Strongest Programs:
Accounting
Human Development
Chemistry
Engineering
English

While a lesser school might get lost in the trappings of the world's largest university system, that's not a concern at Binghamton University. Considered by many the shining star of the SUNY system, Binghamton offers students challenging, high-quality academics and unlimited opportunities for growth. It is the best public university in the country that never gets any respect—except from students. "I find the university is large enough to get super professors and to have cutting-edge resources, but small enough that I have had the opportunity to get to know some professors very well," says a junior. "I can get personal attention when needed."

Binghamton University is situated on over 800 acres of open grassy areas that include a large nature preserve, trails, fountains, and a pond. "The surrounding countryside is breathtaking," one woman notes. The campus itself isn't bad either, if you like modern, "functional" buildings (all structures have been built since 1958). Some students say that from an aerial view the circular campus bears a striking resemblance to the human brain—a total coincidence and not a secret plan of the architects, the administration asserts. Recent construction includes the $20-million academic complex that houses three of the four professional schools.

The first thing that greets students who do gain admission is the general education program. This comprehensive curriculum requires new students to take courses in discipline-based writing, global interdependencies, pluralism in the U.S., math, lab science, aesthetic perspective, and physical activity/wellness.

Engineering receives high marks from students, as do the Decker School of Nursing, which offers an accelerated bachelor's degree program for students with degrees in other fields, and the school of management, which offers a five-year BS/MBA program. In addition, qualified students enrolled in any undergraduate program may pursue the baccalaureate/MBA in a five-year program. Biological science, chemistry, and English win rave reviews in Harpur College. Interdisciplinary fields of study include women's studies, medieval studies, Africana studies, Judaic studies, and Latin American and Caribbean area studies. If these don't satisfy a student's intellectual cravings, the Innovational Projects

Board will oversee and help students design not only their own majors but courses as well. Internship possibilities exist, as do numerous study abroad programs. Undergraduate students are also encouraged to participate in faculty research projects. The new Binghamton Scholars Program offers students of exceptional merit a chance to participate in a special four-year program that includes experiential and capstone courses. For students choosing to do their studying on campus, the university provides six different libraries with excellent resources and study areas as well as a data network allowing access to computer workstations. Students cite sociology, music, and women's studies as being weak.

Although there are complaints that research sometimes receives higher priority than teaching, professors generally receive good marks from students, and the university has benefited from the hiring of new professors thanks to increased state funds. "Professors are known in their fields but have not lost touch with how to teach," says a sophomore. Graduate teaching assistants (mainly those in the natural sciences) hold smaller group meetings to supplement large lecture courses that sometimes seat close to 500 students. According to students, getting into needed courses can sometimes be difficult. Binghamton's strong academic reputation has been enhanced by a tough grading policy in which students are given an F rather than no credit, and pluses and minuses as well as straight letter grades. "You're not spoon-fed," says a student, "yet it's not rocket science." Students agree that the courses are challenging, yet competition among students is not heated. "Students work together quite often in study groups and also use online study groups, which professors set up through the email system," says a student.

Binghamton ranks as one of the best public arts and sciences schools in the nation, although word of this is slow to cross state lines. Ninety-four percent of the students are New Yorkers, with the heaviest proportion of students from New York City and its surroundings, especially Long Island. The traditional upstate-downstate divisions of New York State politics are reflected in the student body, with upstaters complaining about provincial peers who think that "New York City is the only city in the world."

African Americans make up 6 percent of the student body, Hispanics 6 percent, and Asian Americans 17 percent. Binghamton students are a bright bunch when it comes to academic prowess: 96 percent come from the top quarter of their high school class. The school does guarantee to meet full demonstrated financial need, and there's tough competition for the 551 merit scholarships of $325 to $8,000 doled out every year. More than 160 athletic awards are given in a variety of sports.

To help make the university seem a little smaller, residence halls are grouped into five residential areas. Dickinson is the oldest and most stately, but each area has its own personality and reputation. Fifty-three percent of the students live on campus. It pays to get your housing application in early; a student says, "Students who are mindful of the deadlines are guaranteed housing." The majority of juniors and seniors move off campus, where housing is plentiful and "moderately priced." Those who stay on campus say that the residence halls are "pretty modern and really well kept."

Binghamton enforces the state's 21-and-over drinking law. "Campus alcohol policies prohibit minors from possessing alcohol," says a student. "However, this simply moves the drinking scene off campus." This has not damaged the social life for nondrinkers, however, as there is plenty of fun to be had at neighborhood bars, movies, concerts, quiet dinners off campus, and occasional campus-wide parties in the residence areas. Annual events among the dorms include the Passing of the Vegetables to bring in the winter season, Stepping on the Coat to

For students choosing to do their studying on campus, the university provides six different libraries with excellent resources and study areas as well as a data network allowing access to computer workstations.

The optional Freshman Program offers first-year students an interdisciplinary corelike program in the liberal arts.

usher in spring, and dorm wars. Another senior notes, "Homecoming usually comes and goes with little involvement from the students."

Binghamton the town gets mixed reviews from the students, but students agree that townies are friendly and there is a growing trend of community service and volunteer work. There is an expanding, though houseless, fraternity and sorority presence on campus—a total of 33—with about 18 percent of the men and 14 percent of the women as members. Few students take major road trips on the weekends, but for those who need an escape, Syracuse, Ithaca, Cortland, and Oneonta are about an hour by car. The toughest part about road trips may be finding a parking space when you get back—permits currently outnumber spaces by about three to one.

Several Binghamton teams have brought home SUNYAC championships recently, and varsity sports have made the move to the NCAA Division I. On the wish list of many students is big-time football. For now, students must make do with co-rec football, where teams of three men and three women (always a female quarterback) stir up intense rivalries, and "traying" (downhill snow sledding on trays).

Binghamton is proud of its growing reputation as a public alternative to the Ivy League, and the school's reputation for value and excellence attracts an overwhelming number of highly qualified students. One says, "I've had some really good classes, but more than anything else I've connected with some of the greatest people I've ever met." Though some may argue that college is not the "real world," few can dispute the fact that Binghamton grads have a real education that will serve them well in the world.

Overlaps

NYU, SUNY–Albany, SUNY–Stony Brook, Cornell University, SUNY–Buffalo.

If You Apply To ➢

Binghamton University…Early action: Nov. 15. Regular admissions: Feb. 15. Financial aid: Mar. 1. Guarantees to meet full demonstrated need. No campus or alumni interviews. SATs or ACTs: required. No SAT IIs: optional. Accepts electronic applications. Essay question: thoughts about violence; or benefits of higher education.

SUNY–Buffalo

17 Capen Hall, Buffalo, NY 14260

Website: www.buffalo.edu
Location: Suburban
Total Enrollment: 24,257
Undergraduates: 16,259
Male/Female: 53/47
SAT Ranges: V 490–600 M 510–620
ACT Range: 21–27
Financial Aid: 70%
Expense: Pub $ $ $
Phi Beta Kappa: Yes
Applicants: 14,836

In the world of higher learning, SUNY–Buffalo is a big fish in the big pond. As part of the mammoth State University of New York system, UB's resources are large enough to warrant two campuses—North and South. "The outstanding faculty and facilities that are available to students in this 'Ivy League SUNY' are amazing," says a psychology major. This former private university maintains a strong reputation in the life sciences and geography and is the most comprehensive of the SUNY schools. The resources are vast and the size is staggering; UB students must take care not to get eaten alive.

The North campus of SUNY–Buffalo, less than 20 years old and home to most undergraduate programs, stretches across 1,200 acres in the suburbs just outside the city line and boasts buildings designed by world-renowned architects such as I. M. Pei. Meanwhile, the South campus, along Main Street, favors collegiate ivy-covered buildings and the schools of architecture and health sciences, including the highly rated programs in medicine and dentistry.

On the academic front, the engineering and business management schools are nationally prominent, and architecture is strong. Occupational and physical therapy programs are also quite good. The English department is very strong, and notable for its emphasis on poetry. Real poets visit the campus frequently, and students not only compose and read poetry, but study the art of performing it as well. French, physiology, geography, and music are highly regarded, but other humanities vary in quality. Math is also on the weak side, and physics is the least impressive among the sciences. Complaints occasionally surface about the lack of major programs in journalism and broadcasting, although courses in both disciplines are offered. UB has a multitude of special programs, joint degrees (such as a five-year BS/MBA), and interdisciplinary majors as well as opportunities for self-designed majors and study abroad. Students accepted into the honors program enjoy smaller classes, priority in class registration, individual faculty mentors, and special scholarships regardless of need. Freshmen must also take University Experience 101, which orients students to UB's academic life, general social experience, and resources. The university's newest programs include majors in dance, music theatre, computational physics, and computer engineering.

Class size can be a problem, especially for freshmen. Smaller recitation sessions humanize the largest courses. Scheduling conflicts are not unusual, and required courses are often the most difficult to get into. "Classes are registered for by phone," says a student. "It makes registering easier than standing in line, but a constant busy signal can delay your registration and sometimes close you out of a class." Students seem to accept that some degree of faculty unavailability is the necessary trade-off for having professors who are experts in their fields at a school where graduate education and research get lots of the attention. This may also account for faculty counselors seeming "unconcerned and misinformed," according to a senior. The general education program requires students to complete a sequence of multidisciplinary courses dependent on the major, as well as basic classes in math and writing skills. The academically oriented student body spends plenty of time in UB's six main libraries, or one of the several branches, which are for the most part comfortable and well stocked at 3 million volumes.

Once upon a time, a large majority of UB's student body went straight into the job market after graduation, but today a third go on to graduate school. With only 2 percent of the students from out of state, the biggest contingent of home-grown New York Staters, apart from the locals, is from New York City and Long Island. As a large public university, UB has "everything from the all-American coed to the active radical." African Americans and Hispanics account for 13 percent of the student body, and Asian Americans represent another 11 percent. UB's considerable efforts in increasing awareness of diversity include a Committee on Campus Tolerance, Office of Student Multi-Cultural Affairs, and Multi-Cultural Leadership Council. Over 850 students receive merit scholarships ranging from $500 to full cost, and there are also 308 athletic scholarships available in a variety of sports.

Twenty-one percent of students live on campus; the rest commute from home or find apartments near the Main Street campus. Students warn that potential renters should shuffle off to Buffalo a couple of months early to secure a place. There is a new apartment-style residence hall for undergraduates featuring cable, computer connections, and central airconditioning. Most of the on-campus dwellers are housed on the Amherst campus in modern coed dorms. The Main Street campus dorms are smaller, older, and of a more traditional collegiate design, which upperclassmen tend to prefer, and three all-freshmen dorms house extremely sociable freshmen. Security on campus is generally good, "as long as

(Continued)
Accepted: 74%
Enrolled: 29%
Grad in 6 Years: 56%
Returning Freshmen: 84%
Academics: ✍ ✍ ✍ ✍
Social: ☎ ☎
Q of L: ★ ★
Admissions: (716) 645-6900
Email Address:
 ub-admissions@
 admissions.buffalo.cdu

Strongest Programs:
 Biological Sciences
 Business Administration
 Computer Engineering
 English
 Engineering
 Geography
 Occupational Therapy

The English department is very strong, and notable for its emphasis on poetry. Real poets visit the campus frequently, and students not only compose and read poetry, but study the art of performing it as well.

Freshmen must also take University Experience 101, which orients students to UB's academic life, general social experience, and resources.

An increase in enrollment has caused problems with overcrowding and excess roommates, but now that the university is adding townhouses, the housing crunch may be alleviated.

students use their heads," says a junior. The cafeteria food gets so-so reviews, but most dorms are equipped with kitchens for those inclined to cook for themselves.

The large number of commuters and the split campus put a damper on social life, but students seem to manage. "[Buffalo] is a very comfortable, friendly town with a lot to do" says one student who's found her way to the city's many movie theaters, concerts, shopping malls, restaurants, nightclubs, bars, and bowling alleys. Friday night happy hours center on beer and the chicken wings that spread the fame of Buffalo cuisine. Also popular are the Albright-Knox Art Gallery, with its world-renowned collection of modern art, and the Triple-A baseball Bisons, who play downtown. The two major pro teams, the Buffalo Bills and the Sabres in hockey, are both top draws. Open drinking is banned in the dorms, but that doesn't stop students from staging "progressive parties" with a different drink in each room (and we don't mean Cherry Coke and 7-Up). Off-campus bars are another favorite spot for underagers. "The bars are known as 'baby bars' because everyone and their mother can get into them," says a junior.

Having a car might be a great idea, though parking is a problem on campus. Students without cars can get trapped when the intercampus bus stops running after 2:00 A.M. on weekends. The winters are cold in Buffalo. (One student claims the best thing about his school is "the tunnels that connect every building and every dorm so we can walk indoors during winter.") But the flip side is that the outlying areas of the city offer great skiing and snowshoeing—and the ski club even offers free rides to the slopes. UB supports over 500 other student organizations ranging from jugglers to math enthusiasts. Students can preview their honeymoons by darting over to Niagara Falls, just half an hour away, or flee the country altogether by driving to nearby Canada, where the drinking age is lower.

School spirit is sometimes generated at the Student Union and UB's impressive sports complex. "We have the fourth-largest pool in the world, as well as a 10,000-seat arena, squash and racquetball courts, a jogging track, weight rooms," brags one student. The men's and women's cross-country teams are among Buffalo's championship-caliber squads, as are women's basketball and men's and women's swimming. Intramural sports are popular, and earthy types appreciate the annual Oozefest—a mud-bound sports competition that is part of SpringFest.

The largest of SUNY centers, UB offers the most comprehensive education of all the New York state schools but depends on its students to come and find it. UB students sometimes lose patience with the crowds and inconvenience of two campuses. "You have to be your own advocate," advises a Spanish major. As one veteran so appropriately points out, "If you are not a go-getter, you might miss it all."

Overlaps

SUNY–Albany, SUNY–Binghamton, SUNY–Stony Brook, Cornell University, NYU.

If You Apply To ➤ | **SUNY–Buffalo**…Early decision: Nov. 1. Regular admissions: Nov. 1 (priority). Financial aid: Mar. 1. Housing: May 1. Campus interviews: optional, informational. No alumni interviews. SATs or ACTs: required. SAT IIs: optional. Accepts the Common Application and electronic applications. No essay question.

For those seeking a public alternative to private liberal arts colleges, SUNY–Geneseo offers a comprehensive educational experience that emphasizes strong professional programs and a traditional liberal arts core. "Geneseo has a great reputation as a competitive, successful institution at a fair price," says a junior. "It has managed to keep its small size and unique atmosphere throughout the years." Students are quick to point out that faculty and staff go out of their way to ensure each student is treated as an individual. "Going to college is supposed to be a huge growing experience," opines a junior, "and for me, Geneseo is the perfect setting to 'grow-up' in."

The campus is located in the scenic Genesee Valley, with its spectacular sunsets, in western New York State. The architectural style is a mix of Gothic and modern buildings, all nestled in a tree-lined, small community that has been designated a National Historic Landmark Community by the U.S. Department of the Interior. A major campus beautification project has recently been completed and a network connects all residence halls to the Internet.

Geneseo operates on the semester system, and the college's offerings balance between several professional programs and the traditional liberal arts. Special education is the most popular major, followed by business, biology, psychology, and English. The John Wiley Jones School of Business boasts a strong program; 3–2 MBA programs are available with Pace, SUNY–Buffalo, and Syracuse; and 3–3 programs are available with the Rochester Institute of Technology. History, English, and biology are also good, and, true to its roots as a teachers training institution, Geneseo still has an outstanding education program that offers a teaching certificate. There is also a 3–2 program in engineering. New to the curriculum is a major in international relations; medical technology has been dropped. The flexible core curriculum requires two interdisciplinary humanities courses and two courses in each of four categories: natural sciences, social sciences, fine arts, and critical reasoning, as well as one course in non-Western traditions.

On the whole, students feel at home in Geneseo's competitive academic climate. "Courses are demanding, requiring students to have a good liberal arts background," says a junior. "Geneseo is a difficult college." The quality of teaching receives raves. "Geneseo does a spectacular job at hiring professors that are at the top of their fields," says a sociology and psychology double major. Students also praise the academic advising and the career counseling. A student claims that "one-on-one attention is a Geneseo standard." The vast majority of classes have 50 or fewer, and upperclassmen have almost no trouble getting into courses: "Students may not get the class time or professor they want but will almost always get into the class," says a management major.

Almost all the students are from New York State, and 92 percent of them attended public high school. Ninety-two percent graduated in the top quarter of their high school class. "Because the campus is relatively relaxed and conservative," one communications major says, "students with a radical view on life and issues may not be happy at Geneseo." Minority students together account for only 9 percent of the student body. One student reports that there is "no outward hostility between racial and ethnic groups; it's more of a peaceful segregation." The school offers merit scholarships, ranging from $100 to $9,500.

Fifty-seven percent of the students, including all freshmen, live in on-campus

Website: www.geneseo.edu

Location: Small town

Total Enrollment: 5,603

Undergraduates: 5,321

Male/Female: 34/66

SAT Ranges: V 550–640 M 560–640

ACT Range: 24–28

Financial Aid: 85%

Expense: Pub $ $ $

Phi Beta Kappa: No

Applicants: 7,974

Accepted: 52%

Enrolled: 28%

Grad in 6 Years: 79%

Returning Freshmen: 92%

Academics: ✍ ✍ ✍

Social: ☎ ☎ ☎

Q of L: ★ ★ ★ ★

Admissions: (716) 245-5571

Email Address: N/A

Strongest Programs:
Business
Education
Natural Sciences
Music
Communicative Disorders and Sciences
Psychology

housing, which is guaranteed for all four years. The school hired a health educator who integrates programs regarding problems of drug and alcohol abuse, eating disorders, and other health-related issues into residence hall living. Rooms are determined by lottery, and "many students remain on campus due to the clean, highly maintained, and safe living conditions," reports a senior. Campus security is described as "excellent" by many. Says a senior: "Students look out for one another, university police make regular patrols, and the student government runs an escort system."

Small and idyllic, the neighboring village is considered by many students a perfect setting. "It's a typical college town," reports a senior, "there are lots of opportunities to get involved with the community." Hiking and skiing are both nearby, and beautiful Conesus Lake is only a 10-minute drive away. As for the social life, one junior says "there is so much to do at Geneseo...that I never want to go home!" For those aching to hit the road, Rochester lies 30 miles to the north, and Buffalo 60 miles west. Six percent of the men and 4 percent of the women belong to fraternities and sororities, which keep life on campus from getting too humdrum. Only students over 21 may have alcohol in the residence halls, but "enforcement of policies is pretty weak unless the violation is obvious and blatant," says a political science major.

Sports are extremely popular, and Geneseo fields several excellent teams. Women's and men's basketball, cross-country, indoor/outdoor track, soccer, and men's and women's swimming are very strong. Intramurals are popular, and there are nearly 200 other student-run organizations, including a newspaper and radio and television stations.

"[Geneseo] is a place where students come to learn and grow," raves a junior. "I have changed tremendously over my three years here and I look forward to discovering more about myself in the years to come." A more practical senior adds that Geneseo "offers students an excellent, quality education for a very reasonable tuition fee."

Overlaps

SUNY–Binghamton, SUNY–Buffalo, Cornell University, SUNY–Albany, SUNY–Oswego.

If You Apply To ➤ **SUNY–Geneseo**...Early decision: Nov. 15. Regular admissions: Feb. 1. Financial aid: Feb. 15. Does not guarantee to meet demonstrated need. Campus interviews: recommended, informational. No alumni interviews. SATs or ACTs: required. SAT IIs: optional. Essay question: write your own recommendation for admission; impact of computer technology; unpublished writing sample.

SUNY–Purchase College

735 Anderson Hill Road, Purchase, NY 10577-1400

Website: www.purchase.edu
Location: Suburban
Total Enrollment: 3,956
Undergraduates: 3,837
Male/Female: 44/56
SAT Ranges: V 490–590

SUNY–Purchase College is a dream come true for aspiring artists of all kinds—an academic environment that provides a strong sense of community and support, yet celebrates individuals for their unique talents and contributions; it's okay to be an individual here. A senior says the best thing about Purchase is "the freedom to focus on whatever you want without feeling pressured to join anything to fit in."

Set on a 500-acre wooded estate in an area of Westchester's most scenic suburbia, Purchase has a campus described by one student as "sleek, modern, ominous, and brick." The college has earned a national reputation for its instruction in music, dance, visual arts, theater, and film. Almost all the faculty members in the School of the Arts are professionals who perform or exhibit regularly in the New York metropolitan area, and the spacious, dazzling facilities rank among the best in the world. Purchase College boasts of the Neuberger Museum, the sixth-largest public college museum. The four-theater Performing Arts Center is huge, and dance students, whose building contains a dozen studios, whirlpool rooms, and a "body-correction" facility, may never again work in such splendid and well-equipped surroundings. A $50 million capital campaign will have new facilities dotting the campus for years to come.

Mingling with highly motivated and talented performers and artists can make some students in the liberal arts and sciences feel a little drab and out of place. "Dancers, actors, visual artists, and music students pull the most weight as far as campus life is concerned," says a student. Still, Purchase is a fine place to study humanities and the natural sciences, particularly literature, psychology, art history, environmental sciences, and biology. Most of the shaky liberal arts and sciences programs are confined to some majors in the social sciences and language and culture, where offerings are limited.

All students in the Liberal Arts and Sciences spend one-third of their time at Purchase fulfilling the newly-revised general education requirements. Students now take a writing course, two Western Society and Culture courses, and an advising seminar, among others. All students complete a senior project. Students in the arts divisions usually have many more required courses, culminating in a senior recital or show. There are two separate sets of degree requirements, one for the Liberal Arts and Sciences and one for the performing and visual arts. BFA students in the performing and visual arts are required to sample the liberal arts; BA and BS students in the liberal arts and sciences are required to sample fine arts courses. The college also offers several certificate programs including computer science, arts management, and early child development. New majors include creative writing, journalism, dramatic writing, women's studies, and new media.

The atmosphere at Purchase seems to vary between programs. "The academic climate of the visual arts is competitive," reports a sophomore. "Professors are constantly pushing and challenging your creative levels creating a battleground for constant trials and errors." Students tend to be very serious about their own personal achievements. Professors tend to be accessible and friendly. "Absolutely the best possible training for the performing arts," claims an acting major. Eighty-four percent of the students are from New York State, most from New York City and Westchester County. Others are from Long Island, New Jersey, and Connecticut, but all are different and very political (that means very liberal). "It is sort of a melting pot where city kids and upstate country kids all come together," says a visual arts student. Indeed, the largest student organization on this politically active campus is the gay and lesbian union.

In addition to need-based aid, 890 merit scholarships ranging from $200 to $4,000 are awarded each year on the basis of academic achievements, auditions, and portfolios. Past budget cuts hurt the school, but SUNY's new budget has increased available funds, easing the pain somewhat.

The living facilities have undergone renovations, but continue to receive mixed reviews. A sophomore says, "Dorms are generally over-crowded, although the cleaning staff works extremely hard to keep the bathrooms and hallways clean." A new residence hall should ease the burden. The two eating facilities offer decent fare, and for those who tire of institutional cuisine, there is a student-run co-op that specializes in health food. Forty-two percent of the student body

(Continued)

M 450–570

Financial Aid: 60%

Expense: Pub $ $ $

Phi Beta Kappa: No

Applicants: 5,398

Accepted: 35%

Enrolled: 12%

Grad in 6 Years: 49%

Returning Freshmen: 71%

Academics: ✍ ✍ ✍

Social: ☎ ☎ ☎

Q of L: ★ ★ ★

Admissions: (914) 251-6300

Email Address:

admissn@purchase.edu

Strongest Programs:

Acting

Art History

Dance

Environmental Science

Film

Psychology

The four-theater Performing Arts Center is huge, and dance students, whose building contains a dozen studios, whirlpool rooms, and a "body-correction" facility, may never again work in such splendid and well-equipped surroundings.

Overlaps

**SUNY–New Paltz,
SUNY–Stony Brook,
SUNY–Albany,
SUNY–Oneonta,
SUNY–Binghamton.**

commute from nearby communities, though housing in the surrounding suburbs is expensive and hard to find.

The campus is a neighbor to the world headquarters of IBM, Texaco, AMF, General Foods, and Pepsico, but while sharing the "billion-dollar mile" with a few *Fortune* 500s might excite students at some other SUNY schools, "it doesn't do much for us except provide convenient antiapartheid demonstration locations," admits one Purchase activist. No college town exists per se at Purchase, so "we tend to think of our campus as our community," a senior psych major attests. "Purchase is one of those 'if you blink, you'll miss it' towns," says another student. The Big Apple provides a regular weekend distraction that inhibits the formation of a tight campus community. Since the campus shuttle bus runs only once on the weekend, students started their own van service, which goes into Manhattan three times a day. Still, "a car is a definite must at Purchase," admits one student. The Performing Arts Center is host to at least two student or faculty performances every weekend, and there is a constant flow of New York artists and celebrities. Notes a literature major, "Most of the social life on campus takes the form of parties thrown by apartment residents," and the over-21 crowd often frequents the Pub. Fraternities and sororities are definitely out. "The closest we come to Greek are the two guys from Athens who go here," quips a staunch independent. Besides, as one artist explains, "individuality is far more important to the artist than being part of a group." Despite the unconventional aura of the place, Purchase is not without its traditions. There's an annual autumn dance, a Spring Semiformal, and an April Showers campus festival, and on Halloween there are ghost stories told at a historic graveyard on campus.

Purchase is not a member of the NCAA, and the few competitive teams include men's basketball and women's volleyball. Perhaps that is why the administration lends out the renovated gym to the NBA's New York Knicks for its practice sessions. Intramural programs and an excellent athletic facility exist, but informal Frisbee tossing remains more popular than organized sports. Says a student: "Our 'teams' are our dancers, our vocalists, our musicians, our theater companies."

Despite a conspicuous "lack of a college-town atmosphere," Purchase is a perfect place to study the arts and still be able to indulge in academics of all kinds, or vice versa. Those willing to put up with what a senior calls "an isolated campus full of ugly architecture," may find that Purchase offers the opportunity for a personalized, diverse education unique within the SUNY system.

If You Apply To ➤

SUNY–Purchase College...Rolling admissions. Does not guarantee to meet demonstrated need. Campus and alumni interviews: optional, informational (required of theatre design/technology and film program applicants). SATs or ACTs: required. SAT IIs: optional. Accepts the Common Application and electronic applications. Essay question: personal or historical event of impact; personal influences; describe a time you took a leadership role. Apply to particular school or program. Auditions held for acting, dance, and music.

118 Administration Building, Stony Brook, NY 11794-1901

Although SUNY–Stony Brook is most noted for its top-notch programs in the hard sciences, students are quick to point out that the school's other programs demand the same criteria for success: dedication, hard work, and a desire for learning. In return, students take part in an educational experience that leaves a lasting impression.

The school's location on Long Island's plush North Shore (Gatsby's stomping grounds) is a wonderful drawing point. Sitting on about 1,000 wooded acres just outside of the small, picturesque village of Stony Brook, and only 90 minutes from New York City and half an hour from the beaches of the South Shore, the campus architecture is a conglomeration of redbrick Federal-style buildings interspersed with several modern brick and concrete designs. Campus beautification is now a priority, and much of the uninspiring campus concrete is being replaced by grass and trees. Recently completed facilities include the 85,000-square-foot Center for Molecular Medicines and Life Sciences.

Coming of age in the high-tech era, Stony Brook quickly became widely known and respected for its science departments. Facilities are extensive, and the science faculty includes a number of internationally known researchers. The comprehensive university hospital and research center make health sciences strong, especially physical therapy. The hospital, which has been ranked among the nation's best for teaching, attracts grants to the campus and offers a lot of opportunities for various research programs for undergrads as well as graduate students. Students report that engineering is also strong, although it lacks civil and chemical concentrations. There are complaints that the emphasis on science overshadows the school's best social science and humanities programs, but at least efforts have been made to boost the arts with a fine arts center, complete with studios and a reference library. The center complements Stony Brook's beautiful five-theater Staller Center for the Arts. The music department faculty boasts the American pianist Gilbert Kalish. Journalism and philosophy are cited as weak.

The College of Arts and Sciences, the College of Engineering and Applied Sciences, and the Health Science Center each has its own general education requirement, but all cover writing and quantitative reasoning skills, literary and philosophic analysis, exposure to the arts, disciplinary diversity, the interrelationship of science and society, and three culminating multicultural requirements, including one course each in the European tradition, non-Western cultures, and American pluralism. Everyone in the arts and sciences must also satisfy a language requirement. New majors include women's studies, computer engineering, and cinema and cultural studies.

Liberal arts students are less stressed academically than their peers in the sciences, but this may change somewhat with additions of major writing-intensive courses. "The science courses appear to be a bit more cutthroat because so many students want to be doctors," says a senior. As professors delve into their own research projects, undergraduates must struggle for the attention of their teachers. Students who do take the considerable initiative to contact professors report that they are often met with responsive attitudes. "The professors always make you think and keep you interested," says a student. Academic advising is described as weak. A junior says "you need to be aggressive to get good counseling." Since freshmen are the last to register, they sometimes have to wait a semester or two

Website: www.sunysb.edu
Location: City outskirts
Total Enrollment: 19,128
Undergraduates: 12,692
Male/Female: 50/50
SAT Ranges: V 470–580 M 510–630
Financial Aid: 61%
Expense: Pub $ $ $
Phi Beta Kappa: Yes
Applicants: 14,892
Accepted: 58%
Enrolled: 15%
Grad in 6 Years: 51%
Returning Freshmen: 81%
Academics: ✍ ✍ ✍ ✍
Social: ☎ ☎ ☎
Q of L: ★ ★
Admissions: (631) 632-6868
Email Address:
ugadmissions@notes.cc.sunysb.edu

Strongest Programs:
Chemistry
Music
Physics
Philosophy
Biological Sciences
Political Science
Computer Science
History
Psychology

to get into the most popular electives. But bolder students find that "usually you can manipulate your way into classes."

An Undergraduate Research and Creative Activities program (URECA) offers undergraduates the opportunity to work on research projects with faculty members from the time they are freshmen until they graduate. Women in Science and Engineering (WISE) is a multifaceted program for women who show promise in math, science, or engineering. There's also the Federated Learning Communities (FLC) program, in which students take a preplanned block of courses in one general area such as The United States in Perspective, which then becomes their minor. A residential studies program links dormitories to fields of study, and interested students may live in the French, Italian, engineering, or wellness halls, to name a few. Some students take time abroad in Stony Brook's excellent travel programs (France, Poland, Bolivia, and Italy are some possibilities), while others plug into established internships in the fields of policy analysis, political science, psychology, foreign language, and social welfare. Combined BA/MA or BS/MS programs are available in engineering, the teaching of math, and management and policy.

Stony Brook students are 95 percent in-staters, and about half commute from Long Island homes. Sixty-three percent graduated in the top quarter of their high school class, and more than half of Stony Brook's graduates go on to graduate and professional schools. Besides the 16 percent total of African Americans and Hispanics, Stony Brook enrolls 22 percent Asian Americans. The university contributes to the general awareness on campus with programs addressing sexual harassment, a mentor program for students from underrepresented groups, and a host family program for African American students. The university does not guarantee to meet the demonstrated financial need of all accepted applicants. Approximately 100 merit scholarships of $250 to $5,000 are parceled out each year.

Stony Brook has one of the largest residential facilities in the SUNY system, and a major rehabilitation will give resident students access to state-of-the-art fitness centers, computing facilities, Internet access, and wide-screen TV. The consensus is that Mendelsohn and H quads, "very sociable and a good eye-opener for incoming students," are best for freshmen, and that the halls (as opposed to suites) are preferable, a political science major says, because "you meet more people." Commuters are given a social facility of their own, "the commuter commons." While residential freshmen must take a meal plan, upperclassmen who live on campus either opt for a flexible food service plan or pay a nominal fee to cook for themselves. The suites come equipped with dishwashers and ranges, and each hall has a lounge and kitchen area, all of which, students say, could be kept a lot cleaner. Kosher and vegetarian food co-ops keep interested students well supplied with cheap eats.

Stony Brook's present preprofessional student body has long since shaken off the druggie reputation its forefathers earned in the 1960s. "Before the drinking age went to 21 the campus was more open. Now students do things in smaller numbers," one student says. Another student remarks that for underage students to be served alcohol "is as easy here as it would be anywhere." The longtime ban on fraternities and sororities has been lifted, so a fledgling Greek system (with no houses) is another option. Current and classic movies are screened during the week, and other entertainment is available in the form of frequent concerts, plays, and other performances. Annual festivals in the fall and spring and the football game with Hofstra are among the biggest social events of the year. Since many students go home on the weekends, Thursday is a big party night.

The students who remain on the weekends often go beachcombing on the nearby North Shore or the Atlantic Ocean shore of Long Island or head into New York City. Cars are desirable, but many students make do with trains, and a station is conveniently located at the edge of campus. The local community is a "beautiful, wealthy area of Long Island," says a senior. "It's not much of a college town, because there are so many things to do on campus." Nearby Port Jefferson offers small shops and interesting restaurants. Sports facilities have been upgraded, and all 20 varsity teams compete in Division I. Intramurals provide one of the school's greatest rallying points, and competition in oozeball (a mud-caked variant of volleyball) is especially fierce.

Though Stony Brook is not old enough to have ivy-covered walls, it does offer some of the best academic opportunities in the SUNY system. Students have to maneuver around lots of rough spots, including increasing class sizes and decreasing course offerings. Yet despite these budget-crisis-induced problems, students share in the promise of Stony Brook's future. In the meantime, they boast of their school's diversity and creativity as well as the feeling of hospitality that pervades campus life.

Overlaps

NYU,
SUNY–Binghamton,
Cornell University,
Boston University,
Columbia.

If You Apply To > **SUNY–Stony Brook**...Rolling admissions. Early decision: Nov. 1. Regular admission: July 10. Housing: June 30. Does not guarantee to meet demonstrated need. Campus interviews: recommended, evaluative. No alumni interviews. SATs or ACTs: required. SAT IIs: recommended. Apply to particular school or program. Accepts electronic applications. No essay question.

Stetson University

Campus Box 8378, DeLand, FL 32720

Stetson University hopes students take their hats off and stay awhile. All the better if the hats are of the cowboy variety. Stetson gets its name from the maker of the 10-gallon hat, but it's hardly a rustic school. Exceptional programs in music and business administration accentuate a uniformly solid curriculum, and small classes foster a community atmosphere. Don't worry: you won't be herding cattle across a prairie here. "The best aspect about Stetson is the closeness among the community here," says a junior.

Located halfway between Walt Disney World and Daytona Beach, the 165-acre campus features mostly brick structures in a wide range of architectural styles—Gothic to Moorish to Southern Colonial—with a few eccentric wood buildings scattered about. The theme is decidedly old-fashioned with some modern nuances. Students claim that part of the university's allure lies in the beautiful landscaping of royal palms and oak trees. A recent addition to campus architecture is the Hollis Wellness Center, a $3.5-million structure that houses a 14,000-square-foot gymnasium, a dance studio, weight rooms, a juice bar, and student life offices. Also recently completed was an addition to the duPont-Ball library, which includes distance learning technology and space for more books.

All Stetson undergraduates enroll in one of three schools: music, business administration, or arts and sciences. Required curriculums for each major vary, but all students take one religion course and two English courses along with a

Website: www.stetson.edu
Location: Suburban
Total Enrollment: 3,053
Undergraduates: 2,062
Male/Female: 42/58
SAT Ranges: V 510–620 M 500–620
ACT Range: 21–27
Financial Aid: 59%
Expense: Pr $ $ $
Phi Beta Kappa: Yes
Applicants: 1,913
Accepted: 80%
Enrolled: 37%
Grad in 6 Years: 60%
Returning Freshmen: 81%
Academics: ✍ ✍ ✍
Social: ☎ ☎ ☎

(Continued)

Q of L: ★ ★ ★

Admissions: (800) 688-0101

Email Address:

admissions@stetson.edu

Strongest Programs:

Accounting and Finance

Music Performance

Psychology

Sport and Exercise Science

Religious Studies

Education

Psychology

freshman seminar during their first year. The music program is noted for quality instruction in brass instruments, organ, and voice. Business is the most popular major, and students enjoy the resources of the Lynn Business Center, home of the School of Business Administration. Accounting is especially strong. An unusual year-long program for hands-on money management experience is the Roland George Investments program, where students manage an actual cash portfolio worth more than $2 million. Another unique program is the Prince Entrepreneurial Program, which gives students the opportunity to speak with successful entrepreneurs, create their own business plans, and run their own businesses. The Digital Arts Program prepares students for careers in the rapidly expanding field of computer-based graphics, video and music, and the multimedia-based World Wide Web. The Stetson Undergraduate Research Experience allows students to complete a summer research project in the field of their choice, with a stipend. A newly added marine biology major allows those with sea-faring legs to dive into aquatic studies.

While it's hard to imagine spending more time in Florida at the library than at the beach, that's the norm for many Stetson students. "There's definitely value placed on doing well academically, but it's a not a high-pressure environment," says one student. Academic and professional aspirations permeate the student body, and the school's small size helps people achieve. Ninety-nine percent of classes have fewer than 50 students. "My experience here has been awesome," says a music education major. "The professors really seem to enjoy what they do."

An honors program in the liberal arts and business allows the brightest students to replace distribution requirements with interdisciplinary seminars, and many an honors student will undertake an independent contract study with professors of his or her choice. The year abroad program operates out of centers in France, Germany, England, Spain, Mexico, and Russia. Business students can also spend a summer in Innsbruck, Austria. Stetson's education department has become a partner with Walt Disney Corporation and Osceola County School Board to develop a state-of-the-art school and teaching academy in the city of Celebration, Florida. Students offer high praise for their academic and career advisors.

Once affiliated with the Baptist Church, Stetson is now an independent institution. The motto of Stetson is "For God and truth," though chapel worship services have been replaced by nondenominational presentations on ethics and social responsibility. In general, the school attracts a religiously and socially diverse student body, less than 20 percent of whom are Baptists. More than three-quarters of the students graduated from public high school, and 11 percent represent minority groups. Seventy-four percent of Stetson undergraduates are Floridians, 7 percent are from foreign countries, and the rest have migrated south from the North and the Midwest. The big campus issue is race relations, according to students. "Hatters" are generally conservative and Republican-leaning. In addition to need-based aid, the university awards academic and talent scholarships to undergraduates each year and 158 athletic scholarships in baseball, basketball, tennis, cross-country, golf, soccer, softball, and women's volleyball.

Stetson is a predominantly residential college, with 73 percent of the undergraduates living on campus (many of whom clear out on weekends). The dorms get upbeat reviews, as does the staff that cleans them. "The dorms are comfortable and well maintained," one student says. "Some of the nicer ones have been around since the 1800s." All but two of the dorms are coed. Students report that the nicest dorms are Emily Hall, Chaudoin, Stetson, and Conrad. Singles are reserved for juniors and seniors. The quality of cafeteria food, once judged as

An unusual year–long program for hands-on money management experience is the Roland George Investments program, where students manage an actual cash portfolio worth more than $2 million.

average by college standards, is on the upswing after the renovation of the cafeteria, which now resembles a food court with a variety of culinary options (students can even stir-fry their own meals). Three meal plans (21, 15, and 7 meals) are offered. For variety, you can spend your meal tickets at the campus coffee shop, the Hat Rack.

With dorms off limits to alcohol for underage students and DeLand almost as dry as the campus, Stetson's Greek organizations have become central to undergraduate social life. More than one-third of men and one-quarter of women are members of Greek organizations. "A lot of the social life on campus revolves around fraternities and sororities," says a junior. The Council for Student Activities also sponsors comedians, concerts, and movies by the pool. Music majors stage frequent concerts. Major celebrations on campus include Homecoming and Greenfeather, a week when student groups compete to raise money for charity organizations. There is also a campus tradition of throwing students in the fountain in the middle of campus on their birthdays.

DeLand, known by students as Deadland, is not much of a college town. "It is a very quiet town, with not a lot for college students to do," a sophomore says. Community service is high on many students' agendas, particularly youth mentoring. With Orlando and Daytona nearby, there's always plenty of surfing or just slumming on the beach. Other favorite recreational destinations include Disney World, Epcot, and the space center (for an occasional shuttle launch).

As you might expect in Florida, baseball is the most exciting sport on campus, and the varsity squad is almost always competitive. There is no football team, however, inspiring students to don this T-shirt: "Stetson football: still undefeated." Besides baseball, the most successful varsity Hatter teams are basketball, soccer, and women's tennis, softball, and volleyball. Students get fired up to partake in the action themselves; intramurals are competitive and involve much of the student body. The university also has ample recreational facilities, including a health and physical education center, playing fields and courts, and an outdoor pool.

After all the hat jokes and disbelief that people can actually study in such close proximity to scantily-clad beachgoers, students at Stetson know their education is far more important than their tan. Instead, Hatters bask in the one-on-one attention they get at this Sunshine State university. Says an education major, "You are a name and a face and not just a social security number."

Overlaps

University of Florida, Florida State, University of Central Florida, Rollins, University of Miami (FL).

If You Apply To ➤ **Stetson**…Early decision: Nov. 1. Regular admissions and financial aid: Mar. 1. Housing: June 1. Does not guarantee to meet demonstrated financial need. Campus interviews: recommended, evaluative. No alumni interviews. SATs or ACTs: required. SAT IIs: optional. Accepts the Common Application and electronic applications. Essay question: significant experience, important issue, or influential person.

Stevens Institute of Technology

Castle Point on the Hudson, Hoboken, NJ 07030

For most students at the Stevens Institute of Technology, the question isn't whether to pursue an engineering degree: that's a given. The real question is how to choose from the long list of engineering degrees that are available at this

Website:
www.stevens-tech.edu

quality institution. In any case, if you're looking for an educational experience with emphasis on caring faculty, close-knit community, and excellent engineering programs, Stevens could be the answer.

Stevens' 55-acre parklike campus is punctuated by an eclectic mix of architecture. Many of the residence halls and administrative buildings are red brick, while classrooms and labs range from historical ivy-covered brownstones to modern glass-and-steel structures. Campus construction includes a new state-of-the-art multimedia center and extensive renovations to classrooms, labs, and residence halls. Students are also enjoying use of the James C. Nicoll Lab, after its $18.8-million renovations, with its state-of-the-art facilities for surface, electrical, environmental, and concurrent engineering, as well as telecommunications and laser optics.

Stevens was the first college in the country to offer the degree of Mechanical Engineering and now offers majors in the fields of business, engineering, science, computer science, and even the humanities (degrees are offered in English and American lit, history, and philosophy). But engineering, be it mechanical, chemical, civil, electrical, environmental, or computer, is the indisputable king of the campus. Computer science has become a major in and of itself, and the school tries to ensure that all students are computer fluent, not just literate, by the time they leave. Last year, as part of a pilot program, all freshmen received a new personal notebook computer.

Stevens is organized into three schools: the Charles V. Schaefer School of Engineering, the Wesley J. Howe School of Technology, and the School of Applied Sciences and Liberal Arts. This organization is intended to allow Stevens to better meet the changing technological needs of business and industry by fostering collaboration across academic departments. For the first two years in the engineering school, students must follow a core curriculum stressing courses in the sciences and in broad areas of engineering, followed by technical electives that culminate in a senior design project. The business program and the applied sciences each have their own curriculum guidelines. In addition, students must complete four semesters of calculus, eight semesters of humanities, and six semesters of physical education. But never fear, there are ways to get around this predestined courseload. For example, students not quite up to the intensity of Stevens' academic prescription may arrange for a five-year program, without extra tuition charges. Freshmen follow a core program in their chosen curriculum. Juniors can attend the school's program in Scotland, or can study abroad in one of over 50 countries through the International Student Exchange Program. Stevens has initiated a cooperative education program, which offers all students a chance to earn on-the-job training (and earn more than $45,000 in some cases) over a five-year period. Stevens also has an active recruiting program with major corporations, entrepreneurial firms, and the government.

Students are satisfied with the teaching ability of most professors and comfortable in the close-knit environment that develops between students and faculty members. "Most professors have a love for the material they teach which is apparent in their lectures," says a junior. Courses are usually taught in "recitations" of fewer than 25 students, and exams are taken under a successful student-run honor system. Given the subject matter, no one considers the workload unreasonable, and tutorial help is readily available. Small classes encourage study groups, but the academic challenges can raise stress levels to unpleasant heights, and a computer science major warns that if students "don't take advantage of the free time to unwind, they'll go crazy."

Stevens draws half of its students from the greater New York area, and 20 percent of the students commute. Seventy percent come from public high school, and 84 percent graduated in the top tenth of their class. Minorities make up 39 percent of the student body; 22 percent are Asian Americans, 12 percent are Hispanic, and 5 percent are African American. Female student enrollment is 22 percent, a high percentage for a technical school. And when men and women do get together here, they have no trouble finding something to talk about. "The majority of Stevens students wants to be engineers, lawyers, doctors, etc.," says one student. Admissions staffers look more closely at high school grades, especially in math and science, than at test scores; interviews are required; and letters of recommendation from teachers are helpful. Applicants with computers can apply via the Internet and save the application fee. Students praise the school's financial aid policy, and with 85 percent of the student body receiving some sort of aid, most speak from experience. In addition to need-based funding, Stevens also awards academic merit scholarships, ranging from $1,000 to full tuition.

Eighty percent of students live in the dorms, forgoing the almost impossible, very expensive housing hunt in the Hoboken area. Students say housing at Stevens is adequate and well maintained, and each room is hooked into the campus-wide computer network. The five undergraduate residence halls are conveniently located at the center of campus. As for looks, Tech Hall stands out among the crowd. An ultramodern dorm with carpets, telephones, and private bathrooms in each room, it has "all the conveniences of a modern hotel," says one student. The only difference is you can't make reservations at Stevens. Rooms are assigned by lottery or by squatter's rights. After the first year, students can, and often do, move into fraternities, old brownstones off campus, or nearby university-owned apartments. As for dining services, students report that the cafeteria food isn't anything to write home about, although there is a variety to chose from. One student dryly remarks that the variety involves "the same stuff day in and day out."

Previously, weekend activities at Stevens weren't overly exciting, but things are picking up as more people choose to live on campus. Those who don't go home can take advantage of the "extensive pleasures" of Manhattan, just across the Hudson, or kill time until the evening fraternity parties, which are the most popular of the on-campus weekend activities. A third of the student body go Greek, but they don't necessarily rule the campus. Students are also benefiting from the revitalization of Hoboken. "Hoboken is a great college town packed with little coffee shops, restaurants, cool clothing stores, and bars." The 21-year-old drinking age, of course, has put a crimp in the social life, forcing many students out of the campus pub and away from the kegs at parties.

Sports are popular at Stevens, especially intramurals, for which "everyone gets together on ridiculously named teams and blows off steam," in games such as floor hockey and bombardment. Stevens's competitive academic spirit does not always translate to the varsity playing field. But look on the bright side: according to one junior, when Stevens loses an athletic competition, students chant "That's all right, that's okay, you'll be working for us someday!" The new women's swim team remains undefeated, and women's soccer and volleyball are playing stronger than ever. Being at a small school with a lot of engineers also gives students a chance to be editor of the college newspaper or deejay on the campus radio station without being edged out by a journalism or communications major. Fifteen minutes and a dollar for the PATH train will land you in the middle of Manhattan's Greenwich Village. Beaches and ski slopes are within a 90-minute drive.

At Stevens, there are ultimate rewards for suffering through the dining hall,

Stevens has initiated a cooperative education program, which offers all students a chance to earn on-the-job training (and earn more than $45,000 in some cases) over a five-year period.

Last year, as part of a pilot program, all freshmen received a new personal notebook computer.

tolerating the mostly male social scene, accepting the rigid schedule, and surviving the workload. The Stevens degree provides its graduates with good job opportunities in a variety of technical fields and the satisfaction that they can handle it. "You learn a lot technically, of course," says one student, "but you also learn a lot about industry and how to survive out there socially, mentally, and physically."

If You Apply To ➢ **Stevens**...Rolling admissions. Early decision: Nov. 15. Regular admissions: Feb. 15. Financial aid: Feb. 15. Housing: May. 1. Guarantees to meet demonstrated need. Campus and alumni interviews: required, evaluative. SATs: required. SAT IIs: recommended. Accepts the Common Application and electronic applications. Essay question: personal statement.

Susquehanna University

Selinsgrove, PA 17870

Website: www.susqu.edu
Location: Small town
Total Enrollment: 1,722
Undergraduates: 1,722
Male/Female: 43/57
SAT Ranges: V 520–620 M 520–620
Financial Aid: 69%
Expense: Pr $ $
Phi Beta Kappa: No
Applicants: 2,143
Accepted: 75%
Enrolled: 29%
Grad in 6 Years: 75%
Returning Freshmen: 86%
Academics: ✍ ✍ ✍
Social: ☎ ☎ ☎
Q of L: ★ ★ ★ ★
Admissions: (800) 326-9672 or (570) 372-4260
Email Address: suadmiss@susqu.edu

Strongest Programs:
Biology/Biochemistry
Business
Music
Psychology

"Susquewho?" That's the question many students ask when they're first introduced to this undergraduate institution. While it may not be a household name, Susquehanna University is making a name for itself. Challenging courses, friendly faculty, and an increasing emphasis on our global community make SU a good place to expand your mind and enjoy lush scenery. "SU is gorgeous year-round," says a junior. "It's a place that makes me feel at home and puts me at ease when I'm stressed."

Susquehanna's campus is beautiful, over 200 lush acres located on the banks of the Susquehanna River. Most of the 50 buildings on campus are brick; the predominant architectural style is Georgian. Selinsgrove Hall, built in 1858, and Seibert Hall, built in 1901, are on the National Register of Historic Places. The campus is compact and serene. Multimedia classrooms have been added in several departments and the school is in the midst of a $14 million renovation to the sports and fitness facilities.

SU's best academic programs are in business and the sciences. The Sigmund Weis School of Business is not only one of the most striking building on campus, but a prestigious accredited business program as well, which attracts the most majors on campus. The Weis School also sponsors a semester in London exclusively for its junior business majors. The Business school, along with the other majors, encourages SU students to take summer internships as a crucial part of their educational and future job search. Susquehanna is becoming increasingly recognized for its science programs, especially biology, biochemistry, and environmental science. Weaker departments at SU include classical languages and art, which are hampered by their small size and lack of funds. The Write Option program allows qualified applicants (those in the top fifth of their class) the option to submit two graded writing samples in place of SAT or ACT scores.

Susquehanna's unusual core curriculum consists of three components: personal development (wellness/fitness and career development); transition skills (including computer proficiency, logical reasoning, and foreign languages); and world perspectives (social sciences, humanities, and sciences). All freshmen must take a writing seminar (or its honors equivalent) that involves small-group readings and discussion of a particular author. Reading centers around a common contemporary work, with the author often visiting campus to partake in the seminar. A seven-week orientation experience is offered to first-year students; topics include study skills, stress management, and interpersonal communication. Freshmen also have access to the Susquehanna Education in Leadership program, which begins with an all-day retreat and is followed by four seminars throughout the fall semester that focus on leadership styles, listening skills, time management, dealing with conflict, and team building.

For about 50 students a year, the academic experience is embodied by the Susquehanna Honors Program. Unlike other programs in schools of similar size, SU's program does not separate its students from the rest of the campus. Instead it allows students to take most of their classes in other classes with the general student body, thus creating a balance between freedom of choice and a challenging education. Honors students or not, most agree that SU offers a rigorous academic climate. "Depending on the major you select, your courseload can be moderately easy to close to impossible," says a math major.

Student-faculty interaction is one of Susquehanna's strong points, and students have high praise for their professors. "The faculty is committed to Susquehanna's concept of education: student-centered, undergraduate only. They are committed to their students," says a senior. SU students may take classes at nearby Bucknell University and study abroad on almost every continent. The school also offers several study programs in Washington, D.C., as well as a 3–2 engineering program with the University of Pennsylvania. SU offers scholarships, but there are no athletic scholarships. An assistantship program for outstanding first-year students combines a $10,500 scholarship with hands-on work with a professor or staff member (10 hours per week). Past positions have included university archivist, international education, choir manager, wetlands research, and computer modeling of liquid surfaces. Families also have the option of making monthly tuition payments, available through outside vendors.

SU students are down-to-earth, hardworking kids. Sixty-three percent are from Pennsylvania, and 84 percent attended public high school. At a school in which 91 percent of the students are white, and which is "dominated by middle- and upper-class conservative Republicans," most agree that ethnic diversity is lacking. A communications major offers, "Diversity and multiculturalism are big issues. The university wants the student body to be more diverse."

Residence halls are described as "comfortable." A senior says, "Dorm rooms are big with great closets. All housing is pretty equal." Students must get permission to live off campus, and the 20 percent of students who have that privilege are selected by lottery. Cafeteria food is considered average, although a senior claims the "quality has declined sharply over the past three semesters." Campus security receives mixed reviews. "I feel safe because I'm on a small campus," says a student, "not because of campus security."

Greeks dominate the nightlife of Susquehanna, where 25 percent of the men and women each belong to fraternities or sororities. Students 21 and over are allowed to drink on campus, but most acknowledge that underage drinking is "as easy as asking." Favorite campus traditions include a candlelight Christmas service, a pumpkin that mysteriously appears at Halloween, and a Thanksgiving dinner at which faculty members serve traditional fare to the students. Sports are popular among Susquehanna students, especially when the football team plays Lycoming College. Recent MAC championships were won by men's golf and baseball and women's indoor track.

(Continued)
English
Communication
Environmental Science

The Write Option program allows qualified applicants (those in the top fifth of their class) the option to submit two graded writing samples in place of SAT or ACT scores.

Favorite campus traditions include a candlelight Christmas service, a pumpkin that mysteriously appears at Halloween, and a Thanksgiving dinner at which faculty members serve traditional fare to the students.

Outside the university, Selinsgrove is "a small, rural, quaint town" with several restaurants and stores. A biochemistry major says, "We are not located in a 'college town.'" For those with cars, New York and Philadelphia are three hours away, and Penn State is an hour away. SU began by preparing students for the ministry and the university's commitment to the community has remained strong. Each year two-thirds of the student population volunteer on major community service projects.

At Susquehanna, "the professors care about their students," a biochemistry major says. A classmate adds that the "personal atmosphere, great faculty-student relationships, and beautiful campus" make Susquehanna worthwhile—and make it a name worth remembering among strong regional colleges.

If You Apply To ➤ **Susquehanna**…Rolling admissions: Mar. 1. Early decision: Dec. 15. Financial aid: Mar. 1 (priority), May 1. Housing: May 1. Meets demonstrated need of 52%. Campus interviews: recommended, evaluative. Alumni interviews: optional, informational. SAT I or ACT: required; optional for students in top 20% of their class. Accepts the Common Application and electronic applications. Essay question: significant experience; issue of concern; accomplishments since high school (if applicable); or graded high school paper.

Swarthmore College

500 College Avenue, Swarthmore, PA 19081-1397

Website: www.swarthmore.edu
Location: Suburban
Total Enrollment: 1,467
Undergraduates: 1,467
Male/Female: 47/53
SAT Ranges: V 655–770 M 660–750
Financial Aid: 48%
Expense: Pr $ $ $ $
Phi Beta Kappa: Yes
Applicants: 4,163
Accepted: 22%
Enrolled: 41%
Grad in 6 Years: 92%
Returning Freshmen: 95%
Academics: ⚏ ⚏ ⚏ ⚏ ⚏
Social: ☎ ☎ ☎
Q of L: ★ ★ ★ ★
Admissions: (610) 328-8300
Email Address:
admissions@swarthmore.edu

Strongest Programs:
Biology

Swarthmore College, located only 11 miles from Philadelphia, has long been regarded as one of the most intense schools in the nation; a school that prides itself on demanding the best from the best. Just thinking about the workload involved makes students at other top liberal arts schools shake in their Birkenstocks. As one Swattie puts it, "As long as you like to work and like intellectual strenuousness, you will find the academic climate at Swarthmore to be very well suited to your personality."

The campus occupies 330 acres of rolling wooded land that is a nationally registered arboretum. The outdoors defines the character of the campus and serves as the unifying element for its varied but well-designed buildings. Residential scale buildings with natural stone exteriors predominate, and the campus skyline is defined by shaped roofs and cornices. The best of both worlds, students enjoy the quiet, collegiate atmosphere of the college as well as the excitement of the nearby busy city of Philly. Kohlberg Hall houses three departments, many faculty offices, 13 classrooms, a state-of-the-art language lab, and even a commons with an espresso bar.

An academic powerhouse, Swarthmore is challenging. "Anywhere else it would have been an 'A,'" is the unofficial campus motto that best summarizes the astonishingly rigorous academic climate. But there is little cutthroat competition among students. Grades here are secondary; discussion, class time, learning, and enjoying studying are primary. One junior says that "Swarthmore is not competitive at all. It is considered against the social rules to ever discuss grades with other students." Swarthmore has strong departments all across campus, including standouts such as English, biology, engineering, economics, political science, history, and drama. Biology is the most popular major, followed by economics, English, and sociology/anthropology. Even in a strong liberal arts environment, the engineering department offers an outstanding program; the department believes in a "holistic" approach, and students take more than a third of their courses outside of engineering and science. Latin American Studies and Francophone Studies are available as concentrations, too. Among more unusual programs are Peace and Conflict Studies and Interpretation Theory.

Swarthmore's general education requirements center on three courses each from three divisions: science, social science, and humanities. Two choices in each division must be selected from among those courses listed as Primary Distribution Courses, which are specially designed courses that place particular emphasis on the mode of inquiry in a particular discipline. While there are no special requirements for freshmen, seminars are available in various departments, and first-semester grades are pass/fail.

Faculty advisors are initially assigned to freshmen by area of interest, and students feel advising is adequate. Swarthmore profs garner high marks for teaching as well as attitude, and all agree that teaching is one of Swarthmore's greatest strengths. Students have enormous respect for the faculty, and note that the quality of teaching is, "superb, outstanding, second-to-none, excellent beyond compare." The unique corollary is that professors have equally high respect for their students. "Teachers know our names and our work, they listen to what is said and students listen to and hear from one another," says one English and economics major. "They are constantly doing their own research and writing and are always looking for students to collaborate with them." There are no teaching assistants.

Swarthmore offers a unique honors program called the External Examination Program. Candidates attend eight intense seminars during their last four terms, each with four to eight students. Though honors seminars require extensive reading and writing, there are no exams or grades until the end of senior year. At that point, external examiners—faculty members from other universities—administer a series of final exams, oral and written, on four to six areas of study. Good academic standing and a student's demonstrated capacity for assuming the responsibility for the heavy workload are required for entrance, and about a third of juniors and seniors enroll in the program. The new wrinkle is an increase in curriculum areas, including studio and performing arts and study abroad, in which eligible students may study.

As you might imagine, the Swarthmore library (1 million volumes) is a place for serious studying. The exception to the rule is the ever popular annual winter event known as the McCabe Mile, when students race 18 laps amid the bookshelves in the basement of the library; the starting gun is the slam of a book and the prize is a roll of toilet paper. On a more serious note, if a student can't find research materials in the campus library, the interlibrary loan system can help. The solution is cross-registration with nearby Haverford, Bryn Mawr, and the University of Pennsylvania, and the semester exchange program with schools in other parts of the country (including Brandeis, Harvey Mudd, Middlebury, Mills, Pomona, Rice, and Tufts). Swarthmore also sponsors study abroad programs in France, Germany, Spain, Colombia, Italy, and Sri Lanka. The Office of Foreign Study offers support to students in arranging programs almost anywhere in the world, while the Venture Program* allows students to take time off for short-term, full-time jobs in a related interest.

Swatties come from all across the country with only 11 percent from Pennsylvania. The student body is 61 percent Caucasian, with Asian Americans accounting for 13 percent, African Americans for 9 percent, and Hispanics 9 percent. Race and other issues such as homelessness, gay rights, and abortion are heated topics in this very intellectual atmosphere. Swarthmore's Quaker roots

(Continued)
Economics
English Literature
Sociology/Anthropology
History
Political Science

The thought of the workload at Swarthmore makes students at most top liberal arts schools shake in their Birkenstocks.

Even in a strong liberal arts environment, the engineering department offers an outstanding program; the department believes in a "holistic" approach, and students take more than a third of their courses outside of engineering and science.

come through in the concern and respect that students have for others. "Students care about the Quaker values of tolerance and honoring the good in every person and this means that hate speech and nonpolitically correct statements and attitudes are taken seriously." Students at this school care about the world around them and want to make it a better place. "What isn't an issue?" asks one junior.

Swarthmore is committed to making decisions by consensus (students have an active voice in many administrative actions) and is also committed to equal access: all activities on campus—dances, parties, movies, and so on—are free. With one of the largest endowments per student of any college in the nation, Swarthmore is need-blind in admissions and meets the full demonstrated need of all accepted applicants. In addition, 16 merit scholarships are awarded to particularly qualified students.

The college's 12 dorms are home for 93 percent of the student body, and all students are guaranteed housing for four years if they want it. The biggest problem lately has been rising enrollment, causing a bit of a housing crunch for everyone. All but two of the dorms are coed by room, and many have been renovated. "Most dorms are spacious and all are well-maintained," coos a junior. Freshmen usually live in doubles, while upperclassmen choose among singles, two-room doubles, or suites. The full meal plan is the only one offered, and the food is said to be fair to average.

The social life at Swarthmore is less raucous than at a big school, and is described by students as "balanced" and "what you make it." Says a student, "Regarding on-campus social life, that most everything at Swat is fully sponsored and free to students." Another student adds that "It's not a state school so drunkenness and noise don't equal fun here." Swarthmore's administration has always taken a permissive attitude toward students' private lives (each dorm is stocked with condoms), and this extends to drinking as well. "The college's policy is to treat students as adults, and we are expected to behave accordingly," says one student. Most often, social life takes a backseat to academics, and it's not uncommon for people study until 10:00 or 11:00 P.M., then hit the parties. Most of the Swarthmore social life occurs on campus, where there are free dance parties, movies, concerts, performances, and the student-run café. Thursday night is Pub Night.

For students who hanker for the bright lights of the big city, Philly is close (and accessible by commuter rail) and New York isn't too far away. Greeks attract only a small portion of the student body—there are no sororities, and 6 percent of the men join fraternities. Most students prefer Philly to the nearby village of Swarthmore, which offers not much more than a pizza place and a few shops. Many students volunteer in both nearby Chester and Philadelphia.

As for outdoor recreation, intramurals are as popular as varsity sports, and the highlight of the year is the Crum Regatta, in which student-made boats float in nearby Crum Creek—Swarthmore's answer to the America's Cup. Also popular is "primal" scream on the eve of finals. Any athletic competition against Haverford is a beloved tradition. The school's board of trustees recently abolished the football team, explaining that the need to give preference in admissions to football players was undermining the academic quality of the school. Though they may be sparsely supported, many varsity teams are successful, with lacrosse, men's and women's tennis and swimming, and women's field hockey and cross-country as top teams.

Swarthmore is, ultimately, a collection of bright students, each relentlessly pursuing their intellectual or academic Holy Grail. The school works to make sure that each of the students has what they need to succeed. According to one satisfied student, "There's a certain bond among students that comes from the uniquely intense academic experience. You'll never find a group of people with such a sense of community anywhere else."

If You Apply To ➤ Swarthmore…Early decision: Nov. 15, Jan. 1. Regular admissions: Jan. 1. Guarantees to meet demonstrated need. Campus and alumni interviews: optional, evaluative. SATs or ACTs: required. SAT IIs: required (writing and two others; math IIc for engineering students). Accepts the Common Application and electronic applications. Essay question: activities or personal interest to which you feel particularly committed; personal statement.

Sweet Briar College

Box B, Sweet Briar, VA 24595

Sweet Briar College has evolved considerably since its inception in 1901. Founder Indiana Fletcher Williams envisioned a school that would educate young women "to be useful members of society." These days, this college—in the heart of beautiful, rural Virginia—produces more career women than homemakers. Of course, a few men are actually coming to Sweet Briar as nondegree or exchange students. But heed the popular bumper sticker: Sweet Briar remains a place "Where women are leaders and men are guests." And with a slew of academic changes on the horizon, Sweet Briar is working hard to distinguish itself even more.

Set on 3,300 acres of rolling green lawns dotted with small lakes and surrounded by the Blue Ridge Mountains, Sweet Briar's campus of early 20th-century redbrick charmers is a picture of pastoral beauty. Sweet Briar House, now the president's residence, was the 18th-century home of the college's founders, and is listed on the National Register of Historic Places. The new Florence Elston Inn and Conference Center includes high-tech meeting rooms, and a new student center is on the way.

SBC's curriculum is strong in the sciences, boasting state-of-the-art equipment such as a digital scanning electron microscope, modular LASER lab, and a gas chromatograph/mass spectrograph. English, with its strong creative writing program, is one of the better academic departments. Popular majors at Sweet Briar include psychology, history, and government. Dance, philosophy, German, and Italian are cited as weak because of their small size. The college recently added majors in computer science and environmental studies, as well as a minor in Law and Society.

Students agree that academics are rigorous. "The competition is always friendly and supportive, not ever mean. Everybody is happy for you when you do well," reports a sophomore. Faculty members receive much praise from students. "If somebody could make me understand English lit, they must be terrific," admits a chemistry/biology double major. "My professors care deeply about whether I succeed in their classes, and they want to make sure you know the material. They celebrate our achievements," says another sophomore. And with 40 percent of the faculty living on campus, "You get to know the faculty's spouses,

Website: www.sbc.edu

Location: Rural

Total Enrollment: 710

Undergraduates: 710

Male/Female: 3/97

SAT Ranges: V 520–620 M 470–580

ACT Range: 24–27

Financial Aid: 53%

Expense: Pr $

Phi Beta Kappa: Yes

Applicants: 499

Accepted: 89%

Enrolled: 42%

Grad in 6 Years: 68%

Returning Freshmen: 81%

Academics: 🖎 🖎 🖎

Social: ☎ ☎

Q of L: ★ ★ ★ ★

Admissions: (804) 381-6142 or (800) 381-6142

Email Address: admissions@sbc.edu

Strongest Programs:
  Sciences
  Computer Science
  Math
  History

(Continued)
Art History
Modern Languages and
Literatures

kids, and dogs," says one woman. Self-scheduled exams and take-home tests increase the atmosphere of mutual respect. An honors program and self-designed majors allow some students to further challenge themselves at Sweet Briar.

Sweet Briar's Junior Year in France is the oldest and best known of its study abroad programs. And the younger Junior Year in Spain program is quickly gaining in popularity, as are exchanges with Heidelberg University in Germany, Oxford University, and London University. Students can also spend time on other campuses through the Seven-College Exchange, the Tri-College Exchange, or 3–2 liberal arts and engineering programs. It is not unusual for faculty to offer short courses abroad, such as a theater course in London or an antiquities course in Italy. Classes end in early May, providing the perfect opportunity for internships, and SBC's unusually strong alumnae network is helpful in arranging positions and housing in large cities across the country. The college has added many courses to its distribution requirement to broaden students' horizons. All students are required to take classes in English, oral communications, writing, quantitative reasoning, research, physical education, Western culture, literature, foreign language, global cultures, arts, and scientific theory and experimentation/observations. First-year seminars are designed for 15 students and an advisor to discuss topics such as Alien Worlds: Fantasy and Reality and Diva: The Portrayal of Women in Opera. Sweet Briar requires senior seminars in lieu of dreaded comprehensive exams. Outstanding students can qualify for more than 100 merit scholarships that range from $500 to $15,000 each.

Over the years, the face of the SBC student body has changed. African Americans make up 5 percent of the student body, Asian Americans 2 percent, and Hispanics 4 percent. An increasing number of older "turning point" students contribute a valued perspective. Diversity is generally valued. "When 700 women live together in the middle of 3,000 acres for five days a week, they tend to become very tolerant neighbors," explains one student.

The college's vintage dorms, with their polished hardwood floors, sweeping wooden staircases, fireplaces, and furnished parlors, have aged gracefully. They're "positively sumptuous," says one enthusiastic resident. Reid was listed as the dorm of choice for freshmen, along with Grammer and Randolph. To make sure the dorms stay immaculate, the college renovates and restores one each year. Every hall has a fair share of students from all four classes, though student leaders are given the first shot at singles, and upperclassmen get to choose rooms by lottery. Several dorms have 24-hour male visitation hours. Housing is guaranteed to all, and 93 percent of the students live on campus. All residents eat in the common dining hall, which provides freshly baked bread.

SBC is a 1-mile walk from the one-traffic-light town of Amherst ("not a college town") and 12 miles from Lynchburg ("not a happening place"). SBC is only an hour away from Roanoke and Charlottesville. Many students volunteer at local schools and for Habitat for Humanity. The successful Sweet Briar Outdoor Program (SWEBOP) has converted hundreds of students to the joys of backpacking, canoeing, and white-water rafting on weekly expeditions. Organized sports for the Vixens (the school mascot), such as swimming, soccer, and field hockey, are strong in Division III. The equestrienne squad (backed by the largest private indoor ring in the country) has snagged eight national championships.

The $150 annual fee for the Sweet Briar Social Committee goes a long way, covering concerts, mixers with other colleges, theater performances, formal dances, and yearbooks. As at most colleges, underage drinking goes on mainly behind closed doors.

SBC hosts a number of big weekend social events that attract men "like flies from all over." If that's not enough, students say that frat parties at Washington and Lee, Hampden-Sydney, and the University of Virginia, each about an hour away, are the most common destinations. One woman warns, however, that "I spent a lot of time at other colleges last year, but I didn't like it after a while, and I decided I'd rather hang on campus." Lots of people roadtrip to the beach. Students also lovingly nurture traditions—Founder's Day, lantern bearing, step singing, "tapping" for clubs—and appreciate the genteel image that clings to the school and its graduates. The junior banquet is also a major event, at which class members receive their rings, worn on the left pinkie.

The women of Sweet Briar value the blend of academics, friendliness, and career preparation they receive. SBC has found a way to support the goals of the future career woman without shedding the benefits of traditional women's education. "Everything here is small, so you don't ever feel like you're on the assembly line," a sophomore says. The attitude that an all-women's college must be a finishing school has faded as more women graduate from SBC ready to conquer the world, or at least a portion of it.

One woman mentions a popular campus slogan: "When you're ready to believe in yourself, Sweet Briar believes in you."

Overlaps

Hollins, Randolph-Macon Woman's College, James Madison, Mary Washington, Mary Baldwin.

If You Apply To ➤ **Sweet Briar**…Early decision: Dec. 1. Regular admissions: Feb. 15. Meets demonstrated need of 33%. Campus interviews: recommended, evaluative. Alumni interviews: optional, evaluative. ACTs or SATs: required. SAT IIs: recommended. Accepts the Common Application and electronic applications. Essay question: Why Sweet Briar; significant event; choose four women to invite for dinner; personal or national issue; role in multicultural community.

Syracuse University

201 Tolley Administration Bldg., Syracuse, NY 13244-1140

While Syracuse's excellence on the playing field and in America's media gives it a proud past, all eyes are on the future. A renewed emphasis on teaching and learning at the undergraduate level, combined with the facilities and dedication of a major research center, means that the best may be yet to come for the Orangemen. The school recently redefined itself as a student-centered research university, giving students the support they need to excel. "The students and faculty at Syracuse make you feel at home from the very first day," says an education major.

The Syracuse campus is located on a hill overlooking the town of Syracuse, in central New York State. The Carrier Dome sits on the hillside like an oversized alien spacecraft. The character and mixture of architectural styles depict a continuously changing campus, which is grassy, full of trees, and bordered by residential neighborhoods. Fifteen of SU's 140 buildings are listed in the National Register of Historic Places. Many schools and colleges have restructured facilities to accommodate more faculty/student research, as well as social interaction between the two groups. All the dorms are wired with a high-speed communications network. The School of Management links finance students to the stock markets in real-time and the School of Information Studies has a new hands-on, cutting-edge learning center.

Website: www.syracuse.edu

Location: City center

Total Enrollment: 14,668

Undergraduates: 10,685

Male/Female: 46/54

SAT Ranges: V 540–640 M 560–660

Financial Aid: 60%

Expense: Pr $ $

Phi Beta Kappa: Yes

Applicants: 12,663

Accepted: 59%

Enrolled: 37%

Grad in 6 Years: 72%

Returning Freshmen: 91%

Academics: ✍ ✍ ✍

Social: ☎ ☎ ☎

(Continued)

Q of L: ★ ★ ★

Admissions: (315) 443-3611

Email Address:
orange@syr.edu

Strongest Programs:
Communications
Film
Information Management
and Technology
Chemistry
Geography
Aerospace Engineering
Drama
Political Science

The academic programs here are diverse. The Newhouse School of Public Communications, which has produced such media celebrities as *NBC Sports* announcer Bob Costas and *Nightline* host Ted Koppel, is undoubtedly Syracuse's flagship division. It offers leading programs in newspaper, magazine, and broadcast journalism, and is home to four cutting-edge computerized lab facilities for reporting and digital editing. Newhouse introduced graphics as a major and has new labs offering the latest technology in integrating sound, photos and video in productions. Also well known is the Maxwell School of Citizenship and Public Affairs, whose faculty members teach undergraduate economics, history, geography, political science, and social sciences. The College of Arts and Sciences is the largest college at Syracuse, and offers recognized programs in creative writing, philosophy, geography, and chemistry. Students mention mathematics, foreign languages, and nursing as weaker SU programs. The most popular majors are psychology, information management and technology, political science, speech communication, and television/radio/film.

General education requirements at Syracuse vary by school and college. All students are expected to take writing and literature courses. Several schools and colleges subscribe to the Arts and Sciences core requirements, which specify a need to complete coursework in the sciences, math, social sciences, and humanities. Entering freshmen must complete a writing seminar during their first year, and each school and college offers a small-group experience course, known as the Freshman Forum, to share common first-year experiences and provide a forum for discussion of academic and personal issues. The Gateway program is another strong offering for freshmen, which allows students to take introductory classes with senior faculty members in a small classroom setting. For upperclassmen, Syracuse offers a strong honors program based on seminars and independent research. Some students are involved in worldwide humanitarian efforts through the School for Social Work and the College of Nursing. New additions to the curriculum include a BS in economics, a BS in acting, a BA in art history, and a new major in biochemistry.

As is true with most large schools, individual initiative is the key to success. Students generally lavish praise on their professors. "The professors at SU are very interested in helping students," says a speech communications major. "They are never too busy to answer questions or offer advice." Academic advising is adequate, but students have to find a faculty member with whom they interact well. Classes are usually small (fewer than 25 students) and registration relatively painless.

Admissions standards differ among the various schools and are most rigorous in the professional schools, especially architecture, communications, and engineering. Thirty-eight percent of Syracuse's undergraduates come from the top ten percent of their high school class, and 84 percent attended public high school. African Americans and Hispanics account for 7 and 4 percent of the student body, respectively, and Asian Americans make up another 5 percent. The campus is not divisive, one student notes. "With such a diverse population, it is surprising to find that Syracuse is a campus of little social and political conflict." The diversity of students' backgrounds extends to their politics as well; all political ideologies are represented on campus. Hot issues run the gamut from financial aid cuts to the role of unions. More than 40 percent of the students are from New York State, and most of those hail from New York City and Long Island. There are about 300 athletic scholarships in sports ranging from football and basketball to crew and lacrosse. Merit scholarships are also available, ranging from $1,000 to $10,000. There also is a 12-month tuition payment plan available.

The Newhouse School of Public Communications, which has produced such media celebrities as NBC Sports announcer Bob Costas and Nightline host Ted Koppel, is undoubtedly Syracuse's flagship division.

Housing on campus is clean and comfortable, and is provided all four years in modern and well-maintained halls. Seventy-two percent of the undergraduates live in university housing. One senior moved off campus, but missed the familiarity of the dorms. "I moved back my senior year because of the social aspects the dorms offer." Syracuse is continually upgrading dorm facilities as part of a 10-year renovation plan, and students appreciate the efforts made to help them feel comfortable. Freshmen are required to live in the dorms, and should check out Brewster-Boland, Day, and Flint halls. Rooms for upperclassmen are assigned by a lottery, and most everyone who wants a room gets one. Living and dining in fraternity or sorority houses is another popular option, because 20 percent of the men and 30 percent of the women go Greek. As for campus safety, SU has a series of emergency alarms throughout the campus, and a card-key access system in all dorms. A bus service is available for students studying late at the library or in labs.

Most students enjoy the town of Syracuse, which has a refreshing life of its own—independent of the university. Many students are involved in the community through internships in the corporations and student teaching in the schools, notes a student. Downtown is within easy reach on foot or by public transportation, which runs every few minutes. Once there, the opportunities include an excellent art museum, a resident opera company, a symphony, and a string of movie theaters and restaurants. If you tire of the city life, several quaint country towns, complete with orchards, lakes, and waterfalls, are nearby, as are several ski resorts. Carrousel Mall, about 10 minutes away, has an 18-theater cinema, Erie Boulevard is home to big chains such as Wal-Mart and Barnes & Noble, and the city's Armory Square is flanked with coffee shops, a great music store, clubs, and eateries.

The social life tends to stay on campus for freshmen and sophomores, and move off campus for upperclassmen. There are always activities available such as movies, bowling, skating, and dancing. Students over 21 spend many an evening bar-hopping on Marshall Street, a lively strip near campus. For underage students, there is a campus club where student bands play and nonalcoholic drinks and snacks are free. Coffee shops are also popular at Syracuse. Drama productions are frequent on the weekends, and popular road trips include Ithaca, Niagara Falls, Canada, and Rochester.

The spacious Carrier Dome rocks every time the Orangemen take the field or the court. Football games against Miami and a basketball rivalry with Georgetown make for great fun and much enthusiasm during the year. Though the Dome seats 33,000 for basketball—enough to shatter NCAA attendance records—tickets must still be parceled out by a lottery, to the disdain of some. "Athletic tickets are expensive and for basketball we get crummy seats," an advertising/foreign language double major laments. Though receiving less attention, the men's lacrosse team has won a national championship, and the wrestling and field hockey teams have won conference championships.

Syracuse is working to change its reputation as a party school punctuated by impersonally huge seminar classes. By focusing on individual student research, modernizing and expanding its facilities, and promoting close advising relationships, Orangemen really are getting a solid education for their money.

Also well known is the Maxwell School of Citizenship and Public Affairs, whose faculty members teach undergraduate economics, history, geography, political science, and social sciences.

Overlaps

Boston University, NYU, Penn State, Cornell University, University of Massachusetts.

University of Tennessee at Knoxville

Knoxville, TN 37996-0230

Website: www.utk.edu
Location: City center
Total Enrollment: 26,437
Undergraduates: 20,259
Male/Female: 49/51
SAT Ranges: V 500–600 M 490–610
ACT Range: 21–26
Financial Aid: 67%
Expense: Pub $ $
Phi Beta Kappa: Yes
Applicants: 10,605
Accepted: 67%
Enrolled: 58%
Grad in 6 Years: 57%
Returning Freshmen: 79%
Academics: 🐙 🐙 🐙
Social: ☎ ☎ ☎ ☎
Q of L: ★ ★ ★
Admissions: (865) 974-2184
Email Address:
admissions@utk.edu

Strongest Programs:
Accounting
Architecture
Forestry
Biology
Business
Engineering
Communications

When you enter "Big Orange Country," you find University of Tennessee students who put a premium on school spirit, athletics, and academics—usually in that order. In the fall, more than 100,000 boisterous fans pack into one of the nation's largest on-campus football stadiums to watch the Volunteers play against national powerhouses like Florida, Alabama, and Arkansas. And in the winter and spring, the SEC-dominating women's basketball and men's baseball teams spring into action. Amid this excitement, it's easy to forget that UT prides itself on having a strong academic program that receives accolades throughout the Southeast.

Set in the foothills of the Great Smoky Mountains, UT is in the heart of east Tennessee's urban hub and only a few miles away from Oak Ridge, Tennessee, home to the prominent Oak Ridge National Laboratory. The 511-acre campus has an array of architectural styles ranging from Gothic to Georgian to modern. Particularly noteworthy is the John C. Hodges Library—the largest one in the state—built in the shape of a ziggurat. Newest construction on campus includes a geography building and an addition to the Claxton Education Building.

The university's strongest programs are in preprofessional fields, most notably business, architecture, accounting, and engineering. On the liberal arts side, psychology and communications are popular majors. Several majors in French, German, and Spanish incorporate a concentration in international business. A cooperative arrangement with nearby Oak Ridge National Laboratory—the federal government's largest nonweapons lab—bolsters science and technology offerings, and involves more than 400 students and faculty in majors as diverse as English and physics. The honors program at UT is a campus-wide program that offers qualified students scholarships, honors courses, and seminars, and a chance to complete an original research project in collaboration with a faculty member. Students who participate in the Whittle Scholars Program are encouraged to pursue their leadership skills through campus and community organizations, and are given the opportunity to travel to a variety of different countries including Argentina, Australia, France, Mexico, and the Netherlands. The humanities, foreign languages, and philosophy programs are reportedly weak.

Competition varies, depending on the class. "The academic climate is challenging in that the coursework is difficult but competition between students is rare," says an accounting major. Most students agree that the UT has a solid faculty. "The good thing about this school is that it is pretty big and offers a variety of teachers," says one student. "If I don't like my first impression of a teacher, I can drop the class and find a different teacher who teaches the same subject." Coursework varies in terms of difficulty, depending on the major, and students say that they spend 15 to 20 hours per week studying. Students report occasional problems with registration because preference is given to seniors, but none that would extend a four-year stay. Advising is said to be terrific, and students are expected to meet with their advisors each semester before registering. UT's general education requirements are fairly extensive and include two courses each in English composition, math, humanities and arts, history, social sciences, and natural sciences, plus intermediate proficiency in a foreign language or integrated studies. Business majors are immersed in a broad liberal arts program, including a foreign language requirement, during their first two years of study.

Eighty-two percent of the student body are made up of homegrown Tennesseans, and 26 percent of the undergrads graduated in the top tenth of their high school class. Minority enrollment is low; African Americans account for 6 percent of the students, while Asian Americans and Hispanics combine for 3 percent. The university sponsors programs to increase awareness of race and gender issues for faculty and staff. The big issues on campus are state funding, student government, and a four-lane bridge that has been proposed to run through campus. Students also warn that the campus's size can lead to a phenomenon called the "Big Orange Screw," in which the impersonal bureaucratic system makes students' lives miserable. Financial aid opportunities are generous: more than 800 merit scholarships are available, including 10 Whittle Scholarships, which are offered annually. An additional 366 athletic scholarships are awarded in 18 sports.

Dorm space is plentiful, as only 37 percent of UT students live on campus. "Dorms are...small but bearable. No problem getting a room on campus, but hard to get into certain dorms," says a senior. The dorms are for the most part comfortable and well-maintained, and about the only hitch is that some don't have air-conditioning (that can be brutal in August). Each of the dorms has a residence hall association, which for a token fee provides check-out of sports equipment, games, cooking utensils, and other useful items. The university goes out of its way to ensure the security of the campus and the students. To this end, UT has installed remote alarm units that allow students to report a crime from anywhere on campus.

Students say that the social life is "very active" both on and off campus. The social calendar is dotted with numerous major events, including River Fest on the nearby Tennessee, Saturday Night on the Town, and the Dogwood Arts Festival. Greeks control much of the campus life—though only 8 percent of UT men and women go Greek. "You don't have to be a part of the Greek/football/beer scene! You really can be completely happy with your own friends," a senior College Scholar says. Alcohol flows freely, even for underage students. But nothing compares to the sea of orange that engulfs the campus on Saturday afternoons in the fall. More than 100,000 people jam the football stadium to see their Vols take on Southeast Conference rivals ("Alabama is a four-letter word" in these parts). Denizens liken football to religion in Knoxville, and the Volunteers didn't disappoint in the 1998 season, bringing home a national championship. Coach Pat Summit's Lady Vols basketball team has won a record-breaking number of NCAA championships in recent years, and enjoys tremendous crowds (drawing more fans than many NBA teams).

The University of Tennessee is well known for its athletics, and administrators and students are hoping that it can develop the same reputation for academics. Though some may be turned off by the oft-sluggish beauracracy, many will find the myriad of opportunities here at the "Big Orange" to be well worth the hassle.

Overlaps

Middle Tennessee State, Auburn, Vanderbilt, Georgia, East Tennessee State.

UT…Regular admissions: Jan. 15. Financial aid: March 1. Housing: Jan. 15. Campus and alumni interviews: optional, evaluative. SATs or ACTs: required. SAT IIs: optional. No essay question.

Texas A&M University

College Station, TX 77843-0100

Website: www.tamu.edu

Location: Small city

Total Enrollment: 43,389

Undergraduates: 35,889

Male/Female: 53/47

SAT Ranges: V 520–620 M 550–650

ACT Range: 23–28

Financial Aid: 35%

Expense: Pub $ $

Phi Beta Kappa: No

Applicants: 13,258

Accepted: 86%

Enrolled: 55%

Grad in 6 Years: 70%

Returning Freshmen: 88%

Academics: ✑ ✑ ✑

Social: ☎ ☎ ☎

Q of L: ★ ★ ★

Admissions: (409) 845-3741

Email Address

admissions@tamu.edu

Strongest Programs:

Engineering

Psychology

Chemistry

Business

The state of Texas is known for big things, but Texas A&M is one of its biggest. This school of 43,000 students is huge; it boasts a massive endowment of and more traditions than Vatican City. Since its inception as a military academy, Texas A&M has become known for its top-notch engineering program and its unsurpassed school spirit. When they're not studying for rigorous technical courses, Aggies are likely to be found at "yell practice" before each home football game or cheering for their teams at other high-energy athletic events. In any case, A&M students have much to cheer about.

Texas A&M is now the largest university campus in the country—and students remember that every time they walk to class. The A&M campus combines historic brick buildings from the turn of the century with newer structures in more modern styles, and it is pulled together by its heavy cover of live-oak trees. Newer buildings include the George Bush Presidential Library and Museum Complex, featuring open lawns and a pond with bridges for pedestrians and bikers.

Texas A&M is best known for its agriculture and engineering colleges, and for veterinary medicine, although the university is cultivating a strong liberal arts program and an even stronger business school. Aggies also stand by science programs, especially chemistry and physics. Technical programs of virtually all kinds are heartily supported at A&M, especially nuclear, space, and biotechnical research. A&M has become a sea-grant college due to its outstanding research in oceanography, and is also a "space-grant" college. Add that to the college's land-grant status, and the whole universe seems covered by A&M. Coursework sometimes takes students far from Aggieland. Participants in the Nautical Archaeology Program conduct research all over the world, delving into time periods from prehistory to the recent past. The Academy for Future International Leaders trains 15 students per year in international business and cultural issues, followed by a summer international internship. Weaker programs include music performance, ancient languages, and religious studies.

Incoming Aggies can expect some heavy coursework in general education requirements, which consist of speech and writing, mathematics/logical reasoning, science, humanities, social science, physical education, and citizenship (political science and history). They are also expected to have at least two years of language background and demonstrated computer literacy. To help trim the cost of earning a degree, an athlete can compete for one of more than 300 scholarships parceled out each year, while an academic scholar can vie for one of 8,500 merit awards, ranging from $200 to $12,000. Students generally agree that academics are taken seriously at A&M. "Some classes are hard, some are not, but it really all depends on how much time you put into them," says a senior marketing major. And the professors also receive rave reviews. "Every teacher I have encountered has gone above and beyond the call of duty that you would expect from a large university such as Texas A&M," a classmate reports. Because of the school's size, it's sometimes hard to enroll in a required class. But one student suggests, "You just have to go to the professor and get forced in."

Diversity is not a hallmark at A&M, and some students sense this: 94 percent of the student body hail from Texas, and 80 percent are white. Though the school is slowly shedding the image that A&M students are awkward, unrefined hayseeds, students still endure countless Aggie jokes. (Question: "How do you get a one-armed Aggie out of a tree?" Answer: "Wave.") The school's departments of Multicultural Services and Student Life offer numerous programs to enhance minority student recruitment and retention. But a recent court ruling has challenged A&M and other Texas schools because it prohibits the use of affirmative action in admissions decisions. Still, for many students, the one unifying characteristic of the A&M experience is the university spirit. "Aggies look out for other Aggies. Everyone is an Aggie," a senior history major says.

The Academy for Future International Leaders trains 15 students per year in international business and cultural issues, followed by a summer international internship.

Thirty-eight single-sex and coed dorms range from the cheap and not so comfortable to the expensive and cushy (with air-conditioning and private bathrooms). "All dorms are full. In fact they are generally too full," one senior observes. "Freshmen must request a dorm as soon as they are accepted in order to get a dorm of choice or any dorm for that matter." Because of the ever-growing student population, the school's dorms provide only enough space for 26 percent of those enrolled. Most upperclassmen end up living in the numerous apartments and houses in College Station or its twin city, Bryan. These students needn't fear being cut off from campus life, though, as the entire town is filled with fervent Aggies. Several meal plans are offered in the dining halls, and there are snack shops all over campus.

Although College Station may appear uninspiring at first glance, most of the students fall in love with it. "College Station is a model college town," a senior explains. "Every restaurant has an 'Aggie special,' the radio stations play our 'war hymn' at times throughout the day." Students are actively involved in the community, including the largest single-day service project in the nation annually, the Big Event. Although the Texas Alcohol Board is stationed in town, "those who choose to drink have no problem getting alcohol." Those with more sophisticated tastes can drive an hour and a half to either Houston or Austin or three hours to Dallas. Greeks are growing in popularity, with 6 percent of the men and 14 percent of the women in the student body joining up. In addition, there are more than 700 organizations available for interested students.

Athletics, whether on the varsity level or for recreation, is the number-one activity on campus. Football fans rock Kyle Field with cries of "Gig 'em, Aggies," or "Hump it, Ags." After touchdowns are scored, Aggie fans kiss their dates. Still, the annual game against the University of Texas stirs up the Aggies and their fans all season long. Men's baseball routinely fields outstanding teams, and the women's golf and soccer teams have brought home a few championships of their own. The well-organized and extensive intramural program includes hundreds of softball teams.

Favorite traditions include "Twelfth Man," for which all students stand for the entirety of every football game as a symbol of their loyalty and readiness to take part, and the Aggie Muster, a memorial service for A&M alumni around the world who died within the year. There's also the 300-plus member Fightin' Texas Aggie Band and the senior "boot line" at the end of the halftime show. The

Because of the ever-growing student population, the school's dorms provide only enough space for 26 percent of those enrolled.

treasured Corps of Cadets, one of the largest military training programs in the country, is structured like a military unit; students lead other cadets. While less than 10 percent of the school belong to the Corps, it remains the single most important conservator of the spirit and tradition in Aggieland. The famed Aggie Bonfire has been discontinued due to the recent tragedy that resulted in students' deaths.

Texas A&M, while extremely large, is uniquely familial. Being a student here is being a part of something seemingly so much bigger, which is what the Aggie Spirit embodies. Students get the best of both worlds at A&M—a large school with tons of people surrounded by a small community. A&M's no longer just a military school, it's a potpourri of varied educational opportunities—and that's something to cheer about. Boasts one senior, "We have the same traditions as were created years ago and, young or old, Aggies know them all."

> ### Overlaps
>
> **University of Texas, Baylor, Texas Tech, Southwest Texas State, Rice.**

> ### If You Apply To ➤
>
> **Texas A&M**…Early action: Dec. 4. Regular admissions: Mar. 1. Financial aid: April 1. Does not guarantee to meet demonstrated need. Campus interviews: optional, informational. No alumni interviews. SATs or ACTs: required. No SAT IIs. Essay question: response to a challenge, important experience or personal statement. Apply to particular schools or programs. Primarily committed to state residents.

Texas Christian University

TCU Box 297013, Fort Worth, TX 76129

Website: www.tcu.edu
Location: Suburban
Total Enrollment: 7,551
Undergraduates: 6,456
Male/Female: 42/58
SAT Ranges: V 520–620 M 520–640
ACT Range: 23–28
Financial Aid: 94%
Expense: Pr $
Phi Beta Kappa: Yes
Applicants: 5,028
Accepted: 75%
Enrolled: 38%
Grad in 6 Years: 63%
Returning Freshmen: 82%
Academics: ✑ ✑ ✑
Social: ☎ ☎ ☎
Q of L: ★ ★ ★
Admissions: (817) 257-7490

You know a school has spirit when its students paint themselves purple to cheer raucously for something called a Horned Frog. Texans know these folks are TCU fans cheering for the home team (known officially as the Texas Christian University Horned Frogs) at a Saturday afternoon football game. There's a true sense of solidarity and school spirit that extends far past athletics at TCU. The best thing about TCU, according to one senior, is "its dedication to being the best and always taking the students' needs as first priority."

The spacious 237-acre campus is kept in almost perfect condition, and features a small lake, several fountains, and a jogging track. Nearby is a lovely residential neighborhood not too far from the shops and restaurants of downtown Fort Worth. The campus features an eclectic mix of architecture, ranging from neo-Georgian to contemporary. Newer facilities include the Taylor Recreational Track and the Walsh Center for Performing Arts, a 56,000-square-foot performance hall, and theater complex.

Students can choose their majors from about 80 disciplines, with the core curriculum counting for 47 semester hours. The core emphasizes critical thinking and is divided into three areas: foundations (writing and math); explorations (natural and social sciences, cultural heritage, language, and literature); and physical education. There are freshman seminar courses, along with a new student orientation and Frog Camp (an optional summer camp that emphasizes team building and school spirit). New additions to the curriculum include majors in English as a second language in education, advertising/public relations, and news/editorial journalism. Medical technology, fashion, and fashion design have been dropped.

Programs that are strongest at TCU are business, nursing, communications, psychology, and fine arts. Some business majors manage a $1.5-million investment portfolio that is one of the largest student-run investment funds in the nation. The university also offers an innovative dance program with a ballet major and a strong theater internship program. The communications program offers hands-on experience at the two fully operational TV studios, a 5,000-watt radio station, and a Center for Productive Communication. The campus also features a geological center for remote sensing, a nuclear magnetic resonance facility, an observatory, and an art gallery, along with a state-of-the-art electrical engineering lab.

The academic climate at TCU is challenging but not overwhelming. "TCU students are definitely concerned about academics and grades, but there is also a feeling of support and open cooperation between students," says an English major. Professors are well liked and respected. "All of my professors have been enthusiastic, highly knowledgeable, compassionate, and real," reports one student. One student said, "I am a freshman, and three of my teachers are department chairs. That is so cool!" Another freshman said, "The profs are great and have a desire to know and help the students."

TCU's student body is fairly homogeneous; about 70 percent of the student body are from Texas, many from affluent, conservative families. TCU is affiliated with the Christian Church (Disciples of Christ), but the atmosphere is not overtly religious. Social issues generally take a backseat to maintaining the status quo, but political correctness is prevalent. "TCU should be called 'PCU,'" says a junior. The student body is 5 percent Hispanic, 4 percent black, and 2 percent Asian American. TCU offers over 1,300 academic merit scholarships ranging from $2,000 to full tuition, and over 300 athletic scholarships for talented athletes.

Dorm life is a good experience for the 50 percent of students who live on campus. Cable and free Internet access are available in all rooms. Students describe them as comfortable and clean. An escort service, Froggy 5-0, takes you wherever you want to go on campus. "There are also plenty of lights and emergency phones," one freshman says, "so students feel physically safe."

Many juniors and seniors move off campus, and fraternity and sorority members may live in their Greek houses after freshman year. Dorm residents must take the meal plan, which does not receive very high marks. The alcohol rules on campus are fairly strict for minors: resident advisors even perform occasional "fridge checks" looking for alcohol in students' rooms. "If you're caught you are ticketed and have to go to Alcohol Abuse meetings," one student says. "But we're all smart enough to find a way around it," another retorts.

Greek life is important at TCU; 27 percent of the men and 33 percent of the women join Greek organizations. They party in the esprit de corps tradition, but there's plenty of fun left in Fort Worth and on campus for everyone else. Fort Worth "has all the benefits of a big city without feeling like one," a sophomore says. Bars, restaurants, clubs, and off-campus parties keep most students busy on weekends. Dallas is only 45 minutes to the east. Parents' Weekend, Siblings' Weekend, Homecoming, and the traditional lighting of the Christmas tree are all special events. Road trips include Austin, San Antonio, and the Gulf Coast.

As for athletics, the school recently joined the ranks of Conference USA. The football team's resurgence has given championship-hungry fans a reason to cheer, and big rivalries include SMU and Rice. Championship teams in the past few years include football, men's basketball, and men's and women's tennis. On-campus sports facilities feature two indoor pools, weight rooms, a track, and tennis, basketball, sand volleyball, and racquetball courts.

(Continued)

Email Address:
frogmail@tcu.edu

Strongest Programs:
Business
Nursing
Communications
Fine Arts
Psychology
Premed

The university also offers an innovative dance program with a ballet major and a strong theater internship program.

Greek life is important at TCU; 27 percent of the men and 33 percent of the women join Greek organizations. They party in the esprit de corps tradition, but there's plenty of fun left in Fort Worth and on campus for everyone else.

There's a quiet sense of accomplishment at TCU, and an appreciation for the personal attention that is given to the students. TCU provides multiple opportunities to prosper both academically and socially. "I love TCU because it is a small campus and you get to really know the faculty and student body," says a junior. "We all really love our school and what it stands for." Like the beloved Horned Frog, TCU graduates have taken a giant leap toward their futures.

Texas Tech University

Lubbock, TX 79409-2022

Website: www.texastech.edu
Location: Suburban
Total Enrollment: 24,249
Undergraduates: 20,227
Male/Female: 54/46
SAT Ranges: V 480–580
  M 490–600
ACT Range: 20–26
Financial Aid: 30%
Expense: Pr $ $ $ $
Phi Beta Kappa: Yes
Applicants: 8,100
Accepted: 75%
Enrolled: 58%
Grad in 6 Years: 46%
Returning Freshmen: 78%
Academics: ✍ ✍ ✍
Social: ☎ ☎ ☎
Q of L: ★ ★ ★
Admissions: (806) 742-1480
Email Address: nrs@ttu.edu

Strongest Programs:
  Communications
  Chemistry
  Electrical Engineering
  Finance

Texas Tech University is a study in Texan tenacity. Originally intended as a branch of Texas A&M University, TTU has blossomed into a full-blown university serving nearly 25,000 students. The university has committed itself to becoming one of the top 100 research institutions in the country, and administrators have launched a comprehensive capital campaign, hired new faculty, upgraded facilities, and become more selective in an effort to attract the nation's best and brightest. "The addition of a chancellor and reorganization of administration has revolutionized Tech," says a senior. Once a tiny academic outpost in rural Texas, this rising institution is now staking out a legacy worthy of its Texas-sized aspirations.

Located in the West Texas city of Lubbock, Tech's 1,839-acre university campus is home to more than 24,000 students as well as the medical and law schools. Expansive lawns and impressive landscaping complement the campus architecture, which features Spanish Renaissance-style red tile-roofed buildings. The university is in the midst of a $500-million building program that has resulted in new facilities sprouting up around campus, including an alumni center and a student apartment complex. Future projects include an immense English, philosophy, and education building and a science laboratory.

Founded in 1923, Texas Tech was intended to be a western branch of Texas A&M University until governmental red tape and rancor led to the establishment of an entirely new school. Texas Tech University opened its doors in 1925 with less than 1,000 students studying liberal arts, agriculture, engineering, and home economics. These days, the university has its sights set on becoming a top-tier research institution and the school of choice in Texas for undergraduate students.

Students select from more than 150 undergraduate degree programs. Engineering is highly regarded, as are chemistry, human sciences (especially family financial planning), agriculture, and technical writing. The most popular majors are business, mass communications, engineering, agriculture, and applied economics. Newer programs include computer engineering, environmental toxicology, software engineering, and visual studies. Students tend to avoid the math departments due to its highly technical nature, and the administration candidly admits that French and German could be strengthened.

(Continued)
Psychology
Technical Writing

Tech's extensive general education requirements include courses in communications, mathematics, natural science, technology and applied science, humanities, arts, and social and behavioral sciences. Students must also fulfill a 3-hour multicultural course. Freshmen can participate in Tech Transitions, a freshman seminar designed to ease high school students into college life by educating them on the philosophy and scope of higher education. The academic climate varies by program, and students admit that competition becomes more intense in upper level courses. "The academic climate is competitive because of the class sizes," says a computer science major. "You find yourself needing to focus more in larger classes, especially if the course is already complicated." Classes of 100-plus students do exist, but most freshman classes average less than 50. Professors are praised for being accessible and caring, and teaching assistants are few and far between even for freshmen.

Outstanding students can take part in the Honors College, which features special academic courses and extensive student involvement. Students sit on committees, engage in recruiting, help make decisions concerning course content, and evaluate the faculty. Undergraduate research is a high priority at Texas Tech, and students have abundant opportunities to work side-by-side with renowned faculty on a variety of projects. Recent research has included the study of pain management, wind engineering, and sick building syndrome. Those yearning to leave behind the hardscrabble plains of Texas can opt to study abroad, while Type-A personalities might want to investigate the MD/MBA Joint Degree Program.

Tech's student body is primarily homegrown, with only 5 percent from outside the Lone Star State. Twenty-three percent graduated in the top tenth of their high school class, and most hail from public schools. Overall, they are a friendly and conservative group. "The students are more open and likely to introduce themselves to people they don't know," says a junior. "They are quick to want to help one another." The student body is overwhelmingly white, with Asian Americans accounting for 2 percent, African Americans 3 percent, and Hispanics 10 percent. "I have not come across too many 'PC' issues," says a student. More than 2,100 merit scholarships of $500 to $8,000 are available to outstanding students, and 227 scholarships are awarded each year in nine sports.

Twenty-six percent of students live in the residence halls, which are described as "small but comfortable." Freshmen are required to live on campus; upperclassmen generally flee the dorms in search of off-campus alternatives. Housing comes in a variety of options, including coed, single-sex, and quiet study, and each room has its own Ethernet connection. Campus security is adequate and includes emergency telephones, safety lighting, and late-night shuttle buses. "I believe walking around any campus at night is not the safest thing," says a student, "but Tech has enough security to make me feel safe."

When students want to let their hair down, they tend to stay on-campus. School-sponsored activities, including concerts and lectures, are popular pastimes. "Student organizations are always very active," says a senior. "Social life is one of the factors that draws students to Tech." Alcohol is banned on campus, and students say that alcohol policies are enforced. Still, those under 21 can find a way to imbibe with little difficulty. "The campus has pretty strict alcohol rules," says a junior, "but students can get alcohol very easily." Thirty-six fraternities and sororities attract 14 percent of the men and 20 percent of the women, respectively, and Greek parties are a sure bet for a good time. "Tradition is also a huge part of Tech life," a student says. Popular traditions include the Carol of Lights held each December and the famed Masked Rider, who can be found galloping up and down the sidelines during Texas Tech football games clad in Levis, a red and black cape, and black cowboy hat.

Those yearning to leave behind the hardscrabble plains of Texas can opt to study abroad, while Type-A personalities might want to investigate the MD/MBA Joint Degree Program.

Lubbock, with nearly 200,000 residents, is "too quiet" and "in the middle of nowhere," according to students. Still, "the community and TTU wouldn't be the same without each other," admits a Latin American/Iberian Studies major. Students interact with the community through a variety of service projects, and town-gown relations are friendly. "Lubbock and Tech support one another whole-heartedly," says a senior. Popular road trips include Dallas (320 miles away), New Mexico, and Mexico.

The Texas Tech Red Raiders compete in Division I athletics as members of the Big 12 Conference. When it comes to sports, Texas Tech is the school "where men are men and the women are national champions," according to a junior. Women's basketball is strong, and the Lady Raiders have won the Big 12 championship for the past three years. The men's basketball program faces dramatic changes with the hiring of a new head coach: the high-strung and always-controversial Bobby Knight. The football team draws hordes of rabid fans (remember, this is the South!) who are especially frenzied when Texas A&M or the Texas Longhorns are in town. Other popular sports include men's baseball, golf, and tennis, and women's soccer, track and field, and volleyball. Intramurals attract a dedicated number of weekend athletes.

Administrators at this West Texas university are working hard to put TTU in the nation's academic spotlight. "Our West Texas location makes us distinct and unique from other centrally-located universities," says a senior. Students here take advantage of abundant research opportunities and solid academics while reveling in tradition. For those seeking a dynamic education in a Southern setting, Texas Tech may be worth a look.

Overlaps

N/A.

If You Apply To ➤ **Texas Tech**...Rolling admissions. Financial aid and housing: May 1. Does not guarantee to meet demonstrated need. Campus and alumni interviews: optional, informational. SATs or ACTs: required. SAT IIs: optional. Accepts the Common Application. No essay question.

University of Texas at Austin

John Hargis Hall, Austin, TX 78712-1157

Website: utexas.edu
Location: Urban
Total Enrollment: 48,857
Undergraduates: 35,701
Male/Female: 51/49
SAT Ranges: V 540–650 M 560–660
ACT Range: 23–28
Financial Aid: 46%
Expense: Pub $ $

The University of Texas at Austin has come a long way from where it began as a small school with only one building, eight teachers, two departments, and 221 students. Today, the UT campus is enormous and home to over 48,000 students and 2,700 professors. One of the most popular dorms—Jester Center—even has its own zip code. From its extensive academic programs to its powerful athletic teams to its location in one of the nation's ultimate college towns, the University of Texas has it all.

A 350-acre oasis near downtown Austin, replete with rolling hills, trees, creeks, and fountains, the campus features buildings ranging from "old, distinguished" limestone structures to "contemporary" Southwest architecture. Statues of famous Texans line the mall, and the fabled UT Tower is adorned with a large clock and chimes (a lifesaver for the unorganized). From the steps of the tower, one can see the verdant Austin hills. The outstanding library system at the University of Texas has 6.7 million volumes located in 19 different libraries across campus and is the sixth-largest academic library system in the United States.

UT–Austin is one of the nation's largest single-campus universities. This is great after graduation, if your résumé finds its way to a fellow Longhorn in the workplace. But bigger is not always better, even in Texas. Some undergraduates feel they are treated like livestock; long lines are commonplace, despite a telephone registration system. Many classes are extremely large, and smaller sections fill up quickly. Says a fine arts major, "Sometimes there is difficulty getting into classes, but it usually has to do with not getting the desired prof or schedule." Some students attend summer school, which offers slightly reduced class sizes, in order to graduate in four years. "A few majors actually require five years of school, but an extra year only strengthens your knowledge and educates you more completely," says an architecture major. UT is a research-oriented institution, so the professors are often busy in the laboratories or the library. They do, however, have office hours. "The UT professors are intelligent and communicate well with their students," says a senior. Academic counseling draws praise.

The list of academic strengths at University of Texas is impressive for such a large school. Undergraduate offerings in accounting, architecture, botany, biology, business, foreign languages, and history are first-rate. The engineering and computer science departments are excellent and continue to expand. The English department is huge (95 tenure-track professors) and students give it high marks, but say the art/photography department needs improvement. A new molecular biology building is in the works, and a new telescope is under construction for the prestigious Institute for Fusion Studies which already boasts the world's largest telescope.

The late Pulitzer Prize–winning author James Michener was the major force behind the establishment of the Texas Center for Writers at UT, an interdisciplinary graduate program in fiction, poetry, playwriting, and screenwriting. The Plan II liberal arts honors program, a national model, is one of the oldest honors programs in the country, and one of the best academic deals anywhere. It offers qualified students a flexible curriculum, top-notch professors, small seminar courses, and individualized counseling, and provides them with all of the advantages of a large university in a small-college atmosphere. Business and natural sciences honors programs are also available. Engineering majors can alternate work and study in the co-op program, while education and health majors hold term-time internships. Almost 200 UT undergrads work for lawmakers in the Texas State House, only a 20-minute walk from campus. A strong Reading and Study Skills Lab services students in need of remedial help. Students say the academic climate overall is competitive and rigorous. "You must keep up with your studies in order to be successful," a junior admonishes. Every freshman and transfer student must pass the Texas Academic Skills Program test, followed by courses in English composition, English literature, U.S. history and government, and Texas government. Freshmen can take University 101, which covers everything from major requirements to healthy lifestyle choices and cultural diversity. In addition, the colleges within the university have established the following basic requirements for all majors: four English courses, with two writing-intensive; five courses in social sciences; four courses in natural sciences and math; and one course in the fine arts or humanities.

Four out of every five UT students are Texans. Students say there is no dominant political pattern on campus—despite the fact that historically UT has been integral in the careers of big-time (conservative) Texas politicians. There definitely

(Continued)

Phi Beta Kappa: Yes
Applicants: 14,682
Accepted: 78%
Enrolled: 56%
Grad in 6 Years: N/A
Returning Freshmen: 87%
Academics: ✍ ✍ ✍ ✍
Social: ☎ ☎ ☎ ☎
Q of L: ★ ★ ★ ★
Admissions: (512) 475-7399
Email Address:
  admit@utxdp.dp.utexas.edu

Strongest Programs:
  Business
  Architecture
  Engineering
  Natural Sciences
  Computer Science
  Dance
  Film and Television

The Plan II liberal arts honors program, a national model, is one of the oldest honors programs in the country.

Pulitzer Prize–winning author James Michener, who passed away in 1997, was the major force behind establishing the Texas Center for Writers at UT, an interdisciplinary graduate program in fiction, poetry, playwriting, and screenwriting.

are monied students on campus, along with "nutty granola types" and the jeans-and-sneakers crowd. Austin is the most "liberal" of Texas cities, and there is a little bit of everything both on campus and across the street along "the Drag." "Environmental earthy stuff" is one hot issue these days, and another undergrad mentions that "PC is a must on campus." Hispanics account for 14 percent of students, Asian Americans 13 percent, and African Americans 4 percent. Race has been a touchy issue recently due to court decisions outlawing affirmative action. The university now offers special "welcome programs" for African American and Hispanic students, with social and educational events and peer mentoring. The university also provides thousands of merit scholarships based on academic performance (some set aside for minorities) ranging from $2,000 to $7,000, as well as athletic scholarships in a range of sports.

The university houses only 22 percent of undergraduates because of the student body's sheer size. Once in the dorms, students are guaranteed a room for four years. Accommodations range from functional to plush, and dormies have a variety of living options based on common social and educational interests. "The community showers are always clean," gushes one junior. There are a variety of dining facilities and meal plans, plus numerous fast-food joints within walking distance. Most students live off campus; apartments and condos closest to campus are lovely—and very expensive. More reasonably priced digs can be found in other parts of town, a free shuttle ride away. But be forewarned: UT life requires lots of walking, especially for commuters, with 110 buildings and bus stops and parking lots scattered about. You might not even need to go to the gym!

While not a typical college town (it's the state capital), says a senior, "Austin is a great place to socialize." A senior adds, "Austin is a very student-friendly town. Student discounts are abundant and everywhere feels like a college hang-out." Nightlife centers on nearby Sixth Street, full of pubs and restaurants of all types, and a well-known music scene, with everything from jazz to rock to blues to folk. Numerous microbreweries have opened their doors in the past few years. Halloween draws an estimated 10,000 costumed revelers to Sixth Street (and sometimes up its lampposts). Annual festivals include 40 Acres, a sprawling carnival of all the campus organizations and Eeyore's birthday party, where students pay homage to the A. A. Milne character with food and live music. Two pep rallies get students psyched before the Longhorns play Texas A&M or Oklahoma, their biggest rivals. And Texas Independence Day provides an occasion for celebration in March.

On campus, the Texas Union sponsors movies and social events, and boasts the world's only collection of orange-top pool tables. For those more interested in octaves than eight-balls, the Performing Arts Center has two concert halls that attract nationally known performers. Students hang out at the union's coffee shop or café and the on-campus pub draws top local talent to the stage (but you must be 21 to drink). When the weather gets too muggy (quite often in spring and summer), students head for off-campus campgrounds, lakes, and parks. The most popular road trips are to San Antonio or Dallas. For Spring Break, the students travel to Padre Island, if not New Orleans. Although only 11 percent of the men and 13 percent of the women go Greek, members of fraternities and sororities are "probably highest on the social totem pole," says one student. The chapters tend to be choosy and have high visibility, and have increased in size dramatically over the past year.

Athletics is the lifeblood of most Texans. In fact, the UT Tower is lit in Longhorn orange whenever any school team wins. The students look forward to the annual Texas–Oklahoma football game played in the Cotton Bowl in Dallas,

Almost 200 UT undergrads work for lawmakers in the Texas State House, only a 20-minute walk from campus.

and the Texas A&M–UT game is an incredibly noisy experience you have to see to believe. "Football games pull the student body together and give us a chance to show our school spirit," says one student. Basketball is also popular, and the men's and women's teams regularly reach their respective NCAA tournaments. The baseball program has many alumni in the major leagues, and the annual spring game between UT's baseball alumni and the current college squad is quite a contest. Other top programs nationally for men and women include swimming and diving, and track and field. UT's intramural program is the largest in the nation, and offers weekend athletes access to the same great facilities that the big-time jocks use.

The University of Texas may seem overwhelming because of its imposing size, but students say the school spirit and sense of community found here make it feel smaller. UT also prides itself in having one of the most reasonably priced tuitions in the country, and provides the best all-around educational experience a student could ask for.

Overlaps

Texas A&M, Baylor, Texas Tech, Rice, Southwest Texas State.

If You Apply To ➤

UT…Rolling admissions: Feb. 1. No campus or alumni interviews. Apply either to institution as a whole or particular program. SATs or ACTs: required. SAT IIs: recommended (for placement purposes). Essay question: an event that gives insight into your character; a fictional character who has affected you.

Toronto, University of, Canada—See CANADIAN UNIVERSITIES

Trinity College

300 Summit Street, Hartford, CT 06106

Though it's smack-dab in the middle of decidedly urban—and gritty—Hartford, Connecticut, many of the students at Trinity College have dubbed their little liberal arts institution "Camp Trin-Trin." Whether the moniker stems from the huge "Tropical" party one fraternity throws each year, filling its house basement with sand and digging a pool in its backyard, or from the relaxed week of reading days that precede exams, Trinity offers a unique mix of work and play not in vogue at neighboring Yale or rival Wesleyan. Trinity's academic rigor, caring faculty, and independent students are well known, but its students also take pride in being "wacky" more than once a year.

Splendid Gothic-style stone buildings behind wrought-iron fences decorate this 100-acre campus. There's a large, grassy quadrangle known as the Long Walk, where students play hackeysack, hang out on sunny afternoons, and appreciate the spaciousness and serenity of Trinity's collegiate setting. A current revitalization project will include a new admissions building, new residence halls, and renovations to the library and arts center.

Traditional liberal arts departments win rave reviews from Trin's undergraduates, and the university's 1998 curriculum review has brought sweeping improvements. Trinity is home to the newly minted Jewish Studies major, as well as the BEACON program, which allows biomedical engineering students to enroll in courses at UConn, UConn Health Center, or the University of Hartford, while

Website: www.trincoll.edu
Location: Urban
Total Enrollment: 2,371
Undergraduates: 2,169
Male/Female: 50/50
SAT Ranges: V 590–680 M 590–680
ACT Range: 26–29
Financial Aid: 47%
Expense: Pr $ $ $ $
Phi Beta Kappa: Yes
Applicants: 4,850
Accepted: 38%
Enrolled: 30%
Grad in 6 Years: 85%
Returning Freshmen: 92%
Academics: ✍ ✍ ✍ ✍
Social: ☎ ☎ ☎ ☎

(Continued)

Q of L: ★ ★ ★

Admissions: (860) 297-2180

Email Address:

admissions.office@trincoll
.edu

Strongest Programs:

American Studies

Chemistry

Economics

Engineering

English

History

Philosophy

Political Science

*The InterArts Program
enables a limited number of
first- and second-year
students to study, practice,
and discuss art in an
environment that involves
professors, guest artists, and
a plethora of campus
resources.*

conducting research at three area health centers. The Global Sites program allows students to study with Trinity profs while living in Cape Town, St. Augustine, or Katmandu. A Tutorial College program affords 60 lucky sophomores the opportunity to live with five professors in a close-knit residential college setting. Faculty/student collaboration is something of a tradition at Trinity; last year over 30 percent of the graduating class had collaborated in one form or another with a professor. The Department of Theater and Dance offers an unusually integrated major in these disciplines, and sponsors the related LaMaMa arts study abroad program (in New York City and Europe) for all interested juniors and seniors. Interdisciplinary programs in neuroscience and women's studies win praise, too. But offerings in the educational studies department are limited, and students must utilize the resources of the Hartford higher-education consortium to take the methods courses needed for certification.

To graduate from Trinity, students must demonstrate proficiency in writing and math, and pass a five-part distribution requirement, taking one course in each of the following fields: arts, humanities, natural sciences, numerical and symbolic reasoning, and social sciences. Freshmen have the option of taking First-Year Seminars, which explore modes of thought and methods of analysis, emphasizing writing, speaking, and critical thinking. All the participants in a particular First-Year Seminar live in the same dorm, and their instructor serves as their academic advisor until they declare their majors two years later.

Qualified freshmen may also enter one of three demanding, cross-disciplinary guided-studies programs in the humanities, natural sciences, or the history, culture, and future of cities. Upperclassmen may devote a full semester to intensive study of a single broad theme within their major, taking either three related courses and an integrating seminar or simply setting up a series of group tutorials and independent studies. Trinity's small but professionally and educationally accredited engineering program, rare at small colleges, sponsors the Fire-Fighting Home Robot Contest, the largest public robotics competition in the U.S., open to entrants of any age, ability, and experience. In addition, the school runs an extensive internship program with Hartford businesses and government agencies, in which 60 percent of students participate. Visiting arrangements are made through the Twelve-College Exchange Program.* Trinity students may also opt to participate in the Mystic Seaport term,* study Italian language and art history at the college's own campus in Rome, or try out their Spanish at the University of Cordoba. In fact, travel abroad to more than 40 countries is a popular option, and nearly half of each class studies overseas. The InterArts Program enables a limited number of first- and second-year students to study, practice, and discuss art in an environment that involves professors, guest artists, and a plethora of campus resources.

Despite its high-powered resources, the scholastic climate at Trinity is somewhat mixed. Professors are stern graders, and the student body has its share of overachievers. As one senior explains, "Students decide exactly how hard they will study, but all are expected to do so with intensity and earnest effort." A classmate agrees, saying, "I do not feel excessive competitiveness." Part of this attitude is due to the quality of the faculty, to whom students give the thumbs-up. " All students are taught by full professors and the quality of teaching is above and beyond the call of duty," says an English major. The 1 million-volume library, which operates on an open-stack basis, is good but can get noisy in the evening, as some students prefer socializing to studying.

Important issues on Trinity's campus these days include respect for alternative sexualities, racism, sexual assault, and the Greek system, which is now coed.

People of color constitute 16 percent of the student body (including 6 percent African American, 5 percent Hispanic, and 5 percent Asian American). A senior says that's not enough: "Trinity is still a very preppy and conservative school with too little diversity." Those concerned about expenses might be interested to note that Trinity not only carries an expensive price tag, but is still not need-blind in its admissions, though the school guarantees to meet the full demonstrated need of every admit. No scholarships, be they merit or athletic, are available.

Ninety-six percent of undergraduates live in the dorms, all of which are coed. The housing situation is a mixed bag, which the sophomores, curiously, are left holding. (All students are guaranteed rooms, but lottery numbers are assigned on the basis of seniority and quality of previous rooms, and sophomores can get squeezed.) Room options include singles, doubles, quads, kitchen units, and theme houses for those interested in music, community service, wellness, art, and quiet. Living off campus is another option, but in the words of an economics major, "I tried it, regretted it, and am now back on campus." Best bets for freshmen include Elton and Jones, and freshmen must eat in Trinity's dining hall, but dining facilities and options have been significantly upgraded in recent years. The Bistro, an upscale but reasonable café, is another choice for students wishing to use their meal plans. Others hibernate in the Cave, a campus sandwich and grill spot.

When studying is over, or even when it isn't, there's plenty to do for fun here. Minutes away by bus or college-sponsored "culture van" is downtown Hartford, with its symphony and the nation's oldest public art museum. Students have mixed feelings about the city—"surrounding blocks, while not bad, can turn students away," admits a senior—and the school makes sure students consider safety, even on campus. The school has plenty of security officers (on 24-hour patrol), good lighting, a shuttle service in the evenings, and safety education programs. "Campus safety is proactive [that's their buzzword]," says a poli sci major. "In four years here, I have never, ever felt threatened on my campus." More than two-thirds of the student body take part in a Community Outreach volunteer program, the largest student activity group on campus.

The coed Greek organizations command the allegiance of about 19 percent of the student population. Affiliated students and independents party on what one sophomore bio major described as Trinity's "wet" booze-ridden campus or make excursions to local cafés and bars—including the Tap, the Brickyard, No Name, Voodoo Lounge, and ZuZu's. More restrained partyers frequent the Underground Coffeehouse or the weekly comedy nights at the Bistro, and more than 70 extracurricular organizations also beckon, including the newspaper, a ski club, a theater club, and Cinestudio, a popular student-run movie theater.

Athletics are a top priority for most students, especially when Williams or Wesleyan or Amherst is the opponent, and Trinity boasts championship teams in men's and women's basketball and squash, football, field hockey, and men's ice hockey. The school also boasts gym facilities specifically for women, including locker rooms, crew tanks, and weight rooms, and there is a new pool and squash courts.

Despite its image as a fall-back for prestigious peers like Amherst and Wesleyan, Trinity remains ahead of the curve in liberal arts education. Its urban location, high-quality faculty, superb facilities, and motivated students make Trinity an exciting, energizing place to spend four years. "You can have a very balanced life here at Trinity—socialize, join clubs, participate in a sport—while still achieving good grades," says a senior. "It's a place where you are encouraged to do or try everything."

A multilevel, interdisciplinary program on decolonization started in 1997, involving 40 courses in 15 disciplines, a film series, and a lecture-panel discussion series.

Overlaps

Boston College, Tufts, Connecticut College, Boston University, Wesleyan.

Trinity University

715 Stadium Drive, San Antonio, TX 78212-7200

Website: www.trinity.edu
Location: Suburban
Total Enrollment: 2,571
Undergraduates: 2,323
Male/Female: 47/53
SAT Ranges: V 580–680 M 590–690
ACT Range: 26–30
Financial Aid: 42%
Expense: Pr $
Phi Beta Kappa: Yes
Applicants: 2,811
Accepted: 75%
Enrolled: 31%
Grad in 6 Years: 77%
Returning Freshmen: 86%
Academics: ✍ ✍ ✍
Social: ☎ ☎ ☎
Q of L: ★ ★ ★
Admissions: (800) TRINITY
Email Address:
admissions@trinity.edu

Strongest Programs:
Business
Economics
History
English
Biology
Education
Engineering

Trinity University is a small school with big bucks. Thanks to bequests from benevolent Texas oilmen, Trinity has one of the nation's largest and fastest-growing educational endowments for a school its size. The wealth is used unashamedly to lure capable students with bargain tuition rates, and to entice talented professors with Texas-sized salaries. The result? A student body comprised of smart, ambitious men and women, and a faculty that is knowledgeable and caring. Students here enjoy challenges, but still manage a laid-back Texas attitude. "It's not 'work hard, party hard,'" says a student. "It's more like 'have fun while working.'"

Founded around the time of the Civil War, Trinity began in the tiny central Texas town of Tehuacana, moved to Waxahachie, and then, in 1942, pulled up stakes and settled on a campus on the west side of San Antonio. Ten years later, the school moved to its current location, in a residential area about three miles from downtown San Antonio, one of the most beautiful cities in the Southwest. The 117-acre campus, filled with the Southern architecture of O'Neill Ford, is located on what was once a rock quarry. Everything fits the school's somewhat well-to-do image, from the uniform redbrick buildings to the cobblestones in pathways that wind along gorgeous green lawns and through immaculate gardens spotted with Henry Moore sculptures. Trinity's most dominant landmark is Murchison Tower, which rises in the center of campus and is visible from numerous vantage points throughout San Antonio.

The school makes a strong effort to maintain its strict admissions standards, keeping a small enrollment, tightening the grading system, and recruiting high achievers with greater energy than is possible from larger universities. The university has set its sights on becoming the premier small liberal arts school in the Southwest. "Trinity is extremely committed to providing the best possible education for its students," says an English and biology double major. Students report that the academics are very rigorous. "Courses are demanding, especially in the humanities," confides a student. "All of the classes require enormous amounts of study time." Forty-eight percent of students come from the top tenth of their high school class. The professors at Trinity are described as "knowledgeable" and "accessible." "Professors here truly care and go beyond the call of duty to make sure the students have every possible opportunity to succeed," says a religion major. Another student adds, "The professors I have experienced have been extremely qualified and enlightening, and many hold national distinctions for research in their field." Trinity has a highly praised education department, with a five-year MAT program, and a good premed program. Other strong departments include English, economics, business, and engineering. The communications department offers students hands-on training with television equipment or the chance to produce a newscast. Accounting majors are offered a chance to serve an internship with the Big-Six accounting firms in San Antonio, Houston, Dallas, or Austin, while earning a salary and receiving college credit. Students say the art, drama, psychology, and physical education departments are weak.

Trinity's answer to general education requirements is the Common Curriculum, an extensive list of mandatory courses including a first-year seminar dealing with a common theme, such as Justice and Human Rights or Freedom and Responsibility, and a writing seminar. Students must also take courses from five fundamental areas, called "Understandings," which include Western and one other culture, the role of values, and human social context. The common curriculum is popular with students, especially because its courses are taught by full-time faculty. As a member of the Twelve-College Exchange* and the Associated Colleges of the South* programs, Trinity approves a number of study abroad programs and encourages premed and prelaw students, as well as history and English majors, to take advantage of them. Another feature of Trinity's curriculum is an opportunity for students to participate in research projects with faculty mentors. Some students even present their findings at professional conferences or have them published in professional journals.

Almost all classes at Trinity have 50 or fewer students, and freshmen are assigned to mentor groups of 10 to 15 students for academic and guidance counseling, as well as peer tutoring from upperclassmen. "My advisors bend over backward to help me (I'm clueless as to what I want to do)," a senior chemistry major reports. Most students get the courses they want at registration and can be "pink-slipped" in if a class is closed, though they may have to wait a semester or two for a common curriculum course.

Sixty-seven percent of Trinity students are Texans. About 20 percent of the student body represent minority groups; Hispanics alone account for slightly above 9 percent, Asian Americans another 9 percent, and African Americans 3 percent. "The typical student was your above-average overachiever in high school," says a junior. A senior adds, "Students are involved and tend to over-extend themselves." Hot campus issues include gender issues, gay and lesbian rights, and abortion.

Seventy-eight percent of Trinity's students live on campus, but that's partly because Trinity requires students to do so through their junior year. Still, the residence halls are beautiful and spacious; most rooms are two-person suites with balconies, and maids clean the bathroom (which two suites share) and vacuum the floor once a week. Dorms are coed, with one single-sex residence hall that is off-limits to freshmen; all dorms are now wired for cable and the Internet. Most seniors move off campus so that they can have single rooms. Students say San Antonio is a tourist town, not a college town, but it boasts a Sea World, outdoor shops, and cafés at the Riverwalk, and many cultural and musical attractions. Students get involved in city life through the Trinity University Volunteer Action Center.

Soccer and volleyball are popular on campus, and football draws decent crowds, especially because the team improved of late. But students really get a kick out of intramurals. With athletic fields and a renovated and expanded athletic facility, there's lots of room to frolic and play. In fact, a junior laments, with so many things going on, "people get spread too thin—so many activities, difficult classes, and not enough sleep!"

Weekends find students at local bars, fraternity parties, or other on-campus events. Twenty-six percent of the men and 28 percent of the women in the

Accounting majors are offered a chance to serve an internship with the Big-Six accounting firms in San Antonio, Houston, Dallas, or Austin, while earning a salary and receiving college credit.

The communications department offers students hands-on training with television equipment or the chance to produce a newscast.

student body join the local fraternity and sorority organizations, but "it is not necessary to be Greek to be social." Country line-dancing is also a popular activity, and the university sponsors an excellent lecture series that brings notable politicians and public figures to campus. Alcohol may not be consumed on campus except by those of legal age in one of four "wet" dorms, but "it's easy to get away with it in your dorms if you don't draw attention to yourself," a student says. Underage students caught drinking must go before a student court, but punishments tend to be lenient.

San Antonio's warm weather provides ample opportunities for spring fever—even in January. The Texas Hill Country, with its trees, rivers, wildflowers, and charming small towns, is an hour's drive northwest of San Antonio and is a popular destination for weekend adventures. The funky state capital of Austin is 70 miles north, and students also can roadtrip internationally—to nearby Mexico. An annual event most students look forward to is Fiesta, a weeklong celebration of San Antonio's mixed culture that features bands, dancing, food, and drink. They also anticipate the Tigerfest dance and parade on homecoming weekend, the "Spontaneous Erections" of art by various student groups, and a Chili Cook-Off that pits Greek and other clubs against one another. The school year kicks off with a party at the school's bell tower, which students can climb to get a knockout view of San Antonio.

Trinity University offers its students a small-school atmosphere along with all the advantages of a much larger institution: challenging academics, top-notch professors, and abundant social activities all wrapped up with a hefty endowment.

> ## Overlaps
>
> **University of Texas, Texas A&M, Rice, Tulane, Vanderbilt.**

If You Apply To ➤ **Trinity University**...Early decision: Nov. 15. Early action: Dec. 15. Regular admissions: Jan. 15. Financial aid: Feb. 1. Guarantees to meet demonstrated need. Campus interviews: optional, informative. No alumni interviews. SATs or ACT: required. SAT IIs: optional. Accepts the Common Application. Essay question: describe a person, place, or event that has had a significant impact on you.

Truman State University

(formerly Northeast Missouri State University)

McClain Hall, Room 205, Kirksville, MO 63501

Website: www.truman.edu
Location: Small town
Total Enrollment: 6,236
Undergraduates: 5,963
Male/Female: 41/59
SAT Ranges: V 560–670 M 560–670
ACT Range: 25–30
Financial Aid: 34%
Expense: Pub $ $
Phi Beta Kappa: No

While students at Truman State University were growing up, their future school was undergoing a major metamorphosis. The campus was transformed from a regional comprehensive university to the state's flagship liberal arts institution. In 1996, the school's name was changed (from Northeast Missouri State University) to honor one of the state's favorite sons, former President Harry S. Truman. Students and faculty say this institution is on a quest for academic excellence and increased personal attention. "The staff and faculty delight in your success," says a senior. "You are not just a number here—you are a name, a face, a success story."

Truman is located in northeast Missouri, approximately 200 miles from both Kansas City and St. Louis. The campus is spread over 140 acres and includes 39 buildings that reflect aesthetic details of the Georgian style. The oldest portion of the campus, which dates back to 1873, is based on Thomas Jefferson's University of Virginia. Renovations are currently under way on the Ophelia Parrish classroom building to transform it into the Truman Fine Arts Center. This $20-million facility will include an art gallery, performing arts center, art studios, practice facilities, and a black box theater. In addition, Truman just opened Violette Hall, its largest academic facility with state-of-the-art classrooms that have laptop connections at each seat.

Although Truman is a preprofessional school, liberal arts studies form the cornerstone of its educational philosophy. The foundation consists of courses in communications, mathematics and science, humanities, foreign language, and social science. Students must also complete courses that are specific to their chosen academic program, and freshmen are required to attend an orientation program known as Freshmen Week. Strong programs include hard sciences such as chemistry and biology, and the education department. Students say they try to avoid the math department. The university, striving to strengthen its weaker programs, trimmed its offerings from 140 programs in 1986 to 43 today. Undergrads are encouraged to participate in research with faculty members. More than 270 students presented their research projects at the 1999 Undergraduate Research Symposium. For study abroad opportunities, Truman is a member of the College Consortium for International Studies and the Council on International Educational Exchange. The college also offers hands-on internships in Washington, D.C.

A business and computer science dual major describes the academic climate this way: "The courses at Truman are very challenging, and it takes a great deal of work to keep up." Still, students are pleased with the quality of teaching. "The professors truly care about their students and want them to succeed," says a psychology major. Another student adds, "The professors are accessible and want to get to know their students." Students offer mixed reviews of academic advisors, saying some faculty members can't help them navigate the system. Career counseling, though, receives positive feedback.

Nearly three-quarters of the student body hail from Missouri, and 45 percent graduated in the top tenth of their high school class. Minority students make up 7 percent of the student body. "Some students are concerned with diversity on campus, however there isn't a big push to improve," says one junior. "It is a somewhat conservative campus, making political correctness not a huge concern." A variety of multicultural awareness programs have been integrated into the freshman orientation week and throughout the school year. Truman offers more than 3,100 merit scholarships ranging from $250 to full tuition. The school does not guarantee to meet the full demonstrated financial need of every admit, but 83 percent of those who apply for aid are offered a substantial package. Either way, the school's annual price tag is a bargain by most standards.

All freshmen must live on campus, and the dorms are said to be comfortable if not a little small. Accommodations in the eight residence halls and three apartment complexes vary widely. Several dorms are even considered "residential colleges," where students and faculty live and interact together. Although some of the dorms are old and that has been problem in the past, the housing situation is starting to improve. Renovations have provided the dorms with new bathrooms, carpeting, and movable furniture. Fifty-seven percent of students choose to live off campus. "The cost of living in Kirksville is not very high, so for students paying room and board, it is sometimes cheaper to live off campus," a sophomore says.

Students say Kirksville is not really a college town. "The town is a small, farming community," says a business/computer science major. "Not a very happening college town, but you find things to do if you are creative. There are lots of ways

(Continued)
Applicants: 5,159
Accepted: 81%
Enrolled: 35%
Grad in 6 Years: 64%
Returning Freshmen: 84%
Academics: ✍ ✍ ✍
Social: ☎ ☎ ☎
Q of L: ★ ★ ★
Admissions: (660) 785-4114
Email Address:
  admissions@truman.edu

Strongest Programs:
  Accounting
  Political Science
  Education
  Business
  Math
  Nursing
  Biology
  English

Undergrads are encouraged to participate in research with faculty members.

For study abroad opportunities, Truman is a member of the College Consortium for International Studies and the Council on International Educational Exchange.

to get involved in the community." The social activities are plentiful both on campus and off. Greek organizations claim 30 percent of the men and 21 percent of the women, and dominate the nightlife, especially since the campus is dry. But independents need not fear: the Student Activities Board regularly sponsors concerts, movies, dances, and excursions. Upperclassmen tend to go drinking and dancing off campus, where the liquor is more readily available. Truman Day, Homecoming, and Dog Days are three annual events the students look forward to. Most students are able to find entertainment nearby. If not, there are always road trips to St. Louis or Chicago.

Sports are popular at Truman, and the Bulldog basketball team never fails to draw a large crowd. Football does, too, but bragging rights for best squads on campus go to women's tennis, men's cross-country, and men's soccer, who all finished first in the MIAA Conference recently. The oldest Division II rivalry, called the "Hickory stick game" is between Truman and Northwest Missouri. Nonvarsity types stretch their muscles in one of the many intramural events sponsored by the university. Some other traditions: seniors like to play in the campus fountain before they graduate, and many students stick chewing gum on the gum tree in hopes of getting an "A" on their next test. That is, until the tree was recently stolen.

For variety and personal atmosphere, Truman is a good choice. With a new name and a new attitude, it has aptly proved that it's an up-and-coming university, looking to make a solid reputation for itself.

Overlaps

University of Missouri, Saint Louis University, Southwest Missouri State, University of Illinois, Washington University (MO).

If You Apply To ➤ **Truman State University**…Early action: Nov. 15. Regular admissions: Mar. 1. Financial aid: Apr. 1. Housing: May 1. Meets demonstrated need of 83%. Campus interviews: recommended, informational. No alumni interviews. SAT I or ACTs: required. SAT IIs: optional. Accepts the Common Application and electronic applications. Essay question: important change in American education; benefits and problems of computer technology; living person whom you would nominate as a "national living treasure" and why.

Tufts University

Bendetson Hall, Medford, MA 02155

Website: www.tufts.edu
Location: Suburban
Total Enrollment: 8,876
Undergraduates: 4,791
Male/Female: 48/52
SAT Ranges: V 610–700 M 640–720
ACT Range: 27–31
Financial Aid: 39%
Expense: Pr $ $ $ $
Phi Beta Kappa: Yes
Applicants: 12,366
Accepted: 33%

Some academic superstars used to consider Tufts University a safety school, a respectable place to go if you didn't get into Penn or Cornell. But Tufts isn't so safe anymore, at least not when it comes to admissions. Applications are up dramatically, propelling Tufts into the ranks of the most competitive schools in the country (only one in three applicants are accepted). With its strong academics, high-achieving student body, and an attractive setting, some would say that not much more separates Tufts University from its illustrious neighbors, Harvard and MIT, than a few stops on the "T."

Tufts's 150-acre tree-lined, hilltop campus overlooks the heart of nearby Boston and is a striking scene. The main campus, with its brick and stone buildings, sits on the Medford/Somerville boundary. Medford, the fifth-oldest city in the country, was a powerful shipbuilding center during the 19th century. Somerville, the historic Revolutionary powder house, lies adjacent to the Tufts campus, and in 1776, the first American flag was raised on its Prospect Hill. Recent construction includes a five-story parking garage and $20 million field house.

For years, Tufts has devoted resources to traditional areas of graduate strength—medicine, dentistry, law, and diplomacy—as well as new ventures, such as a Nutrition Research Center. Such additions had only a peripheral impact on the liberal arts and engineering colleges, but Tufts has made a noticeable commitment to facilities that primarily benefit undergraduates. Recent additions include the high-tech project development laboratory for student design projects, a $21-million addition to the Tisch library, which doubled its size, and the renovation of the chemistry research building, which allowed more lab space for undergraduate research. On the nonacademic but all-important quality-of-life side, Tufts renovated the Dewick/Macphie Dining Hall, which added a food court with 13 individual prep stations, such as a noodle bar, wok station, and vegetarian grill, built a new intramural gymnasium, and hardwired all dormitory rooms for Internet, email, and voice mail access. Tufts is conspicuously committed to self-improvement.

Despite the recent flurry of expansion, undergraduate teaching is what attracts students. They get highly personalized attention from faculty, and they enjoy wide freedom to design their own majors, pursue independent study, and do research and internships for credit. Strong departments include international relations, political science, biology, engineering, drama, and languages, and there is an excellent child-study program. The most popular major is international relations, followed by biology, economics, English, and psychology.

While upper-level courses are reasonably sized (with an average of about 25 students), intro lectures can be quite large. Tufts has two popular programs in which students who need a break from being students can develop and teach courses: the 31-year-old Experimental College, which annually offers more than 100 nontraditional, full-credit courses taught by students, faculty, and outside lecturers; and the Freshman Explorations seminars, each taught by two upperclassmen and a faculty member to between 10 and 15 students. With topics ranging from media and politics to juggling, Exploration courses are a way for freshmen to get to know each other and ease into the college experience, since the teachers double as advisors.

Tufts students also get a healthy diet of traditional academic fare. Distribution requirements include a new World Civilization course in addition to art, English and foreign languages, social sciences, humanities, natural sciences, and math. Engineers only have an English requirement in addition to the standard math, science, and technically oriented curriculum, but they must complete 38 credits compared to the liberal arts students' 34. According to the administration, preparing students "to make the Global Village safe" is a central goal, and annually 35 to 40 percent of the junior class studies abroad. Ambitious students may enroll in five-year joint-degree programs with the university's School of the Museum of Fine Arts, the New England Conservatory of Music, and the famed Fletcher School of Law and Diplomacy, or they may pack their suitcases for engineering and liberal arts programs in England, Germany, France, Spain, and Russia. Back home, Tufts offers the Washington Semester,* the Mystic Seaport program,* an exchange with Swarthmore, and cross-registration at a number of Boston schools.

The biggest homeland of the student body is Massachusetts (21 percent). New Jersey, New York, and California are also well represented, but students hail from all 50 states and 61 countries. The university's reputation in international relations also attracts a substantial number of foreign students (8 percent) and Americans living abroad. Asian Americans make up 14 percent of the population, Hispanics 6 percent, and African Americans 5 percent. Political liberals outnumber conservatives. In general, Tufts undergraduates tend to be a little less

(Continued)

Enrolled: 30%
Grad in 6 Years: 87%
Returning Freshmen: 95%
Academics: ✍ ✍ ✍ ✍
Social: ☎ ☎ ☎
Q of L: ★ ★ ★
Admissions: (617) 627-3170
Email Address:
  uadmiss-inquiry
  @infonet.tufts.edu

Strongest Programs:
  Engineering Technology
  Center
  Center for Environmental
  Management
  Center for Materials and
  Interfaces
  Electro-Optics Technology
  Center
  Experimental College
  International Relations

competitive and a bit more easygoing than their counterparts at places like Harvard. You are expected to do more than absorb, memorize, and regurgitate. Professors are looking for thoughtfulness, and "many students compete with themselves but not with each other," says one student. No merit or athletic scholarships are available, but several prepayment and loan options are, and in the past, the school has met the full demonstrated need of all admits.

Accommodations in the Uphill and Downhill (the two quads joined by a great expanse of grass and trees) campus dorms vary from long hallways of double rooms to apartment-like suites, old houses, and co-ops. A good-natured rivalry exists between the two areas; Uphill is closer to the humanities and social sciences classrooms and supposedly a little more social, while Downhill is nearer the science facilities. Freshmen and sophomores must live on campus in the dorms, while upperclassmen compete in a lottery. Students and administration agree that the addition of South Hall makes housing available to just about anyone who wants a room. Apartments are plentiful and, according to at least one student, "affordable." Still, 20 percent of the students live off campus. All but one of the dorms are coed by floor or suite or alternating rooms. Food plans for 5, 10, 14, or 20 meals a week are offered to everyone but freshmen, who must choose one of the last two options. Kosher and vegetarian meals are available, and occasional special meals (e.g., Italian night and Mexican night) spice up standard college cuisine.

While suburban Medford is not very exciting for those of the college class, the "T" metro system extends to the Tufts campus, so it's easy to make a quick jaunt to "student city" (a.k.a. Boston) for work or play. Harvard Square is even nearer and provides plenty of restaurants, nightlife, and music stores. For those with valid IDs, the campus pub has become an "in" place to hang out, especially Monday through Thursday nights. Tufts, incidentally, has earned a national reputation for its programs to promote the "responsible" use of alcohol.

A small band of 13 fraternities and 3 sororities provides many of the on-campus weekend parties, though only 15 percent of the men and 3 percent of the women join the Greek system, and there is talk of getting rid of it altogether. University-sponsored activities include concerts, plays (there are 15 to 20 productions each year at Aidekman Arts Center), parties, etc., and there are $2 movies on Wednesday and weekend nights. Major campus events in the fall include Homecoming and Halloween on the Hill, the latter of which is a carnival for children in the community. At the end of finals week in December, the "students turn out by the hundreds and watch and participate in the Naked Quad Run!" confesses one student. In the spring, there is Tuftsfest, a month–long affair with festivals, an interdorm Olympics, a semiformal dance, and Spring Fling, an end-of-year hurrah. Of all student activities, the largest by far, with more than 500 students, is the Leonard Carmichael Society, the umbrella group for all volunteer activities. The students are involved in programs of adult literacy, blood drives, elderly outreach, English as a second language teaching, hunger projects, tutoring, low-income housing construction, and active work with the homeless and battered women.

The Tufts sailing team has won the Fowle trophy for the best overall collegiate sailing team in North America numerous times, the baseball team is strong, too. As a Division III school, Tufts is no sports powerhouse, but many of its 33 varsity teams are competitive on the regional level, and the school boasts an impressive number of all-American athletes. The intramural gym and athletic facility upgrades make sports more accessible to jocks of all stripes.

Tufts is in the midst of a modern day renaissance, or what many universities know as a capital campaign. Money raised already is allowing Tufts to improve campus facilities and financial aid for students. This, along with a swelling applicant pool, makes Tufts a much hotter school than it was just a few years ago. And its proximity to Boston, an intellectual and educational Mecca, makes it even more attractive than were it in, say, Detroit. Tufts gives every indication that it's going to keep scaling the university ranks until it reaches the summit—and that's not too far from Prospect Hill.

If You Apply To ➤

Tufts…Early decision: Nov. 15, Jan. 1. Regular admissions: Jan. 1. Financial aid: Mar. 1. Housing: June 1. No campus interviews. Alumni interviews: recommended, informational. ACTs or SATs and 3 SAT IIs: required. Guarantees to meet demonstrated need. Accepts the Common Application and electronic applications. Essay question: two Common Application essays or choose from following: how you were shaped by your environment; why have you chosen to be a leader; how have you demonstrated citizenship. Apply directly to either the College of Liberal Arts or Engineering.

Tulane University

6823 St. Charles Avenue, New Orleans, LA 70118

New Orleans—a diverse metropolitan city with much excitement and a rich history. Not to mention the exotic foods, soulful jazz, and lively people. And nowhere is the playful flavor of this city more evident than on the campus of Tulane University. "New Orleans is the dream college town," says an enthusiastic junior. "The students more or less own the city." Aside from its prime location, Tulane offers all the charm of the South, and all the charge of a quality education.

The school's lovely 110-acre campus is located in an attractive residential area of uptown New Orleans, about 15 minutes from the French Quarter and the business district. Tulane's administration building, Gibson Hall, faces St. Charles Avenue, where one of the nation's last streetcar lines still clatters past mansions. Across the street is Audubon Park, a 385-acre spread where students jog, walk, study, or feed the ducks in the lagoon. The buildings of gray stone and pillared brick are modeled after the neocollegiate/Creole mixture indigenous to Louisiana institutional-type structures. One particular point of pride is the university's 13 Tiffany windows, one of the largest collections in existence.

Tulane's strength lies in the natural sciences, environmental sciences, and the humanities; international studies and Latin American studies in particular are especially strong. The Stone Center for Latin American studies includes the 200,000-volume Latin American Library and offers more than 150 courses taught by 80 faculty members. An interdisciplinary program in political economy (economics, political science, and philosophy) stands out among the social sciences and is very popular with prelaw students. Those undergraduates ready to focus on a career may apply to Tulane's respected schools of engineering (biomedical engineering is particularly good), architecture, and business, as well as the highly acclaimed medical and law schools. Environmental studies majors benefit from the Tulane/Xavier Center for Bioenvironmental Research, where faculty members and students work together on research projects that include hazardous waste remediation and the ecological effects of environmental contaminants. Tulane offers several study abroad options, including one-semester programs to locations such as Japan to study sociology and culture, Mexico City to delve into the

Website: www.tulane.edu
Location: Urban
Total Enrollment: 11,945
Undergraduates: 7,170
Male/Female: 47/53
SAT Ranges: V 600–690 M 590–680
Financial Aid: 55%
Expense: Pr $ $ $ $
Phi Beta Kappa: Yes
Applicants: 8,189
Accepted: 78%
Enrolled: 24%
Grad in 6 Years: 72%
Returning Freshmen: 86%
Academics: ✍ ✍ ✍
Social: ☎ ☎ ☎ ☎
Q of L: ★ ★ ★
Admissions: (504) 865-5000
Email Address: undergrad.admission@tulane.edu

Strongest Programs:
Engineering
Business
Psychology
History

language, and London to study liberal arts. In addition, the Tulane/Newcomb Junior Year Abroad program is one of the country's oldest and most prestigious programs, in which the student is fully immersed in the language and culture of the particular country. Other academic programs include Religious Traditions in the West, an interdisciplinary major designed to introduce students to the study of Western religion traditions, and a major in Music Performance or Composition. For students looking to go into medical or law school, approximately 66 percent of graduates are accepted.

Here's something else to consider: Tulane lavishes its academic and physical resources on an undergraduate student body of fewer than 8,000. Perhaps that's one reason why Tulane has produced seven Marshall scholars in as many years. Sixty-five percent of the classes at Tulane have fewer than 25 students, while an additional one-fourth have fewer than 50, making it difficult for students to get into the classes of their choice. About 60 percent of those classes are taught by full professors. Graduate instructors are most likely to teach the beginning-level classes in English, foreign languages, and math, and are rarely found in the schools of business, architecture, or engineering. Overall, students praise Tulane's faculty. "The one thing I have found is that teaching is student-oriented, professors are always available to review material a different way to help you understand it," explains a junior. As you might expect, the academic atmosphere can be very intense, depending on the class.

All Tulane liberal arts majors must complete a rigorous set of general education requirements. Besides demonstrating competency in English, math, and a foreign language, these requirements mandate that students take distribution requirements in the humanities and fine arts, the social sciences, and mathematics and the sciences. In the process of satisfying the requirements, students must take at least one course in Western and non-Western civilization, as well as a writing intensive class. Each year the university's highly acclaimed honors program invites about 700 outstanding students, known as Tulane Scholars, to partake in accelerated courses taught by top professors and never exceeding 20 students. These select scholars also have the opportunity to design their own major and spend their junior year abroad.

While Tulane has a somewhat Southern feel, it is a sophisticated and cosmopolitan institution. Says one student, "There is a large Northeastern constituency here who have brought their Type-A personalities and racial tolerance down to a Southern city. If you're a Northerner, it's impossible to escape the Southern influence of the city, and if you're a Southerner, it's impossible to escape the Northern influence that exists on campus." Over 20 percent of the students are minorities, about half of whom are African American. Tulane awards merit scholarships, ranging from $10,000 up to full tuition, and another 210 athletic scholarships for student athletes. For those concerned about the high price tag, take note: the financial aid office offers a variety of "creative financing" methods.

Though residence halls are not given rave reviews, students say they are improving and the university has spent $70 million on the construction and renovation of new dorms. "With a new dorm every other year, the housing situation is getting better," explains one junior. "Three years ago freshman housing was the oldest rooms on campus, now they are among the newest." Except for local students, freshmen must live on campus and leave their cars at home. After freshman year, housing is by lottery, and choices include Stadium Place, a student apartment complex. Many students opt to move off campus, claiming that it's much cheaper than university housing, but others are concerned about the safety factor of living in New Orleans. Amenities are numerous for the 89 percent who

The Tulane/Newcomb Junior Year Abroad program is one of the country's oldest and most prestigious programs, in which the student is fully immersed in the language and culture of the particular country.

stay on campus, including air conditioners and VCRs that can be checked out with a student ID. There are also special-interest floors, such as Healthy Lifestyles or Women in Science. Some men live in their fraternity houses, but sororities only have social halls due to an old New Orleans law that makes it immoral to have more than four unrelated women living in one house. Freshmen have to stomach the cost of Tulane's meal plan, but alternatives exist at the remodeled University Center food court.

While schoolwork is taken seriously at Tulane, so are sports. The campus-wide acclaim for men's basketball borders on hysteria. Because the basketball arena seats only 3,600, causing students to camp out to buy tickets for big games, Tulane basketball benefits from a new arena adjacent to the Louisiana Superdome. The football team isn't as talented, but draws a loyal following nonetheless. Women's tennis and volleyball and men's baseball traditionally have winning teams, and the women's basketball team has made several NCAA appearances. Club sports are big and students can also opt for weight work, squash, or swimming among other options at the Reily Recreational Center.

Social life at Tulane goes almost without saying. "New Orleans itself never stops partying!" boasts a junior. Fraternities and sororities are strong—16 percent of the men and 19 percent of the women join—but do not "dominate" the social life. With the nightlife of New Orleans just 15 minutes away, students can head off campus to the many offbeat cafés and clubs in the French Quarter. Though you're supposed to be 21 to buy alcohol or enjoy the bar scene, a sophomore explains that "alcohol is accessible." Mardi Gras is such a celebration that classes are suspended for two days and students from all over the country pour in to celebrate. An annual Jazzfest in the spring also draws wide participation. Road-trip destinations include the Gulf Coast, Mississippi, Houston, Atlanta, and Memphis.

While Tulane is rich in Southern tradition, it is a forward-looking school where the possibilities seem endless. And like its hometown, it is a diverse, energetic melting pot of interests and activity with caring professors and eager minds. And when the work is done: *Laissez les bon temps roulet!* (Let the good times roll!)

Mardi Gras is such a celebration that classes are suspended for two days and students from all over the country pour in to celebrate.

Overlaps

Emory, Boston University, Vanderbilt, Duke, University of Texas.

If You Apply To ➤ **Tulane**…Early action: Nov. 1. Regular admissions: Jan. 15. Financial aid: Jan. 15. Housing: May 1. Meets demonstrated need of 77%. Campus and alumni interviews: optional, informational. SATs or ACTs: required. SAT IIs: recommended (home-schooled applicants only). Accepts the Common Application and electronic applications. Essay question: personal statement.

University of Tulsa

600 South College Avenue, Tulsa, OK 74104

The University of Tulsa has an unusual predicament: A private liberal arts college in an area of the country where most education is public, it's closer in size to small Northeastern institutions than to the large, Midwestern state schools that surround it. And compared to its public competition, Tulsa's tuition is relatively low. So the school is stuck in a battle over its future: should it stress traditional liberal arts or more easily marketed career programs? It has settled on a mixture of the two.

TU's 230-acre campus is just three miles from downtown Tulsa, and there's a

Website: www.utulsa.edu
Location: Suburban
Total Enrollment: 4,192
Undergraduates: 2,924
Male/Female: 48/52

(Continued)

SAT Ranges: V 540–670 M
  540–680

ACT Range: 23–29

Financial Aid: 63%

Expense: Pr $

Phi Beta Kappa: Yes

Applicants: 2,037

Accepted: 80%

Enrolled: 38%

Grad in 6 Years: 54%

Returning Freshmen: 81%

Academics: 🖉 🖉 🖉

Social: ☎ ☎ ☎

Q of L: ★ ★

Admissions: (918) 631-2307
  or (800) 331-3050

Email Address:
  admission@utulsa.edu

Strongest Programs:
  Engineering
  Finance/Accounting
  Communicative Disorders
  Biological Sciences
  English
  Psychology

The Tulsa Undergraduate Research Challenge offers outstanding opportunities for cutting-edge scientific research, and has produced 19 Goldwater Scholarship winners since its 1995 founding.

striking view of the city's skyline from the steps of the neo-Gothic McFarlin Library. The university's more than 50 buildings run the architectural gamut from 1930s-vintage neo-Gothic to contemporary, all variations on a theme of yellow Tennessee limestone dubbed "TU brick." Recently completed facilities include the 8,000-seat Donald W. Reynolds Center, a basketball arena and convocation center that also boasts state-of-the-art sports medicine, and strength-conditioning facilities for athletic training, exercise, and sport science majors. Construction has also been completed on the TU Legal Information Center, a $10.5-million renovation and expansion of the law library. Plans are in the works for a new music building and an addition to the Engineering and Natural Sciences complex.

In addition to its well-established and internationally recognized petroleum and geosciences engineering programs, TU offers solid majors in finance, accounting, and computer science. The rapidly growing English department has some impressive resources at its disposal in McFarlin Library's special collections. The collections boast original works by 19th- and 20th-century American and British authors, including books, letters, manuscripts, and even a stained necktie that once belonged to James Joyce, and more than 50,000 items representing author V. S. Naipaul's life and work from the 1950s to the present. TU's Naipaul Archive is the only comprehensive collection of Naipaul manuscripts, correspondence, and family memorabilia in the world. The school's graphic arts program operates a design studio that produces projects for nonprofit organizations at low cost.

In accordance with the Tulsa Curriculum, the cornerstone of the school's emphasis on liberal arts, all undergraduates take three writing courses, at least one mathematics course, and one or two years of foreign language, depending on the degree. In addition, each student completes at least 25 credit hours of general curriculum classes: six hours from aesthetic inquiry and creative experience, 12 hours from historical and social interpretation, and seven hours from scientific investigation. All freshmen take one semester of Argumentation and Exposition, followed by Writing for the Professions (for business students and future engineers) or First Seminar (for everyone else). American sign language may be used to fulfill the language requirement for the College of Arts and Sciences.

Fourteen interdisciplinary programs allow students and professionals to follow up cross-departmental interests. Honors students take exclusive seminars, complete a thesis or advanced project, and have the option of living together in a computer-equipped house. The Tulsa Undergraduate Research Challenge offers outstanding opportunities for cutting-edge scientific research, and has produced 19 Goldwater Scholarship winners since its 1995 founding. A five-year BA/MBA option draws aspiring entrepreneurs, and a six-year BA/JD program trains legal eagles.

Sixty-six percent of Tulsa's students are from Oklahoma; most others are from the Midwest and Southwest, with many hailing from Dallas and St. Louis. Ten percent of the students are foreign, coming from the Middle East, East Asia, and Scandinavia. The student body is mildly diverse, with 7 percent African American, 2 percent Asian American, 3 percent Hispanic, and 6 percent Native American. "TU is a very politically correct campus," says a marketing major. "All races, sexes and lifestyles are represented and respected here." Another student adds, "This campus encourages people to be open-minded." Athletes can compete for 283 scholarships in 16 sports, ranging from women's crew to men's golf. TU also offers 1,029 merit scholarships, ranging from $560 to $18,060.

At Tulsa, freshmen and sophomores are required to live on campus, but only 46 percent of the student population use campus housing. Students have plenty of living options, including three mixed-sex dorms (two coed by wing and the other coed by suite), one women's dorm, one men's dorm, fraternity and sorority houses, and campus apartments. All of the dorms are equipped with free cable television, and connections to the campus mainframe and the Internet are available for a nominal charge. The single-sex dorms are quieter and more attractive to upperclassmen, but "all of the residence halls have been renovated in the last five years, and the rooms are bigger than average," says a sophomore mechanical engineering major.

The social life at TU is pretty good, students say. The Student Association has a large budget and brings top-name comedians, speakers, and entertainers to campus. "There is always something to do on campus, and a lot of people go off campus into the city of Tulsa, which has everything," a senior says. Greek organizations claim 21 percent of TU men and 23 percent of the women, and the frats host campus-wide house parties. Student-initiated policies govern drinking on campus; administrators say this self-policing has led to responsible imbibing.

Campus traditions include the ringing of the college bell in the Alumni Center cupola by each senior after his or her last class, and Springfest, a wild week of games, food, and entertainment that celebrates the changing of seasons. Other big events include Reggaefest, Homecoming, and Greek events such as the Kappa Sigma Olympics, the Sigma Chi Derby Days, and the Delta Gamma Anchor Splash. Nearby parks, lakes, and a huge recreational water park please outdoor enthusiasts. Even better, downtown Tulsa is just a hop, skip, and a jump away, and the city offers symphony, ballet, and opera, and an annual Oktoberfest. Students are very active in community service, volunteering and tutoring in town through programs like TU Cares.

Here in the home state of J. C. Watts and Steve Largent, pro football players turned congressmen, sports are fairly important. Tulsa's basketball team is strong, and the women's golf team recently won conference championships. The school places a heavy emphasis on games against football rivals Oklahoma and Oklahoma State, and basketball games against Arkansas and OSU get students riled up.

Though its mission and identity still appear somewhat in flux, TU seeks to provide students with diverse learning experiences, a balance between career preparation and liberal education, and an appreciation of the value of continual learning. Students appreciate all of that—along with the school's urban location, small size, and emphasis on close relationships with professors.

A five-year BA/MBA option draws aspiring entrepreneurs, and a six-year BA/JD program trains legal eagles.

Overlaps

Texas Christian, Southern Methodist, Washington University (MO), University of Oklahoma, Oklahoma State.

If You Apply To ➤ | **Tulsa**…Rolling admissions. Early action: Oct. 1. Meets demonstrated need of 67%. Campus interviews: recommended, evaluative. No alumni interviews. SATs or ACTs: required. SAT IIs: optional. Accepts the Common Application and electronic applications. Essay question: challenge you have faced; world issue that will impact your future; significant life event.

Union College

807 Union Street, Schenectady, NY 12308

If you're a trendsetter, come join the Union! The first to follow a formal architectural plan, first to have Greek fraternities, and the first nondenominational college, this small school continues to make a big impression. Union students work

Website: www.union.edu
Location: City outskirts

(Continued)

Total Enrollment: 2,150

Undergraduates: 2,084

Male/Female: 52/48

SAT Ranges: V 560–650 M
  580–670

Financial Aid: 60%

Expense: Pr $ $ $ $

Phi Beta Kappa: Yes

Applicants: 3,761

Accepted: 46%

Enrolled: 31%

Grad in 6 Years: 83%

Returning Freshmen: 94%

Academics: ✍ ✍ ✍ ✍

Social: ☎ ☎ ☎

Q of L: ★ ★ ★

Admissions: (518) 388-6112

Email Address:
  admissions@union.edu

Strongest Programs:
  Engineering
  Psychology
  Economics
  Political Science
  Biology
  Mechanical Engineering
  English

Union is at the forefront of national efforts to use computers throughout the academic spectrum. The college links all dorm rooms to its system, and students have used the school's computing facilities for everything from foreign language drills to writing haiku to designing the most complicated engineering models.

hard, whether it's in fraternizing with fellow engineers or engineering a fraternity party. Few liberal arts colleges offer engineering in the context of a strong liberal arts program. Princeton and Swarthmore are among them, as is Union, which offers solid engineering and computer science as "liberal education for a technological world."

The 100-acre Union campus sits on a hill overlooking the city of Schenectady. Its unified campus plan, another college first, was designed by French architect and landscaper Joseph Jacques Ramée back in 1813, and includes eight formal gardens and woodland. His vision took shape in brownstone and red brick, with white arches, pilasters, and rows of lacy trees. The 16-sided Nott Memorial, a National Historic Landmark, is a meeting, study, and display center for students and alumni. The college has recently invested $10 million to revitalize an adjacent neighborhood.

Union's general education standards include studies in Western and foreign cultures. Everyone must take a five-course history, literature, and civilization sequence that includes a freshman preceptorial based on a close reading of classic and multicultural texts, and close faculty interaction. Liberal arts majors must take one social or behavioral science course; one math course; two courses in basic or applied science; and either three semesters of a foreign language, three nonwestern area studies courses or one term of study abroad with associated prerequisites. Freshmen can participate in small-group advising that includes discussion about successful transitions to college life. A writing-across-the-curriculum program ensures that students at all levels work on their prose.

Among the liberal arts majors, psychology, biology, and political science draw student raves. The engineering program is also legendary at Union; it, and the computer science program, were recently redesigned as the "liberal education for a technological world." The history department is home to Union's most esteemed lecturer, Stephen Berk, whose course on the Holocaust and 20th-century Europe is a hot ticket. The Educational Studies Program allows students to complete the courses and fieldwork required to become certified as secondary schoolteachers in fourteen subjects while giving them a strong liberal arts grounding. Interdisciplinary majors are a popular option at Union, and include programs such as Russian and Eastern European Studies, industrial economics, and law and public policy. According to the administration, environmental studies, studio and performing arts, and electrical engineering are the weakest of Union's offerings.

Union operates on a trimester system, which is a mixed blessing. On the downside, the system means the joys of exams three times a year, and a late start to summer jobs, since school doesn't finish until June. "The trimester calendar really prevents a laid-back atmosphere," says one senior. "Classes move quickly, so students must keep up." On the upside, some students feel that learning on trimesters allows them to concentrate on just three courses a term. More terms also mean more opportunities for independent study and internships, either in Albany, the state capital, 20 minutes away, or in Washington, D.C. More than 50 percent of Union students study abroad at some point, some taking advantage of a unique summer program examining national health care systems in England, Holland, and Hungary; others participate in the sea study program in Bermuda, Woods Hole, and Newfoundland.

Back on campus, students give professors high marks. Sophomore and junior honors students participate in interdisciplinary seminars team-taught by faculty members, as well as private meetings with visiting luminaries. Union's Internal Education Foundation funds special academic projects, and the relatively new Union Scholars Program provides an enriched four-year program for entering freshmen with unusual academic capabilities. "The professors are superb," says a sophomore. "Professors are always available, they're eager to help and easy to talk to." Some students say that even at three in the morning, professors can be found working in their offices, accessible to students. The professionally minded aren't out of luck, either; they can take advantage of accelerated degree programs with the Albany School of Law or Medicine to receive a JD or MD at the end of six and eight years, respectively. Five-year BS/MS and BA/MBA programs are also available.

Union is at the forefront of national efforts to use computers throughout the academic spectrum. The college links all dorm rooms to its system, and students have used the school's computing facilities for everything from foreign language drills to writing haiku to designing the most complicated engineering models. The library's collection draws a few complaints, but it is adequately supplemented by an efficient program of interlibrary loans ad extensive online materials.

Everyone, including the engineers, must take a five-course history, literature, and civilization sequence that includes a freshman preceptorial based on a close reading of classic and multicultural texts, and close faculty interaction.

Just under half of Union's students are New York State residents. The student body has a mix of liberals and conservatives, but the hottest issue seems to be the status of the Greek system. African Americans and Hispanics account for 8 percent of the Union student body, Asian Americans another 5 percent. The school's Multicultural Affairs Council, made up of faculty, administrators, and students, and the President's Commission on Diversity both work to strengthen this area at Union. Also, an affirmative action officer and community outreach director was hired to help with relations. Union does not award merit scholarships but guarantees to meet the demonstrated financial needs of all admits who apply within the deadline. The Chester Arthur Undergraduate Support for Excellence (CAUSE) award offers loans to students interested in public service, which are forgiven at 20 percent per year if the student enters a service career.

Housing options include single-sex, coed, and theme houses, which are popular alternatives to fraternities and sororities. The college has recently renovated several houses in a neighborhood revitalization project, providing apartment style housing for up to 160 upperclassmen. "Dorm rooms are comfortable and well-maintained," describes one senior. Eighty percent of students live on campus. Students recommend West, which is considered by many to be the most social place for freshmen since it is coed by room. A student recalls, "My freshman year I lived in West, which is the social mecca for a new student. " Also drawing praise are Fox and Davidson, where freshmen and sophomores live in suites: four people to two bedrooms and a "huge" common room. Everyone eats at one of two dining halls, with freshmen eating together in West College.

At Union, 31 percent of the men and 26 percent of the women go Greek. As expected, the fraternities play a significant role in campus social life. "Greek life dominates the social scene," says a sophomore. "Aside from the fraternity parties, there are also alcohol-free events which tend to change every weekend." The on-campus pub is a popular hangout, perhaps because campus alcohol policies are "strict, but widely disregarded," says a senior. "It is very easy for underage students to be served." University-sponsored events such as movies, a regular coffee-house, dances, and guest speakers provide nonalcoholic outlets.

More than half of Union students study abroad at some point, some taking advantage of a unique summer program examining national health care systems in England, Holland, and Hungary.

The college's picturesque campus lends a touch of sophistication to Schenectady, an old-line industrial city that's becoming more high-tech but is not a typical college town. "Schenectady really doesn't affect us," says a senior. Many students do volunteer in town, especially through Big Brothers/Big Sisters and We Care About U Schenectady, a program that builds houses for the homeless. Also, all freshmen participate in a community clean-up project during orientation. What Schenectady lacks can be found in resort-like Saratoga Springs and the

Adirondacks, to the north, and the Catskills, to the south. Fall Fest and Spring Fest feature all-campus picnics and live music; only hard-core geeks miss the home football or Division I ice hockey games against Rensselaer Polytechnic Institute. Painting the Idol, a really ugly campus statue, is another tradition, as is rooting for the women's field hockey, tennis, and lacrosse teams, and the men's basketball, football, and soccer teams, which compete in Division III.

Students at Union gush about the social and academic experience. One student says "I chose Union because everyone seemed so happy and it seemed like a great place to grow and learn." "Union students are real go-getters," exclaims a transfer student. With praise like that, it's clear that despite its small size, Union makes a big impression on its students.

Overlaps

Hamilton, Colgate, Lafayette, Trinity, Cornell University.

If You Apply To ➤ Union…Early decision: Nov. 15, Jan. 15. Regular admissions, financial aid, and housing: Feb. 1. Guarantees to meet demonstrated need. Campus interviews: recommended, evaluative. Alumni interviews: recommended, informational. SAT I or three SAT IIs (writing and two others) or ACT: required. Accepts the Common Application. Essay question: significant experience or achievement; important issue of personal, local, national, or international concern; influential person; or a topic of own choosing.

Ursinus College

Box 1000, Collegeville, PA 19426

Website: www.ursinus.edu
Location: Suburban
Total Enrollment: 1,240
Undergraduates: 1,240
Male/Female: 47/53
SAT Ranges: V 520–620 M 540–640
ACT Range: 26–28
Financial Aid: 81%
Expense: Pr $ $ $
Phi Beta Kappa: Yes
Applicants: 1,491
Accepted: 78%
Enrolled: 29%
Grad in 6 Years: 75%
Returning Freshmen: 92%
Academics: ✑ ✑ ✑
Social: ☎ ☎ ☎
Q of L: ★ ★ ★
Admissions: (610) 409-3200
Email Address: admissions@ursinus.edu

Ursinus College was established as a school where, in the words of founder Zacharias Ursinus, students would "examine all things and retain what is good." For many years, the college emphasized solid training in practical fields ranging from business administration to sports science, but it is now returning with a vengeance to its liberal arts roots. All new students and faculty members must now take part in a course called the Common Intellectual Experience that explores topics ranging from Plato to Buddhist scripture, and there is a new requirement that each student have an independent learning experience. Though Ursinus (pronounced Ur-SIGN-nus) is small, students are happy at this college in the cornfields of Pennsylvania, thanks largely to close contact with professors and a cozy atmosphere where everyone knows everyone else. There is even a weekly common hour for the entire community.

Ursinus is located in Collegeville, about 40 minutes west of Philadelphia, and only 10 miles from the green, rolling hills of Valley Forge National Park. The 140-acre campus is mostly Pennsylvania fieldstone with a variety of restored buildings. The campus walkway includes the F. W. Olin Center for the Humanities and the Berman Museum of Art. Ursinus completed a $16 million renovation and expansion of Pfahler Science Hall, which houses chemistry, computer science, mathematics, and physics. A $1 million bookstore was added to the back of the Student Center as well as a new addition to the field house.

The school offers more than 20 fields of study, with the sciences garnering the most praise. Ursinus has cultivated a strong minor in East Asian Studies, and it has a viable classics program as well as solid strength in history, English and politics. Biology is still the most popular major, though faculty members have shifted the emphasis of instruction from premed to science. Ursinus was the first college in Pennsylvania approved by the state to certify secondary teachers of Japanese.

Other language programs are popular, but the number of economics/business administration majors has declined since the economists began requiring calculus. Almost 20 percent of the rising senior class will have paid summer academic fellowships where they work fulltime with a faculty mentor. For the academically motivated who want a change from the Pennsylvania countryside, Ursinus offers opportunities around the globe as part of the Bradley University Consortium. The college also offers programs with its own faculty in France, Japan, Mexico, Spain, and Germany. Students can study at other U.S. universities, including Howard and American in Washington, D.C. Prospective engineers may choose 3-2 programs at the University of Pennsylvania and elsewhere.

Every freshman is issued a laptop computer. In four years, all Ursinus students will be so equipped. A new graduation requirement will be added, the Independent Learning Experience, where every student must either complete an independent research project, become an intern, study abroad, or student teach. Two new majors have been added, including the single major of Biochemistry and Molecular Biology.

General education requirements under the Ursinus Plan revolve around a Liberal Studies Seminar, which include a Freshman Seminar, English composition, two foreign language courses, two math or science courses, two courses in different social sciences, and two humanities courses. The Common Intellectual Experience for freshmen, which is taught by faculty members from all disciplines, is designed to give students a common basis for academic discussions that will spill over into the cafeteria and dorms. Honors students complete an independent research project that is evaluated by outside examiners. Ursinus students work hard for their grades. "Ursinus has a very competitive environment, especially in the sciences," a sophomore says. In fact, nearly half of students at the school come from the top tenth of their class. Classes at the college are small and professors are outstanding. "All students are taught by professors, never graduate students. Professors get to know students and are always available outside the classroom," says one junior communications major. Academic advising also receives high marks; freshmen meet their advisors once a week during the first half of their first semester. "Advisors are there whenever you need them," one student says. Financial aid is similarly praised, with 80 percent of students receiving some sort of financial aid, and 80 merit scholarships available each year, ranging from $500 to full tuition. The library has 185,000 volumes, but the school is connected to OCLC, a consortium of more that 18,000 libraries, and most books are accessible within a few days. Ursinus students may also use the Penn libraries.

Sixty-five percent of the students at Ursinus are from Pennsylvania, with others hailing from New York or New Jersey. Eighty-three percent of students are white, with blacks making up 7 percent, Asian Americans another 4 percent, and foreign students and Hispanics 2 percent each. Racial tension is minimal. The school's excellent student life staff includes several key members who are African American. Race relations, sexual harassment, and physical safety are covered in "Ursinus in Community," which begins with freshman orientation. At an intimate school where 20 percent of the men and 30 percent of the women belong to Greek organizations, politics give way to more pressing issues: sorority pledging and fraternity parties. "Ursinus is not a politically active school at all," a sophomore says. "Too laid back." But the Greeks do more than just drink; they also participate in the community. The campus is very safe, one student says; the security guards are always available for anything. "If it's raining, they will bring you an umbrella. If you're locked out of your room, they will get you in." Other

For the academically motivated who want a change from the Pennsylvania countryside, Ursinus has joined the Bradley University Consortium, opening to students opportunities spanning the globe.

students say Ursinus makes it easy to succeed. "Just about everyone graduates in four years, unless you are a real slacker," says a sophomore.

Housing options at Ursinus run the gamut from typical to modern, and most students live in the dorms, adding to the college's community feel. "Rooms are big, especially for freshmen," a student raves. Upperclassmen quickly grab the Main Street houses, a string of Victorian-era homes across the street from campus, while many first-year men take up residence in Old Men's (BWC), which has generously sized rooms. The college recently finished renovations on two of the 30 Victorian-era student residences that the college owns. Dorm food isn't great, and the required three-squares-a-day plan gets mediocre reviews.

Collegeville is a tiny town, only eight blocks long, and Ursinus takes up six of them. While the town has little that the students want, it does have some of what they need, including late-night pizza delivery. As for social life, students stick close to home. "Most parties are on campus," a student says. "Parties get crazy. Not many road trips." But Ursinus is not isolated: Philadelphia is just a half-hour away, and because many students have cars, they retreat to the Jersey shore during the warmer months. Other social activities include free movies every night, lectures, and dances. Finally, there are five malls within a 20-minute radius of Ursinus, including the King of Prussia complex, the second-largest mall in the country.

Students here love sports, and 60 percent of the student body play on an NCAA Division III varsity team. For women determined to pursue careers in athletics, Ursinus is a well-known stepping-stone to collegiate coaching posts; more than 50 colleges have hired Ursinus alumnae. The lacrosse team is recognized as a perennial contender for the national championship. The longest-running football rivalry in the Philadelphia area belongs to Ursinus and Swarthmore. Among other contributions in the world of sports, Ursinus is in the *Guinness Book of World Records* for having a tree in the end zone of the football field.

Ursinus may not be in the center of some great metropolitan area, or be big enough to have a big town built around it. But to the students who attend, the college offers a solid education within a close-knit community. Says an amiable lawyer-to-be, "It is a small, comfortable atmosphere where everyone knows everyone."

Overlaps

Muhlenberg, Gettysburg, Dickinson, Franklin and Marshall.

If You Apply To ➤ **Ursinus**…Early decision: Jan. 15. Regular admissions and housing: Feb. 15. Financial aid: Feb.1 (early decision), Apr. 1. Does not guarantee to meet demonstrated need. Campus interviews: recommended, informational. No alumni interviews. SATs: required. SAT IIs: recommended. Accepts the Common Application and electronic applications. Essay question: significant experience; personal issue; or significant person.

University of Utah

250 SSB, Salt Lake City, UT 84112

Website: www.utah.edu
Location: City outskirts
Total Enrollment: 26,193

Founded in 1850, the University of Utah is also unique in its ability to offer students the advantages of living in a city while at the same time maintaining a connection with nature.

Set in the foothills of the Rocky Mountains, near the shores of the Great Salt Lake, the university enjoys a picturesque location a half-hour's drive from "the greatest snow on earth." Though not the aesthetic equal of its stunning backdrop, the Utah campus is extremely attractive. Occupying 1,500 well-landscaped acres with nearly as many different kinds of trees as undergraduates, the campus is the state's arboretum. The architectural style of the university's structures ranges from 19th-century, ivy-covered buildings to state-of-the-art athletic facilities. The Marriott Library renovation, a project that doubled the library's size, was completed in 1998, and a new supercomputing facility has recently been completed.

The U operates on a semester calendar with a full summer session. There is a slate of general education requirements that students must fulfill including courses in writing, American institutions, intellectual explorations, and quantitative reasoning. Utah provides a blend of strong professional training with a solid program in liberal arts. Renowned for its research in biomedical engineering, Utah's Health Sciences Center hosted the first mechanical heart transplant. Engineering, computer science, business, and chemistry are the most popular majors. Dance programs (both ballet and modern) and physical therapy are also noteworthy, while students say the sociology department needs improvement. Utah's honors program, the third-oldest in the nation, features top faculty and small classes, and routinely receives high praise. The Undergraduate Research Program gives students the chance to join faculty members in research projects and allows them to receive either academic credit or a stipend for their participation. The academic climate is competitive, but not cutthroat. "The courses are challenging but students tend to their own circumstances instead of worrying about what others are doing," says a psychology major.

To make it easier to sign up for classes, the school now has computerized telephone registration, with freshmen getting first priority. Introductory courses often enroll hundreds of students, and classes can be overcrowded. Utah's professors generally receive high marks from the students. "The professors are well versed in their subjects and eager to help their students," says one senior.

Utah's students are a middle-class, fairly homogeneous lot; out-of-staters make up 23 percent of the student body, while minority students are barely represented, with African Americans, Hispanics, and Asian Americans combining for less than 7 percent. Nevertheless, there seems to be little overt racial hostility. "If there is a confrontation, it's usually between the university and Mormon leaders," says one student. Many of the Mormons are of the "returned missionary" variety, older than most undergraduates and married. Despite Utah's buttoned-down image, there are at least a handful of liberals lurking around, and the Mormon influence is not as all-pervasive as at neighboring Brigham Young. Utah offers more than 1,600 scholarships for academic achievement, some reserved for state residents, along with 300 athletic scholarships, distributed among 21 NCAA Division I teams.

According to one student, the U is "determined to be the largest commuter campus in the United States." Just 10 percent of students live on campus. "The dorms are old but serve their purpose," says a senior. Students who live in residence halls can grab a bite at the Trading Post convenience area or at one of the six restaurants located in the student union. As for social life, it's as good as a commuter school's can be: low key. Still, one student states, "There's a lot of fun to be had, if you know where to look." The Outdoor Recreation Program offers excursions into nature and also has a storehouse of more than 1,500 different items to rent to students. Still, while the university does sponsors symposiums and lectures, and students do support a variety of movie houses and clubs with live acts, most socializing at this "suitcase school" takes place off campus. Road trips to bowl games (Utah won the Freedom Bowl in 1994), Las Vegas, Seattle, or

(Continued)
Undergraduates: 21,095
Male/Female: 53/46
SAT Ranges: V 460–620
M 470–630
ACT Range: 20–27
Financial Aid: 30%
Expense: Pub $
Phi Beta Kappa: Yes
Applicants: 5,663
Accepted: 90%
Enrolled: 47%
Grad in 6 Years: 28%
Returning Freshmen: 59%
Academics: ✍ ✍ ✍
Social: ☎ ☎ ☎
Q of L: ★ ★ ★
Admissions: (801) 581-7281
Email Address: N/A

Strongest Programs:
  Business
  Psychology
  Communications
  Mining
  Chemistry
  Engineering
  Computer Science

The U recently moved from a quarter system to a semester calendar with a full summer session.

Renowned for its research in biomedical engineering, Utah's Health Sciences Center hosted the first mechanical heart transplant.

any of the nearby ski resorts (the school provides slopeside bus service) is very popular. Only 3 percent of the men and 2 percent of the women go Greek and the city council recently clamped down on Greek growth in order to keep the system small.

The few students who don't go home on weekends warn that "a car is requisite" to navigate the sprawling metro area surrounding the U. Adjacent to campus, the Latter-Day Saints Institute of Religion sponsors dances and other social activities, though the conservative social attitudes may dampen the spirits of the party animals. The Lowell Bennion Community Service Center has received one of four national awards for community service. "The volunteer program is exceptional, very well organized, and supported," notes an economics major. The campus sits on a hill overlooking downtown Salt Lake City, which will host the 2002 Olympic Winter Games. "Salt Lake City offers a lot of entertainment including restaurants, movie theaters, and all kinds of outdoor activities," says a chemistry/English major. The flourishing cultural scene is regional in scope and includes the respected Utah Symphony, several dance companies, opera, the NBA's Utah Jazz, the minor league Utah Buzz, and of course, the Mormon Tabernacle Choir.

Football and basketball are the most popular sports on campus, and both draw an enthusiastic following. The women's gymnastics team has won 10 NCAA titles in the past 14 years, and the men's basketball team is always strong. Available athletic amenities include indoor tennis, racquetball and squash courts, saunas, swimming pools, an indoor track, and weight machines. Intramurals in nearly 100 sports, a quarter of which are coed, are an important student activity. And any match against rival BYU usually sells out. Students also rave about the three-day Mayfest, celebrated every spring, which brings the campus together for dances, plays, movies, and speakers, as well as edible delights.

If you're looking for a campus that rages with raucous parties on weekends, complemented by crowded dorms that encourage the formation of a real community, the University of Utah probably won't fulfill your expectations. On the other hand, if you are looking for top-notch professors, excellent academics, and a beautiful campus at a reasonable price, the U might just be the place.

Overlaps

Brigham Young, Utah State, Stanford, University of Arizona.

If You Apply To ➤

University of Utah…Regular admissions: June 1. Financial aid: Feb. 15. Does not guarantee to meet demonstrated need. No campus or alumni interviews. SATs or ACTs: required; ACT preferred. No essay question.

Vanderbilt University

2305 West End Avenue, Nashville, TN 37240

Website: www.vanderbilt.edu
Location: City outskirts
Total Enrollment: 10,022
Undergraduates: 5,780

Vanderbilt University used to be a quiet, conservative school in the heart of the South. But no longer. Vanderbilt is working to diversify its student body and has gained an impressive national reputation. Sure, football games still require dressing up and finding a date, but the flip side of that formality is a Southern ease and friendliness that make rigorous academics easier to swallow.

The 330-acre Nashville campus, named a national arboretum in the late

1980s, is park-like. Art and sculptures dot the campus, and architectural styles range from gothic to modern glass and brick. Vandy's campus also includes 60-acre Peabody College, the central section of which is listed on the National Register of Historic Places. As it tries to preserve its roots, the campus is also growing at an incredibly fast pace. Recent construction has left little of the campus untouched and includes additions to academic buildings and the Hill Student, plus new lots and garages to ease the campus' tight parking situation.

Vanderbilt undergraduates choose from among four schools—arts and science, engineering, music, and education/human development—with all undergraduates taking their core liberal arts courses in the College of Arts and Science. Specific distribution requirements vary from school to school, but most students get a good dose of writing, math, foreign language, humanities, and natural science courses. "I've taken a wide variety of liberal arts courses and come away with the impression that all of Vanderbilt's academic offerings are well above average," a junior reports. Freshmen in the College of Arts and Science benefit from one of the best writing programs anywhere, and the university's freshman seminars offer small settings and discussion on topics ranging from Country Music in Social Context to Women and Work in the U.S.

Popular majors are engineering, psychology, education, and English. The Peabody College of education and human development—which requires its teacher licensure candidates to double major, usually in a liberal arts field—offers strong programs in elementary and special education, including the opportunity to spend a summer at England's Cambridge University and teach at a British school. Though Vandy has no undergraduate major in business administration, many students make do as economics majors with a business minor. There is also a 3–2 program with the Owen Graduate School of Business. New majors include neuroscience and a 5-year joint BMus/MEd degree in cooperation with Peabody College (for those who wish to teach music).

Vanderbilt's popular study abroad program features instruction in England, France, Germany, Spain, China, Japan, and Australia. The optional May session allows students to spend four weeks on one concentrated project—helping some graduate with two majors in four years. Drama classes have been known to tour London theaters during the May term, while some students work at regional archeological digs. Thanks to a multiyear dorm renovation project, students in dorms are networked to the campus library computers. The state-of-the-art library also has one of the country's best videotape collections of network evening news, a special help to students majoring in history and political science.

When it comes to academic etiquette, Vanderbilt students are governed by the school's honor system, which makes possible unproctored exams. First instituted in 1875, this system governs all aspects of a student's academic conduct. Students rave about the faculty. "First rate: my experiences with professors have been extremely positive," says a biomedical engineering major. Another student says, "Even small discussion-oriented seminars are led by Ph.D.s." A senior double major says the professors "have the ability to change a student's life or motivate us to achieve our academic potential."

While a mixture of conservative Republicans and fraternity and sorority types has set the tone at Vanderbilt in the past, students say the college is slowly becoming more liberal. The changes may be due to the fact that more students are coming from outside the state of Tennessee and the suburban Birmingham-Atlanta corridor and public school graduates now constitute about 55 percent of the student body. Still, Vandy has a much more Southern feel than Duke, the South's other leading private university.

(Continued)
Male/Female: 47/53
SAT Ranges: V 600–690
M 620–710
ACT Range: 27–31
Financial Aid: 36%
Expense: Pr $ $ $ $
Phi Beta Kappa: Yes
Applicants: 8,494
Accepted: 61%
Enrolled: 31%
Grad in 6 Years: 83%
Returning Freshmen: 92%
Academics: ✍ ✍ ✍ ✍
Social: ☎ ☎ ☎ ☎
Q of L: ★ ★ ★
Admissions: (615) 322-2561
Email Address:
admissions@vanderbilt.edu

Strongest Programs:
English
Natural Sciences
Engineering
Philosophy
Musical Arts
Education

The number of minorities is increasing (Asian Americans constitute 6 percent, African Americans 5 percent, and Hispanics 3 percent) as is their acceptance by the student body. One student says, "Racial and gender issues are very pivotal on this campus. Political correctness is very important for many people." "Many would unfairly characterize the stereotypical Vanderbilt student as rich, white, and Greek," a philosophy/psych double major says. "Admittedly, Vanderbilt has some growing to do, but it would be a mistake to ignore the great strides we continue to make in this area." The administration is also heeding the call, creating the Visiting Minority Faculty Program to bring minority faculty to the campus and upping financial support for minority programs including the Black Cultural Center and the Office for Intercultural Affairs. The Vandy's need-based financial aid program is complemented by numerous merit scholarships and more than 227 athletic scholarships.

Eighty-three percent of Vandy's undergraduates live in the dorms. According to the students, the dorms are "relatively nice" and "well-maintained." Freshmen occupy singles or doubles in their own special dorms; other accommodations include 10-person town houses, six-room suites, theme dorms (wellness, environmental awareness, philosophy, foreign language), and apartments. Seniors can live off campus but report that housing is not easy to find, and that the on-campus lottery system—in which seniors get first priority—is a better bet. There are 13 different dining facilities on campus. Freshmen are required to buy the Dinner Plan; upperclassmen can purchase the Dinner Plan or use other dining facilities. Fraternity houses have cooks, but sorority kitchens are used only once a week. Campus security is tight.

Fifty percent of the women and 34 percent of the men join the Greek system, which is a very active force on the campus. Interaction between the Greeks and non-Greeks is encouraged, although not always successfully, by making many functions open to the whole campus. "Fraternities have parties almost every weekend," a senior says. The Vandy Late Night Program provides free entertainment opportunities off campus from ice-skating to trips to the Grand Ol' Opry. Dating is big at Vandy; the most coveted invitation is the Accolade formal that precedes Homecoming, tickets to which are both expensive and limited. (Funds from the Accolade benefit scholarships for minority students.) Another favorite Vandy tradition is the Rites of Spring festival, a carnival and music festival that takes place on the main lawn. Though Vandy students drink as much alcohol as those at any other school, they have to work to get their hands on it. Open containers are banned in public, and kegs are taboo. "The policy is fairly effective, but underage students can find loopholes," a worldly senior says.

Vanderbilt's proximity to Music City USA (and the Grand Ol' Opry) provides "something for pretty much everyone": a rich supply of bluegrass, country, and rock music and an abundance of good restaurants and theaters—all within walking distance. Walk in one direction and there are fajitas and buckets of beer at the San Antonio Taco Company; walk the other way and it's CDs galore at Tower Records. For country music fans, the wax museum in town is a must-see, and there is an ever-increasing amount of brew pubs in the city. Beyond Nashville's borders are the Smokies, state parks with picnic facilities, beautiful lakes, and skiing in the winter. The best road trips are to Memphis (home of Elvis!), New Orleans (for Mardi Gras), the Kentucky Derby, and Atlanta.

Vanderbilt is the smallest—and the only private—institution in the competitive and football-crazy Southeastern Conference (Division IA). Among the campus sports events, basketball is the hot ticket and both the men's and women's teams draw raves from Vanderbilt fans. The women's team won the conference championship in 1994–95, and the men's team won the 1993 Southeastern Conference Championship and advanced to the NCAA postseason tournament's "Sweet 16." Women's soccer has also done quite well, winning the conference for two years straight. Rivals include Alabama, Georgia, and Tennessee, though Vanderbilt almost always comes up on the losing end against these schools in football.

Vanderbilt is quietly building a reputation for excellence that extends beyond its Southern heritage. Its talented students, who enjoy working hard and playing harder, thrive in its uniquely Southern atmosphere. It's not a cheap alternative, exemplified by one of its slogans: "Vanderbilt: It Even Sounds Expensive." But for many, it's money well spent. One student says after he had visited all the schools on his list, he felt "most at home" at Vanderbilt. It's this easy-going charm that makes the Vandy experience so unique.

If You Apply To ➤

Vanderbilt…Early decision: Nov. 1, Jan. 15. Regular admissions: Jan. 15. Financial aid: Nov. 1 and Jan. 1 (early decision), Feb. 1. Housing: May 1. No campus or alumni interviews. SATs or ACTs: required (SAT preferred). SAT IIs: optional. Apply to particular school or program. Accepts the common application and electronic applications. Essay question: applicant's choice of topic.

Vassar College

Poughkeepsie, NY 12604

Once known as the most liberal of the Seven Sisters, and still a bastion of the left even though men are now common on campus, Vassar stands out among its small-college peers because of its curricular flexibility, proximity to city life, and untypical undergraduates. A Vassar diploma, whether held by a man or a woman, is well respected in the job market, and a strong Vassar GPA is highly regarded at graduate schools. But even more important is the experience behind the sheepskin and transcript.

The college's 1,000-acre campus, just outside the town of Poughkeepsie, New York, is beautifully landscaped. Daffodils circle the two lakes in springtime and foliage is inescapable in the fall. Encircled by a fieldstone wall, the campus includes an astronomical observatory with one of the largest telescopes in the Northeast, a state-of-the-art chemistry building, a farm with an ecological field station, and an art center boasting 13,500 works from Ancient Egypt to modern art. The architecture is varied, with neo-Gothic overtones, and includes buildings designed by such notables as Marcel Breuer, Eero Saarinen, and James Renwick. The most recent additions to campus include a coffeehouse with plenty of performance space for those wanting to showcase their talents and $25-million expansion and technology upgrade of the main library.

English and drama are on almost everyone's list of best departments, though history, psychology, and the sciences are also applauded by students. Newer on campus are a computer science degree program, enhanced astronomy and geology programs, and strengthened aspects of the curriculum through the Asian Studies, international studies, and Francophone literature courses taught in French. In addition, environmental studies and Jewish studies have recently

There is great curricular freedom at Vassar: there is no core curriculum, which allows students to construct their own multidisciplinary area of interest.

Environmental studies and Jewish studies have recently become full-fledged majors.

become full-fledged majors. Russian is weak, though, and students describe the studio art department as small. There is great curricular freedom at Vassar: there is no core curriculum, which allows students to construct their own multidisciplinary area of interest. But to graduate, students are required to complete one course emphasizing oral and written expression and another requiring significant quantitative analysis, in addition to demonstrating foreign language proficiency at the first-year level. Students agree that professors encourage group study and outside-the classroom instruction. "The academic climate here is cooperative," says a music major. "I find I'm constantly collaborating with my peers, not competing against them." Vassar strikes a happy median between being a competitive or laid-back environment by keeping students sincerely motivated. The professors are accomplished in their fields, having written acclaimed books and edited major works. There also are team-taught courses that bring together experts in various fields (for example, in Caribbean literature and Judaism in the course Miami in the American Imagination).

Seminars and tutorials are the rule here, even for introductory courses. Popular classes fill up quickly, but on the positive side, friendships with faculty members develop easily (80 percent of the professors live on campus). "I am on a first-name basis with several professors, and they go out of their way to work with students," a junior says. "Vassar's courses are very demanding, but not at all competitive or cutthroat." Exams run on an honor system. Most people study in the Gothic-style library, with its delightful decor and 24-hour study room for those all-night crams.

The biology building houses two electron microscopes, and music students are spoiled by a grand collection of Steinway pianos, sprinkled all over campus, and their own superb library of scores and books. Vassar runs the Powerhouse Summer Theater program in which apprentices are accepted from around the country to take classes, perform Shakespeare, and work in some capacities with a professional company from New York City. Participants can earn academic as well as Actors Equity points through the program. Also highly regarded, the Undergraduate Research Summer Institute (URSI) pays students a stipend to work one-on-one with faculty members on scientific research projects, either at Vassar or at off-campus sites. The Ford Scholars program offers similar opportunities for student-faculty collaboration in the humanities and social sciences. Study abroad is popular and encouraged, with a large number of programs available under the auspices of other colleges. Vassar also sponsors programs in England, Germany, France, Spain, Morocco, Ireland, and Italy. For domestic study, Vassar has an agreement with the Bank Street College in NYC for students interested in urban education. There are programs with the other 11 members of the Twelve College Exchange* or at any of four historically black colleges, as well as opportunities to participate in a drama production at the Eugene O'Neil Theater and a maritime studies program at the Mystic Seaport*, both in Connecticut.

Sixty-five percent of Vassar's students come from the top tenth of their class; only 28 percent are New York natives. Minorities account for a substantial subset of the student population: Asian Americans make up 10 percent, African Americans 6 percent, and Hispanics 5 percent. Vassar has a commitment to its Intercultural Center, which supports and recognizes students of color and other ethnic and cultural groups. However, issues of race are hardly the only hot topics on campus; free speech, women's issues, animal rights, sweatshop labor, and alternative sexuality are all at the top of the agenda. "There are touches of P.C. here, but most students tend to have open minds," a junior says.

Ninety-eight percent of the students live on campus, most in singles after freshman year, and housing is guaranteed for all four years. "The dorms are decent and there's plenty of single rooms available," says an economics major. Another student adds, "I was surprised by how beautiful and spacious the rooms are here." All but one of the nine dorms are coed. The word is that Lathrop is the best dorm for freshmen, but no halls are reserved strictly for first-year students. Juniors and seniors favor the college-owned town houses (five-person suites) or the four-person Terrace Apartments, both with kitchens and living rooms, while some prefer the communal living in Ferry House. Dorm dwellers eat in relative splendor in the All-Campus Dining Center (a.k.a. ACDC) overlooking pine groves and rolling lawns.

One student suggests that, given the nature and interests of its undergraduate body, "Vassar should be located in Greenwich Village." But reality is far from this vision: Poughkeepsie is an old industrial town that leaves, as far as many of Vassar's more cosmopolitan students are concerned, much to be desired. Still, the town is the seat of Duchess County government, so internships with law firms and political offices are easy to come by, a student says. And 50 percent of Vassar students do some kind of community work in Poughkeepsie, through the Step Beyond program—programs like "I Won't Grow Up Day" bring kids from the area to campus to get a taste of college life. However, most social activities—films, drama, and musical entertainment—are found on campus. Campus dances feature the latest music from the East Village, and one student suggests that art is a valuable topic to be fluent in around here. Considering founder Matthew Vassar was a brewer, it's no surprise that Matthew's Mug, the campus dance club/bar, is packed on weekends, as is the Aula coffeehouse for those not yet of legal age. According to one Brewer, "Vassar is fairly self-contained so most weekends take place on campus." Vassar is not a big drinking school, but underage students can get served booze. In other words, Vassar isn't "dry," but drinking doesn't dictate what students do when classes have ceased for the week. Non-alcohol-centered activities include worthwhile jaunts to Roosevelt's Hyde Park and the Culinary Institute of America (for gourmet meals). The Bardavon Theater and Hudson Valley Philharmonic also help curb a student exodus to New York.

The annual gala formals bring high society to Vassar twice a year. There are many other social traditions, including the Founders Day carnival in May, and Serenading, a ritual in which the classes sing to one another in a competitive yet congenial way. Afternoon teatime—yes, tea—in the Rose Parlor of historic Main Building remains a popular ritual for unwinding after a day of classes.

Varsity athletics are experiencing a renaissance; tennis and volleyball are among the strongest offerings. A $12 million expansion of the athletic facilities resulted in a new basketball gym with an elevated running track and new fitness center. The men's soccer and volleyball teams have won conference championships over the past few years, while the women's tennis and volleyball squads have captured Seven Sisters crowns. The women's soccer team recently won the New York State championship. The up-and-coming crew team works out on the Hudson River, which, at this distance from Manhattan, is still beautiful. Those who choose to leave their idyllic home on weekends usually head for Manhattan, about one-and-a-half hours away. But one chemistry major assures "this isn't a suitcase school."

Students are generally curious and inquisitive, and not at all shy about expressing their views. Boasts one Brewer, "It's a Vassar tradition." For those seeking a place where it's okay to color outside the lines—or erase the lines entirely—this educational oasis abutting the grit of Poughkeepsie could be paradise found.

Vassar runs the Powerhouse Summer Theater program in which apprentices are accepted from around the country to take classes, perform Shakespeare, and work in some capacities with a professional company from New York City.

Overlaps
Brown, Wesleyan, Tufts, Yale, Columbia.

University of Vermont

194 South Prospect Street, Burlington, VT 05401

Website: www.uvm.edu

Location: Small city

Total Enrollment: 10,206

Undergraduates: 7,520

Male/Female: 45/55

SAT Ranges: V 510–610 M 520–620

ACT Range: 21-26

Financial Aid: 55%

Expense: Pub $ $ $

Phi Beta Kappa: Yes

Applicants: 7,877

Accepted: 80%

Enrolled: 30%

Grad in 6 Years: 67%

Returning Freshmen: 81%

Academics: ✑ ✑ ✑

Social: ☎ ☎ ☎ ☎ ☎

Q of L: ★ ★ ★ ★ ★

Admissions: (802) 656-3370

Email Address:
admissions@uvm.edu

Strongest Programs:
Environmental Studies
Business
English
History
Natural and Life Sciences
Psychology
Political Science

The product of a merger of a private college and public university, UVM is not your typical school. Its acronym, which doubles for *Universitas Viridis Montis*, is Latin for "University of the Green Mountains." Its admissions standards are stringent, particularly for nonresidents, and its price tag is high, even for Vermont natives. (Vermont's state legislature gives UVM the lowest rate of state funding in the nation, so it is, for all practical purposes, a private school.) With just 7,500 highly able and motivated undergraduates, UVM can even feel like an elite liberal-arts college, complete with strong academics, mellow milieu, and concern for the earth and others that never gets old. With a new emphasis on diversity and academic excellence, this unique fusion of public and private educational models may finally be coming into its own.

Nestled on the picturesque shores of Lake Champlain, the UVM campus, a pleasant mix of Colonial, high Victorian Gothic, and functional modern buildings, is located in Burlington (the state's largest city and cultural mecca, virtually on Canada's doorstep). In the heart of the campus, each building surrounding the manicured park is recognized in the National Registry of Historic Places. The school recently completed several projects: the 15,000 square foot Center for Food Sciences; a 22-horse barn for the Equine Sciences Program; a state-of-the art health research facility; a fitness and recreation complex; a $4.5 million ecosystems lab for the Natural Resources school; and renovations to the historic Allen House, where the multicultural center is located.

Like the architecture, UVM's academic atmosphere varies. The school has a "laid-back atmosphere with challenging and quite rigorous courses," says one business administration major. Business and physical therapy are said to be much more demanding than liberal arts, but in general, "UVM is far more academically oriented than it is widely perceived to be,"a student notes. There are no university-wide general education requirements, though most students must enroll in at least 30 credits (10 courses) in the arts, humanities, social sciences, languages, literature, mathematics, and the sciences. A three-credit Race and Culture course is also required. Among the best of UVM's 100-plus majors are the hard sciences (particularly environmental studies), business, and physical therapy. Premeds and physical therapy students benefit from UVM's fine medical school, and learning disabled students are supported in all majors. Computer science and information systems have been added as majors. Weaknesses appear in a few social science areas, such as anthropology and the fine arts.

At UVM, you can design your own major. You can also participate in the Living and Learning Center, an imaginative residential-academic program where like-minded students live together in suites and create their own programs with a faculty advisor's help. Freshmen in Arts and Sciences may participate in the Teacher-Advisor Program (TAP), a special seminar where the professor also serves as the enrolled students' advisor. Roughly two-thirds of first year liberal arts students enroll in a TAP seminar. The internship program is popular, and co-ops are available in engineering, business, recreation management, and agriculture. About 400 students per year partake in UVM study abroad programs in South America, Western Europe, and Asia and the Pacific Rim.

Students report that classes fill up quickly, which can be hard on freshmen (who register last), but graduating in four years is no problem. By junior year, most students are in classes with 25 or fewer students, which helps foster relationships with UVM's outstanding faculty. Students also heap praise on the various advising programs: "If you wanted to see your advisor every day, you could," crows one student.

UVM students have much in common: 95 percent are white, and most are New Englanders. Asian Americans are the largest minority group on campus, at 2 percent, while African Americans and Hispanics combined comprise another 2 percent. The campus political climate is unabashedly liberal, and recycling and other environmental concerns are big issues on campus, say students. "Most students are 'granola,'" a sophomore says. Between 200 and 300 merit-based scholarships are available to students who also demonstrate financial need, and administrators say that number is growing. UVM also offers 150 athletic scholarships each year in nine women's and eight men's sports.

There are 26 residence halls on campus, each with its own flavor. That's a good thing, since freshmen and sophomores are required to live on campus, and they select rooms by lottery. Dorms are situated in three residential areas separated by 10-minute walks. Other on-campus options include the Living and Learning suites, co-ops, and apartments. Redstone Campus is described as the rowdiest area, while the best freshman dorms are said to be Chittenden or Buckham, which feature tiny rooms and great atmosphere. Still, most juniors and seniors rent apartments in town.

A popular campus T-shirt warns: "If you want to party, come to UVM. If you want to stay, study!" While students here buckle down when they have to, they also know how to have fun when the week's studying is done. Skiing takes the prize as the most popular pastime. "Every weekend, every student goes...it is a blast," one student exclaims. College-sponsored movies, dances, bars, and coffeehouses are all big draws. Eight percent of students join Greek organizations, but the frat scene has quieted down in recent years. Another annual festival of sorts is the Primal Scream, a collective scream on campus every midnight during finals week. Underage students caught drinking openly in the dorms risk being sent before the school judiciary committee—but that hasn't stopped illegal imbibing, students say. One religion major warns that the alcohol policies have gotten very strict in recent years, making students "much more aware and cautious" and less likely to throw wild parties.

As a venue, students say Burlington is a "100 percent college town." It's stylish, with symphonies, art galleries, chic shopping, and lively bars and restaurants, as well as ample community service opportunities. "Burlington is the greatest college town I could ask for," says a senior. But as much as they love their little city, students look forward to getting out of town. The Outing Club is one of UVM's most popular student organizations, since the nearby Green Mountains, White Mountains, and Adirondacks offer prime hiking, skiing, and backpacking. The best road trips are Montreal (90 minutes) and Boston (four hours).

The hockey team competes in the ECAC, has ranked as high as second

All majors require a three-credit course in race and culture that explores race relations and ethnic diversity in the United States.

Freshmen are now eligible for the John Dewey Honors Program through the College of Arts & Sciences. These scholars participate in special seminars and high-level courses in their majors and complete a senior thesis.

One thing UVM students know about is snow. Every year during the first snowfall, the snowball fight between the main campus and the east campus draws students into the winter wonderland.

nationally, and is the pride and joy of UVM sports. Catamount games are always sold out; students get access to tickets before the general public, and there is a lengthy waiting list for community members. Soccer is king in the fall—as student T-shirts say, the football team's been "Undefeated since 1974," the last year of its existence. Men's and women's basketball are solid programs, as are field hockey and men's and women's track, and the ski teams are NCAA powerhouses. Students love intramural sports, especially tennis and broomball (ice hockey played with brooms, on shoes instead of skates) "Groovy Uvey" is definitely the product of its homegrown, laid-back Vermont environment, where students hit the books and the slopes with equal abandon. Though the high price tag may scare away some potential students, those who call this university home seem to enjoy UVM's special blend of work and play.

If You Apply To ➤ **UVM**…Early decision: Nov. 1. Regular admissions: Jan. 15. Financial aid: Feb. 10. Does not guarantee to meet demonstrated need. Campus and alumni interviews: optional, informational. SATs or ACTs: required. SAT IIs: optional. Apply to individual schools or programs. Accepts electronic applications. Essay questions: significant experience, academic interests, outside interests; long essays: one of three: person you admire, why your major, topic of your choice.

Villanova University

800 Lancaster Avenue, Villanova, PA 19085-1672

Website: www.villanova.edu
Location: Suburban
Total Enrollment: 9,968
Undergraduates: 7,144
Male/Female: 50/50
SAT Ranges: V 550–640 M 570–670
Financial Aid: 63%
Expense: Pr $ $ $
Phi Beta Kappa: Yes
Applicants: 9,826
Accepted: 56%
Enrolled: 30%
Grad in 6 Years: 83%
Returning Freshmen: 93%
Academics: ✍ ✍ ✍
Social: ☎ ☎ ☎
Q of L: ★ ★ ★
Admissions: (800) 338-7927
Email Address:
gotovu@email.villanova.edu

Villanova University offers all the trappings of a traditional Roman Catholic university: strong academics (including nationally-recognized programs in business and nursing), unrivaled traditions, and a student body that is dedicated to their faith. Says one senior, "You will be involved in campus ministry at one point in your four years at Villanova, if not every day."

Situated in a suburb on Philadelphia's posh Main Line, the Villanova University campus occupies more than 220 acres of beautiful grounds that were once the estate of a Revolutionary War officer. The buildings range from ivy-covered stone to modern, with plenty of secluded, tree-lined walkways connecting them. The atmosphere is tranquil with wide lawns, pleasant walks, and modern terracing, and the traditions of Roman Catholicism are as prevalent now as when Villanova was founded by Augustinians over 150 years ago. "I believe it is the Catholic aspect of the school that gives it such a friendly, personal feel," says one happy Wildcat.

Students universally cite the College of Commerce and Finance as the best on campus, so it's no wonder that business administration and accounting are national draws. In fact, finance is the most popular major on campus, followed by accounting, nursing, biology, and management. Students also give thumbs-up to the College of Engineering, which enjoys strong regional recognition. In the College of Liberal Arts and Sciences, most departments are considered adequate, if not great, but offerings that fall under the arts part of the equation are less than spectacular. Villanova's fourth academic unit, the College of Nursing, is also regionally recognized. A whole squadron of ROTC options are available. General education requirements vary by program, but all majors participate in a seminar program, which includes small classes taught by select members of the English, history, philosophy, and religious studies departments. The seminars stress discussion, intensive writing, readings from primary texts, and close working relationships between students and faculty. These integrative courses allow students to choose a topic or theme from the perspective of several disciplines with an emphasis on Villanova's Christian character.

Students describe the quality of teaching at Villanova as "very high," and report that professors are accessible. "I have experienced many excellent professors who are extremely knowledgeable in their fields," says one junior. Students also say that professors are always available for outside help and personal attention. Some students admit there is difficulty getting into the courses taught by the preferred professors but explain that scheduling is very flexible and students don't have a problem graduating within four years. Approximately 200 students participate in Villanova's honors program, with enrollment by invitation only. The 629,000-volume library is adequate for most needs, though certain areas have the reputation of being more for socializing than studying. The St. Augustine Center for the Liberal Arts houses most of the liberal arts faculty and provides seminar rooms.

Twenty-nine percent of the student body are native, noncommuting Pennsylvanians. The campus is home to a large number of affluent white Catholics (hence the nickname Vanillanova), and faith plays an important role for most students. "We have three different masses on Sunday nights," explains a student, "and each time there is barely any standing room...forget about sitting." Three percent of the student body are African American; Hispanics and Asian Americans comprise another 8 percent. Villanova requires students to take a class on diversity, whether it be a course in United States or international culture. Additionally, the Multicultural Affairs office focuses the drive toward diversity, which has been increasing in recent years. For what little diversity there is, though, students report that there is little hostility among the groups.

'Nova students are as preprofessional as any you'll find, and they praise the Career and Planning Center for helping them prepare résumés, perfect interviewing skills, obtain internships, and investigate various careers. In addition to need-based financial aid, Villanova awards more than 800 merit scholarships every year, ranging from $1,000 to full tuition, room, and board. Athletic scholarships are earmarked for several men's and women's sports.

Housing ranges from excellent to grim, although one honors student is quick to add that the older dorms are in great locations, and four apartment complexes for juniors and seniors are available. Sixty-five percent of undergrads live on campus. Housing is guaranteed for three years, but upperclassmen most often choose to live off campus. Students usually get the housing they request through a lottery system, and freshmen are housed on the South Campus Circle. The housing situation is still a little cramped, though, since off-campus housing can be expensive and limited and the neighborhood folks aren't terribly friendly to college types. One junior says that the lack of guaranteed housing is the school's biggest problem. About 10 percent of the students from the Philadelphia area avoid the hassle by commuting from home. Everyone who lives on campus is required to buy one of the three meal plans and eat in one of the three dining halls.

Most socializing revolves around weekend parties on or off campus, some sponsored by Greek groups, which claim 18 percent of the men and 34 percent of the women. The campus is dry, and policies strictly enforce the under-21 Pennsylvania law. But an education major says the campus is actually "slightly damp." A row of local bars on Lancaster Avenue caters to students over 21, and partying at the apartments or houses of upperclassmen is frequent. On-campus alternatives to drinking include movies and dances, usually held in Connelly

(Continued)
Strongest Programs:
Accounting
Biology
Engineering
Business

Students universally cite the College of Commerce and Finance as the best on campus, so it's no wonder that business administration and accounting are national draws.

Men's and women's track continue to be national powerhouses, sometimes supplying the United States Olympic team with the best runners in the world.

Center, a multimillion-dollar student activities building, and a nightclub. Those who tire of Villanova's suburban setting can hop the train for a short 12-mile ride into Philly, where myriad cultural and social opportunities, ranging from museums to hockey games, await them. Ski resorts, the Jersey shore, Atlantic City, and the Poconos are all within a two-hour drive.

'Novan prayers were answered one spring night in 1985 when the Wildcats stunned Catholic rival Georgetown in the NCAA basketball tournament championship game. That victory put Villanova's varsity sports on the national map. The women's swim and cross-country teams are also strong, while the football team (Division I-AA) plays to sold-out crowds. Men's and women's track continue to be national powerhouses, sometimes supplying the United States Olympic team with the best runners in the world. The entire athletic program benefits from a massive athletic complex, which includes a swimming center and an indoor track. For ex-high school jocks not up to varsity status, the thriving intramural program offers competition in three different leagues, ranging from serious to slapstick. Extracurricular activities are as numerous as the intramurals.

Spiritual commitments aside, many Villanova students seem to believe a little worldly success wouldn't do them any everlasting harm. The university likens itself to a happy family with strong Catholic principles, and a strong bond of love and respect crossing the divides between the faculty, staff, and student communities.

Overlaps

Penn State, Boston College, Lehigh, Loyola, Notre Dame.

If You Apply To ➢ **Villanova**...Early action: Nov. 15. Regular admissions: Jan. 7. Financial aid: Mar. 15. Does not guarantee to meet demonstrated need. No campus or alumni interviews. SATs or ACTs: required. No SAT IIs. Apply to a particular school or program. Accepts electronic applications. Essay question: What you would tell your Villanova classmates at your tenth reunion.

Virginia Polytechnic Institute and State University

Blacksburg, VA 24061

Website: www.vt.edu
Location: Small town
Total Enrollment: 25,783
Undergraduates: 21,810
Male/Female: 58/42
SAT Ranges: V 520–620 M 540–650
Financial Aid: 63%
Expense: Pub $ $
Phi Beta Kappa: Yes
Applicants: 15,883
Accepted: 73%
Enrolled: 30%
Grad in 6 Years: 74%

Though it's full name is the Virginia Polytechnic Institute and State University, those in the know just call it Virginia Tech. Long known for its solid engineering and architecture programs, this Southern university has recently garnered more national attention for its athletics than its academics. It's no wonder students want to spend four years at the "Hokie Pokie."

Set on a plateau in the scenic Blue Ridge mountains, Tech's campus occupies 3,000 acres and comes complete with a duck pond, hiking trails, and a 200-year-old plantation that is a local landmark. Students enjoy unlimited outdoor recreation thanks to the proximity of the Jefferson National Forest, the Appalachian Trail, the scenic Blue Ridge Parkway, and the majestic old New River. The campus buildings are an attractive mix of gray limestone structures and Colonial-style brick and modern cement buildings. Newer facilities include the 150,000-square-foot Advanced Communications and Information Technology Center.

Virginia Tech is best known for its first-rate technical and professional training. For undergrads with an appetite for engineering, Tech has programs for every taste, including aerospace, ocean, biological systems, civil, chemical, computer, electrical, industrial and systems, materials, mechanical (the most popular), and mining. The Pamplin College of Business is also prominent, and the five-year architecture program is considered one of the nation's best. Though no longer Tech's centerpiece, the College of Agriculture and Life Sciences remains strong, especially in animal science. Students in the College of Natural Resources can choose from such concentrations as environmental conservation, fisheries science, forestry, and wildlife management. The College of Education merged with the College of Human Resources, where Hospitality and Tourism is the best known program.

Tech's offerings in the liberal arts are spotty. Students in the sciences reap the benefits of their high-tech environment; other disciplines do not fare so well. The humanities have been hard hit by budget cuts. In particular, "religious studies, foreign languages, and philosophy are dwindling away," says a senior. One bright spot is internationally known poet Nikki Giovanni, who teaches creative writing and advanced poetry. The university also has a tradition of excellence in the performing arts, and the school's theater group has received more awards from the American College Theater Arts Festival than any other college in the Southeast. The music department boasts the most advanced digital music facilities in the region.

Introductory class size tends to be large—sometimes well into the hundreds—and the budget ax has only made matters worse. Most of the big lecture classes are taught by full-time faculty, though discussions and grading are generally handled by TAs. Nevertheless, a communications major says her professors "keep you on the edge of your seat." A senior adds, "The classes are large, but the professors are always accessible, I have been taught mostly by full professors for all of my four years." All students are required to take courses in English, math, humanities, and social and natural science. There is also a foreign language requirement, though high school coursework may cover this requirement. The 1,500 or so students who participate in the University Honors Program are guaranteed access to top faculty and research opportunities.

Each year, more than 1,000 students take advantage of Tech's co-op opportunities, available in almost all majors. The nationally acclaimed Small Business Institute program enables faculty-led groups of business majors to work with local merchants, analyze their problems, and make suggestions on how to increase profits. The Corps of Cadets, a tradition once on the verge of extinction, has made a comeback. Cadets earn a minor in leadership and can choose from three tracks: military/ROTC, civic professions, or a combination of the two.

Students looking at pricey Northeastern technical schools will find Tech a real bargain. Not surprisingly, the admissions office is inundated with out-of-state applicants, which means stiff competition for the 25 percent of the slots available to non-Virginians. Tech's relative isolation from major cities is a drag on minority recruitment: Blacks and Hispanics account for only 6 percent of the student body, Asian Americans account for another 6 percent. Students with financial need who apply for aid before the deadline receive priority consideration; those who apply later are likely to be out of luck. Tech hands out a total of about 280 athletic scholarships, and several hundred students, including lots of future engineers, are granted merit awards that are generally $5,000 or less. Tech is among the nation's leaders in the integration of computers into all facets of life. All freshmen are required to own a computer. Says an engineering major, "On campus you can do anything from handing in homework to checking grades to checking out what movies are playing, all by computer."

(Continued)
Returning Freshmen: 97%
Academics: ✍ ✍ ✍
Social: ☎ ☎ ☎
Q of L: ★ ★ ★ ★
Admissions: (540) 231-6267
Email Address:
vtadmiss@vt.edu

Strongest Programs:
Engineering
Architecture and Urban
Studies
Business
Sciences
Human Resources and
Education
Mathematics
Forestry and Wildlife
Resources
Humanities / Arts

For undergrads with an appetite for engineering, Tech has programs for every taste, including aerospace, ocean, biological systems, civil, chemical, computer, electrical, industrial and systems, materials, mechanical (the most popular), and mining.

"Rooms are on the small side, but they provide all you need to live," says a freshman. Some 25 undergraduate dorms serve 8,400 students; 43 percent of the student body live on campus, though only freshmen and the Corps of Cadets are required to. Most upperclassmen live off campus in nearby apartment complexes. Dietrick's Depot, the largest dining hall on campus, was recently renovated. Three specialty lines supplement the standard dining-hall fare to create an intimate, café-style atmosphere. Students who are committed to a healthy lifestyle can opt to reside in the W.E.L.L. (Wellness Environment for Living and Learning), which will provide them with a substance-free atmosphere, and includes special healthy living courses and is overseen by a specially trained wellness staff.

Leisure-time activities often involve the outdoors. The nearby Cascades National Park is an especially popular retreat for lovers and camping jocks alike, and tubing down the New River is a ritual for summer students. Blacksburg has the usual assortment of college town bars and a quaint downtown shopping area. Tech's varsity athletics program struggled for years to make the big time—and never succeeded—but the football team's recent shot at the national title have cheered alumni and hiked applications by several thousand. The annual "big game" pits the backwoodsy Hokies against the aristocratic (snobby?) Cavaliers of the University of Virginia. (In case you're wondering, "Hokie" is taken from a nonsense lyric in the school fight song: "Hokie, Hokie, Hokie Hi—We're the Boys from V.P.I.") Tech has one of the nation's most extensive intramural programs, with everything from football to horseshoes and underwater hockey—a recent rage—and more than 400 softball teams each spring, many of them coed. Weekend athletes benefit from the addition of a fitness center.

Aside from sports, leisure-time favorites include school-sponsored plays, jazz concerts, arts and crafts fairs, and dances. Thirteen percent of the men and 23 percent of the women join fraternities and sororities, which set the tone of the social life. If going Greek isn't for you, don't worry, as one student says, "There is a place for every person at VT. There are so many organizations and everyone is so friendly that any person who comes here and wants to get involved can do so without any trouble." The most important annual event is the Ring Dance (when the juniors receive their school rings), the German Club's Midwinter's Dance, and the Corps of Cadets military ball. For real big-city action, Washington, D.C., and Richmond are four and three hours away by car, respectively.

Anyone looking for a high-tech education garnished with Southern hospitality will find Virginia Tech just right. "I think Tech is pretty personal considering the number of students it serves," says a junior.

Overlaps

University of Virginia, Radford, George Mason, James Madison.

Easily one of the most prestigious public schools in the nation, the University of Virginia blends rich tradition with progressive attitudes. Perhaps that's a mark of its founder. UVA is known to all in Charlottesville as Mister Jefferson's University. Not just any Mister Jefferson, mind you, but *the* Mister Jefferson, author of the Declaration of Independence. Though he passed away over 150 years ago, he is referred to here as if he ran down to the apothecary shop for a bit of snuff and will be back momentarily. Of all his accomplishments, Jefferson was arguably proudest of UVA—he even asked that his epitaph speak to his role in creating the university rather than his presidency.

Located just east of the Blue Ridge Mountains in central Virginia, UVA's campus was designed by Mister Jefferson himself, and still uses many of its original buildings today. At the core of the university is Jefferson's "academical village," with its majestic white pillars, serpentine walls, and extensive brickwork. The village is built around a rectangular terraced green—called the Lawn—that is flanked by two rows of identical one-story rooms that are reserved for undergraduate student leaders. Five pavilions, each in a different style, accent each side of the Lawn. Both the rooms and the pavilions enter into a colonnaded walkway that fronts the Lawn. Behind the rows of buildings are public gardens. The Rotunda, a half-scale model of the Roman Pantheon, overlooks the Lawn. New construction is adding modern facilities to the existing neoclassical buildings. In the planning or construction phase is a residence hall, an addition to the architecture school, a special collections library, a parking garage for 600 vehicles, an addition to the student health center, and an expansion of the football stadium.

Elite among public institutions of higher education, UVA also holds its own against the best of the private schools, too. Students are accepted into the four-year schools of engineering, nursing, and architecture, but the vast majority enter the liberal arts college. According to students, the best departments are history, English, religious studies, and the School of Commerce. Students steer clear of visual, dramatic, and musical arts, which are considered to be the weakest. The university, however, continues to make improvements to the fine and performing arts departments. The most popular majors are commerce, psychology, economics and biology. UVA's school of education offers a five-year program that culminates in a BA from the College of Arts and Sciences and a Master of Teaching degree from the education school.

After their second year, about 300 Arts and Sciences students transfer into the commerce school, but competition for these spots is tough. Virginia requires students in the College of Arts and Sciences and the commerce school to master a foreign language. Arts and Sciences students must also take courses in humanities and fine arts, social science, natural sciences and mathematics, non-Western studies, and composition. All freshmen in the College are required to take English composition. The emphasis is on top-level academic programs taught within nationally recognized departments. With more than 4 million volumes and one of the nation's largest collections of online materials in six digital centers, the library is more than adequate. The computer science department also has a state-of-the-art virtual reality lab.

A number of special programs are offered in addition to the regular curriculum. The most prestigious of these is the Echols Scholars program, which exempts

Website: www.virginia.edu
Location: Small city
Total Enrollment: 22,433
Undergraduates: 13,570
Male/Female: 46/54
SAT Ranges: V 600–700 M 610–710
ACT Range: 26–31
Financial Aid: 23%
Expense: Pub $ $ $
Phi Beta Kappa: Yes
Applicants: 16,461
Accepted: 34%
Enrolled: 52%
Grad in 6 Years: 91%
Returning Freshmen: 96%
Academics: ✍ ✍ ✍ ✍ ✍
Social: ☎ ☎ ☎ ☎
Q of L: ★ ★ ★ ★ ★
Admissions: (804) 982-3200
Email Address: undergrad-admission@ virginia.edu

Strongest Programs:
English
Foreign Languages
Physiology
Government
Economics
History
Biochemistry
Religious Studies

Though he passed away over 150 years ago, Thomas Jefferson is referred to here as if he ran down to the apothecary shop for a bit of snuff and will be back momentarily.

students from distribution and major-field requirements and lets them loose to explore the academic disciplines as they see fit. The school invites about 180 top freshmen (plan on total SATs solidly above 1400) into the program and houses them together for their first year. The Distinguished Majors Program enables qualified students to pursue an independent study during their third and fourth years. Two residential colleges house approximately 800 students, mostly upper-classmen, with 100 faculty members participating (a handful even living in the student housing). The Interdisciplinary Majors program allows students to combine three disciplines and integrate them into a year-long senior thesis. Professors are said to be highly accessible and friendly. "The professors here make learning fun and intriguing," says a French major. Another student adds, "The professors are knowledgeable and very approachable." To encourage more professor/student interaction, the university instituted a University Seminar program, in which prominent faculty teach 15 or fewer first-year students in a seminar learning environment. It also offers a number of one-credit courses called University Topics, which focus on current events. The school has added a coffee bar in the library and a fund subsidizing faculty-student lunches, both aimed at fostering informal conversations.

Virginia is noted for its honor system, which was instituted by students in 1842 after no one owned up to shooting a professor on the Lawn. Students are expected to "have the moral fortitude to abide by the community's standards of moral conduct," and the penalty for infractions is a swift dismissal from campus. A number of controversial cases recently produced a measure of reform, and discussions continue about the appropriateness of the single-sanction system and even the continued existence of the student-run honor system. But rest assured, some form of the honor code will remain a way of life here, as many students say they feel comfortable leaving backpacks and calculators unattended without worry of thieves. "Students here are kicked out if they are caught lying, cheating or stealing, which makes for a really unique community of trust," a second-year says.

Admission for out-of-state students,—31 percent of the undergraduate body, —is more competitive than for in-staters, but nearly everyone who gets in is highly qualified. Ninety-six percent of the freshmen were in the top quarter of their high school class. Many students hail from Washington, D.C., and suburbs of northern Virginia, while most out-of-staters come from New York, New Jersey, Pennsylvania, and Maryland. Among the few merit scholarships offered at Virginia are 20 to 25 highly prized Jefferson Scholarships, which are awarded by the alumni association and are good for full tuition, as well as room and board. Administrators also award 50 in-state applicants who will advance the university's pursuit of diversity with renewable grants for full tuition. Up to seven out-of-state blacks get renewable stipends of $10,000 a year. About 400 athletes in 12 men's sports and 12 women's sports get athletic scholarships.

The student body is somewhat diverse, with 10 percent African American students, 10 percent Asian American students, and a growing number of students from abroad. The consensus here is that while race relations are not overly hostile, there is a sense that black students "self-segregate," as one student says. In the past, the university has been recognized as having the highest graduation rate for blacks of any state-supported college in the country; 88 percent of black students who started school between 1986 and 1989 graduated within six years, according to *The Journal of Blacks in Higher Education.*

A conspicuous exception to the historic graciousness of most of the Virginia campus is the Hereford College, a residential and dining complex that features

The university continues to make improvements to the fine and performing arts departments and plans are in the works to construct a new studio art building, a new museum, a fine arts library, and a concert hall.

contemporary architecture described by *The New York Times* as "proudly, almost defiantly modern." All first-year students live "on grounds," as do some top fourth-year leaders and honors students, who qualify for coveted singles in the academic village. Others (53 percent) trek off campus, but still stay involved with the university. Commuters praise the university's bus system, which is important since campus parking is extremely limited. Meal plans are required for first-year students, while many upperclassmen either cook for themselves or take meals at their Greek houses. Thirty percent of men and women make up the Greek system, which has a fairly prominent role in campus social life.

Mr. Jefferson founded UVA as a place where students could come together to "drink the cup of knowledge," but today's undergraduates seem to favor a different sort of brew. Studious Virginians by day can metamorphose into the Rowdy Wahoos (a nickname derived from one of the college cheers about the fish that can drink twice its weight) by night. As with most college students, drinking is a favorite pastime, and underage students have little problem obtaining alcohol. The administration has made major efforts to curtail such rowdiness by enforcing drinking rules, such as no kegs or grain alcohol in the dorms, and students under 21 can attend parties where booze is served only if "Tips"—trained alcohol supervisors—are present. Though taps have been known to run freely on Rugby Road, where some 33 fraternity houses have set up shop, the administration has cracked down in recent years. UVA has a dry rush, and guest lists are now required for all fraternity parties. The fraternities assume an obligation to provide social activities not only for their own members but for the campus at large, and the "big weekends" are still big, though far less legendary than in the early '80s. The student-run University Union and more than 300 student organizations offer movies, concerts, social hours, and other extracurricular activities. Students also tend to immerse themselves in community service activities. One traditional local event is Foxfield, in which students dress up and host catered parties prior to attending a horse race. Other famous traditions include streaking the Lawn, doing the "Corner Crawl" on your 21st birthday, Midwinters and Midsummers, dressing up for football games, and an annual visit by a hypnotist that draws more than 10,000 people.

The town of Charlottesville gets high marks from students. One computer science/engineering major calls the city "off the beaten bath, but not far away from the flow of the world." If the city limits of Charlottesville get too confining, students roadtrip two hours to Washington or head to Richmond for concerts and other events. Ski slopes are an hour away, and Virginia Beach is less than four hours in the opposite direction. Big-time Atlantic Coast Conference basketball has long been an integral part of UVA life.

Ultimately, this quintessentially Virginian institution can take pride in its paternal lineage and its powerful present, as it defends its title as one of the premier public institutions in the country, holding its own against the top privates as well.

No doubt, strong programs and a one-of-a-kind atmosphere will allow Mister Jefferson's university to hold on to its "budget Ivy League" reputation well into the next millennium.

UVA's school of education offers a five-year program that culminates in a BA from the College of Arts and Sciences and a Master of Teaching degree from the education school.

Overlaps

William and Mary, Duke, Virginia Tech, University of Pennsylvania, Cornell University.

Wabash College

301 West Wabash, Crawfordsville, IN 47933

Website: www.wabash.edu

Location: Small town

Total Enrollment: 861

Undergraduates: 861

Male/Female: 100/0

SAT Ranges: V 520–630 M 540–650

Financial Aid: 70%

Expense: Pr $ $

Phi Beta Kappa: Yes

Applicants: 894

Accepted: 75%

Enrolled: 33%

Grad in 6 Years: 69%

Returning Freshmen: 81%

Academics: ✍ ✍ ✍

Social: ☎ ☎

Q of L: ★ ★ ★

Admissions: (800) 345-5385

Email Address:
admissions@wabash.edu

Strongest Programs:
Religion
Premed
Prelaw
Economics
Biology

In keeping with its reputation in the sciences, Wabash has an electron microscope and a laser spectrometer, a 180-acre biological field station, and a cell culture lab.

At Wabash College, an all-male school in Indiana, students follow the Gentleman's Rule: "Wabash men are expected to behave like gentlemen at all times," says a senior history and speech major. "This rule encompasses alcohol, women, academics, and all other areas of college life." Indeed, stepping onto the Wabash campus is much like stepping back in history to a time when men were men and the world was theirs. Wabash was founded in 1832 by transplanted Ivy Leaguers, who most certainly held a positive view of a man's future.

The Wabash campus is characterized by redbrick, white-pillared Federal-style buildings (three are originals from the 1830s). Located in the heart of tiny Crawfordsville, a small town of about 15,000, Wabash is surrounded by grass and tall trees that are part of the gorgeous Fuller Arboretum. Current construction includes a 170,000-square-foot athletics and recreation center.

The Wabash educational program has certainly proved itself over the years. This small college has amassed quite an impressive list of alumni: executives of major corporations, doctors, lawyers, and a large proportion of Ph.D.s. Most Wabash alumni are faithful to their school in the form of generous donations. On a per capita basis, the school's $315-million endowment makes it one of the wealthiest in the nation. This financial security enables Wabash to refuse any federal aid, with the exception of Pell Grants, which go directly to students.

History and economics draw the most majors at Wabash, and the highest accolades go to the biology (premed) and chemistry departments, which are among the most challenging and produce many successful grads. In keeping with its reputation in the sciences, Wabash has an electron microscope and a laser spectrometer, a 180-acre biological field station, and a cell culture lab. Political science and the religion/philosophy department are also popular, but students say the speech department could be improved. A 42,600-square-foot fine arts center provides more studio space and practice rooms and is a pleasant addition to the music and art departments. The newest additions to the curriculum include international studies, gender studies, and multicultural American studies.

The academic climate at Wabash is intense, and people are serious about their studies. "The academic climate is very challenging and you have to put in a lot of time and effort to get a good grade," says a senior. The students are very focused during the week on the academic challenges presented to them. General education requirements include courses from a wide variety of fields—natural and behavioral sciences, literature and fine arts, mathematics, language studies, and a course on cultures and traditions. In addition, a freshman tutorial, which is limited to a maximum of 15 students, is designed to improve class participation and reading and writing skills. A special writing center is available for all Wabash students who demonstrate a weakness in written communication skills. The ability to write well is definitely an asset, as many tests feature essay questions. Juniors are encouraged to study on continents throughout the world or in various domestic programs through the Great Lakes College Association.* Those who can't satisfy their high-tech interests at Wabash can opt for a 3–2 program in engineering with Columbia University or Washington University of St. Louis. Wabash also offers a tuition-free semester after graduation to train students to become teachers. Students use the words "outstanding" and "fantastic" to describe their professors. Advising is also considered excellent, and students say they have no problems getting into required courses.

Most of Wabash's students come from public high schools in Indiana, and 68 percent were in the top quarter of their high school class. Many were active in athletics and student government and continue that tradition in college. The campus is mostly conservative, through both Republican and Democratic student organizations are strong. The administration is working with a grant to improve diversity on campus. It has expanded the freshman orientation program to include diversity and community issues, focusing on making choices and accepting the consequences. However, students agree there's still a ways to go. African American, Hispanic, Asian American, and foreign students combined account for 13 percent of the campus population. "There tend to be very few pressures on campus caused by diversity," one sophomore says. "All students, regardless of race, are Wabash brothers."

Residential life for the temporary denizens of small-town Crawfordsville revolves around the 10 fraternities, each with its own house. Seventy percent of the students join up and many end up living with their brothers. As an alternative to Greek life, there are three modern dorms, two of which have all single rooms. Dorm residents must eat in the dining hall, while fraternities have private cooks who prepare "meals that are really not that bad." Those living in the dorms (and the 9 percent who live off campus) may feel excluded from what there is of campus social life, since the fraternities "ship in" sorority members from Purdue, Indiana, DePauw, and Butler for parties. "Many people make the mistake [of thinking] that since Wabash has no women...we don't have good parties," says a senior history major. A wise freshman, however, points out that "the absence of women on weekdays helps some to concentrate on their studies." As for drinking on campus, students agree that policies are loose. A sophomore says, "Alcohol is fairly accessible.... The big difference is that at Wabash, students behave responsibly. No one is stupid enough to drink and then decide to drive around."

Wallies are tough in athletics. The football, baseball, basketball, swimming, and the cross-country teams are very competitive. When they're not studying or partying, students are likely to be found working out in the gym or running. Most nonvarsity athletes participate in intramurals, which encompass 22 sports, including pool and horseshoes. School spirit is abundant, especially when the opponent is long-standing rival DePauw. The annual Monon Bell football game against the hated "Dannies" (DePauw Tigers) is "a great game, steeped in tradition." Another popular though less sweaty event is Chapel Sing, where all the freshmen sing the lengthy school song in unison. "Actually, we yell until we go hoarse," a participant says.

Just as it is at an all-women's school, tradition is an important part of the lives of the men at Wabash. "It is almost impossible to put into words why Wabash is special," a senior says. "You have to experience it to understand why generations of Wabash men continue to support and love the school. The traditions of Wabash have remained almost unchanged since its founding in 1832." Students here accept the workload and the social sacrifices to be part of the Wabash tradition.

A 42,600-square-foot fine arts center provides more studio space and practice rooms and is a pleasant addition to the music and art departments.

Those who can't satisfy their high-tech interests at Wabash can opt for a 3–2 program in engineering with Columbia University or Washington University of St. Louis.

Overlaps

Indiana University, Purdue, Ball State, Hanover, DePauw.

Wake Forest University

P.O. Box 7305, Winston-Salem, NC 27109

Website: www.wfu.edu

Location: City outskirts

Total Enrollment: 6,082

Undergraduates: 3,990

Male/Female: 51/49

SAT Ranges: V 600–690 M 610–700

Financial Aid: 33%

Expense: Pr $ $ $

Phi Beta Kappa: Yes

Applicants: 4,982

Accepted: 49%

Enrolled: 40%

Grad in 6 Years: 86%

Returning Freshmen: 91%

Academics: ✍ ✍ ✍

Social: ☎ ☎ ☎

Q of L: ★ ★ ★

Admissions: (336) 758-5201

Email Address:
admissions@wfu.edu

Strongest Programs:
Psychology
Business
English
Biology

You wouldn't assume that a small liberal arts school in North Carolina would be at the forefront of the technology revolution. But Wake Forest University is committed to integrating computers into its curriculum and into students' lives. The university provides each freshman with an laptop computer when they arrive on campus. And at the beginning of their junior year, students receive a second new computer, which they take with them upon graduation. Already well established as one of the top private schools in the Southeast, Wake is working hard to develop a national reputation. "The college has focused its energy—providing students the tools, knowledge, and experience to work in a world where computers and technology are so prevalent," says one junior.

Located in the lovely Piedmont region of North Carolina, the 340-acre campus features flower gardens, wooded trails, and stately magnolias. The architecture consists of more than 40 Georgian-style buildings of old Virginia brick and granite trim. In the fall of 1999, Wake finished construction on a new 80,000-square-foot academic building and an addition to Wingate Hall to house its new Divinity School. All of the new mortar and stone complements some of the delightful facets of the school's physical plant, such as the Reynolda Gardens annex—150 acres of woods, gardens, and a shopping village—and the Graylyn International Conference Center. Just three miles south of the campus is downtown Winston-Salem, a town rich in North Carolina history.

Competition is fierce at Wake Forest, and grade inflation is kept to a minimum, say students. "All of the courses are very rigorous—there are no slack classes," says a sophomore pre-med student. "Everyone is motivated and competes with themselves to do the best." All students are required to take a first-year seminar, a writing seminar, two semesters of foreign language, and two classes in health and exercise science. Students then select courses in each of five basic divisions, including literature, natural sciences, social sciences, history, and fine arts. Those in the innovative honors program participate in small seminars focusing on major thinkers and artists. Faculty draws high praise from students. "I still haven't figured out when professors do their research—all are published authors and research professors, yet they are always in their offices and willing to help or simply chat with students," a senior says. Students say the majority of classes are taught by full professors, and well over 95 percent of their classes have fewer than 25 students.

Business is the most popular major, followed by psychology, English, communications, and biology. Students tend to avoid philosophy, math, and religion. Wake Forest's future accountants rank in the top five in the nation in passing the CPA exam. New programs include the Hewlett initiative, which offers stipends to 14 students who are willing to engage in critical dialogue about historical and current issues related to diversity in their respective disciplines. The school owns residential study centers on the Grand Canal in Venice and in London and Vienna. It also offers programs in France, Spain, China, Japan, and Russia. About 35 percent of Wake graduates study abroad.

But while Wake Forest students traipse around the world sampling foreign cultures, life on campus is fairly homogeneous, with (mostly upper-class, conservative) whites making up 88 percent of the student body. Sixty-nine percent of the student body are from outside North Carolina, with many others coming from Southern states. Blacks represent 8 percent of the student body, while Hispanics and Asian Americans constitute 3 percent combined. "I wouldn't describe Wake as segregated or racist, but we do need to work on intermingling to appreciate the diverse cultural and religious backgrounds represented at Wake," says a senior politics major. Wake offers athletic scholarships and merit scholarships that range from $350 to full tuition.

Life on campus is good for Wake Forest students, who describe the dorms as "small but comfortable." Recently installed gates around the campus have made students feels safe and cozy. Eighty percent of undergraduates live on campus, and students are guaranteed housing on campus for all four years. But once a student chooses to move off campus, the university rescinds the dorm privileges. Rooms are assigned by a lottery that gives seniors priority; but few report problems getting a room. As far as campus dining, students select a meal plan to suit their appetites and are charged only for what they eat. Dining options include a fairly typical cafeteria, the food court, and the Magnolia Room, which dishes out classier food and is also more expensive than the other options. Students use a debit card to pay for meals at all three locations, debiting their yearly account.

Fraternities and sororities dominate much of the social scene; Greeks draw 37 percent of the men and 51 percent of the women. "Fraternities and sororities dominate the party scene on campus," a senior says. "But all on-campus parties open up at 10:00 P.M. and anyone is welcome." Students agree that the "open party" system, which keeps all parties open to Greeks and non-Greeks alike, adds to the social life on campus. The university has approximately 100 campus groups, including theater troupes, religious organizations, volunteer service corps, a student-run newspaper, radio and television stations, and special-interest groups, such as the Black Student Alliance and the Women's Issues Network. Those students who choose to eschew the Greek scene go to off-campus bars or restaurants or to plays and other cultural events on campus. Winston-Salem has a strong music scene, with Ziggy's and Freddy B's serving as the cornerstones of the local concert circuit.

Winston-Salem is rich in culture, with a symphony, a Christmastime "Moravian love feast," and the well-known North Carolina School of the Arts. In addition to the on-campus Museum of Anthropology, two art museums are within a three-mile walk from campus. Still, the city is not what most consider a college town. "Wake Forest is separated from the city and does not have much contact with the community except for certain events during the year," a junior French major says. Another adds, "Students actually refer to Wake as 'the bubble.'" Nonetheless, students are involved in the community through churches and volunteer activities. Top road-trip destinations include the Carolina beaches, about four hours away; Atlanta and Washington, about five hours away; and the Blue Ridge Mountains, two hours away. (Wake even offers a ski class.)

In the South, basketball is king, and the Demon Deacons are perennial powerhouses in the incredibly tough Atlantic Coast Conference. Wake Forest prides itself on its ability to play with the big boys of the ACC and won the NIT

Students say the majority of classes are taught by full professors, and well over 95 percent of their classes have fewer than 25 students. Only one class has more than 100 students.

The school owns residential study centers on the Grand Canal in Venice and in London and Vienna. It also offers programs in France, Spain, China, Japan, and Russia. About 35 percent of Wake graduates study abroad.

Students agree that the "open party" system, which keeps all parties open to Greeks and non-Greeks alike, adds to the social life on campus.

Invitational Tournament in 2000. "Following a victory, the entire campus raids the bathrooms and covers the quad in toilet paper," says a sophomore, referring to the "Rolling the Quad" tradition. The football team draws big crowds, too, and were victorious in the 1999 Aloha Bowl. In 1998 and 1999, men's baseball won the ACC championship, and a year later, it won the NCAA regional championships. Wake Forest offers stellar athletic facilities, including seven playing fields, four gymnasiums, a first-rate baseball stadium, a new soccer stadium, and a fine golf course.

Wake Forest offers a combination that few other schools can match—championship caliber athletics, competitive academics, outstanding faculty and facilities, and a name with clout. Other than some concerns about the lack of diversity at the school, students seem contented as Wake Forest works to make its name known outside the southeast. No doubt, as more Wake Forest students graduate with fond memories and positive feelings for their alma mater, the school's reputation will continue to grow.

If You Apply To ➤

Wake Forest…Early decision: Nov. 15. Regular admissions: Jan. 15. Financial aid: Feb. 1. Guarantees to meet demonstrated need. Campus interviews: optional, informational. No alumni interviews. SATs or ACTs: required. SAT IIs: recommended (writing and math). Accepts the Common Application and electronic applications. Essay question: identify with a character in literature; explain Wake Forest's motto of *Pro Humanitate*; define your personal perception of honor.

Washington and Jefferson College

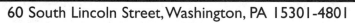

60 South Lincoln Street, Washington, PA 15301-4801

Website: www.washjeff.edu
Location: Small town
Total Enrollment: 1,217
Undergraduates: 1,217
Male/Female: 51/49
SAT Ranges: V 500–600 M 500–600
ACT Range: 21–26
Financial Aid: 76%
Expense: Pr $ $ $
Phi Beta Kappa: Yes
Applicants: 1,261
Accepted: 80%
Enrolled: 31%
Grad in 6 Years: 72%
Returning Freshmen: 85%
Academics:
Social: ☎ ☎ ☎
Q of L: ★ ★
Admissions: (724) 223-6025

Future professionals will be happy to discover that there is a college tailored for their career-centered needs. Washington and Jefferson College provides solid preprofessional programs, small classes, and impressive placement rates at medical and law schools. Students appreciate the closeness among those on campus at this tiny Pennsylvania school and believe it is crucial to their learning experience. "One of the best things about W&J is the small class size and the personal attention received from professors," one satisfied student boasts. "It's easy to develop a friendship with a professor when there are only ten students in a class!"

The campus, like the student body, is tight-knit: 31 buildings residing on 42 acres in a small town about 30 miles outside of Pittsburgh. W&J is the 11th-oldest college in the country, and houses the 8th-oldest college building, which was built in 1793. The prevailing architectural style is traditional Colonial/Georgian, though modern structures have been added at a rapid pace during the past two decades. On the way is the Burnett Center, with new classrooms for business and language majors, as well as the Vilar Technology Center for the new Advanced Information Technology Program.

W&J's formula for success starts with individual attention in small classes, half of which are limited to 25 students. The academic climate is said to be rigorous by most students, especially those on the premed and prelaw track. According to an English and psychology major, "Students here are stereotypical overachievers, but they're not cutthroat." Most classes are taught by tenured professors who are eager to help them understand the requirements and assist them if they fall behind in classwork. Students agree that the quality of teaching is "very high" and "very intense." Academic advising gets good reviews, but career counseling is cited as "moderately successful" to "terrible."

New graduation requirements require students to complete 34 courses and demonstrate proficiency in writing, speaking, reading, quantitative reasoning, and use of information technology. Students also must take credits in culture and intellectual tradition, fine arts, language and literature, science and mathematics, and social sciences. An innovative program called Entrepreneurial Studies allows students to major in any subject and then supplement their studies with special courses on the importance of ambition, energy, poise, and integrity. A thematic major allows students to design their own course of study, while double majors produce such types as a biologist well versed in literature. Rare among liberal arts colleges are the 3–4 programs with the Pennsylvania Colleges of Optometry and Podiatry. More technically minded students can take advantage of the 3–2 engineering programs with Case Western Reserve and Washington University in St. Louis. Among the standard departments, anything premed or prelaw, especially chemistry, biology, political science, and history, is highly praised and popular. Students cite the philosophy, music, and foreign languages departments as weak.

During the January intercession, students find brief apprenticeships in prospective career areas, take a school tour abroad (marine biology trips to the Bahamas or Australia, English theater trips to London, history trips to Russia or China, and biology trips to Africa), or engage in nontraditional coursework. There is also a junior year abroad option at the Royal Holloway College at the University of London that is available at no additional cost to the student, and a semester exchange program with American University in Washington for economics and politics majors.

W&J maintains its conservative atmosphere and students say political correctness is a nonissue. More than 80 percent of the students hail from Pennsylvania—the biggest contingent from "the better areas of Pittsburgh"—and many are from neighboring states in the Northeast. The campus is not terribly diverse: only 3 percent of students are African American, less than 1 percent Hispanic, and less than 2 percent Asian American. Because of this, students admit that "racism is here but quiet." Excellent students get a bargain if they win one of the 495 academic scholarships that range from $2,500 to $18,675. There are no athletic scholarships, and the school no longer guarantees to meet the full demonstrated need of all admits.

Most students live in either the one coed dorm or one of the four that are single-sex (two male and two female). Women's dorms are the newest and the nicest, according to most. All rooms are spacious, and a maid service ensures that the facilities are kept clean. On-campus apartments are available based on GPA, activities, and need. Fraternity brothers and a few overflow freshmen reside in renovated houses. Sororities obtain block-housing within the dormitories and, like the fraternities, have territorial tables in the dining rooms. The administration does have plans to build new townhouses and specialty housing. In order to live off campus, students need an excuse from a parent or doctor. An aggressive security program includes 24-hour patrols, escorts, and call boxes.

The social life at W&J is centered around the Greeks, which attract 38 percent of the men and 32 percent of the women. "This has become one of the major avenues for a good time," reports a junior English major. Those who dodge the Greek system tend to feel left out, for there are "few other alternatives on campus," says a sophomore. Fraternities need a party permit to serve alcohol, and no one is permitted outdoors with an open container. A fraternity council keeps a

(Continued)
Email Address:
admission@washjeff.edu

Strongest Programs:
Prelaw
Premed
English
Political Science
Psychology
English
Business Administration

W&J's formula for success starts with individual attention in small classes, half of which are limited to 25 students.

During the January intercession, students find brief apprenticeships in prospective career areas, take a school tour abroad (marine biology trips to the Bahamas or Australia, English theater trips to London, history trips to Russia or China, and biology trips to Africa), or engage in nontraditional coursework.

watchful eye on alcohol use, and students over 21 don colored bands that are only removable by scissors. A nonalcoholic pub called George & Tom's has become quite a popular diversion, as has the Campus Center. During the course of the year, Carnival Weekend and Spring Concert are the most popular.

Students head home on the weekends or explore dating opportunities at nearby colleges, most notably Penn State and Pitt. One of the most popular excursions is a 30-minute commute to Pittsburgh. Still, not all students share the administration's appreciation for "the unique characteristics of the western Pennsylvania milieu." "The town is very bitter toward the school after losing a major legal battle," reports a sophomore commenting on the college's relationship with the small, sleepy town of Washington. The town is a former steel/mining town, hit by hard times but trying to make a comeback in high-tech industry. Townies tend to be a bit resentful of dressy W&J undergrads, but students try to assuage this attitude by actively volunteering in the community.

Just about anyone has a shot at varsity sports, and athletics play an important role in the lives of many W&J students. Football has competed for the Division III national championship three of the last four years, generating the most student enthusiasm. Men's and women's basketball, women's swimming and volleyball, and wrestling all boast their own successes. For the nonvarsity type, there are numerous clubs to join, everything from the cycling association to the karate club.

W&J offers a solid education that is one of the best small-school bets for students who are seriously considering a professional or graduate school. A W&J degree may not make you famous, but it almost guarantees a few distinguished initials to tie on to the end of your name.

Overlaps

Allegheny, Penn State, Westminster, University of Pittsburgh, Duquesne.

If You Apply To ➤

W&J...Early decision: Nov. 1. Regular admissions: Mar. 1. Financial aid: Feb. 15. Does not guarantee to meet demonstrated need. Campus interviews: recommended, evaluative. Alumni interviews: optional, evaluative. SATs and SAT IIs (writing and two others) or ACTs: required. Accepts the Common Application and electronic applications. Essay: Significant experience, influential person, fictional character, or free topic.

Washington and Lee University

Lexington, VA 24450

Website: www.wlu.edu
Location: Small town
Total Enrollment: 2,066
Undergraduates: 1,696
Male/Female: 55/45
SAT Ranges: V 630–710 M 630–710
ACT Range: 28–31
Financial Aid: 30%
Expense: Pr $ $

Washington and Lee University, which shares the town of Lexington, Virginia, with the Virginia Military Institute, is about as genteel as Southern schools come. The Fancy Dress Ball is a highlight of each year, and a "speaking tradition" mandates at least casual communication between students and professors when they pass one another on the well-manicured grounds. But behind the frills and fun lies an honor code that students cite as one of their school's best features. "It's not a set of rules and regulations but a general way of living—do not lie, cheat, or steal and behave in the manner of a gentleman," explains a European history major. Adds a freshman, "This system leaves you a tremendous amount of freedom."

W&L's wooded campus sits atop a hill of lush green lawns, sweeping from one national landmark to another. Redbrick buildings feature white Doric columns and the prevailing architectural style is Greek Revival. A $23-million science center houses all science departments and facilities, and the school has completed major additions to the athletic facilities as well.

Though Washington and Lee is a school steeped in tradition, it is also working hard to find the future. The number of women on campus is growing, and though they were first admitted only about a decade ago, they now account for 45 percent of the student body. W&L boasts an impressive list of alumni, including writer Tom Wolfe.

Although a standard liberal arts program remains the foundation of the school's curriculum, it offers excellent preprofessional programs, particularly business, economics, public policy, and accounting through the Williams School of Commerce, Economics, and Politics. Journalism and mass communications are popular, as are biology (for pre-meds) and English. W&L also has bachelor's degree programs in fields as diverse as Russian Studies, cognitive science (computer science, philosophy, and psychology), and marine science education, where students can work at the Duke University Marine Laboratory for a semester. The East Asian Studies program has ties to universities in Taiwan and Japan. Fine arts and theater are on the weaker side.

Distribution requirements at W&L include varying numbers of credits in English composition, humanities, social sciences, math and science, and literature, plus two years of a foreign language and five terms of physical education. A class on the history of Washington and Lee University is immensely popular. There are no required courses for the freshman year, but orientation week activities are popular and some spring-term seminars are limited to freshmen and sophomores.

The academic climate ranges from intense to casual, depending on the student. "The courseload can be tough at times because of the trimester system," says a chemistry major, "but it's never unbearable. People definitely work well together." Classes tend to be small, and freshmen can count on getting full professors; there are no teaching assistants. "I have adored all my professors," says a satisfied sophomore, "and they really challenge me." Tests and final exams are taken without faculty supervision; doors remain unlocked, calculators stay on desks, and library stacks are open 24 hours a day. Online registration helps quell any potential scheduling disasters. "If there are any problems, you can always call up your dean and talk to them," says a student. "Usually they can fix it and get you in." The modern library, like most W&L facilities, is superb and offers 800 individual study areas as well as private rooms for honors students. Well-qualified students can apply for the Robert E. Lee Undergraduate Research Program, which offers students paid fellowships for assisting professors in research or doing their own.

Just as General Lee refused to march in step here during his years as the school's president after the Civil War, so Washington and Lee University refuses to march in step with some current trends in public higher education. The emphasis is still on undergraduate teaching, for example. And recently, there's been an "attempt by some higher power to make our very unique school more like Amherst, Middlebury, etc. [i.e., more liberal and diverse]," gripes a senior. However, since most students are politically conservative (and proud of it), they're happy with things as they are. This sentiment comes through in a popular campus T-shirt: "We're not snobs, we're just better than you." "Most students here are rather preppy," says a junior. "It's a fairly homogeneous crowd." Blacks account for a mere 3 percent of the student body, despite the school's argument that it is strongly committed to recruiting African American students; Hispanics and Asian Americans, meanwhile, combine for 2 percent. Less than 12 percent of

(Continued)

Phi Beta Kappa: Yes
Applicants: 3,330
Accepted: 33%
Enrolled: 42%
Grad in 6 Years: 84%
Returning Freshmen: 95%
Academics: ✍ ✍ ✍ ✍
Social: ☎ ☎ ☎
Q of L: ★ ★ ★
Admissions: (540) 463-8710
Email Address:
   admissions@wlu.edu

Strongest Programs:
   Business
   History
   Politics
   English
   Journalism
   Natural Sciences

Though Washington and Lee is a school steeped in tradition, it is also working hard to find the future. The number of women on campus is growing, and though they were first admitted about a decade ago, they now account for 45 percent of the student body.

students are native Virginians, but the university's geographic diversity has not prompted much other differentiation. The school offers about 30 merit scholarships every year, ranging from $2,000 to $16,950.

There are no athletic scholarships. Coeducation has been a godsend for the admissions office; applications are way up for the past several years, the median SAT scores of each freshman class are on the rise, and the acceptance rate is much lower than it was five or six years ago.

Students spend their first year at W&L in "modest but comfortable" coed dorms, and some freshmen may reserve singles. "Most of the rooms on campus for freshman and sophomores are singles, which is great!" says a sophomore. Freshmen are required to buy the meal plan, and the food is reportedly good. Sophomores are also required to live on campus, although upperclass dorms and apartments are available, and many students move into country houses when they are juniors or seniors.

With its scenic location in the midst of the Appalachian Mountains, the university provides an abundance of activities for nature lovers, including hunting, fishing, camping, and tubing in the rivers, as well as skiing. Washington, D.C., Richmond, and Roanoke are easily reached by car for weekend trips. Lexington, a quaint Old Virginia town," has a few bars, two movie theaters, several restaurants, and a lot of history. A thriving intramural program is a staple of W&L life, bringing fraternities and independents together in friendly rivalry. Football sparks some interest in the fall, with its attendant tailgate parties, but W&L students live for the spring and the Lee Jackson Lacrosse Classic against VMI. In general, "Athletic rivalries are not that important, but no one here likes to lose," reports a freshman. Other strong teams include men's tennis, golf and indoor track, and women's swimming, tennis, volleyball, and cross-country.

Eighty-one percent of the men join fraternities, which along with newly created sororities that claim 71 percent of the women, dominate the social scene. "The first thing anyone wants to know about you is what house you're in," says one student. Underage drinking is banned in the dorms and strictly avoided because it's against the honor code, but students insist that "it's never a problem to get alcohol at a fraternity party." No underage student would ever stoop so low as actually to purchase the necessary alcohol, for "that would be dishonorable" and would net the buyer dining hall duty, mandatory alcohol school, and a stiff fine. Nor would students use a fake ID; that would violate the honor code.

W&L's social life focuses on Greek bashes, which often feature live bands, although the aforementioned Fancy Dress Ball, or "$100,000 prom," also draws raves. Equally well known is W&L's mock political convention for the party out of power, held every four years, which has predicted past presidential nominees with uncanny accuracy. Aside from trips to the four women's colleges in the surrounding area and the University of Virginia, the Foxfield races near Charlottesville and the Kentucky Derby are popular road-trip destinations.

Most students are proud to look back on their college careers and point to the progress their alma mater has made in the intervening years, but not those from Washington and Lee. "W&L is resistant to change," says one senior. Budding liberals be warned, a senior notes: "W&L is a historically conservative school, and most students choose it for that reason." The culture favors men of honor who can hold their liquor. But those who choose Washington and Lee because of their reverence and appreciation for Southern tradition—and their desire to "work hard and play hard" while getting a solid grounding in the liberal arts or business— won't be disappointed.

Overlaps

University of Virginia, Wake Forest, Duke, William and Mary, Davidson.

<table>
<tr><td>

If You

Apply

To ➤
</td><td>

W&L...Early decision: Dec. 1. Regular admissions: Jan. 15. Financial aid: Feb. 1. Does not guarantee to meet demonstrated need. Campus and alumni interviews: recommended, informational. ACTs or SATs: required. SAT IIs: required (writing and two others). Accepts the Common Application. Essay question: significant experience or achievement with special meaning; best advice received; issue of personal, national, or local concern and its importance.
</td></tr>
</table>

Washington University in St. Louis

Campus Box 1089, One Brookings Drive, St. Louis, MO 63130-4899

One of higher education's rising stars, Washington University is arguably the best private university between Chicago and San Francisco. Though it has always been strong in its region, Wash U is becoming a truly national university. With a hefty endowment, strong preprofessional programs, and an emphasis on research, it's not hard to see why this school is held in such high regard.

Wash U's charming 169-acre campus abuts Forest Park, one of the three largest urban parks in the nation. It's also close to the St. Louis Zoo, the Art Museum, the History Museum, and the Science Center. The Collegiate Gothic architecture, executed in red Missouri granite and white limestone, sports plenty of climbing ivy, gargoyles, and arches. The campus is continually growing, with the recent opening of three new residence halls and three more under construction. The school has also constructed a new building for the George Warren Brown School of Social Work and the law school. A new biomedical engineering building is under way, as are an education center and a lab sciences building. Finally, plans are being drawn up to build new space for visual arts, executive education, and engineering departments.

Undergraduates may enroll in one or more of Wash U's five schools—arts and sciences, architecture, art, business, or engineering. Double majors or specially-tailored interdisciplinary majors, like environmental studies, are easily arranged. General education requirements for liberal arts include quantitative reasoning, physical and life sciences, social or behavioral sciences, minority or gender studies, language or the arts, and the famous—some say infamous—freshman English composition course (a.k.a. E Comp). Requirements for other divisions vary; first-year students in specific majors often have specialized courses required in addition to their liberal arts classes.

The natural sciences, especially biology and chemistry, have long been notable, especially among premeds. The outstanding medical school runs a faculty exchange program with the undergraduate biology department, which affords bio majors inordinate opportunities to conduct advanced laboratory research. An interdisciplinary program in social thought and analysis links several schools. Recently added programs include a biomedical engineering major, a robotics minor, and a philosophy/neuroscience/psychology concentration. Students say the academic atmosphere is not kill or be killed. "The courses are difficult and the workload is heavy," a junior notes, "but the students are not cut-throat or overly competitive. They work hard, but not just to be better than their friends."

To strike a balance between the drawing-card science and preprofessional

Website:
www.admissions.wustl.edu
Location: Suburban
Total Enrollment: 12,088
Undergraduates: 6,509
Male/Female: 50/50
SAT Ranges: V 620–710 M 650–730
ACT Range: 28–32
Financial Aid: 49%
Expense: Pr $ $ $ $
Phi Beta Kappa: Yes
Applicants: 17,109
Accepted: 34%
Enrolled: 24%
Grad in 6 Years: 86%
Returning Freshmen: 96%
Academics: 🖉 🖉 🖉 🖉
Social: ☎ ☎ ☎
Q of L: ★ ★ ★ ★
Admissions: (314) 935-6000 or (800) 638-0700
Email Address:
admissions@wustl.edu

Strongest Programs:
Biology and Natural Sciences
Premed
Foreign Languages
English
Chemistry
Accounting
Business

programs and the university's desire to provide a broad and deep educational experience, a freshman FOCUS program option has been installed. In FOCUS, a single theme, such as law and society or cultural assimilation into American society, is explored in different courses and brought into focus through a weekly seminar. The program lets first-year students work closely with faculty members—including at least one Nobel Prize winner—and sample offerings from various departments. Other notable programs include the Summer Scholars Program in Biology and Biomedical Research and the Hewlet Program, which allows groups of students to focus on an interdisciplinary area of study, such as environmental studies, during their first two years on campus. About 60 percent of Wash U students graduate with more than a single degree in four years.

As Wash U's applicant pool has gotten bigger, the admissions committee has become much more selective and classes more rigorous. "The goal here is to think, not just repeat information learned in class," one student says. Students point to numerous resources for those having trouble keeping up, including teaching assistants, help sessions, and study groups. One freshman political science major calls the quality of teaching "marvelous," adding, "The professors are very approachable."

Diversity is an issue that most schools face, and Washington University is no exception. Seven percent of students are African American, 2 percent Hispanic, and 12 percent Asian American. Organizations such as STAR (Students Together Against Racism) and ADHOC (Against Discrimination and Hatred on Campus) educate students on multicultural awareness. But change is slow in coming, laments one student: "Students tend to congregate with others of similar religious, racial, and ethnic backgrounds. Unique subcultures are created, but this polarization can lead to negative feelings and friction among factions." Perhaps this clash stems from the high percentages of Wash U's students who come from the East (especially New York and New Jersey) mixing with the native Midwesterners.

Many students say they wouldn't be at Wash U without the university's generous financial aid offerings. The Partners in Education with Parents (PEP) is an innovative financing program that allows parents to prepay all 4 years at the entering rate or to borrow up to 4 years of charges at the entering-year rate.

Two high-rise and 14 low-rise buildings collected in an area called South 40, a 40-acre plot adjoining the campus, offer comfortable, air-conditioned accommodations. All dorms are coed, with some divided into single-sex suites for six to eight students. The dorms are wired for direct Internet and campus network access, and freshmen and sophomores are guaranteed rooms. There is no trouble getting a room. Many upperclassmen live off campus, but in university-owned apartments. Until the recent growth of the freshman class, virtually all upperclassmen who wished to remain on campus could. But the many reasonably priced apartments in the bordering neighborhoods of University City and Clayton attract lots of juniors and seniors every year. Students can use their meal-plan credit cards in any of 12 dining centers, and the cards also work in vending machines and laundry rooms.

With Forest Park in its front yard, Wash U offers incredible recreational options: a golf course, an ice-skating rink, a zoo, a lake with boat rentals, art and history museums, an outdoor theater, and a science center. Multiple professional sporting events and a wide variety of clubs and restaurants are also nearby. St. Louis is also one of the best shopping cities in the nation, and home of the addictive Ted Drewes frozen custard. As one student sees it: "From the Arch to Six Flags to the Blues (hockey), Cardinals (baseball), and Rams (football), there is always something to do." Popular road trips include Chicago, Kansas City, and Indianapolis, all roughly four hours away.

On weekends, movies, fraternity parties, plays, and concerts combine to tear students away from their books. "Students take their social lives as seriously as they do their academics," says a psychology and music double major. One century-old Wash U tradition everyone wants to take part in is the annual Thurtene Carnival, billed as one of the nation's oldest and largest student-run carnivals. Another big event is the Walk-In-Lay-Down (WILD) Theater, held the first and last Fridays of the academic year, where everyone brings a blanket to the main quad, assumes a horizontal position and listens to live bands until late at night. When it comes to typical college partying, the Greek system is a healthy social force; a third of the men and half of the women belong. Alcohol policies are not too strict: no kegs and no open containers in public places. The policies work somewhat. "This is a wet campus," a junior says. "Students are given the privilege to drink as long as they respect their community. The lenient policy leads to fewer alcohol-related incidents because students learn to drink responsibly." Varsity sports, though not quite in the limelight, have generated a good deal of interest here in recent years. The women's volleyball team has captured seven of the last 11 NCAA national championships. Other strong programs include football, men's soccer, basketball, and baseball, and women's soccer and basketball. The range of all-important intramural sports runs from badminton, arm wrestling, and floor hockey to pocket billiards and Ultimate Frisbee.

Wash U continues to gain national recognition as a fine liberal arts school and attracts hard-working students from around the world. Students here are expected to work hard, but Wash U is not the place for all-work-and-no-play types. "People are open, friendly, and laid-back," a junior explains, "and they want to have fun!"

Overlaps

Northwestern, Duke, Emory, Penn, Harvard.

If You Apply To ➤ **Wash U**…Early decision I: Nov. 15. Early decision II: Jan. 1. Regular admissions: Jan. 15. Financial aid: Nov. 1 (early decision applicants), Feb. 15. Housing: May 1. Meets demonstrated need of 80%. Campus interviews: optional, evaluative. Alumni interviews: recommended, evaluative (where available). SATs or ACTs: required. SAT IIs: optional. Apply to one of five undergraduate schools. Accepts the Common Application and electronic applications. Essay question: creative work and its effect on you; write your own recommendation letter; write your own essay question and answer it.

University of Washington

1410 N.E. Campus Parkway, Seattle, WA 98195

In recent years, the University of Washington has come on strong as a solid research institution. It is a gem of a school that many in the Northwest regard as one of the best deals around. And with funds pouring in from Microsoft multimillionaires (including head honcho Bill Gates), this public university promises to become even stronger in the future. Students on this campus understand that anonymity and size are the prices that must be paid for the wealth of opportunities that await them. Those looking for the extra, personal touch might want to investigate the school's two branch campuses in Tacoma and Bothell, where class sizes average 25 students. But if the Seattle campus is your focus, as one senior hints, "learn to work the system."

Washington's Seattle campus features a number of distinctive landmarks. Red

Website: www.washington.edu

Location: Urban

Total Enrollment: 35,559

Undergraduates: 25,638

Male/Female: 59/51

SAT Ranges: V 510–630 M 530–650

ACT Range: 22–27

Financial Aid: 30%

(Continued)

Expense: Pub $ $

Phi Beta Kappa: Yes

Applicants: 12,785

Accepted: 76%

Enrolled: 43%

Grad in 6 Years: 62%

Returning Freshmen: 91%

Academics: ✍ ✍ ✍ ✍

Social: ☎ ☎ ☎

Q of L: ★ ★ ★

Admissions: (206) 543-9686

Email Address:
askuwadm@u.washington
.edu

Strongest Programs:

Business

Art

English

Psychology

Drama

Engineering

Architecture

Environmental Studies

Square sits atop the Central Plaza parking garage and features the Broken Obelisk, a 26-foot-high steel sculpture gifted to the university by the Virginia Wright Fund.

Many of Washington's diverse undergraduate strengths correspond with its excellent graduate programs. The ultracompetitive business major, for example, benefits from the university's highly regarded business school and is the most popular undergraduate major, followed by biology, art, English, and accounting. Similarly, students majoring in public health, community medicine, pharmacy, and nursing profit from access to facilities and faculty at the medical school, an international leader in cancer and heart research, cell biology, and organ transplants. Also recommended for undergraduates are biological and life sciences (pumped up even more by a new physics/astronomy building), and most engineering programs, especially aero- and astronautical engineering, which are generously funded by Boeing and NASA. Reflecting the focus on natural resources in Washington's economy, the programs in fisheries and forestry are excellent, as are earth and atmospheric sciences, including oceanography. Washington has dropped its major in environmental studies and added a major in community and environmental planning.

Undergraduates in both professional and liberal arts programs must take five credits in English composition, seven credits in writing beyond composition, and one course in quantitative and symbolic reasoning. Students must also fulfill 40 credits in general education requirements, including the arts, individuals and societies, and the natural world. Schools and colleges also have their own requirements that must be met. Many Washington professors are tops in their field, but students may have to be patient about seeing professors after class. As for academic advising, a student advises, "The key is to take the bull by the horns and find out which advisors are better than others." While students once complained that classes were difficult to get into, that problem seems to have been solved, except for large 100- and 200-level courses. Ninety percent of the classes have fewer than 50 students. "It is very common to be taught by teaching assistants, but overall the quality is good in both senior faculty and graduate student teachers," a business major says.

For those interested in skirting the masses, UW sports an honors program that offers small classes on interesting subjects taught by fine professors. The academic environment at UW is "very much centered on learning. Part of that comes from the fact that this is a research institution." And if students get the itch to see some different scenery, there are 60 different study abroad programs offered in 20 countries, including China, Denmark, and Russia. A program in experiential learning encourages students to find internships and participate in community service. This fits in with a variety of classes that give students the opportunity to volunteer as part of their coursework. A senior says, "There's simply no better way to learn than by combining challenging courses with 'real-world' experience. When you're learning in the classroom, you can't always apply it. Experience adds to your learning, and it helps you remember it."

Part of the reason for UW's national anonymity is the fact that it turns away large numbers of out-of-state applicants, preferring to keep its focus on the home folks. Ninety percent of undergraduates are state residents, and an unusually large proportion are over the age of 25. The student body is 59 percent white and 22 percent Asian American, with Hispanics and blacks comprising 7 percent. Students say the school strives for diversity by offering Valuing Diversity workshops to foster increased awareness of and sensitivity to individual differences; one student calls it "the administration's way of giving lip service to issues they can't or won't deal with." The campus is very active politically, as one junior reports: "Political correctness is very big here and students find very creative ways to make their points."

Students say budget cuts have decreased the number of course offerings and programs like Society and Justice. Merit scholarships are awarded to Washington residents with good high school records and test scores. Athletic scholarships are awarded to men and women in a wide variety of sports, including swimming, women's gymnastics, golf, tennis, and track and field. Freshmen are given special attention via the Freshman Interest Group (FIG) program, which offers freshmen a chance to meet, discuss, and study with other freshmen who have similar interests. Each FIG consists of 20 to 24 students who share a cluster of classes (which meet graduation requirements) and includes a weekly seminar led by a junior or senior peer advisor. Also of interest to freshmen are General Studies 101, an optional two-credit course designed to help students meet the demands and expectations of college life, and Freshman Seminars, one-credit courses with 10 or 12 other freshmen.

Fifty-six percent of the students live in the school's seven coed dorms. Hagget provides a comfortable setting for freshmen, and McMahon is recommended for those inclined to party. Housing is also available for married students, and the fraternity and sorority organizations are home to another 11 percent of the men and 12 percent of the women. The rest live off campus in Seattle or other parts of King County. Each dorm has its own cafeteria and fast-food line based on a debit card system. The Husky Union Building also offers a dining hall, espresso bar, writing center, sun deck, and lounges. "Great" is how one student describes campus security, while others also report that they feel "100 percent safe" on campus.

Given the large number of commuters, it's no surprise that most of Washington's social life takes place away from campus, except for the Greeks (members of a combined total of 48 fraternities and sororities). "The dorms and fraternities seem to contain the most social activity, and what they lack is made up for by the proximity to downtown Seattle," says one student. There are also free movies and drama productions for those who must find entertainment on campus. Both dormies and Greeks are not supposed to drink if they're under 21. Sooner or later most students hit the "Ave.," University Way, where shops and top restaurants await them.

And that's true of Seattle, too. A 10-minute bus ride connects students to a full array of urban offerings. The Seattle Center hosts outstanding operas, symphonies, and touring shows, while the Kingdome houses the Seahawks and the Mariners. But who needs pro football with Washington's Huskies around? Husky Fever breaks out on every football weekend, and the stands are always packed for UW's top-rated team. Despite some off-the-field problems among football players, the Huskies are much loved on Saturday afternoons. The team has won the Rose Bowl several times in the past few years and is consistently in the hunt for the PAC 10 athletic crown. While students get fired up for the trip to Pasadena, they're equally excited when Washington State comes to town to vie for the coveted Apple Cup. Other strong UW teams include women's basketball, crew, cross-country, and tennis, and men's crew, baseball, soccer, and tennis.

More than anything else, the great outdoors define the University of Washington. The campus offers breathtaking views of Lake Washington and the Olympic Mountains. Outdoor pastimes for students include boating, hiking, camping, and skiing, all found nearby, and Canada is close enough for road trips to Vancouver. The weather is consistently temperate, and natives insist that the city's reputation for rain is undeserved. Then again, the sports stadium has an overhang to protect spectators from showers.

While students once complained that classes were difficult to get into, that problem seems to have been solved, except for large 100- and 200-level courses. Ninety percent of the classes have fewer than 50 students.

Part of the reason for UW's national anonymity is the fact that it turns away large numbers of out-of-state applicants, preferring to keep its focus on the home folks.

While some students won't appreciate the no-nonsense and often impersonal academic programs and the lack of a centralized social life, many students can overlook these obstacles for the big picture of the up-and-coming University of Washington. And that involves more than just the beautiful scenery.

Wellesley College

Wellesley, MA 02481

Website: www.wellesley.edu
Location: Suburban
Total Enrollment: 2,333
Undergraduates: 2,333
Male/Female: 0/100
SAT Ranges: V 630–720 M 630–720
ACT Range: 28–31
Financial Aid: 52%
Expense: Pr $ $ $ $
Phi Beta Kappa: Yes
Applicants: 2,862
Accepted: 46%
Enrolled: 46%
Grad in 6 Years: 90%
Returning Freshmen: 95%
Academics: ✍ ✍ ✍ ✍ ✍
Social: ☎ ☎ ☎
Q of L: ★ ★ ★ ★
Admissions: (781) 283-2270
Email Address:
admission@wellesley.edu

Strongest Programs:
Economics
Political Science
Biological Sciences
Computer Sciences
Chinese Language

Wellesley is not just the best women's college in the nation, it's one of the best colleges in the nation, period. With an alumni roster that includes Senator Hillary Rodham Clinton, Madame Chiang Kai-shek, Madeleine Albright, and Diane Sawyer, Wellesley College is the at the top of the list for those who are seeking an all-women's education. Wellesley women excel in whatever field they choose, including traditional male bastions like economics and business. "It is a wonderful place to grow," says a senior.

Nestled in a corner of a wealthy Boston suburb, the Wellesley campus, one of the most beautiful anywhere, occupies 500 rolling acres of cultivated and natural areas, including Lake Waban. Campus buildings range in architectural style from Gothic (with stone towers and brick quadrangles) to state-of-the-art science, arts, and sports facilities. A 22-acre arboretum and botanical garden features a wide variety of trees and plants.

With its hefty endowment and top-notch facilities, Wellesley offers a top-of-the-line educational experience. The most popular majors are English, psychology, economics, political science, and international relations, though economics is known as the biggest powerhouse. In fact, Wellesley has produced virtually all of the country's high-ranking female economists. Students in molecular biology work with faculty on DNA research, and a high-tech science center houses two electron microscopes, two NMR spectrometers, ultracentrifuges, two lasers, and other such equipment. A comprehensive renovation of the social science building added videoconferencing, computer labs, and a research facility.

In the past, Theater Studies was considered a weak department, but the school has gone to great lengths to remedy the situation by building a department students can brag about. The Ruth Nagel Jones Theater provides performance space for mainstage productions and experimental theater. The Davis Museum and Cultural Center houses 11 galleries, a cinema, and a café. The students at Wellesley will find an academic art museum to their benefit, along with more than a million volumes in the campus libraries. The five libraries sport a computerized catalog system that is accessible on or off campus. Anything Wellesley women find lacking in their facilities or curriculum can probably be found at MIT, where they have full cross-registration privileges. Wellesley students can also take courses at Brandeis University and Babson College, or participate in exchange programs with Spelman College in Atlanta or Mills College in Oakland, California.

Wellesley has distribution requirements that include three units drawn from Language and Literature and Visual Arts, Music, Theater, Film and Video; one unit from Social and Behavioral Analysis; a unit each from two of the following: Epistemology and Cognition, Religion, Ethics and Moral Philosophy, and Historical Studies; and three units from Natural and Physical Science and Mathematical Modeling and Problem Solving. In addition, students must take a first-year writing class, a foreign language, and a course on multiculturalism as well. Academics are taken very seriously at Wellesley. "The classes can seem competitive," says a senior, "especially when the top women from high schools are placed together on the same campus." Professors are highly respected and make themselves available through email, voice mail, office hours, and by appointment. "The quality of teaching is excellent," says a senior. "All students are taught by professors and class sizes are small, so we get individual attention. Profs here are dedicated to teaching their students, and that makes a big difference."

A five-course technology studies concentration gives liberal arts students the skills necessary to understand and use technological innovations in their future studies as well as in the professional world. Grants from private foundations have allowed Wellesley to add other innovative programs, including independent research tutorials for advanced science students and fellowship funding for joint student–faculty projects. Students can participate in the Twelve-College Exchange, including the National Theater Institute, the Maritime Studies Program, or they can travel and study abroad through one of Wellesley's recently-expanded international programs, including the Summer Internship Program in Washington, D.C.

Under the honor system, students may take their finals, unsupervised, at any time during exam week. Class sizes are almost always small (they average 18 to 23 students per class). First-years (as they are exclusively called here) and upperclasswomen alike have faculty advisors. First-years also have a dean of first-year students to offer additional advice on courses and other academic matters. "There are good counseling resources available, but students must seek them out," explains a sophomore.

To a degree, the college is dogged by its reputation as "a haven for rich white girls," but actually 60 percent graduate from public high school and almost half represent minority groups. Twenty-three percent of Wellesley's students are Asian American. Although the Northeast is the best-represented geographical area (though only 18 percent are from Massachusetts), students also come from every state and more than 70 countries. Ninety-seven percent ranked in the top quarter of their high school class. Whatever their background, most have a fair amount of social aplomb. Issues on campus run the gamut from multiculturalism and racism to gender questions and national politics. "Political correctness is a huge issue," says a psychology and economics double major. "We have such a diverse campus racially, culturally, geographically, and religiously that the major issues address creating a supportive environment for all." There are no athletic or academic scholarships, but students don't seem to mind, rating the recently enhanced financial aid packages as "constant and fair."

Dorm life at Wellesley is a step ahead of most institutions, to say the least. Virtually every student lives on campus, in rooms that are described as "immaculate." Dorms feature high-ceilinged living rooms, hardwood floors, fireplaces, computers and laser printers, television annexes with VCRs, walk-in closets,

Economics is known as the biggest powerhouse. In fact, Wellesley has produced virtually all of the country's high-ranking female economists.

kitchenettes with microwaves, and even grand pianos. The dorms are renovated every five years or so and all are well maintained, students say. "Nice dorms—most of them have early-20th-century architecture and beautiful windows to look out on a beautiful campus," says an anthropology senior. All residence halls are smoke-free.

There are no dorms specifically for first-years—all classes live on all floors. Peer tutors also live in each dorm. These students, called APT advisors, are trained to tutor in specific subjects and in study skills and time management. Juniors and seniors are granted single rooms. Two co-ops, one with a feminist bent, present an educational housing option. Meal cards are valid in every dorm, and at the campus snack bar, which is stocked with everything from milk and flour to Twinkies.

When it comes to weekend fun, Wellesley is in a prime location. Or more accurately, it's close to a prime location: Boston. Not even half an hour away, Boston is the place where Wellesley women can mingle with lots of other students—specifically male—from Harvard and MIT. Cambridge—with Harvard Square, MIT frat parties, and lots of jazz clubs—is accessible by an hourly school shuttle that runs on weekdays and weekends. There is also a trolley stop located a short walk from school. By car, Cape Cod, Providence, and the Vermont and New Hampshire ski slopes are close by.

The town of Wellesley is an upper-crust Boston suburb, without many amenities for students. "The town is not a college town," gripes a junior, due to "unfriendly residents and expensive stores." For campus-bound students (like many first-years, who cannot have cars on campus), dorm parties and movies are the featured attractions. "Wellesley students decide their own social lives, and there is no one way or outlet," one student notes. Wellesley is a dry town, although the school is in the process of trying to get liquor licenses for the dorms. When alcohol is served, campus police check IDs. Students enjoy going to the student-run Café Hoop, the campus coffeehouse, to sip tea or share a fro-yo or a chocolate croissant. The closest thing Wellesley has to sororities are societies for arts and music, literature, Shakespeare, and general lectures. These societies also sometimes hold parties.

Wellesley is chock-full of traditions, but the most endearing ones include Flower Sunday, step-singing, an all-campus sing-along on the chapel steps, the sophomore class planting a tree, a junior class variety show, Spring Weekend (with a big-name band and comedian), and a hoop-rolling contest by seniors in their graduation robes. The winner of this contest will supposedly be the first in her class to become a CEO, and she gets off to a flying start when her classmates toss her in the lake. Speaking of the lake, students mention their unofficial campus event, Lake Day, where students take breaks between (or from) classes to enjoy a festival held on the lawn near the lake.

Students balance their academic schedule with athletics to become "Healthy, Wellesley, and Wise." Lacrosse and tennis are among the top varsity sports and cross-country made the NEWMAC Conference championships for four consecutive years. Field hockey, soccer, and volleyball have also claimed championships. The sports "palace," recently renamed the Nannerl Sports Center in honor of Wellesley's 11th president (who now runs Duke University), offers an Olympic-size pool, squash, racquetball and tennis courts, dance studios, a weight room, and an indoor track. Harvard's Head of the Charles crew race takes honors as the most popular spectator sport of the year. The big athletic rival is Smith College, another of the Seven Sisters group of great women's colleges.

When it comes to academics, Wellesley women are no joke. Their school is competitive with all but the top three Ivies. Many of them enjoy the quaint traditions of the school and appreciate the idyllic atmosphere for contemplation, but know they are poised to dominate whatever field they enter. The graduates of this incredible school are smart, self-confident, capable, and unstoppable in their drive to the top. As one contented senior says: "It's a wonderful place to grow as individuals, as students, and as women." Another senior adds, "I know the friendships I made here will last the rest of my life."

If You Apply To ➤	**Wellesley**…Early decision: Nov. 1. Regular admissions and financial aid: Jan. 15. Guarantees to meet demonstrated need. Campus and alumni interviews: recommended, evaluative. SATs and SAT IIs (writing and two others) or ACTs: required. Accepts the Common Application and electronic applications. Essay question: Significant experience or achievement; issue of personal concern; influential person. Students participate on admissions board.

Wells College

Aurora, NY 13026

At a time when most colleges are increasing tuition, students at Wells College are actually paying less for their education than in previous years. In an effort to attract top-notch students, the all-women's college has cut its tuition and embarked on an aggressive marketing campaign. According to students, Wells is placing a major emphasis on educating and empowering women for leadership roles in the 21st century. But there are a few throwbacks to the past: seniors still ride to graduation in beautiful old Wells Fargo stagecoaches.

A few dramatic additions on campus, such as the renovation and rededication of Weld House in the Greek Revival style, have maintained the classic collegiate atmosphere created by the school's massive old, ivy-covered buildings. The rolling 365-acre lakeside campus has been named to the National Register of Historic Places. With Cayuga Lake affording beautiful sunsets, boating, and fishing opportunities, students can juxtapose the rigor of their studies with relaxation in a gorgeous environment.

The liberal arts provide the basic framework for a Wells education. In addition to standard distribution requirements, all students must complete two courses in a foreign language, one course in formal reasoning, three courses in the arts, three courses in natural or social sciences, one wellness course, and three physical education activities. Wells 101, a core course required for all freshwomen, covers the basics of college writing, speech, and analytical thinking. The most popular majors (biological and chemical sciences, English, performing arts, sociology and anthropology, and psychology) are generally the strongest academic departments, according to students, while the art history and physical education programs need improvement. Those who major in biology are able to use the local environment—Cayuga Lake and surrounding lands—for ecology and botany fieldwork. Accredited elementary and secondary education programs are available, and interdisciplinary minors are offered in such fields as management studies, secondary education, communications, and public policy. Wells recently added an international studies minor and dropped its Italian concentration.

Wells also offers a variety of integrated majors, all of which require coursework across traditional disciplinary boundaries. Specialized areas include

Website: www.wells.edu

Location: Small town

Total Enrollment: 404

Undergraduates: 404

Male/Female: 0/100

SAT Ranges: V 520–630 M 490–600

ACT Range: 22–27

Financial Aid: 81%

Expense: Pr $

Phi Beta Kappa: Yes

Applicants: 410

Accepted: 90%

Enrolled: 37%

Grad in 6 Years: 60%

Returning Freshmen: 80%

Academics: ✍ ✍ ✍

Social: ☎ ☎

Q of L: ★ ★ ★ ★

Admissions: (315) 364-3264

Email Address:
admissions@wells.edu

Strongest Programs:
Biological and Chemical Sciences
English
Performing Arts

American Studies; foreign languages, literature, and cultures; history; and sociology and anthropology. Qualified students may design their own majors. Wells also offers 3–2 dual degree programs in community health and business administration with the University of Rochester, in veterinary medicine with Cornell, and in engineering with Case Western Reserve, Cornell, Columbia, Clarkson, and Washington University in St. Louis. For a change of pace, students can take one nonmajor course per semester on a pass/fail basis and cross-register to take up to four courses at nearby Cornell University.

The college operates on a semester calendar, with January being used as a time for internships, study abroad, independent study projects, or Leadership Week. In addition, Wells College sponsors a popular corporate affiliate program that is aimed at preparing women for the business and financial professions through special courses and lectures, portfolio management experience, and corporate internships. Foreign study is available for either a semester or a year.

The faculty at Wells is unusually accessible and friendly, even by small-college standards. "The faculty is excellent in both knowledge and enthusiasm brought to the job," says one junior. "They develop a true rapport with the students and are always available outside of class for additional help." And size is far from a problem at this school of a little more than 400. Classes virtually always number fewer than 25 students, which means a personalized education for each student. An honor system is enforced by the student-run collegiate association, and take-home and self-scheduled tests are the rule rather than the exception.

On the first and last day of classes, professors serve the seniors a champagne breakfast; sophomores give them roses on the last day of classes and dance around the sycamore tree.

The students pride themselves on their open-mindedness and variety of philosophies, and say that the school values diversity. Sixty-two percent of the students are state residents, and foreign students account for only 3 percent of the population. Asian Americans make up 6 percent of the student body, African Americans 4 percent, and Hispanics 2 percent. A wider range of courses with a minority focus, workshops on racial issues, and a support network for new minority students are used to educate students about diversity. Homosexual rights is a big issue on campus. The school does not guarantee to meet the full demonstrated financial need of every admit, but there are a variety of scholarships of up to $20,000 awarded each year.

All students are guaranteed housing on campus, and 84 percent of the student body take advantage of this option. The dorms range from the founder's 19th-century mansion to a modern dorm setup with a suite system. Weld House is the newest dorm with two computer labs. Accommodations are described as "comfortable" and "well maintained," but some students complain that the college has been slow to add Internet connections to each room. Upperclasswomen participate in a lottery for housing (most prefer singles), and freshwomen are usually assigned doubles. There are only five dorms on campus, and none is specifically dedicated to freshwomen. Each dorm has a lake view, and some boast bay windows and winding staircases. There is virtually no off-campus housing in Aurora, where the total population is equal to the tiny student body at Wells. Meals are served in a magnificent Tudor-style dining hall complete with two working fireplaces. The school is so small that "security knows all of us and will always approach unescorted people and ask them where they belong," a junior psychology major says.

An honor system is enforced by the student-run collegiate association, and take-home and self-scheduled tests are the rule rather than the exception

The college owns a great deal of waterfront property and maintains a dock and boathouse for its students, which translates into plenty of opportunities for camping and fun in the water. Meanwhile, the ski slopes of Greek Peak are less than an hour away, and the golf course and tennis and paddle courts are usually full of lively players. A field house provides indoor tennis courts, a pool, and other facilities. Aurora itself offers almost no entertainment, as the entire town basically consists of a pizza parlor, a nice restaurant, a mini-grocery store, two churches, and a bar. "Aurora is a pretty town but much too quiet," says a psychology major. But Ithaca to the south and Syracuse to the east provide more diversions, and a Wells van runs between the school and Ithaca eight times a day. When students flee on weekends, they usually travel to nearby Cornell University or Ithaca College, where fraternity parties and mixers are the main attractions. As far as drinking is concerned, no one under 21 is served on campus or at the local bars, but students say it's still possible for an underage student to get alcohol. "It is very easy for underage students to get access to alcohol through upperclasswomen," admits one student, "but local bars have lists of students and will not serve underage."

The soccer and field hockey teams do fairly well, and other sporting events are crowd pleasers. Softball was recently added. The college's penchant for tradition carries over into athletics in the Oddline/Evenline competition, which culminates in a basketball game between the freshwomen and the sophomores. Intramurals are available for those with the initiative, but they take a backseat to the more popular and numerous nonsports clubs.

The school is very high on traditions. Bells are rung every evening to announce dinner and when the first snow of the season falls. And alumnae may request that they be rung on the occasion of their marriage. On the first and last day of classes, professors serve the seniors a champagne breakfast; sophomores give them roses on the last day of classes and dance around the sycamore tree. A popular t-shirt on campus these days boasts, "We aren't at an all-girl's school without men; we're at an all women's college without the boys."

Wells lacks some of the facilities and academic programs that large universities can offer because of its size and the social isolation may pose problems for some. But students say the sorority-like atmosphere more than makes up for these minor concerns. Brags one senior, "Wells women are going places! We know what we want to do and set out to get it done."

Overlaps

Cornell University, NYU, Smith, Mount Holyoke, Syracuse.

If You Apply To ➤ **Wells**...Early action: Dec. 15. Regular admissions: Mar. 1. Financial aid: May 15. Housing: July 15. Meets demonstrated need of 35%. Campus interviews: recommended, evaluative. Alumni interviews: recommended, informational. SATs or ACTs: required. SAT IIs: optional. Essay question: write about a significant achievement, important issue, or a person who influenced you.

Wesleyan University

North College, Middletown, CT 06457

Wesleyan is one of a handful of colleges that can stake a legitimate claim to the title "tops in the nation." It has engaging faculty members who care deeply about student performance. It has students that are driven by an innate desire to learn for learning's sake. And it has an administration that is firmly committed to preparing the college for the challenges of the 21st century. Whether they're engrossed in academics, debating and demonstrating over various issues, or engaged in community service, Wes students seem to do things with a passion

Website: www.wesleyan.edu
Location: Small town
Total Enrollment: 3,204
Undergraduates: 2,750
Male/Female: 49/51

(Continued)

SAT Ranges: V 620–720 M
  610–710

ACT Range: N/A

Financial Aid: 41%

Expense: Pr $ $ $ $

Phi Beta Kappa: Yes

Applicants: 6,400

Accepted: 29%

Enrolled: 39%

Grad in 6 Years: 88%

Returning Freshmen: 96%

Academics: 🖎 🖎 🖎 🖎 🖎

Social: ☎ ☎ ☎

Q of L: ★ ★ ★

Admissions: (860) 685-3000

Email Address:

  admissions@wesleyan.edu

Strongest Programs:

  East Asian Studies

  English/Creative Writing

  Biology

  History

  American Studies

  Music

  Film

and intensity that helps set this school apart from tamer institutions. "Wes students take an in-your-face approach to life," says a government major.

If there's any mold at all at Wesleyan, it's probably shaped by the excitement and fervor with which students in this diverse academic community view their education. This New England college offers more academic and extracurricular options than almost any school its size, and the Wesleyan experience means liberal learning in a climate of individual freedom. "Students work very hard, but the academic climate is not competitive," an American Studies major says. "Students help each other in classes, rather than try to get ahead by inhibiting them." Another student agrees, "The courses are rigorous but the climate is supportive and conducive to sharing ideas." The freedom at Wesleyan requires motivated students who stay on task despite the laid-back atmosphere. There are many opportunities open to students willing to take advantage of them, which is precisely what these doers do.

It begins with the Wesleyan campus architecture, which is as diverse as the student body. The nucleus of this stately university is a century-old row of lovely ivy-covered brownstones that look out over the football field. The rest of the buildings can be described as "eclectic" and range from mod-looking dorms of the '50s and '60s to the early 19th-century architecture of many academic buildings to the beautiful and modern Center for the Arts. The Wesleyan-owned student residences look freshly plucked from Main Street, USA. The most recent additions to campus have been a new admissions building and a home for the new Center for the Americas.

One of the most richly endowed institutions per capita, Wesleyan has used its wealth to attract highly-rated faculty members. These professors are expected to be scholar-teachers: academic supermen who juggle groundbreaking research, enthusiastic lectures, and personal student attention at the same time. And they seem to pull it off. "The professors here are active individuals who bring passion to their classes," says a junior. "They have an open-door policy and are extremely accessible." Another student adds, "The teachers at Wes are amazing and because of the smaller class sizes, you have the opportunity to really develop a friendship with them." Among Wesleyan's strongest departments are music, economics, biology, American Studies, and English, which for years has been the most popular degree. But even the smaller departments attract attention. Ethnomusicology, including African drumming and dance, is a particular specialty; students can be found reclining on the wide, carpeted bleachers at the Third World Music Hall or watching a dozen musicians play the Indonesian gamelan. The film department is first-rate. The East Asian Studies Center has both a strong program and an authentic Japanese tea room. Even the math department, which has been a source of criticism for years, has made significant changes to emphasize problem solving in small groups rather than interminable lectures dedicated to theory.

Wesleyan's curriculum renewal program ensures the relevance of liberal arts education in the 21st century by adding more professors for first- and second-year students and clustering courses to help students reach their academic goals. Students are expected in their first two years to take a minimum of two courses in each of three areas—humanities and the arts, social and behavioral sciences, and natural sciences and mathematics. During their second two years, students must take one course in each of the three areas. At the end of their freshman year, Wesleyan students can apply to major in one of three competitive, interdisciplinary seminar colleges: the College of Letters (literature, politics, history with a leftist bent), the College of Social Studies (politics, economics, history with a conservative bent), and the Science in Society program (concerned with the humane use of scientific knowledge, a la Buckminster Fuller). New students can take First-Year Initiative courses designed just for them. The university also has installed a Web-based course selection and registration system to ease the process.

Wesleyan students are marked by an unusual commitment to debate, from political to cultural to intellectual. "One thing about Wesleyan, people aren't afraid to speak their mind or challenge someone else's idea," a student reports. "This creates an environment that is constantly debating and discussing things." It is hands-down an activist campus. One sophomore lists rallies and protests alongside parties and concerts as part of the campus social life. "This is a politically aware and active campus," a history major says. "Anything and everything can be an issue." Another student adds, "You'll have a hard time finding a more politically correct and socially active campus than Wes." But students level their smarts against topics close to home, mostly the university administration. "There's an energy on this campus, for me it's a spirit of creativity and political energy," a sophomore explains.

Wesleyan strives to keep its classes small and only 6 percent of the courses have 50 or more students. Some students claim they sometimes have trouble getting into the "hot" courses. "With popular classes, you have to be persistent, but you can get in," a history major says. If beseeching is not your style, studying abroad may be a temporary tonic to registration headaches. Programs are available in Israel, Germany, Africa, Japan, Latin America, France, Spain, and China. Students can also participate in the Venture Program,* study at Mystic Seaport,* or take a semester at another Twelve-College Exchange* school. Internships are popular, and students can also take advantage of 3–2 engineering programs with Columbia and Caltech.

Wesleyan likes to describe itself as "a small college with university resources." The libraries have over a million volumes, practically unheard of at a school this size. Students claim that whenever you happen to walk past the brightly lit, glass-walled study room of Sci-Li (the science library), you're apt to see numerous students huddled over their books. Wesleyan's excellent reputation and strong recruiting network attract students from all over, ensuring the clash of viewpoints that makes it such a vital place. Of the student body, enrollment figures indicate the makeup as 9 percent black, 6 percent Hispanic, and 12 percent Asian American. Students report that diversity is cherished at Wes. As one student puts it, "We have a huge percentage of racial minorities, but it's not just racial diversity, it's also geographical diversity, political diversity, economic diversity.... I end up learning just as much from the people around me as I do in the classroom." Another student adds, "Wes students are tolerant because there's an open dialogue both in and outside of the classroom that creates a high level of awareness and acceptance." Fifty-seven percent of the students graduated from public school, 37 percent from private school, and 6 percent from parochial. No academic or athletic merit scholarships are offered, but Wesleyan does guarantee to meet the financial need of all admits. In late 1999, the university endorsed a nearly 30 percent reduction in the total debt students receiving financial aid will incur after four years, from $28,000 to $20,000. Freshman orientation, which gets rave reviews, consists of a week of standard preregistration fare, plus comedy nights, movies, and square dancing.

For housing, most freshmen are consigned to the newly renovated singles or doubles in the campus dorms. Popular opinion indicates that the Butterfield complex is the choice for quiet study, while Clark Hall is where the party people go. Ninety-three percent of undergraduates live in university housing, and housing is guaranteed for four years. Juniors and seniors enjoy numerous housing options:

Ethnomusicology, including African drumming and dance, is a particular specialty; students can be found reclining on the wide, carpeted bleachers at the Third World Music Hall or watching a dozen musicians play the Indonesian gamelan.

The East Asian Studies Center has both a strong program and an authentic Japanese tea room.

townhouses for four or five students, fraternities, college-owned houses and apartments, or special-interest houses organized around concerns such as ecology, feminism, or minority-student unity. Upperclass students who want to live off campus must apply for permission. Those who move off have the option of eating at home, in the school grill, or at the fraternity eating clubs. Everyone else takes meals in Mocon, the glass-walled main dining hall, or two smaller cafeterias, and complains about the mandatory meal plan.

Middletown is a small city within easy driving distance of Hartford and New Haven, but it is off the beaten track of steady public transportation. Often students contend that "it may have everything you need, but nothing you want." Still, Wes students contribute a great deal of time to community service, and help maintain a peaceful, beneficial relationship with the town. And Wesleyan's rural surroundings afford the much-appreciated opportunity to jog through the countryside, swim at nearby Wadsworth Falls, or pick apples in the local orchards. Good road trips include New York and Boston, each two hours away, and decent ski areas and beaches, just under an hour away. Wesleyan sports tend to be for scholar-athletes rather than spectators. In any sport, annual encounters with "Little Three" rivals Williams and Amherst get even the most bookwormish student out of the library and into the heat of the action. The Ultimate Frisbee club (the Nietzsche Factor) almost always whips challengers, and intramurals are extremely popular. Athletics are enhanced by a much-needed $20-million complex that comes complete with a 200-meter indoor track, fitness center, and a 50-meter pool.

Although two former fraternities have turned into coed literary societies, Greek life at the remaining three is a jock preserve. Only 12 percent of the men and a scant 4 percent of the women go Greek. Wesleyan's enforcement of the 21-year-old drinking age is moderate compared with most schools. Consistent with the university's encouragement of independence, students bear a large part of the responsibility for policing themselves. "To the University's credit, they are really stressing alcohol awareness, so to speak," says a neuroscience and behavioral studies major. Students who throw a party for 75 or more people must attend a workshop that stresses safe drinking. Still, most students concur that it is quite easy for the underaged to imbibe. "You can get alcohol if you want to," notes a sophomore. It seems, however, that drinking alcohol is a minor event when compared to the multitude of other things happening on campus. Activities abound from comedy performances to a cappella groups, films, plays, bands, lectures, parties, and events planned by the more than 200 student groups. "There's tons going on right on campus," raves a sophomore, "so much that you feel like you're missing out if you leave." Major events on the social calendar include Spring Fling and Fall Ball—two outdoor festivals—and Uncle Duke Day and Zonker Harris Day, two similar events with a more psychedelic, 1960s flavor, in which students pay tribute to the infamous Doonesbury characters.

With so much to do, so much to learn, students at Wesleyan take it all in stride. The key to Wesleyan's success seems to be the fostering of an intellectual milieu where independent thinking and an appreciation of differences are omnipresent. So different, in fact, that a sophomore describes the typical Wesleyan student as "sarcastic, dramatic, poetic, athletic, creative, proactive, open-minded, caring, loud, and polite." And if you're still not convinced, take it from a veteran: "We would make any liberal arts college proud, but you can only find us here."

Overlaps

Brown, Yale, Harvard, Amherst, Williams.

West Virginia University

P.O. Box 6009, Morgantown, WV 26506-6009

Even though West Virginia University continues to be the state's flagship land-grant college, its mission has broadened considerably since its founding in 1867. The school offers students a choice of 166 degree programs at the undergraduate, graduate, and professional levels. It features 265 student organizations, including Greek houses and honor societies. And WVU also boasts 21 intercollegiate varsity athletic programs, including the national powerhouse rifle team. Clearly, this school is no longer just for coal miners and country folks. It is now a solid choice for scholars, researchers, and athletes.

WVU is situated in the picturesque mountains of north-central West Virginia, a few miles from the Pennsylvania border and overlooking the Monongahela River. A futuristic, driverless rail system bridges the school's two campuses, Morgantown and Evansdale, which are 1.5 miles apart. The buildings downtown are of ivy-covered brick, dating mainly from the 19th century, while the Evansdale campus is more modern. Ten campus buildings are listed on the National Register of Historic Places, and many of those structures have been restored or renovated. A computing center is the newest addition to the campus and construction is underway on an addition to the library, student recreation center, and life sciences building.

The university offers a total of 166 degree programs in 14 different schools, the best of which are engineering (particularly energy-related fields) and health sciences. WVU also boasts solid programs in journalism, physical education, agriculture and forestry, and the creative arts. Education, psychology, and business are also popular majors. An honors program, open to students with a 3.5 high school GPA and stiff 1360 on the SAT (or a 3.8 and an 1240), offers small classes and early registration, enabling students to get spots in the most sought-after courses. The BS in pharmacy has been converted to a six-year, first-professional, entry-level Pharm D program. WVU also now offers a BS in Forensic Identification, the first degree program of its kind in the world.

General education requirements call for 12 credits in each of three areas: humanities and fine arts, social and behavioral sciences, and natural sciences and math. Everyone must take courses that stress math and writing skills, as well as a course in foreign culture and minority or gender studies. New students are encouraged to enroll in "Orientation to University Life." This pass-fail course helps students make the transition from high school to college by addressing the academic, social, and emotional expectations of the college experience. Topics covered include study skills, university and community support services, goal setting, and career planning. Professors receive high marks from students. "My professors have been great," says a biology major. "They really care about what they teach." As for academic climate, courses are generally challenging. "For the

Website: www.wvu.edu
Location: Small city
Total Enrollment: 22,315
Undergraduates: 15,417
Male/Female: 54/46
SAT Ranges: V 460–560 M 460–560
ACT Range: 19–25
Financial Aid: 55%
Expense: Pub $
Phi Beta Kappa: Yes
Applicants: 8,124
Accepted: 94%
Enrolled: 47%
Grad in 6 Years: 55%
Returning Freshmen: 78%
Academics: ✍ ✍
Social: ☎ ☎ ☎ ☎
Q of L: ★ ★ ★
Admissions: (800) 344-WVU1
Email Address:
wvuadmissions@arc.wvu.edu

Strongest Programs:
Engineering
Political Science
Health Sciences
Psychology
Pharmacy
Journalism

WVU also now offers a BS in Forensic Identification, the first degree program of its kind in the world.

competitive student, the Honors Program provides an outlet for their competitive drive. The rest of the university provides challenging classes in a friendly atmosphere," says a law major.

Though West Virginia attracts students from 48 states and 84 other countries, it is primarily a regional university. State residents account for 62 percent of the students, and WVU lures a sizable contingent from western Pennsylvania. Minorities total a meager 7 percent, and the university offers specific programs to help minority students adjust. The university offers 3,000 merit scholarships that range from $500 to the full cost of a four-year program. Five University Foundation Scholarships for in-staters cover all expenses, plus up to $2,000 for travel, study abroad, internships, and the like. Athletic scholarships are also plentiful; there are over 200 in 21 different sports (including cheerleading). And at West Virginia you could be better off knowing your pigs and cows than your p's and q's, since the list of special interests in which merit scholarships are offered includes livestock and animal judging.

Only 20 percent of the students live on campus, but dorms do provide academic support services such as computer rooms, tutoring centers, and courses in career options and college-survival skills. Freshmen also participate in Operation Jump Start, which pairs each class with a faculty member who represents them to the community. For upperclassmen, housing is first-come, first-served, and rising enrollments are making rooms harder to get. Many opt for nearby apartments, though about 20 percent choose Greek houses. Most dorms are coed; the older ones are known for their character, and the newer residential complexes on the Evansdale campus are desirable to those who seek larger rooms and luxuries like air-conditioning. The renovated Stalnaker Hall, which contains the honors program, is probably the choicest of all. Each hall has its own cafeteria offering meal plans to all on- and off-campus students; the fraternities and sororities have their own cooks. The shuttle runs only until midnight, so late-night partyers should arrange for their own wheels.

WVU boasts solid programs in journalism, physical education, agriculture and forestry, and the creative arts.

West Virginia fields almost two dozen men's and women's varsity teams, including conference champions in baseball, gymnastics, wrestling, track, and swimming. The women's basketball team is one of the best in the Big East Conference, and the rifle team has won numerous NCAA national championships. But football is the hands-down favorite, and whenever the Mountaineers earn a victory over archrival Pittsburgh, delirious fans storm the field, sometimes before the game ends. "For social life," one student reports, "we go to sporting events: football and basketball." When the cheers at WVU's 63,500-seat stadium or 14,000-seat basketball coliseum die down, the action usually moves to downtown or fraternity houses, where Homecoming Week and Mountaineer Week, celebrating the virtues of the state, highlight the social season. Alcohol is banned in the dorms, and frats are responsible for limiting their events to 300 members and guests, as well as having a carding system at the door.

In any case, the campus stays buzzing on weekends, and this, along with the school's picturesque location and rising athletic and academic scenes, makes "Mo-town" a great place to spend four years.

Overlaps

Penn State, Virginia Tech, Pittsburgh, University of Maryland, Marshall.

If You Apply To ➤ **West Virginia**…Rolling admissions. Financial aid: Mar. 1 (Jan. 15 for freshman scholarships). Meets demonstrated need of 25%. Campus and alumni interviews: optional, informational. SATs or ACTs: required. SAT IIs: optional. Accepts the Common Application and electronic applications. No essay question.

Wheaton College

501 College Avenue, Wheaton, IL 60187

A deep love for learning and for Jesus Christ is reflected in every aspect of the Wheaton College experience. Wheaton is arguably the finest evangelical college in the country because it provides its students with the knowledge they need to grow intellectually and spiritually. "The unique combination of spiritual commitment and intellectual ability make Wheaton a wonderful place to grow," says a senior Biblical studies major. "You are free to discover truth for yourself in a caring and safe environment." The school's motto, "For Christ and His Kingdom," demonstrates its deep commitment to the nurturing of one's mind and soul. Known as Wheaties, Wheaton students are well respected; the alumni roster reads like a "Who's Who" among American Evangelical Protestants.

Wheaton's 80-acre campus is an oasis of sorts: Blanchard Hall, built in the last century, looks like a castle perched atop the front campus hill. Down the hill from the Old Main campus is the $13.5-million Billy Graham Center (named after the school's most famous alumnus), a museum and library that has become a cornerstone in research on American evangelicalism. The mall area provides room for strolls through the wooded campus, which sits right in the middle of one of Chicago's oldest and most established suburbs. The newest addition to the campus is the student life facility, complete with an aerobics studio.

Wheaton is a Christian, liberal arts institution that is committed to the principle that truth is revealed by God through Christ, in whom is hidden all the treasures of wisdom and knowledge. The school's deep dedication to spirituality only strengthens its commitment to education. Wheaton has managed to attract enough National Merit Scholars to put it on par with the best secular colleges of its size. Ethics is applied to disciplines across the curriculum, which is built around extensive distribution requirements that include studies in faith, reason, society, nature, literature, and the arts. Students are also expected to be competent in knowledge of the Bible, communications, English, foreign language, and mathematics. Fourteen credit hours of Bible studies and theology are required of all students, and all freshmen must take the Freshman Experience Seminar. Students describe the quality of teaching as exceptional. "Although the professors set high standards and expect a great deal from their students, they are also more than willing to assist them when they need help." Another student adds, "The professors here are some of the brightest people in their fields." The academic climate is considered very competitive and rigorous. "The professors demand a lot from their students," says a freshman elementary education major. "The students, in turn, are very hard-working and highly motivated. It has taken learning to a whole new tier."

Any fears about the gap between Christianity and science have been overcome at Wheaton, where most of the natural sciences are strong—biology and chemistry in particular. English, music, Biblical studies, business/economics, and communications are the most popular majors. In addition to major programs in the liberal arts and sciences, students can opt for the 3-2 liberal arts/nursing program or liberal arts/engineering double degree. Wheaton recently added an anthropology major. Studying abroad in East Asia, England, France, Germany, Spain, or the Holy Land is an option for Wheaton undergraduates, as is spending a semester at one of 12 other evangelical schools in the Christian College Consortium.* The Human Needs and Global Resources (HNGR) program coordinates studies in Third World development, with six-month internships in a

Website: www.wheaton.edu

Location: Suburban

Total Enrollment: 2,732

Undergraduates: 2,338

Male/Female: 49/52

SAT Ranges: V 610–720 M 600–700

ACT Range: 27–31

Financial Aid: 60%

Expense: Pr $

Phi Beta Kappa: No

Applicants: 1,964

Accepted: 54%

Enrolled: 55%

Grad in 6 Years: 83%

Returning Freshmen: 94%

Academics: 🖉 🖉 🖉

Social: ☎ ☎ ☎

Q of L: ★ ★ ★ ★

Admissions: (630) 752-5005 or (800) 222-2419

Email Address: admissions@wheaton.edu

Strongest Programs:
Literature
Psychology
Music
Bible/Theology

In addition to major programs in the liberal arts and sciences, students can opt for the 3-2 liberal arts/nursing program or liberal arts/engineering double degree.

There is also the Black Hills Science Station for summer study in botany and zoology and Honey Rock Camp for leadership training.

development project in a Third World country.

The High Road Wilderness Program provides an Outward Bound-type experience in the woods of northern Wisconsin. There is also the Black Hills Science Station for summer study in botany and zoology and Honey Rock Camp for leadership training. Other options include those offered through the Christian College Coalition.* Students in science, math, and computer science have the opportunity to perform research at Argonne National Laboratory.

Most Wheaties share a fairly similar middle-class, public school background. Eighty percent graduated in the top quarter of their high school class, a fact that adds to the academic pressures. Minorities make up 11 percent of the student body, and all agree that diversity is valued. About one-fifth of the students are from Illinois. People at Wheaton for the most part are educated about issues, and discussions often center on abortion, euthanasia, and genetic cloning. The political bent is definitely toward the right. The financial aid office offers a range of scholarships, but there are no athletic free rides. A large percentage of students spend their time volunteering in inner-city Chicago, tutoring, visiting nursing homes, visiting AIDS patients, and running church youth groups.

Students are pleased with their dorm rooms, which one student describes as comfortable and a decent size. And "recent renovations have improved many of the older dorms," says a senior. A high percentage of juniors and seniors live in college-owned apartments off campus, and most of the rest are granted permission to move off campus. Wheaton offers a beautiful dining hall with fireplaces and a variety of spaces in which to eat. Students even find room to praise the food as pretty good for institutional fare.

The Human Needs and Global Resources (HNGR) program coordinates studies in Third World development, with six-month internships in a development project in a Third World country.

Fraternities and sororities are not part of the social scene on this campus. Most students are committed to the pledge, which they reaffirm every semester, "to maintain a lifestyle pleasing to Christ," which includes abstaining from alcohol, on or off campus. Most students adhere to the policy, but of course, there are some who don't. One student says the policy works, for the most part, and anyone who is caught drinking is confronted by the administration. Wheaton's social scene is active, albeit mostly on campus. The College Union organizes movies, late-night skating parties, and other activities almost every weekend. The school's administration has loosened its ban on social dancing, pleasing students. Also popular are treks to the movies and local coffee shops. A quick half-hour train ride transports Wheaton undergrads to Chicago's Loop, which offers restaurants, blues clubs, museums, shopping, and professional sporting events. Major annual events include Fall and Spring fests, the annual Air-Jam, and the annual Christmas screening of Jimmy Stewart in *It's a Wonderful Life*.

The calm of Wheaton's mild-mannered Christian ambiance is periodically shattered by the interclass scramble for the Bench, a reinforced slab of concrete that is the subject of an ongoing and often rough-and-tumble game of keep-away. A gentler Wheaton tradition is that engaged couples climb to the top of Blanchard Hall and ring the bell. Wheaton athletic teams, known for 70 years as the Crusaders, are now the Thunder. Critics claimed the old mascot glorified medieval Christians who killed thousands of people in the name of Jesus. The new mascot was chosen from 1,300 suggestions because it sounds strong and is one of the natural phenomena associated with God.

Wheaton's motto inspires its students to make a positive impact on the world before and after graduation. One senior comments: "Wheaton is carving out its identity as a place where thinking Christians can come and grow." This makes for an incredible balance of high-quality academics and a dedicated, Christian-centered body of believers.

Overlaps

Taylor, Calvin, Messiah, Grove City, Harvard.

Wheaton College

Norton, MA 02766

More than a decade has passed since Wheaton converted to a coed campus and admitted its first male student. Since then, the college has developed a reputation for its progressive programs, emphasis on gender equality, and efforts to help students grasp the controversies of the day. Like many of the small liberal arts colleges that dot the Northeast, Wheaton provides a sheltered arena where students can step back and contemplate the larger world. "Learning for life," one senior says, "is a central theme for most students."

Tucked into 385 acres of picturesque, rural landscape, Wheaton offers few distractions from intellectual pursuits. The campus is a pretty blend of ivy-covered Georgian brick (the old campus) and ivy-covered modern architecture (the new) set among beautiful lawns and numerous shade trees. The two halves of the campus are separated by Peacock Pond, which probably qualifies as the only heated duck pond on any American campus. A number of campus houses have been renovated in recent years and a new dormitory has been built.

No matter what your gender, Wheaton has much to offer academically. There are scores of major programs in the liberal arts, most of them quite solid, with foreign languages, political science, psychology, English, economics, and Hispanic studies considered especially good. A major in women's studies has been recently added to the curriculum, and faculty efforts to renew interest in mathematics and French appear to be working. While few students point to any weak departments at Wheaton, its small size has raised some complaints about understaffing. Independent study courses and individualized majors are also encouraged. Wheaton offers dual degree programs in journalism, business administration, engineering, religion, optometry, and studio art in conjunction with other schools, and allows students to take semesters on other campuses through the Twelve-College Exchange Program.* Students may also take classes at nearby Brown University if they are not offered at Wheaton. For those tired of being landlubbers, Wheaton is also part of the Maritime Studies Program.*

For a small college, Wheaton gives its students a wide range of opportunities. The highly praised Filene Center for Work and Learning provides exceptional help to all eager students. Courses are regarded as fairly competitive, but pressure is largely imposed from within. "The professors are amazing and the courses are great, but it is easy to 'just get by' if that is what you want to do," says a political science major. "The challenge is there. You just need to be responsible enough to make the most of it."

The cornerstone of Wheaton's general education requirements is the popular First-Year Seminar, an interdisciplinary course focused on different "controversies" that have generated debate or heralded changes in the ways students

Website: www.wheatonma.edu
Location: Suburban
Total Enrollment: 1,451
Undergraduates: 1,451
Male/Female: 34/66
SAT Ranges: V 560–640 M 550–680
ACT Range: 25–28
Financial Aid: 63%
Expense: Pr $
Phi Beta Kappa: Yes
Applicants: 2,417
Accepted: 72%
Enrolled: 28%
Grad in 6 Years: 74%
Returning Freshmen: 84%
Academics: ✍ ✍ ✍
Social: ☎ ☎ ☎
Q of L: ★ ★ ★ ★
Admissions: (508) 286-8251 or (800) 394-6003
Email Address: admission@wheatonma.edu

Strongest Programs:
  Psychology
  English
  Economics
  Hispanic Studies
  Studio Art

experience and understand the world. Other requirements include two semesters of foreign language, two courses in the arts and humanities, two semesters in the natural sciences, one social science, one western history, and a course in cultural diversity. Also required are one course in math, English 101, and one course in the non-Western world.

Small classes encourage close ties between students and teachers. And the school says only one class has more than 100 students. "The professors are so intelligent, but so down to earth," a senior says. "When you walk into the classroom, you can feel their energy and their love for the subject." And because the teacher of the First-Year Seminar is also a student's faculty advisor, students need not worry about being lost in the shuffle. Students who accumulate a 3.75 average are rewarded with a $1,000 scholarship.

Sixty-two percent of the Wheaties are from public school, and 57 percent come from outside Massachusetts. The student body is largely Caucasian, with blacks accounting for 4 percent, Hispanics 3 percent, and Asian-Americans another 3 percent. "While political correctness is conscious on the minds of most students, it isn't to the point where it becomes an issue," reports a junior psychology major. "For the most part, Wheaton students are very accepting of the diversity of thinking and values each student brings." The college's decision to go coed sparked a financial growth spurt. Student applications and enrollment have increased dramatically, allowing the administration to launch a massive capital campaign and hire more minority scholars.

Wheaton is rich in tradition. The first night after arriving, freshmen are given candles and taken to the chapel. There they are instructed in college lore and told to keep their candles until Sentimental Night, when, as seniors, they float them on Peacock Pond. Only seniors are allowed to sit on the steps of the library or go into the front door of the chapel. And bashful boys beware: tradition dictates that if a Wheatie walks with a date three times around the pond and he doesn't kiss her, she is perfectly justified to push him in. Only time will tell if Wheaton men will claim the same prerogative.

Virtually everyone lives on campus in dorms or houses (1 all-women, 26 coed) monitored by teams of upperclassmen. Gebbie Hall regularly hosts panels, presentations, and colloquia on gender issues, and the 51 residents of this self-governing hall are selected on the basis of applications that speak to a student's commitment to gender equality. Freshmen live in doubles, triples, or quads; upperclassmen head straight for spacious singles with wood floors on the old campus. Meals in the bright and spacious dining halls are first-rate, at least by college standards, and dining hall policies provide students with an "unlimited meal plan." But the biggest winners of all are the ducks, who thrive on leftover bread and hang around Peacock Pond all winter long.

Norton is nobody's idea of a college town and most social life is centered on campus in the form of plays, movies, dances, concerts, or parties. The alcohol policy, which students in recent years had seen as lax, has been strengthened recently. "They've really cracked down this year," says a sophomore English major. "but it just has made us a group of closet drinkers." The student center offers a cafe, dance studio, and sun deck for afternoon study breaks. Students looking for a good time generally head for Boston or Providence (35 and 15 miles away, respectively). And many Wheaton students do find time for community service, when studying or socializing time isn't occupied.

Wheaton's calendar is punctuated by a number of big weekend events, including AutumnFest, the Champagne Christmas Dance, and the "Head of the Peacock," where students build boats and race them across the pond. "We all sink, or at least voluntarily end up in the pond," one student jokes. Biggest of all is the Spring Weekend, which features live bands and outdoor barbecues. Athletic events also tend to draw cheerful crowds. In varsity sports, the soccer teams, volleyball teams, men's basketball, and synchronized swimming all fare well. The women's indoor track and field team won the NCAA championship in 1998-99. A huge athletic facility with an eight-lane swimming pool, a field house, and an 850-seat arena for basketball or volleyball provides Wheaton students, fans and athletes alike, with a home-court advantage.

Most current Wheaton students were just starting elementary school when the college decided to admit men. But in the years that have elapsed since that decision, the presence of testosterone has become a nonissue. Few students mention it and that might be because now the school is simply focused on providing its students with the best education.

If You Apply To > **Wheaton**...Early decision: Nov. 15. Early action: Dec. 15. Regular admissions: Feb. 1. Financial aid: Nov. 15 (early decision), Feb. 1 (early action and regular admissions). Campus and alumni interviews: recommended, evaluative. SATs or ACTs: optional. SAT IIs: optional. Essay question: letter to an old friend upon being notified about your tenth high school reunion. Graded writing sample required.

Whitman College

345 Boyer Avenue, Walla Walla, WA 99362-2083

Nestled amid the onion and wheat fields of southern Washington, Whitman College began as the dream of a husband-and-wife team of medical missionaries on the Northwest frontier. Many students refer to some "unquantifiable essence" when they try to describe how they feel at this small school. They love the one-on-one attention lavished by their professors and say the sense of community at Whitman is "a blessing." All in all, these Whitties are pretty contented folks.

Everything important is within walking distance of campus, including the main drag of Walla Walla (a.k.a. Walla Squared), only three blocks away. If a picturesque setting is your thing, you'll feel right at home at Whitman, with its 55-acre campus blending of Colonial buildings and modern facilities, all covered in New England ivy. The campus stands in contrast to the rolling expanse of Northwestern terrain nearby, inhabited primarily by farmers and ranch hands. Beyond Walla Walla (which means "many waters"), and as far as the eye can see, are scenic mountains, rivers, fields, and forests. Recent construction includes a major renovation and expansion of the Penrose Memorial Library and plans are underway for a new campus center, which will also house a dance hall and cyber-lounge.

Without a doubt, Whitman's faculty is its biggest academic asset. "Professors are extremely accessible, and it's not uncommon for students to call them at home or to go to dinner at their houses to discuss assignments," says a chemistry/biology double major. A sophomore adds, "The professors here are entertaining, give meaningful assignments, and facilitate great discussions." Many students consider their teachers friends, not just people droning in front of a podium. "My econ prof offered to take some friends and I snowboarding," a

Website: www.whitman.edu
Location: Small city
Total Enrollment: 1,400
Undergraduates: 1,400
Male/Female: 43/57
SAT Ranges: V 610–720
  M 600–700
Financial Aid: 75%
Expense: Pr $ $ $
Phi Beta Kappa: Yes
Applicants: 2,151
Accepted: 50%
Enrolled: 34%
Grad in 6 Years: 80%
Returning Freshmen: 91%
Academics: ✍ ✍ ✍ ✍
Social: ☎ ☎ ☎
Q of L: ★ ★ ★ ★
Admissions: (509) 527-5176
Email Address:
  admission@whitman.edu

(Continued)

Strongest Programs:

Politics

Biology

History

English

Theater

freshman says. The school's small size translates into relatively limited course offerings, but students with far-flung interests can find a supportive faculty mentor and put together combination majors. Seniors get first dibs at registration, but most professors allow students to enroll in full classes if students approach them.

Most students agree that the academic climate at Whitman is challenging. "Whitman College is an academically rigorous institution," says a psychology/philosophy double major. "The classes tend to be small and discussion intensive so if you plan on sitting in the back row and never raising your hand, Whitman is probably not the place for you." Still, the students insist that the atmosphere is not overly competitive. "Although the students here strive to do their best, they are also more than willing to help each other out," says a senior. Impressive academic departments are politics, biology, chemistry, and history, and Whitman has the most active small-college theater program in the country. Recent additions to the curriculum include a major in Classics and a new minor in Latin American studies. A new one-semester extension of the Core, Critical and Alternative Voices, which offers an examination of non-Western world views, has also been added. Some students complain because there isn't a religion major and the physics and computer science departments are cited as weak.

All Whitman students must complete the General Studies Program, divided into the freshman core and distribution requirements. The program helps freshmen learn to read analytically and write effectively. Also, all students take at least six credits in the following areas: fine arts; history and literature; language, writing and rhetoric; physical science and mathematics; philosophy and religion; descriptive science; and social science. Seniors also must pass comprehensive written and oral exams in their major—the first college or university in the nation to require undergrads to do so.

Whitman boasts an extensive Asian art collection and expanded Asian Studies and art history programs. The library, with 355,000 volumes, is a great place to catch up on the latest campus news as well as study. Whitman has 3–2 or 3–3 programs in engineering (with the University of Washington, Caltech, Columbia, Washington University, and Duke), forestry (Duke), international studies and international business (Monterey Institute of International Studies), computer science and oceanography (University of Washington), and law (Columbia). There are also numerous study abroad programs and a slate of internships. Many students work on special projects or work with faculty members collaborating in professional research.

Forty-five percent of the Whitman student body come from Washington, the rest are primarily from the suburbs of Western cities, notably San Francisco and Portland. Seven percent are Asian American, while African Americans and Hispanics make up only 4 percent of the students. Despite the apparent lack of diversity, attempts are being made to improve the situation—the college has established a full-time director of multicultural student affairs to get the ball rolling. As for any big political issues, one students says "I think a lot of Whitties were born with tattoos that read 'Reduce, Reuse, Recycle.'"

Jock types are in short supply at Whitman, and devotees of alternative lifestyles may feel outnumbered. A large portion of the students come from public high school, and 63 percent were in the top tenth of their class. Whitman awards merit scholarships based on academic performance each year, ranging from $2,000 to $8,000, but there are no athletic scholarships.

All freshmen and sophomores must live in campus housing, which includes some lovely old buildings with large, comfortable rooms. Prentiss Hall and Lyman House, both built in 1926, have received multimillion-dollar face-lifts including

Whitman offers theme housing for students interested in foreign languages, fine arts, writing, community service, and environmental studies, as well as a multiethnic house.

computer hookups, an aerobics room, central air and heating, new furniture and carpeting, and a conference room. Seventy-one percent of the student body live in campus housing, and some students say it's difficult for upperclassmen to get rooms since dorm spots are in such high demand. There's also theme housing for students interested in foreign languages, fine arts, writing, community service, and environmental studies, as well as a multiethnic house. Overall, students seem quite pleased with housing: "The dorms are very plush and well-maintained. I almost wish I still lived on campus," a junior sighs. Thirty-seven percent of the men belong to the four fraternities, which have their own houses. The four sororities, which claim 34 percent of the women, stake out sections in the all-female residence hall. In a break from tradition, Bon Appetit (a small corporation based in Menlo Park, California) runs the food service and catering operations, and students appreciate the café and bistro styles of food.

Whitman boasts an extensive Asian art collection and expanded Asian Studies and art history programs.

Outdoor attractions are important in this area of the country, where autumn is gorgeous, winter sporadically snowy, and spring delightfully warm. Walla Walla (pop. 30,000) is located in the center of agricultural southeastern Washington near the Blue Mountains. Hiking, biking, and backpacking are minutes away, and white-water rafting and rock climbing are popular on weekends. Two ski centers and other recreational areas are within an hour's drive of campus. Students who get antsy in this remote location feel that weekend trips to Seattle (260 miles) and Portland (235 miles) can be lifesavers.

Whitman scrapped varsity football in the late 1970s, but the "Fighting Missionaries" maintain an active interest in physical exertion. Highly popular intramural football (both men and women participate) has filled the void nicely, and 75 percent of the student body competes in the vigorous intramural club program. Sherwood Center, the athletic complex, underwent a $500,000 renovation in 1997 that transformed it into a modern fitness center. The project included a new dance studio and aerobic and weight-lifting equipment that are utilized by fitness-conscious students, faculty, and staff. Rock climbers can challenge themselves on two walls, one outdoors and one indoors. Men's and women's teams in skiing, swimming, tennis, and lacrosse are especially strong.

"The campus is an oasis of activity. One student sums it up this way: "If you can't find something to do at Whitman, you're not looking hard enough." Several students mention the very active drama department, which stages about 12 plays a year, as important to on-campus life. The lack of a football team doesn't stop Whitties from celebrating Homecoming, complete with cultural events, nostalgic alumni, and a campus-wide dance. In the spring, Whitman shows its intellectual side with Renaissance Faire. There are also budget-priced movies, and a student coffeehouse featuring live music weekly from various local or out-of-town bands. While hardly a cultural mecca, Walla Walla supports a resident symphony, community theater, numerous art galleries, two rodeos, and a hot-air balloon festival in the spring. "Whitman students are more likely to say 'What should I do?' rather than 'There is nothing to do,'" one student notes.

While Whitman's small size and out-there location may not appeal to more cosmopolitan students, those looking to bond with peers and professors alike will probably feel at home here. "Whitman offers the best of both worlds," says an economics major, "a challenging academic program as well as plenty of personal attention."

Overlaps

University of Washington, Puget Sound, Pomona College, Stanford, Lewis and Clark.

Whittier College

13406 East Philadelphia, P.O. Box 634, Whittier, CA 90608

Website: www.whittier.edu

Location: Suburban

Total Enrollment: 2,198

Undergraduates: 1,291

Male/Female: 43/57

SAT Ranges: V 460–590 M 460–590

ACT Range: 19–24

Financial Aid: 70%

Expense: Pr $ $ $

Phi Beta Kappa: No

Applicants: 1,345

Accepted: 87%

Enrolled: 32%

Grad in 6 Years: 63%

Returning Freshmen: 74%

Academics: 🖎 🖎 🖎

Social: ☎ ☎ ☎

Q of L: ★ ★ ★ ★

Admissions: (562) 907-4238

Email Address:
admissions@whittier.edu

Strongest Programs:
Business Administration
Political Science
Biology
English
Whittier Scholar Program

Outwardly, Whittier College doesn't look much different from when its most famous alum, Richard Nixon, strolled the campus. But the school is making major strides toward becoming a global training ground—a move Mr. Nixon would surely endorse. Students can study in 30 foreign countries and even design their entire curriculum. "In the last five years, we have come to a point of financial success, as well as academic success," says a senior English major. "Our curriculum has been revised and our ethnic, as well as socioeconomic diversity, is at its best."

Located just 18 miles away from the Los Angeles area, the college is perched on a hill overlooking the town of Whittier, California, with the San Gabriel Mountains rising up from the horizon. The 95-acre campus is a pleasant mixture of modern buildings tucked between the red-roofed, white-walled Spanish traditionals. Whittier recently completed work on its landmark building (Diehl Hall) to include a digital audio/video computer lab for languages.

Founded in 1887 by members of the Society of Friends, Whittier officially ended its affiliation with the Quakers in the 1940s, but the prevailing spirit of community harkens back to their traditions. Faculty wins high marks for their concern and accessibility. "The professors here don't just want to teach, they want to inspire—and do so," remarks a sophomore theater and English major. While classes are somewhat competitive, students still work together. "The courses are challenging but the students are always willing to help each other out," says a senior.

Whittier offers its students two major programs: the liberal education program and the Whittier Scholars Program. About 80 percent of the students take the revised liberal education track, in which they fulfill distribution requirements in writing skills, mathematics, natural sciences, global perspectives, comparative knowledge, and creative and kinesthetic performance. The emphasis of the liberal education program is on interdisciplinary focus, globalism, and critical and quantitative thinking. These liberally educated Whittierans next choose a major from among 26 departments, the strongest and most popular of which include English, biology, political science, and business administration. The college added a major in earth and environmental sciences. Students feel that anthropology, music, and women's studies are weak.

Whittier's strongest reputation is for the Whittier Scholars Program, a path taken by 20 percent of the undergraduates, who choose to bypass the traditional liberal education program. They are relieved of most general requirements and start from square one with an "educational design" process. With the help of an academic advisor, the scholars carve their majors out of standard offerings by taking a bit of this and a bit of that. Majors have included such names as Symbol

Systems, Visual Studies and Business, and Dynamics of Politics and Urban Life. The program is highly regarded (even by those who don't elect to take it) because of the more active role it allows students to play and the freedom it affords them in pursuing their interests. All students, no matter which curriculum they choose, must fulfill a yearlong freshman writing requirement. In an attempt to help freshmen develop both their critical thinking skills and their ability to communicate clearly in writing, Whittier lets students choose their preferences from a variety of seminars. They are also encouraged to take an additional writing course, mathematics, and lab science during their freshman year.

Study abroad options include programs in Denmark, India, Mexico, and Asia, and undergraduates may also take foreign study tours during the January interim. Sixty-two percent of the students come from California, and the rest are from all over the United States and the world (8 percent are foreign). On campus the word is this: "Your roommate can be from another state, another country, or another state of mind. The key here is tolerance." Diversity plays a major role on this campus. While African Americans make up only 6 percent of the students, Hispanic enrollment is an impressive 27 percent, and Asian Americans constitute another 8 percent. "Whittier College is so diverse in every way that there really isn't a political correctness issue," a business administration major says. "People here are so accepting of everyone else." One club, called Eliminating Campus Homophobia (ECHO), is quite vocal on campus, as are the Black Student Union and Hispanic Student Association. An on-campus cultural center focuses on diversity programming and resources. In addition to need-based aid, the college grants some students talent awards of half tuition in art, drama, music, and writing, as well as more than 200 merit scholarships, ranging from $3,500 to full tuition.

Forty percent of the students seek off-campus shelter, but the Turner Residence Hall entices many students to stay on campus and vie for a chance to get a room with a panoramic view of Los Angeles and campus computer network access in every room. Most freshmen are assigned rooms, though Whittier Scholars, athletes, and members of Whittier's social societies tend to cluster in selected dorms and houses. All dorms are equally suited for freshmen, says one student, because each is its own little community. "There is an atmosphere suited to every personality," says a social work senior. "Rooms are large with lots of closet space and clean bathrooms." All campus residents must take at least 10 meals at the Campus Inn dining hall, where the food is said to be typical college fare. The Spot (Whittier's popular campus coffeehouse) was recently expanded to include a state-of-the-art nightclub called—what else?—the Club.

Nine social societies (they're not called fraternities or sororities here) attract 15 percent of the men and women and tend to be identified by certain interests. These societies don't dominate the social scene at Whittier, but their dances, which frequently feature live entertainment, are welcomed by all. For many, entertainment takes the form of road trips to exciting destinations such as Las Vegas, Mexico, Joshua Tree, Hollywood, San Diego, and northern California. Whittier has a fairly strict alcohol policy and underage drinking is not permitted. Nevertheless, a senior contends that "it is not a problem for underage students to get alcohol." Popular annual events include a Spring Sing talent show, the football game against archrival Occidental College, and Sportsfest, which is a campus-wide competition in which dorms compete in a variety of athletic, intellectual, and wacky games and events. A favorite among students is Mona Kai, a Hawaiian party put on by the Lancer Society where tons of sand are shipped in for the event. The most important campus landmark is the Rock, which sits near the front of campus and is given a fresh coat of paint by countless aspiring artists. The

Whittier's strongest reputation is for the Whittier Scholars Program, a path taken by 20 percent of the undergraduates, who choose to bypass the traditional liberal education program.

Study abroad options include programs in Denmark, India, Mexico, and Asia, and undergraduates may also take foreign study tours during the January interim.

In an attempt to help freshmen develop both their critical thinking skills and their ability to communicate clearly in writing, Whittier lets students choose their preferences from a variety of seminars.

beach is a frequent destination, and for nightlife, Los Angeles looms large. The local community, known as Uptown Whittier, offers quaint shops, restaurants, and cobblestone sidewalks but little in the way of entertainment.

Men's lacrosse is the biggest sports team on campus, having won the 1997 WCLL championship and maintaining a perfect winning record in the process. Men's football and basketball, women's basketball, softball, and volleyball, and intramurals are also strong.

All in all, most students agree that Whittier is a supportive, intimate environment where people cooperate and take an active role in education. According to one student, the atmosphere is what makes Whittier unique. "Professors, students, and administrators know who you are and really care about you," says a business/political science double major. "It feels like home."

Willamette University

900 State Street, Salem, OR 97301

Willamette attracts students who are eager to be onboard as the school shifts into overdrive and makes a run for the big leagues. For many, the school provides a more personal atmosphere than some of the larger universities in the area and is a better-endowed alternative to the smaller private colleges. Indeed, the school might be one of the few in the nation that can successfully maintain a laid-back feeling while ratcheting up the intellectual intensity. "The academic climate at Willamette is fairly rigorous in that the classes are challenging, and you must strive to do your best," says an English literature major. Another student adds, "Students care about their academics and studying usually has a huge priority over partying." Strong offerings in political science and economics and an unusually robust study abroad program help make this small college one of the nation's best-kept secrets.

The Willamette campus, with a profusion of trees, small wildlife, and a clean, clear brook running amid old redbrick buildings, offers the advantages of a small college—low student/faculty ratio, lots of individual attention, and a cohesive intellectual community—plus some of the resources of a larger, research-oriented university. Willamette recently dedicated the Hallie Ford Museum of Art, the Collins Legal Center, the $7.1-million Olin Science Center, and a $1.1-million addition to the school's athletic center.

The oldest college in the West, Willamette has graduate schools of law, management, and education, and boasts 34 undergraduate degree programs. The Willamette way of life blends the beauty of the West Coast with the intensity of better known schools in the Northeast. "Students are very laid-back and down-to-earth," reports a Japanese studies major, "but are also very hard workers." The $7.4-million Mark O. Hatfield Library (named for the former U.S. senator) boasts a computerized card catalog system and enough study space to create a climate conducive to hitting the books. Professors get high marks from students. "Professors are very close with the students and take time to personally help," a junior says. "All of my professors have been passionate about their subject and about teaching." It's not uncommon for profs to invite their classes home for dinner, either, since the great majority have 25 or fewer students.

Willamette now only offers Bachelor of Arts and Bachelor of Music degrees. A set of newly redesigned general education requirements supports this change, including courses in six modes of inquiry: Creating in the Arts; Understanding the Natural World; Interpreting Texts; Analyzing Arguments, Reasons and Values; Viewing Cultures Historically; and Understanding Society. In addition, students must satisfy a foreign language requirement, take two quantitative analysis courses, complete the Writing Program (an intensive undergraduate program designed to foster a campus-wide writing culture), and take the freshman seminar World Views.

Among the most popular programs at Willamette are biology, economics, English, politics, art, and psychology. Future politicos benefit from having the state capitol complex available nearby as a laboratory. Business, premed, and prelaw tracks are popular, and Willamette boasts good acceptance rates at corresponding professional schools. Students say dance and philosophy suffer because of their small size and low student interest, and they add that freshman sometimes have trouble getting into certain classes. Faculty members have been added recently in history and the history of science, and foreign language programs have been expanded and upgraded. The latter benefit from Willamette's proximity to the U.S. campus of Tokyo International University, WU's sister college. WU also has extensive programs for study abroad, from Western Europe to Scandinavia, Asia and the Pacific Rim, South America, and even Cuba. The Simiferopol exchange, in what was once the USSR, continues to be popular. Students also can study in Chicago, Washington, D.C., and at the United Nations. Opportunities for undergraduate research are more numerous than ever, and support has more than doubled with the creation of the Carson Undergraduate Research Awards, the Science Collaborate Research Program, and a newly organized humanities center.

For the most part, students come to Willamette from Oregon (37 percent) and other Western states, such as California and Washington. Three-quarters ranked in the top tenth of their high school class. The school is 82 percent white; minorities account for 17 percent of the population. In a change from recent years, students say that race is not as important on campus as homosexual rights, humane treatment of farm workers, sexual assault, and state politics. However, many students admit that the "Willamette bubble" can be frustrating at times. "The outside world is perceived by many as something that exists far beyond and that we learn about only through classes." In addition to need-based financial aid, Willamette offers talent and academic merit scholarships each year, ranging from $500 to full tuition. Athletes, however, score no points in the scholarship department.

Freshmen and sophomores must live on campus, but many juniors and seniors live in off-campus housing. All residential housing is coed, and a small percentage of the students live in fraternity and sorority houses. Housing is generally "well-maintained" and "fun." The prime dorm for freshmen seems to be the quiet and mellow Lausanne, while Kaneko Hall, the Japanese exchange dorm, is recommended for sophomores and juniors. The student-owned-and-operated bistro offers a popular and tasty alternative to cafeteria fare. An active campus

(Continued)
Strongest Programs:
Politics
Biology
Economics
English
Art
Psychology
Rhetoric and Media Studies

security initiative includes 24-hour patrols and keeps students feeling safe.

Students say the Greeks have an undeniable effect on the social scene; 33 percent of men and 25 percent of women sign up. Most socializing takes place on campus, and while guidelines for alcoholic functions are changing, students aren't. "Underage college students will always drink, it's just a question of how easy or difficult it is," a senior says, adding that the alcohol policies seem to get stricter each year. Movies, barbecues, dances, Monday night football on the big-screen TV, coffeehouses featuring local performers, and gatherings with friends are high on students' lists of favorite leisure-time activities. Then there are the traditional events, such as Senior Skits, Spirit Week, and a Drag Dance sponsored by the lesbian, gay, and bisexual students' group. Willapalooza is a music festival.

While Salem is not a college town, the school makes up for it with some of its own flavor. Students are dumped into a shallow campus brook when they are "Mill-Streamed" on their birthdays, and they partake in genuine, spit-roasted pig during the annual Luau. Besides, Salem is just an hour from the Cascade Mountain Range and the ruggedly beautiful Oregon Coast, and only 40 minutes from wicked cool Portland. When Willamette students aren't roadtripping to Seattle (about four hours north) or San Francisco (eight to nine hours south), most seem to enjoy the activities and resources of the Oregon state capital, especially parks, restaurants, and movies. Volunteer work through the Community Outreach Program is also high on many students' lists.

As for sports, Willamette fields strong varsity teams in golf, track and cross-country, soccer, football, and volleyball. The school made history in October 1997, when junior soccer star Liz Heaston kicked her way into the record books as the first woman to play intercollegiate football. (She made the two extra points she attempted.) The women's soccer team has won the conference title for seven consecutive years and advanced to the final four in the 1998 NCAA II tournament.

Willamette may be a tad too homogeneous for some, but the school is making headway in its quest to eclipse the nation's other liberal arts universities. As with many schools, success at Willamette depends on the student's willingness to work. Says a rhetoric and media studies major, "If the student is up to the challenge, they will find encouragement in every phase of their experience, but they will also be pushed to go way beyond their comfort zone."

Overlaps

Puget Sound, Lewis and Clark, Whitman, University of Oregon, Colorado College.

If You Apply To ➤ | **Willamette**…Early action: Dec. 1. Regular admissions and financial aid: Feb. 1. Does not guarantee to meet demonstrated need. Campus and alumni interviews: recommended, evaluative. SATs or ACTs: required. SAT IIs: optional. Accepts the Common Application and electronic applications. Essay question: why attend Willamette; one of three: comment on school motto, discuss importance of diversity in academia; compare yourself from sixth grade to now; which historic event would you like to attend.

College of William and Mary

P.O. Box 8795, Williamsburg, VA 23187

Website: www.wm.edu
Location: Small city

Though the physical campus might seem stuck in a time warp, students say everything about William and Mary—from the amazing faculty to the picturesque grounds—is up to date. Traditions abound, yet this historic public university—the second-oldest in the nation—continues to evolve in its pursuit of academic excellence. The W&M formula of blending the old and the new has been working for more than 300 years, and it's only getting better with age.

A profusion of azaleas and crape myrtle add splashes of color to William and Mary's finely manicured campus, located about 150 miles southeast of Washington, D.C. The campus is divided into three sections, and includes a lake and wooded wildlife preserve, which is filled with trails and widely used by the science departments. The Ancient Campus is a grouping of three Colonial structures, the oldest being Wren Hall, which has been in continuous use since 1695 and is one of the most visually pleasing buildings in American higher education. The Old Campus, where the buildings date from the '20s and '30s, is a little farther out, and next to it is New Campus, where ground was first broken in the '60s. The W&M campus boasts one of the most romantic spots of any in the nation: Crim Dell, a wooded area with a small pond spanned by an old-style wooden bridge. The 95,000-square-foot university center includes a bookstore, auditorium, game room, post office, conference rooms, and student lounge. Students say the center has enhanced campus social life by providing bands and comedians with a great performance space. Renovations to the biology department building are under way.

William and Mary created Phi Beta Kappa in December of 1776, and the honor code demands much from the college's students. There are no "easy A" classes at the college, and the academic climate is demanding and competitive, but not cutthroat. The business school especially emphasizes teamwork. "Professors truly push students to perform at their highest level," a sophomore says. "Courses are rigorous enough to help students reach their full academic potential."

Fittingly, the history department, a joint sponsor with Colonial Williamsburg of the Institute for Early American History and Culture, is among William and Mary's best departments. Business, biology, psychology, English, and government are the five most popular majors. The accounting program ranks in the top 20 nationwide, causing one government major to grumble that "accounting majors don't seek employment, employers seek them." Music has been a weak spot, but renovated facilities have given it a boost. State-mandated restructuring eliminated "master's only" programs in English, government, mathematics, and sociology, but undergraduate programs haven't yet felt the pinch. New on the academic menu are majors in biological psychology and black studies, and minors in biochemistry and film studies. There are summer and yearlong study abroad programs around the globe, from Europe to China, the Philippines, Australia, and Mexico, and summer field schools in archeology, including one in St. Eustatius in the Caribbean. The College's International Relations center is internationally acclaimed.

Relations between students and professors are considered excellent. "I have been very impressed and often amazed at the professors' knowledge and abilities," says a marketing and religion double major. "Our professors are here to teach, not do research. We are being led and constantly motivated by passionate people," claims a junior majoring in English and government. Sixty percent of the classes have 25 or fewer students, although a few introductory lectures may have a couple hundred. Virtually every class is taught by a full professor, and TAs are used for grading or lab purposes only. The college established freshman seminars limited to 15 students each that provide even closer faculty interaction. A computerized registration system has taken the headaches out of the once hellish scheduling process.

(Continued)

Total Enrollment: 7,553
Undergraduates: 5,552
Male/Female: 42/58
SAT Ranges: V 620–710 M 610–700
Financial Aid: 26%
Expense: Pub $ $ $ $
Phi Beta Kappa: Yes
Applicants: 6,878
Accepted: 45%
Enrolled: 42%
Grad in 6 Years: 89%
Returning Freshmen: 95%
Academics: ✑ ✑ ✑ ✑ ✑
Social: ☎ ☎ ☎
Q of L: ★ ★ ★
Admissions: (757) 221-4223
Email Address:
  admiss@facstaff.wm.edu

Strongest Programs:
  Biology
  Business
  History
  English
  Government
  International Relations
  International Studies

There are summer and yearlong study abroad programs around the globe, from Europe to China, the Philippines, Australia, and Mexico, and summer field schools in archeology, including one in St. Eustatius in the Caribbean.

Graduation requirements are thorough and include proficiency in a foreign language, writing, computing (concentration-specific), and physical education. More specific distribution requirements include a course in mathematics and quantitative reasoning, two courses in the natural sciences, two in the social sciences, one each in literature and history of the arts and creative and performing arts, and one course in philosophical, religious, and social thought. The Center for Honors and Interdisciplinary Studies allows outstanding students four semesters of intensive liberal arts seminars, with lectures by top scholars from around the country, and also facilitates interdisciplinary majors like American Studies, environmental science, and women's studies.

Because W&M is a state-supported university, two-thirds of its students are Virginians. Competition for the nonresident spots is stiff, with most out-of-staters from the Mid-Atlantic and farther north. Ninety-seven percent of freshmen ranked in the top quarter of their high school class. The college has made a major effort to recruit and retain more minorities; Asian Americans now account for 7 percent of the students, and Hispanics make up 3 percent. "For the most part, students like diversity, but there have been a few cases of racial tension, usually a result of bad judgment," notes a government major. And it's his opinion that "unfortunately, the school capitalizes on these incidents with a PC multicultural effort that seems to impede campus unity and encourage separatism." An ongoing series of programs in the residence halls addresses physical safety issues as well as diversity and gender communication.

W&M has its share of eagerly recruited jocks; about 220 athletic scholarships are offered each year, in almost all sports. More than one hundred academic merit scholarships are awarded annually, and 12 percent of freshmen are designated Monroe Scholars and receive a $2,000 summer research stipend; one student used his to distribute his band's CD, and another traveled to Paris to sketch and study.

Seventy-seven percent of the undergraduates live on campus in mostly coed dorms that range from stately old halls with high ceilings to modern buildings equipped with air-conditioning. All freshmen are guaranteed a room on campus (with both cable and Internet connections), but after that students try their luck with the infamous lottery, which can spin against sophomores. Some students, usually soph men, draw the Dillard Complex—two dorms located a couple miles off campus. "Getting a room is annoying, but it works out," a senior says. Special-interest housing is available—there are four language houses and an International Studies House—and life in a fraternity or sorority house is also an option. Students give the three campus cafeterias mixed reviews, but all freshmen must purchase a 19-meal plan. Others have a variety of options, including cooking in the dorms and dinner plans open to Greeks and non-Greeks alike in sorority and fraternity houses.

W&M isn't known as a social school, but "because W&M students are so uptight academically, when they unwind...they unwind," a student says. Thirty-two percent of the men and 29 percent of the women join Greek organizations, which host most of the on-campus parties. The few local bars and delis pick up the rest. It seems relatively easy to obtain alcohol on this campus, even if you are under 21. "The school is very strict and has added new policies this year," says a senior. "They work for the most part, but people still drink." The Student Association sponsors mixers, band and tailgate parties, and a film series. Campus security is regarded as tight, although crime is not a big issue.

Anyone who gets restless can always step across the street to Colonial Williamsburg to picnic in the restored area, walk or jog down Duke of Gloucester Street (called "Dog Street"), or study in one of the beautiful gardens. Substantial job opportunities exist for students at Colonial Williamsburg, Busch Gardens, and other tourist-oriented attractions in the area. Although the "tourons" can be trying, says one student, "Colonial Williamsburg offers some very unique entertainment opportunities that would not be available at most colleges." Richmond and Norfolk, each an hour's drive, are top road trips; the University of Virginia, although an archrival, is also popular; and Virginia Beach, a favorite springtime mecca, is a little farther away.

Traditions are the stuff of which William and Mary is made, and perhaps the most cherished is the annual Yule Log Ceremony in Wren Hall, where students sing carols and hear the president, dressed in a Santa Claus outfit, read the Dr. Seuss story, *The Grinch Who Stole Christmas*. Grand Illumination is a great Christmas fireworks display, and on Charter Day, bells chime and students celebrate the distinguished history of their 300-year-old institution. On Sorority Acceptance Day, the pledges must all cross the sunken garden barricaded by fraternity men, and romantics will be happy to learn that any couple who kisses at the top of Crim Dell Bridge will be married by the end of the year. The 13 Club, a secret society of students dedicated to the college, provides students and professors with a helping hand (like missed class notes) or a pat on the back when they're feeling low—all delivered anonymously, with nothing to identify the helper but his or her number. One activity, though illegal, is always popular: jumping the wall at the Governor's Mansion at the end of Dog Street.

William and Mary isn't a football powerhouse like most southern state schools, but the athletic program is strong nonetheless. The football team plays in Division I-AA and always stirs enthusiasm, especially on Homecoming Weekend, while basketball and soccer are other popular men's sports. Men's gymnastics have won the state championships for 25 consecutive years and the women's tennis team brought home the CAA championship 11 years in a row. Other championship teams include men's and women's cross-country and women's soccer. Intramurals, from skydiving to Ultimate Frisbee, attract two-thirds of the student body, and a $6-million recreational athletic complex provides excellent facilities. The old gym is now the home of the graduate school of business and undergraduate student services, including admissions and career planning.

William & Mary's tradition stretches back to the dawn of this nation, and its grand old campus and stirring history makes it a distinguished and cherished part of many student's lives. And on the last day of classes, seniors return to the Wren. They climb the old stairs and reach for a cord to ring the building's bell high above. And they announce to the world, here we come!

> *The college's broad general education requirements mean every student must take courses in math, science, history, literature, arts, and physical education.*

Overlaps

University of Virginia, Georgetown, Richmond, Duke, Virginia Tech.

If You Apply To ➢   **William and Mary**...Early decision: Nov. 1. Regular admissions: Jan. 5. Financial aid: March 15. Meets demonstrated need of 38%. Campus and alumni interviews: optional, informational. ACTs or SATs: required. SAT IIs: recommended (writing plus two others). Accepts electronic applications. Essay question: how a particular work of music, literature or art has inspired you; historical figure you most identify with; an invention you would patent; what about you needs improving.

Williams College

Williamstown, MA 01267

Website: www.williams.edu

Location: Small town

Total Enrollment: 2,162

Undergraduates: 2,113

Male/Female: 51/49

SAT Ranges: V 650–760 M
  660–750

ACT Range: N/A

Financial Aid: 41%

Expense: Pr $ $ $ $

Phi Beta Kappa: Yes

Applicants: 5,007

Accepted: 23%

Enrolled: 47%

Grad in 6 Years: 94%

Returning Freshmen: 98%

Academics: ✍ ✍ ✍ ✍ ✍

Social: ☎ ☎ ☎

Q of L: ★ ★ ★ ★

Admissions: (413) 597-2211

Email Address:
  admission@williams.edu

Strongest Programs:
  Art
  Environmental Science
  History
  Political Science
  Economics
  Art History
  English
  Natural Sciences

The backdrop of gentle mountains and wooded countryside is a perfect setting for Williams College, a top-notch school that excels across the academic spectrum. Both the dramatic beauty of the campus and the academic excellence associated with it have remained steady since its founding in 1793. Williams is known as one of the finest liberal arts schools in the country, where students are pushed hard and have immense school spirit. Once a haven for preppies, Williams has changed in its student body but not in its intellectual rigor. Boasts one junior: "The courses are rigorous, and it is difficult to get the A, but students seem to exhibit a sense of 'being in this together,' helping each other out as much as possible."

Nestled in the small village of Williamstown, the college takes full advantage of the Berkshires' rich history and natural resources. The wooded countryside acts as a perfect backdrop for the skiing, cycling, and backpacking for which Williams students are famous. Nearly every window looks out over the purple mountains—the same mountains that moved Henry David Thoreau during his travels through the Massachusetts wilderness. Williams buildings constitute a virtual museum of architectural styles, from the elegantly simple Federal design of the original West College to contemporary designs by Charles Moore and Carlos Jimenez. Many of the buildings of brick and gray stone are arranged around loosely organized quads that provide both a sense of enclosure and of openness to nature. Students can also take advantage of MASS MoCA, a new center for visual, performing, and media arts.

Williams's greatest strengths are in art history, environmental science, history, political science, economics, English, chemistry, and biology, all of which contribute directly to an acceptance rate of about 90 percent at business, law, and medical schools. Says one junior, "With one of the finest college art museums in America and one of the best impressionistic collections in the world, we have tremendous resources for an outstanding (art history) program." Most everything is good here, students say, but the Romance languages are cited by many as needing improvement. Interdisciplinary programs in Afro-American studies, area studies, and women's studies are increasingly popular. Environmental studies, based in the 2,000-acre, college-owned Hopkins Forest, makes full use of the campus's natural resources. For future engineers, 3–2 BA/BS programs are offered in conjunction with Columbia and Washington Universities (although most students are quite satisfied with Williams's offerings).

The Williams curriculum places an emphasis on interdisciplinary studies and personalized teaching. The distribution requirements consist of three courses in each of three areas—arts and languages, social studies, and sciences and mathematics—two of which must be completed by the end of the sophomore year. Students must also take at least one course that deals with "issues of cultural pluralism in American society and the world at large" by the end of junior year. Entering first-years have the option of taking the First-Year Residential Seminar, in which they live together in the same residential unit and take a team-taught or interdisciplinary course together. When asked how the college's mission is evolving, an administrator says, "It's perfect already."

A required winter study period in January is spent completing a project in a variety of academic areas. There is also Free University, in which students teach one another anything from Chinese cooking to the jitterbug. In recent years, students have explored India, the Soviet Union, West Africa, and Western Europe with the college's unusual and relatively inexpensive faculty-guided tours. Opportunities for off-campus study are also available during the fall and spring. The many options include Williams at Mystic Seaport,* the Twelve-College Exchange,* and an innovative program in conjunction with Exeter College of Oxford University in England. The college recently developed a cluster of courses in leadership studies and another cluster that stresses clinical reasoning and analytical skills.

Williams's faculty is its greatest educational asset, and all students have access to top professors. States one senior, "The professors are ours and ours only. They are very accessible after hours and take an interest in all their students." Most professors live right in Williamstown, giving students the opportunity to see them not just in class, but at the bank, on Main Street, and even in their homes. Additionally, the college provides a stipend with which advisors sometimes take their advisees out to lunch or dinner (yet another personal touch). "Counselors guide the student's course selection carefully and enthusiastically," says one freshman. The computer center is impressively equipped, and Sawyer Library reportedly has ample accommodations to offer the wearied but inspired. The entire campus, including all residences, is networked, providing access from student rooms to the Internet. It's not surprising that the area become known in the media as "Silicon Village," referring to the growing number of successful technology companies started by Williams alumni.

The typical Williams student is a bright, enthusiastic, extremely energetic, well-rounded extrovert. One junior describes the campus as "politically liberal." Another student says, "People are so involved in the college community, and interesting, and friendly." In-state residents only account for about 14 percent of the student body, while foreign students make up 6 percent. Eighty-four percent graduated in the top tenth of their high school class. In making admissions decisions, Williams looks for diversity in prospective students; students who are strong in more than one area tend to stand out. Blacks and Hispanics account for 13 percent of the students, and Asian Americans constitute another 9 percent. "People are very open here," says a psychology major. But a classmate warns, "Sometimes it seems hard to relate to people if you aren't an athlete or a social partyer." Nearly a third of the students are bona fide preppies; the rest just look that way. The campus uniform seems to include relatively little makeup for women and Williams sweatshirts and jeans for all. The school's mascot is a purple cow, so cows and purple naturally dominate clothes and signs. There are no athletic or merit scholarships, but Williams guarantees to design a financial aid package that meets the full demonstrated financial need of every admit. First-year students arrive on campus four days early for First-Year Days, during which they meet each other and are assigned to their junior advisors.

"Phenomenal" and "definitely above the norm" is how students describe the housing at Williams. Dorms are spacious and well maintained, and housing is guaranteed for all four years. One dormitory was once a fine old inn, with fireplaces and mahogany paneling; several others look as if they should have been. "Every dorm has lots of common space with couches, TV, VCR, fireplace, and some even have ballrooms," says an English major. Living options range from two modern complexes to the lovely row houses that were fraternities before Greek organizations were abolished in 1962. New arrivals reside in first-year-only dorms known as "entries," where the highly praised junior advisor system works to provide advice and support. Says a history major, "The minute you get here you

Most professors live right in Williamstown, giving students the opportunity to see them not just in class, but at the bank, on Main Street, and even in their homes.

In making admissions decisions, Williams looks for diversity in prospective students; well-rounded students who are strong in more than one area tend to stand out.

know about 20 other people with whom to hang out." Small co-op houses are available for students who want to cook and play house. Upperclassmen, virtually ensured a single, may enter the housing lottery individually or in groups. The college permits only a handful of students to move off campus. The best first-year dorm is said to be the quad. Beware: thin walls are a complaint. Food is another area where Williams's resident overachievers are pampered. Except for the much-feared tofu pie, the food is considered quite good, and nearly everyone buys the meal plan, which is usable in any of the five campus dining halls.

Williams' Berkshires setting can seem isolated at times, yet civilization—Albany, New York—is only an hour away. The gentle mountains and serene wooded countryside of Williamstown are the perfect tonic for the fatigued and tense Williams College student. Even the most focused of scholars would find the peaceful Williamstown backdrop a refreshing distraction. Despite its relative isolation, the town is far from a cultural desert. The Clark Art Institute, within walking distance of campus, possesses one of the finest collections of Renoir and Degas in the nation, as well as a fine library. The modern college music center attracts top classical musicians, and the college theater is home to a renowned summer festival that often features Broadway stars. Films, lectures, and concerts abound on most weekends, as do the usual number of parties.

Fraternities and sororities have long since been banned, but that hasn't created a dearth of drinking opportunities. The administration has taken a much tougher stance on drinking since last year. "Our policy has recently become a lot stricter, so now it's very hard for underaged students to drink at a party, and the consequences are more severe," says one senior. "This is not necessarily a good thing." Still, students find plenty of other things to do. The college brings in lots of cultural groups, popular concerts, and speakers, and there are always student performances or organized activities. An organization called Connections strives to distract keg-seeking students and emphasize alcohol-free alternatives, of which there are many. All parties must serve food and nonalcoholic beverages whenever alcohol is present.

Sports are more like a religion than an extracurricular activity, and Williams has become a perennial winner of the Division III Sears Cup, awarded annually to the school with the strongest overall athletic program. One reason is that student-athletes are strongly favored in admissions decisions. Everyone seems to play on some team, and any contest with archrival Amherst ensures a big crowd. After all, Amherst was founded in 1821 by a defecting Williams president and part of the student body. And the insults tend to go beyond the athletic field and consistent high scores. T-shirts can be seen around campus offering the following sentiment regarding its rivals in the Little Three: "The good: Williams. The bad: Wesleyan. The ugly: Amherst." Both the men's and women's swim teams are nationally ranked, and the men's tennis, basketball, and cross-country teams have been among the top in the nation. Women's tennis, field hockey, and lacrosse teams are also strong contenders. The men's indoor track and field team has won 122 straight Quad Cup competitions. The Taconic golf course, rated among the best collegiate facilities, has been host to several national college championships. The college helps maintain a cross-country ski trail located 10 miles from town, and two alpine ski resorts within 10 miles of campus are also popular. The one knock against the Williams sports program is the charge from some quarters that women's sports get less support than men's. Homecoming is always popular at Williams, as are Mountain Day, Winter Carnival, and Spring Fling. Every winter there is also a campus-wide snowsculpting contest.

Even four long, cold winters in a small New England town fail to chill most

Ephs' love for their school (that's pronounced Eefs, as in school founder Ephraim Williams). Those who are hardy enough to survive the wilderness, the workload, and the weather can move quite comfortably into loyal Williams alumnihood—a stage of life that comes complete with a respected degree, professional contacts, and an ability to do something for their alma mater.

Overlaps

Harvard, Princeton, Dartmouth, Brown, Yale.

If You Apply To ➤ | **Williams**…Early decision: Nov. 15. Regular admissions: Jan. 1. Financial aid: Feb. 1. Guarantees to meet demonstrated need. Campus and alumni interviews: optional, informational. SATs or ACTs: required. SAT IIs: required (any three). Accepts the Common Application. Essay question: experience that defined a value.

University of Wisconsin–Madison

140 Peterson Building, 750 University Avenue, Madison, WI 53706-1490

At the University of Wisconsin at Madison, two things are a sure bet: very cold weather and red-hot academics. On a campus where the mercury often dips below zero, you're likely to be too busy studying to notice. With nearly 27,000 undergraduates and enormous resources, Madison offers something for virtually everyone. All that's required is a desire to learn. And a very warm coat.

Described by one student as "architecturally olden with a modern touch," Madison's mainly brick campus is distinctive. It spreads out over 903 hilly, tree-covered acres and across an isthmus between two glacial lakes, Mendota and Monona, named by prehistoric Indians who once lived along their shores. From atop Bascom Hill, the center of campus, you look east past the statue of Lincoln and the liberal arts buildings, down to a library mall that was the scene of many a political demonstration during the '60s. Farther east you see rows of State Street pubs and restaurants and the bleached dome of the Wisconsin state capitol. On the other side of the hill, another campus, dedicated to the sciences, twists along Lake Mendota. But students from both sides of the hill drink beer elbow to elbow in the old student union, the Rathskeller, where political arguments and backgammon games can rage all night. Outside on the union's veranda, students can look out at the sailboats in summer or iceboats in winter. The icy wind that blows off the lakes in winter is vicious, and the academic climate is not exactly tropical either. Coursework is demanding and in many ways akin to graduate school elsewhere. Predictably, grading is tough and inflexible and often figured on a strict curve. "There are a lot of smart people studying here," observes one student.

A list of first-rate academic programs at Madison would constitute a college catalog elsewhere. There are 70 programs considered in the top 10 nationally. Some highlights include education, agriculture, communications, biological sciences, and social studies. The most popular majors are history, engineering, political science, psychology, and business, in that order. The math department is cited as lacking faculty, and letters and science could use better advising, according to some. Due to overcrowding, some popular fields, such as engineering and business, have had to restrict entry to their majors by requiring high GPAs. But with a smaller freshman class, students are finding it a bit easier to get into the courses

Website: www.wisc.edu
Location: Center city
Total Enrollment: 40,196
Undergraduates: 27,533
Male/Female: 48/52
SAT Ranges: V 520–650 M 550–670
ACT Range: 25–29
Financial Aid: 55%
Expense: Pub $
Phi Beta Kappa: Yes
Applicants: 16,290
Accepted: 77%
Enrolled: 47%
Grad in 6 Years: N/A
Returning Freshmen: 95%
Academics: ✐ ✐ ✐ ✐ ✐
Social: ☎ ☎ ☎ ☎
Q of L: ★ ★ ★ ★
Admissions: (608) 262-3961
Email Address:
on.wisconsin@mail.admin
.wisc.edu

Strongest Programs:
Agriculture
Biological Sciences
Education
Communications
Social Studies

of their choice. Several improvements made over the last couple of years have helped to relieve the overload. First, an automated system makes the headaches of registration a bit less severe. Second, the Grainger Hall of Business Administration, a $35-million complex, quadrupled the space in the current school of business. The biotechnology building supports research and undergraduate teaching.

Distribution requirements vary among the different schools and academic departments, but they are uniformly rigorous, with science and math courses required for BA students, and a foreign language for virtually everyone. All students must fulfill a two-part graduation requirement in both quantitative reasoning and communication. For students who prefer the academic road less traveled, options include the Institute for Environmental Studies and the Integrated Liberal Studies (ILS), which consists of related courses introducing the achievements of Western culture. An elite Medical Scholars program allows 50 select high school seniors guaranteed admission to the Madison medical school after completing three years of undergraduate work. A variety of internships are available, as are study abroad programs all over the world, including Europe, Brazil, India, Israel, and Thailand.

Professors at Madison are certainly among the nation's best, with Nobel laureates, National Academy of Science members, and Guggenheim fellows scattered liberally among the departments. The English program boasts such young, vibrant faculty as highly acclaimed writers Lorrie Moore and Debra Spark. Along with downsizing, Madison has taken a number of steps to strengthen the freshman experience in particular. They have emphasized more small classes, with 15 to 20 students, to help entering freshmen adjust to college-level coursework; more comprehensive orientation and mentoring for freshmen; and more student-faculty contact. Advising has received a booster shot, too. For undergrads who find it difficult to choose one of the vast array of majors available, the university has developed a plan called Cross-College Advising System, which features a 10-member team of academic staff advisors. The idea is to help students refine their educational and career goals, so their interests, majors, and professional aspirations mesh into a complete package. Upon admission, every student is assigned an advisor to meet with at least three times in the first year.

If there is one common characteristic among the undergraduates, it is aggressiveness. "It's easy to get lost in the crowd here, so you have to be fairly strong and confident," declares one student. "No one holds your hand." The flip side is that "anyone can fit in, you just have to find your own niche." Almost two-thirds of the students are from Wisconsin. The school is a heartland of progressive politics, and Madison's reputation as a haven for liberals remains intact. "Students here are called liberal because they are eager and willing to change and are continually looking for newer and better ideas," explains an activist. The university has implemented a racial awareness program to make the campus more hospitable to minorities. Blacks and Hispanics currently make up 4 percent of the student body, while Asian Americans constitute another 4 percent. CIA recruiting, women's rights, and tuition increases have all been issues recently. Thousands of academic merit scholarships ranging from $500 to $7,000 are awarded each year, and most of the sports on campus offer full scholarships to their athletes. Need-based financial aid packages meet 100 percent of need for all in-staters, but out-of-state applicants get no guarantees. The two-day orientation program, known as SOAR, welcomes incoming freshmen in groups staggered throughout the summer.

Housing, once the bane of many a student's existence, is no longer a problem now that housing is guaranteed for all. For a school this size, that's quite an accomplishment. Dorms are either coed or single-sex and come equipped with laundry facilities, game rooms, and lounges. Most also have a cafeteria. The student union also offers two meal plans, and there are plenty of restaurants and fast-food places nearby. Campus safety is always an issue, but the school offers a variety of services for those on campus. There are escort services for those walking and those needing a ride, and a free shuttle system that operates seven days a week. Madison (a.k.a. Madtown) has been the stomping ground for many fine rock 'n' roll or blues bands on the road to fame.

There are more film clubs than anyone can follow, and everyone has a favorite bar. "This is Wisconsin, don't forget, and everybody drinks a lot of beer. If you don't drink, then you'll have to be quite comfortable with that," says one teetotaler, "because peer pressure can be quite overwhelming." About 10 percent of the men and 18 percent of the women go Greek. "Frat parties are a very popular break from the bar scene," reports one expert on both options. One old standby that is still as popular as ever is the student union, which hosts bands, shows, and so forth and provides a great atmosphere in which to hang out. Nature enthusiasts can lose themselves in the university's 12,000-acre nature preserve. Ski slopes are close at hand, but be prepared to confront thermometers that read 20 below zero.

The students at this Big 10 school show "tons of interest" in sports, especially hockey and football, and especially when the Badgers try to rout the University of Minnesota's Gophers. And don't forget that the football squad beat UCLA in the 1994 Rose Bowl! Bucky Badger apparel, emblazoned with slogans ranging from the urbane to the decidedly uncouth, is ubiquitous. However, the much-acclaimed marching band known as Fifth Quarter may outdo all the teams in popularity. The Badgers are recent Big 10 champions in a number of sports, notably women's cross-country and men's indoor and outdoor track. The men's soccer team won the NCAA Division I championship recently, a feat that will undoubtedly draw attention to the school's athletic program.

All in all, Madison is a school that students sum up as "diverse, intellectual, fashionable, and moderately hedonistic." And these are the qualities that attract bright and energetic students from everywhere. "You feel you're accepted for who you are no matter what," says one student. "It's so nice to just be yourself." Perhaps one of the best and most well-rounded state schools around, Madison is truly a best buy.

Overlaps

University of Michigan, Northwestern, University of Illinois, Indiana, Boston University.

If You Apply To ➤ | **Wisconsin**...Rolling admissions: Feb. 1. Financial aid: Mar. 1. Guarantees to meet the demonstrated need of in-state admits. Campus interviews: recommended, informational. No alumni interviews. SATs or ACTs: required (ACTs required for Wisconsin residents). SAT IIs: optional. Essay question: personal statement. Special consideration given to students from disadvantaged backgrounds. Apply to particular school.

P.O. Box 720, Springfield, OH 45501

Website: www.wittenberg.edu
Location: City outskirts
Total Enrollment: 2,150
Undergraduates: 2,150
Male/Female: 45/55
SAT Ranges: V 545–630 M 538–625
ACT Range: 22–27
Financial Aid: 75%
Expense: Pr $ $ $
Phi Beta Kappa: Yes
Applicants: 2,515
Accepted: 85%
Enrolled: 33%
Grad in 6 Years: 71%
Returning Freshmen: 86%
Academics: ✍ ✍ ✍
Social: ☎ ☎ ☎
Q of L: ★ ★ ★
Admissions: (800) 677-7558
Email Address:
admission@wittenberg.edu

Strongest Programs:
Special Education
English
Education
Business
Biology
Management

Wittenberg offers a comprehensive, well-rounded academic program and is committed to assisting its students in reaching their full intellectual, social, physical, spiritual, and aesthetic potential. In addition, Wittenberg not only nurtures a sense of community between its students and faculty members, but it teaches compassion for others. "One of the general education requirements of this institution is the completion of 30 hours of community service," says a psychology major. "It can really change your outlook on life." This friendly Ohio campus sparks intense loyalty from students who appreciate the school's All-American flavor.

The Wittenberg campus is classic collegiate: plenty of trees surround the 70 rolling acres in hilly southwestern Ohio. The architectural style is a mixture of Gothic and the '60s. At the center stands the picturesque brick 19th-century Myers residence hall with its white pillars and an open-air dome. The Matthies House provides a home for the Wittenberg Honors Program and construction has been completed on Hollenbeck Hall, a state-of-the-art learning facility.

Founded in 1845 by German Lutherans, Wittenberg is committed to providing a quality liberal arts education with a forward-looking agenda. The Wittenberg Plan helps students coordinate the broad liberal arts portion of their degree and consists of 16 learning goals, 12 of which include course, competency, or participation requirements for each student. Students choose from a variety of courses such as writing, research, mathematics, and foreign language, along with natural and social sciences, to fulfill the learning goals. Students also must take courses in religion or philosophy, non-Western cultures, and physical education and must participate in community service in Springfield. All first-year students take the interdisciplinary Common Learning Course, taught by their faculty advisor and focused on contemporary social issues like civility. There is also a University Scholars Program for outstanding freshmen and a new Wittenberg Fellows Program, which offers students an opportunity to work with faculty members on research.

Wittenberg students look forward to the challenges that await them after college, knowing they are well prepared for the teamwork that is becoming so common in the workplace. "The academic climate is competitive in the sense that the coursework is difficult and the workload is challenging, but it's also laid-back when it comes to competition between the students," says an elementary education major. Students praise their school's offerings in education, business, psychology, marine sciences, and East Asian Studies, but admit that physics, philosophy, and theater could use improvement. Students praise the advising system, and according to a senior elementary education major, "It's not uncommon for students to go to their advisor's house for dinner." The Career Development and Placement Center offers help in preparing résumés and prepping for interviews. The newest additions to the curriculum include a BS in science and a MA in education.

Professors at Wittenberg receive high marks from students. "The professors here are wonderful," says a management/psychology double major. "They are enthusiastic, provide first-class instruction, and are eager to meet their students' needs.

"Another student adds, "The professors care about students, not just academics. They are committed to lives, not just lectures." Teaching assistants are unheard of, and professors' doors are always open, students agree. If students declare their majors on time and complete the proper coursework in the correct order, the college guarantees a degree in four years—and will pay for additional time on campus if it's necessary. Wittenberg also encourages students to take a semester or a year off campus, either in this country or abroad. Options include the international Student Exchange Program, field studies in the Bahamas and Costa Rica, the National Institutes of Health in Washington, D.C., or a term at the United Nations. Wittenberg also offers a 3–2 program for engineering with the School of Engineering at Columbia University, Case Western Reserve University, and Sever Institute of Washington University.

Thirty-five percent of the Wittenberg student body is from out-of-state. Unfortunately, minority students make up only 10 percent of the student body, but the school has a multicultural affairs director who is working diligently to increase that number through changes in minority recruiting and advising. The school offers 250 merit scholarships, ranging from $2,500 to full tuition. There are also several tuition payment plans available.

Wittenberg students are required to live on campus their first two years, and dorms feature cable, modem hookups, and some even have air-conditioning. "The dorms are comfortable and there are specialty dorms that cater to specific types of students," says a senior. Almost everyone gets a double, but freshman assignments are processed in the order that room deposits are received. Most older students live in the Greek houses or in off-campus apartments in Springfield. Food service in Witt's dining hall is provided by Marriott and runs the culinary gamut from burgers to made-to-order breakfasts to once-a-month theme dinners. Wittenberg's dining halls have been rated Marriott's best college food service.

The Witt social life centers on campus. The Union Board, Residence Hall Association, and many campus organizations sponsor activities that include guest speakers, movies, comedians, and concerts. "Students definitely reward themselves on the weekend for their hard work during the week," an upperclassman says. "If there's not something happening on campus, there's always something going on at the off-campus housing of juniors and seniors," says a psychology major. Fifteen percent of the men and 30 percent of the women join Greek organizations, which hold regular bashes. The students say they look forward to Greek Week and Homecoming each year and also to "Wittstock" (a takeoff on you-know-what), a traditional daylong party featuring bands, volleyball, and "lots of bubbles." Overall, the college is pretty strict concerning alcohol on campus, but underage students can find it if they want it. "It's very easy for an underage student to get alcohol at parties," says a political science major.

As for other entertainment, Springfield has movie theaters, a mall, and plenty of restaurants, along with a $15-million performing arts center. Students generally like the town. When the weather is conducive, nearby state parks are popular for swimming, camping, and picnics. The best road trips are to Dayton (30 minutes), Columbus (one hour), or Cincinnati (an hour and a half).

While not as well known as many of its bigger, Midwestern brethren, Wittenberg's athletic teams are quite competitive in Division III play. Both the men's football and women's basketball teams have participated in the national championships, and volleyball, football, men's golf, baseball, and soccer are good squads. The college recently won the All-Sports trophy recognizing combined men's and women's athletic performance in the North Coast Athletic Conference. The Bill Edwards Athletic and Recreational Complex sports a stadium and an

If students declare their majors on time and complete the proper coursework in the correct order, the college guarantees a degree in four years—and will pay for additional time on campus if it's necessary.

Wittenberg also encourages students to take a semester or a year off campus, either in this country or abroad.

eight-lane track, football and soccer fields, 12 lighted tennis courts, and weight facilities, as well as a pool and racquetball courts.

Wittenberg's motto showcases the school's can-do spirit: "Having the light, we pass it on to others." Ambitious? Yes. Unrealistic? Students say no. With a move to semesters and the implementation of learning goals, the administration is leading the effort to excel. Technological improvements and facilities growth have marked the past few years, but these changes have not affected the friendliness and close-knit feel of the campus. Says a management major: "The overall friendly atmosphere of the campus helps students to feel as if they belong from their first day here."

If You Apply To > Wittenberg…Rolling admissions. Early decision: Nov. 15. Early action: Dec. 1. Regular admissions and financial aid: Mar. 15. Guarantees to meet demonstrated need. Campus interviews: recommended, evaluative. No alumni interviews. SATs or ACTs: required. SAT IIs: recommended. Accepts the Common Application and electronic applications. Essay question: significant experience or relationship; or issue of concern.

Wofford College

429 North Church Street, Spartanburg, SC 29303-3663

Website: www.wofford.edu
Location: Small city
Total Enrollment: 1,100
Undergraduates: 1,100
Male/Female: 53/47
SAT Ranges: V 540–610 M 540–650
ACT Range: 22–27
Financial Aid: 55%
Expense: Pr $ $
Phi Beta Kappa: Yes
Applicants: 1,592
Accepted: 85%
Enrolled: 28%
Grad in 6 Years: 83%
Returning Freshmen: 90%
Academics: ✍ ✍ ✍
Social: ☎ ☎
Q of L: ★ ★ ★
Admissions: (864) 597-4130
Email Address:
admissions@wofford.edu

Strongest Programs:
Biology

The case for Wofford is fairly clear: sound academics, Southern hospitality, and an excellent chance to move on to graduate school or a good job after graduation. More than one student notes the warm "family" atmosphere that permeates Wofford, and virtually all take pride in their school and the Wofford way. The Wofford Way means a well-rounded curriculum, career-related internships, study abroad options, and, of course, solid liberal arts and preprofessional programs. "The interconnectedness of every part of the community is clear from the get-go," says a sophomore.

The school is near the heart of Spartanburg, a moderate-size city perched on the northwest corner of South Carolina. Founded in 1854, Wofford is one of fewer than 200 existing American colleges that opened before the Civil War. The college operates on its original 140-acre campus, with the distinctive, twin-towered Main Building and four original faculty homes surrounded by azaleas, magnolias, and dogwoods. More than 700 trees were recently planted to further beautify the leafy campus. The college recently completed a $10-million modernization and expansion of the Milliken Science Building.

Wofford has received national recognition for its programs in the humanities: English, history, fine arts, foreign languages, religion, and philosophy. Also strong are the natural sciences, though they are known for being difficult. "In other words, no one takes Organic Chemistry or Cell Biology as an elective," notes an amused bio major. Faculty and administration alike boast about the $5.5-million F. W. Olin academic building, which houses the departments of mathematics, computer science, foreign languages, and education, as well as the campus media center. The building's computer center is the hub of a campus-wide technology network that links classrooms, offices, and residence halls with computer, video, and library resources. Typically, about 11 percent of Wofford's students go on to medical, dental, or vet school after graduation. The business program also attracts loyal followers, and aspiring engineers can apply for a combined 3–2 program with Clemson University. On the other side of the ledger, social sciences and fine arts could stand some improvement. Wofford is run on the 4–1–4 academic calendar, in which students study a single topic during a January term between the two semesters. Most students find the academic climate sufficiently challenging. "The academic climate is fair with occasional showers," says a religion major. "Wofford students are expected to work but more importantly to learn and inwardly digest material in all classes. Students are not competitive, but collaborative in learning." Almost one in five students earns academic credit abroad. The newest addition to the curriculum is the Japanese language program.

Wofford's distribution requirements are fairly stiff and include two semesters each of English, a foreign language, natural science, and physical education, as well as one each of fine arts and math, and a total of four from history, philosophy, and religion. "The liberal arts emphasis virtually forces students to try a well-rounded smattering of courses," a student says. Most freshmen take the two-semester sequence in the required natural science and foreign language courses, plus the humanities seminar and an English course, along with electives from required courses. The faculty gets high marks for helpfulness and accessibility. "The professors here are very dedicated and will go the extra mile for their students," says an English/religion double major. The vast majority of classes have fewer than 25 students; registering is mostly painless. Advisement is good, especially after you've chosen a major. Students are now required to take a class through the career services center, although counseling there is still lacking somewhat.

Sixty-five percent of the Wofford student body are in-staters, a large number considering the fact that the college is within spitting distance of both Georgia and North Carolina. Most students are hardworking types used to success in the classroom; 85 percent of freshmen graduated in the top quarter of their class. The student population is 88 percent white, with an African American population of 9 percent; Asian Americans, Hispanics, and international students comprise 2 percent. While students agree that there is mixing among races, some say there is still a lack of diversity: "It has been said that we seek students from the 'middle half' of society," a sophomore says. "A majority of students are khaki pants/collar shirt folks, and yet we have our share of distinct personalities and styles." Wofford has implemented a summer program, led by an African American, female faculty member, to attract more Spartanburg County minorities and women to the sciences.

The college offers 15 to 20 merit scholarships ranging from $1,000 to $25,000. Moreover, the college also makes available athletic awards for nearly all sports. In addition to the standard scholarship opportunities, each year one lucky upperclassman is chosen to be a Presidential International Scholar and sent around the world all-expenses-paid to study an issue of global importance. Upon return as a senior, this student spends the year helping the faculty enhance the international content of courses across the curriculum.

Students seem pleased with the dorms, and 90 percent live in university housing. First-year women stay in Greene Hall, with their male counterparts at Marsh Hall. Students aren't too keen on the college cafeteria—other than as a social hour—but they praise the Canteen, a lunchtime option that serves southern cooking. One student said the food has gotten better since the ARAmark company took over. Students agree that campus security has been greatly improved during the past few years, and most feel safe on campus.

According to the administration, Wofford's mission is "fostering a romance,

(Continued)
Premed
Chemistry
English
History
Foreign Languages
Religion

The newest addition to the curriculum is the Japanese language program.

courtship, engagement, and lifelong marriage between a student and the liberal arts." "Students are serious, but also fun," a senior says. "We understand the importance of the weekends and the weekdays." In conformance with the law, the administration prohibits students under 21 from drinking on campus, and the policy generally works. Over half the student body pledges the Greek system, which practically dominates the social scene. But that's not all there is, if students work on other options. "If a student leads and capitalizes on those opportunities, it can be a rewarding experience," a student says. "Many students are working for a more vibrant non-Greek social life. We need explorers in this area." Social and service organizations attract loyal followings, and rare is the student who does not participate in at least one extracurricular activity. Those who tire of the campus scene can venture out to Atlanta, the mountains, or the beach. "Wofford is a place that prohibits a student from idly sitting in their room alone for four years," a religion major says. Though not a typical college town, Spartanburg is home to several other schools (most notably Converse College) and is part of the Greenville-Spartanburg metro area.

Wofford's sports teams are unusually strong for a small college and have been featured in *Sports Illustrated*.

The varsity teams recently became a member of NCAA Division I. People get fired up for football, especially when the opponent is the Citadel. The basketball schedule includes such top Division I teams as Clemson. Yet it's the golf team that earns top honors, placing in the top 20 nationally. When not in the stands cheering, students take the field themselves in the ever popular intramural program.

Wofford's academic threads are woven through its small population via a broad liberal arts foundation and multitude of extra-curricular activities. The faculty works closely with students, both in the classroom and on their own time. While most Wofford students are "seeking a traditional four-year experience," many are determined to grow as individuals before jumping into the real world. "Excellent professors, challenging academic coursework, varying social activities, service and leadership opportunities make Wofford a well-rounded small college," a senior reports. "It just has a lot to offer."

Overlaps

Clemson, University of South Carolina, Furman, UNC-Chapel Hill, Wake Forest.

If You Apply To ➤ **Wofford**…Early decision: Nov. 15. Regular admissions: Feb. 1. Financial aid: Mar. 15. Housing: May 1. Meets demonstrated need of 90%. Campus interviews: recommended, informational. Alumni interviews: optional, informational. SATs or ACTs: required. SAT IIs: optional. Accepts the Common Application. Essay question: significant event, interest, experience, goal, or person.

The College of Wooster

Wooster, OH 44691

Website: www.wooster.edu
Location: Small town
Total Enrollment: 1,709
Undergraduates: 1,709
Male/Female: 47/53

How many Wooster students does it take to change a lightbulb? "None, because you're never in the dark at the College of Wooster." If you think that's funny, then you'll see that the amusing quirks of this remarkable little school don't end with the administration's lightbulb jokes. "Woo" prides itself on fostering individuality and a close-knit environment. Hardworking students, difficult but rewarding independent studies, a beautiful campus, and plenty of fun are all things you can expect from this small Ohio college. And there's plenty of humor and high spirits to go around. This is, after all, a college where the school mascot is a bagpiping Scotsman.

Located in the city of Wooster, C.O.W. is situated on a 320-acre campus atop a hill. The carefully planned campus features 35 buildings, many designed in the English-Collegiate Gothic style and constructed principally of cream-colored brick, with most of the recent buildings trimmed with Indiana limestone or Ohio sandstone. Kauke Hall, the central building in Quinby Quadrangle (the square around which the college grew), is easy to spot with its central arch and two towers. The new Flo K. Gault Library for Independent Study offers each senior in the humanities and social sciences a private carrel. The Ebert Fine Arts Center was recently completed and includes classrooms, work space, lecture halls, and public galleries. The new Timken Science Library in Frick Hall features a natural science collection and access to major scientific databases. The $11.2-million project to enlarge Severance Chemistry Building resulted in an additional 14,000 square feet of classrooms, labs, lecture halls, and study space.

While visitors marvel at the beauty of the campus, they also find a lot going on inside the Wooster buildings. Students must complete a first-year seminar, limited to 15 students per section, and composed of classical reading, critical writing, and heated discussions. The freshman seminar is linked to the Wooster Forum, a series of lectures and events held throughout the first semester concerning a broad issue. This broad exploration is followed by an interdisciplinary seminar for sophomores, juniors, and seniors that links the first-year seminar and the independent study program. The academic environment is somewhat competitive, but "your peers keep you on your toes with constant new ideas about the way the world works," says one junior.

Wooster's curriculum is built around the required Independent Study experience for juniors and seniors. This unique approach provides each student with a chance to explore a particular problem in his or her major with a faculty mentor, and usually results in theses, scientific research, creative writing projects, or theatrical productions. Independent Study has become such a part of C.O.W. that each year seniors celebrate their successful completion of the requirement by staging the annual IS Parade across the campus. Completion of the IS earns you a Tootsie Roll. You can either eat it or keep it for posterity next to your diploma. The college even awards $60,000 each year to support students in their research, by underwriting travel, purchasing special materials, or paying for conference registration.

A third of each student's transcript reflects an array of liberal arts courses from outside the chosen or self-constructed major; proficiency in a foreign language, one religion course, and writing proficiency are also required. Dedicated professors win praise for their devotion to teaching and advising. One student notes proudly that "professors always know their students' names and have a genuine passion to teach." Freshmen are taught by full professors—not teaching assistants. Science majors have been known to coauthor faculty papers, while students in economics collaborate with professors in managing a portion of the college's assets. Computers are also big here: Wooster has been recognized as a leader in the development of computerization in liberal arts colleges. WoosterNet is a computer network that links every academic and administrative building and residence hall on campus and provides users with 24-hour access to more than 150 microcomputers and terminals. Sections of the first-year seminar have created their own homepages on the World Wide Web to facilitate out-of-class discussions and participation.

(Continued)

SAT Ranges: V 540–650 M 540–650

ACT Range: 24–28

Financial Aid: 65%

Expense: Pr $ $ $

Phi Beta Kappa: Yes

Applicants: 2,195

Accepted: 79%

Enrolled: 30%

Grad in 6 Years: 71%

Returning Freshmen: 80%

Academics: ✍ ✍ ✍

Social: ☎ ☎ ☎

Q of L: ★ ★ ★

Admissions: (800) 877-9905

Email Address:
admissions@wooster.edu

Strongest Programs:
English
Chemistry
Biology
Geology
History
Music

Chemistry tends to be rated at the top of the academic pyramid by administrators and students alike, along with geology, biology, and music. History is now the most popular major, followed by English, communication, psychology, and political science. Students sometimes find the foreign language department small and wish it were more extensive. Recently, though, the college appointed its first fulltime faculty in the area of Chinese language and added a professor in the archeology program. Economics and music theory are tough, with the latter requiring a large time commitment, a junior says. The college offers many out-of-classroom experiences, including local internships to study tours. A leadership and liberal learning program includes a seminar class and a weeklong acquaintanceship, in which participants attach themselves to a prominent politician, businessperson, or other professional. Wooster also sponsors a range of off-campus and overseas programs on five continents, whether as a member of the Great Lakes Colleges Association* or through its own programs.

The admissions office strives to assemble a diverse group of scholars each year. In fact, a substantial increase in applicants in the past couple of years has pushed Wooster toward becoming a more selective school. In the financial aid department, Wooster awards 140 merit scholarships ranging from $6,000 to $16,000. Eighty-four percent of the students are white, and the majority attended public school. Blacks constitute 4 percent of the student body, Asian Americans 2 percent, and Hispanics 1 percent. One women's studies major says, "A bigger collection of raging psychos has never been assembled...I mean that in a nice way, though. We're just unique, uncharacterizable." Wooster and about a quarter of its students are affiliated with the Presbyterian Church, and the Scottish heritage is reincarnated in the school band, complete with bagpipes and kilts, as well as Scottish dancers—all on display at Scot Spirit Day in the fall and spring. Volunteering is big at Wooster, and through the Wooster Volunteer Network, students stay connected with the community. Groups of community service volunteers can apply for one of 26 college-owned program houses, where they can plan and organize groups ranging from a local juvenile boys' home to Habitat for Humanity.

Ninety-five percent of students live on campus in nine coed and two single-sex dorms with small rooms but great maid service. There are two dining halls on campus where the food is relatively well rated. The campus is described as generally very safe. Security provides escorts to students and security phones are located around campus.

Social life is definitely campus-based, though students roadtrip to the Flats in Cleveland or to Columbus, both about an hour away. Wooster is "in the middle of cornfields," so a trip to the 24-hour Wal-Mart is considered "a rush of fun—for 30 minutes." The college has no national Greek societies, but there are local "sections" for men and "clubs" for women that provide a large part of the weekend social scene. Thirty percent of students belong, equally split between men and women. One major hangout for the weekends is the Underground, a bar/dance place that brings in bands and comedians. Ohio's drinking age of 21 is strictly enforced at campus events. Plenty of nonalcoholic events are sponsored by a student activities board. Annual traditions include the fall Party on the Green and the formal Winter Gala for students, faculty, and staff. For those seeking constant urban stimulation, Wooster could be dullsville. One student says that it is the people, however, who make up for the town's lack of urban excitement.

Wooster fields a number of competitive Division III teams. The men's tennis, men's basketball, women's soccer, and baseball teams have each won recent North Coast Atlantic Conference championships.

Winter can be a drag in this snowy region of the country, but students at Wooster are warmed by the school's caring and close community. And when the white stuff really comes down, there is one tradition to bring up your temperature. "There's this old legend that if you can fill the arch of Kauke, our largest academic building, with snow, all classes will be canceled," one junior explains. "The arch is HUGE, but every time there's a big snow, hundreds of people show up to pack the thing!"

If You Apply To ➤ **Wooster**...Early decision: Dec. 1. Regular admissions and financial aid: Feb. 15. Housing: May 1. Meets demonstrated need of 90%. Campus interviews: recommended, evaluative. Alumni interviews: optional, informational. SATs or ACTs: required. SAT IIs: optional. Accepts the Common Application and electronic applications. Essay question: significant historical event; describe how you are an independent thinker; discuss a creative work.

Worcester Polytechnic Institute

100 Institute Road, Worcester, MA 01609-2280

Students at Worcester Polytechnic Institute value the WPI way of life: the real-world practicality of their education, the easy association with professors, and the successful job-placement program. The innovative and fast-paced curriculum creates a competitive yet cooperative environment where teamwork is vital and academics paramount at a school where students classify one another as "creative, analytical logical problem-solvers."

WPI is the third-oldest independent science and engineering school in the nation. Its compact 80-acre campus is set atop one of Worcester's "seven hills" on the residential outskirts of town. Worcester is an industrial city (second-largest in New England) and the home of 10 colleges, most notably WPI, Clark University, and Holy Cross. Though WPI is less well-known, one biotech major says the university is small enough that students are "faces, not just names. WPI allows you to really find yourself by becoming anything you want to be." These schools are brought together by the WPI-initiated Social Web (http: //social.wpi.edu/) for the Colleges of Worcester Consortium.* This program is a one-stop academic and social gathering place on the World Wide Web where students can discover what is happening on each campus associated with the consortium.

The city is also a base for the rapidly growing Northeast biotechnology industry, and the region has a considerable number of high-tech firms that support WPI's project and research programs. The university also plans to open a project center in the Silicon Valley where students can work with area colleges and businesses. WPI's campus borders on two parks and the historic Highland Street District, where local merchants and students come together to form the neighborhood community. Old English stone buildings, complete with creeping ivy, dominate the architecture, but modern facilities dot the immaculately kept grounds. Recent changes include the $8.5-million renovation of Higgins Laboratories, the $2-million renovation of Life Sciences building including new biotechnology and biochemistry labs, and a revamped football field and track facility. The renovated Higgins building houses a design center, where students learn modern engineering theory and practice by designing and manufacturing

Website: www.wpi.edu
Location: City outskirts
Total Enrollment: 3,875
Undergraduates: 2,784
Male/Female: 77/23
SAT Ranges: V 560–660 M 620–700
Financial Aid: 90%
Expense: Pr $ $ $
Phi Beta Kappa: No
Applicants: 3,231
Accepted: 79%
Enrolled: 26%
Grad in 6 Years: 75%
Returning Freshmen: 91%
Academics: ✍ ✍ ✍ ✍
Social: ☎ ☎ ☎
Q of L: ★ ★ ★ ★
Admissions: (508) 831-5286
Email Address: admissions@wpi.edu

Strongest Programs:
Mechanical, Electrical, and Computer Engineering
Computer Science
Biology and Biotech

(Continued)
Biomedical Engineering
Fire Protection Engineering

products. Classrooms are constantly upgraded, with 75 percent now multimedia equipped.

At the center of Worcester's academic program is the WPI Plan, which established the school as a pioneer in engineering education. This flexible program gives undergraduates hands-on experience in their chosen field and an awareness of the social impact of technology. Students must complete three projects, including the Interactive Qualifying Project, a creative application of technical knowledge to one of society's problems, which is supervised by a science and/or a humanities professor from any discipline in science, engineering, humanities, or social science; or the Major Qualifying Project, a student's first chance to work on a truly professional-level problem in his or her major field. Many courses are project oriented, bringing student teams and professors in close contact as problem-solving colleagues. "The professors at WPI really care about their students and will go out of their way to make themselves available to them," says an electrical engineering major. Another student adds, "The professors work hard to make their courses interesting." Courses provide the information students need to complete their projects, reemphasizing WPI's curriculum as one driven by knowledge and not credit. Other resources include the library of videotaped lectures on specific topics. There are four terms per academic year at WPI, each lasting seven weeks. When students are not completing projects, they take three courses per term.

Students warn that the seven-week quarters mean the "pace of classes is so fast, and you have to have each class almost every day." But the set-up allows them to speed through tough classes and enjoy an extended summer vacation. The intent of WPI's unique grading system and educational philosophy is to polish social skills and develop teamwork abilities. The curriculum remains remarkably flexible for a high-powered engineering school. Standard course distribution requirements vary by major but include courses in engineering, math, and science. To promote cooperation and cohesiveness, the only recorded grades are A, B, C, or No Record. Failing grades do not appear on transcripts, and the school does not compute GPA's or class ranks.

The humanities department gets mixed reviews from students: "They are not as strong due to the extremely technical nature of the school and the nontechnical nature of these programs," says one senior. Technical writing, which was once seen as a somewhat anemic program, is growing swiftly. The most popular departments are, not surprisingly, mechanical, electrical/computer engineering, civil/environmental engineering, computer science, and biology/biotechnology. There are also a number of interdisciplinary programs such as prelaw and international studies. An unusual program in biomedical engineering is offered in conjunction with the University of Massachusetts Medical School, located about two and a half miles away. WPI also offers a rare Fire Protection Engineering program and a system dynamics major and minor. Scholarship can only be enhanced by the Fuller Labs Informational Sciences building, a $10-million computer center and a state-of-the-art bioprocess center, the first in the country dedicated to undergraduate education.

In light of an increasingly interdependent global economy, WPI offers many students unusual internships at one of the school's residential project centers in San Francisco, Washington, D.C., England, Denmark, Holland, Italy, Puerto Rico, or Thailand. These centers provide students with the opportunity to tackle current problems for a sponsor and spend their term working independently on a specific socio-technical assignment under the direction of one or more faculty members. Roughly one-third of students participate in this program, which is part of the "increased emphasis on learning about the world as a whole," says a

WPI also offers a rare Fire Protection Engineering program and a system dynamics major and minor.

biology and theater tech double major. The co-op program offers upperclassmen two eight-month work experiences and adds an extra half or full year to the degree program.

Most Worcester students come from Northeast public high schools, and all have a scientific bent. Eighty-two percent ranked in the top quarter of their high school class. African Americans and Hispanics together account for only 5 percent of the students, and Asian Americans represent an additional 7 percent. The school offers 491 merit scholarships, ranging from $5,000 to a full ride each year, but there are no athletic scholarships.

Only first-year students are guaranteed spots in the university residence halls; however, the room assignment process usually allows upperclassmen their first, second, or third choice. There are five coed-by-floor or coed-by-wing units, and one single-sex unit, including a spacious 220-bed residence hall that houses upperclassmen in suites of four or six. Forty-five percent of students move off campus, sometimes to nearby, "reasonably priced, close to school, off-campus" apartments that are within a mile of the college grounds. Upperclassmen who are in fraternities can live in their houses, and the two sororities are residential. The two dining halls offer multiple meal plans along with a choice of grill, healthy entrées, pizza, or wok items.

Twenty-four percent of the men join fraternities, and 21 percent of the women enter sororities. Students over 21 may have alcohol, provided it is kept in their rooms, but underage students do find a way to get alcohol. Even though one resident advisor reports his charges are teetotalers, a sophomore says, "If you want it, you can get it." BYOB is the required (and accepted) partying rule. In addition to Greek parties, there are student-organized coffeehouses, concerts, poetry readings, movies, and pub shows. Nearby colleges such as Holy Cross, Assumption, and Clark University are linked to WPI through shuttle buses, which provide even more social and academic opportunities. Boston and Hartford are both an hour's drive away, as are ski resorts and beaches.

One of WPI's more notable campus traditions is the Goat's Head Rivalry, a grudge match between the freshman and sophomore classes that includes the Pennant Rush, a rope pull across Institute Pond, and a WPI trivia competition. There is also an annual festival of international culture. Students say the new student center ("We're finally getting one!" a biotech major gushes) is desperately needed to encourage cohesiveness across the campus and offer a viable alternative to the Greek domination of the social scene. One major gripe about WPI is its gender ratio: 3-to-1 male. "No women," says one student bluntly.

While not particularly scenic, Worcester does offer a large number of clubs and restaurants and an art museum, as well as an upscale outlet shopping mall. A large multipurpose arena, the Centrum, is host to frequent concerts (Phish, Puff Daddy, the Beach Boys, to name a few) and occasional visits from Boston's Bruins and Celtics and a minor league hockey team. The newly opened Convention Center—attached to the Centrum—is expected to add a new level of vitality to the area. On campus, an extremely large proportion of the student body takes part in the intercollegiate athletic activity. In recent years, field hockey, football, and men's soccer have qualified for NCAA postseason competition. The women's tennis and men's wrestling are title holders and women's soccer was added to the list of 19 varsity sports.

One of WPI's chants is fittingly mathematic: "E to the x, dydx, e to the xdx, cosine secant tangent sine, 3.14159, e, i, radical Pi, fight 'em fight 'em WPI!" There's only one response to that: if you know what any of that stuff means, you'll fit right in at WPI.

An unusual program in biomedical engineering is offered in conjunction with the University of Massachusetts Medical School, located about two and a half miles away.

Overlaps

Rensselaer Polytechnic, MIT, Boston University, Cornell, Tufts.

Xavier University of Louisiana

7325 Palmetto Street, New Orleans, LA 70125

Website: www.xula.edu

Location: City center

Total Enrollment: 3,820

Undergraduates: 2,942

Male/Female: 28/72

SAT Ranges: V 450–560 M 420–540

ACT Range: 18–23

Financial Aid: 87%

Expense: Pr $

Phi Beta Kappa: No

Applicants: 3,143

Accepted: 92%

Enrolled: 31%

Grad in 6 Years: 54%

Returning Freshmen: 74%

Academics: 🖉 🖉 🖉

Social: ☎ ☎ ☎

Q of L: ★ ★ ★

Admissions: (504) 483-7388

Email Address:

apply@xula.edu

Strongest Programs:

Biology

Chemistry

Psychology

Business Administration

Prepharmacy

Premed

Xavier University of Louisiana is truly one of a kind. As the nation's only historically black Roman Catholic college, XU strives to combine the best features of both its faith and its cultural heritage. While the university's ultimate purpose is "the promotion of a more just and humane society," it's true strength lies in its proactive teaching style, which emphasizes the nurturing of minority high school students. The sciences are especially strong here, and this small school has a big reputation for turning out many of tomorrow's most successful scientists.

Founded in 1915, Xavier is located near the heart of the Big Easy in a quiet neighborhood that is dotted with bungalows. The focal point of the campus is the Library Resource, which, with its green roof and stately neo-Gothic architectural style, has become a landmark for those traveling by car from the New Orleans airport to the French Quarter. A closed campus green mutes the urban feel of the encroaching city, and yellow brick buildings have been erected among the older limestone structures.

Xavier's U-shaped administration building marks the geographic center of the campus. Most recently, a student lounge and playing field have been constructed, as have a new science complex annex and resource center.

"The departments that are important in setting the tone of the campus are biology, chemistry, and pharmacy," explains a student, "because more than half of Xavier's students major in these areas." It's true—in fact, nearly two-thirds of the student body majors in a science-related field. For the last three years, Xavier has led the nation in the number of undergraduate physical science degrees awarded to African Americans, as well as the number of African Americans placed into medical school. Xavier is also credited with educating 25 percent of all black pharmacists nationally. The university has built a national reputation as one of the most effective teaching institutions anywhere, and has been designated as one of only a few Model Institutions for Excellence by the National Science Foundation. Political science is a small but good department, and the psychology and education departments have been traditional strengths. Recently programs in German and economics have been eliminated due to waning student interest, whereas most other departments are constantly revising their curriculums to accommodate the evolving demands of the students. In addition to the many internships available, Xavier offers cooperative education programs in all fields and study abroad programs throughout North, Central, and South America, Europe, Africa, and Japan. The new Center for the Advancement of Teaching works to improve pedagogy across the curriculum and encourages African American students to become teachers and researchers.

Xavier's undergraduate curriculum is centered on the liberal arts. All students are required to take a core of prescribed courses in theology and philosophy, the arts and humanities, communications, history and the social sciences, mathematics, and the natural sciences; freshmen also take a mandatory seminar titled "The Student and the University." The academic climate is competitive and challenging. "There are a lot of students here who came from private or Catholic schools, which contributes to their outstanding educational background," says a psychology major. Priests and nuns teach and help run the school, though the faculty and staff are composed mainly of multiracial laypeople. "Freshmen are rarely taught by anyone less than full professors," says a student. Another says that the "majority of teachers here are very thorough in what they teach, and they tend to follow a regular syllabus." Academic and career advising are well received, and registration doesn't present any major concerns.

For a historically black Catholic college, Xavier's student body is quite diverse. More than 60 percent of the students are non-Catholic and close to 10 percent are not African American. Students come mostly from the Deep South; half are from parochial high schools, and a high percentage are second- or third-generation Xavierites. While school and career are priorities, social issues such as abortion, contraception, and the environment are not forgotten. "Political correctness is a big issue here because it is a Catholic institution with moral religious values," says a freshman. Merit scholarships are available for those who qualify, but financial aid is a sore point with many. "Financial aid packages are nowhere near adequate," says a student, "but it's better than nothing."

Three of the four contemporary-looking residence halls are single-sex, and "housing is very limited," says a psychology major. "Many students live off campus because dorm rooms are scarce and the rules are very strict." Though the housing situation is far from perfect, students admit that dorm rooms are comfortable and well kept. New Orleans has one of the highest crime rates in the nation so campus security is always an issue. "Campus security is very good," says a student. "They frequently patrol the grounds and set up posts to ensure student safety." A classmate adds, "Campus security seems to be adequate, but the security officers might be too obsessed with parking policies when spaces are limited."

When students tire of microscopes and Mass, they can trek into the Crescent City for a good time. "Students often go out for a night on the town where they can enjoy good music, fine dining, or great clubs," says a biology/premed major. New Orleans is home to Mardi Gras, the French Quarter, and a boundless buffet of smoky clubs and one-of-a-kind eateries. "It is a major college town," says a student. Back on campus, fraternities and sororities play a leading role in extracurricular and social life, though less than 10 percent of the student body goes Greek. Popular events include Culture Fest, Spring Fest, and Homecoming. "These events contain fashion shows, concerts, balls, dances, Greek shows, food, and rides," explains a freshman. Alcohol is prohibited on campus, so underage drinkers return to the city where nearly anything goes. Basketball for men and women—the Gold Rush and Gold Nugget teams—is the only varsity sport, and the teams are enthusiastically supported, especially when the opponent is rival Dillard.

Xavier is a school where achievement has been the rule and beating the odds a routine occurrence. More important, it's a place where perseverance and dedication are rewarded. "The best thing about Xavier University is that they give students space to successfully grow in responsibility and dependability, developing for themselves a philosophy of life and a sense of values," says a student. That's been Xavier's unique mission since day one.

For the last three years, Xavier has led the nation in the number of undergraduate physical science degrees awarded to African Americans, as well as the number of African Americans placed into medical school.

The new Center for the Advancement of Teaching works to improve pedagogy across the curriculum and encourages African American students to become teachers and researchers.

Overlaps
Howard, Spelman, Clark Atlanta, Hampton, Florida A&M.

Yale University

38 Hillhouse Avenue, New Haven, CT 06520

Website: www.yale.edu

Location: Urban

Total Enrollment: 11,017

Undergraduates: 5,266

Male/Female: 52/48

SAT Ranges: V 690–780 M 690–770

Financial Aid: 41%

Expense: Pr $ $ $ $

Phi Beta Kappa: Yes

Applicants: 13,270

Accepted: 16%

Enrolled: 65%

Grad in 6 Years: 94%

Returning Freshmen: 98%

Academics: ✐ ✐ ✐ ✐ ✐

Social: ☎ ☎ ☎

Q of L: ★ ★ ★

Admissions: (203) 432-9300

Email Address:

undergraduate.admissions@ yale.edu

Strongest Programs:

Art and Architecture

History

English

Biology

Economics

Political Science

Psychology

Music

Drama

Architecture

For decades, Yale has had a sterling reputation as one of the finest private universities in the nation, if not the world. Known as the Ivy League university that cares about undergraduate teaching, its name has long been synonymous with prestige. In recent years, Yale has been plagued by a variety of troubles including urban problems, well-publicized strikes by university workers and graduate students, and the long struggle to revive its aging physical plant. Once in danger of crumbling, this ivory tower of education has taken dramatic steps to reverse the decline, including a selective excellence policy and the largest construction and renovation project ever undertaken at an American university.

Yale's campus is a triumph of collegiate architecture, featuring magnificent courtyards, imposing quadrangles, Gothic architecture designed by James Gamble Rogers, and Harkness Tower, an imposing spire that was once washed with acid to create its aged, stately look. A massive $2.6-billion construction and renovation project is slowly transforming the university's aging physical plant and is expected to be completed in 2010. Leaking roofs, chipping paint, and drafty corridors are being replaced by state-of-the-art facilities, including science and engineering buildings. Renovations are underway in every corner of the campus, and facelifts are planned for the gymnasium, Sterling Library, the law school, and residence halls.

Once inside Yale's wrought-iron gates, students find a galaxy of academic opportunities that few institutions can rival. Though Yale's offerings are superb across the board, its programs in the arts and humanities are without equal among the elite national universities (just ask Meryl Streep or Jodie Foster). The prominence of the arts programs makes for an interesting juxtaposition: while the campus echoes with nearly three centuries of hallowed tradition, today's Yale attracts one of the most liberal and free-thinking student bodies in the Ivy League.

Yale University was founded in 1701 by Connecticut Congregationalists who, the story goes, were concerned about "backsliding" tendencies among their counterparts at a certain school in Cambridge, Massachusetts. Though secular liberalism has replaced the strident Puritanism of centuries past, the ancient work ethic remains a Yale hallmark. For students that means one of the heaviest workloads of any major university: thirty-six rather than the usual 32 courses are required for graduation. Yalies also cover their material in a shorter time; the reading period and exams are compressed into two weeks at the end of each semester, so work can't be left to the end of the term. These demands contribute to an academic atmosphere that ranges from intense to manic. Pressure is internally generated and the courses are extremely difficult. "I spend every waking hour studying," says one Yalie with only slight exaggeration. Incidentally, people at

Yale who work all rather than most of their waking hours are not called nerds as they are elsewhere. Here they are "weenies."

The "Selective Excellence" policy recently adopted by Yale's president, Dr. Richard Levin, has been controversial. The purpose of the plan is to focus the university's resources on its largest and strongest departments such as history, law, and biomedical sciences, leaving the smaller departments, like engineering and physical sciences, to seek excellence through specialization. Some have expressed concern that the success of the plan will be at the expense of some of the university's most valuable programs, but most agree that a change must be made.

Education is the university's primary task. Although it has 12 graduate schools, Yale College, the undergraduate arts and sciences division, remains the heart of the university. Virtually all faculty members teach undergraduate courses, and even the resources of professional schools—especially architecture, fine arts, drama, and music—are put at the disposal of undergraduates. Yale's history department is superb, a judgment confirmed by the fact that students have traditionally made it one of the most popular undergraduate majors. History also has one of the most demanding programs: A 30- to 50-page senior essay is required by the department. The English department routinely blazes a trail as the vanguard of literary theory, and the psychology and American Studies majors are quite popular. There's also an outstanding interdisciplinary humanities major that entails study of the medieval, Renaissance, and modern periods. Sociology, philosophy, and environmental science departments get the thumbs-down from students, and one student confides that the math department is fraught with bad lecturers.

Yale has a long-boasted excellence in drama and music at the undergraduate as well as the graduate levels. Architecture and modern languages, especially French, are also top-notch. Although science majors complain about the walk to Science Hill, where most labs and science classrooms are situated, it's worth the trip The biology department is excellent, as is a major called molecular biochemistry and biophysics, known as MB&B. (Both fields consist mainly of premeds.) Chemistry and marine biology have been nourished by several investments. Elite students with a particularly strong appetite for the humanities can enroll in Directed Studies, which examines the literature, philosophy, history, and politics of Western tradition. Prospective DSers should be prepared for some serious weenie-ing—they don't call it "Directed Suicide" for nothing.

Despite its traditionalism, Yale does not have a core curriculum. Instead, students are required to take three classes of their choosing in each of four broad areas: language and literature; humanities (other than literature); social sciences; and natural sciences and math. Yale also mandates intermediate-level mastery of a foreign language, though it has never been keen on study abroad because of the belief that every Yalie should spend four full years "'neath the elms" of campus. In lieu of preregistration, students have what is known as a "shopping period": two weeks at the beginning of each term to sample morsels of the various offerings before handing in their schedules.

Introductory-level classes at Yale are usually large lectures, which are typically broken down into small sections with teaching assistants. Some of the most popular, such as Paul Kennedy's course on European history, seem more like performances than lectures. Upper-level seminars are small and plentiful, though especially popular ones often turn away even juniors and seniors. Fortunately, this normally doesn't hinder one's chances to graduate within four years. With the exception of a few mammoth introductory courses, the accessibility of professors is unusually good for a major research university. "The professors at Yale are outstanding," says one economics major. "They have a lot of office hours and

In lieu of preregistration, students have what is known as a "shopping period": two weeks at the beginning of each term to sample morsels of the various offerings before handing in their schedules.

An array of cultural houses maintains a high campus profile and sponsors popular parties and dances as well as assorted newsmagazines.

some will even give out their phone number or invite students to dinner at their home."

Yale's library holdings are second in size only to Harvard's and contain more than 10 million volumes. Age, heavy use, and environmental conditions contributed to the deterioration of the main library, and at one point many people worried about the future of its impressive holdings, but extensive renovations are under way to correct the problem. The flash-cube-shaped Beinecke Rare Book Library houses many extraordinary manuscripts, including a Gutenberg Bible and some music manuscripts penned by Bach, and the most frequently used books are found underground in the Cross Campus Library. Also located in CCL are rows of "tiny beige boxes that look like phone booths with desks in them." To Yalies, these are "weenie bins," where many a tired student has dozed on an open book.

Nearly half the student body is from the Northeast, 42 percent come from private and parochial schools, and 99 percent come from the top fifth of their high school class. Yale is also consistently more popular with women than most of its rivals, most notably Princeton, and its gender ratio is nearing 50/50. Most of the traditions that make Yale—singing groups like the Whiffenpoofs, drinking at "the tables down at Mory's"—are either coed or have female counterparts, and there is a vocal gay and lesbian community. Diversity is a major issue on campus. Although African Americans make up only 7 percent of the students and Hispanics only 6 percent, Asian American enrollment is fairly large at 14 percent. An array of cultural houses maintains a high campus profile and sponsors popular parties and dances as well as assorted newsmagazines. Though more liberal than counterparts at either Harvard or Princeton, Yalies are a diverse lot and not shy to express an opinion.

Undoubtedly, Yale's most distinctive feature is its residential college housing system. Endowed by a Yale graduate (who also began the house system at Harvard) and modeled on those at Oxford and Cambridge, Yale's colleges provide intimate living and learning communities. "The residential colleges create a small liberal arts college atmosphere at a big research university," explains one senior. Each college has a library, dining hall, and special facilities such as photographic labs or tree swings—one is even said to have an endowment used solely for whipped cream. All have their own dean, which makes for a more decentralized administrative structure, a nice security blanket for undergraduates struggling to adapt to academic or other rigors. Still, "prospective students should realize that the quality of their freshman year will depend on how compatible they are with their roommates," says one student. "The residential colleges and an uncooperative administration make it impossible to switch rooms or roommates." Each college also has its own affiliated faculty members (a few of whom actually live there) and offers its own seminars. These, along with plays, concerts, lectures, and other events sponsored by the colleges, are integral to the cultural life of the university as a whole. Much of the residential college's distinctive identity is drawn from their architecture. Some are fashioned in craggy, fortresslike Gothic, while others are done in the more open Colonial style, with redbrick and green shutters the prevailing motif. All have their own special nooks and crannies with cryptic inscriptions that pay tribute to illustrious Yalies of generations past. Despite their history and charm, many of the residential colleges are in serious need of maintenance, and a major project to renovate them is under way. In addition, the university has also made security one of its biggest priorities, offering an elaborate minivan system and a free escort service. Most freshmen live together in the Old Campus, the historic 19th-century quadrangle, before moving into their colleges as sophomores. Sophomores and juniors generally live in suites of single and double rooms, while many seniors get a room of their own.

When Yale is winning the annual Yale-Harvard football extravaganza, the Harvard side has been known to taunt them by shouting across the stadium, "You may be winning, but you have to go back to New Haven." That prospect is not an enticing one to either current or prospective students—the main reason Yale's applications have failed to keep pace with those at Harvard and Princeton in recent years. However, an effort to revitalize the city is under way and New Haven does have its virtues. A summer jazz festival brings thousands to the historic town green, as do occasional food fairs and performances of Shakespeare's comedies. The city's long-standing tradition of theater—it was once the place to try out plays headed for Broadway—has been brought back with the renovation and reopening of two grand old theater/concert halls just a block from campus. Locals will swear that Pepe's on Wooster Street was the first pizza parlor in the country, and Louis's Lunch the first true hamburger joint. Closer to campus, a number of cafés have sprouted up to cater to the afternoon coffee and tea crowd. Relations between students and the locals have been improving. "The Yale–New Haven partnership is becoming much stronger as they work together for the betterment of the community," says an anthropology major. Every year more than 2,000 students temporarily vacate their sophisticated fortress to volunteer their time in community service organizations. One student boasts, "Yale has the largest collegiate umbrella organization for community service in the country."

Though studying takes the lion's share of their time, Yalies also find plenty of ways to unwind. With the drinking age enforced at larger university-sponsored bashes, most socializing takes place at private parties in the colleges or off campus. A handful of Greek organizations have yet to enter the social mainstream. A potpourri of film societies offers numerous weekend screenings. The Yale Repertory Theater is an excellent, innovative professional company that depends heavily on graduate school talent but always brings in a few top stage stars each season. Natural history and art museums on and near campus, especially the British Art Center, are excellent. For those who want more excitement, the typical Yalie refrain on New Haven—"It's halfway between New York and Boston"— tells it all. Metro North trains run almost hourly to New York, and visiting Boston is nearly as easy.

Many Yale students identify strongly with their extracurricular groups and spend most of their waking hours at the newspaper office, radio station, or computer center. Particularly clubby are members of the a cappella singing groups, who do everything from drink together on a certain night of the week to tour together during spring vacation. Students whose social tastes range to the arcane can investigate Yale's secret societies, those mysterious clubs for seniors, some with their own mausoleum-like clubhouses.

Yale fields a full complement of athletic teams. Men's hockey, squash, soccer, and crew routinely post winning seasons, and the golf and fencing teams have recently brought home Ivy League championships. The football team isn't the power it once was (decade by decade, Yale has won more games than any other school), and basketball has also struggled. Women's sports are strong across the board, but especially in gymnastics, swimming, fencing, and lacrosse. Thousands of students take part each year in intramural competition among the 12 colleges. Like most of its physical plant, Yale's athletic facilities are aging, though much-needed renovations are currently moving forward.

The intensity of a Yale education leaves an indelible mark on the lives of its alumni. They are heirs to the loyal breed that originated the phrase, "For God, for country, and for Yale." Yalies take justifiable pride in their school, as much for its

The biology department is excellent, as is a major called molecular biochemistry and biophysics, known as MB&B.

lack of snobbery and pretense as for its well-known academic excellence. Perhaps, this is the reason the Yale community is so dedicated to removing the tarnish from its reputation and committed to keeping it in its spot near the pinnacle of the Ivy League pecking order.

If You Apply To ➤ **Yale**…Early decision: Nov. 1. Regular admissions: Dec. 31. Financial aid: Feb. 1. Guarantees to meet demonstrated need. Campus interviews: optional, evaluative. Alumni interviews: recommended, evaluative. SATs and SAT IIs (any three) or ACTs: required. Essay question: most important activity; and personal statement.

Consortia

Students who feel that attending a small college might limit their college experiences should realize that many of these schools have banded together to offer unusual programs that they could not support on their own. Offerings range from exchange programs—trading places with a student on another campus—to a semester or two anywhere in the world on one of the seven continents or somewhere out at sea.

The following is a list of some of the largest and oldest of these programs, some sponsored by groups of colleges, and others by independent agencies. An asterisk (*) after the name of a college indicates that the institution is the subject of a write-up in *The Fiske Guide*. An asterisk following the name of a program in the college write-ups means that it is described below.

The **Associated Colleges of the Midwest** comprises 14 institutions in five states: Beloit,* Lawrence,* and Ripon* in Wisconsin; Carleton,* Macalester,* and St. Olaf* in Minnesota; the University of Chicago,* Knox,* Lake Forest,* and Monmouth in Illinois; Coe, Cornell,* and Grinnell* in Iowa; and Colorado College.*

The consortium offers its students semester-long programs to study art in London and Florence; culture and society in Florence, the Czech Republic, and Zimbabwe; language and culture in Costa Rica and Russia; and tropical field research in Costa Rica. Yearlong programs include Chinese studies in Hong Kong, India studies, and study in Japan. The Arts of London and the Florence program are the most popular with students. Language study is a component of all the ACM overseas programs. Prior language study is required for the programs in Costa Rica, Japan, and Russia. Domestic off-campus programs include Humanities at the Newberry Library (an in-depth research project) or a semester in Chicago in the arts, urban education, or urban studies. Scientists can study at the Oak Ridge National Laboratory in Tennessee, or there's a wilderness field station in northern Minnesota.

Living arrangements vary with the program and region. Students in programs in Chicago live in apartments and residential hotels; Minnesota's wilderness enthusiasts must rough it in cabins, and Oak Ridge scientists are on their own. There are no comprehensive costs for any of the ACM programs, domestic or foreign, and tuition is based on the home school's standard fees. The programs are open to sophomores, juniors, and seniors majoring in all fields. The only programs that tend to be especially strict with admissions are the Oak Ridge, Newberry, and Russian arrangements. For information, contact Associated Colleges of the Midwest, 18 South Michigan Ave., Chicago, IL 60603, (312) 263-5000.

The **Associated Colleges of the South**, incorporated in 1991, is composed of 12 Southern schools (Birmingham-Southern,* Centenary, Centre,* Millsaps,* Rhodes,* University of the South,* Furman University, Hendrix College, Morehouse College,* Southwestern University, Trinity University,* and the University of Richmond*). Established to strengthen liberal education in the South, the consortium focuses on academic program development (with attention to international programs), faculty, staff, and student development. Overseas courses are offered year-round. Affiliated and ACS-managed programs are offered at Oxford, in Central Europe, and in Brazil. For information, contact the Associated Colleges of the South, 17 Executive Park Dr., Suite 420, Atlanta, GA 30329, (404) 636-9533.

The **Atlanta Regional Consortium for Higher Education** comprises 20 public and private colleges and universities in the Atlanta area, as well as several specialized institutions of higher education. Members are Agnes Scott College,* Atlanta College of Art, Clark Atlanta University,* Clayton College and State University, Columbia Theological Seminary, Emory University,* Georgia Institute of Technology,* Georgia State University, State University of West Georgia, Institute of Paper Science and Technology, Interdenominational Theological Center, Kennesaw State University, Mercer University, Morehouse College,* Morehouse School of Medicine, Morris Brown College,* Oglethorpe University,* Southern Polytechnic State University, Spelman College,* and the University of Georgia.*

Students from member colleges and universities may register for approved courses at any of the other institutions, including those with highly specialized courses. The consortium's interlibrary lending program uses a daily truck delivery service to put more than 10 million books and other resources at students' disposal.

The **Christian College Coalition** promotes cooperation among more than 80 liberal arts colleges from across the nation, each enthusiastic in Christian commitment. Members include Calvin,* Gordon,* Houghton,* King, Taylor, Westmont, and Wheaton (IL).*

The Washington, D.C., national headquarters of the coalition coordinates a variety of cooperative student programs, including semester-long internship/seminar programs in Costa Rica and the nation's capital, a film studies center in Hollywood, and a six-week summer school program at Oxford: Renaissance and Reformation in Europe. Fourteen of the coalition campuses have been designated model site campuses for a minority concerns project, with special attention given to campus climate and curricular issues. In addition, approximately a dozen campuses have been involved in a Russian initiative, with exchanges of students and faculty between member colleges and Russian universities. Other cooperative projects offer opportunities for students who seek to combine a solid liberal arts education with a dynamic, thoughtful Christian faith.

The **Christian College Consortium** comprises 13 of the nation's top evangelical liberal arts schools: Asbury, Bethel (MN), George Fox, Gordon,* Greenville, Houghton,* Malone, Messiah, Seattle Pacific, Taylor, Trinity (IL), Westmont, and Wheaton (IL).*

The consortium offers a "student visitors program" whereby students can spend a semester—with little paper pushing—at any of the member schools. More than a hundred students (not including freshmen) participate each year, and the cost is strictly the home school's regular fees. Other than a reasonably good grade average, there are no special requirements. Consortium schools share a wide array of international programs on a space-available basis, and the consortium has cooperative arrangements with Daystar University College in Nairobi, Kenya, and Han Nam University in Taejon, Korea.

The **Five College Consortium** is a nonprofit organization that comprises Amherst,* Hampshire,* Mount Holyoke,* Smith,* and the University of Massachusetts at Amherst,* and is designed to enhance the social and cultural life of the 30,000 students attending these Connecticut Valley colleges. Legally known as Five Colleges Inc., this cooperative arrangement allows any undergraduate at the four private liberal arts colleges and UMass to take courses for credit and use the library facilities of any of the other four schools. A free bus service shuttles among the schools.

The consortium sponsors joint departments in dance and astronomy, as well as a number of interdisciplinary programs including black studies, East Asian languages, coastal and marine sciences, Near Eastern Studies, peace and world security studies, Canadian Studies, and Irish Studies. Certificate programs are available in African Studies and Latin American Studies. There are five college centers for East Asian Studies, women's studies research, and foreign language resources. Students from the four smaller colleges benefit from the large number of course choices available at the university. The undergrads from UMass, in turn, take advantage of the small-college atmosphere as well as particularly strong departments, such as art at Smith, sculpture at Mount Holyoke, and film and photography at Hampshire. There is also a Five College Orchestra and an open theater auditions policy that allows students to audition for parts in productions at any of the colleges. The social and cultural aspects of the Five College Consortium are more informal than the academic structure. The consortium puts out a calendar listing art shows, lectures, concerts, and films at the five schools, as well as the bus schedules. In addition, student-sponsored parties are advertised on all campuses, and there is a good deal of informal meeting of students from the various schools.

For those students taking courses on other campuses, one's home-school meal ticket is valid on any of the five member campuses for lunch. Dinners are available with special permission. Taking classes at other schools is encouraged, but not usually for first-semester freshmen. The consortium is a big drawing card for all schools involved.

The **Great Lakes Colleges Association** comprises 12 independent liberal arts institutions in three states: Antioch,* Denison,* Kenyon,* Oberlin,* Ohio Wesleyan,* and the College of Wooster* in Ohio; DePauw,* Earlham,* and Wabash* in Indiana; and Albion,* Hope,* and Kalamazoo* in Michigan. Like ACM, the Great Lakes group offers students off-campus opportunities both in the U.S. and overseas.

For adventures abroad, there are African studies programs in Sierra Leone, Senegal, and Kenya. Students can spend a year studying in Scotland or Japan, or a semester comparing socioeconomic changes in Poland, the United Kingdom, and Germany (European Academic Term). GLCA cosponsors five programs mentioned in the ACM write-up above, but these sometimes cost more: a fall or a year at a People's Republic of China university;

study in Hong Kong, Russia, or the Czech Republic; and programs at the Newberry Library in Chicago and Oak Ridge National Laboratory in Tennessee. Other domestic programs include a one-semester arts internship in New York City and a liberal arts urban study semester in Philadelphia.

Primarily juniors participate, but the programs are open to sophomores and seniors. New York and Philadelphia are the most popular domestic plans, and Scotland is the largest of those abroad. There are language requirements to meet in several of the programs, such as a year of Mandarin for China, a year of Japanese for Japan, and two years of Russian for Russia. Sometimes, however, an intensive summer language program can be substituted. Contact GLCA, 2929 Plymouth Rd., Suite 207, Ann Arbor, MI 48105-3206, (313) 761-4833.

The **Lehigh Valley Association of Independent Colleges** is a 23-year-old cooperative effort among six colleges in the same area of Pennsylvania: Allentown College of St. Francis de Sales, Cedar Crest College, Lafayette College,* Lehigh University,* Moravian College, and Muhlenberg College.*

Approximately 400 students each year cross-register at member campuses, although the bulk of the activity occurs between schools that are closest to each other. A Jewish studies program, headquartered at Lehigh, draws on the faculties of Lehigh, Lafayette, and Muhlenberg. Faculty members travel from college to college in order to offer students a variety of courses in this field. The association's Consortium Professors program puts faculty on two other member campuses each year to teach unusual or special-interest courses. Several members exchange courses by video conference. Special seminars are arranged at central locations for selected students, with transportation provided. The association offers a cooperative cultural program sponsoring nationally known visiting dance companies. Students at each college are eligible for reduced-rate tickets to plays and other events on campuses of association schools. But the most frequently used service of the association is its interlibrary loan program, which permits students at one institution to use the research facilities of the others. Summer study abroad programs take students to Germany, Spain, Mexico, or Israel.

The **Maritime Studies Program** of Williams College and Mystic Seaport Museum is an interdisciplinary semester designed for 22 undergraduates (primarily juniors, but some second-semester sophomores and seniors) who are eager to augment liberal arts education with an in-depth study of the sea. Participants take four Williams College courses (maritime history, literature of the sea, marine policy, and oceanography or marine ecology). Classes are taught with an emphasis on independent research in the setting of the Mystic Seaport Museum. Classroom lectures are enhanced by hands-on experience in celestial navigation, boat building, sailing, blacksmithing, and other historic crafts. Students spend two weeks offshore in deep-sea oceanographic research aboard a traditionally rigged schooner, highlighting the purpose of the program: to understand our relationship with the sea—past, present, and future.

Most students are drawn from 20 affiliate colleges: Amherst,* Bates,* Bowdoin,* Colby,* Colgate,* Connecticut,* Dartmouth,* Hamilton,* Middlebury,* Mount Holyoke,* Oberlin,* Smith,* Trinity,* Tufts,* Union,* Vassar,* Wellesley,* Wesleyan,* Wheaton,* and Williams.* Credit is granted through Williams College, and financial aid is transferable. Students from all four-year liberal arts colleges are encouraged to apply. Write to the Maritime Studies Program, Box 6000 Mystic Seaport Museum, Mystic, CT 06355-09 90, (302) 572-5359.

Sea Semester (not to be confused with Semester at Sea) is a similar venture for water lovers, but it is designed for students geared more toward the theoretical and practical applications of the subject. Five 12-week sessions are offered each year, and there are 48 students in each session. One prerequisite for the program is a course in college-level lab science or the equivalent. All majors are considered, as long as they're in good academic standing, submit transcripts and recommendations, and have an interview with an alumnus in their area.

Students spend the first half of the term living on Sea's campus in the Woods Hole area and immersing themselves in oceanography and maritime and nautical studies. Independent study projects begun ashore are completed during the sea component aboard either a schooner or a brigantine, which cruises along the Eastern seaboard and out into the Atlantic, North Atlantic, or Caribbean, depending on the season. Six weeks on the ocean is when theory becomes reality, and the usual mission consists of enough navigation, oceanographic data collection, and record keeping to keep even Columbus on the right course.

Students from affiliated colleges (Boston U,* College of Charleston,* Colgate,* Cornell,* Drexel,* Eckerd,* Franklin and Marshall,* the U. of Pennsylvania,* and Rice University*) receive a semester's worth of credit directly through their school. Students from other schools must receive credit through Boston U. Write to the Sea Education Association, P.O. Box 6, Woods Hole, MA 02543.

Semester at Sea takes qualified students from any college and whisks them around the globe on a study/cruise odyssey. Based at the University of Pittsburgh, this nonprofit group takes 450 students each term (from second-semester freshmen to grads) and puts them on a ship bound for almost everywhere. The vessel itself is a college campus in its own right. Sixty courses are taught by two dozen professors in subjects ranging from anthropology to marketing, and usually stressing the international scene as well as the sea itself. What's more, art, theater, music, and other extras can be found on board. When students aren't at sea, they're in port in any of 12 foreign countries throughout India, the Middle East, the Commonwealth of Russian States, the Far East, Africa, South America, and the Mediterranean, and it's not uncommon for leaders and diplomats to meet them along the way.

Students must be in good standing at their home colleges to be considered, which often means a GPA of 2.5 or better. Some financial aid is available in the form of the usual federal grants and loans, and 30 eligible students can use a work/study plan to pay for half the trip. Most colleges do recognize the Semester at Sea program and will provide participating students with a full term's worth of credits. Information may be obtained by writing to Semester at Sea, University of Pittsburgh, 811 William Pitt Union, Pittsburgh, PA 15260, (800) 854-0195 or (412) 648-7490.

The **Seven-College Exchange** consists of four women's colleges (Hollins,* Mary Baldwin, Randolph-Macon Woman's,* and Sweet Briar*), one men's school (Hampden-Sydney*), and two coed (Randolph-Macon College and Washington and Lee*). The exchange program was more popular when it began almost two decades ago and was utilized mainly for social reasons. Today the exchange program is used mainly for academic reasons, and enables students to take advantage of courses offered on the other campuses. Eligibility for participation is determined by the home institution, and except for special fees, rates are those of the home institution. Designed primarily for juniors, the program also considers sophomores and seniors as applicants. Several participating members sponsor study abroad programs.

The **Twelve-College Exchange Program** comprises a dozen selective schools in the Northeast: Amherst,* Bowdoin,* Connecticut College,* Dartmouth,* Mount Holyoke,* Smith,* Trinity,* Vassar,* Wellesley,* Wesleyan,* Wheaton (MA),* and Williams.*

The federation means that students enrolled in any of these schools can visit for a semester or two (usually the latter) with a minimum of red tape. Approximately 300 students utilize the opportunity each year; most of them are juniors. Placement is determined mainly by available space, but students need also display good academic standing. While the home college arranges the exchange, students must meet the fees and standards of the host school. Financial aid holders can usually carry their packages with them. Also available through this exchange is participation in the Williams College–Mystic Seaport Program in American Maritime Studies or study at the Eugene O'Neill National Theater Institute.

The **Venture Program** is based at Brown University, but has at various times counted many of the most prestigious East Coast and Midwestern colleges and universities in its membership. The eight current member institutions include Bates,* Brown,* Connecticut College,* Hobart and William Smith,* College of the Holy Cross,* Swarthmore College,* Vassar,* and Wesleyan.*

Venture, established in 1973, places students who want to take time off from college in short-term, full-time jobs in many fields of interest and geographic locations. Venture provides students with an opportunity to test academic, career, and personal interests on the job. There is no cost to students or employers for participation. Venture is supported by member institutions. About 200 students apply to the program, and about half of them are eventually placed in positions. All students attending a member college are eligible to participate. Venture also works with students who want to take time off between high school and college. In 1987, the consortium initiated the Venture II program, which encourages graduating seniors from member schools to explore work opportunities in the not-for-profit sector. The consortium also operates the Urban Education Semester in collaboration with the Bank Street College of Education and Community School District Number 4 in New York City, introducing liberal arts undergraduates to issues and practice in urban education. All of Venture's programs aim to foster social awareness and responsibility among students and build connections between higher education and the community.

The **Washington Semester** of American University takes about 750 students each year from hundreds of colleges across the country (who meet minimum academic qualifications of a 2.75 GPA) and gives them unbeatable academic and political opportunities in the nation's capital. The program is the oldest of its kind in Washington.

Students take part in a semester of seminars with policymakers and lobbyists, an internship, and a choice between an elective course at the university or a self-designed, in-depth research project. Students live in dorms on the campus, and are guided by a staff of 20 American University professors.

Ninety percent of the students are drawn from 192 affiliated schools. Although admissions competition depends on the home school and how many it chooses to nominate, the average GPA hovers around a 3.3. Most who participate are juniors, but second-semester sophomores and seniors get equal consideration, and the cost is either American University's tuition, room, board, and fees or that of the home school. Just over a third of the affiliated colleges are profiled in the *Guide*.

The **Worcester Consortium** is made up of 10 institutions nestled in and about Worcester, Massachusetts: Anna Maria, Assumption, Becker Junior, Clark University,* Holy Cross,* Quinsigamond Community, Tufts University of Veterinary Medicine, the University of Massachusetts Medical Center, Worcester Polytechnic Institute,* and Worcester State. Member schools coordinate activities ranging from purchasing light bulbs to sharing libraries, and a bus transports scholars to the various campuses as well as public libraries. Academic cross-registration is offered, as are two special programs: a health studies option and a certificate in gerontology. The consortium calendar lists upcoming events on each campus and encourages community service with a special emphasis on college/school collaboration. The consortium also provides free academic and financial aid counseling to low-income, first-generation students thinking about college. Write the Educational Opportunity Center, 26 Franklin St., Worcester, MA 01608.

Index

Acknowledgments

The Fiske Guide to Colleges Staff

Editor: Edward B. Fiske
Managing Editor: Robert Logue
Contributing Editor: Bruce G. Hammond
Production Coordinator: Julia Fiske Hogan

Writers: Eva DuBuisson, Rose Fatton, Angela Fernandes,
Nicole Hess, Ann Jackson, Samantha Levine, Noah Wilker

College Counselor Advisory Group

Nancy Beane, Atlanta, GA

Margaret Johnson, San Antonio, TX

Eileen Blattner, Shaker Heights, OH

William Mason, Southborough, MA

Susan Case, Milton, MA

Judy Muir, Houston, TX

Angela Connor, Raleigh, NC

Susan Moriarty Paton, New Haven, CT

Debra Craig, Austin, TX

Alice Purinton, Andover, MA

Anne Ferguson, Shaker Heights, OH

Phyllis Steinbrecher, Westport, CT

Bruce Hammond, Albuquerque, NM

The Fiske Guide to Colleges reflects the talents, energy, and ideas of many people. Chief among them are Robert Logue, the managing editor, and Julia Fiske Hogan, the production coordinator. The three of us are grateful for the dedicated work of our intrepid team of writers, as well as the formidable editorial assistance of Todd Stocke, Kelley Thornton, and their colleagues at Sourcebooks, Inc.

In the final analysis, *The Fiske Guide* reflects the contributions of the thousands of students and college administrators who took the time to answer detailed and demanding questionnaires. Their candor and cooperation are deeply appreciated, and while I, of course, accept full responsibility for the final product, the quality of the book is a testimony to their thoughtful reflections on the institutions they have chosen to attend.

About the Author

In 1980, when he was Education Editor of *The New York Times*, Edward B. Fiske sensed that college-bound students and their families needed better information on which to base their educational choices. Thus was born *The Fiske Guide to Colleges*. A graduate of Wesleyan University, Fiske did graduate work at Columbia University and assorted other bastions of higher learning. He left the *Times* in 1991 to pursue a variety of educational and journalistic interests, which included writing a book on school reform, *Smart Schools, Smart Kids*. When not visiting colleges, he can be found playing squash, sailing, or doing research on the educational problems of Third World countries for UNESCO and other international organizations. Fiske lives in Durham, North Carolina, near the campus of Duke University, where his wife is a member of the faculty.

Notes

Notes

Notes

Notes

Notes